The Developing Person

Through Childhood

Maurice Brazil Prendergast, *Low Tide*, ca. 1895–1897.

The Developing Person
Through Childhood

KATHLEEN STASSEN BERGER

Bronx Community College

City University of New York

ROSS A. THOMPSON

University of Nebraska—Lincoln

WORTH PUBLISHERS

The Developing Person Through Childhood

Copyright © 1996 by Worth Publishers, Inc.

All rights reserved

Printed in the United States of America

Library of Congress Catalog Card Number: 94–62217

ISBN: 1–57259–016-5

Printing: 1 2 3 4 5 – 99 98 97 96

Developmental Editor: Peter Deane

Design: Malcolm Grear Designers

Art Director: George Touloumes

Production Editor: Toni Ann Scaramuzzo

Production Supervisor: Barbara Anne Seixas

Layout: Heriberto Lugo

Picture Editor: Barbara Salz

Line art: Demetrios Zangos

Composition and separations: TSI Graphics, Inc.

Printing and binding: R.R. Donnelley & Sons Company

Cover: Maurice Brazil Prendergast, *Low Tide,* ca. 1895–1897. Oil on
    panel. Height: 13½ in. Width: 18 in. Williams College Museum of
    Art, Williamstown, Massachusetts. Gift of Mrs. Charles
    Prendergast.

Photo acknowledgments begin on page PA-1, and constitute an
extension of the copyright page.

Worth Publishers

33 Irving Place

New York, NY 10003

Contents in Brief

Contents

CHAPTER 3 **Heredity and Environment** 77

The Beginning of Development 78

The Genetic Code 79

CHAPTER 4 **Prenatal Development** 109

From Zygote to Newborn 110

Preface

I began the first edition of this book eighteen years ago with a single goal in mind: to convey the study of child development as the intriguing, exciting, and critically important discipline that it is. Years of teaching had convinced me that it was possible to communicate the fascinating complexities and the immediate impact of this subject without being simplistic or, alternatively, so overburdening the reader with theoretical and academic details as to become dull and inaccessible. I wanted to present theory and research, practical examples and policy implications, controversial issues and unanswered questions, all in a manner that inspired critical thinking, deepened insight, and gave pleasure. The enthusiastic response of instructors and students has been enormously gratifying, encouraging me to believe that the book is reaching its goal and at the same time making me eager to improve, as well as update, each new edition.

However, with my original goal in mind, I have become increasingly concerned that the field of child development is moving much too rapidly across an ever broadening range of disciplines for a single author to keep abreast of it all *and* produce meaningful textbook revisions on a timely schedule. Therefore, the first step I took to improve this and future editions of the *Developing Person Through Childhood* was to ask Ross Thompson, professor of psychology at the University of Nebraska—Lincoln, to be my coauthor. Over the years, Ross's role as a generous reviewer and straightforward critic of this book has grown into that of a friend and collaborator, who made valuable contributions to several chapters of the third edition. As a coauthor, Ross brings to the book not only his highly respected scholarship in many areas, including attachment, public policy, and family relationships, but also, through his work as an editor of *Child Development*, a wide-ranging familiarity with the newest research and latest perspectives across the entire discipline. In addition, he brings personal insights as a teacher at a leading university in the Midwest—nicely complementing my own as a teacher at an urban community college. He also brings his experiences as the father of two boys, complementing mine as the mother of four girls. All told, I believe our collaboration on this edition has resulted in a deeper and more inclusive view of the developing child than that in any of the previous editions.

Kathleen Stassen Berger

The Present Edition

As developmentalists and coauthors, we share a deep respect for children and for the families, educators, and communities who nurture them. Equally, we share an abiding commitment to teaching and communicating the latest scientific understanding of human growth and development in a way that is accessible and relevant to students. Given our mutual interests, goals, and vision of the field, it was inevitable that we would see eye to eye on the major changes that needed to be made for this edition. Consequently, much of our effort has been devoted to expanding and strengthening the contextual perspective on development. Between the first edition and this one, a sea change has occurred in the study of human development, with the old debate between nature and nurture being dramatically, and sometimes stormily, recast. As scientists have come to realize that genetic influences play a far more extensive role in human development than had previously been thought, so too have they recognized the crucial importance of the specific environmental contexts in which human development occurs. Developmentalists now view the interaction between heredity and environment as intensely dynamic and fascinatingly diverse, an ever changing constellation of influences that affect each person differently.

Thus, while the focus in this edition, as always, is on the developing individual, more explicit attention is now called to the rich and powerful panoply of biological, political, and social forces—from the protein codes of the DNA molecule to far-reaching shifts in the world economy—that affect each person's development. Most especially, we focus on the ways children's growth is affected by the opportunities and challenges presented by their key surrounding contexts—the family, the school, and the community.

Throughout this edition, you will see the deeper insights gained from this heightened contextual perspective, insights evident in areas ranging from the implications that parent-infant attachment has for later development to the social sensitivities of children as young as age 2, the impact of cultural differences regarding the disciplining of children, the links between family structure and developmental outcome, and the effects of various approaches to education. Further, our deeper cross-cultural and cross-historical perspective has led us to devote more attention in this edition to some of the controversial social issues of our time, such as DNA testing, prenatal drug abuse, the effects of day care, maltreated children, the acculturation of immigrant families, and the consequences of poverty. Often an international and cross-cultural perspective reveals that developmental problems commonly associated with such issues are not inevitable and that, once causes are understood and various options are studied, solutions emerge. In addition to the regular text discussion, a new feature, Public Policy boxes, has been added to highlight certain of these contextual issues.

A second major shift in this edition is in the depiction of cognitive growth, especially that of the infant and the preschooler. Whereas Jean Piaget's insightful formulations were once the mainstay of developmentalists' understanding of early cognitive growth, over the past decade an explosion of research and theory has revealed that young children possess many cognitive capacities that Piaget, because of the limited research methods and cultural perspective of his time, was unaware of. Infants' perceptual concepts and memory capacities, and preschoolers' theory of mind, social reasoning, number abilities, and problem-solving potential, are all, quite properly, foremost in any current presentation of infant or child thinking. Accordingly, each of the cognitive chapters in this edition begins with current research on the child's intellectual potential, and Piagetian theory is seen within a wider view provided by insights from information-processing and sociocultural theory. The emphasis is thus more on what children *can* do cognitively, given the appropriate materials and encouragement, and less on the traditional depiction of what they cannot yet understand.

Finally, with increased attention to context and to children's cognitive potential has come a third shift: an appreciation, much deeper and more thrilling than ever before, of learning as an interactive, social process. As developmentalists have gained access to the work of Lev Vygotsky, a Russian psychologist who was a contemporary of Piaget and Freud, as well as to cross-cultural research from around the globe, they have developed a fuller appreciation of the role of "guided participation," the apprenticeship process through which children acquire the skills, customs, and values of their culture. This apprenticeship process is given particular attention as we explore such topics as the various ways in which parents foster language development and problem-solving skills in their young offspring, the peer interactions through which children develop social skills, and the specific educational practices that bring out the excitement of learning. True to Vygotsky, we emphasize the individual learner's active participation in eliciting and shaping his or her social and academic education.

The interactive nature of the learning process is also reflected in this text overall. We have sought to make this textbook an accessible learning tool and a continual prompt to critical thinking. Controversies are discussed not with moral conclusions or "correct" values but in all the complexity that available space allows, encouraging readers to strive for objectivity in their assessments and to be ever alert to the potential for bias, distortion, and confounding factors in their reasoning. Current research is explained not as received wisdom but as refined possibility, charged with the excitement of new discoveries yet to come. Here is a sample of some of the current and controversial topics, new or expanded, in this edition:

> the Human Genome Project and the implications of genetic engineering/mandated prenatal care for drug abusers/bilingual, bicultural education/ability tracking within elementary schools/blood-lead levels and intelligence/the effects of family structure, including single-parent and blended families/the effects of spanking as a discipline technique/the reliability of children as eyewitnesses/what IQ tests really measure/drug treatment for attention-deficit hyperactivity disorder/ the effects of maternal employment on infants/long-term effects of breast-feeding/autism as a developmental disorder/the relationship between brain maturation and cognitive abilities/contrasts between fathers' and mothers' care/the scientific achievement of East Asian students/cultural differences in what constitutes child abuse/the troubles of, and help for, the rejected child/the advantages and disadvantages of the only-child/long-term implications of low birthweight/special problems of homeless children/injury control and overprotection/ insights from developmental psychopathology/ prevention of AIDS in newborns/the genetics and social contexts of schizophrenia, alcoholism, and other illnesses/new views on the

causes of dyslexia/risks and precautions for sudden infant death syndrome/young children's "hidden" memory abilities

In a number of important ways, the book remains unchanged, including its basic organization. Two introductory chapters, one on the goals, definitions, and methodology of developmental study and one on four major theories, are followed by four parts that correspond to the four major periods of child development—the prenatal period, infancy, early childhood, and middle childhood. With the exception of the prenatal section, each part consists of a trio of chapters dealing with, respectively, biosocial development, cognitive development, and psychosocial development. This topical organization within a chronological framework fosters students' appreciation of how the various aspects of development are interrelated—of how body, mind, and personality develop through interaction rather than separately. In this edition, we have also made a concerted effort to more tightly integrate our discussion of development in the three domains, and we have presented more extensive reiterations of, and comparisons between, development at different ages. The net result, we hope, is that students will have a sense of actually seeing the developing person growing before their eyes.

The pedagogical aids have also been retained. Thus, at the end of each chapter there is a chapter summary, a list of key terms (along with page numbers indicating where the term was introduced), and a series of key questions for reviewing important concepts. At the end of each part there is a full-page chart that provides an overview of the significant biosocial, cognitive, and psychosocial events covered in that part. A comprehensive glossary at the back of the book lists all the key terms in the text, along with the page number for each term's initial use. One important new pedagogical aid is the addition of an on-page glossary, with definitions of key terms occurring in the margin of the page on which the terms first appear.

Supplementary Materials

The new *Study Guide* by Richard Straub (University of Michigan, Dearborn) and Joan Winer Brown uses the *PPTR: Preview/Read/Think Critically/Review* format to guide students at each step of their study. Each chapter includes a review of the key concepts, guided study questions, and section reviews that make students active participants in the learning process. Two practice tests and a challenge test of multiple-choice, true/false, and matching questions help students to determine their degree of mastery of the material. The correct answers to test questions are explained to ensure understanding. The study guide is also computerized in a highly interactive program for use on IBM PC and Macintosh computers.

Each chapter of the *Instructor's Resources* by Richard Straub features a chapter preview and lecture guide, learning objectives, lecture/discussion/debate topics, handouts for group and individual student projects, and supplementary readings from journal articles with introductions and questions. The general resources include course planning suggestions, ideas for term projects, including observational activities, and a guide to commercially available audiovisual materials.

A set of acetate transparencies of key illustrations, charts, tables, and summary information from the textbook is available to adopters.

An extensive *Test Bank,* revised by Carolyn Meyer (Lake Sumter Community College) includes approximately 80 multiple-choice questions and 50 fill-in, true/false, and essay questions for each chapter. Each question is keyed to the textbook topic and page numbers, and its level of difficulty is noted. The *Test Bank* questions are also available with test-generation systems for IBM PC, Macintosh, and Apple II.

The Authors

Kathleen Stassen Berger: My theoretical roots are diverse. My graduate-school mentors included gifted teachers who studied directly with Erik Erikson, B. F. Skinner, and Jean Piaget, and I continue to have great respect for each of these theorists. However, like most developmentalists today, my overall approach is eclectic, influenced by all the theories rather than adhering to any one. The abiding influence of my academic study and training is in my respect for knowledge attained through the scientific method: I believe that the more we know about development, the better we can help all people fulfill their potential.

As great an influence on my thinking as those who have taught me have been those whom I have taught, for my students have had a powerful effect on how I interpret and envision the material I study and write about. I have taught at a variety of institutions, ranging from the United Nations High School to Fordham University Graduate School to Sing Sing Prison, and I have been a member of the psychology department at Bronx Community College of the City University of New York for the past twenty years. My students have come from a great diversity of ethnic, economic, and educational backgrounds, and my work with them and my close observation of their interests and concerns have greatly broadened my own understanding of human development.

Ross A. Thompson: I became a developmental psychologist because I was fascinated by young children, and wanted to understand how their experiences form the foundation for what they become as adults. Having always been interested in the law, my developmental interests are closely united with concerns about how public policies affect children and families. As a graduate student, I studied moral development with Martin Hoffman and was introduced to attachment theory by Michael Lamb, and both scholars (particularly the latter) have continued to influence my thinking and research on parent-child relationships and emotional growth.

My entire professional career has been at the University of Nebraska, where I teach in the Department of Psychology and also in the College of Law and direct research on early attachment, infant cries, and the development of emotional regulation. I have also been Associate Director of the Center on Children, Families, and the Law, where my efforts to apply developmental research to policy problems concerning child maltreatment, grandparent rights, divorce and custody, and family support programs have been nurtured. I have enjoyed editing a major research journal, collaborating with international scholars, and reviewing research grant proposals—but most all, I enjoy teaching undergraduates, who continue to surprise me with the perspectives and applications they bring to their interests in psychology and human development.

Thanks

This book has benefited from the work of the entire community of scholars involved in human development. We have learned much from conferences, journals, and conversations with fellow developmentalists. Of course, we are particularly indebted to the many academic reviewers who have read various drafts of this book in each edition, providing suggestions, criticism, references, and encouragement. Each of them has made the book a better one, and we thank them all. We especially wish to thank those who reviewed this new edition or offered suggestions for its improvement:

Susan Barrett, *Lehigh University*

Judith Bernhard, *Ryerson Polytechnic University*

Lois Bloom, *Columbia University, Teacher's College*

Angela Pratts Buchanan, *DeAnza College*

Lily Chu, *New Mexico State University*

E. Mark Cummings, *West Virginia University*

Peggy A. DeCooke, *State University of New York at Purchase*

Judy DeLoache, *University of Illinois at Urbana-Champaign*

Gene V. Elliott, *Rowan College of New Jersey*

Jeffrey Fagen, *St. John's University*

Beverly I. Fagot, *University of Oregon*

Hill Goldsmith, *University of Wisconsin, Madison*

Jan V. Goodsitt, *Minnesota School of Professional Psychology*

George W. Holden, *University of Texas at Austin*

Shelley Hymel, *University of British Columbia*

Russell A. Isabella, *University of Utah*

Philip Mohan, *University of Idaho*

David Moshman, *University of Nebraska at Lincoln*

Scott Paris, *University of Michigan*

Susan A. Rose, *Albert Einstein College of Medicine*

Anita Miller Sostek, *National Institutes of Health*

Linda A. Stoner, *San Joaquin Delta College*

Douglas Teti, *University of Maryland*

Laura A. Thompson, *New Mexico State University*

Mary Trepanier-Street, *University of Michigan at Dearborn*

The editorial, production, and marketing people at Worth Publishers are dedicated to meeting the highest standards of excellence. Their devotion of time, effort, and talent to every aspect of publishing is a model for the industry. We especially appreciate the efforts of the production staff, and of Toni Ann Scaramuzzo, the production editor, who are responsible for the high quality of the book's appearance. We are also very much indebted to Barbara Anne Seixas for her heroic efforts to keep this book on schedule, to Laura Rubin for her smooth and skillful management of the reviewing process, and to Alana Trafford for her dedicated editorial assistance.

Dedication

In many ways that should be readily apparent, the collaboration between us has been a rewarding experience that has resulted in a better book. However, true joint authorship also entails complications, as the efforts of two headstrong individuals, each contributing the full force of his or her own perspective, knowledge, and style must be brought together in such a way that their shared creation shows none of the disjointed or contradictory strains that naturally occur. The final product must be both smooth and strong, consistent but not watered-down. The secret behind the seamless integrity of our work is our editor, Peter Deane, who has been an integral part of every page of every edition of this book, maintaining his perseverance, brilliance, creativity, and humor throughout. This edition taxed all those qualities and called forth another, wisdom. For all those reasons, we dedicate this 4th edition to him. Thank you, Peter.

Kathleen Stassen Berger
Ross A. Thompson
January, 1995

The Developing Person

Through Childhood

Introduction

You are about to begin a fascinating journey through the study of human development. To help prepare you for this journey—which explores development from the moment of conception to the threshold of adulthood—Chapter 1 will serve as a kind of roadmap, outlining your route and familiarizing you with the general terrain. More specifically, it will introduce you to the goals, values, and methods that are involved in the scientific study of human development and suggest some of the practical applications that developmental study can produce. Among the questions this chapter addresses are the following:

What are the primary concerns and goals of developmental scientists?

What innate and environmental factors help shape an individual's ongoing development?

What is the relationship between development in the early stages of life and development in later years?

How do variations in cultural context, socioeconomic status, and historical setting affect the course of development?

What methods and strategies do researchers use to ensure that their findings are as valid and objective as possible?

What ethical values guide the study of human development?

We would like to begin our journey into the study of human development with an unusual personal story. It involves a young man named David, the nephew of Professor Berger.

In many ways, David's childhood and adolescence were typical: he had a family that cared for him from the moment he was born; schools and teachers that brought out his best, and sometimes his worst; and a social life with peers and the community that gave him both joy and pain. David is now in his final year of college, and, in some respects, he is similar to many of you. After a struggle in his freshman year, he has settled down to become a serious student, earning a 3.7 grade point average this past semester and gaining mastery of two foreign languages, Russian and German. He is also deeply intrigued by politics and will eagerly debate current issues with anyone. Like a few of you, he is a late-bloomer socially: he is self-conscious about his appearance (he is slight of build and must wear thick glasses), and he has yet to develop a serious romantic relationship, although he wishes it were otherwise. In certain essential facts of his life, then, David is not unlike many members of his generation.

In one very basic way, however, David's development is far from typical. He began life severely handicapped, with little hope for survival, let alone for a life approaching normality. His childhood and adolescence were filled with harsh, often heartbreaking obstacles to normal development, and he still struggles against unusual odds as his life unfolds.

Most of this book is, of course, about "normal" development—that is, the usual patterns of growth and change that everyone follows to some degree and that no one follows exactly. But in this chapter we will examine David's unusual story for two reasons.

First, David's struggles and triumphs offer a poignant illustration of the underlying goal of developmental study: to help each person develop throughout life as fully as possible.

Second, David's example illuminates, with unusual vividness, the basic definitions and central questions that frame the study of human development. Just as suddenly being thrust into an unfamiliar culture can help us see more clearly our own daily routines, habits, and assumptions, which we tend to overlook precisely because they are so familiar, so, too, can David's story highlight the major factors that influence more typical human development. Let us begin, then, with a brief look at those definitions and questions that underlie the study of human development, and then return to David's story.

The Study of Human Development

Briefly, *the study of human development explores how and why people change as they grow older and how and why they remain the same.*

Developmental scientists examine all kinds of change—simple growth, radical transformation, improvement, and decline—and all sources of continuity from one day, year, or generation to the next. They consider everything from the genetic codes that lay down the foundations of growth to the countless environmental factors that shape development. And they examine all these factors—and untold others—in light of the ever-changing social and cultural contexts that give them meaning and force. The study of human development thus involves many academic disciplines, especially biology, education, and psychology, but also history, sociology, anthropology, medicine, economics, and subspecialties such as developmental genetics, public health, developmental psychopathology, and demography.

The study of human development covers the entire life span—from conception until death—because people change every moment they are alive. But most developmentalists focus, as this text does, on the years leading to adulthood. The reason is obvious: during the first two decades of life, growth and change in every area are at their most dramatic and distinctive, forming the foundation for lifelong development.

Developmentalists study two quite different sets of changes: age-typical developments—changes that most people experience in a predictable manner after a certain amount of maturation; and individual developments—often atypical and idiosyncratic changes that make each life unique. They seek to understand, for instance, how most infants learn to crawl and why some babies never do; how most 5-year-olds painstakingly sound out a written word or two and why some 5-year-olds already read fluently; how almost all 10-year-olds master the social skills they need to make friends and why some 10-year-olds are unusually popular, or isolated, or rejected. Both the general patterns of development and the many exceptions and variations to those patterns are part of our developmental study.

The Three Domains

To make it easier to undertake this vast interdisciplinary study of developmental change, human development is often separated into three domains: the **biosocial domain**, including brain and body changes and the social influences that guide them; the **cognitive domain**, including thought processes, perceptual abilities, and language mastery, as well as the educational institutions that encourage them; and the **psychosocial domain**, including emotions, personality, and interpersonal relationships, and the complex social contexts in which they occur.

FIGURE 1.1 Every aspect of human behavior reflects all three domains. Obviously biosocial factors—such as hormones and body strength—are at work here, but so are cognitive and psychosocial ones. For instance, each student's mental concentration or lack of it is critical to karate success, as is the culture's message about who should learn the marital arts, a message that seems to have made this a nearly all-male class.

biosocial domain Includes physical growth and development as well as the family, community, and cultural factors that affect that growth and development.

cognitive domain Includes all the mental processes through which the individual thinks, learns, and communicates.

psychosocial domain Includes emotions, personality characteristics, and relationships with other people.

All three domains are important at every age. For instance, understanding an infant involves studying his or her health, curiosity, and temperament, as well as dozens of other aspects of biosocial, cognitive, and psychosocial development. Similarly, to understand an adolescent, we consider physical changes that mark the bodily transition from child to adult; intellectual development that leads to efforts to think logically about such issues as sexual passion and future goals; and the emerging patterns of friendship and courtship that prepare for the intimate relationships of adulthood.

FIGURE 1.2 The division of development into three domains makes it easier to study, but we must remember that very few factors belong exclusively to one domain or another. Development is not piecemeal but holistic: each aspect of development is related to all three domains.

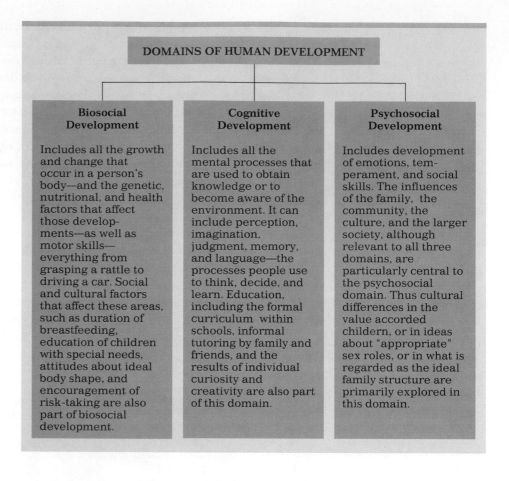

DOMAINS OF HUMAN DEVELOPMENT

Biosocial Development	Cognitive Development	Psychosocial Development
Includes all the growth and change that occur in a person's body—and the genetic, nutritional, and health factors that affect those developments—as well as motor skills—everything from grasping a rattle to driving a car. Social and cultural factors that affect these areas, such as duration of breastfeeding, education of children with special needs, attitudes about ideal body shape, and encouragement of risk-taking are also part of biosocial development.	Includes all the mental processes that are used to obtain knowledge or to become aware of the environment. It can include perception, imagination, judgment, memory, and language—the processes people use to think, decide, and learn. Education, including the formal curriculum within schools, informal tutoring by family and friends, and the results of individual curiosity and creativity are also part of this domain.	Includes development of emotions, temperament, and social skills. The influences of the family, the community, the culture, and the larger society, although relevant to all three domains, are particularly central to the psychosocial domain. Thus cultural differences in the value accorded childern, or in ideas about "appropriate" sex roles, or in what is regarded as the ideal family structure are primarily explored in this domain.

Inevitably, each domain is affected by the other two: whether or not an infant is well-nourished, for instance, may well affect the baby's learning ability and social experiences. For many adolescents, their perception of their bodies—the way they *think* their bodies look—affects their eating and exercise habits, and these, in turn, affect their physical health and their emotional and social development.

The Many Contexts of Development

We often think of development as originating *within* the individual—the result of such internal factors as genetic programming, physical maturation, cognitive growth, and personal choices. However, development is also greatly influenced by forces *outside* the individual, by the physical surroundings and social interactions that provide incentives, opportunities, and pathways for growth. Taken as a whole, these external forces are the *context* of development.

Describing these external influences more than twenty-five years ago, Urie Bronfenbrenner, a leading developmental researcher, began to emphasize what he calls an **ecological approach** to the study of human development (Bronfenbrenner, 1977, 1979, 1986). Just as a naturalist studying a flower or a fish needs to examine the organism's supporting ecosystems, Bronfenbrenner argues, developmentalists need to study the ecological systems, or contexts, in which each human being seeks to thrive.

ecological approach A perspective on development that takes into account the various physical and social settings in which development occurs.

Bronfenbrenner's ecological model of human development is depicted in Figure 1.3, which organizes the broad contexts of development in terms of the relative immediacy of their impact. At the center of this model is the individual. Each immediate social setting that surrounds and shapes that individual is called a *microsystem*. Examples of microsystems include the family, the peer group, the classroom, the workplace, and so on. The *mesosystem* is the connections between various microsystems—such as parent-teacher conferences that link home and school. Next comes the *exosystem*, the specific economic, political, educational, and cultural institutions and practices that directly affect the various microsystems, and, in so doing, indirectly, but often powerfully, affect everyone in those microsystems. Surrounding and permeating all these developmental contexts is the *macrosystem*, the overarching traditions, beliefs, and values of the society.

FIGURE 1.3 Each person is significantly affected by interactions between and among a number of overlapping ecosystems. Microsystems are those social systems that intimately and immediately shape human development. For a typical child, the primary microsystems include the family, the classroom, and the neighborhood peer group, and sometimes a church, temple, or mosque as well. The specific interaction between the social systems takes place through the mesosystem, as when parents and teachers coordinate their efforts to educate the child. Surrounding the microsystems is the exosystem, which includes all those external networks, such as the community structures and the local educational, medical, employment, and communications systems, that influence the microsystems. And influencing the entire process on a grand scale is the macrosystem, which includes the overarching cultural values, political philosophies, economic patterns, and social conditions that affect all the other systems.

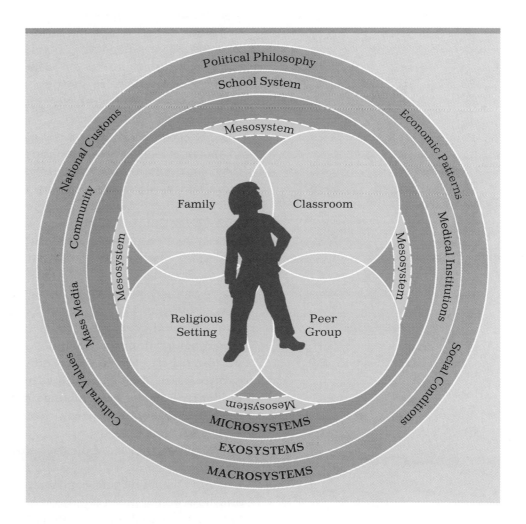

The influences within and between these systems are multidirectional and interactive. For example, research has shown that the quality of life in the family microsystem directly affects a worker's productivity on the job. At the same time, the microsystem of the workplace—specifically the stresses and satisfactions at the office, store, factory, or farm—affects the quality of life at home, including how satisfied a couple is with their marriage and how responsive they are to their children (Greenberger & Goldberg, 1989; Hoffman, 1989; Zedek, 1992). These reciprocal interactions between home and work are also affected by factors in the surrounding exosystem and macrosystem. In North America, for example, hard work and pioneer self-sufficiency are bedrock values, and for most Americans, being productive and independent is key to their sense of self-worth. Consequently, if the family breadwinner loses a job, that loss may affect family life not only through the financial strain it causes but also through the psychological stress it creates. This link among systems is dramatically reflected during times of economic recession: as unemployment in a community increases, domestic violence and divorce typically increase as well (Dooley & Catalano, 1988).

Bronfenbrenner's ecological approach to development is very useful in highlighting the complex influences, both immediate and distant, on any one person's development. However, it has been the authors' experience that Bronfenbrenner's terminology, and his depiction of spheres of influence, nested one inside the other, often lead students to think of these ecosystems as discrete entities, with clear boundaries between them—when, in fact, the various systems are inextricably intermeshed, their effects dynamic, fluid, and overlapping.

To avoid this confusion, we have chosen to use the term **social context** to encompass all the ecosystems delineated by Bronfenbrenner. We will thus focus on the many specific contexts of development without trying to locate them specifically within a given ecosystem. Bear in mind, however, that whatever the nomenclature—contexts or systems—the core concept is the same: every individual develops within, is influenced by, and in turn influences, the dynamic relationships that exist among many interlocking social settings.

An Example: The Family in Social Context

The critical importance of the overall social context is, of course, obvious throughout childhood. A newborn baby could not survive, even for a day, without nurture from others, and young children do not learn to talk, or to express affection, or even to care for themselves without years of social guidance from parents, siblings, teachers, and friends. However, in our everyday thinking, the dynamic complexity of each social system sometimes eludes us.

Consider, for example, the most basic social context, the family. Universally, the family context is the primary setting for nurturing children to become competent and contributing members of society. In what manner, and how well, a given family does this, depend on a wide array of factors. Some of these factors are rooted directly in the specific family setting—from the number and age of children, parents, and other adults in the family to the emotional climate the interactions of these individuals create. Each family relationship (such as that between husband and wife, parent and child, brother and sister, spouse and in-law) affects all the other family members, and all these relationships are mutually influential, affecting everyone involved.

social context The entire spectrum of social milieux—including the people, the customs, and the beliefs—that surround each developing person.

FIGURE 1.4 The influence of the social context on the family is sometimes most apparent in families who are potentially vulnerable to unusual stress. The nature of the relationship between a single mother and her child, for example, depends not just on the interaction between them but also on such factors as the financial and emotional support of the father, the encouragement of grandparents and other relatives, the positive and negative effects of the school and the workplace, and the attitude of the community (which now accepts single motherhood much more than thirty years ago).

Some of the factors influencing family relationships are less immediate, such as the values of the community regarding gender roles, or the ways in which the structure of the neighborhood institutions might affect family functioning, or the past and current experiences of the grandparents, who, in turn, are influenced by the customs and core beliefs of earlier times. While universally the family is the basic setting for intimacy and growth, the complexity of contexts and histories that affect each family makes the family one of the most varied institutions on earth (Altergott, 1993).

A "Difficult" Child

To sharpen our focus a bit, let us look at the contextual interactions of the family in the case of a young boy who is "difficult"—disobedient, hostile, demanding, impulsive. A noncontextual approach to this problem behavior might focus on the mother, finding her to be self-absorbed, or cold, or indulgent. Such an explanation would be flawed, however, because it is one-dimensional. As a leading family therapist explains:

> It may be relatively easy to discover that a little boy who misbehaves in school has a mother who doesn't make him behave at home. On closer examination we might see that she doesn't discipline the boy because she is overly involved with him. They're constantly together and interact more like playmates than parent and child. But why is the mother so close to the boy? Why does she need a playmate? Is it because she's emotionally distant from her husband? . . . Perhaps she is deliberately lenient with the boy to counterbalance her husband's overly harsh control. The reason so many family dilemmas defeat us is that we fail to recognize that every family member's behavior is influencing and influenced by the behavior of the rest. [Minuchin, 1993]

Increasingly, developmentalists recognize that not only the nature of the marital relationship but also such factors as the father's involvement in caregiving and the rivalries and tensions of the other siblings are implicated in the child's behavior. And of course, the child, too, is a central player. In the case of the difficult child, the mother's apparent caregiving flaws might be the *result* of the child's intractable behavior more than the *cause* of it. Thus, when considering development within the family setting, the contextual approach attempts to consider the totality of family interactions, with each family member likely to be both "a victim and an architect" of whatever problems the family might have (Patterson, 1982; Patterson & Capaldi, 1991).

A contextual view does not stop there, however, for just as each family member is affected by the interactions of all its members, each family is reciprocally influenced by other social contexts (Bronfenbrenner, 1986). As already noted, the stresses and satisfactions of the workplace can have a significant impact on family interactions. Whether the difficult child's parents feel secure and fulfilled in their work or anxious and frustrated can obviously affect the quality of attention they give their son, as well as their tolerance for certain of his disruptive antics.

Other relevant influences can be found in the contexts of the peer group and the school. The difficult child's friends, for example, may admire and thus encourage his unruly behavior, while the school's demand for obedience and conformity may create tensions that spill out at home. Of course, the influences of these contexts could also be positive: the peer group might provide a setting in which the child learns needed social skills, and the school might provide avenues of success in the classroom or the playground that enhance self-esteem, thus mitigating the child's hostility.

Typically, the contexts of peer group and school affect the family only indirectly, through their influence on the behavior of the child. Sometimes, however, these other contexts have a direct impact on the family. For example, if the parents come to see that their son is actually less rowdy than most of the neighborhood boys, or if they hear from a teacher that he is unusually creative, their perceptions of the boy may change, as they come to appreciate certain of his behaviors that once made them angry.

The same multicontextual, multidirectional analysis could be applied to almost any specific behavior in almost any developing person. In every case, the individual's actions are both cause and consequence of the social context in which development occurs.

As you might imagine, it is impossible to consider simultaneously all the contextual factors that can have an impact at any given moment for any developing person. Mindful of this complexity, we will, throughout the book, primarily focus on several contexts that developmentalists have found to be most influential in patterning a life. In addition to the more obvious contexts we have already mentioned, such as family and school, recent research has highlighted four broad contexts that we will preview here.

The Historical Context

In every era, prevailing assumptions, critical public events, current technologies, and popular trends shape the lives and thoughts of individuals living in that time period. If your attitudes about hard work and job security, or the relative importance of money in the bank and independence in one's personal life, are quite different from those of your parents or grandparents, for instance, one reason is that such attitudes are affected by the economic and social picture that existed when a person first reached adulthood—whether that was during the Great Depression of the 1930s, the affluent 1950s, or the more financially troubled 1990s.

Research into the historical context reveals not only that profound economic, political, and technological changes occur over the years, but that even basic concepts about how things "should be" are readily influenced by the times. Often one or another of our most cherished assumptions is, in fact, a *social construction,* that is, an idea built more on shared perceptions of the members of a society than on objective reality. The obligations of women to be docile housewives and of men to be strong and independent are two obvious examples of social constructions that, in many cultures and contexts, have lost their consensus in recent times.

Even the most basic ideas about patterns of development change. For example, most readers of this book probably take it for granted that children have some legal rights, including protection from physical labor and harsh punishment, as well as access to nourishing food, nurturing love, and formal education. Taking an historical view, however, it seems clear that these are relatively recent ideas, and that, before they took hold, the daily life of a great many children in the Western world was, by current standards, often brutal. Physical beatings were a routine part of child-rearing, and many children, especially from poorer families, worked at "adult" jobs that were often dangerous. And through all this no one—neighbor, social worker, or police officer—believed he or she had the right to interfere. This was reflected in the law of the land: the first legal requirement that all children should have at least a basic education was not enacted in the United States until the late nineteenth century, and laws prohibiting child abuse and child labor came even later, appearing only about eighty years ago (Pizzo, 1983; Takanishi, 1978).

In fact, the very concept of *childhood* as we know it, that is, as a special and extended stage of life, is a social construction that was virtually nonexistent throughout much of history. In many historical contexts, children were cared for until they could take care of themselves (at about age 7) and then they entered the adult world, working in the fields or at home, and spending their leisure time engaged in the activities of grownups.

Likewise, the notion of *adolescence*—as a period between childhood and adulthood when teenagers rebel against authorities, unite with their peers, and seek their own identities—is largely a social construction that is the product of the past fifty years (Boxer et al., 1984).

In societies characterized by rapid social change, each new **cohort**—defined as all those persons born within a few years of each other—grows up within a context of inventions and ideas unlike that of earlier cohorts. In fact, the specific behaviors expected of teenagers—from matters of musical taste and hairstyle to more serious concerns about their relationship with the adult world—change with every generation, a transformation much more apparent to the young person experiencing it than to the older generations witnessing it. When a 15-year-old rejects advice from a 30-year-old with words such as "You don't understand, everything is different now," there is more than a grain of truth in this retort.

Similarly, the current cohort of school-age children is affected by television, computer technologies, firearms violence, and the consumer culture in ways that their grandparents and sometimes even their parents never experienced. Indeed, because today's current events quickly become tomorrow's history, your own children—who will no doubt be veteran voyagers through cyberspace and virtual reality—will undoubtedly listen to stories of your childhood with wonder and amusement. And you will learn from them even as you wax nostalgic over "the good old days" of the 1990s.

FIGURE 1.5 The current view of childhood as a special period given over to formal education and play is a fairly recent one. As late as 1900, one out of every five children between the ages of 10 and 16 in the United States worked, often at dirty and dangerous jobs in factories, mills, and mines. These breaker boys, who usually started their work at age 10, had the task of picking out slate and rubble from crushed coal as it came down shutes from giant processors. Their hours were long; their environment was choked with coal dust; and their pay was less than a dollar a day.

cohort A group of people who, because they were born within a few years of each other, experience many of the same historical and social conditions.

The Cultural Context

As we shall see in the chapters that follow, the cultural context also provides direction and meaning to a person's developmental path. When social scientists use the term **culture**, they refer to the set of values, assumptions, and customs, as well as the physical objects—everything from clothing, dwellings, and cuisine to technologies and works of art—that a group of people have developed over the years *as a design for living* to structure their life together.

When we look closely at the impact of the cultural context on child development, it becomes clear that culture guides child-rearing practices and goals in a multitude of interrelated ways, setting guidelines for what and when to feed children, how strictly and for what misdeeds to discipline them, what toys and educational experiences to provide them, what values and skills to teach them, and so on. Overall, these customs prepare children for their roles as adults. Some cultures, for example, prescribe distinct gender-related child-rearing—such that a boy would never be given a doll and a girl would never be dressed in pants. In effect, such gender restrictions in childhood serve to socialize children into patterns of gender segregation that pervade the culture, not only in work and family roles, but in sexual behavior, access to education, religious worship, and so on (Whiting & Edwards, 1988; Triandis, 1994).

FIGURE 1.6 One obvious way cultures differ is in the activities and objects—toys, artifacts, living things—they make available to their young, as suggested by these roller-bladers in the United States and these shepherds in Lesotho, South Africa. Spending daily leisure time speeding down a street with the latest thrill-producing possessions may foster quite different values and expectations in children than spending "leisure time" sharing in the responsibility of tending the family flocks. However, speculations about the specific developmental effects of such cultural differences need the confirmation of scientific research.

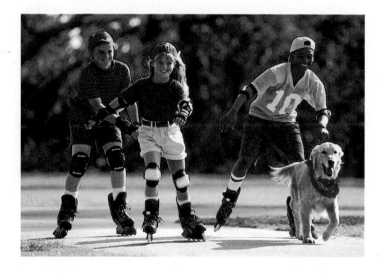 

Understanding the cultural context of human development requires much more than marveling at cultural differences in children and their care. It involves an understanding of how specific practices arise from deeper values and traditions, which, in turn, are part of the entire overall social context.

Here is an example. Robert LeVine (1980, 1988) has noted that in many developing agricultural communities, children are an economic asset because they can contribute to the family's farming and, later, to forming a strong family unit to preserve the family land and to caring for aging parents. Thus, every child who survives to adulthood benefits the entire family group. But in many of these communities, nutrition and medical care are

culture The set of shared values, attitudes, customs, and physical objects that are maintained by people in a specific setting as part of a design for living one's daily life.

poor, leading to high mortality rates, particularly among young children. Therefore child-rearing is designed to maximize survival and emphasize family cooperation: its typical features include intensive physical care, feeding on demand, immediate response to crying, close body contact, and constant care by siblings and other relatives as well as by the mother. All these measures protect the fragile infant from an early death, and work to establish such values as the interdependence of family members.

By contrast, according to LeVine, American middle-class parents do not have to be so concerned about infant mortality. Instead, hoping to ensure their children's future success in a technological and urbanized society, they focus their child-rearing efforts on fostering emotional independence and cognitive growth. Middle-class American parents thus emphasize individual accomplishments and self-sufficiency through child-rearing practices such as cognitive and social stimulation, talking to their infants more than touching them, having them sleep by themselves in their own cribs in their own rooms, and teaching tolerance of frustration by scheduling meal and sleep times. Not surprisingly, these contrasting parental strategies produce children with quite different capacities, goals, and expectations, but in both cases, the children become relatively well-prepared for the culture in which they have been raised.

The Ethnic Context

An **ethnic group** is a collection of people who share certain attributes, such as ancestry, national origin, religion, and/or language and, as a result, tend to identify with each other and have similar daily encounters with the social world. Racial identity is sometimes an element of ethnicity, but as social scientists emphatically point out, biological tendencies (such as hair or skin coloring, facial features, and body type) that distinguish one "race" from another are much less significant to development than the sense of common identity—and the attitudes and experiences resulting from minority or majority status—that may arise from ethnic or racial consciousness.

Ethnicity is similar to culture, in that it provides people with shared beliefs, values, and assumptions that can significantly affect their own development as well as how they raise their children. Indeed, sometimes ethnicity and culture overlap. However, people of many ethnic groups can all share one culture, yet maintain their ethnic identities. Within multiethnic cultures, such as those found in most large nations today, ethnic differences are most apparent in matters such as whether children are raised in large extended families or smaller nuclear families; whether they are encouraged toward independence, dependence, or interdependence; whether they view education as all-important or as secondary to social obligations; whether they defer to family elders or assert their autonomy; as well as in many other beliefs, values, and behaviors (Harrison et al., 1990).

The Socioeconomic Context

A fourth major contextual influence on development is **socioeconomic status**, sometimes called "social class" (as in "middle class" or "underclass"). Socioeconomic status, abbreviated as **SES**, is most accurately measured through a combination of several overlapping variables, including income,

ethnic group A collection of people who share certain background characteristics, such as national origin, religion, upbringing, and language, and who, as a result, tend to have similar beliefs, values, and cultural experiences.

socioeconomic status (SES) An indicator of social class that is based primarily on income, education, and occupation.

education, residence, and occupation. As measured by social scientists, then, the SES of a family consisting of an infant, a full-time mother, and an employed father who earns $10,000 a year could be either lower or middle class, depending on whether the household head is an illiterate dishwasher living in an urban slum or a graduate student living on campus and teaching part-time. The point of the distinction between these cases, as should be obvious, is not just financial: it entails *all* the advantages and disadvantages, opportunities and limitations, that may be associated with either status. Social class is as much a product of the mind as of the wallet.

Nonetheless, in official government statistics, SES is often measured solely by family income (adjusted for inflation and family size). For example, in 1994 in the United States, a family of four with an annual income under about $15,000 was considered to have the lowest SES, below the poverty level.

Looking only at family income is simplistic, but nevertheless useful, especially when children from low-income families are concerned. The reason is that inadequate family income both signals and creates a social context of limited opportunities and heightened pressures that conspire to make growing up much more difficult than it is higher up on the socioeconomic ladder (Huston et al., 1994). For example, infant mortality, child neglect, and adolescent violence are each much more common among the poor than among the nonpoor. Further, partly in response to the stresses in their own lives, especially those associated with the dangers and fears of inner-city life, parents of low SES tend to raise their children differently than do parents of higher SES—employing stricter emphasis on obedience, more physical punishment, and less encouragement of imagination and verbal expressiveness (McLoyd, 1990; Hashima & Amato, 1994).

The Individual and the Social Context

Since each individual develops within many contexts, it is obviously important to understand the special impact that each context has. But it is also important to be cautious about any explanations of personality traits, abilities, or actions that link individual behavior exclusively to any one of these contexts. As the lead article in a recent issue of *The American Psychologist* emphasizes,

> scientists should think carefully about the group of interest, whether it be cultural, racial, ethnic, or social, and go beyond the group category to the specific factors that underlie the group category. By doing so, studies will be able to identify what about culture, race, ethnicity, or social class is related to the psychological phenomena of interest. [Betancourt & Lopez, 1993]

When the phenomena of interest are broad patterns of child-rearing, social context is certainly relevant. But when studying any individual's development, it quickly becomes obvious that each of us is often pulled in divergent directions by various contextual influences. In short, no one is exactly like the statistically "average" person of his or her generation, ethnic group, culture, or socioeconomic status. Each of us differs in unexpected ways from any stereotypes or generalities that might seem pertinent, and these individual idiosyncrasies demand as much scientific respect and scrutiny as any of the commonalities that link us to any given group.

Now let us return to David, a person clearly affected by the social contexts that structured and continue to shape his development, yet who is, just as obviously, unique.

David's Story: Domains and Contexts at Work

David's story begins in 1967, with an event that seems clearly from the biosocial domain. In the spring of that year, in Appalachia, an epidemic of rubella (German measles) struck two more victims—David's mother, who had a rash and a sore throat for a couple of days, and her 4-week-old embryo, who was damaged for life. David was born in November, with a life-threatening heart defect and thick cataracts covering both eyes. Other damage caused by the virus became apparent as time went on, including minor malformations of the thumbs, feet, jaw, and teeth, as well as brain injury.

From a contextual perspective, the larger medical and political contexts had already had a major impact, one determined partly by the particular point in historical time at which David entered the world. Had David been conceived a decade later, the development and widespread use of the rubella vaccine would probably have prevented his mother's contracting the disease. On the other hand, had he been born a few years earlier, or in a different part of the world, he would have died, because the medical technology that saved his life would not have been available.

The Early Years: Heartbreaking Handicaps, Slow Progress

As it happened, heart surgery in the first days of life was successful, and it was thought that David would have at least a few years of life. However, surgery to open a channel around one of the cataracts failed, completely blinding that eye.

It soon became apparent that David's physical handicaps were contributing to cognitive and psychosocial liabilities as well. Not only did his blindness make it impossible for him to learn by looking at his world, but his parents overprotected him to the point that he spent almost all his early months in their arms or in his crib. An analysis of the family context would have revealed that David's impact on his family, and their effect on him, were harmful in many unintended ways. Like most parents of seriously impaired infants, David's felt guilt, anger, and despair (Featherstone, 1980), and they were initially unable to make constructive plans to foster David's normal development.

Fortunately, however, David's parents came from a socioeconomic background that encouraged them to seek outside help. The first step occurred when a teacher from the Kentucky School for the Blind visited David's home and gave his parents some much-needed encouragement and advice. They were told to stop blaming themselves for David's condition and to stop overprotecting him because of it. If their son was going to learn about his world, he was going to have to explore it. To this end, they were told that, rather than confining David to a crib or playpen, they should provide him with a large rug for a play area. Whenever he crawled off the rug, they were to say "No" and place him back in the middle of it, thus enabling him to use his sense of touch to learn where he could explore safely without bumping

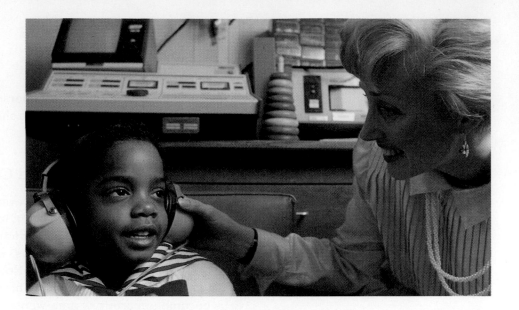

FIGURE 1.7 Today's generation of children have many advantages over earlier generations, especially with regard to technological health benefits. The hearing tests this boy is receiving are far more sophisticated than those even a decade ago, and certain other tests can detect hearing impairments even in infants. When David was a baby, by contrast, hearing tests were such that no one knew how well he could hear until he was about 4 years old.

into walls or furniture. David's mother dedicated herself to this and the many other tasks that various other specialists suggested, including exercising his twisted feet and cradling him frequently in her arms as she sang lullabies to provide extra tactile and auditory stimulation.

His father helped, too, taking over much of the housework and care of the two older boys, who were 2 and 4 at the time. When he found an opportunity to work in Boston, he took it, partly because the Perkins School for the Blind had just begun an experimental program for blind toddlers and their mothers. At Perkins, David's mother learned specific methods for developing physical and language skills in multihandicapped children, and she, in turn, taught the techniques to David's father and brothers. Every day the family spent hours rolling balls, doing puzzles, and singing with David.

Thus, a smooth collaboration between the family and the educational contexts helped young David develop. However, progress was slow. It became painfully apparent that rubella had damaged much more than his eyes and heart. At age 3, David could not talk, nor chew solid food, nor use the toilet, nor coordinate his fingers well, nor even walk normally. An IQ test showed him to be severely mentally retarded. Fortunately, although most children with rubella syndrome have hearing defects, David's hearing was normal. However, the only intelligible sounds he made mimicked the noises of the buses and trucks that passed by the house.

At age 4, David said his first word, "Dada." Open-heart surgery corrected the last of his heart damage, and an operation brought partial vision to his remaining eye. While sight in that eye was far from perfect, David could now recognize his family by sight as well as by sound, and could look at picture books. By age 5, when the family returned to Kentucky, further progress was obvious: he no longer needed diapers or baby food.

David's fifth birthday occurred in 1972, just when the idea that severely handicapped children could be educated in school rather than at home was beginning to take hold. David's parents found four schools that would accept him and enrolled him in all of them. He attended two schools for victims of cerebral palsy: one had morning classes, and the other—forty miles away—afternoon classes. (David ate lunch in the car with his mother on the daily trip.) On Fridays these schools were closed, so he attended a school for the mentally retarded. On Sundays, he spent two hours in church school, his first experience with "mainstreaming"—the then-new idea that children with special needs should be educated with normal children.

Childhood and Adolescence: Heartening Progress

By age 7, David's intellectual development had progressed to the point considered adequate for the normal educational system. In some skills, he was advanced; he could multiply and divide in his head. He entered first grade in a public school, one of the first severely handicapped children to be mainstreamed. However, he was far from being a normal first-grader, for rubella continued to have an obvious impact on his physical, cognitive, and social development. His motor skills were poor (among other things, he had difficulty controlling a pencil); his efforts to learn to read were greatly hampered by the fact that he was legally blind even in his "good" eye; and his social skills were seriously deficient (he pinched people he didn't like and cried and laughed at inappropriate times).

During the next several years, David's cognitive development proceeded rapidly. By age 10, he had skipped a year of school and was a fifth-grader. He could read with a magnifying glass—at the eleventh-grade level—and was labeled "intellectually gifted" according to tests of verbal and math skills. At home he began to learn a second language and to play the violin. In both areas, he proved to have extraordinary auditory acuity and memory.

FIGURE 1.8 The efforts of these Special Olympians reflect not only the thrill of competition but also the satisfaction of having one's abilities and interests recognized and accepted. In a highly competitive society like the United States, being forced to the sidelines by social attitudes can be far more devastating psychologically than the limitations imposed by a particular disability.

David's greatest problem was in the psychosocial domain. Schools generally ignored the social skills of mainstreamed children (Gottlieb & Leyser, 1981), and David's experience was no exception. For instance, David was required to sit on the sidelines during most physical-education classes, and to stay inside during most recess periods. Without a chance to experience the normal give-and-take of schoolyard play, David remained more childish than his years. His classmates were not helped to understand his problems, and some of them teased him because he still looked and acted "different."

Because of David's problems with outsiders and classmates, his parents decided to send him to a special school when he was ready for junior high. In the Kentucky School for the Blind, his physical, cognitive, and psychosocial development all advanced: David learned to wrestle and swim, mastered algebra with large-print books, and made friends whose vision was as bad as his or even worse. For his high school years, David remained at the Kentucky School, where he mastered not only the regular curriculum but also specialized skills, such as how to travel independently in the city and how to cook and clean for himself. In his senior year he was accepted for admission by a large university in his home state.

Looking Back and Looking Forward

Now many of David's worst problems are behind him. In the biosocial domain, he seems certain of a long life, and doctors have helped to improve its quality: an artificial eye has replaced the blind one; a back brace has helped his posture; and surgery has corrected a misaligned jaw, improving his appearance and his speech. In the cognitive domain, the once severely "retarded" preschooler is a bright, articulate college student, who is looking forward to a career as a linguist and translator (an interesting choice for someone who has learned to listen very carefully to what people say because he is unable to read their facial expressions). And in the psychosocial domain, the formerly self-absorbed child is now an outgoing young man, eager for friendship.

This is not to suggest that David's life is all smooth sailing. In fact, every day presents its struggles, and David, like everyone, has his moments of self-doubt and depression. As he once confided:

> I sometimes have extremely pejorative thoughts . . . dreams of vivid symbolism. In one, I am playing on a pinball machine that is all broken—glass besmirched, legs tilted and wobbly, the plunger knob loose. I have to really work at it to get a decent score.

Yet David never loses heart, at least not for long. He continues to "really work" on his life, no matter what, and bit by bit, his "score" improves.

In looking at David's life thus far, we can see how the domains and various social contexts interact to affect development, both positively and negatively. We can also see the importance of research and the application of developmental principles. For example, without research that demonstrated the crucial role of sensory stimulation in infant development, David's parents might not have been taught how to keep his young mind actively learning. Nor would David have been educated in schools had not the previous efforts of hundreds of developmental scientists proved that schools could provide effective teaching even for severely handicapped children. David might instead have led an overly sheltered and restricted life, as many children born with his problems once did. Indeed, many children with David's initial level of disability formerly spent their lives in institutions that provided only custodial care.

David's immediate future will likewise be influenced by various social contexts. Changes in the historical context, for instance, have led to increasing sensitivity to the needs of the disabled: the laws of the land now safeguard the right to a normal life in college, in housing, and in employment. And David will continue to draw love and support from the family context.

However, as he ventures through adulthood, he will need to find his own social world—a difficult task for most young American adults, especially for those who have an unusual life history and appearance.

At the same time that David's story highlights the influence of developmental domains and social contexts, it also serves to remind us of a universal truth: none of us is simply a product of these influences. Each person is a unique individual who uniquely reacts to, and acts upon, the constellation of contexts that impinges on his or her development. Thus the most important factor in David's past successes may have been David himself, for his determination and stoic courage helped him weather the physical trauma of repeated surgery and the psychological devastation of social rejection. Of all those who should be proud of David's accomplishments—including the scientists, teachers, and family members who directly and indirectly contributed to his growth—the one who should be most proud is David himself. More than anyone else, in the final analysis, David, like each of us, directs his own development.

Three Controversies

As David's case makes abundantly clear, the study of development requires taking into account the interplay of the biosocial, cognitive, and psychosocial domains, within a particular historical time, influenced by familial, cultural, ethnic, and economic forces. Not surprisingly, assessing the relative impact of all these factors is no simple matter. In fact, developmentalists often find themselves on one side or another of three controversies that have been debated since the scientific study of human development began.

Nature and Nurture

The central dispute in the study of human development is the nature-nurture controversy. It is the continuing debate over the relative impact of hereditary and environmental influences in shaping various personal traits and characteristics.

Nature refers to the range of traits, capacities, and limitations that each person inherits genetically from his or her parents at the moment of conception. Body type, eye color, and inherited diseases are obvious examples. Nature also includes those largely inherited traits, such as activity level or verbal ability, that appear after a certain amount of maturation has occurred.

Nurture refers to all the environmental influences that come into play after conception, beginning with the mother's health during pregnancy and running through all one's experience with the outside world—in the family, school, community, and the culture at large.

The controversy about nature and nurture has taken on many names, among them *heredity versus environment* and *maturation versus learning.* Under whatever name, however, the basic question remains: How much of any given characteristic, behavior, or pattern of development is determined by genetic influences and how much is the result of the myriad experiences that occur after conception? Note that the question is "How much?"—implying that with all characteristics, behaviors, and patterns of development,

nature All the genetic influences on development, including those that affect physical characteristics as well as psychological traits, capacities, and limitations.

nurture All the environmental influences on development, from prenatal influences on the embryo to the cultural context at death.

both nature and nurture are influential. All developmentalists agree that, at every point, the *interaction* between nature and nurture is the crucial influence on any particular aspect of development. They note, for example, that intelligence is determined by the interplay of heredity and such aspects of the social and physical environment as schooling and nutrition. Despite their acknowledgment of the interaction between nature and nurture, however, developmentalists can get into heated arguments about the relative importance of each (see Scarr, 1992; Baumrind, 1993; Jackson, 1993).

One of the reasons the controversy over the relative importance of heredity and environment is very much alive is that the practical implications of the controversy are enormous. Consider one example. Although boys and girls in elementary school show similar math aptitude, the mathematical achievement of the typical teenage boy is higher than that of the average teenage girl. Furthermore, high school students who are gifted in math are usually boys, by a 4-to-1 ratio, according to one American study (Benbow and Stanley, 1983). A closer analysis of the male advantage reveals that, beginning at about age 10, boys are better at spatial skills—the kind required for geometry—and this accounts for much of the difference in math achievement (Johnson & Meade, 1987). In addition, boys are better prepared in math, in that they take more geometry and calculus classes than girls do (Beal, 1994).

FIGURE 1.9 It's all in the family, Whitney Houston on the right, her aunt Dionne Warwick on the left, and her mother, Cissy, a gospel singer, in the middle—all descendants of the same woman, a mother and grandmother who sang to her children. But is the musical bond that unites these three women the result of nature or nurture? Perhaps they inherited extraordinary vocal cords and melodic sensitivity, or perhaps long hours in church choirs and family gatherings encouraged them to sing. The answer, of course, is that both nature and nurture made essential contributions, as is always true for talents and abilities.

Is nature responsible for these differences? Perhaps some hormonal difference causes early brain differentiation that, at puberty, gives males an advantage (Jacklin et al., 1988), and in turn, leads them to take more math. Or is nurture the key factor? Perhaps girls learn that math ability is not considered feminine, and perhaps their parents, teachers, or boyfriends, sharing this view, subtly—or not so subtly—discourage their interest and efforts in math (Eccles & Jacobs, 1986). Support for the latter hypothesis comes from cross-cultural research on women scientists, which shows that the percentage of physics faculty members who are women ranges from about 1 percent in Japan to 47 percent in Hungary (see Figure 1.10), a diversity that suggests that in this particular example, at least, social factors are much more influential than biological ones (Barinaga, 1994).

Whatever the answer, the implications are significant. If boys are naturally better at math than girls, it may be neither wise nor desirable to push girls to study math and related subjects such as physics and engineering.

FIGURE 1.10 Nations differ dramatically in how many of their university instructors are women, particularly in the natural sciences and math. The data in this chart, for example, reflects the percentage of female physics professors worldwide. Notice that even within continents, and within ethnic groups, the rates vary by nation. Obviously, nurture—especially the political and economic patterns of each country—is much more at work here than nature.

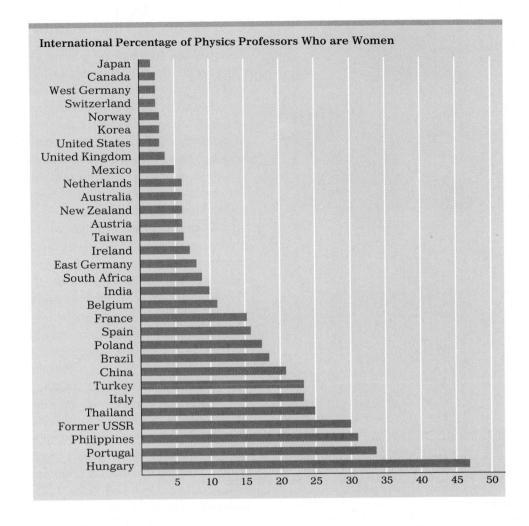

On the other hand, if such gender differences are the result of nurture, we are wasting a major portion of our mathematical potential, as well as limiting the career options for many female workers, by not encouraging girls to develop their full math abilities.

Another of the many controversial issues that pivots on the nature-nurture debate is the question of sexual orientation. Whereas psychologists once assumed that adult homosexuality resulted from unusual patterns in the mother-father-child relationship, many now believe that homosexuality is at least partly genetic. Included in the growing evidence for this view is research showing that a man is more likely to be gay if his mother's brother or his own brother—especially his identical twin—is homosexual (Pool, 1993; Whitam et al., 1993; Hamer et al., 1993).

But disagreement remains as to whether the evidence for genetic influence on homosexuality is conclusive, and if so, how great a role nature plays (Bailey et al., 1993; Maddox, 1993). Once again, the implications are profound. If homosexuality is primarily the result of nurture, then those who are concerned about the future sexual orientation of the young have reason to examine the influence of school curriculum and television programming regarding this issue. On the other hand, if the primary influences on a person's eventual sexual orientation are genetic, then the issues debated—and perhaps even the need for a debate at all—will change.

Continuity or Discontinuity?

How would you describe human growth? Would you say we develop gradually and continually, the way a seedling becomes a tree? Or do you think we undergo sudden changes, like a caterpillar becoming a butterfly?

Many developmental researchers emphasize the **continuity** of development. They believe that there is a gradual, continual progression from the beginning of life to the end. Accomplishments that may seem abrupt, such as a baby's first step, can actually be viewed as the final event in weeks of growth and practice. In the same way, learning to talk or read, or the physical changes that occur in adolescence, can be seen as gradual processes rather than as abrupt changes.

Other theorists emphasize the **discontinuity** of development. They see growth as occurring in identifiable stages, each with distinct challenges, changes, and characteristics. Terms such as the "terrible twos" or "teenage rebellion" or "midlife crisis" reflect the popular version of the stage concept. Those who focus on stages of development believe that, at certain times during life, a person moves from one level to another, as though climbing a flight of stairs. Often pivotal events—such as beginning to walk, learning to talk, or beginning the sexual changes of puberty—signal the beginning of a new stage. Such events are thought to change the individual quite suddenly and in many specific ways, leading to new patterns of thought and behavior.

The stage view of development has been the dominant one in the twentieth century. Indeed, this textbook, like most of its kind, reflects the stage view by treating development in terms of distinct periods—infancy, early childhood, middle childhood, and adolescence. There is, of course, good reason for this organization. To begin with, maturation occurs according to a biologically determined timetable, with the result that people of roughly the same age have in common many physical abilities and limitations, as well as age-related patterns in the way they think about their world and about themselves. Correspondingly, at various ages, many people also experience similar kinds of psychosocial needs and conflicts. Moreover, society treats people (especially children) in stagelike ways by grouping them according to their age in schools, recreational activities, and access to rights and privileges (such as driving a car, voting, and serving in the military).

However, a number of developmentalists have cautioned against overemphasizing distinct stages of development. As Flavell (1982) expresses it, strict stage views "gloss over differences, inconsistencies, irregularities, and other real but complexity-adding features." Although it would be convenient to approach human development as a "neat 'ages and stages' development story," Flavell notes, actual development is much more complex, for children grow in varied ways—sometimes in sudden leaps and bounds, sometimes step by step, and sometimes with such continuity that they seem not to change at all. Further, age may not be the most influential factor. In predicting the activities, interests, and abilities of a particular child, it is sometimes more useful to know the child's cultural, ethnic, or family background than the child's chronological age. A 12-year-old may have much more in common with a younger or older child of a similar background than with another 12-year-old of a different background.

As with the nature-nurture controversy, taking one side or the other of the continuity-discontinuity question can have profound practical conse-

continuity Refers to development that is gradual, steady, and predictable over time.

discontinuity Refers to development that is characterized by relatively abrupt, sudden, or surprising changes, often occurring in stages.

quences. Consider the impact on adolescents, for instance, of the assumption that there is substantial discontinuity between adolescence and adulthood. In many nations, teenagers are prohibited from purchasing alcohol and cigarettes, from watching certain movies, from engaging in sexual intercourse, from obtaining medical care without their parents' consent, or, in a growing number of cities, from even being outside after a particular curfew. At the same time, the assumption of discontinuity may protect teenagers in a number of respects, even as it restricts their freedom. This is most obvious if they commit a crime: in many nations, police traditionally tend to treat most adolescents more leniently, judges give them lighter sentences, and, if incarcerated, teenagers escape the worst of prison life. The discontinuity theory behind all these legal practices views adolescents as much more vulnerable, foolish, and impulsive than they will be after the magically maturing age of 18 or 21.

The controversial implications of the continuity-discontinuity debate are particularly obvious in the two current, hotly debated issues: whether pregnant teens should be allowed to obtain abortions without their parents' consent, and whether violent juvenile offenders should be punished as though they were adults.

The First Years of Life: Determining Force or Fading Influence?

A third controversy at the heart of developmental psychology concerns the extent to which the experiences of early childhood affect later emotional and intellectual development. Are our individual personality characteristics rooted in the events and emotional patterns of our first few years, shaping us for life? Or is personality fluid and malleable, shifting in response to different experiences and perceptions? Is the developmental process like that of a building, with the initial foundation and framework determining the form of the eventual structure? Or is it more like that of a painting, in which the initial sketch may be completely altered as subsequent brushstrokes create the picture?

For much of its history, developmental study endorsed the former view, contending that the first five years of life provide the basic structure for the individual's later personality development. And in many ways, various theories that emphasize the importance of early experiences have been substantiated by careful research. For example, some years ago Erik Erikson (1963) and John Bowlby (1969), building on the earlier ideas of Sigmund Freud, hypothesized that the nature of an infant's trust in, and attachment to, his or her mother determines whether that person can later sustain other close relationships, such as those with friends or lovers. Recent studies of infant-mother attachment have, in fact, confirmed that the security or insecurity of this first human bond can have long-term consequences, not only for the child's future relationships but also for the child's own self-esteem (Egeland et al., 1993; Lamb et al., 1985).

Research in other areas has likewise shown that certain early experiences can have lasting effects. Children who experience devastating poverty or the crushing instabilities and anxieties of homelessness tend to have such extensive early cognitive delays that they are likely to remain intellectually behind for many years to come, even when their circumstances have improved (Rafferty & Shinn, 1991; Ramey & Campbell, 1991). Long-term negative effects, extending well into adulthood, can be even more apparent when young children have undergone acute trauma, such as being severely abused or neglected (Cicchetti, 1990).

For some developmentalists, findings such as these confirm their belief that the early years, good or bad, are far more crucial than the later years for the development of capabilities and dispositions. In their view, our first experiences in early childhood provide the thrust and direction of our "launching" into life, establishing a trajectory that irrevocably determines the nature of our journey and our eventual destination.

Many other developmentalists, however, hold quite a different view. They believe that our early developmental paths can be changed, even reversed, by our later experiences. Their view is also supported by extensive research, especially by studies showing that children can rebound from difficult early experiences, if they have at least minimal amounts of emotional and cognitive support. Even after years of a troubled infancy and childhood, marred by medical problems, extreme poverty, mentally disturbed parents, family disruptions, or abuse, some resilient individuals become quite successful and well-adjusted adults (Elder et al., 1985; Furstenberg et al., 1987; Masten et al., 1990; Rutter, 1989).

For these people, certain protective factors and opportunities—among them finding close friends, attaining higher education, mastering vocational skills, developing a supportive marriage, and maintaining spiritual faith— seem to have acted as buffers against devastation. As one study that followed troubled children from birth to age 32 concludes:

> . . . these buffers make a more profound impact on the life course of children who grow up under adverse conditions than do specific risk factors or stressful life events. They appear to transcend ethnic, social class, geographical, and historical boundaries. Most of all, they offer us a more optimistic outlook than the perspective that can be gleaned from the literature on the negative consequences of perinatal trauma, caregiving deficits, and chronic poverty. They provide us with a corrective lens—an awareness of self-righting tendencies that move children toward normal adult development under all but the most persistent adverse circumstances. [Werner & Smith, 1992]

Increasingly, developmental psychologists are coming to agree with the view that life pathways are shaped by later experiences as well as by early ones, and that the first years of life *influence*—but rarely *determine*— later personality and behavior.

Nonetheless, the issue remains controversial because many practical decisions in child development hinge on the relative importance of the early or later years. The debate can become especially sharp with respect to public policy, when advocates of "early prevention" find themselves in a tug of war with believers in "targeted remediation." For instance, some child advocates argue that to help prevent juvenile delinquency and other antisocial or violent behavior thought to be associated with inadequate child-rearing, families "at risk" should be provided with help very early on, starting with well-trained nurses who would visit the home frequently, not only to provide medical care for the infant but also to teach the parents how to be responsive and responsible caregivers. Others argue that it is more cost-effective to wait until a child or adolescent actually appears headed for serious trouble, and then to intervene with such measures as personal counseling, intensive job training, and subsidized employment.

In disputes such as this, the evidence, far from settling the issues, generally corroborates many points of view, because, at every age, most observable adult traits can be linked to an intertwining web of immediate and distant events. In most cases, teasing apart the strands of this web, and assessing the relative impact of each, is an extremely difficult task that involves subjective interpretation as well as objective judgment—so the controversy continues.

The Scientific Method

As the three preceding controversies show, developmentalists, like everyone else, have opinions, opinions that are partly the result of their own background and biases. However, as scientists, they are committed to consider insights and evidence from the available research before they draw conclusions and to change their view when new data indicate they should. When doing research, they are expected to follow a general procedural model often called the **scientific method**, which helps them overcome whatever biases they have. Procedures and techniques, not theories and assumptions, are what make the study of development a science (Scarr, 1985).

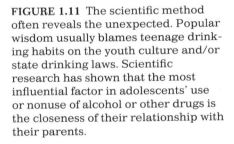

FIGURE 1.11 The scientific method often reveals the unexpected. Popular wisdom usually blames teenage drinking habits on the youth culture and/or state drinking laws. Scientific research has shown that the most influential factor in adolescents' use or nonuse of alcohol or other drugs is the closeness of their relationship with their parents.

The scientific method involves four basic steps, and sometimes a fifth:

1. *Formulate a research question.* Build on previous research, or on a particular developmental theory, or on personal observation and reflection, and pose a question that has relevance for the study of development.

2. *Develop a hypothesis.* Reformulate the question into a hypothesis, which is a specific prediction that can be tested.

3. *Test the hypothesis.* Design and conduct a scientific research project that will provide evidence about the truth or falsity of the hypothesis. As the Research Report on pages 26–27 indicates, the research design often includes many specific elements that help make the test of the hypothesis a valid one.

scientific method The sequence and procedures of scientific investigation (formulating questions, collecting data, testing hypotheses, and drawing conclusions) designed to reduce subjective reasoning, biased assumptions, and unfounded conclusions.

4. *Draw conclusions.* Formulate conclusions directly from the results of the test, avoiding general conclusions that are not substantiated by the test data.

5. *Make the findings available.* Publishing the results of the test is often the fifth step in the scientific method. In this step, the scientist must describe the test procedures and the resulting data in sufficient detail so that other scientists can evaluate the conclusions and, perhaps, **replicate** the test of the hypothesis—that is, repeat it and obtain the same results—or extend it, using a different but related set of subjects or procedures. Through replication, the conclusions from each test of every hypothesis accumulate, leading to more definitive and extensive conclusions and generalizations.

In actual practice, scientific investigation is less straightforward than these five steps would make it appear to be. The link between testing a hypothesis and drawing conclusions is bound to include some speculation and uncertainty (Bauer, 1992). For this reason, scientists use various research methods, sometimes in combination, to test hypotheses, because the accumulated results are likely to provide a clearer picture of the puzzles of human development than any one method alone. This is because each method has advantages and disadvantages.

Observation

replicate To repeat, with a different population, the specific design and procedures of a previous scientific study in order to test the validity of that study's conclusions.

observation The unobtrusive watching and recording of the behavior of subjects in certain situations, either in the laboratory or in natural settings.

Scientists can test hypotheses by using **observation**, that is, by observing and recording what people do in specific circumstances. Observations can occur either in a laboratory setting that has been especially designed for this purpose or in a naturalistic setting, such as a home, school, playground, or neighborhood street. Typically, the scientist tries to be as unobtrusive as possible, so that the people being observed will act as they normally do.

In *laboratory* observation, scientists (situated behind one-way windows, where they can observe unseen) study topics ranging from the rate

FIGURE 1.12 Developmentalists are currently investigating many aspects of children's social behavior. One way they do this is to observe children from behind a one-way window in a laboratory. In this photo, a researcher is observing children in a simulated day-care setting, noting such things as how their play patterns, ability to share, and negotiation strategies are affected by different factors, such as the presence or absence of the teacher.

and duration of eye contact between infant and caregiver in specific contexts, to the play patterns of 3-year-olds in a mixed-sex playroom, to the way adolescents and parents negotiate a family issue.

In *naturalistic* observation, scientists observe people in their natural environment. In one study of this type, researchers wanted to test the hypothesis that "maternal responsiveness is affected by cross-cultural differences" (Richman et al., 1992). Accordingly, they arranged for trained observers, familiar with the local language and culture, to compare mothers and their second and later-born babies in several communities, among them the Gusii in rural Kenya and middle-class whites in suburban Boston. The observations, which spanned several months, were made in the subjects' homes, with the mothers going about their normal household activities and each observer taking the part of a visiting neighbor, trying to be as casual and unintrusive as possible while recording the mother's and child's behaviors as each responded to the other.

There were, of course, many cross-cultural similarities in maternal responsiveness that were observed: when the infants cried, for example, mothers in both locations were attentive, rarely ignoring their infant's signs of distress and usually responding to them with some form of social interaction—holding, touching, or talking. (As experienced caregivers, they did not assume that every cry signaled hunger; they offered a breast or bottle to their crying infants less than 10 percent of the time.) In both locations, mothers also took the baby's developmental stage into account: they were more likely to cradle their crying 4-month-olds than they were to cradle their older babies.

Confirming the researchers' hypothesis, the observers also noted many cultural differences. One of the more intriguing was that American mothers communicated much more with words and much less with physical contact than Kenyan mothers did. This was apparent not only when the babies cried (see Figure 1.13) but also when they made other sounds, played with objects, or merely looked at their mothers.

FIGURE 1.13 As is apparent from these data and from other research, African mothers are more physical, and North American mothers more verbal, in raising their children. This does not mean that one group is better than the other. For instance, for 10-month-olds, both touching and talking are quite successful methods of hushing an unhappy baby, and mothers from both groups are equally responsive—albeit in different ways. However, the fact that every child is raised within a culture that encourages some aspects of development more than others is one reason adults have the particular values, abilities, and desires that they do.

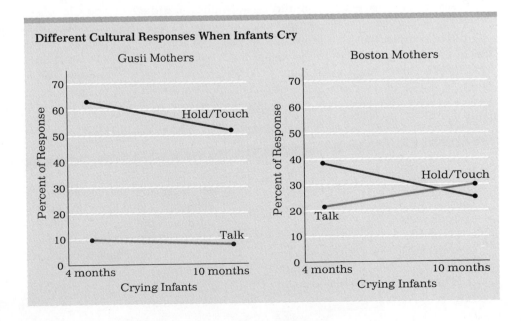

Ways to Make Research More Valid

In scientific investigation, there is always the possibility that the researchers' procedures and/or biases can compromise the validity of their findings. Consequently, scientists often take a number of steps to ensure that their research is as valid as possible. Six of these steps are explained here.

Sample Size

To begin with, in order to make any valid statement about people in general, the scientist must study a group of individuals that is large enough that a few extreme cases will not distort the picture of the group as a whole. Suppose, for instance, that researchers wanted to know the age at which the average American child begins to walk. Since they could not include every American infant in their study, they would work with a large sample group—a *sample population*—determining the age of walking for each member of the sample and then calculating the average for the group.

The importance of an adequate **sample size** can be seen if we assume for the moment that one of the infants in the sample had an undetected disability and did not walk until age 24 months. If the sample size were less than ten infants, that one late walker would, relative to the current standard of 12 months, add more than a month to the age when the "average" child was said to walk. However, if the sample were more than 500 children, one abnormally late walker would not change the results by even one day.

Representative Sample

Since the data collected on one group of individuals might not be valid for other people who are different in significant ways, such as gender, ethnic background, and the like, it is important that the sample population be a **representative sample**, that is, a group of subjects who are typical of the general population the researchers wish to learn about. In a study of when the average American infant begins to walk, the sample population should reflect—in terms of sex ratio, economic and ethnic background, and

so forth—the entire population of American children. Ideally, other factors might be taken into consideration as well. For instance, if there is some evidence that first-born children walk earlier than later- or last-born children, then the sample should include a representative sample of each birth order.

The importance of representative sampling is revealed by its absence in two studies of age of walking (Gesell, 1926; Shirley, 1933) undertaken in the 1920s. Both studies used a relatively small and unrepresentative sample (all the children were white and most were middle-class), and, consequently, both arrived at a norm that is 3 months later than the current one, which was derived from a much more representative sample.

"Blind" Experimenters

A substantial body of evidence suggests that when experimenters have specific expectations of the outcome of their research, those expectations can affect the research results. As much as possible, then, the people who are carrying out the actual testing should be "**blind**," that is, unaware of the purpose of the research. Suppose one hypothesis is that first-born infants walk sooner than later-borns. Ideally, the examiner who tests the infants' walking ability would not know what the hypothesis is, and would not even know the age or birth order of the toddlers under study.

Operational Definitions

When planning a study, researchers must establish **operational definitions** of whatever phenomena they will be examining. That is, they must define each variable in terms of specific, observable behavior that can be measured with precision. Even a simple variable such as whether or not a toddler is walking requires an operational definition. For example, does "walking" include steps while holding onto someone or something, or must it occur without support? Is one unsteady step enough to meet the definition, or must the infant be able to move a certain distance without

---

sample size The number of individuals who are being studied in a research project.

representative sample A select group of research subjects who reflect the relevant characteristics of the larger population that is under study.

blind Refers to researchers who are deliberately kept ignorant of the purpose of the research, or of relevant traits of the research subjects, in order to avoid biasing their data collection.

operational definition A precise definition of a research variable that is intended to make the variable easier to observe and measure.

Drawing by Sempé; © 1986 The New Yorker Magazine, Inc.

"I'm walking."

Do babies walk (or talk) when they are ready, no matter how little attention their parents provide? Only careful research can provide the answer.

faltering? For a study on age of first walking to be meaningful, the researchers would need to resolve questions like these in a clear and thorough definition.

Understandably, operational definitions become much harder to establish when personality or intellectual variables are being studied, but it is essential that researchers who are investigating, say, "aggression" or "linguistic ability" or "hyperactivity" define the trait in as precise and measurable terms as possible. Obviously, the more closely operational definitions reflect conceptual definitions, the more objective, valid, and reliable the results of the study will be.

Experimental and Control Groups

In order to test a hypothesis adequately in an experiment, researchers must compare two study groups that are simi-lar in every important way except one: they must compare an **experimental group**, which receives some special experimental treatment, and a **control group**, which does not receive the experimental treatment.

Suppose a researcher hypothesized that infants who are provided with regular exercises that strengthen their legs walk earlier than babies who do not receive such exercise. In order to find out if this is true, the researcher would select two representative groups of children and arrange that one group (the experimental group) receive daily "workouts" devoted to leg-strengthening between their third and twelfth months, while the other group (the control group) would be given no special treatment.

Determining Statistical Significance

Whenever researchers find a difference between two groups, they have to consider the possibility that the difference occurred purely by chance. For instance, in any group of infants, some will walk relatively early and some relatively late. When the researchers in the study divide the sample population into the experimental and control groups, it is possible that, by chance, a preponderance of early walkers ends up in one group or the other.

To determine whether their results are simply the result of chance, researchers use a statistical test, called a test of **statistical significance**. This test takes into account many statistical factors, including the sample size and the average difference between the groups, and yields the *level of significance,* a numerical indication of exactly how likely it is that the particular difference occurred by chance. (Note that the word "significance" here means something quite different from its usual sense; that is, it refers to the validity of a study, not to its value.) Generally, in order to be called statistically significant, the possibility that results occurred by chance has to be less than one in twenty, which is written in decimals as a significance of .05. Often the likelihood of a particular finding's occurring by chance is even rarer, perhaps one chance in a hundred (the .01 level) or one in a thousand (the .001 level).

experimental group Research subjects who experience special conditions or treatments that the control group does not experience.

control group Research subjects who are comparable to the experimental group in every relevant dimension except that they do not experience the special experimental conditions.

statistical significance A mathematical calculation, derived from such factors as sample size and differences between groups, that indicates the likelihood that a particular research result occurred by chance.

The difference is clearly related to cultural views of the mother's role, as the researchers explain:

> Both groups of mothers are responsive to infant signals, but their different behaviors indicate divergent goals and styles. The responsiveness of the Gusii mothers is directed toward soothing and quieting infants rather than arousing them . . . The responsiveness of the Boston mothers, especially as their infants become more communicative later in the first year, is designed to engage the infants in emotionally arousing conversational interaction. Gusii mothers see themselves as protecting their infants, not as playing with or educating them. [Richman et al., 1992]

Limitations of Observation

But what more specific factors might underlie these differing cultural practices? There are several possible explanations, and they reveal the chief drawback of observation—the difficulty of pinpointing the variable that is the direct cause of the behaviors that are observed. A **variable** is any factor or condition that can change or vary from one person or group or situation to another and thus affect behavior. The problem for researchers is that any given human behavior is surrounded by many variables that may or may not be influential. For example, one plausible hypothesis for the above findings points to infant mortality as the key variable. As noted earlier, in a society in which adequate food and survival are in doubt, as is the case in much of Africa, good parenting may place higher value on immediate soothing and physical nurturance. In contrast, in an amply fed group with a relatively low mortality rate, such as the suburban Bostonians, a parental priority is likely to be providing the infant with cognitive stimulation (Nugent et al., 1989; Le Vine, 1988).

Another likely hypothesis, posited by the researchers, is that maternal education may be the key variable, since is likely to influence attitudes about verbal communication: if the mothers are well-educated and literate, as the Boston mothers were, they may encourage verbal interactions even before the babies can speak a word. Some support for this hypothesis comes from a study of Mexican mothers, who were all from the same low-income neighborhood but who had varying levels of education (Richman et al., 1992). This study found that, indeed, the more education the mothers had, the more verbal they were with their babies. In other words, the study found a *correlation* between maternal education and verbalization with infant offspring.

However, we need to be very careful in interpreting such findings: a **correlation** is a statistic that merely indicates whether two variables are related to each other—specifically, whether changes in one are likely to be accompanied by changes in the other. But in and of itself, *correlation does not indicate causation* (see A Closer Look on p. 29). While it seems logical that being more educated might lead women to be more verbal with their infants, it is possible that some third variable was the underlying cause of the correlation. It could be, for example, that people who are higher in verbal skills tend to spend more years in formal education, and that because of their verbal skills, rather than their education, they tend to talk more to everyone—babies included.

Obviously, then, observation can provide fascinating data and can often generate a number of explanations for the results that it produces. But just as obviously, it cannot definitively link cause and effect, because obser-

variable   Any factor or condition that can change or vary from one individual or group or situation to another and thus affect behavior.

correlation   A statistical term that indicates a corresponding relation between two variables (when both variables either increase or decrease together, the correlation is positive; when one variable increases as the other decreases, the correlation is negative).

Correlation: What It Does, and Does Not, Mean

Correlation is a statistical term that indicates that two variables are somehow related; that is, that one particular variable is likely, or unlikely, to occur when another particular variable occurs. For instance, there is a correlation between height and weight, because, usually, the taller a person is, the more he or she weighs. There is also a correlation between wealth and education, and perhaps even between springtime and falling in love.

Note that the fact that two variables are correlated does not mean that they are related in every instance. Some tall people weigh less than people of average height; some wealthy people never finished high school; some people fall in love in the depths of winter.

Nor does correlation indicate cause. The correlation between education and wealth does not necessarily imply that more education leads to greater wealth. It may be instead that more wealth leads to greater education, since wealthier people can better afford the expense of college. Or there may be a third variable, perhaps intelligence or family background, that accounts for the level of both income and education.

Positive, Negative, and Zero Correlation

There are two types of correlation, positive and negative. Whenever one variable changes in the same direction as another variable changes (for example, both increase or both decrease), the correlation is said to be *positive*. All the examples given so far are examples of positive correlation. Thus, when education increases, income tends to increase as well; when education is low, so is income likely to be.

When two variables are inversely related (one increasing while the other decreases), the correlation is said to be *negative*. Warm weather and snow, middle-age and childbirth, and hostility and popularity are negatively correlated.

When there is no relationship between the two variables, the correlation is said to be *zero*. It is hard to think of any two variables that have no relationship to each other at all. Probably the correlation between eye color and age is zero (except in infancy, when many babies temporarily have blue eyes), as is the correlation between how much milk you drank yesterday and whether it is raining today (unless your thrist is somehow related to seasonal variations in rainfall).

Correlations can be expressed numerically. They range from plus one (+ 1.0), the highest positive correlation, to minus one (– 1.0), the most negative correlation. Halfway between plus one and minus one is zero, indicating no correlation at all.

Like all single parents, this single father is confronted with the research finding that single parenthood correlates with developmental problems for the children involved. However, it must be remembered that correlations nearly always reflect tendencies, not inevitabilities. Nor do they indicate causation. The developmental problems associated with single parenthood may arise from variables other than single parenthood itself—such as reduced family income or ongoing conflict between ex-spouses.

Correlations are one of the most useful tools in psychology and, at the same time, one of the most misused. They are useful because knowing how variables are related helps us understand the world we live in. However, as the respected researcher Sandra Scarr (1985) notes, "the psychological world . . . is a cloud of correlated events to which we as human observers give meaning."

Unless we are cautious in giving that meaning, we are likely to seize on one or another particular correlation as an explanation, without looking for other possible explanations. For instance, in the 1960s many psychologists noted the correlation between "broken" homes and maladjustment in children and concluded that single parents necessarily put their children at risk. In the 1990s, psychologists looking at the same kinds of homes (now called single-parent families) note that many children in them do quite well, and that other factors that correlate with such homes (e.g., low income, parenting stress) may be the explanation for children's problems when they occur (see Chapter 14). The lesson here is clear: we need to be very careful not to jump from the discovery of correlations to conclusions about causes.

vational settings, especially naturalistic ones, contain numerous variables that are beyond the researcher's control. To be certain that a particular observation is the result of one variable and not another, and to prove that their speculations are not simply creative hypotheses, scientists must go beyond observation to the experiment.

The Experiment

Unlike observation, an **experiment** tests a hypothesis in a controlled manner, in which the relevant variables are limited and therefore can be manipulated by the experimenter. Typically, the experimenter exposes a group of subjects to the particular variable that is under investigation (for instance, a specific behavior on the part of a caregiver, a new teaching technique, a special diet, a particular social setting, a memory strategy) and then evaluates how they react.

Let's take a simple example. Everyday observation reveals that children are much more likely to follow their parents' suggestions at certain moments than at others. You can probably think of dozens of explanations for this variation, but without an experiment, it is impossible to know which are valid. One hypothesis is that children's moods directly affect how they respond to their parents' directives.

To test this hypothesis, twenty-eight 4-year-old children and their mothers were studied in a laboratory playroom (Lay et al, 1989). Half the children were put into a positive mood by being asked to think of some event that had made them feel happy, good, or excited, and the other half were put into a negative mood by being asked to recall some event that had made them upset, scared, or angry. After thinking of the experience, the children were asked to relate it to the experimenter, and then to go over it again in their minds, remembering how it made them feel. Such guided memories have, in previous experiments, been shown to affect a person's mood.

Then the experimenter left, and each mother (as directed) asked her child to sort and put away 153 blocks that were scattered on the floor. The mothers were told not to praise or help the child but to simply repeat the instructions if the child stopped sorting. Four minutes later, the experiment was over. The influence of mood on the two groups was striking. All the children in a positive mood began sorting the blocks quickly—averaging only a 15-second delay before beginning. Even the slowest among them started within half a minute after the initial instructions. By contrast, the children in a negative mood were much slower to comply, typically waiting 90 seconds to begin and sometimes refusing to begin at all. By the end of the 4 minutes, the children in a positive mood had sorted and put away an average of 93 blocks each, whereas the children in a negative mood had sorted and put away an average of only 42.

Limitations of the Experiment

As you can see, experiments of this sort, done under very controlled conditions that compare two groups of subjects, can make the link between cause and effect quite clear. The question is, To what degree do findings from an artificial experimental situation apply in the real world? In the normal give-and-take at home, for instance, can children be put into a particular mood as easily, and with the same effect, as they were in this experiment? Proba-

FIGURE 1.14 Naturalistic observation reveals that children are sometimes cruel to animals as well as to each other, but it does not reveal why. Laboratory experiments, however, have shown that one factor is the observation of cruelty and aggression in others. Chances are these children have seen someone else try to settle a dispute over a possession in a similar fashion.

experiment A research method in which the scientist deliberately changes one variable and then observes the results in some other variable.

bly not. In addition, the actual experimental task—sorting the blocks—was an easy and neutral one. All the children could do it, and neither mother nor child had any personal interest in whether or not it got done. In actual life, parents generally ask their children to do things that the parents want them to do, and that the children may not want to do, or may not be able to do. The influence of mood may therefore not be as straightforward at home as it is in the experimental setting.

The experiment is subject to an additional limitation when it involves older children, who may alter their behavior in the experimental setting because they know that they are being studied. Subjects sometimes behave in ways that they think will please the experimenter or will make them look good, and, occasionally, some subjects (usually college students) may try to undermine the experiment—all of which adds an additional layer of possible artificiality to this type of research. Nonetheless, experiments can provide invaluable clues regarding cause and effect.

The Interview or Survey

In an **interview** or **survey**, the researcher asks a series of questions of people and records their answers in order to determine those individuals' knowledge, opinions, or personal characteristics. This seems to be an easy, quick, and direct research method. However, it is more difficult to get valid data through an interview or survey than it seems, because these methods, even more than an experiment, are vulnerable to bias, on the part of the researcher and the respondents. To begin with, the very phrasing of the questions can influence the answers. A survey of teenagers on the issue of abortion, for instance, might prompt different responses depending on whether it asked about "terminating an unwanted pregnancy" or "taking the life of an unborn child."

In addition, many people who are interviewed—including children—give answers that they think the researcher expects, or that they think will make them seem mature or "good." Even when people wish to give completely accurate information, their responses may be flawed because their opinion on a particular question varies from day to day, or because their recollection of events is distorted. Interviews can be particularly difficult when they involve young children, who may misunderstand the interviewer's questions, be uneasy with the questioning process, or confuse reality with fantasy. Indeed, it is easy for researchers to mistakenly conclude that a young child's brief response to an interview question reveals limited understanding when, in fact, it may well reflect discomfort with the interview.

Sometimes an interview or survey consists of a performance measure, such as a personality inventory or an intelligence test, that is designed to reveal specific personal characteristics. In such cases, the questions are posed precisely and in a predetermined sequence, so that the assessment will be consistent for each person. Because the conclusions that are drawn about an individual—whether they involve the person's intellectual capability or memory or personality makeup—can have significant consequences for the person being tested, performance measures must be painstakingly designed to ensure that these conclusions are valid and reliable. As we shall see in Chapter 13, there is considerable controversy over how to best design performance measures to evaluate an important individual characteristic such as intelligence.

interview A research method in which people are asked specific questions to discover their opinions or experiences.

survey A research method that collects interview information on a large number of people, either through written questionnaires or through personal interviews.

"You are fair, compassionate, and intelligent, but you are perceived as biased, callous, and dumb."

FIGURE 1.15 Reconciling the many possible, sometimes conflicting, views about the subject of a case study requires a talented interpreter, whose views and possible biases must also be taken into account.

case study A research method that focuses on the life history, attitudes, behavior, and emotions of a single individual.

reports from secondary sources A research method in which the scientist obtains information about a research subject indirectly, usually from people who know the individual.

The Case Study

An additional research tool is the **case study**, an intensive study of one individual. David's story, which opened this chapter, exemplifies the case study. Typically, the case study is based on interviews with the subject regarding his or her background, present thinking, and actions, and often utilizes interviews of others who know the individual. Observation and standardized tests may furnish additional case-study material.

Case studies can provide a wealth of detail and therefore are rich in possible insights. However, the interpretation of case-study data depends on the wisdom as well as the biases of the researcher. In particular, the insights revealed by a case study may not be generalizable to others, but may instead apply only to the particular individual being studied. (The case study of David's encouraging progress over his particular handicaps, for example, applies only to David and might give a misleading picture if used to predict the future outcomes for others with rubella syndrome.) For the most part, then, the case study is not used to do basic research, because no confident conclusions about people in general can be drawn from a sample size of one.

Reports from Secondary Sources

At times, the most valuable information researchers can obtain about people consists of reports provided by others who know them well. In these instances, researchers are using **reports from secondary sources**. Secondary source reports are especially useful in developmental research because children may be too young to provide a valid account of their own behavior, and informants can often provide insights that observation or experiments may not yield. Developmentalists who study early temperament, for example, commonly rely on parental reports of the child's activity level, adaptability, ability to be soothed, and other temperamental traits, because to assess these traits directly would require many hours of intensive observation. In similar fashion, researchers often evaluate children's popularity or acceptance among their peers by asking other children to identify their friends.

Of course, secondary reports can be biased. Parents usually want to portray both themselves and their children in the best possible manner, for example, and temperament researchers commonly find that the proportion of parents reporting that their children have an easy temperament is far higher than direct observation—or common sense—can support (Mebert, 1991). Consequently, it is wise to supplement secondary source reports with other, more direct, measures that enable researchers to confirm the accuracy of these reports.

Clearly, there are many ways to test hypotheses. Researchers can observe people in naturalistic or laboratory settings, or experimentally alter their reactions under controlled conditions; they can compare one group with another to find significant differences, or correlate one characteristic with another to discover if they are somehow related; they can survey hundreds or even thousands of people about their opinions or knowledge, or interview a smaller number in great depth; they can study one life in detail, or talk to secondary sources. Because each method has weaknesses, none of these ways of examining a hypothesis is sufficient in itself, but each can bring researchers closer to an understanding of the question being investigated.

Good developmental research thus requires careful consideration of the relative advantages and disadvantages of each method in relation to the hypothesis to be tested. It requires thoughtful attention to the selection of a research sample of suitable size, the choice of an appropriate research setting, and the use of statistical tests of significance. And, as the Public Policy box on page 34 points out, developmental research likewise requires attention to the ethics of research with children.

All this methodological carefulness and attention to detail does not mean that developmental research is dry and mechanical, however. Good research also involves creativity, because discovering new insights into developmental processes requires innovative and ingenious research strategies. Having to be creative is what makes it fun to be a researcher, and as you read through the pages of this text, you will be struck, time and again, by the ingenuity of developmental researchers as they seek to reveal the complexities of human development.

Designing Developmental Research

For research to be truly developmental, scientists must discover how and why people change or remain the same *over time*. To learn about the pace and process of change, developmentalists use two basic research designs, cross-sectional and longitudinal.

Cross-Sectional Research

The more convenient, and thus more common, way researchers study development is by doing a **cross-sectional** comparison of people of various ages. In this kind of study, groups of people who are different in age but similar in other important ways (such as their level of education, socioeconomic status, ethnic background, and so forth) are compared on the characteristic under investigation. Any differences on this characteristic that exist between the people of one age and the people of another are, presumably, the result of age-related developmental processes.

One cross-sectional study compared infants, toddlers, and preschoolers (average ages, 9, 12, and 24 months) to see whether distress at being dropped off at day care fluctuated with the child's age (Field et al., 1984). Children in all three groups attended the same all-day day-care center and came from middle-class families of a range of ethnic backgrounds. The ratio of boys to girls was about the same for all three age groups. An observer who was "blind" to the purpose of the study noted precisely how the children behaved when their parents dropped them off. The results showed definite age differences: the 12-month-olds were significantly more likely than younger or older children to cry, cling, and complain when their parents left.

cross-sectional research In the study of development, research that compares groups of people who are different in age but who are similar in other important ways.

Ethics of Research with Chidren

Every scientist must be concerned with the ethics of conducting and reporting research. At the most basic level, researchers who study human behavior and development must pursue their studies in an ethical manner, ensuring that their research subjects are not harmed by the research process and that their participation is voluntary and confidential. This is particularly crucial when the subjects are children, as reflected in the following precautions urged by the Society for Research in Child Development (1990):

> The investigator should use no research operation that may harm the child either physically or psychologically. . . . When in doubt about the possible harmful effects, consultation should be sought from others.
>
> Before seeking consent or assent from the child, the investigator should inform the child of all features of the research that may affect his or her willingness to participate and should answer the child's questions in terms appropriate to the child's comprehension. [The child is free to] discontinue participation at any time. . . . Investigators working with infants should take special effort to explain the research procedures to the parents and be especially sensitive to any indicators of discomfort in the infant.
>
> Informed consent requires that parents or other responsible adults be informed of all the features of the research that may affect their willingness to allow the child to participate.
>
> When, in the course of research, information comes to the investigator's attention that may jeopardize the child's well-being, the investigator has a responsibility to discuss the information with the parents or guardians and with those expert in the field in order that they may arrange the necessary assistance for the child.
>
> The investigators should keep in confidence all information obtained about research participants.

All these goals are ones that developmental researchers endorse. However, it is easier to enunciate these ethical principles governing research than it is to resolve some of the thorny dilemmas that they may entail (Fisher, 1993; Stanley & Sieber, 1992; Thompson, 1992). How can a developmentalist know, for example, that a child wishes to end his or her participation in a research project when many children are afraid to voice their reservations to an authority figure like a researcher? Does the confidentiality of research data include restricting parental access to this information? (This question may be of particular concern to adolescents who participate in developmental studies.) What is the best way to inform young children about the research, and to ensure that they understand what they have been told? Some ethicists, like Paul Ramsey (1976), have argued that infants and young children cannot meaningfully consent to research participation and thus should not be used as research subjects (even though their parents grant permission). But if young children were to be excluded from research efforts, researchers would be prohibited from pursuing many important questions with potentially critical practical applications.

The most complex matter of all is ensuring that the benefits of research outweigh the risks. One reason is that the risks that children may experience vary with the child's age: a young child may be most vulnerable to stress in research that involves a separation from caregivers, while older children are more susceptible to loss of self-esteem and privacy violations (Thompson, 1990). In addition, different children are affected by research procedures in different ways. Another reason is that studies with the greatest potential for social benefit necessarily involve children who are most vulnerable to emotional stress, such as children who have been maltreated or who have behavioral disorders. Balancing the risks and benefits of research in these cases can be extremely tricky.

Because of all these considerations, all universities sponsoring research with human participants create review committees to ensure that research subjects will be treated in an ethical and humane manner. Before any developmental researcher at a university can begin a study involving children, therefore, she or he must submit for approval detailed information concerning the research procedures to be used.

Once the research has been completed, additional ethical issues arise concerning the use of research findings. The Society for Research in Child Development (1990) stipulates that "caution should be exercised in reporting results [and] making evaluative statements or giving advice" and that "the investigator should be mindful of the social, political, and human implications of his [or her] research." This is essential because controversial issues such as infant day care, sex education, and child custody are often argued on the basis of research that is carelessly interpreted and deliberately overstated. Many scientists now are trying to explain to the media and to the general public the complex process of scientific research. Indeed, one of the ethical principles of the Society for Research in Child Development is that textbooks such as this one make every effort to explain the implications of the research process. This obligation sometimes includes pointing out the weaknesses of particular pieces of research and of exploring alternative explanations for various research findings.

This difference in the behavior of the three groups of children presumably occurred because of some age-related developmental processes that made the toddlers less willing to be parted from their parents than infants or preschoolers were. It might be, for instance, that the attachment of these 12-month-olds to their parents was sufficiently developed to cause them to protest being separated from their parents, and that, unlike the preschoolers, they were not yet mature enough to become easily involved in play with classmates and teachers to quickly deter or relieve their distress.

However, in a cross-sectional study, it is always possible that some variable other than age differentiated the groups of children: perhaps the toddlers were, as a group, more temperamentally fussy children, or perhaps the manner in which their parents dropped them off triggered anxiety. Moreover, because cross-sectional research compares *different* children of each age, it is impossible to know whether individual differences among children of a given age would persist over time. For example, were the infants in this study who did not fuss when their parents dropped them off likely to become fussy toddlers? To answer questions like this, researchers turn to longitudinal research.

FIGURE 1.16 The apparent similarity of these two groups in terms of gender and ethnic composition makes them seem potential candidates for cross-sectional research. However, before we could be sure that any differences between the two groups on any given dimension are the result of age, we would have to be sure the groups are alike in other ways, such as socioeconomic background, religious upbringing, and so forth.

Longitudinal Research

longitudinal research In the study of development, research that follows the same people over time in order to measure both change and stability with age.

To help discover if developmental processes—rather than other personal or situational influences—account for differences in behavior with age, researchers sometimes study the *same* people over a period of time. This type of research, known as **longitudinal research**, allows information about people at one age to be compared with information about them at another age, thus enabling researchers to find out how these particular individuals changed or remained the same over time. As you can see, this approach also enables researchers to determine whether individual differences among these people persist over this period.

In the study of the day-care children discussed above, the researchers added a longitudinal component: they reexamined the children in all three groups six months after the initial observation. They found that the relatively quiet infants of the first study had become toddlers who were likely to protest at being left, and that those who had been protesting toddlers earlier had, after the six-month period, become less likely to fuss when their parents departed. This longitudinal research confirms the developmental picture suggested by the cross-sectional research: as children approach their first birthday, they become more likely to cry and cling when their parents leave them in day care and then, after about age 2, they gradually take these separations in stride.

Longitudinal research is particularly useful in studying developmental trends that occur over a long age span. It has produced valuable and sometimes surprising findings on such questions as children's adjustment to divorce (the negative effects linger, especially for school-age and older boys [Hetherington et al., 1989]); the long-term effects of serious birth problems (remarkable resiliency is often apparent [Werner & Smith, 1992]); and the adult lives of "genius" children (contrary to the popular wisdom that geniuses are maladjusted eccentrics, these individuals are happier and more successful than most adults [Terman & Oden, 1959; Shur Kin, 1992]). Longitudinal studies have also been used to evaluate the long-term consistency of individual differences on characteristics ranging from emotionality to intelligence to coping with stress.

FIGURE 1.17 Long-term longitudinal research can provide a revealing view of how individuals change and how they remain the same over time. Longitudinal research on this boy, for example, might indicate whether his seeming placidness remained constant from one period of childhood to another, and whether his sense of self-esteem as an adolescent varies notably from what it was in earlier years.

However, although longitudinal research is "the lifeblood of developmental science," the actual number of studies that cover more than a few years is "woefully small" (Appelbaum & McCall, 1983). The primary reason for this is a very practical one: to follow the development of a group of people over a number of years usually requires great effort, considerable foresight, and substantial funding. Sometimes researchers use *short-term* longitudinal studies in which they follow the growth of individuals over a period of months or a year, rather than over many years. (The longitudinal component added to the study of separation distress in day care is an example of this variety of longitudinal research.) But for many kinds of questions, short-term longitudinal studies are not adequate. Thus, while most developmental researchers consider longitudinal research to be far more revealing than cross-sectional studies, they are forced to rely quite heavily on cross-sectional research.

Shifting Historical Contexts

One fact that both longitudinal and cross-sectional researchers must bear in mind as they evaluate their findings is that, as noted earlier, each cohort may experience social conditions and attitudes that are different from those of other cohorts. Thus, research on people developing in one era may not be valid for people developing during an earlier, or later, generation. This is particularly true in a society in which rapid social change occurs. For example, research on American children born twenty or thirty years ago may not be valid for today's children, who are more likely to live with a single parent, are more significantly influenced by television, and are more likely to grow up poor than earlier generations.

This means that our conclusions about developmental processes must constantly be updated by new studies reexamining old assumptions, and by an awareness of how each generational cohort is affected by changing social conditions. As we have seen, children have been viewed much differently by different generations throughout history—from the eighteenth-century radicals led by Jean Jacques Rousseau, who thought that children should be allowed to grow "naturally" without adult direction, to the Pilgrims in Massachusetts who believed that a child's "natural pride must be broken and beaten down"—and such shifting views have helped shape the way children were reared by their caregivers. Just as the contextual view reminds us that development occurs differently in different historical, cultural, ethnic, and socioeconomic conditions, so it also reminds us that the contexts of human development continue to change and evolve and to affect development accordingly.

As we examine the mechanisms and patterns of development throughout this text, you will, time and time again, be confronted with the changing contextual features of human development, whether they involve infant day care, early education, the popular media, computers in schools, the growth of single parenting, or any number of other crucial issues. Because these conditions constitute the environment in which the next generation will grow and develop, your own increasing understanding of the practical and scientific questions of developmental psychology is important whether you plan to become a researcher or a practitioner, a teacher or a parent, or simply a more involved and better-informed member of the human family.

SUMMARY

The Study of Human Development

1. The study of human development explores how and why people change in systematic ways with increasing age, and how and why they remain the same. Developmentalists include researchers from many academic and practical disciplines, especially biology, education, and psychology, who study people of every age and in every social group.

2. Development is often divided into three domains, the biosocial, the cognitive, and the psychosocial. While this division makes it easier to study the intricacies of development, researchers note that development in each domain is influenced by the other two, as body, mind, and emotion always affect each other, and the social context always guides all three.

3. An ecological, or contextual, approach stresses the influences of the various settings in which development occurs, particularly the influence of family, community, and culture, as well as the historical, ethnic, and socioeconomic features that pervade any given developmental context. Each individual is seen as being affected by, as well as affecting, many interacting contexts.

4. The interaction of domains is clearly seen in the example of David, whose handicaps originating in the biosocial domain quickly affected the other two domains. His example also shows how the individual is affected by, and also affects, the surrounding contexts of family, society, and culture.

Three Controversies

5. All aspects of development are guided by the interaction of hereditary forces and the particular experiences a person has. The relative importance of these factors is a topic of debate, called the nature-nurture controversy.

6. Another controversy exists between those who think that development is smooth and continuous, and those who think it occurs in stages. While the stage view is common, many developmentalists caution against assuming that a child's stage of growth best predicts the child's behaviors and abilities.

7. The theory that the early years determine later development is much less influential than it once was, as most developmentalists now recognize that development is shaped and reshaped throughout life. Nevertheless, there are still moments of intense controversy over the relative influence of the early years, especially regarding matters of public policy.

The Scientific Method

8. The scientific method is used, in some form, by most developmental researchers. They observe, pose a question, develop a hypothesis, test the hypothesis, and draw conclusions based on the results of the tests.

9. To check their conclusions and to try to remain as objective as possible, researchers use a variety of methods, among them, adequate sample size, selection of a representative sample population, operational definitions, "blind" experimenters, control groups, and tests of statistical significance.

10. One common method of testing hypotheses is observation, which provides valid information but does not pinpoint cause and effect. The laboratory experiment pinpoints causes but is not necessarily applicable to daily life. Surveys, interviews, case studies, and secondary source reports are also useful.

11. In developmental research, ways are needed to detect change over time. Cross-sectional research compares people of different ages; longitudinal research (which is preferable but more difficult) studies the same individuals over a long time period. Both are valid for the cohorts under examination, but not necessarily for other age groups.

12. Contemporary researchers in the social sciences give considerable thought and attention to safeguarding the rights and well-being of the participants in their research. A more difficult ethical problem is the accurate reporting of research and understanding and dealing with all of its implications.

KEY TERMS

biosocial domain (3)

cognitive domain (3)

psychosocial domain (3)

ecological approach (4)

social context (6)

cohort (9)

culture (10)

ethnic group (11)

socioeconomic status (SES) (11)

nature (17)

nurture (17)

continuity (20)

discontinuity (20)

scientific method (23)

replicate (24)

observation (24)

sample size (26)

representative sample (26)

blind (26)

operational definition (26)

experimental group (27)

control group (27)

statistical significance (27)

variable (28)

correlation (28)

experiment (30)

interview (31)

survey (31)   cross-sectional research
case study (32)   (33)
reports from secondary   longitudinal research (35)
   sources (32)

KEY QUESTIONS

1. What is the main focus of the study of human development?

2. What are the three domains into which the study of human development is usually divided?

3. Give examples of the interaction among the various contexts that affect an individual's development.

4. Name and give examples of three broad contextual factors that developmentalists recognize as powerful influences on human development.

5. What are the steps of the scientific method?

6. What are the advantages of the scientific method?

7. What are the advantages and disadvantages of testing a hypothesis by observation?

8. What are the advantages and disadvantages of testing a hypothesis by experiment?

9. Compare the advantages of longitudinal research and cross-sectional research.

10. What ethical precautions should developmental researchers take?

Theories

CHAPTER

2

The patterns of development in everyday life are often complex and not simply explained. Over the past hundred years, social scientists have devised several theoretical perspectives that offer insight into why individuals develop as they do and how they learn to act in new ways. In this chapter, we will see how these different perspectives suggest answers to questions such as the following:

Are humans, including children, motivated by unconscious impulses?

In what ways do we learn the specific behaviors we enact?

How do children and adults influence their own development?

How is the human mind like a computer, and how is it different?

How do others guide developing persons to new achievements and growth?

As we saw in Chapter 1, the scientific effort to understand human development usually begins with questions. How do we, as individuals, develop into the kind of person we ultimately become? How significant and long-lasting are influences from early childhood? To what degree are we the products of our genetic inheritance, or of our environment? How do we learn to think, reason, create, and understand as we do? What are the unique challenges for personality growth at each stage of the life span?

What Theories Do

To begin to answer these questions and many others, we need some way to select significant facts and organize them in a manner that will take us deeper than our first speculations. In short, we need a theory. A **developmental theory** is a systematic statement of principles that explains behavior and development and guides developmentalists' investigations of new questions. To be more specific, in developmental research, theories have several purposes.

    1. Theories provide a broad and coherent view of the complex influences on human development, and thus they offer guidance for practical issues encountered by parents, teachers, therapists, and others

developmental theory A systematic set of hypotheses and principles that attempts to explain development and provide a framework for future research.

concerned with development. They distinguish certain influences as paramount and others as peripheral, for example, and suggest how to optimize human growth.

2. Theories form the basis for hypotheses—or educated guesses—about behavior and development that can be tested by research studies and either supported or disconfirmed by their results (as you learned in Chapter 1).

3. As theories are constantly modified by research findings, they provide a current summary of our knowledge about development. In this respect, developmental study is never complete, because updated theories give rise to new questions and new hypotheses meriting further investigation. Theories thus help us to ask important and relevant questions as well as lead us to useful answers.

Theories are central to understanding development. Consider why, for example, parents devote such time and energy to caring for their children. Is it because parenting is a basic stage of adult development? Does parental devotion derive from the rewards and reinforcement that children provide, or does it arise from an understanding of, and empathy for, children's needs? Does it occur because of cultural expectations? Different theories provide different answers to these questions, and lead us to view parenting in different ways. Furthermore, the answers provided by developmental theories often have important practical applications, such as determining how best to provide preventive intervention with parents who abuse or neglect their offspring, or whether it is best to have children at the very beginning of adulthood or closer to middle age, or what qualities would make a person a good foster parent.

Many theories are relevant to the study of development, but in this chapter we will focus on four kinds of theories that have been most influential and useful to developmental psychology—psychoanalytic theories, learning theories, cognitive theories, and sociocultural theories. Remember that their purpose is to provide a broad understanding of human development that integrates our knowledge and leads us to ask important questions and make relevant applications of this knowledge.

FIGURE 2.1 No matter what interaction developmentalists study, they can make their observations from various theoretical perspectives—psychoanalytic, which emphasizes unconscious drives and motives; learning, which emphasizes learned responses to particular situations; cognitive, which emphasizes the individual's understanding of self and others; and sociocultural, which emphasizes the cultural influences on the growth of individual learning and competencies.

Psychoanalytic Theories

Psychoanalytic theories interpret human development in terms of intrinsic drives and motives, many of which are unconscious, hidden from our awareness. These basic, underlying forces are viewed as influencing every aspect of a person's thinking and behavior, from the smallest details of daily life to the crucial choices of a lifetime. Psychoanalytic theories also see these drives and motives as providing the foundation for universal stages of development and for specific developmental tasks within those stages, from the formation of human attachments in infancy to the quest for emotional and sexual fulfillment. As a consequence, psychoanalytic theories provide a fascinating window into age-typical developmental processes as well as into the growth of individual differences in personality and behavior.

Origins

The psychoanalytic perspective provided the first comprehensive view of human behavior for the field of psychology. Because of this, the questions it posed and the answers it offered have intrigued psychologists ever since. To understand the tenets of this perspective, it is helpful to know something about the intellectual climate that it challenged. In Europe during the late 1800s, prevailing thought about human behavior included the ideas that people are governed for the most part by reason and mature judgment, and that children are "innocent," devoid of all sexual feelings.

FIGURE 2.2 In addition to being the world's first psychoanalyst, Sigmund Freud was a prolific writer whose many papers and case histories, based largely on his patients' bizarre symptoms and unconscious sexual urges, helped make the psychoanalytic perspective a dominant force for much of the twentieth century.

psychoanalytic theory A theory originated by Sigmund Freud that stresses unconscious forces that underlie human behavior.

By the 1870s, against the grain of these notions, a number of European intellectuals were developing an explanation of human behavior that emphasized the controlling power of emotional forces and the subordinate role of reason. In Vienna, Sigmund Freud (1856–1939), the founder of the psychoanalytic approach, began to evolve a theory that pointed specifically to the irrational basis of human behavior. Most notably, Freud called attention to the hidden emotional content of our everyday actions, to the ways the individual is driven by unconscious but powerful sexual and aggressive impulses, to the inner conflicts surrounding these impulses, and to the ways these conflicts arise in childhood and shape the individual's personality. Freud's depiction of the irrational and destructive forces at work in the normal personality shocked most of his contemporaries, but his view was soon to become a major influence in the field of psychology.

Freud was a medical doctor who formulated his theory while treating people with various physical disorders. Freud suspected that the origin of their symptoms was in the mind. In an effort to uncover the hidden causes of their problems, Freud would have his patients recline on his office couch and talk about anything and everything that came to mind—daily events, dreams, childhood memories, fears, desires—no matter how seemingly trivial or how unpleasant. From these disclosures and such things as the patients' slips of the tongue and unexpected associations between one idea and another, Freud discerned clues to the deep-seated, and usually unconscious, emotional conflicts that paralyzed one person or terrified another. Once the patient, under Freud's guidance, came to understand the nature of these hidden conflicts, the patient's symptoms would frequently diminish or disappear.

The medical establishment ridiculed Freud's "talking cure," especially when he reported that many physical and emotional problems were caused by unconscious sexual desires, some of which originated in infancy. This idea was contrary to the prevailing view that children are asexual, and that early life events have little influence on adult personality. But as patients revealed their problems and fantasies, Freud listened, interpreted, and formulated an influential theory of human personality development.

Freud's Ideas

One of Freud's basic ideas is that, long before they reach adolescence, children have sexual—or sensual—pleasures and fantasies, derived from stimulation of various parts of their bodies. According to his theory of **childhood sexuality**, development in the first six years occurs in three **psychosexual stages** (see Table 2.1, p. 47). Each stage is characterized by the focusing of sexual interest and pleasure on a particular part of the body. In infancy, it is the mouth (the **oral stage**); in early childhood, it is the anus (the **anal stage**); in the preschool years, it is the penis (the **phallic stage**).

Freud maintained that in each stage, the sensual satisfaction associated with these body regions is linked to the major developmental needs and challenges that are typical of various ages in childhood. During the oral stage, for example, the baby not only gains physical nurturance through sucking but also experiences sensual pleasure in the process and becomes emotionally attached to the person who provides these oral gratifications. During the anal stage, pleasures related to control and self-control—initially in connection with defecation and toilet training—are paramount. During the phallic stage, pleasure is derived from genital stimulation, and the young child's interest in physical differences between the sexes leads to the development of gender identity and sexual orientation and to the child's identification with the moral standards of his or her same-sex parent.

childhood sexuality The idea that infants and children experience sexual fantasies and erotic pleasures.

psychosexual stages A series of developmental stages, each originating in sexual interest in, and gratification through, a particular part of the body.

oral stage The first stage of psychosexual development in which the mouth is the source of erotic pleasure for the infant.

anal stage The second stage of psychosexual development in which the anus becomes the source of bodily pleasure for the toddler.

phallic stage The third stage of psychosexual development, occurring in early childhood, in which the penis becomes the focus of psychological concern as well as of physiological pleasure.

FIGURE 2.3 The girl's interest in the statue's anatomy may reflect simple curiosity, but Freudian theory would maintain that it is a clear manifestation of the phallic stage of psychosexual development, in which girls are said to feel deprived because they lack a penis.

It was Freud's contention that each stage also has its own potential conflicts between child and parent, such as those that typically arise during weaning or toilet training. Freud also contended that how the child experiences and resolves those conflicts influences his or her basic personality and lifelong patterns of behavior.

The first three of Freud's stages are followed by a five- or six-year period of sexual **latency**, during which sexual forces are dormant. Then, at about age 12, the individual enters a final psychosexual stage, the **genital stage**, which is characterized by mature sexual interests and lasts throughout adulthood.

Id, Ego, and Superego

To help explain the dynamics of psychological development, Freud identified three components of personality: the id, the ego, and the superego. The **id**, which is present at birth, is the source of our unconscious impulses toward fulfillment of our needs. It operates according to the *pleasure principle*; that is, it strives for immediate gratification. In other words, the id wants whatever seems satisfying and enjoyable—and wants it *now*. The impatient, greedy infant screaming for food in the middle of the night is all id.

Gradually, as babies learn that other people have needs of their own and that gratification must sometimes wait, the **ego** begins to develop. This rational aspect of personality, which emerges because of frustrating experiences like weaning and toilet training, has the role of mediating between the unbridled demands of the id and the limits imposed by the real world. The ego operates according to the *reality principle*; that is, it attempts to satisfy the id's demands in realistic and appropriate ways that recognize life as it is, not as the id wants it to be.

The ego also strives to keep another irrational force at bay. At about age 4 or 5, the **superego** starts to develop, as children begin to identify with their parents' moral standards during the phallic stage. The superego is like a relentless conscience that distinguishes right from wrong in unrealistically moralistic terms. Its prime objective is to strive for perfection and to keep the id in check. In this regard, it is the function of the ego to mediate between the primal desires of the id and the superego's unbending effort to inhibit those desires. How successful the ego will be depends, in part, on the specific moral training and the cultural taboos that the developing child experiences.

latency The period in middle childhood when sexual interests and pleasures are relatively quiet.

genital stage The final stage of psychosexual development, beginning at adolescence and continuing throughout adulthood, in which the primary source of sexual pleasure is in the genitals.

id The part of the personality that contains unconscious sexual and aggressive impulses striving for immediate gratification.

ego The part of the personality that attempts to deal, rationally and consciously, with reality.

superego The part of the personality that is self-critical and judgmental and that internalizes the moral standards set by parents and society.

The Ego and Development

According to psychoanalytic theory, the ego guides the course of developmental changes that are initiated by physical maturation, pressures and opportunities in the environment, and the child's own internal conflicts. The development of new skills, understanding, and competence is largely an outgrowth of the ego's striving for mastery over intrapsychic and environmental challenges (Loevinger, 1976).

Psychologically healthy individuals develop strong egos that can also competently manage the demands of the id and superego. However, in some circumstances, the ego may rely on *defense mechanisms* to cope with internal conflict or with demands from the environment. One of the most commonly referred to of these defense mechanisms is **repression**—that is, the pushing of a disturbing memory, idea, or impulse out of awareness and into the unconscious, where it is no longer actively threatening. Because of repression, for example, a traumatized child may not remember witnessing a terrifying accident, and thus will not be troubled by explicit recollections of the event. At the same time, however, repression prevents the individual from confronting a disturbing experience thoughtfully and rationally. Moreover, memory of that experience remains in the unconscious, where it may continually distort behavior and thinking (for example, the child may have an irrational fear of places and objects associated with the accident). According to Freud, a repressed memory, impulse, or emotion can endure throughout life, undermining healthy personality.

Psychoanalytic theory thus holds that each person inherits a legacy of conflicts from his or her childhood, along with particular ways of coping with them. Depending on our early experiences and our cultural milieu, some of us are more able to cope with the stresses of daily life than others.

Erikson's Ideas

Dozens of Freud's students became famous psychoanalytic theorists in their own right. Although they all acknowledged the importance of the unconscious, of irrational urges, and of early childhood, each in his or her own way expanded and modified Freud's ideas. Many of these neo-Freudians are mentioned at various points in this book. One of them, Erik Erikson (1902–1994), formulated a comprehensive theory of development that we will briefly outline here.

Psychosocial Development

Erikson spent his childhood in Germany, his adolescence wandering through Italy, his young adulthood in Austria under the tutelage of Freud and Freud's daughter Anna, and his later life in the United States. In America, he studied a wide array of subjects, including students at Harvard, soldiers who suffered emotional breakdowns during World War II, civil rights workers in the South, disturbed and normal children at play, and Native American tribes. Partly as a result of this diversity of experience, Erikson began to think of Freud's stages as too limited and too few. He proposed, instead, eight developmental stages, spanning the entire life span, each one characterized by a particular challenge, or developmental **crisis**, that is central to the stage of life in question and must be resolved.

FIGURE 2.4 Until his death in 1994, at the age of 92, Erik Erikson continued to write and lecture on psychosocial development. An important feature of his work is its emphasis on psychohistory—the relationship between historical factors and personality development.

repression A defense mechanism in which disturbing thoughts or impulses are excluded from consciousness.

crisis In psychosocial theory, the central conflict of each developmental stage.

TABLE 2.1

Comparison of Psychosexual and Psychosocial Stages

Approximate Age	Freud (Psychosexual)	Erikson* (Psychosocial)
Birth to 1 year	*Oral Stage* The mouth, tongue, and gums are the focus of pleasurable sensations in the baby's body, and feeding is the most stimulating activity.	*Trust vs. Mistrust* Babies learn either to trust that others will care for their basic needs, including nourishment, warmth, cleanliness, and physical contact, or to lack confidence in the care of others.
1–3 years	*Anal Stage* The anus is the focus of pleasurable sensations in the baby's body, and toilet training is the most important activity.	*Autonomy vs. Shame and Doubt* Children learn either to be self-sufficient in many activities, including toileting, feeding, walking, exploring, and talking, or to doubt their own abilities.
3–6 years	*Phallic Stage* The phallus, or penis, is the most important body part, and pleasure is derived from genital stimulation. Boys are proud of their penis, and girls wonder why they don't have one.	*Initiative vs. Guilt* Children want to undertake many adultlike activities, sometimes overstepping the limits set by parents and feeling guilty.
7–11 years	*Latency* Not a stage but an interlude, when sexual needs are quiet and children put psychic energy into conventional activities like schoolwork and sports.	*Industry vs. Inferiority* Children busily learn to be competent and productive in mastering new skills, or feel inferior and unable to do anything well.
Adolescence	*Genital Stage* The genitals are the focus of pleasurable sensations, and the young person seeks sexual stimulation and sexual satisfaction in heterosexual relationships.	*Identity vs. Role Confusion* Adolescents try to figure out "Who am I?" They establish sexual, political, and career identities or are confused about what roles to play.
Adulthood	Freud believed that the genital stage lasts throughout adulthood. He also said that the goal of a healthy life is "to love and to work well."	*Intimacy vs. Isolation* Young adults seek companionship and love with another person or become isolated from others by fearing rejection and disappointment. *Generativity vs. Stagnation* Middle-aged adults contribute to the next generation through meaningful work, creative activities, and/or raising a family, or they stagnate. *Integrity vs. Despair* Older adults try to make sense out of their lives, either seeing life as a meaningful whole or despairing at goals never reached.

*Although Erikson described two extreme resolutions to each crisis, he recognized that there is a wide range of outcomes between these extremes and that, for most people, the best resolution to a crisis is neither extreme but a middle course.

As you can see from Table 2.1, although Erikson's first five stages are closely related to Freud's stages, Erikson proposed three additional stages that occur in adulthood. Another significant difference is that, rather than centering on a body part, as Freud's stages do, each of Erikson's stages focuses on the person's relationship to the social environment. To highlight this emphasis on social and cultural influences, Erikson called his theory the **psychosocial theory** of human development.

In this psychosocial theory, the resolution of each developmental crisis depends on the interaction of the individual's characteristics and the support provided by the social environment. In the stage of *initiative versus guilt,* for example, children between ages 3 and 6 often want to undertake activities that exceed their abilities and/or the limits set down by their parents. Their efforts to act independently can thus leave them open to feelings of either pride or failure, depending in part on the reactions of their parents and on their culture's expectations regarding children's behavior. Similarly,

psychosocial theory A theory that stresses the interaction between internal psychological forces and external social influences. Erikson's theory is a psychosocial one.

FIGURE 2.5 It seems quite clear that the toddler here is well into the psychosocial stage Erikson referred to as *autonomy versus shame and doubt*. Whether he emerges from this stage feeling independent or inept depends, in part, on whether his parents encourage his various efforts at self-control or, instead, regularly criticize him for his failures. It seems equally clear that this young girl is trying to negotiate the stage Erikson called *identity versus role confusion*. In this stage, teenagers try out a number of roles (often focusing on appearance) in an effort to discover who they really are.

while all adolescents everywhere must negotiate the crisis of *identity versus role confusion,* how quickly they resolve this crisis depends partly on their own inclination toward conformity or rebelliousness and partly on the society's ability to provide guidance and support. How a child resolves the challenges of each stage thus depends on both the child's competencies and the response of others to the child's successes and failures.

Evaluations of Psychoanalytic Theories

All developmentalists owe a debt of gratitude both to Freud and to the neo-Freudians who extended and refined his concepts. Many of Freud's ideas are so widely accepted today that they are no longer thought of as his—for example, that unconscious motives affect our behavior, that development occurs in a series of stages, and that the early years are a formative period of personality development. While few accept Freud's ideas completely, many have learned from his insights.

Moreover, the psychoanalytic approach continues to shape current thinking about topics as diverse as mother-infant attachment, the effects of parental discipline, gender identity, moral development, adolescent identity, and a variety of other issues that you will study in subsequent chapters. Although the ideas of Freud and his followers have been modified considerably, they remain suggestive and insightful, and many current formulations originate in psychoanalytic ideas (Emde, 1992).

There are, however, many aspects of Freud's psychosexual approach that most contemporary developmentalists find to be inadequate or wrong. For instance, Freud's notion that the child's oral and anal experiences during the first two psychosexual stages form the basis for character structure and personality problems in adulthood has found little support in studies of normal children. Similarly, specifics of the phallic stage seem only marginally related to whether a person is heterosexual, homosexual, or bisexual. Most researchers agree that, throughout life, personality characteristics and behavior are affected much more by genetic traits, current life events, and the overarching sociocultural context than by the psychosexual dynamics of early childhood (Bengston et al., 1985; Ingleby, 1987; Vandenberg et al., 1986; Whitbourne, 1985a). Also lacking support is Freud's depiction of the struggle between the id and the superego—that is, between a torrent of impulses seeking immediate release and a ceaselessly judgmental monitor trying to check those impulses—a notion that seems more an outgrowth of the Victorian morality of nineteenth-century Vienna than a valid depiction of a universal process.

Erikson's interpretation of development has fared better than Freud's, perhaps because Erikson's ideas, though arising from Freudian theory, are more comprehensive, contemporary, and apply to a wider range of behavior. Even so, most of the sources of Erikson's theory are, like Freud's, grounded in his own experiences, the recollections of his patients in therapy, and his insights from literature, film, and historical circumstances. In general, psychoanalytic theories do not lend themselves easily to laboratory testing under controlled conditions, which leads to the accusation by some that the validity of psychoanalytic ideas is "evaluated by dogma, not data" (Cairns, 1983). Consequently, some psychologists find psychoanalytic theories illuminating and insightful; others find them provocative nonsense; most think they are somewhere in between.

Learning Theories

Early in the twentieth century, John B. Watson (1878–1958) argued that if psychology was to be a true science, psychologists should study only what they could see and measure. In Watson's words: "Why don't we make what we can *observe* the real field of psychology? Let us limit ourselves to things that can be observed, and formulate laws concerned only with those things. . . . We can observe behavior—what the organism does or says" (Watson, 1930/1967). Many American psychologists agreed with Watson, partly because of the difficulty of trying to study unconscious motives and impulses identified in psychoanalytic theory. Behavior, by contrast, could be studied far more objectively and scientifically. Thus developed a major theory of American psychology, **behaviorism**. This theory formed the basis for a variety of contemporary **learning theories** that share an emphasis on how we learn specific behaviors.

Laws of Behavior

Learning theorists have formulated laws of behavior that can be applied to any individual at any age, from newborn to octogenarian. These laws provide insights into how mature competencies are fashioned from simple skills, and how environmental influences shape individual development. In this view, all development is a process of learning.

The basic laws of learning theory explore the relationship between **stimulus** and **response**, that is, between any experience or event (the stimulus) and the behavioral reaction (the response) with which it is associated. Some responses are automatic, like reflexes. If someone suddenly waves a hand in your face, you will blink; if a hungry dog smells food, it will salivate. But most responses do not occur spontaneously; they are learned. Learning

behaviorism   A theory that emphasizes the systematic study of observable behavior, especially how it is conditioned.

learning theory   A theory that emphasizes the sequences and processes of conditioning that underlie most of human and animal behavior.

stimulus   Anything that elicits a response, such as a reflex or a voluntary action.

response   Any behavior (either instinctual or learned) that is elicited by a specific stimulus.

theorists emphasize that life is a continual learning process: new events and experiences evoke new behavior patterns, while old, unproductive responses tend to fade away. One part of this learning process involves **conditioning**, through which a particular response comes to be triggered by a particular stimulus. There are two basic types of conditioning: classical and operant.

Classical Conditioning

More than ninety years ago, a Russian scientist named Ivan Pavlov (1849–1936) began to study the link between stimulus and response. While doing research on salivation in dogs, Pavlov noted that his experimental dogs began to salivate not only at the sight of food but, eventually, at the sound of the approaching attendants who brought the food. This observation led him to perform his famous experiment in which he taught a dog to salivate at the sound of a bell. Pavlov began by ringing the bell just before feeding the dog. After several repetitions of this association, the dog began salivating at the sound of the bell even when there was no food in sight.

This simple experiment in learning was one of the first scientific demonstrations of **classical conditioning** (also called *respondent conditioning*). In classical conditioning, an organism (any type of living creature) comes to associate a neutral stimulus with a meaningful one, and then *responds* to the former stimulus as if it were the latter. In Pavlov's original experiment, the dog associated the bell (the neutral stimulus) with food and responded to the sound as though it were the food itself.

Many everyday examples suggest classical conditioning that you yourself have probably experienced: imagining a succulent pizza might make your mouth water; reading a final-exam schedule might make your palms sweat; seeing an erotic photograph might make your heart beat faster. In each instance, the stimulus is connected, or associated, with another stimulus that regularly produced the physiological response in the past. Classical conditioning is also apparent when a child who has been badly frightened by some event—say an attack by a snarling dog—is returned to the scene of the incident and begins crying, because he or she now associates the location with previous feelings of terror. As Watson (1927) himself noted, emotional responses are especially susceptible to learning through classical conditioning, particularly in childhood.

Operant Conditioning

The most influential American proponent of learning theory was B. F. Skinner (1904–1990). Skinner agreed with Pavlov that classical conditioning explains some types of behavior. However, Skinner believed that another type of conditioning—**operant conditioning**—plays a much greater role, especially in more complex learning. In operant conditioning, the organism learns that a particular behavior produces a particular consequence. If the consequence is useful or pleasurable, the organism subsequently repeats the behavior to achieve that consequence again. If the consequence is unpleasant, the organism will not repeat the behavior.

In operant conditioning, then, a system of pleasurable consequences (such as rewards) might be used to train an organism to perform a specific

FIGURE 2.6 Pavlov was a physiologist who received the Nobel Prize in 1904 for his research on digestive processes. It was this line of study that led to his discovery of classical conditioning.

conditioning The process of learning, either through the association of two stimuli or through reinforcement or punishment.

classical conditioning The learning process in which a meaningful stimulus is linked to a neutral one, so that the latter elicits a response similar to that previously elicited by the former.

operant conditioning The learning process in which a person or animal becomes more, or less, likely to perform a certain behavior because of past reinforcement or punishment for similar behavior. (Also called *instrumental conditioning*.)

FIGURE 2.7 B. F. Skinner is best known for his experiments with rats and pigeons, but he also applied his knowledge to a wide range of human problems. For his daughter, he designed a glass-enclosed crib in which temperature, humidity, and perceptual stimulation could be controlled to make time spent in the crib as enjoyable and educational as possible. He also conceptualized and wrote about an ideal society based on principles of operant conditioning, where, for example, workers at the less desirable jobs earn greater rewards.

behavior that is not in the organism's natural repertoire. (A simple example of this is training a dog to fetch newspapers or jump through a hoop by giving it a treat every time it performs the behavior.) Once the behavior has been learned, the organism will continue to perform the activity even when the pleasurable consequences occur only occasionally rather than consistently. (Sometimes the behavior can become rewarding in itself.) Almost all a person's daily behavior, from socializing with others to earning a paycheck, can be the result of operant conditioning. (Operant conditioning is also called *instrumental conditioning,* bringing attention to the fact that the behavior in question has become an instrument for achieving a particular consequence.) Children likewise respond to operant conditioning, from the toddler who learns to "stay dry" to obtain parental approval to the adolescent who takes up the latest fad in order to be accepted by peers.

Types of Reinforcement

In operant conditioning, the pleasurable or useful consequence that makes it more likely that the behavior in question will recur is called **reinforcement** (Skinner, 1953). A stimulus that increases the likelihood that a behavior will be repeated is therefore called a **reinforcer**. Reinforcers may be either positive or negative. A **positive reinforcer** is something pleasant—a good feeling, say, or the satisfaction of a need, or a reward from another, such as a piece of candy or a word of praise. For a grade-conscious student who has studied hard for an exam, getting an "A" would be a positive reinforcer of scholarly effort. A **negative reinforcer** is the *removal* of an unpleasant stimulus as the result of a particular behavior. When a student's anxiety about test-taking is reduced by extra preparation or, counterproductively, by "getting high," the reduction of anxiety is a negative reinforcer. That is, the anxiety-reduction increases the probability that the next time the student is worried about a test, he or she will again prepare well, or take drugs.

reinforcement The process whereby a particular behavior is strengthened, making it more likely that the behavior will be repeated.

reinforcer Anything that increases the likelihood that a given response will occur again.

positive reinforcer Anything (such as a reward or positive event) that follows a behavior and increases the likelihood that that behavior will occur again.

negative reinforcer The removal of an unpleasant stimulus following a particular behavior, which removal increases the likelihood that the behavior will be repeated should the unpleasant stimulus recur.

Figure 2.8 According to learning theory, the girl in the upper photo is likely to develop an understanding of basic nutrition requirements, largely because she is reinforced for her efforts at menu planning and is aware of the link between behavior and consequence. The girl below is obviously thrilled with her accomplishment. Her feelings of satisfaction and self-competence are self-reinforcing.

punishment An unpleasant event that follows from a particular behavior, making it less likely that the behavior will be repeated.

extrinsic reinforcer A reinforcer that comes from the environment, such as a word of praise (positive reinforcer) or the cessation of a disturbing noise (negative reinforcer).

intrinsic reinforcer A reinforcer that comes from within the individual, such as a feeling of pride (positive reinforcer) or the reduction of hunger pangs (negative reinforcer).

Note that a negative reinforcer differs from a **punishment**, because punishment is an unpleasant event that makes behavior *less* likely to be repeated. For the grade-conscious student, a failing grade on a test might be a punishment that would make the individual subsequently avoid the particular circumstances (like skipping class) that led to the failure.

Reinforcers may also be either extrinsic or intrinsic. **Extrinsic reinforcers** come from the environment in such varied forms as payment for work, a special privilege for behaving a certain way, good grades, and so forth. **Intrinsic reinforcers** come from within the individual, and typically involve feelings of satisfaction for a job well done and perceptions of self-competence. Thus individuals not only obtain reinforcement from others but are also *self-reinforcing* when they act in particular ways (see Figure 2.8).

It is important to recognize that not all reinforcers have equal significance for those experiencing them. For some people, money is a potent reinforcer; for others, obtaining a special privilege is; and for others, praise and appreciation are most influential. As every student knows, the value of getting an "A" varies tremendously, depending on the student's goals, needs, and past experiences. Indeed, for some students an "A" might lead to less studying rather than more, if the student feels the grade was obtained too easily or if it provokes mockery from classmates for being a bookworm. Learning theorists judge the effectiveness of a reinforcer by how strongly it affects behavior.

When extrinsic reinforcers are used, the timing and consistency of reinforcement are important. To establish the behavior as a learned response, reinforcement initially should follow the behavior every time it occurs. If a mother wants to foster cooperation between siblings, for example, she would be wise to praise the children whenever she sees them cooperate, even though this would require considerable effort on her part. Later, when the children seem to be cooperating most of the time, reinforcement could be provided less frequently and still remain effective. Over time, in fact, the siblings may discover that cooperating is more enjoyable than fighting and makes each child feel good—and then their cooperation would be partially maintained by intrinsic reinforcement rather than by extrinsic reinforcement alone. Cooperation would, in other words, become self-reinforcing.

When behaviorists weigh the methods of creating lasting changes in behavior, they prefer reinforcers to punishments. Harshly criticizing or penalizing someone might immediately change behavior, but research has shown that, for two reasons, these are not the best ways to alter behavior permanently. First, punishment does not teach a desirable alternative behavior to replace the one that is being punished. More important, punishment can also have destructive side effects: someone who is punished frequently can become an apathetic, frustrated, or aggressive person (Skinner, 1972).

Social Learning Theory

Learning theorists have traditionally sought to explain behavior primarily in terms of the organism's direct experience, for they believe that each individual's current behavior results from the accumulated bits of learning acquired through past conditioning, whether classical or operant. These conditioning processes can explain complex patterns of human interaction, as well as simpler behaviors (Bijou, 1989). However, contemporary learning theorists also focus on less direct, though equally potent, forms of learning. They emphasize that people learn new behaviors merely by observing the behavior of others, without directly experiencing any conditioning. These theorists have developed an extension of learning theory called **social learning theory**.

Modeling

An integral part of social learning is **modeling**, in which we observe other people's behavior and then pattern our own after it. This is not simply a case of "monkey see, monkey do." We are more likely to model certain aspects of our behavior, in certain contexts, after that of certain people. Generally, modeling of a particular behavior is most likely to occur in situations in which we are uncertain or inexperienced and the behavior has been previously enacted by someone we consider admirable or powerful or much like ourselves (Bandura, 1977). Often the modeling process is patently obvious, particularly in children. A child who sees another child disobey a command, or share a snack, or play with a toy in an unusual way is likely to imitate the example. The effects of modeling can be particularly apparent when children go off to visit with another family for a few days—and return with a repertoire of new behaviors, in everything from speech mannerisms to table etiquette to moral stances.

Figure 2.9 Social learning theory tends to validate the old maxim "Examples speak louder than words." If the moments here are typical for each child, the girl on the left is likely to grow up with a ready sense of the importance of this particular chore of child care. Unfortunately, the boy on the right may become a cigarette smoker like his father—even if his father warns him of the dangers of this habit.

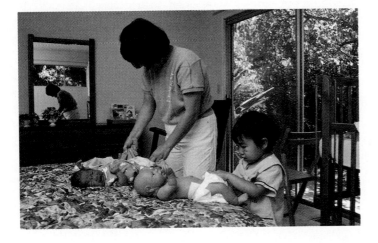 

Cognitive and Motivational Processes

Of course, social learning involves much more than just observing a model and imitating his or her behavior. A person must be motivated to attend to the modeled behavior, to store information about it in memory (perhaps by mentally rehearsing it), and to later retrieve that information when opportunities to use that behavior arise (Bandura, 1977, 1986, 1989). These cognitive and motivational processes help to explain why children's susceptibility to modeling changes as they mature. With increasing age, for example, children become more discriminating observers of other people, and are better able to extract general rules of behavior from the specific examples they observe. This is why young children tend to imitate the most obvious behaviors

social learning theory   The theory that learning occurs through imitation of, and identification with, other people.

modeling   The process in which one person learns from the example of another.

Children Who Are Out of Control

One of the most serious problems that developmentalists have been called upon to solve is that of disruptive, antisocial children. Such children cause havoc at home and trouble at school and also tend to become juvenile delinquents and even career criminals (Farrington, et al., 1990).

One social learning researcher, Gerald Patterson, has spent his career trying to understand and help "out-of-control" children, that is, children who behave in aggressive and antisocial ways that neither the family nor school seems able to control. For the past three decades, Patterson has led a team of scientists at the Oregon Social Learning Center in providing behavioral analysis as well as practical help to families in which one child is disruptively aggressive (Patterson et al., 1967, 1989).

In the tradition of learning theorists, Patterson and his research team have spent thousands of hours observing the moment-by-moment sequences of behavior in hundreds of normal families and in families with an out-of-control child. They have produced a vast amount of data on the frequency of aversive behavior (defined as unpleasant acts such as hitting, yelling, teasing, scolding), as well as on the events leading up to, and the consequences of, such behavior.

Their research found that out-of-control children behave aversively at least three times as often as normal children (the record for frequency was set by a 6-year-old boy who behaved aversively, on average, four times a minute). Patterson determined that the problem is in not just the child but also in the social learning provided by the family.

For one thing, in problem families, the other family members also have higher-than-average rates of aversive behavior, often responding to aggression with aggression in a way that sets up an escalating cycle of retaliation. For example, a problem child and a sibling might begin exchanging increasingly nasty names with each other and end up exchanging blows. In time, these patterns of attack and counterattack become so well learned that the parties involved become blind to alternative ways of resolving conflict. Siblings also provide each other with potent aggressive models to imitate.

Another factor highlighted by Patterson's research is that mothers of problem children are often unwitting perpetuators of aversive behavior once it occurs. When a child does something aversive, mothers of problem children are twice as likely to end up responding positively—that is, by giving in to the child—or neutrally (allowing the child to continue the aversive behavior) than they are to respond negatively by punishing the behavior. Thus they buy their children candy to stop them from screaming and crying in the supermarket, or they let a child stay up later if he or she vehemently refuses to go to bed. As Patterson analyzes it, the immediate result of such maternal behavior is reinforcing for both the child and the mother. The child gets what he or she wants (positive reinforcement), and the mother avoids further unmanageable behavior that calls attention to her ineffectiveness (negative reinforcement). In essence, the child becomes operantly conditioned to go out of control in order to get his or her way, and the mother becomes operantly conditioned to acquiesce in order to avoid intensifying the child's behavior.

The mother's short-term solution creates a long-term problem, however. Patterson found that mothers are the victims of aversive behavior ten times as often as fathers and three times as often as siblings. As his research clearly shows, the mother's role is typically that of family caretaker and "crisis manager," the one who is almost always at the front lines when problems occur. This is in marked contrast to the role taken by the typical father.:

> The role most appropriate for fathers might be that of "guest." They expend much effort on activities which they find reinforcing (e.g., reading the newspaper). They may

of a wide range of people, whereas adolescents and adults reproduce more subtle behaviors and styles of conduct (such as a "laid-back air" or a "scholarly manner") from their observations of selected individuals.

Observing others also enables people to anticipate likely consequences of their actions. With these expectancies, they can mentally test alternative behaviors and choose the one with the most desirable probable outcome. Not surprisingly, children acquire considerable skill in this capacity for "forethought" as they get older (Bandura, 1986, 1989). Whereas preschoolers may act impulsively and regret the consequences, school-age children can, on the basis of memories of past experiences and their obser-

function as reinforcer, spectator, and participant in games, that is, "the resident good guy." They may even enter into some lightweight child management activities. However, given real crisis or high rate of aversives, they tend to drop out. [Patterson, 1980]

Patterson also notes that mothers who do not generally deal effectively with aversive behavior also tend to respond inappropriately to good behavior, either ignoring it or, about 20 percent of the time, actually punishing it. (One explanation for this involves classical conditioning: the mother becomes so conditioned to interpret her child's behavior as negative that she interprets all the child's behavior that way.) Since the child is neither reinforced for good behavior nor punished for bad, the child doesn't learn to do anything differently.

The solution, as Patterson sees it, is for the mothers to become more skilled at conditioning techniques. They must reinforce positive behavior in their children, and, when punishing negative behavior, they must make sure that the punishment is sufficient to stop the outburst, rather than simply escalating and extending it. Here is an observer's account of Patterson's approach to training mothers in appropriate management techniques:

> The child went to bed early only when he felt like it, insisted on sleeping with his mother (she had no husband), rarely obeyed even the most reasonable commands, spread his excrement all over the living room walls, was a terror to other children who tried to play with him, and seemed destined to be a terror to his teachers. The first task was to make the mother realize that he was not minding her in important ways because he was not minding her in small ones. Every day for one hour she was to count the number of times the boy failed to obey an order within fifteen seconds of its being issued and report the results to the therapist. This led the mother to become aware of how many times she was issuing orders and how long she was waiting to get results. . . .

At the third session, the mother was taught how to use "time out" as a means of discipline. She was told that whenever her son did something wrong she should immediately tell him why it was wrong and order him to go to time out—five minutes alone in the bathroom. She resisted doing this, because it forced her to confront all of her son's rule-breaking, and to do so immediately. She preferred to avoid the conflicts and the angry protests. She especially resisted using this means to enforce her son's going to bed at a stated, appropriate time; she was . . . lonely, . . . and it was clear to the therapist that she wanted her son to sleep with her. In time, the woman was persuaded to try this new form of discipline and to back up a failure to go to time out by the withdrawal of some privilege ("no TV tonight"). As the weeks went by the woman became excited about the improvement in the boy's behavior and came to value having him sleep alone in his own room. [Wilson, 1983]

However, retraining is not easy. In many families, the parents have developed a marriage relationship that works to encourage aggression rather than to limit it (Morton, 1987). For instance, if standard family disputes (over whether a child should have a new bike, or where to go for vacation, or if the television can be on during dinner) are typically resolved by one parent outshouting the other, the children never learn how conflicts can be resolved in an amicable way. It takes a skilled trainer and several weeks or months to undo the habits learned over many years. Ideally, mother, father, and siblings should be brought into the project to change the social network of the family and to become models of appropriate, rather than inappropriate, behavior. They can also practice specific techniques to condition the problem child to behave in a more compliant fashion. If the entire family works to improve their interaction, a family that has been at war with itself can learn to function in a supportive way for every member.

vations of others, anticipate the results of their impulses and perhaps act differently.

Finally, social learning is also affected by perceptions of **self-efficacy**, that is, a person's sense of his or her own aspirations and capabilities (Bandura, 1986, 1989). Because people have different goals, standards, and expectations for themselves, they are naturally drawn to certain social influences, and to certain models, more than to others. Perceptions of self-efficacy also influence how motivated people are to learn certain behaviors (like dribbling a basketball or playing a musical instrument) and to act on what they have learned.

self-efficacy One's feelings of competency, capability, and effectiveness.

Figure 2.10 Whether children strive to imitate Eric Clapton's moves on an air guitar or Shaquille O'Neal's moves on a basketball court depends, in part, on perceptions of self-efficacy—what people aspire for themselves and believe they can accomplish.

Learning is thus affected by self-understanding, because the standards you set for yourself, and your confidence in your ability to meet them, influence your motivation to learn from various sources—whether they be peers, mentors, or media stars. Differences in perceptions of self-efficacy can help explain, for example, why one 10-year-old with good coordination and past athletic successes can be found imitating Shaquille O'Neal's moves on a basketball court, while another 10-year-old whose inclinations are more musical is likelier to be found practicing Eric Clapton's moves on an air guitar. In short, much of our social learning depends on the directions in which our perception of self-efficacy points us.

Reciprocal Determinism

Because of these cognitive and motivational influences on social learning, theorists like Albert Bandura (1986, 1989) regard behavior as an outcome of **reciprocal determinism**—that is, the mutual interaction of the person's internal characteristics, the environment, and behavior itself. One's internal characteristics, such as personal expectations, self-perceptions, and goals, are affected by the social environment, as we have seen, but they also influence that environment. Extroverted individuals, for example, evoke different reactions from others than do withdrawn persons. These reactions, in turn, reinforce the personal qualities in question. Behavior is jointly the result of personal and environmental factors, but also influences each. In this concept of reciprocal determinism, social learning theorists seek to include the significant personal and environmental determinants of individual development within a comprehensive theory—a far cry from the early behaviorist focus on salivating dogs or rats running mazes.

Evaluations of Learning Theories

The study of human development has benefited from learning theory in at least two ways. First, the emphasis on the causes and consequences of observed behavior has led researchers to see that many behavior patterns that may seem to be inborn or the result of deeply rooted emotional problems may actually be the result of the immediate environment. As the Research Report (pp. 54–55) on children who are out of control clearly shows, an

reciprocal determinism Refers to the idea that an individual's internal characteristics, environment, and behavior are mutually interactive in determining the individual's specific behaviors.

analysis of environmental influences can sometimes reveal the origins of otherwise perplexing behavioral problems. And even when the immediate environment cannot explain a problem completely, altering that environment may nevertheless significantly remedy the problem by providing new reinforcements and new expectations. Indeed, contrary to the tenets of psychoanalysis, there is sometimes no need to uncover the deep and tangled roots of a particular problem, if some reshaping of behavior will fix it.

This realization has encouraged many scientists to approach particular problem behaviors, such as temper tantrums, phobic reactions, and drug addiction, by analyzing and attempting to change the stimulus-response patterns they entail. A similar approach has been adopted by programs that help parents to understand how they unintentionally reinforce or model problem behavior in offspring and to learn more successful child-rearing skills. Teachers, too, have benefited from this insight, developing classroom environments that promote learning and cooperation through reinforcements and modeling influences.

Second, learning theory has contributed considerable scientific rigor to developmental study. Learning theorists have challenged researchers to define terms precisely, test hypotheses critically, explore alternative explanations for research findings (especially explanations involving environmental influences), and avoid reliance on theoretical concepts (such as unconscious drives or reasoning structures) that cannot be observed and directly tested. This emphasis has made developmental psychology a more scientific—and less speculative and intuitive—field of study (Horowitz, 1992).

At the same time, learning theory is often criticized for being inadequate to the task of explaining complex cognitive, emotional, and perceptual dimensions of human development (Grusec, 1992). Critics point out that these developmental processes are influenced not just by the environment, but also by biological maturation, internal structures of thought, and the developing person's own efforts to comprehend new experiences. From this perspective, behavioral and social learning theories that focus primarily on learning from the environment provide an important but very incomplete picture of the full range of developmental influences at work throughout life.

Cognitive Theories

Cognitive theories focus primarily on the structure and development of the individual's thought processes and the way those processes affect the person's understanding of the world. Further, cognitive theories consider how this understanding, and the expectations it creates, affect the individual's behavior.

Piaget's Theory

Jean Piaget (1896–1980), a major pioneer of cognitive theory, first became interested in thought processes while field-testing questions that were being considered for a standard intelligence test for children. Piaget was supposed to find the age at which most children could answer each question correctly, but eventually he became more interested in the children's *wrong*

FIGURE 2.11 All his life Jean Piaget was absorbed with studying the way children think. He called himself a "genetic epistemologist"—one who studies how children gain knowledge about the world as they grow up.

cognitive theory The theory that the way people understand and think shapes their behavior and personality.

answers. What intrigued him was that children who were the same age made similar types of mistakes, suggesting that there is a developmental sequence to intellectual growth. He began to believe that *how* children think is much more important, and more revealing of their mental ability, than what they know. Moreover, understanding how children think also reveals how they interpret their experiences and gradually construct their understanding of the world.

Stages of Cognitive Development

Piaget held that there are four major stages of cognitive development. Each one is age-related, and each has structural features that permit certain types of knowing and understanding (see Table 2.2).

According to Piaget, infants in the **sensorimotor stage** know the world exclusively through their senses and motor abilities: their understanding of the objects in their world is limited to the immediate actions they can perform on them and their sensory experiences of them. This is a very practical, experience-based kind of early intelligence, but it is limited to the here and now.

By contrast, preschool children in the **preoperational stage** can begin to think symbolically; that is, they can think about and understand objects using mental processes that are independent of immediate experience. This is reflected in their ability to use language, to think of past and future events, and to pretend. However, they cannot think logically in a consistent way, and thus their reasoning is subjective and intuitive.

School-age children in the **concrete operational stage** can begin to think logically in a consistent way, but only with regard to real and concrete

sensorimotor stage   Piaget's first stage of cognitive development (from birth to about age 2) in which infants use their senses and motor skills to understand their world.

preoperational stage   Piaget's second stage of cognitive development (from age 2 to about 7) in which children are unable to grasp logical concepts such as conservation, reversibility, or classification.

concrete operational stage   Piaget's third stage of cognitive development in which a child can reason logically about concrete events and problems but cannot reason about abstract ideas and possibilities.

TABLE 2.2

Piaget's Stages of Cognitive Development

Approximate Age	Stage	Characteristics	Major Acquisitions
Birth to 2 years	Sensorimotor	Infant uses senses and motor abilities to understand the world. There is no conceptual or reflective thought; an object is "known" in terms of what an infant can *do* to it.	The infant learns that an object still exists when it is out of sight (*object permanence*) and begins to think by using mental as well as physical actions.
2–6 years	Preoperational	The child uses *symbolic thinking*, including language, to understand the world. Sometimes the child's thinking is *egocentric*, causing the child to understand the world from only one perspective, his or her own.	The imagination flourishes, and language becomes a significant means of self-expression and of influence from others. Children gradually begin to *decenter*, that is, become less egocentric, and to understand and coordinate multiple points of view.
7–11 years	Concrete Operational	The child understands and applies logical operations, or principles, to help interpret experiences objectively and rationally rather than intuitively.	By applying logical abilities, children learn to understand the basic concepts of conservation, number, classification, and many other scientific ideas.
From 12 on	Formal Operational	The adolescent or adult is able to think about abstractions and hypothetical concepts and is able to speculate in thought from the real to the possible.	Ethics, politics, and social and moral issues become more interesting and involving as the adolescent becomes able to take a broader and more theoretical approach to experience.

FIGURE 2.12 To Piaget, a child's stage of cognitive growth influences how the world is experienced and understood. Each of these children is thinking about a plant, but they are thinking in much different ways. To the baby in the sensorimotor stage, the flower is "known" as something that can be looked at and tasted. To the child in the preoperational stage, plants can be named and their needs can be understood through language. To the grade-school child, plants can be analyzed through logical reasoning skills, such as classification.

formal operational stage Piaget's fourth stage of cognitive development, characterized by hypothetical, logical, and abstract thought.

equilibrium Cognitive balance achieved through the assimilation and accommodation of conflicting experiences and perceptions.

scheme A general way of thinking about, or interacting with, objects and ideas in the environment.

disequilibrium Cognitive uncertainty and imbalance that arises when new information does not fit into existing schemes.

features of their world, not abstract situations. Nevertheless, logical reasoning abilities make the school-age child a more systematic, objective, and scientific kind of thinker.

In the final, **formal operational stage**, adolescents and adults, in varying degrees, are able to think hypothetically and abstractly: they can think about thinking and speculate about the possible as well as the real. Each of these ways of thinking is explained in detail later in this book.

How Cognitive Development Occurs

Underlying Piaget's stage theory is his basic view of cognitive development as a process that follows universal patterns. This process is guided, according to Piaget, by the need in everyone for **equilibrium**, that is, a state of mental balance (Piaget, 1970b). What he meant is that each person needs to, and continually attempts to, reconcile new experiences with his or her existing understanding in order to make sense of them.

Equilibrium is achieved when a person's mental concepts—or, in Piaget's terms, **schemes**—accord well with his or her current experiences. A scheme is a general way of thinking about, or interacting with, ideas and objects in the environment. The infant first comes to know the world through schemes involving sensorimotor activities—a sucking scheme, a grasping scheme, a listening scheme, and the like. By adulthood the schemes through which the individual knows the world are innumerable, ranging from something as simple as the scheme for buttoning and unbuttoning to the abstract moral scheme that a human life is more valuable than any material possession. Equilibrium is experienced when one's present schemes "fit" new experiences, whether this involves a baby's discovery that new objects can be grasped in accustomed ways or an adult's being able to explain current events in terms of his or her political philosophy. When existing schemes do not seem to fit present experiences, the individual falls into a state of **disequilibrium**, a kind of imbalance that initially produces confusion and then leads to growth, as the person modifies old schemes and constructs new ones to fit the new experience. You may experience disequilibrium, for example, when a friend's argument reveals inconsistencies in your views, when your favorite chess strategy fails against a skilled opponent, or when your mother does or says something you never expected her to.

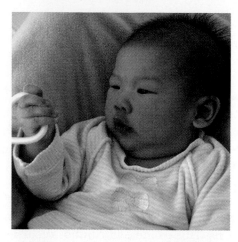

FIGURE 2.13 One indication of cognitive growth in infancy is how the baby's inborn grasping scheme is used and adapted to different objects. Infants will assimilate just about any object to this scheme, whether it is their blanket, a rattle, or Daddy's nose! They also accommodate this scheme to the size and shape of the object. In this manner, grasping becomes better adapted to the environment—and the baby grows intellectually.

Periods of disequilibrium can be disquieting to a child or an adult who suspects that accepted ideas no longer hold true. But they are also exciting periods of mental growth, which is one reason why people of all ages seek new, challenging experiences. By seeking out novel experiences, children are constantly putting their current schemes to the test. Babies poke, pull, and taste everything they get their hands on; preschool children ask thousands of questions; school-age children become avid readers and information collectors; adolescents try out a wide variety of roles and experiences; and adults continually increase their knowledge and expertise in areas that interest them—all because people at every age seek cognitive challenges. Recognition of this active searching for knowledge is the very essence of Piaget's theory of human cognitive development.

The search for knowledge (provoked, in part, by disequilibrium) is accomplished through two innate, interrelated processes that are, according to Piaget, the core of intelligence. These processes are **organization** and **adaptation**. People organize their thoughts so that they make sense, establishing links between one idea and another and integrating their knowledge in systematic, cohesive ways. In the process of learning about various animals, for example, a child may organize them mentally in clusters according to whether they are birds, mammals, or fishes. At the same time, people adapt their thinking to include new ideas as new experiences provide additional information.

This adaptation occurs in two ways, through *assimilation* and *accommodation*. In the process of **assimilation**, new information is incorporated into a current scheme; that is, it is simply added to the cognitive organization already in place. In the process of **accommodation**, the intellectual organization has to adjust to the new information. Thus, in watching a nature film on whales, a child may *extend* his or her scheme for classifying mammals by learning that whales, like cats and elephants, are members of this class (assimilation). Simultaneously, the child may also *change* the scheme through the realization that, like fish, some mammals live in the sea (accommodation). As in this example, assimilation and accommodation work in tandem, because a scheme is both expanded and modified when something new is learned.

These basic processes of cognitive change are at work even in the first weeks of life. Consider the act of grasping, for instance. Newborns curl their fingers tightly around anything that crosses their palm. Soon, however, grasping becomes organized in specific ways as their particular experiences provide them with new knowledge: they grasp Mother's sweater one way, their bottle another way, a rattle another, and the cat's tail not at all. They have thus adapted their inborn grasping to their environment, first by assimilation (grasping everything that comes their way) and then by accommodation (adjusting their grasp to the "graspability" of the object).

The processes of assimilation and accommodation continue throughout life, and help to account for cognitive growth. As a final example, consider one of Piaget's famous experiments, in which a child is first shown two identical glasses, each containing the same amount of liquid (Piaget & Inhelder, 1974). Next, the liquid from one of the glasses is poured into a third glass, which is taller and narrower than the other two, resulting, naturally, in the liquid's reaching a higher level than in the original glass. The experi-

FIGURE 2.14 Professor Berger's daughter Sarah, here at aged 5¾, demonstrates Piaget's conservation-of-liquids experiment. First she examines both short glasses to be sure they contain the same amount of milk. Then, after the contents of one is poured into the tall glass and she is asked "Which has more?" she points to the tall glass, just as Piaget would have expected.

organization The process of synthesizing and analyzing perceptions and thoughts.

adaptation Cognitive processes that lead to adjustment of new and existing ideas and experiences. Adaptation takes two forms, assimilation and accommodation.

assimilation The process of including new information into already existing schemes.

accommodation The process of shifting or enlarging current ideas, or schemes, in order to encompass new information.

conservation of liquids The concept that a given amount of liquid remains constant regardless of the shape of its container.

information-processing theory A theory of learning that focuses on the steps of thinking—such as sorting, categorizing, storing, and retrieving—that are similar to the functions of a computer.

menter then asks the child which glass contains more. Most children younger than 5 consider the relative levels of liquid and say the taller glass contains more, using the simple scheme that "taller is more." They are unshakable in this conviction, even when the experimenter tries to persuade them otherwise (see Figure 2.14).

By the age of 7 or 8, however, most children have developed the scheme that Piaget called **conservation of liquids**—the realization that the amount of liquid does not change even though a different container (in this case, a taller glass) changes the liquid's appearance. They remain steadfast in this conviction, even in the face of contrary arguments.

In both cases, the children's ideas and perceptions are in a state of equilibrium: their mental concepts enable them to make sense of what they see. However, in the transition from the first state of equilibrium to the second, children experience disequilibrium, during which they begin to recognize that some of their ideas conflict with their experiences. They become increasingly aware, for example, of the inconsistency between their perception that the identical glasses originally contained the same amount of liquid and their scheme that "taller is more." During this transitional period, the dual processes of assimilation and accommodation yield interim resolutions to this dilemma, such as the idea that the tall glass actually contains *less* liquid because it is narrower.

Taken together, Piaget's portrayal of the child is of a "little scientist" who develops new organizations of thought by exploring the world and modifying his or her understanding accordingly. Piaget's theory also describes the comprehensive changes that occur in thinking and reasoning as children proceed through stages of mental growth that increase their capacity to view the world symbolically, logically, and then abstractly.

Information-Processing Theory

In recent years, another perspective on cognitive growth has influenced a growing number of developmental researchers. Taking its inspiration from modern technology, **information-processing theory** likens many aspects of human thinking to the way computers analyze and process data. In many ways, of course, the human mind is far more sophisticated than the most advanced computer: no computer can match the mind's capacity for reflection, creativity, and intuition. However, information-processing theorists suggest that by focusing on the step-by-step mechanics of human thinking, we might derive a more precise understanding of cognitive development (Klahr, 1989, 1992; Siegler, 1983, 1991). Like computers, for example, humans must store large amounts of information, get access to that information when it is needed, and analyze situations in terms of the particular problem-solving strategies that will yield a correct solution.

Steps of Processing

One example of how researchers portray the information-processing system can be seen in Figure 2.15. Notice that, like the learning theorists, information-processing theorists are interested in the relationship between stimulus and response. But they differ from learning theorists because of their interest in internal mental processes—specifically, in the flow of information between cognitive processes—and in the developmental changes that occur in each of these processes.

The first step in information processing occurs in the **sensory register**, which stores incoming stimulus information for a split second after it is received to allow it to be selectively processed. (You may have noticed that whenever you close your eyes, you retain a fleeting visual image of what you were last looking at. This is an example of the sensory register at work.)

Most information that comes into the sensory register is lost or discarded, but what is meaningful is transferred to working memory for further analysis. It is in **working memory** (sometimes called *short-term memory*) that your current, conscious mental activity occurs. This includes, at this moment, your understanding of this paragraph, any previous knowledge you recall that is related to it, and also, perhaps, distracting thoughts about your weekend plans or the interesting person who sat next to you in class today. Working memory is constantly replenished with new information, so thoughts and memories are usually not retained for very long. Some are discarded, while a few are transferred to your knowledge base.

The **knowledge base** (also called *long-term memory*) stores information for days, months, or years, and has a virtually limitless capacity. Together with influences from the sensory register and working memory, the knowledge base assists in organizing your reactions to environmental stimuli through the **response generator**, a network of mental processes that organize behavior.

Although we do not usually think of our minds as sophisticated computers, the information-processing flow chart depicted in Figure 2.15 helps to explain many features of mental activity. Suppose the radio is playing while you are studying, and a call-in phone number for a contest is announced. If you are distracted or uninterested, this auditory information will get no further than the sensory register, and you will not consciously think about it. If you pay attention to the number, however, it will enter working memory and remain there temporarily—probably long enough for you to call the number. If you get a busy signal, however, and can't find a pencil, you must decide how to retain the number for a longer period of time, perhaps by transferring it to your knowledge base. You might mentally rehearse it, by repeating it a number of times, or divide the digits into

sensory register A memory system that functions for only a fraction of a second, retaining a fleeting impression of a stimulus on a particular sense organ.

working memory The part of memory that handles current, conscious mental activity. (Also called *short-term memory*.)

knowledge base The part of memory that stores information over a long time, from minutes to decades. (Also called *long-term memory*.)

response generator A network of mental processes, involving the sensory register, working memory, and knowledge base, that organizes reactions to the environment.

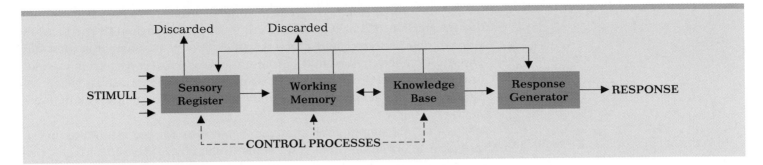

FIGURE 2.15 This is a flow chart of the information-processing system. Solid arrows refer to the transfer of information between system components. Broken arrows refer to influences within the system that affect how information is processed and transferred. (Adapted from Shiffrin and Atkinson, 1969.)

groups to make them more memorable, or use some other memory strategy. Thus as you analyze sensory information (in this case, the phone number) further, additional components of the information-processing system are enlisted.

Developmental Changes

The various components of the information-processing system function differently as children and adults mature, which explains in part why learning and memory skills change with development. One obvious change is that the knowledge base expands throughout childhood and adolescence, as children acquire more information about the world. This speeds new learning because it is easier to process new information when it relates to what one already knows.

With development, pivotal changes also occur in the component called **control processes**, which regulate the analysis and flow of information within the system. When you deliberately use rehearsal or another strategy to remember a phone number, for example, you are using a control process. Control processes are also involved when you try to retrieve someone's name or other specific information from your knowledge base, or listen for a familiar voice in a crowd, or use a rule-of-thumb to solve a problem. In a sense, control processes assume an executive role in the information-processing system, regulating the analysis and transfer of information within the system.

The developing efficiency of the control processes is most noticeable in young children, as they acquire more sophisticated memory and retrieval strategies, learn to use selective attention, become capable of automatically performing mental activities that formerly required considerable effort (like reading), and develop more effective rules or strategies for problem solving (Kuhn, 1992; Sternberg, 1988). Consider what happens, for example, when a 5-year-old is faced with a simple problem—like trying to remember what she did after kindergarten the day before yesterday. Her retrieval of that information from her knowledge base may be limited because she does not yet know how to search her memory thoroughly or deeply. She may remember pieces of events from that time period ("I came home and had a snack"), but may be distracted by other, associated knowledge ("I really like my teacher"). Her account is likely to be piecemeal, partly irrelevant, and probably misleading. By contrast, at age 10, she will approach this problem far more effectively, perhaps by bringing to mind her usual after-school routine

control processes That part of the information-processing system that regulates the analysis and flow of information, including memory and retrieval strategies, selective attention, and rules or strategies for problem solving.

(or "script") and trying to recall any events that may have modified it on the day in question. She will probably also focus on this task until she can provide a coherent, complete account of her after-school activities that day. These differences in the child's problem solving arise, in part, from the maturation of control processes, which contributes to the more strategic and efficient learning that occurs at the end of primary school compared to that of the beginning.

Other developmental changes contribute to age-related improvements in information-processing skills (Kuhn, 1992; Flavell, 1992). As they mature, children develop richer associations among their knowledge networks, making it possible for an idea in one area of their thinking to trigger additional related thoughts and ideas in other knowledge domains. A grade-schooler studying about government, for example, might spontaneously recall things he heard about Congress during a TV news show. In contrast with a younger child's tendency to acquire knowledge in more piecemeal fashion, the integration and association of different knowledge networks in the older child's thinking contributes to greater cognitive depth and flexibility. Finally, older children are also more capable of monitoring and regulating their own thinking processes: they can spontaneously evaluate their performance on an intellectual task (whether remembering information for a test or reasoning about a personal dilemma), and can often use remedial strategies to improve it.

To study these developmental changes, researchers present children with tasks that are carefully designed to measure specific features of their information-processing skills—their use of a control process related to memory, for example, or their capacity to spontaneously evaluate their own problem-solving strategies. Sometimes the researchers measure the length of time children require to complete the task successfully, or analyze the patterns of errors children tend to make. Information-processing theorists often employ a "task analysis" to understand the particular skills that are necessary to successfully solve a specific problem. Recall our earlier discussion of Piaget's conservation-of-liquids experiment, for example. To an information-processing theorist, successful performance would require at least five distinct cognitive components: understanding the experimenter's question; searching memory for past experiences that are pertinent to the task; devising a correct rule or strategy to apply to the three liquid containers; spontaneously evaluating the suitability of that strategy to this particular task; and, finally, reporting a solution to the experimenter. Indeed, some information-processing theorists have been able to write computer programs that mimic the reasoning processes of children of various ages on this conservation experiment (Klahr, 1989; Klahr & Wallace, 1976), underscoring how these information-processing components resemble a computer's analysis of complex problems.

As you can see, information-processing theorists view cognitive development differently than Piaget did. Whereas Piaget characterized cognitive development as a series of broad stages of mental growth, information-processing theorists tend to think of development as a more gradual process involving the acquisition of specific strategies, rules, and skills that affect memory, learning, and problem solving.

Evaluations of Cognitive Theories

Cognitive theories have revolutionized developmental psychology by focusing attention on active mental processes (Beilin, 1992). The attempt to understand the mental structures and strategies of thought, and to appreciate the internal need for new ones when the old ones become outmoded, has led to a new understanding of certain aspects of human behavior. Thanks to the insights provided by cognitive theories, we now have a greater appreciation of the capacities and limitations of the types of thinking that are possible at various ages—and of the ways in which these capacities and limitations can affect behavior.

Cognitive theories have also profoundly affected education in many countries, allowing teachers and students to become partners in the educational process once the child's own capacities and needs are recognized. Learning through personal discovery, acquiring effective learning strategies, and acting on objects rather than merely being told about them are all contemporary features of educational practice drawn from cognitive theories.

For instance, today elementary-school math is taught with objects the child can manipulate, because educators now realize that the thinking of school-age children is better suited to working out and understanding solutions through concrete activities, such as measuring blocks or counting pennies, than to using the more abstract learning tasks involved in reading about, and memorizing, mathematical facts. Children can also be helped in developing learning and problem-solving strategies that improve their classroom performance.

Finally, and perhaps most obviously, cognitive theories remind us that "intelligence" involves many factors that are not easily summarized in an IQ score and reflects the remarkably diverse and complex skills and strategies that people evolve through their interactions with the surrounding world.

While Piaget's studies have made a profound contribution to educational practices, his work has met with some criticism. Many people think Piaget was so absorbed by the individual's active search for knowledge that he ignored the influence of external motivation and instruction. While it is comforting to think that children can develop their own schemes when they are ready, this implies that teachers should not intervene if a child seems uninterested in learning to add or spell. And even some of those who most admire Piaget believe that he underestimated the role of society and home in fostering cognitive development. As we shall see in the next section, sociocultural theorists believe that culture and education can be crucial in providing the proper mix of incentives to cognitive growth (Flavell, 1992).

Critics have also found fault with Piaget's depiction of cognitive stages. For example, there are many adults who are very inconsistent in using the skills of abstract thinking that Piaget described as typically developing in adolescence. In addition, new research has shown that infants and preschoolers are far more competent intellectually than Piaget believed (Flavell, 1992). A number of researchers have also pointed out that Piaget's description of cognitive development tends to make it seem comprehensive, as though once a new stage of cognition has been achieved, it will be re-

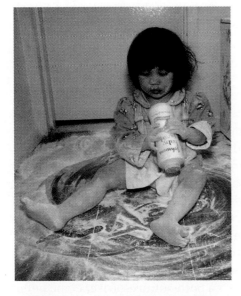

FIGURE 2.16 Are children more like scientists or computers in their cognitive growth? Elements of each are apparent in this preschooler's enthusiasm for discovering how baby powder looks, feels, and tastes, and in her attempts to relate these discoveries to prior experiences and events (like tasting and touching snow). Unfortunately, her parents are likely to see her efforts at intellectual discovery as nothing more than making a mess.

flected in all aspects of the individual's thinking. In fact, the cognitive advance may occur in some areas of thinking and not in others, or may appear on one occasion and not on another. Most cognitive theorists now generally believe that with regard to the pace of cognitive growth in specific areas, each child has "a unique rate of development and possesses his or her own idiosyncrasies" (Thomas, 1993). Information-processing theorists in particular emphasize that the skills and strategies children acquire may be task-specific and do not generalize to other situations (Case, 1985; Fischer, 1980).

Of course, information-processing theory has its critics as well. Some take issue with the use of the computer metaphor as a model of human thinking. Computers do not have the capacity for reflection, insight, or self-change that people do, and using this metaphor may mislead researchers into neglecting these essential features of human reasoning. These critics find Piaget's portrayal of the child as a little scientist, eagerly generating new understanding by acting on the world, to be a far more attractive image of children's thinking. Moreover, because the focus of information-processing theorists has been primarily on the development of specific skills and abilities in the context of specific tasks, some critics wonder whether the information-processing approach will lead to useful, general conclusions about the nature of children's thinking as a whole and its development over time. In essence, then, Piaget has been faulted for overgeneralizing the nature and progression of cognitive development in four broad stages, while information-processing theorists have been criticized for offering explanations of cognitive change that are too particularized.

Sociocultural Theory

Whether they are living in a society that is urban and industrialized, rural and agricultural, or nomadic and hunter-gatherer, all children must acquire the skills and knowledge essential to their culture. For children in a small rural Kenyan community, for example, this may mean learning the skills needed for managing farmland and animals, for anticipating and reading seasonal rhythms, and for contributing to the well-being of their family and community. In contrast, for children growing up in urban America, acquiring essential cultural knowledge may mean learning the literary, logistical, and mathematical skills required in a technological society and developing the social alertness and self-assertion needed to remain safe while interacting with strangers. Underlying such skills in both cultures are specific belief structures that children must also acquire, such as the value of respecting one's elders without question and of putting the needs of one's family and social group ahead of one's own—or, alternatively, the value of routinely questioning the authority of others and of steadfastly securing one's independence and self-interests.

sociocultural theory A theory that seeks to explain the growth of individual knowledge and competencies in terms of the guidance, support, and structure provided by the broader cultural context.

Recognizing these crucial aspects of cultural influence, **sociocultural theory**, a contextual perspective, seeks to explain the growth of individual knowledge and competencies in terms of the guidance, support, and structure provided by the broader cultural context. The central thesis of sociocultural theory is that human development is the result of a dynamic interaction between developing persons and their surrounding culture. This

FIGURE 2.17 The sociocultural theory of development is changing the nature of classroom education today, especially in multiethnic schools such as this one. Increasingly, teachers are recognizing that the most effective methods of instruction take into account the values, practices, and interests of the student's particular culture.

view goes beyond mere descriptions of contrasting developmental patterns and looks at the processes through which children develop in a cultural context: it recognizes not only the importance of learning and instruction from parents, teachers, and peers in one's immediate environment but also the ways in which these influences are shaped by the beliefs and goals shared by members of the community and the larger society.

Vygotsky's Theory

A major pioneer of the sociocultural perspective was Lev Vygotsky (1896–1934), a psychologist from the former Soviet Union who was a contemporary of Pavlov, Freud, and Piaget. Although his writings have only recently become available in the West (Vygotsky, 1978, 1987), they have attracted a wide audience, and many current researchers in developmental psychology take a sociocultural view that is deeply influenced by Vygotsky's ideas.

Vygotsky was primarily interested in the development of cognitive competencies. In his view, these competencies result from the interaction between children and more mature members of the society, in what has been called an "apprenticeship in thinking" (Rogoff, 1990). The implicit goal of this apprenticeship is to provide children with instruction and support for acquiring the knowledge and capabilities that are valued by the culture. By engaging children in a context of guided participation, parents and other teachers tutor them in practical skills (such as casting a fishing net, or sewing a button on a shirt, or using a TV remote control), social skills (such as shaking hands, or showing deference to elders, or expressing one's wishes in an acceptable manner), and intellectual skills (such as writing in one's native language, or being able to gain new knowledge by consulting a village elder or an encyclopedia). This apprenticeship may take the form of explicit instruction, or it may occur informally, as children observe older friends or family members carry out the activities of everyday life.

Such social interaction also provides the context for mastering the culture's tools for further learning, whether they include an alphabet, a computer, Roman numerals, an abacus, a telephone, or a slide rule. Vygotsky believed that, universally, the most important learning tool is the specific *language* of each society, because language provides a powerful means of learning through social interaction. With the mastering of language, children's thinking acquires unique potential, enabling them to express their thoughts and ideas to social partners and, in turn, to absorb the ideas of others—and the culture at large—into their own thinking (Vygotsky, 1978, 1987).

FIGURE 2.18 Lev Vygotsky is now recognized as a seminal thinker, whose ideas on the role of culture and history are revolutionizing education as well as expanding the conception of developmental processes. A contemporary of Freud, Skinner, Pavlov, and Piaget, Vygotsky did not attain their eminence in his lifetime, partly because his work, conducted in Stalinist Russia, was largely inaccessible, and partly because he died prematurely at age 38.

In both skill learning and language mastery, the process of social apprenticeship is similar. Typically, a mentor senses the child's readiness for new challenges and arranges social interactions that help push the child's skills in new directions. In Vygotsky's terms, the mentor draws the child into the **zone of proximal development**, which is the range of skills that the child can exercise with assistance but cannot perform independently. Through sensitive assessment of the child's abilities and capacity for potential growth, the adult offers guidance that engages the child's participation and gradually facilitates the child's transition from assisted performance to independent performance.

To make this rather abstract-seeming process more concrete, let's take a simple example—a father teaching his 5-year-old daughter to ride a bicycle. He will probably begin by helping his daughter to get the feel of the bicycle, as he slowly rolls her along, firmly supporting her weight and holding her upright while encouraging her to keep her feet on the pedals and to look straight ahead. When she says she feels that she is going to fall, he reassures her that he is right there and suggests that she lean forward a little bit and relax her arms. As she becomes more comfortable and confident, he begins to roll her along more quickly, noting that she is now able to keep her legs pumping in a steady rhythm. Within another lesson or two he is jogging beside her, holding on to just the handlebar, as he feels her control gradually go from dangerously wobbly to slightly shaky. Then comes the moment when he senses that, with a little more momentum, she could maintain her balance by herself. Accordingly, he urges her to pedal faster and slowly loosens his grip on the handlebar until, without her even realizing it, she is riding on her own.

Such excursions in the zone of proximal development are commonplace: children experience dozens of them daily as various tutors—parents, siblings, friends, teachers—help them learn everything from how to dress themselves to how to solve complex problems of logical reasoning. In each instance, ideally, the learning process follows the same overall pattern, with the mentor, sensitively attuned to the child's continually shifting abilities, urging the child on to new levels of competence, and in turn, to new challenges.

Evaluation of Sociocultural Theory

Sociocultural theory has helped developmentalists deepen their understanding of the diversity in the pathways of growth, leading them to recognize the ways in which the skills, challenges, and opportunities involved in human development vary depending on the values and structures of the society in question. It has also reinforced the idea that in order to understand developmental processes in different cultures, developmental psychologists must understand the values and beliefs of the particular culture, how they affect children, and how particular competencies fit into the child's cultural context.

In the wake of this recognition, developmental researchers have become more cautious about trying to generalize the findings of research on children in one culture to children in another culture (Cole, 1992; Rogoff & Morelli, 1989). They have also come to recognize the need for evaluating developmental competence with procedures that are relevant to the child's

zone of proximal development The knowledge and understanding that a child does not yet comprehend on his or her own but could master with guidance.

specific culture. The importance of this was highlighted by a study in which researchers tested the mathematical abilities of unschooled Brazilian children who worked as market vendors. When the researchers used a testing format like that typically used in schools, the children performed quite poorly. But when the researchers retested the children with problems common to buying and selling in the marketplace, the children displayed remarkable mathematical competence (Carraher et al., 1985).

In many ways, therefore, sociocultural theory has contributed to a broadening of developmental theory and research, as well as to a deeper appreciation of the cultural specificity of human interactions and growth. Sociocultural theorists have been criticized, however, for overlooking developmental processes that are not primarily social. Vygotsky's theory, in particular, has been viewed as neglecting the role of biological maturation in guiding development, especially with regard to neurological maturation in mental processes (Wertsch, 1985; Wertsch & Tulviste, 1992).

Barbara Rogoff (1990), a leading sociocultural theorist, has noted that Vygotsky did not recognize how much children affect the context of their own development by, for instance, choosing their own mentors, activities, and settings for learning, or, sometimes, by refusing the guided assistance of others when mastering new skills ("Let me do it myself!"). No doubt, sociocultural theory provides valuable insights into the social transmission of knowledge, but, as is true of all the other theories, by opening up new vistas on the developmental processes, it may simultaneously obscure others.

The Theories Compared

Each of the theories presented in this chapter has contributed a great deal to the study of human development. Psychoanalytic theories have made us aware of the importance of early childhood experiences and of the impact of the "hidden dramas" that influence our daily lives. Learning theories have shown us the effect that the immediate environment can have on our behavior. Cognitive theories have brought us to a greater understanding of how our thinking affects our actions. And sociocultural theory has reminded us of how our development is embedded in a rich and multifaceted cultural context.

Each theory has also been criticized. Psychoanalytic theory has been faulted for being too subjective; learning theory, for being too mechanistic; cognitive theory, for undervaluing the power of direct instruction and overemphasizing rational, logical thought; and sociocultural theory, for neglecting the intrinsic incentives for development.

In reviewing the theories, consider how they differ in their portrayals of the child and of human development. As we have seen, each theory offers its own unique portrait of what the child is like—a cauldron of unconscious impulses, a little scientist, a computer, an apprentice. Similarly, the theories also vary in how they describe the process of human development. Some theories, like those from the psychoanalytic perspective and Piaget's cognitive theory, view development as a succession of stages of growth, with each stage characterized by its own unique challenges and achievements. For other theories, however, development is a much more gradual and continuous process, and the factors that govern human development (such as learn-

A CLOSER LOOK

Developmental Theories and Child-Rearing Advice

Theories of human development have had considerable and widespread impact throughout the twentieth century. They have guided researchers in their study of children and adults and have shaped policy in education, pediatrics, and the treatment of troubled children. More noticeably, though sometimes less successfully, they have influenced the advice offered to the public by various child-rearing experts.

Americans have always been drawn to learning theories because they seem to provide straightforward solutions to common child-rearing dilemmas. It is not surprising, therefore, that early in this century John Watson was both a leading theoretician in academic psychology and a popular writer in parents' magazines. In one article, "What to Do When Your Child Is Afraid," Watson (1927) applied principles of classical conditioning to the problem of children's fears.

> No child is afraid, at first, to be put to bed alone in the dark, but suppose the wind blows over a screen with a loud bang or causes a shutter to slam, or suppose the wind catches the door and bangs it behind you as you leave the room. You have almost an ideal situation for making the child afraid of the dark. . . .
>
> Suppose this fear of the dark has developed in your child. How will you handle it? You can treat or 'recondition' as we say, the child in a very simple way. When you put him to bed tonight, leave the door partly open and a dim light burning in the hall. The child will go to sleep. Then, gradually, close the door a little and dim the light a little every night. If you work patiently, four or five nights will enable you to recondition the child so that the door can be closed and the light turned out.

Such advice was influential because it offered practical, easy-to-apply solutions and came from a recognized scientific authority. But it also encouraged parents to feel responsible (perhaps too responsible) for their child's development because they controlled many of the environmental influences affecting their offspring. In a sense, Watson gave parents a double message: that they could substantially shape their child's growth through principles of conditioning, but that this also made them responsible for the result.

Following World War II, and the immigration to this country of many of Europe's leading psychoanalysts, popular advice to parents began to reflect Freud's ideas about the emotional, irrational forces within children and the role of parents in understanding and supporting their offspring. Consider this passage from the classic source of parental advice, *The Common Sense Book of Baby and Child Care,* by the leading child-rearing expert of his time, Benjamin Spock (1945):

> New types of fears crop up fairly often around the age of 3 or 4—fears of the dark, of dogs, of fire engines, of death, of cripples. The child's imagination has now developed to the stage where he can put himself in other people's shoes and picture dangers that he hasn't actually experienced. His curiosity is pushing out in all directions. He not only wants to know the cause of everything, but what these things have to do with him. . . .
>
> These fears are commoner in children who have been made tense through battles over such matters as feeding and toilet training, children whose imaginations have been overstimulated by scary stories or too many warnings, children who haven't had enough chance to develop their independence and outgoingness.
>
> Don't make fun of him, or be impatient with him, or try to argue him out of his fear. If he wants to talk about it, as a

ing processes or structures of information-processing) remain more consistent throughout life. The theories also vary in how each addresses the controversies described in Chapter 1, such as the relative importance of nature and nurture or the relative importance of the early years to overall development. Comparing developmental theories in these ways can highlight the unique contributions of each and how each theory alerts us to important features of the developmental process (see Table 2.3, p. 72).

Each theory by itself is, in fact, too restricted to grasp the breadth and diversity of human development (Cairns, 1983; Thomas, 1981). As one researcher explains, developmentalists see human beings as

> so complex and multifaceted as to defy easy classification . . . [and] multiply influenced by a host of interacting determinants. . . . It is an image that highlights the shortcomings of all simplistic theories that view behavior as the exclusive

few children do, let him. Give him the feeling that you want to understand, but that you are sure nothing bad will happen to him. This is the time for extra hugs and comforting reminders that you love him very much and will always protect him.

Notice that Spock analyzed the reasons for children's fears much differently than Watson did: in keeping with the psychoanalytic view, he depicted them as the natural outgrowth of children's irrational imaginative thinking rather than of prior learning experiences. Consequently, his advice to parents was different: they should provide reassurance, security, and emotional support rather than try to recondition the child.

More recent child-rearing advice has drawn from Spock's legacy, but has also been influenced by cognitive views. Parents are now encouraged to accept children's needs and desires—however unreasonable they might appear—by respecting the limitations in the young child's intellectual understanding and experience. Consider this excerpt from the highly popular volume for parents, *Babyhood,* by Penelope Leach (1989):

> Unfortunately where fears are concerned we tend to treat toddlers as if they were miniature versions of adults. When a child is afraid of something which many adults fear, he is usually sympathetically handled. . . . But when the toddler expresses a fear that seems to the adult to be simply silly, it is often treated with bossiness, irritation, or even shame. We forget that the toddler has an intrinsic fear of the strange; we forget that he does not have our experience or our knowledge to call on. Meeting his first tortoise, an 18-month-old boy reacted immediately with pure horror: "Way, way," he said, scarlet-faced. "It's a tortoise, darling," said his mother, picking it up and moving toward him. "Notty," wailed the toddler, exploding into tears and backing up against the wall. . . . The mother could not see that the child *could* be afraid of a tortoise. He had never met one before; had had no nasty experiences with tortoises; it made no noise. . . . Yet she herself disliked spiders. I wonder how many spiders had bitten or roared at her? . . .
>
> Perhaps we need to rethink our attitudes to two separate issues: fearlessness and bravery. Fearlessness is simply not being afraid. It comes from not feeling fear. Logically, then, the less we frighten children, the more fearless they will be.

The idea that many fears are both natural (including, according to Leach, adults' fears of spiders), and intensified by children's limited understanding, implies that it is probably fruitless to try to talk children out of them. Whereas Watson would seek to recondition the frightened child and Spock would provide reassurance, Leach suggests completely avoiding situations that provoke fear until the child has acquired the cognitive skills necessary for approaching these situations more maturely. In a sense, she argues, a child's fears should be respected by the parents as a natural outgrowth of the child's stage of development.

In these examples, popular advice to children reflects influential theories of development that guide researchers. As new views of children and their growth continue to emerge within developmental psychology, it is fascinating and provocative to speculate about how these new perspectives will find their way into the next generation of child-rearing manuals.

result of any narrow set of determinants, whether these are habits, traits, drives, reinforcers, constructs, instincts, or genes, and whether they are exclusively inside or outside the person. [Mischel, 1977]

Because no one theory can encompass all of human behavior, most developmentalists today would describe themselves as having an **eclectic perspective**, meaning that rather than adopting any of these theories exclusively, they make use of all of them.

In subsequent chapters, as echoes and elaborations of the psychoanalytic, learning, cognitive, and sociocultural theories appear, you can form your own opinion of the validity of each theory, developing an eclectic view of your own. The best challenge you can set for yourself—the same one facing developmentalists—is the integration of theory, research, and applications into an increasingly comprehensive picture of human development.

eclectic perspective A view that, instead of adhering to a single perspective, incorporates what seems to be the best, or most useful, elements from various theories.

TABLE 2.3

Summary of Major Developmental Theories

	Freud	Erikson	Learning Theories	Piaget	Information-Processing	Sociocultural
Major focus	Psychosexual development	Psychosocial development	Environmental influences	Thinking and reasoning	Components of processing information	Cultural guidance
Portrayal of child	Cauldron of unconscious impulses	Guided by universal challenges	Passive—shaped by environment	Scientist	Computer	Apprentice
Nature or nurture	Both	Both	Nurture	Both	Both	Nurture emphasized
Continuity or discontinuity	Stages	Stages	Continuity	Stages	Continuity	Continuity
Early experiences shape later development	Yes	Yes	No (early and later experiences are both important)	No (impact limited by stage of development)	No (early and later experiences are both important)	No (early and later experiences are both important)

SUMMARY

What Theories Do

1. A theory provides a framework of general principles that can be used to interpret observations. Each theory interprets human development from a somewhat different perspective, but all theories attempt to provide a context in which to understand individual experiences and behavior.

Psychoanalytic Theories

2. Psychoanalytic theories emphasize that our actions are largely ruled by the unconscious—the source of powerful impulses and conflicts that usually lie below the level of our conscious awareness. They also propose that early experiences can have significant, long-term effects on personality.

3. Freud, the founder of psychoanalytic theory, developed the theory of psychosexual stages to explain how unconscious impulses arise and how they affect behavior during the oral, anal, phallic, and genital stages of psychosexual development of the child.

4. Freud interpreted behavior in terms of three components of personality: the id seeks immediate gratification of its desires; the superego acts as a relentless conscience to suppress the id; the ego moderates the demands of the id and the superego and copes with the recognition that one must seek satisfaction by realistic and appropriate ways in view of the limitations of the real world. Developmental growth results from these efforts of the ego.

5. Erikson proposed a theory of psychosocial development that describes individuals as being shaped by the interaction of personal characteristics and social forces. In this theory, Erikson depicts eight successive stages of psychosocial development, each of which involves a particular developmental crisis.

Learning Theories

6. Learning theorists believe that the focus of psychologists' study should be behavior that can be observed and measured and the environmental bases of that behavior. They are especially interested in the relationship between events and the reactions they are associated with, that is, between the stimulus and response.

7. Learning theory emphasizes the importance of various forms of conditioning, a process by which particular stimuli become linked with particular responses. In classical conditioning, one stimulus becomes associated with another to produce a particular response. In operant conditioning, reinforcement makes a behavior more likely to occur.

8. Social learning theory recognizes that much of human behavior is modeled after the behavior of others, and that various cognitive and motivational processes influence how we are affected by the behavior of others.

Cognitive Theories

9. Cognitive theorists believe that a person's thought processes—the understanding and analysis of a particular situation—have an important effect on behavior and development.

10. Piaget proposed that people develop schemes—general ways of thinking about ideas and objects. When a person becomes aware of perceptions or experiences that do not fit an existing scheme, the scheme changes or a new one is created, and cognitive growth occurs. Learning is accomplished by a process of organization and adaptation through each of several stages of cognitive development: sensorimotor, preoperational, concrete operational, and formal operational.

11. Information-processing theorists study cognitive development in terms of changes in internal cognitive processes such as working memory and the knowledge base. Growth and refinement of control processes are especially important to cognitive development.

Sociocultural Theory

12. Sociocultural theory explains human development in terms of the guidance, support, and structure provided by the culture. For Vygotsky, children mature intellectually through the social interactions they share with more mature members of the society, who provide challenges for the child in the zone of proximal development.

The Theories Compared

13. Psychoanalytic, learning, cognitive, and sociocultural theories have all contributed to the understanding of human development, yet no one theory is adequate to describe the complexity and diversity of human experience. Most developmentalists incorporate ideas from several developmental perspectives into their thinking.

KEY TERMS

developmental theory (41)
psychoanalytic theory (43)
childhood sexuality (44)
psychosexual stages (44)
oral stage (44)
anal stage (44)
phallic stage (44)
latency (45)
genital stage (45)
id (45)
ego (45)
superego (45)
repression (46)
crisis (46)
psychosocial theory (47)
behaviorism (49)

learning theory (49)
stimulus (49)
response (49)
conditioning (50)
classical conditioning (50)
operant conditioning (50)
reinforcement (51)
reinforcer (51)
positive reinforcer (51)
negative reinforcer (51)
punishment (52)
extrinsic reinforcers (52)
intrinsic reinforcers (52)
social learning theory (53)
modeling (53)

self-efficacy (55)
reciprocal determinism (56)
cognitive theory (57)
sensorimotor stage (58)
preoperational stage (58)
concrete operational stage (58)
formal operational stage (59)
equilibrium (59)
scheme (59)
disequilibrium (59)
organization (61)
adaptation (61)

assimilation (61)
accommodation (61)
conservation of liquids (61)
information-processing theory (61)
sensory register (62)
working memory (62)
knowledge base (62)
response generator (62)
control processes (63)
sociocultural theory (66)
zone of proximal development (68)
eclectic perspective (71)

KEY QUESTIONS

1. What functions does a good theory perform?

2. What is the major premise of psychoanalytic theories?

3. According to Freud's theory, what is the function of the ego?

4. What is the major difference between Freud's theory and Erikson's theory?

5. What is the major premise of learning theories?

6. What are the differences between classical and operant conditioning?

7. What are some of the cognitive processes in social learning?

8. What is the major premise of cognitive theories?

9. According to Piaget, how do periods of disequilibrium lead to mental growth?

10. What is the difference between assimilation and accommodation?

11. How do information-processing theorists describe cognitive growth?

12. How do sociocultural theories view development?

13. What are the main differences among the psychoanalytic, learning, cognitive, and sociocultural theories?

14. Why do most developmentalists describe themselves as having an eclectic perspective?

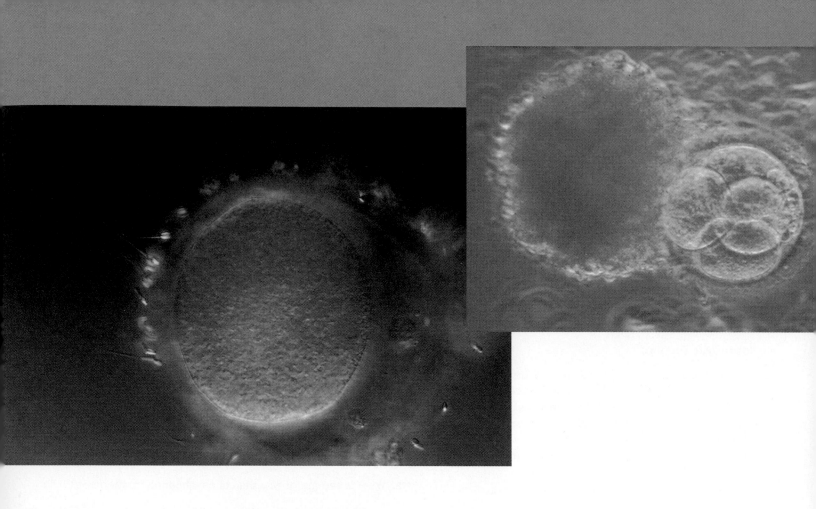

PART I The Beginnings

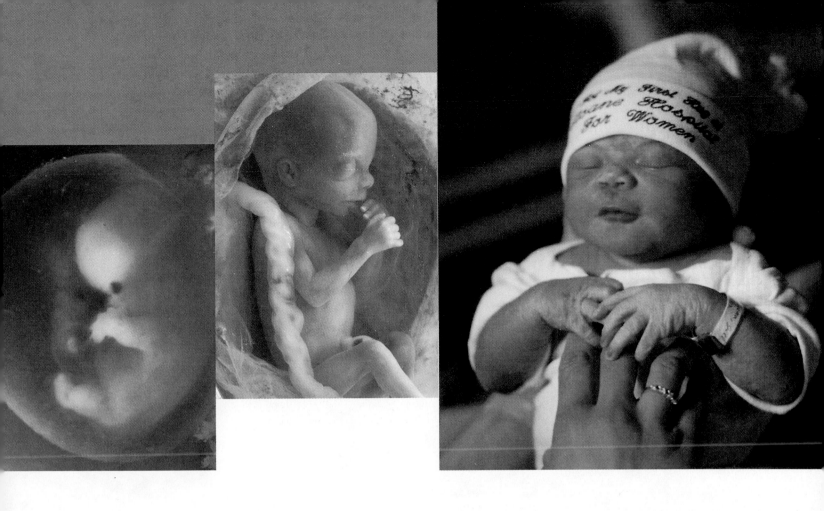

When considering the human life span, most people ignore or take for granted the time from conception through birth. Indeed, among all the cultures of the world, China seems to have been the only one to have ever included the prenatal period when reckoning age. Yet these 266 or so days could not be more crucial. On the very first day, for instance, our entire genetic heritage is set, affecting not only what we see when we look in the mirror but also many of the abilities, talents, and disabilities that characterize each of us. Survival is much more doubtful and growth much more rapid during the prenatal period than at any other time in our lives. At the end of this period, the day of birth usually provides the occasion for more anticipation, worry, excitement, and joy on the part of parents than any other day of childhood. Indeed, the impact of the physiological and emotional events of that day can be felt for weeks, months, even years.

These early days, usually uncounted and underemphasized, are the focus of the next three chapters.

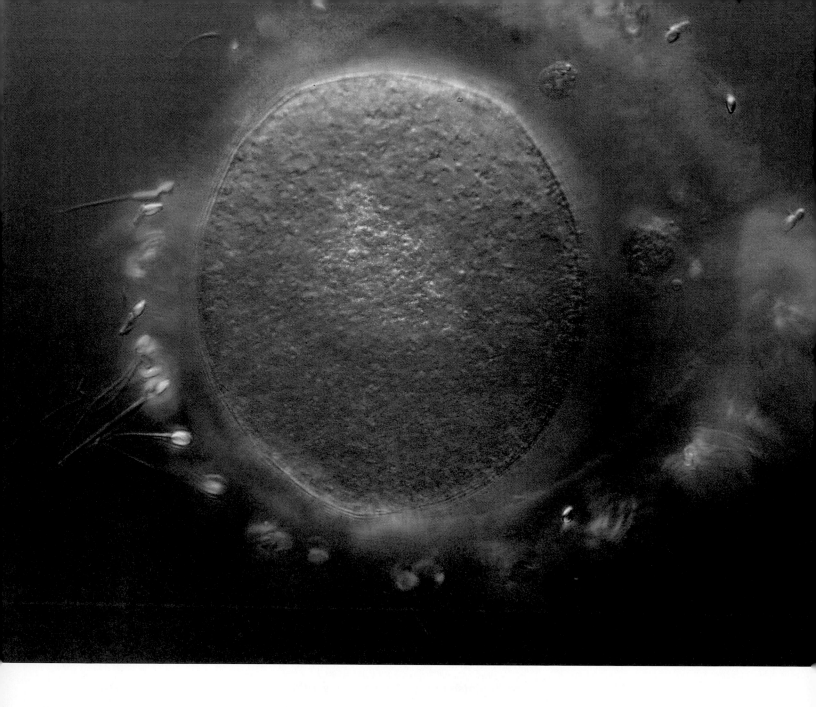

Heredity and Environment

CHAPTER

3

When a sperm and an ovum unite in conception, genetic instructions from both parents combine to direct the growth and development of a unique person. This genetic inheritance influences the course of the individual's entire life, from the moment of conception until the moment of death. However, the ultimate unfolding of that life depends, not on genetic influences alone, but on the interaction that occurs between those influences and an endless array of environmental factors—everything from the mother-to-be's health during the first days of pregnancy to the society's economic policies regarding families, from the cultural routines that regulate everyday life to the unique events that each individual experiences. In this chapter, we will discuss the interactions between genetic inheritance and environment that continually affect every developing person, focusing on questions such as the following:

What does it mean to say that a trait is genetic?

Is personality the result of genes, or individual experience, or culture, or all three?

Why do children from the same family sometimes seem so different?

Are some couples more likely than others to have a child with a genetic or chromosomal abnormality?

From the very beginning, individual development is driven by the interaction of two prime forces, heredity and environment. At conception, a complex set of genetic instructions takes form to influence every aspect of development, affecting not only obvious characteristics such as sex, coloring, and body shape but also less visible traits, psychological as well as physical—from blood type to bashfulness, from metabolic rate to moodiness, from voice tone to verbal fluency. Even the timing and pace of certain developmental changes are genetically guided.

As we will see throughout this chapter, however, just as no human characteristic is untouched by heredity, no genetic instruction—including those for basic traits such as physical structure and intellectual potential—is unaffected by the environment. Indeed, each person's genetic inheritance and individual experiences are so intertwined that it is virtually impossible to isolate the specific effects of one from the other. The interaction between these two factors is lifelong, shaping the individual from the moment of conception until the moment of death.

The Beginning of Development

Human reproductive cells are called **gametes**. Human development is initiated when a male gamete, or **sperm**, penetrates the membrane of a female gamete, or **ovum**. Each of these gametes contains more than a billion chemically coded genetic messages, which, taken together, represent one half of a rough blueprint for human development. When the two reproductive cells subsequently fuse, the two blueprint halves combine, interacting to form a complete set of developmental guidelines.

At first, the two gametes maintain their separate identities, side by side, enclosed within the ovum's membrane. Then, after an hour or more, they suddenly merge, their genetic material combines, and a one-celled **zygote** is formed.

FIGURE 3.1 The ovum shown here is about to become a zygote. It has been penetrated by a single sperm, whose nucleus now lies next to the nucleus of the ovum. Shortly, the two nuclei will fuse, bringing together several billion genetic codes that will guide future development.

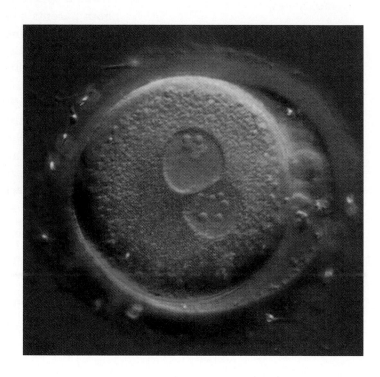

gamete A reproductive cell, that is, a cell that can reproduce a new human being if it combines with a gamete from the other sex. Female gametes are called ova, or eggs; male gametes are called spermatozoa, or sperm.

sperm The reproductive cells of a male, which begin to be produced in a young man's testicles at puberty.

ovum (plural, ova) The reproductive cells of a female, which are present from birth in the ovaries.

zygote The single cell formed from the union of two gametes, a sperm and an ovum.

Within hours after its formation, the zygote initiates human development through the processes of duplication and division. Just before the zygote divides, all the combined genetic material from both gametes duplicates itself, forming two complete sets of genetic instructions. These two sets move toward opposite sides of the cell; the cell then divides neatly down the middle, and the zygote thus becomes two cells. In identical fashion, these two cells duplicate themselves and divide to become four; these four, in turn, duplicate and divide to become eight; and so on.

Soon, a third process, differentiation, is added to the simple duplication and division. Following a genetic timetable, various cells begin to specialize and reproduce at different rates, according to their programmed function. Following the same timetable, some cells will die early in life and others will continually reproduce for decades; still others will remain dormant until puberty, or adulthood, or old age.

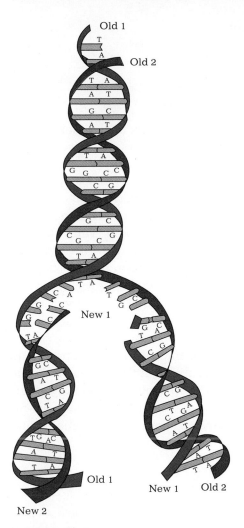

Old 1
Old 2
New 1
Old 1
New 1   Old 2
New 2

FIGURE 3.2 The structure of DNA is like a ladder, with the rungs composed of a pair of bases, some combination of A (adenine), T (thymine), C (cytosine), and G (guanine). Shown here is a DNA molecule in the process of duplicating the code as it creates two new copies. From such a simple but elegant uncoupling and reconnecting, the entire genetic code for a life is transmitted.

gene A basic unit of heredity. Genes, which number about 100,000 in humans, direct the growth and development of every living creature.

chromosome Molecules of DNA that carry the genes transmitted from parents to children.

DNA (deoxyribonucleic acid) Molecules containing genetic information.

genetic code The sequence of chemical bases in DNA; referred to as a code because it determines the amino acid sequence in the enzymes and other protein molecules synthesized by the organism.

At birth, a baby is made up of about 10 trillion cells. By adulthood, the number of cells has increased to between 300 and 500 trillion. But no matter how many cells a person may have, and no matter how much differentiation and specialization has occurred, each body cell carries a copy of the genetic instructions inherited by the one-celled zygote at the moment of conception.

The Genetic Code

The basic unit of these genetic instructions is the **gene**. Genes are discrete segments of a **chromosome**, which is a **DNA (deoxyribonucleic acid)** molecule that typically contains thousands of genes as well as other material. Every normal human being has twenty-three pairs of chromosomes (forty-six chromosomes in all), which collectively carry about 100,000 distinct genes.

The instructions on each gene are "written" in a chemical code, or alphabet, made up of four bases, adenine, guanine, cytosine, and thymine, abbreviated A, G, C, and T. These chemical bases occur in only four pairings, A-T, T-A, G-C, and C-G, which at first would seem to provide a very limited genetic vocabulary. In fact, however, what determines the precise nature of a gene's instructions, called the **genetic code**, is the overall sequence of these base pairs along their segment of the DNA strand (see Figure 3.2). And since there are approximately 3 billion base pairs in the DNA of every human, and thousands of base pairs in every gene, the genetic vocabulary is extremely rich and extensive. Indeed, scientists now engaged in deciphering the complete genetic code (see pp. 104–105) estimate that, when fully transcribed, it will cover at least as many pages as thirteen full sets of the *Encyclopedia Britannica* (Lee, 1993).

In essence, what this multitude of genetic instructions does is provide the body's cells with directions for the synthesis of hundreds of different kinds of proteins, including enzymes, that are the body's building blocks and regulators. Thus, following these instructions, certain cells become part of the neurons of the brain; others become part of the lens of the eye; others become part of the valves of the heart, and so on—even though every cell contains the entire genetic code of the organism.

In addition to directing the form and location of cells, genes also influence their specific function. That is, the enzymes created through genetic instructions direct the cells' behavior—influencing, for example, how rapidly the neurons in each particular area of the brain process information and what kind of information that particular area attends to; how quickly and sharply the lens of the eye focuses on diverse forms in various lightings, contrasts, and distances; how readily blood flows through the heart when the body is exerted and when it is at rest. The process doesn't stop there. Through some on-off switching mechanism not yet understood, genes control life itself, instructing cells to grow, to repair damage, to take in nourishment, to multiply, to die. Even certain advances in cognitive development may involve genes that switch on at a certain age (Gottesman & Goldsmith, 1993; Plomin et al., 1993).

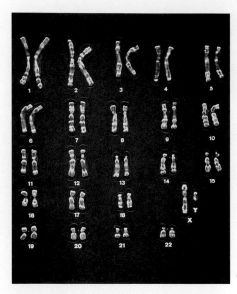

FIGURE 3.3 This picture, called a karyotype, shows the forty-six chromosomes from one individual, in this case a normal male. In order to produce a chromosomal portrait such as this one, a cell is removed from the person's body (usually from inside the mouth), processed so that the chromosomes become visible, magnified many times, photographed, and then arranged in pairs according to the length of the upper "arms."

twenty-third pair   In humans, the chromosome pair that determines the person's sex.

Chromosomes

As you already know, each normal human has forty-six chromosomes. The chromosomes are arranged in twenty-three distinct pairs, one chromosome in each pair being from the mother and the other being from the father. Each pair member serves as the designated location for a particular portion of genetic material that corresponds to the genetic material on its chromosome mate (see Figure 3.3). For the most part, genes are positioned quite precisely on a particular "arm" of a certain chromosome. Thus chromosomes not only carry the genes; they also furnish each gene with a niche opposite a corresponding gene on the matching chromosome, thereby allowing each gene pair to perform its mission in directing development.

The matching of the chromosome pairs occurs at conception. Every human sperm carries twenty-three chromosomes, each one of which corresponds in functioning to one of the twenty-three chromosomes carried in every ovum. Collectively, the twenty-three chromosomes in the sperm and the twenty-three chromosomes in the ovum represent the two halves of the genetic blueprint referred to earlier. When the sperm and ovum unite, their corresponding chromosomes link up, providing complete instructions for the development of a new person. The chromosomal pairing remains lifelong.

The Sex Chromosomes

Twenty-two of the twenty-three pairs of human chromosomes are closely matched pairs, each half containing similar genes in almost identical positions and sequence. The **twenty-third pair**, which is the one that determines the individual's sex, is a different case. In the female, the twenty-third pair of chromosomes is composed of two large, X-shaped chromosomes. Accordingly, it is designated XX. In the male, the twenty-third pair is composed of one large X-shaped chromosome and one, much smaller, Y-shaped chromosome. It is designated XY.

FIGURE 3.4 Whether a fertilized ovum will develop into a male or female depends on whether the ovum, which always has an X chromosome, is fertilized by a sperm carrying an X chromosome (a female will result) or a sperm carrying a Y chromosome (a male will result).

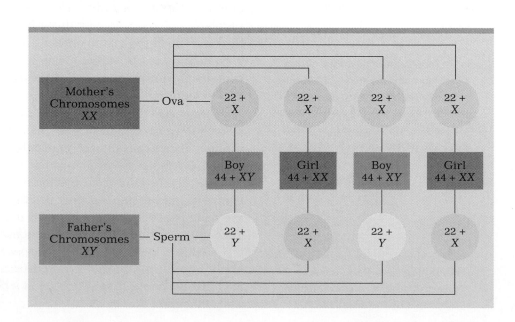

The reason for this unusual pair is that the duplication-and-division process in the production of gametes differs from that in the production of all other cells. When cells make gametes, they do so in such a way that each sperm or ovum receives only one member of each chromosome pair. Thus each sperm or ovum has only twenty-three chromosomes, half as many as the forty-six in every other body cell. This assures that when the chromosomes of a sperm and an ovum combine at conception, the total chromosome number for the new organism will still be forty-six.

Obviously, since a female's twenty-third chromosome pair is XX, every gamete she makes will have either one X or the other. And since a male's twenty-third pair is XY, half his sperm will have an X chromosome and half will have a Y. Thus the critical factor in the determination of a zygote's sex will be which sperm reaches the ovum first, a Y sperm, creating a male (XY), or an X sperm, creating a female (XX).

Human Diversity

Genes accomplish two goals that are each essential to the survival of the human race: they ensure both genetic continuity across the species and genetic diversity within it. The vast majority of each person's genes are identical to those of any unrelated person (Plomin et al., 1990). As a result of the instructions carried by these genes, each new member of the human race shares with every other human common physical structures (such as the pelvic alignment that allows us to walk upright), behavioral tendencies (such as vocalization), and reproductive potential, allowing each new generation to perpetuate the human species. These characteristics have been fashioned throughout our long evolutionary history, promoting our survival as a species by enabling humans to live successfully in the environment.

The remainder of each person's genes differ in various ways from those of other individuals. The diversity these genes provide over the generations is essential to the ability of our species to adapt to changing environments and needs. The fact that humans differ genetically means that, as a species, we retain the potential to change and evolve. Thus our individual uniqueness fosters the survival of the entire human race.

Given that each sperm or ovum from a particular parent contains only twenty-three chromosomes, you may be wondering how it is possible that every conception represents the potential for a genetically unique individual. The answer is that when the chromosome pairs divide up during the formation of gametes, which one of each pair will wind up in a particular gamete is a matter of chance, and many combinations of chromosomes are possible. The laws of probability show that there are 2^{23}—that is, about 8 million—possible outcomes. In other words, approximately 8 million genetically different ova or sperm can be produced by a single individual.

In addition, just before a chromosome pair divides during the formation of gametes, corresponding segments of the pair are sometimes exchanged, altering the genetic composition of both pair members. Through the recombinations it produces, this crossing-over of genes adds greatly to genetic diversity. And finally, when the sperm and ovum unite, the interaction of their chemically coded instructions forms combinations not present in either parent. All things considered, any given mother and father can

FIGURE 3.5 Since monozygotic twins (top) share the same genes, their similarity is apparent in every detail, from the curve of their eyebrows to the shape of their fingers, as well as more obvious features such as their body type and hair pattern. Dizygotic twins (bottom) sometimes look quite different, as these sisters do.

monozygotic twins Twins who have identical genes because they were formed from one zygote that split into two identical organisms very early in development.

dizygotic twins Twins formed when two separate ova are fertilized by separate sperm at roughly the same time. Such twins share about half of their genes, just like any other siblings.

polygenic traits Characteristics produced by the interaction of many genes.

multifactorial traits Characteristics produced by the interaction of several genetic and environmental influences.

genotype A person's entire genetic inheritance including those characteristics carried by the recessive genes but not expressed in the phenotype.

form over 64 trillion genetically different offspring. Thus it is no exaggeration to say that every conception is, potentially, the beginning of a genetically unique individual.

Twins

Although every zygote is genetically unique, not every newborn is. In about 1 in every 270 pregnancies, the growing cluster of cells splits apart during the first two weeks of development, creating two identical, independent clusters (Bryan, 1992). These cell clusters become **monozygotic twins** (identical twins), so named because they originated from one (mono) zygote. Since they originated from the same zygote, they share identical genetic instructions for physical appearance, psychological traits, vulnerability to certain diseases, and so forth.

Of course, not all twins are monozygotic. In fact, **dizygotic twins** (fraternal twins), who begin life as two separate zygotes created by the fertilization of two ova that were ovulated at roughly the same time, are more common. They occur naturally about once in every sixty births, with considerable variation among different racial and ethnic groups (Bryan, 1992). Moreover, when fertility drugs are used, fraternal twinning is much more common, occurring about once in every ten births. Dizygotic twins share no more genes than do any other two offspring of the same parents; that is, they share about 50 percent of the genes governing individual differences. They may be of different sexes and very different in their appearance. Or they may look a great deal alike, just as nontwin brothers and sisters sometimes do. Other multiple births, such as triplets and quadruplets, can likewise be monozygotic, dizygotic, trizygotic, quadrazygotic, and so forth (or even some combination of these).

From Genotype to Phenotype

As we have seen, conception brings together genetic instructions from both parents for every human characteristic. How do these instructions work to influence the specific characteristics a given offspring will inherit? The answer is usually quite complex, because most traits are both **polygenic**—that is, affected by many genes—and **multifactorial**—that is, influenced by many factors, including factors in the environment.

To grasp the complexity of genetic influences we must first distinguish between a person's genetic inheritance—his or her genetic *potential*—and the actual *expression* of that inheritance in the person's physical appearance and behavioral tendencies. The sum total of all the genes a person inherits for any particular trait—that is, the person's genetic potential for that trait—is called the **genotype**. The actual expression of the trait is called the **phenotype**. The phenotype of any given characteristic arises from two levels of genetic interaction: (1) the interaction of the proteins synthesized from the specific genes that make up the genotype of the characteristic and (2) the ongoing interaction between the genotype and the environment. Let us look first at the types of interaction that can occur among the genes themselves. Then we will consider some of the ways the phenotype is shaped by environmental factors.

FIGURE 3.6 Using terms such as black, white, yellow, red, or brown to denote skin color is misleading, for humans actually exhibit thousands of skin tones, each resulting from the combination of many genes. Depending on which half of their mother's and father's skin color genes children happen to inherit, offspring can be (and in modern nations, often are) paler, ruddier, lighter, darker, more sallow, more olive, or more freckled than either parent. This variation is apparent in many African-American families whose heritage includes ancestors from various parts of both Europe and Africa, and often Asia and pre-Columbian America as well.

phenotype An individual's observable characteristics that result from the interaction of the genes with each other and with the environment.

additive pattern A common pattern of genetic inheritance in which each gene affecting a specific trait makes an active contribution to the final outcome. Skin color and height are additive.

nonadditive pattern A pattern of genetic inheritance in which the outcome depends much more on the influence of one gene than of another.

dominant-recessive pattern A pattern of genetic inheritance in which one member of a gene pair (referred to as dominant) acts in a controlling manner, hiding the influence of the other (recessive) gene.

Gene-Gene Interaction

One common pattern of interaction among genes is called **additive** because in this pattern the phenotype reflects the sum of the contributions of each of the genes involved. The many genes affecting height and skin color, for instance, probably contribute in an additive fashion.

To simplify, if a particular tall man, whose parents and grandparents were all very tall, married a short woman, whose parents and grandparents were all very short, their children would all be of middling height. None of them would be as tall as their father or as short as their mother, because the sum total of all their genes for tallness and all their genes for shortness, when averaged together, would be halfway between the two. Of course, in actuality, many people have both kinds of ancestors, relatively tall ones and relatively short ones, which means that many children are notably taller or shorter than either of their parents, depending on which genes from each parent's varied genotype they happened to inherit.

Less often, genes interact in a **nonadditive** fashion: their interaction is either/or, winner/loser, rather than compromise. To be more precise, when a gene pair acts in a nonadditive pattern, the outcome depends much more on the influence of one gene than of the other.

One kind of nonadditive pattern you may be familiar with is the **dominant-recessive** pattern. In a pair of genes with this pattern, the phenotype reflects the influence of one gene, the *dominant gene,* while the effects of the other gene, the *recessive gene,* are masked. Indeed, often the dominant gene completely controls the characteristic in question, and the recessive gene is invisible in the phenotype. In other instances, the outcome reflects *incomplete dominance,* with the phenotype influenced primarily, but not exclusively, by the dominant gene.

It is through nonadditive genetic patterns that offspring may be much different from their parents, especially if they happen to inherit a recessive gene from each parent's genotype that, because of the parent's dominant gene, was not part of the parent's phenotype.

Hundreds of physical characteristics follow the dominant-recessive pattern. Eye color is one of them. In actuality, eye color involves quite complex interactions among many genes, but for the sake of illustration, let's simplify greatly and say for the moment that a person inherits two eye-color genes, one from each parent, and that the gene for brown eyes is dominant and that the gene for blue eyes is recessive. (Following traditional practice, we will indicate the dominant gene with an upper-case letter—"B" for dominant brown—and the recessive gene with a lower-case letter—"b" for recessive blue.) If both genes are for brown eyes (BB), the person's eyes will be brown. If one gene is for brown eyes and the other for blue (Bb), the person's eyes will be brown, since the brown-eye gene is dominant. If both genes are for blue eyes (bb), the person will have blue eyes.

Through the dominant-recessive pattern, then, it is possible for parents to have offspring whose phenotype for a particular characteristic is completely different from theirs, if both parents both have the necessary recessive genes. For example, if each of two brown-eyed parents has a recessive gene for blue eyes (Bb and Bb), there is 1 chance in 4 that a particular child of theirs will inherit the recessive blue-eye gene from both of them and will therefore have blue eyes. (The four possible combinations in their offspring would be BB, Bb, Bb—all yielding brown eyes—and bb, yielding blue eyes.)

A person who has a recessive gene as a part of his or her genotype is called a **carrier** of that gene. In fact, we are all carriers of dozens of recessive genes that are in our genotypes but not in our phenotypes. Usually we are unaware of which recessive genes we carry until we have a child with a surprising phenotype (see Figure 3.7).

FIGURE 3.7 Two brown-eyed parents who are both carriers for blue eyes can have a blue-eyed child. As shown here, the odds are 1 in 4 that a child will inherit the brown-eye genes from both parents, 2 in 4 that a child will inherit one brown-eye gene and one blue-eye gene (one child got the blue gene from the mother and the other from the father, but the outcome is the same), and 1 chance in 4 that a child will inherit two recessive blue-eye genes and thus have blue eyes. Of course, "chance has no memory," and despite the neatness of this table, a family of four children born to two brown-eyed carriers for blue eyes might not include any children with blue eyes, or might have two, three, or—in one such family in 256—four blue-eyed offspring.

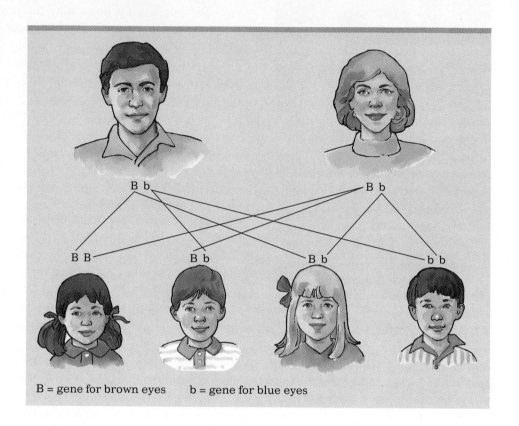

B = gene for brown eyes   b = gene for blue eyes

carrier An individual who has a recessive gene on his or her genotype that is not expressed on his or her phenotype. Carriers can pass the gene on to their children, who will express the gene if they receive a similar recessive gene from the other parent.

X-linked genes Genes that are carried on the X chromosome. X-linked genes are more likely to appear on the phenotype of males, even though women are more likely to have them on their genotype.

X-Linked Genes

Some genes are called **X-linked** because they are located only on the X chromosome. If such a gene is dominant, the fact that it is on the twenty-third pair is irrelevant to its effect. But if an X-linked gene is recessive, as are the genes for most forms of color blindness, many allergies, several diseases, and some learning disabilities, the fact that it is on the X chromosome can be critical. Since males have only one X chromosome, the recessive genes they inherit on that chromosome will be expressed in their phenotype, because they have no second X chromosome that might carry the counterbalancing gene. This explains why some traits are passed from mother to son (via the X), but not from father to son (since the Y does not carry the trait).

For example, suppose a man is color-blind. We know that he inherited the color blindness from his mother, since the X chromosome comes from the mother. If that man has children, none of his sons will inherit his gene for color blindness (because they receive his Y chromosome), but all his daughters will (because they receive his X chromosome). However, unless his wife is a carrier of X-linked color blindness, causing the daughters to have the recessive gene on both X chromosomes, the daughters will not themselves be color-blind—but all their sons will be. This pattern holds true for all X-linked traits: while people of both sexes have them on their genotype, males are far more likely to have them on their phenotype.

As complex as the preceding descriptions of additive, dominant, and recessive gene interaction may seem, they in fact make gene interaction appear much simpler than it actually is. This is because, of practical necessity, we are forced to discuss genes as though they were discretely functioning entities. But as we have seen, what genes actually do is direct the synthesis of hundreds of kinds of proteins that form the body's structures and direct its biochemical functions. In a sense, each body cell is "nothing more than a sea of chemicals" that is continually affected by other proteins and by the enzymes that direct the cell's functioning (Lee, 1993). Thus, no single gene directly determines even simple traits, such as eye color or height.

In addition, the patterns of gene interaction are seldom straightforward. Some additive genes contribute more substantially than others, either because they are naturally partially dominant, or because their influence is amplified by the presence of certain other genes. When additive genes combine, their final product is not always the simple total of all the contributions.

Nor are recessive genes always completely suppressed by the presence of their dominant gene counterparts. For example, although eye color is listed in many textbooks as either dominant brown or recessive blue, in reality, eyes are many shades of brown, blue, and even green or gray, each revealing the influence of several genes of varied dominance. Many a hazel-eyed child has one parent with blue eyes and the other with brown. In this case, the child's light-brown eyes bear witness to the recessive gene in his or her genotype.

Finally, geneticists have recently discovered that certain genes behave differently depending on whether they are inherited from the mother or the father (Hoffman, 1991). While the full scope and significance of this parental "imprinting" have yet to be determined, it is known that certain of the genes influencing height, insulin production, and several forms of mental retardation affect a child differently—even in opposite ways—depending on which parent they came from.

Such polygenic complexity is particularly apparent in psychological characteristics, including everything from personality traits, such as sociability, assertiveness, moodiness, and fearfulness, to cognitive traits, such as memory for numbers, spatial perception, and fluency of expression. Typically, many pairs of genes, some interacting in the dominant-recessive mode, some additive, and some creating new combinations, affect every behavioral tendency (Eaves et al., 1989; Plomin, 1990).

Gene-Environment Interaction

Polygenic complexity is only one of the difficulties in understanding the relationship between genotype and phenotype. Another key source of complexity is the environment in all its forms.

In order to understand the wide-ranging impact of the environment on genetic inheritance, you need to know that when social scientists discuss the effects of the **environment**, they are referring to a multitude of variables.

environment All the nongenetic factors that can affect the individual's development—everything from the impact of the immediate cell environment on the genes themselves to the effects of nutrition, medical care, socioeconomic status, family dynamics, and the broader economic, political, and cultural contexts.

Indeed, the environment includes everything that can interact with the person's genetic inheritance at every point of life, from the first prenatal moments to the last heartbeat, from the impact of uterine acidity on the first cells as they begin to multiply to all the ways the elements in the external world impinge on the individual. These external elements include direct effects, such as those of nutrition, climate, medical care, and family interaction, and indirect effects, such as those of the broad economic, political, and cultural contexts. They also include varying degrees of permanence, from irreversible effects such as the lifelong toll of severe brain injury on cognitive ability to transitory effects such as the impact of immediate stress on an individual's temper.

Distinguishing Hereditary and Environmental Influences

Before we examine the complex interplay of heredity and the environment, we first need to distinguish the developmental impact of these two forces. This is not easy to do, because, with any given trait, both are intertwined at every moment of a person's life. When the trait in question is an obvious and lifelong physical one, as reflected in family resemblances in facial features, eye color, or body type, the impact of genes on the phenotype is fairly easy to identify. But when the trait is a psychological one, such as an intellectual ability, artistic talent, or personality trait, the fact that the trait seems to run in families could be explained by nurture just as easily as by nature. How, then, do scientists distinguish genetic from environmental influences on personality characteristics?

Studying children in their birth families is not much help, precisely because of the confounding of genetic inheritance and environmental family influences. For instance, if children of highly intelligent parents excel in school, their school performance could, theoretically, be attributed entirely to their genetic inheritance, or entirely to the family environment (which is likely to encourage reading, intellectual curiosity, and high academic standards) or to any combination of the two.

One approach to this puzzle has been to study twins. As we have seen, monozygotic twins share all the same genes, while dizygotic twins share only half their genes, just like any other two siblings from the same parents. Thus, if monozygotic twins, on the whole, are found to be much more similar on a particular trait than dizygotic twins are, it seems likely that genes play a significant role in the appearance of that trait. Of course, this approach assumes (among other things) that each twin growing up in a particular family shares the same environment, an assumption that is not necessarily true (Emde et al., 1992; Loehlin, 1992).

Another way to distinguish the impact of genes from that of upbringing is to study large numbers of adopted children, comparing their traits with those of both their biological and adoptive parents. Traits that show a strong correlation between adopted children and their biological parents suggest a genetic basis for those characteristics; traits that show a strong correlation between adopted children and their adoptive parents suggest environmental influence. The difficulty with this approach is that adopted children are often placed in families whose socioeconomic, educational, and religious backgrounds are similar to those of their birth families. As a consequence, some of the similarity found between adopted children and their biological parents may be the result of shared culture rather than shared genes (Plomin, 1990).

The most telling way to try to separate the effects of genes and environment is to combine both strategies, studying identical twins who have been separated at birth and raised in different families. Although it requires painstaking searching in order to find enough twin pairs to make statistically significant conclusions, several groups of researchers in the United States, Sweden, England, Denmark, Finland, and Australia have done just that, finding altogether close to 1,000 twins raised apart. The results (see A Closer Look, pp. 88–89) provide dramatic confirmation for the general conclusion reached by more conventional research on thousands of single-born adopted children and on twins raised by their biological parents—and that conclusion is that virtually every psychological characteristic and personal trait is genetically influenced (Bouchard, 1994; Bouchard et al., 1990; Eaves et al., 1989; Pederson et al., 1988; Shaw, 1994).

At the same time, these very same studies reinforce another, equally important conclusion: that virtually every psychological characteristic and personal trait is affected, throughout the life span, by one's environment.

Physical Traits

Environment, as broadly defined above, affects every human characteristic—even physical traits that show a strong genetic influence. Take height, for example. An individual's height potential is genetically directed, yet most adults in developed countries are, on average, taller than their grandparents ever were but virtually the same height as their full-grown children. Why? Because to reach his or her genetically based height potential, a person must have adequate nutrition and good health. In the nineteenth century, these two factors were much less common than they are now, and Americans, for example, were, on average, about 6 inches shorter than they are today (Tanner, 1971). Throughout the twentieth century, however, as nutrition and medical care improved, each generation grew slightly taller than the previous one. Over the past several decades, this trend has stopped, because the prevailing levels of health and nutrition have permitted the vast majority of the population to reach their genetically set height limits, and most children reaching adulthood in the 1990s will, on average, be about as tall as their parents. Of course, in individual cases, environmental factors such as malnutrition, chronic illness, and stress can make a child considerably shorter than his or her heredity allows for.

Psychological Traits

Environmental influences such as nutrition are fairly simple to understand as they affect physical traits. More varied, hidden, and intriguing are the effects of the interactions of environmental influences on psychological traits.

A CLOSER LOOK

Personal Choices, Private Tastes, Individual Preferences, and . . . . Genes?

Your chosen friends, favorite foods, individual idiosyncrasies, and lifestyle preferences all seem a matter of personal choice, part of what makes any given moment of your life uniquely yours to live. To the extent that you think of your personal choices as being subject to influences outside your control, you probably regard environmental circumstances—such as childhood experiences, social pressures, and cultural context—as much more powerful than any particular sequence of DNA in your genetic code. That may be *how it seems*, but is that *how it is*? If, in the early days of prenatal life, the zygote that contained your genes had happened to split, and if you and your twin had happened to be separated at birth and raised by different families, and if you were to one day run into your twin, you might discover that many of your supposedly unique personal choices had also been made by someone else.

Consider the case of Robert Shafran, who, while walking across the campus of the university in which he had recently enrolled, was suddenly greeted by a young woman who kissed him warmly on the mouth and exclaimed, "Where have you been?" That Robert didn't even know this woman was a fact he admitted somewhat reluctantly, since she was just his type. As it turned out, she was also his brother Eddy Galland's type; in fact, it was Eddy, Robert's long-lost twin, whom the woman had taken Robert to be. When Eddy and Robert were reunited, it was soon clear that the resemblance between them was not limited to physical characteristics. Among other striking similarities, the brothers wore the same kinds of clothes; had similar hairstyles; laughed in the same way at the same jokes; drank the same brand of beer; smoked the same brand of cigarettes (which they held in the same way); engaged in the same sports, including team wrestling (in which they had almost identical records); and listened to the same music, at similar volumes.

When the story of Robert and Eddy hit the press, David Kellman looked at their photo and thought he was seeing mirror images of himself—and, in fact, he was, for in this case, monozygotic triplets rather than twins had been separated at birth. When the three brothers were reunited, they (and the psychologists who studied them) were amazed at the number of experiences, tastes, and interests they had in common (*New York Times*, 1980).

Similar amazement was registered, a bit less publicly, by a group of researchers beginning the Minnesota Study of Twins Reared Apart, an extensive study of monozygotic twins who were separated early in life (Bouchard, 1994; Bouchard et al., 1990; Holden, 1980). One pair of identical twins, Oskar Stohr and Jack Yufe, were born of a Jewish father and Christian mother in Trinidad in the 1930s. Soon after their birth, Oskar was taken to Nazi Germany by his

The sources of triple confusion, from top to bottom: Edward Galland, David Kellman, Robert Shafran.

mother to be raised as a Catholic in a household consisting mostly of women. Jack was raised as a Jew by his father, spending his childhood in the Caribbean and some of his adolescence in Israel.

On the face of it, it would be difficult to imagine more disparate cultural backgrounds. In addition, when they were reunited in middle age, the twins certainly had their differences. Oskar was married and a devoted union member. Jack was divorced and owned a clothing store in southern California. But, when the brothers met for the first time in Minnesota,

similarities started cropping up as soon as Oskar arrived at the airport. Both were wearing wire-rimmed glasses and mustaches, both sported two-pocket shirts with epaulets. They share idiosyncrasies galore: they like spicy foods and sweet liqueurs, are absentminded, have a habit of falling asleep in front of the television, think it's funny to sneeze in a crowd of strangers, flush the toilet before using it, store rubber bands on their wrists, read magazines from back to front, dip buttered toast in their coffee. Oskar is domineering toward women and yells at his wife, which Jack did before he was separated. [Holden, 1980]

Since Oskar Stohr (left) and Jack Yufe (right) are monozygotic twins, it is not surprising that they look very much alike. However, since they have been separated almost from birth, it is more difficult to explain their similarities in many of those characteristics that are usually considered to be acquired, for example, their preference for moustaches and their tastes in food and drink.

Their scores on several psychological tests were very similar, and they struck the investigator as remarkably similar in temperament and tempo. Other pairs of twins in this study likewise startled the observers by their similarities, not only in appearance and on test scores, but also in mannerisms and dress. One pair of female twins, separated since infancy, arrived in Minnesota, each wearing seven rings (on the same fingers) and three bracelets, a coincidence that might be explained by pure chance, but more likely was partly genetic—that is, genes endowed both women with beautiful hands and, possibly, contributed to an interest in self-adornment.

The evidence from monozygotic twins suggests that genes affect a much greater number of characteristics than most psychologists, including the leader of the Minnesota study, Thomas Bouchard, originally suspected. As Bouchard has noted (Cassill, 1982), he once believed it was "foolish" to think that genes affect almost every trait, but he now finds that the idea is "no longer subject to debate" and that genetic variation is significant for "almost every behavioral trait so far investigated from reaction time to religiosity" (Bouchard et al., 1990).

This does not mean that the seemingly uncanny similarities between monozygotic twins raised in separate homes should automatically be attributed to genetics. For instance, the triplets' taste in cigarettes and beer was also shared by a million or so other young men, who had little in common genetically but a great deal in common culturally, including exposure to advertising messages extolling the manly virtues of particular brands.

Further, most twins reared apart have quite similar home experiences. Typically, they are raised by close relatives in neighboring communities. A review of the research found that in every case in which separated twins were raised in markedly different homes, such that one twin experienced "extreme deprivation or unusual enrichment," the resemblance between the twins lessened (Scarr & McCartney, 1983).

Only rarely are identical twins separated by language, culture, and religion, as Oskar and Jack were. Even in their case, says Bouchard, beneath the more dramatic differences in background, their upbringing was basically quite similar. Moreover, personality similarities may foster environmental similarities, as much as vice versa. Large-scale research finds that monozygotic twins tend to evoke similar degrees of warmth and encouragement from the adults who interact with them (Plomin, 1990a). Thus a pair of identical twins, making their way in different families, may be similarly influenced by the similar family patterns they themselves help create.

All these caveats and cautions notwithstanding, most researchers are astonished at the similarities they find in monozygotic twins raised separately (Lykken et al., 1992). Indeed, these twins are sometimes more alike than twins raised together (Juel-Nielsen, 1980). It seems that, when they grow up in the same home, some monozygotic twins deliberately create or emphasize differences between themselves in order to preserve a sense of individuality.

Such findings make one wonder anew about the sources of our own individuality. Are our life choices—large and small—mostly an outgrowth of experience and cultural background, or do the roots go much deeper? Could many of the habits, patterns, and values that distinguish each of us be not so much a matter of personal choice as a matter of genetic push? It is an intriguing question to which we may never have a definitive answer.

By the way, how many rings do you have on your fingers, and why?

Take shyness, for instance. No doubt shyness is partly inherited: study after study finds that the levels of a personality trait called inhibition (or its opposite, extroversion or sociability) are more similar in monozygotic than dizygotic twins (Bouchard et al., 1990; Eaves et al., 1989; Plomin et al., 1990; Robinson et al., 1992). In addition, there are biological differences between inhibited and extroverted children (Kagan, 1992; Kagan et al., 1993). Shy children, for example, show quicker startle reactions as infants, show less activity overall as young children, and, among Caucasians, are more likely to be of northern- rather than southern-European ancestry. However, research on adopted children shows that shyness is affected both by the genetic heritage of the biological parents and the social atmosphere provided by the adoptive parents (Loehlin et al., 1982).

As this research suggests, a child with a genetic disposition to shyness raised by outgoing parents would have many contacts with other people, and would observe his or her parents greeting strangers with a friendly hello and socializing freely. Although such a child might cling to his or her parents in the beginning, gradually the child would learn to relax and would become less observably shy. It is not that as life experiences accumulate, genetically based tendencies disappear: a shy child would always feel twinges of inhibition when entering a new school, or when arriving at a party full of strangers, for instance. But some shy people are able to build on childhood experiences and know how to warm up to others and feel more at ease. Alternatively, of course, if this same shy child's parents were also very shy and socially isolated, the child might grow up much more timid socially than he or she would have been with outgoing parents—and considerably more so than most other children.

Thus the expression of shyness will depend on the interactions between parental example, cultural encouragement, school milieu, cognitive awareness, self-understanding, and adult experiences—each of which may exacerbate, diminish, or redirect the impact of the others. The same conclusion applies to other psychological traits that have been found to have strong genetic influences, including intelligence, emotionality, activity level, and even neuroticism (Loehlin, 1992; Loehlin et al., 1988; Plomin, 1989, 1990). In each case, various dimensions of the individual's environment can enhance, inhibit, or alter the expression of hereditary predispositions in his or her phenotype.

Mental Illness

Overall, research reveals that, as in the case of shyness, genes are never the exclusive determinant of any psychological characteristic. This is also true with regard to psychopathologies such as depression, antisocial behavior, and affective disorders: here, too, both genes and environment are influential (Gottesman, 1990; Plomin, 1989, 1990).

The most extensive research on this question has been done on schizophrenia, and it shows that relatives of schizophrenics have a higher-than-normal risk of becoming schizophrenic themselves (Gottesman, 1991) (see Figure 3.8). Most striking is the fact that if one monozygotic twin becomes schizophrenic, the chances are about 50 percent that the other will too, a rate far above the 1 percent incidence in the overall population. Looked at another way, however, the same evidence reveals the importance of the environment: among identical twins, half of those whose twin is schizophrenic

FIGURE 3.8 If a person has a relative who is schizophrenic, that person's lifetime risk of being diagnosed as schizophrenic begins rising from the 1-in-100 chance for the population at large, depending on how genetically close he or she is to the afflicted relative. The highest risk occurs for monozygotic twins: when one twin is diagnosed as being schizophrenic, the other has almost a 50 percent chance of eventually being so diagnosed. Note, however, that while this chart shows a clear genetic influence on schizophrenia, the odds also show the effects of environment. For instance, over half the monozygotic siblings whose twin is schizophrenic are not schizophrenic themselves.

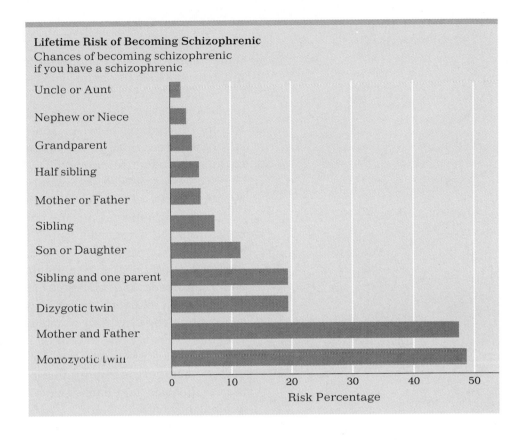

Lifetime Risk of Becoming Schizophrenic
Chances of becoming schizophrenic if you have a schizophrenic

Uncle or Aunt
Nephew or Niece
Grandparent
Half sibling
Mother or Father
Sibling
Son or Daughter
Sibling and one parent
Dizygotic twin
Mother and Father
Monozyotic twin

Risk Percentage

are not themselves afflicted. Moreover, most diagnosed schizophrenics have no close relatives with the illness (Cromwell, 1993). Obviously, schizophrenia is multifactorial, with environmental elements—possibly a slow virus, head injury, or overall stress—playing a pivotal role.

Alcoholism: A Clear Example of Gene-Environment Interaction

One particularly clear example of the way the environment moderates genetic potential in psychological characteristics can be seen in the case of alcoholism. At various times alcoholism was thought to be a moral weakness, a personality flaw, or a sign of psychopathology. We now know that alcoholism is at least partly genetic, although the specific genes involved, the nature of their interaction, and their precise power have yet to be determined (McClearn et al., 1991). We do know that some people's biochemistry makes them highly susceptible to alcoholism; others' biochemistry makes them much less so.

Thus, while anyone can abuse alcohol, the addictive pull can be immensely strong or very weak, depending on the person's genetic makeup. In addition to quite specific metabolic patterns, certain temperamental traits, themselves partly genetic, also correlate with abusive drinking. Among these are a quick temper, a willingness to take risks, and a high level of anxiety. Thus alcoholism is polygenic, with alcoholics inheriting different genetic dispositions, but with almost every alcoholic inheriting biochemical or temperamental traits that push toward abusive drinking.

Obviously, however, environment plays a critical role in the expression of alcoholism (McGue, 1993). If a person with a strong genetic affinity to alcoholism spends a lifetime in an environment where alcohol is unavailable, the alcoholic tendency in the genotype will never become manifest in the phenotype. On the other hand, if the same person is raised in a dysfunctional family within a culture that promotes the use of alcohol, he or she is much more likely to become an active alcoholic. Even in that situation, however, social influences and individual choices can dramatically alter the outcome. Some alcoholics die of the disease before they are 30; others spend a lifetime fluctuating between abuse, controlled drinking, and abstinence; still others recognize the problem by early adulthood, get help, and are sober and productive throughout a long life.

The example of alcoholism also illustrates a final factor influencing the interaction between genes and the environment—the individual's age and the particular expectancies the culture holds for persons of that age. Alcoholism may be genetically "present" at birth, but since few cultures allow children to consume alcohol, it is rarely expressed before adolescence. Many other traits become more apparent as children mature and their capabilities, needs, and interests change, while at the same time, parental restrictions and influence wane (Caspi & Moffitt, 1991; McGue et al., 1993). This is especially the case with adopted children, whose genetic predispositions are sometimes at odds with those of their adoptive parents. When they are very young, adoptees reflect many of their adoptive parents' interests, behaviors, and personality traits. However, with maturity, they often choose friends, hobbies, and habits that express their biological, rather than their familial, heritage.

In summary, then, it is quite clear that both genes and environment are powerful influences on development, that their interaction is involved in every aspect of development, and that their interaction is complex. On a practical level, this means we should not ignore the fact that there is a genetic component in any given trait—whether it be something wonderful, such as a wacky sense of humor, or something fearful, such as a violent temper, or something quite ordinary, such as the tendency to tire of the same routine. At the same time, we must always recognize that the environment affects every trait in every individual in ways that change as developmental processes unfold. Genes are always part of the tale, influential on every page, but they never determine the plot or the final story.

Genetic and Chromosomal Abnormalities

In studying human development, we give particular attention to genetic and chromosomal abnormalities, for three reasons. One reason is that, by investigating genetic disruptions of normal development, we can gain a fuller appreciation of the complexities of genetic interaction. A second reason is that an understanding of those who inherit genetic or chromosomal abnormalities is essential to everyone concerned about fostering human development. A lack of such understanding can lead to misinformation and prejudice, which only compound the problems of those affected by such disorders. The third reason is the most practical: the more we know about the origins of genetic and chromosomal abnormalities, the better we understand the risks of their occurring and the better prepared we are to limit their harmful effects. We will begin by looking at those problems caused directly by the chromosomes. Such genetic abnormalities are, in general, the most serious, but they are also the easiest to detect and prevent.

Chromosomal Abnormalities

Sometimes when gametes are formed, the forty-six chromosomes divide unevenly, producing a sperm or ovum that does not have the normal complement of twenty-three chromosomes. If such a gamete fuses with a normal gamete, the result is a zygote with more or less than forty-six chromosomes. This is not unusual. An estimated half of all zygotes have an odd number of chromosomes. Most of these do not even begin to develop, and most of the rest never come to term, usually because a spontaneous abortion occurs. Once in every 200 births, however, a baby is born with forty-five, forty-seven, or even more chromosomes (Gilbert et al., 1987). In every case, these chromosomal abnormalities lead to a recognizable **syndrome**—a cluster of distinct characteristics that tend to occur together. Individuals who have a particular syndrome do not necessarily have all the distinguishing characteristics, and in any given syndrome, the severity of the symptoms varies from person to person.

In most such cases, the presence of an extra chromosome is lethal within the first days or months after birth. There are two major exceptions in which affected individuals often live to adulthood—when the extra chromosome is at the twenty-first pair, where the smallest nonsex chromosome pair is located, or when it occurs at the twenty-third pair.

Down Syndrome

The most common of the extra-chromosome syndromes is **trisomy-21**, or **Down syndrome**, in which the individual inherits a third chromosome at the twenty-first pair. Some 300 distinct characteristics can result from the presence of that extra chromosome, but as with all syndromes, no individual with Down syndrome is quite like another, either in the specific symptoms he or she has or in their severity (Cicchetti & Beeghly, 1990). Despite this variability, almost all people with trisomy-21 have certain facial characteristics—a thick tongue, round face, slanted eyes—as well as distinctive hands, feet, and fingerprints. Many also have hearing problems, heart abnormalities, muscle weakness, and short stature.

syndrome A cluster of distinct characteristics that tend to occur together in a given disorder, although the number of characteristics exhibited, and their intensity, vary from individual to individual.

trisomy-21 (Down syndrome) A chromosomal abnormality caused by an extra chromosome at the twenty-first pair. Individuals with this syndrome tend, with much variation, to have round faces, short limbs, and to be slow to develop.

FIGURE 3-9 Many of the athletes in this Special Olympics competition have Down syndrome, as one can tell from their distinctive facial features. Other characteristics of Down syndrome show much wide variation, and the intellectual growth and personality development of these individuals will depend on many factors besides the impact of their extra chromosome. Events such as this, for instance, can foster self-esteem and social congeniality.

In terms of psychological development, almost all individuals with Down syndrome experience some mental slowness, but their eventual intellectual attainment varies, from severely retarded to average or even above average. Often—but not always—those who are raised at home and given appropriate cognitive stimulation progress to the point of being able to read and write and care for themselves (and often much more), while those who are institutionalized tend to be, and to remain, much more retarded. In their socioemotional qualities, many children with trisomy-21 are considered unusually sweet-tempered. By middle adulthood, however, individuals with Down syndrome are more likely to develop a form of dementia similar to Alzheimer's disease, severely impairing their intellectual and social skills. They are also prone to a host of other problems more commonly found in older persons, including cataracts and certain forms of cancer.

Abnormalities of the Sex Chromosomes

Every newborn infant has at least one X chromosome. About 1 in every 500 infants, however, has either a missing sex chromosome, so that the X stands alone, or has the X chromosome complemented by two or more sex chromosomes. As you can see from Table 3.1, these abnormalities can impair cognitive and psychosocial development, as well as sexual maturation, with each particular syndrome having a specific effect. In many cases, treatment with hormone supplements can alleviate some of the physical problems, and special education may remedy some of the deficits related to psychological functioning.

TABLE 3.1

Common Abnormalities Involving the Sex Chromosomes

Name	Chromosomal Pattern	Physical Appearance*	Psychological Characteristics*	Incidence
Kleinfelter syndrome	XXY	Male. Secondary sex characteristics do not develop. For example, the penis does not grow, the voice does not change. Breasts may develop.	Learning disabled, especially in language skills.	3 in 1,000 males
(No name)	XYY	Male. Prone to acne. Unusually tall.	Tend to be more aggressive than most males. Mildly retarded, especially in language skills.	1 in 1,000 males
Fra-X (Fragile X)	Usually XY	Male or female. Often, large head, prominent ears. Occasionally, enlarged testicles in males.	Variable. Some individuals apparently normal; others severely retarded.	1 in 1,000 males 1 in 2,500 females
(No name)	XXX, XXXX	Female. Normal appearance.	Retarded in almost all intellectual skills.	2 in 1,000 females
Turner syndrome	XO (only one sex chromosome)	Female. Short in stature, often "webbed" neck. Secondary sex characteristics (breasts, menstruation) do not develop.	Learning disabled, especially in abilities related to math and science and in recognition of facial expressions of emotion.	1 in 2,000 females

*There is some variation in the physical appearance and considerable variation in the intellectual and temperamental characteristics of these individuals. With regard to psychological characteristics, much depends on the family environment of the child.

Sources: Gardner & Sutherland, 1989; Kaplan et al., 1987; Lee, 1993; McCauley et al., 1987; Moore, 1989; Vandenberg, 1987.

Again, however, remember that the specific features of any syndrome vary considerably from one individual to another. In fact, in many cases, the presence of abnormal sex chromosomes goes undetected until a seemingly normal childhood is followed by an abnormally delayed puberty. Many specialists recommend chromosomal analysis as soon as a problem is suspected, followed by carefully individualized counseling and treatment for those with a problem.

Other Chromosomal Problems

Sometimes during the formation of gametes, a piece of a chromosome breaks off and reattaches itself to another chromosome. Depending on the particular gamete that created the zygote, as well as on the specific pattern of early cell division, the result can be a zygote with some genetic material missing or with extra material. Indeed, Down syndrome is sometimes caused by chromosome 21 having an extra arm rather than an entire additional chromosome. Individuals with this pattern often have the facial features of Down syndrome but are less likely to experience serious cognitive deficits. Recently researchers discovered that a small extra piece on chromosome 17 is the cause of an inherited degenerative weakness in the hands and feet, called Charcot-Marie-Tooth syndrome (Patel & Lupski, 1991).

As you might expect, more severe problems are caused when genetic material is missing than when additional material is present. Usually the zygote does not grow and develop, and thus is spontaneously aborted. One exception is *cri du chat* syndrome—so named because the newborn's cry resembles that of a cat—which is caused by a deletion on chromosome 4 or 5. Typically the baby survives, but is severely retarded, requiring lifelong total care.

The Fragile X

One of the most common problems associated with chromosomes is actually genetic in origin. In some individuals, part of the X chromosome is attached by such a thin string of molecules that it seems about to break off, and thus the problem is called **fragile-X syndrome**. This abnormality in the chromosome is caused by the mutation of a single gene. Unlike all other known mutations, the mutation involved in fragile X can intensify as it is passed from one generation to the next (Jacobs, 1991; Oberlé et al., 1991).

Overall fragile-X syndrome is highly variable in its effects. Of the females who carry it, most are normal (perhaps because they also carry one normal X chromosome), but a third show some mental deficiency. Among the males who inherit a fragile-X chromosome, there is considerable variation in effect: contrary to all the usual laws of X-linked inheritance, about 20 percent are apparently completely normal; about 33 percent are somewhat retarded; and the rest are severely retarded. The last group is sufficiently large that about half the residents in most homes for the retarded have the fragile X (Brown et al., 1987). While the extreme variability in the effects of this disorder are somewhat unusual, some geneticists believe that the more we learn about other abnormal genes and their interactions, the more diversity in the expression of the phenotype we will find (McKusick, 1990).

fragile-X syndrome A genetically based chromosomal abnormality in the twenty-third pair (sex chromosomes) that causes mental deficiency in about 30 percent of the women who carry it and in an even larger percentage of the men who carry it.

FIGURE 3.10 The fact that older parents have a higher risk of conceiving an embryo with chromosomal abnormalities should not obscure another reality. With modern medical care and prenatal testing, pregnancies that occur when the parents are in their 40s can, and almost always do, result in healthy babies.

Causes of Chromosomal Abnormalities

Chromosomal abnormalities are caused by many factors, some genetic and some environmental (such as viruses contracted by the mother). However, among the most common correlates of chromosomal abnormalities, especially Down syndrome and Kleinfelter syndrome, is parental age. According to one detailed estimate, for example, a 20-year-old woman has 1 chance in 500 of having a child with chromosomal abnormalities; a 39-year-old woman has 1 chance in 100; and a 48-year-old woman has 1 chance in 9 (Cefalo & Moos, 1988). One possible explanation for this increasing rate is the aging of the gametes. Since a female is born with all the ova she will ever have, a 48-year-old woman has ova that are 48 years old. Perhaps degeneration of the ova leads to chromosomal abnormalities. However, this cannot be the only reason older parents have more offspring with chromosomal problems, because, no matter how old the mother, the father's age correlates with the birth of a child with an extra chromosome. Perhaps as the male reproductive system ages, it produces a higher percentage of malformed sperm.

Harmful Genes

While relatively few people have abnormal chromosomes, everyone is a carrier of at least twenty genes that could produce serious diseases or handicaps in one's offspring (Milunsky, 1989). To date, roughly 5,000 genetic disorders have been identified, many of them exceedingly rare (Mukusick, 1990).

Among the more common genetic disorders are cystic fibrosis, spinal defects, cleft palate, and club feet (see Table 3.2, pp. 98–99, for a detailed listing of genetic disorders). Fortunately, many genetic problems are recessive, so a person will not have a particular condition unless he or she has inherited the genes for it from both parents. In addition, some serious genetic conditions are polygenic, including autism, diabetes, and depression (Rutter et al., 1993), so several specific genes must be present in the genotype before the problem appears in the phenotype (Caskey et al., 1992). Still others are multifactorial; they do not become apparent unless something in the prenatal or postnatal environment fosters their expression. Thus, most babies have no apparent genetic problems, although all carry some of the abnormal genes that their parents have. About one baby in every thirty, however, is born with a serious genetic problem (Wheale & McNally, 1988).

In most cases, the parents are completely unprepared for the birth of such a child, which compounds the problem. As we will now see, a better understanding of genetics, and a more widespread use of genetic counseling, can make such births less likely and better prepare families and physicians for those births that do occur.

Genetic Counseling

For most of human history, couples at risk for having a child with a chromosomal or genetic problem did not know it. Today, a combination of testing and counseling before and during pregnancy, as well as immediate medical attention at birth, has transformed the dilemmas faced by many such couples. Through **genetic counseling**, couples can learn more about their genes, and make informed decisions about their childbearing future.

Who Should Be Tested?

Who should receive genetic counseling? Certainly everyone who plans to become a parent should probably know something about his or her genetic inheritance. Ideally, all couples should have preconceptual counseling, not only exploring their family histories for possible warning signs but also learning about factors in their lifestyle—nutrition, drugs, work, and so forth—that might affect a fetus (Cefalo & Moos, 1989). However, genetic counseling is strongly recommended for couples in any of five situations:

1. those who already have a child with a genetic disease;

2. those who have relatives with genetic problems;

3. those who have had previous pregnancies that ended in spontaneous abortion;

4. those who have a history of infertility;

5. those in which the woman is over 34 or the man is over 44.

FIGURE 3.11 The first step in genetic counseling is usually the taking of a detailed family history, searching not only for ancestors and descendants with known genetic diseases, but also for relatives with unexplained problems such as infertility, stillborn children, or a seemingly innocuous mental or physical "peculiarity" that might be a marker for a more serious genetic anomaly. The history is typically interpreted as a chart, such as the one here, that helps elucidate inheritance patterns.

genetic counseling Consultation and testing that enables couples to learn about their genetic heritage and to make decisions about childbearing.

Another group of couples who may be at risk are those whose ancestors came from particular regions of the world where matings almost always occurred between members of the same small ethnic group. Such group inbreeding causes the gene pool to become closed, and the odds of the identical harmful gene being present in both mother and father increase. As indicated in Table 3.2, virtually every ethnic group has an elevated risk for at least one inherited disease. At even greater risk are those couples whose ancestors were from one of the many parts of the world where young people are encouraged to marry cousins or other relatives. Obviously, the more ancestors a particular couple have in common, the more likely they are to carry similar harmful genes, making genetic testing all the more important (Bittles et al., 1991).

TABLE 3.2

Common Genetic Diseases and Conditions

Name	Description	Prognosis	Method of Inheritance	Incidence*	Carrier Detection†	Prenatal Detection?
Alzheimer's disease	Loss of memory and increasing mental impairment	Eventual death, often after years of dependency.	Some forms are definitely genetic; others are not.	Less than one in 100 middle-aged adults; nearly half of all adults over age 80.	No.	No.
Cleft palate, cleft lip	The two sides of the upper lip or palate are not joined.	Correctable by surgery.	Multifactorial. Drugs taken during pregnancy or stress may be involved.	One baby in every 700. More common in Asian-Americans and Native Americans; rare in African-Americans.	No.	Yes, in some cases.
Club foot	The foot and ankle are twisted, making it impossible to walk normally.	Correctable by surgery.	Multifactorial.	One baby in every 200. More common in boys.	No.	Yes.
Cystic fibrosis	Lack of an enzyme. Mucous obstructions in body, especially in lungs and digestive organs.	Most live to middle adulthood.	Recessive gene. Also spontaneous mutations.	One white baby in every 2,500. One in 20 white Americans is a carrier.	Usually.	Yes, in some cases.
Diabetes	Abnormal metabolism of sugar because body does not produce enough insulin.	Early onset is fatal unless controlled by insulin. Diabetes in later adulthood increases the risk of other diseases. Controllable by insulin and diet.	Multifactorial. Exact pattern hard to predict because environment is curcial.	About 10 million Americans. Most develop it in late adulthood. One child in 500 is diabetic. More common in Native Americans.	No.	No.
Hemophilia	Absence of clotting factor in blood.	Crippling and death from internal bleeding. Blood transfusions can lessen or even prevent damage.	X-linked recessive. Also spontaneous mutations.	One in 10,000 males. Royal families of England, Russia, and Germany had it.	Yes.	Yes.
Hydrocephalus	Obstruction causes excess water in brain.	Can produce brain damage and death. Surgery can sometimes make survival and normal intelligence possible.	Multifactorial.	One baby in every 100.	No.	Yes.
Muscular dystrophy (13 separate diseases)	Weakening of muscles. Some forms begin in childhood, others in adulthood.	Inability to walk, move; wasting away and sometimes death.	Duchenne's is X-linked; other forms are recessive or multifactorial.	One in every 3,500 males will develop Duchenne's; about 10,000 Americans have some form of MD.	Yes, for some forms.	Yes, for some forms.

*Incidence statistics vary from country to country; those given here are for the United States. All these diseases can occur in any ethnic group. When certain groups have a higher incidence, it is noted here.

Name	Description	Prognosis	Method of Inheritance	Incidence*	Carrier Detection†	Prenatal Detection?
Neural tube defects (open spine)	Two main forms: anencephaly (parts of the brain and skull are missing) and spina bifida (the lower portion of the spine is not closed).	Often, early death. Anencephalic children are severely retarded; children with spina bifida have trouble with walking and with bowel and bladder control.	Multifactorial; defect occurs in first weeks of pregnancy.	Anencephaly: 1 in 1,000 births; spina bifida: 3 in 1,000. More common in those of Welsh and Scottish descent.	No.	Yes.
Phenylketonuria (PKU)	Abnormal digestion of protein.	Mental retardation, hyperactivity. Preventable by diet.	Recessive gene.	One in 15,000 births. One in 100 European-Americans is a carrier; more common among those of Norwegian and Irish ancestry.	Yes.	Yes.
Pyloric stenosis	Overgrowth of muscle in intestine.	Vomiting, loss of weight, eventual death; correctable by surgery.	Multifactorial.	One male in 200; 1 female in 1,000. Less common in African-Americans.	No.	No.
Sickle-cell anemia	Abnormal blood cells.	Possible painful "crisis"; heart and kidney failure.	Recessive gene.	One in 500 African-American babies is affected. One in 10 African-Americans is a carrier, as is 1 in 20 Latinos.	Yes.	Yes.
Tay-Sachs disease	Enzyme disease.	Apparently healthy infant becomes progressively weaker, usually dying by age 5.	Recessive gene.	One in 4,000 births. One in 30 American Jews is a carrier, as is an estimated 1 in 20 French-Canadians and 1 in 200 non-Jewish Americans.	Yes.	Yes.
Thalassemia	Abnormal blood cells.	Paleness and listlessness, low resistance to infection; treatment by blood transfusion.	Recessive gene.	As many as 1 in 10 Greek-, Italian-, Thai-, and Indian-Americans is a carrier.	Yes.	Yes.
Tourette syndrome	Uncontrollable tics, body jerking, verbal obscenities.	Often imperceptible in children; worsens with age. Can be treated with drugs.	Probably dominant gene.	One in 500 births.	Sometimes.	No.

†Studying the family tree can help geneticists spot a possible carrier of many genetic diseases or, in some cases, a definite carrier. However, here "Yes" means that a carrier can be detected even without knowledge of family history.
Sources: Bowman & Murray, 1990; Caskey, 1992; Connor & Ferguson-Smith, 1991; Lee, 1993; McKusick, 1990; Milunsky, 1989; Moore, 1989.

FIGURE 3.12 Being born with six fingers is a rare, minor genetic abnormality, of no consequence if it occurs alone. However, it sometimes is a marker for more serious recessive problems including dwarfism.

markers   In genetic testing, particular physiological characteristics or gene clusters that suggest that an individual is a carrier of a harmful gene.

alphafetoprotein (AFP) assay   A blood test that reveals if a pregnant woman might have a fetus who has Down syndrome or defects in the central nervous system.

sonogram   A prenatal-screening technique, akin to an x-ray, that uses ultrasound waves to reveal the size and skeletal structure of the fetus.

amniocentesis   A test that takes cells from amniotic fluid to be examined for chromosomal abnormalities.

Predicting Genetic Problems

The ease and accuracy of predicting genetic problems varies from condition to condition. In some cases, both the test and the interpretation of it are quite simple. A blood test is all that is needed, for example, for carrier detection of the genes for sickle-cell anemia, Tay-Sachs, PKU, hemophilia, and thalassemia. Chromosomal analysis can readily reveal fragile X and the inherited form of Down syndrome, as well as many other, less common, abnormalities.

With many other disorders, the specific harmful genes involved have yet to be located, but **markers** for the presence of such genes have been identified. Such markers, usually harmless in themselves, suggest, but do not prove, that the individual is a carrier. In some cases, the marker is in the carrier's phenotype, such as an oddly shaped earlobe or finger, or a particular pattern of eye movement (Holzman & Matthysse, 1990; Kurnit et al., 1987). Other markers involve specific clusters of genes that are typically linked with a specific disease gene. These markers can be detected only through DNA analysis of several family members, ideally through several generations (Lee, 1993).

Knowing the carrier status of a particular set of prospective parents can pin down the odds of their children's inheriting a genetic disease. If the potential problem involves recessive genes, the odds are clear. When two carriers of the same recessive gene procreate, each of their children has 1 chance in 4 of having the disease, because each child has 1 chance in 4 of inheriting the recessive gene from both parents. (The principle is the same as that in the case [p. 84] of two brown-eyed parents who have recessive genes for blue eyes and a 1-in-4 probability of having blue-eyed offspring.) It is important in this respect to remember that "chance has no memory," which means that *each time* two carriers have another child, the odds of that child's inheriting the disease are 1 in 4. Each child born into the family also stands a 1-in-4 chance of avoiding the gene altogether, as well as a 50-50 chance of inheriting one recessive gene, thereby making the child a carrier like the parents.

Most single-gene diseases are carried by a dominant rather than a recessive gene. In fact, there are almost twice as many known dominant-gene disorders as recessive ones (McKusick, 1990). Each offspring of a carrier of a dominant-gene disorder has a 50-50 chance of inheriting the disorder if the other parent is not also a carrier.

Once pregnancy has begun, further testing can often reveal definitively if a particular fetus has beaten the odds or not (see Research Report, p. 101). Some of these tests, such as the **alphafetoprotein (AFP) assay** and the **sonogram**, are routine for all pregnancies in certain countries. Others, such as **amniocentesis**, are suggested whenever the mother is older than 35 or when both parents are carriers of certain genetic diseases. Indeed, in the United States, an obstetrician who fails to advise a high-risk patient about prenatal testing can be sued if the patient gives birth to a severely impaired child (Blank, 1988).

This fact may lead to the erroneous impression that all genetic diseases are predictable. They are not. There are many genetic diseases for

Prenatal Diagnosis

Within the past twenty years, researchers have refined literally dozens of tests to determine if a fetus is developing well. Many of these are now routine, recommended for every pregnancy. For example, blood tests reveal whether the mother has had diseases that might harm the fetus; various measurements tell whether fetal growth and development are occurring on schedule; urine analysis and blood-pressure readings indicate how well the mother's system is coping with pregnancy.

Many other tests are not routine. They are used selectively, especially when there is some likelihood of genetic, chromosomal, or prenatal damage. Five of these tests demonstrate the amazing sophistication, and awesome implications, of prenatal diagnosis today.

Alphafetoprotein Assay

Analyzing the level of alphafetoprotein (AFP) in the mother's blood is useful for indicating neural-tube defects, Down syndrome, or the presence of multiple embryos. The actual test is a simple blood test. However, not all women or doctors choose to employ this test, unless they are ready to undergo further tests if indicated. The reason is that, while about 10 percent of all pregnancies have an unexpected AFP level, many of these are false alarms, caused by miscalculations of the age of the fetus or some other normal variations (Evans et al., 1989). Thus unexpected AFP levels indicate that more tests are needed; usually, the new tests reveal a normal pregnancy.

Sonogram

The sonogram, or ultrasound, uses high-frequency sound waves to outline the shape of the fetus. Sonograms can reveal problems such as an abnormally small head or other body malformations, excess spinal fluid accumulating on the brain, and several diseases (for instance, of the kidney). In addition, sonograms are used to diagnose twins, estimate fetal age, locate the position of the placenta, and reveal the rate of fetal growth. About half of all North American pregnancies are now scanned with sonogram because it provides a valuable and low-risk means of monitoring the pregnancy throughout its duration.

Fetoscopy

Fetoscopy is performed by inserting a very narrow tube into the woman's abdomen, piercing the uterus. Then a fetoscope is inserted, allowing the physician to observe the fetus and the inside of the placenta directly. Fetoscopy is most often performed when a malformation is suspected. It is also used to take a blood sample from the placenta or the umbilicus, or a blood, skin, or liver sample directly from the fetus, to diagnose suspected abnormalities of the blood, immune, or organ systems (Carlson, 1994).

Amniocentesis

In amniocentesis, about half an ounce of the amniotic fluid is withdrawn through the mother's abdominal wall with a syringe. The fluid contains sloughed-off fetal cells that can be analyzed to detect chromosomal abnormalities as well as many other genetic and prenatal problems. The amniotic fluid also reveals the sex of the fetus (useful knowledge if an X-linked disorder is likely) and provides clues about fetal age and health. Amniocentesis has been the "mainstay" of prenatal diagnosis since 1973 (Evans et al., 1989). However, it has one decided disadvantage: it cannot be performed until mid-pregnancy, about fourteen weeks after conception, when there is sufficient fluid available for sampling.

Chorionic Villi Sampling

In chorionic villi sampling (CVS), a sample of the placental tissue that surrounds the fetus is obtained and analyzed. This test provides the same information as that obtained through amniocentesis, with close to the same accuracy, but CVS has one decided advantage: it can be performed as early as the sixth week of pregnancy (Carlson, 1994).

Risks and Benefits

Nearly all these tests are regarded as low-risk for both the mother and the fetus. Nevertheless, even a low risk should be avoided if possible. The AFP is completely safe, and there are no proven risks for the sonogram either. However, 1 in every 200 amniocentesis and between 1 and 2 percent of chorionic villi samplings and fetoscopies have been associated with spontaneous abortions that probably would not otherwise have occurred (Mennuti, 1989). Thus the risk of unexpected abortion must be weighed carefully against the need to know if a particular pregnancy might result in a seriously handicapped child, or if special prenatal care is needed to reduce the risk of birth complications.

which the culprit genes or their markers have yet to be identified. With some other genetic diseases, such as cystic fibrosis, there are various sets of markers, which can make carrier detection uncertain. Even more problematic, cystic fibrosis, as well as many other genetic diseases, can arise from a spontaneous mutation, an event that is impossible to predict. And because most genetic diseases are rare, many high-risk couples, with no known problems in their family history, never imagine that they are both carriers of the same defective gene.

Although scientists have a long way to go before being able to predict every genetic disease, advances are being reported each year. In addition, for couples who know that their progeny are at risk for a disease involving an identified gene, a new technique, called *implantation testing*, may soon be available (Lee, 1993). This procedure is a variation of *in vitro* fertilization: the couple's ova and sperm are mixed in the laboratory (see the Research Report on alternative reproductive approaches, pp. 112–113), and the resulting zygotes are tested for the presence of the problem gene. If the zygotes are free of the gene, they are inserted into the woman's uterus, as in a regular *in vitro* procedure, and if all goes well, at least one of them will implant and develop just as any other embryo would.

Overall, genetic testing is one of the most innovative areas in all of developmental research, raising hopes that within the next decade researchers will be able to detect elevated genetic vulnerability in both fetus and adult for an increasing number of conditions, including not only dominant and recessive diseases but multifactorial ones, among them cancer, heart disease, and diabetes, as well as many types of mental retardation and psychopathology (Marx, 1991). As scientists focus on particular harmful genes, both prevention and treatment will improve. In some cases, genetic disease will be cured by inserting a healthy gene into the affected person's DNA—a practice already in the experimental stage for cystic fibrosis. Aided by exciting new knowledge arising from the Human Genome Project (see Public Policy, pp. 103–104), advances in experimental techniques of gene splicing and gene-replacement therapy offer hope of permanent solutions to certain genetic disorders.

Many Alternatives

Fortunately, with proper counseling, those who undergo genetic testing because they are concerned about their potential offspring learn that they have many choices. Often testing reveals that neither partner, or only one, is a carrier of a harmful trait, or reveals that the odds of that couple's having offspring with a serious illness are not much higher than they are for any other couple. If a couple learn that they both are carriers of a recessive disease, or are high-risk in other ways, they have several alternatives—from avoiding pregnancy and, perhaps, planning adoption, to having amniocentesis and, perhaps, considering abortion, to determining how they will care for their infant if he or she is born with a disorder. Moreover, recent experimental (and sometimes controversial) advances in medical technology offer the possibility, in the future, of treating some fetal disorders prenatally, whether through drugs delivered directly to the fetus, or surgery performed on the fetus, or in other ways. The specifics will vary, not only by couple, but also by disease.

The Human Genome Project

Imagine a time when the mysteries of your heredity could be revealed by analyzing a drop of blood or saliva, or even a snippet of hair. Analyzing a cell from anywhere on your body, a laboratory might be able to provide a complete report of the physiological and psychological characteristics encoded within your DNA.

When going for a medical checkup, you would bring along a computer disk that fully described your hereditary features for the physician to consult while diagnosing or treating your ailments. And when making the most important decisions of your life—whom to marry, where to live, what career to pursue—detailed information about your heredity would shed important light on your options.

Does this sound like a wonderful new world, or a nightmare? In either case, certain aspects of this world are fast approaching, partly as a result of the **Human Genome Project**, a $3 billion, fifteen-year initiative that formally began in 1991. It has been described as biology's equivalent of putting a man on the moon, or of exploding the first atom bomb (Angier, 1989; Watson, 1990). The goal of this worldwide research effort is, quite simply, to map all the 100,000 genes of the human body, indexing the exact chemical instructions of each of the 3 billion base pairs and locating every gene on its carrier chromosome. In this way, scientists hope to crack the genetic code of all our human characteristics, from the hereditary origins of physical structures and physiological systems to the genetic foundations of behavioral tendencies and psychological disorders.

The knowledge yielded by this project will have wide-ranging applications, in medicine, criminal justice, public health, education, psychotherapy, and other related fields. Already researchers have located the genetic defects that cause cystic fibrosis, Duchenne's muscular dystrophy, fragile-X syndrome, and many forms of cancer. Scientists believe that with every passing year, the genes associated with other hereditary disorders will be identified, including those for mental illnesses such as depression, dementia, and schizophrenia and for multifactorial disorders such as heart disease, hypertension, and stroke.

In addition, scientists already know much more about those genes that allow people to live longer and healthier lives. One recent discovery, the gene for a protein called P53, was dubbed "molecule of the year" by *Science* magazine (Culotta & Koshland, 1993). P53 suppresses the growth of tumors and might soon lead to treatment—even prevention and cure—for some fifty-one types of cancer. Other "protective" genes that scientists may soon identify include genes that create the vitamin D receptors essential to preventing osteoporosis; genes that enhance the growth of neural axons, slowing the development of senility; genes that reduce a person's unhealthy appetite for fat; and genes that foster the production of neurotransmitters that

The actual work of mapping genes for the Human Genome Project is tedious and time-consuming, as well as expensive. However, the worldwide cooperation in this mapping effort has already paid off, not only in locating some particularly critical genes but also in developing techniques to speed the search. Assisted by the robot in the background, this scientist at Genethon in Paris is cloning thousands of copies of a particular gene colony as part of the process of building a "gene library."

help a person cope with stress efficiently (Depue et al., 1994; Morrison et al.; 1994; Leibowitz & Kim, 1992).

The excitement brought about by these discoveries comes with fear as well as hope, however. Our current difficulties safeguarding privacy in a computer-connected world are like a spring breeze compared to the tornados that might be unleashed if access to each person's genetic code is not carefully restricted.

The dangers are most apparent with regard to medical insurance. In any nation that does not have universal medical coverage, insurance companies might require a drop of blood upon application for a policy, analyze its DNA messages, and then charge exorbitant rates, or deny coverage altogether, to anyone who appears to have a risk of a serious, chronic illness, or who has a harmful recessive gene that might someday be passed on to a dependent child.

Another potential problem relates to employment. Instead of assessing job-related experience or skills, a prospective employer might ask for a genetic reading to determine a candidate's suitability for a job. Educational opportunities might be restricted as well. Even the most simple adult privileges, like getting a driver's license or renting an apartment, might require a DNA check and might be denied to those with genetic vulnerability to, say, alcoholism, even if the person in question has never shown any inclination to drink. Obviously, any attempt to discrim-

The Human Genome Project (continued)

inate against a particular person because of generalizations based on other people with similar genes should be made illegal. The best way to prevent abuse in this area is to protect such personal information with clear laws and guidelines for its use.

Another area with great potential for healing, and for harm, is "gene therapy," that is the insertion of a healthy gene in a person who lacks it (Thompson, 1994). The first human to benefit from such therapy was a 5-year-old girl, Ashanthi DeSilva, who was suffering from severe combined immune deficiency, known as SCID. Her disease was caused by a mutation in a gene on chromosome 20, which made her body incapable of producing a specific enzyme called adenosine deaminase, or ADA. SCID is the same disease that eventually killed the famous "boy in the bubble," who spent his twelve years of life sealed in a germ-free plastic world, "a lifeboat shielding him from a sea of germs" that prevented play with other children or even the comfort of his mother's touch (Thompson, 1994).

Partly because of the development of new drugs, Ashanthi DeSilva's childhood was not that limited, although her parents kept her homebound and isolated as much as possible. By age 4, however, she was becoming sicker and weaker; survival to adulthood was unlikely, and a normal childhood was impossible. In a courageous decision, her parents gave permission to scientists at the frontier of gene therapy to try a revolutionary treatment. On the morning of September 14, 1990, doctors removed some of Ashanthi's blood, treated it with a virus carrying the gene that her body lacked, and returned the blood to her body. Not only did Ashanthi endure the treatment with no ill effects (asking only if she could return to the hospital playroom after the transfusion was over) but the treatment stimulated her body to produce the missing ADA enzyme. The cure was not permanent, however; Ashanthi needed repeated transfusions for three years.

Then, in 1993, another type of gene therapy began for Ashanthi, with the missing gene inserted into her bone marrow cells. The hope—not yet confirmed but becoming brighter with every passing day—is that this gene therapy is a permanent cure for her genetic disease. Meanwhile, Ashanthi goes to school, plays with other children, and experiences all the normal scrapes and sniffles of childhood without life-threatening reactions (Thompson, 1994).

Almost no one would quarrel with gene therapy to save a life of a gravely ill child such as Ashanthi. However, there are other applications of gene therapy that demand thoughtful, ethical analysis. According to a 1992 Harris poll sponsored by the March of Dimes, almost half of the general public would approve of gene therapy to improve children's inherited physical characteristics (43 percent) and intelligence levels (42 percent). Already, more than 10,000 children have been treated with a precursor of genetic therapy, a hormone to stimulate growth in children who seem to be much shorter than average.

Such high acceptance for changing individual traits alarms many scientists, including those responsible for the Human Genome Project, who have set aside millions of dollars to explore and publicize the ethical dilemmas of genetic research. Their concerns are two. First, that the individual children who receive genetic correction will also receive a destructive message—that their normal development is so unacceptable that considerable money must be spent to ensure that they conform to a particular social standard. (Most scientists believe that we should change the standard rather than change the child.) Second, geneticists stress that wide variation in inherited human characteristics, including traits that a particular parent may prefer not to see in his or her own child, helps keep the entire human community healthy and strong.

Consequently, most scientists and doctors prefer to use genetic therapy only when serious illness is imminent. As the March of Dimes, an organization that advocates for prevention and treatment of birth defects of every kind, explains, the goal of gene therapy is "to make sick babies healthy, not normal babies perfect."

Human Genome Project   A worldwide effort to construct and decipher a chromosomal map of all 3 billion codes of the 100,000 human genes.

Preventive measures are usually chosen when the risk is high for a devastating disease. For example, no one would willingly have a child with Tay-Sachs (see Table 3.2) because the disease progressively destroys the infant's mind and body, leading to death by age 5. Between 1970 and 1990, extensive testing and counseling of engaged Jewish couples led to a 95 percent reduction in Tay-Sachs among North American Jews (Zeiger, 1990). This dramatic turnaround involved some very painful decisions for the carrier couples involved. Some broke off their engagements; some decided not to bear

FIGURE 3.13 With the help of a genetic counselor, even couples who know they run a risk of having a baby with a genetic defect might decide to have a child. Although the process of making that decision is more complicated for them than it is for a couple with no family genetic illness and no positive tests for harmful recessive genes, the outcome is usually a healthy baby. In each case, the genetic counselor provides facts and alternatives: every couple must make their own decision. In fact, two couples who have the same potential for producing a child with a genetic defect, and are aware of the same facts regarding the situation, sometimes make opposite decisions because they differ in their attitudes about abortion, in their willingness to raise a child with a genetic abnormality, or in their desire to have their own child rather than an adopted one.

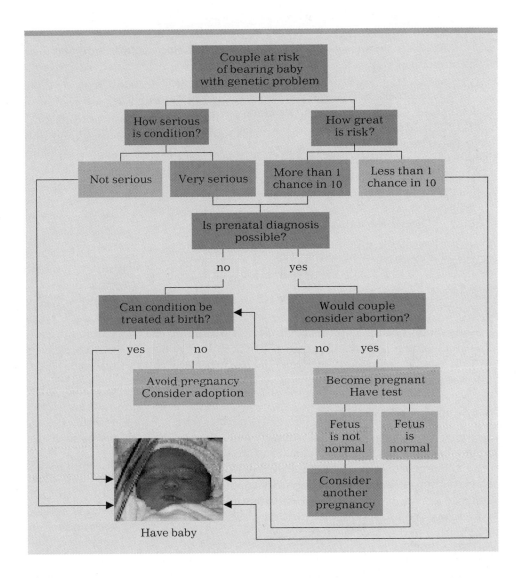

children; some decided to try pregnancy, with abortion as an option if their fetus was found to have Tay-Sachs. But as a result, almost none had to watch their child suffer a short and ravaged life.

In cases where the consequences of a genetic disease are variable, the decision-making process is even more difficult. For example, some infants born with sickle-cell anemia (see Table 3.2) die in childhood after suffering frequent "crises," in which they experience great pain; others live relatively normal lives into adulthood, with occasional bouts of illness.

Couples at risk of any particular problem should talk with parents who have, or have had, children with the same problem. Almost always, they will gain an important perspective and insight, including a sense of the unanticipated anguish and unexpected fulfillment that having a seriously disabled child can represent. Most genetic counselors believe very strongly that the final choice should be made by the individuals concerned, whose values must be respected, even if their decision is not what the counselor, or their family members, would make. Indeed, couples with identical genetic risks often make quite different decisions, depending on their personal relationship, religious beliefs, ethical views, values, temperaments, and financial resources.

As the decision tree in Figure 3.13 makes clear, the goal of genetic counseling—and a major goal of this chapter—is to get prospective parents to think through their options step by step, so that the outcome of their procreation decisions is not only one they can live with but one that will, as much as possible, result in a welcomed addition to the human family who will live a long and happy life.

SUMMARY

The Beginning of Development

1. Conception occurs when a sperm penetrates an ovum, creating a single cell called a zygote. The zygote contains all the genetic material—half from each of the two gametes—needed to create a unique developing person.

The Genetic Code

2. Genes, which provide the information cells need to specialize and perform specific functions in the body, are arranged on chromosomes. With the exception of gametes, every human cell contains twenty-three pairs of chromosomes, one member of each pair contributed by each parent. Every cell contains a duplicate of the genetic information in the first cell, the zygote.

3. Twenty-two pairs of chromosomes control the development of most of the body. The twenty-third pair determines the individual's sex: zygotes with an XY combination will become males; those with an XX combination will become females.

4. Each person has a unique combination of genes, with one important exception. Sometimes a zygote separates completely into two or more genetically identical organisms, creating monozygotic (identical) twins, triplets, and so on.

5. The totality of genes a person has for any given trait—that is, the genetic potential for that trait—is the genotype. The trait that the individual actually develops is the phenotype.

From Genotype to Phenotype

6. While sometimes one pair of genes is the major influence on one particular aspect of the phenotype, most human characteristics are polygenic and multifactorial, the result of the interaction of many genetic and environmental influences.

7. Genes can interact in many ways, as the various genes on the genotype work to influence the phenotype. Most often genes from both parents contribute to the trait in an additive fashion, but sometimes genes act in a dominant-recessive pattern. In this case, the presence of only one dominant gene is sufficient to direct the phenotype, while two recessive genes are required for the trait to be expressed.

8. Males inherit just one X chromosome, from their mother, while females inherit two, one from each parent. For this reason, males are more likely to have recessive traits, such as color blindness, that are X-linked.

9. Multiple genes affect almost every human trait, including intellectual abilities, personality patterns, and mental illness. At the same time, the environment—from the moment of conception throughout life—constantly influences genetic tendencies. Gene-environment interaction is thus ongoing and complex.

Genetic and Chromosomal Abnormalities

10. Chromosomal abnormalities occur when the zygote has too few or too many chromosomes, or when a chromosome has a missing, a nonfunctioning, or an extra piece of genetic material. While most embryos with chromosomal abnormalities are spontaneously aborted early in pregnancy, many of the babies who survive with such defects have extra or missing material on their sex chromosomes. The most common chromosomal abnormality that does not involve the sex chromosomes occurs when an extra chromosome is attached to the twenty-first pair. This causes trisomy-21, or Down syndrome, a varying cluster of problems in physical and intellectual functioning.

11. Every individual carries some genes for genetic handicaps and diseases. However, since many of those genes are recessive, and many of the diseases involved are polygenic, or multifactorial, most babies will not inherit a serious genetic defect.

Genetic Counseling

12. Genetic testing and an evaluation of family background can help predict whether a couple will have a child with a genetic problem. If there is a high probability that they will, they can consider several options, such as adoption, remaining childless, or obtaining prenatal diagnosis and, if necessary, abortion. In some cases, appropriate postnatal treatment may remedy or alleviate the problem.

KEY TERMS

gamete (78)
sperm (78)
ovum (78)
zygote (78)
gene (79)
chromosome (79)
DNA (deoxyribonucleic acid) (79)
genetic code (79)
twenty-third pair (80)
monozygotic twins (82)
dizygotic twins (82)
polygenic traits (82)
multifactorial traits (82)
genotype (82)
phenotype (83)
additive pattern (83)
nonadditive pattern (83)

dominant-recessive pattern (84)
carrier (84)
X-linked genes (84)
environment (85)
syndrome (93)
trisomy-21 (Down syndrome) (93)
fragile-X syndrome (95)
genetic counseling (97)
markers (100)
alphafetoprotein (AFP) assay (100)
sonogram (100)
amniocentesis (100)
Human Genome Project (104)

KEY QUESTIONS

1. How do genes influence one's physical characteristics and behavior?

2. How is each person's genetic uniqueness ensured, and why is this important?

3. What are the differences between additive and nonadditive patterns and dominant and recessive genes?

4. What research strategies are used to determine genetic and environmental influences on psychological characteristics?

5. How does the interaction between heredity and environment occur for physical traits, such as height, and psychological traits, such as shyness?

6. Why is it that some people who have a genetic predisposition for schizophrenia or alcoholism never develop these conditions?

7. What are some of the effects of chromosomal defects?

8. What are some of the factors that determine if a couple is at risk for bearing a child with genetic abnormalities?

9. How can genetic counseling help those parents who are at risk for bearing a child with genetic problems?

Prenatal Development

CHAPTER

4

The nine months that precede birth are the time of the most rapid growth, the greatest transformation, and the most hazardous development of the entire life span. Although the dramatic events of the prenatal period are hidden from ordinary view, much is now known about these crucial nine months. Among the questions we will answer in this chapter are the following:

What is the normal process of growth from a single-celled zygote to a newborn infant?

At what prenatal age does a fetus have some chance of surviving outside the womb, and what factors contribute to the likelihood of survival?

In what ways can the fetus sense and respond to events in the outside world?

What factors in prenatal development can cause birth defects or result in later problems?

What factors can increase the chances that prenatal development will result in a healthy baby?

As you learned in Chapter 1, a contextual perspective encourages us to look at any moment of development as a complex interaction among developmental domains and the social context. This is no less true for the nine months that precede birth than for the 900 or so that follow it.

Obviously, the primary focus of a chapter on prenatal development is the astounding physical growth that transforms a single-celled zygote into a fully formed human baby. However, the specifics of this growth, and its bearing on later cognitive and psychosocial development, are deeply influenced by the social context, because the family, the community, and the culture all have the power to enhance or inhibit prenatal development. The influence of the mother's health habits and activities, for example, and of her culture's customs and laws regarding health, disease, and various harmful substances, makes some newborns much better prepared for a long and healthy life than others. These various contextual factors will be discussed in this chapter, which describes what is arguably the most important developmental period of life.

From Zygote to Newborn

The process of human growth from a single-celled zygote into a fully developed baby is generally discussed in terms of three main periods. The first two weeks of development are called the **germinal period**; from the third week through the eighth week is the **period of the embryo**; and from the ninth week until birth is the **period of the fetus**.[*]

The Germinal Period: The First Fourteen Days

Within hours after conception, the one-celled zygote starts to travel further down the Fallopian tube toward the uterus and begins the process of cell division and growth, first dividing into two cells, which soon become four, then eight, then sixteen, and so on (see Figure 4.1). At least through the fourth doubling, each of these cells is identical, and any one of them could become a complete human being. In fact, as explained in Chapter 3, nature sometimes splits the cluster of cells into two or even four distinct segments, and then each segment becomes a monozygotic twin or quadruplet.

FIGURE 4.1 The very first stages of prenatal development are shown here, as the original zygote is dividing into two cells (*a*), four cells (*b*), and (*c*) eight cells. Occasionally at this early stage, the cells separate completely, forming the beginning of a monozygotic twin, quadruplet, or octuplet.

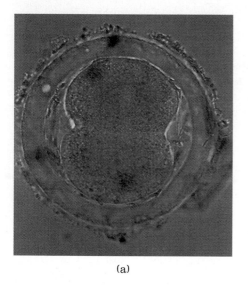

(a)

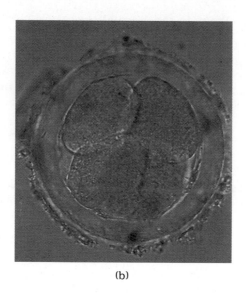

(b)

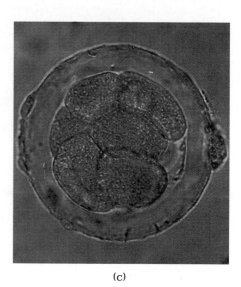

(c)

Soon, however, the process of **differentiation** occurs, causing clusters of cells to begin to take on distinct traits and gravitate toward particular locations that foreshadow the types of cells they will become. The first clear sign of differentiation occurs about a week after conception, when the multiplying cells (now numbering more than a hundred) separate into two distinct masses, the outer cells forming a protective circle that will become the placenta, and the inner cells forming a nucleus that will become the embryo.

germinal period The first two weeks of development after conception, characterized by rapid cell division and the beginning of cell differentiation.

period of the embryo From approximately the third through the eighth week after conception, when the rudimentary forms of all anatomical structures develop.

---

[*] Technically speaking, the name of the developing human organism changes several times depending on the precise stage of development. While there is no need for the student to know all the terms, the curious might be interested to know that the organism that begins as a zygote becomes a morula, a blastocyst, a gastrula, a neurula, an embryo, and a fetus before it finally becomes an infant (Moore, 1988).

The first task of the outer cells is to achieve **implantation**, that is, to plant themselves into the nurturant environment of the uterus. This is accomplished as the cells nestle into the uterine lining, rupturing tiny blood vessels in order to obtain nourishment and to build a connective web of membranes and blood vessels that links the mother and the developing organism, allowing the growth of the next nine months or so. Implantation is far from automatic, however: an estimated 58 percent of all naturally occurring conceptions fail to become properly implanted (Gilbert et al., 1987) (see Table 4.1), thereby ending the new life even before the embryo begins to form or the woman suspects she is pregnant.

TABLE 4.1

The Vulnerability of Prenatal Development

The Germinal Period
From the moment of conception until 14 days later, 58 percent of all developing organisms fail to grow or implant properly, and thus do not survive the germinal period. Most of these organisms were grossly abnormal.

The Period of the Embryo
From 14 days until 56 days after conception, during which time all the major external and internal body structures begin to form, about 20 percent of all embryos are aborted spontaneously.

The Period of the Fetus
From the eighth week after conception on, about 5 percent of all fetuses are aborted spontaneously before viability at 22 weeks, or are stillborn after 22 weeks.

Birth
Only 31 percent of all conceptions survive prenatal development to become living newborn babies.

Source: Gilbert et al., 1987; Moore, 1988; Volpe, 1987.

Once accomplished, implantation triggers hormonal changes that halt the woman's usual menstrual cycle, elevate her body temperature slightly, increase the supply of blood to her breasts, as well as cause many other body changes that will help to nurture the new life. For many women, some of the very earliest of these changes cause cigarette smoke to nauseate them and coffee to taste suddenly bitter, which may be nature's way to encourage pregnant women to adopt more healthful habits even before they know, or even suspect, that they are pregnant. Successful implantation marks the end of the most rapid growth and the most hazardous transition of the entire life span, and the beginning of the woman's interaction with her future child.

That early interaction—including maintaining a healthy diet, getting prenatal care, and the like—depends, in part, on the couple's relationship, their economic status, and the mother's age. It may also depend on how wanted and planned the pregnancy is. For example, almost all pregnancies under age 15 are unintended (85 percent are aborted), while most pregnancies of women between ages 30–35 are welcomed (only 19 percent are aborted) (Koonin et al., 1993). And for a small but increasing number, pregnancy is the long hoped-for reward after years of disappointment, effort, and expense (see A Closer Look: Infertility and Alternative Reproductive Approaches, pp. 112–114).

period of the fetus From the ninth week after conception until birth, when the organs grow in size and complexity.

differentiation The developmental process by which a relatively unspecified cell or tissue undergoes a progressive change to a more specialized cell or tissue.

implantation Beginning about a week after conception, the burrowing of the organism into the lining of the uterus, where it can be nourished and protected during growth.

A CLOSER LOOK

Infertility and Alternative Reproductive Approaches

For many couples, the confirmation of pregnancy culminates a long, sometimes painstaking journey to overcome the challenges of infertility. In fact, about 15 percent of all married couples experience **infertility**—usually defined as being unable to conceive a child after a year or more of trying. Since many couples today are waiting until their thirties before deciding to start their families, age is often a contributing factor to this problem. One statistic in particular makes the point: about one couple in twenty is infertile when the woman is in her early twenties, whereas about one couple in seven has this problem when the woman is in her early thirties (Menken et al., 1986).

It should be noted that although fertility statistics are often given in terms of the age of the woman, until middle age, both sexes contribute about equally to fertility problems: in 40 percent of cases the source of the infertility lies with the man, in another 40 percent, with the woman, and in 20 percent, with both partners (Davajan & Israel, 1991). In men, infertility can be the result of inadequate sperm production, or the sperm's poor functioning (for example, the sperm may lack the ability to swim quickly and far enough to reach the ovum). Sperm production is affected by age, but it is also influenced by other factors that can impair normal body functioning, such as an illness with high fever, medical therapy involving radiation, a high dosage of prescription drugs, drug abuse, or exposure to environmental toxins (Bardin, 1986; Newton, 1984). For women, infertility can derive from numerous sources, the most common being difficulties with ovulation or blocked Fallopian tubes. Another fairly common cause of female fertility problems is **endometriosis**, a condition in which fragments of the uterine lining become implanted and grow on the surface of the ovaries or the Fallopian tubes, blocking the reproductive tract. Endometriosis is most likely to occur between the ages of 25 and 35, and about a third of those who have it are infertile (Davajan & Israel, 1991).

Many of these fertility problems are remediable. In women, difficulties with ovulation can often be treated with drugs to stimulate the ovaries. When blocked Fallopian tubes are the result of endometriosis, they can usually be opened surgically. Men with a low sperm count are often urged to abstain from intercourse for several days to build up their store of sperm prior to the next effort at conception. If this fails, another alternative is **artificial insemination**, in which the husband's sperm are collected in a laboratory and injected directly into the woman's cervix, increasing the likelihood that they will reach the ovum. (When the problem is the poor quality of the husband's sperm, sperm from a donor is sometimes used for this procedure.)

For many couples, these solutions are helpful. Recent technological innovations have provided new hope for others (Nachtigall & Mehran, 1991; Zoldbrod, 1992). With **in vitro fertilization** (IVF), for example, ova are surgically removed from the ovaries and fertilized by sperm in the laboratory. The resulting embryos are then inserted into the uterus with the hope that one or more will implant into the uterine lining and establish a pregnancy. (Sometimes embryos created through IVF are frozen for later use.) This technique, experimental in 1978 when the first "test tube baby" was born, is now widely available, with a success rate of about one baby in seven attempts. Two recent variations of IVF, *GIFT* (gamete intra-Fallopian transfer) and *ZIFT* (zygote intra-Fallopian transfer), which involve inserting either sperm and unfertilized ova (gametes) or fertilized ova (zygotes) into a Fallopian tube, have success rates of about one in five attempts.

In addition to these approaches, a variety of "third-party" contributions might be considered: donor sperm (as may occur with artificial insemination), donor ova (as with GIFT or ZIFT), and even donor wombs. In the last case, also known as **surrogate motherhood**, a woman volunteers to become impregnated by the father-to-be (usually through artificial insemination) and carries the baby to term. After-

---

infertility Defined by medical doctors as failure to conceive a child after one year of trying.

endometriosis A condition in which fragments of the uterine lining become implanted and grow on the surface of the ovaries or the Fallopian tubes, often causing fertility problems.

artificial insemination Alternative method to normal conception in which sperm is inserted with a syringe into a woman's vagina, either on or near the cervix.

Although they obviously differ in age, brothers David and Nicholas might be called "twins," since they were conceived at the same time. Because their mother had a blocked Fallopian tube that prevented normal conception, the boys' parents turned to IVF. One of the embryos that resulted from the procedure (David) was used immediately; another embryo (Nicholas) was kept frozen and then used about a year later.

ward, the father and his wife raise the child as their own.

Needless to say, these alternative reproductive approaches come with profound ethical and legal questions, not the least of which is, Who really are the child's parents? In any of the "donor" conceptions described above, several adults may legitimately stake a claim to parenthood, as has been made painfully apparent in well-publicized cases of surrogate mothers who decide not to relinquish the baby to the father and his wife, but instead seek to raise the child as their own. Also raising a thicket of tangled issues are situations in which a married couple undergo *in vitro* fertilization and the freezing of their embryos for future childbearing—and then divorce and battle for legal "custody" of the embryos or ask a court to decide on whether the embryos should be destroyed or not. Although courts are usually required to address such legal dilemmas, they

cannot resolve the profound ethical issues that the new reproductive techniques entail. Added to these dilemmas are considerations concerning the child's interests. Should children be informed of their parentage if it involved a third-party donor? Should they be legally permitted a chance to learn who their biological parents are upon request?

There are a variety of costs as well as benefits to these new reproductive approaches. The most obvious cost is the economic one: in the United States the expense of the various fertility therapies can range from $1,000 for artificial insemination to upwards of $100,000 for all the expenses related to a series of *in vitro* fertilizations, making some of these avenues toward childbearing inaccessible to all but the most affluent couples. The psychological costs of treating infertility can also be high. The treatment process itself can be lengthy and emotionally draining, and, as indicated, the success rates are modest. People who spend years of their lives and thousands of dollars on medical measures without success often find their marital relationship sorely strained and their self-concept badly damaged (Dunkel-Schetter & Lobel, 1991).

More broadly, some ethicists question why couples would go to such great lengths to have their own (or partially their own) biological offspring in a world where millions of unwanted newborns seem destined to suffer neglect and abuse. They acknowledge that the desire to reproduce oneself biologically can indeed be powerful, but they also point out that, to a developing child, the biology of parenthood is likely to be far less meaningful than the parenting role assumed by the adult or adults who provide the child with love and nurturance. Adoption is, of course, an alternative approach for couples who find that they are unable to have children on their own. Taken together with the alternative reproductive approaches discussed here, there are clearly multiple options to be considered by adults who experience fertility problems.

in vitro fertilization Alternative method to normal conception in which ova are removed from a woman and fertilized with sperm in a laboratory dish. After the resulting zygotes have begun normal cell division, they are inserted into a woman's uterus for implantation or are frozen for later use.

surrogate motherhood Alternative method to normal conception in which sperm from the husband is inserted with a syringe into a woman who has agreed to bear the child for the infertile wife.

The Period of the Embryo: The Third Through the Eighth Week

The beginning of the third week after conception initiates the *period of the embryo,* as some of the inner cells of the organism form a structure known as the **embryonic disk,** which consists of three layers. The outer layer, the **ectoderm,** will become the skin and the nervous system; the middle layer, the **mesoderm,** will become the muscles, bones, and the circulatory, excretory, and reproductive systems; the inner layer, the **endoderm,** will become key elements of the digestive and respiratory systems (Carlson, 1994). As this process begins, the first perceptible sign of body formation appears: a fold in the ectoderm becomes the **neural tube,** which will later become the central nervous system, including the brain and spinal column.

During the embryonic period, growth proceeds in two directions: from the head downward—called **cephalo-caudal development** (literally, "from head to tail")—and from the center (that is, the spine) outward—called **proximo-distal development** (literally, "from near to far"). Thus the most vital organs and body parts form first, before the extremities.

embryonic disk   A flat inner structure of cells that, during the third week after conception, forms into three embryonic layers (the ectoderm, mesoderm, and endoderm).

ectoderm   The outer layer of the embryonic disk, which becomes the outer skin, the nails, part of the teeth, the lens of the eye, and the central nervous system.

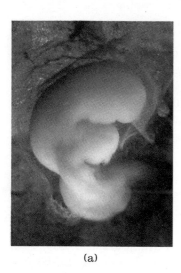

(a)

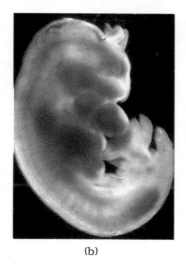

(b)

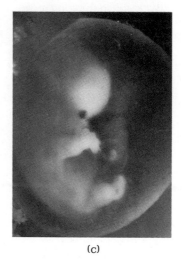

(c)

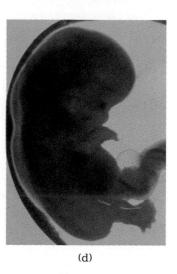

(d)

FIGURE 4.2 At 4 weeks past conception (*a*), the embryo is only about ⅕ inch long (5 millimeters), but already the head (top right) has taken shape. (*b*) At 5 weeks past conception, the embryo has grown to twice the size it was at 4 weeks. Its heart, which has been beating for a week now, is visible, as is what appears to be a primitive tail, which will soon be enclosed by skin and protective tissue at the tip of the backbone (the coccyx). (*c*) By 7 weeks, the organism is about an inch long (2 centimeters). Eyes, nose, the digestive system, and even the first stage of toe formation can be seen. (*d*) At 8 weeks, the 1½-inch-long (4-centimeter) organism is clearly recognizable as a human fetus.

Following this pattern, in the fourth week after conception the head and blood vessels begin to develop. Most significant, the primitive heart begins to beat, making the cardiovascular system the first organ system to begin to function (Moore, 1988). At the end of the first month, eyes, ears, nose, and mouth start to form, and buds that will become arms and legs appear, as does a tail-like appendage extending from the spine. The embryo is now about ⅕ of an inch long (5 millimeters), about 7,000 times the size of the zygote it was twenty-eight days before.

During the early weeks of life, rapid growth is also occurring in the **placenta,** an organ consisting of (1) blood vessels that lead to both the mother's and the embryo's circulatory systems and (2) membranes that prevent the mixture of the two blood supplies. The structure of the placenta thus enables the developing organism to have its own independent bloodstream and, at the same time, to obtain nourishment from the mother's bloodstream and to excrete wastes into it. For example, oxygen, carbohy-

FIGURE 4.3 This diagram shows the placenta and the fetus in the last months of pregnancy. At full term, the fetus weighs about five times as much as the placenta. In the first weeks of development, the ratio is reversed.

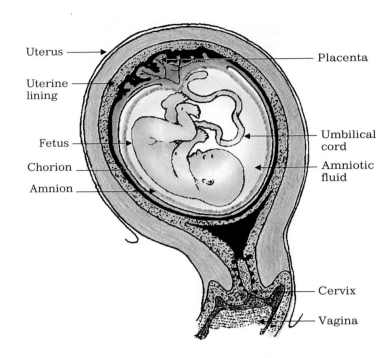

placenta An organ made up of blood vessels that delivers oxygen and nutrients from the mother's bloodstream to the fetus and enables the fetus's waste products to be excreted through the mother's system.

mesoderm The middle layer of the embryonic disk, which becomes muscles, bones, and the circulatory, excretory, and reproductive systems.

endoderm The inner layer of the embryonic disk, which becomes key elements of the digestive and respiratory systems.

neural tube The fold of cells that appears in the embryonic disk about three weeks after conception, later developing into the central nervous system.

cephalo-caudal development The sequence of body growth and maturation from head to foot. Human growth, from the embryonic period throughout early childhood, follows this pattern.

proximo-distal development The sequence of body growth and maturation from the spine toward the extremities. Human growth, from the embryonic period through early childhood, follows this pattern.

drates, and vitamins from the mother diffuse through the placental membranes into the embryo's bloodstream, while carbon dioxide and other waste products from the developing organism similarly diffuse into the mother's bloodstream and are then removed through her lungs and kidneys. Thus a pregnant woman is literally breathing, eating, and urinating for two.

The developing organism is connected to the placenta by the umbilical cord, which contains three blood vessels, one that transports nourishment and two that remove waste products. The movement of blood through the umbilical cord acts like water at high pressure in a hose, keeping the cord taut and making it almost impossible for the cord to become knotted, tangled, or squeezed during prenatal development, no matter how many somersaults the developing baby (or its mother) does.

The Second Month

About five weeks after conception, following the proximo-distal sequence, the upper arms, then the forearms, the hands, and the fingers appear. Legs, feet, and toes, in that order, follow a few days later, each having the beginning of a skeletal structure. By the end of the second month, the fingers and toes, which originally were webbed together, are separate.

Eight weeks after conception, the embryo weighs about 1/30 of an ounce (1 gram) and is about 1 inch (2.5 centimeters) long. The head has become more rounded, and the features of the face are fully formed. The embryo has all the basic organs (except sex organs) and features of a human being, including elbows and knees, fingers and toes, and even buds for the first baby teeth. The tail is no longer visible, having become incorporated into the lower spine at about fifty-five days after conception (Moore, 1988). The organism is now ready for another name, the fetus.

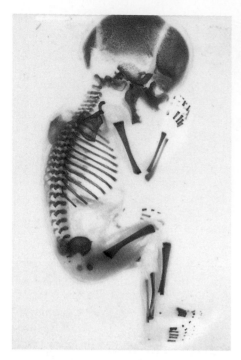

FIGURE 4.4 During the fetal period, cartilage becomes bone, as can be seen in this x-ray of a fetus at 18 weeks. The skull and the spine are most clearly developed, and the bones of the fingers and toes are visible. Even buds for the teeth will soon begin to harden, although the first "baby" tooth will not emerge from the gum until 6 months after birth.

The Period of the Fetus: The Ninth Week to Birth

During the third month, muscles develop and cartilage begins to be replaced by bone. All the major organs complete their formation, including stomach, heart, lungs, and kidneys.

It is also during this period that the sex organs take discernible shape. The first stage of their development actually occurs in the sixth week, with the appearance of the *indifferent gonad,* a cluster of cells that can develop into male or female sex organs. If the fetus is male (*XY*), a gene on the *Y* chromosome sends a biochemical signal late in the embryonic period that triggers the development of male sex organs, first the testes at about seven weeks and then the other male organs during the early fetal period. If the embryo is female and therefore has no *Y* chromosome, no signal is sent, and the fetus begins to develop female sex organs at about the ninth week (Koopman et al., 1991). Not until the twelfth week after conception are the external male or female genital organs fully formed (Moore, 1988).

By the end of the third month, the fetus can and does move almost every part of its body, kicking its legs, sucking its thumb, and even squinting and frowning. The 3-month-old fetus swallows amniotic fluid, digests it, and urinates, providing its tiny organs with practice for the day when it will take in nourishment on its own. This remarkably active little creature is now fully formed—including its fingerprint pattern—and weighs approximately 3 ounces (87 grams) and is about 3 inches (7.5 centimeters) long.[*]

The Second Trimester

In addition to the periods of pregnancy related specifically to prenatal growth, pregnancy is often divided into 3-month-long segments, each called a **trimester**. Our discussion of the germinal, embryonic, and fetal periods so far has concerned only the events of the first trimester, when basic body structures and organs begin to form. In the second trimester (the fourth, fifth, and sixth months), hair, including eyebrows and eyelashes, begins to grow, and fingernails, toenails, and buds for adult teeth begin to form.

The major advances of the second trimester are in the functioning of the developing body organs. The heart beat becomes much stronger during this period (it can be heard with a stethoscope), and the digestive and excretory systems develop more fully. As a result of overall growth, the fetus's weight increases tenfold: a typical fetus weighs about 3 ounces (87 grams) at the beginning of this trimester and 30 ounces (870 grams) at the end. This increasing body mass means that most women feel first the flutter, and then the thump, of fetal arms and legs during the second trimester.

The most appreciable development of this period involves the brain. From the beginning to the end of the second trimester, the brain increases sixfold in size and exhibits dramatic maturation (Moore, 1988). By the end of this period, the brain's electrical impulses, which had formerly registered a flat wave pattern, begin to show occasional bursts of activity similar to that

trimester One of the three-month periods in the nine months of pregnancy.

[*] During early prenatal development, growth is very rapid and considerable variation occurs between one fetus and another, so numbers given for length and especially for weight are only rough guidelines. For example, at 12 weeks after conception the average fetus weighs 45 grams (about 1½ ounces), while at 14 weeks the average weight is 110 grams (about 4 ounces) (Moore, 1989).

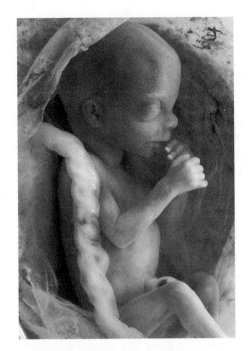

FIGURE 4.5 At the end of 4 months, this fetus, now 6 inches long, looks fully formed, down to the details of eyebrows and fingernails. However, brain development is not yet sufficient to sustain life outside the uterus. For many more weeks, the fetus must depend on the translucent membranes of the placenta and umbilicus (the white cord in the foreground) for survival.

in a newborn (Parmelee & Sigman, 1983). This development, which is essential to the regulation of basic body functions such as breathing, sleep patterns, and so forth, may be the critical factor in the fetus's attaining the **age of viability** sometime between the twentieth and twenty-sixth week after conception. At this point, the fetus has at least some slight chance of survival outside the uterus, if expert care is available. Weight is also crucial to viability: a 22-week-old fetus typically weighs about 22 ounces (about 600 grams) and has a 20 percent chance of survival, whereas a 26-week-old fetus weighs about 2 pounds (900 grams) and has an 80 percent chance of survival (Behrman, 1992).

The Third Trimester

While the first trimester is the time for building basic body structures, and the second is the time for the essential organ and brain maturation that makes survival possible, the third trimester is a period of final prenatal maturation that is truly transforming. An infant born at the beginning of this trimester is a tiny creature requiring intensive hospital care, dependent on life-support systems for nourishment and for every breath. The typical newborn born at the end of this period is a vigorous baby, ready to thrive at home with mother's milk—no expert help, concentrated air, special food, or technical assistance required. As you can imagine, this change is important psychologically as well as biologically, since an uncomplicated full-term birth is less stressful for the infant, and more joyful for the parents. (Preterm infants are discussed further on pp. 145–146.)

Two important developments underlying this transformation occur in the respiratory and the cardiovascular systems (Moore, 1988). In the last months of prenatal life, the lungs begin to expand and contract, exercising the muscles that will be needed to breathe by using the amniotic fluid surrounding the fetus as a substitute for air. At the same time, the valves of the heart go through a final maturation that, at birth, will enable the newborn's circulatory system to function independently.

Brain development is also notable in this period. Beginning about twenty-nine weeks after conception, the brain is rarely completely inactive. By about thirty-four weeks, measurement of the brain's electrical activity reveals distinct sleeping and waking patterns (Parmelee & Sigman, 1983).

In addition, during these final months, the fetus gains substantial weight, increasing, on average, from about 2 pounds (900 grams) at the beginning of this trimester to 7½ pounds (3,400 grams) at the end. An important part of this weight gain is fat, which will provide a protective layer of insulation when the developing person no longer is surrounded by the mother's body warmth. The weight gain of the last weeks also stores nourishment and vitamins that will be used in the early days after birth, when the mother's supply of breast milk is not yet fully established. Thus, until the due date is reached, thirty-eight weeks, or 266 days, after conception,[*] every week of prenatal life increases the likelihood, not only of survival, but of healthy infancy.

age of viability The age (usually between twenty and twenty-six weeks after conception) at which a fetus can possibly survive outside the mother's uterus if specialized medical care is available.

---

[*] Sometimes a full-term pregnancy is said to be forty weeks, or 280 days. These numbers arise when calculations are based on the first day of the woman's last menstrual period, approximately fourteen days prior to ovulation.

Responding to the World Outside

As the foregoing discussion suggests, the fetus is far from passive during development. Beginning at about nine weeks, the fetus moves its body in response to the mother's movements and her shifts in body positions. At first, the movements of tiny heels, fists, elbows, and buttocks are imperceptible to the mother, and then are felt as faint flutters; but by the last months before birth, a sudden kick or somersault can occur with such vigor that the mother's delight at feeling new life turns to dismay at a sore rib. In the last months before birth, the fetus begins to develop sleeping and waking patterns that may carry over to the first months of infancy. At about the fourteenth week, in preparation for the smooth functioning of various organ systems at birth, the 3-inch-long fetus begins to breathe in and spit out or swallow amniotic fluid, eventually even hiccuping if it swallows too fast. It digests amniotic fluid as well, urinating most of it but also storing solid matter in the form of meconium, to be excreted as the first bowel movement after birth.

Toward the end of prenatal development, the sensory systems begin to function as well. At about the twenty-seventh week, the eyelids open and the eyes begin to function, perceiving the faint reddish glow of sunlight or other bright illumination that diffuses through the mother's belly (Kitzinger, 1989). The most remarkable response to the immediate environment involves hearing. Most mothers-to-be are certain that their fetus can hear, having felt it quiet down when they sing a lullaby and startle with a kick when a car backfires or a door slams. In addition, newborns seem to retain associations with particular prenatal noises: they typically stop crying, for example, when they are held with an ear close to the mother's heart, presumably because they are comforted by the familiar rhythm they have known for months.

Researchers have confirmed that fetuses not only can hear but, as newborns, can recognize some of what they heard while in the womb. In a series of experiments, pregnant women read a particular children's book aloud every day during the last weeks before birth. Three days after birth, the infants were exposed to tape recordings of the story being read by their own mother and by another baby's mother. Laboratory monitoring of their behavioral reactions indicated that they paid greater attention to the recording of their own mother's reading. What's more, they showed greater responsiveness to the recording of their mother reading the familiar story than to a recording of her reading an unfamiliar text (DeCasper & Spence, 1986; Moon & Fifer, 1990). Such results suggest that, at least in some ways, fetuses not only prepare their reflexes and organ systems for physiological functioning at birth; they also begin to learn about the social world they will soon join.

Preventing Complications

The remarkable nine-month transformation from a single-cell zygote to a viable human newborn is not only a period of amazing developmental change but, as indicated earlier, it is also a period of great vulnerability. In this section, we will examine a number of potential prenatal complications in detail, but as we proceed, we need to keep several facts in mind. First, it is essential to remember that despite the complexity of prenatal development and the many hazards to the developing organism, the large majority of babies are born healthy and capable. Moreover, medical advances can now help many of those who are born with serious problems, allowing them happy and productive years of life. Furthermore, many potential prenatal hazards to healthy development can be prevented or corrected through the care taken by the expectant mother, and by those around her.

The current successes in preventing or treating prenatal complications make scientists want to improve the odds for every newborn. This is the goal of **teratology**[*], which is the study of the factors that can contribute to, or protect against, birth defects. We now understand a great deal about **teratogens**—that is, substances or conditions that can lead to prenatal abnormalities—and this understanding helps in preventing many kinds of birth defects as well as in reducing the impact of those problems that occur. In the preceding chapter we examined those congenital problems that have definite chromosomal or genetic origins. Now we turn our attention to those congenital problems that are significantly influenced by the intrauterine environment of prenatal growth.

Determining Risk

Until about the middle of this century, it was thought that the placenta and other systems supporting prenatal growth protected the developing organism from most potential hazards. However, the findings of teratology have revealed that, in fact, hundreds of harmful agents can reach the embryo and the fetus and cause significant damage. These agents range from many viruses and bacteria to various drugs, chemicals, and types of radiation and environmental pollutants. The effects of these agents vary greatly, from obvious defects, such as physical malformations, to less visible problems, such as language retardation or poor impulse control.

But while exposure to these teratogens increases the risk of prenatal damage, few of them are *always* damaging. Many pregnant women use drugs of one sort or another, and virtually all are exposed to various pollutants and diseases, yet most newborns seem normal in body and mind. Even when it is definite that a particular fetus has been exposed to a known teratogen, it can rarely be predicted with certainty that a specific defect will result. This is because the ultimate effects of a given teratogen depend on the complex interplay of many factors, both destructive and protective.

The science of teratology is thus a science of **risk analysis**, which attempts to take into account not only the developing organism's exposure to harmful agents but also the factors that can increase or lessen the potential for harm. Depending on the specific mix of both destructive and protective factors, exposure to a teratogen can result in one baby being born problem-free while another is born with several disabilities. To understand better

teratology The scientific study of birth defects caused by genetic or prenatal problems, or by birth complications.

teratogens External agents, such as viruses, drugs, chemicals, and radiation, that can impair prenatal development and lead to abnormalities, disabilities, or even death.

risk analysis In teratology, the attempt to evaluate all the exacerbating and ameliorating factors surrounding exposure to teratogens, in order to assess the potential for prenatal damage.

---

[*] "Teratology" stems from the Greek word *tera*, meaning "monster." Coined over a century and a half ago, the term was born out of ignorance of the true nature of birth defects and is no longer read literally. Today, teratology includes the study of all substances that might harm prenatal development, including not only those that lead to visible physical abnormalities but also those that do invisible damage to the brain or to other internal organs.

TABLE 4.2	
Teratogenic Risk Factors	
	A specific teratogen is more likely to harm a particular embryo or fetus if several of the following conditions prevail.
Family Background	Stress within the family. Low socioeconomic status.
Fetal Characteristics	Genetic predisposition to certain problems. The fetus is *XY* (male).
Mother's Characteristics	Undernourished. Over 40 or under 18. Previous pregnancy ended less than a year before current pregnancy began.
Nature of Teratogen	Occurs early in pregnancy. High dose or exposure. Occurs over a period of several days or weeks. Other teratogens also present.
Nature of Prenatal Care	Woman is more than three months pregnant before prenatal care begins.

how risk analysis in teratology occurs, we will first examine the factors that most directly affect a teratogen's potential for causing harm. We will then survey some specific teratogens, and the key protective influences, that can affect prenatal growth.

Timing of Exposure

critical period The period of prenatal development during which a particular organ or body part is most susceptible to teratogenic damage. In many cases the critical period occurs in the first eight weeks of development, when the basic organs and body structures are forming.

One crucial factor that determines whether a specific teratogen will cause harm, and of what nature, is the timing of the developing organism's exposure to it. This is because the vulnerability that a given organ or other body part has to a particular teratogen often depends on its stage of development at the time of exposure. Some teratogens, for example, will cause damage only if exposure occurs during a particular time span early in pregnancy, when the organ or body part in question is going through its formation and most rapid growth. This time span, called the **critical period**, is consequently

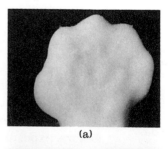

(a)

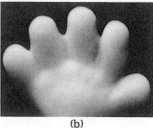

(b)

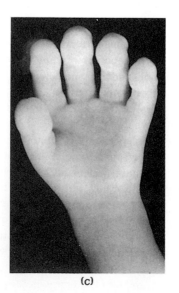

(c)

FIGURE 4.6 As you will see in the discussions that follow, the impact of a potential teratogen partially depends on when the developing organism is exposed to it. This is because there is a critical period in the formation of every body part during which it is especially vulnerable. Shown here is the critical period of hand development: Three stages in finger development: *(a)* notches appear in the hand at day 44; *(b)* fingers are growing but webbed together at day 50; and *(c)* fingers have separated and lengthened at day 52. By day 56, fingers are completely formed, and the critical period for hand development is over. Other parts of the body, including the eyes, heart, and central nervous system, take much longer to complete development, so the critical period when they are vulnerable to teratogens lasts for months rather than days.

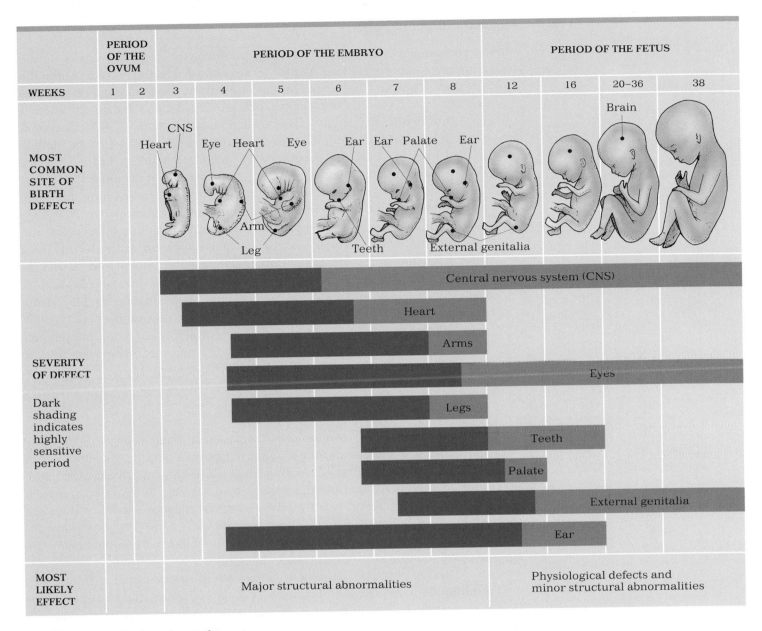

	PERIOD OF THE OVUM		PERIOD OF THE EMBRYO						PERIOD OF THE FETUS			
WEEKS	1	2	3	4	5	6	7	8	12	16	20–36	38

FIGURE 4.7 As this chart shows, the most serious damage from teratogens is likely to occur in the first eight weeks after conception. However, damage to many vital parts of the body, including the brain, eyes, and genitals, can occur during the last months of pregnancy as well.

behavioral teratogens Teratogens that tend to damage neural networks in the prenatal brain, affecting the future child's intellectual and emotional functioning.

the time when that part of the body is most susceptible to damage. As can be seen in Figure 4.7, each body structure has its own most critical time: the eyes at about four weeks, the ears and arms at about six weeks, the legs and palate at about seven weeks, and so on. Exposure before or after the critical period generally causes little or no damage to that body part.

However, with some teratogens, the entire prenatal period is critical. This is particularly true for teratogens that affect the brain and nervous system, impairing the child's intellectual and emotional functioning. Such hazards are called **behavioral teratogens**, because they chiefly affect the way the child behaves rather than how he or she looks (Brackbill et al., 1985; Kopp & Kaler, 1989). A 5-year-old who cannot sit quietly and concentrate for more than a minute, or an 8-year-old who cannot control aggressive impulses, may be suffering the effects of a teratogen to which he or she was exposed at any time during prenatal development.

Amount of Exposure

A second important factor affecting potential teratogenic damage is the amount of exposure. Especially for teratogenic drugs, the more frequent the exposures and the higher the amount on any one occasion, the greater the likelihood and severity of damage. For some drugs, like tobacco, the effect is straightforward and cumulative: each cigarette smoked by a pregnant woman reduces birthweight by several milligrams. For other drugs, there is a threshold: that is, the substance is virtually harmless until exposure reaches a certain frequency or amount, at which time it becomes damaging. Indeed, many substances that are actually beneficial in small amounts (such as certain vitamins) can be teratogenic in large quantities.

Compounding the issue of the amount of teratogenic exposure is the possible interaction *between* teratogens. Sometimes, for example, one drug intensifies the effects of another. Both marijuana and alcohol may be threshold drugs—that is, teratogenic only at a certain level (Waterson & Murray-Lyon, 1990). However, when taken together, their thresholds may drop, making them potentially harmful in combination at an amount that, for each drug taken separately, would be inconsequential. Similar compounding effects are likely to occur with all drugs that affect the central nervous system, from nicotine to cocaine (Robins & Mills, 1993).

Genetic Vulnerability

A third factor that determines whether a specific teratogen will be harmful, and to what extent, is the developing organism's genetic vulnerability to damage from this substance. Among fraternal twins who are exposed to the same amount of alcohol in the mother's bloodstream, for example, one will usually be more severely affected by prenatal alcohol exposure than the other (Sokol & Abel, 1992). The likely explanation is that dizygotic twins differ in their genetic susceptibility to the harmful effects of alcohol during the prenatal months.

The sex of the developing organism also presents certain genetic vulnerabilities to teratogenic hazards. Probably because the Y chromosome carries fewer genes, and is thus less well defended than the much larger X chromosome, male embryos and fetuses generally are more vulnerable to teratogens. This is evident both in the higher rate of teratogenic birth defects and later teratogen-related behavioral problems for males and in the higher rate of spontaneous abortions and stillbirths for male embryos and fetuses.

However, it is important to recall the lesson of the previous chapter: namely, that while genetic vulnerability increases the risk of certain disorders, it does not ensure that they will occur. As with the other components of the risk analysis of teratology, it is impossible to predict precisely how genetic vulnerabilities interact with teratogenic exposure and protective factors in the prenatal environment.

Further complicating teratogenic risk analysis is the recent realization that hazards to the developing organism can be conveyed by the father as well as by the mother. Preliminary research has revealed that the health and functioning of sperm, or of the semen carrying sperm, can be affected by paternal drug and alcohol abuse, smoking, or exposure to environmental toxins (Merewood, 1991). These teratogens can impair prenatal growth either directly, through hazards incorporated within the sperm, or indirectly, through their effects on the intrauterine environment. One large study found, for example, that the offspring of men who were exposed to pesticides, herbicides, or fungicides were twice as likely as the children of nonexposed fathers to be born smaller than normal—although it was impossible to tell if this hazard came directly from the sperm, less directly via the seminal fluid throughout pregnancy, or through the pregnant woman's touching or inhaling the pesticides on the father's skin, hair, or clothes (Savitz et al., 1989). Similar complexities surround the possible prenatal effects of paternal drug use. It has been shown, for example, that newborns whose fathers smoke have lowered birthweights, but the pathway of this effect is not yet known (Zhang & Ratcliffe, 1993).

Specific Teratogens

Despite the fact that risk analysis is challenging, decades of research in teratology have revealed the likely effects of some of the more damaging common teratogens. Looking at these will help clarify the complexity inherent in preventing birth defects.

Diseases

One of the first teratogens to be recognized was **rubella** (sometimes called German measles), which had long been considered a harmless childhood disease. It is now well established that rubella, if contracted by the expectant mother early in pregnancy, is very likely to cause birth handicaps, among them blindness, deafness, heart abnormalities, and brain damage. (Some of these problems and their effects were apparent in David's story in Chapter 1.) In contrast with rubella's damaging effects in the early stages of pregnancy, if an expectant mother contracts the disease during the second trimester, the fetus often escapes structural damage but suffers emotional and intellectual impairments, reflecting nervous system damage to the brain. These different consequences occur because of the different critical periods for the physical systems involved. If rubella occurs during the last months of pregnancy, typically no discernible damage occurs (Enkin et al., 1989).

The seriousness of this teratogen became all too evident in a worldwide rubella epidemic in the mid-1960s. In the United States alone, 20,000 infants had obvious rubella-caused impairments, including hundreds who were born both deaf and blind (Franklin, 1984). Since that epidemic, widespread immunization—either of preschool children (as in the United States) or of all adolescent girls who are not naturally immune and are not pregnant (as in England)—has helped to reduce the rubella threat. In addition, there is a simple blood test that can be administered to any woman before she becomes pregnant to determine whether she is immune to rubella. If she is not, she can be immunized and then wait several months before trying to conceive. As a consequence, during the 1980s, an annual average of only twenty-three rubella-syndrome infants were born in the United States (Eschenbach, 1988), and even fewer were born in England (Enkin et al., 1989).

rubella A form of measles that, if contracted during pregnancy, can harm the fetus, including causing blindness, deafness, and damage to the central nervous system.

However, about a third of all American preschoolers and 10 to 15 percent of all pregnant American women lack immunity to rubella because they have never had the disease or been inoculated (Eschenbach, 1988)—raising the specter of a future rubella epidemic, with thousands of birth defects that could have been prevented.

The effects of rubella were first recognized in the 1940s. Once medical researchers realized that a virus could cross the placenta and harm the fetus, they began looking for other diseases that might also be teratogenic. They found dozens, including mumps, chicken pox, polio, and measles. Like rubella, all these diseases can now be curbed by immunization.

No such protection is available, however, for the most devastating viral teratogen of all: **human immunodeficiency virus (HIV)**. HIV gradually overwhelms the body's natural immune responses, making the individual vulnerable to a host of diseases and infections including, inevitably, the fatal cancers, pneumonias, and other pathologies that together constitute **acquired immune deficiency syndrome (AIDS)**. The HIV virus is transmitted from an infected adult to an uninfected one chiefly through sexual intercourse or through direct blood contact, such as that which occurs in the sharing of unsterilized needles for drug injections.

FIGURE 4.8 These children, all born to HIV-positive mothers, do not all have the deadly virus, but they have suffered from the disease nonetheless. Although those who are HIV-negative will survive, their mothers are unable to care for them because they are dying, or already dead, of the disease. Nonetheless, these children are more fortunate than many others in their condition: they are residents of Hale House, founded by a grandmother in Harlem who opened her home and heart to children with AIDS.

**human immunodeficiency virus
(HIV)** A viral disease agent that gradually overwhelms the body's immune responses, leaving the individual defenseless against a host of pathologies that eventually manifest themselves as AIDS. HIV is carried in the blood and certain other bodily fluids of an infected person and is transmitted chiefly through sexual or direct blood contact.

**acquired immune deficiency syndrome
(AIDS)** The final, terminal stage of HIV degradation of the immune system, which typically appears as serious infections, specific cancers, and the like.

Although most of the first reported cases of AIDS in North America and Europe involved homosexual men, heterosexual women are now the fastest-growing group of victims in those two continents (Chin et al., 1990). When a woman with HIV becomes pregnant, she risks passing the virus on to her fetus during pregnancy or childbirth: about one in every four infants born to an HIV-positive woman has the virus (Ades et al., 1991; Goedert et al., 1989). Infants who have the virus will, like adults, eventually develop AIDS and die—about a third during infancy, another third before kindergarten, and the remaining third before adolescence.

Obviously, the best way to prevent pediatric AIDS is to prevent adult AIDS or, barring that, to prevent pregnancy or birth in HIV-positive women. Both goals are complicated by the disease's long incubation period—up to ten years or more—during which time a person can transmit the virus without showing any symptoms of the disease, and thus without knowing that he or she is infected. Unfortunately, even more than men, many women are unaware that they carry the HIV virus, until one day their infant is tested for an unexplained fever or other illness and is found to be HIV-positive. In one Bronx, New York, hospital everyone coming to the emergency room over a three-week period in 1989 was anonymously tested for HIV. Of the females between the ages of 13 and 39 who were tested, 12 percent were found to be HIV-positive, with five out of six not knowing that they were infected (Schoenbaum et al., 1993).

Early knowledge of the mother-to-be's HIV infection is key to reducing the chances of HIV transmission to the fetus. Such knowledge would allow for a Cesarean delivery, eliminating the possibility of exposure during the birth process. In addition, it has recently been discovered that giving HIV-positive pregnant women AZT (zidovudine), a drug that slows the onset of adult AIDS, dramatically reduces prenatal transmission. Indeed, *if* all newly pregnant women obtained early prenatal care and agreed to be tested for the HIV virus, and *if* those found to be positive were given AZT, the proportion of their infants born with the virus would be reduced from 1 in 4 to 1 in 12. This remarkable result can be achieved, however, only if outreach to women at risk of HIV is much improved (*MMWR,* April 29, 1994).

Syphilis is another sexually transmitted disease that can cause devastating harm to the fetus. Unlike AIDS, however, syphilis can be cured. In the first months of pregnancy, the organisms that produce the disease cannot cross the placenta, so if a blood test in the first weeks of pregnancy reveals that a woman has syphilis, the antibiotic penicillin can halt the disease before her fetus is harmed. But if the woman does not get early treatment, her fetus may die or suffer severe bone, liver, and brain damage (Grossman, 1986).

Another disease that can be lethal for the fetus is **toxoplasmosis**, which is caused by a parasite that humans can acquire by eating raw meat or by not washing their hands after touching cat feces or yard dirt. Toxoplasmosis causes only mild symptoms in adults but it can severely damage the fetal brain, causing death, retardation, and blindness. If early prenatal testing reveals that a woman is not immune (70 percent of American women are not), she is advised to take some simple precautions: eat meat that is well cooked, use gloves in the garden, and find someone else to change the cat's litter box.

Medicinal Drugs

In 1960, thousands of pregnant women were delighted by the introduction of **thalidomide**, a mild tranquilizer to reduce nausea and insomnia, such as that experienced in early pregnancy. Their delight soon became despair, however, as virtually every woman who took thalidomide in her second month of pregnancy gave birth to a seriously deformed baby. As a result of their mothers' taking thalidomide, approximately 8,000 malformed babies were born in twenty-eight countries, some with no ears, others with deformed or missing arms or legs (Schardein, 1976). The thalidomide disaster was especially apparent in Western Europe, where the drug could be purchased without a prescription; in the United States, restrictions by the Food and Drug Administration limited the availability of thalidomide and, thus, the extent of the tragedy.

toxoplasmosis A disease caused by a parasite present in uncooked meat, cat feces, and yard dirt. If a pregnant woman contracts this disease, her fetus may suffer eye or brain damage.

thalidomide A tranquilizer—now banned in many countries—which, when taken early in pregnancy, causes malformations of the fetus's arms, legs, and ears.

Research following the thalidomide episode identified other prescription drugs that can be teratogenic—including such common medications as tetracycline, anticoagulants, bromides, phenobarbital, retinoic acid (a common treatment for acne), most psychotherapeutic drugs (including lithium and Valium), and most hormones. As a result, physicians are advised not only to avoid prescribing these specific drugs to a pregnant woman but to be "exquisitely discriminating" in the use of any medication during pregnancy (Anderson & Golbus, 1989). For the most part, medication is warranted only when it is essential for the mother's health, and only when possible harm to the fetus is negligible. This caution is also warranted with nonprescription drugs, which an estimated four out of five women take during pregnancy (Brackbill et al., 1985). Although most of these appear to be harmless, a few, including aspirin, antacids, and megadoses of vitamins A and D, have been implicated in birth defects.

Psychoactive Drugs

Not only medicinal drugs but also so-called social drugs—psychoactive agents such as alcohol, tobacco, marijuana, cocaine, heroin, and the like—can harm prenatal growth. While some of these drugs—notably alcohol—can cause physical abnormalities, the most insidious teratogenic effects of psychoactive drugs are chiefly behavioral, including long-term learning difficulties, impaired self-control, and irritability. Such behavioral effects occur because these drugs inflict damage on the brain and nervous system of the developing organism, probably by reducing the oxygen and nutrition provided through the placenta, as well as by directly impairing brain growth. These teratogens also impair the physical growth of the fetus, increase the likelihood of premature birth, and heighten the probability of postnatal complications. Unfortunately, if a woman regularly uses a psychoactive drug prior to pregnancy, as most women do (about 80 percent drink alcohol, 25 percent smoke cigarettes, 18 percent use marijuana, and 5 percent use cocaine), she is likely to be using some such drug in the first weeks of pregnancy, before she knows she is pregnant, and may continue that drug use throughout pregnancy (Adams et al., 1989; Robins & Mills, 1993).

As we shall see, teratogenic risk analysis of exposure to any specific drug is especially complex because the ultimate impact of such exposure is influenced by many factors not directly related to the drug itself, such as the mother's nutrition before pregnancy, her exposure to other teratogenic substances during pregnancy, and the quality of care the child receives after birth (Johnson et al., 1990; Robins & Mills, 1993). As a consequence, the teratogenic effects of the various psychoactive drugs are much more variable than those of other types of teratogens.

Alcohol

The most prevalent drug in American society is alcohol, and it may also be the most pervasive teratogen. An estimated 1 in every 550 babies is born with the distinctive symptoms of **fetal alcohol syndrome (FAS)**: growth retardation, behavior problems (including poor concentration and poor social

fetal alcohol syndrome (FAS) A cluster of birth defects, including abnormal facial characteristics, slow physical growth, and retarded mental development, that is caused by the mother's drinking excessive quantities of alcohol when pregnant.

skills), and abnormal facial characteristics (including such features as a small head, abnormally wide-spaced eyes, and a flattened nose). FAS is also the leading known prenatal cause of mental retardation in the industrialized world (Abel & Sokol, 1987).

Fetal alcohol syndrome does not occur in every fetus exposed to alcohol: likely victims are those who are genetically vulnerable and whose mothers are heavy drinkers (that is, who ingest more than five cocktails or five glasses of wine or beer daily) during pregnancy (Sokol & Abel, 1992). Unfortunately, the greatest damage from prenatal alcohol consumption occurs early in pregnancy, often before a woman has become aware that she is pregnant and should restrict her drinking.

FIGURE 4.9 These two children are quite different in age and ethnicity. But this African-American teenager and this Swedish toddler have a great deal in common: both have the distinctive facial features and the retarded mental development of persons with FAS.

Even moderate drinking may be harmful to the developing organism. In a study of fifty-four women who were social drinkers, nine gave birth to babies with at least two of the half dozen or so facial characteristics of FAS (Hanson et al., 1978). Most of these women had no more than three or four drinks per day during the month before they knew they were pregnant. More recent research has similarly shown that while the consumption of three or more drinks a day during pregnancy (perhaps a beer with lunch and two glasses of wine with dinner) may not lead to FAS, it can nevertheless cause long-term deficits, including motor, emotional, and intellectual impairments (Olson et al., 1992). Further cautions are raised by Harriett Barr and her colleagues (1990), who asked mothers about their drinking practices during pregnancy and later studied their children. By age 4, when compared to children whose mothers had abstained entirely from alcohol use, children whose mothers had had an average of one or more drinks daily early in pregnancy performed less well on measures of motor-skill abilities. These researchers concluded that studies have yet to establish a level of safe prenatal alcohol exposure, bolstering the advice offered by many medical experts and obstetricians that expectant mothers abstain entirely from alcohol as soon as they know they are pregnant. This advice seems especially worthwhile given that most people—including pregnant women—believe that their drinking practices are more moderate than they actually are (Ernhart et al., 1989).

FIGURE 4.10 This woman's daydreams about her future baby may not be realized if she smokes heavily throughout her pregnancy. Every puff slows nutrition to the fetus, a cumulative effect that can result in a newborn who weighs a pound or more less than he or she otherwise would have. When a mother-to-be smokes, she always puts her fetus at risk for a number of other prenatal complications, and may also be compromising her child's later health and intellectual functioning.

Tobacco

Tobacco has been well documented as a hazard that is significantly detrimental to prenatal development (Martin, 1992). A wealth of studies show, for example, that cigarette smoking impairs fetal growth. Babies born to regular smokers weigh, on average, 9 ounces (about 250 grams) less than would otherwise be expected, and they are shorter, both at birth and in the years to come. In addition, smoking increases the chances of ectopic (tubal) pregnancy (Coste et al., 1991), stillbirth, premature separation of the placenta from the uterus, and premature birth (Tisi, 1988).

There is also evidence that the offspring of cigarette smokers have behavioral problems, including learning disabilities and temperamental irritability (Butler & Golding, 1986; Fried & Watkinson, 1990). However, it is often difficult to establish clearly that these long-term effects are caused by prenatal exposure to tobacco, since pregnant women who smoke are more likely to be young, poorly educated women who have other characteristics (such as poor health habits or a tendency toward high-strung impatience) that may account for these physical and cognitive problems in their offspring (Rush & Callahan, 1989).

Marijuana

Marijuana is another teratogen whose damage (like alcohol's) is dose-related. Heavy marijuana use can produce notable effects on the fetus. In one study in Jamaica, where marijuana smoking is generally acceptable, the infants born to heavy users of marijuana showed impairment to their central nervous systems, including a kind of abnormal, high-pitched crying that often denotes brain damage (Lester & Dreher, 1989). Research on the effects of mild marijuana use has yielded more equivocal findings, however, with the likelihood of serious and/or long-term effects increasing when marijuana use is accompanied by cigarette smoking, alcohol use, or exposure to other hazards to prenatal growth (Dalterio & Fried, 1992).

Heroin

Maternal use of heroin poses many hazards to the developing organism. During pregnancy, the mother's experiencing of the physiological effects of the typical highs and lows of opiate addiction—shortness of breath, irregularity of heart rate, and sweating and chills during withdrawal—pose significant challenges to the fetus (Kaltenbach & Finnegan, 1992). Moreover, the addicted mother's typically poor appetite may threaten the nutritional status of the developing child. In addition, heroin is powerfully addictive to the fetus. Addicted newborns show evidence of an unstable central nervous system—manifested in tremors, sleeplessness, voracious sucking, and hyperactive reflexes—and must be withdrawn from the drug carefully to avoid seizures that can cause lasting brain damage. Heroin-exposed infants also tend to have a variety of other immediate medical problems, including low birthweight, jaundice, and breathing difficulties. Several longitudinal studies of addicted newborns have also found extensive long-term effects, including mental retardation, poor motor development, and behavioral problems like aggression, tantrums, hyperactivity, and poor concentration (Hans, 1989; Wilson, 1989). However, these long-term effects may be attributable—at least in part—to the erratic and neglectful care provided by addicted parents and to the continued stress of poverty, malnutrition, and poor medical care that tend to be associated with heroin use (Wilson, 1992).

Cocaine

Recently, considerable attention has been devoted to the consequences of maternal cocaine use—especially in its devastatingly addictive form of "crack," which largely accounted for a 300 percent increase in the number of drug-exposed births reported by hospitals in the United States from 1986 to 1989 (Weston et al., 1989). Cocaine use affects the fetus throughout pregnancy as well as immediately before and after birth. In early pregnancy, the use of cocaine seems to increase the risk of structural damage, especially to the sex organs (Chasnoff et al., 1988). In addition, cocaine use causes overall growth retardation (especially of head size) even more dramatically than other social drugs do, and it may directly cause certain kinds of brain damage (Neuspiel & Hamel, 1991). In later pregnancy, cocaine use causes additional problems for the fetus. The sudden rush and crash of cocaine—especially when it is smoked—can cause fetal convulsions, because the fetus's brain and heart cannot withstand the stress of such rapid changes. In early labor, maternal cocaine consumption extends the birth process and increases the risk of prematurity and birth complications, especially premature separation of the placenta from the uterus, resulting in a potentially fatal deprivation of oxygen (Skolnick, 1990). Newborns who still have cocaine in their bloodstreams after birth, when they must adjust to breathing on their own, are especially vulnerable to seizures that can cause lasting brain damage. They also show evidence of an unstable central nervous system by trembling, startling, or crying at the slightest disturbance or, alternatively, being unusually sleepy and sluggish in their responses to stimulation (Lester et al., 1991).

Once again, we need to be cautious before naming cocaine as the cause for all these effects. For example, one study of infants who were prenatally exposed to cocaine found that 83 percent were also exposed to tobacco, 43 percent to heavy doses of alcohol, and 7.5 percent to syphilis. Further, 29 percent of the pregnant mothers in the study received no prenatal care of any kind (Bateman et al., 1993).

The Fetus as a Developing Person: Parental Rights and Responsibilities

The implications and imperatives of the fetus's approaching personhood are a complex matter, psychologically, legally, and medically. In particular, the growing powers of medical technology and our increasing understanding of teratogenic effects raise complicated questions regarding the balance between the mother-to-be's personal rights and her responsibilities to the developing organism she is carrying.

For example, in many cases, doctors can, and do, treat the fetus itself as a patient, with separate medical needs from those of the mother. If the fetus is ailing, direct intervention, including surgery within the uterus, may be attempted. A fetoscope allows the surgeon to see into the hidden world of the amniotic sac and, using microsurgery techniques, perform such procedures as repairing heart or kidney defects; transfusing blood through the wall of the uterus and placenta if antibodies are destroying the fetal blood supply; and implanting a shunt, or drainage tube, into the fetal skull to drain abnormal collections of fluid on the brain.

At the moment, such surgery is at the frontier of medicine, rescuing fetuses who otherwise would either die before birth or survive with serious physical or cognitive handicaps. *At the moment*, successful treatment of an unborn patient whose weight is registered in ounces, not pounds, is heralded as miraculous, a victory of nurture over nature. *At the moment*, the demand for fetal surgery far exceeds the supply of surgeons trained to perform it.

But what will happen when such surgery becomes readily available, and improved sonograms, fetoscopes, and other diagnostic techniques reveal more and more fetuses who might benefit from direct intervention? Would women be expected, even legally required, to submit to surgery? Already judges have compelled pregnant women to have blood transfusions and Cesarean sections, even when these procedures are contrary to the woman's religion or personal desire (Tomkins & Kepfield, 1992). And what if medical intervention might save the fetus but risk a woman's life? Morally and legally, treating the fetus as a patient can be a morass as well as a miracle (Fletcher, 1989).

Even more problematic is the question of the mother's endangering her fetus through her own behavior. This question was forcefully raised some years ago by a medical team that was confronted with a pregnant woman who had a sixteen-year history of alcohol and phenobarbital abuse (Mackenzie et al., 1982). The woman had been hospitalized in a state of stuporous intoxication, with bruises and other signs that she might have been physically abused. In response to the medical staff's concerns, she denied that she was trying to get rid of the fetus, saying she and her husband wanted the baby "very much." Nevertheless she admitted to two phenobarbital overdoses during the first two months of pregnancy.

Two months later the woman was hospitalized because of premature labor. The pregnancy was successfully prolonged, but the medical staff became more concerned about the fetus, for blood tests revealed that the woman was continuing to abuse phenobarbital, and while she was in the hospital, she covertly took an overdose of diuretics.

With their fears for the well-being of the fetus mounting, the medical team referred the woman to the local Child Protection Service. She attended several counseling sessions, and thereafter no further episodes of drug abuse were reported. The woman subsequently gave birth to a girl who, though low in birthweight, was full-term and seemingly healthy.

As the medical team made clear, a case such as this is likely to have aspects that make the decision to intervene prenatally a highly complex one:

> At no time could fetal damage be demonstrated. Further, it could not be established conclusively that [the mother's] behavior, if continued, would have caused significant harm to the fetus. Yet this behavior indisputably increased the risk of neonatal morbidity and mortality and threatened to compromise the child's developmental capacities.

The medical team concluded that "protective custody" laws should be extended to allow physicians to safeguard the developing fetus in whatever way seems necessary. Although this baby may have escaped harm, and although the woman attended counseling sessions, the authors feel that they should have had the power to intervene earlier and more aggressively.

Since this case, some steps toward prenatal "protective custody" have been made, raising a number of unanticipated problems. Some states require official reporting of any evidence of illegal drug use during pregnancy, even if there is no sign that the fetus is being harmed and even if the newborn seems to be drug-free. In some states, fetal alcohol syndrome constitutes evidence of child maltreatment. And in many jurisdictions, expectant mothers have been prosecuted under child abuse laws for drug abuse during pregnancy (Tomkins & Kepfield, 1992). Because of such laws, some women who most need prenatal care avoid it, fearing that they will be arrested or forced to give up their baby after it is born (Robins & Mills, 1993; Skolnick, 1990). Moreover, it is hard to know how far to extend such protections for the developing person. Women have been prosecuted not only for abusing illegal drugs during pregnancy but also for abusing legal drugs (like alcohol). Should pregnant women be prohibited from smoking, required to eat nutritious foods, and forced to abstain from drinking altogether? Certainly many people would regard these restrictions as undue infringements on a woman's rights to privacy and self-determination, even though they might enhance the probability of healthy fetal growth. As one woman who had been voluntarily hospitalized to protect her developing fetus complained, "I'm a person too, not just something that happens to be wrapped around a baby" (quoted in Snyder, 1985).

The idea of prenatal "protective custody" is not, of course, limited to mothers-to-be. As evidence that drug use, smoking, and drinking can also affect the health and functioning of male sperm cells and contribute to prenatal damage (Merewood, 1991), men may also be required to curtail their freedoms when anticipating fatherhood.

Yet it is an inescapable fact that a parent's right to self-determination can sometimes threaten a child's future. Consider another example, one from a Native American community in which genetics and prejudice conspire to make alcoholism an epidemic. A Native American man adopted Adam, a Sioux from the Pine Ridge reservation in South Dakota. Adam had been neglected, first by his mother, who died of alcoholism when he was 2, and then by state institutions and foster parents. His new father recalls diapering 3-year-old Adam for the first time:

> I . . . lay him on the floor, and pulled open the snaps of his pants. Then, while he contemplated the ceiling, I wiped and I powdered. It was impossible to see his thin legs, dominated by the thick balls of his knee joints, without making resolutions. He needed nourishment, care, encouragement, stability. I was determined that his development in every area would match his age before another year had passed. [Dorris, 1989]

These resolutions were tragically impossible to keep. Adam was slow to talk, to feed himself, to read. Even as a young adult he could not do math, tell time, plan ahead, keep a job, or think for himself. The cause: severe fetal alcohol syndrome.

The case of Adam leads to the central issue: At what point, in what ways, and with what sanctions can community concern for the well-being of the unborn supersede parents' rights to live as they choose? The urgency of this question is brought home by Adam's adoptive mother:

> Because his mother drank, Adam is one of the earth's damaged. Did she have the right to take away Adam's curiosity, the right to take away the joy he could have felt at receiving a high math score, in reading a book, in wondering at the complexity and quirks of nature? Did she have the right to make him an outcast among children, to make him friendless, to make of his sexuality a problem more than a pleasure, to slit his brain, to give him violent seizures? . . .
>
> On some American Indian reservations, the situation has grown so serious that a jail internment during pregnancy has been the only answer possible . . . Some people have . . . called for the forced sterilization of women who, after previously blunting the lives of several children like Adam, refuse to stop drinking while they are pregnant. This will outrage some women, and men, good people who believe that it is the right of individuals to put themselves in harm's way, that drinking is a choice we make, that a person's liberty to court either happiness or despair is sacrosanct. I believed this too, and yet the poignancy and frustration of Adam's life has fed my doubts, has convinced me that some of my principles were smug, untested. After all, where is the measure of responsibility here? Where, exactly, is the demarcation between self-harm and child abuse? . . . Where do we draw the line? [Erdrich, 1989]

The most devastating effects of cocaine may arise from the mother's use of it after her baby's birth. More than any other drug, crack cocaine makes maternal feelings virtually disappear (Revkin, 1989). As one pregnant ex-addict explains it:

> I've got three cousins, they're on crack. One is nine months pregnant. She's got three other kids. She stays out like three or four days at a time. I used to do the same thing. Didn't care about nothing or nobody. That's just the way it is when you're on crack. You just don't care about nothing. [quoted in Revkin, 1989]

Thus with cocaine, as with other psychoactive drugs, the long-term consequences of prenatal use may depend as much on the conditions associated with the drug use as on the effects of the drug itself. Women who abuse cocaine are likely, for example, to abuse other drugs, to be clinically depressed, and to be living with their offspring in poor, unstable environments (Hawley & Disney, 1992). Not surprisingly, their children often are emotionally and physically neglected. Since all these factors can contribute to poor developmental outcomes, trying to isolate prenatal cocaine exposure as the primary cause of later difficulties can be tricky, and even misleading. This is an important point in view of sensational media stories about "crack babies" who, as young children, are reported by day-care workers and teachers to be irritable, hard to please, in constant motion, disorganized, and antisocial—all due, allegedly, to irrevocable brain damage caused by prenatal exposure to cocaine (Hutchinson, 1991). Clearly, however, to attribute these behaviors entirely to prenatal cocaine exposure is to ignore the many ways in which the initial effects of prenatal exposure can be exacerbated—or reduced—by the specific environmental conditions in which these children grow up (Mayes et al., 1992). Indeed, promising treatment programs are showing that these children are not irrevocably "lost" because of their prenatal exposure to drugs but, instead, show considerable gains in a supportive, healthy environment (Hawley & Disney, 1992).

As all the foregoing examples remind us, sensitive risk analysis of the effects of psychoactive drugs on prenatal growth is a difficult task. Consequently, the wisest course for a pregnant woman is to avoid such drugs entirely. However, as long as these drugs are socially accepted and their use encouraged, this lonely wisdom may be difficult for many people to follow. Public education efforts are sometimes ignored by the women most in need of learning about the hazards of prenatal drug use, and many obstetricians neglect their responsibility to counsel expectant mothers about the use of licit and illicit substances during pregnancy (Chasnoff, 1989; Waterson & Murray-Lyon, 1990). This raises the thorny issue of how to establish personal and social responsibility for fetal drug exposure, a topic that is discussed in the Public Policy box on pages 130–131.

Environmental Hazards

Pregnant women who are sufficiently cautious can avoid taking drugs. With a little luck and planning, they may even avoid getting sick. But without adopting a very unusual lifestyle, it would be virtually impossible for most expectant mothers to avoid all environmental hazards, including pollutants in the air and water and possible contaminants in the workplace.

FIGURE 4.11 Definitive links between teratogens and birth defects are usually impossible to prove. However, this boy's mother is convinced that her exposure to pesticides when she was five weeks pregnant is the reason her son, pictured here at age 7, has no arms or legs. Many pesticides are sprayed extensively by modern agribusiness to increase the yield of crops per acre. Typically, such chemicals are not tested regarding birth defects, since they are not classified as food or drugs.

A few of these environmental teratogens are known to cause serious damage. For example, extensive exposure to carbon monoxide, lead, and mercury can be teratogenic to the developing organism. Because some of these chemicals can be stored in the body for long periods, even exposure *before* pregnancy can be hazardous to prenatal growth. A combination of both prenatal and postnatal exposure to lead can cause greater deficits in the child than would either alone (Jacobson & Jacobson, 1990).

Another example involves the manufacturing chemicals known as PCBs, which, in high levels, have been proven to be teratogenic (Rogan, 1986). Even low levels of PCBs may have a teratogenic effect in some cases. Pregnant women in Michigan were compared on their levels of consumption of PCB-polluted fish from Lake Michigan, and then their newborns were examined. Women who had eaten more fish had newborns with more problems: their infants tended to be smaller and to have slowed and depressed reactions to stimuli (Jacobson et al., 1984).

Because many future mothers are employed, a good deal of attention has been focused on potential teratogens in the workplace environment. Not surprisingly, the risks appear to be greatest for women who actually work with teratogenic chemicals—not only PCBs but also paints and solvents widely used in cleaning and manufacturing, and pesticides used in farming. Risks may also be high for women who are constantly exposed to radiation, as x-ray technicians may be. However, contrary to concern in recent years about a possible link between miscarriage and prenatal exposure to the radiation from video display terminals (VDTs), the thousands of mothers-to-be who regularly use computers do not appear to be at risk. A comprehensive study found no significant difference in miscarriages or pregnancy problems between women who did all their work in front of VDTs and those in the same occupation who did not (Schnorr et al., 1991).

The developing organism may also be at risk if the mother's occupation is unusually physically stressful, or if that stress continues up to the due date. A number of studies over the years have suggested that shift work involving physical and psychological stress, as well as irregular sleep—the kind of work often experienced by doctors in residencies, rookie police officers, airline attendants, and coal miners, for example—may increase the risk of pregnancy complications (McDonald et al., 1988). However, there is also evidence that these risks are significantly reduced if the mother-to-be has good health habits and receives regular prenatal care: under these conditions, risks tend to increase only if the woman works more than eighty hours a week (Klebanoff et al., 1990). The lesson, it seems, is that as long as they maintain careful health and work habits with regard for the developing fetus, expectant mothers can safely continue to work throughout most of their pregnancy if they wish. Indeed, most research finds that employed women have healthier pregnancies and births than do unemployed women (Silbergeld et al., 1989).

Protective Factors

The story thus far has been cautionary, because many substances can pose surprising hazards to the developing organism. But it is important to remember that prenatal risk analysis takes into account protective factors as well as hazards. There are, of course, many innate protections provided by the processes of prenatal development themselves. Many spontaneous abortions—especially those that occur in the first weeks of pregnancy, when widespread structural damage to the fetus is possible—are part of a natural process that tends to promote normal development. Further, the fact that growth (especially brain growth) is a lengthy process means that, in most cases, harm at one point of pregnancy can be overcome if the rest of pregnancy and infancy are healthy. Behavioral teratogens, in particular, usually do not do serious damage unless they are one component of a variety of risk factors, including extensive teratogenic exposure, birth complications, and a neglectful pattern of child-rearing (Kopp & Kraler, 1989).

We will now examine three additional protective factors in pregnancy: adequate nutrition, prenatal care, and social support.

Nutrition

Sound nutrition for the expectant mother, obtained from eating a variety of fresh foods with ample calories, is an essential element of a successful pregnancy. Besides serving as the growing organism's own nutritional source, the mother's diet of adequate calories, vitamins, and minerals acts as a first line of defense against low birthweight and as a protective screen against various birth defects. Indeed, many of the drug-related teratogenic effects that we have examined may occur primarily through malnutrition that is commonly associated with abuse of drugs, rather than directly from the substance in question (Robins & Mills, 1993). The higher rate of birth complications in young mothers may, likewise, be primarily the direct result of inadequate and imbalanced diets of many teenage girls (Hayes, 1987).

In the beginning of pregnancy, it is critical that the embryo obtain sufficient quantities of specific nutrients needed for basic body formation, such as calcium for bones and teeth and vitamin A for eyes. Adequate nourishment at the end of pregnancy is even more important for overall development of the fetal body and brain than at the beginning. Studies of malnourished women who were given nutritional supplements in the last three months of pregnancy found that the odds of their having a healthy birth and normally intelligent children were significantly improved (Salt et al., 1988).

Fortunately, good basic nutrition is not hard to obtain in most developed countries, and most pregnant women consume more than enough calcium and vitamin A and gain sufficient weight to sustain a healthy pregnancy (Enkin et al., 1989). Optimal weight gain in pregnancy depends partly on the woman's prepregnancy weight: underweight women should gain between 28 and 40 pounds; normal-weight women, between 25 and 35 pounds; and overweight women, between 15 and 25 pounds (Institute of Medicine, 1990). If a woman gains much more than the ideal amount, the main concern is not for the fetus, which usually suffers no ill effects, but for the mother, who is at greater risk of high blood pressure and diabetes and often has trouble losing the extra weight after the baby is born (Keppel & Taffel, 1993). In developing countries, of course, many women begin pregnancy poorly fed, and it is critical for them to eat well and gain at least 15 pounds (Enkin et al., 1989).

It is important to note, however, that while adequate nutrition, especially adequate calories toward the end of pregnancy, is protective, too

FIGURE 4.12 A balanced diet is important throughout pregnancy, but especially toward the end, when among other special requirements, calcium is needed for bones and teeth. Taking calcium pills is usually not recommended; drinking milk or eating other calcium-rich foods—yogurt, cheese, and sardines, for instance—is much better.

much vitamin supplementation can be destructive. Megadoses of vitamin A, for instance, cause defects in body formation, and taking an excess of iron can deplete the body of zinc, a deficiency associated with many birth complications (Kitzinger, 1989). Consequently, pregnant women should *never* undertake an intense regimen of self-prescribed vitamin supplements in a mistaken effort to "play it safe." Especially since scientists are still discovering which nutrients are linked to which aspects of prenatal development, the safest course is a varied diet rich in foods that contain the nutrients known to be protective, since such a diet is also likely to contain additional protective substances not yet discovered.

Within the past decade, research has revealed the importance of one protective nutrient that many women do not get in adequate amounts from the typical diet. That is **folic acid**, found especially in dark-green leafy vegetables, as well as certain fruits, grains, and organ meats, especially liver.

The role of folic acid was forcefully evidenced by two recent studies of *neural tube defects*. As you may remember from Chapter 3, in about 1 in every 500 embryos, the neural tube does not grow properly: either the lower spine does not close, causing spina bifida, or the upper part of the central nervous system does not develop, causing anencephaly. The cause is partly genetic, as evidenced not only by ethnic differences in the rate of the defect (fetuses of British descent, for example, are more vulnerable than those of African or Asian descent), but also by the fact that if a given couple has an infant with a neural tube defect, the chance of their next child having the problem is 1 in 30.

Folic acid, however, can sometimes prevent this defect. In one study in England, close to 2,000 pregnant women who had already had one child with a neural tube defect were randomly assigned to one of four conditions: vitamins including folic acid; vitamins without folic acid; folic acid but no other vitamins; or no special dietary supplements at all. Those women who received additional folic acid, with or without the other vitamins, had far fewer infants with a neural tube defect: their risk was reduced from 1 in 30 to 1 in 100 (Ward et al., 1991).

The crucial role of folic acid was shown even more clearly in a study in Jamaica, where, ordinarily, the incidence of infants with neural tube defects is quite low. In the last half of 1989, however, the rate of Jamaican newborns with spina bifida or anencephaly more than doubled (Duff & Cooper, 1994). Attempts to find the cause traced back to Hurricane Gilbert, which on Sep-

folic acid A nutrient, found in dark-green leafy vegetables as well as certain fruits, grains, and organ meats, that helps protect against neural tube defects.

tember 12, 1988, devastated the island's crops and livestock. In the months following the hurricane, Jamaicans were deprived of their usual diet, which is typically high in folic acid—including ripe bananas and oranges that contain appreciable amounts of folate and ascorbate, vegetables such as the local callaloo, which is similar to spinach, and such meats as beef and chicken liver and kidney. Instead, their daily staples consisted of relief supplies of prepared and packaged foods such as rice, flour, sugar, cornmeal, tinned corned beef, sausage, sardines, and mackerel. As a result, women who became pregnant in the months following the hurricane tended to begin pregnancy deficient in folic acid and to maintain that deficiency in the critical first few months. (It should be noted that before the researchers concluded that folic acid deficiency was the cause of the Jamaican tragedy, they examined and eliminated other possible explanations, including a temporary rise in substance abuse, exposure to pesticides, trauma related to the hurricane, overall malnutrition, and interrupted health care.)

Studies such as these lead some experts to conclude that folic acid should be added to the general diet, perhaps as an ingredient in bread, in much the way vitamin D is added to milk. However, considerable disagreement remains as to how much supplementation would be protective without posing the dangers of overdosing for those who happen to consume a great deal of whatever foods happen to be fortified (Beresford, 1994).

Overall, then, medical advice on preconceptual and prenatal nutrition agrees with common sense: a varied and plentiful diet of all the basic foods, especially fruits, vegetables, and grains, provides the best overall protection for the developing fetus.

Prenatal Care

Medical care that begins in the early months of pregnancy and includes prenatal counseling as well as basic screening tests is one of the best predictors of a healthy pregnancy, an easy birth, and a normal newborn (Enkin et al., 1989). This is true whether a mother is of high socioeconomic status (in which case income and education provide additional contributions to a healthy pregnancy) or is of low SES. In China, for example, a network of workers trained in basic medicine—the "barefoot doctors"—provide prenatal care in even the most remote and impoverished areas of the country.

FIGURE 4.13 Both these birth attendants—the obstetrician in New York City and the midwife in Rajastan, India—are assessing the size, position, and heartbeat of a developing fetus. Which pregnancy is more likely to result in a healthy baby? If the birth is high-risk, then the high-tech equipment on the left might be critical. However, if the pregnancy is a normal one, as most pregnancies are, the experience and empathy of the trained attendant is more important than the diagnostic tools he or she uses.

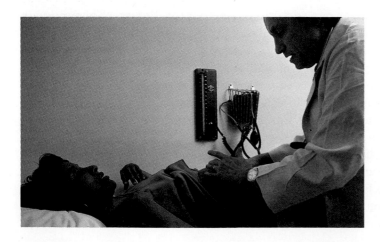

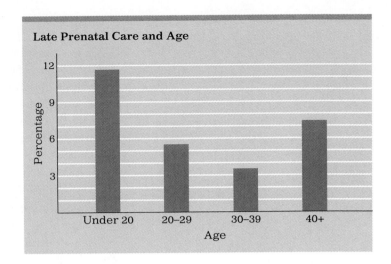

FIGURE 4.14 This figure shows the percentage of women in the United States who receive very late (after the sixth month) prenatal care, or none at all. Ironically, but not surprisingly, in a nation in which the individual is primarily responsible for paying for medical care, those women who need good obstetrical attention the most are often the least likely to get it.

Consequently, China has achieved a lower rate of birth defects and complications than many wealthier nations (United Nations, 1990). Even more telling, in the United States, Mississippi, one of the lowest-ranking states in both education and income, is ahead of many richer states in the prevention of birth complications and infant mortality—because almost every pregnant resident is entitled to free prenatal care (DeParle, 1991). Ironically, in most of the United States, those who need early prenatal care the most—the poor, the addicted, and the relatively young or old—are the least likely to get it (Johnson, 1992) (see Figure 4.14).

Social Support

A final important protective factor in pregnancy is **social support** (Norbeck & Tilden, 1983; Pagel et al., 1990). This term refers to the emotional and material assistance provided by members of the social networks to which a person has access. Someone who has extensive social support has several people to depend on for encouragement, advice, and practical help. However, the key factor in the social network's promotion of a healthy birth is not so much the network's size and density—how many relatives live nearby, whether or not the woman is married, and so forth—as it is how helpful the woman feels her relatives and friends are or how often she has experienced support from them in the past (Thompson, 1992).

There are many ways that supportive social networks can reduce prenatal complications, including directly easing the financial and material stresses of life during pregnancy, as well as facilitating the expectant mother's efforts to maintain good health habits and regular prenatal care. In some traditional societies, the support network for pregnant women and new mothers includes all their female relatives, particularly mothers and aunts, as well as other women in the community. In industrialized countries, this extended kin network is often absent because of residential mobility, and the woman's mate becomes a more crucial source of social support, along with close friends. If the woman feels that her mate is positive about the pregnancy and actively supportive of it (attending prenatal classes with her, encouraging her to eat well, and helping her to maintain nonrisky health practices), she is more likely to have a healthy baby. On the other hand, if he responds negatively to the pregnancy or is abusive, she is at greater risk of complications (Amaro et al., 1990).

social support Emotional encouragement and practical assistance provided by other people, particularly friends and family, to a person in need.

In considering how protective factors can buffer prenatal growth against some of the risks that inevitably occur, it is also helpful to remember that their effects (like those of teratogens) are compounding. In other words, the combined effects of good nutrition, social support, and prenatal care in the life of a pregnant woman and her developing fetus are greater than the positive influence of each taken alone. One reason this is true is that each of these protective factors is mutually reinforcing: prenatal examinations are often a context for expectant mothers to learn about their dietary requirements, and social support helps to facilitate the mother's commitment to good health habits.

As we have seen, human development commences with a single cell that begins to grow imperceptibly, deep inside the uterus, according to a precise biological timetable. While there are many known and unknown hazards that may lie ahead, almost every zygote that manages to multiply, implant, and grow has the potential to become a healthy newborn, with the capacity for decades of intellectual growth and emotional well-being.

Whether that possibility is fulfilled depends not only on the mother-to-be but also on the support provided by her immediate social network and the larger community. For example, whether the prenatal environment that nourishes the fetus is drug-free depends on the culture's drug use generally and on its policies and attitudes regarding treatment for abuse and addiction. It also depends on the encouragement or indifference that comes from the father, the community, and the medical establishment regarding the practice of good prenatal health habits. Similarly, whether or not the embryo is harmed by a disease agent depends on the adequacy of various public health measures, from immunization programs for preschoolers to safe-sex education for adolescents. These factors, in turn, are influenced by the overall cultural attitudes regarding the younger generation.

Thus, although prenatal development might seem at first to be a purely biological topic, it quickly becomes apparent that it can be understood only in terms of the specific social context in which it occurs, with all the influences that socioeconomic status, ethnic values, and cultural traditions bring to bear on it. As you will soon learn, the same is even more apparent for birth, an event surrounded by "a proliferation of rituals" that convey the core values of each society (Davis-Floyd, 1992). At every moment of development for any one individual, the values of the family, the community, and the entire society close off some possibilities while opening others.

SUMMARY

From Zygote to Newborn

1. The first two weeks of prenatal growth are the germinal period. During this period, the single-celled zygote grows to an organism more than a hundred cells in size, travels down the Fallopian tube, and implants itself in the uterine lining, where it continues to grow.

2. The developing organism divides into inner and outer cells. The outer cells form the membranes that will provide nourishment and protection during the prenatal period. The inner cells will become the embryo.

3. The period from the third through the eighth week after conception is the period of the embryo. The development of the embryo is cephalo-caudal (from the head downward) and proximo-distal (from the inner organs outward). During this period the heart begins to beat and the eyes, ears, nose, and mouth begin to form.

4. The placenta, formed from the outer cells of the developing organism, enables fetal nourishment to be provided, and fetal waste products to be removed, by the mother's bloodstream. Although the placenta allows substances to pass between the two bloodstreams, it keeps the blood supplies of mother and fetus separate.

5. At eight weeks after conception, the future baby is only about an inch long. Yet it already has the organs and features of a human baby, with the exception of the sex organs, which take a few more weeks to develop.

6. The fetal period extends from the ninth week after conception until birth. The fetus grows rapidly; muscles develop and bones begin to harden. The sex organs take shape, and the other organs complete their formation.

7. The fetus attains viability when the brain is sufficiently mature, between the twentieth and twenty-sixth week after conception. The average fetus weighs 2 pounds at the beginning of the third trimester and 7½ pounds at the end. The additional pounds, plus maturation of brain, lungs, and heart, ensure survival for more than 99 percent of all full-term babies.

8. Brain growth, especially toward the close of the fetal period, is reflected in the organism's increased responsiveness to stimulation from within and outside the womb.

Preventing Complications

9. It was once believed that the placenta protects the fetus from any harmful substances, but now we know that many teratogens (substances that can cause birth defects) can affect the embryo and fetus. Diseases, drugs, and pollutants can all cause birth defects.

10. In understanding teratology, it is critical to realize that teratogens are risk factors, not inevitable destroyers. Whether a particular teratogen will harm a particular embryo or fetus depends on many factors, including the timing and amount of exposure. It also depends on protective factors in prenatal growth. For example, for many teratogens, harm is more likely if exposure to the teratogen occurs early in pregnancy and less likely if the mother-to-be is healthy and well nourished.

11. As a result of the knowledge derived from teratology, many serious teratogens, including rubella and some prescription drugs, now rarely reach the fetus. However, certain other diseases and psychoactive drugs remain hazards that require prevention on the part of the woman. HIV is the most deadly of these teratogens; alcohol is the most common.

12. A diet providing adequate protein and calories is especially important during prenatal growth. So also are regular prenatal medical care and social support to the expectant mother.

KEY TERMS

germinal period (110)
period of the embryo (110)
period of the fetus (111)
differentiation (111)
implantation (111)
infertility (112)
endometriosis (112)
artificial insemination (112)
in vitro fertilization (113)
surrogate motherhood (113)
embryonic disk (114)
ectoderm (114)
placenta (115)
mesoderm (115)
endoderm (115)
neural tube (115)
cephalo-caudal development (115)
proximo-distal development (115)

trimester (116)
age of viability (117)
teratology (119)
teratogens (119)
risk analysis (119)
critical period (120)
behavioral teratogens (121)
rubella (123)
human immunodeficiency virus (HIV) (124)
acquired immune deficiency syndrome (AIDS) (124)
toxoplasmosis (125)
thalidomide (125)
fetal alcohol syndrome (FAS) (126)
folic acid (135)
social support (137)

KEY QUESTIONS

1. What developments occur during the germinal period?

2. What major developments occur during the period of the embryo?

3. What major developments occur during the period of the fetus?

4. In what ways is the fetus capable of responding to the outside world?

5. To which teratogens is the developing organism most vulnerable?

6. What are the effects of maternal drinking on the fetus?

7. What are the effects of drug abuse on the fetus?

8. What are some of the environmental hazards to prenatal growth?

9. What factors make a fetus more likely to be harmed by teratogens?

10. What are the three primary protective factors that promote a healthy birth?

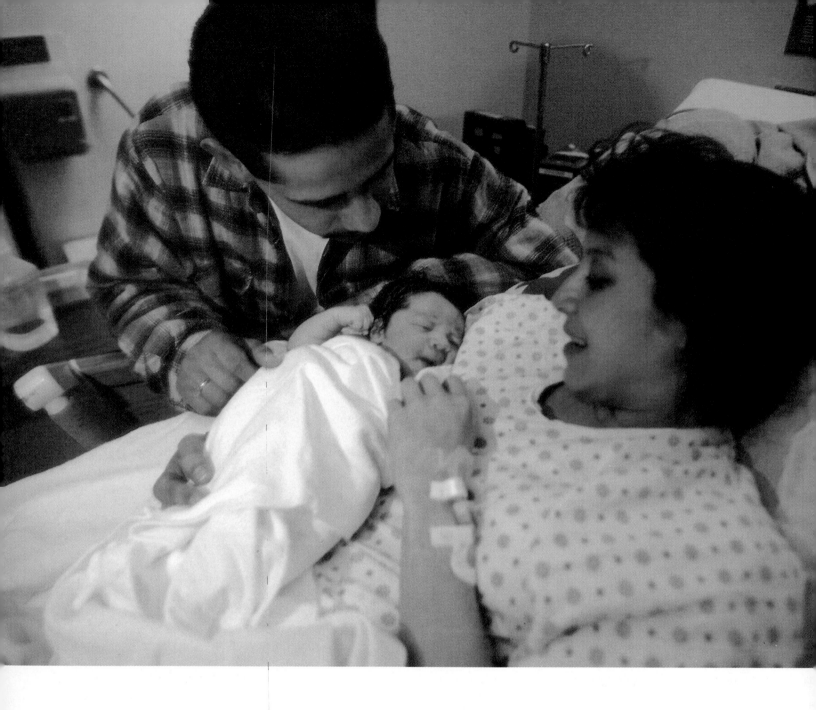

Birth

Although birth is a universal human expe
birth can vary greatly, with consequences
event, affecting child, mother, father, an
and months ahead. The process of birth,
nificance for participants will be examin
following questions:

If birth takes place several weeks early, l
appearance differ from that of an infant b

What are some of the factors that may m;
child?

Why do some critics object to routine birt}

What are some of the cultural differences
birth in various nations?

What are the benefits of prepared chil
parents?

How do siblings' reactions to the birth
differ from those of the parents?

Is there a critical period for the bond
form?

The moment of birth marks the most rap
tire life span. No longer insulated from t
world, no longer guaranteed the nouris}
provided through the umbilical cord, the
ment where needs and desires will only
thus becomes a newborn, a separate hu
his or her worldly existence almost entir

Birth is also a transforming experi
members. For parents having their first
ization "I am a mother" or "I am a father
sponsibilities, worries, sorrows, and joy
arrival of a second, third, or later-born c
and changes the status of the other c
brother or sister; the "baby" of the fam
changes in rank may have important cor

and self-understanding. Each birth also adds a grandchild, cousin, niece, or nephew to the extended family, sometimes affecting the self-concept of older relatives. As one man newly elevated to the status of grandfather put it, "Now I'm immortal" (Kornhaber & Woodward, 1981).

We will now look more closely at this moment of transition, and at the first days of life for newborns and their families.

The Normal Birth

In the last months of pregnancy, the fetus and the uterus prepare for the birth process. The muscles of the uterus contract and relax at irregular intervals, gaining tone and widening the cervix a centimeter or two. Sometime during the last month, most fetuses change position for the final time, turning so that their heads are in the mother's pelvic cavity. They are now in position to be born in the usual way, headfirst.

The actual birth process begins with uterine contractions that most women think are just movements of the fetus or the irregular contractions they have recently been experiencing. But when the contractions become strong and regular, it is clear that the **first stage of labor** has begun. During this stage the uterine muscles tighten and release, gradually pushing the fetus downward until the cervix dilates to a width of about 4 inches (10 centimeters), allowing the fetus's head to squeeze through (see Figure 5.1).

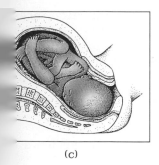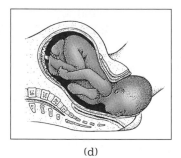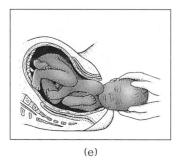

(c)   (d)   (e)

From the first tentative contractions until full dilatation of the cervix, the first stage of labor lasts eight to twelve hours in first births and four to seven hours in subsequent births, although there is much variation—from a few minutes to a few days (Friedman & Neff, 1987).

When the cervix is almost fully dilated, a process called **transition** begins, as the fetus's head descends from the uterus into the birth canal, or vagina. During this descent, contractions often come very rapidly, and the woman may feel nauseated, or chilled, or ready to quit. Luckily, transition usually lasts only a few minutes.

Technically, the **second stage of labor** begins as soon as the first stage ends. After transition, the baby's head appears at the opening of the vagina. The skin surrounding the vagina stretches with each contraction until the head emerges. Within a few seconds of the next contraction, the baby is fully born. This stage may last as long as one to two hours for first pregnancies but as little as a few minutes for subsequent ones.

FIGURE 5.2 A minute after birth, this newborn is undergoing his first exam, the Apgar. From the newborn's ruddy color and obvious muscle tone, it looks as if he will pass with a score of 7 or higher.

third stage of labor The expulsion of the placenta after a child is born.

neonate A newborn baby. Infants are neonates from the moment of birth to the end of the first month of life.

Apgar A test devised by Dr. Virginia Apgar to quickly assess the newborn's color, heart rate, reflex irritability, muscle tone, and respiratory effort. This simple method is used 1 minute and 5 minutes after birth to determine whether a newborn needs immediate medical care.

The birth process, however, is no baby is born, the **third stage of labor** placenta.

The Newborn's First Minutes

People who have never witnessed a birt held upside-down and spanked by the at the baby start breathing. Actually, this is **neonates**, usually breathe and cry on the fact, sometimes babies cry as soon as t canal. As the first spontaneous cries occu begins to function fully, and soon the in tinge to pink, as oxygen circulates thro there is much for those attending the bir in the throat is removed, the umbilical c dry and wrapped to preserve body heat.

If birth is assisted by a trained he births in industrialized nations and 51 p [United Nations, 1994]), the newborn is ir tioning. One common method of assessin sure called the **Apgar**, which assigns a s rate, breathing, muscle tone, color, and i birth and again at 5 minutes (see Table 5 ter, the newborn is not in danger; if the help establishing normal breathing; if the ical condition and needs immediate me tory distress and death.

Next the infant is carefully examine as a cleft palate, a spinal defect, or a hip is typically alert and wide-eyed, is usual perhaps breast-feed. Fathers also can h taking care to keep the infant warm. The pecially if they are not interrupted by fu very special time for the family. In one fa

> Christopher was placed in my wife's a shortly after it was cut, he was wrapped a chick out of an egg) and given to me back. He was very alert, apparently at other objects in the room; as I held hi parts of his body turning from deep pu was fascinated by the colors; time stopp

TABLE 5.1

Criteria and Scoring of the Apgar Test

Score	Color	Heartbeat	Reflex Irritability	M
0	blue, pale	absent	no response	fla
1	body pink, extremities blue	slow (below 100)	grimace	w
2	entirely pink	rapid (over 100)	coughing, sneezing, crying	st

Source: Apgar, 1953

Usually after the initial contact, silver nitrate or erythromycin drops are put into the infant's eyes to prevent infection from any bacteria picked up in the birth canal, the infant's body temperature is checked to make sure the baby is warm enough, and various other hospital routines (footprinting, vitamin-K injections, blood sampling) are completed. Soon thereafter the newborn goes to sleep (Behrman, 1992).

The Newborn's Appearance

The news that the newborn's health is good is always reassuring, especially since many normal newborns look abnormal to someone who has never seen one before. Newborns' heads, especially the upper portion, seem disproportionately large relative to their trunks and short, sometimes quite skinny, limbs. Often their heads are elongated and sometimes even pointy, because the bones of the skull overlap during birth as the head squeezes through the birth canal. This overlapping causes no lasting damage, since the bones of a baby's skull do not fuse together until the *fontanelles* ("soft spots") on the head close, several months after birth. Sometimes newborns have hair on their faces and bodies as well as on their heads.

Most newborns have flat noses and virtually no chin, a fact that makes it easier for them to get milk from the mother's breast. Their skin also might look strange: especially if the baby is born a bit early, the skin may be covered with a waxy white substance called *vernix*; if the baby is a bit late, the skin is often red, splotchy, and wrinkled. All of these characteristics are temporary.

Variations, Problems, and Solutions

As we have seen, birth is usually a short and natural process that results in a healthy newborn. However, this is not always so. Birth can be long and complicated, or a medical emergency during the birth process may sometimes result in a lifelong handicap for the newborn. Because the possible physical and psychological consequences of birth complications can be important factors in development, we will review some of the variations of the birth process that can cause difficulties. They fall into two main categories: birth that occurs too early and birth that causes too much stress for the fetus.

The Low-Birthweight Infant

The average newborn is born 266 days after conception (forty weeks after the mother's last menstrual period) and weighs 3,400 grams (7½ pounds). As is usually the case in human development, however, few individuals are precisely average: a newborn is considered normal weight if he or she weighs between 2,500 and 4,000 grams (5½ to 8¾ pounds) and is labeled "on time" if born no more than three weeks early or two weeks late. In fact, fewer than one baby in twenty arrives precisely on day 266, the "official" due date (Carlson, 1994).

About one newborn in seven, however, is sufficiently below the average birthweight to be considered **low birthweight**, defined internationally as less than 2,500 grams (5½ pounds). Worldwide, the incidence of low birthweight

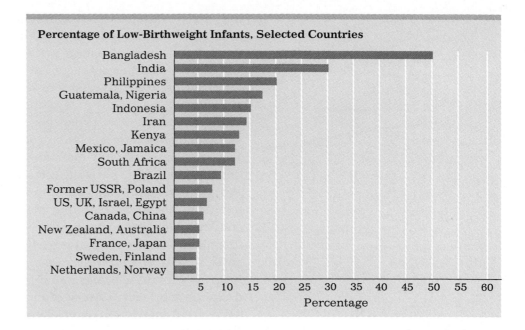

Percentage of Low-Birthweight Infants, Selected Countries

FIGURE 5.4 Poor nutrition and lack of prenatal care are the major reasons that some nations have a much higher percentage of low-birthweight babies than others. In the United States, this is reflected in the fact that low-birthweight rates are notably higher in inner cities and in poorer rural states.

generally varies from less than 4 percent in several of the most developed nations to about 25 percent in several of the most malnourished, although one nation, Bangladesh, has a low-birthweight rate of 50 percent (United Nations, 1994). Rates of low birthweight also vary within countries, with rates being higher in inner cities and rural areas than in the more affluent suburban areas. Even under ideal conditions, however, some very small infants are born.

No matter what their background, low-birthweight infants are at risk for many immediate and long-term problems, although whether that risk becomes a life-threatening reality or simply a statistical possibility depends a great deal on how these tiny infants are cared for in the first days and months of life, as well as on the reason for their small size.

One cause of low birthweight is simply that birth occurs too early, before the final doubling of body weight that takes place in the last two months of development. In such cases, early-born infants are called **preterm** (a more accurate designation than *premature*), defined as being born three or more weeks before the due date. Other low-birthweight infants are born close to the due date but weigh substantially less than they should, given how much time has passed since conception. They are called *small-for-dates,* or **small for gestational age (SGA)**. A particular baby can be both preterm and small for gestational age, or can be one but not the other, or can be neither. For example, thirty-four weeks after conception, a normal fetus weighs 2,800 grams (slightly over 6 pounds). If born at that point, a month early, the baby would be preterm but neither small for gestational age nor low birthweight. By contrast, a fetus might grow very slowly in the uterus and be born after a full thirty-eight weeks of development weighing only 2,000 grams (about 4½ pounds). Such an infant, while not preterm, would be both small for gestational age and low birthweight.

Many low-birthweight infants are also preterm. As newborns, they show many physical signs of immaturity; for example, they often have fine, downy hair (*lanugo*) and a thick coating of vernix on their faces or bodies, and their nipples may not yet be visible; and, if they are male, the testicles

preterm infant   An infant born three or more weeks before the due date.

small for gestational age (SGA)
   A term applied to newborns who weigh substantially less than they should given how much time has passed since conception.

may not yet have descended into the scrotum. Most of these physical characteristics pose no serious problem. Vernix and lanugo eventually disappear, and the nipples emerge and testicles descend shortly after birth.

However, other characteristics may be critical. The first major challenge facing low-birthweight, preterm infants is survival, because several vital functions are not yet developed enough for life outside the womb. For example, these newborns may have difficulty sucking and digesting food because of the immaturity of their reflexes and of the body's digestive system. They also have difficulty maintaining adequate body heat because they do not have the fat that normally accumulates during the last stages of prenatal growth. Low-birthweight preterm infants are also especially vulnerable to infection. Most important, they may be unable to breathe in sufficient oxygen, especially if they are more than a month preterm. About 60 percent of the infants born three months early, and 20 percent of those born one month early, suffer from *respiratory distress syndrome,* a potentially life-threatening problem caused by the immaturity of the lungs. Respiratory distress syndrome is the leading cause of preterm death, which, in turn, represents between 70 and 85 percent of all neonatal deaths in the United States (Goldenberg, 1992).

This does not mean that most preterm infants die. In fact, within developed countries, medical intervention after birth—isolettes, intravenous feeding, respirators, and so on—now allows most low-birthweight infants to live. Indeed, the increased survival of **very-low-birthweight (VLBW)** infants—those weighing under 1,500 grams (less than 3½ pounds)—is the main reason that, despite the constancy of VLBW rates, infant mortality in the United States had decreased to about 1 in every 110 births in 1992, less than half the rate in 1970, when 1 out of every 50 babies died before age 1. Seventeen other countries—Canada, Japan, and the Scandinavian nations among them—have even lower infant death rates—not primarily because of intensive postnatal care but because of extensive prenatal care, which results in fewer early, underweight births (Hilts, 1991; Schiff, 1992).

In general, the survival of low-birthweight preterm infants depends more on maturation of the brain and lungs than on body weight alone. For example, a 1,000-gram (about 2¼-pound) newborn who is 28 weeks old has about a 90 percent chance of survival; a newborn who is the same weight but only 25 weeks old has only a 50 percent chance. Of course, every day of additional prenatal growth, and every additional gram of body weight, increases the chances for postnatal survival. Whether that survival includes normal development, with no signs of a hazardous beginning, or involves ongoing or repeated medical and psychological effects depends on the causes of the low-birthweight and the treatment of its immediate consequences (Beckwith & Rodning, 1991).

Causes of Low Birthweight

The most common and direct cause of low birthweight is maternal malnutrition, especially during the last trimester of pregnancy. Another leading cause is the mother's poor overall health, or her poor health habits, including smoking, drinking, and drug abuse. Indeed, virtually every social drug impairs fetal nourishment and may precipitate early labor, causing both preterm and SGA births. In addition, fetal nutrition can be affected by ge-

very low birthweight (VLBW)
Birthweight of less than 1,500 grams (3½ pounds) at birth.

netic handicaps, prenatal infections, and malfunctioning of the placenta or umbilical cord. And, as always, the quality of prenatal medical care is an important factor.

The mother's age is also a factor in birthweight (Lee et al., 1988). The incidence of low birthweight is higher among mothers under age 18 or over age 35. This correlation is partly explained by the fact that teenage mothers often have inadequate diets and that older women have more health problems. A more direct reason, however, is the fact that for these two groups, especially mothers-to-be under age 15 or over age 40, the uterus does not sustain pregnancy as well as during the prime childbearing years.

The interval between pregnancies also plays a role in birthweight: the shorter the time between pregnancies, the less the later-born tends to weigh. This is a major reason that a child born less than eighteen months after a previous birth is three times as likely to die before age 5 as is a baby born at least four years after a previous birth (Hobecraft, 1991).

Another common cause of low birthweight, even when the mother and fetus are both healthy, is simultaneous pregnancies. Twins usually gain weight normally until eight weeks before the due date, and then gain more slowly than a single fetus does, partly because of the nutritional and placental difficulties of sharing the same intrauterine environment. They also tend to be born early, by three weeks on average. As a result, the typical newborn twin weighs about 5 pounds. Triplets tend to be born even earlier and to weigh even less.

Of particular concern for those interested in child development is that many of these factors are related to poverty. The link between poverty and maternal nutrition is an obvious example. Poverty is also linked to less education and more stressful living conditions, and these, in turn, are related to poorer health, pregnancies at younger ages, and greater exposure to teratogens of all kinds, from air pollution to crack cocaine. Malfunctions of the placenta and umbilical cord are more likely when pregnancies are closely spaced, and such spacing occurs more often in women of low income. Even for something as seemingly unrelated to socioeconomic influences as simultaneous pregnancy, poverty is a powerful factor. Early and adequate medical care can result in newborn twins who weigh 7 pounds each rather than 2, but especially in countries such as the United States, where most medical care is privately paid for, the likelihood of a pregnant woman obtaining prenatal care in the first half of pregnancy is directly related to her income. Thus social-contextual factors are an underlying cause of low birthweight, and help explain the wide national and international variations in the following statistics:

1. Of the more than 20 million low-birthweight infants born worldwide each year, the overwhelming majority are from developing countries (United Nations, 1994).

2. Developing countries in the same general region, with similar ethnic populations, can have markedly different rates of low birthweight. Colombia's rate, for example, is 50 percent higher than that of Venezuela, whose per capita income is triple that of Colombia.

3. In many developed countries, including the United States, the rate of low birthweight in the inner cities is more than double that of the nearby suburbs.

4. Within the United States, the rate of low birthweight in the poorest states (e.g., Tennessee and South Carolina, more than 9 percent) is almost twice that of some richer states (e.g., Alaska and Oregon, less than 5 percent) (Children's Defense Fund, 1994).

5. Ethnic-group differences in low-birthweight rates within nations tend to follow socioeconomic, rather than genetic, patterns (Kleinman et al., 1991). The most telling example in the United States is the rate of low birthweight for infants of African-American descent, which is 12.4 percent, more than twice the rates for whites and Asian-Americans, who, as a whole, are considerably higher in socioeconomic standing. The socioeconomic influences behind these differences are underscored by the fact that wealthier African-Americans have lower rates of low birthweight than poorer African-Americans do. Similarly, the rate among Hispanic-Americans of Puerto Rican heritage is 9.5 percent, whereas the rate among those of Cuban descent, who tend to be more affluent, is 5.8 percent. Of course, socioeconomic status is only a rough gauge for other factors that may or may not apply in different cases. This is apparent with another Hispanic group—Americans of Mexican descent, whose low-birthweight rate is only 5.6 percent, which is much better than that of other groups having similar levels of income and education (U.S. Bureau of the Census, 1992). One reason for this difference appears to be that the rate of alcohol, tobacco, and drug use among pregnant Chicanas is relatively low (Vega et al., 1993).

Consequences of Low Birthweight

Many factors in the early days and months of life may put the low-birthweight infant at risk, especially if the birth was more than six weeks early and if the birthweight was under 1,500 grams. Many such infants experience brain damage as the result of **anoxia**—a temporary lack of oxygen—or of cerebral hemorrhaging (Beckwith & Rodning, 1991). In addition, as we have seen, the immediate care of such infants is dictated by precaution, to protect them from disease and infections. Often they are confined to isolettes or are continuously hooked up to one or another piece of medical machinery. Consequently, they are deprived of certain kinds of stimulation, such as the gentle rocking they would have experienced if they still were in the womb, or the regular handling involved in feeding and bathing a newborn. At the same time, these infants are subject to a number of experiences unknown to the normal infant, such as breathing with a respirator, being fed intravenously, and sleeping in the bright lights and noise of an intensive-care unit.

Parents are also deprived and stressed. They cannot cradle and care for their infant normally, and they must cope with uncertainty, and perhaps with sorrow, guilt, and anger, as well. This can impede the start of normal parent-infant interactions.

Low birthweight also has consequences for the first months at home. Parents of preterm low-birthweight infants tend to be more protective of them, and more active—rubbing, poking, talking, offering the bottle—than parents of full-term babies are. For their part, preterm babies tend to be

anoxia A temporary lack of fetal oxygen during the birth process; if prolonged, it can cause brain damage or even death.

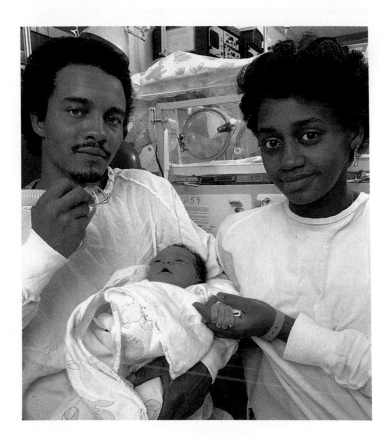

FIGURE 5.5 Pictured here is one of the increasingly lucky low-birthweight infants, who, thanks to medical technologies, have twice the chance of surviving today that they had twenty years ago. The next step is for her parents and community to provide the right mix of attention, patience, and stimulation for her intellectual and social development. She may be fortunate here too: unlike many low-birthweight infants, she seems to have two parents who are ready and able to give her what she needs.

more passive than full-term babies (Brazelton, 1990). It is as if the parent, noticing the baby's relative passivity, tries to push the child into behaving normally, while the infant, in reaction to more stimulation than he or she can comfortably handle, withdraws. Given the nature of this interaction, it is not surprising to find that these parents and infants smile at each other less frequently in the first months than do parents and their full-term infants (Field, 1987).

As time goes by, short- and long-term difficulties in cognitive development may also emerge. Infants who were low birthweight but had no obvious impairments sometimes have problems with early cognitive and language development, being more distractible and slower to talk, for example (Byrne et al., 1993; Lukeman & Melvin, 1993). Long-term learning difficulties, especially distractibility, are likely to occur when low birthweight is accompanied by other medical complications, such as respiratory distress syndrome, anoxia, or cerebral hemorrhaging, but sometimes they occur even in the absence of these complications (Hack et al., 1992; Szatmari et al., 1993). Low birthweight may also lead to later difficulties in social competence and to problems in parent-child interaction, especially when accompanied by medical complications (Landry et al., 1990). In cases where low birthweight is related to poverty and other social and family stresses, the potential long-term decrements of low birthweight are likely to be intensified by the continuing effects of these contextual factors. Thus predicting the future life prospects of low-birthweight infants depends not only on the fact and degree of their low birthweight but also on the added medical and contextual demands with which they must also cope.

RESEARCH REPORT

Early Intervention with Low-Birthweight Babies

Consistent with the contextual view that recognizes the on-going influence that the family, the educational climate, and community support have on every child's development, many clinical and developmental scientists point out the sharp disparity between the high-tech, labor-intensive neonatal care that low-birthweight infants receive in the hospital and the care they receive in their early life at home. Often these infants' mothers are already stressed by poverty, single parenthood, and other small children at home, yet when the infants are discharged from the hospital, the most their mothers usually receive in the way of help and guidance is a week's supply of formula, a clinic appointment, and a list of symptoms that might warrant a call to the doctor. Obviously, given the cognitive and behavioral problems that low-birthweight infants are likely to experience, this "follow-up" is woefully inadequate. At the same time, however, developmentalists do not yet know what specific interventions and supports would be most helpful for such families, nor when they should optimally occur.

One large research project (Ramey et al., 1992) began to answer these questions by studying close to 1,000 low-birthweight babies and their mothers across the United States. About a third of the babies weighed between 2,500 and 2,000 grams at birth, another third weighed between 2,000 and 1,500 grams, and the rest weighed below 1,500 grams. Most of the mothers were quite young, about half in their early 20s and almost a fourth in their teens. They also were usually low in SES: less than half were high school graduates or had incomes above the poverty level. Racially, the group was composed about equally of blacks and whites, reflecting the fact that, even though African-Americans comprise only about 15 percent of the United States population, almost half the VLBW babies born in the United States are of African descent (*Morbidity and Mortality Weekly Report,* April 29, 1994).

The infants were divided into an experimental group and a control group, with both groups having a similar representation of infants with particular backgrounds and medical risk factors. All the babies received good pediatric care and periodic psychological testing, and the mothers were referred to various specialists if problems arose over the three years of the study.

In addition, the experimental group received several special interventions. In the first year, the mothers were visited weekly at home by someone trained to foster good infant care—providing tips regarding nutrition and exercise, demonstrating how to encourage early language development and exploration of the environment, and so on. In addition, the home visitor counseled the mother on whatever problems of daily life might come up, from handling sibling rivalry to finding a better place to live.

When the babies were 1-year-old, the researchers initiated two additional programs to supplement the home visits over the remainder of the study. The children attended a high-quality day-care center (with a developmental curriculum carried out by one teacher for every three 1-year-olds, and one for every four 2-year-olds), and the mothers attended a monthly parent-support meeting.

In the first year, the intervention did not seem to make a difference: both groups of 1-year-olds did equally well on the Bayley Scales of Infant Development, which measures behaviors such as ability to walk, to repeat a sound, to put an object in a box, and so on. By age 2, however, the control group had fallen almost 10 points behind the experimental group in intellectual development, scoring somewhat below average. By age 3, the scores of both groups had declined, but the spread between them still remained about 10 points, which meant that the preschoolers in the experimental group were mostly in the average-intelligence range, while the control-group children were mostly in the slow-learning range.

Other comparisons between the two groups also favored the experimental group. As reported by their parents, the experimental children had fewer behavioral problems (such as hitting other children or being terrified of the dark). As rated by researchers who were blind as to which children were in which group, the experimental group tended to be more persistent and enthusiastic when given a problem to solve (such as connecting two pieces of plastic to remove a toy from under a plexiglass box). In addition, the researchers found that the mothers in the experimental group were more responsive teachers, offering their children just the right amount of encouragement and assistance (Spiker et al., 1993).

The sample size was large enough, and the study long enough, that the researchers could detect whether children with particular characteristics were more likely to benefit from the intervention than were other children.

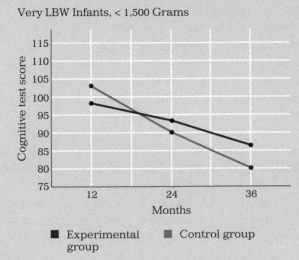

Very LBW Infants, < 1,500 Grams

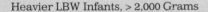

■ Experimental   ■ Control group
group

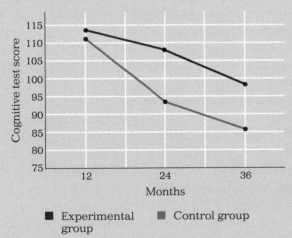

Heavier LBW Infants, > 2,000 Grams

■ Experimental   ■ Control group
group

These charts show the experimental effects that home visitation and good nursery school education had on the intellectual growth of low-birthweight infants. As you can see, the intervention had significant benefits for the infants who weighed between 2,000 and 2,500 grams at birth, but had no effect on the intellectual decline of the infants whose birthweight was less than 2,000 grams.

Overall background characteristics (such as the child's sex or the mother's age or race) did not appear to be crucial to outcome. For instance, while the girls generally scored higher than the boys, the overall average of the experimental-group girls was about 10 points higher than that of the control-group girls, the same differential as existed between the two groups overall. Even the child's medical status as a newborn did not predict how effective the intervention would be. In the end, only one factor seemed important: the infant's birthweight. The special experimental efforts did not seem to benefit the VLBW infants who weighed less than 1,500 grams (3 pounds, 4 ounces) as much as it did their heavier peers (see charts) (Brooks-Gunn et al., 1993).

Several conclusions can be drawn from this project. The most obvious one has been confirmed by other less extensive research: very early childhood education can significantly improve the cognitive ability and social behavior of high-risk infants (Campbell & Ramey, 1994). Another conclusion is more tentative: since the noticeable improvements occurred only after the high-quality day care began at age 1, it may be that providing structured education in a group setting for toddlers who were low birthweight is a more powerful intervention than visiting the mothers of younger infants at home. One possible explanation is that, as long as good medical help was available, most of the mothers in both groups were able to provide adequate care for their infants, so that the addition of the home visitors during the first year of life did not make much difference. Alternatively, it may be that the weekly home visitation was too slight an intervention to have any substantial impact over a period of twelve months. However, it is clear that the day-care education program had a decided intellectual impact, and that, by the time the children reached age 3, the mothers in the intervention group had become more responsive than the other mothers.

The final conclusion is that, educationally as well as medically, the smaller a low-birthweight baby is, the harder it is to prevent the cognitive detriments that sometimes ensue. This finding underscores the overall conclusion drawn from the medical research: prenatal care that manages to add as little as a few hundred grams or a few ounces to a fetus is a more effective use of public health resources than emergency care after birth or educational intervention in childhood.

What Can Be Done?

Recognizing the deprivations that early intensive medical intervention can represent for these infants, many hospitals now provide substitutes for the soothing experiences and regular stimulation that these infants miss because of their precautionary care. The benefits of this approach have been shown experimentally. For example, in one study, infants born six or more weeks early were rocked mechanically while being exposed to the sound of a recorded heartbeat for fifteen-minute sessions many times a day. These infants showed immediate improvements in activity level compared to that of a control group who received normal hospital treatment. Two years later they were significantly ahead of the control group in intellectual ability. The authors of this study speculate that the lulling quality of the stimulation, as well as its regularity, "may have aided in the development of crucial, but subtle, aspects of the central nervous system" (Barnard & Bee, 1983). In another experiment, preterm infants were gently massaged, and their arms and legs moved rhythmically, for fifteen minutes a day. These infants were more alert and more active than those in a control group, and they gained weight more quickly. This was particularly apparent in those infants who had experienced more medical complications and thus had endured more invasive, destabilizing procedures (Scafidi et al., 1993).

Hospitals are also increasingly recognizing the parents' role in the early days of a preterm, low-birthweight infant's life, even if the infant is in intensive care. Whereas once they were banned from entering intensive-care nurseries, parents are now encouraged to be with their baby as soon as medically possible, perhaps holding and feeding the infant, perhaps simply visiting through the plastic of the isolette (Behrman, 1992).

With time, most parents and preterm infants adjust to each other, just as parents and full-term infants do. For example, parent-infant attachment (explained on pp. 269–284) is often considered a sensitive indication of the overall relationship between a child and parent. One longitudinal study of middle-class families found that, even with infants who weighed less than 1,500 grams at birth, secure attachment was just as likely to develop by 18 months as it was with normal-birthweight infants (Easterbrooks, 1989).

Also with time, most of the learning problems that these children exhibit in the first years become less problematic, although much depends on the particular family, school, and community. Sadly, but not surprisingly, children born into families of lower socioeconomic status are more likely to continue to have learning problems than are children raised in middle-class families (Beckwith & Rodning, 1991; Butler & Golding, 1986). This is largely because families with little education or income have fewer resources of their own, and the quality of preschool education or of additional medical help available is, apparently, not enough to make up the difference. When such families are provided with intensive, long-term assistance, the result can be substantial intellectual gains for the low-birthweight child, and benefits for the mother-child interaction (see Research Report, pp. 150–151).

Overall, then, unless low birthweight is actually a symptom of some genetic disorder or teratogenic impairment, or is associated with other medical problems soon after birth, the deficits related to it can usually be overcome. As with so much of development, responsive caregiving can make the difference. Only when the infant is very, very tiny—under 1,000 grams—are early problems unlikely to disappear (see Public Policy, p. 153).

PUBLIC POLICY

Very-Very-Low-Birthweight Infants

A dramatic improvement has occurred over the past twenty-five years in the survival rate of very tiny infants—those under 1,000 grams (about 2¼ pounds). In 1970, virtually all of them died; now about 50 percent survive. Some of the survivors will live essentially normal lives. Unfortunately, some will not. About one-third will be severely handicapped, and another third will likely have learning difficulties in primary school (Beckwith & Rodning, 1991).

Ironically, the very same medical interventions that save lives sometimes create lifelong handicaps, among them blindness (from the administering of high concentrations of oxygen to aid breathing), cerebral palsy (from brain damage that occurred during the emergency assisted birth), and cognitive deficits (from hemorrhaging during surgery required by heart or respiratory failure). With very-very-low-birthweight infants, a choice must sometimes be made between two risks: the risk of visual and intellectual impairment versus the risk of early death. For all concerned, the choice can be agonizing.

One example makes the point:

Debbie and Bill Lonstein's daughter Joan was born fifteen weeks prematurely . . . During her four months in Georgetown's Intensive Care Nursery, she suffered the most serious degree of brain hemorrhaging, and her lungs were badly damaged. Joan is home now, but the uncertainty continues. She may have severe brain damage and cerebral palsy. She may never be able to swallow or suck. "When I hold her in my arms, she's my baby and I want her to live," says Debbie. "We appreciate every day we have with her, but sometimes you can't help but wonder whether this is the best for her. We don't know that she'll ever be able to enjoy her life. . . ."

Her husband adds: "There was a time when we were afraid she would die. Now there are times when we're afraid she'll live. Without this technology, she would have died naturally, and we wouldn't have had to ask ourselves these questions. Maybe that would have been better." [Kantrowitz et al., 1988]

This harsh reality has raised a social dilemma. Parents and doctors alike obviously wish every newborn the fullest chance of survival. But some experts question "the practice of providing highly sophisticated and very costly therapies to the extremely small newborns . . . when the probability of intact survival remains very low" (Nordio et al., 1986). Including the costs of immediate neonatal care, repeated hospitalizations and medications over the first year, and a prorated portion of the expenses for every very-very-low-birthweight infant who dies, the cost of saving a newborn under 1,000 grams is close to half a million dollars. Hospital expenses alone for an infant with respiratory distress syndrome exceed those for an adult's kidney transplant and rival those for heart or bone marrow transplantation (Paneth, 1992). If the same money were spent on the prevention of very-very-low birthweight, there is no doubt that many more lives would be saved and the total hardship and disability would be much less.

Further, the intensive effort to save the life of a tiny baby is seldom matched in the care of the infant once the crisis is over. Few parents are prepared to understand the needs of the very tiny, immature infant, or to cope with the demands of the special infant at home. Medical insurance does not usually cover at-home care, and specialized education for children is sometimes unavailable until they are preschool age—years after such help is required. Many such children spend months, even years, in custodial care in hospitals because no other alternative is available.

Most developmentalists feel that the choice should not be between ensuring the survival of one tiny infant and providing early prenatal care for a dozen high-risk pregnancies or specialized infant care for a disabled child. Moreover, it is unclear who (or how) such choices would be made in a social context of limited public resources. No one would want to suggest that ensuring the survival of any child's life is not worth the cost, but many question the moral myopia of narrowly focusing on high-tech heroics. As one physician put it, "Our ability to offer expensive, cutting-edge technological support to 1-kilogram infants of homeless mothers contrasts sadly with our inability (or unwillingness) to provide housing for their mothers" (Paneth, 1992). Perhaps the best approach to this policy dilemma is to recognize that in the earliest stages of life, as at any point in the life span, the best medicine is preventive medicine.

h

common complications of birth is that labor does not
ly as it should. Sometimes contractions seem to weaken,
r; sometimes, despite strong contractions, the cervix di-
entimeter per hour; sometimes the fetus does not move
he birth canal.

for a long labor are many. For instance, the fetus's head
ative to the woman's pelvis, or the woman might be over-
, or overmedicated. The difficulty can also be in the posi-
or instance, about one labor in four begins with the fetus's
st the mother's back, allowing less flexibility than the
o-front position. In this case, appropriately called "back
ually rotates spontaneously just at transition. However, if
facing in the wrong direction, the second stage of labor
d more difficult. Another difficulty arises when the fetus
birth in a **breech position**, that is, buttocks-first instead of
it difficult for the head to follow quickly. Breech births
ercent of all births.

stresses necessarily causes problems for the fetus. How-
n a long and stressful birth, there is the possibility of
anoxia, the lack of oxygen referred to earlier. Moments of anoxia occur even
in a normal birth, as strong contractions temporarily squeeze the umbilical
cord. This is not harmful to the fetus, any more than momentarily holding
one's breath is. As we have seen, however, repeated and prolonged anoxia
can cause brain damage and even death, especially if the fetus is undernourished or preterm. In this respect, breech births pose a particular risk:
the fact that the head is the last part to be born means that breathing problems are more likely to occur.

Monitoring Labor

In recent years, various medical techniques have helped to reduce the number of long and stressful labors (Charlish, 1991; American College of Obstetricians, 1992). For example, in virtually all hospital births, the condition of
the fetus and the progression of labor are closely monitored every few minutes as labor intensifies. This can be done by a birth attendant, who measures the dilatation of the cervix, checks the fetal heart rate with a
stethoscope, clocks the frequency and duration of contractions, and checks
on the mother in other ways, including assessing her energy, mood, and desires. Observation can also be done continuously with an electronic **fetal
monitor** that automatically charts the fetal heart rate, the frequency of contractions, and other information. Fetal monitoring of the heart rate can help
detect anoxia, for example, thus indicating when delivery should occur
quickly so serious damage does not occur. Fetal monitoring also reveals
when a labor that appears to be difficult is actually creating no unusual
stress for the fetus and therefore can continue without intervention.

The most commonly used fetal monitor is an external one, which is
strapped around the mother's belly and attached to a screen that shows a
continuous record of fetal heart rate and uterine contractions. A newer external method, telemetry, which employs a battery strapped to the woman's

breech position A birth in which the
newborn emerges from the uterus
buttocks-first instead of headfirst.

fetal monitor An electronic instrument that charts fetal heart rate,
frequency of contractions, and
other information.

thigh, has the added advantage of allowing the woman to walk around. Fetal monitors can also be internal. The most common internal monitor involves the use of a tiny electrode that is inserted through the vagina and attached to the fetus's skull. This intrusive measure gives a more accurate indication of fetal stress but can also be a cause of maternal distress.

Although electronic fetal monitoring provides an effective and "high-tech" means of continuously checking the birth process, recent research suggests the old-fashioned stethoscope method of monitoring labor may actually contribute to better outcomes, as indexed by higher Apgar scores and lower infant mortality (Shy et al., 1990). One possible explanation of this surprising finding is that medical personnel respond more quickly when they actually hear a fading fetal heart beat, or see the woman overwhelmed by cascading contractions, than when they simply notice trouble being registered on a monitor.

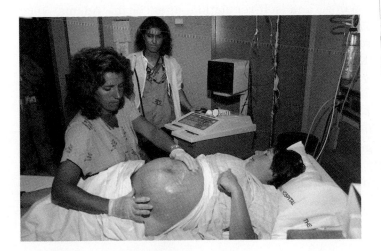 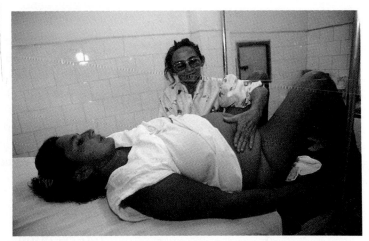

FIGURE 5.6 The Brazilian midwife on the right and the North American obstetrician on the left both use an experienced hand, rather than a fetal monitor, to examine the position of the fetus and the strength of the contraction as labor begins. Research suggests that the practiced touch of a skilled birth attendant helps the mother to relax, and thus makes contractions more effective and less painful.

Another explanation of the benefits of the stethoscope method is that the direct personal attention provided by traditional monitoring of birth is itself a positive influence. Many studies have found that mothers in labor are more comfortable when they have constant companionship, and that such comfort translates into shorter, easier labors (Enkin et al., 1989). In Guatemala, for example, the continuous emotional support provided by a *doula,* an experienced woman who offers guidance, encouragement, and companionship during labor, has been associated with shorter labors and fewer medical complications during birth (Sosa et al., 1980). Indeed, a survey of nonindustrialized societies found that in 96 percent of the cultures, companionship in labor was believed to be so important that women were never allowed to labor alone (Lozoff, 1992). A study in the United States revealed similar findings: women who had been randomly assigned a *doula* upon their arrival at the hospital had shorter labors, used fewer medications during labor, and delivered infants with fewer complications than women who had not received the support of a labor assistant (Kennell et al., 1991; Rosen, 1991). For many women, of course, a husband, mother, or close friend is able to provide encouragement and help throughout labor and delivery.

When monitoring reveals a weak or erratic fetal heart rate, or birth is not progressing as rapidly as it should, or the mother becomes exhausted or shows signs of physical stress (e.g., high blood pressure), assistance can be provided in several ways. In each case, the benefits of these procedures must be thoughtfully weighed against the potential risks they pose for either the mother or the fetus, or both.

Medication

For many mothers, anesthetic medications ease the experience of labor and delivery, and most women expect that birth would be assisted with such drugs. It has long been known, however, that anesthetics cross the placenta and enter the bloodstream of the fetus. Consequently, many of the anesthetics, analgesics, and sedatives that are intended to relax the mother and reduce her discomfort during labor have a significant effect on the fetus before it is born, resulting in diminished alertness, greater irritability, and poorer reflexes, feeding, and self-regulation after birth (Adams, 1989; Brackbill et al., 1985; Lester et al., 1982). These effects are enhanced if multiple medications are used, or if medications are used early in labor (Friedman & Neff, 1987). Moreover, because the baby's immature liver and kidney do not rid the tiny body of toxins as quickly as mature organs do, these drugs accumulate and remain in the baby's body long after birth, and exert a continuing effect on the newborn's alertness and irritability. Thus many parents who look forward to an alert, responsive newborn discover instead that their baby is groggy or agitated. Fortunately, any such aftereffects are temporary, usually lasting a day or two, unless the dose of the medication was unusually high, or the newborn was unexpectedly vulnerable (Rosenblith, 1992).

Intervention

Once labor has reached the second stage, other techniques can hasten delivery if there are signs of difficulty. These include the use of **forceps**, an instrument that fits around the fetal head, or a **vacuum extractor**, a special suction cup that fits over the top of the fetal head and can be used to pull the fetus through the birth canal. These devices do not pose significant risks to the baby, although they can result in bruises that disappear within a few days or a week. Once the fetal head begins to emerge, an **episiotomy**—a surgical incision in the skin surrounding the vagina (usually done under a local anesthetic) is often performed to speed birth by a few minutes.

When the fetus or mother is in more immediate danger, or when a normal vaginal delivery is likely to be hazardous, a doctor may recommend a **Cesarean section**, in which the mother's abdomen and uterus are surgically cut and the fetus is removed. Because it is a major surgical procedure, Cesarean delivery significantly prolongs the mother's recovery from childbirth and impairs her ability to care for the newborn immediately after birth, partly owing to her prolonged hospitalization. Even after returning home, she is less likely to feel up to cradling, feeding, and bathing her infant when recovering from a "C-section." Nevertheless, Cesareans now account for nearly one birth bin four in the United States, a dramatic increase from the 5 percent rate in 1968. Cesarean surgery is the most common surgical proce-

forceps   A large, spoonlike medical instrument sometimes used to facilitate or hasten birth. The forceps hold the fetal head and allow the fetus to be pulled through the birth canal.

vacuum extractor   A special suction cup, used to facilitate or hasten birth, that fits over the top of the fetal head and allows the fetus to be pulled through the birth canal.

episiotomy   A small surgical incision that is made in the skin surrounding the vagina to allow the fetal head to emerge without tearing the vaginal opening.

Cesarean section   A surgical procedure in which an obstetrician cuts open the abdomen and uterus to deliver the baby. This technique is used when the fetus or mother is in immediate danger or when the fetus is unable to travel safely through the birth canal.

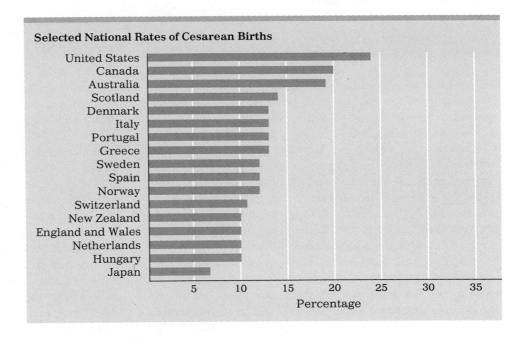

FIGURE 5.7 The United States spends more money on obstetrics than any other nation in the world, largely because of its high-tech, hospital-based approach to birth. This is clearly reflected in its rate of Cesarean births. Given that the United States has higher low-birthweight rates than fourteen other industrialized nations and higher infant mortality rates than twenty-one other nations, many public health experts believe that much of the obstetric expenditure should be directed instead toward improved family planning and prenatal care.

dure in the United States, which ranks highest among the world's nations in the rate of Cesarean deliveries (see Figure 5.7) (Notzon, 1990).

Some Cesarean deliveries are performed because of emergencies that arise during labor. Many others are performed even before labor begins, when sonograms and stress tests reveal that vaginal birth will probably be too stressful—as is likely to be the case with a breech birth in a relatively young or old first-time mother, or when the fetus's head is too large to pass through the birth canal, or when the newborn is known to be medically at risk. But many experts as well as laypeople are now convinced that a considerable proportion of Cesarean deliveries are not medically necessary but are performed for the sake of convenience—the doctor's and the hospital's, as well as the patient's. Since this benefit comes at the cost of a prolonged recovery for the mother, efforts to reserve Cesarean deliveries for medically warranted occasions have strengthened in recent years (Stafford, 1990).

All observers agree that, worldwide, medical intervention at birth saves millions of lives (see Table 5.2)—those of mothers as well as infants—and that its absence is a major reason the maternal mortality rate in the developing and least developed nations is nearly ten times that of developed countries (United Nations, 1994).

TABLE 5.2

Maternal Mortality and Assisted Birth

	Maternal deaths per 10,000 births	Percentage of births with no trained health worker
Industrialized nations	1	2 percent
Developing nations	35	45 percent
Least developed nations	59	72 percent

Source: United Nations, 1994.

A CLOSER LOOK

The Medicalization of Birth

As recently as a century ago, everywhere in the world, childbirth was the leading cause of death for women between the ages of 15 and 50, killing 1 in every 10 delivering women. At the same time, 1 in every 10 babies failed to survive the birth process. Now, thanks to hundreds of medical indicators, precautions, practices, and interventions that can be performed immediately before, during, or after birth, the maternal death rate in developed nations has plummeted to 1 in every 10,000, while newborn death has decreased to 1 in every 100 (Goldenberg, 1992).

But many aspects of the medicalization that has produced this turnaround are under serious attack, not only by feminists, midwives, and home-birth advocates (Gaskin, 1990; Inch, 1984; Mitford, 1992; Rothman, 1989), but also by some developmental psychologists and medical doctors (Campbell & MacFarlene, 1987; Enkin et al., 1989). Essentially the critics contend that by treating every birth as a medical emergency waiting to happen rather than as a normal, natural event, the emotional development of the new family suffers needlessly.

Let us look at some of the specifics of birth within the United States. About 98 percent of American births occur in a hospital, and include most, if not all, of the following particulars. As soon as a woman in labor walks into the hospital, she is placed in a wheel chair and taken to be "prepped" (typically she has her pubic hair shaved), is given an enema, and has her vital signs (blood pressure, temperature, heart rate) checked and recorded. Then she receives a glucose IV inserted in her wrist, has a fetal monitor strapped around her belly, and receives an internal examination to see how far the cervix has dilated—along with instructions and warnings about the need to stay in bed without food or drink while labor progresses. The message of all these initial procedures is clear: once she crosses the hospital threshold, the mother-to-be is not a healthy person undergoing a natural process but a fragile and helpless person, in potential need of emergency intervention and totally under the control of others.

As the hours pass by, an estimated 80 percent of women are given a pitocin IV drip to intensify and speed up contractions, and 90 percent are given some sort of anesthesia, either through the IV or by means of an epidural, a spinal injection that usually deadens all sensations in the lower body (Davis-Floyd, 1992). As the moment of birth nears, the woman's wishes are increasingly subordinated to the orders of the doctors and nurses, who warn her of the damage she might inflict on her baby if she does not obey. They examine her frequently to check on the dilatation of the cervix; they tell her to push or not push as the fetal head begins to move through the birth canal; they respond to their own interpretations of what they see on the fetal monitor rather than to the woman's perceptions

of what is occurring within her or to her wishes regarding medication, examination, surgery, and the like. For one American woman in four, these various procedures ultimately result in a Cesarean birth. For the remaining 75 percent, an episiotomy is performed, and after birth, more drugs are administered to the mother to aid delivery of the placenta and repair of the episiotomy.

From several perspectives, there seems little to fault in this medicalized, technological approach to birth, especially since most American women choose to give birth in a hospital rather than at home, want relief of pain instead of a drug-free birth, and expect to be given a certain amount of medical attention rather than to be left alone. Indeed, contrary to the notion that doctors invariably insist on medical procedures despite the wishes of their patients, some women demand anesthesia and even Cesarean sections from medical staff who sometimes are reluctant to give them (Davis-Floyd, 1992).

Further, in many cases, medications make births easier and safer than they would otherwise be, with few long-lasting risks to the mother or newborn. Most important, when a fetus is known to be vulnerable, as a preterm fetus might be, to the stresses of a vaginal birth or to the suppressing effects that anesthesia has on the immature central nervous system, the physician can quickly perform a Cesarean, surgery that is stress-free for the baby. Indeed, some obstetricians have argued that every birth would be easier for all concerned if it were done by Cesarean (Beecham, 1989).

But one question is not usually asked by the medical personnel directly involved with the birth event: How will the mother, father, and child be affected by hospital procedures in the hours and days after birth? Some negative effects can arise directly from the use of medications, which inevitably remain in the bloodstream of both mother and child and slow down their ability to focus on each other and enjoy their early interactions (Adams, 1989; Brackbill et al., 1988; Murray et al., 1981). Further, specifics such as the pain of the mother's stitches from the episiotomy or from a C-section, the newborn's eye irritation from the silver nitrate, and the separations imposed on the new family by medical procedures and hospital protocol add to the difficulty of the early family relationship.

The most problematic effect of medicalized birth may result, not directly from the medical procedures themselves, but from the psychological impact they may have on the parents-to-be. When the mother and father are knowledgeable and instrumental participants in the birth of their child, they tend to feel powerful as well as "full of love and compassion and support" (Davis-Floyd, 1992). Although such feelings are most likely to arise from a home birth, or one in which medical intervention is minimal, they can also develop in highly technological births if the parents feel that the technologies and medications are serving them rather than dominating them. On the other hand, if the hospital authorities and procedures make parents feel helpless and ignorant and convince mothers-to-be that they are incapable of giving birth properly and safely without expert intervention, then the postnatal result can be depression and anger that last for days, even weeks, disrupting the family's relationships.

Of course, medical interventions that are disruptive to the family formation can be justified when they are used in response to unavoidable medical emergencies. However, many routine obstetrical procedures are not medically warranted: shaving the pubic hair, for example, is actually more likely to lead to infection; having the mother lie down during labor actually slows the birth process; fetal monitoring and pitocin are often used routinely, even with no indications of their being needed, and often lead to unnecessary intervention. Many other labor practices are likewise rooted in tradition rather than in true medical necessity (Enkin et al., 1989; Tew, 1990).

This is most clearly seen in international comparisons, which reveal the extreme variability of obstetrical practice, a variability that must be caused more by cultural differences than by differences in the rate of emergency conditions. In a study of twenty-three European nations, for example, the rate of obstetrical intervention (e.g., Cesarean sections or forceps deliveries) ranged from 6 to 20 percent. Further, in some countries, women were denied anesthesia that they wanted and that is routinely given elsewhere; in other countries, women were given drugs they did not want. Similar disparities were evident in whether or not the woman could move during labor, whether she could deliver her baby in a squatting position, and whether she could have her husband, mother, or friends present at birth (Phaff, 1986). Although medical research now affirms that most women can have a vaginal birth in a subsequent pregnancy following a Cesarean section, in the United States and Canada, only 8 percent do so, compared to 40 percent in Norway and Scotland (Goldman et al., 1993).

Notable variation occurs not only between countries but within them. The study of European nations found that in Italy, for instance, the episiotomy rate was 90 percent in Rome but only 25 percent in rural areas (Phaff, 1986). In Brazil, the rate of Cesarean sections reaches 90 percent in some of the private hospitals in Rio, while it is only about 5 percent in the poorest areas of the northeast.

Within the United States, a careful look at interventions in the birth process, hospital by hospital and doctor by doctor, makes the case even clearer. In the state of Washington, the rate of Cesareans in church and military hospitals is half that in private hospitals, even though private patients are more likely to be in good health and to have had excellent prenatal care. Clearly the explanation for much of this disparity is that American doctors have a "financial disincentive" to perform Cesareans on poorer patients, because their medical insurance is less likely to cover it (McKenzie & Stephenson, 1993). Even among wealthier patients, the rates vary for reasons that are not medical. A study that compared obstetricians in one Detroit hospital found that their rate of Cesarean sections for private, low-risk patients ranged from 19 to 42 percent. One doctor delivered virtually all his breech babies by C-section, whereas another delivered none of them that way unless other complications occurred (e.g., a premature fetus with anoxia) (Goyent et al., 1989).

A related reason for the extensive use of monitoring, medication, and surgery is that many doctors practice aggressive "defensive medicine," because they are wary of being sued, especially by their better-educated, private patients. Their fears are justified: more than two out of every three American obstetricians have, in fact, been sued, and consequently malpractice insurance for obstetricians typically exceeds $200,000 per year. It is not that obstetricians are more negligent than other physicians but rather that, when unexpected birth problems do occur, parents often seek to blame some expert rather than accept the possibility that some elusive factor, such as inherited vulnerability, or prenatal teratogens, or the inherent risks of birth, may have been the cause. Further, in cases of birth mishaps, juries are inclined to find doctors guilty for not marshaling the entire arsenal of medical technology rather than to credit them for letting nature take its course, even though research suggests the latter route is often wisest. Given the financial odds against them, it is no wonder that doctors err on the side of active intervention.

Obviously, the costs and benefits of medicalized childbirth vary from birth to birth, and ensuring a long and healthy life for mother and child must outweigh other considerations. However, from a developmental perspective, the cost-benefit equation seems off in its timing: medical emergencies are anticipated and treated long before they occur, while normal births are not allowed to proceed without intervention, even though natural births result in less pain and more joy for the new family in the days ahead. A step toward a more balanced equation would be to treat each birth as the unique beginning that it actually is. Then parents-to-be, as well as medical personnel, would analyze and weigh each routine, each medication, and each intervention for its impact—negative and positive—on the prospective newborn. They would act, or simply wait, accordingly.

At the same time, many critics (including some doctors) believe that medical procedures tend to be overused in typical hospital settings, resulting in more expensive and less humane birth experiences (see A Closer Look, pp. 158–159). If birth is routinely treated as a medical emergency that must be medically managed lest disaster occur, rather than as a natural event that typically needs little assistance, the inadvertent casualty may be the new family, whose emotional needs are sacrificed for medical precautions, protocols, and procedures (Davis-Floyd, 1992).

Birth as a Family Event

Simply describing the sequence and procedures of birth tells little about how all the participants are affected by their experience. The psychological and social effects of birth and the days thereafter may have profound and long-lasting influences on all family members.

The Baby's Experience

How does it feel to be born? Buddha called birth one of the inevitable sufferings of human existence. Otto Rank, a psychoanalyst, thought of birth as a traumatic event that affects all of later life. He reasoned that the experience of being thrust from the comfort and security of the uterus into a harsh world of hunger, cold, and noise causes lifelong fear and anxiety, and a continuing effort—at least symbolically—to return to the womb (Rank, 1929). Although this idea caught the imagination of a good many theorists and brought the term "birth trauma" into common use, there is no scientific evidence to support such a theory. In fact, some specifics support the opposite conclusion—that nature protects newborns from birth trauma in several ways. The newborn's head bones, for example, are flexible and can overlap to facilitate passage through the birth canal. In addition, as the mother labors to give birth, especially if her breathing is in sync with the rhythmic contractions, her body produces hormones similar to those that uplift athletes in competition, making them resistant to stress and pain. These hormones flow through the umbilicus and reach the fetus.

The notion that newborns are traumatized by birth is also contradicted by close observation of them in the first minutes after birth. If they are kept warm and held securely or wrapped snugly in a soft blanket, babies who are only a few seconds old quickly become peaceful, alert, and curious—a far cry from the reaction one would expect after a traumatic experience.

Indeed, newborns' wide-eyed interest at their first glimpse of the world outside the uterus suggests that—barring crisis or exhaustion—infants are born, not traumatized, but energized and ready to experience and learn about their new environment. One indicator of this is the typical baby's response to the **Brazelton Neonatal Behavioral Assessment Scale (NBAS)** (Brazelton, 1983). This twenty-six item test, developed by T. Berry Brazelton, a noted pediatrician and developmentalist, assesses the infant's skill and style in responding to the environment through social interaction, sensory exploration, and the like. Behaviors such as putting a hand to the mouth, startling to a sudden noise, cuddling into the mother's body,

Brazelton Neonatal Behavioral Assessment Scale (NBAS) A rating of twenty-six items of a newborn's behavior, such as responsiveness, strength of reflexes, and irritability.

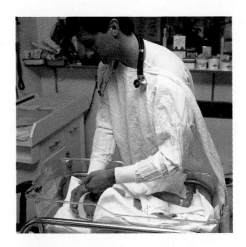

FIGURE 5.8 This doctor is using his finger to test the newborn's sucking reflex. Estimating the strength of that reflex is one part of the Brazelton Neonatal Behavioral Assessment Scale, which measures twenty-five other capabilities in the typical newborn's repertoire—many of which are surprising to parents.

staring at a bright light, or grabbing an adult's finger are elicited, measured, and scored in the NBAS. Changes of state, such as from sleeping to waking or from alertness to crying, are particularly significant, as is the ability to "self-soothe," that is, to return to a state of alertness after a burst of crying. Built into the administration of the test is the recognition that all babies are different: the examiner is trained to elicit the best performance from each particular baby, and to stop the test midway, or to reschedule another session, if a newborn seems too tired, irritable, or distracted to do his or her best.

The Brazelton test is time-consuming and thus is not usually administered unless there is a special concern. However, maybe it should be routine. When parents observe their newborn being tested on the NBAS, their usual reaction is amazement at the brand-new infant's many capacities. Indeed, one use of the test is to demonstrate to parents the nuances of their child's capabilities and temperament, so that parents can more quickly "read" the complexity of their baby's behavior style (Brazelton, 1990).

The NBAS is also used to indicate the baby's overall birth experience (Brazelton et al., 1987). It is particularly useful in detecting reduced responsiveness that may have resulted from a heavy dose of certain drugs—either illegal substances or alcohol ingested right before labor or medications administered during birth. Finally, the NBAS sometimes provides the first sign that something may be neurologically amiss with the infant, requiring additional medical intervention or parental counseling. For the most part, however, the Brazelton indicates that newborns are ready and eager to experience their world, especially the social interactions that it provides.

The Parents' Experience

As we have seen, a number of biological and medical factors interact to determine whether a birth is simple and quick or complicated and lengthy. However, social and contextual factors, much more than physiological ones, determine both the mother's and father's overall experience of birth. Such factors can make a long labor exhilarating or a short one terrifying. They can make both parents swear "never again" after what physicians would call an easy birth, or can make even an emergency Cesarean so rewarding that the parents are ready to plan their next pregnancy. Two contextual factors are particularly important: preparation for birth and social support.

Preparation for Childbirth

Until a decade or two ago, first-time parents-to-be often approached childbirth with negative feelings picked up from other women or popular culture. Indeed, one study of women who were pregnant for the first time in the 1970s found that almost all had negative attitudes about giving birth (Leifer, 1980). Some attributed their apprehension to television programs in which, as one woman put it, "whenever they have a woman bearing a child, it seems like she's screaming horribly or she's fainting, she can't control herself." Others had picked up their attitudes from their mothers and older women whose view generally seemed to be "It's horrible at the time but . . . you soon forget it."

Fortunately, today more and more future parents are preparing for birth, by gathering knowledge, interviewing and choosing doctors, attending birth classes, and talking to friends who have recently had babies. Even a generation ago, such friends would not have been able to report much, since fathers were excluded from the delivery room and mothers were usually unconscious at the critical moments. But now almost every new parent has a birth story he or she is eager to tell.

One reason for the change is that, over the past thirty years, feminists and others have advocated that women should be involved in their own health care, and that birth—as a normal female experience—belongs to the woman and her family as much as to the doctor (Arms, 1975; Rothman, 1989). Men also have become much more assertive of their rights as fathers, and this has led to their greater supportive involvement in the overall birth process.

Another reason for the newer active role parents take in preparing for childbirth is directly tied to one of the theories of psychology explained in Chapter 2, namely the Pavlovian theory of conditioned response. In 1951 a French obstetrician named Fernald Lamaze was visiting the Soviet Union, where he observed doctors there applying Pavlov's theories of classical conditioning to childbirth. The Soviet doctors were teaching women to associate birth with pleasant feelings and relaxing mental images, such as a peaceful rural scene, and to lessen discomfort by using specific breathing techniques. To Lamaze's amazement, many women who were thus prepared gave birth without medication and without the screams of agony that were standard in Western Europe and North America.

Lamaze refined these breathing and relaxation practices into what is now known as the **Lamaze method** (Lamaze, 1958). These techniques are taught in a series of prenatal classes, where expectant mothers practice them so often that they became a conditioned response. A key feature of the Lamaze method is the presence of a labor coach, often the father, who learns how to direct and guide the woman as she employs these techniques. Ideally, certain sights, sensations, breathing patterns, and the touch of one's labor coach become associated with self-control and peaceful thoughts. In short, these techniques allow women to concentrate on the work and control, rather than the pain, of having a baby.

Many other methods of birth are possible, including birth under water, birth that emphasizes moving in harmony with contractions rather than attempting to control them, birth in which the father's role (coaching, massaging, monitoring, and providing support and encouragement) is almost as important as the mother's, and so on (Kitzinger, 1989). Study after study shows that, with all these techniques, it is the woman's knowledge and emotional preparation, as well as the specific breathing and relaxation methods, that make the birth process quicker, less medicated, and easier on both mother and baby (Ball, 1987).

One recent study of one hundred middle-class women giving birth for the first time found that those whose expectations, preparation, and understanding of birth corresponded with their actual birth experiences tended to feel proud of themselves and happy with their babies (Davis-Floyd, 1992). Interestingly, their expectations were quite varied. At one extreme were women who expected nothing short of a completely natural birth (one such woman quit her obstetrician when he told her that a sonogram was a stan-

Lamaze method A childbirth technique involving breathing and relaxation exercises that reduce the pain of labor and allow the mother to help control the birth process.

FIGURE 5.9 The woman on the right is a Lamaze coach. When the Lamaze method first came into practice, such coaches accompanied women in the labor room themselves. Now most Lamaze coaches instruct the father in the art of coaching, which includes helping to pace and monitor breathing, as shown here.

dard and necessary procedure: she subsequently gave birth at home, with almost no medical assistance). At the other extreme were women who expected birth to be a highly technological event but anticipated that they themselves would decide what specific technologies were needed (one such woman refused to allow an internal monitor to be attached to her fetus's scalp and demanded, and got, a Cesarean-section). Most of the women in this study, however, fell somewhere between these extremes, undergoing a modified form of natural childbirth that used some of the standard medications and routines of the hospital. These women knew what to expect, and they felt quite happy with the birth process. By contrast, the women who knew almost nothing about the process (there were nine) tended to be terri-

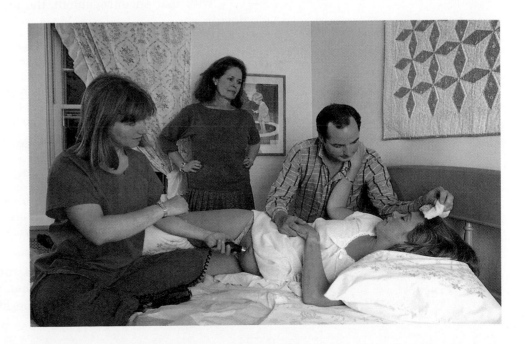

FIGURE 5.10 While the birth attendant checks the fetal heart, the husband wipes the brow of the laboring woman as her mother looks on. This is a cultural switch: in earlier generations of home births, the mother was the main caregiver during labor, while the future father waited anxiously in another room.

fied and needed a great deal of medical assistance. Those who fared worst of all were another nine who had wanted to have natural childbirth but, because of some lapse in their knowledge or in their communication with their doctor, had not been able to (one woman had accepted pitocin not realizing that it might—and did—cause her to lose control of her contractions; the doctor of another planned a Cesarean without informing the mother-to-be). These women tended to feel "miserable, agonizing miserable" or "devastated by the whole experience" (Davis-Floyd, 1992).

Birth Attendants

The sensitivity of doctors, nurses, and midwives to the psychological needs of the mother and father can be essential to making birth a satisfying experience. Encouraging words can ease a lengthy labor, while impersonal and sarcastic comments can spoil the entire event.

The interplay of the various individuals involved in a hospital birth is shown in the following account, provided by a woman who, soon after she had entered the hospital, heard the doctor tell the nurse:

> "Prep her, we're going to cut it out." I said, "Hold it, hold it—you're not going to do anything until you tell me what is going on here." He said, "Baby time. You're not dilating; you need a C-section." I said, "That will be fine as long as you can write down a medical reason why I need a section."

This woman explains that she knew that the doctor could be sued if he did a C-section without a medical reason, and she knew that there was no reason apparent yet. She also found out later that she

> was the only patient in labor on Saturday, and I don't think he wanted to hang around all night, but we called our Lamaze teacher, Fran, and she came to the hospital. I had supportive nurses, but even though they couldn't contradict him they could say "You're doing fine, the baby's fine, everything's fine."

With that encouragement, the mother-to-be was, in fact, fine, but the doctor

> was very nasty. He would come in, send my husband out, check me, yell at me because I wasn't doing what he told me to do. He made my husband sign a paper saying that we would take full responsibility for the death of my child and all this. "You know," he said, "you're killing this baby because you won't have a section." I said, "I'll have one if you tell me why." He said "Just because I say you need one," and I said "That's not good enough." . . .
>
> If I can block him out of the picture, then everything was wonderful, 'cause my husband was great . . . as soon as he would come back into the room everything would be okay . . . and the doctor thought Fran was a nurse, and so when he would send Steve out, she couldn't say anything, but she would stand there and hold my hand and squeeze it all the time he was yelling and screaming and being really nasty, and then as soon as the guy would leave she would hurry Steve back in [quoted in Davis-Floyd, 1992].

This story ends happily, with the birth of a fine, 8½-pound baby, and a mother delighted with her husband and baby, glad she "just refused to let the doctor ruin it." But it is clear that, without the help of the nurses, the Lamaze teacher and, most of all, the husband, the birth story would have been very different.

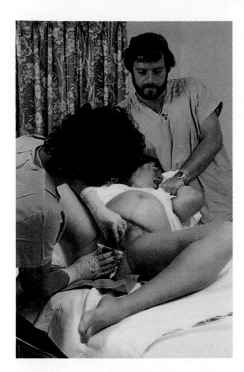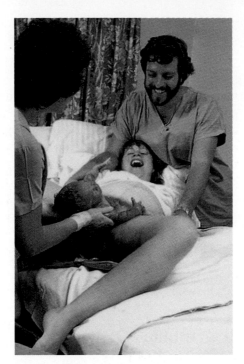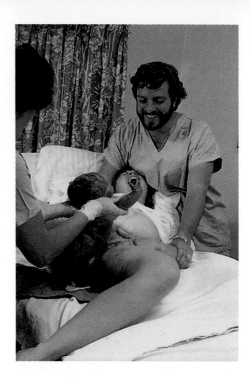

FIGURE 5.11 Many hospitals have tried to make hospital births more homelike, as in this "birthing room." This birth occurs on a bed, not a steel table, and the mother is aided by a midwife and her husband rather than by unfamiliar doctors and nurses.

In truth, the diversity of attitude and approach among medical attendants at birth is vast, and many new parents laud their doctors and midwives to the heavens. However, given the variability of human-relations skills and cultural values that can surround hospital birth, it seems that the personal traits and attitudes of the particular birth attendants can be a powerful determinant in how smooth and satisfying the birth process is for all concerned. One study of postnatal depression (experienced by about 10 percent of all mothers in the days and weeks after birth) found that the degree of support from doctors, nurses, and midwives was much more influential on the occurrence of "baby blues" than any physical variables such as ease of labor or use of anesthesia (Ball, 1987).

The Father's Participation

Before 1970 fathers in most Western cultures were rarely allowed in the delivery room. It was thought that, at best, they would merely be in the way and might even disrupt the birth process by becoming faint or ill. This was in striking contrast to the role of fathers in other, non-Western cultures, who sometimes assume a crucial place in the rituals surrounding childbirth and in the birth process itself (Parke, 1981). Over the past generation, however, it has become generally recognized in many Western cultures that the father can have a highly positive impact during birth, not only as a help to his partner but also as an informed participant in the birth process. Accordingly, hospital regulations are changing. Increasingly, fathers are present when their infants are born, even when medical intervention, such as a Cesarean, is needed. This is true in many countries around the world (Lamb, 1987). A review of fatherhood in Britain explains:

> The presence of the father at birth is so clearly expected in Britain that it is probably as hard for a man to stay out of the delivery room as it was for him to get in it only a decade ago. The extent to which this has now become conventional was underlined by the widely reported presence of the Prince of Wales at the birth of both his sons. At the time of the Prince's own birth, as several newspapers remarked, the Duke of Edinburgh was playing squash. [Jackson, 1987]

The results of such participation by the father are generally very positive, for the father as well as for the mother. For some fathers, being part of the birth process is an indelible, deeply moving experience, as the following quotation suggests:

> I . . . coached her on pushing, holding her around the shoulders as support during each push. She was magnificent. Slowly I began to feel a kind of holiness about all of us there, performing an ageless human drama, a grand ritual of life. The trigger was probably the emergence of the baby's head—coughing, twisting, covered with blood, as purple as error, so eager for life—that set me into such intensities of joy and excitement that I cannot possibly adequately describe them. It was all so powerful I felt as though my head might come off, that I might simply explode with joy and a sense of participation in a profound mystery . . . [quoted by Tanzer & Block, 1976]

The Sibling's Experience

For many children, the birth of a younger brother or sister is a stressful, unhappy event, but several factors can influence whether or not this is the case (Vandell, 1987). One factor is preparation. If the child is told what to expect in the days surrounding the birth, and is reassured that becoming a big brother or sister will have its benefits, adjustment will be easier.

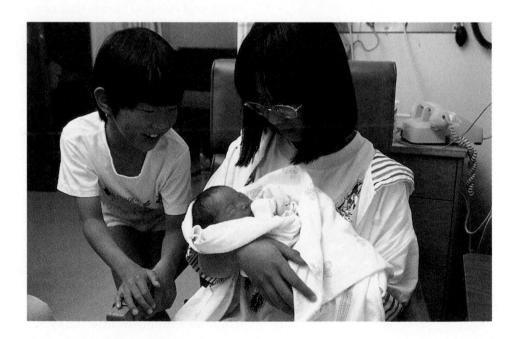

FIGURE 5.12 From the looks of things here, sibling rivalry will not be much of a problem for this newborn's 9-year-old brother and 12-year-old sister (holding the infant). This is so, in part, because of their age, but their being included in the baby's nurturance from the start will also be a factor.

The birth itself can be traumatic for a young sibling. If the mother goes to the hospital, the child at home may feel abandoned and frightened, especially if the child associates hospitals with sickness and death. Showing the child photographs of his or her own early days at the hospital, and making plans for a special outing with the father when the mother is away, may relieve some of the child's anxieties. Many hospitals now allow young siblings to visit soon after a birth, and planning trips to see Mom and the new baby can also be reassuring.

If the birth occurs at home, the adults' excitement about the event might make them forget the young child's perspective. As you will see in Chapter 9, most preschool children judge an event by appearances, and thus a joyous, arduous, and naturally bloody birth might be viewed by the child as a frightening trauma. An important part of preparing for home birth, then, might be arranging for young siblings to be cared for away from the home during labor—or, at least, having a close adult with them to help them interpret and understand what they are witnessing.

In addition to intellectual and emotional preparation, children benefit from practical preparation as well. If the older child will need to sleep in a new bed, or have a new babysitter, or adjust to a new routine of any sort, it is helpful to initiate the change months before the new baby arrives.

However, even when the child is prepared for the new arrival, and even when the birth itself is not frightening, difficulties often arise. The parents inevitably spend substantial time and effort on the new infant, and less on the older child. They are likely to be more tired, and to have less patience and energy, than usual. Understandably, they hope that the older child will be quiet, self-sufficient, and even helpful. Understandably, the older child may feel slighted and disappoint those hopes. Especially if the big brother or sister was an only-child, or if the new sibling requires extraordinary attention because of a handicap, the older child may be considerably disturbed by the birth of a baby. Indeed, some psychologists refer to the only-child's adjustment to the arrival of a sibling as a process of **dethronement**, in which the former little king or queen of the household must suddenly relinquish his or her autocratic power.

The Beginning of Bonding

One of the topics of human development that has captured much popular attention is the concept of the **parent-newborn bond**, the almost instant connection that can occur between parents and their newborn children as they share physical contact in the first hours after birth. Over the past decade, hundreds of newspaper and magazine articles have waxed rhapsodic over the joy and the necessity of forming this special bond. Without it, it has been claimed, the long-term love between parent and child will be diminished, and the child will suffer. Many people have come to believe that bonding is a critically important "magical social glue." As one mother who was deprived of early contact said, "It made me feel like a rotten mother when I didn't get to bond with my first two children. Made me feel they were going to go out and rob a bank" (Eyer, 1992).

The best evidence for a parent-newborn bond comes from studies that reveal the formation of a quite specific and powerful bond between mother and newborn in various species of mammals. Many animal mothers, for instance, nourish and nurture their own young and ignore, reject, or mistreat the young of others.

At least three factors have been identified as contributing to this animal bond: hormones released during and after birth that trigger maternal feelings; the mother's identification of her particular infant by its smell; and the timing of the first physical contact between mother and newborn. The

dethronement Adjustment of an only-child to the arrival of a new sibling (the former little autocrat of the household having to suddenly relinquish his or her power).

parent-infant bond The strong feelings of attachment between parents and newborns that are said to arise from their initial contact after birth. The long-term importance of this postpartem bond has been greatly, and dangerously, overblown by the popular media.

FIGURE 5.13 Smell and touch are essential components for mother-infant bonding for many animals, including the nuzzling lions seen here. Fortunately, bonding between humans can occur in varied ways, with early contact not at all essential—though physical intimacy, from breast-feeding at infancy to hugs at adolescence, can obviously foster close attachments between parent and child.

third of these factors can be remarkably precise: in some species, contact must occur within a specific "critical period" in order for bonding to take place. For example, if a baby goat is removed from its mother immediately after birth and returned a few hours later, the mother sometimes rejects it, kicking it and butting it away no matter how pitifully it bleats or how persistently it tries to nurse. However, if the newborn goat remains with the mother who nuzzles and suckles it for the critical first five minutes, and is then separated and later returned, the mother goat welcomes it back (Klopfer, 1971). Sheep and cows react in like fashion, with other species displaying a less pronounced form of the same behavior (Rosenblatt, 1982).

Does a corresponding sensitive time period exist for bonding in humans? Some early research on a few dozen mothers suggested that it does. In these studies, both initial contact in the moments immediately after birth and opportunities for extended contact over the first several days of life were shown to have a positive effect over the first year. This was especially true for first-time mothers who were very young, poor, or otherwise stressed, or who had preterm infants who, by traditional standards, would have been deemed too forbiddingly frail, or too dependent on life-support, to be held or played with. The mothers in these studies who had held their infants soon after birth were more attentive and attached to them at age 1 than were the mothers who had barely seen their infants in the early days (Klaus & Kennell, 1976; Leifer et al., 1972; Grossman et al., 1981).

This research is credited with ending several postpartum hospital practices that were once routine, including whisking newborns away to the nursery right after birth, preventing mothers from seeing and holding their newborns for the first twenty-four hours, and barring parents from setting foot in intensive-care units, much less actually touching their preterm babies. All these practices were originally thought to protect mother and child from infection: all are now seen as unnecessary.

Almost no one now questions the wisdom of early contact between mother and child. It can provide a wondrous beginning to the parent-child relationship, as suggested by this mother's account:

> . . . the second he came out, they put him on my skin and I reached down and I felt him and it was something about having that sticky stuff on my fingers . . . it was really important to feel that waxy stuff and he was crying and I made soothing sounds to him . . . And he started calming down and somehow that makes you feel—like he already knows you, he knows who you are—like animals or something, perhaps the smell of each other . . . it was marvelous to hold him and I just touched him for a really long time and then they took him over but something had already happened. Just instant love. [quoted in Davis-Floyd, 1992]

But is this early contact, as has been claimed, essential for the formation of a positive and healthy mother-child bond? Extensive later research finds that immediate or extended skin-to-skin togetherness makes no specific long-term differences in the mother-child relationship (Lamb, 1982; Myers, 1987).

One social scientist, Diane Eyer, has raised an interesting query: Why was the concept of bonding so quickly accepted, when the research evidence was so sparse? She has concluded that the entire concept of bonding is a social construction, an idea formed as a rally cry against the medicalization, depersonalization, and patriarchy of the traditional hospital birth. Eyer argues that women and developmental experts were ready to believe that newborns and mothers need to be together from the start, and that therefore it took only a tiny nudge from scientific research for the mystique of early bonding to spring forth into general acceptance. She fears that this zealous acceptance comes at a high price, a standard of instant affection and "active love right after birth . . . that many women find impossible to meet" (Eyer, 1992).

Indeed, some developmentalists argue that too rigidly applying the idea of bonding is hardly better than not promoting it at all. If a medicated mother, exhausted from the birth process, is handed her infant for ten minutes or so while the episiotomy is stitched, and then the baby is removed because "bonding" has occurred, she may well feel guilty if she has not experienced the surge of emotion that the mystique of mother love prescribes. Even worse, if an inexperienced mother who believes in bonding is not allowed to hold her infant, all her fears about her own ability to be a good mother may overwhelm her. The same mother who described touching the sticky vernix of her newborn's skin had a quite different experience with her first child:

> They put the baby on my tummy but told me *not* to touch it. They didn't want my hands anywhere near down there . . . Then they took it away and I just turned off like a clam. It was awful . . . I didn't want anything to do with it. . . . It was six weeks before I felt like I really loved him.

Notice that the critical factor here is not the fact of whether or not she held the baby, but the entire social context—with the message that she could contaminate her own baby, and that others could care for it better out of her sight.

Fortunately, the evidence now confirms that the formation of family bonds is flexible. Immediate contact is neither necessary nor sufficient for bonding, as evidenced by the millions of very affectionate and dedicated biological, adoptive, or foster parents who never touched their children when they were newborns. The mother above reports about her first child, "Now I wouldn't part with him . . . he's great." Further, to whatever extent the early postpartum experiences can have an impact, it is not primarily through mother-infant contact per se but through the entire emotional and cognitive context of the birth.

Does this mean that hospital routines can go back to the old ways, separating mother and newborn? No. As one leading developmentalist states:

> I hope that the weakness of the findings for bonding will not be used as an excuse to keep mothers and their infants separated in the hospital. Although such separation may do no permanent harm for most mother-infant pairs, providing contact in a way that is acceptable to the mother surely does not harm and gives much pleasure to many. It is my belief that anything that may make the postpartum period more pleasurable surely is worthwhile. [Rosenblith, 1992]

Overall the ebb and flow of bonding research and practice reminds us that there is no quick fix or single solution to the potential problems of family relationships. Love between parent and child often begins months before birth, and is affected by ongoing parent-infant interactions throughout infancy, childhood, and beyond, as well as by the manifold social contexts in which their relationship flourishes. As the following chapters reveal, while the nature of the parent-infant relationship is critical for healthy development, the specifics of its formation are not.

SUMMARY

The Normal Birth

1. Birth typically begins with contractions that push the fetus, headfirst, out from the uterus and then through the vagina. Birth occurs in three stages with an added phase, called transition, intervening between stages one and two.

2. The Apgar, which rates the neonate's vital signs at 1 minute after birth, and again at 5 minutes after birth, provides a quick evaluation of the infant's health. Although neonates may sometimes look misshapen, most are healthy, as revealed by a combined Apgar score of 7 or more.

Variations, Problems, and Solutions

3. Preterm or small-for-gestational-age babies are more likely than full-term babies to suffer from stress during the birth process and to experience medical difficulties, especially breathing problems, in the days after birth. Some long-term developmental difficulties may occur as well, depending on the presence of added medical problems or social-contextual challenges.

4. Low birthweight arises from a variety of causes, including the mother's poor health or nutritional status, smoking, drinking, drug use, and age. Many of these factors are associated with poverty. Clinical researchers have learned that a number of approaches—including better prenatal care and enhanced postnatal support for families—can provide assistance to such low-birthweight infants.

5. Variations in the birth process—such as breech births—can result in a birth that is stressful for mother and child, and in some cases cause anoxia. However, fetal monitoring can provide early warning of this and other problems, and

if necessary, delivery can be hastened by Cesarean section or the use of forceps or a vacuum extractor. None of these procedures is completely risk-free, but they may, in some cases, save lives and prevent possible brain damage.

Birth as a Family Event

6. While biological factors are the primary determinants of birth complications and the length of labor, factors in the social context play a large role in the parents' overall experience of birth. Women who are prepared for birth—knowing what to expect and how to make labor easier—and who have the support of their husbands and/or other sensitive birth attendants are most likely to find the birth experience satisfying.

7. The father's participation in the birth process generally has several positive effects. Women whose husbands or partners are present throughout delivery often experience emotional support and are provided with valuable assistance. Fathers, in turn, are often thrilled at being involved in the birth of their child.

8. The arrival of a newborn brother or sister is not necessarily a happy experience. An older sibling's emotional adjustment can be eased somewhat if the birth itself is not frightening and if the child is given extra attention in the days and weeks after the event. Nonetheless, considerable adjustment is almost inevitable.

The Beginning of Bonding

9. Although the idea of early parent-infant bonding has received much popular attention, most developmentalists downplay its importance, stressing that the formation of the parent-infant bond develops continuously over a long period of time. The moments after birth contribute to, but do not determine, the success of the parent-infant relationship.

KEY TERMS

first stage of labor (142)

transition (142)

second stage of labor (142)

third stage of labor (143)

neonate (143)

Apgar (143)

low-birthweight infant (144)

preterm infant (145)

small-for-gestational-age
   (SGA) infant (145)

very-low-birthweight
   (VLBW) infant (146)

anoxia (148)

breech position (154)

fetal monitor (154)

forceps (156)

vacuum extractor (156)

episiotomy (156)

Cesarean section (156)

Brazelton Neonatal
   Behavioral Assessment
   Scale (NBAS) (160)

Lamaze method (162)

dethronement (167)

parent-infant bond (167)

KEY QUESTIONS

1. What are the three stages of a normal birth? What occurs in each stage?

2. What vital body signs does the Apgar measure? What does the Apgar score tell about the health of the newborn?

3. What are the most serious problems of low-birthweight infants?

4. What are the causes of low birthweight?

5. What factors predict the long-term consequences of low birthweight and other birth problems?

6. What medical techniques can be used to speed up delivery if birth becomes too stressful for the fetus or mother?

7. What are the advantages and disadvantages of medication administered during childbirth?

8. What are the advantages of prepared-birth courses for parents-to-be?

9. What are the benefits of the father's presence during the delivery?

10. How does the arrival of the newborn affect the older children in a family?

11. How is the formation of the parent-infant bond different in animals than it is in humans?

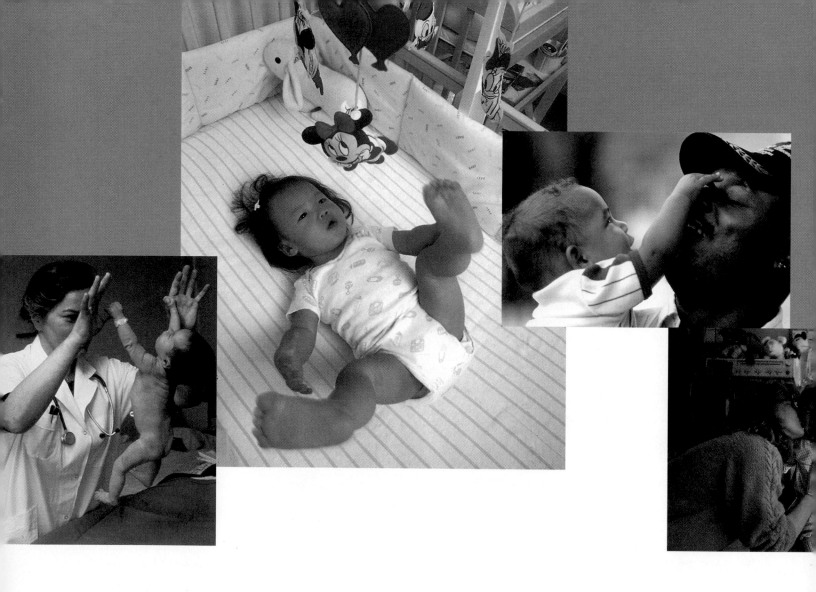

PART II The First Two Years: Infants and Toddlers

Adults usually don't change much in a year or two. Sometimes their hair gets longer or grows thinner, or they gain or lose a few pounds, or they become a little wiser or more mature. But if you were to be reunited with some friends you hadn't seen for several years, you would no doubt recognize them immediately.

If, on the other hand, you were to care for a newborn twenty-four hours a day for the first month, and then did not see the baby until a year or two later, the chances of your recognizing that child are similar to those of recognizing a best friend who had quadrupled in weight, grown 14 inches, and sprouted a new head of hair. Nor would you find the toddler's way of thinking, talking, or playing familiar. A hungry newborn just cries; a hungry toddler says "more food" or climbs up on the kitchen counter to reach the cookies.

While two years seem short compared to the almost eighty years of the average life span, children in their first two years reach half their adult height, possess cognitive abilities that have surprised even researchers, and express almost any emotion, from jealousy to shame. Two of the most important human abilities, talking and loving, are already apparent. The next three chapters describe these radical and rapid changes.

The First Two Years:
Biosocial Development

CHAPTER

6

The biological changes that occur in the child's first two years are swift and dramatic. At birth, infants are totally dependent on others, with a very limited repertoire of abilities for coping with life's demands. By the end of infancy, changes in size, motor skills, and brain maturation have transformed newborns into resourceful, highly mobile adventurers, able to hold their own on a playground. This chapter traces the impressive physical development of infancy and addresses, among others, the following questions:

What is the relationship between brain maturation and the infant's increasing behavioral competencies?

How well can infants see and hear, and what captures their interest?

How does experience affect early sensory and perceptual growth?

How do a newborn's reflexes indicate brain maturation?

Why might one infant take his or her first steps several months before another?

Why is it often better for an infant to be breast-fed rather than bottle-fed?

Are there long-lasting consequences if an infant is malnourished?

The forces of biosocial growth and development in the first two years of life are very powerful. Proof of this is visible to any observer, as infants quickly outgrow one set of clothes after another, attempt new behaviors almost daily, and display a rapidly increasing mastery of emerging skills. Evidence is also apparent from laboratory data on brain development, which shows increasing density and complexity of neural networks that are vital to the maturing of physical and mental capacities. All these changes, of course, are biologically rooted, but they are also facilitated by the social context, as parents and others nourish, protect, and encourage the infant's development. In this chapter we will look first at the physical developments in the child's body and brain, and then at the social environment—particularly factors in nutrition—that can either enhance or inhibit those developments.

Physical Growth and Health

Monitoring growth and protecting health are critical throughout childhood, but they are particularly so during infancy, when growth, as well as vulnerability to growth problems and disease, are most pronounced. Throughout childhood, visits to the doctor for a checkup are an annual affair, but in early infancy, visits should occur monthly, not only to keep tabs on the infant's physical progress and to spot the first signs if something is amiss, but also, as you will see, to meet the recommended schedule of immunizations.

Size and Shape

With the exception of prenatal development, infancy is the period of the fastest and most notable increases in size and changes in body proportion. Especially in the first few months of life, babies grow so rapidly that even their own parents might have difficulty recognizing a photo of their newborn after a few weeks have past.

The average North American newborn measures 20 inches (51 centimeters) and weighs a little more than 7 pounds (3.2 kilograms). This means that the average newborn is lighter than a gallon of milk, and about as long as the distance from a man's elbow to the tips of his fingers. In the first days of life, most newborns lose between 5 and 10 percent of their body weight, mostly in water, before their bodies adjust to sucking, swallowing, and digesting on their own. Once they have made these adjustments, most infants grow rapidly, doubling their birthweight by the fourth month, tripling it by the end of the first year, and growing about an inch longer each month for the first twelve months. Much of the weight gain in the early months of life is fat, which provides insulation for warmth and a store of nourishment. After 8 months or so, weight gain derives more from growth in bone, muscle, and body organs. By age 1, the typical baby weighs about 22 pounds (10 kilograms) and measures almost 30 inches (75 centimeters) (Behrman, 1992).

Growth in the second year proceeds at a slower rate. By 24 months of age most children weigh almost 30 pounds (13 kilograms) and measure between 32 and 36 inches (81 to 91 centimeters), with boys being slightly taller and heavier than girls. In other words, typical 2-year-olds are almost a fifth of their adult weight and half their adult height (see Figure 6.1).

As infants grow, their body proportions change. Most newborns seem top-heavy because their heads are equivalent to about one-fourth of their total length, compared to one-fifth at 1 year and one-eighth in adulthood. Their legs, in turn, represent only about a quarter of their total body length, whereas an adult's legs account for about half of it. Proportionally, the smallest part of a newborn's body is that part farthest from the head and most distant from the center, namely, the feet. Over the course of childhood and adolescence, as the body lengthens, the relative size of each part changes. By adulthood, a person's feet, for example, will be about five times as long as they were at birth, while the head will have only doubled in size.

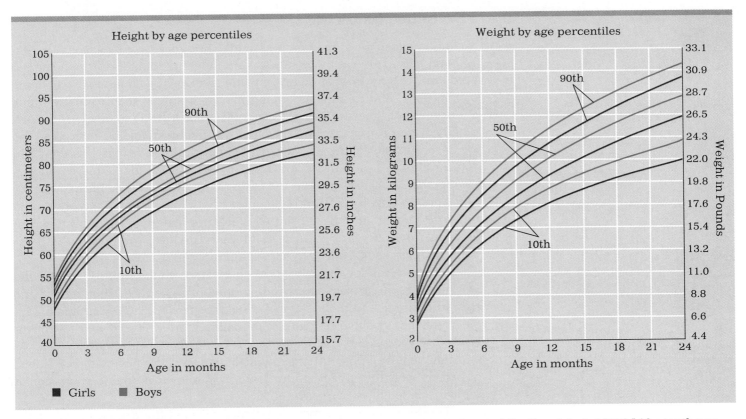

Height by age percentiles

Weight by age percentiles

■ Girls   ■ Boys

FIGURE 6.1 These figures show the range of height and weight of American children during their first two years. The lines labeled "50th" (the fiftieth percentile) show the average; the lines labeled "90th" (the ninetieth percentile) show the size of children taller and heavier than 90 percent of their contemporaries; and the lines labeled "10th" (the tenth percentile) show the size of children who are taller or heavier than only 10 percent of their peers. Note that girls (red lines) are slightly shorter and lighter, on the average, than boys (blue lines).

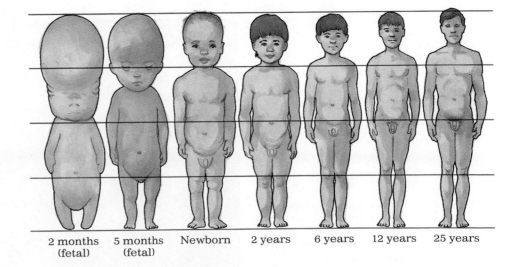

2 months (fetal)   5 months (fetal)   Newborn   2 years   6 years   12 years   25 years

FIGURE 6.2 As shown in this figure, the proportions of the human body change dramatically with maturation, especially in the first years of life. For instance, the percentage of total body length below the belly button is 25 percent at two months past conception, about 45 percent at birth, 50 percent by age 2, and 60 percent by adulthood.

Preventive Medicine

A century ago in developed nations, and only a decade or two ago in less developed ones, survival to age 5 was very much in doubt, because a sudden epidemic of any one of many infectious diseases—smallpox, whooping cough, polio, and diphtheria among them—rapidly spread to many young children, sometimes with serious complications leading to death. Now such deadly diseases are rare, and the chance of infants dying in North America, Western Europe, Japan, or Australia within the first year is less than 1 in 100, down from 1 in 20 fifty years ago (UNICEF, 1990). Indeed, increased survival in the early years of life is the main reason that average life expectancy has increased over the twentieth century, both in developed nations and in underdeveloped ones. In the United States, for instance, life expectancy increased from 55 years in 1920 to 75 years in 1990; in Tanzania, life expectancy increased from 45 to 51 years in just one decade, 1975–1985.

The reasons for the increased survival of young children worldwide are many, ranging from improved sanitation procedures that reduce the spread of disease to technological breakthroughs for high-risk infants, including hypersensitive respirators to maintain breathing in very-low-birth-weight newborns and microsurgery for babies born with heart defects. In addition, in developing nations, public health workers have taught millions of parents how to prevent infant death from dehydration and starvation, a topic discussed later in this chapter.

However, the single most important cause of the dramatic twentieth-century improvement in child survival is immunization. In less developed nations during the 1980s, the rate of immunization against the leading fatal childhood diseases—diphtheria, pertussis (whooping cough), tetanus, measles, polio, and tuberculosis—improved from about 20 percent to 80 percent, reducing deaths from these diseases by three-fourths (UNICEF, 1990). (Much remains to be done, however: measles, for instance, is the cause of

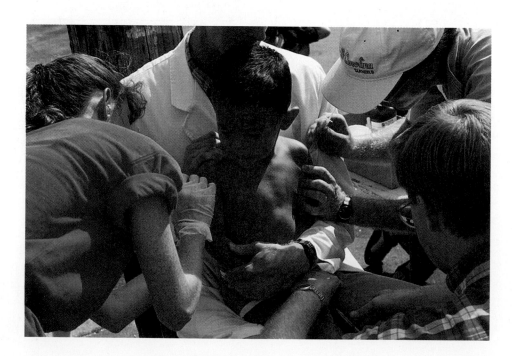

FIGURE 6.3 This brave inner-city boy is getting three shots at once because he had had none of the earlier immunizations recommended for infants. His lack of preventive medical care not only put him at high risk for childhood diseases but made him a potential vector for viruses that could prove deadly for unborn fetuses and people with lowered immune systems.

death for almost 1 million children worldwide per year [*MMWR,* December 31, 1993].)

In developed nations, both the quality and the scope of immunization have improved every decade, such that more than 90 percent of all infants are now immunized against diphtheria, pertussis, tetanus, measles, polio, and mumps. Many are immunized against hepatitis B, hemophilus influenza type-B, rubella, and chicken pox as well (see Table 6.1). (Some developed countries also immunize children against tuberculosis, while others, including the United States, test children for exposure and then follow up with further testing and treatment if needed.)

TABLE 6.1

Immunizations Recommended in the First Five Years

	Birth	2 mo	4 mo	6 mo	15 mo	5 yr
DPT (diphtheria, pertussis, tetanus)		X	X	X	X	X
HIB (hemophilus influenza type-B)		X	X	X	X	
Hepatitis B	X	X			X	
MMR (measles, mumps, rubella)					X	X
Oral Polio Vaccine		X	X		X	X
BCG* (antituberculosis)	X					

* BCG is not recommended in some developed nations.
Sources: Centers for Disease Control, 1994; UNICEF, 1990.

Immunization is undoubtedly effective, and side effects are increasingly rare. Although complete protection is not guaranteed to any one child, the result of widespread immunization eradicated smallpox worldwide by 1977, and, if current immunization rates continue, polio is expected to disappear by the year 2000.

Unfortunately, immunization programs are in danger of becoming victims of their own success. As the once-common diseases of childhood have receded, so has the public's awareness of, and attention to, them:

> Most parents of infants and preschoolers have no memory of summers when children were kept out of swimming pools for fear of catching polio . . . . Nor do they know firsthand the terrors of breath-robbing whooping cough, the often fatal paralysis of tetanus, or the sometimes fatal throat infection caused by diphtheria . . . [or that] measles can cause life-threatening encephalitis and mental retardation. [Brody, 1993]

As a result, many parents and policy makers take immunization lightly. This is particularly true in the United States, which ranks seventieth worldwide in the proportion of preschoolers fully immunized (Brody, 1993). In 1992, only 69 percent of American 2-year-olds had all their recommended vaccines against DPT, polio, and measles, and only 28 percent received protection against hemophilus influenza type-B (*MMWR,* April 22, 1994). These low rates have already caused a miniepidemic of measles (which rose from a low of less than 5,000 cases per year in the 1980s to almost 30,000 cases in 1990), as well as unexpected increases in rubella and whooping cough (*MMWR*, September 24, 1993; May 6, 1994).

While the cost of repeated pediatric visits and of vaccines is one impediment to complete childhood immunization within the United States, ignorance and/or indifference appears to be a much larger problem, given that three-fourths of the families with underimmunized children have incomes above the poverty line. Most parents in this group use private physicians when their children get sick, but postpone well-baby visits and inoculations. Many believe that if their child does get a "childhood" disease, it will swiftly run its course, with no important aftereffects. In most cases, with most diseases, this is probably true, especially if the child is well-nourished and if good medical care keeps fever down and infections limited. However, some childhood diseases, including diphtheria and whooping cough, often prove deadly, and others such as measles, while usually not fatal, nonetheless can be. Many childhood diseases have side effects that endure throughout life. For example, mumps can cause nerve deafness; even a slight case of polio can weaken muscle control later in life; and hemophilus influenza type-B is the leading cause of childhood meningitis, which can produce permanent brain damage.

In addition, lack of complete immunization not only puts the child, as well as his or her playmates, at risk, but also jeopardizes the well-being of others in the child's world: new babies too young to be immunized who catch a disease from an older child may die; pregnant women who catch rubella may transmit it to their fetuses causing blindness, deafness, and brain damage; healthy adults may suffer much worse consequences than a child might from mumps or measles; and the particularly vulnerable, such as those who are elderly, who have AIDS, or who have cancer, may die. Chicken pox, for instance, can kill a person whose immune system is depleted by chemotherapy. Moreover, from a public health perspective, the uneven rates of immunization signal a deficient delivery of medical care. As one physician warns:

> A case of measles or diphtheria in a child is like the death of the miner's canary—both signal problems in the environment. The miner's canary dies because gases are present that might affect the miner. Cases of a vaccine-preventable disease signal problems in the health care environment. [Klerman, quoted in Leary, 1994]

Indeed, for most of the ills of infancy and childhood, prevention is much easier, cheaper, and less painful than remedy, but sometimes seems surprisingly difficult to put into practice. As we shall see later in this and subsequent chapters, the same is true with a number of other childhood risks, including malnutrition, accidents, and abuse.

Sudden Infant Death Syndrome

sudden infant death syndrome (SIDS)
Death of a seemingly healthy baby who, without apparent cause, stops breathing during sleep.

Most infant deaths occur in the first month of life and are related to problems that are obvious at birth, such as heart defects or other inborn abnormalities, very low birthweight, and so on. However, there is one common cause of infant death that is not related to any obvious problem, **sudden infant death syndrome**, or **SIDS**. SIDS typically kills infants who are at least 2 months old and seemingly completely healthy—already gaining weight, learning to shake a rattle, starting to roll over, smiling at their caregivers. In the United States, SIDS is the second leading cause of infant death (see Table 6.2). Each year more than 5,000 American babies go to sleep and never wake up, victims of a sudden failure to breathe.

The term "sudden infant death" (also called *crib death* or *cot death*) is more a description than a diagnosis, because, despite decades of research, the actual cause of SIDS is still unknown. The diagnosis of sudden infant death is assigned when autopsy suggests that the infant simply stopped breathing, with other possible causes, such as deliberate or accidental suffocation, ruled out (Reece, 1993). Such determinations need to be done speedily and carefully, since crib deaths sometimes provoke unfounded suspicions from neighbors and police, who assume that the parents must have done something wrong. In recent years, as the diagnosis has become more definitive, many scientists have searched for a cause—perhaps a subtle neurological or physiological abnormality or some disease agent that is particularly harmful to young infants—that, if detected, might lead to prevention of SIDS. Despite decades of speculation and research, however, the cause remains a mystery.

TABLE 6.2

Infant Deaths in the United States, 1991

Leading Causes	Total
Congenital anomalies	7,685
Sudden infant death syndrome	5,349
Disorders related to short gestation and low birthweight	4,139
Respiratory distress syndrome	2,569
Maternal complications of pregnancy	1,536
Complications of placenta, cord, and membranes	962
Accidents and adverse effects	961
Infections specific to the perinatal period	881
Pneumonia and influenza	607
Intrauterine hypoxia and birth asphyxia	599

Source: National Center for Health Statistics, 1993.

In fact, SIDS may have no single cause, but instead may result from a combination of factors (see Table 6.3), which, as they accumulate, make *certain* infants, for unknown reasons, vulnerable. Drawing a profile from the table of risk factors, for example, we can say that a particular (but unidentifiable) 4-month-old boy, born in September weighing 5 pounds, who lives with several siblings in a low-income neighborhood, who has a slight case of the sniffles, and whose mother smokes cigarettes and does not breast-feed him, is more likely to die of SIDS than both a baby who does not have any of those characteristics and most infants who share all those traits (but who do not also share some as-yet-unknown critical factor). As with all risk analysis, scientists can spot vulnerability but cannot predict actual cases, and they unfortunately cannot rule out a risk for SIDS for infants with no known risk factors at all.

TABLE 6.3

SIDS Risk Factors

	SIDS More Likely	SIDS Less Likely
Characteristics of the Mother		
Age	under 20	over 25
Blood type	O, B, or AB	A
Personal habits	smoker	nonsmoker
Income	poverty-level	middle-class
Education	grade school only	college or higher
Ethnic background	African descent	Asian descent
Characteristics at Birth		
Sex	male	female
Birth order	later-born	first born
Multiple birth?	yes (twin or triplet)	no (single-born)
Apgar score at 5 min.	7 or lower	8 or higher
Heart beat	some irregularity	normal
Situation at Death		
Time of year	winter	summer
Age in months	2 to 4	under 1, over 6
Health	has a stuffy nose	no cold, no runny nose
Feeding	bottle-fed	breast-fed
Sleeping Conditions		
Position	sleeps on stomach	sleeps on back
Mattress	soft, natural fibers	firm, synthetic
Blankets, nightclothes	swaddled, tight	allow free movement
Bedroom temperature	heated	cool

Sources: Guilleminault et al., 1982; Haas et al., 1991; Meny et al., 1994; Mitchel et al., 1993; Ponsoby et al., 1993.

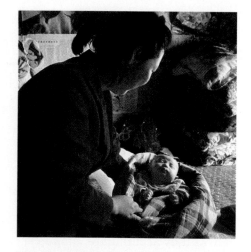

FIGURE 6.4 Infants in China are traditionally placed on their backs for sleeping. They also tend to be constantly in the presence of the mother or some other relative, who regularly checks on them as they sleep, adjusting their covers, making them comfortable, and the like. These two factors may help account for the low rate of SIDS in China. The woman in this photo, a seamstress, keeps her baby beside her as she works, a practice, incidentally, that is allowed by many employers in China and is encouraged by the government.

However, one important contributing factor has recently been discovered: the infant's sleeping position. All controlled research finds that there is less of a risk for SIDS when healthy infants sleep on their back than when they sleep on their stomach (Beal & Finch, 1993). Indeed, one comparison study found that an infant's risk of SIDS quadruples if the baby is put to sleep in a prone rather than in a supine position (Ponsoby et al., 1993). Additional evidence for the importance of sleeping position comes from China, where infants are almost always put to sleep on their back, and where SIDS rates are unusually low, even though babies are generally swaddled as they sleep (a risk factor) (Beal & Porter, 1991). Ironically, putting infants to sleep on their stomach has been recommended by Western pediatricians for decades, on the assumption that, when babies spit up (as almost all sometimes do), they might choke if they are lying on their back (Spock, 1976). While this idea makes sense, and may occasionally be borne out, it is now accepted that putting babies to sleep on their back is the safer course.

Another key factor reflected in Table 6.3 is ethnic background. Generally, within ethnically diverse nations such as the United States, Canada, Great Britain, Australia, and New Zealand, babies of African descent are more likely, and babies of Asian descent less likely, to succumb to SIDS than are babies of European descent. The reasons for this difference are not known. Certainly, genetic factors may play a role in the maturation and strength of the breathing reflex, although no specific connection has been found. At the same time, background variables that correlate with ethnicity, but are not caused by it, may be relevant. Within the United States, for instance, African-American infants have higher rates of low birthweight than those of other groups and are five times as likely as Asian-American infants to be born to teenage mothers (23 percent compared to 4 percent), with the rates for European-American infants being halfway between the two (11 percent). These two risk factors alone may be the critical variables that produce higher rates of SIDS among African-Americans. Similarly, in New Zealand, higher rates of SIDS among the indigenous Maori may be explained by the greater prevalence of socioeconomic and medical risk factors among that group than among New Zealanders of European descent (Allen et al., 1993).

An alternative explanation for the correlation between ethnicity and SIDS focuses on potentially relevant infant-care routines that are widespread in one culture and rare in another. Bengladeshi infants in England, for instance, tend to be low in birthweight and socioeconomic status but nonetheless have lower rates of SIDS than British infants, despite the fact that white British infants are more often of normal birthweight and middle-class. One possible reason for this difference may be that Bengladeshi infants tend to be surrounded by many family members in a rich sensory environment, continually hearing noises and feeling the gentle touch of their caregivers, and they therefore do not sleep too deeply for very long. By contrast, their white age-mates tend to sleep in their own private space in an environment of enforced quiet, and "long periods of lone sleep may contribute to the higher rates of SIDS among white infants" (Gantley et al., 1993).

A similar pattern of child care may also account for the low SIDS rate among Chinese-American infants, whose parents not only place their babies to sleep on their back but also tend to them periodically as they sleep, caressing a cheek, repositioning a limb, and so on. Specific practices that vary from one culture to another have only recently been examined as something other than curiosities, but it is easy to imagine that many specifics—perhaps in frequency of feeding, or in sleeping garments, or even in the parents' reaction to thumb-sucking—may likewise have an impact on SIDS (Davis & Gantley, 1993; Farooqi et al., 1994).

As you can see, simple answers to the SIDS tragedy are elusive: risk factors are many, alternative explanations abound, and the search for definitive causes—perhaps in brain functioning or breathing reflexes, perhaps in a quick virus or spoiled food—has been fruitless. However, even without a known cause, the prevalence of SIDS can be reduced by limiting exposure to risk factors—reducing low birthweight, encouraging breast-feeding, advising mothers to put their infants to sleep on their back, and so on.

Brain Growth and Maturation

As we saw earlier, the newborn's skull is disproportionately large. One reason is that it must accommodate the brain, which at birth has already attained 25 percent of its adult weight. The neonate's body weight, by comparison, is only about 5 percent of its adult weight. By age 2 the brain is about 75 percent of its adult weight, while the 2-year-old's body weight is only about 20 percent of what it will be in adulthood (Lowrey, 1986).

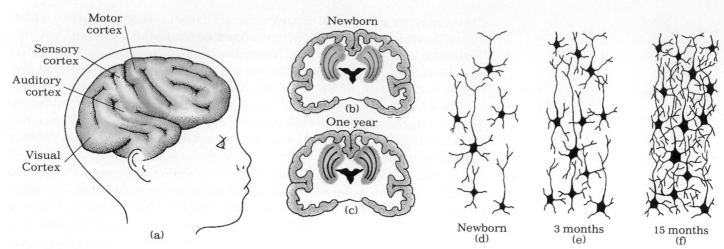

FIGURE 6.5 (*a*) Areas of the brain are specialized for the reception and transmission of different types of information. Research has shown that both experience and maturation play important roles in brain development. For example, myelination of the nerve fibers in the visual cortex of the brain will not proceed normally unless the infant has had sufficient visual experience in a lighted environment. The role of maturation is apparent in the growth and development of the neurons that make up the nerve fibers. These cells increase in size and in the number of connections among them as the infant matures, enabling impressive increases in the control and refinement of actions. The cross-sectional drawings in (*b*) and (*c*) show the development of nerve fibers in the visual cortex between birth and 1 year. Drawings (*d*), (*e*), and (*f*) illustrate changes in the neurons themselves.

neurons Nerve cells of the central nervous system.

dendrites Communication networks among the neurons in the cortex of the brain.

myelin A fatty insulating substance that coats the neurons, facilitating quicker, more efficient transmission of neural impulses.

Weight, of course, provides only a crude index of brain development. More significant are the changes in the maturing nervous system, which consists of the brain, the spinal cord, and the nerves. The nervous system is made up of long, thin, nerve cells called **neurons**. At birth, this system contains most of the neurons it will ever have—far more than it will ever need.

During the first months and years, the brain undergoes important changes that greatly enhance its functioning. These changes are particularly notable in the cortex, the outer layer of the brain (about an eighth of an inch of "gray matter") that controls perception and thinking. As you can see in Figure 6.5, specific portions of the cortex are specialized for particular sensory and motor functions, with the remainder of the cortex committed to processing and integrating many different kinds of information. The most important change that occurs in the cortex involves the growth and refinement of the communication networks among its billions of neurons (Greenough, 1993; Greenough et al., 1987). Neurons communicate by means of their thin, branchlike structures called **dendrites**, which form communication pathways among various neurons. From birth to age 2, there is an estimated fivefold increase in the density of dendrites in the cortex (Diamond, 1990), a proliferation that enables neurons to become connected to a greatly enlarging variety of other neurons within the brain. At the same time, these communication networks become more refined and specialized because, with maturation and experience, new connections emerge and others disappear, enhancing the efficiency of neural communication and economizing the brain's overall organization (Huttenlocher, 1990; Kolb, 1989). Thus the developing brain becomes simultaneously more densely interconnected and also more specialized.

The functioning of the brain's communication networks is also enhanced by a process in which neurons and dendrites become coated with **myelin**, a fatty, insulating substance that speeds the transmission of neural impulses. This process of *myelination*, which proceeds most rapidly from birth to age 4 (but continues through adolescence), allows children to gain increasing neurological control over their motor functions and sensory abilities and facilitates their intellectual functioning as well.

Advances also occur as different brain processes mature. For example, the frontal areas of the cortex (located behind the forehead) assists in self-control and self-regulation. This area is immature in the newborn, but as the neurons of the frontal area become myelinated and interconnected during the first year, infants show greater regulation of their physiological states and sleep-wake patterns and increasing control over their early reflexes (see below and p. 188). Somewhat later, cognitive skills requiring deliberation begin to emerge, along with a basic capacity for emotional self-control (Bell & Fox, 1992; Dawson, in press; Diamond, 1990; Fox, 1991). Other types of brain maturation lead to greater regularity in the baby's arousal patterns (Fox & Fitzgerald, 1991; Izard et al., 1991; Porges, 1991). As parents well know, infants in their first months display "all-or-nothing" swings of arousal, going from peaceful contentment to noisy crying in a few seconds. By age 1, the child's emotions are much more nuanced and predictable, as we shall see in more detail in Chapter 8.

Regulation of Physiological States

An important function of the brain throughout life is the regulation of physiological conditions, or **states**. Just like an older child or adult, a full-term infant normally exhibits several regularly occurring states, the most distinct being *quiet sleep,* in which breathing is regular and slow (about thirty-six breaths per minute) and muscles seem relaxed; *active sleep,* in which the facial muscles move and breathing is less regular and more rapid (forty-six or more breaths per minute); *alert wakefulness,* in which the eyes are bright and breathing is relatively regular and rapid; and *active crying*—which every parent can recognize (Thoman & Whitney, 1990).

Because each state produces a particular pattern of electrical activity in the brain, the patterns can be measured and recorded as an **electroencephalogram (EEG)**, a graphic readout of the electrical impulses, or brain waves, from the neurons. Brain waves change rapidly from about 3 months before term to about 3 months after, reflecting the maturation that is taking place (see Figure 6.6).

As the brain develops, physiological states become more cyclical and distinct. With each passing week, for instance, infants are asleep and awake for longer, more regular periods, because their brain maturation allows deeper sleep, more definite wakefulness, and greater self-regulation of alertness, noted above. Between birth and age 1, the infant's total daily sleep does not change all that much—from about 16 hours a day for the newborn to 13 for the toddler—but the length and timing of sleep episodes more closely match the day-night activities of the family. About a third of all 3-month-olds and 80 percent of all 1-year-olds "sleep through the night," defined as sleeping for at least 6 straight hours during the night. The remainder of each group continue to wake up wanting food and attention (Bamford et al., 1990; Michelsson et al., 1990). However, patterns of infant care can significantly influence the development of sleep-wake cycles in the first year (see Research Report, pp. 186–187). As one might expect, preterm newborns sleep more, but less regularly, throughout the first year.

FIGURE 6.6 The more mature pattern of brain-wave activity shows many more bursts of electrical activity and greater overall intensity, as can be seen in this electroencephalogram of quiet sleep.

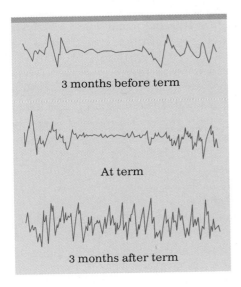

3 months before term

At term

3 months after term

physiological states   Refers to various levels of physiological arousal, such as quiet sleep and alert wakefulness.

electroencephalogram (EEG)   A graphic recording of the waves of electrical activity that sweep across the brain's surface. These waves are measured by placing electrodes on the scalp.

Schedules and the Culture of Infant Care

As the brain matures, the infant's developing ability to regulate alertness and arousal has important implications for the family system. Universally, newborns tend to be notoriously unpredictable: they sleep, wake, and cry with hunger at different hours and varying intervals, day and night. This erratic pattern gradually changes, to one of longer and more stable periods of sleep and wakefulness, and longer intervals between feedings—a welcome relief to the family. Parents who had run themselves ragged by trying to protect and please their disorganized little person find that they begin to relax and enjoy their baby much more once the child's states become more manageable and predictable, by 3 months or so. Furthermore, after the child has begun to show regular sleep-wake patterns, parents begin to look forward to a good night's sleep of their own, rather than to mere snatches of rest interrupted by feeding, diapering, and calming the baby. Experienced parents know how important the child's "getting on a schedule" can be: it is one of the first questions they ask new parents about, and they are quick to offer sympathy and reassurance if the response is an exhausted sigh.

But while physiological states become longer and more predictable with maturity in all infants, these universal processes are molded by specific child-rearing practices, which, in turn, reflect the values and assumptions of the family's particular culture. One such value is the importance of schedules *per se*. Most industrialized cultures place great importance on schedules, and on the punctual and predictable meeting of them, while many less developed, more rural cultures tend to be flexible and relaxed about making and meeting schedules. These different approaches to scheduling affect the way parents attempt to "manage" the infant's early months (Triandis, 1994).

For example, the majority of parents in the United States are locked into a rigid workplace schedule, and usually make concerted efforts to program their infant's sleeping accordingly, carefully scheduling naps and offering relaxing enticements for sleep, such as gentle rocking, a backrub, or a soft lullaby. Typically, the infant's mealtimes are also scheduled, usually to mesh with sleep and waking, so that soon the infant is having "breakfast," "lunch," "dinner," and "snacks" in coordination with evening sleep and day-time nap patterns.

Such concerns about scheduling are much less apparent in nonindustrialized countries, where infant care is often integrated into the stream of daily work activities around the home. For example, among the Kipsigis, a farming and herding community in Kokwet, Kenya, young infants regularly accompany their mother as she performs her farming, household, and social activities. In the early months, babies are carried around on a front sling, then on the mother's back, and later they crawl around and play close to their mother. At night, they sleep beside her. This overall pattern allows Kipsigis infants to sleep and nurse at any hour without disturbing the mother's daily activities or rousing her from bed at night.

These diverse cultural attitudes about infant schedules become reflected in the baby's own body rhythms. When Charles Super and Sara Harkness (1982) compared the daily routines of Kipsigis infants with those of babies from middle-class homes in the United States, they found that although newborns from both groups initially exhibited similar patterns of sleep, by the end of the first year, the American babies were, on average, sleeping much more per day than were the Kipsigis (15½ hours compared to 11), and for longer stretches at a time (see figure). In addition, by age 1, the American babies slept about 7 hours at night, while the unbroken nighttime sleep of the Kipsigis 1-year-olds was only about half that amount. In a sense, middle-class American infants had learned to be "good babies" as defined by their culture, permitting their parents uninterrupted nighttime rest, while a "good" Kipsigis baby could still wake up several times a night.

These differences caution against drawing universal conclusions about "normal" maturation, even for something as basic as attaining regularity in states of arousal.

Motor Skills

We now come to the most visible and dramatic of the physical changes that occur in infancy, those that ultimately allow the child to "stand tall and walk proud." Thanks largely to the changes in body size and proportion and the increasing brain maturation that we have outlined, infants gain dramatically in their ability to move and control their bodies. Consider the transition from the excited, undirected flapping of arms that 2-month-olds exhibit

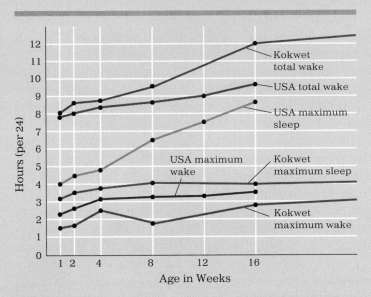

As you can see, the difference in the sleep patterns of Kipsigis infants in Kokwet, Kenya, and infants in the United States is not inborn. For the first month of life, the sleep patterns are almost identical. Then cultural differences in infant-care practices begin to have an impact, as American infants are awake for less total time per day than Kipsigis infants and sleep for longer intervals. By 16 weeks of age, American infants are sleeping notably more per day than the Kipsigis infants, in segments of up to 8 hours, while the Kipsigis babies tend to sleep no more than 4 hours at a stretch.

While greater regularity is a useful indicator of brain maturation, the degree of regularity a particular infant displays is affected not only by biological development but also by child-rearing practices, as well as by the infant's own temperament. The interaction of these factors can make it much harder for some babies to conform to a schedule than it is for others. Further, it is not necessarily true that the longer infants can sleep at a stretch, or the closer they approach a three-meal-a-day schedule, the further along their maturation and the better their parents' management skills. In some cases, an emphasis on sustained nighttime sleeping may overstress the young infant's self-regulatory capacities. As Michael Cole (1992) has noted,

the rather rigid schedule imposed by modern industrialized lifestyles may be pushing the limits of what the immature human brain can sustain; hence, while the length of a longest sleep period may be a good indicator of physical maturity, pushing those limits may be a source of stress with negative consequences for children who cannot measure up to parental expectations.

Indeed, if parents expect their infants to sleep soundly through the night, and instead their offspring wake at all hours, the parents are likely to blame both the child and themselves, and to become sleep-deprived as well. This makes them irritable at home, drowsy on the job, and too tired to have a social life. It also is likely to make them obsessed with sleep, talking about it "the way a hungry person talks about food" (Hochschild, 1989). Most American parents, in fact, feel that their infants' sleep patterns are problematic and search for solutions that will make the child sleep longer and awaken less often (Johnson, 1991).

The research we have been examining suggests, however, that at least some of the adaptation should be on the part of the parents—anything from trying to arrange some flextime shift in their work schedule to simply providing a midnight feeding months after the "good" baby is supposed to sleep through the night. Even if such practical adjustments are impossible or inadvisable, changes in attitude and expectations are warranted. An infant's natural rhythms of sleep and arousal may be problematic only in the cultural context of an adult's highly organized, tightly scheduled, sleep-deprived life, and should not be taken as a sign of either the baby's willfulness or the parent's inadequacy.

when a toy is dangled in front of them to the typical response of a 6-month-old—a smooth, efficient movement of the arm and shoulder muscles to intercept the toy, together with the finger movements that effectively close around the object. In the course of this four-month transition, infants have learned to (1) scale muscle movement against gravity to hit the target and not overshoot it; (2) compensate for the inertial forces that are transmitted from one muscle group (say, the shoulder) to other muscles (say, in the arm); (3) anticipate the trajectory of the arm in motion to enable the hand to intercept the target; (4) coordinate moving and braking forces in different muscle groups; and (5) organize these various components into a smooth motor action—while all the time their body is changing in size and strength! Researchers who have studied these "developmental biodynamics" have become convinced not only that this is a remarkable achievement but that its development is a painstaking process of trial-and-error accomplishments that gradually assembles and fine-tunes a sequence of smooth motor actions (Goldfield et al., 1993; Lockman & Thelen, 1993; Thelen et al., 1993). Thus the development of skilled motor behavior—whether it involves learning to walk or to grasp small objects with the fingers—is not simply a matter of waiting for a maturational timetable to unfold, but instead involves the active efforts of the infant to attain competence by mastering and coordinating successive components of each complex skill.

Because of the growing independence they afford the child, motor skills become a "catalyst for developmental change" (Thelen, 1987), as they open new possibilities for the child's discovery of the world. For this reason, especially, it is important to understand the development of these skills—including the usual sequence and timing of their emergence—and the various factors that might cause one child to develop certain skills "behind" or "ahead of" schedule.

Reflexes

The infant's first motor skills are not, technically, skills at all, but are **reflexes**, that is, involuntary responses to particular stimuli. The newborn has dozens of reflexes. Some are essential to life itself; others disappear completely in the months after birth; still others provide the foundation for later motor skills. All are important as signs of neurological health and behavioral competence.

Three sets of reflexes are critical for survival and become stronger as the baby matures. One set works to maintain an adequate supply of oxygen. The most obvious reflex in this group is the **breathing reflex**. Normal newborns take their first breath even before the umbilical cord, with its supply of oxygen, is cut. For the first few days, breathing is somewhat irregular, and reflexive *hiccups, sneezes,* and *spit-ups* are common, as the newborn tries to coordinate breathing, sucking, and swallowing.

Another set of reflexes helps to maintain constant body temperature: when infants are cold, they *cry, shiver,* and *tuck in their legs* close to their bodies, thereby helping to keep themselves warm. A third set of reflexes fosters feeding. One of these is the **sucking reflex**: newborns suck anything that touches their lips—fingers, toes, blankets, and rattles, as well as natural and artificial nipples of various shapes. Another is the **rooting reflex**, which helps babies find a nipple by causing them to turn their heads and start to suck when something brushes against their cheek. *Swallowing* is another important reflex that aids feeding, as is *crying* when the stomach is empty.

Other reflexes are not necessary for survival, but they are important signs of normal brain and body functioning. For example, the following five reflexes are present in normal, full-term newborns:

reflexes Involuntary physical responses to stimuli.

breathing reflex A reflex that ensures an adequate supply of oxygen and the discharge of carbon dioxide by causing the individual to inhale and exhale.

sucking reflex A reflex that causes newborns to suck anything that touches their lips.

rooting reflex A reflex that helps babies find a nipple by causing them to turn their heads toward anything that brushes against their cheek and to attempt to suck on it.

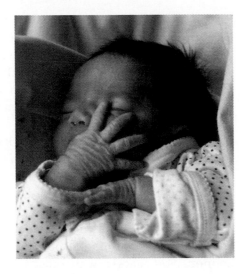

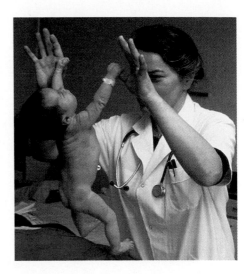

FIGURE 6.7 For developmentalists, newborn reflexes are mechanisms for survival, indicators of brain maturation, and vestiges of evolutionary history. For parents, they are mostly delightful and sometimes amazing. This is demonstrated by three star performers: a 2½-week-old infant stepping eagerly forward on legs too tiny to support her body, a 3-day-old infant, still wrinkled from amniotic fluid, contentedly sucking his thumb; and a newborn grasping so tightly that his legs dangle in space.

1. When their feet are stroked, their toes fan upward (*Babinski reflex*).

2. When they are held upright with their feet touching a flat surface, they move their legs as if to walk (*stepping reflex*).

3. When they are held horizontally on their stomachs, their arms and legs stretch out (*swimming reflex*).

4. When something touches their palms, their hands grip tightly (*Palmar grasping reflex*).

5. When someone bangs on the table they are lying on, newborns usually fling their arms outward and then bring them together on their chests, as if to hold on to something, and they may cry and open their eyes wide (*Moro reflex*).

None of these reflexes remain as involuntary responses after the first few months of life. Why, then, do they exist at all? Some may be vestiges of earlier evolutionary development. The Moro and Palmar grasp reflexes, for example, may have been crucial ways for the young infant to remain close to the mother, especially during startling or unexpected events. Others are the precursors of voluntary movements, or motor skills.

Gross Motor Skills

Gross motor skills, which involve large body movements, begin to emerge early. Even as newborns, infants placed on their stomachs move their arms and legs swim-fashion and attempt to lift their heads to look around. As they gain muscle strength, they start to wiggle, attempting to move forward by pushing their arms, shoulders, and upper body against the surface they are on. Although these initial efforts usually get them nowhere, or even move them backward, infants persist, and over the next two months or so, they become able to use their arms, and then legs, to inch forward. By 6 months, most infants succeed at this type of locomotion (Chandler, 1990). A few months later, usually between 8 and 10 months after birth, most infants are crawling on "all fours" (sometimes called creeping), coordinating the movement of their hands and knees in a smooth, balanced manner. Within a cou-

gross motor skills Physical skills involving large body movements such as waving the arms, walking, and jumping.

ple of months, most infants also learn to climb up onto couches and chairs—as well as ledges, window sills, and the like. Some babies do not crawl at all, achieving mobility instead by either scooting along on their buttocks, rolling over and over, doing the "bear walk" (on all four "paws," without letting their knees or elbows touch the ground), or even cruising unsteadily on two feet, moving from place to place by holding onto tables, chairs, or bystanders.

As with every new skill, crawling opens new opportunities and challenges. Once infants can locomote on their own, they can propel themselves toward intriguing objects, whether nearby or across the room. They can even leave the room, exploring new areas and gaining a sense of their own independent actions. New hazards are also within reach, from the stairs they might tumble down to the floor polish they might taste. (The prudent parent seals off all dangerous places and substances by 6 months, if not sooner.) Fortunately, with most infants, the advent of crawling coincides with an emerging sense of wariness about the unfamiliar (see Chapter 8), producing a new measure of caution that tempers their curiosity: infants in-

(a)

(b)

(c)

(d)

FIGURE 6.8 Nicholas and Daniel are monozygotic twins, and consequently reach various stages of motor skills virtually together. The abilities shown here are (a) lifting the head and shoulders at 4 months, (b) preparing to crawl at 6 months, (c) standing with one supporting hand at 8 months, and (d) finally walking at 12 months—right on schedule.

vestigate a novel situation tentatively, frequently interrupting their explorations to glance at a parent for signs of encouragement or disapproval. Thus, a combination of motor skills, cognitive awareness, social interaction, and access to new surroundings makes the crawling 9-month-old a quite different baby from the precrawler (Bertenthal & Campos, 1990).

Walking shows a similar progression, from reflexive, hesitant newborn stepping to a smooth, speedy, coordinated gait (Thelen & Ulrich, 1991). On average, a child can walk while holding a hand at 9 months, can stand alone momentarily at 10 months, and can walk well unassisted at 12 months. In recognition of their accomplishment of walking, infants at this stage are given the additional name **toddler**, for the characteristic way they move their bodies, toddling from side to side. Since their heads and stomachs are relatively heavy and large, they spread out their short little legs for stability, making them seem bowlegged, flatfooted, and unbalanced. Interestingly, once an infant can take steps, walking becomes the preferred mode of movement—except when speed is an issue, and then many new walkers quickly drop to their hands and knees to crawl. Within a short time, mastery of walking leads to mastery of running; 2-year-olds are proficient walkers and almost never crawl except when, with a mocking grin on their face, they pretend to be babies.

In addition to allowing infants freedom of movement, crawling and walking aid their development in other ways. It is no coincidence that with infants' increased mobility and independence comes a forward leap in their cognitive awareness (detailed in Chapter 7) and the opening of new dimensions in parent-infant interaction (described in Chapter 8). In addition, in purely practical terms, upright mobility not only raises the child's vistas figuratively but literally gives the child a new perspective on his or her world. It also frees up the child's hands, fostering the development of fine motor skills.

Fine Motor Skills

Fine motor skills, which mostly involve small movements of the arms, hands, and fingers, are more challenging to master because they require the coordination of complex muscle groups. As we have seen, infants are born with a reflexive grasp, but they seem to have no control of it. During their first 2 months, babies will stare and wave their arms at an object dangling within reach, and by 3 months, they can usually touch it. But they cannot yet grab and hold on unless the object is placed in their hands, partly because their eye-hand coordination is so limited. By 4 months, they sometimes grab, but their timing is often off, causing them to close their hand too early or too late, and their grasp tends to be of short duration. Finally, by 6 months, with a concentrated stare and deliberate movements, most babies can reach for, grab, and hold onto almost any object that is the right size, whether it is a bottle, a rattle, or a sister's braids.

Once grabbing is possible, infants explore everything within reach, mastering fine motor skills while they learn about the physical properties of their immediate world. As Eleanor Gibson, a leading researcher in infant perception, describes it, the infant at 6 months has "a wonderful eye-hand-mouth exploratory system," which before age 1 is sufficiently developed that

toddler A child, usually between the ages of 1 and 2, who has just begun to master the art of walking.

fine motor skills Physical skills involving small body movements, especially with the hands and fingers, such as picking up a coin and drawing.

FIGURE 6.9 Motor skills develop rapidly during the first two years, partly because infants take advantage of every opportunity to use whatever abilities they have. Climbing, perching, and grasping are just some of the motor skills this young muralist is currently refining.

the infant can "hold an object in one hand and finger it with the other, and turn it around while examining it. This is an ideal way to learn about the distinctive features of an object" and, bit by bit, about the tangible world (Gibson, 1988).

Other developing skills contribute to the child's ability to explore. By 4 to 8 months, most infants can transfer objects from one hand to the other. By 8 or 9 months, they can adjust their reach in an effort to catch objects that are tossed toward them, even when the object is thrown fairly fast and from an unusual angle (von Hofsten, 1983).

At the same time, the skill of picking up and manipulating small objects develops. At first, infants use their whole hand, especially the palm and the fourth and fifth fingers to grasp. Later they use the middle fingers and center of the palm or the index finger and the side of the palm. Finally, they use thumb and forefinger together, a skill mastered sometime between 9 and 14 months (Frankenburg et al., 1981). At this point, infants delight in picking up every tiny object within sight, including bits of fuzz from the carpet and bugs from the lawn.

Variations in Timing

Although all healthy infants develop the same motor skills in the same sequence, the age at which these skills are acquired can vary greatly from infant to infant and still be considered normal. Table 6.4 shows the age at which half of all infants in the United States master each major motor skill, and the age at which 90 percent master each skill.

These averages, or **norms**, are based on a large representative sample of infants from a wide range of ethnic groups. Such representativeness is important because norms vary from group to group, as well as from place to

norms The overall usual, or average, standard for a particular behavior. Norms are generally the result of research done on a large sample of a given population.

TABLE 6.4

Age Norms (in Months) for Motor Skills

Skill	When 50% of All Babies Master the Skill	When 90% of All Babies Master the Skill
Lifts head 90° when lying on stomach	2.2	3.2
Rolls over	2.8	4.7
Sits propped up (head steady)	2.9	4.2
Sits without support	5.5	7.8
Stands holding on	5.8	10.0
Walks holding on	9.2	12.7
Stands momentarily	9.8	13.0
Stands alone well	11.5	13.9
Walks well	12.1	14.3
Walks backward	14.3	21.5
Walks up steps (with help)	17.0	22.0
Kicks ball forward	20.0	24.0

Source: The Denver Developmental Screening Test (Frankenburg et al., 1981).

place. For example, throughout infancy, African-Americans are more advanced in motor skills than Americans of European ancestry (Rosser & Rudolph, 1989). Internationally, the earliest walkers in the world seem to be in Uganda, where, if well nourished and healthy, the typical baby walks at 10 months; some of the latest walkers are in France, where taking one's first unaided steps at 15 months is not unusual.

What factors account for this variation in the acquisition of motor skills? Of primary importance are inherited factors, such as activity level, rate of physical maturation, and body type. The power of this genetic component is suggested by the fact that identical twins are far more likely to sit up, and to walk, on the same day than fraternal twins are. Moreover, there are striking individual differences in the strategies by which infants gradually master and coordinate the various components of motor actions—whether learning to walk or smoothly grasp a toy—that can also affect the timing of these achievements (Thelen et al., 1993). Particular patterns of infant care may also be influential. Indeed, among the Kipsigis of Kenya and other African groups, infants are held next to an adult's body virtually all day long, cradled and rocked as the adult works. This kind of stimulation allows the infant to practice movement while in an upright position and to continually feel the rhythm of an adult's gait, which may well give African babies an advantage in gross motor skills over the typical Western infant who spends much of each day in a crib (Bril, 1986).

Given the evidence, most developmentalists would say that the age at which a *particular* baby first displays a *particular* skill depends on the interaction between inherited and environmental factors. Each infant has a genetic timetable for maturation, which can be faster or slower than that of other infants from the same ethnic group and even from the same family; and each infant also has a family and culture that provide varying amounts of encouragement, nutrition, and opportunity to practice.

FIGURE 6.10 Some practice is essential for development of motor skills, but extensive experience is not necessary, as proven by Algonquin infants from Quebec, Canada, who spend much of their first year in cradle boards but typically sit up, walk, and run within the same age ranges as infants from other cultures.

Although some variation in the development of motor skills is normal and to be expected, a pattern of slow development, especially if the infant does not seem curious and motivated to attempt new skills, may signal a serious problem. Indeed, most tests of infant development, from the Brazelton Neonatal Assessment Scale to the Bayley Scales of Infant Development for older babies, include many measures of movement skills. While babies who seem somewhat slow in gaining motor abilities generally develop quite well, those who are markedly below the norm need special professional attention to determine whether their unusually slow development is the result of neurological or family problems.

Sensory and Perceptual Capacities

Psychologists draw an important distinction between sensation and perception. **Sensation** occurs when a sensory system detects a particular stimulus. **Perception** occurs when the brain tries to make sense out of that stimulus, such that the individual becomes aware of it. This distinction may be clear to you if you have ever done your homework while playing the stereo and realized that you had worked through an entire recording but had actually "heard" only snatches of it. During the gaps in your "hearing," your auditory system was sensing the music—your tympanic membranes, hammer, anvils, stirrups, and the like were vibrating in response to the sound waves coming from the speakers—but you were not perceiving the music; that is, you were not consciously aware of it.

At birth, both sensation and perception are apparent. Newborns see, hear, smell, and taste, and they respond to pressure, motion, temperature, and pain. Most of these sensory abilities are immature and somewhat selective, responding to a fairly narrow range of stimuli. Thus newborns' perceived world is not at all the "great, blooming, buzzing confusion" psychologists once believed it to be (James, 1950). Further, the stimuli they do respond to—such as visual patterns, the sound of a human voice, and sweet and sour tastes—reveal much about their growing comprehension of the surrounding world.

In this section, we will briefly consider the infant's sensory capacities and basic perceptual abilities. In Chapter 7, we will examine the cognitive dimensions of infant perception.

Research on Infant Perception

Over the past twenty years, there has been an explosion of research into infant sensory and perceptual skills. Technological breakthroughs—from brain scans to computer measurement of the eyes' ability to focus—have enabled researchers to measure the capacities of infants' senses and to gain a greater understanding of the relationship between perception and physiology.

The basis of this research is the fact that the perception of an unfamiliar stimulus elicits simple responses, for example, changed heart rate, concentrated gazing, and in the case of infants who have a pacifier in their mouths, intensified sucking. When the new stimulus becomes so familiar that these responses no longer occur, the infant is said to be *habituated* to

sensation   The response of a sensory system to a particular stimulus.

perception   The mental processing of sensory information.

that stimulus. Employing this phenomenon of **habituation**, researchers have been able to assess infants' ability to perceive by testing their ability to discriminate between very similar stimuli (Bornstein, 1985). Typically, they present the infant with a stimulus—say a plain circle—until habituation occurs. Then they present another stimulus similar to the first but different in some detail—say a circle with a dot in the middle. If the infant reacts in some measurable way to the new stimulus (a change of heart rate, a refocusing of gaze), that indicates that the difference in stimulus has been perceived.

Vision

At birth, vision is the least developed of the senses. Newborns focus most readily on objects between 4 and 30 inches (10 and 75 centimeters) away. Their distance vision is about 20/400, which means the baby sees an object 20 feet (6.1 meters) away no better than an adult with 20/20 vision sees the same object 400 feet (122 meters) away. However, distance vision develops rapidly, improving in the first months and reaching 20/40 by 6 months and 20/20 by 12 months (Haith, 1990, 1993). This improvement results more from changes in the brain than from changes in the eye. Distance focusing is not impossible for the newborn (as it would be for an adult with 20/400 vision), but the immaturity of the brain's neural networks makes such focusing slow and difficult (Braddick & Atkinson, 1988). As neurological maturation and myelination allow better coordination of eye movements and more efficient transmission of information between the eyes and the brain, focusing improves. By 6 months, the visual system has matured considerably and more closely approximates adult capacities.

FIGURE 6.11 How well can newborns really see? In the first weeks, their vision of Mom is closer to the picture on the left than to the one on the right. The ability to focus improves gradually, and it is not until about the end of the first year that a baby with normal eyesight develops 20/20 vision.

habituation The process of becoming so familiar with a particular stimulus that it no longer elicits the physiological responses it did when it was originally experienced.

During the same time period, increasing maturation of the visual cortex accounts for improvements in other visual abilities. When 1-month-olds look at something, their gaze often wanders, and their ability to scan the object and attend to the critical areas is quite imperfect. When looking at a face, for example, they look at the peripheral features, such as the hairline. However, by 3 months of age, scanning is more organized, efficient, and centered on important aspects of a stimulus. Thus, when 3-month-olds look at a face, they scan the eyes and mouth regions, which contain more information

FIGURE 6.12 Scientists, aided by Donald Duck, monitor a 7-month-old girl's responses to visual stimuli. As various pictures flash on the screen, the infant's brain activity is recorded by means of the head-band device she is wearing, indicating not only what she sees and how well she sees it, but also which parts of her developing brain are processing visual stimuli.

(Aslin, 1988; Braddick & Atkinson, 1988). **Binocular vision**, that is, the ability to use both eyes together to focus on one object, also develops in the early months, occurring at about 14 weeks, on average.

As a result of these achievements, depth and motion perception improve dramatically. Evidence of this comes from infants' ability to "track" a moving object, that is, to visually follow its movement (Nelson & Horowitz, 1987). Although some instances of tracking are apparent in the first days of life, this ability is erratic. Most very young babies "lose sight" of an object that moves slowly right in front of their face. One reason for this is that, even with stationary objects, newborns' eyes do not remain focused for long, and they do not focus on edges (Bronson, 1990). Thus continual, smooth tracking of a moving object is virtually impossible. In the months after birth, tracking improves week by week, with large, fast-moving, high-contrast objects being tracked more readily than small, slow-moving, low-contrast objects.

Color vision is apparent from birth, and rapidly becomes refined during the early months. Newborn infants can distinguish among red, green, and white, but are limited in detecting other colors (Adams, 1989; Adams et al., 1986). By 3 to 4 months of age, however, infants can distinguish many more colors and can also differentiate them more acutely, perceiving aqua, for example, as bluish rather than greenish (Bornstein & Lamb, 1992; Haith, 1990).

Infant Visual Preferences

So far we have described what young infants are *able* to see. But what do they *prefer* to see when given a choice? One clear conclusion from the research on infant visual preferences is that babies seek visual stimulation that offers complexity within their range of perceptual ability. They prefer to look, for example, at novel images rather than at familiar ones, at complex visual patterns rather than at solid colors, and at stimuli with contrast and contour density (like a three-dimensional mask of a face) rather than at something two-dimensional (like a picture of a face). In addition, infants increasingly enjoy visual events that represent incongruity or discrepancy

binocular vision The ability to use both eyes together to focus on a single object.

from the usual, such as seeing a familiar crib toy turned upside down (Haith, 1980, 1990). This preference for visual stimulation may arise from the fact that, as we will shortly see, visual stimulation is necessary for the full development of the visual system in the early months of life. It may also occur because visual complexity contains more information that provokes the baby's interest—and will stimulate cognitive growth.

These findings have led to a new appreciation of the young infant as a stimulus-seeker who strives to make sense out of his or her surroundings. As Marshall Haith (1990), who has studied infant visual perception for more than thirty years, comments,

> this creature is actively processing whatever lies within its visual province and even looks for more, rather than simply choosing one stimulus or another. It is important for investigators to appreciate the infant as an active processor rather than a selector and to try to figure out what the baby is trying to accomplish rather than how dimensions of the world control its activity.

Hearing

Relative to their vision, newborns' hearing is quite sensitively attuned. Sudden noises startle newborns, making them cry; rhythmic sounds, such as a lullabye or a heartbeat, soothe them and put them to sleep. When they are awake, they turn their heads in an effort to locate the source of a noise (Clarkson et al., 1985), and they are particularly attentive to the sound of conversation. Indeed, as we saw in Chapter 4, newborns can distinguish their mother's voice from the voice of other mothers soon after birth.

By the age of 1 month, infants can also perceive differences between very similar speech sounds. In one experiment, 1-month-old babies activated a recording of the "bah" sound whenever they sucked on a nipple. At first, they sucked diligently, but as they habituated to the sound, their sucking decreased. At this point, the experimenters changed the sound from "bah" to "pah." Immediately the babies sucked harder, indicating by this sign of interest that they had perceived the difference (Eimas et al., 1971). It may even be that newborns have some ability to discriminate between vowels (Clarkson & Berg, 1983). More important, young infants can distinguish between speech sounds that are not used in their native language—and that are indistinguishable to adult speakers of their native language. For example, whereas English-speaking adults cannot distinguish between different

FIGURE 6.13 The procedure pictured here tests an infant's ability to detect changes in speech sounds. While the child is focused on a toy held by the experimenter (a), a single speech sound is played repetitively through a loudspeaker. At random intervals the speech sound is changed, and shortly thereafter one of the toys on the infant's right lights up and begins to move (b). After this routine is repeated a number of times, the infant learns that a change in speech sounds signals a delightful sideshow across the room. Thereafter, researchers can tell whether the infant discriminates between other speech sounds by whether or not the child looks expectantly over to the showcase after a particular sound is changed. (The experimenter and the child's mother are wearing special headphones that prevent them from hearing the speech sounds, thereby eliminating the possibility of their unwittingly cuing the child to the changes in sound.)

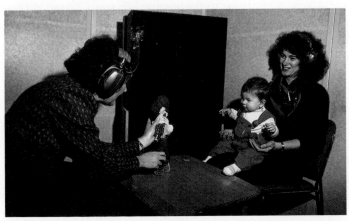

(a)

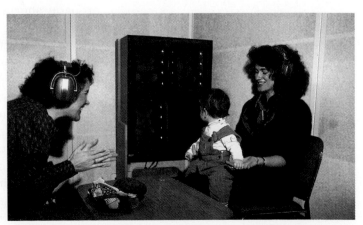

(b)

"t" sounds that are used in Hindi speech, or between various glottal consonants used in some Native American dialects, their infants would be able to
differentiate these sounds. This suggests to some researchers that there
may be certain innate features to early speech perception (Werker, 1989).

Although very young infants can discriminate among a wide variety of
sounds, their hearing is not as acute as that of an older child (Trehub et al.,
1991). Even at 6 months, when infants can hear high-frequency sounds as
well as older children can, their hearing for low-frequency sounds is much
less acute (Olsho, 1984; Olsho et al., 1988). Undoubtedly this is one reason
most adults use a higher pitch when talking to babies than when talking to
other people, as discussed in Chapter 7, and why infants prefer listening to
"baby talk" over adult styles of conversation (Cooper & Aslin, 1990; Fernald,
1985; Fernald & Kuhl, 1987). Infant hearing differs in another way from that
of older children: infants are less capable of locating sounds in space. Most
older children can intuitively determine the location of a sound (say, off to
the right or left) based on which ear receives the auditory signal first. But
because infants have smaller heads, their ears are closer together, significantly limiting their ability to make this determination. Sound localization
ability improves gradually throughout infancy (Morrongiello & Rocca, 1990).

Other Senses

Although less developed than their hearing, neonates' sense of taste is
clearly functioning. This was vividly shown in a demonstration with a dozen
2-hour-old infants who were each given tastes of sweet, sour, salty, and bitter
water (Rosenstein & Oster, 1988). Careful analysis of their video-taped facial
expressions revealed distinctive reactions to all the samples except the
salty one, with infants preferring sweet tastes.

Newborns' sense of smell is even more acute, especially for odors that
are particularly meaningful to them—like those associated with feeding
(Porter et al., 1992). In a number of experiments, breast-fed infants a few
days old have been positioned in a crib between two gauze pads, one worn
by their own mother in her bra for several hours, the other similarly worn by
another breast-feeding mother. In trial after trial, infants tended to turn
their heads toward their own mother's pad, preferring her smell to that of
another woman (Schaal, 1986).

Together, taste and smell continue to develop during the early months,
and become quite acute by age 1. Indeed, by late infancy, these senses are
probably sharper than at any other time in the entire life span. Experts recommend giving infants a wide variety of foods, not because nutrition demands it, but because taste preferences develop so rapidly that introduction
of new foods becomes more problematic with each passing year (Birch,
1990).

Finally, the sense of touch is remarkably acute during the first year
(Bushnell & Boudreau, 1993). From their early months, long before their limited visual skills permit careful visual examination, babies manipulate objects (often transferring them to their mouths for exploration with their
tongue, gums, cheeks, and lips, which are very sensitive to touch). By 6
months of age, infants distinguish objects on the basis of their temperature,
size, hardness, and texture; somewhat later, they are able to differentiate
weight. The ability to make such tactile distinctions is an important skill be-

cause most of these characteristics cannot be assessed on the basis of sight alone, yet they are essential to a baby's knowledge of the surrounding world, as we shall see in the next chapter.

The Role of Sensory Experience

One of the most intriguing issues in infant development is how important sensory experience is to the development of the infant's sensory abilities, particularly with regard to the establishment of the brain's neural networks. To a great extent, of course, the basic elements of infants' sensory systems are already established at birth. There is no doubt, however, that at least a minimal amount of sensory experience is essential, not only in the development of perceptual abilities, but even in the development of the dendrites and other brain structures that make seeing, hearing, and other sensory abilities possible.

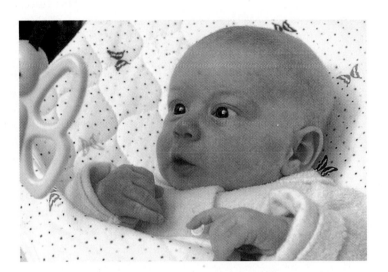

FIGURE 6.14 This 7-week-old's concentrated gaze is a sign that her brain is hard at work processing the visual information provided by her crib toy. Experiences such as this are not only fascinating to infants but are essential for the normal development of the visual pathways of the cortex.

This fact is most clearly shown by research in which animals that were prevented from using their senses or moving their bodies in infancy became permanently handicapped (Parmelee & Sigman, 1983). Kittens who are blindfolded for the first several weeks of life, for example, do not develop the visual pathways in their brains to allow normal vision, even if their blindfolds are removed when they are just a few months old. Indeed, if only one eye is temporarily blinded and the other left normal, kittens can see but will never develop the binocular vision that plays a role in depth vision (Mitchell, 1988). Significantly, such atrophy of brain pathways occurs only when blindness takes place in the early weeks of life; kittens who have had some normal visual experiences, as well as older cats who are subjected to longer periods of temporary blindness, recover quite well once the sight deprivation is over.

In very simple terms, these abnormalities occur because the deprivation of certain basic sensory experiences prevents the development of the normal neural pathways that transmit sensory information. As researchers explain it metaphorically, the "wiring" of the brain—that is, the basic structures that allow the development of specific capacities—is genetically pro-grammed and present at birth. What is required is the "fine-tuning" that oc-curs with the development of the connective networks, and it is this fine-tuning process that can be affected by the individual's experience or the lack of it.

As best we know, the brain development that permits seeing and hear-ing in humans likewise becomes "fine-tuned" through visual and auditory experiences in the first months (Imbert, 1985; Parmelee & Sigman, 1983). This is not to say that an infant would not be able to see colors or understand speech unless he or she had an opportunity to experience them in the first days of life. Nor does it mean that intensive exposure to visual, auditory, and motor stimulation is desirable in the first weeks. (Indeed, many newborns would react to such stimulation by shutting it out with crying or sleep.) How-ever, it does mean that even in the case of a biologically programmed event such as early brain maturation and sensory-system development, experi-ence also plays a role.

The cultural context in which the child develops may be one important feature of this early experience. Recall that young infants can distinguish between different speech sounds that are not part of the language they overhear and that mature speakers of the language cannot differentiate. However, over the course of the first year, and especially with the emer-gence of early language skills, infants gradually lose this ability (Werker, 1989), and by late childhood, many children simply cannot perceive nuances of pronunciation that are irrelevant to their mother tongue. In a sense, their speech perception becomes developmentally fine-tuned to learning the lan-guage sounds of the culture in which they are being raised. Thus, sensory experience changes the child's capacity to perceive speech. Similar contex-tual fine-tuning may occur in many other areas of perception, a possibility that is further explored in Chapter 7.

Nutrition

As we have seen, under normal circumstances, infants double their birth-weight in the first months, a growth rate that sometimes requires feeding every three or four hours, day and night. The actual feeding "schedule," which can vary considerably from one child to another, is not the crucial fac-tor, however. What matters is the overall quality and quantity of the infant's nutritional intake. Adequate nutrition is essential not only to physical growth but to brain development and skill mastery as well.

The Ideal Diet

At first, infants are unable to eat or digest solid food, but their rooting, suck-ing, swallowing, and breathing reflexes make them well adapted for con-suming the quantities of liquid nourishment that they need. In these early months, breast milk is the ideal infant food (Lawrence, 1989). It is always sterile and at body temperature; it contains more iron, vitamin C, and vita-min A than cow's milk; and it also contains antibodies that provide the in-

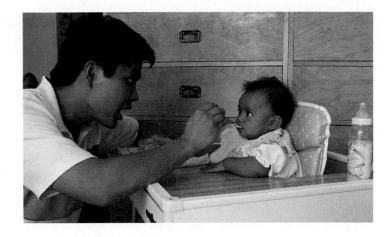

FIGURE 6.15 Feeding an infant "solid" foods usually begins in earnest at about 6 months of age, as the baby's digestive system matures and his or her nutritional needs become more complex. The father of this 7-month-old is obviously an experienced feeder, having mastered the "open wide" expression to signal the arrival of the spoon.

fant some protection against disease. In addition, the specific fats and sugars in breast milk make it more digestible than any formula, which means that breast-fed babies have fewer allergies and stomach upsets than bottle-fed babies, even when both groups of babies have similar family backgrounds and excellent medical care. Finally, research is now discovering many new and possibly crucial substances in breast milk. As one scientist explained, "It's a cocktail of potent hormones and growth factors, most of which we are just beginning to understand" (Frawley, quoted in Angier, 1994). Among the newly discovered ingredients in breast milk are various hormones believed to help regulate growth, encourage attachment, reduce pain, and regulate the brain, liver, intestines, and pancreas. There is also one hormone in breast milk that may affect the timing of sexual maturation.

Despite the advantages of breast milk, breast-feeding is no longer the most common method of feeding infants. The advent of the rubber nipple, the plastic bottle, canned milk, powdered milk, and premixed infant formulas available in handy six-packs has meant that many infants now survive and thrive without ever tasting breast milk (see A Closer Look, p. 202–203). Fewer than a fifth of all babies born in the United States are breast-fed for six months or more, despite evidence that breast milk is beneficial throughout the infant's first year (Rush & Ryan, 1991).

Although breast milk or formula can be the exclusive food in the first six months, by 6 months or so, "solid" foods should gradually be added to the diet. Cereals are needed for iron and B vitamins, fruits for vitamins A and C, and when these first solids are well-tolerated, vegetables, meat, and fish can be introduced to provide additional nutrition (Purvis & Bartholmey, 1988). By the time the infant is a year old, the diet should include all the nutritious foods that the rest of the family consumes.

In most developed countries, an ample and varied diet is fairly easy to obtain. When problems occur, they are usually due to parents' either allowing children to eat when, what, and how much they choose, or being overly restrictive, like putting an infant on a fat-free diet (babies need fat for normal brain development) (Eichorn, 1979). Unfortunately, in many other areas of the world, inadequate nutrition results instead from an inadequate food supply, and the consequences for the individual's development can be extremely serious.

A CLOSER LOOK

Breast versus Bottle

If breast milk is best, why do many women choose to give their infants formula? The reasons have little to do with nutrition directly, but are greatly influenced by the cultural attitudes and social pressures of our modern world and by the mother's socioeconomic status. Ironically, since the practice of breast-feeding in developed countries decreases as the level of maternal education and maternal income decreases, breast-feeding occurs less often among women who would greatly benefit from it in terms of both health protection for their infant and financial savings for themselves (While, 1989).

Many women find that, even if they want to breast-feed, it may not be easy. Problems may begin in the hospital if procedures make it impossible for the mother to have her newborn near her day and night, so that she can nurse whenever the infant is hungry. Outside the hospital, cultural attitudes may make breast-feeding inconvenient, if not impossible, except in the privacy of one's own home. Even in some cultures that have traditionally regarded breast-feeding in public as completely normal, there has been, as a result of Westernizing influences, a growing trend toward "modern modesty."

Increasing time pressures in many cultures have added to the problem. In order for breast-feeding to succeed, especially in the early weeks, nursing should occur every two or three hours or even more often if the baby demands it (Jones, 1993; Lawrence, 1989), with each feeding lasting twenty minutes or more. Such a schedule is important because the supply of breast milk is closely linked to demand, and the infant's frequent sucking helps establish ample production of the mother's milk. For many women who work outside the home or whose daily activities require them to be out in public much of the time, meeting this kind of schedule is difficult. (In response to the growing number of new mothers in the work force, a few U.S. employers now provide the time, privacy, and even breast pumps to allow nursing mothers to express milk in the workplace for their infants' consumption at home during the next day's work hours (Tousigant, 1993).

In addition, most women today are aware that traces of whatever drugs a breast-feeding mother ingests—cigarettes, alcohol, birth-control pills, and so forth—will show up in her milk. Furthermore, the quantity and quality of the milk are affected by what the woman eats, so weight-loss diets are inadvisable for nursing mothers. Consequently, some women decide that they would rather feed their baby formula in order to have greater freedom and flexibility to their own lives.

Fathers are influential, too. Some contemporary fathers want to be involved in all aspects of infant care right from the start, and, especially if they are unaware of the advantages of breast-feeding, prefer that their child be bottle-fed so they can sometimes do the feeding.

Practical advice can also be pivotal. When infant formulas and rubber nipples first became widely available in the 1930s, many hospitals encouraged bottle-feeding as the more "reliable" and convenient method, a trend that accelerated as hospitals and pediatricians endorsed the idea that newborns should be fed every four hours (Apple, 1988). Consequently, breast-feeding became less common, and by 1960 in the United States, three-fourths of all infants were exclusively formula-fed. Then, as the nutritional and health benefits of mother's milk became better understood, expert advice and hospital practices shifted, and by 1980, almost two-thirds of all American newborns were breast-fed. But over the next decade, as more and more mothers of infants entered the labor force, breast-feeding declined, dropping in 1992 to 52 percent during the hospital stay (Brody, 1994). Even fewer babies were breast-fed at 6 months, between 18 and 20 percent in the period 1986–1992.

One reason for these low rates is the reduced avail-

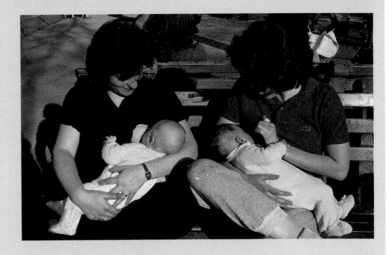

In the 1990s, breast-feeding in public has become more common in the United States. One reason is that mothers are more aware of the importance of nursing when the baby is hungry rather than adhering to a fixed feeding schedule. Another reason is that, in some parts of the country, pioneering women who have been arrested for indecent exposure because they breast-fed their infants in public have challenged the law and won.

ability of early help and encouragement. As one physician explains:

> Mothers are now discharged so fast from the hospital they leave even before their milk comes in. They are just handed a package of formula on the way out the door. At home, if their mother didn't breast feed, they have no support. [Lawrence, quoted in Hilts, 1991]

Further, "most people assume, incorrectly, that breast-feeding comes naturally," when, in fact, it is a "learned skill" (Brody, 1994). Without practical guidance, many women do not know how to handle all the specifics of breast-feeding—such as positioning the infant, getting the full nipple into the mouth, increasing milk supply, coping with a fussy feeder, relieving sore nipples, protecting against teething—and they give up when the first problem arises. The fact that even most of those who start out nursing quit before their infant is 6 months old is unfortunate, since experts now recommend that breast-feeding continue much longer for every infant worldwide. According to an extensive study sponsored by the United Nations,

all infants should be fed exclusively on breast milk for the first four to six months of life. Children should continue to be breast-fed, while receiving adequate complementary foods, through the second year of life and beyond. [UNICEF, 1990]

The reason for long breast-feeding is not only for optimal nutrition and protection against diseases but also for the mutual pleasure and intimacy that helps build a close mother-child relationship. Breast-feeding, of course, does not guarantee infant health or a good mother-child relationship—any more than bottle-feeding precludes it. And while the consensus among developmentalists is that breast-feeding generally fosters good maternal care, as well as good health and nutrition, it must be remembered that the choice between breast- and bottle-feeding is a personal and sometimes complicated one. Breast-feeding for at least one year may well be ideal, but the practical needs of the mother, father, and other children may mean that the best overall pattern for the entire household entails at least some bottle-feeding for the newest family member.

Nutritional Deficiencies

"Nutritional deficiency" covers a wide range of problems and consequences, from anemia and fatigue to outright starvation. In some cases, these conditions are the result of catastrophic circumstances, such as prolonged drought or civil war. In many cases, however, the underlying causes are ignorance or indifference in the family, culture, and community.

Severe Malnutrition

It is estimated that, overall, roughly 7 percent of children in developing nations are severely malnourished during their early years, with rates running above 60 percent in countries like Ethiopia, Pakistan, and Niger (United Nations, 1990). In the first year of life, severe protein-calorie deficiency can cause **marasmus**, a disease that occurs when infants are severely undernourished. Growth stops, body tissues waste away, and the infant dies. During toddlerhood, protein-calorie deficiency is more likely to cause **kwashiorkor**, a condition in which the child's face, legs, and abdomen swell with water, sometimes making the child appear well-fed to anyone who doesn't know the real cause of the bloating. Because in this condition the essential organs claim whatever nutrients are available, other parts of the body are degraded, including the child's hair, which usually becomes thin, brittle, and colorless.

The primary cause of malnutrition in developing countries is early cessation of breast-feeding. In many of these countries, breast-feeding was usually continued for at least two years, but now is often stopped much earlier in favor of bottle-feeding, usually with powdered formulas. Under normal circumstances, such formulas are adequate and safe. However,

> for many people in the developing world . . . the hygienic conditions for the proper use of infant formula just do not exist. Their water is unclean, the bottles are dirty, the formula is diluted to make a tin of powdered milk last longer than it should. What happens? The baby is fed a contaminated mixture and soon becomes ill, with diarrhea, which leads to dehydration, malnutrition, and, very often, death. [Relucio-Clavano, quoted in Grant, 1986]

A decline in breast-feeding, and a consequent increase in infant mortality, are apparent in many nations throughout the world (UNICEF, 1990). Many countries have tried to combat severe infant malnutrition by encouraging breast-feeding. Their efforts are proving successful in some cases. In Brazil, for example, infant mortality was cut in half between 1973 and 1983, even though overall nutrition and living standards did not improve. Longer duration of breast-feeding was one critical factor (Monteiro et al., 1989). In other countries, extensive efforts to promote breast-feeding seem to have had little or no impact. One reason may be that in-hospital campaigns to educate new mothers about breast-feeding through lectures and pamphlets are often undermined by such simultaneous in-hospital practices as separating mother and newborn for lengthy periods and providing new mothers with free samples of infant formula (Cunningham & Segree, 1990; Hull et al., 1990). The latter might be interpreted as the hospital's endorsement of infant formula, despite physicians' preference for breast-feeding.

In developed countries, severe malnutrition in infancy is not widespread, even among families with very low income. This is because social

marasmus   A disease that afflicts young infants suffering from severe malnutrition. Growth stops, the skin wrinkles, body tissues waste away, and death may eventually occur.

kwashiorkor   A disease resulting from protein-calorie deficiency in children. The symptoms include thinning hair, paleness, and bloating of the stomach, face, and legs.

programs, though often inadequate in many ways, tend to meet the essential nourishment needs of infants. Even when a particular impoverished family cannot obtain welfare, food stamps, or other governmental assistance, enough help is usually available from neighbors, relatives, and religious groups to prevent the extremes of marasmus or kwashiorkor. However, isolated cases of severe malnutrition during infancy do occur, when emotional and physical stresses on the caregivers (or the devastating effects of drug addiction on parenting) are so overwhelming that the adults ignore the infant's feeding needs or prepare food improperly, and the malnutrition of such an infant is not noticed by the larger community.

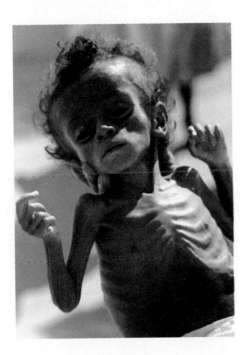 

FIGURE 6.16 Starving children, such as the Brazilian infant on the left or the Ethiopian refugees on the right, are suffering in many ways. Not only are their bellies empty and their bones visible; they also have depleted immune systems and stunted brain growth.

Undernutrition

Undernutrition is far more prevalent than severe malnutrition, both in developing and developed countries. Worldwide, according to United Nations statistics, 190 million children are undernourished, including 56 percent of all children in the least developed countries (UNICEF, 1994) (see Figure 6.17). The criteria for undernutrition vary, but usually include weight that is substantially below normal coupled with a failure to gain weight over time.

Most commonly, undernutrition is caused by a complex interaction of factors, with social and/or family problems being prime underlying factors. This is most obvious in regions of the world where everyone is undernourished: typically, the society's socioeconomic policies do not reflect the importance of infant nutrition, and parents may not even realize that a somewhat thin offspring is undernourished.

In developed countries, problems contributing to undernourishment are generally centered in the home. Mothers who are depressed, for example, tend to feed their children erratically and to be highly arbitrary in deciding when an infant has had enough to eat (Drotan et al., 1990). In infancy, as well as later in childhood, emotional stress brought about by conflict at home, or changes in a child's life, can also cause undernutrition (Sinclair,

1978). A previously well-nourished toddler who suddenly fails to gain weight probably has experienced a disruption in his or her life—such as an upsetting entry into day care, or the arrival of a new baby, or the departure of the father—that is expressed in mealtimes that are less frequent, or less healthy, or less pleasant.

Another cause of undernutrition in developed countries is ignorance of the infant's nutritional needs. For example, one common form of undernutrition in the United States is "milk anemia," so named because it arises from parents' giving their toddler a bottle of milk (which has no iron) before every nap and with every meal, inadvertently destroying the child's appetite for other foods that are iron-rich.

Because of these complexities, programs that see undernutrition as a problem of poor families exclusively, and seek to solve the problem by providing poor families with free food, are too narrowly focused (Ricciuti, 1991). To be successful in staving off the harm of inadequate nutrition, social policy must consider the entire context, including the need to raise parents' "nutritional consciousness."

FIGURE 6.17 If it continues throughout childhood, undernutrition not only makes a child smaller and shorter than his or her genetic potential would allow, but also undermines intellectual development, resistance to disease, and eventually, reproductive fitness. For example, even if they are well-fed in adulthood, women who were undernourished as children tend to have more difficult pregnancies and to have a higher rate of low-birthweight infants than women who were well nourished as children. Given the consequences and pervasiveness of undernutrition, public health officials contend that relief efforts should center as readily on undernourished children as on the emaciated, listless, severely malnourished children who easily capture public sympathy.

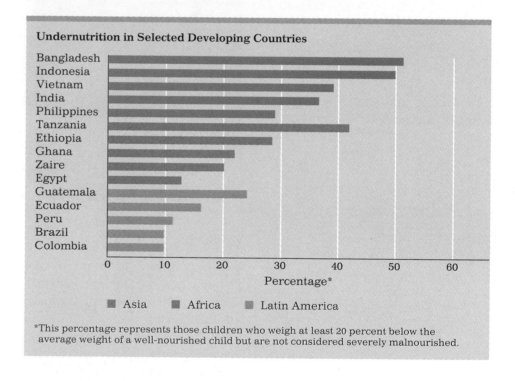

Undernutrition in Selected Developing Countries

Bangladesh
Indonesia
Vietnam
India
Philippines
Tanzania
Ethiopia
Ghana
Zaire
Egypt
Guatemala
Ecuador
Peru
Brazil
Colombia

0   10   20   30   40   50   60
Percentage*

■ Asia   ■ Africa   ■ Latin America

*This percentage represents those children who weigh at least 20 percent below the average weight of a well-nourished child but are not considered severely malnourished.

Consequences of Undernutrition

While severe malnutrition in infancy brings obvious physical and cognitive problems, the toll of less serious undernutrition is not so apparent: it may be manifested in a child's being smaller than normal, or being listless or apathetic, or having diminished resistance to disease. However, these characteristics are quite variable (Lozoff, 1989). Moreover, research suggests that even when undernourishment occurs during the brain's most rapid growth period, children's intellectual abilities can recover.

FIGURE 6.18 Normal genetic variation is apparent here, in appearance, activity level, and body size. However, if this is a typical sample of American infants, at least one infant is undernourished and one is overnourished. Infants who are undernourished have insufficient energy for normal growth and the expression of curiosity; infants who are overfed are slower to develop motor skills and are more likely to have a variety of health problems—ranging from asthma to heart disease—later in life.

Such recovery is not automatic, however. It is influenced by the duration of the undernutrition and the quality of intellectual stimulation experienced after infancy. Longitudinal research on undernourished children in Mexico, Kenya, and Barbados, as well as in Europe and North America (Dobbing, 1987; Galler, 1989), reveals that if they receive only minimal stimulation from family members or the school, children who were malnourished as infants show impaired learning—especially in their ability to concentrate and in language skills—throughout childhood and adolescence. Not surprisingly, these effects are more apparent when the early nutritional deprivation continues into childhood. Thus marginal nutrition in infancy is a risk factor, not necessarily causing deficits, but making problems more likely to occur if other stresses are present (Riccuiti, 1991). On the other hand, enhanced nutrition coupled with social support to the child and family (in the course of a home visitation program by a trained worker) has yielded long-term gains in physical growth as well as cognitive development for infants at risk of malnutrition (Super et al., 1990).

This research demonstrates one of the themes of biosocial growth illustrated throughout this chapter: the remarkable accomplishments of brain maturation, physical growth, and perceptual development are guided by a genetic plan but require a supportive environment to realize maturational potential. This theme should be kept in mind as we proceed to the next chapter, because the equally remarkable achievements of cognitive development also reflect the dual requirements of biological endowment and social support.

SUMMARY

Physical Growth and Health

1. In their first two years, most babies gain about 20 pounds (9 kilograms) and grow about 15 inches (38 centimeters). The proportions of the body change. The newborn is top-heavy, for the head takes up one-fourth of the body length, partly because the brain, at birth, has attained a high proportion of its adult size in comparison to other parts of the body. In adulthood, the head is about one-eighth of the body length.

2. Infants who are born full-term and healthy usually remain so during the first two years of life. However, to ensure a healthy childhood, all babies should receive regular immunization against the diseases that once sickened almost every child and killed many.

3. One cause of infant mortality remains unexplained and unpredictable—sudden infant death syndrome. While the precise cause and ultimate cure of SIDS are yet to be discovered, various measures can be taken to reduce its risk.

Brain Growth and Maturation

4. Although at birth the nervous system has virtually all the nerve cells it will ever have, these neurons form branching networks that grow and become refined and specialized during infancy and childhood. The result is increasing efficiency of communication between the brain and the rest of the body. As different areas of the brain mature, new capabilities emerge, including, in early infancy, the growth of self-regulation.

5. Brain maturation is responsible for the infant's increasingly regular patterns of sleep and wakefulness, and also for changes in the infant's ability to respond to, and control responses to, the environment.

Motor Skills

6. The development of motor abilities during the first two years allows the infant new possibilities in discovering the world. Gross motor skills involve large movements, such as running and jumping; fine motor skills involve small precise movements, such as picking up a penny.

7. At first, the newborn's motor abilities consist of reflexes. Some reflexes are essential for survival; some provide the foundation for later motor skills; others simply disappear in the first months. However, all reflexes are indexes of brain development.

8. Although the sequence of motor-skill development is the same for all healthy infants, babies—for both hereditary, developmental, and environmental reasons—vary in the ages at which they master specific skills.

Sensory and Perceptual Capacities

9. Both sensation and perception are apparent at birth, and both become more developed with time. Newborns are capable of virtually all modes of sensory experience and show early preferences for some types of events over others. Some senses—notably hearing—seem very acute within the first months of life; others—notably vision—develop more slowly throughout the first year.

10. The development of perceptual abilities involves the interaction between brain maturation and the infant's experience.

Nutrition

11. Breast milk is the ideal food for most babies. A mother's choice to breast-feed or bottle-feed typically depends on many factors, including education, lifestyle, and cultural pressures.

12. In developing countries, severe malnutrition can often be attributed to the early cessation of breast-feeding and improper preparation of commercial formulas. Marasmus and kwashiorkor, two major diseases caused by long-term protein-calorie deficiencies, can result in early death. When not fatal, chronic malnourishment may result in intellectual deficits and in shorter physical stature.

13. Undernutrition is quite common in developing countries and is often apparent in developed countries as well. The consequences vary, depending in part on the child's intellectual stimulation at home and in school.

..KEY TERMS

sudden infant death syn-
   drome (SIDS) (180)
neurons (184)
dendrites (184)
myelin (184)
physiological states (185)
electroencephalogram
   (EEG) (185)
reflexes (188)
breathing reflex (188)
sucking reflex (188)

rooting reflex (188)
gross motor skills (189)
toddler (191)
fine motor skills (191)
norms (192)
sensation (194)
perception (194)
habituation (195)
binocular vision (196)
marasmus (204)
kwashiorkor (204)

KEY QUESTIONS

1. How do the proportions of the infant's body change during the first two years?

2. What are the benefits of immunizations in infancy, in addition to preventing certain illnesses in infants?

3. What are the leading risk factors for sudden infant
death syndrome?

4. What are the primary maturational processes that take
place in the infant's brain and how do they affect the infant's physical functioning?

5. How do the baby's capacities to regulate alertness and
arousal change during the first year?

6. Which reflexes are critical to an infant's survival?

7. What is the general sequence of the development of
motor skills?

8. What factors account for individual differences in the
timing of motor achievements?

9. How do researchers determine whether an infant perceives a difference between two stimuli?

10. What are the sensory capabilities of a young infant?
How do they change over the first year of life?

11. What kinds of sensory experiences do babies typically
prefer in early infancy?

12. Give one example of how early experience fine-tunes
sensory and perceptual skills.

13. What are the advantages and disadvantages of breast-
feeding?

14. What are some of the consequences of serious, long-
term malnutrition?

15. Why does undernutrition occur?

The First Two Years:
Cognitive Development

CHAPTER 7

The pace of cognitive development in infancy is dramatic. An infant begins life capable of learning about the world only through such basic activities as sucking, grabbing, staring, and listening, and yet within two years, he or she will be capable of anticipating future events, deducing the causes of events, experimenting with objects (and people), and pretending. The development of language is similarly remarkable: for a young infant, crying and smiling are the major modes of expression, yet by age 2, the average toddler will be able to converse simply but effectively with others. In this chapter, we will discuss how these significant accomplishments occur, and look for answers to a number of intriguing questions, including the following:

How do infants perceive the world, and what particular things do they notice?

Do young infants have any awareness of number?

In what ways can babies think?

Can infants remember past experiences?

How do infants' actions reveal their growing intelligence?

Are children born with some of the abilities required for using language, or are all language abilities learned?

Imagine, for a moment, that you are a newborn infant, and then consider some of the elementary things you have yet to learn about the world around you. Enveloped in a swirl of constantly changing images, sounds, smells, and physical sensations, you must, in the weeks and months ahead, begin determining how these surrounding events fit together, enabling you to develop perceptions of objects, people, and even parts of your own body. You must begin deducing which of these events are enduring features of your everyday experience, and which change from moment to moment, or day to day. You must start figuring out the characteristics of the objects in your world—where they exist relative to you, where and how they move, and whether they are hard or soft, solid or flexible, and so forth. You must begin intuiting the sequences of events, linking causes and the effects they produce, and predicting the consequences of the events you can observe. And these are just the beginning of the incredible variety of cognitive tasks that babies must begin to achieve. No wonder that the grandfather of American psychology, William James, described the young infant's world as a "blooming, buzzing confusion!"

If you are now impressed with the remarkable cognitive growth that must occur early in infancy, consider another thing that has left developmental psychologists in awe: the speed and apparent ease with which this growth occurs. By the end of the first year—and often much sooner—infants have a basic grasp of the nature of objects and people around them and of their fundamental attributes (such as their boundaries, their permanence over time and in space, and other properties). They also have developed an understanding of the nature of distance and depth, have a rudimentary concept of number, demonstrate simple problem-solving capacities, and have begun to use language. It is as if the newborn infant is biologically endowed with the necessary intellectual tools for beginning to take in, and understand, the world in all its daunting complexity, and is supremely motivated from birth to do so. The young infant is not a passive recipient of experience but, rather, is a highly active and surprisingly competent processor of information.

The goal of this chapter is to explore how and why these accomplishments occur during the first two years of life. We will begin where we left off in our discussion of perception in Chapter 6, with the interpretive processes by which infants comprehend sensory experience and make it useful intellectually. To complete our portrayal of the infant's remarkable cognitive accomplishments, we will then consider the growth of memory and cognition, as well as the development of sensorimotor intelligence and the emergence of language.

Perception

As you learned in Chapter 6, infants possess remarkably acute sensory abilities from their first days: they can see, hear, taste, smell, and otherwise sense with far greater skill than was earlier believed. They also develop early *preferences* for what they experience, showing a hunger for novelty and stimulation, and discriminating easily between familiar and unfamiliar events. But how do infants interpret and make sense of what they experience? This side of perception—which is closely related to cognitive growth—is our topic for this chapter, and our examination will reveal an infant who is an active and eager interpreter of the world.

The first major theorist to realize that infants are active learners, and that early learning is based partly on sensory abilities, was Jean Piaget, who was introduced in Chapter 2 and whose depiction of infants' *sensorimotor development* is presented later in this chapter. We begin now, however, with the work of Eleanor and James Gibson, a husband-and-wife team whose understanding of the links between perception and cognition has inspired much of the current research on infants' cognitive growth.

The Gibsons' Contextual View

The central insight of Eleanor and James Gibson is that perception is far from being an automatic phenomenon that everyone, everywhere, experiences in the same way. Rather, perception is, essentially, an active cognitive process, in which each individual selectively interacts with a dense and richly varied field of perceptual possibilities (Gibson, 1969, 1982; Gibson, 1979).

In the Gibsons' view, all objects have many **affordances**; that is, they "afford," or invite, various activities by the perceiver. What affordances a person actually perceives in any given object depends partly on the individual's developmental level and past experiences, partly on his or her present needs, and partly on the person's cognitive awareness of what the object might be used for. To take a simple example, a lemon, among many other possibilities, affords smelling, tasting, touching, viewing, throwing, and squeezing. Which of these affordances a person perceives depends on the individual and the situation: a lemon might elicit a quite different perceptual response from an artist about to paint a still-life, a thirsty adult in need of a cool, refreshing drink, and a teething baby wanting something to gnaw on.

The idea of affordances thus emphasizes that there is an ecological fit between individual perceptions and the environment, such that affordances do not reside solely in the objective qualities of the object itself but arise in large measure from how the individual subjectively perceives the object (Ruff, 1984). As one psychologist explains:

> With affordances, a function is defined not by an essence but by its functional use to an organism. For example, if I want to sit down in a sparsely furnished bus station, a floor or a stack of books or a not-too-hot radiator might afford sitting. None of these are chairs, and thus their affordance of "sit-ability" is in relationship to my perception. [Gauvain, 1990]

How does the idea of affordances relate to infants? First of all, it alerts us to consider what the infant has a need to perceive from the environment. One such affordance is *graspability,* that is, whether an object is the right size, shape, and texture for grasping, and whether it is within reach. This is vital information for infants, since they learn a great deal about their world by handling various objects (Palmer, 1989; Rochat, 1989). Extensive research has shown that infants perceive graspability long before their manual dexterity enables them to actually grasp successfully. For instance, when 3-month-olds view objects, some graspable and some not, they reach for those that are the right size and distance for grasping and merely follow the others with their eyes (Bower, 1989).

The fact that babies perceive graspability so early helps explain how they explore a face. Once they have some control over their arm and hand movements, and a face comes within their reach, they immediately grab at it. But their grabbing is not haphazard: they do not grab at the eyes or mouth (although they might poke at them), for they already perceive that these objects are embedded, and thus do not afford grasping. A pull at the nose or ears is more likely, because these features do afford grasping. Even better, however, are glasses, or earrings, or a long mustache—all of which are quickly yanked by most babies, who perceive at a glance the graspability these objects afford.

Similarly, from a very early age, infants understand which objects afford suckability, which afford noise-making, which afford movability, and so forth. An impressive feature of this perceptual capacity is the infant's ability to distinguish affordance similarities in dissimilar objects (rattles, flowers, and pacifiers are all graspable) and affordance differences in similar ob-

affordances The various opportunities for interaction that an object offers. These opportunities are perceived differently by each person depending on his or her past experiences and present needs.

jects (among objects the same color, size, and shape, furry ones are more likely to be squeezed and plastic ones more likely to be sucked) (Palmer, 1989).

Second, the idea of affordances also has relevance for the infant's increasing perceptual maturity. Perceptual growth is partly a process of detecting and discriminating the most meaningful features of the environment, and the affordances infants perceive in the common objects around them evolve as babies gain experience with those objects. A gently sloping ramp, for example, may afford ascent and descent—but it may also afford falling, depending on the prior experience and locomotor skills of the infant. In one experiment, Karen Adolph and her colleagues observed two groups of infants as they moved up and down ramps pitched at different inclines: one group consisted of 14-month-olds with plenty of walking experience; the other consisted of 8½-month-olds with crawling (but not walking) experience (Adolph et al., 1993a, 1993b). The researchers had expected that the older infants would respond more cautiously to the incline because they could better perceive the affordance of falling due to their prior experience of walking—and falling—over various surfaces. And they were correct, the 14-month-olds confidently walked down gentle slopes, but when the slopes were made more steep, they negotiated the descent instead by sliding down in a sitting position (some courageous toddlers went down backward!), often after much hesitation and searching for alternative positions in which to make the descent. By contrast, the 8½-month-olds, regardless of the steepness of the slope, tried to make the descent by crawling rather than sliding, often falling headlong (their mothers were standing by to catch them). They never tried alternative means of descent and, even after falling, would often be ready to take another plunge down the ramp on the next trial. Thus, although infants of both ages could perceive the ramp's affordance of descent, only the older infants (with prior walking experience) could perceive its affordance of falling, and respond more cautiously as a result.

FIGURE 7.1 Like the other 14-month-olds in Karen Adolph's study, Lauren perceives that a gently sloping ramp (a) affords walking and confidently descends it. When later confronted with a steep slope (b), Lauren, like the other experienced walkers in the study, perceives the affordance of falling, and consequently descends the slope by sliding down it. (c) This is in marked contrast to the inexperienced 8-month-olds, who, like Jack, try to descend every slope, no matter how steep, by crawling, sometimes ending up in a nose dive.

(a)

(b)

(c)

The Gibsons' ecological view emphasizes, therefore, that early perceptual development involves a growing knowledge of affordances that is acquired through infants' active interactions with the objects and events around them.

Perceiving the Constancy of Objects

A task that is obviously essential to perceiving affordances, and to the infant's overall cognitive growth, is gaining an understanding about the constancy of objects. This is a surprisingly complex accomplishment, as illustrated in this example:

> Consider what we see when we gaze at the family cat stretched out before the fireplace. We see a single, solid, three-dimensional object, located in a particular region of space and separate from both the objects it touches (e.g., the rug on which it lies) and the object it occludes (e.g., the fireplace behind it). We see an object of a particular size, shape, and color, and do so regardless of the distance between us and the cat, the angle of viewing, or the lighting in the room (all factors that change the image in our retina). If an object comes between the cat and us, blocking all except head and tail, we do not perceive the cat as being bisected; rather, our perception is still of a continuous, indivisible object. . . . If the cat stirs itself and strolls from the room we do not expect its [tail] or any other part to remain behind; instead, we realize that the parts of an animate object move together in predictable unison. If the movement takes the cat away from us we correctly perceive that it is receding from us (but not changing size, despite changes in the size of the retinal image); on the other hand, if the cat suddenly makes a run for our lap we perceive not only that it is approaching but that its course guarantees contact within a very short time. (Of course, how we feel about such contact depends more on our attitude toward cats than on perception per se.) [Flavell et al., 1993]

How long does it take a newborn infant to master these complex interpretations of the sensory world? Not long (Flavell et al., 1993; Haith, 1980; Spelke, 1988, 1991). By the age of 3 months, for example, infants are able to distinguish the boundaries of separate three-dimensional objects, and a few months later they can do so even when one object partly overlaps another. This is especially true when the objects are in motion, as they typically are in everyday life. It seems that one way young infants can deduce the boundaries of an object is by observing how the parts of the object move together through space (Spelke, 1988). In other words, a cat's head, tail, and legs move in coordinated unison as the cat strolls across the room. Infants begin to realize that these body parts are each components of a single entity.

FIGURE 7.2 From the angle of her arm and the bend of her hand, it appears that this infant recognizes the constancy of this furry mass, perceiving it as a single entity whether it is standing still, rolling in the sand, or walking along the beach.

During the first half-year of life, moreover, infants also begin to develop an understanding of **perceptual constancy**, that is, the awareness that the size and shape of an object remain the same despite changes in the object's appearance. Thus, even though objects (like cats) look smaller when seen from a distance, and look different when perceived from different viewpoints, infants quickly grasp that they are the same objects nevertheless.

Dynamic Perception

As we have seen in a number of instances, movement plays a key role in infants' perception of the property of objects, and in the development of their perceptual and cognitive skills generally (Bornstein & Lamb, 1992; Flavell et al., 1993). Babies prefer to look at things in motion, whether those objects are a mobile rotating overhead, their own flexing fingers, or their favorite bobbing, talking human face. They also use movement cues from an early age to discern not only the boundaries of objects but also their rigidity, wholeness, shape, and size. Infants can even form simple expectations of the path that a moving object will follow (Haith et al., 1993; Nelson & Horowitz, 1987). The fact that infants have **dynamic perception**, that is, perception primed to focus on movement and change, works well in a world in which stimuli are constantly moving within the infant's field of vision. Movement captures the baby's attention, enhances the salience of certain attributes of an object (like its boundaries), and produces changes in the infant's perception of the object that enable the infant to learn about its other qualities.

FIGURE 7.3 One indication of dynamic perception is a baby's reaction to the "visual cliff," a surface constructed to look as if there is a sudden drop-off halfway across it. As shown here, when infants who are 8 or more months old are placed on a visual cliff, they hesitate, their heart rate increases, and they typically refuse to crawl over it, even if their mother encourages them to. In contrast, when younger infants with no experience at crawling are placed atop a visual cliff, they show no such signs of trepidation.

perceptual constancy   The awareness that the size and shape of an object remain the same despite changes in the object's appearance due to changes in viewing distance or perspective.

dynamic perception   Perception primed to focus on movement and change.

Not only objects' movements but also the baby's own movement enhances sensory and perceptual skills (Bertenthal & Campos, 1990). As babies scoot, crawl, creep, walk, and climb around the living room, they pay closer attention to their surroundings than when they are carried because they must navigate their own way; and they can be more goal-directed because their pursuit of interesting objects or people is not dependent on the person carrying them.

Further, as they move around their perceptual world, infants undergo a refinement of their **depth perception**, that is, the ability to perceive where objects exist relative to each other in a three-dimensional world. Depth perception becomes especially important, of course, once infants have begun crawling and (later) walking, because it aids in their safe navigation.

Researchers have discovered that self-locomotion also creates important changes in infants' reactions to their perception of vertical depths. When 3-month-olds are placed on a laboratory "visual cliff" (which is actually a glass surface several feet above an apparent drop [see Figure 7.3]), their eyes usually open wide and their heart rate decreases, an indication of curiosity and interest. This suggests that the very young infant perceives that something unusual is happening but does not yet realize that it might be dangerous to be suspended in air, seemingly several feet above solid ground. However, once babies have mastered crawling—whether early (perhaps at 7 months) or late (perhaps at 12 months)—it becomes apparent that they perceive not only vertical depth but also its danger. Probably owing to their all-too-common experience of crawling off the edges of beds, steps, and other drop-offs at home, they display fear when placed on the visual cliff (as shown by their facial expressions, vocalizations, and faster heart beat), and they will even refuse to come toward their beckoning mother if getting to her means crawling over that seemingly dangerous drop (Bertenthal & Campos, 1990).

Coordination Between Sensory Systems

Once researchers were alerted to the early development of the infant's perceptual skills, they also began to look closely at the infant's ability to integrate perceptual information from different sensory systems.

One aspect of this is **intermodal perception**, the ability to associate information from one sensory modality (like vision) with information from another (say, hearing). For example, when we sit near a lighted fireplace, it is through intermodal perception that we realize that the heat, the crackling, the smokey odor, and the flickering light all come from the same source.

Even newborns exhibit some intermodal perception, as when they look to see the source of a sound—though not always in the right direction. By 3 months, however, they not only look in the right direction for the source of what they hear but also have a notion of which sounds are likely to accompany what events. This has been demonstrated in various experiments that test whether infants can "match up" a film they are watching with an appropriate soundtrack. In one such experiment (Spelke, 1979), 4-month-old infants were shown two films simultaneously, each one displaying a stuffed animal puppet jumping up and down. At the same time, the infants heard a percussion soundtrack, keyed to the dancing movements of one of the puppets. By carefully monitoring the direction of the infants' gaze, the experimenter discovered that the infants looked more often at the film that matched the soundtrack.

What do these results mean? Were the infants simply responding in a visceral way to the beat of the drum and the accompanying visual rhythm of the puppet's jumping, or were they actually making a mental link between a particular sound and a particular sight?

FIGURE 7.4 This infant is coordinating an intermodal perception by linking the sight of the sponge with its texture and affordance of squeezability. From the looks of it, the next mode of perception to be coordinated may be taste.

depth perception   The ability to perceive where objects exist relative to each other in a three-dimensional world.

intermodal perception   The ability to associate information from one sensory modality (like vision) with information from another (like hearing).

To answer these questions, variations of this experiment have been repeated many times, usually with infants less than 6 months old. Even when there is no obvious visual or auditory rhythm, infants typically focus most on the film that matches the soundtrack, whether the sound is music, a voice, or simply noises—such as squishing sounds (matched with a film of a sponge being squeezed) or clacking sounds (matched with a film of wooden blocks hitting one another) (Bahrick, 1983). In one variation, infants about 6 months old simultaneously viewed two films of a person talking, in one film, with a happy expression, in the other, with a sad expression. At the same time, they heard the soundtrack of one of the films, which conveyed either a happy or sad mood. Although the infants at first looked equally at both films, they soon began looking more intently at the one that matched the mood of the soundtrack (Walker, 1982).

Perhaps unsurprisingly, infants make similar discriminations based on the speaker's sex, looking more at the film of a man talking when the soundtrack is of a male voice and more at the film of a woman talking when the soundtrack is of a female voice (Walker-Andrews et al., 1991). Quite startling, however, is the fact that infants look more at speakers whose lip movements match the speech sounds the infants are hearing (Kuhl & Meltzofe, 1988). Basically, the infants are "reading lips" before they understand words!

The fact that infants 6 months and younger are able to match pictures with sounds in so many different examples suggests that the babies are not simply making a primitive match between visual and auditory rhythms. Rather, they seem to be doing something more complex and more cerebral, turning information from one sensory modality into an expectancy and then matching that expectancy with information from another sensory modality.

Evidence for such cognitive integration of perceptual information also comes from research on a related ability known as **cross-modal perception**, the ability to use information from one sensory modality to imagine something in another—as when you hear the voice of a stranger on the phone and picture the person who is talking, or see a food and imagine how it tastes. In infants, of course, cross-modal perception is extremely rudimentary, but it has nevertheless been demonstrated many times (Rose & Ruff, 1987; Spelke, 1987).

The most convincing evidence that very young infants can translate information from one sensory system to another comes from experiments in which infants create a visual expectancy through their sense of touch. Essentially, experimenters allow infants to manipulate an object that is hidden from view and then show them two objects, one of which is the object they have just touched. By analyzing the infants' gaze, researchers can tell whether the infants distinguish the object they manipulated from the one they didn't. In one such experiment, for example, 2½-month-olds touched either a plastic ring or a flat disk and then were shown both objects. The duration of their gazing revealed that most of the infants "recognized" the object they had just manipulated (Streri, 1987).

Startlingly, even 1-month-olds have some cross-modal perceptual abilities. Again, visual expectancy derived from touch is involved, but the touch is by mouth, not by hand. In one experiment, infants sucked for 1 minute on an object, either a rigid one (a lucite cylinder) or a flexible one (a piece of

FIGURE 7.5 The earliest verifiable instances of cross-modal perception occur when 1-month-olds put something in their mouths and form a concept of how it might look. With experience, infants can reverse the process, imagining how something will taste from the way it looks.

cross-modal perception   The ability to use information from one sensory modality to imagine something in another.

wet sponge). They then observed both objects being manipulated by a pair of black-gloved hands. Analysis of their gazing suggested that they could distinguish the familiar object from the novel one: in other words, just by sucking an object they had gained some understanding of how it might look and move (Gibson & Walker, 1984). This rudimentary cross-modal perceptual skill improves significantly during the first-year as infants deduce the qualities of objects more quickly and sensitively with increasing age (Rose & Ruff, 1987).

The remarkable speed and apparent ease with which infants attain all these perceptual accomplishments has led some researchers to conclude either that these basic perceptual skills are innate or that newborns are biologically endowed with powerful capacities and motivation to quickly acquire these skills (Spelke, 1991). However the remarkable perceptual development of early infancy is explained, it is quite clear that very young infants do not merely passively absorb sights, sounds, and sensory impressions, but also (in a simple way) analyze, interpret, and integrate these perceptions to learn about the world around them. Their early skill in doing so provides the foundation for the equally impressive emergence of early cognitive abilities.

Cognition, Memory, and Intelligence

From our discussion so far, it is clear that a considerable portion of infants' knowledge of the world is built upon the development of their perceptual skills. As these skills become further enlisted for simple conceptualizing, thinking, and even problem solving, the infant clearly demonstrates the growth of cognition, memory, and intelligence.

Categories

You have seen that, from a very early age, infants coordinate and organize their perceptions into categories, such as soft, hard, flat, round, rigid, flexible, and so forth. For the preverbal infant, of course, these categories do not have labels such as "soft" and "hard," but they nonetheless represent useful and important ways of conceptualizing the world. Once an object is mentally placed in a category, for example, the infant has a ready set of expectations about it, and can distinguish it from objects that belong to other categories.

How do developmental researchers learn about an infant's categorization abilities when the child cannot verbally label them? Often they measure the infant's habituation, which (as you learned in the preceding chapter) is the gradual subsiding of a baby's initial responses to a novel stimulus as the stimulus becomes more familiar. Young infants usually stare wide-eyed at a new object, for example, but if the object continues to be presented to them, this initial expression of interest wanes, and the baby will, eventually, become uninterested and look away. If, however, a new and different object is presented, the infant will show renewed attention.

As you will recall from Chapter 6, researchers capitalize on this phenomenon to study whether infants can perceptually discriminate between different shapes, colors, sounds, and other sensations. In a similar manner, investigators can explore infant categorization skills by showing a baby several different objects in a particular category (say, circles of different sizes) until habituation occurs. Subsequently, two new objects are presented, one a member of the previous category (that is, another circle), and the other a member of a totally different category (like a square). If the infant shows such signs as an intensified gaze and a change in heart rate, or looks significantly longer at the new object, it can be inferred that the child has discriminated between the objects on the basis of their shape. In a sense, the child seems to be saying, in the example of the circles, "Here's one of those round things I saw before. But what is *this* with the angles and lines?" The discrimination seems to be based on the infant's developing a *category* of some kind from the earlier experience with differently sized circles.

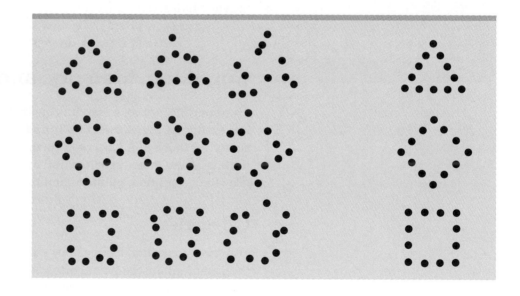

FIGURE 7.6 In one test of infant concepts, babies are shown a series of somewhat triangularly arranged dots, such as those at the top of this figure When they are next shown both a true triangle and a true square or a true diamond, infants as young as 3 months old tend to look longer at the square, or the diamond, a sign that they have developed a concept of triangularity from the previous viewings and find the novelty of the square or the diamond more intriguing. The same variations with the other shapes produce the same results.

A strategy like this was used in a study of 3- and 4-month-olds (Bomba & Siqueland, 1983), who were shown dot patterns that resembled either triangles, squares, or diamonds (see Figure 7.6). Some infants, for example, saw several dot patterns that were "squarish" in shape. When habituation occurred, the infants were shown two new dot patterns: one was a true square, and the other was a true triangle or diamond. Infants looked longer at the latter—suggesting that they had acquired some category of "squarishness" from the preceding dot patterns that caused them to view the triangle or diamond as more novel and interesting to look at.

Young infants also seem to form categories on the basis of the relationships between objects. In one study, a group of 4-month-olds were shown several pairs of geometric forms, with the members of each pair identical in shape but different in size. In each pair, the smaller shape was pictured above the larger one. After seeing several instances of this arrangement, the infants gradually habituated to it. Next, two pairs of new shapes were presented: in one case, the smaller shape was above the larger shape (as before); in the other case, the smaller shape was underneath the larger one. Infants looked much longer at the latter, suggesting that they had extrapolated a general concept of the relationships between, or the ordering of, objects (Caron & Caron, 1981).

The same general research format reveals that infants younger than 8 months can also categorize objects based on their angularity, shape, and density. They can similarly categorize different kinds of speech sounds they hear (Quinn & Eimas, 1988). Taken as a whole, the evidence suggests that young infants are not merely perceiving the difference between shapes like squares and triangles, or relative sizes like larger or smaller, or speech sounds like "ba" and "pa"; they are also applying some underlying organizing principles that enable them to develop a concept of what is, or is not, relevant for inclusion in a particular category. Although many researchers believe that a rudimentary understanding of certain categories in the natural world may be biologically based, experience with different kinds of objects and events also plays an important role.

This becomes especially apparent when we observe that as infants get older, they can categorize in increasingly complex ways. By the end of the first year, they can categorize and discriminate faces (based on features like hair length and nose size) (Sherman, 1985), animals (based on tail width or leg length) (Younger, 1990, 1993), and even birds (perceiving parakeets and hawks as similar to each other, but distinct from horses) (Roberts, 1988).

Discriminations like these enable young infants to conceptualize their world in increasingly more meaningful ways that are relevant to their day-to-day encounters with objects and people. Not surprisingly, categorical distinctions between male and female also occur, based on differences between the two sexes that are biological as well as cultural. As the Research Report on page 222 demonstrates, even young infants show some ability to distinguish male and female and, by age 1, can begin to apply cultural cues to these categories.

Although the simple categories that infants construct and recognize are nothing like the verbally labeled, and often highly ordered, categories that older children use, they nevertheless form a conceptual foundation for later cognitive accomplishments. Thus, it may be that, in part, language development progresses so rapidly during the second year (as we will see later) because infants are learning words for concepts that they may have understood for some time. As we will now see, their categorization skills may also explain why their capacities for understanding number and the causes of events on a preverbal level are so much more sophisticated than was once believed.

Is It a Boy or a Girl?

Very early in life infants have some beginning understanding that people are subdivided into male and female. By 3 months of age, babies seem to realize that male voices and faces are different from female voices and faces. For instance, an infant who is shown a series of photographs of male faces is likely to habituate to the series, even if each face is obviously different. Then, if a female face appears, the infant suddenly pays more attention.

Studies of intermodal perception demonstrate that infants are soon able to coordinate their knowledge of sex-specific voices and faces. One study showed 6-month-olds two photographs, one of a woman and one of a man, and simultaneously played a tape of a person talking. At first the infants scanned both faces equally. Then, gradually, sex expectancies were revealed: the babies looked longer at the male face when the speaker was male, and longer at the female face when the speaker was female (Francis & McCroy, 1983).

By 1 year of age, infants seem to have a firm ability to distinguish male from female, even among young children. In fact, whereas adults frequently have trouble distinguishing the sex of 1-year-olds, especially when the infants are dressed in unisex clothes, 1-year-olds themselves do not share this difficulty (Bower, 1989). When playing with unfamiliar peers, dressed in unisex clothes, boys are much more likely to play with boys, and girls, with girls. Even in looking at video tapes of toddlers, boys pay more attention to the boys, and girls, to the girls.

In one experiment, reported by Bower (1989), researchers made several brief films with a very simple basic script: a toddler walks over to a toy, picks it up, and sits down. The only variations were the sex of the toddler, how he or she was dressed (either in boyish pants and shirt or a frilly dress), and the toy (a drum or a doll). When 1-year-olds were shown two of these films, different only in the actor's biological sex, they looked more intently at the film that showed someone of their own sex, no matter what the other variables. Thus, a girl would tend to look more intently at a girl in pants and shirt playing with a drum than at a boy in a dress playing with a doll. The most interesting specific finding was that boys "spent proportionally far more time" looking at cross-dressed boys than at traditionally dressed boys or cross-dressed girls.

> Their typical pattern of looks at the cross-dressed boy was a long stare, a glance off at nothing, followed by short looks, interspersed with looking off. It was almost as if the boys found the sight of a boy dressed in girls' clothing extremely puzzling, almost shocking. No such pattern was found in girls. [Bower, 1989]

Is this child a boy or a girl? You may not be able to tell, but most 1-year-olds would be able to, especially after watching the child move around. (If you guessed a girl, you're wrong.)

How do these infants detect biological sex when the external clues are deceptive? Bower hypothesized that movement patterns seemed the likely answer. To test his idea, he dressed boy and girl models in black jumpsuits and placed a band of reflective tape on each shoulder, elbow, wrist, hip, knee, and ankle. He then filmed the infants in special lighting that revealed nothing but the movement of the reflective bands. According to Bower, when toddlers are shown these films, "the familiar pattern emerges, with boy babies looking more at boy babies and girl babies looking more at girl babies." On analyzing the films, Bower found that girls take shorter steps, swing their hips more, and seem more fluid in their movements. In addition, boys almost always bend from the waist to pick up a toy, whereas girls bend from the knees.

The fact that 1-year-olds are sensitive to all these subtle differences that escape most adults suggests that they have formed their own version of gender categories, based more on perception of body movement than on culturally determined differences in clothing or playthings. At the same time, the fact that the boys were highly alert to boys in frilly dresses, whereas the girls took no special notice of girls in boyish garb, suggests that by age 1 children may have already begun to absorb cultural norms regarding "sex-appropriate" attire among their peers.

Number

Through studies using habituation techniques, researchers have discovered a remarkable early sensitivity to number in infants—at least with small quantities. For example, after babies age 4 months or older are habituated to pictures of a standard number of items (say, three stars, then three houses, then three mops, etc.), they suddenly begin looking more intently when the number of items in a picture is different (such as two dogs) (Strauss & Curtis, 1984; Treiber & Wilcox, 1984; van Loosbroek & Smitsman, 1990). Obviously this sensitivity to number is evident long before children begin to count: what can explain it? Many researchers believe that small quantities can be perceived at a glance without having to be counted, and this is why infants respond to differences in small amounts (up to four or five) but are unable to differentiate larger quantities.

More startling are some preliminary findings suggesting that 5-month-olds possess not only basic number awareness but also some capacity to count. In one experiment, Karen Wynn (1992) showed individual infants a Mickey Mouse doll that danced across a stage. When the doll stopped, a screen was raised over part of the stage, concealing the doll from the child's view. Then, while the infant watched, another Mickey Mouse doll danced across the stage and behind the screen to join its partner. When the screen was lowered, infants saw either two Mickey Mouse dolls (which would be expected by a person who could count) or only one (which would be unexpected). Infants looked significantly longer at the unexpected display of a single doll, indicating that they had "counted up" the number of dolls that should have been behind the screen. The same outcome resulted from a subtraction experiment in which infants first saw two dolls placed behind the screen and then saw one doll being removed. Infants stared longer when the screen was lowered to reveal two Mickey Mouse dolls rather than one.

How may we account for these surprising findings? Scientists are divided in their opinions. Some have suggested that a basic appreciation of quantity, like some of the other perceptual skills we have surveyed, may be part of the biological endowment of the young infant (there is even some evidence that newborns perceive small quantities; see Antell & Keating, 1983). Others argue that these findings reveal that infants may distinguish between perceptions of one or more than one but have no real appreciation of number. Further research is required to clarify the extent of young infants' understanding of number and how this understanding relates to the more mature number concepts used by older children.

Object Permanence

Certainly one of the most important cognitive accomplishments of infancy is the ability to understand that objects (and people) exist independently of one's perception of them. With this understanding, referred to as **object permanence**, infants realize that even when objects like a familiar toy, the family cat, or Mommy cannot be seen or heard, they exist somewhere else in the world; they do not cease to exist simply because they are not immediately apparent. Although this understanding no doubt seems obvious to you, it is not obvious to young infants, whose early awareness of reality is strictly connected to what they can see, hear, and otherwise sense at a given mo-

FIGURE 7.7 Infants have demonstrated a firm concept of the difference between one and two objects, and sometimes even between two and three. This 5-month-old is registering surprise that there are only two dolls in front of her, because seconds before there were three. (The third, as you can see, was surreptitiously removed by the experimenter while the dolls were momentarily hidden behind a screen.) A number of researchers believe that this kind of surprised reaction reflects an innate numerical understanding.

object permanence   Piaget's term for the realization in infants, at about 8 months of age, that objects and people still exist even when they cannot be seen.

FIGURE 7.8 One nonexperimental demonstration of object permanence is the delight that 8-month-olds take in simple forms of peek-a-boo. By 11 months of age, the child's firmer grasp of object permanence may lead parents to engage in more sophisticated variations of the game.

ment. Consequently, the development of an awareness of object permanence has been especially interesting to researchers concerned with cognitive growth in infancy.

One way of testing for awareness of object permanence is to see whether an infant will search for a hidden object. In an experiment that was pioneered by Piaget, an infant is shown an interesting toy, which is then covered up with a blanket or cloth. If the infant searches under the covering for the toy, he or she realizes the toy still exists, even though it cannot be seen at the moment. Various forms of this experiment have been carried out by many researchers, with fairly consistent results: infants do not search for hidden objects until about 8 months of age. Even then, their search abilities are limited; they cannot easily find an object that has been concealed in one hiding place and then visibly transferred to a second hiding place (they tend to look for the object in the first hiding place). Thus their understanding of object permanence is slow to develop over the first year of life.

But does a failure to search necessarily reflect the absence of object permanence? After all, many skills are required for an infant to search competently for a hidden object (Harris, 1987; Ruff, 1982). For example, removing a cover to reveal a familiar toy requires the ability to set a goal and to know how to achieve it, and such means-ends understanding does not emerge until sometime in the second half-year of life. In addition, whether or not an infant searches for a hidden toy can depend on the infant's prior experience with searching and on the child's motivation to search. (The infant may have no interest in the toy, or may be tired or distracted by some other event.) The nature of the hiding place can also affect searching, as can the length of the delay between when the object is hidden and when the child is allowed to begin searching. Is it possible, then, that younger babies have an awareness of object permanence that is concealed by other factors when they are given Piaget's test of object permanence?

This intriguing possibility was explored by Renée Baillargeon and her colleagues in a series of experiments using the habituation technique. In one of these, Baillargeon (1987) placed 3½- and 4½-month-old infants directly in front of a large screen that was hinged along its base to the center of a table top. The screen was then repeatedly swung back and forth

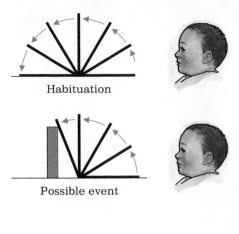

Habituation

Possible event

Impossible event

FIGURE 7.9 This illustration shows the basic steps of Renée Baillargeons's test of object permanence—a test that doesn't depend on the infant's searching abilities or motivation to search. First the infant is habituated to the movement of a hinged screen through a 180-degree arc. Next, with the infant observing, a box is placed in the path of the screen. Then the infant witnesses two events, the "possible event," in which the screen's movement through the arc is stopped by the box, and the "impossible event," in which the screen completes its movement through the arc as though the box did not exist. Infants as young as 4½ months old register surprise at the "impossible event," indicating that they are aware that the box does exist even though they can't see it behind the screen.

through a 180-degree arc (see Figure 7.9) until, as habituation occurred, the infants began to look away. At this point, a box was placed directly in the path of the screen's backward descent. Then the screen began to rise again until it reached its full vertical height, concealing the box. Thereafter followed two experimental conditions. In the first, named the "possible event," the screen continued to move until it was intercepted by the box and stopped, as one would expect. In the second experimental condition, named the "impossible event," the screen continued to move through its entire 180-degree arc, as though there were no box to block it. In fact there wasn't: it had been surreptitiously dropped out of the way through a trap door before the screen could hit it. Baillargeon found that 4½-month-old infants stared significantly longer at the "impossible event" than at the "possible event," as if they recognized that this was a novel, unexpected occurrence. She subsequently noted that infants could not have been surprised by this event unless they simultaneously

> (a) believed that the box continued to exist behind the screen, (b) understood that the screen could not rotate through the space occupied by the box, and hence (c) expected the screen to stop in the impossible event and were surprised that it did not. [Baillargeon & DeVos, 1992]

Baillargeon and her colleagues have devised a variety of different procedures to substantiate their view that infants possess a basic understanding of object permanence months before they can demonstrate this understanding on a hidden-object task (Baillargeon, 1991, in press; Baillargeon & DeVos, 1992; Baillargeon et al., 1990). In each case, young infants have looked significantly longer at "impossible events" that violated an expectation that objects cannot move through other hidden, solid objects. In addition, these experiments have revealed further aspects of infants' understanding of objects, including an awareness that although hidden, objects retain their original size, rigidity, and location, and that they can support other, visible, objects. All told, these findings suggest that young infants understand many things about the permanence of objects long before they acquire the motor skills to effectively demonstrate their understanding by searching for a hidden toy.

Memory

You have already seen some evidence for the memory skills of infants, ranging from their performance in habituation studies (requiring their ability to remember certain objects as familiar) to their skills in hidden-object tasks (in which they must remember the toy that is concealed by a blanket). But these cases involve memory, sometimes fragmentary, over fairly short spans. The real question is: How good are infants' long-term memory abilities? Both common sense and research experience have concluded that infants' long-term memory is generally very poor. A baby's trip to the pediatrician for an inoculation at age 2 months is forgotten a month later, when the same doctor in the same setting is likely to be greeted with a grin. Most of us have wondered why we cannot recall personal events that occurred during our early years, and developmental researchers concluded long ago that "infantile amnesia" arises from the weak memory skills of infancy. It isn't until the growth of language, most believed, that memory could be organized and stored in a way that facilitates retrieval.

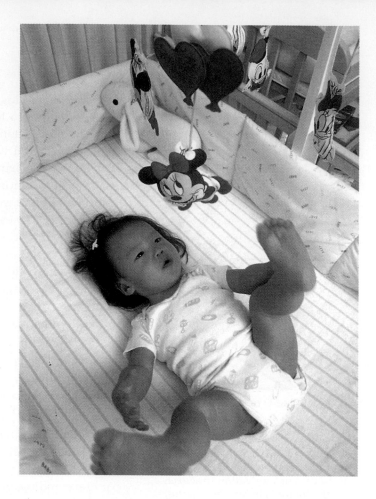

FIGURE 7.10 Mobiles, especially moving, musical, colorful ones, are fascinating to infants, because such objects offer exactly the kind of dynamic, intermodal perceptual experience the infant seeks to comprehend. Unfortunately for the parents, infant memory is far better than was once believed, which means that this expensive mobile is likely to become much less captivating in a few days.

But consistent with the story of much of this chapter, researchers have recently acquired a fuller appreciation of infants' memory abilities. To be sure, new research has not discovered young babies to be reliable recollectors: they have greater difficulty storing new memories, and forget them more easily, than they will by the end of their first year. But this research has shown that infants' early memory abilities can be much better than was formerly believed, *if* (1) situations are carefully tailored to the young infant's memory capacity as it might be demonstrated in real life; (2) the infant's motivation to remember is high; and (3) special measures are taken to aid retrieval.

Notable among this new research has been a series of experiments with 3-month-olds, in which infants learned to make a mobile move by kicking their legs (Rovee-Collier, 1987, 1990; Rovee-Collier & Hayne, 1987). This is a highly reinforcing event for young babies, who delight in controlling colorful, moving objects within easy focusing distance. The infants were tested at home, in their own cribs. A brightly colored mobile was placed overhead, and the infants were connected to the mobile by means of a ribbon tied to one of their feet. In this situation, virtually every infant quickly learned to kick to make the mobile move.

Would they later remember this experience? When the mobile-and-ribbon set-up was reinstalled in their cribs one week later, most infants started to kick, indicating that they remembered the connection between their kicking and the mobile's spinning. But another group of infants who were initially retested *two* weeks later had seemingly forgotten the connection. However, a further experiment demonstrated a remarkable effect: infants *could* remember after two weeks if they were given a brief "reminder" session prior to the retesting. In this reminder session, the infants were not tied to the ribbon, and were positioned so they could not kick. They merely watched as the mobile, activated by a hidden experimenter, moved. The next day, when they were tethered to the mobile and positioned so that they could move their legs, the infants remembered to kick as they had learned to do two weeks before. In a sense, their memory had been "reactivated" by the experience of having watched the mobile move a day earlier.

Similar experiments have been performed with younger infants (as young as 8 weeks) after a longer interval (up to eighteen days) with the same result (Davis & Rovee-Collier, 1983; Linde et al., 1985): a brief "reactivation" of their memory prolonged young infants' retention of an earlier event. Moreover, these researchers have also found that early memory improves with extra training or with less time separating training and recall, or with familiar cues (such as a distinctive crib bumper) to help bring to mind the earlier training (Borovsky & Rovee-Collier, 1990; Butler & Rovee-Collier, 1989). Carolyn Rovee-Collier thinks that this kind of "training" occurs quite frequently in an infant's daily experiences, since babies typically experience the same basic events day after day, and in familiar circumstances that aid memory renewal. When, for example, a parent regularly shakes a rattle or spins a toy to make it move for the baby, this may help to renew the child's memory for how to create these effects on his or her own.

At times, the events that will reactivate a baby's memory are surprisingly specific. This was revealed in another set of experiments in which 3-month-olds were again conditioned to kick their feet to make a mobile move. The mobile consisted of a series of blocks embossed with either the letter A or the number 2. Two weeks after the original training, infants who had been trained and reminded with an A mobile were more likely to activate an A mobile by kicking than they were to activate a 2 mobile, and vice versa. However, infants who had been trained on one mobile, and reminded with the other, were not likely to activate either (Hayne et al., 1987).

As they mature, older infants are capable of retaining information for longer periods of time than younger babies, and can do so with less initial training and less need for memory "reactivation." By 9 months of age, for example, babies can imitate behavior they saw modeled a day earlier (Meltzoff, 1988). A 9-month-old, for instance, who sees a playmate push a button on a toy to make an interesting sound may do the same thing the next day if she is at the playmate's house and has access to the toy. It appears that older infants can also retain more of the details surrounding an earlier experience or modeled behavior, including information about the sequence of events, and thus can use diverse aspects of the event—a sound, or a part of the setting—as a retrieval cue later on (Bauer & Mandler, 1992). The 9-month-old who observed her playmate push the button on the toy may later have that action called to mind by hearing the sound of the toy again or by being back in her playmate's room. Older infants can also begin to use other memory aids, like someone's referring to a past event, to assist their recall (Bauer & Hertsgaard, 1993). On the basis of the research, it seems possible that our inability to recall events from early in life may be due not only to the immaturity of our storage abilities in infancy but also to shortcomings in the ability to retrieve these recollections many years later. This realization is now causing researchers to reexamine the possibility of long-term storage—and retrieval—of memory from infancy, as A Closer Look on pages 228–229 explains.

Long-Term Memory in Infancy?

Most adults cannot remember specific events from their very early years (the experiences they think they recall are often ones that they were later told about by relatives or friends, or that have been memorialized in family photographs, home movies, and the like). Many explanations for this "infantile amnesia" emphasize the differences between memory processes in infancy and in later years (Siegler, 1991). In infancy, for example, memories are probably stored and retrieved according to the sensations (smells, sights, sounds) and motor skills associated with specific events or objects, while memories in later childhood and beyond are usually tied to more complex, language-based concepts. Consequently, even if experiences in infancy have been stored in mind, it may be very difficult to gain access to these memories in later years.

Is it possible, however, that infants store long-term memories that can be recalled when the recall process involves meaningful cues that "reactivate" dormant memories. Inspired by their new appreciation of infant memory, researchers have recently begun exploring whether young children can recall specific experiences that occurred when they were infants. The results have been intriguing.

One study, conducted in a university laboratory, began with 6-month-olds being trained during a single, 20-minute session, to reach for a dangling Big Bird toy when it made a noise, first in normal lighting and then in the dark (Perris et al., 1990). Two years later, the children were brought back to the lab and retested on this reaching task, along with a control group of age-mates who had received no training. Prior to the retesting, the trained children were interviewed to see if they had any overt memory of the laboratory setting or the training experience. They did not. Then, 30 minutes before testing, half of all the children who were to participate were randomly selected and given a 3-second exposure to the sound of the toy in the dark—intended as a possible "reactivation" of memory for those in the trained group.

In the retesting that followed, the conditions of the original test were repeated: each child sat in his or her mother's lap and was told the lights would go out. Then, in the dark, the experimenter dangled the noise-making toy in front of the child. Compared with the untrained children, those who had been trained at 6 months were more likely to reach and grab the toy—just as they had been trained to do long ago! In fact, among those who experienced the 3-second "reactivation" session, the trained children reached for the toy almost four times as often as the untrained children. Moreover, their reaction to suddenly being in the dark was "an almost global emotional acceptance," a marked contrast to the discomfort and fussiness exhibited by many children from the control group (and, indeed, by most 2½-year-olds who suddenly find themselves in a dark, unfamiliar room!). Thus, not only the specific behaviors of a single training experience at 6 months, but also its emotional tone, can remain in the memory of a young child for two full years.

Causes and Effects

Another important cognitive accomplishment in infancy is the ability to recognize, and associate, the causes of events with the effects they produce. Infants' ability to understand and anticipate the events they observe (whether shoving one toy into another to send the second toy flying, or clinging to Mommy while she puts on her coat and heads toward the door), as well as to act effectively in the world (whether kicking their legs to make a mobile move or lifting a blanket to find a concealed toy), hinges on the capacity to identify what actions lead to what results. One way of studying an infant's understanding of cause-effect relations is to closely observe the child's behavior to see if the child intentionally repeats some action that has produced an interesting result. If, for example, a child squeezes a rubber duck, producing a squeak, and, delighted by the noise, squeezes the duck again, the child has made a cause-and-effect connection between the squeeze and the squeak. But this method of study requires that infants possess the motor

It is important to remember that long-term recall was facilitated in many ways in this study—by the children's return to a distinctive testing room, by their reacquaintance with unique procedures and materials, and, ultimately, by a memory reactivation procedure for some of the children. Nevertheless, findings like these, which have been reported by other researchers (Myers et al., 1987), put to rest the idea that all infant memories inevitably disappear completely, and are causing developmentalists to reexamine infant memory to discover exactly how it functions (Lipsitt, 1990). So far, they have come to some of the following conclusions:

Early in life, even under the best of conditions, memory storage and retrieval appear to be fragile and uncertain. Infant recognition and recall of past events is facilitated by reminder events that help to reactivate memory.

The specific learning situation and the infant's motivation to remember are extremely important to later recall. Also, recall is more likely to occur when the task and the situation have some ecological familiarity and personal relevance for the baby.

Very young infants can and do remember, but their recollections probably consist not of words but of sensations and actions—images, smells, movements, and sounds—that are unlikely to be measured by traditional tests of memory.

Improvement in memory ability seems tied to brain maturation and language development, with notable increases in memory capacity and duration occurring at about 8 months of age, and again at around 18 months.

Much more needs to be understood, however, including answers to the following questions:

Are there several forms of memory, perhaps a type for basic sensory experiences, another for physical movement, and still another (or others) for more conceptual processes, such as those involving language?

Is the fragility of infant memory primarily a problem of encoding and storage—that is, getting the event into memory—or of retrieval—that is, recalling it after it has been stored?

Do older children and adults seem unable to remember their infancy because these memories are processed primarily through the senses and physical actions, rather than through language and other higher conceptual skills?

Much more research in this area is now underway, promising to yield further revisions in our understandings of what infants retain, and remember, from their earliest experiences.

skills that many young infants do not yet have. (Even deliberately squeezing a rubber duck demands a degree of hand control that is beyond many young infants.) To overcome this problem in studying young infants' awareness of the connection between causes and effects, researchers have again turned to the familiar habituation procedure.

One commonly used technique presents infants with a **launching event**. In this procedure, the infant sees an object, say, a square, move to the right across a table until it bumps into another object, say, a rectangle: the square stops moving, and the rectangle begins moving to the right. Most adults would view such an event as causal: the square appears to "launch" the rectangle into motion. By contrast, if the rectangle begins to move before it is bumped by the square, or if it doesn't move until a second or two after it is hit, most of us would not regard this as a causal sequence of events. In such cases, the rectangle appears to be moving for other reasons.

launching event A habituation technique used to determine if a young infant understands the connection between causes and effects.

Can young babies draw similar inferences? Studies in which infants are first habituated to the initial launching sequence and then shown variations of it (such as the rectangle moving before contact, or after a delay) reveal that 6-month-olds seem to have only a very rudimentary understanding of causal relations but that 10-month-olds can properly interpret the causality of simple launching events like this (Cohen & Oakes, 1993; Leslie, 1984; Leslie & Keeble, 1987; Oakes & Cohen, 1990). As we shall see in our discussion of Piaget's theory, this accomplishment coincides with a period in which infants are very busily engaged in manipulating and interrelating objects in their explorations of their world.

An understanding of cause-and-effect relations is basic to problem-solving ability, and some research has elicited displays of certain simple deductive skills in infants at about the same time that their causal awareness is blossoming. In one study, Peter Willatts (1984, 1989) presented 9-month-olds with a formidable challenge: to obtain an attractive toy that was out of reach on a table in front of them. Fortunately, the toy was resting on a cloth that was within reach; unfortunately, their access to the cloth was blocked by a foam-block barrier. Infants as young as 9 months old skillfully removed the barrier, then deliberately pulled the cloth to obtain the toy. Their strategic behavior contrasts with the actions of a comparison group of infants who were presented with the same situation, except that the out-of-reach toy was *not* resting on cloth. These infants tended to play with the foam block, but showed no interest in the cloth, since it provided no access to the toy.

Intelligence

As you no doubt have already surmised, the surprising competencies we have surveyed—intermodal and cross-modal integration of perceptions, categorical knowledge, simple number understanding, object permanence, memory skill, a capacity for expectations, delayed imitation, an awareness of causal relations, and even simple problem-solving capabilities—can all be considered markers of intelligence in infancy. Although this kind of intelligence is obviously much different from the symbolic, language-based forms of intelligence used by older children and adults, it reflects astonishing abilities in a young being whom earlier researchers had regarded as cognitively very simple. And these skills may provide the foundation for more sophisticated forms of conceptualizing, thinking, and reasoning in later years.

One question that has long intrigued cognitive developmentalists is whether measures of infant intelligence can predict later intellectual ability. In the past, efforts to establish a correlation between the results of traditional tests of infant intelligence and those of child and adult IQ measures have proven fruitless (Bornstein & Lamb, 1992). Developmentalists have usually explained this by pointing to important differences between intelligence in infancy and at later ages, the chief difference being that the former is based on a baby's actions, sensations, and other features of direct experience, while the latter is based on more abstract, symbolic, representational abilities. Reflecting this, traditional tests of infant intelligence have measured the kinds of motor skills and perceptual abilities that were presumed to be the cornerstone of infant intelligence but that may not have links to later forms of intelligence and reasoning.

However, in the more recent efforts to study infant cognition through habituation procedures, a number of researchers have noticed that infants differ in the speed of their habituation—that is, in how quickly they begin to lose interest when repeatedly presented with the same stimulus—and that these differences are associated with their performance on other measures of cognitive skill (e.g., Baillargeon, 1987). This finding led them to ask if individual differences in habituation speed would provide a better basis for predicting later intelligence in childhood.

The answer is a tentative yes. Infants who are faster in habituating to familiar stimuli—and who show a preference for new events in similar tests—tend to score higher on tests of childhood IQ and other measures of cognitive performance (Bornstein, 1989; McCall, 1990; Rose & Feldman, 1990; Slater et al., 1989). This holds true even when researchers have accounted for various influences that could affect both early habituation speed and later intelligence, such as differences in family influences. Taken together, therefore, it appears that one key feature of early cognitive ability—namely, the speed with which infants recognize familiarity and seek something novel—is related to later cognitive skill.

Many researchers believe that infants who habituate faster are, in other ways, quicker and more efficient in how they analyze incoming information (Colombo et al., 1991), an ability that would also benefit children as they grow up and encounter different, and more abstract, cognitive challenges. At the same time, it is important to recognize that differences in intelligence are only partly innate and therefore are not fixed for life: studies indicate that there is also considerable flexibility in intellectual growth from infancy to childhood, as new abilities are mastered and new skills are refined. That infant cognition is predictive of later intelligence underscores that the growth of cognition, memory, and thinking in the early years provides an important foundation for later mental abilities. That cognitive abilities continue to change suggests that nurture—such as parents' readiness to provide varied stimulation and encouragement of the infant's curiosity—is important as well.

Piaget's Theory of Sensorimotor Intelligence

In reading the foregoing account of cognitive development, it is easy to picture the infant as a young scholar who carefully observes surrounding events to deduce an understanding of how the world functions. However, such an image omits one of the most important characteristics of young babies: their activity and its central role in learning. Infants are not only constantly observing but also reaching, grasping, shaking, tossing, banging, and otherwise manipulating and interacting with objects and people around them. Sometimes their activity serves the purpose of sensory analysis, such as when infants mouth interesting toys to explore their texture, taste, rigidity, and other attributes. Sometimes it aids conceptual growth, as infants gain an understanding of object constancy and depth perception. Any description of early cognitive growth that ignores the ceaseless activity of infants in their pursuit of understanding misses a critical aspect of how intelligence develops.

This aspect of intelligence is central to Jean Piaget's theory of infants' cognitive development, first described sixty years ago as Piaget studied his own three children. Piaget believed that children actively seek to comprehend their world, constructing understandings of it that reflect specific, age-related cognitive stages. He showed that this process begins at birth and accelerates rapidly in the early months of life. To Piaget, infants lack concepts and ideas but are nevertheless intelligent; their intelligence functions exclusively in terms of their senses and motor skills (Gratch & Schatz, 1987). Consequently, Piaget called the first stage of cognitive development **sensorimotor intelligence**.

What does it mean to say that infants think exclusively with their senses and motor skills? As Flavell (1985) expresses it, the infant "exhibits a wholly practical, perceiving-and-doing, action-bound kind of intellectual functioning: he does not exhibit the more contemplative, reflective, symbol-manipulating kind we usually think of in connection with cognition." Although Piaget was incorrect in his belief that infants do not have concepts and ideas—as we have seen, infants have a fairly rich conceptual life—and some of his other proposals have been revised by recent findings, his portrayal of the "practical, perceiving-and-doing" side of early intelligence remains valid, and serves as a step-by-step encapsulation and illustration of much of the cognitive development already described in this chapter.

The Six Stages of Sensorimotor Intelligence

According to Piaget, sensorimotor intelligence develops through six stages, each characterized by a somewhat different way of understanding the world (see Table 7.1).

FIGURE 7.11 At the sensorimotor stage of cognitive development, even Father's face is a site for active exploration by all the infant's senses and motor skills.

sensorimotor intelligence Piaget's term for the first stage of cognitive development (from birth to about 2 years old). Children in this stage primarily use their senses and motor skills to explore and manipulate the environment.

TABLE 7.1

The Six Stages of Sensorimotor Intelligence

To get an overview of the stages of sensorimotor thought, it helps to group the six stages into pairs.
The first two stages involve the infant's own body.

Stage One (birth to 1 month)	*Reflexes*—sucking, grasping, staring, listening.
Stage Two (1–4 months)	*The first acquired adaptations*—accommodation and co-ordination of reflexes—sucking a pacifier differently from a nipple; grabbing a bottle to suck it.

The next two involve objects and people.

Stage Three (4–8 months)	*Procedures for making interesting sights last*—responding to people and objects.
Stage Four (8–12 months)	*New adaptation and anticipation*—becoming more deliberate and purposeful in responding to people and objects.

The last two are the most creative, first with action and then with ideas.

Stage Five (12–18 months)	*New means through active experimentation*—experimentation and creativity in the actions of "the little scientist."
Stage Six (18–24 months)	*New means through mental combinations*—thinking before doing provides the child with new ways of achieving a goal without resorting to trial-and-error experiments.

Stage One: Reflexes (Birth to 1 Month)

Sensorimotor intelligence begins with newborns' reflexes, such as sucking, grasping, looking, and listening. In Piaget's terms, these reflexes represent the only *schemes* that neonates have. (As you learned in Chapter 2, a scheme is a general way of thinking about, and interacting with, the environment.) Take sucking as an example. One of the most powerful inborn abilities of the newborn is the *sucking reflex:* newborns suck everything that touches their lips, using the scheme that all objects are to be sucked. Similarly, infants grasp at everything that touches the center of their palm, stare at everything that comes within focus, and so forth. Through the repeated exercise of these reflexes, newborns gain information about the world, information that will be used to develop the next stage of learning.

Stage Two: The First Acquired Adaptations (1 Month to 4 Months)

The second stage of sensorimotor intelligence begins when infants adapt their reflexes to the environment. These are *acquired adaptations* because they are learned as a result of particular experiences the infant has.

Again, let us take the sucking reflex as an example. Infants first show signs of adapting their sucking to specific objects at about 1 month, according to Piaget, and by 3 months they have organized their world into objects to be sucked for nourishment (breasts or bottles), objects to be sucked for pleasure (fingers or pacifiers), and objects not to be sucked at all (fuzzy blankets and large balls). They also learn that efficient breast-sucking requires squeezing or suction sucking, whereas efficient finger- and pacifier-sucking do not. In addition, once infants learn that some objects satisfy hunger and others do not, they will suck contentedly on a pacifier when their stomach is full but will usually spit one out when they are hungry.

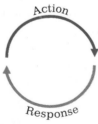

Circular Reaction

Primary Circular Reaction

circular reaction Piaget's term for an action that an infant repeats because it triggers a pleasing response.

primary circular reactions Piaget's term for circular reactions in which infants repeat actions that involve their bodies—for example, sucking their thumbs or kicking their legs.

Modifying or adapting reflexes reveals important growth in intelligence. So also does the appearance of **circular reactions**, which is Piaget's term for situations in which a baby's action triggers a reaction (in the baby or in someone or something else) that, in turn, makes the baby repeat the action. In the first stage of sensorimotor intelligence, **primary circular reactions**, in which the baby's own body is the source of the reaction, are typical: babies suck their thumbs, kick their legs, or stare at their hands again and again. As they grow, their primary circular reactions might include playing with their tongue or with the saliva that can accumulate on the lips, or making sounds.

As you can see from these examples, the intelligence reflected in primary circular reactions is entirely self-absorbed: infants play with their bodies, seemingly for the pleasure of doing so. In the process, however, they gain valuable information. They learn, for instance, that those wiggly little things that regularly come into view and often wind up in their mouths are actually attached to them, and that these things, which they will later know as fingers and toes, are within their control. Information such as this is basic to developing an awareness of body integrity—that is, an awareness of one's body as a whole. The emergence of this awareness is one of the first steps in understanding the world of other people and objects.

Stage Three: Procedures for Making Interesting Sights Last (4 Months to 8 Months)

In the third stage, infants become more aware of objects and other people, and they begin to recognize some of the specific characteristics of the things in their environment, particularly how objects respond to their actions on them. One way infants show this new awareness is by repeating a specific action that has just elicited a pleasing response from some person or thing. Piaget called this a **secondary circular reaction**. As noted ealier, for example, a baby might accidentally squeeze a rubber duck, hear a quack, and squeeze the duck again. If the quack is repeated, the infant will probably laugh and give another squeeze, delighted to be able to control the toy's actions.

Piaget called stage three "procedures for making interesting sights last," because babies interact diligently with people and objects to produce exciting experiences. Realizing that rattles make noise, for example, babies at this stage shake their arms and laugh when someone puts a rattle in their hands. And as you earlier saw in our discussion of memory, infants will excitedly kick their legs in a crib again and again to make an overhead mobile dance and spin. In fact, even the sight of something that normally delights the infant—a favorite toy, a favorite food, a smiling parent—can trigger an active attempt at interaction. Vocalization of all sorts increases a great deal, for now that babies realize that other people can respond, they love to make a noise, listen for a response, and answer back.

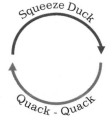

Squeeze Duck

Quack - Quack

Secondary Circular Reaction

secondary circular reactions   Piaget's term for infants' tendency to repeat actions to produce responses from objects or people.

FIGURE 7.12 This 7½ month-old knows that a squeal of delight is one way to make the interesting experience of a-tickle-from-Daddy last.

FIGURE 7.13 What do you see in this photo? Instead of a mess that needs to be cleaned up, you might discern a demonstration of intellectual ability. Brandon has a goal firmly in mind, and is wielding the tools to attain it—an achievement beyond most younger babies. At age 12 months he is about to enter a more elaborate stage of goal-directedness, one in which he might deliberately drop a few peas on the floor, or smash a few noodles on his head, or turn his plate upside down—all as "experiments in order to see."

Stage Four: New Adaptation and Anticipation (8 Months to 12 Months)

In stage four, babies adapt in new, more deliberate ways. They can better anticipate events that will fulfill their needs and wishes and can set about initiating them. A 10-month-old girl who enjoys playing in the tub might see a bar of soap and bring it to her mother as a signal to start her bath, squealing with delight when she hears the bath water turned on. Similarly, if a 10-month-old boy sees his mother putting on her coat to go out without him, he might begin tugging at it to stop her, or he might signal that he wants her to get his coat too.

Both of these examples reveal anticipation and, even more noteworthy, **goal-directed behavior**—that is, purposeful actions. The baby's greater goal-directedness stems from an enhanced awareness of causes and their effects that develops during this stage, together with the emergence of the motor skills needed to achieve the infant's goals. Thus, stage-four babies might see something clear across the room and crawl toward it, ignoring many interesting distractions along the way. Or they might grab a forbidden object—a box of matches, a thumbtack, a cigarette—and cry with rage when it is taken away, even if they are offered a substitute that they normally find fascinating.

Stage Five: New Means Through Active Experimentation (12 Months to 18 Months)

Stage five builds directly on the accomplishments of stage four, as the infant's goal-directed and purposeful activities become more expansive and creative. It is a time of active exploration and experimentation, a time when infants "get into everything," as though trying to discover all the possibilities their world has to offer.

Typical of the exploration and experimentation that occur in this stage are **tertiary circular reactions**. Unlike the primary and secondary circular reactions, in which babies repeat the same action again and again, tertiary circular reactions are distinguished by variations of a given behavior. A tod-

goal-directed behavior Purposeful actions initiated by infants in anticipation of events that will fulfill their needs and wishes.

tertiary circular reactions Piaget's term for circular reactions that infants repeat with slight variations.

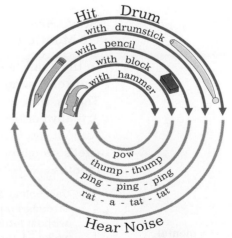

Tertiary Circular Reaction

dler might first hit a toy drum with a drumstick and then hit it again, in turn, with a pencil, a block, and finally a hammer. The different effects produced by each instrument—a light tap, a heavy bang, and so forth—evoke interest. Similarly, the toddler might first pat a lump of clay, then squeeze it, then pound it, and then rub it into the carpet to see what happens.

Because of the explorations that characterize this stage, Piaget referred to the stage-five toddler as a "little scientist" who "experiments in order to see." Having discovered some action or set of actions that is possible with a given object, stage-five infants seem to ask, "What else can I do with this? What happens if I take the nipple off the bottle, or turn over the trash basket, or pour water on the cat?" Their "scientific method" is trial and error. As parents of toddlers can readily attest, a little scientist's experiments can often wreak havoc. Remembering that these explorations are signs of developing intelligence may help a parent maintain a sense of humor, or at least a sense of perspective, when an infant combines baby powder and vaseline and uses the mixture to "paint" the wall, or takes out all the eggs in the refrigerator and throws them one by one on the floor, or, in a single flush, tries to send toothbrushes, hairbrushes, and a roll of paper down the toilet.

FIGURE 7.14 This is a perfect set-up for a little scientist: something inside something inside something, and all of it pullable.

Stage Six: New Means Through Mental Combinations (18 Months to 24 Months)

In the final stage of sensorimotor intelligence, toddlers begin to anticipate and solve simple problems by using **mental combinations** before they act. That is, they are able to try out various actions mentally without having to actually perform them. Thus the child can invent new ways to achieve a goal without resorting to physical trial-and-error experiments. Consider how Piaget's daughter Jacqueline solved the following problem at the age of 20 months:

> Jacqueline arrives at a closed door with a blade of grass in each hand. She stretches out her right hand toward the knob but sees that she cannot turn it without letting go of the grass. She puts the grass on the floor, opens the door, picks up the grass again and enters. But when she wants to leave the room, things become complicated. She puts the grass on the floor and grasps the doorknob. But then she perceives that in pulling the door toward her she will si-

mental combinations The mental playing out of a course of action before actually enacting it.

multaneously chase away the grass which she placed between the door and the threshold. She therefore picks it up in order to put it outside the door's zone of movement. [Piaget, 1952a]

The growth of mental combinations leads to far more than better problem-solving skills. It enables the child to think more flexibly about past and future events, to anticipate what can occur in a particular situation, and to enjoy a broader range of pretend activities.

These stage-six behaviors all share an important characteristic. They are a step beyond the simple motor responses of sensorimotor thought and a step toward "the more contemplative, reflective, symbol-manipulating activity" (Flavell, 1985) that we usually associate with cognition. As you will see in Chapter 10, these capacities will blossom into the symbolic thought typical of the next period of cognitive development.

Taken as a whole, Piaget's view underscores an essential feature of early cognitive growth that we saw in our discussion of perceptual affordances: infants learn about the world not as passive observers but as active (and highly motivated) scientists who strive, through experience, for greater understanding. Piaget was among the first developmental scientists to emphasize that early intelligence is constructed through these moment-by-moment encounters with the world. His depiction of sensorimotor intelligence reveals how, in each stage, increasingly sophisticated transactions with objects and people form the foundation for new understanding and more complex sensorimotor activities and lay a path to the next stage. And although infants do not always proceed through each of these stages quite as uniformly and discretely as his portrayal might imply—largely because their growth is often affected by aspects of cultural and familial experience (LeVine, 1989)—Piaget's theory provides a step-by-step view of the construction of knowledge through sensorimotor activity that most developmentalists and practitioners continue to find useful and thought-provoking.

Language Development

Mastering the sounds and meanings of one's first language is "doubtless the greatest intellectual feat any one of us is ever required to perform," according to one early developmental scholar (Bloomfield, 1933). Before dismissing this claim as hyperbole, imagine yourself as a tourist in a foreign land, surrounded by natives chattering rapidly in a language quite different from your own. Without extensive experience with that language, you cannot even decipher where one word stops and another begins; which nuances of tone and pronunciation are significant and which are merely individual variations; how the string of sounds is put together to make statements or questions; and most important, if the content of conversation should make you embarrassed, frightened, or delighted.

Lost as you might be, however, at least you know that spoken sounds have specific meaning, and you can figure out how to begin to learn those meanings in a different language—perhaps by nodding and smiling to the strangers to get their attention and then pointing to an object while gesturing in a manner that signals "What?" The infant does not even know this.

Nevertheless, by age 2, "children, bright and dull, pampered or neglected, exposed to Tlingit or to English," all learn language (Wanner & Gleitman, 1982). Consider the words, grammar, and conversational skill of one 24-month-old, Sarah, determined to distract her mother, who at the time was intently revising an earlier edition of this textbook.

> Uh, oh. Kitty jumping down.
> What drawing? Numbers? [said as her words were being transcribed]
> Want it, paper.
> Wipe it, pencil.
> What time it is? [said upon seeing a watch]

These sentences show that Sarah has a varied vocabulary and a basic understanding of word order. For example, Sarah said "Kitty jumping down" rather than "Down jumping kitty," or "Jumping kitty down," or "Kitty down jumping." They also show that she has much to learn, for she incorrectly uses the pronoun "it" and its referent together, omits personal pronouns, and uses reverse word order in asking the time.

Beyond the specifics of English vocabulary and grammar, this excerpt shows that Sarah has learned the universal function of language—to express one's thoughts and wishes to another, and to elicit a response. Despite her mother's preoccupation and attempt to ignore the distraction, Sarah produced seven successive sentences crafted to entice her mother into a dialogue. The final question, "What time it is?", reveals considerable sophistication about the rules of polite conversation: Sarah must have noticed that almost any adult, even a stranger on the street, usually answers that particular question.

Sarah's impressive but imperfect language is quite similar to that of 2-year-olds in many families and cultures. On the basis of detailed studies of hundreds of babies, we know quite a bit about the power of infants' drive to communicate and about the sequence of their emerging verbal skills in the first two years, and Sarah at age 2 is typical.

Steps in Language Development

It seems as if infants are equipped to learn language from birth, partly due to innate readiness and partly because of their auditory experiences during the final prenatal months. Newborns, for example, show a preference for hearing speech over other sounds, for hearing baby talk over normal speech, and for hearing their mother's voice over the voices of other adults (Cooper & Aslin, 1990; DeCasper & Fifer, 1980). (As we saw in Chapter 4, in one experiment, babies even showed a greater preference for hearing a story that their mother had regularly recited during pregnancy than for her reading of an unfamiliar story [DeCasper & Spence, 1986]). Moreover, young infants can distinguish among many different speech sounds, and can even differentiate between sounds that speakers of their native language cannot differentiate (Werker, 1989). As we saw earlier, they also quickly learn to recognize that certain speech sounds go with specific mouth positions. Rounded lips go with the "oo" sound, for example, while "aah" is associated with a more open mouth, and young infants may show surprise when they perceive an "oo" coming from a mouth positioned by an "aah" (Kuhl & Meltzoff, 1988). To a young infant, the sound of human speech—whether it comes from Mommy or Daddy, a doting grandparent, or an older sibling—creates special interest and curiosity.

Children the world over follow the same sequence of accomplishments in early language development, although their timing may vary considerably (see Table 7.2). Prior to their being able to verbalize, of course, infants are very effective at communicating their emotions, preferences, and ideas through grunts, cries, squeals, body movements, gestures, and facial expressions. These early communication skills serve the primary role of *language function:* to understand, and be understood by, others. As you will see, within the first two years of life, this rudimentary ability to communicate evolves into an impressive command of *language structure,* that is, the particular words and rules of the infant's native tongue.

TABLE 7.2

The Development of Spoken Language: The First Two Years*

Newborn	Reflexive communication—cries, movements, facial expressions.
2 months	A range of meaningful noises—cooing, fussing, crying, laughing.
3–6 months	New sounds, including squeals, growls, croons, trills, vowel sounds.
6–10 months	Babbling, including both consonant and vowel sounds repeated in syllables.
10–12 months	Comprehension of simple words: simple intonations; specific vocalizations that have meaning to those who know the infant well. Deaf babies express their first sign: hearing babies use specific gestures (e.g., pointing) to communicate.
13 months	First spoken words that are recognizably part of the native language.
13–18 months	Slow growth of vocabulary, up to 50 words.
18 months	Vocabulary spurt—three or more words learned per week.
21 months	First two-word sentence.
24 months	Multiword sentences. Half of the infant's utterances are two or more words long.

* The ages of accomplishment in this table reflect norms. Many healthy and intelligent children attain these steps in language development earlier or later than indicated here.
Source: Bloom, 1993; Lenneberg, 1967

Cries, Coos, and Babbling

Infants are noisy creatures, crying, cooing, and making a variety of other sounds even in the first weeks of life. These noises gradually become more varied over the first months, so that by 5 months, squeals, growls, grunts, croons, and yells, as well as some speechlike sounds, are part of most babies' verbal repertoire. Then, at 6 or 7 months, babies' utterances begin to include the repetition of certain syllables ("ma-ma-ma," "da-da-da," "ba-ba-ba"), a phenomenon referred to as **babbling** because of the way it sounds. In some respects, babbling is universal—all babies do it, and the sounds they make are similar no matter what language their parents speak. However, over the next few months, babbling begins to incorporate more and more sounds from the native language, perhaps as infants imitate the sounds they hear (Boysson-Bardies et al., 1989; Masataka, 1992). Many cultures assign important meanings to some of these sounds, with "ma-ma-ma," "da-da-da," and the like usually being applied to significant people in the infant's life (see Table 7.3).

babbling Extended repetition of certain syllables, such as "ba, ba, ba," that begins at about 6 or 7 months of age.

TABLE 7.3

First Sounds and First Words: Cross-Linguistic Similarities

	Mother	Father
English	mama, mommy	dada, daddy
Spanish	mama	papa
French	maman, mama	papa
Italian	mamma	babbo, papa
Latvian	mama	tēte
Syrian Arabic	mama	baba
Bantu	ba-mama	taata
Swahili	mama	baba
Sanskrit	nana	tata
Hebrew	ema	abba
Korean	oma	apa

Babbling in Deaf Infants

Deaf babies begin to make babbling sounds several months later than other infants do (Oller & Eilers, 1988). However, recent research suggests that deaf infants may actually begin a type of babbling—manually—at about the same time hearing infants begin babbling orally (Pettito, 1991). Analysis of video tapes of deaf children whose parents communicate in sign language reveals that before the tenth month, the infants use about a dozen distinct hand gestures—most of which resemble basic elements of the American Sign Language used by their parents—in a rhythmic, repetitive manner analogous to normal babbling. The similar timing of babbling among hearing babies exposed to spoken language and deaf babies exposed to signed language suggests that brain maturation, more than specific maturation of the vocal apparatus, underlies the universal human ability to develop language.

Gestures

During the same months that babbling appears, gestures become part of the baby's deliberate efforts to communicate (Bates et al., 1987; Oller & Eilers, 1988). Often the first gesture to be used is *pointing*. When desired objects are out of reach, even very young infants may extend an arm and fuss. But by 9 months they begin to point, vocalize, and look from the object toward an adult, leaving no doubt about their message. By 12 months, other gestures appear, usually modeled after those used by caregivers. Interestingly, during this period (6 to 12 months), deaf babies tend to show superiority over hearing babies in communicating through gestures and facial expressions.

Comprehension

At every stage of development, including the preverbal stage, children understand more than they express (Kuczaj, 1986). When asked "Where's Mommy?" for instance, many 10-month-olds will look in her direction; or when asked "Do you want Daddy to pick you up?" will reach out their arms. In addition, as the infant learns to better anticipate events (stage four of sen-

FIGURE 7.15 Infants' verbal understanding advances well ahead of their abilities at verbal production. "Fishee" is probably one of dozens of words that this child readily recognizes even though he has yet to say them himself.

sorimotor development), words such as "hot!" "no!" or "bye-bye" take on meaning. Of course, context and tone help significantly to supply that meaning (Fernald, 1993). For example, when parents see their crawling infant about to touch the electrical outlet, they say "No!" sufficiently sharply to startle and thus halt the infant in his or her tracks. Typically, they then move the child away, pointing to the danger and repeating "No. No." Given the frequency with which the mobile infant's behavior produces this response, it is no wonder that many infants understand "No" months before they can talk.

First Spoken Words

At about 1 year of age, the average baby speaks one or two words, not pronounced very clearly or used very precisely. Usually caregivers hear, and understand, the first word before strangers do, which makes it hard to pinpoint, specifically, exactly what a 12-month-old can say (Bloom, 1993).

Vocabulary increases gradually, perhaps a few words a month. By 18 months of age, the average baby speaks about fifty words and comprehends many more. Most of these early words are names of specific people and objects in the child's daily world, although some "action" words are included as well (Barrett, 1986; Kuczaj, 1986). At about the fifty-word milestone, vocabulary suddenly begins to build rapidly, a hundred or more words a month (Bloom, 1973). Toddlers differ in their vocabulary growth: some (called "referential") children primarily learn naming words (such as "dog," "cup," and "ball"), while others (called "expressive") acquire a higher proportion of words that can be used in social interaction (such as "please," "want," and "stop") (Nelson, 1981).

At first, infants show marked inaccuracies in the way they connect the few words they know to the people, objects, and events around them. Initially, they tend toward **underextension** of word meanings, applying a word more narrowly than an adult would. "Cat" may be used to name only the family cat, for example, and no other feline. A bit later, the opposite may occur, and words are applied far more broadly than their meaning allows. This characteristic, known as **overextension**, or overgeneralization, might lead one child to call anything round "ball," and another to call every four-legged creature "doggie." But once vocabulary begins to expand, toddlers seem to "experiment in order to see" with words just as they do with objects. The "little scientist" becomes the "little linguist," exploring hypotheses and reaching conclusions. It is not unusual for 18-month-olds to walk down the street pointing to every animal, asking "doggie?" or "horsie?" or "kitty?"— perhaps to confirm their hypotheses about which words go with which specific animals.

As children learn their first words, they usually become adept at expressing intention. Even a single word, amplified by intonation and gestures, can express a whole thought. When a toddler pushes at a closed door and says "bye-bye" in a demanding tone, it is clear that the child wishes to go out. When a toddler holds on to Mother's legs and plaintively says "bye-bye" as soon as the babysitter arrives, it is equally clear that the child is asking Mommy not to leave. A single word that expresses a complete thought in this manner is called a **holophrase**. In the early stages of language development, almost every single-word utterance is a holophrase, making toddlers much more proficient linguists than their limited vocabulary would suggest.

underextension The use of a word to refer to a narrower category of objects or events than the term signifies.

overextension The application of a word to several objects that share a particular characteristic.

holophrase A single word that expresses a complete thought.

Indeed, it is important to note that vocabulary size is not the only, nor the best, measure of early language learning. Rather, the crux of early language is communication, not vocabulary. If parents are concerned about their nonverbal 1-year-old son, they should look at his ability and willingness to make his needs known and to understand what others say. If those skills seem to be normal, and if the child hears enough simple language addressed to him every day (through someone's reading to him, singing to him, talking about the food he is eating and the sights he sees), he will probably be speaking in sentences before age 2 (Eisenson, 1986). In fact, one in-depth study of infant language development found that infants who were most adept at expressing their emotions nonverbally (through frowns, smiles, cries, and laughter) were generally slower to talk, but once they began, they progressed to multiword sentences just as rapidly as early talkers (Bloom, 1993). On the other hand, infants who show signs of language delay (for example, not babbling back when parents babble to them, or not responding to any specific words by age 1) should have their hearing examined as soon as possible. Even a moderate early hearing loss can delay speech acquisition (Butler & Golding, 1986). Further, an unwillingness to communicate can be a sign of serious emotional trouble. Again, early consultation with a professional is recommended.

Combining Words

Within about six months of speaking his or her first words, a child begins to learn new words more rapidly, and soon after this vocabulary spurt, starts to put words together. As a general rule, the first two-word sentence appears at about 21 months. Combining words demands considerable linguistic understanding because, in most languages, word order affects the meaning of the sentence. However, even in their first sentences, toddlers demonstrate that they have figured out the basics of subject-predicate order, declaring "Baby cry" or asking "More juice" rather than the reverse. (We will explore other features of language learning in the preschool years in Chapter 10.)

Teamwork: Adults and Babies Teach Each Other to Talk

How do babies learn to talk? Early research on language development tended to take one of two directions, focusing either on the ways parents teach language to their infants or on the emergence of the infant's innate language abilities.

The focus on teaching arose from B. F. Skinner's learning theory, which held that conditioning processes could explain verbal behavior just as well as it could other types of behavior (Skinner, 1957). According to this theory, for example, if babies are reinforced with food and attention when they utter their first babbling sounds, they will soon call "mama," "dada," and "baba" whenever they want their mother, father, or bottle. Similarly, many learning theorists believed that the quantity and quality of parents' talking to their child affects the rate of the child's language development, from the first words through complex sentences.

The focus on innate language ability came from the theories of Noam Chomsky (1968, 1980) and his followers, who believe that language is too complex to be mastered so early and so easily through conditioning. Ac-

FIGURE 7.16 If his infancy is like that of most babies raised in the relatively taciturn Ottavado culture in Ecuador, this 2-month-old will hear significantly less conversation than infants from most other regions of the world, including other localities in South America. According to many learning theorists, such a lack of reinforcement will result in a child who is much less verbal than most children from other cultures. However, each culture tends to encourage the qualities most needed and valued in the culture, and verbal fluency among children is not a priority in this community.

cording to Chomsky, the fact that children master the rudiments of grammar so rapidly, and at approximately the same age, implies that there is an innate facilitator of language, called a **language acquisition device** (abbreviated **LAD**), in the human brain. The LAD enables children to quickly and efficiently derive rules of grammar from the speech they hear every day, regardless of whether their native language is English, Chinese, or Urdu. Other theorists have proposed other innate structures to facilitate different features of language learning.

Research in recent years has suggested that both Skinner's and Chomsky's theories have some validity, yet both miss the mark (Bates & Carnevale, 1994; Bloom, 1991; Golinkoff & Hirsh-Pasek, 1990). One reason is because the actual language-learning process occurs in a social context, framed by the adult's teaching sensitivity and the child's learning ability. Infants are genetically primed to pick up language, and, on the whole, caregivers are surprisingly skilled at facilitating the infant's language learning.

The language-learning process begins in the first days of life, as infants turn their heads and open their eyes wide when they hear voices, express excitement when someone talks to them, and show preferences for certain voices. As time goes on, infants become attuned to the specific intonations, timing, and phonetic distinctions of the language they hear daily (Golinkoff & Hirsh-Pasek, 1990; Kuhl et al., 1992). Japanese infants, for example, become less attentive to the difference between "l" and "r" because there is no "l" sound in the Japanese language. Babies raised hearing English, on the other hand, become highly attuned to the distinction between these two letters, noticing the difference long before they can articulate it themselves.

FIGURE 7.17 Conversations rich with facial expressions, gestures, and dramatic intonation of a few words are universally found between mothers and toddlers, illustrated here by this winning pair in a Mexican market.

language acquisition device (LAD)
　Chomsky's term for the innate ability to acquire language, including an innate knowledge of basic aspects of grammar and an innate predisposition to attend to and remember the critical, unique aspects of the language.

baby talk　A term for the special form of language typically used by adults to speak with infants. Adults' baby talk is high pitched, with many low-to-high intonations, is simple in vocabulary, and employs many questions and repetitions.

For their part, adults talk to infants even in the first days of life, using a special form of language called **baby talk**, nicknamed *Motherese*. As used by researchers, the term "baby talk" or "Motherese" does not refer to the way people think babies talk—the "goo-goo-ga-ga" that few infants actually say. Rather, it refers to the particular way people talk to infants. Motherese differs from adult talk in a number of features that are consistent throughout all language communities (Ferguson, 1977): it is distinct in its pitch (higher), intonation (more low-to-high fluctuations), vocabulary (simpler and more concrete), and sentence length (shorter). It also employs more questions, commands, and repetitions, and fewer past tenses, pronouns, and complex sentences, than adult talk does.

People of all ages, parents and nonparents alike, speak baby talk with infants (Jacobson et al., 1983), and preverbal infants prefer listening to Motherese over normal speech (Cooper, 1993; Fernald, 1985), even if the Motherese is in a language the infant has never heard (Fernald, 1993). Part of the appeal, and the impact, of baby talk may lie in its energy and exaggerated expressiveness. Research has shown that the baby talk of depressed mothers is too flat in intonation and too slow in its conversational responses to hold the baby's interest (Bettes, 1988).

The function of baby talk is clearly to facilitate early language learning, for the sounds and words of baby talk are those that infants attend to, and speak, most readily. In addition, difficult sounds are avoided: consonants like "l" and "r" are regularly omitted, and hard-to-say words are given simple forms, often with a "-y" ending. Thus, father becomes "daddy," stomach becomes "tummy," and rabbit becomes "bunny," because if they didn't, infants and parents would have difficulty talking about them. Moreover, the intonations and special emphases of baby talk help infants make connections between specific words and the objects or events to which they refer (Fernald & Mazzie, 1991).

In the earliest stages of baby talk, the conversation is, of course, rather one-sided. However, as the child grows more responsive and communicative, the general interaction between parent and child becomes more like a conversation in its give and take, with turn-taking games such as peek-a-boo becoming more common.

The "conversational" aspect of the parent-child interaction is strengthened between 5 and 7 months, as parents begin to treat burps, smiles, yawns, gestures, and babbling as part of a dialogue. Even when the baby seems to do nothing, the parent is likely to carry on the conversation as though it were actively two-way (Bremner, 1988). A mother might say, "Don't you want to take a nap now?", pause a second or two as though allowing the baby to answer, and then say, "Of course you do."

In fact, the response is not all in the mind of the mother. Babies show with facial expressions that they listen to maternal speech, and they indicate when they are ready to hear more. By 9 months, many babies have developed the conversational skill of taking turns, just as adults do, both in vocalization and in gaze (looking intently at the mother when listening, averting the eyes somewhat while "talking"). This skill becomes more efficient and rapid as infants mature, with the number of turns taken per minute increasing from seven at 9 months to sixteen at 24 months (Rutter & Durkin, 1987).

Motherese promotes early language learning also because each partner shares the same focus of attention. When the child looks at his or her hands, the mother tends to make a comment using the word "hand"; if the child's focus shifts suddenly to a nearby toy, the mother is likely to comment about the toy. Talking to a child about whatever the child is focusing attention on at a given moment is an important contributor to vocabulary growth (Akhtar et al., 1991; Bloom, 1993; Tomasello, 1988).

Once the child begins to talk, many conversations between parent and child show the parent interpreting the child's imperfect speech and then responding with short, clear sentences the child can understand, often with special emphasis on important words. Particularly with firstborns, the child's vocabulary expands in the process (Jones & Adamson, 1987). Naturalistic observation is the best way to study this interaction, for facial expression and intonation are as much a part of baby talk as the words spoken. However, recorded dialogues like the following one between a mother and her toddler son at bedtime help give the flavor (Halliday, 1979):

> Mother: And when you get up in the morning, you'll go for a walk.
> *Nigel:* *Tik.*
> And you'll see some sticks, yes.
> *Hoo.*
> And some holes, yes.
> *Da.*
> Yes, now it's getting dark.
> *I wa [repeated thirteen times].*
> What?
> *I wa [repeated seven times]. Peaz.*
> What do you want in bed? Jamie? [his doll]
> *No!*
> You want your eiderdown? [quilt]
> *(grins) Yeah!*
> Why didn't you say so? Your eiderdown.
> *Ella [three times]*

In most episodes of baby talk, the child is an active participant, responding to the speaker and making his or her needs known. In this one, Nigel asked for his quilt a total of twenty times, persisting until his mother got the point. An analysis of toddlers' speech shows that, especially after the vocabulary spurt begins, early speech is almost never idle conversation. Babies seem intent on communicating their needs and desires, as well as commenting on their own actions.

More generally, the many ways in which adults support early language acquisition—from their use of baby talk, to their nonlinguistic "conversations" with the infant, to the persistent naming of objects and events that capture the child's attention, to their expansion of the child's sounds and words into meaningful communications—are, taken together, part of the structured guidance that theorists like Vygotsky believe to be the basis for cognitive and language growth. As you recall from Chapter 2, Vygotsky and his followers maintain that the child's intellectual competencies emerge through an "apprenticeship in thinking," as skilled mentors provide the child not only active instruction but also guided participation in shared activities that facilitate the development of skills. In many ways, early language development provides an example *par excellence* of how an important feature of intellectual growth—specifically, mastery of one's native tongue—is structured, guided, and nurtured under the sensitive tutelage of the adults in the child's world.

A Social Interaction

As we have seen repeatedly, infants are motivated to understand the world: the same motivation that makes toddlers resemble little scientists makes

FIGURE 7.18 Having completed these first two chapters on infancy, you can probably spot a number of signs that this baby in Nairobi is well nurtured by her family and culture—among them, the delight on both parents' faces, the "breast is best" shirt, the surrounding objects that stimulate exploration and conceptualization, and the language of gesture that obviously communicates to all three.

infants seek to understand the noises, gestures, words, and grammatical systems that describe the world in which they live, as well as to use words to engage in social relationships. Central to the achievement of understanding language is verbal interaction. As one researcher writes:

> language . . . could not emerge in any species, and would not develop in any individual, without a special kind of fit between adult behavior and infant behavior. That fit is pre-adapted: It comes to each child as a birthright, both as a result of biological propensities and as a result of social processes learned and transmitted by each new generation. [Kaye, 1982]

The idea that language develops as the outcome of "biological propensities" and "a special kind of fit" highlights the fact that both innate processes and the social context are prerequisites for language development. Humans are biologically destined to communicate, and their brains are primed to develop language. At the same time, verbal interaction between adult and infant is essential, for without a sensitive and responsive conversational partner, a child's language learning will be impeded. Thus parent and baby together accomplish what neither could do alone: teach a person to talk. The same is true of the other cognitive accomplishments discussed in this chapter. And as we will see in the next chapter, the same parent-infant relationship is at the core of the psychosocial development of the infant.

SUMMARY

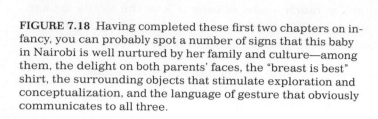

1. The interaction of the infant's early perceptual, cognitive, and linguistic abilities leads to impressive changes in the baby's capacity to understand and communicate with the world and forms the initial foundation for thinking and learning.

Perception

2. Infants quickly grasp the affordances of objects, that is, the activities one can do with them, such as grasping, sucking, squeezing, rolling, shaking, and the like. Affordances change for the infant as his or her experience and repertoire of skills and abilities increase.

3. Infants' perceptual skills contribute to such cognitive understandings as their grasp of the boundaries of objects, of depth and distance, of perceptual constancy, and other physical properties of objects.

4. Both intermodal perception (such as listening to a sound and knowing which object is likely to be the source) and cross-modal perception (such as touching an object and imagining how it might look) are evident in the first months of life.

Cognition, Memory, and Intelligence

5. Habituation research has provided important insights into the early growth of categorization skills, as well as into other abilities in infancy. Early categories of shape and sound quickly evolve into categories for faces, animals, and other objects. Young infants also show evidence of very simple number skills.

6. Young infants have a basic appreciation for object permanence in the early months of life, even though they will not effectively search for a hidden object until later in their first year.

7. Early memory is fragile yet surprisingly capable. Infants easily forget, but their memory can also be "reactivated" to help them remember past events. There is also intriguing evidence for long-term memory capacity in infancy.

8. Using measures of habituation speed, researchers have found that infants who habituate faster tend to score higher on cognitive measures later in childhood.

Sensorimotor Intelligence

9. From birth to age 2, the period of sensorimotor intelligence in Piaget's theory, infants use their senses and motor skills to understand their environment. They begin by adapting their reflexes, coordinating their actions, and interacting with people and objects. By the end of the first year, they know what they want and have the knowledge and ability to achieve simple goals.

10. In the second year, toddlers find new ways to achieve their goals, first by actively experimenting with physical objects, and then, toward the end of the second year, by manipulating mental images of objects and actions that are not in view.

Language Development

11. Language skills begin to develop as babies communicate with noises and gestures, and then practice babbling. Infants say a few words after the end of the first year, and they understand more words than they speak. By age 2, most toddlers can combine two words to make a simple sentence.

12. Children vary in how rapidly they learn vocabulary, as well as in the ways they use words. In the first two years, a child's comprehension of simple words and gestures, and willingness and ability to communicate, are more significant than the size of the child's vocabulary.

13. Language learning is partly the result of the interaction between parent and child. The child is innately primed to learn language, and adults all over the world facilitate language development by communicating with children using a simplified form of language called baby talk, which suits the child's abilities to understand and use language.

KEY TERMS

affordances (213)
perceptual constancy (216)
dynamic perception (216)
depth perception (217)
intermodal perception (217)
cross-modal perception (218)
object permanence (223)
launching event (229)
sensorimotor intelligence (232)
circular reactions (233)
primary circular reactions (233)

secondary circular reactions (234)
goal-directed behavior (235)
tertiary circular reactions (235)
mental combinations (236)
babbling (239)
underextension (241)
overextension (241)
holophrase (241)
language acquisition device (LAD) (243)
baby talk (243)

KEY QUESTIONS

1. How does an understanding of affordances affect perceptual ability?

2. What are the crucial accomplishments of perceptual growth in the early months of life?

3. Describe the early growth of categorization and number skills.

4. Why do developmentalists believe that young infants have an awareness of object permanence even though they cannot search well for a hidden object?

5. How good are the memory abilities of young infants? What factors can strengthen their memory?

6. What is the relationship between infant intelligence and later intellectual ability?

7. What perspective does Piaget's theory bring to the study of cognitive development in infancy?

8. Describe how changes in a baby's actions over time reveal the growth of sensorimotor intelligence.

9. What are the major milestones in the growth of language in infancy? Do all children reach these accomplishments at the same age?

10. How do experiences of social interaction in infancy facilitate language learning?

The First Two Years:
Psychosocial Development

CHAPTER

8

The social life of the developing person begins very early, earlier even than many researchers have believed. In the very first month, infants can express a number of emotions and can, in turn, respond to the moods, emotions, and attention of others. One reason these communications are so readily exchanged is that humans seem to be born with a universal language of emotional expression—a basic understanding of the meaning of each other's smiles, tears, and quizzical glances. Which other aspects of our personalities are we born with, and which develop as we mature and interact with others? This question and the ones that follow reflect some of the topics that will be examined in Chapter 8.

How does the infant's increasing sense of self-awareness affect his or her emotions and relationships with others?

What factors help a child to develop a basic sense of trust?

What are the implications of an infant's attachment, or lack of attachment, to his or her mother?

What are the differences in the ways mothers and fathers play with their infants and what are the effects of these differences?

What are the possible effects of an infant's being in day care on a regular basis during the first year?

When researchers first began to study the early social development of infants, they assumed that the emotional bonds babies develop with their caregivers are rooted in the benefits these people provide, such as food, physical warmth, and other direct satisfaction of needs. In this view, infants are born with no social tendencies at all, but eventually learn to enjoy the social stimulation that is associated with the caregiving they receive.

As we shall see, current analyses of early psychosocial growth still emphasize the importance of nurturance, but they add a new perspective—the view that infants are innately *predisposed* to be social. The research underlying this perspective has contributed to a much greater appreciation of the emotional needs and social competencies of young infants and of the sensitivity that caregivers demonstrate in responding to these needs and competencies. We now know that infants are remarkably attuned to social events from a surprisingly early age and that, just as they do in motor skills and cognitive achievements, infants show impressive psychosocial accomplishments during the first two years of life.

The Ethological Perspective

In Chapters 6 and 7, we saw that babies are born with impressive sensory, perceptual, and cognitive competencies that defy the once-traditional view that their minds are "blank slates" at birth. Infants, in fact, enter the world already equipped to respond to the events that will be most meaningful and relevant to their growth and development. But newborns require more than just perceptual and cognitive skills to thrive. Throughout the long evolution of our species, babies have depended on close social contact with those who feed, clothe, clean, and otherwise care for them. A baby's nurturance is thus tied to social interaction, and in this respect, infants likewise come into the world "preequipped," with basic social predispositions and skills that can contribute to their growth and development.

The source of these basic insights about the social infant is the ethological perspective (Hinde, 1983). **Ethology** is the study of patterns of animal behavior, particularly as that behavior is related to evolutionary origins and species survival. Typically, ethologists study such phenomena as the behaviors that trigger aggression in various species, the particular rituals that precede mating, the means by which certain species communicate the presence of food or of danger, the behaviors that are included in a species' care and raising of its young, and so on. After collecting detailed data on the relevant behaviors, ethologists attempt to determine how these behaviors evolved to contribute to the perpetuation of the species in question. For all species, including *Homo sapiens,* ethologists believe that to fully appreciate the meaning and significance of typical behaviors, we must look for their origins in the species' evolutionary heritage and understand what role these behaviors have played in its survival over the millennia (Hinde, 1989).

In the study of human development, the ethological perspective has particular relevance for infancy, because many of the behaviors of young infants tend to promote their nurturance and survival. Imagine that you can hear an infant crying, for example. No matter where you are, no matter what you are doing, your attention will most likely be diverted immediately, and you will probably feel concerned, sympathetic, and then troubled if someone does not make the child feel better. Such reactions are typical because, universally, adults recognize the infant's cry as a signal that the baby may be cold, hungry, or otherwise in need or in danger. Indeed, adults are quite adept at interpreting the infant's broad repertoire of cries, which in their varying intensity, duration, and change of pitch can alternately signal hunger, pain, fear, and so on (Wolff, 1969). Researchers have discovered that adults, even if they have never cared for a baby, become physiologically aroused, with focused attention and more rapid heart beat, upon hearing the sound of a baby's cry (Thompson & Frodi, 1984). Moreover, caregivers respond with greater urgency and more sensitive care the more distressed the baby sounds (Gustafson & Harris, 1990; Zeskind & Collins, 1987). The cry thus contributes to the baby's survival by signaling conditions that may harm the child.

Human infants, otherwise immobile and helpless, display additional behaviors, including reaching, clinging, and grunting that also summon

ethology   The scientific study of animal behavior in the natural environment, including its evolutionary origins and impact on survival. Ethological studies often shed light on human behavior.

adults, or keep them nearby, to provide nurturance. As we shall shortly see, by the time they are able to crawl, infants become emotionally attached to their caregivers, as well as fearful of unfamiliar situations that might represent potential dangers. At a time in development when the infant might otherwise wander away, both attachment and fear trigger a new set of dependent behaviors in the infant (such as regularly glancing in the caregiver's direction to confirm his or her presence), as well as increase the baby's motivation to stay close to the adult (Lieberman, 1993). In short, because, over the course of human evolution, infants who stayed near nurturing and protecting adults were more likely to survive, a broad repertoire of actions and feelings evolved in infants to keep them near their caregivers. At the same time, another set of complementary behaviors and emotions evolved in caregivers to ensure infants' nurturance and protection. In addition to responding to infants' cries, for example, adults become emotionally and physiologically aroused by the sight of a baby's smile or by the sound of an infant's laughter. In general, adults seem magnetically attracted to their infant's or toddler's simplest actions, noting, and doting on, the child's every move. This attention obviously serves a survival function, for adults will be more likely to notice when something is amiss with their offspring if they are drawn to them for hours on end. Even the baby's appearance—fat cheeks, round face, button nose, small chin, and big eyes—elicits innate nurturing urges in adults. (Indeed, the "babyish" appearance of almost anything, from a kitten to a cuddly cartoon character to the Pillsbury "dough boy," is a compelling and heart-warming sight for almost any human—which explains why advertisers use such images to sell everything from toilet tissue to car tires.) Over countless generations, this reciprocal attraction and affection between babies and adults has contributed to the survival and success of the human species, in climates ranging from tropical to arctic, and in situations where the dangers could be anything from marauding tigers to moving automobiles.

FIGURE 8.1 Everywhere in the world, adults' eyes seem to light up at the sight of an infant. Research has shown that almost anything that evokes a sense of babyishness excites an adult's attention, and this response seems to be part of an evolutionary mechanism that helps ensure infants' survival.

The four major theoretical perspectives in Chapter 2—psychoanalytic, learning, cognitive, and sociocultural—are all relevant to understanding the psychosocial development of the child at every age. For an understanding of infants, however, the additional insights of the ethological perspective are particularly illuminating. An infant's wariness of an approaching stranger, for example, or distress when the mother leaves, may arise not from previous fearful experiences with strangers or from anticipated abandonment by the mother (as a learning or psychoanalytic theorist might claim) but from an evolved predisposition to be wary of potentially dangerous situations, especially if one's own protector is not present. A toddler's clinging to the mother in an unfamiliar setting may reflect not an excessive "dependency" but, rather, a natural tendency to seek security through closeness to a trusted caregiver. Similarly, a parent's delight at a baby's smile, or worry when an infant crawls out of sight, may be as much an instinctual reaction as a rational response. Let us now look closely at early emotions in young infants, paying particular attention to how these emotions serve to connect each new baby to the larger human family.

Emotional Development

An examination of infants' emotional development provides a valuable window into early psychological growth because it reveals how young infants begin to perceive, understand, and respond to their surroundings. It also shows infants' emotions as important contributors to parent-infant interaction, for, as we have just seen, a baby's cry, smile, and other expressions are very significant social signals.

Recently, researchers have taken a new look at infant emotions, partly in response to the surprising discoveries that have been made concerning infant perception and cognition (see Chapters 6 and 7). Using sophisticated systems for deciphering the emotional content of facial expressions, they have analyzed videotapes of hundreds of infants, frame-by-frame, and found that even very young infants express many emotions—including joy, surprise, anger, fear, disgust, interest, and sadness (Campos et al., 1983; Izard, 1991). (See Research Report, pp. 254–255.) Indeed, it seems as if there is a developmental "schedule" by which infants acquire the capacity for specific emotions. This capacity appears to be related to brain maturation (Fox & Davidson, 1984) and to infants' growing abilities to understand the events around them.

The First Days and Months

The first emotion that can be reliably discerned is distress, most obviously registered in the crying of the infant who is hungry or otherwise uncomfortable. In addition, when newborns a few days or even a few hours old hear a loud noise, or feel a sudden loss of support, or see an object looming toward them, they often cry and look upset (Izard & Malatesta, 1987; Sroufe, 1979). By 4 to 7 months of age, babies exhibit more pronounced distress reactions that are combined increasingly with anger, such as when something attractive is taken away from them or they are prevented from moving (Stenberg & Campos, 1990).

Sadness, or at least a sensitivity to it, is also apparent early in infancy. In an experiment in which mothers of infants between 1 month and 3 months old were told to look sad and appear downcast, their infants responded by looking away and fussing (Cohn & Tronick, 1983; Tronick et al., 1986). Sadness expressions are even more apparent in the infants of depressed mothers (Cohn et al., 1990; Field et al., 1988). Other negative caregiving conditions can also give rise to the expression of sadness in infants. In one experiment, the facial expressions of a 3-month-old girl who had been severely abused by her parents were filmed and later shown to "blind" judges for assessment: without knowing anything about her condition, the judges rated the infant as undeniably sad (Gaensbauer, 1980).

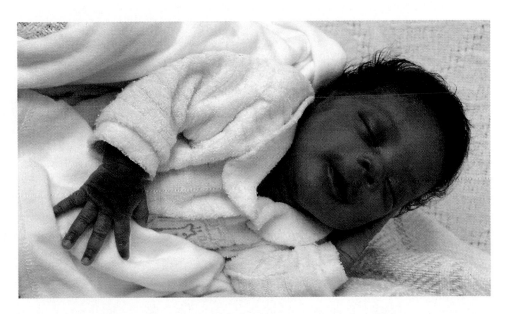

FIGURE 8.2 Toni at 1 month of age smiles in her sleep, as many very young babies do in response to the inner satisfaction of a full belly and a comfortable bed. However, not until about 6 weeks of age do babies smile in response to outside stimuli, such as a caregiver's face. Since Toni was born a month preterm, her social smile is likely to occur at 10 weeks of age, for neurological maturation rather than experience outside the womb seems to be the main prerequisite for the first appearance of the social smile.

social smile An infant's smile in response to a human face or voice. In full-term infants, this smile first appears at about 6 weeks after birth.

On the positive side, newborns show the wide-eyed looks of interest and surprise when something catches their attention (Field, 1982). Smiles also begin early: a half-smile at a pleasant noise or a full stomach appears in the first days of life. A **social smile**—a smile in response to a moving face or a human voice—begins to appear at about 6 weeks (Emde & Harmon, 1972). By 3 or 4 months, smiles become broader, and babies laugh rather than grin if something is particularly pleasing, especially during social interaction (Malatesta et al., 1989). These patterns are universal, as evident among, say, the hunter-gatherers of the Kalahari as among the upper class of Boston or Paris (Bakeman et al., 1990). Interestingly, some of the most potent elicitors of smiling and laughter in young infants are events (such as shaking a rattle to make a noise) whose occurrence the infant can control (Ellsworth et al., 1993; Lewis et al., 1990). Not surprisingly, some of the earliest anger expressions are observed when changes in circumstances end the infant's control of such an event (such as when a sibling takes a rattle away).

RESEARCH REPORT

Measuring Emotion

The measurement of emotions in infants is, obviously, a difficult task. Since babies can't say what it is they are feeling, researchers have had to rely on their own interpretations of infants' behaviors and expressions—a task equivalent to your having to determine the precise emotion that is being displayed by each of the infants in the accompanying series of photographs. However, researchers have discovered that, in fact, many facial expressions are universally understood: people from one society are able to look at photographs of people from quite distinct and distant societies and recognize expressions of anger, joy, sadness, disgust, surprise, and fear (Ekman et al., 1969; Izard, 1991). Further, there is a strong tendency for facial expressions to be significantly correlated with physiological, situational, and verbal signs of emotion. Despite obvious cultural differences, the facial cues of the common basic emotions are similar throughout the world.

This commonality implies that basic emotional expression is, at least in part, innate: there is "a prewired communication process, a process now known to require no social learning either for the reception . . . or production . . . of at least some facial and gestural signals" (Campos et al., 1983).

The discovery of the universality of many facial expressions led scientists to search for ways to achieve an objective analysis of emotional expressions, free of cultural biases. Some researchers developed systematic categorizations of facial positions that signal specific emotions. For example, in one system called MAX (Izard, 1980), twenty-seven distinct positions of the facial features are described. Some of these are listed in the table on the next page.

Looking at a videotape, advanced frame by frame, or examining a photograph, the scientist can note which of the twenty-seven positions are present and compare them to a numbered list of facial positions. Various combinations of these positions reveal specific emotions. Thus 20 + 30 + 50 is surprise; 21 + 31 + 53 is fear; 38 + 52 is happiness, and so on. An even more comprehensive system, called FACS, scores fifty-eight possible facial and head movements (Ekman & Friesen, 1976, 1978) and has been adopted for the special facial characteristics (e.g., the sucking lip) of the very young infant (Oster & Rosenstein, in press).

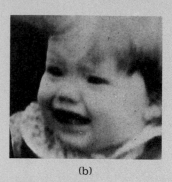

(a)   (b)

Can you tell what emotions these infants are expressing? Check your answers against those of the experts who analyze infant emotional expression. Shown here are (a) joy (mouth forming smile, cheeks lifted, twinkle in eye); (b) anger (brows drawn together and downward, eyes fixed, mouth squarish); (c) interest (brows raised or knitted, mouth softly rounded, lips may be pursed); (d) disgust (nose wrinkled, upper lip raised,

However, facial expressions alone are not foolproof indicators of emotion. As every mother knows, infants sometimes seem to grimace when yawning, or look disgusted during a pleasant bath. Developmentalists, too, have found that infants' facial expressions are sometimes incongruous with what they were likely to be feeling in a particular situation (Matias & Cohn, 1993; Oster et al., 1992). Consequently, many researchers are studying facial expressions in conjunction with other simultaneous expressions of emotion—such as vocalizations (laughing, cooing, and different forms of crying, for example) and body movements (such as turning away from a stimulus, or motionless gazing)—to deduce what a baby is truly feeling. Combined, these research tools have advanced the study of infant emotion in the past decade, for researchers now have an objective way to determine what a particular infant expresses. They would be able to agree, for instance, on what emotions the infants in the accompanying photos are experiencing (see caption).

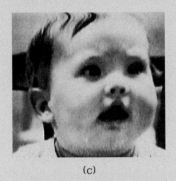

(c)

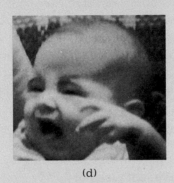

(d)

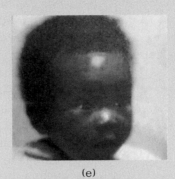

(e)

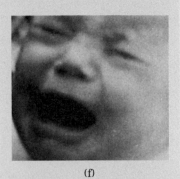

(f)

tongue pushed outward); (e) surprise (brows raised, eyes widened, mouth rounded in oval shape); (f) distress (eyes tightly closed; mouth, as in anger, squared); (g) sadness (brows' inner corners raised, mouth corner drawn down); and (h) fear (brows level, drawn in and up, eyelids lifted, mouth corners retracted).

(g)

Maximally Discriminative Facial Movements (MAX) Codes

Brows (B), Forehead (F); Nasal root (N)

20. *B:* Raised in arched or normal shape. (*F:* Long transverse furrows or thickening; *N:* Narrowed.)

21. *B:* One brow raised higher than other (other one may be slightly lowered).

22. *B:* Raised; drawn together, straight or normal shape. (*F:* Short transverse furrows or thickening in mid-region; *N:* Narrowed.)

23. *B:* Inner corners raised; shape under inner corner. (*F:* Bulge or furrows in center above brow corners; *N:* Narrowed.)

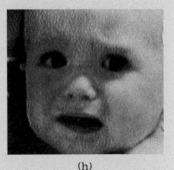

(h)

Eyes/Nose/Cheeks

30. Enlarged, roundish appearance of eye region owing to tissue between upper lid and brow being stretched (upper eye furrow may be visible); upper eyelids not raised.

31. Eye fissure widened, upper lid raised (white shows more than normal).

33. Narrowed or squinted (by action of eye sphincters or brow depressors).

36. Gaze downward, askance.

37. Cheeks raised.

Mouth/Lips

50. Opened, roundish or oval.

51. Opened, relaxed.

52. Corners pulled back and slightly up (open or closed).

53. Opened, tense, corners retracted straight back.

54. Angular, squarish (open).

Further Growth in Emotionality

After these early developments, sometime between 6 and 9 months of age, all the basic infant emotions become more differentiated and distinct. Emotions also show greater range and selectivity, owing to the child's growing cognitive skills and more varied experiences.

This shift is most evident in the various fears and anxieties that the infant experiences. One common reaction, **stranger wariness**, or fear of strangers, is first noticeable at about 6 months of age and is usually full-blown by 10 to 14 months. Perhaps you have observed this fear yourself when offering a 1-year-old a friendly greeting in a supermarket—only to have the child erupt in loud wailing! Contrary to popular belief, however, not all infants experience wariness with every stranger, and those who do vary considerably in the intensity of their reactions. Moreover, many infants respond positively to unfamiliar adults, and some mingle wary and friendly reactions in an unmistakably "coy" demeanor.

How a baby responds to a stranger depends on aspects of the infant (such as temperament and the security of the mother-infant relationship), the stranger (including gender and behavior toward the baby), and the situation (such as the mother's proximity or the infant's current mood) (Thompson & Limber, 1990). A baby may be friendly toward a stranger who keeps at a distance in the mother's presence, but react fearfully if the same stranger looms suddenly when the mother is away.

FIGURE 8.3 For most toddlers, the approach of a stranger with a buzzing razor triggers a full-blown case of stranger wariness—one that even reassurances and kisses from Mom can't quiet. Had the boy here encountered the stranger in a different context—say in a friendly conversation with Mom on the street—his reaction might have been a bit different.

stranger wariness Fear of unfamiliar people, first noticeable in infants at about 6 months of age and usually full-blown by 10 to 14 months.

separation anxiety A child's fear of being left by the caregiver. This emotion emerges at about 8 or 9 months, peaks at about 14 months, then gradually subsides.

A related reaction is **separation anxiety**, the fear of being left by the mother or other caregiver. Separation anxiety emerges at about 8 or 9 months of age, peaks at about 14 months, and then gradually subsides. Whether or not infants will be distressed by separation depends on such factors as the baby's prior experiences with separation and the manner in which the parent departs—leaving abruptly, for example, or in a relaxed fashion with good-byes and reassurance (Thompson & Limber, 1990). Stranger wariness and separation anxiety each reveal how the older infant's emotions are based not on a single event (such as the approach of an unfamiliar person) but on various contextual features of the event in question.

As every parent knows, anger also intensifies in toddlerhood. For example, when videotapes of infants being inoculated between the ages of 2 and 19 months were categorized by "blind" raters who could see only the children's faces, ratings of anger increased dramatically for infants between ages 7 and 19 months. In addition, the duration of anger increased, from a fleeting expression in early infancy to a lengthy demonstration at 19 months (Izard et al., 1987).

As infants become older, they smile and laugh more selectively, as well as more quickly (Lewis & Michalson, 1983). For instance, the sight of almost any human face produces a stare and then a smile in the typical 3-month-old, but the typical 9-month-old may grin immediately at the sight of certain faces—and might remain impassive or burst into tears at the sight of certain others. At 12 months of age, the infant's immediate smile at seeing a parent's face may be swiftly followed by an explosion of loud squeals if the parent's behavior signals the beginning of a playful interaction.

The overall effect of the many specific changes in the infant's emotional life is that the baby appears to have greater emotional vitality toward the end of the first year (Thompson, 1990). Whether they are expressions of pleasure, fear, distress, or anger, the most striking difference between the emotions of a 6-month-old and those of a 12-month-old is that the older infant's emotions are manifested more quickly, more intensely, and more persistently. As a result, the older infant's emotions become easier for an adult to read and respond to, which allows a more stimulating and mutual emotional exchange.

Emotion and Cognition

As you can see, in many ways the infant's emotional life in the second half of the first year is quite different from that of the first half, and the period between ages 8 and 9 months seems one of particular emotional growth. What might explain these changes in emotional development that cause the toddler at 12 months to be quite a different creature from the infant at 5 months? Since this is the same time that new cognitive and memory abilities appear (see Chapter 7), the emotional changes may be the result of a "cognitive metamorphosis" (Zelazo, 1979). In other words, being able to think and remember in a much more efficient and mature way, the infant can recognize more reasons to be happy or afraid, and be quicker to show anger or sorrow. For example, the emergence of anticipation and goal-directed behavior means that the infant can respond emotionally to *expectations,* such as crying when seeing Mommy putting on her coat to leave the house or laughing excitedly when she brings out the baby's ice-cream bowl. The infant's growing awareness of *causality* transforms the simple distress reactions of an earlier age into the emotion of anger, which is directed to the frustrating object or person (Stenberg & Campos, 1990).

Moreover, emotional growth is influenced by the infant's developing capacity to read the emotional expressions of others. Recall that 2-month-olds respond to their mothers' downcast appearance with their own expressions of sadness. Prior to this time, the emotional expressions of the mother have little impact on the baby's feelings (partly because the infant's limited visual skills make it difficult to detect facial expressions) (Klinnert et al., 1983; Nelson, 1987). After 2 months of age, however, infants do react in distinct ways to the facial expressions of emotion they can observe, but it is not clear that they are responding to the *emotional* meaning of those expressions: a baby may look sad when the mother is downcast because she is acting in an atypical manner, and not because of her sad mood. Beginning at age 4 months, however, infants begin to associate emotional meaning with different facial expressions, and by 8 or 9 months, they start to recognize that these emotional expressions are connected to particular events or objects. Similarly, at about 8 months of age, they become much more attuned to the "emotional messages" conveyed in the tone, pitch, and timing of spoken language, sometimes crying in response to the *sounds* of criticism—especially if it is accompanied by an angry face (Caron et al., 1988).

Social Referencing

At this point the emotional expressions of others begin to assume new meaning because infants engage in **social referencing**; that is, they look to trusted adults for emotional cues in uncertain situations (Feinman, 1985; Klinnert et al., 1983), darting glances at, or running to, their caregiver for signals that will help them to interpret unfamiliar or ambiguous events. The cues infants receive through social referencing—a look of calm reassurance, a vocal warning, or an expression of fear or dismay—affect how they feel about, and react to, unfamiliar people, unusual toys, a novel play setting, or other situations and events that provoke uncertainty (Rosen et al., 1992; Walden & Ogan, 1988). In one experiment, for example, 12-month-old infants were less likely to play with a toy robot or a moving, cymbal-clapping monkey when their mothers showed disgust as opposed to pleasure, and they continued to avoid the toy even when their mothers were no longer providing these emotional cues (Hornik et al., 1987). This suggests that infants remember what they learn from these emotional signals, and use this knowledge repeatedly. In addition, when encountering a novel situation, infants often spontaneously share whatever emotions their mothers communicate, sometimes even laughing after they fall down if that is what their mother does (Haviland & Lelwica, 1987; Termine & Izard, 1988). Fathers are also the focus of social referencing, as are other adults whom the infant has learned to trust (Camras & Sachs, 1991; Dickstein & Parke, 1988; Hirshberg & Svejda, 1990).

As indicated, from an ethological perspective, the fact that social referencing also becomes much more evident at just about the time infants become more mobile can be explained as an innate protection strategy against the dangers the exploring infant might encounter. This strategy is particularly adaptive

> in a highly technological society, where the biologically based cues to danger (darkness, sudden loud noises, animals, being alone) are only a subsample of the myriad threats to a child's safety. Dangers may lurk in speeding cars, seemingly friendly strangers, stairs, elevators. This means that, in spite of their innate competence in seeking protection, children's safety depends largely on the adult's more developed capacity to anticipate danger. [Lieberman, 1993]

social referencing Looking to trusted adults for emotional cues in interpreting a strange or ambiguous event.

The adult must signal anticipated danger and the child must read and heed that signal, which explains why most 12-month-olds repeatedly check on their caregivers' emotional messages and respond by mirroring the fear or pleasure they see.

New Emotions of Toddlerhood

One-year-olds continue to express all the basic emotions, such as joy, sadness, and fear, with increasing vigor, speed, and selectivity. In addition, new emotions emerge. These are linked to the changing world of the toddler, now a person who can move independently, use spoken language, and anticipate events in ways infants cannot.

Self-Awareness

One pivotal cognitive accomplishment of later infancy is the development of **self-awareness**. The emerging sense of "me and mine" becomes the fertile ground that allows many self-conscious emotions—from pride and confidence to guilt, shame, and embarrassment—to grow. Simultaneously, self-awareness allows a new consciousness of others, which fosters such emotions as defiance and jealousy, as well as empathy and feelings of affection that go beyond the pleasure of seeing a familiar face.

The development of this self-awareness is striking when infants of various ages are compared. Young infants have no sense of self: in fact, they do not even have an awareness of their bodies as *theirs* (Lewis, 1990). To them, for example, their hands are interesting objects that appear and disappear: 2-month-olds, in effect, "discover" their hands each time they catch sight of them, become fascinated with their movements, then "lose" them as they slip out of view. Even 8-month-olds often don't seem to know where their bodies end and someone else's body begins, as can be seen when a child grabs a toy in another child's hand and reacts with surprise when the toy "resists." By age 1, however, most infants would be more aware that the other child is a distinct person, and might show this awareness with a smile or a shove if the coveted toy is not immediately forthcoming.

Evidence of the emerging sense of self was shown in a classic experiment in which babies looked in a mirror after a dot of rouge had been surreptitiously put on their nose (Lewis & Brooks, 1978). If they babies reacted to the mirror images by touching their nose, it was clear that they knew they were seeing their own face. After trying this experiment with ninety-six babies between the ages of 9 and 24 months, the experimenters found a distinct developmental shift. None of the babies under a year reacted to the mark, whereas most of those between 15 and 24 months did. Before their second birthday, most infants can point to themselves when asked "Where's [child's name]?" and they can use their own name appropriately when pointed at and asked "Who's that?" (Pipp et al., 1987).

The link between the advent of self-awareness and the emergence of certain self-conscious emotions was shown in an extension of the rouge-and-mirror experiment (Lewis et al., 1989). In this study, 15- to 24-month olds who showed self-recognition in the rouge task described above also looked embarrassed when they were effusively praised by an adult; that is, they smiled and looked away, covered their face with their hands, and so forth. Infants who did not show self-recognition were not embarrassed. These changes from lack of self-recognition to coy smiles seem universal, occurring at about the same time among toddlers from varied backgrounds (Schneider-Rosen & Cicchetti, 1991).

Self-awareness also changes the intensity and conditions of the toddler's reactions to others, including affection and jealousy. Indeed, the infamous toddler temper develops partly because, when children become more

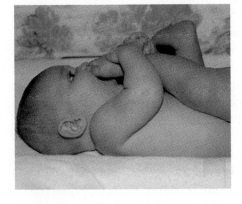

FIGURE 8.4 Although Alexandra at 4 months has enviable agility in being able to get her foot to her mouth, she probably does not yet realize that what she is trying to chew on is part of her—a cognitive gap that may result in unexpected discomfort.

self-awareness A person's sense of himself or herself as a being distinct from others, with particular characteristics.

FIGURE 8.5 Mirror images make young infants smile and try to touch "the baby." It is not until after they are a year old that children realize that they are looking at themselves.

aware of themselves, they take frustration and hurt much more personally, and realize, in turn, that they are more able to respond in kind (Dunn & Munn, 1985).

Developing self-awareness also enables toddlers to be self-critical and to have emotional responses such as guilt (Emde et al., 1991). By age 2, for example, most children are aware of the basic "do's" and "don'ts" they should follow, and sometimes show distress or anxiety when they have misbehaved, even when no adult is present. In one experimental demonstration of this, 2-year-olds were "set up" to experience two mild mishaps: they were left alone in a playroom with (1) a doll whose leg was rigged to fall off when the doll was picked up, and (2) a juice drink in a trick cup that dribbled when drunk from. Many of the children responded to their "accidents" with expressions of sadness or tension, accompanied by efforts to repair the damage (Cole et al., 1992). Such reactions are evident at home as well as in the laboratory: mothers report that the toddler's sense of shame and guilt appears for the first time after self-awareness develops (Stipek et al., 1990). With the growth of self-awareness, anger at an injustice (such as another child's getting the first slice of pie), as well as being "sorry" for a misdeed, become part of the child's developing moral sense (Zahn-Waxler et al., 1992).

The relationship between self-awareness and emotions is evident in other ways as well. Toddlers become notably more proud of their accomplishments, and as their ability to interpret others' emotional expressions continues to grow, children in their second year respond more sensitively and thoughtfully to the feelings of others. At times, this expanding emotional awareness is manifested in helpful, sympathetic responses to people who are hurt or distressed (Zahn-Waxler et al., 1992). On other occasions, it becomes a weapon enlisted in teasing, bragging, and conflicts with siblings and other family members (Dunn, 1988; Dunn & Munn, 1985).

In short, the emergence of self-awareness is crucial to the infant's social comprehension of the world and enables the child to become a more active partner in the community in which he or she is being nurtured.

Emotions and Social Interaction

Social interaction not only provides a context for emotional expression but also shapes emotional development. When playing with their babies, mothers mimic the baby's positive emotional expressions as if to enhance them; and when the baby shows sadness or distress, they tend to ignore these expressions, as though to avoid encouraging them, or they may briefly imitate the baby's sadness and then quickly switch to a more positive expression, as if to change the baby's feelings (Malatesta, 1990; Malatesta et al., 1989). As we have seen, these social influences can also have a negative impact on emotional development—such as when the offspring of depressed mothers themselves show more sadness and distress (Pickens & Field, 1993).

Cultural influences also shape emotional development by ordaining the kinds of experiences parents provide their offspring. Some cultures and subcultures, for example, stress the need to pacify infants when they are distressed, whereas others allow them to cry (so they won't become spoiled); some cultures promote nearly continuous contact between mother and infant, whereas others encourage separation in daily care and nighttime sleeping arrangements; some freely indulge the infant's dependency needs, whereas others foster the growth of self-control and self-reliance; some ex-

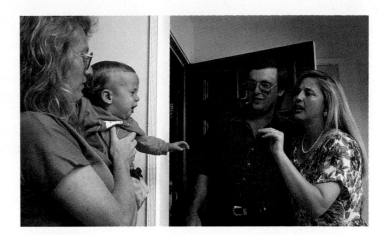

FIGURE 8.6 One of the many ways that cultural values influence child-rearing practices is in determining how much time infants spend with their mothers, day in and day out. In Japan, where young children's dependency on their mothers is encouraged—and where few mothers are in the workforce—children are with or near their mothers almost constantly. In the United States, where the development of the child's independence is a prime goal of child-rearing—and where the majority of mothers with young children are in the workforce—children are apart from their mothers a good deal more, whether in some form of day care or in the occasional care of a hired babysitter. Such differences in child-rearing patterns, and in the values that underlie them, help shape the infant's emotional growth.

pose infants to a rich variety of social partners, whereas others tend to keep infants' contact with others strictly limited (Tronick, 1992). In these and hundreds of other ways, emotional growth is shaped by social practices that derive from the values of the culture in which the family lives.

The Origins of Personality

Now that we have seen how emotional capacities develop during infancy, the next questions are: How do the infant's emotional and behavioral responses begin to take on the various patterns that form personality? What happens to evoke or create personality traits and social skills during infancy, leading to the emergence of a distinct individual?

Psychological Theory: The Importance of Nurture

In the first half of the twentieth century, the prevailing view among psychologists was that the individual's personality is permanently molded by the actions of his or her parents—most especially the mother—in the early years of childhood. There were two major theoretical versions of how this comes about.

Behaviorist Theory

Those who favored the behaviorist perspective (see Chapter 2) maintained that personality is molded as parents reinforce or punish their child's various spontaneous behaviors. Behaviorists proposed for example, that if parents smile and pick up their baby at every glimmer of an infant grin, the baby will become a child, and later an adult, with a sunny disposition. Similarly, if parents continually tease the child by, say, removing the nipple as the child is contentedly sucking, or by pretending to take away a favorite toy that a toddler is clutching, that child will be likely to develop a suspicious, possessive nature.

Once conditioned, claimed the behaviorists, early habits of personality tend to be self-reinforcing, and thus persist unless something disrupts them. Of course, the laws of behavior are such that any pattern of behavior can be changed if new conditioning occurs, but, according to the behaviorist view, the old pattern is never entirely erased. This means that old personality traits, first developed in the nursery but then altered by later experiences, might reappear in a situation that evokes the old circumstances. Thus, a baby who had learned to be suspicious might become more trusting later on, but a single episode of betrayal might reawaken all the person's former suspiciousness.

The strongest statement of this early view came from John Watson, the leading behaviorist of the time, who cautioned:

> Failure to bring up a happy child, a well-adjusted child—assuming bodily health—falls squarely upon the parents' shoulders. [By the time the child is 3] parents have already determined . . . whether . . . [the child] is to grow into a happy person, wholesome and good-natured, whether he is to be a whining, complaining, neurotic, an anger-driven, vindictive, over-bearing slave driver, or one whose every move in life is definitely controlled by fear. [Watson, 1928]

Watson even claimed that he could train any healthy baby to be "any type of specialist I might select—doctor, lawyer, artists, merchant, chief, and yes, even beggar man and thief, regardless of his talents, penchants, tendencies, abilities, vocations, and race of his ancestors" (Watson, 1924).

Later theorists in the behaviorist tradition incorporated the role of social learning, finding that infants tend to imitate personality traits of their parents, even if they are not directly reinforced for doing so. A child might develop a quick temper, for instance, if he or she sees a parent regularly display anger and get respect or obedience from other family members in return. Although these theorists accepted that not all personality traits are directly reinforced in babyhood, "the guiding belief of social learning theorists was that personality is learned" (Miller, 1993).

The most recent formulations of learning theory recognize two additional constraints on the pure conditioning process: innate biological and maturational limits, and the wider social context (Bandura, 1986; Bijou, 1989). Given this wider perspective, few learning theorists today would agree with Watson's bold boast, but most continue to emphasize the importance of early experiences, which, they contend, stamp a quite specific personality pattern onto an infant born with many possible personality traits. As one of the leading social theorists has explained, "human nature is characterized as a vast potentiality that can be fashioned by direct and vicarious experience into a variety of forms" (Bandura, 1977).

In infancy, the mother traditionally is in charge of most of the experiences the infant might have, and therefore, according to learning theorists, her moment-by-moment responses are primarily responsible for whatever personality traits might emerge.

Psychoanalytic Theory

Beginning with a different set of assumptions about human nature, psychoanalytic theorists (see Chapter 2) reached very similar conclusions about the early, and permanent, formation of the individual's personality. Sigmund Freud, who established the framework for their view, felt that the experiences of the first four years of life "play a decisive part in determining whether and at what point the individual shall fail to master the real problems of life" (Freud, 1963). He also thought that the child's relationship with the mother was "unique, without parallel, established unalterably for a whole lifetime as the first and strongest love-object and as the prototype of all later love relations" (Freud, 1940/1964).

Freud: Oral and Anal Stages

As we noted in Chapter 2, Freud viewed human development in terms of psychosexual stages that occur at specific ages. According to Freud (1935), psychological development begins with the **oral stage**, so named because in the first year of life the mouth is the infant's prime source of gratification. Not only is the mouth the instrument for attaining nourishment; it is also the main source of pleasure: sucking, especially at the mother's breast, is a joyous, sensual activity for babies, partly because the mouth, tongue, and cheeks are so sensitive to stimulation.

In the second year, Freud maintained, the infant's prime focus of gratification shifts to the anus, particularly the sensual pleasure taken in stimulation of the bowels, and eventually, the psychological pleasure in controlling them. Accordingly, Freud referred to this period as the **anal stage**. This change is more than a simple shift of locus; it is a shift in the mode of interaction, from the passive, dependent mode of orality to the more active, controlling mode of anality, in which the child has some power. Parents at this time are striving to foster the toddler's self-control in many ways in addition to toileting, a goal that can lead to a power struggle between adult and child.

Indeed, according to Freud, both these stages are fraught with potential conflict for the infant, conflict that can have long-term consequences. If a mother frustrates her infant's urge to suck—by making nursing a hurried, tense event, or by weaning the infant from the nipple too early, or by continually preventing the child from sucking on fingers, toes, and other objects—the child may be made distressed and anxious. Moreover, the child may become an adult who is "fixated," or stuck, at the oral stage, excessively eating, drinking, chewing, biting, smoking, or talking in quest of the oral satisfaction denied in infancy. Similarly, if toilet training is overly strict or premature (occurring before the age of 1½ or 2, when children are physiologically, as well as psychologically, mature enough to participate in the toilet-training process), parent-child interaction may become locked into conflict over the toddler's resistance or inability to comply.

Although Freud's ideas concerning orality and anality have been extremely influential, research has failed to support the linking of specific conflicts during these stages to later personality traits. Rather, it has shown that the parents' overall pattern of warmth and sensitivity or strict domination is much more important to the child's emotional development than the particulars of either feeding and weaning or toilet training (Maccoby & Martin, 1983). This broader perspective is reflected in the theories of Erik Erikson and Margaret Mahler, two contemporary psychoanalytic theorists who have studied infancy.

Erikson: Trust and Autonomy

As you will remember from Chapter 2, Erik Erikson believed that development occurs through a series of basic crises, or issues, throughout the life span (see p. 47). The first crisis of infancy, in Erikson's view, is one of **trust versus mistrust** in which the infant learns whether the world is essentially a secure place where basic needs will be met. Erikson contended that babies begin to develop a sense of security when their mothers sensitively provide food and comfort with "consistency, continuity, and sameness of experi-

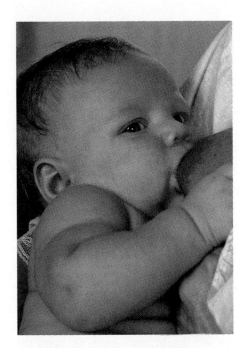

FIGURE 8.7 To psychoanalytic theorists, breast-feeding is important not just because it is a source of nourishment but also because the pleasurable, intimate contact it affords strengthens the infant's attachment to the mother and fosters a feeling of "basic trust" in the world.

oral stage Freud's term for the first stage of psychosexual development, in which the infant gains erotic pleasure through sucking and biting.

anal stage Freud's second stage of psychosexual development, in which the anus becomes the main source of bodily pleasure, and defecation and toilet training are therefore important activities.

trust versus mistrust Erikson's first stage of psychosocial development, in which the infant experiences the world as either good and comfortable or as threatening and uncomfortable.

FIGURE 8.8 How will this young child's parents react to her explorations? According to Erikson, parent strictness or permissiveness can shape how young children resolve the psychosocial crisis of *autonomy versus shame and doubt.*

FIGURE 8.9 Typical of children at the separation-individuation phase, this little girl loves to slide down on her own, but she still wants her mother to climb up the slide with her to get her started.

ence." When the relationship with the mother inspires trust and security, the child experiences confidence in engaging and exploring the world.

The next crisis, which occurs in toddlerhood, is the crisis of **autonomy versus shame and doubt**. Toddlers want to rule their own actions and bodies. If they fail in their efforts to do so, either because they are incapable or because their caregivers are too restrictive and forbidding, they come to feel shame and to doubt their abilities. According to Erikson, the key to the child's successfully meeting this crisis and gaining a sense of autonomy is parental firmness:

> Firmness must protect him [the toddler] against the potential anarchy of his as yet untrained sense of discrimination, his inability to hold on and let go with discretion. As his environment encourages him to "stand on his own feet," it must protect him against meaningless and arbitrary experiences of shame and of early doubt. [Erikson, 1963]

If parents accomplish this, the child is likely to become increasingly self-confident when encountering new challenges as an independent being.

Like Freud, Erikson believed that problems arising in early infancy can last a lifetime. He maintained that the adult who is suspicious and pessimistic, or who always seems burdened by self-doubt, may have been an infant who did not develop sufficient trust, or a toddler who did not achieve sufficient autonomy. However, Erikson also emphasized that experiences later in life can alter or transform the effects of early experiences, and that earlier crises can be taken up again and resolved later in life.

Mahler: Separation-Individuation

The need for a proper balance between protection and freedom is also central to Margaret Mahler's theory of infancy. In the first months of life, according to Mahler, the mother-child relationship is symbiotic. The nursing infant feels literally a part of the mother's body, and the mother, ideally, welcomes this temporary intrusion and dependency. At about 5 months, a new period begins that lasts until about age 3. This is **separation-individuation**, when the infant gradually develops a sense of self, apart from the mother. Mahler refers to this as the time of "psychological birth," when babies break out of the "protective membrane" that had symbiotically enclosed them and "hatch" by crawling and walking away from the mother (Mahler et al., 1975).

Toddlers attempt greater psychological separation from their mothers, but then become frightened by the independence they have gained, perhaps regressing to a period of babyish clinging. Because they are caught between two opposing needs, toddlers can be moody, showing sorrow and dependence, or anger and aggression. Even well-adjusted 1-year-olds show their ambivalence by darting away, hoping to be chased, or following their mother around, hoping to be noticed. Ideally, the mother will recognize the child's needs for both independence and dependence allowing a measure of freedom as well as providing comforting reassurance.

Like Freud and Erikson, Mahler (1968) believes that each stage of development is important for later psychological health. Indeed, Mahler thinks severe mental illness results directly from maladaptive mothering in the first six months of life. She also maintains that the resolution of the separation-individuation stage likewise has lasting implications: adults who avoid intimacy, or fear independence may still be trying to resolve the tension of separation-individuation and achieve a proper sense of self.

The Importance of Sensitivity

Each of these traditional psychological views maintains that personality is primarily shaped by early nurture, particularly the mother's caregiving. They share another feature in common: an emphasis on the **sensitivity** of caregiving as a crucial component of healthy nurturance. Whether it involves fostering a sense of trust, measuring demands for self-control against the child's capacity to comply, or recognizing the toddler's needs for both independence and support, the parent's sensitivity to the child's needs, desires, and abilities is an important contribution to healthy personality growth.

Such sensitivity involves a number of related components (Lamb & Easterbrooks, 1981), including the capacity to interpret the infant's signals appropriately and to respond to them in a nurturing way. This dimension of sensitivity also entails consistency: infants gradually develop expectations leading to trust and confidence in a parent who responds in a consistently helpful manner. Another key element of sensitivity is the ability to perceive situations from the infant's point of view so that, even when parents cannot comply with the baby's desires (because doing so might be dangerous or inappropriate), they can understand and respond to the child's feelings. Obviously, no parent can always meet this ideal of sensitivity, because in real life many things compete with a parent's attention to the child's needs and desires. And, of course, the parents' sensitivity is greatly affected by characteristics of the infant: it is a different task to be sensitive to an easy-going, sociable 1-year-old than it is to a fussy, difficult toddler. Thus, in assessing the role of parental sensitivity, or of any other influence on the infant's personality development, it is necessary to consider the infant's own contributions to the process—which now brings us to the study of temperament.

Temperament: The Importance of Nature

As you read in Chapter 3, researchers have determined that each individual has his or her own distinct, genetically based temperament, which permeates virtually every aspect of the person's developing personality. **Temperament** is defined as "relatively consistent, basic dispositions inherent in the person that underlie and modulate the expression of activity, reactivity, emotionality, and sociability" (McCall, in Goldsmith et al., 1987).

Temperament begins in the multitude of genetic codes that guide the development of the brain and is affected by many prenatal experiences, especially those relating to the nutrition and health of the mother. Elements of temperament are evident from birth, and within the first months, temperamental individuality is clearly established. However, although temperament is apparent in the first months of life, as the person develops, the social context and the individual's experiences increasingly influence the nature and expression of temperament.

Dimensions of Temperament

Given the centrality of temperament in determining the kind of individual each person is and how a person interacts with others, many researchers have set out to describe and measure the various dimensions of temperament. Among the leading scientists working in this area is Mary Rothbart (1981, 1991; Rothbart & Derryberry, 1981), who sees the elements of tempera-

autonomy versus shame and doubt Erikson's second stage of psychosocial development, in which the toddler struggles between the drive for self-control and shame and doubt about oneself and one's abilities.

separation-individuation Mahler's term to describe the child's gradual development of a sense of self, apart from the mother. This process begins at about 5 months of age and is completed at about 3 years.

sensitivity The capacity to notice and interpret the infant's signals appropriately and to respond to them in a nurturing way.

temperament Inherent dispositions, such as activity level, intensity of reaction, emotionality, and sociability, that underlie and affect a person's responses to people and things.

ment as clustering into two basic features—how people react to events and others, and how they control their own behavior. Rothbart assesses temperament by measuring such dimensions as smiling and laughing, fear, soothability, distress when thwarted, persistence at one task, and activity level. Another prominent researcher, Arnold Buss (1991; Buss & Plomin, 1984), examines temperament in terms of three dimensions—activity, emotionality, and sociability—which can be measured through detailed surveys of those who know the person best. Thus parents are asked about their infant's every action and reaction.

The most famous, comprehensive, and durable study of temperament remains the classic New York Longitudinal Study (NYLS), conducted by Alexander Thomas, Stella Chess, and Herbert Birch (Thomas et al., 1963). The researchers interviewed parents of new infants repeatedly and extensively, noting in detail various aspects of infants' behavior and taking measures to reduce the possibility of parental bias:

> During the first three years we relied on interviews with the parents, for the obvious reason that no one else is in a position to supply as detailed and comprehensive a picture of the child as they can. We took many precautions to insure both objectivity and accuracy. The interviews took place often enough so that the parents' reports covered events in the child's life that were still close enough in time and memory to be clearly remembered.
>
> Descriptive reports of what children did, rather than interpretive accounts of their behavior, also improved the accuracy and objectivity of the information. For example, if a mother said that her child did not like his first solid food, we asked her to describe his actual behavior. We were satisfied only when she gave a description such as, "When I put the food into his mouth he cried loudly, twisted his head away, and let it drool out."
>
> If we asked what a six-month-old baby did when his father came home in the evening, and his mother said, "He was happy to see him," we pressed for a detailed description: "As soon as he saw his father he smiled and reached out his arms."
>
> Our interviewers are always receptive, and they are trained never to express a critical attitude toward the parent. This is essential in getting forthright reports from parents. [Chess et al., 1965]

According to the researchers' initial findings (Thomas et al., 1963), babies in the first days and months of life differ in nine temperament characteristics:

1. *Activity level.* Some babies are active. They kick a lot in the uterus before they are born, they move around a great deal in their bassinets, and, as toddlers, they are nearly always running. Other babies are much less active.

2. *Rhythmicity.* Some babies have regular cycles of activity. They eat, sleep, and defecate on schedule almost from birth. Other babies are much less predictable.

3. *Approach-withdrawal.* Some babies delight in everything new; others withdraw from every new situation. The first bath makes some babies react in wide-eyed wonder while others tense up and scream; the first spoonful of cereal is gobbled up by one baby and spit out by the next.

4. *Adaptability.* Some babies adjust quickly to change; others are unhappy at every disruption of their normal routine.

FIGURE 8.10 Confronting their first experience in a wading pool, these twins are showing such a difference on the approach-withdrawal dimension of temperament that one would have to guess that they are dizygotic.

5. *Intensity of reaction.* Some babies chortle when they laugh and howl when they cry. Others are much calmer, responding with a smile or a whimper.

6. *Threshold of responsiveness.* Some babies seem to sense every sight, sound, and touch. For instance, they waken at a slight noise, or turn away from a distant light. Others seem unaware even of bright lights, loud street noises, or wet diapers.

7. *Quality of mood.* Some babies seem constantly happy, smiling at almost everything. Others seem chronically unhappy: they are ready to complain at any moment.

8. *Distractibility.* All babies fuss when they are hungry, but some will stop if someone gives them a pacifier or sings them a song, while others keep fussing. Similarly, some babies can easily be distracted from their interest in an attractive but dangerous object and diverted to a safer plaything, while others are more single-minded.

9. *Attention span.* Some babies play happily with one toy for a long time. Others quickly drop one activity for another.

Thomas and Chess (1977) believe that "temperamental individuality is well established by the time the infant is two to three months old." In terms of various combinations of personality traits, most young infants can be described as one of three types: *easy* (about 40 percent), *slow-to-warm-up* (about 15 percent), and *difficult* (about 10 percent). Note, however, that about 35 percent of normal infants do not fit into these well-defined groups.

Stability and Change in Temperament

In a series of follow-up studies carried into adolescence and adulthood (Carey & McDevitt, 1978; Chess & Thomas, 1990; Thomas et al., 1968), temperamental characteristics showed some stability: the easy baby remains a relatively easy child, while the difficult one is more likely to give his or her parents problems. Similarly, the slow-to-warm-up infant who cried on seeing strangers at 8 months may well hide behind Mother's skirt on arriving at nursery school and avoid the crowd in the halls of junior high.

This does not mean that temperament remains the same throughout life. Temperament changes and develops. Indeed, some of the NYLS characteristics are not particularly stable. Rhythmicity and quality of mood, for instance, are quite variable, meaning that the infant who has been taking naps on schedule might not do so a few months later, and the baby who seemed consistently happy might become a malcontent if life circumstances change

RESEARCH REPORT

Early Signs of Shyness

One dimension of infant temperament, extroversion (or sociability) and its opposite, shyness, has been the focus of extensive research, partly because extroversion/shyness has proven to be one of the most durable and significant traits of the human personality. This trait, which relates to such personality dimensions as friendliness, fearfulness, self-confidence, and introspection, has been linked with a variety of life-course events. For example, shy men tend to date, marry, and become fathers later than other men, and shy women are more likely to become full-time homemakers rather than pursue a career. In general, extroverts are more likely to attain higher-paid, stable management positions (Caspi et al., 1990; Caspi et al., 1988).

Although every ethnic and racial group has a portion of individuals who are very outgoing and another portion who are unusually shy, the most detailed research concerning extroversion/shyness has been carried out with white American children. Among this group, about 25 percent are "consistently sociable, affectively spontaneous, and minimally fearful," while about 10 percent are "consistently shy, cautious, and emotionally reserved" (Kagan & Snidman, 1991).

Although social shyness is difficult to ascertain in very young infants, the personality trait of extroversion/shyness is readily observable by age 1, and continues to be apparent in childhood. For example, while many toddlers are somewhat cautious when a stranger appears, some hide their faces or even cry and run away. By the time children join a preschool, differences are even more evident: some children immediately make friends, while others stand quietly on the periphery of a group of children, watching and waiting. In addition, shy children are often unusually fearful in certain nonsocial situations, such as seeing the ocean for the first time or watching a scary movie (Honig, 1987).

Such tendencies have led researchers to theorize that the extroversion/shyness trait might manifest itself even in the first months of life as a general inhibition to unfamiliar objects and experiences. To test this hypothesis, ninety-four healthy middle-class infants were tested longitudinally (Kagan & Snidman, 1991). At 4 months they were videotaped for 10 minutes as they reacted to several new toys, mobiles, and sounds. Blind observers, watching the tapes, rated the infants as high or low on two behaviors: motor activity (for instance, how much they kicked or waved their arms) and crying (including how quickly they could be soothed if they began to fret). Twenty-three percent of the infants were high in both activities, 37 percent were low in both, and the remaining 40 percent were high in one but not the other.

Then, at 9 months and 14 months, the infants were tested again with several possibly unsettling situations, such as a stranger's inviting the child to play with a metal robot, or the child's being given unusual things to taste. All the children showed wariness, but some of them were notably more fearful than others—crying and refusing to play with the novel toy, for instance. Again blind observers rated the number of times each infant showed apparent fear. Given the normal variability of infants, and the difficulties in testing them, the results were amazingly clearcut: those high or low in both crying and motor activity at 4 months were, respectively, high or low in fear at 9 and 14 months. When individual patterns were examined, results were most marked for those who were unusually fearful or fearless. Of the fourteen toddlers who had the lowest fear scores, none had been in the high/high category as infants. Similarly, of the five toddlers who were most fearful, none had been in the low/low category.

Results such as these extend the general finding that extroversion/shyness is an inherited trait (see p. 87); they also provide two further details. First, they suggest that so-

In Mongolia and many other Asian countries, females are expected to display shyness as a sign of respect to elders and strangers. Consequently, if this younger sister is truly as shy as she seems, her parents are less likely to be distressed about her withdrawn behavior than the typical North American parent would be. On the other hand, they may consider the relative boldness of her older sister to be a serious problem.

cial shyness is only one manifestation of a more general, physiological pattern of inhibition to new stimuli, apparent in infancy. Second, the fact that the behavior of a specific group of infants was, over time, distinctly more shy or more sociable than the average infant suggests that extroversion/shyness is inherited not only in an additive fashion, producing a simple continuum from very social to very shy, with every gradation in between. In addition, the presence or absence of a certain gene, or genes, may produce unusual neurological reactions to novelty. Thus the trait may also be inherited discretely, as blood type is, for instance (Kagan, 1989). In either case, other studies, with identical and fraternal twins, indicate that shyness is strongly influenced by heredity (Emde et al., 1992; Robinson et al., 1992).

Of course, as with all inherited tendencies, the reaction of others can modify or exacerbate a person's tendency toward extroversion or shyness. For instance, children who are genetically predisposed to be timid are more likely to become extremely shy if they have a dominating older brother or sister. Parents also make a difference: even if a child becomes an extremely shy toddler, he or she has about a 50/50 chance of no longer behaving with unusual timidness at age 7, with family encouragement of social play with other children being one deciding factor. Even with parental guidance and preschool experience, however, very few shy toddlers become such spontaneous and social 7-year-olds that they would be mistaken for extroverts (Galvin, 1992; Kagan, 1989).

This research has a very practical application. In cultures in which shyness is considered a fault, the realization that some children may be genetically inhibited should make everyone more accepting and reassuring when a child seems unusually fearful, timid, or quiet.

for the worse. The age of the child is also important. In the first few years, stability is more evident from month to month than from year to year (Bronson, 1985; Peters-Martin & Wachs, 1984). Temperamental qualities tend to remain stable over the course of a particular developmental stage but to shift as the child makes the transition to a new stage and faces different challenges. Change itself may follow genetic timetables, and inborn traits may be more apparent during particular developmental periods and under certain conditions (Chess & Thomas, 1990; Plomin et al., 1993).

In addition, there are several ways the environment can affect a child's temperamental characteristics. One way is through the **goodness of fit**, or "match," between the child's temperamental pattern and the demands of the environment (Buss & Plomin, 1984; Lerner & Lerner, 1983; Thomas & Chess, 1977). When parents accommodate their child-rearing expectations to their offspring's temperamental style, for example, the result is a more harmonious "fit" between them, with good outcomes for both child and family. For some parents, this may involve setting up a "child-proof" play area in which their high-activity-level child can run off excess energy without trouble; for other parents, it may require allowing extra time for a slow-to-warm-up child to adjust to new situations. By contrast, when the child's temperamental pattern and the caregiving expectations are significantly out of sync, parents and offspring are likely to experience greater conflict, and the child's temperamental style may become more difficult. The same is true of the fit between temperament and other environmental demands. In these ways, both nature and nurture contribute to temperamental individuality. Consider the effects of "goodness of fit" on one of the original subjects from the NYLS:

> Carl was one of our most extreme cases of difficult temperament from the first months of life through 5 years of age. However, he did not develop a behavior disorder, primarily due to optimal handling by his parents and stability of his environment. His father, who himself had an easy temperament, took delight in his son's "lusty" characteristics, recognized on his own Carl's tendencies to have intense negative reactions to the new, and had the patience to wait for eventual adaptability to occur. He was clear, without any orientation by us, that these characteristics were in no way due to his or his wife's influences. His wife tended to be anxious and self-accusatory over Carl's tempestuous course. However, her husband was supportive and reassuring and this enabled her to take an appropriately objective and patient approach to her son's development.
>
> By middle childhood and early adolescent years, few new situations arose which provoked the difficult temperament responses. The family, school, and social environment was stable and Carl flourished and appeared to be temperamentally easy rather than difficult. . . .
>
> When Carl went off to college, however, he was faced simultaneously with a host of new situations and demands—an unfamiliar locale, a different living arrangement, new academic subjects and expectations, and a totally new peer group. Within a few weeks his temperamentally difficult traits reappeared in full force. He felt negative about the school, his courses, the other students, couldn't motivate himself to study, and was constantly irritable. Carl knew something was wrong, and discussed the situation with his family and us and developed an appropriate strategy to cope with his problem. He limited the new demands by dropping several extracurricular activities, limited his social contact, and policed his studying. Gradually he adapted, his distress disappeared, and he was able to expand his activities and social contacts. . . . [I]n the most recent follow-up at age 29 . . . his intensity remains but is now an asset rather than a liability. [Chess & Thomas, 1990]

goodness of fit The quality of the "match" between the child's temperament and the demands of the surrounding environment.

As in this example, most parents soon learn that how their parenting style affects their child depends on how it "fits" with the child's temperamental style. A parenting style that provides lots of opportunities for learning and stimulation at home, for instance, may help a child with a low activity level to explore, but that same approach may overwhelm a highly active child (Gandour, 1989). The quality of sibling interaction is also affected by the "fit" between each child's temperament (especially for emotional intensity and negative mood), and sibling conflict often occurs because of a collision between the children's emotional styles (Munn & Dunn, 1989). As a consequence, the effects of many early experiences depend on the individual's characteristics, including temperament (Wachs & Gruen, 1982). In essence, everyone approaches the world differently—and is affected by it differently—depending on his or her temperamental style.

Parent-Infant Interaction

As the discussion of temperament makes clear, the traditional psychological view of parents as the sole shapers of the child's personality was clearly in error. At the same time, it is also clear that psychological development is not determined solely by the individual's innate characteristics. As developmentalists now emphasize, it is the interaction between the parent and the child that is crucial. This interaction is affected by the personality of the parent and the temperament of the child, as well as by the child's stage of development.

Becoming Social Partners

As you read earlier, even very young infants communicate emotionally, through sounds, movements, and facial expressions. And they are interested in social events virtually from birth: the sound of a human voice, the sight of a human face, and other social stimuli are among the earliest events to capture a young baby's attention, interest, and emotion. But although infants are social from birth, they initially are not ready to play their part in social interactions. First-time parents who look forward to the birth of their child, eagerly anticipating joyous episodes of social exchange after the baby's arrival, are often disappointed to discover that their newborn spends most of the day sleeping, and is often unresponsive even when awake!

The skills of social interaction develop slowly, but inevitably, during the early weeks and months of life. As the infant acquires greater behavioral self-control, periods of alertness and attention become more frequent, and the opportunities for social interaction grow. Although infants are capable of recognizing the sound of their mother's voice (and sometimes her smell) very early, further growth in visual and intermodal perception (see Chapter 7) gradually enables infants to integrate perceptions of their mother's face, voice, and other characteristics into a recognizable human partner. Other kinds of learning also occur during these early weeks: the recurrent experience of being in distress and having that distress relieved by a caregiver enables the infant to progressively associate the sight, sound, smell, and other features of the adult with the experience of soothing and the pleasant alertness that follows it (Lamb & Malkin, 1986).

By the age of 2 to 3 months, these developments in the baby converge to create a change that parents recognize and rejoice in: the baby begins to respond especially to them. To be sure, other adults can also elicit smiles from the infant, but the appearance of the mother, father, or another familiar caregiver can provoke widened grins, lilting cooing, and other reactions that signify the person's special status to the child. Many parents report a deepening of their own attachment to the baby at this time, as they proceed from the newborn phase, when they tended to perceive the child as a delicate guest requiring careful treatment, to a new phase of their relationship, when they perceive the child as a social partner who can reciprocate their love and attention. This, in turn, provokes a new kind of interaction. Instead of merely gazing intently over the crib rails at the baby, trying to decipher what the infant's needs are, caregivers begin to initiate focused episodes of face-to-face play.

These episodes may occur in a variety of contexts—during a feeding, a diaper change, a bath, or in any other situation. They may be initiated by either the adult or the infant: the caregiver might notice the baby's expression or vocalization and mirror it with his or her own (such as smiling when the baby smiles) or the baby might notice the adult's wide-eyed beaming and break into a grin. What really distinguishes these episodes of social play are the moment-by-moment actions and reactions of both partners. To complement the infant's animated but quite limited expressive repertoire, adults use dozens of behaviors that seem to be reserved exclusively for infants. Typically, caregivers open their eyes and mouths wide in exaggerated expressions of mock delight or surprise, make rapid clucking noises or repeated one-syllable sounds ("ba-ba-ba-ba-ba," "di-di-di-di," "bo-bo-bo-bo," etc.), raise and lower the pitch of their voice, change the pace of their movements (gradually speeding up or slowing down), imitate the infant's actions, bring their face close to the baby's and then pull back, tickle, pat, poke, lift, and rock the baby, and do many other simple things. (If you are reading thoughtfully, you probably recognize some of these behaviors as your own natural response when in the presence of a baby—sometimes to your own embarrassment when you catch yourself acting these ways, and especially to the amusement of those around you!) The infant's responses typically complement those of the adult: they stare at their partners or look away, vocalize, widen their eyes, smile, move their heads forward or back, or turn aside (Stern, 1985).

It appears that episodes of face-to-face play are a universal feature of the early interaction between caregivers and infants, although the frequency and duration of these episodes, as well as the goals of the adults who initiate them, may differ in various cultures. One cross-cultural study of mothers at play with their infants found, for example, that American mothers most often directed the infant's attention to a nearby toy, object, or event, while Japanese mothers focused on establishing mutual intimacy by maintaining eye contact with the infant as well as kissing, hugging, and so on (Bornstein et al., 1992). In another cross-cultural comparison, researchers noted that whereas American mothers employed social overtures that stimulated and excited their babies (such as tickling the baby), mothers from the Gusii community in rural Kenya were more soothing and quieting in their initiatives (Richman et al., 1992). Of course, mothers are not the only ones who engage infants in face-to-face play: fathers are active partners in play (see A Closer Look, pp. 274–275), and in many non-Western cultures, older siblings and other adults assume an active role in infant care, and participate in social play with babies (Tronick et al., 1992; West, 1988).

Developing and Maintaining Synchrony

What accounts for the pleasure that adults and infants both experience from their face-to-face interactions? Many researchers believe that it is the mutual experience of being "in sync"—that is, being socially and emotionally coordinated with the partner. In this respect, therefore, one of the goals of face-to-face play is to develop and maintain **synchrony**, or coordinated interaction between infant and caregiver. Synchrony has been variously described by researchers as the meshing of a finely tuned machine (Snow, 1984), a patterned dance or "dialogue" of exquisite precision (Schaffer, 1984), and an emotional "attunement" of an improvised musical duet (Stern, 1985). It is partly through synchrony that infants learn to express and read emotions (Bremner, 1988) and begin to develop some of the basic skills of social interaction—such as turn-taking—that they will use throughout life.

Even in the early months, synchrony is a partnership. Infants modify their social and emotional expressiveness (smiling, looking, cooing) to match or complement their caregiver's overtures, while adults sensitively modify the timing and pace of their initiatives to accord with their baby's readiness to respond (Cohn & Tronick, 1987). Such coordination, of course, is not necessarily common or constant. In fact, episodes of synchrony occur less than 30 percent of the time in normal mother-infant play. Much of the time, the pair is jointly reestablishing coordinated play following periods of dyssynchrony, caused by the baby's becoming fussy, or by the mother's becoming distracted, or by any number of other factors (Tronick, 1989; Tronick & Cohn, 1989). Thus infants are learning not only how to socialize during periods of interaction but also, with the caregiver's assistance, how to remedy or "repair" social encounters that are not going well (Gianino & Tronick, 1988).

synchrony Carefully coordinated interaction between infant and parent (or any other two people) in which each individual responds to and influences the other's movements and rhythms.

FIGURE 8.11 A moment of perfect synchrony!

Traditional views of infant development focused almost exclusively on mothers, partly because the received wisdom in most cultures was that fathers are naturally "remote and authoritarian," too busy with other matters for an intimate relationship with their young children (Poussaint, 1990). And in Western cultures fathers were, historically, removed from most caregiving activities, in response to the cultural expectations as well as to the practical necessities of working long hours away from home while the mothers tended house, children, and garden.

Recently, however, as family size has shrunk and mothers have increasingly become employed outside the home, many fathers have taken on a "significant share of the nurturing responsibilities" for their offspring (Poussaint, 1990). This shift is apparent worldwide, including countries such as Ireland and Mexico, where the stereotype is that fathers are above changing diapers or spooning baby food (Bronstein, 1984; Lamb, 1987; Nugent, 1991). Virtually all developmentalists applaud this trend, for fathers who share the child-care responsibilities probably enhance the development of their children more than the remote fathers of old did.

As this change began to occur, it raised some interesting questions about the relationship between fathers and their infants. The first and most urgent was: Could fathers provide adequate care for newborns and young infants? The answer, quick in coming, was a resounding "yes": research found that babies drank just as much formula, emerged from the bath just as clean, and seemed just as content with the caregiving of fathers as with the caregiving of mothers. It was further determined that fathers can provide the necessary emotional and cognitive nurturing as well, coordinating their facial expressions in synchrony, speaking Motherese like a native, and forming secure attachments (Parke, 1981). Overall, researchers found "no evidence that women are biologically predisposed to be better parents than men are" (Lamb, 1981). As one psychiatrist emphatically expressed it:

> There is perhaps no mystique of motherhood that a man cannot master except for the physical realities of pregnancy, delivery, and breast feeding. [Poussaint, 1990]

Given that fathers *can* master caregiving, the next question was: Why don't more fathers develop this skill? Worldwide, women spend far more time in child care than men do, especially in the early months and particularly if the child is a girl (Lamb, 1987). Even in contemporary marriages, even when both parents work outside the home on weekdays, and even when both agree that child care is a shared responsibility, the reality is that, although fathers do some basic caregiving in the evenings and on weekends, mothers do a great deal more (Belsky et al., 1984; Pleck, 1985; Thompson & Walker, 1989).

Surprisingly, although the media, and many mothers, tend to blame the fathers, mothers may be as responsible for this unequal distribution of labor as fathers. Indeed, many mothers assume the status of the family child-care authority: they serve as a kind of gatekeeper and judge of the father's performance, forbidding or criticizing certain behaviors, permitting and praising others (Kranichfeld, 1987; Pollack & Grossman, 1985). Fathers' limited involvement with babies may be a joint result of maternal and paternal preferences.

In addition, the general social context often works against fathers' being intensely involved in caregiving with infants. The traditional view of child-rearing roles, for example, is reinforced by many cultural pressures—from that of older relatives, who may encourage the mother to provide most of the nitty-gritty child care, to that of the father's friends and colleagues, who may deride the idea of Daddy's changing diapers. Employers, too, are more likely to recognize, and make allowances for, the woman's role as caregiver than they are the man's. Even when paternity leave is an option, for example, many men do not take advantage of this opportunity because of the stigma—and career sacrifices—they think might occur. Finally, the marriage relationship can affect the father-child relationship: when the couple are happy with their relationship, they are more likely to share child-care duties (Belsky et al., 1991).

As researchers looked more closely at the amount of time mothers and fathers spend with their infants, they discovered another curious difference between the caregiving of mothers and fathers: although fathers provide less basic care, they play more with infants. Moreover, compared to mother's play, father's play is noisier, more boisterous, and idiosyncratic, as fathers make up active and exciting games on the spur of the moment (MacDonald & Parke, 1986).

Even in the first months of the baby's life, fathers are more likely to play by moving baby's legs and arms in imi-

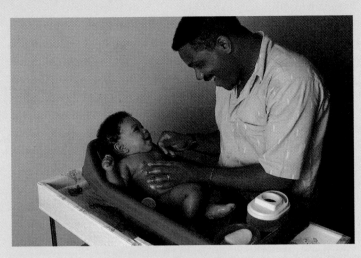

In many modern families, bathing is the caregiving task most often assumed by father. The reason is illustrated by 4-month-old Christopher and his dad: bathing is not only a necessary, nurturant task; it also offers opportunities for joyous physical play, a father's specialty.

tation of walking, kicking, or climbing, or by zooming the baby through the air ("airplane"), or by tapping and tickling the baby's stomach; mothers, on the other hand, are more likely to talk or sing soothingly, or to combine play with caretaking routines such as diapering and bathing (Parke & Tinsley, 1981).

These differences between mothers' and fathers' play are not lost on infants. Even young infants typically react with more visible excitement when approached by their fathers than when approached by their mothers. In the first months of life, infants are more likely to laugh—and more likely to cry—in episodes of play with Daddy.

As infants grow older, fathers generally increase the time they spend with them, and their tendency to engage in physical play becomes more pronounced. Fathers are likely to swing their toddlers around, or "wrestle" with them on the floor, or crawl after them in a "chase."

Mothers, on the other hand, when "playing," are more likely to read to their toddlers, help them play with toys, or play conventional games such as patty cake or peek-a-boo (MacDonald & Parke, 1986). These differences continue to be reflected in infants' reactions. According to one study (Clarke-Stewart, 1978), 20-month-olds are more responsive during play with their fathers than with their mothers. By 30 months, differences are even more apparent: children at this age are generally more cooperative, involved, and interested in their fathers' games than in their mothers' play, and judging by their smiles and laughter, they have more fun.

What do infants gain from playing with their fathers in addition to having fun? Many things. Most important, playing is a direct avenue to attachment. Remember that play with an infant requires mutual engagement and synchronous responsiveness—precisely those qualities that help build a secure attachment. Indeed, it is almost impossible for an adult and a baby to succeed at the challenging and rewarding task of shared play without becoming responsive and attached partners as time goes by. Play with father may also contribute to the growth of unique social skills and tendencies. In one study, 18-month-olds who were securely attached to both parents met a stranger while either their father or their mother sat passively nearby. The father's presence made the toddlers much more likely to smile and play with the new person than the mother's presence did, a result especially apparent for the boys. The authors of this study speculated that the child's experience of boisterous, idiosyncratic play with Dad may make the father's presence a cue for playfulness and embolden the child to engage the stranger.

Findings such as this raise anew the question of whether or not gender-specific caregiving with infants may be best. At the moment, researchers have no definitive answers, but some are beginning to shift the emphasis of the question, suggesting that the division of child-rearing labor that may be best for infants is whatever division is best for the parents. Indeed, when their relationship is good, each parent complements, encourages, and enhances the other in "a balanced system of interactive effects between husbands and wives" (Grossman et al., 1988). Even in today's changing world, mothers and fathers together are more likely to meet all their infant's needs—biological, cognitive, and social—than either one alone is.

Generally, repair is not difficult: the signs of dyssynchrony are obvious—averted eyes, stiffening or abrupt shifting of the body, an unhappy noise—and the alert caregiver can quickly make adjustments, allowing the infant to "recover." Depending on various aspects of their temperament and maturity, of course, some infants take longer than others to recover and to resume synchronous interaction. Since development of the central nervous system improves awareness and timing, 5-month-olds lead the "dance" notably better than do 3-month-olds (Lester et al., 1985).

When initiation and repair of synchrony are difficult, it is usually because the caregiver regularly overstimulates the baby who wants to pause, or ignores the infant's invitation to interact (Isabella & Belsky, 1991). If the infant is repeatedly ignored, he or she may not try as much to respond: offspring of depressed mothers, for example, are less likely to smile and vocalize, not only when interacting with their mothers but also when responding to a nondepressed adult (Field, 1987). Infants with an intrusive, overstimulating caregiver defend themselves more obviously, by turning away or even "shutting down" completely, such as by crying inconsolably. Unfortunately, some caregivers still do not notice the cues, as in this example:

> Whenever a moment of mutual gaze occurred, the mother went immediately into high-gear stimulating behaviors, producing a profusion of fully displayed, high-intensity, facial and vocal . . . social behavior. Jenny invariably broke gaze rapidly. Her mother never interpreted this temporary face and gaze aversion as a cue to lower her level of behavior, nor would she let Jenny self-control the level by gaining distance. Instead she would swing her head around following Jenny's to reestablish the full-face position. Jenny again turned away, pushing her face further into the pillow to try to break all visual contact. Again, instead of holding back, the mother continued to chase Jenny. . . . She also escalated the level of her stimulation more by adding touching and tickling to the unabated flow of vocal and facial behavior . . . Jenny closed her eyes to avoid any mutual visual contact and only reopened them after [she had moved her head to the other side]. All of these behaviors on Jenny's part were performed with a sober face or at times a grimace. [Stern, 1977]

While this example clearly shows the effects of the caregiver's personality, it should be noted that the infant's personality and predispositions also affect the ease of synchrony. For example, some infants are constitutionally

FIGURE 8.12 Adults typically use special social behaviors (a) with their young infants—leaning in close, opening their eyes and mouths wide in exaggerated expressions of surprise or delight, maintaining eye contact—because they elicit the baby's attention and pleasure. But these behaviors are subdued or absent when the adult is depressed or stressed (b), and this makes social interaction much less enjoyable for each partner.

(a)

(b)

more sensitive to stimulation than others; such babies would have particular problems with an intrusive caregiver like Jenny's mother. Fortunately, even with such a mismatch, repair is possible. Sometimes a helpful outsider can teach the caregiver how to more sensitively read the baby's signals, and sometimes the baby and caregiver begin to adjust to each other spontaneously (Stern, 1985). In this case, Jenny eventually became more able to adjust to the mother's sudden overstimulation, and the mother, finding her infant more responsive, no longer felt the need to bombard her with stimulation as she had earlier. With time, Jenny and her mother established a mutually rewarding relationship.

Attachment

Just as the moment-by-moment harmony between parents and young infants has captured scientific attention, so has the **attachment** between parents and slightly older infants been the subject of extensive research. "Attachment," according to Mary Ainsworth (1973), "may be defined as an affectional tie that one person or animal forms between himself and another specific one—a tie that binds them together in space and endures over time." Not surprisingly, when people are attached to each other, they try to be near one another, and they interact with each other often. Thus infants show attachment through "proximity-seeking" behaviors—such as approaching, following, and climbing into the lap—and "contact-maintaining" behaviors—such as clinging and resisting being put down (Ainsworth & Bell, 1970). Parents show their attachment by keeping a watchful eye on their infant, even when safety does not require it, and by responding affectionately and sensitively to the infant's vocalizations, expressions, and gestures. As we noted at the outset of this chapter, the attachment bond not only deepens the parent-infant relationship, but over our long evolutionary history, may also have contributed to human survival by keeping infants near their caregivers and keeping caregivers vigilant.

Measuring Attachment

In studying attachment in England, Uganda, and the United States, Ainsworth discovered that virtually all normal infants develop special attachments to the people who care for them, with some infants much more secure in those attachments than others, a fact confirmed by hundreds of other researchers (Bretherton, 1992).

A **secure attachment** is one in which the infant derives comfort and confidence from the caregiver, as evidenced by the infant's attempts to be close to the caregiver and readiness to explore the environment. The caregiver acts as a "secure base," enabling the child to venture forth, perhaps scrambling down from mother's lap to play with a toy while periodically looking back, vocalizing, or returning for a hug.

By contrast, **insecure attachment** is characterized by the infant's fear, anger, or seeming indifference toward the caregiver. The infant has much less confidence, perhaps being unwilling to let go of the mother's arms, or perhaps playing aimlessly with no signs of trying to maintain contact.

attachment The emotional connection between a person and other people, animals, or objects that produces a desire for consistent contact as well as feelings of distress during separation.

secure attachment A healthy parent-child connection, signaled by the child's being confident when the parent is present, distressed at the parent's absence, and comforted by the parent's return.

insecure attachment A troubled parent-child connection signaled by the child's overdependence on, or lack of interest in, the parent. Insecurely attached children are not readily comforted by the parent and are less likely to explore their environment than are children who are securely attached.

While there are many ways to measure attachment, Ainsworth developed a classic laboratory procedure, called the **Strange Situation**, which is designed to evoke the infant's reactions to the caregiver under somewhat stressful conditions. Infants are closely observed in a well-equipped playroom, in several successive episodes of about three minutes, with their mother and/or a stranger, and alone. These conditions are designed to measure the baby's motivation to be near the caregiver, and to reveal how much the caregiver's presence reestablishes security and confidence.

About two-thirds of all American infants tested in the Strange Situation demonstrate secure attachment. Their mother's presence in the playroom is enough to give them courage to explore the room and investigate the toys; her departure may cause some distress (usually expressed through verbal protest and a pause in playing); and her return is a signal to reestablish positive social contact (with a smile or by climbing into the mother's arms) and then resume playing.

  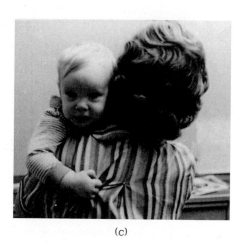

(a)   (b)   (c)

FIGURE 8.13 In this trial of the Strange Situation test, Brian shows every sign of secure attachment. (*a*) He explores the playroom happily when his mother is present, (*b*) cries when she leaves, (*c*) and is readily comforted when she returns.

Other infants, however, show one of three types of insecure attachment. Some are anxious and *resistant*: they cling nervously to their mother even before her initial departure and thus are unwilling to explore the playroom; they cry loudly each time she leaves; they refuse to be comforted when she returns, perhaps continuing to sob angrily even when back in her arms. Others are *avoidant*: they engage in little interaction with their mother; they often show no apparent distress when she leaves; and on her return, they tend to avoid reestablishing contact, sometimes even turning their backs. Others are *disoriented,* or disorganized: they show an inconsistent mixture of behavior toward the mother, such as avoiding her just after seeking to be close to her (Main & Solomon, 1986).

Attachment and Context

Ainsworth's procedure for measuring attachment has been used in hundreds of studies. From these we have learned that attachment is affected by the quality of care in early infancy (Bretherton & Waters, 1985; Lamb et al., 1985; Thompson, 1991). Among the caregiving features that affect the quality

Strange Situation An experimental condition devised by Mary Ainsworth to assess an infant's attachment. The infant's behavior is observed in an unfamiliar room while a caregiver (usually the mother) and a stranger move in and out of the room.

of attachment are (1) general sensitivity to the infant's needs, (2) responsiveness to the infant's specific signals, and (3) talking and playing with the infant in ways that actively encourage the child's growth and development (Ainsworth, 1993; Isabella, 1993). Not surprisingly, the interactions between mothers and infants who are securely attached have been found to exhibit greater synchrony than those between mothers and infants who are insecurely attached (Isabella & Belsky, 1991). Thus sensitive and responsive caregiving in the early months leads naturally to secure attachment in the later months.

Attachment may also be influenced by the broader context in which infant and mother live. It may be affected, for example, by the extent and quality of the father's involvement in the care of the child, and by the nature of the marital relationship (Easterbrooks & Goldberg, 1984; Goldberg & Easterbrooks, 1984; Pianta et al., 1989). Furthermore, significant changes in family circumstances—such as a parent's losing a job—alter the attachment relationship between infant and mother by altering familiar patterns of interaction. This can result in a new relationship that may be more or less secure than before (Thompson et al., 1982). Such influences can affect attachment in diverse ways, so it is not surprising that when researchers have tried to explain why infants become securely or insecurely attached, measures of maternal care alone provide only a partial explanation. Measures of infant temperament likewise tell a part of the story (Belsky & Rovine, 1987; Vaughn et al., 1992). As you read earlier, the "goodness of fit" or "match" between infant temperament and parenting style is a key developmental factor, and it may be the quality of this fit that best predicts whether a secure or insecure attachment will develop (Mangelsdorf et al., 1990). In essence, attachment relationships take shape from the *interaction* of mother and infant within a complex social ecology.

As part of the ecology of care, cultural context can also affect the development of attachment, or at least the measurement of it (Sagi & Lewkowicz, 1987; van Ijzendoorn & Kroonenberg, 1988). In cross-cultural comparisons of the Strange Situation, for example, Japanese and Israeli children show a higher rate of anxiety and resistance than American infants do, while infants from some Western European countries show higher rates of avoidance. Why do these differences exist? Some researchers believe that particular cultural backgrounds may make the Strange Situation too demanding for certain infants, causing them to exhibit insecure behavior. Japanese mothers, for instance, rarely leave their infants with babysitters, and their offspring are thus less prepared to cope with being with a stranger or alone in the Strange Situation than American infants are (Chen & Miyake, 1986). However, an extensive analysis of cross-cultural data on attachment reveals that, in the Strange Situation, the majority of infants of various nationalities are securely attached (van Ijzendoorn & Kroonenberg, 1988). Most infants worldwide consider their mother's presence a reassuring sign that it is safe to explore the environment, and most infants come back to her for comfort under stress (Sagi et al., 1991). Most infants also show signs of secure attachments to other caregivers—fathers, siblings, day-care providers—although this obviously varies from culture to culture.

Attachment Theory and the Infant-Day-Care Controversy

When Laura's daughter Heather was 12 months old, her mother began to have serious doubts about Heather's being in a day-care center every weekday. She confided her concerns to a psychologist. "Yesterday was typical," Laura said. "Heather began fussing in the morning when it was time for me to leave, but the teacher said she settled down fine shortly after. But when I came to pick her up at 5, Heather seemed to be more interested in the toys than in me!" Laura needed the income of her job, and she knew that the particular day-care center was safe and that the staff were responsive and stimulating. But she could not help wondering if day care was undermining Heather's attachment to her.

Concerns like Laura's were given articulate and forceful voice in 1986, when Jay Belsky, a prominent developmental psychologist, published a review of the research on day care and attachment entitled, "Infant Day Care: A Cause for Concern?" Summarizing the findings of his own research and other studies, Belsky (1986) concluded that extended day-care experience (that is, more than 20 hours weekly) during the infant's first year is a "risk factor" for the development of insecure attachments with parents. In particular, infants with early and extended day-care experience are more likely to avoid and ignore their mothers when observed in the Strange Situation. Furthermore, he argued, the effects of early day-care experience are long-term, contributing to aggression and noncompliance in the preschool years. These consequences arise, according to Belsky, because young infants are not prepared to cope psychologically with extended separations from their mother while attachments are still developing in the first year.

Belsky's views provoked considerable attention, partly because they were consistent with what many people intuitively believed about infant day care, and they also fed into more general fears about the consequences of mothers working outside the home and the overall impact of changes in the family's roles and structure.

At the same time, Belsky's conclusions were criticized by many developmentalists for several reasons. First, the rate of insecure attachment for infants in day care was only 8 to 15 percent higher than for "home-reared" infants, so it is probably unwarranted to call day care a "risk factor" for insecure attachment. The majority of infants with early, extended day-care experience are, in fact, securely attached (Thompson, 1991). Second, when attachment behavior is measured in the Strange Situation, day-care infants may behave differently—that is, seeming blasé about their mother's comings and goings—because of their prior experience of separation and reunion, not because of insecure attachment. As Clarke-Stewart (1989) noted, in the Strange Situation

the infant plays with someone else's toys in a room that is not his or her own; the infant is left by his or her mother with a woman who is a stranger; the infant plays with and is comforted by that woman in the mother's absence; the mother returns to pick the infant up. Although at least some infants of nonworking mothers undoubtedly have had experiences like these before their assessment in the Strange Situation, infants of working mothers are more likely to have had them regularly and routinely and, therefore, to be more accustomed to them.

Whether concerns about infant day care and insecure attachment prove well-founded or not, the debate has highlighted the need for affordable, high-quality care for infants and toddlers. As Belsky (1990) himself has noted:

Because it is unknown whether infant day-care experi-

The Importance of Attachment

Why is attachment considered so important? Part of the reason lies in longitudinal research that documents the results of secure and insecure attachment. Studies clearly show that secure attachment at age 1 provides a preview to the child's social and personality development in the years to come. For example, observations in nursery school reveal that 3-year-olds who were rated securely attached at age 1 are significantly more competent in certain social and cognitive skills: they are more curious, outgoing, and self-directed than those who were rated insecurely attached (Sroufe et al., 1983). The 3-year-olds who were securely attached as toddlers are also more likely to be sought out as friends and chosen as leaders. Furthermore, securely attached infants tend to become children who interact with teachers in friendly and appropriate ways, seeking their help when needed.

Although researchers disagree about the effects of early day-care experience on attachment, they all concur that infants benefit from high-quality centers with a low adult-child ratio, well-qualified staff, and lots of age-appropriate toys.

ence is a cause or just a correlate of insecurity, aggression and noncompliance, and because we know that affordable, high-quality day care is by no means nearly as available as it needs to be, it is totally inappropriate to conclude that only mothers can care for their infants or that day care is bad for babies. . . .

Developmental research has convincingly established that high-quality care in the preschool years not only does not carry any risks, but actually serves to enhance child development. Although comparable evidence in the case of day care in the first year is sorely lacking, there is good reason to believe that when care in this developmental period is of high quality there should be little reason to anticipate negative developmental outcomes.

Other research has confirmed these views. There is increasing evidence from this country and Sweden (where

high-quality infant day care is readily available) that when infants experience early and extended amounts of high-quality day care (with perhaps two regular and responsive caregivers for a group of five infants), they show more positive long-term outcomes than children without such experience (Andersson, 1989; Field, 1991). One reason may be that in quality centers, infants develop secure attachments to their professional caregivers (Howes & Hamilton, 1992; Howes et al., 1992).

It would certainly seem, then, that in the United States, where more than half the mothers of young children are employed, high-quality day care would provide a valuable benefit for families. The issue of infant day care thus underscores the need for parents, researchers, and policymakers to discover how to optimize infant development in the context of present-day social realities.

By contrast, infants who show anxious insecure attachment tend to become preschoolers who are overly dependent on teachers, demanding their attention unnecessarily and clinging to them instead of playing with other children or exploring the environment (Sroufe et al., 1983). At age 4, boys who were rated insecurely attached tend to be aggressive, while girls who were rated insecurely attached tend to be overly dependent (Turner, 1991). Even at ages 5 and 6, differences are apparent between children who were securely and insecurely attached as infants (Arend et al., 1979; Main & George, 1985).

Does this mean that a secure or insecure attachment in infancy determines whether a child will grow up to be sociable or aggressive, self-directed or dependent, curious or withdrawing? Probably not by itself. Certainly it is true that a sensitive caregiver who fosters a secure attachment in his or her infant is likely to maintain this kind of caregiving as the child matures, encouraging the development of sociability, curiosity, and independence. And it is also true, unfortunately, that the insensitive care that contributes to an insecure attachment is also likely to be maintained, making the child more inclined to be cautious, aggressive, or dependent. But remember that attachment relationships are sometimes altered as changing family circumstances (a divorce, a new job, a new baby) establish new patterns of interaction. In addition, as children mature, they make new friends, face new developmental challenges, and experience new social settings, all of which may alter the long-term effects of a secure or insecure attachment in infancy. Thus while an insecure attachment may lead a young child to approach new relationships skeptically and cautiously, later relationships may encourage trust and security that provide the child with new confidence and openness.

This view that early attachment biases, but does not inevitably determine, later social relationships also provides the basis for helpful interventions with children whose early attachment is insecure. In one study with Spanish-speaking immigrant families in the United States, for example, three groups of 1-year-olds were compared: a securely attached group, an insecurely attached control group, and an insecurely attached experimental group who were visited weekly by an empathic bilingual and bicultural adviser. Within a year, the experimental group of mothers and infants were relating to each other almost as well as the group who were originally securely attached—and far better than the control group on measures of infant anger, maternal responsiveness, and the like (Lieberman et al., 1991). Happy outcomes like these alert us to the fact that although early experiences provide a foundation for later growth, they rarely create developmental pathways that are inevitable and cannot be altered.

The Parents' Side of Attachment

By the time an adult becomes a parent, he or she has a long history of attachment experiences, including relationships with his or her parents, romantic partners, and friends. As you yourself probably know from experience, each new attachment can inspire trust and security or, instead, feelings of insecurity and anxiety—and each relationship further refines the expectations with which one approaches new relationships (Simpson, 1990). Recently, researchers have begin examining the parents' side of attachment to see whether the security or insecurity of parents' own past relationships has any bearing on their attachment with their children.

To explore the parents' side of attachment, Mary Main and her colleagues have devised the Adult Attachment interview, an hour-long series of questions related to parents' memories of their childhood attachment experiences, their perceptions of trust and security in their early years, and their views of their own parents as well as of their adult relationships (Main & Goldwyn, in press; Main et al., 1985). Based on what the parents say, and how they say it, they are classified into one of four categories:

Autonomous. Adults who are classified as autonomous value attachment relationships and regard them as influential, but they are also capable of discussing them objectively, whether their own early attachments were positive or negative in quality.

Dismissing. Adults who are dismissing tend to devalue the importance and influence of attachment relationships in their own lives, and tend to idealize their parents without being able to provide specific examples of positive interactions in the past to support their view.

Preoccupied. Adults in this category seem to be very preoccupied with the past, and are unable to discuss early attachment experiences objectively, often showing considerable emotion while talking about their relationships with their parents.

Unresolved. Adults who are unresolved have not yet reconciled their past attachment experiences with the present; these parents are sometimes still coping with parental loss and related experiences.

If these four adult attachment classifications appear to parallel those of infancy (secure, avoidant, resistant, and disorganized), it is not a coincidence: researchers have discovered that parents' adult-attachment ratings closely parallel the kind of attachment they form with their children (Crowell & Feldman, 1988, 1991; Fonagy et al., 1991; Main & Goldwyn, 1992). Autonomous mothers tend to have securely attached infants; dismissing mothers tend to have avoidant babies; and preoccupied mothers tend to have resistant infants. (The parallel is less clear for the unresolved classification, partly because it is often a transitional status for many adults.)

FIGURE 8.14 Research suggests that this baby's future attachment to her mother (on left) may depend partly on the kind of attachment her mother had with her own mother many years before. Judging by the grandmother's evident delight at watching her daughter and granddaughter play together, this family appears to be enjoying three generations of secure attachment.

The link between adults' attachment histories and their attachment with their own children could occur for several reasons. It may be that parents who value attachment and can reflect objectively on their own experiences are more sensitive to their offspring, and inspire a secure attachment as a result; or it may be that innate temperament predisposes individuals to certain attachment patterns across most of their personal relationships, including those with parents and with children; or it may be that the nature of parents' attachment with their children influences their memories of, and attitudes about, their other attachments. Whatever the reason for the link, it appears that one important contribution to the development of a secure attachment in infants is the parent's views of his or her own early attachment experiences.

Exploring the Environment and New Relationships

The synchrony of the early months, and the emergence of attachment as the first birthday approaches, set the stage for the next phase of parent-infant interaction. At home, as infants become more mobile, as well as more secure, they explore the environment with ever greater scope. Whether this exploration is regarded as a process of separation-individuation, or as the experimentation carried out by the curious "little scientist," its effect is to significantly widen the toddler's mastery of the home setting. At the same time, most toddlers in the United States experience some form of out-of-home care, whether at a day-care center, family day-care home, nursery school, babysitting cooperative, or play group. In these settings, toddlers begin to negotiate the demands of peer relationships and expand their repertoire of social skills.

These changes pose a new challenge for caregivers as well—keeping the infant's exploration within safe and tolerable bounds while including whatever toys, experiences, and people will lead to the development of the typical toddler's enormous potential for intellectual growth, skills mastery, and self-esteem. Let us first look at the environmental conditions that foster development.

The Best Setting for Toddler Curiosity

It is not easy to fashion a good place for a toddler to play and learn. Safety alone is a concern, since toddlerhood is the most accident-prone period of childhood. But safety is only the first step toward creating an environment that is ideal for development. Toddlers need to explore and discover, to run and to climb, to experience new things that they can touch and smell, think about and remember, each day. Consider some of the activities of a typical 1-year-old:

> Her legs can accomplish wonders: walk, climb, jump, run. And the legs, in turn, are at the service of eager little hands. She can now climb on the dresser to reach that colorful porcelain doll that had always beckoned to her. She can drag all the stuffed animals from her room to join Mom in the kitchen. She can squeeze herself under a cabinet to find a long-lost marble and put it in her mouth. She can be silent and out of sight for a long time, only to be found carefully tearing the pages of a book that she found by climbing on Mommy's desk. [Lieberman, 1993]

What specific aspects of a home setting help toddlers learn? To put it more bluntly, how can a caregiver prevent a toddler from breaking an heirloom, disrupting home furnishings, choking on a marble, and destroying a book while still encouraging the child's exploration as the prime pathway to intellectual development? Opinions abound on this issue, and each culture has somewhat different approaches (Rogoff et al., 1993), but one group of American researchers has developed a tool to answer that question. The tool is called **HOME** (an acronym for Home Observation for the Measurement of the Environment). HOME is a list of forty-five family and household characteristics that have been shown to correlate with children's development (Bradley, 1988; Caldwell & Bradley, 1984). These characteristics, divided into six subscales, are rated by a trained observer while visiting an infant and caregiver at home.

HOME has been used to evaluate the environment of young children from many racial, cultural, and socioeconomic groups, with better success in predicting children's later cognitive development than conventional intelligence tests (Bradley & Rock, 1985; Mitchell et al., 1985) or ratings of socioeconomic status (Bradley et al., 1988; Johnson et al., 1993). Contrary to the traditional methods of predicting an infant's competence, HOME suggests that a toddler who is of average IQ and from a lower-income home, but who has a responsive, involved mother and a safe, stimulating play environment, is likely to become a more competent preschooler than a middle-class infant who seems more advanced, but whose HOME scores are low.

TABLE 8.1

The Six Subscales of HOME

1. *Emotional and verbal responsiveness of mother.* Example: Mother responds to child's vocalizations with vocal or verbal response.

2. *Avoidance of restriction and punishment.* Example: Mother does not interfere with the child's actions or restrict child's movements more than three times during the visit.

3. *Organization of the physical environment.* Example: Child's play environment appears safe and free of hazards.

4. *Provision of appropriate play materials.* Example: Child has one or more toys or pieces of equipment that promote muscle activity.

5. *Maternal involvement with child.* Example: Mother tends to keep child within visual range and to look at the child often.

6. *Opportunities for variety in daily stimulation.* Example: Mother reads stories to child at least three times weekly.

HOME A method that evaluates how well the home environment of a child fosters development. HOME looks at maternal responsiveness and involvement with the child, the child's freedom of movement, the play environment, the play materials, and the variety of activities in the child's day.

Each of the six subscales of HOME are important. However, analysis of which aspects of HOME correlate best with later development reveals that, particularly for boys, the best predictor of future competence is "provision of appropriate play materials" that encourage the child's motor and cognitive development (Bradley & Caldwell, 1980, 1984). These play materials do not need to be expensive "educational" toys: large cardboard boxes, pots and pans, a collection of stones (too big to swallow) and plastic bottles can be great toys for toddlers. The next most important predictors of future achievement are "variety in daily stimulation" and "maternal involvement."

Parental Influences on Exploration

Not surprisingly, then, it seems that parents' greatest impact on early personality development as well as cognitive development occurs as they foster play in a variety of ways—with materials as well as personal involvement with their toddlers. You will note that this observation appears to bring us back to the idea that the caregiver's behavior is crucial. In fact, there is no denying the importance of the caregiver's role in fostering synchrony, or attachment, or exploration. The difference between the evidence of recent studies and the thrust of traditional theory, however, is the current emphasis on the infant's active participation in the process and the ways it can affect both the caregiver's behavior and the impacts of the ecological settings they share. This is clear in two contrasting examples from a study of mother-toddler interaction (Carew, 1980).

The first example is of a mother and her 24-month-old daughter Sonja, who has just begun the interaction by saying that she went to a circus:

Mother:	No, you didn't go to the circus—you went to the parade.
Sonja:	*I went to the parade.*
	What did you see?
	I saw . . .
	What?
	Big girls.
Mother smiles:	Big girls and what else?
	Drums.
Mother chuckles.	
Sonja laughs, as if remembering the parade.	
Mother blows up	
a balloon:	What made all the loud noise at the end?
	Trumpets.
	Yes and fire engines. Do you remember the fire engines?
	You hold my ears a little bit.
Mother smiles:	Yes, I did, just like this. (Puts her hands on Sonja's ears.)
Sonja laughs.	

In this case, Sonja begins the interaction, and the mother helps her remember and recount her experiences. Indeed, each partner escalates mutual enjoyment, as when Sonja says, "You hold my ears a little bit" and then the mother playfully holds the child's ears again. Thus both mother and daughter are creators of this interchange and, judging by their laughter, each enjoys the interaction they are developing together.

The other example comes from 18-month-old Terry, who begins the interaction by his active exploration:

Terry sits in front of the bookshelf, pulling books out. He pulls out a book and picks up a piece of paper (his sister's school worksheet) and looks at it. Terry pulls out another book. Mother comes over and says "Terry, No" and removes him saying "Don't touch again," and slaps his hand. Terry babbles something back.

Terry goes back and touches the books. Mother "No." Terry throws himself on the floor and whines. He gets up and picks up a doll and throws it on the floor. He throws it again. Terry marches back to the shelf and pulls at the books again. Mother yells "No," and goes to remove him. Terry marches around and then picks up a framed picture from the shelf. Mother: "Terry!" and comes to remove him. "Don't touch." Terry laughs. Mother: "I am not playing with you!" He goes and picks up another picture. Mother tells his sister to get it from him and she does so. Terry tries to get it back. Mother goes and pulls him away from the shelf. Mother: "Don't touch it again, you know it. Don't laugh, fresh kid." Terry laughs and walks to the TV. [Carew, 1980]

One way to analyze this episode is to take the traditional stance and criticize the mother. Terry gave clear signals that he wanted his mother's attention (taking the books down, throwing the doll, and taking the pictures), and his mother's reaction was, at best, ineffectual, and at worst, destructive. Ideally, Terry's mother should have seen that he needed distraction and attention as well as restriction and prohibition. She should have moved him, not only away from the books, but also toward something he would like—perhaps reading to him from one of his own books, or looking at a family photo album with him.

However, instead of simply blaming the mother, as traditional approaches would do, consider Terry's contribution to this interaction, as well as the overall context. Terry stubbornly persists in doing what his mother doesn't want him to do and laughs at his mother's rebuke. As you remember from the description of infant emotions, Terry's reaction is not unusual for a toddler, though that fact may be of little comfort to his mother. Further, Terry's temperament may be a "difficult" one. At least in this incident, he is difficult to distract and quick to complain and express anger. Finally, for obvious reasons, many mothers are less able to be patient and creative with their second child than with their first, especially if the first is still relatively young and there is intense sibling rivalry.

Thus the interaction of caregiver, child, and the overall context is as important to a toddler's healthy development as it is to a young infant's. The difference, of course, is that the toddler is a more adept, complex, and assertive child. The toddler is also widening his or her social world to include peer relationships developed in play groups at home, or in various out-of-home settings. As every parent has witnessed, peers can have a profound effect on the developing toddler.

Developing Peer Relations

Historically, most toddlers' first experiences in developing peer relations occurred in the home, with slightly older brothers and sisters, or in the backyard or playground with neighbor children. Today, smaller family size, greater spacing between births, and, most significant, the fact that the majority of mothers with young children work outside the home, mean that most toddlers begin to relate to peers in a play group or organized day-care setting. Such social relationships are now coming under study, and the re-

FIGURE 8.15 "Your pail is better than my pail" seems to be a typical theme in toddler peer play. What happens next depends on the playmates' temperaments, past relationships, and current negotiating skills. Fortunately, even young toddlers have some social sense, and the interaction pictured here seems more likely to end in shared play than in a tug of war.

sults echo a note already sounded many times in this chapter: young children are far more complex social beings than most theorists once realized.

Infants proceed through several stages in their ability to engage in social interaction with other infants (Howes, 1987). Even as young as 6 months of age, infants are capable of very simple social responses to their age-mates: gazing intently at another child's activity, vocalizing animatedly when that child does something interesting, or smiling and touching that child. These overtures and responses tend to be brief and fleeting, but over the rest of the first year, longer and more complex interactions begin to occur. One-year-olds may gesture to each other or exchange words when referring to toys or people, and they may offer toys to, or take toys from, each other. In addition, infants begin to distinguish between familiar and unfamiliar peers, preferring to be with familiar ones and interacting in a more complex fashion with them. Not surprisingly, infants tend to be less skilled when interacting with another infant than with an adult because an infant partner cannot provide the structure and support for the child's social skills that the adult can.

With the growth of self-awareness and emotional vitality in the second year, peer encounters flourish. Toddlers become capable of a broader range of more cooperative and complex social skills, such as turn-taking on a slide, playing elementary coordinated games such as run and chase, and joining in simple forms of pretend play. Toddlers begin to imitate each other, often to the delight of both the model and the imitator (Hanna & Meltzoff, 1993). They also spontaneously share toys, territory (such as a sand box), and even food (such as half-eaten cookies) (Hay et al., 1991).

Of course, toddlers are not always prepared to share, and frequently one toddler seems to covet an object to the degree that another is unwilling to give it up. Often the result is shouts of "No!" and "Mine!" followed by pulling, crying, and hitting. As they play together, however, toddlers develop simple strategies for avoiding such conflicts. Some toddlers become quite skilled tacticians, keeping a favorite toy out of sight, for instance, or distracting a peer by calling attention to some other object.

Increasingly, toddlers recognize each other's individuality, and friendships between two children begin to form even in day-care clusters of six or so toddlers. Signs of obvious affection—hugs, kisses, and big smiles—are sometimes exchanged between 2-year-olds who have not seen each other for a while. Apparently, attachment already begins to extend beyond the home in toddlers who have steady playmates.

Of course, toddlers still have much to learn in the social sphere. However, taken together, their personality development, emotional maturation, and peer relationships over the first two years of life represent a time of notable psychosocial growth, providing a foundation for the more complex socioemotional achievements to come. The first two years of life comprise a time when a child, who is born with social stirrings, learns to connect those inclinations with the particular emotional expressions and specific people of the social world.

SUMMARY

The Ethological Perspective

1. The ethological perspective argues that the significance of many behaviors is revealed in light of human evolution. Especially in infancy, many behaviors are relevant to the baby's nurturance and survival.

2. Infant crying, smiling, and other behaviors help to alert caregivers to the baby's needs and keep them nearby to provide nurturance and protection. Complementary behaviors may also have evolved in adults to promote the baby's well-being, such as warmth to cues of babyishness.

Emotional Development

3. In the first weeks and months of life, infants are capable of expressing many emotions, including fear, anger, sadness, happiness, and surprise. Toward the end of the first year, the typical infant expresses emotions more readily, more frequently, and more distinctly.

4. In the second year, cognitive advances allow infants to become more aware of the causes of events, and more conscious of the distinctions between themselves and others. Thus new emotions emerge, such as guilt, pride, and embarrassment, and social referencing begins to occur as one means by which emotions are shaped by social interaction.

The Origins of Personality

5. In the first half of the twentieth century, the prevailing view among psychologists was that the individual's personality is permanently molded by the actions of his or her parents in the early years of childhood. The early behaviorists as well as later social learning theorists believed this occurred as the child experienced or witnessed reinforcing events, day by day, that accumulated to create habits of attitude and action.

6. Freud argued that the child-rearing practices encountered in the oral and the anal psychosexual stages had a lasting impact on the person's personality and mental health. The mother's love—whether freely given or withheld—was central in this process.

7. Erikson and Mahler built on Freud's ideas, broadening his concept of the first two stages. According to Erikson, the infant first experiences the crises of first *trust versus mistrust*, discovering whether the immediate world is secure or insecure, and then the crisis of *autonomy versus shame and doubt*, as the infant tries to achieve some measure of independence. Mahler describes a period of separation-individuation, in which the infant, with much ambivalence, develops a sense of self apart from the mother. Like Freud, both of these psychoanalytic thinkers stress the lifelong impact of the caregiver's actions during the first two years, and the importance of maternal sensitivity.

8. Temperament—a group of basic, early dispositions, some largely influenced by genetics, others more susceptible to environmental influences—is another factor in psychosocial development. Individual temperament tends to be stable over time but can change, sometimes because of changes in the "goodness of fit" between temperament and environmental demands.

Parent-Infant Interaction

9. In addition to the parents' actions and the infant's temperament, developmentalists stress the social partnership between parent and child and its growth during the early months of life.

10. The early parent-child interaction is sometimes characterized by synchrony, a harmony of gesture, expression, and timing that can make early nonverbal play a fascinating interchange. Attachment between parent and child becomes apparent toward the end of the first year. Secure attachment tends to predict curiosity, social competence, and self-assurance later in childhood; insecure attachment tends to correlate with less successful adaptation in these areas.

Exploring the Environment and New Relationships

11. In the second year, the toddler's world widens through exploration of the home environment. Parental guidance and support remain important to these new developmental challenges. Through peer interactions, children expand their social understanding and repertoire of social skills.

KEY TERMS

ethology (250)
social smile (253)
stranger wariness (256)
separation anxiety (256)
social referencing (258)
self-awareness (259)
oral stage (263)
anal stage (263)
trust versus mistrust (263)
autonomy versus shame
 and doubt (265)

separation-individuation
 (265)
sensitivity (265)
temperament (265)
goodness of fit (270)
synchrony (273)
attachment (277)
secure attachment (277)
insecure attachment (277)
Strange Situation (278)
HOME (285)

KEY QUESTIONS

1. What does the ethological perspective contribute to our understanding of early development?

2. Which emotions develop in the first year?

3. Which factors influence whether a baby will be afraid of, or friendly toward, a stranger?

4. What are some consequences of the toddler's growing cognitive skills and developing sense of self?

5. According to behaviorists, how do parents affect the formation of personality?

6. What are the similarities among the theories of Freud, Erikson, and Mahler?

7. What are the three most common temperamental patterns in infancy, and how does nurture affect them?

8. Why does temperament sometimes change over time?

9. What are the similarities and differences between mother-infant and father-infant interactions?

10. What do infants learn from parent-infant interaction?

11. What contributes to a secure attachment?

12. Does early attachment determine later psychosocial growth? Why or why not?

13. What are the major developmental challenges of the second year of life?

Biosocial Development	Cognitive Development	Psychosocial Development

Body, Brain, and Nervous System

Over the first two years, the body quadruples in weight and the brain triples in weight. Neurons branch and grow into increasingly dense connective networks between the brain and the rest of the body. As neurons become coated with an insulating layer of myelin, they send messages faster and more efficiently. The infant's experiences are essential in "fine tuning" the brain's responses to stimulation.

Motor Abilities

Brain maturation allows the development of motor skills from reflexes to coordinated voluntary actions, including grasping and walking. At birth, the infant's senses of smell and hearing are quite acute, and although vision at first is sharp only for objects that are about 10 inches away, by 1 year, acuity approaches 20/20.

Perceptual Skills

Sensory abilities are linked in both intermodal and cross-modal perception, and the various affordances of objects and people are understood.

Cognitive Skills

The infant's active curiosity and inborn abilities interact with various experiences to develop early categories, such as object size, gender differences, and even number as well as an understanding of object permanence. Memory capacity, while fragile, grows during the first years, although retrieval is sometimes difficult. The infant progresses from knowing his or her world through immediate sensorimotor experiences to being able to "experiment" on that world mentally, through the use of mental combinations.

Language

Babies' cries are their first communication; they then progress through cooing and babbling. Interaction with adults through "baby talk" teaches them the surface structure of language. By age 1, an infant can usually speak a word or two, and by age 2 is talking in short sentences.

Emotions and Personality Development

Emotions change from quite basic reactions to complex, self-conscious responses. Infants become increasingly independent, a transition explained by Freud in terms of the oral and anal stages, by Erikson in terms of the crises of trust versus mistrust and autonomy versus shame and doubt, and by Mahler in terms of separation-individuation. While these theories emphasize the parents' role, research finds that much of basic temperament and mood is inborn, and apparent lifelong.

Parent-Infant Interaction

Parents and infants respond to each other first by synchronizing their behavior. Toward the end of the first year, secure attachment between child and parent sets the stage for the child's increasingly independent exploration of the world. Some cultures emphasize an exclusive mother-infant bond; others encourage wider social interaction with the father and other caregivers.

PART III The Play Years

The period from age 2 to 6 is usually called early childhood, or the preschool period. Here, however, these years are called the play years to underscore the importance of play. Play occurs at every age, of course. But the years of early childhood are the most playful of all, for young children spend most of their waking hours at play, acquiring the skills, ideas, and values that are crucial for growing up. They chase each other and dare themselves to attempt new tasks, developing their bodies; they play with words and ideas, developing their minds; they invent games and dramatize fantasies, learning social skills and moral rules.

The playfulness of young children can cause them to be delightful or exasperating. To them, growing up is a game, and their enthusiasm for it seems unlimited, whether they are quietly tracking a beetle through the grass or riotously turning their play area into a shambles. Their minds seem playful too, for the immaturity of their thinking enables them to explain that "a bald man has a barefoot head," or that "the sun shines so children can go outside to play."

If you expect them to sit quietly, think logically, or act realistically, you are bound to be disappointed. But if you enjoy playfulness, you might enjoy caring for, listening to, and even reading about children between 2 and 6 years old.

The Play Years: Biosocial
Development

CHAPTER

9

Between the ages of 2 and 6, increases in children's strength and motor skills, along with their more adultlike body proportions, allow children's exploration and mastery of their world to proceed by leaps and bounds, both literally and figuratively. This growth also, unfortunately, increases their vulnerability to biosocial hazards, including accidental injury and, for some children, abuse. In this chapter we will examine not only the biosocial changes that occur in the play years but also the implications these changes have for behavior and learning, including topics such as the following:

What are some of the reasons one child grows markedly taller and heavier than another?

What changes occur in brain growth, and how does this affect the child's behavior and thinking?

What motor skills can children develop before age 6?

What personality traits and past experiences might put parents at risk of maltreating their children?

How can child abuse and neglect best be prevented?

Between ages 2 and 6, significant biosocial development occurs on several fronts. The most obvious aspect of this development during early childhood, of course, is the striking changes that occur in size and shape, changes that cause many 6-year-olds to find photos of themselves as chubby toddlers unrecognizable. Less obvious but more crucial changes involve the maturation of the brain and central nervous system. This maturation allows the mastery of motor skills that clearly sets the 6-year-old apart from the clumsy toddler and also makes possible the cognitive development that we will discuss in the next chapter. Let us begin our examination of biosocial development in the preschool years by looking at the way children's body proportions change.

Size and Shape

During the preschool years, children generally become slimmer as the lower body lengthens and some of the fat accumulated during infancy is burned off (Rallison, 1986). The kindergarten child no longer has the protruding stomach, round face, and disproportionately short limbs and large head that are characteristic of the toddler. By age 6, the proportions of a child's body are not very different from those of an adult.

Steady increases in height and weight accompany the changes in body proportions. From age 2 through 6, well-fed children add almost 3 inches (7 centimeters) and gain about 4½ pounds (2 kilograms) per year. By age 6, the average child in a developed nation weighs about 46 pounds (21 kilograms) and measures 46 inches (117 centimeters).

The range of normal development is quite broad. Many children are notably taller or shorter than average, and the spread among age-mates becomes greater with every passing preschool year (see Figure 9.1). Weight is especially variable. For example, by age 6, about 10 percent of American children weigh less than 38 pounds (17 kilograms) and another 10 percent weigh more than 53 pounds (24 kilograms) (Behrman, 1992).

Of the many factors that influence growth (see Table 9.1), the three most influential are the child's genetic background, health care, and nutrition. This last factor is largely responsible for the dramatic differences that exist between children in developed and underdeveloped nations: the average 4-year-old in Sweden, for example, is as tall or taller than the average 6-year-old in Bangladesh, where 65 percent of the children experience stunted growth due to poor nutrition (United Nations, 1994). Within developed nations, however, most of the variations that one sees among preschoolers are due to genetic factors.

FIGURE 9.1 As these charts show, preschool boys (blue line) and girls (red line) grow more slowly and steadily than they did in the first two years of life. Most children actually lose body fat during these years. The weight that is gained is usually bone and muscle.

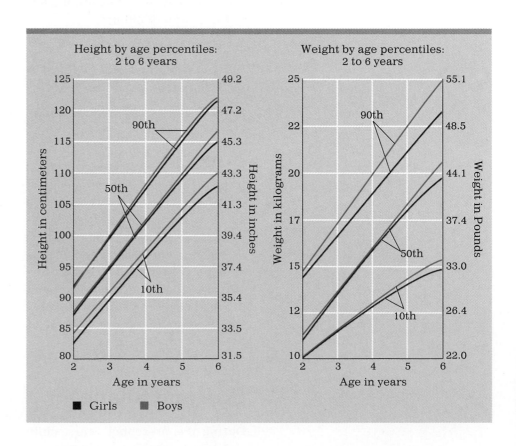

Generally, boys are more muscular, have less body fat, and are slightly taller and heavier than girls throughout childhood, although this varies depending on the culture and the child's age. For example, even in the early years, boys in India are markedly taller and heavier than girls, because boys are more highly valued by the society and therefore are more likely to have their nutritional needs taken care of first when food is scarce (Poffenberger, 1981). In North America, by contrast, children who are in the heaviest 10th percentile are more likely to be girls than boys, primarily because girls in general have a higher proportion of body fat when they have access to ample food (Lowrey, 1986).

TABLE 9.1

Factors Affecting the Height of Preschoolers

Taller Than Average If	Shorter Than Average If
well nourished	malnourished
rarely sick	frequently or chronically sick
African or northern European ancestors	Asian ancestors
mother is nonsmoker	mother smoked during pregnancy
upper SES	lower SES
lives in urban area	lives in rural area
lives at sea level	lives high above sea level
first-born in small family	third- or later-born, large family
male	female

Source: Eveleth and Tanner, 1976; Meredith, 1978; Lowrey, 1986.

Eating Habits

Whether a child is short or tall, his or her annual height and weight gains are much less from age 2 to 6 than during the first two years of life. In fact, between ages 2 and 3, an average child adds fewer pounds than during any other twelve-month period until age 17 (Rallison, 1986). Since growth is slower during the preschool years, children need fewer calories per pound during this period than they did from birth through toddlerhood, especially if they are among the modern sedentary children who spend much of their time indoors. Consequently, their appetites seem smaller, a fact that causes many parents to worry. In most cases, however, this relative decline in appetite does not represent a medical problem unless the child is unusually thin or is not gaining weight at all. Most parents report a noticeable increase in their children's appetite by age 8 (Achenback & Edelbrock, 1981).

Of course, as at any age, the diet during the preschool years should be a healthful one. The most prevalent specific nutritional deficiency in developed countries during the preschool years is iron deficiency anemia, a chief symptom of which is chronic fatigue. This problem, which stems from an insufficiency of quality meats, whole grains, and dark-green vegetables, is three times more common among poor families than among nonpoor ones. Although limited financial resources make it harder to purchase high-iron foods, it should also be noted that families of every social class are likely to contribute to the problem by giving their children candy, soda, sweetened cereals, and the like. These items can spoil a small appetite faster than they can a large one, and therefore may keep a child from consuming enough of the foods that contain essential vitamins and minerals.

FIGURE 9.2 Lifelong food preferences are formed during early childhood, which may be one reason why the two children on the right seem dubious about the contents of the pink lunch-box, broccoli and all. Nevertheless, each of these children appears to be a model of healthful eating.

An additional problem for most American children is that they, like most American adults, eat too few fruits and vegetables and consume too much fat. Whereas preschoolers should obtain no more than 30 percent of their daily calories from fat, the daily diet of six out of seven preschoolers exceeds that limit. Interestingly, both children whose family income is at the poverty level and those whose family income is three times the poverty level are more likely to eat too much fat than those whose family income lies somewhere in between (Thompson & Dennison, 1994).

Brain Maturation

The most important physiological development during early childhood is the continued maturation of the central nervous system. This maturation underlies children's rapidly expanding cognitive abilities as well as their increasing control and coordination of their bodies.

As explained in Chapter 6, during childhood the brain develops faster than any other part of the body. One simple indication of this is weight: by age 5, the brain has attained about 90 percent of its adult weight, even though the average 5-year-old's total body weight is only about 30 percent that of the average adult (Lowrey, 1986). Part of this increase in brain size is due to the continued proliferation of dendrite networks, enhancing communication among the brain's various specialized areas, and to the ongoing process of myelination, which provides the nerves with an insulating sheathing that speeds up the transmission of neural impulses. Myelination thus bears significantly on the child's developing abilities. For instance, because the areas of the brain associated with the control of eye movement and focusing undergo myelination throughout the preschool years, children gradually become much better at recognizing letters and numbers, and eventually words, as their eyes move across a printed page (Aslin, 1987; Mitchell & Timney, 1984). By age 6, most children can focus on letters and scan a line of print reasonably well, though, of course, they are still much less skilled at scanning than adults are (Van Oeffelen & Vos, 1984). Increasing myelination also improves the child's hand-eye coordination during the play years, enabling older preschoolers to copy a letter or number that they recognize on a printed page, or to catch a ball that is tossed toward them.

This myelination process continues beyond the preschool years and is closely related to the ongoing improvement of certain skills. Myelination in the brain areas associated with language and reasoning, for example, continues until the end of childhood, enhancing communication among the brain's neural networks and allowing the processing of more abstract thought.

Also of major importance is the myelination process—complete at around age 8—that occurs in the **corpus callosum**, a band of nerve fibers that connects the two halves of the brain.

The Two Halves of the Brain

The brain is divided into two similar halves, the left brain and the right brain. Each half controls the functioning of the opposite side of the body as well as being primarily responsible for certain specialized tasks. In 95 percent of right-handed adults and about 70 percent of left-handed adults, the left brain is the location of several key areas associated with logical analysis and language development, including speech; the right brain, meanwhile, is the location of areas associated with various visual and artistic skills, among them recognizing faces, responding to music, and perceiving various types of spatial relations.

Obviously, for a person to be fully functioning, both halves of the brain, as well as both sides of the body, need to work together, which is why the myelination and maturation of the corpus callosum is a critical factor for advanced motor skills and higher-order cognition (Springer & Deutsch, 1989). Indeed, when the corpus callosum is surgically severed, as it sometimes must be to halt chronic brain seizures, people show dramatic deficits in particular tasks involving left-brain–right-brain coordination (Gazzaniga, 1983). For example, they can see a familiar object with the right eye but are unable to name it, or, given the title of a popular song, they can readily recite the words but have great difficulty recognizing the correct melody.

In the early years, considerable flexibility in the functioning of the two halves of the brain and body is apparent. In infancy and early childhood, many fewer areas of the brain seem to be dedicated to specific functions than in adulthood. Consequently, when damage occurs to an area that has only begun to specialize, the functions of that area can usually be taken over by some other area. By contrast, functioning that is lost in a given area in adulthood is much harder to remedy, and often remains deficient.

This developmental change is notable when damage occurs in the language area of the brain. In children, such damage is more likely to lower overall cognition than to impair specific language abilities (O'Leary, 1990), while in adults, the identical damage might cause the loss of a specific set of verbal abilities. In some cases, an adult might be unable to retrieve whole

corpus callosum A network of nerves connecting the left and right hemispheres of the brain.

categories of vocabulary (such as prepositions, or the names of fruits) but otherwise show no language impairment. Similarly, some brain-damaged adults lack other particular skills—such as the ability to move one part of the body or to respond appropriately to social nuances—while young children are less precisely affected.

This early flexibility of brain functioning and specialization is evident in handedness: even by age 5, when more than 90 percent of all children are clearly right- or left-handed, a child can be taught to use his or her nonpreferred hand for certain skills. In fact, in times past, most lefties, under pressure from misguided teachers and parents, learned to write with their right hand. Once any pattern of brain functioning and specialization is firmly set, by the end of childhood, it is more difficult to switch sides or to learn new patterns. Adults find it much harder to learn to hammer a nail, or knit, or write with their nonpreferred hand than young children do, because bodily coordination patterns in the brain have become localized and habitual.

FIGURE 9.3 Both of these young artists are producing colorful work with great concentration, and, given their age, probably with their preferred hand. The specialization in brain functioning that is related to handedness is related to other aspects of development as well; some research suggests that while lefties are generally at a disadvantage in writing languages that read from right to left, they may have an advantage in artistic skills.

Precisely how the two halves and the various sections of the brain function as a whole, and how this relationship changes with time, are a matter of great interest and practical import but little knowledge. It does seem clear that, even at birth, the two halves of the brain are already specialized to some degree, and that smooth coordination of the many parts of the brain underlies many intellectual skills (Molfese & Segalowitz, 1988). For example, analysis of the brain's electrical activity reveals that several areas in both sides of the brain are involved in reading, and that some children who are poor readers use one side of the brain considerably more than the other, preventing them from properly connecting visual symbols, phonetic sounds, and verbal meanings (Bakker & Veinke, 1985). Similarly, the left and right sides have different roles in emotional arousal and its regulation as early as the first year of life (Dawson, 1994; Fox, 1991). While various researchers disagree about the particulars of specialization and coordination within the brain, all agree that much more research is needed before we understand how the two halves of the brain interact (Molfese & Segalowitz, 1988; Springer & Deutsch, 1989).

Activity Level

Developmental studies of **activity level**, concerning how much and how often a person moves his or her body, show definite age-related patterns that are assumed to be linked to brain maturation. Although the precise mechanisms are not well understood, they are thought to be related to neurological development, to the brain's production of certain hormones, and to the mind's need for a certain level of outside stimulation, a need that changes as a person grows older.

We do know that, in the first two or three years of life, activity level increases in all children, and then decreases throughout childhood (Eaton & Yu, 1989). Thus a 2½-year-old is more likely than a 1-year-old, but less likely than a 5-year-old, to display signs of high activity level, such as fidgeting while being read to, moving about while being dressed and groomed, and being continually on the run, indoors and out (Fullard et al., 1984).

This developmental trend in activity level is universal, but a number of factors contribute to wide variation among individuals. One such factor is heredity: variations in activity level are one of the abiding distinctions between one person and another (Goldsmith et al., 1987). The genetic component of activity level has been highlighted by studies of monozygotic and dizygotic infant twins. In one, measurements taken by motion meters attached to the infants' arms and legs for two days revealed that activity level for monozygotic twins was almost identical, whereas for dizygotic twins it was no more similar than for regular siblings (Saudino & Eaton, 1989).

Activity level can also be affected by environmental factors. For example, family and cultural differences regarding "acceptable" levels of activity in various contexts can intensify or dampen the child's rate of activity. Specific contexts, such as a raucous playground or a quiet religious service, can likewise affect a child's activity level, temporarily. (In a context such as the latter, children with naturally high activity levels tend to become fidgety.)

In practical terms, what is the relevance of this developmental trend? First, it suggests that it is a mistake to expect young children to sit quietly for very long, whether at home or in nursery school. Nor should anyone expect every child to be as quiet as his or her peers. Some children are naturally much more active than others, as well as more active than the typical younger child (though they are, fortunately, likely to be less active than they themselves were a few years before). Since activity level is sometimes associated with the ability the concentrate and to think before acting, expectations should be tempered in these respects as well, especially for preschoolers. As with many developmental patterns, a combination of patience and an appreciation for individual differences is likely to be more productive than merely ordering a child to stay still or pay attention.

Mastering Motor Skills

As their bodies grow slimmer, stronger, and less top-heavy, and as their brain maturation permits greater control and coordination of their extremities, children between ages 2 and 6 are able to move with greater speed and grace, and become more capable of focusing and refining their activity. The result is an impressive improvement in their various motor skills.

activity level A measure of how much and how often a person moves his or her body.

Gross Motor Skills

Gross motor skills, involving large body movements such as running, climbing, jumping, and throwing, improve dramatically during the preschool years (Clark & Phillips, 1985; Du Randt, 1985; Kerr, 1985). The improvement is obvious to anyone who watches a group of children at play.

Two-year-olds are quite clumsy, falling down frequently and sometimes bumping into stationary objects. But by age 5, many children are both skilled and graceful. Most North American 5-year-olds can ride a tricycle, climb a ladder, pump a swing, and throw, catch, and kick a ball. Some of them can even ice skate, ski, roller-blade, and ride a bicycle, activities that demand balance as well as coordination. These specialized abilities obviously require practice, as every parent knows. However, a certain level of brain maturation is also necessary. This is readily apparent in hopping on one foot, a skill that requires fluid coordination between the two halves of the brain. It is a skill very few 3-year-olds can master, no matter how often they try, and one almost all 5-year-olds can perform (Sutherland et al., 1988).

Most young children practice their gross motor skills wherever they are, whether in a well-equipped nursery school with climbing ladders, balance boards, and sandboxes, or on their own, with furniture for climbing, fences for balancing, and gardens or empty lots for digging up. Indeed, their active exploration and curiosity, combined with their developing motor skills, can lead to injury and other physical hazards (see Public Policy, pages 304–306). Generally, preschool children learn basic motor skills by teaching themselves and learning from other children, rather than by specific adult instruction. So long as a child has the opportunity to play with other children in an adequate space and with suitable play structures (none of which is to be taken for granted in today's neighborhoods, especially in large cities [Garbarino, 1989]), gross motor skills will develop as rapidly as maturation, body size, and innate ability allow.

FIGURE 9.4 In mastering their gross motor skills, children, of every group, in all settings, seem to obey a universal command: "If it can be climbed, climb it."

Fine Motor Skills

Fine motor skills, involving small body movements, especially those of the hands and fingers, are much harder for preschoolers to master than gross motor skills. Such things as pouring juice from a pitcher into a glass without spilling, cutting food with a knife and fork, and achieving anything more artful than a scribble with a pencil are difficult even with great concentration and effort. Preschoolers can spend hours trying to tie a bow with their shoelaces, often producing knot upon knot instead. The chief reason many children experience these difficulties is simply that they have not developed the muscular control, patience, and judgment needed for the exercise of fine motor skills, in part because the myelination of the central nervous system is not complete. For many preschoolers, this liability is compounded by their still having short, fat fingers. Unless these limitations are kept in mind when selecting utensils, toys, and clothes for the preschool child, frustration and destruction can result: preschool children may burst into tears when they cannot button their sweaters, or mash a puzzle piece into place when they are unable to position it correctly.

FIGURE 9.5 The papier-mâché animals produced by this girl and her preschool classmates are more likely to be mushy and misshapen than artistic. However, the real product here, in addition to fun and a sense of accomplishment, is the development of eye-hand coordination and fine motor skills. With intensive, dedicated practice, such as that evidenced here, such skills are mastered by the school-age years, when children's art work is sometimes truly remarkable.

Fortunately, such frustrations usually fade as the child's persistence at practicing fine motor skills gradually leads to mastery. One fine motor skill that seems particularly linked to later success in school is easy for parents and teachers to encourage—the skill of making meaningful marks on paper.

Children's Art

Drawing is an important form of play. On the simplest level, "the child who first wields a marker is learning in many areas of his young life about tool use" (Gardner, 1980). In addition, in thinking about what to draw, manipulating the pencil, crayon, or brush to execute the thought, and then viewing, and perhaps explaining, the end product, the child is experiencing a sequence of events that not only provides practice with fine motor skills but also enhances his or her sense of accomplishment.

Children's artwork also provides a testing ground for another important skill, self-correction. A developmental study of children's paintings found that whereas 3-year-olds often just plunked their brushes into the paint, pulled them out dripping wet, then pushed them across the paper without much forethought or skill, by age 5 most children took care to get just enough paint on their brushes, planned just where to put each stroke, and stood back from their work to examine the final result (Allison, 1985). Older children also show an eagerness to practice their skills, drawing essentially the same picture again and again.

Such mastery of drawing skills is related to overall intellectual growth. In general, as children become more skilled and detailed in their drawing, their level of cognitive development rises as well (Bensur & Eliot, 1993; Chappell & Steitz, 1993). While there is no way of knowing to what degree the mastering of drawing skills contributes to cognitive advances—as well as arises from them—it may be that a sketch pad and a box of markers are as much an "educational toy" as traditional alphabet blocks or counting games.

Injury Control Is No Accident

As children gain control of their motor skills, they practice them continually, wherever and however they can. They climb trees and fences; they run along open fields and busy streets; they find ways to play with almost anything they can get their hands on. All this activity and exploration is healthy in many ways, but it also poses dangers, exposing children to far greater risks than those parents usually worry about, such as abduction or leukemia (MacDonald, 1990).

In fact, in all but the most disease-ridden or war-torn countries of the world, accidents are, by far, the number-one cause of childhood death. In the United States, a child has about 1 chance in 500 of dying due to an accident before age 15—four times the risk of dying of cancer, the second-leading cause of childhood death. More than a third of the children who are killed in accidents each year die as a result of auto accidents, either as passengers or pedestrians. The other most common accidental fatalities in childhood primarily involve falls, choking, suffocating, burning, drowning, and poisoning. Accidental death from these nonvehicular causes is particularly prevalent among preschool children, pushing their *annual* death rate even higher than that of school-age children (18 per 100,000 compared with 10 per 100,000) (U.S. Bureau of the Census, 1994).

Injuries, of course, are even more common. In the United States, a preschool boy has more than 1 chance in 3 each year of having an injury that needs medical attention, while a girl has 1 chance in 4 (U.S. Bureau of the Census, 1993). Virtually every child will need stitches or a cast sometime before adolescence, and 44 percent of all serious injuries that require hospitalization, including a disproportionate number of serious brain injuries, occur among children under age 15.

The accident risk for any particular child depends on several factors, some within the child and some within the surrounding family, community, and culture. Naturally, the child's own judgment, motor skills, and activity level are crucial, as are caregivers' knowledge of, and attentiveness to, potential hazards, along with the quality of their supervision. Also of major importance are community standards and cultural norms that either foster or impede safety practices. For instance, walkers for infants are much less common in most nations than in the United States, where some new parents consider them essential baby equipment—and where they injure one out of every three babies who use them (Simon, 1992). Something in American culture—perhaps the eagerness to have one's children walking "on time" or even early, or perhaps the wish to have all the baby furniture that others have—drives the purchase of this dangerous device.

Family and community factors also play a role with another group of American children at particular risk, rural youngsters. Farm equipment, especially corn augers, tractors, and gravity boxes, injure 20,000 children and kill 300 each year, with deaths more likely during harvest time, when equipment use is heavy and supervision light (Salmi et al., 1989).

A child's gender, ethnicity, and family income also affect accident risk. For instance, no matter where they live, boys, as a group, tend to take more risks and have more injuries and accidental deaths than girls—about one-third more between ages 1 and 5, twice as many between ages 5 and 14. Asian-Americans, the most closely supervised among American ethnic groups, have the lowest accident rate of any American children, while African-Americans and Native Americans have the highest. The clearest risk factor of all is socioeconomic status. One study of all childhood deaths in North Carolina found that low-SES children were three times as likely to die an accidental death as other children, with income disparity being particularly pronounced in the fatality rates for preschool children. For example, 1- to 4-year-olds whose families were on welfare were at least four times as likely to be fatally hit by a car, four times as likely to die by choking, and nine times as likely to burn to death, compared with children whose families did not need welfare assistance. Among the reasons cited for these differences were the substandard housing, hazard-filled neighborhoods, and inferior medical care that are typically associated with low socioeconomic status. For reasons that are not clear, when black and white children of the same income were compared, poverty increased the risk of accidental death for white children even more than for black children (Nelson, 1992).

For all children, however, the risk of accidental injury, especially serious injury, could be much lower than it is. With forethought, certain accidents can be avoided completely; and while some accidents are inevitable in a normal childhood, proper precautions could significantly reduce their severity. The first step in reducing injury risks, many believe, is to approach the problem in terms of **injury control** instead of "accident prevention." The word "accident," advocates of injury control point out, misleadingly implies that no one was at fault, whereas most serious accidents involve someone's lack of forethought (Christophersen, 1989).

Sometimes forethought means little more than providing adequate adult supervision. But what is "adequate" to controlling injury? There are no absolutes and no guarantees: children sometimes get hurt even when they are being closely watched in their own homes, and sometimes they may be alone in dangerous places all day long without incident. There is also the risk that being overly protected might keep children from developing the independence and self-confidence they need. Nonetheless, there is some consensus on what adequate supervision entails, at least in the case of infants and young children. Pediatricians, child-protection workers, and parents agree that a crawling baby cannot be safely left alone anywhere, even for a minute, and that children between the ages of 4 and 8 should never be unsupervised in a neighborhood that has attractive dangers, such as accessible bodies of water (creeks, ponds, or swimming pools). Between the ages of 4 and 8, children should be able to play unwatched at home for at least ten minutes; older children should be able to do so for half an hour or more (Peterson et al., 1993). Especially for older children, temperament and past history are important indicators of how long a particular child can safely go unsupervised.

Forethought also involves instituting safety measures in advance to reduce the need for vigilant supervision and to prevent serious injuries when accidents do occur. For instance, compared with adults, children are more likely to drown, choke on a nonfood object, fall off a bicycle, or suffocate in a fire. Advance precautions, such as teaching children to swim, or removing all swallowable objects from their reach, or requiring them to wear a helmet when bicycling, or installing working smoke alarms in the house, could prevent most such deaths.

One obstacle to injury control is that many parents are not always sure which particular objects or activities represent potential hazards, or which preventive measures work. For example, many parents give their children balloons to play with, not knowing that chewing popped balloons is a common cause of asphyxiation among preschoolers. With many toys, items of juvenile furniture, and children's activities, parents, on their own, have no good way to judge risk. Not until accurate nationwide data become available did most parents realize the extent of the hazards associated with, for example, cribs with widely spaced slats, playgrounds surfaced with concrete, or roller-blading without head gear and protective pads. *(continued on next page)*

(a)

(b)

(c)

In order for parents to safeguard their children from injury, they first need to be aware of safety hazards, and then need to take whatever action is necessary. In two of these photos, the parents are to be commended: the parents in (b) not only put a helmet on their child but demonstrate by example the importance of this measure; and as suggested by the smiles in (c), the mother probably has been securing her child in a safety seat from early infancy. However, the boy in (a), apparently left unattended for a moment, has managed to scramble up onto a piece of sculpture that was obviously intended to be viewed, not crawled across.

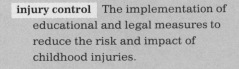 **injury control** The implementation of educational and legal measures to reduce the risk and impact of childhood injuries.

Injury Control Is No Accident (continued)

Obviously, the responsibility of injury control should not be left to parents alone. Research is needed to identify potential hazards, and information about demonstrated risks needs to be made readily available. In addition, schools, community groups, and legislators can take many educational and legal measures to reduce injuries. The question is, which measures work best? Overall, broad-based safety education, such as television announcements and poster campaigns, rarely have a direct impact on children's risk-taking, although they may foster a general climate that makes more specific measures likely to work. Similarly, educational programs in schools and preschools may be successful to the extent that they enable children to verbalize safety rules, but they appear to have little effect on children's actual behavior.

If neither public advertisement nor classroom instruction is very effective in changing behavior, are all educational efforts in vain? Not necessarily. The best approaches to safety education are those that reach both parents and children, individually or in small groups, in situations where motivation is high (as when a child known to those involved has been injured) (Garbarino, 1988). Motivation may be the reason that new and expectant parents are much more likely than experienced parents to heed the safety suggestions of pediatricians and other experts, such as to use an infant car seat, to set the household water heater below 120 degrees to avoid accidental scalding, to place all poisons in locked cabinets, and so forth (Christophersen, 1989). Apparently, experienced parents whose children have not yet had serious injuries become complacent, reasoning "We've never had a car accident . . . no one we know has ever been scalded . . . our kids don't play with detergents, medicines, or matches—so why worry?" Such attitudes, which send chills up the spine of emergency workers, may be one reason that the risk of accidental injury rises as family size increases.

However, even more effective than targeted educational measures in reducing the overall injury rate are safety laws that include penalties for noncompliance. Among such measures that have led to significant reductions in accidental death rates for children in the United States are

1. a federal law requiring child-proof safety caps on medicine bottles—credited with an 80 percent reduction in poisoning deaths of 1- to 4-year-olds;

2. a federal law requiring flame-retardant sleepwear for children, decreasing deaths from burning pajamas and nightgowns 97 percent;

3. local laws requiring fencing around swimming pools, reducing childhood drowning by 51 percent;

4. state laws requiring car safety seats for infants and children, credited as a significant factor in the 26 percent decline in motor-vehicle deaths of children under age 5 from 1980 to 1991;

5. city laws requiring window guards on every apartment where children live, credited for a dramatic decline in the number of deadly falls from windows in New York City—from more than 30 per year in the 1960s to 4 per year in the 1980s (National Center for Injury Prevention and Control, 1992, 1993).

Largely as a result of laws like these, the accidental death rate for children between the ages of 1 and 5 in the United States has been cut in half in the past two decades. Nevertheless, this means that nearly 2,600 children in this age group and 3,700 children between the ages of 5 and 14 are still being killed by accidents each year.

Much remains to be done. For example, although child-safety restraints, when properly employed, can reduce children's auto-crash deaths by 90 percent, only about a third of all parents use them, possibly because local laws requiring their use are underenforced (Garbarino, 1988). Similarly, about half of all children who are killed in car accidents are pedestrians, yet in most heavily trafficked areas, safe outdoor play spaces for young children are probably even more scarce now than they have ever been. Guns are widely purchased for home protection, but it is estimated that six times as many friends and family members are accidentally shot to death in the home as are criminals killed. Many of these fatalities involve children. In 1988, 277 children were accidentally killed by a gun, and up to six times as many were injured by one (Weil & Hemenway, 1992; Wintemute et al., 1987).

The issue of injury control is now capturing the attention of many experts—pediatricians, developmental psychologists, teachers, and lawmakers alike. It is increasingly apparent that the child who escapes serious injury in childhood is not *just lucky*, and that accidents are not *just an accident*. But while we know general statistics regarding accidental death, such as age, sex, and immediate cause of death, we have much to learn about specific circumstances that could be changed. The lessons already learned have reduced accidental death dramatically, but good statistics on, and expert analysis of, precisely what causes and prevents accidents are just beginning to be collected (National Center for Injury Prevention and Control, 1992, 1993). As adults become more knowledgeable about the hazards facing children and the ways to reduce their impact, more children will survive the risks of their early years intact.

Child Maltreatment

Throughout this chapter and elsewhere in this text, we have assumed that parents naturally want to foster their children's development and protect them from every danger. Yet daily, it seems, the news media report stories of parents who actually cause harm to their offspring. Accounts like the following are all too familiar:

> 8-month-old Yessana "began crying and would not stop." The mother . . . had been drinking and could stand the crying no more. She said in a videotaped statement that she shook and struck the baby and twice dropped her on the floor . . . less than 12 hours later, the infant died, apparently of multiple fractures of the skull. [McFadden, 1990]

> 7-month-old Daniel died of starvation and dehydration after five days without food or water. After his father beat his mother, she . . . "went on a six-day crack binge." The next day his father "left the baby alone in the unlocked apartment. . . ." According to the police, neither parent intended for the child to die; they were "both remorseful." The mother was known to authorities, because she had several other children, all in foster care. [Duggar, 1991]

The public is horrified by the brutality and senselessness of cases like these, and appalled at the pathological perpetrators, indifferent neighbors, and overworked child-welfare workers who often seem to share the blame. Yet sensational cases like these represent only a minor portion of all maltreatment cases. And as experts in child-maltreatment research point out, while the media's focus on the lurid and inexplicably brutal instances of maltreatment triggers justifiable outrage, it also distracts us from our collective responsibility to remedy the underlying causes of the more typical, and far-too-common, cases of maltreatment (Scheper-Hughes & Stein, 1987).

More specifically, most maltreatment does *not* involve serious physical abuse: only 25 percent of all new cases reported and accepted for protective services for 1993 involved physical abuse, with a fatality occurring in roughly 1 in 1,000 cases (McCurdy & Daro, 1994). Much more common is a persistent

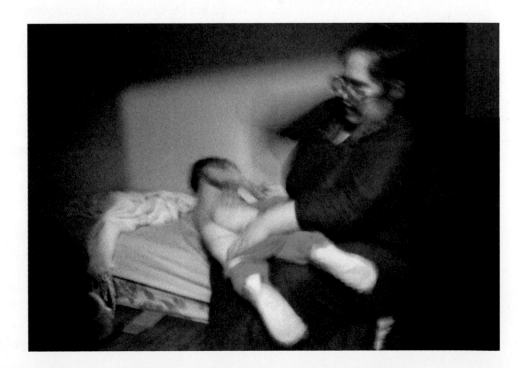

FIGURE 9.6 Like that of many child abusers, this mother's abusive behavior may be intensified by her poverty and the difficulty of raising two children alone. However, unlike most abusive parents, she not only admits her problem, but is getting counseling to overcome it. (See Figure 9.10.)

pattern of neglect and psychological abuse that often begins in infancy and, accumulating over the years, harms the child's self-concept, social interactions, and intellectual growth, sometimes permanently. Instead of the uncontrolled rage or total indifference of the parents cited above, more frequent are the actions of caregivers who do not understand how to love and guide a child, reasoning, for example, like this mother of a 6-month-old:

> If he spits up his food at me I slap his leg. No time to learn like the present—if he is old enough to do it, he is old enough to learn not to do it. [Gelles, 1987]

or this father, who has set ideas of how children should behave and believes that his son should be "kept on his toes":

> So his dad teases him a lot . . . [and] plays games with him. If Jon wins, his dad makes fun of him for being an egghead; if he loses, he makes fun of him for being a dummy. It is the same with affection. Jon's dad will call him over for a hug; when Jon responds, his dad pushes him away, telling him not to be a sissy. . . . Jon is tense, sucks his thumb, and is tongue-tied (which his dad teases him about). [Garbarino et al., 1986]

Often a child is neglected partly because of the family's poverty, when inadequate income, dangerous housing, perfunctory medical care, threatening neighborhoods, and an inability to provide the basic necessities combine to put children at risk. These stresses help explain why neglect is more common in single-parent households than in households with two parents. As Leroy Pelton (1994) has noted, "In some cases a mother does not have much choice but to provide her children with inadequate supervision or to deprive them of necessities. A low-income mother with many children cannot easily obtain or pay for a babysitter every time she wants or needs to leave the house. If she leaves her children alone, she is gambling with their safety" and can be arrested for neglect.

The task of social scientists, then, is to get beyond sensationalism and blame and to discover the underlying causes and remedies of all types of child maltreatment. As you will see, compared with a few decades ago, experts today, as well as the general public, are becoming much more aware of the scope, causes, and consequences of maltreatment.

Changing Definitions of Maltreatment

Only forty years ago, the concept of child maltreatment was primarily limited to physical abuse, which was generally thought to be the rare, violent outburst of a mentally disturbed person (Zigler & Hall, 1989). It is now recognized that child maltreatment is neither rare nor sudden, that its perpetrators usually are not deranged, and that serious physical injury is only one of several forms of maltreatment (Annerman & Hersen, 1990; Cicchetti & Carlson, 1989; McGee & Wolfe, 1991). With this recognition has come a broadened definition of maltreatment. Currently the term **child maltreatment** includes all intentional harm to, or avoidable endangerment of, anyone under age 18. Child maltreatment thus includes both **abuse**—actions that are deliberately harmful to a child's well-being—and **neglect**—failure to appropriately meet a child's basic needs. Abuse and neglect are both further subdivided into more specific categories (Barnett et al., 1993; Panel on Research on Child Abuse and Neglect, 1993):

1. *Physical abuse*—deliberate, harsh injury to the body. Signs of physical abuse include broken limbs and battered bodies, as well as less ob-

child maltreatment Includes all intentional harm to, or avoidable endangerment of, someone under age 18.

abuse All actions that are deliberately harmful to an individual's well-being.

neglect A form of child maltreatment in which parents or caregivers fail to meet a child's basic needs.

vious symptoms, such as old, poorly knit fractures (revealed by x-rays), bleeding in the brain (revealed by CAT-scan), and burn marks that are small and round (from lit cigarettes), lattice-like (from hot radiators), or that stop part-way up the body (from scalding bathwater).

2. *Physical neglect*—failure to meet the child's basic physical needs. This includes the failure to provide adequate food, warmth, or medical care, as well as reasonable supervision and protection from harm or injury.

3. *Sexual abuse*—deliberate involvement in, or exposure to, sexual activities. Because of their immaturity and vulnerability to the power of adults, children and adolescents are considered unable to give free consent to sexual activities. Thus any erotic activity that arouses an adult and excites, shames, or confuses a child—whether or not the child protests and whether or not genital contact is involved—can be sexual abuse.

4. *Psychological abuse*—deliberate destruction of a child's self-esteem and equanimity. The most common type is repeated verbal abuse, ranging from angry threats to incessant criticism. Another type is social isolation, such as shutting a small child in a dark closet or keeping an adolescent housebound and friendless. Overall, any terrorizing, isolating, degrading, or belittling of the child can become emotional abuse.

5. *Psychological neglect*—failure to meet basic needs for emotional sustenance. Distant, cold, indifferent, and unaffectionate caregivers are emotionally neglectful. So are those who capriciously withdraw love or comfort, who allow the child's self-abuse with drugs or by other means, who ignore the child's need for basic education, or who do not shield a child from witnessing violence between adults.

To some extent, each of these five forms is distinct, with somewhat different causes and consequences. However, while distinguishing specific forms of abuse helps untangle the web of causes and consequences, the unfortunate reality is that most children who come to the attention of authorities usually suffer from several forms of maltreatment.

For a number of reasons, estimating the frequency and severity of the various types of child maltreatment, as well as their fluctuating rates over time, is very difficult. The chief problem is that the reporting process itself is flawed in many ways. As A Closer Look (p. 310) and the Research Report (pp. 312–313) make clear, there is no certain way to measure prevalence. However, even if we take the most conservative approach, counting only those children who are officially reported as being maltreated (2,989,000 in 1993) and then confirmed (1,016,000), the rate of maltreatment is appallingly high—about 15 cases in every 1,000 children (McCurdy & Daro, 1994).

Causes of Maltreatment

At first it is hard to imagine any reason why someone would hurt a child entrusted to his or her care. However, research has shown that virtually everything—from the community values to the caregiver's history, from the family culture to the child's temperament—can contribute to the causes of child maltreatment.

A CLOSER LOOK

Child Maltreatment in Context

As emphasized throughout this book, every behavior needs to be considered in context. This is especially true when assessing parental nurturance, a topic that involves our deepest and most personal emotions. Developmentalists increasingly believe that "behaviors per se can seldom be defined as harmful or beneficial—the immediate, relational, familial, and cultural contexts in which they occur all play a crucial role in determining what effects the behavior may have" (Sternberg & Lamb, 1991).

Understanding child maltreatment in context begins by considering *community standards*. Each community has somewhat different customs and goals regarding child-rearing, which means that sometimes what is maltreatment in one place is not maltreatment in another. For example, while more than 90 percent of American parents sometimes spank, slap, or push their 3-year-olds, and think such behavior is justified, in Sweden any physical punishment of children at any age is considered abusive and is against the law (Daro, 1988). In some Asian, African, and Caribbean countries, by contrast, to never hit a child is tantamount to neglect (Arnold, 1982; Rohner, 1984; Rohner et al., 1991). Physical punishment—administered by mothers as well as fathers—may be especially commonplace and accepted in cultures where men are expected to be aggressive and dominant, where the father's role is that of an "authoritarian tyrant," and where child-rearing styles are highly controlling and nonnurturant. A punitive style of child-rearing in such cultures "may have little connection with the general value accorded to children. Rather, parents may use this style of child-rearing to teach children the code of conduct and behavior they will need to become responsible adults" (Deyoung & Zigler, 1994).

Thus in many cases, before concluding that a particular behavior or practice represents maltreatment, we need to take community standards into account. This is especially important in light of the fact that children everywhere feel loved when their parents raise them not too differently from other children in the same family, neighborhood, and culture, and that parents judge their own child-rearing partly on the basis of the collective wisdom and practice of their peers. Given the diversity of the world's communities, it is "imperative to disentangle the natural from the cultural," distinguishing those practices that hurt any child anywhere from those that are harmful only in a particular place (Woodhead, 1991). Administering a beating is one example: for children in the West Indies, being hit for misbehaving is commonplace, and is taken as a sign of the parent's love and concern. But for these children, as for children everywhere, frequent and severe physical beatings result in feelings of rejection and low self-esteem (Rohner et al., 1991).

Understanding maltreatment in context also requires taking into account the impact of a behavior on the particular child. Since each child is unique, and every child changes over time, a practice that harms one child may not negatively affect another, or may not hurt either of them a few years later. For example, some children need much more supervision than others; some wither more quickly under criticism; some are more likely to be injured, physically or emotionally, by corporal punishment. Thus the seriousness of any specific act of maltreatment depends partly on the age, temperament, and abilities of the child (McGee & Wolfe, 1991).

At what point, then, does imperfect parenting become maltreatment? There is no clear line of demarcation. Every case should be judged in terms of its context and developmental history (Cicchetti, 1991; Zigler & Hall, 1989). Beyond that, the question becomes: Who is judging the behavior, and for what purpose? When the issue is whether a particular case should be legally labeled as maltreatment, only those cases in which maltreatment seems clearly dangerous and ongoing, as well as completely unacceptable to the community, merit official intervention (Thompson & Jacobs, 1991). On the other hand, when caregivers wonder if they are crossing the line, they need to remember that every parent's caregiving is, indeed, sometimes potentially harmful, no matter what the context, and that whenever doubts about the severity of disciplining arise, it is far better to trust those doubts and err on the side of leniency.

The Cultural and Community Context

According to the United Nations, overall concern and protection for the well-being of children varies markedly worldwide. Even countries in the same region of the world, with similar per capita income, differ markedly in measures of children's general health, education, and overall well-being

(United Nations, 1994). In addition, day-to-day caregiving is influenced by broad cultural values (Korbin, 1994; Sigler, 1989). Four such values appear to be especially important in protecting children from maltreatment:

1. Children are highly valued, as a psychological joy and fulfillment, as well as an economic asset.

2. Child care is considered the responsibility of the community. If parents are unwilling or unable to care for their child, other relatives or neighbors are ready to take over.

3. Young children are not expected to be responsible for their actions. In some cultures, almost any punishment of children younger than age 3, or even age 7, is considered abusive and unnecessary.

4. Violence in any context—between adults, between children, and between caregiver and child—is disapproved of.

The role of social values in child maltreatment is dramatically highlighted by the different rates of child abuse among the Polynesian people who live in their traditional home, the Pacific Islands, and those who have emigrated to New Zealand. Among the former, maltreatment is virtually nonexistent (Ritchie & Ritchie, 1981), for their society meets the four criteria listed above: children are highly respected, are cared for by many adults, are considered unteachable until they are at least 2 years old, and adults rarely express their anger through physical aggression (Reid, 1989; Ritchie & Ritchie, 1981).

However, when Polynesians move to New Zealand, the rate of child abuse skyrockets, surpassing the rate of the European New Zealanders many times over. The demands of the new lifestyle, designed for nuclear rather than extended families, make it impossible for the parents to continue their relaxed permissiveness, communal authority, and informal, shared child care. Like every immigrant group entering a radically different culture, these Polynesian parents experience considerable stress until they develop viable new coping strategies, such as learning how to guide children's behavior without resorting to physical punishment, how to replace the freely available caregivers of the past, and how to limit family size so that children are not an overwhelming financial burden. These contextual stresses often lead to a loss of perspective, and abuse results.

FIGURE 9.7 Child maltreatment, a serious social problem in industrialized nations, is rare in Micronesia. One reason, reflected in this photo of a community on Pulap Island, is that family life occurs largely in the open rather than behind closed doors. Neighbors and relatives immediately notice any lapse of care or outbursts of temper, and remedy the problem before it becomes neglect or abuse.

RESEARCH REPORT

Child Maltreatment: How Common in the United States?

Nobody knows the true prevalence of child maltreatment, since it usually occurs behind closed doors, with the caregiver unwilling, and the child unable, to acknowledge it. However, there are four methods commonly used to estimate prevalence: official reports, professional surveys, general surveys, and retrospective accounts. The problem is that each of these methods can yield quite different results, as can be seen by comparing estimates of maltreatment in the United States derived from each method for the same time period, the mid-1980s.

The simplest method is to count the number of complaints received by official agencies. In 1985, about 2 million reports were logged in the United States—which represents a reporting rate of one in every thirty children, double that of ten years before.

However, tallying complaints is probably the least accurate method of estimating the incidence of maltreatment: while many instances are not reported, others are reported more than once, and of those that are reported, only about a third are substantiated—sometimes because the report was completely false, but more often because the seriousness of the offense was insufficient to warrant an official recognition (Finkelhor, 1992; McCurdy & Daro, 1994). Further, maltreatment reporting rates are notoriously subject to the public's awareness of the problem and to varying laws and customs regarding the designation of maltreatment and the necessity of reporting it. Thus the dramatic increase in reported cases of child maltreatment cited above may actually reflect increased *reporting* more than an increased frequency of maltreatment.

A better method of estimating maltreatment is to ask all the trained professionals—judges, probation officers, police, doctors, nurses, teachers, day-care-center staff, child-welfare workers—in representative communities to name every child they are quite sure has been maltreated, and then extrapolate the results to the nation as a whole. This approach, taken by the National Center for Child Abuse and Neglect, produced the results shown in the first table on the next page, indicating that about 1 child in 40 (about 1.5 million) was known to suffer maltreatment of some kind in 1986, with physical abuse affecting 1 child in about 175 (NCCAN, 1988).

A third method is to ask caregivers, confidentially, about their behavior with their children. One study that used this approach conducted a telephone survey of more than 3,000 representative American families from all fifty states (Straus & Gelles, 1986). (If a surveyed family had two parents or several children, only one parent was asked about his or her behavior with one child, in order to get an accurate incidence rate per caregiver and child rather than per family.) The results, shown in the second table, suggest that about one child in forty was abused very violently (kicked, bitten, beaten, burned, hit with a fist, cut with a knife, and/or shot at)—a much higher figure than the estimates derived from cases of physical abuse known to professionals. Even so, this figure is undoubtedly an underestimate. Not only would some caregivers report less violence than they actually committed, but, as indicated, they were not asked about their abuse of other children in the household or about abuse by other family members. In addition, parents who refused to answer questions or who were without telephones were, obviously, not part of the study. Since being without a telephone is a sign of both poverty and social isolation, the latter group, especially, represents an important missing segment of the population most at risk. Moreover, while this method may be fairly accurate for most forms of physical punishment, it cannot validly assess sexual abuse, about which most per-

Cultural Factors Affecting Maltreatment in the United States

Comparing the four characteristics of nonmaltreating cultures with the patterns common in the United States explains, to a great extent, why child maltreatment is so prevalent in the United States, and why some U.S. communities have higher rates than others. First, children are often considered to be both a financial and personal burden. Not surprisingly, no matter how maltreatment is defined or counted, it occurs more frequently as family income falls (Pelton, 1994). This is particularly true for neglect and physical abuse, which fall most heavily on children between the ages of 3 and 6 who live in families with an income below the poverty line, an unemployed father, and four or more children. In such families, children obviously add to

Incidence of Child Maltreatment Known to Professionals, per 100 Children: United States, 1986

Rate of Abuse	1.07
Physical	0.57
Sexual	0.25
Emotional	0.34
Rate of Neglect	1.59
Physical	0.91
Educational	0.46
Emotional	0.35
Overall Rate	2.52

Totals of subcategories exceed the overall rate because about 10 percent of the children were known to have experienced more than one type of maltreatment.
Source: National Center for Child Abuse and Neglect, 1988.

Parents' Reporting of Their Own Violence with Offspring

Type of Violence	Percent Reporting
Cursed or insulted child	63
Slapped or spanked child	55
Pushed, grabbed, shoved child	31
Hit child with something (e.g., belt, stick)	11
Kicked, bit, hit with fist, beat up, burned	3
Used gun or knife	0.2

Source: Gelles, 1987, 1989.

petrators are ashamed and secretive, or neglect, since many caregivers do not know when they seriously neglect their children.

Finally, a fourth method—asking adults if they have ever been abused or neglected—leads to the highest incidence statistics of all. For example, in one study of families, 30 percent of the fathers and 17 percent of the mothers reported having been regularly hit with a belt, paddle, or other object by their parents when they were about age 12 (Simons et al., 1991). This rate well exceeds the 11 percent rate of hitting acknowledged by parents in the second table. The discrepancy between the rates of maltreatment reflected in self-reports and those from any other source is particularly apparent with regard to sexual abuse, where even the *lowest* rates of childhood abuse recalled by adults are more than twenty times the rates reported or known to professionals (Peters et al., 1986).

Among the reasons that this last method produces notably higher abuse rates is, obviously, that it accounts for victims whose cases never came to official attention and helps compensate for the unwillingness of some parents to be candid about their maltreatment of their children. Another important reason is that the retrospective survey usually asks about a person's entire childhood, while the other techniques focus on a single year. At the same time, however, the higher retrospective rates could reflect a higher actual rate of abuse in previous generations, as suggested by many studies that find maltreatment decreasing (Besharov, 1992; Gelles, 1987; Simons et al., 1991). In addition, some adults may have distorted or exaggerated memories of their mistreatment in childhood.

Thus each method of estimating maltreatment has its drawbacks. Each reflects a part of the picture, and therefore each has some validity and purpose, but none is completely accurate. Nevertheless, taken together, they make it starkly clear that child maltreatment is the most common of the serious developmental problems American children encounter.

the financial stress, and are more likely to become victims because of it (Wolfner & Gelles, 1993).

Second, in the United States, social support for parents and young children is scarce. For a variety of reasons, ranging from geographic separation of family members to the cultural emphasis on "looking out for number one," few relatives, neighbors, and friends are willing and able to help with child care. Grandmothers, for instance, once the mainstay of practical help, are now much more likely to live a distance away and to have their lives taken up with careers and friends outside the family. Lacking a supportive network, overburdened parents often take out their problems on their chil-

FIGURE 9.8 Poverty often sets the stage for neglect: for some parents, it is hard to give their children the individual love and attention that each needs when they can't even afford to give them a bed of their own. At the same time, many parents are able to be loving and nurturing no matter how difficult their circumstances.

dren, with the problems escalating, undetected, until considerable harm has been done. The likelihood of maltreatment is especially high when lack of support results in social isolation, with those who are most isolated being among the most abusive (Corse et al., 1990; Thompson, 1994). Neighborhoods in which there is a strong sense of community and in which there is a network of support through religious groups, schools, and community centers tend to have lower rates of abuse (Garbarino & Kostelny, 1992).

Third, the culture's views concerning the speed with which young children should "grow up" may add to the problem. The emphasis on the infant's and preschooler's ability to learn may cause some parents to forget that young children are also immature and dependent on others. For example, exaggerated expectations can lead some parents to consider irritating but normal behavior to be deliberate and therefore amenable to correction: they punish their infants for "crying too much" or punish toddlers for being unable to control urination or defecation or punish older children for "immature" behavior, expecting them to get themselves up, dressed, fed and to school, as well as to avoid "trouble" of all kinds, long before they are sufficiently mature to do so.

Finally, as many have observed, "violence is as American as apple pie." Indeed, by almost any measure, from the prevalence and prominence of aggression on television to the rate of spouse abuse, from the rates of violent crime to the rate of homicide, the United States is one of the most violent nations of the world (Benedek, 1989; Gelles & Straus, 1988; Sigler, 1989).

The Family Context

Each family has its own private culture, including habits, coping styles, and values that affect every family member. Many experts believe that the way these are structured in the individual family system can be pivotal in allowing maltreatment to occur. For example, the daily routine of most families is somewhat flexible, with adults and older children being able to make minor adjustments in their schedules and established roles as the occasion requires. However, the routines of maltreating families are typically at one of two extremes: they are either so rigid in their schedules and role demands that no one can measure up, or they are so chaotic and disorganized that no one can be certain of what is expected, or under what circumstances one can count on receiving appreciation, encouragement, protection—or even food and a clean bed. In such families, hostility and neglect are inevitable (Dickerson & Nadelson, 1989).

Similarly, while almost every family experiences crises that disrupt their harmony, most also have ways of coping and readjusting so that the family once again functions well. One crucial element in this restabilization is the family's ability and willingness to avail themselves of social support when needed. As already noted, however, maltreating families tend to shun social support, and problems are especially likely to worsen if a particular family's code includes isolation and distrust of all outsiders, from the neighbor next door to members of the local clergy (Polansky et al., 1985). If family stresses then erupt in violence, children are stuck within

> a family system in which exploitation, loyalty, secrecy and self-sacrifice form the core of the family's value system. In a sense, the victim's survival is dependent on adjusting to a psychotic world where abusive behavior is acceptable but telling the truth about it is sinful. [Carmen, 1989]

Another element within the family system that exacerbates maltreatment is dysfunctional relationships between members other than the perpetrator-victim pair. Child maltreatment is most likely within a home where the relationship between the resident adults—especially that between mother and father or between grandparents and children—is either extremely hostile or emotionally neglectful or both. Further, that climate of hostility adds significantly to the child's psychological stress, intensifying the effects of whatever direct abuse there may be (Cummings et al., 1994; Fantuzzo et al., 1991).

Another factor that clearly affects the intensity of dysfunctional family relationships is family size and the adult-to-child ratio: when there are more than three young children, maltreatment is more common (see Figure 9.9), partly because each new child means less money, less space, and less attention for other family members and greater stress for parents. These effects are more pronounced in single-parent families, since it is even harder for one adult to meet all the needs of several children.

FIGURE 9.9 As suggested by the nursery rhyme about the "old woman who lived in a shoe, she had so many children she didn't know what to do," large families increase the risk of neglecting the children's basic needs.

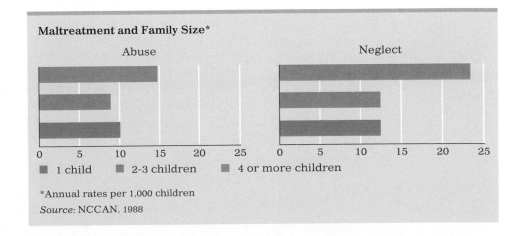

Not surprisingly, low-income single mothers are more likely to mal-treat their children than are their married counterparts, presumably be-cause the former are often isolated and overwhelmed by being the only adult supporting the family. However, once income rises, single mothers are no more maltreating than married mothers, perhaps because the additional income makes supportive social networks more likely, as well as allowing the mother to pay for care by babysitters, day-care centers, and so forth (Gelles, 1987, 1988).

Problems in the Parents

Contrary to popular misconceptions, most maltreating parents are not markedly different from average parents. Like other parents, they love their children and want the best for them. Fewer than 10 percent of them are pathological—so deluded or emotionally and cognitively dysfunctional that they never recognize the basic needs and vulnerabilities of their children.

Overall, however, abusive parents do tend to have personality traits that, in combination with stressful situations in a hostile ecosystem, form a volatile constellation likely to lead to an injured child. Personality tests of abusive parents find that they tend to be less trusting, less self-assured, and less adaptable than other parents. They are also less mature, which makes them more concerned with their own needs and less patient with, or even aware of, the needs of others (Belsky & Vondra, 1989).

Maltreating parents are also likely to show cognitive patterns that are somewhat distorted. They tend to view the world in negative ways that affect not so much their general attitudes about child-rearing as their attributions for a child's specific behaviors (Newberger & White, 1989). They tend to see the world as hostile and difficult, which leads them to interpret any signs of their child's discomfort or distress as a personal attack. This negative attri-bution, especially when combined with immaturity, makes normal coping with the demands and needs of children very difficult (Heap, 1991). Thus two mothers may have similar child-rearing attitudes; they may, for instance, both agree that a deliberately disobedient child should be spanked. How-ever, when a particular 4-year-old knocks over the milk, one considers it an accident, while the other "knows" that the "fresh kid" did it out of spite.

Compounding the problem is the fact that some maltreating parents completely misread their child's communications. For instance, they are likely to misinterpret the facial expressions and cries of an infant in distress as displays of anger (Kropp & Haynes, 1987), or to mistake the fearful cling-ing of a genuinely frightened preschooler as a manipulative demand for at-tention. Alternatively, they may view a child's typical behavior as sexually seductive, or fail to perceive the child's cues of hunger, cold, or fatigue as needs requiring attention. The effects of this misattribution and miscommu-nication can be disastrous:

> An average mother will regard a crying or fussy baby as hungry or wet or full of gas. She will proceed to feed, change, burp him, and then put him down in the crib and say, "Baby, you're tired," close the door, then turn on the radio or talk to a friend. The abusive parent is unable to leave the crying child, and tries harder and harder to pacify him until in a moment of utter frustration she is over-whelmed by the thought that this baby, even at two weeks of age, is saying, "If

you were a good mother I wouldn't be crying like this." It is precisely because the parent tries to be extra good, to be loved and earn the love of the child, that intractable crying is seen as total rejection and leads to sudden rage. The abuse is clearly not a rational act. It is not premeditated, and it is often followed by deep grief and great guilt. Such parents are seen by doctors and nurses as being very solicitous. Third parties find it hard to believe that so loving a parent could have inflicted such serious injury. [Kempe & Kempe, 1978]

An additional factor that increases the likelihood of maltreatment is drug dependency. According to official investigation of reported maltreatment, substance abuse is an apparent contributing factor in at least one case in four (McCurdy & Daro, 1994). Undoubtedly, the actual number is higher, given the difficulty any adult has in meeting the insistent, ongoing, and often unpredictable needs of a young child while in the grip of psychoactive drugs.

"Problems" in the Child

Finally, children themselves sometimes inadvertently contribute to their neglect or abuse. Children who were unwanted, who were born too early, who were the product of an unhappy love affair or a difficult pregnancy, who are the "wrong" sex, or who have physical problems can become victims of their parents' disappointment. Even the child's appearance, as in the case of the little boy who looks just like the father who left the mother early in pregnancy, or the little girl who reminds her father of his abusive mother, can trigger rejection instead of love. Parents may also be unhappy and frustrated over their child's temperament, wanting a quieter child, or a less active one, or a less difficult one. All these disappointments may lead to unresponsive and rejecting parenting, which, as we have seen, is likely to make a child much more difficult than he or she would otherwise have been.

Because the child's nature or behavior can sometimes be a precipitating factor in cases of maltreatment, it is important to stress the obvious: maltreated children are not to be blamed for their fate. While most high-risk children—especially demanding, irritable ones—cause stress in their parents, most parents cope well enough without mistreating the child. Problems arise when the difficult or disappointing child is in a family that is already under strain and unable to function well (Belsky & Vondra, 1989). In addition, although many abused and neglected children are difficult—immature, hyperactive, or deceitful—their difficulties are often a result of maltreatment more than a cause of it. Most important, even when a child's actions provoke justifiable anger and merit punishment, abusive punishment is never acceptable, for the consequences of abuse, as well as of neglect, can be devastating.

Consequences of Maltreatment

The more we learn about child maltreatment, the clearer it becomes that its consequences extend far beyond any immediate injuries or deprivation. For the victim, maltreatment often results in impaired development. Compared to well-cared-for children, chronically abused and neglected children tend to be slower to talk, underweight, less able to concentrate, and delayed in academics (Cicchetti et al., 1993; Eckenrode et al., 1993; Hanson et al., 1989; Vondra et al., 1990). Deficits are particularly apparent in social skills: maltreated children tend to regard other children and adults as hostile and exploitative, and hence they are less friendly, more aggressive, and more isolated than other children (Dodge et al., 1994; Hart & Brassard, 1989; Haskell & Kistner, 1991; Mueller & Silverman, 1989; Salzinger et al., 1993). As adolescents and adults, those who were severely maltreated in childhood, either physically or emotionally, often engage in self-destructive and/or other destructive behaviors.

The human and financial costs, both to the victim and to society, are virtually impossible to measure. In the United States in the 1980s, the *annual* cost of immediate care (investigation, medical treatment, court costs, emergency shelter) for all reported cases of serious maltreatment was around $500 million, with another $700 million spent on therapeutic services and long-term foster care (Daro, 1988). Additional costs result when victims of maltreatment later require special education for learning disabilities, therapy or institutionalization for emotional problems, and, in some cases, imprisonment for acts of misdirected anger.

In assessing the outcomes of maltreatment, we must neither minimize nor exaggerate. On the one hand, virtually every child who experiences serious, ongoing maltreatment is likely to bear some lifelong scars, including depression, fear of intimacy, difficulty controlling emotions, and low self-esteem (Rutter, 1989). On the other hand, many adults who were victims of childhood abuse or neglect live relatively normal lives, working, marrying, and raising a family.

One potential consequence that must be carefully considered is **intergenerational transmission**, that is, maltreated children growing up to become abusive or neglectful parents themselves. Many people erroneously believe that the transmission of maltreatment from one generation to the next is automatic and unalterable. This assumption is not only false but may be destructive. As one review explains:

> Uncritical acceptance of the intergenerational hypothesis has caused undue anxiety in many victims of abuse, led to biased response by mental health workers, and influenced the outcome of court decisions, even in routine divorce child custody cases. In one such case . . . a judge refused a mother custody rights because it was discovered during the trial that the mother had been abused as a child. Despite the fact that much of the evidence supported the children's placement with their mother, the judge concluded that the mother was an unfit guardian, since everyone "knows" abused children become abusive parents. [Kaufman & Zigler, 1989]

intergenerational transmission The phenomenon of mistreated children growing up to become abusive or neglectful parents themselves, a phenomenon that is less common than is generally supposed.

In determining the actual rate of intergenerational transmission, it is critical to study the problem longitudinally rather than retrospectively. Retrospective analyses invariably show high rates of transmission because almost every adult who seriously mistreats his or her child does, in fact, remember a very difficult and sometimes neglectful or abusive childhood. But these analyses, by definition, omit the victims of abuse who do not themselves become abusers. And there are many, many such people.

On the basis of longitudinal studies that begin before the abused individual becomes a parent, experts believe that only about 30 percent of adults who were abused as children actually become child abusers themselves, a rate about six times that of the general population but much less than that generally assumed to be the case (Kaufman & Zigler, 1989). Those parents least likely to perpetuate abuse they endured as children are those who subsequently had someone who loved and cared for them, such as the other parent or a foster caregiver in childhood or their spouse in adulthood. In addition, those who are able to remember their maltreatment and understand its effects are much better able to avoid abusing their own children.

Treatment and Prevention

As the scope and consequences of child maltreatment have become better recognized, efforts at treatment and prevention have greatly expanded, particularly in the area of public awareness. In most countries worldwide—as well as throughout the United States—laws have been passed over the past thirty years requiring the reporting of child maltreatment; several public and private national organizations tally reports of abuse and neglect, monitor treatment, and fund research; attention by the popular press has increased dramatically; and a professional journal, *Child Abuse and Neglect*, has been in publication for more than a decade. As a result, professionals and the general public have become much more aware of the problem, and are more likely to report it.

Treatment

Reporting, investigating, and substantiating maltreatment, and even punishing the perpetrator, do not necessarily stop the harm (Finkelhor, 1992). Even with documented cases, between a third and a half of all victims experience another episode of maltreatment (Daro, 1989). While great strides have been made in recognizing and defining maltreatment, and in understanding the causes and consequences, researchers and practitioners are still struggling with the application of these findings to treatment and prevention.

One of the major challenges is how to tailor treatment to fit the particular family context (Wolfe, 1994). According to one useful analysis, families involved in maltreatment can be subdivided into four categories: vulnerable to crisis; restorable; supportable; and inadequate (Crittenden, 1992).

Those families that are *vulnerable to crisis* are experiencing unusual problems and need temporary help to resolve them. For example, a divorce, the loss of a job, the death of a family member, or the birth of a handicapped infant can severely strain some adults' ability to cope with the normal demands and frustrations of child-rearing. Especially if other relatives or friends are unable to relieve the pressure, the relationship between parents and children may deteriorate to the point of abuse or neglect.

About a fourth of all maltreating families fall into this vulnerable-to-

FIGURE 9.10 This mother's display of affection is not inconsistent with her abusive behavior in Figure 9.6. Most abusive parents love their children, but need to learn how to use encouragement and guidance to control their children rather than harsh criticism and punishment.

crisis category. They are relatively easy to help, with services such as crisis counseling and parent training that are already available in some parts of the country. In the majority of cases, once the parents learn to cope with the specific difficulty more effectively, a process that usually takes less than a year, they are once again able to provide adequate child-rearing.

Less easily reached are the *restorable families*, who make up about half of all maltreating families. The caregivers in these families seem to have the potential to provide adequate care, and perhaps have done so in the past, but they have many problems, caused by their immediate situation, their past history, and their temperament, that seriously impair their parenting abilities. A single mother, for example, might have untreated medical problems, inadequate housing, and poor job skills, all fraying against a quick temper, which tends to explode when her child is difficult or disobeys her. Or a binge-drinking husband might periodically beat his children, perhaps with the tacit permission of his overly dependent and isolated wife, who herself may have come from an abusive home. Or a teenage couple might be both emotionally immature and addicted to drugs, causing them to sometimes disregard their infant's basic needs or to seriously overestimate the baby's abilities.

Treatment with restorable families requires a case worker who has the time and commitment to become a family advocate, mediating and coordinating various services, finding help for every family member who needs it, and providing essential emotional support. In actuality, however, few case workers are trained as, or have the time to be, such advocates. Indeed, one study of child-protection workers found that they spent only 11 percent of their time working directly with families—usually in their offices rather than in the family's home—and that half of the approved treatment plans were not implemented, usually because the case worker or referral agency was too busy (Crittenden, 1992).

Supportable families, who make up about a fifth of all maltreating families, will probably never be able to function adequately and independently until the children are grown. However, with ongoing support, ranging from periodic home visits by a nurse or housekeeper to special residences that include a variety of services—such as free clinics, day-care centers, recreation programs, social workers, and therapists—these families could meet their children's basic needs for physical, educational, and emotional care. Unfortunately, this range of support services is rarely available, and affordable, to the families that need them most.

Finally, nearly 10 percent of families are so *inadequate*, so impaired by deep emotional problems or serious cognitive deficiencies, that they may never be able to meet the needs of their children. For children born into these families, long-term foster care is the best solution.

Foster Care

Historically, many children have been raised by "foster parents"—usually relatives or neighbors—because their biological parents died or were too poor or too ill to care for them. However, in contemporary society, **foster care** generally refers to a legally sanctioned, publicly supported arrangement in which children are officially removed from their original parents and given—usually temporarily—to another adult to nurture.

FIGURE 9.11 Foster care works well as a response to a crisis of short duration—a few weeks or less—or as a permanent solution to an inadequate home. Unfortunately, many foster families are in limbo between the two. Three-year-old Sharmaine has been with her foster parents, shown here, since she was placed with them as an agitated, inconsolable, crack-exposed newborn. She developed into a happy, spunky daughter until at age 2½, a court ordered her to begin weekend visits with her biological mother and four older siblings in preparation for her eventual return to them. Before each visit, Sharmaine holds on tightly to her foster father and says, over and over, "Daddy, I don't want to go," and when she returns, her preschool teachers report that she becomes clingy, insecure, and sad. Such children, torn between two opposing principles, number in the hundreds of thousands in the United States.

foster care A legally sanctioned, publicly supported arrangement in which children are removed from their original parents and temporarily given to another caregiver.

The quality of foster care is controversial. Indeed, foster care has long been stereotyped as inadequate care. This stereotype is partly based on the myth that, no matter what, children are always better off with their biological parents. It is also partly based on the reality that, compared with children overall, foster children tend to do less well in school and have fewer friends, and are more likely to become delinquents and, later, criminals. However, it is not valid to compare foster children with children overall:

they should be compared instead with children who are left in the care of severely abusive or neglectful biological parents. When this more valid comparison is made, foster children come out ahead.

Research over the past decade has demonstrated that, while it is not good for children to be moved frequently from foster family to foster family, consistent long-term foster placement is preferable to many other arrangements. It is better than allowing a child to remain in a severely abusive family, or permitting a child to be shunted from relative to relative, or, even worse, letting a child be put through a series of foster placements interspersed with stays with an unsupportable or unrestorable biological parent (Fein, 1991; Widom, 1991). Indeed, some foster children do very well, catching up on missed education, learning how to respect themselves and others, and eventually becoming good, nonmaltreating parents. A positive outcome is especially likely when the foster parents are committed to the child and are provided with the ongoing resources needed to address whatever special emotional, physical, and social needs the child with a history of inadequate care might have (Daro et al., 1988). Those children who fare worst with foster care tend to be those who have endured such severe and extensive maltreatment in their biological family—and hence have such low self-esteem, such impaired social skills, and so much anger—that they would encounter difficulty no matter where they were raised.

Of course, with foster-care families, as with all families, some are better than others, and some are downright destructive. This is true both for foster families in which parents and child are unrelated by blood and marriage and foster families in which the foster parents and child are relatives, although the frequency of foster abuse is somewhat less when the caregivers are related to the child. Fortunately, destructive foster families can usually be recognized in advance and rejected, if the social workers involved in placement are sufficiently alert to proven risk factors, such as a serious illness of a family member, inadequate income exclusive of the foster-care allowance, frequent moving, too many children per room, a mix of biological and foster children in the household. A recent downturn in household circumstances, such as the father's loss of a job or the illness of the primary caregiver, is a particularly important warning sign that calls for close screening to determine the adequacy of the home (Zuravin et al., 1993).

Although foster care is sometimes the best solution, it is still the treatment of last resort, to be used when other methods to help a family fail. Unfortunately, decisions made about foster care are too often based on bureaucratic expediency, and sometimes cultural insensitivity to variations in family and community standards and values (Lindsey, 1991; Pinderhughes, 1991). Many times a child is hastily placed in foster care as a temporary solution, meant to last only until the parents correct whatever problems led to the child's removal. Such temporary placements work against the critical factor that can make foster care successful: the child and the foster parent becoming committed and attached to each other. Moreover, once a child is removed, fewer services—material or psychological—are provided to the biological family than would have been provided if the child were still at home (Lindsey, 1991). The result is that temporary foster

Say the word and you can break a child's spirit.

Words that demean and insult a child can hit as hard as a fist. And leave scars you can't see. Stop using words that hurt. Start using words that help.

stop using words that hurt.

For helpful information, write National Committee for Prevention of Child Abuse, Box 2866E, Chicago, IL 60690

FIGURE 9.12 Public information campaigns are part of the essential education necessary to begin to prevent child abuse and neglect. The more people recognize the many faces of abuse, the fewer the number of children who will suffer.

care stretches into an uncertain future, and if the child is returned, the family is neither restored nor sufficiently supported. Thus the child is still vulnerable to another cycle of abuse and neglect.

Prevention

The most important goal in dealing with child maltreatment is, obviously, to prevent it before it occurs. This is a daunting task that must take into account a wide array of contextual factors, including the cultural values and practices surrounding the family at risk, the various sources of community stress and support, the family's economic status and social isolation, as well as factors within the particular child and the particular parent that increase the child's vulnerability to maltreatment (U.S. Advisory Board on Child Abuse and Neglect, 1993).

A broad variety of programs attempt to do this. Many developed countries, England and New Zealand among them, provide a network of nurses and social workers who visit all families with young children at home, to encourage good health practices and to screen for potential problems, providing referrals as necessary. Many other nations provide a patchwork of programs, such as parent-newborn bonding sessions, high school classes in parent education, crisis hotlines,* respite care, drop-in centers, special training for teachers and police officers on recognizing abuse and neglect, programs to educate children about sexual abuse, and so on (Willis et al., 1992).

Many of these prevention programs are targeted at families that are considered particularly vulnerable, such as those with teenage parents, low-income families, or families with a child who needs special care. While some early intervention programs are already beginning to show promise (see Public Policy, pp. 324–325), research has generally revealed only suggestive evidence about what works. Finding out what is truly effective in what specific contexts is crucial, because, as one reviewer of early intervention programs notes, "the world of public policy is crowded with examples of results that are unexpected and unwanted by-products of well-meaning legislative or administrative initiatives" (Gallagher, 1990). Among these by-products are the dangers of wrongfully stigmatizing certain families as inadequate, of undermining family or cultural patterns that, contrary to conventional wisdom, work, and of creating a sense of helplessness in the family instead of strengthening its self-confidence, skills, and resourcefulness.

More broadly, the contextual view reminds us that, since poverty, youth, isolation, and ignorance correlate with unwanted births, inadequate parenting, and mistreated children, any public policies that work to raise the lowest family incomes, discourage teenage pregnancies, encourage community involvement, and increase the level of education of prospective parents may be the most effective overall approach to the prevention of maltreatment.

---

* A national hotline, 1-800-422-4453, or 1-800-4 A CHILD, is open in the United States day and night for questions and problems related to child maltreatment of any kind.

Preventing Child Maltreatment

One of the most vexing questions faced by policymakers who are concerned about preventing child abuse is "What works?" Before they are willing to invest public funds in prevention programs, they want hard evidence of these programs' long-term effectiveness. Unfortunately, such evidence is generally lacking, chiefly because it is difficult, and costly, to carry out careful follow-up studies to determine whether families continue to provide appropriate care for offspring long after they have completed a prevention program. However, there is promising preliminary evidence indicating that two kinds of approaches are successful in preventing the incidence, or the recurrence, of child maltreatment.

The first strategy, known as *home visitation*, focuses on first-time mothers who are young and alone and whose child is newborn. Early intervention may be crucial for these mothers because the stress of caring for a very needy and demanding newborn can quickly exhaust their parenting capacities. Several recent research projects in North America and Europe have found that providing these mothers with a trained home visitor who can offer ongoing emotional support throughout the first year benefits both the mothers and their babies (Government Accounting Office, 1990; Olds & Kitzman, 1990, 1993; Wasik et al., 1990). The home visitor can be anyone who cares: a social worker, nurse, paraprofessional, or trained volunteer may be equally helpful. The visits to the home may take place daily at first, and then occur weekly, monthly, or less often as the mother's needs for support change. Researchers have found that unmarried mothers who are depressed and isolated and whose pregnancies were unwanted are particularly likely to feel more confident, and to have better relationships with their children, when they have experienced a supportive relationship with a trained home visitor.

One extensive research project included four groups of women who were at high risk of becoming abusive or neglectful, ranging from a comparison group who were given only a free developmental evaluation of their offspring at 12 and 24 months of age to an extensive-treatment group who received home visits throughout pregnancy and infancy and were provided free transportation to a clinic for pediatric care. The visitor was a specially trained nurse who, among other things, encouraged informal support networks—friends, neighbors, grandparents, and the like—and taught inexperienced mothers how to interpret and respond to their infant's needs and moods. Positive results from visitation were especially apparent for those women who were poor, unmarried, and young: not only did the visited teenagers enjoy motherhood more than their unvisited counterparts, but they were much less likely to scold or hit their babies. This difference was also reflected in an independent source: according to official reports (logged by hospitals, police, and social agencies), when the babies were 2 years old, only 4 percent of the extensive-treatment teenagers had abused or neglected their infants, as opposed to 19 percent of the comparison group (Olds & Henderson, 1989).

Highly promising results have also been found in a more ambitious, state-funded effort in Hawaii, titled Healthy Start. Begun as a small demonstration project in 1985, this program now makes home visitation available to the majority of Hawaii's civilian population (Breakey & Pratt, 1991; Hawaii Department of Health, 1992). Parents participate in home visitation voluntarily, and may continue with the program until their child reaches age 5. During regular visits, trained home visitors provide emotional support, model positive parent-infant interaction, and help the mother get in contact with health-care providers and other community agencies who can offer further assistance. The preliminary evaluation of this program has been astonishing: of the 1,204 high-risk families served by Healthy Start between 1987 and 1989, there were only three cases of abuse and six cases of neglect reported to child-protection caseworkers—indicating a less than 1 percent rate of maltreatment in a select high-risk population that usually averages 18 to 20 percent (Hawaii Department of Health, 1992). Abroad, home visitation is used widely in many European countries as one component of national health care (Government Accounting Office, 1990; Kamerman & Kahn, 1993; Wasik et al., 1990).

Home-visitation approaches may be helpful in preventing maltreatment before it occurs in troubled families, but, clearly, a different kind of prevention strategy is needed with families in which maltreatment has already occurred. One promising strategy is "intensive family preservation" (sometimes called "Homebuilders"), the goal of which is to preserve the family rather than place the child in foster care (Fraser et al., 1991; Wells & Biegel, 1991; Whittaker et al., 1990). Although there are many different kinds of such family-preservation programs, they share several features in common: a caseworker meets with the family frequently and intensively during a limited period of time—often visiting several days weekly (for three to four hours each visit) over a one- to three-month period, while remaining "on call" twenty-four hours a day—and provides both practical and therapeutic assistance. The caseworker may teach new child-rearing skills, provide counseling for parents, arrange for day care, suggest new coping strategies, assist families in obtaining food stamps or medical

Home-visitation programs for Hawaiian families at risk of child maltreatment have had remarkable success, not only in reducing the rate of abuse and neglect but in offering such helpful support that families sometimes refer themselves to the programs. Shown here is a mother with her two children and her home visitor, part of the Hana Like Home Visitor Program, the original prototype for the Healthy Start model.

care, and help parents find jobs or financial aid. The impact of this type of multifaceted assistance is often enhanced by the fact that parents are aware that this may be their last opportunity to keep their child at home.

Intensive family-preservation services have only recently been instituted in several states, so it is still too early to thoroughly evaluate their success. So far, however, these programs have clearly reduced the placement of children in foster homes, without putting the child at significant risk of reabuse (Wells & Biegel, 1992). In one New Jersey program, for example, abusive families received intensive services for five to six weeks after they were identified by child-protection caseworkers. As a result of this intervention, which included counseling, parent education, and assistance in obtaining outside aid, significantly fewer children from these homes were later placed into foster care than was the case with a comparison group of equally troubled families who did not receive such services (Feldman, 1991). In addition to preventing foster care, some programs also document significant increases in the quality of parent-child interaction (Pecora, 1991; Wells & Biegel, 1992). Despite these benefits, however, the families who receive intensive preservation services remain vulnerable, and sometimes later show problems in caring for their offspring that may eventually result in a foster-care placement. Unfortunately, distinguishing those families for whom foster care is best instituted immediately from those

families who, with help, will eventually provide adequate care is usually very difficult. For the most part, then, it seems that although short-term intensive intervention may help some families get back on their feet, it cannot be expected to inoculate them against later difficulties, given the financial, social, and legal problems that are often part of their ongoing life experience.

It is noteworthy that each of these promising prevention efforts—home visitation and intensive family preservation—work directly with troubled families in their homes rather than in a clinic or office. Moreover, each strategy includes parent counseling and education, social support, and parental-skills training. Each type of program also tries to enlist the social resources that may exist in the neighborhood or community, such as the support of relatives or neighbors, a community health clinic, and various social service agencies, so that families continue to receive assistance long after the home visitor or caseworker has ceased paying calls. These strategies are entirely consistent with the contextual perspective, which alerts us to the importance of aiding families in ways that recognize the broad range of ecological troubles, and resources, they may experience.

But neither home visitation nor intensive family preservation is inexpensive: each requires the investment of considerable public funds. Justifying this expense requires assessing the costs to society that child maltreatment poses. In evaluating Hawaii's Healthy Start program—which cost an estimated $7,800 for a full five years of service to a single family in 1993—one important government report put it this way:

> The cost of child abuse includes, but may not be limited to, the costs of the immediate consequences of child abuse, such as hospitalization and foster care. A hospital official in Hawaii said that the cost of hospitalizing an abused child for 1 week would range from $3,000 to $15,000. A Hawaii social services official said that providing foster care for 1 year would cost more than $6,000. Adding the costs of the potential long-term consequences of abuse could raise this amount substantially. For example, the Hawaii program estimates the cost of incarcerating a juvenile for 1 year at about $30,000, the cost of providing foster care to an abused child to age 18 at $123,000, and the cost of institutionalizing a brain-damaged child for life at $720,000. [Government Accounting Office, 1992]

In light of these costs to society, as well as the costs to maltreated children, efforts to prevent maltreatment may well pay for themselves in the long term. What is needed now are further carefully designed, well-targeted, thoroughly researched prevention programs to determine which specific approaches are the most successful and the most cost-effective.

SUMMARY

Size and Shape

1. During early childhood, children grow about 3 inches (7 centimeters) a year. Normal variation in growth is caused primarily by genes, health care, and nutrition.

Brain Maturation

2. Brain maturation, including increased myelination and improved coordination between the two halves of the brain, brings important gains in children's physical abilities and their higher-order cognition. In the early years, considerable flexibility in the functioning of the two halves, as well as in various sections, of the brain is apparent, with compensation for specific brain damage more likely than later on. Once patterns of brain specialization are firmly set by the end of childhood, however, there is much less flexibility.

3. Activity level is assumed to be associated with brain maturation in several ways. It is highest at around age 2 or 3, and then declines throughout the rest of childhood.

Mastering Motor Skills

4. Gross motor skills improve dramatically during early childhood, making it possible for the average 5-year-old to do many things with grace and skill. Fine motor skills, such as holding a pencil or tying a shoelace, improve more gradually over this time. Many tasks, including writing, remain difficult and frustrating.

5. Along with increased motor skills, and the explorations and adventuring that go with them, is an increased risk of accidents and fatalities. Developmentalists emphasize the idea of injury control to contain this danger, stressing that childhood "accidents" are usually the result of a lack of forethought on the part of caregivers.

Child Maltreatment

6. Child maltreatment can take many forms, including abuse or neglect that may be physical and/or psychological. Child abuse and neglect can occur from conception through adolescence, and can have diverse consequences for a child's well-being. About 1 million cases of child maltreatment are reported and confirmed in the United States each year.

7. The causes of child maltreatment are many, including problems in the society (such as negative or exploitative cultural attitudes about children), in the family (such as social isolation and inadequate coping styles), in the parent (such as drug addiction), and in the child (such as being a disappointment in some way to the parents).

8. The consequences of child maltreatment can be far-reaching, impairing the child's learning, self-esteem, social relationships, and emotional management. However, these problems can usually be treated, and it is not inevitable that maltreated children will become maltreating adults.

9. Once maltreatment occurs, careful intervention must support and restore those families that can be helped and provide stable foster care for the minority of families in which the pattern of maltreatment cannot be halted.

10. The most effective strategies for preventing maltreatment emphasize the ecology in which these families live, attempting to enhance community support and address the material as well as emotional needs of troubled families. They also help parents acquire new coping skills and parenting strategies for caring for offspring more competently. One specific method of accomplishing this is home-visitation programs that offer support and assistance to families at risk.

KEY TERMS

corpus callosum (299)
activity level (301)
injury control (305)
child maltreatment (308)
abuse (308)

neglect (308)
intergenerational trans-
   mission (318)
foster care (321)

KEY QUESTIONS

1. How do the size, shape, and proportions of the child's body change during early childhood?

2. What causes variations among children in height and weight during early childhood?

3. How do the two halves of the brain compare in their functioning? How much flexibility exists in these processes in early childhood?

4. Why do young children vary so much in their typical activity level?

5. How do gross motor skills and fine motor skills compare in their development during early childhood?

6. What measures seem most effective in reducing the rate of accidents in childhood?

7. How common is child maltreatment? How does the rate of child neglect compare with the rate of physical abuse?

8. What are some of the factors in the culture, the community, the family, the parent, and the child that can contribute to child maltreatment?

9. What is the estimated probability that a maltreated child will become a maltreated adult? What other long-term consequences of childhood abuse and neglect are likely?

10. What have been found to be the most effective strategies for preventing child maltreatment?

The Play Years:
Cognitive Development

An adult who asks a preschool child "What is it?" or "How does it work?" is likely to hear some surprising answers. Although children at this age are never at a loss for an explanation, sometimes they seem to formulate their ideas according to entirely different rules of logic than those used by adults, while on other occasions they are astonishingly perceptive and insightful. What are the characteristics of children's thinking at this stage and how do mature patterns of thinking develop? These and the following questions will be among the topics discussed in this chapter:

What kinds of number, problem solving, and memory skills do preschoolers possess?

What ideas do preschoolers develop about human thoughts and emotions?

How do children progress from understanding the world through actions and perceptions to using symbols such as words?

How does the social environment contribute to cognitive growth?

What factors are conducive to language development?

How do children use language to help their thinking?

Does preschool education really benefit children?

For developmentalists as well as parents, one of the delights of observing children in their preschool years is seeing how they construct and express their growing understanding of the world around them. Often this understanding seems to be grounded in the kind of fanciful imaginings reflected in the following account by Selma Fraiberg, a child psychoanalyst who is writing about her young niece and her niece's imaginary playmate:

> Let me introduce you to Laughing Tiger. I first met him myself when my niece Jannie was about two years eight months old. One afternoon as I entered the door of her grandparents' house, I found my niece just about to leave with her grand uncle. Jan did not greet me; if anything, she looked a little annoyed at my entrance, like the actress who is interrupted during rehearsal by a clumsy stage-hand who blunders on stage. Still ignoring me, Jan pulled on white cotton gloves and clasped her patent purse in her hand in a fine imitation of a lady leaving for an afternoon engagement. Suddenly she turned and frowned at something behind her. "No!" she said firmly. "No, Laughing Tiger. You *cannot* come with us for an ice-cream cone. You stay right there. But Jannie can come

with us. Come along Jannie!" And she stepped out the door with her uncle, swinging her purse grandly. I thought I saw a shabby and wistful beast slink across the hall and disappear in the shadows. [Fraiberg, 1959]

Fraiberg's description of Jannie and Laughing Tiger captures the imaginative, magical thinking of children between the ages of 2 and 6 that has always amused, delighted, and surprised adults. Children who chatter away with an imaginary playmate, or who wonder where the sun sleeps, or who comfort a sad parent by offering a lollipop, or who confidently claim that they sleep with their eyes open are bound to make us smile. At the same time, we are often startled by how easily confused preschoolers can be by events with which they have little experience (such as hearing that Daddy is "tied up" at the office), and by how illogically and intuitively they attribute the causes of common occurrences (such as believing that the moon follows them as they walk home at night). Clearly, their approach to the world is often dictated more by their own subjective views than by the world's reality.

For many years, this subjective feature of young children's thinking dominated developmental analyses of preschoolers' cognitive abilities. Researchers maintained that those abilities were sorely limited by preschoolers' egocentrism, that is, their prevailing tendency to view the world and others exclusively from their own personal perspective. However, research in recent years has highlighted another important side of preschool thought, a side that is suggested by the following episode between a 2-year-old child and his mother, who has been trying to hold his sweet tooth in check:

> Child sees chocolate cake on table.
>
> Child: Bibby on.
>
> Mother: *You don't want your bibby on. You're not eating.*
>
> Chocolate cake. Chocolate cake.
>
> *You're not having any more chocolate cake either.*
>
> Why? [whines] Tired.
>
> *You tired? Ooh!*
>
> Chocolate cake.
>
> *No chance.* [from Dunn et al., 1987]

The young child in this episode (several months younger than Jannie) is definitely *not* being illogical or oblivious to the constraints of the real world, and shows strategic skill in pursuing his goal—from asking for his bib (a noncontroversial request) to eliciting sympathy by feigning fatigue. Indeed, in countless everyday instances, as well as in the findings of numerous research studies, preschoolers reveal themselves to be remarkably perceptive and insightful thinkers, whose grasp of the causes of everyday events, memory of the past, anticipation of the future, grasp of human psychology, and mastery of language are sometimes astonishing.

These two sides of cognitive growth during the play years are the theme for this chapter. We will begin our examination of them by discussing the growth of basic intellectual skills like number and memory and considering how preschoolers act like theorists in the development of their interpretations of the world. We will then discuss Piaget's depiction of preoperational thinking—which emphasizes young children's intuitive, illogical ways of reasoning—and Vygotsky's depiction of the child as apprentice—

which emphasizes the role of parents and others as mentors. Finally we will consider the remarkable accomplishments of language development, and the cognitive benefits of high-quality preschool education.

How Preschoolers Think

As you learned in Chapter 7, researchers long believed that a baby's world was a "blooming, buzzing confusion"—until new research designs allowed them to look closely at infants' capacities for memory, categorization, and thought. In a similar fashion, developmentalists tended to underestimate the cognitive skills of preschoolers—until new research strategies allowed them to go beyond preschoolers' initial, intuitive responses to experimental queries and to more closely probe what young children know and understand about the world. As researchers have done so, it has led to a new appreciation of preschoolers' cognitive abilities, many of which begin to emerge earlier than had been thought. At the same time, researchers have come to recognize that the emergence of these abilities is partial, fragile—evident in some contexts but not in others. In short, cognitive development in the preschool years is a mixed affair, and very much a case of "Now you see it, now you don't."

Number

FIGURE 10.1 The day, the date, the season, and the weather are all concepts that are part of the curriculum of a good preschool. Young children's ability to grasp these concepts—as well as to develop an understanding of number—is a good deal stronger than researchers or educators once imagined.

Brian, Professor Thompson's younger son, began learning to count several years ago, at the age of 4. However, his halting efforts to enumerate his baseball cards—"one, two, three, eight, ten, elebenteen!"—were derided by his older brother, who claimed that Brian knew nothing about numbers. Until recently, many developmental researchers would have agreed, believing that the growth of true numerical understanding was a school-age accomplishment. Indeed, only two decades ago, scientists "denied the preschooler any arithmetic prowess at all" (Gelman & Massey, 1987). In the past few years, however, researchers have come to recognize that beneath their apparent inability to count, preschoolers like Brian possess number concepts that are actually fairly sophisticated.

Consider *how* Brian counted, for example. Even though he didn't yet know the proper sequence of numbers, he nevertheless assigned each baseball card one and only one value, and omitted no cards from his count. This *one-to-one* principle is usually respected by young children, especially when they are counting small quantities. Another feature of Brian's counting was that he recognized that numbers should always be said in the same order. Complying with the *stable-order principle,* in other words, he consistently enumerated "one, two, three . . . " rather than "three, one, two . . . " or any other order of number terms. Finally, Brian's counting of baseball cards usually ended something like, ". . . eight, ten, elebenteen . . . there are *elebenteen* cards!" That is, he recognized the *cardinal principle,* which is that the last number in a count represents the total amount. A considerable body of research shows that young children have a rudimentary awareness of these principles of counting—especially when they are counting small quantities—even when they have not yet mastered the correct number sequence (Gelman, 1982; Gelman & Gallistel, 1978).

Brian's number awareness is similar to that of most 4-year-olds, and is part of a predictable progression of cognitive growth. As you remember, beginning in early infancy, children have some perceptual awareness of small quantities (such as noticing the difference between two toys and three toys). At about age 2, children begin to use numbers symbolically, by connecting words with the items they are counting. At first, the connection between numbers and quantity is quite tenuous. For example, in one study (Saxe, 1987), 2½- and 4-year-olds were presented with two displays of dots, one of five dots and the other of thirteen, and were asked "to count the dots and touch each dot as you count it" (see Figure 10.2). The younger children seemed to understand the task, but typically failed to touch at least two dots in the five-dot display and missed an average of eight dots in the thirteen-dot display. They also miscounted, some saying only "one, two, three" for both the five- and the thirteen-dot display. Most of the 4-year-olds performed perfectly on the five-dot display and made an average of only two mistakes in counting and only two in pointing on the thirteen-dot display. Indeed, many of the 4-year-olds did the thirteen-dot task with no errors. When the same children were tested in simple arithmetic, similar age differences were found in number ability: most of the 4-year-olds, but virtually none of the 2½-year-olds, for example, could figure out what to subtract when a puppet with four pennies needed to have three.

FIGURE 10.2 In the experimental game of "count the dots," most 2½-year-olds made several errors, even on the five-dot display. But some 4-year-olds did both tasks perfectly. They had already learned the most basic of number rules: count each object once, and only once.

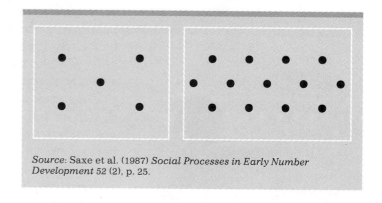

Source: Saxe et al. (1987) *Social Processes in Early Number Development* 52 (2), p. 25.

This is not to say that older preschoolers are masters of simple math. Even if they can count correctly to twenty, and even if they can add and subtract numbers totaling less than four (as many 5-year-olds can), they quickly get confused with larger numbers or more complicated math. A preschooler who can count rapidly and accurately, for instance, might have no idea how many six-packs of soda should be bought to provide one can for each of ten birthday party guests, or might be unable to divide up twelve marbles evenly among four children without distributing them in turn, one at a time. Thus, while older preschoolers may have a good basic grasp of quantity and counting, they frequently become confused about varying quantities and other number operations (Frye et al., 1989; Fuson, 1988).

What contributes to the child's developing understanding of number? One factor is simple maturation: in the dot study above, for example, the eighteen-month age difference between the two groups of children was a much more powerful determinant of math ability than any other factors, including socioeconomic status or gender (both of which were not significant) or how often the mothers said they normally engaged in number activities with their children (which was only marginally significant). This age-related improvement in math involves not only the underlying brain development that is ongoing throughout childhood but also the emergence of language and the ability to use it to conceptualize and express number. Improved number ability also involves maturation in the sense emphasized by Piaget—that is, the flowering of the child's innate curiosity and exploration of the world of objects, which entails spontaneous organizing and counting during the preschool years in much the same way it involves sucking and fingering during the sensorimotor years.

The overall cultural context, especially the importance the particular culture places on number competence, also plays a role. In societies like the United States, the child's mathematical flowering has a rich environment to sustain it. Preschoolers typically

> accompany their parents on shopping trips; hear numbers used in talk about time, birthdays, and how many presents they will or will not get; and ride elevators in buildings with many floors. Long-distance driving and the consequent talk about how far one has gone or has yet to go "to get to Grandma's" is not uncommon. They watch the Count on the television program "Sesame Street" talk about his passion for counting different size sets, or Senor Zero looking for nothing so he can count zero things, or even a puppet dressed up in a black leather jacket singing "Born to Add" set to the tune of a popular rock and roll song. [Gelman & Massey, 1987]

In some cultures, another factor that may promote preschool number competence is the structure of the particular language. Indeed, one hypothesis for the overall superiority of East Asian children over European and American youngsters in math is that languages such as Japanese, Korean, and Chinese are much more logical in their labeling of numbers, for instance, making "eleven, twelve, thirteen," and so on, the equivalent of "ten-one, ten-two, ten-three" (Fuson & Kwon, 1992). This linguistic structuring advances young children's intuitive grasp of their number system as soon as they begin to talk.

A final factor in building number competence—a factor we will emphasize in connection with other cognitive abilities as well—is the structure and support provided by parents, other adults, and older children. Parents and offspring frequently use numbers together—counting small quantities, playing number games ("one, two, button my shoe . . ."), pushing television-channel buttons, sorting coins, and measuring small amounts, such as the allotted spoonfuls of cocoa mix to put in a glass of milk.

Researchers who have studied these activities at home and in the laboratory have noticed that their complexity and sophistication increase steadily as the child gets older and becomes more competent with number (Saxe et al., 1987). When Geoffrey Saxe and his colleagues observed preschoolers and their mothers working together on simple numerical tasks, for example, they noticed that mothers adjusted the amount of help they provided according to the child's skills. Typically, mothers gave 2-year-olds more structured guidance—providing specific instructions, modeling what to do, or simplifying the task—than they did 4-year-olds, and some mothers cut back on the help they gave as their child became more skilled and confident at the tasks. By providing this kind of guided participation in shared activities involving number, parents ensure that the tasks remain challenging to their children but within their capabilities, and help to stimulate the growth of numerical understanding. As we shall see now, this same type of guided participation can help the growth of problem-solving skills.

Problem Solving

Preschoolers are everyday problem solvers, whether the problem requires figuring out how to construct a castle out of blocks, resolve a dispute over toys with a friend, or create a picture that simultaneously shows the inside and outside of one's house. Despite their practical problem-solving experiences, however, preschoolers have considerable difficulty with the kinds of formal problem-solving tasks devised by experimenters, such as problems requiring the use of analogy from one situation to another, or logical deduction, or step-by-step planning. As we will see in Chapter 13, it is not until the early school-age years that children begin to master the kinds of objective, planned, logical reasoning skills that permit them to succeed at problem-solving tasks of a formal nature. This is not very surprising. Efficient problem solving requires many skills—including the ability to use systematic trial-and-error, to plan a sequence of steps toward the solution of a task, and to notice, evaluate, and correct one's errors—and these skills, in turn, require considerable brain maturation, memory ability, mental flexibility, and objectivity.

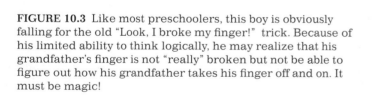

FIGURE 10.3 Like most preschoolers, this boy is obviously falling for the old "Look, I broke my finger!" trick. Because of his limited ability to think logically, he may realize that his grandfather's finger is not "really" broken but not be able to figure out how his grandfather takes his finger off and on. It must be magic!

However, researchers have learned that, just as with number, some rudimentary skills related to problem solving begin to develop during the play years. Consider, for example, a study in which preschoolers were asked to solve a problem by analogy (Brown et al., 1986). The children were first told a story about a genie who succeeded in transferring some jewels across a wall and into a bottle by rolling up his magic carpet to make a tube, and then placing the tube at the mouth of the bottle and rolling the jewels through the tube into the bottle. After hearing the story, the children were presented with a problem involving an Easter-bunny puppet who wanted to transport some eggs across a narrow stream and into a basket. The puppet had available several "tools" to solve the problem, including scissors, sticks, and large sheets of heavy paper. On their own, very few 3-year-olds were capable of generalizing what they had heard in the genie story to the rabbit problem, but some 5-year-olds could do so. However, with the assistance of an experimenter who drew the children's attention to the similarities between the story and the problem, and between the genie's magic carpet and the bunny's sheets of paper, children of both ages could solve the problem.

Like the research on number understanding, the results of this experiment suggest that supportive guidance provided by an adult can facilitate the development of cognitive skills in preschoolers. This was further illustrated by a study in which young children were given a sorting task that involved helping a puppet move into his new home by putting doll-house furniture into the proper rooms (Freund, 1990). The children were randomly divided into two groups and given a practice session: one group worked with their mothers on the sorting task; the other group sorted and installed the furniture by themselves, in the company of an experimenter who corrected any errors by properly relocating misplaced furniture while the children watched. When the children later sorted the furniture entirely on their own, the researchers discovered that those who had worked with their mothers sorted better than those who had only received corrective feedback from the experimenter. It was not hard to see why: mothers carefully structured the task for children based on the child's age, as well as the difficulty of the sorting, to keep the demands on the child challenging but manageable. Mothers of 3-year-olds, for example, offered more concrete, specific suggestions to their offspring ("Here is a bed—it goes in the bedroom") than did the mothers of 5-year-olds, while the latter talked more often about planning and the goals of the task ("Let's move in all the furniture that goes in the living room first"). In short, mothers gave their children as much responsibility for problem solving as they thought their youngsters could handle, while providing an overall structure for the child that promoted success.

The importance of parents' providing cognitive structure and guidance is especially clear when we look at memory, another aspect of preschoolers' cognitive capacities that, while marked with notable lapses, has also been underestimated.

Memory

Preschoolers are notorious for having a poor memory. They forget to deliver urgent phone messages; they go to their room to get their shoes and return with a toy instead; they tell a story and jumble the sequence while leaving out key parts. Ask a school-age child what he or she did during the day and you are likely to get a detailed accounting, complete with reflections about why people acted as they did and how their behavior relates to their actions in the past. Ask a preschooler the same question and you are likely to get a quizzical stare, or a noncommittal "Nothing," or a string of seemingly irrelevant details.

However, it is not that preschoolers have deficient memory *per se*. Rather, they have not yet acquired the skills (described in full in Chapter 13) for deliberately storing memories of past events and efficiently retrieving these memories as needed on later occasions. Just as you know how to remember information that you will later need—whether it involves rehearsing an address or a telephone number, organizing your course notes so that one item calls to mind another, or relating a new experience to some past memory to keep it in mind—you also have strategies for retrieving this information when you need it, say, to perform well on a test or to recount the day's events. Preschoolers, by contrast, are strikingly nonstrategic in their memory: they rarely try deliberately to retain some experience or bit of information in memory, and they seldom know precisely how to recall some hard-to-retrieve bit of past experience (Kail, 1990). As a result, they can sometimes appear strangely incapable of remembering past experiences that older children can recall with ease.

But this does not tell the whole story about memory in young children. In other ways, young children are remarkably capable of storing in mind a representation of past events that they can later use. One way they do so is by retaining **scripts** of familiar, recurrent past experiences. These scripts act as a kind of structure or skeletal outline that facilitates the storage and retrieval of certain memories. By age 3, for example, children can tell you what happens in a restaurant (you order food, eat it, and then pay for it), at a birthday party (you arrive, give presents, play games, have cake and ice cream, and sing "Happy Birthday"), during their bedtime routine (first a bath, then a story, and then lights out), and during other everyday events (Nelson, 1986a). Here is one 5-year-old's description of what happens during grocery shopping:

> Um, we get a cart, uh, and we look for some onions and plums and cookies and tomato sauce, onions, and all that kind of stuff, and when we're finished we go to the paying booth, and um, then we, um, then the lady puts all our food in a bag, then we put it in the cart, walk out to our car, put the bags in our trunk, then leave. [quoted in Nelson, 1986b]

This is a typical script in two key respects: it presents a correct sequence of events and it also recognizes the causal flow of events—reflecting an awareness that some events (like putting food in the cart) must precede other events (like going to the "paying booth") (Bauer & Mandler, 1990; Ratner et al., 1990). Preschoolers use scripts not only when recounting familiar routines but also when they engage in pretend play, enacting everyday events such as dinnertime, shopping, or going to work. They may also use scripts in their telling, or retelling, of a story, building the story around their scripts for familiar routines (Nelson & Hudson, 1988).

Scripts are important to early memory development because they provide a framework of general understanding of common events within which memories for specific experiences can be recalled. When asked what happened on a particular occasion, young children often "bootstrap" their memories for specific past experiences by starting with the most notable and memorable feature of that experience, then consulting the pertinent script with which they are most familiar. For example, when a stranger asked a 2½-year-old about a camping trip, the child first commented about sleeping in a tent (an unusual part of this experience), and then the interview proceeded this way:

scripts Skeletal outlines of the usual sequence of certain common recurrent events. Young children use such scripts to facilitate the storage and retrieval of memories related to specific episodes of these events.

FIGURE 10.4 The fact that preschoolers have scripts for events such as birthdays is especially evident when someone "violates" the script. If this birthday-boy's sister (on his right) had blown out the last candle rather than merely pointing to it, he might have exploded in angry tears.

Interviewer: You slept outside in a tent? Wow, that sounds like a lot of fun.

    Child: *And then we waked up and eat dinner. First we eat dinner, then go to bed, and then wake up and eat breakfast.*

What else did you do when you went camping? What did you do when you got up, and after you ate breakfast?

Umm, in the night, and went to sleep. [quoted in Fivush & Hamon, 1990]

As you can see, reliance on a routine script to recall a particular event may result in an account that is incomplete or faulty. In such cases, the child's account may reflect knowledge of the relevant script much more than it does an accurate remembrance of the event in question, especially when the event was complex or difficult to understand (Farrar & Goodman, 1990; Fivush & Hamond, 1990). Thus, scripts are an aid to memory, but they can also impair recall of specific experiences.

Another reason young children sometimes appear deficient in their memory ability is that they often do not attend to the features of an event that an older person would consider pertinent (Bjorklund & Bjorklund, 1992). Every parent has had the experience of taking a preschooler to a memorable event (a circus, a baseball game, a play), only to find that the child's later account of that experience focused on the ticket-taker, the person sitting in the next row, or the refreshments! To young children, the features of their experience that are most important, and memorable, may depend on what momentarily grabs their attention, or on what their mood is. When observing an event entails complexity—such as watching the right players at the right time during a baseball game, or following the sequence of events in a play—preschoolers may be especially inattentive to the things adults expect them to remember.

Research has shown, however, that parents and other caregivers can play a special role in helping children to attend to, and remember, aspects of their experience that may otherwise escape notice. Consider the following conversation between a mother and her 2-year-old daughter after a day at the zoo.

> Mother: Brittany, what did we see at the zoo?
> Brittany: *Elphunts.*
>   That's right! We saw elephants. What else?
>   *(Shrugs and looks at her mother.)*
>   Panda bear? Did we see a panda bear?
>   *(Smiles and nods.)*
>   Can you say "panda bear"?
>   *Panda bear.*
>   Good! Elephants and panda bears. What else?
>   *Elphunts.*
>   That's right, elephants. And also a gorilla.
>   *Gorilla!* [quoted in Bjorklund & Bjorklund, 1992]

Conversations like this one are part of the everyday exchanges between parents and offspring that review, reconstruct, and consolidate a young child's memory of the day's events. Developmentalists who have studied these conversations believe, however, that they also provide young children with lessons in memory retrieval (Fivush & Hamond, 1990; Hudson, 1990). Parents commonly assist preschoolers' recollections by asking specific questions ("What did you see climbing in the tree?") rather than general ones; by reviewing events in their temporal sequence ("First we saw the monkeys, and *then* what did we see?") rather than out of sequence; and by providing children with memory cues ("And then we had lunch at Burger . . ." Child: "King!"). Each of these approaches not only aids young children's memory search but also provides a model of how to better recall past events and experiences.

Parents, of course, vary in how they guide young children's recall of past events. Some parents ("repetitors") tend to ask children specific questions to cue their memory search, and then repeat the child's answer en route to the next inquiry. Other parents ("elaborators") not only do these things but also supplement the child's recall with additional information about the experience, in a sense, building additional memories into those the child can already recall (Reese & Fivush, 1993). One study that examined these differences in parental recollective style found that 2-year-olds whose mothers used an elaborative style remembered more and could better answer questions about a prior experience—whether they were asked by their mother or an experimenter (Hudson, 1990). The elaborative style apparently not only aided young children's memory retrieval but helped to consolidate a more complete account of their shared experience.

Memories of Mickey Mouse

Despite the many limitations in young children's memory, developmental researchers have recently discovered that, under certain circumstances, children show surprising evidence for their long-term retention of early experiences. In one particularly revealing study (Hamond & Fivush, 1991), researchers assessed the memories of forty-eight children who had visited Disneyworld at about their third or fourth birthday (specifically, between ages 33 and 42 months or between ages 43 and 54 months). The children were interviewed in their homes, either six months or eighteen months after their Disneyworld experience, under the following procedure:

> After a brief warm-up period in which the experimenter and the child got acquainted, mothers left the room and the memory interview began. The experimenter asked each child a structured series of questions about their Disneyworld experience, the first of which was open-ended: "Can you tell me about Disneyworld?" After this question, the experimenter asked a standard series of questions focusing on who went, what rides were ridden, what sights were seen, what was eaten, what presents were bought, and how children felt about their experiences. [The standardized interview is shown in Figure 10.5, p. 340.] When necessary, these questions were followed with nondirective prompts (e.g., "And what else?"; "And then what?"; "Tell me more about that") designed to elicit further information about the Disneyworld experience.

The children's answers to the experimenter's questions were tape-recorded, checked with the parents for accuracy, and then analyzed to determine

> 1. how many units of discrete information the children remembered (a unit of information was considered to consist of any statement that contained an explicit or implicit verb, such as, "I saw Mickey Mouse");
>
> 2. how much elaboration the children's recollections contained (an elaboration was considered to consist of any modifying words or phrases contained in a unit of information (thus the statement "I saw Mickey Mouse in the morning" was scored as a unit of information plus an elaboration;
>
> 3. what kinds of information the children remembered (that is, whether it related to activity, description, emotion, or explanation).

Additionally, the researchers distinguished between *directed recall* and *spontaneous recall*. Directed recall was given in response to the series of directive questions that focused the child's attention on specific aspects of their Disneyworld experience. Spontaneous recall included both the child's responses to the open-ended questions at the start of the interview and information not expressly asked for in the series of directive questions that followed.

All the children responded well in their interviews, recalling an impressive average of forty-two units of information, virtually all of it confirmed as accurate by the parents. Surprisingly, although the older children recalled slightly more information than the younger ones, the age-related differences in the amount of recall were minimal, as were the differences related to the length of time between the Disneyworld visit and the interview. In other words, the children remembered similar amounts of information irrespective of how old they were when they visited Disneyworld, how much time had passed since their visit, and how old they were when they were interviewed!

Although age did not significantly affect the amount of information children remembered, it did play a role in other aspects of their recollection. For example, while both groups were equally likely to remember many activities ("Donald Duck hugged me") and descriptions ("Goofy has funny feet"), the older children remembered more emotions ("I was scared") and more explanations ("Mom said it was too crowded"). More telling, the older children recalled more information spontaneously than the younger children did, and their recollections tended to contain more elaboration.

FIGURE 10.5 Preschool children can remember in much more specific detail when asked directive questions than when asked open-ended ones. In fact, after 3- to 6-year-olds had nothing else to say in response to the open-ended questions in this interview about their visit to Disneyworld, they produced, on average, four times more information in response to the directive questions.

Structured Interview Questions

1. Open-Ended Questions
   I know that you remember a lot about your trip to Disneyworld. I've never gone there before. Can you tell me about Disneyworld?
   What was the very first thing that happened?
      And then what?

2. Directive Questions
   How did you get to Disneyworld?
   Who went with you?
   Where did you stay?
   What did you see at Disneyworld?
      What did you think about that?
   Who did you see there?
      What was that like?
   What rides did you go on at Disneyworld?
      Which one did you like the most?
      What did that feel like?
      What did you like/dislike about it?

   What rides did "X" (other people there) go on?
      What did "X" think of it?
      Did "X" like it?
      What did "X" like about it?
   Did you eat anything there?
      What did you eat?
   Did you buy anything at Disneyworld?
      What did you buy?
   Did anything bad happen at Disneyworld?
      What happened?
      Was there anything you didn't like?
      What didn't you like?
   What was your favorite fun thing at Disneyworld?
      What did you like about it?
   If you got to go to Disneyworld again, what would you want to do the most?

Source: Hammond and Fivush, 1991.

Overriding these age differences, however, was a single commonality: all the children provided much more information in response to directive questions than they did spontaneously. In fact, across both age groups and both retention intervals, nearly 80 percent of all the information elicited from the children came in response to directive questions.

Overall, this study confirms and amplifies other recent research, strongly suggesting that when recollecting personally meaningful material, "even quite young preschoolers can recall a great deal of information if given appropriate cues and prompts" (Hamond & Fivush, 1991). This conclusion is particularly helpful in understanding why preschoolers' memory abilities appear to be so erratic: some of the time, at least, their seemingly vague memories may merely be the result of vague questioning. (The importance of appropriate questioning to young children's ability to provide reliable eye-witness testimony is explored in Public Policy, pp. 341–343.)

Concepts: Preschoolers as Theorists

You learned from Chapter 7 that infants quickly begin categorizing objects in the world according to their perceptual properties, such as shape and sound. By the early preschool years, children are able to richly elaborate this categorical system to include not only the physical attributes of objects and people but also their distinctive characteristics, actions, and origins. A 1-year-old notices the difference between big dogs and little dogs, but a 4-year-old realizes that not every little dog is a puppy and that dogs have different temperaments (some are friendly, while others bark and growl) and different uses (family pets, watchdogs, sheepdogs, and so forth). In essence, the *categorical* understanding of the infant becomes the *conceptual* understanding of the preschooler, and the growth and elaboration of concepts form the basis for young children's expanding knowledge of the world.

Young Children as Eyewitnesses

The legal system has long doubted the credibility of young children's eyewitness accounts. Comparing them to adults who are "mentally incompetent," many judges and legal scholars believed that children are far too prone to suggestion, and too confused about the distinction between fact and fantasy, to be relied on to provide a truthful and accurate account of stressful events they have experienced or witnessed. Indeed, until quite recently, young children in most countries were prohibited from providing courtroom testimony.

However, as a result of the increased awareness of the prevalence of child maltreatment, including sexual abuse, children in the United States and many other countries are now allowed to testify in court after a judge has determined that they are capable of doing so truthfully and accurately. This judicial acceptance of children's testimony seems essential, since many children are the only witnesses to their own devastating abuse. At the same time, however, this change has provoked a backlash from those who argue that, if children are automatically assumed by the legal system to "provide a truthful and accurate account," they are open to being manipulated by adults for their own purposes, such as those of parents feuding over custody, or those of overzealous authorities handling cases involving day-care centers (where, in fact, abuse is actually far less likely to occur than it is in homes).

In light of this controversy, what can developmentalists tell the courts about the reliability of children's eyewitness testimony? To put the question in perspective, the first thing to be noted is that even the eyewitness accounts of adults are almost never completely accurate, and are sometimes startlingly erroneous—especially when the person has been influenced by false information or leading questions (Loftus & Wells, 1984). Thus, the value of children's eyewitness testimony cannot be dismissed out of hand merely because it is likely to be flawed. Second, as our text discussion points out, recent research has shown that, while decidedly uneven in their memory abilities, young children often retain accurate memories of past events and, under the right circumstances, can retrieve them accurately. However, this new research concerning children's impressive early memory abilities does not necessarily predict the accuracy of their courtroom testimony, and in recent years, a large number of studies have explored various facets of young children's eyewitness accounts in order to address questions like the following. How accurate are the reports provided by children immediately after a stressful event they have witnessed or experienced? Does the accuracy of their reports change over time? How susceptible are young children to leading questions and misleading information that may be part of an investigative interview? Do the interviewer's beliefs about what actually happened influence his or her behavior with the child—and does that behavior, in turn, influence the child's account? Does the amount of emotional distress the child experienced during the original event enhance, or undermine, the child's recollection of that event?

In attempting to answer these questions, developmental investigators face a number of formidable challenges. First, there are the ethical dimensions of their research. As you learned in Chapter 1, researchers cannot subject young children to undue stress in their studies, even when exploring a topic as crucial as children's recollection of traumatic experiences. At the same time, it is important to simulate, as closely as possible, the stresses and trauma about which children are often required to testify.

Second, developmental researchers must always recognize the real-life conditions surrounding legal investigations and interviews, especially those involving child abuse, and consider how they might influence the accuracy and credibility of young children's accounts (Ceci & Bruck, 1993; Melton & Thompson, 1987). For example, owing to the delays that commonly accompany child-abuse prosecution, children who testify in court are usually interrogated many weeks, months, or even years after the event in question. Consequently, research should probably focus on children's long-term memory of an event rather than on their immediate recall of what happened. Moreover, the people who interview children for legal proceedings are rarely the kind of supportive, objective investigators who conduct developmental research studies. Instead, the child is interviewed by many different "interested parties"—parents, police officers, therapists, and attorneys—sometimes on more than one occasion, and often each interviewer already has an idea of what "actually" occurred. Consequently, the potential for the child to be asked leading questions, and to be given misinformation and explicit suggestions, is considerable (Ceci & Bruck, 1993).

Finally, these interviews take place in an unfamiliar and unsettling context, including emotional upheaval (the child's as well as that of the adults who are involved), the authority of the police and the judicial system, and the confusions of having to face obviously conflicting points of view and outright lies. Any of these factors can powerfully affect the account a young child gives during pretrial interviews as well as during an actual trial. Young children are particularly likely to be frightened by unfamiliar courtroom procedures, especially if they must testify sitting alone in the witness chair and in the presence of the defendant (Goodman et al., 1992). In the light of all these complexities, it is

Young Children as Eyewitnesses continued

As the only eyewitness to the slaying of a playmate, 4-year-old Jennifer Royal was allowed to testify in open court. Her forthright answers, and the fact that she herself had been wounded, helped convict the accused gunman. While most developmentalists agree that, when questioned properly, children can provide reliable testimony about events they have experienced or witnessed, many advocate arranging a more sheltered way for young children to give testimony.

difficult, if not impossible, for any research study to begin to approximate the real-life features of children's eyewitness testimony in court.

Nevertheless, a number of fruitful efforts have been made in this direction, by examining young children's recall of difficult or painful, but naturally occurring, stressors, such as a medical inoculation, a genital examination, or a dental exam (Baker-Ward et al., 1993; Goodman et al., 1991; Saywitz et al., 1991). In one series of such studies, children between the ages of 3 and 6 were videotaped while undergoing a medical examination that included, among other things, a DPT inoculation administered by a nurse (Goodman et al., 1990).

> The children's reactions varied widely. Most looked frightened, but some were quite stoic, relatively unfazed, and said "It didn't hurt." Others, however, became nearly hysterical. These children had to be physically restrained, often by two or three people. They cried, screamed, yelled for help, tried to run out of the room, and sobbed afterward while complaining that it hurt. In sum, they reacted as if they were being attacked.

Several days after this event, the children were asked first to tell about the experience, then to answer various questions about it, and finally to look at a photo lineup and identify the nurse who had administered the shot. None of the children offered any false information during the free recall, and, contrary to the concern that emotional arousal might scramble a child's memory, those who showed the most distress during the exam were the ones who provided the most detailed, accurate accounts.

When asked specific questions, all the children were quite good witnesses, particularly about what did, and did not, happen. Notably, none of the children answered "yes"

to any of the following four questions: "Did she hit you?" "Did she kiss you?" "Did she put anything in your mouth?" "Did she touch you any place other than your arm?" However, although the children were very clear about what had been done to them, they were less sure about exactly who had done it: on the photo lineup, only half picked the nurse's photograph, while 41 percent picked other photos and 9 percent said they couldn't remember.

The next step in this experiment was to determine the durability of the children's memories of their stressful experience with a stranger. When the children were interviewed again a year later, their overall recall had diminished, but again they reported virtually no significant false memories. For example, none of the children answered that the nurse had hit them, kissed them, or put something in their mouth. Some (14 percent) reported, falsely, that she had touched them elsewhere than on the arm—but when asked where, the children said on the wrist, on the leg, or on their other arm. (One child explicitly stated that there is "good touch" and "bad touch," and that the nurse's had been good touch.) The one long-term memory test that most children failed was the photo-identification task, with only 14 percent correctly identifying the nurse this time around. Most of the rest said they didn't remember what the nurse looked like, but 32 percent picked the wrong photo.

Following up on their finding of impressive long-term recall for a stressful event, these researchers developed several experimental variations that tested whether children's memories can be deliberately distorted. In one, the initial interview after a medical check-up included some questions that were purposely phrased to be misleading

("She touched your bottom, didn't she?" "How many times did she kiss you?" and so on), asked either in a friendly, encouraging manner or in an intimidatingly stern one. The older children (ages 5 to 7) were rarely influenced by these misleading questions, affirming them less than 9 percent of the time whether the interviewer was friendly or stern. The 3- and 4-year-olds, however, were more vulnerable to the adult's tone: although those responding to the friendly questioner affirmed the interviewer's false assumptions only 10 percent of the time, those responding to stern questioning affirmed them 23 percent of the time.

These results accord with other research that finds that, particularly for young children, the social context (including the relationship of the child to the questioner, the age of the questioner, and whether the atmosphere of the interview is intense or relaxed) has a substantial influence on answers offered to memory questions (Baker-Ward et al., 1993; Ceci et al., 1990; Rogoff & Mistrry, 1990). At the same time, this research also corroborates other findings showing that, under a variety of circumstances, the great majority of children resist suggestive questioning.

But what happens if a child is not simply misled by questions but is deliberately given false information? This was the topic of another study that employed a medical-exam format, this time with 5-year-olds (Brock et al., in press). Immediately after they had been examined and inoculated by a pediatrician, each child met Laurie, who had been a bystander during the inoculation. Laurie, who actually was a research assistant in the study, chatted with the child and then, regardless of what the child's actual reaction to the shot had been, randomly responded to each child in one of three ways: (1) she indicated that the child had been brave (saying "Your shot didn't seem to hurt you at all"); (2) she indicated that the child had been appropriately distressed (saying "Your shot seemed to hurt you a lot. But you know, it hurts kids when they get a shot, so it's OK that it hurt a lot"); or she did not mention the shot at all.

One week later the children were interviewed by another researcher, who asked how they had reacted to their shot. The questioning was straightforward, and the children accurately reported how much they had cried, regardless of what they had been told by Laurie. Then, about a year later, the same children went through a series of three interviews about their medical exam. This time some of the questions they were asked contained misleading information about the details of the exam (such as "When Laurie gave you the shot, was your mom or dad with you?") and about what their reaction to the shot had been. In the final interview, many of the children appeared to have been influenced by the misleading information they had heard in the previous interviews. For example, of the children who had been inaccurately "reminded" that the research assistant had given them the shot, more than one-third reported, on their own, that Laurie had given them the inoculation. Likewise, children who had been told they were "brave" during the inoculation (some of whom had actually been quite distressed) reported less crying than children who weren't given this information. Even more interesting, children who had incorporated misinformation into their account altered other details to make their account consistent. For instance, many of the children who reported that Laurie had administered the inoculation also reported that she had performed other parts of the medical examination as well, such as checking their eyes and nose, even though they had not been given misinformation about those aspects of the check-up.

What, then, can we conclude from the varied findings of all this research? As one pair of researchers explain:

> Children are neither as hyper-suggestible and coachable as some pro-defense advocates have alleged, nor as resistant to suggestions about their own bodies as some pro-prosecution advocates have claimed. They can be led, under certain conditions, to incorporate false suggestions into their accounts of even intimate bodily touching, but they can also be amazingly resistant to false suggestions and able to provide highly detailed and accurate reports of events that transpired weeks or months ago. [Ceci & Bruck, 1993]

The research also makes clear that, when children are required to give eyewitness testimony, they should be provided a context that enhances their ability to remember accurately. They should be interviewed by a neutral professional, who encouragingly probes but does not lead in the questioning process, with the interview being videotaped for later use. Or, if testimony must be repeated during the trial, it can occur on closed-circuit television, to spare the child from confronting the accused—a confrontation that can trouble the child for months afterward and does nothing to ensure accuracy (Goodman et al., 1992). Such practices have already been accepted by the United States Supreme Court as fair to defendants (*Coy v. Iowa,* 1988; *Maryland v. Craig,* 1990), but many states and municipalities do not yet allow these child-friendly processes, and many lawyers still argue that young children are invariably confused and unreliable. The evidence is otherwise: children are not necessarily worse witnesses than adults, as long as their vulnerability to intimidation is fully taken into account.

Many developmentalists believe that preschoolers act like scientific theorists in the growth and refinement of their concepts about the world: that is, preschoolers develop rudimentary ideas about the phenomena they discover around them, and they develop expectations about these phenomena that are confirmed or disconfirmed by subsequent experience. In this way, youngsters gradually construct coherent, internally consistent theories about "how things work" that become elaborated and refined as experience, and understanding, contribute to the growth of knowledge.

Preschoolers develop theories about many things, but they theorize especially about the events and phenomena that figure prominently in their everyday experience, such as the physical world of objects (or elementary physics), the animate world of plants and animals (or elementary biology), and the inner workings of human thoughts, emotions, and motives (or elementary psychology) (Wellman & Gelman, 1992). Instead of touching on all the various concepts that develop during this period, we instead will look closely at one that has particular significance for the child's participation in the social world.

FIGURE 10.6 Scientists use data to test hypotheses, and children do too. Almost every child develops a theory regarding what makes a thing alive, and then tests it, with dolls, sleeping dogs, and plants. This child will likely conclude that, although turtles may sit in the sun and look like rocks, they are very much alive.

Children's Theories About Psychology

Human emotions, motives, thoughts, and intentions are among the most complicated and thought-provoking phenomena in a young child's world, whether the child is trying to understand a peer's unexpected display of anger, determine whether a sibling will be generous or selfish, or persuade a parent to purchase a desired toy. As a result of their experiences with others, preschoolers develop informal theories about human psychology that attempt to answer basic questions about mental phenomena, such as how a particular person's knowledge and emotions affect that person's actions, and how particular people can differ so markedly in their thoughts, feelings, and intentions, often in response to the same situations. In other words, young children acquire a **theory of mind** that reflects their developing concepts about human mental processes (Frye & Moore, 1991; Wellman, 1990; Whiten, 1991).

Indeed, developmentalists have discovered that, in contrast with the traditional view of preschoolers as egocentric—that is, preoccupied with their own point of view—young children are not only aware of divergent psy-

theory of mind   An understanding of mental processes, that is, of one's own or another's emotions, perceptions, and thoughts.

chological perspectives but strive hard to understand how, and why, different viewpoints exist. Two-year-olds, for example, have been observed to say things such as "Don't be mad, Mommy," "Mama having a good time?" and even from one precocious 28-month-old boy "Maybe Craig would laugh when he saw Beth do that" (Bretherton & Beeghly, 1982). Each of these statements reveals a nonegocentric awareness that other people can have emotions that are not identical to one's own.

FIGURE 10.7 At age 3, Brittany has already had almost a year of being a big sister to Brian. As a result, her theory of mind—especially with respect to what behaviors please or irritate her baby brother, and which of her behaviors with her brother please or irritate her parents—has advanced considerably.

By age 3 or 4, young children clearly distinguish between mental phenomena and the physical events to which they refer (for example, you can pet a dog that is in front of you, but not one that is in your thoughts); they appreciate how mental states (like beliefs, expectations, and desires) arise from one's experiences in the real world; they understand that mental phenomena are subjective (others cannot "see" what you are imagining); they recognize that people have differing opinions and preferences (someone might like a game that you dislike); and they realize that beliefs and desires can form the basis for human action (Dad is driving the car fast because he doesn't want to be late for Grandma's dinner) (Flavell et al., 1993; Wellman & Gelman, 1992). They also understand that emotion arises not only from physical events but also from one's goals, expectations, and other mental states: a 5-year-old, for example, might eat lunch by himself at day care to avoid his friends' annoying request to share his dessert (Stein & Levine, 1989).

An important advance in preschoolers' theory of mind occurs when they realize that mental states may not accurately reflect reality, and that people can be mistaken or fooled. This concept is especially difficult for young preschoolers to grasp when they have themselves been deceived. Consider this example. An adult shows a 3-year-old a candy box and asks the child what is inside. The child says, naturally, that there is candy. But, in fact, the child has been tricked:

Adult: Let's open it and look inside.
Child: Oh . . . holy moly . . . pencils!
Now I'm going to put them back and close it up again. [does so]
Now . . . when you first saw the box, before we opened it, what did you think was inside it?

Pencils.

Nicky [friend of the child] hasn't seen inside this box. When Nicky comes in and sees it . . . When Nicky sees the box, what will he think is inside it?

Pencils. [adapted from Astington & Gopnik, 1988]

Three-year-olds have considerable difficulty grasping that one's subjective understanding can be different from the way things "really and truly" are—and consequently, when they learn that they have been mistaken, they not only change their mind but also think that they have *always* held the view that they now know to be correct. They even think that others, like Nicky, will intuitively know the "real case." In similar fashion, when 3-year-olds are presented with an extremely realistic fake egg, they are understandably surprised to discover that it is actually a painted stone (Flavell et al., 1983). Once they realize they have been tricked, however, children believe—with the same conviction as earlier—that the egg now actually looks like a stone! (The researchers in this experiment commented, "It is an eerie experience to see a 3-year-old peer at an imitation egg that would fool the most discerning hen and solemnly indicate that it *looks* like a stone to his eyes right now" [Flavell et al., 1983].) For children of this age, there is only one "real and true" reality, and they fail to appreciate that one's subjective understanding of that reality may be mistaken.

As children reach the late preschool years, and their theory of mind becomes more comprehensive, they begin to grasp the distinction between objective reality and subjective understanding. When they discover that the candy box is filled with pencils, for example, they not only acknowledge that they were earlier mistaken, but they take considerable delight in the prospect of their friends' being similarly fooled. This increased awareness of subjective understanding is also demonstrated in an experiment in which children first observe a doll named Sally-Anne put a toy into a cupboard and then, while Sally-Anne is absent, they observe another doll moving the toy to a closet. Whereas 3-year-olds claim that when Sally-Anne returns, she will search for the toy in the closet, both 4- and 5-year-olds know that Sally-Anne will search for the toy in the cupboard (Wimmer & Perner, 1983).

The growth of children's theory of mind has broader implications for social understanding. As they begin to grasp how a person's thinking can be influenced by past experiences and other people's opinions, as well as how a person's thinking may affect his or her behavior, older preschoolers become far more capable of anticipating and affecting the thoughts, emotions, and intentions of others. Not surprisingly, this conceptual growth quickly becomes enlisted for various practical purposes, such as persuasion ("If you buy me a TV for my room, Mom, then I won't be fighting with Susie over what to watch anymore!"), sympathy (consoling a sad friend by reminding her of an upcoming birthday party), and teasing (telling an older brother, who is a Shaquille O'Neal fan, that "Shaq would never wear such a stupid-looking T-shirt!"). Preschoolers' understanding of human psychology is rudimentary, of course, but the theory of mind they begin to develop during the play years provides the foundation for the more sophisticated understanding they will develop in the years to come. Simpler though they are, young children's efforts as psychological theorists are sometimes not very much different from those that adults attempt.

FIGURE 10.8 A preschooler might be told that this is really a person inside a Barney costume, but nonetheless believe that the person becomes Barney once the costume is on. During the play years, the relationship between appearance and reality is a tenuous, tricky one.

We have thus far looked at recent research on preschool thought, particularly in four areas, number, problem solving, memory, and theorizing. In every case, preschoolers show both surprising skill and notable naiveté. Now we will consider the theories of Jean Piaget and Lev Vygotsky, both of whom provide a set of principles that bring important insights to this cognitive mix.

Piaget's Theory of Preoperational Thought

More than sixty years ago, Jean Piaget developed a description of cognitive development during early childhood that highlights some of the major strengths of preschoolers' thinking (especially as compared to infants' sensorimotor intelligence) and some of its major limitations (especially as compared to the operational intelligence of older children and adults). As we have noted on a number of occasions, however, Piaget tended to underestimate certain aspects of young children's cognitive abilities; and as we will see, he also underestimated the power of the social context in eliciting those abilities. Nevertheless, the overall sweep of Piaget's description remains insightful.

Symbolic Thinking

To Piaget, the most important feature of cognitive development during the preschool years is the rapid growth of **symbolic thinking**. This is the ability to use words, objects, and even actions as symbols in one's thinking and communication. The growth in the use of symbolic thinking occurs as the child becomes able to mentally coordinate an increasing number of schemes for the objects and events in his or her world. This progression is particularly clear when children play, using objects to represent something other than what they are (Stambak & Sinclair, 1993).

When children, at about age 1½, first play symbolically with toys, using, say, a doll or stuffed animal to represent a person, their play involves one fairly simple action at a time. For example, a doll might be put to bed and left there, ending that particular episode of pretend play. With time, the child will put the doll through a sequence of related behaviors—making her wash her hands, cook the dinner, and eat it. Finally, at age 3 or 4, the child gives the doll more complex roles, such as talking and interacting with other dolls and toys to form a family or a play group or a situation involving friends and foes. As children become older, they share their symbols in play with others: by age 4 or 5, many children are quite delighted to develop pretend dramas—such as "hospital," "store," or "family"—and act them out with their friends.

As we shall shortly see, the increasing complexity of symbolic thinking reflected in pretend play is accompanied by an increasingly elaborate use of spoken language, itself a manifestation of symbolic thought, since words are the most common symbols we have. Initially, the child's first words are hardly symbols at all, since sounds like "ma, ma, ma" seem, from the child's perspective, to be part of Mommy herself rather than a name that stands for her. But by age 2, words are not only clearly used as symbols but become

symbolic thinking Thinking that involves the use of words, objects, or actions to represent ideas.

FIGURE 10.9 When 5-year-old Peter and 3-year-old Gwen are together, they both love to pretend, but note that the older child appears to be a good deal more "into" his role. Symbolic thinking and dramatic play become increasingly complex as the play years unfold.

playthings themselves, as one child calls another "doo-doo head" and then laughs uproariously, and by age 3 or 4 a child can create extensive dialogue while making toy figures interact. Finally, several children can play various roles together, improvising dialogue with an appropriate accent and tone, and adapting their actions to fit their fluid script. Thus the sequence of symbolic thinking and play, first with objects, then with words, and then with other children, is evidence of increasing cognitive development that distinguishes the preschooler from the infant (Garvey, 1989; Lyytinnen, 1991; Piaget, 1951).

Indeed, the fact that preschool children immerse themselves in pretend play with such concentration and imagination, and that they learn language with such speed and involvement (as we will see later in this chapter), underscores Piaget's central insight regarding cognition—that children are active learners, eager to use whatever burgeoning intellectual abilities they might have to master and explain both the world of ideas and the practical experiences they encounter.

Limits of Logic

In keeping with the overall theme of this chapter, we must quickly point out that despite their rapidly increasing capacity to coordinate symbols in a meaningful way, preschool children are not necessarily able to do so in a way that is consistently logical. This is why Piaget describes thinking between about ages 2 and 6 as **preoperational thought**, referring to the fact that preschool children cannot yet perform logical "operations"; that is, they cannot use ideas and symbols to develop logical principles about their experiences. At the simplest level, they cannot regularly apply a general rule, such as "if this, then that" or "If not this, then not that."

The observation that young children are illogical (or, to Piaget, "prelogical") does not mean that they are stupid or ignorant. Rather, it means that their thinking reflects certain characteristics of preoperational thought (Flavell et al., 1993). First, preschoolers tend to be *irreversible* in their thinking—that is, they fail to apply the logical idea that reversing a process will bring about the original conditions from which the process began. This sounds much more complicated than it actually is: in practical terms it means that the child may know that $3 + 2 = 5$ but not necessarily realize that the reverse is true, that $5 - 2 = 3$. Reversibility is not only a logical feature of

preoperational thought Piaget's term for the second period of cognitive development. This period generally occurs from age 2 to 6, before logical concepts such as conservation, reversibility, or identity are fully understood.

number understanding. It is also basic to many forms of problem solving, enabling a person to undo the steps of a process, or reverse a line of reasoning, back to the point where taking other steps or another line of reasoning might lead to a better solution.

Second, preschoolers sometimes exhibit *centration* in their thinking: they tend to focus their analysis on one aspect of a situation to the exclusion of all the others. They may, for example, insist that lions and tigers are not cats, because in their view, "cats" are house pets. Or they may say that their father is a *daddy* only—not a son, or brother, or uncle as well—because they see family members exclusively in the role those individuals play for them. Or upon meeting, say, a 4-year-old and a 5-year-old, the younger of whom is taller, they may assert that the 4-year-old is actually 6, because "bigger is older."

Finally, preschoolers are sometimes rather *static* in their reasoning, understanding the world in terms of an either/or framework rather than as a flux of possibilities. As we have seen, for example, 3-year-olds have difficulty appreciating that, at different times, one may have correct or incorrect beliefs about the contents of candy boxes, fake eggs, or other aspects of reality. To a child of this age, one's beliefs must be completely consistent with how things "really and truly" are.

These characteristics of preoperational thought were of particular interest to Piaget, and his experiments with conservation illustrate the ways in which they limit young children's ability to reason logically. Conservation, you will recall from Chapter 2, is the simple idea that an amount is unaffected by changes in its shape or placement. This familiar idea, however, is not at all obvious to young children, who often focus precisely, and exclusively, on a change in shape or placement in assessing constancy of amounts. One example is conservation of number: preschool children sometimes fail to realize that a particular quantity of items remains the same quantity no matter how the items are arranged. As Piaget and other researchers have shown, if an experimenter lines up, say, seven pairs of checkers into two rows of equal length and asks a 4-year-old if both rows have the same number of checkers, the child will usually say "Yes." However, if, while the child watches, the experimenter elongates one of the rows by spacing the checkers in it farther apart, and then asks again if the rows have the same number, the child will most likely reply "No," indicating that the longer row has more checkers. In this situation, the child seems to be compelled on the basis of appearance to conclude that the longer row, in fact, contains a larger amount.

Experiments involving conservation of liquid likewise show that, when comparing the amount of liquid in two glasses, young children are impressed solely by the relative height of the fluids. If they are shown two identical glasses containing equal amounts of lemonade, and then watch while the lemonade from one glass is poured into a taller, narrower glass, they will insist that the taller, narrower glass has more lemonade than the remaining original. Other conservation tasks present young children with similar intellectual challenges, and produce similar results (see chart on p. 350).

In all such tests of conservation, Piaget believed, the problem is that preschoolers center on appearances and thus ignore or discount the transformation that has occurred. Instead, they look at the static results of the change and reason intuitively that the longer row, the taller glass, and so on, must contain more. In addition, these tests of conservation also reveal

Tests of Various Types of Conservation

Type of conservation	Initial presentation	Transformation	Question	Preoperational child's answer
Liquids	Two equal glasses of liquid.	Pour one into a taller, narrower glass.	Which glass contains more?	The taller one.
Number	Two equal lines of checkers.	Increase spacing of checkers in one line.	Which line has more checkers?	The longer one.
Matter	Two equal balls of clay.	Squeeze one ball into a long, thin shape.	Which piece has more clay?	The long one.
Length	Two sticks of equal length.	Move one stick.	Which stick is longer?	The one that is farther to the right.

preschoolers' irreversibility in that it apparently does not occur to them to reverse the actions they have observed. They do not visualize, or suggest, pouring the liquid from the taller glass back into the smaller one, for example, to return to the beginning and thus demonstrate that the two glasses contain the same amount.

Piaget believed that it is impossible for preoperational children to grasp the idea of conservation and other logical reasoning processes, no matter how carefully they are explained to them. But some later researchers wondered if perhaps the specific nature of Piaget's conservation experiments—including their formality or testlike features—might be affecting children's performance. And, in fact, they found that in playful, gamelike situations (rather than the formal experimental procedures described above), preschoolers often do reveal an accurate grasp of number conservation (Dockrell et al., 1980; McGarrigle & Donaldson, 1974).

In one example, experimenters used a variation of the checkers test in which the elongation of the row of checkers was caused by the action of a "naughty" teddy bear rather than by the deliberate manipulations of an adult. In this context, preschoolers were more likely to recognize that both rows still contained the same number. The experimenters hypothesized that in the formal experimental situation, young children may assume that if an adult takes the time and trouble to reposition a row of checkers, all the while making sure the child is paying attention, something significant, like the total number of checkers, must be being changed. In the gamelike situation, however, the teddy's "messing up" the display does not lead to this distracting assumption.

Subsequent research has likewise shown that very young children can succeed at other tests of conservation, if the tests are simple and gamelike, and especially if the children are given special training, including explicit verbal instructions with demonstrations. One particularly successful experiment with liquid conservation included both pretend play, in which the children themselves poured liquids from one container to another as part of a game, and specific, step-by-step, explanations of why the amount of liquid is the same no matter what the shape of the containers. As a follow-up to this conservation test, the experimenters asked the children who had succeeded very explicit questions to determine the depth of their understanding, such as "How can the water in this one be so much taller and still have the same amount as this one?" The preschoolers were quick and confident in correctly explaining the rationale for conservation (Golumb & McLean, 1984).

In a variety of training experiments, most preschool children are able, for the moment, to follow the examiner's guided instructions and then apparently, grasp the idea of conservation. Indeed, many 4- and 5-year-olds—though almost no 3-year-olds—still grasp the concept of conservation several weeks after training, demonstrating not only the type of conservation taught to them (such as liquids) but also other types of conservation (such as number or matter) (Field, 1987). Nevertheless, their capacity to exercise these reasoning skills is limited and fragile: when faced with tasks that are more complex or challenging, their tendencies toward centration, egocentrism, and magical thinking reemerge. In other words, despite the impressive evidence for early competency in symbolic thought and reasoning—as well as in number, problem solving, memory, and theory of mind—the thinking and reasoning of the preschooler surely does not approach the systematic, logical, and objective understanding that the typical grade-schooler possesses (Becker, 1989). The "fragile but nonetheless genuine competencies" (Flavell et al., 1993) revealed by recent research highlight how much earlier developmentalists, including Piaget, underestimated the intellectual skills of children during the play years. This recent research also confirms how much children have yet to learn.

Now we turn to another major cognitive theorist, Lev Vygotsky, who explains how the gap between the intellectual skills already evident in preschoolers and the knowledge they have yet to learn is bridged.

Vygotsky's Theory of Children as Apprentices

Whether at any given moment a preschooler's thinking shows surprising competencies, confounding ignorance, seemingly far-fetched intuitive imaginings, or a mixture of all of these, it is apparent that young children strive for understanding in a world that fascinates and sometimes confuses them. But they do not strive for understanding in social isolation. Their efforts are embedded in a social context, where parents, older children, preschool teachers, and many others try to guide a young child's cognitive growth by providing challenges for new learning, offering assistance with tasks that may be too difficult, providing instruction, and supporting the

FIGURE 10.10 Through shared social activity, adults in every culture guide the development of their children's cognition, values, and skills. Typically, the child's curiosity and interests, rather than the adult's planning for some future need, motivate the process. This seems to be the case as this Guatamalan girl eagerly tries to learn the sewing skills of her mother.

guided participation A learning process in which the child learns through social interaction with a "tutor" (a parent, a teacher, a more skilled peer), who offers assistance with difficult tasks, models problem-solving approaches, and provides explicit instruction when needed.

child's interest and motivation (Rogoff, 1990; Rogoff et al., 1993). On their part, children ask endless questions and try to include almost anyone of any age in their cognitive quests. In many ways, then, young children are "apprentices in thinking" whose intellectual growth is stimulated and directed by their **guided participation** in social experiences and explorations of their ecological settings (Rogoff, 1990).

This view of the social context of cognitive development is inspired by the writings of Lev Vygotsky, the Russian psychologist to whom you were first introduced in Chapter 2. As you learned, Vygotsky's ideas have become the basis for several sociocultural theories that emphasize the cultural foundations of growth and development. In contrast to many developmentalists (including Piaget) who tend to regard cognitive growth as a process of *individual* discovery propelled by experience and biological maturation, Vygotsky believed that cognitive growth is driven by cultural processes, which shape the experiences, incentives, and goals involved in children's learning. More specifically, Vygotsky saw cognitive growth less as a process of individual discovery than as a *social* activity advanced by the guidance of parents and other teachers who motivate, channel, and structure a child's learning.

To see how Vygotsky's approach works in practical terms, let's look at an example of a young child's guided participation in a challenging activity. Say that a child quits after trying unsuccessfully to assemble a puzzle. Does that mean the task is beyond the child's ability? Not necessarily—that is, if the child can be given guidance that provides motivation, focuses attention, and restructures the task to make its solution more attainable. In this case, an adult or older child might begin such guidance by encouraging the child to look for a likely piece for a particular section ("Does it need a big piece or a little piece?" "Do you see any blue pieces with a line of red?"). Suppose the child finds some pieces the right size, and then some blue pieces with a red line, but again seems stymied. The tutor might then be more directive, selecting out a piece to be tried next, or rotating a piece so that its proper location is more obvious, or actually putting a piece in place with a smile of satisfaction. Throughout, the teacher praises momentary successes, maintains enthusiasm, and helps the child see their joint progress toward the goal of finishing the puzzle.

The critical element in guided participation is that the adult and child interact to accomplish the task. Eventually, such guided participation enables the child to succeed independently. Once the child puts the puzzle together with adult help, chances are he or she will try it again soon, needing less help, or perhaps none at all. At the same time, the tutor gradually requires the child to do more on his or her own. Each step toward independence is encouraged by the adult. Assuming that puzzle solving is a valued skill in the culture, the adult might also find a new puzzle for the child to attempt, so that skills mastered in the first instance—such as locating pieces of similar coloring or finding and connecting all the edge pieces first—are transferred to the next instance, and then, eventually, generalized to the world of all possible puzzles.

Such interactive apprenticeships are commonplace: in every culture of the world, adults direct children's attention and provide assistance to teach various skills, and, soon, children who are given such guided practice learn to perform the skills on their own (Rogoff, 1990; Rogoff et al., 1993; Tharp & Gallimore, 1988).

FIGURE 10.11 The best way to learn almost any practical or intellectual skill is with the help of a "mentor" who guides one's entry into the zone of proximal development, the area between what one can do alone and what one might do with help. Of course, it is essential that the apprentice be eager to enter that zone, as this intent young carpenter certainly seems to be.

zone of proximal development
Vygotsky's term for the difference between an individual's attained level of development and the person's potential level of development that might be reached with guidance.

scaffold To sensitively structure a child's participation in learning encounters so that the child's learning is facilitated.

The "Zone of Proximal Development"

Key to the success of these apprenticeship experiences is the tutor's sensitivity to the child's abilities and readiness to learn new skills. According to Vygotsky (1986),

> the only good kind of instruction is that which marches ahead of development and leads it. It must be aimed not so much at the ripe as at the ripening functions. It remains necessary to determine the lowest threshold at which instruction may begin, since a certain ripeness of functions is required. But we must consider the upper threshold as well: instruction must be oriented toward the future, not the past.

As we saw in Chapter 2, Vygotsky believed that, for each developing individual, there is a **zone of proximal development**, that is, a range of *potential* development involving skills that the person can accomplish with assistance but is not yet quite able to perform independently. How and when a person masters these cutting-edge skills depends, in part, on the willingness of tutors to **scaffold**, or sensitively structure, the child's participation in learning encounters (Bruner, 1982; Wood et al., 1976). We have already seen several examples of scaffolding, including a parent's helping a child with a puzzle, or providing a supportive structuring with a number of problem-solving tasks, or guiding a young child's recollections of a shared experience. Other examples, among many, might include a parent's encouraging a child to talk about his or her own feelings in order to deepen the child's emotional understanding, or sensitively rephrasing a child's verbal expressions to foster language learning.

Developmentalists who have observed how parents provide this kind of structure for their child's emergent capabilities have identified a number of steps that contribute to effective scaffolding (Bruner, 1982; Rogoff, 1990; Wood et al., 1976):

1. Recruit the child's interest in the task or activity.

2. Simplify the task by reducing the number of steps required for correct solution (perhaps by helping the child focus only on the best strategy, or perhaps by completing certain aspects of the task for the child).

3. Maintain the child's interest in, and enthusiasm for, the task in the face of distraction, waning interest, and/or discouragement.

4. Anticipate and indicate errors as they occur in the child's performance and provide guidance toward correction.

5. Control frustration, both by encouraging the child's desire to achieve and by reducing his or her unhappiness at making mistakes.

6. Demonstrate or model correct solutions—ideally in a manner that shows how to complete each step along the way.

A person's progress through the zone of proximal development is influenced in other ways besides a parent's scaffolding of cognitive skills. Other family members may also offer incentives for new learning, such as when sibling rivalry provokes a child to figure out what an older brother might be thinking and feeling, and to use this information for teasing, self-defense, or negotiation. Beyond the home, a child's experiences in day care or preschool provide similar incentives for the growth of social understanding and cognitive competence, especially as the child begins to compare his or her skills with those of other children the same age. More broadly still, culture influences the development of certain cognitive abilities. Every culture values some cognitive skills more than others, so it is not surprising, for example, that children in the Micronesian islands are much better at interpreting weather and navigation signs than are American children, or that American children are more likely than Micronesian children to acquire skills that are well-suited for abstract and scientific reasoning. As Vygotsky believed, cognitive growth is facilitated by opportunities and incentives at various levels of a child's social ecology.

Talking to Learn

Vygotsky believed that language is essential to cognitive growth in two crucial ways. The first is through **private speech**, the internal dialogue in which a person talks to himself or herself (Vygotsky, 1987). In adults, private speech is usually silent, but in children, especially preschoolers, it is much more likely to be uttered out loud. With time, this self-talk becomes a whisper, and then becomes inner, private speech.

Researchers studying private speech have found that preschoolers use it to help them think, reviewing what they know, deciding what to do, and explaining events to themselves. Interestingly, many researchers have found that children who have learning difficulties tend to be slower to develop private speech, or to use it to guide their behavior (Diaz, 1987). Training in private speech sometimes helps them learn, another sign that language, in this form, aids the learning process.

The second way language advances thinking, according to Vygotsky, is as the *mediator* of the social interaction that is a vital part of learning. Whether it involves explicit instruction or casual conversation, verbal interaction with others helps to refine and extend one's present level of understanding. This function of language is essential to traversing the zone of proximal development, because verbal interaction provides the bridge from the child's current understanding to the almost-understood.

As we will see in the next section, during the preschool years, both private and social language erupt in a verbal explosion, as children spend hour upon hour asking question after question, telling stories that seem endless, or just talking and singing to themselves. From this perspective, a child's language development becomes critically important as a cognitive tool. Now let us look explicitly at the course of language development during the preschool years.

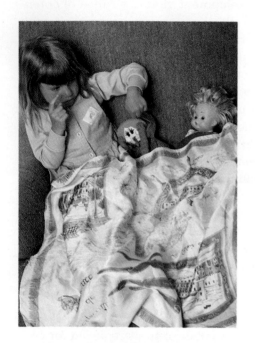

FIGURE 10.12 As 3½-year-old Laura explains the rules for taking a nap to her dolls, she is developing her language skills. Most preschoolers talk all the time, to themselves, to their dolls, to the television, and to their parents, even when none of them answer back.

private speech The use of language to form thoughts and analyze ideas, either silently or by talking to oneself.

Language Development

As noted in Chapter 7, babies normally begin talking at about a year, with language development occurring slowly at first. Toddlers typically add only a few new words to their vocabulary each month, speak in one-word sentences, and sometimes have trouble communicating, frustrating themselves as well as even the most patient caregiver who tries to understand what the 1-year-old wants to say.

During the preschool years, however, as cognitive powers increase, the pace and scope of language learning increase dramatically. Indeed, an "explosion" of language occurs, with vocabulary, grammar, and the practical uses of language showing marked and rapid improvement. As we shall see, the growth of language builds upon, and contributes to, the growth of thinking and reasoning during the preschool years.

Vocabulary

The rapid growth of vocabulary during early childhood is most astonishing, especially when we remember that it takes most infants a year to utter one intelligible word, and several months more before they master a dozen words. Nevertheless, the typical child's vocabulary more than doubles between 18 and 21 months of age, then doubles again over the next three months. By age 6, children's lexicons contain an average of more than 10,000 words (Anglin, 1993). As one summary describes it:

> Children typically produce their first 30 words at a rate of three to five new words per month. The same children learn their next 30,000 words at a rate of 10 to 20 new words per day. [Jones et al., 1991]

Words are often learned after only one hearing, through a process called **fast mapping**, in which the child immediately assimilates new words by connecting them through their assumed meaning to categories of words he or she has already mastered (see A Closer Look, p. 356).

The learning of new words follows a predictable sequence according to parts of speech. Nouns are generally mastered more readily than verbs, which, in turn, are learned more readily than adjectives, adverbs, conjunctions, or interrogatives. Within parts of speech, the order is predictable as well. For instance, basic general nouns, such as "dog," are learned before specific nouns, such as "collie," or more general categories, such as "animal." The first interrogatives children typically learn are "where?" and "what?" then "who?" followed by "how?" and "why?" (Bloom et al., 1982).

fast mapping A way to grasp the essential meaning of new words by quickly connecting them to words and categories that are already understood.

FIGURE 10.13 One of the key features of any good preschool program is the frequent opportunity it affords children to hear and express new vocabulary. While it is of course important for preschool teachers to read to their young students and to regularly engage them in conversation, the best language teachers for children are sometimes other children. With pragmatic skill and personal understanding, they tune into the best topics, and express the most relevant vocabulary, to move language learning along.

A CLOSER LOOK

Fast Mapping: Advantages and Disadvantages

Considerable research has attempted to determine how children master vocabulary so quickly. This inquiry begins with the realization that after the first year or so of language acquisition, learning vocabulary is no longer simply an additive process, with each word, in isolation, being added to the child's current stock of words. After age 2, there is an acceleration of vocabulary growth that soon seems like an explosion, with words being added daily in chunks. How does this happen?

One explanation is that the child's mind seems to develop an interconnected set of categories for vocabulary, a kind of mental map that charts the meanings of various words (Golinkoff et al., 1992). Hearing a new word, the child uses the context in which it is being employed to create a quick, partial understanding and then to categorize it, placing it in his or her existing lexicon. Thus children learn new animal names so quickly, for instance, because new names can be mapped close to the old ones ("zebra" is easy to learn if you know "horse," for example); similarly, they learn new color terms by comparing them with those they already know. This process is called "fast mapping," as if, rather than stopping to figure out an exact definition, and waiting until a word has been understood in several contexts, the child simply hears it once or twice and adds it to his or her mental language map (Heibeck & Markman, 1987).

Young children's fast mapping can be aided by the way adults label new things for them (as when a parent points at an animal the child is watching at the zoo and says "See the *lion* resting by the water. It's a *lion*!"). In addition, children make some basic assumptions that enable them to figure out a new word's meaning. They assume, for example, that words refer to whole objects (rather than to their parts) and that each object has only one label (Clark, 1990; de Villiers & de Villiers, 1992; Markman, 1991). While these assumptions sometimes prove misleading (such as when a child retorts, "That's not an animal. It's a *dog*!"), they usually lead to good, provisional definitions.

The quickness of fast mapping is phenomenal: a word can be learned after a single exposure (Dickinson, 1984). Moreover, several new words can be learned over a short time period. In one experiment, 3- and 5-year-olds were first given a multiple-choice vocabulary test on twenty words they were unlikely to know, such as "gramophone," "nurturant," "artisan," "malicious," and "contentment." Their scores were just about what they would be by chance, between five and six correct of the twenty. Then, in two 15-minute sessions, the children viewed cartoons with the twenty words used in context about ten times each. On retesting, the 3-year-olds averaged eight correct answers and the 5-year-olds averaged eleven right. Object words (e.g., "gramophone," which 93 percent got right) were easiest to learn, and emotional-state words (e.g., "contentment," which only 20 percent got right) were hardest. This is not at all surprising, since the language map for objects is well formed during preschool years, but the map for emotions is not (Rice, 1990; Rice & Woodsmall, 1988).

Fast mapping has obvious advantages, in that it fosters quick vocabulary acquisition. However, it also means that a child might seem to understand a word because he or she uses it in an appropriate context, when, in fact, the child has no real understanding of the word's meaning or understands it only in a limited way. One very simple, common example is the word "big," a word even 2-year-olds use and seem to understand. In fact, however, young preschoolers often use "big" when they mean "tall," or "old," or "great" ("My love is so big!"), and only gradually use "big" correctly (Sena & Smith, 1990).

If adults realize the difficulty children often have in comprehending exactly what the words they use mean, it becomes easier to understand, and sometimes forgive, the mistakes children make. Professor Berger can still vividly recall an example of fast mapping that arose when one of her daughters, then 4, was furious at her.

> Sarah had apparently fast-mapped several insulting words into her vocabulary. However, her fast map did not contain precise definitions, or reflect the nuances. She first called me a "mean witch," and then a "brat." I smiled at her innocent imprecision. Then she let loose with an X-rated epithet that sent me reeling. Struggling to contain my anger, I tried to convince myself that fast mapping had probably left her with no real idea of what she had just said. "Language like that is never to be used in this house!" I sputtered. My appreciation of the quickness of fast mapping was deepened by her response: "Then how come my big sister called me that this morning?"

The speed with which a child acquires words and relates them to categories and concepts depends partly on the particular conversations the child has with adults, who may or may not stress the linkage between one noun and another (Markman, 1989). When adults do describe categories—not in a formal lesson but simply in the course of normal speech—children are able to map new words more quickly, just as Vygotsky's stress on the pivotal role of social interaction would suggest. For example, when a child meets a dog named Lassie, and repeats "Lassie," a parent might say "Yes, Lassie is a dog, a collie dog," helping the child make the connection between the specific name, the breed, and the kind of animal.

The vocabulary-building process happens so quickly that, by age 5, some children seem to understand and use almost any specific term they hear. In fact, 5-year-olds can learn almost any word or phrase, as long as it is explained to them with specific examples and used in context. One 5-year-old surprised his kindergarten teacher by explaining that he was ambidextrous. When queried, he said, "That means I can use my left or my right hand just the same." In fact, preschoolers are able to soak up language like a sponge, an ability that causes most researchers to regard early childhood as a crucial period for language learning.

The spongelike fast mapping that occurs during these years is so impressive that we need to remind ourselves that young children cannot readily grasp *every* word they hear. Abstract nouns, such as "justice" or "government," are difficult to understand because there is no referent in the child's experience to link them to. Metaphors and analogies are also difficult, because the fast-mapping process is often quite literal, allowing only one meaning per word. When a mother, exasperated by her son's frequent inability to find his belongings, told him that someday he would lose his head, he calmly replied, "I'll never lose my head. If I feel it coming off, I'll find it and pick it up."

Further, although young children can quickly grasp words with objective meanings (such as nouns), they have greater difficulty with words expressing comparisons, such as "tall" and "short," "near" and "far," "high" and "low," "deep" and "shallow" (Reich, 1986). The reason is that children do not understand the *relative* nature of these words. Once they know which end of the swimming pool is the deep one, for instance, preschoolers might obey instructions to stay out of deep puddles by splashing through every puddle they see, insisting that none of them are deep. Words expressing relativities of place and time are difficult as well, such as "here" and "there," and "yesterday" and "tomorrow." More than one pajama-clad child has awakened on Christmas morning and asked "Is it tomorrow yet?"

Grammar

Grammar includes the structures, techniques, and rules that a language uses to communicate meaning. Word order and word form, prefixes and suffixes, intonation and pronunciation, all are part of grammar. Grammar is apparent even in toddlers' two-word sentences, since youngsters always put the subject before the verb.

By age 3, children typically demonstrate extensive grammatical knowledge. They not only put the subject before the verb but also put the verb before the object, explaining "I eat apple" rather than using any of the other possible combinations of those three words. They can form the plural of nouns, the past, present, and future tenses of verbs, the subjective, objective, and possessive forms of pronouns. They can rearrange word order to create questions, and can use auxiliary verbs ("I *can* do that.") They are well on their way to mastering the negative, progressing past the simple "no" of the 2-year-old ("No sleepy," "I no want it," "I drink juice no") to more complex negatives such as "I want nothing" or "I am not sleepy."

Children's understanding of grammar is revealed when they create original phrases and expressions, like those in the Table 10.1 on page 359. Each of the words in the chart shows not only children's mastery of grammatical rules but also their ability to apply these rules to create expressions they have never heard before but which convey their thoughts clearly and accurately to others.

How do preschoolers master the basic rules of language so quickly and easily? This impressive accomplishment has inspired many explanations. Recall from Chapter 7 that some developmentalists, following the ideas of Noam Chomsky (1968, 1980), believe that young children are aided in their language learning by a uniquely human brain structure—referred to as a "language acquisition device"—that facilitates their mastery of grammar. This innate mental program provides them with a set of "intuitive" guidelines for quickly deducing the rules of their native language, whether they are learning Russian, French, or Mandarin Chinese. In support of this view, researchers point out that certain areas of the human brain are specifically responsible for language (the part known as Broca's area is associated with language production, while Wernicke's area is associated with language comprehension). They also note that children worldwide proceed through similar stages and sequences in language acquisition, and that there are important characteristics that all the world's languages have in common (Slobin, 1985). The presence of innate, maturational incentives to acquire language is also suggested by the fact that even children who do not otherwise have opportunities to learn language from their environment—such as deaf children being raised by hearing parents who do not use sign language—begin to create their own grammatical language system in the ordering of gestures and self-devised signs at about the time that other children begin to master grammar (Goldin-Meadow, 1979).

This view also suggests that there may be a certain period of development—specifically, from late infancy through late childhood—that is primed for language learning. Even though most skills are more easily mastered by adults than by children, those who have studied a foreign language in high school or later can attest to the fact that acquiring a second language is more difficult than acquiring one's first language as a child. Indeed, even learning a second language appears to be easier for children than for adults. Johnson and Newport (1989) studied the English grammar of Korean- and Chinese-Americans who had emigrated to the United States between the ages of 3 and 39 years old and subsequently started to learn English as a second language. They found that the earlier the person began learning English, the better the person's mastery of English grammar—up to adulthood. Among those who learned English in adulthood, command of the language was uniformly lower. The researchers concluded, "It appears as if language learning ability slowly declines as the human matures, and plateaus at a low level after puberty."

FIGURE 10.14 This boy has been having phone conversations with his grandmother since he was 1-year-old, although at first he mostly listened, and then cried when the phone was taken away. Now, at almost 3, he chatters away unstoppably, revealing an extensive grasp of vocabulary and grammar. However, he still doesn't necessarily provide all the details that would let his grandmother follow the conversation, sometimes referring to events she has no knowledge of and people she does not know, or telling the ending of a story without a beginning, or vice versa.

Although the maturation of an inherent language-learning capability helps to explain why young children so easily master the basic rules of grammar, it does not tell us how they do so. One way preschoolers acquire grammar is by "semantic bootstrapping," in which, over time, they use their knowledge of the meanings of words, as well as the context in which they hear them spoken, to deduce sentence structure (Pinker, 1984, 1987). Say a young child is watching the family cat and hears his mother saying "Kitty is playing with the string." If he recognizes the main words of the sentence—"kitty," "play," and "string"—he can use this sentence, and hundreds like it, to derive a lesson in word order: the agents of an action come first, the actions come next, and the objects come last. In a sense, children's knowledge of semantics (or the meanings of words) provides a scaffold for an early grasp of grammatical rules.

TABLE 10.1

Children's Knowledge of Grammar in Creating Words

Rule Followed	Word	Context
Add "un" to show reversal.	"unhate"	Child tells mother: "I hate you. And I'll never unhate you."
Use a limiting characteristic as an adjective before a noun to distinguish a particular example.	"plate-egg," "cup-egg" "sliverest seat"	Fried eggs, boiled eggs. A wooden bench.
Add "er" to form comparative.	"salter"	Food needs to be more salty.
Create noun by saying what it does.	"tell-wind"	Child pointing to a weather vane.
Add "er" to mean something or someone who does something.	"lessoner" "shorthander"	A teacher who gives lessons. Someone who writes shorthand.
Add "ed" to make a past verb out of a noun (as in punched, dressed).	"nippled"	"Mommy nippled Anna." Reporting that Mother nursed the baby.
	"needled"	"Is it all needled yet?" Asking if Mother has finished mending the pants.
Add "s" to make a noun out of an adjective.	"plumps"	Buttocks.
Add "ing" to make a participle out of a noun.	"crackering"	Child is putting crumbled crackers into soup, thereby crackering it.
Turn a noun into a verb by giving it an object.	"bellhop"	"Bellhop me to Mom!" Asking to be carried to Mother.

Source: Examples come from Bowerman, 1982; Clark, 1982; Reich, 1986; and the Berger and Thompson children.

Children benefit not only when they can overhear conversations at home that are models of good grammar but also when their parents give them helpful feedback about their language use (Farrar, 1992; Hoff-Ginsberg, 1986, 1990; Tomasello, 1992). In one study, for example, 2-year-olds whose mothers frequently asked them questions (such as "Where does the duck live?") and repeated their answers, correctly rephrased (reworking the child's reply of "Wa-wa" into "Yes, the duck lives on the water"), showed better grammatical use six months later compared with children whose mothers rarely used these strategies (Hoff-Ginsberg, 1986). These "lessons" in grammar occur as part of the normal dialogues between parent and child, of course, not as a deliberate effort to instruct children in grammar.

Difficulties with Grammar

Young children learn their grammar "lessons" so well that they often tend to apply the rules of grammar even when they should not. This tendency, called **overregularization**, can create trouble when a child's language is one that has many exceptions to the rules, as English does. For example, one of the first rules of grammar that English-speaking children use is adding "s" to form the plural. Thus many preschoolers, applying this rule, talk about foots, tooths, sheeps, and mouses. They may even put the "s" on adjectives, when the adjectives are acting as nouns, as in this dinner-table exchange between a 3-year-old and her father:

> Sarah: I want somes.
> *Father:*   *You want some what?*
>   I want some mores.
>   *Some more what?*
>   I want some more chickens.

Once preschool children learn a rule, they can be surprisingly stubborn in applying it. Jean Berko Gleason reports the following conversation between herself and a 4-year-old:

> She said: "My teacher *holded* the baby rabbits and we *patted* them." I asked: "Did you say your teacher *held* the baby rabbits?" She answered: "Yes." I then asked: "What did you say she did?" She answered again: "She *holded* the baby rabbits and we *patted* them." "Did you say she *held* them tightly?" I asked. "No," she answered, "she *holded* them loosely." [Gleason, 1967]

Although technically wrong, such overregularization is actually a sign of verbal sophistication, since children are, clearly, applying rules of grammar. Indeed, as preschoolers become more conscious of grammatical usages, they may exhibit increasingly sophisticated misapplications of them (de Villiers & de Villiers, 1986). A child who at age 2 says she "broke" a glass may at age 4 say she "braked" one and then at age 5 say that she "did broked" another. After children hear the correct form often enough, they spontaneously correct their own speech, so parents can probably best help development of grammar by example rather than explanation or criticism—in this case, for example, by simply responding "You mean you broke it?" While few children will immediately correct their grammar, the cumulative effect of correct demonstration will lead to more rapid language mastery (Farrar, 1992).

During the preschool years, children are able to comprehend more complex grammar, and more difficult vocabulary, than they can produce. Thus, while it is a mistake to expect preschoolers to use proper grammar and precise vocabulary, it is also an error to simply mirror the child's speech, "talking down" to his or her level. And while an adultlike understanding of some grammatical forms is beyond many preschoolers, that does not mean that their language-learning abilities are severely limited. Vygotsky's concept of the zone of proximal development is useful here: between the grammar forms that are understood, and those that are, as yet, incomprehensible, lies a zone of potential development that, with adult guidance and the child's natural intellectual curiosity, can be used to expand the child's grammatical comprehension. While adults from various

Drawing by Glenn Bernhardt

No, Timmy, not "I sawed the chair."
It's "I saw the chair" or "I have seen
the chair."

FIGURE 10.15 This mother has obviously become accustomed to her son's use of overregularization.

overregularization   The tendency to apply grammatical rules and structures when they are not called for, or when exceptions to them should be used.

cultures differ in their readiness to teach language to their children, all children, as we will now see, are extraordinarily receptive to whatever communication patterns they experience.

Language in Context

In addition to studying the growth of children's grasp of the meanings and forms of language, developmentalists have also studied **pragmatics**, the practical features of communication between one person and another in terms of the overall context in which language is used (Rice, 1982). The major emphasis of this study is that a person's competence in verbal communication depends on that person's knowing how to adjust vocabulary and grammar to the social situation.

Children learn these practical aspects of language very early. Evidence of such pragmatic understanding of language can be seen, for example, in 2- or 3-year-olds' use of high-pitched "baby talk" when talking with younger children or with dolls and in their use of a deeper, "adult" voice when giving commands to dogs and cats (Dunn & Kendrick, 1982). Similarly, preschoolers use more formal language when playing the role of doctor or teacher or train conductor, and they use "please" more often when addressing someone of higher status (Rice, 1984). Children also gradually master proper listening behavior, such as nodding the head and saying things like "Uh huh" and "Really?" to continue a conversation by indicating that the speaker is heard and understood, even when this is not the case (Garvey, 1984). As every adult knows, this practical skill facilitates social interaction as well as further understanding, and thus smoothes the way for learning.

At the same time, there are sometimes notable shortcomings in young children's communication skills. Frustrating conversations in which a preschooler makes an ambiguous request ("I want a dog just like Tommy has," when the listener has never met Tommy nor seen his dog), or provides a vague description of events ("It was just like in the cartoons!") attest to the fact that young children are inexperienced conversationalists. Their difficulties in clearly communicating their intentions, wishes, or experiences stem, at least in part, from the challenges of simultaneously creating a verbal message and evaluating its communicative clarity to a listener, especially one with different perspectives, background, and experience (Beal, 1988; Beal & Belgrad, 1990). As a consequence, young children frequently become annoyed that the listener just doesn't "get it."

Differences in Language Development

Families and cultures differ in how much they stress language development. Consequently, by the time children enter kindergarten, differences in language skill are great. While one child seems to know the name of almost every object and action within that child's experience, and can converse in complex sentences, another child has only a basic vocabulary and uses only a few words at a time.

To some extent, one can predict which groups of children are likely to be more advanced in language (Bates et al., 1987; Quay & Blaney, 1992). On

FIGURE 10.16 It is obvious from their body language that these two children have different points of view. Their ability to communicate their opinions and come to an agreement is an indication of their pragmatic skills.

pragmatics A term for the practical aspects of communication, such as adjusting vocabulary and grammar to fit the specific situation and audience.

FIGURE 10.17 Why do girls, on average, tend to be more advanced in verbal skills than boys? One reason may be that young girls and their female caregivers tend to spend more time together in close communication, as this Inuit child and her aunt illustrate.

most measures of language production, girls are more proficient than boys; middle-class children are more proficient than lower-income children; first-borns more proficient than later-borns; single-born children are more proficient than twins, who, in turn, tend to be ahead of triplets.

Researchers who try to explain these differences usually look first at the familial and cultural variations in the language children hear. In general, they have found that mothers talk more to daughters than to sons; that middle-SES parents provide their children with more elaborate explanations, more responsive comments, and fewer commands than lower-SES parents do; and that parents talk more to first-borns and single-borns than to later-borns or twins.

Interestingly, research finds that measures of the overall relationship between parent and child, such as strength of attachment and the amount of time spent together, are *not* especially good predictors of a child's language competence. However, the particulars of conversation between adults and children are relevant. Children become more linguistically competent if the significant adults in their lives encourage them to talk, and reply to their comments with specific and contingent responses (Snow, 1984). If, for instance, a child says, "I saw a fire engine," a response like "Was it a long red fire engine?" is much more helpful than "That's nice."

Adults can also provide experiences that act as a scaffold on which to build language skills (Genishi & Dyson, 1984; Schiefelbusch, 1984). Such experiences might include looking at and conversing about picture books together, going on excursions that provide opportunities for new vocabulary and topics of discussion, and pretending together (pragmatic skills can be evoked by almost any imaginary venture, from a tea party to a trip to the moon). Activities like these work as well for learning a second language as they do for learning a first (McLaughlin, 1984).

Language and Thought

What is the relationship between language and thought in the child's cognitive growth? Do children first develop a notion or an idea, and later try to find the words to express it? Or does their language ability enable children to think in new and different ways?

As we have seen in much of this chapter, language and thought are intertwined during the early years. On the one hand, language ability builds on the sensorimotor and conceptual accomplishments of infancy and toddlerhood. As Piaget (1976) noted, children must first have an experience or understand a concept before they are capable of using the words that describe it. This explains, for instance, why the first words that children learn are ones that refer to the objects they can manipulate and explore with their senses, and that fit into the child's early categorical understandings. The noun "ball" is usually used before "crib," for example, because although infants hear the word "crib" more often, they cannot play with it in the same sensorimotor way they can play with a ball. Some developmentalists draw attention to the ways in which the vocabulary explosion is related to the growth of cognitive skills, such as the ability to organize and categorize objects conceptually according to their function or appearance (Gopnik & Meltzoff, 1987).

On the other hand, language growth leads to new ways of conceptualizing experience, and of learning. As we have seen, Vygotsky and other sociocultural theorists believe that language is a crucial means for the social transmission of knowledge, and provides a basis for the shared experiences that contribute to cognitive growth. Moreover, as children rapidly expand their vocabularies, they acquire words that lead them to form new categories, refine earlier ones, and think about events differently. A child who learns the names and distinctive characteristics of different kinds of fish on a visit to an aquarium, for example, is likely to think differently about "fish" in general. New terms for soccer positions, plays, and strategies lead to new ways of viewing the game. And as their emotional lexicon expands, children who thought they only felt "bad" learn to interpret their feelings as "worried" or "depressed."

Vygotsky (1962) believed that initially language and thought may develop independently, but that after age 2, they are mutually influential: the child's cognitive growth leads to linguistic refinements, while the development of language provides a more powerful way for other people and the children themselves to guide and advance thinking.

Having examined preschoolers' cognitive capabilities, their eagerness to learn, and their ability to learn through guided participation, let us now turn to the final topic of this chapter, preschool education.

Preschool Education

The cognitive experiences of preschool-age children are quite different now than they were thirty years ago. Whereas children formerly almost always stayed at home until age 6, now—in almost every industrialized nation and in many of the developing ones—most children experience some form of regular out-of-home care. It may be in a day-care environment such as the kind discussed in Chapter 8, or it may be in a preschool, designed to foster cognitive growth as well as to provide child care.

The overall increase in out-of-home care is attributable primarily to the dramatic shift in maternal work patterns. Whereas once few mothers of young children were employed away from the home, now most are. The rise in preschool care is related more particularly to the findings of research on child development. Over the past thirty years, scientists have shown not only that the years before age 6 are a time of rapid learning but also that young children can learn at least as well outside the home as within it.

The clearest and most extensive evidence for the benefits of preschool education comes from high-quality schools characterized by (1) a low teacher-child ration, (2) a staff with training and credentials in early childhood education, (3) a curriculum geared toward cognitive development rather than behavioral control, and (4) an organization of space that facilitates creative and constructive play. Research has found that preschools that include cognitive development among their goals but do not have all these costly resources can also foster children's learning, though not as much (Burchinal et al., 1989; Lee et al., 1988).

Most of the research on early childhood education comes from the United States and Canada, but similar results have also been found in research conducted in other countries. For example, a large comparison done in Bermuda (McCartney, 1984), where 84 percent of the children between ages 2 and 4 spend their days in some sort of care outside their homes, found that quality of care (particularly the amount of adult-child conversation) had noticeable effects on the children's verbal skills and on their overall intellectual development. The best centers were the ones where teachers spent more time teaching children (usually with small groups of children) and less time controlling them (usually done one child at a time), and where the children engaged in a variety of activities designed to foster motor, social, and language skills.

FIGURE 10.18 While the current figures for preschool enrollment are much higher than those of a decade ago, most developmentalists feel that they are not high enough. In fact, most developmentalists believe that preschool for 3- and 4-year-olds is just as important as school for 5- and 6-year olds, and that trained educators, along with age-appropriate curricula and materials, should be provided for all children.

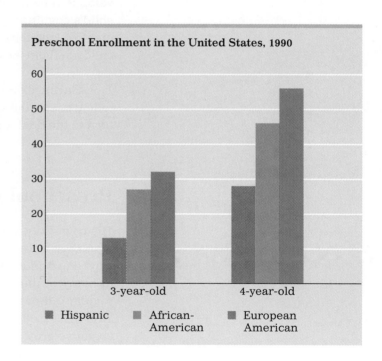

Preschool Enrollment in the United States, 1990

As a result, then, of both the increased need for child care and the proven benefits of preschool education, more and more young children are in some sort of educational milieu. In 1970, only 20 percent of all 3- and 4-year-olds in the United States were in a preschool of some type; in 1990, close to half were (see Figure 10.18). In many other developed countries, the numbers are even higher, because their governments sponsor education in early childhood.

In most cultures, the goals of preschool education go beyond cognitive preparation for later schooling. For example, in Japan, a society that places great emphasis on social consensus and conformity, preschool provides training in the behavior and attitudes appropriate for group activity: children are encouraged to show concern for others and to contribute cooperatively in group activities. These social skills not only prepare young children for their entry into the formal school system but also socialize attitudes and habits that they will later use in work settings (Peak, 1991). In China, an emphasis on learning how to be part of the group is combined with an emphasis on academic skills as well as creativity in self-expression, both drawn from the culture's Confucian ethic of disciplined study. In the United States, by contrast, preschools are often designed to foster self-confidence and self-reliance—qualities that are valued in our society—and to give children a good academic start through emphasis on language skills (Tobin et al., 1989). In this respect, the goals of preschool education—entailing a mixture of cognitive and social skills—reflect cultural values as well as the needs and capabilities of young children.

FIGURE 10.19 These photos show happy kindergartners in teacher-directed exercise in two settings, Tokyo and southern California. If you were a stranger to both cultures, with no data other than what you see in the photos, what would you conclude about the values, habits, and attitudes adults hope to foster in these two groups of children?

An additional goal of at least one form of American preschool—Headstart—is to provide extra assistance and encouragement to children who are disadvantaged by poverty.

Headstart: A Longitudinal Look

In the early 1960s, social scientists and social reformers advocated giving low-income children who might be disadvantaged by their home environment, or "culturally deprived" by their community, some form of compensatory education during the preschool years. Since these years were increasingly being regarded as critical for later cognitive development, such children were thought to need remediation for the deficiencies of their early experiences and a "head start" on the skills required in elementary school (Zigler & Berman, 1983; Zigler et al., 1993).

This idea caught on, and as part of the federal government's "war on poverty," **Project Headstart** was inaugurated in 1965. In its first year some 20,000 children, from many racial and ethnic backgrounds and from virtu-

Project Headstart A preschool educational program designed to give children advance preparation (a "headstart") for the intellectual and social challenges of elementary school.

ally every pocket of rural or urban poverty in the nation, attended a variety of Headstart programs—some full-time, some part-time, some concentrating on classroom activity, some teaching parents how to educate their children in the home. Despite these somewhat improvised and hasty beginnings, the initial results from Project Headstart were encouraging. Children learned a variety of intellectual and social skills between September and June of their Headstart year, averaging a gain of 5 points on intelligence tests.

Although longitudinal research found that the early IQ advantage of Headstart graduates often faded by the time youngsters reached third grade, it also revealed important "sleeper effects," or results that become apparent sometime after the precipitating event (Consortium for Longitudinal Studies, 1983; Haskins, 1989). As they made their way through elementary school, for example, the Headstart graduates scored higher on achievement tests and had more positive school report cards than non-Headstart children from the same backgrounds and neighborhoods. By junior high, they were significantly less likely to be placed in special classes or made to repeat a year. In adolescence, Headstart graduates had higher aspirations and a greater sense of achievement than their non-Headstart peers. As they entered adulthood, Headstart graduates were more likely to be in college and less likely to have a criminal record or a dependent child.

Similar findings to these appear in longitudinal research, begun in the 1960s, on participants in the Perry Preschool Program, a well-financed preschool education project in Ypsilanti, Michigan, that was much like Headstart in design. The latest survey of the Perry subjects, now in their late 20s, indicates that, compared to the study's control group, they have more education, greater earning power, greater family stability, and have required fewer social services. One comparison is particularly striking: only 7 percent of the program group had been arrested for drug-dealing by age 27, compared with 25 percent of the control group (Schweinhart & Weikart, 1993).

Conclusion

While no developmentalist believes that a year or two of preschool education will necessarily transform an impoverished child's life, almost all agree that, on the evidence from Headstart and other programs, most disadvantaged children will benefit from early education beginning at age 3 or even sooner. This education can be in the form of a Headstart program (the program is the only antipoverty measure that survived federal government funding cutoffs in the 1980s) or in another setting, as long as trained teachers implement a child-centered curriculum.

Preschool sleeper effects include economic benefits as well. Various studies comparing the cost of publicly financed preschool in the United States to the later savings from lower rates of special education, crime, and welfare dependency all find that early education is a sound public investment. Indeed, the more intensive, and expensive, the programs, the greater the dividend (Barnett & Escobar, 1987). Not surprisingly, those preschool programs that involve parents and community most intensely are also those that show the strongest long-term benefits for children and families. Too often, unfortunately, those children who most need quality care are least likely to get it, because their parents cannot find or afford it (Hayes et al., 1990). The importance of quality is strongly emphasized by the leading architects and advocates of Headstart, who believe that "it is much wiser to serve fewer children well than to serve more children poorly . . . [and] only high-quality programs can produce meaningful effects" (Zigler et al., 1993).

Do the same generalities hold for children who are not poor? Yes, to a degree. Longitudinal research on more advantaged children in the United States and elsewhere finds that they also benefit from a quality preschool setting, although the better the home environment, the less pronounced the influence of the preschool is likely to be (Anderson, 1989; Larsen & Robinson, 1989). Such benefits are cumulative: the more months and years a child spends in preschool, the more the cognitive and emotional benefits accrue (Field, 1991).

Considering all we now know about cognitive development between ages 2 and 6, we should not be surprised at the benefits of a well-run preschool education program. Children develop cognitive skills as a result of many interactive experiences with adults and children, in settings with many activities and much opportunity to play. That is precisely what a good preschool provides.

SUMMARY

How Preschoolers Think

1. Although young children cannot count large amounts and cannot easily add or subtract, their counting reveals an understanding of basic number principles, such as the "one-to-one principle," the "stable-order principle," and the "cardinal principle." Through the many number activities they engage in with their children, parents play an important role in the development of early number skills.

2. Preschoolers sometimes display considerable practical problem-solving skills in their everyday play and in their relations with peers, but they generally do not succeed at formal problem-solving tasks of the kind experimenters devise. However, some research has shown that children's problem-solving abilities can be enhanced when adults provide supportive guidance that is keyed to the child's ability level.

3. Young children are not skilled at deliberately storing or retrieving memories, although they can use scripts of familiar events to "bootstrap" their recollections of particular experiences. Parents and other adults also aid memory by helping children reconstruct their memories of past events, and by modeling the strategies for retrieving memories. Children sometimes display surprising long-term memory ability when adults use directive questions and prompting to help them focus their attention on specific aspects of past events.

4. Children's concepts reveal elementary theories about various features of their life experiences, including human psychology. A preschooler's theory of mind reflects developing concepts about human mental processes, including an understanding of how and why people have different thoughts, feelings, and intentions. Young children show a surprising awareness that people have different viewpoints and knowledge about events, and that subjective states may not be shared. One aspect of their developing theory of mind that is especially challenging to preschoolers is understanding that mental states may not always accurately reflect reality.

Piaget's Theory of Preoperational Thought

5. To Piaget, the growth of symbolic thought—that is, the ability to use words, objects, and actions as symbols—is the central achievement of the preoperational stage of cognitive development

6. Piaget described preoperational thought as, essentially, prelogical. This is because preschoolers tend to be irreversible in their thought processes, exhibit centration by focusing on one aspect of a situation to the exclusion of others, and reason in a static rather than a dynamic fashion.

7. Although preschoolers do not possess the well-established, systematic logical reasoning skills that they will exhibit during the school-age years, current research reveals that preschoolers are not as illogical as Piaget believed them to be.

Vygotsky's Theory of Children as Apprentices

8. Vygotsky viewed cognitive development as an apprenticeship, in which children acquire cognitive skills through their guided participation in social experiences that stimulate intellectual growth.

9. Vygotsky's view of the zone of proximal development is that there exists, for each child, a range of potential development that is the cutting-edge of new cognitive accomplishments. Social guidance is therefore most helpful in taking the child from what he or she can already do to what he or she is ready to learn next.

10. According to Vygotsky, language fosters cognitive growth by facilitating social interaction that teaches new skills. In addition, children use "private speech" to guide and direct their own actions.

Language Development

11. Language accomplishments during early childhood include learning 10,000 words or more, and understanding basic grammatical forms. Children of this age, however, have difficulty with abstract words and often misunderstand, or overregularize, grammatical rules.

12. Children's language can also be viewed from the perspective of pragmatics—that is, the use of practical communication in a variety of contexts. The ability to make meaningful conversation often develops alongside the acquisition of vocabulary and grammar. As impressive as they are, however, young children's communication skills are often limited.

13. The relationship between thought and language has fascinated developmental theorists, partly because each is likely to mutually influence the other during the early years of life.

Preschool Education

14. Whereas once most children used to stay home until they began formal education at about age 6, over the past thirty years insights from developmental psychology and changes in family composition and work patterns have resulted in increases in preschool education throughout the world.

15. The quality of preschool education varies a great deal. Those programs with an educational curriculum led by trained adults have shown a range of long-term benefits, not only in the child's later schooling but also in successful adult development.

scripts (336)

theory of mind (344)

symbolic thinking (347)

preoperational thought
(348)

guided participation (352)

zone of proximal develop-
ment (353)

scaffold (353)

private speech (354)

fast mapping (355)

overregularization (360)

pragmatics (361)

Project Headstart (365)

1. Which number principles are revealed in a young child's counting?

2. How do young children's scripts aid in their recall of specific past experiences?

3. What role do parents play in the development of number skills and memory and in the growth of problem-solving abilities during the preschool years?

4. What advice might a developmental psychologist give a lawyer who was planning to interview a preschool child who had witnessed a crime?

5. Describe the growth of a young child's grasp of mental processes, or theory of mind, through the preschool years.

6. According to Piaget, what are the central features of preoperational thought?

7. In Piaget's view, what are the strengths and weaknesses of preschoolers' reasoning?

8. How does symbolic thinking expand the cognitive abilities of the preschool child?

9. What key feature of Vygotsky's ideas about cognitive growth sets them apart from those of Piaget and many other developmental psychologists?

10. Give a hypothetical illustration of how a parent fosters a preschool child's new cognitive accomplishments in the zone of proximal development.

11. What explanations do developmental psychologists offer for the extremely rapid acquisition of new words during the preschool years?

12. How do young children so quickly and easily master the basic rules of language, or grammar?

13. How well do preschoolers communicate their thoughts, feelings, and intentions in everyday circumstances?

14. How do preschool education programs such as Project Headstart affect young children's cognitive development?

The Play Years:

Psychosocial Development

In the preschool years, children's self-awareness and understanding of others grows appreciably. Their relationships with their parents and siblings become more complex and multifaceted. At the same time, their growing capacity for social understanding allows preschoolers to participate in ever-more-elaborate play scenarios with other children and to explore various social roles. In this chapter we will consider the ways preschoolers develop their ideas about themselves and their relationships to the social world, as we examine questions such as the following:

How does the development of a child's self-understanding influence his or her ability to form relationships with others?

How do emotional growth and understanding arise from close relationships?

What are the various types of caregiving patterns that parents adopt, and how do these patterns affect children's behavior?

What accounts for differences in how well siblings get along?

What do children learn from playing with their peers?

How do children learn sex roles?

Picture a typical 2-year-old and a typical 6-year-old, and consider the psychosocial differences between them. Chances are the 2-year-old still has many moments of clinging, of tantrums, and of stubbornness, vacillating between dependence and self-determination. Further, many 2-year-olds cannot be trusted alone, even for a few moments, in any place where their relentless curiosity might lead them into destructive or dangerous behavior.

Six-year-olds, by contrast, have the confidence and competence to be relatively independent. They can be trusted to do many things by themselves, perhaps getting their own breakfast before school and even helping to feed and dress a younger sibling. They also can show affection with parents and friends without the obvious clinging or exaggerated self-assertion of the younger child. Six-year-olds are able to say goodbye to their parents at the door of the first-grade classroom, where they go about their business, befriending certain classmates and ignoring others, and respecting and learning from their teachers.

It is apparent that in terms of self-confidence, social skills, and social roles, much develops during early childhood. Cognitive growth permits children a greater appreciation of psychological roles, motives, and feelings, deepening their understanding of themselves and of others. At the same time, their social world becomes more diverse, with the introduction of new social partners (in preschool or in the neighborhood) and richer roles for familiar partners (such as parents, siblings, and peers). Catalysts for psychosocial development thus come from within and around the child, and this chapter examines that development.

The Self and the Social World

Self-concept, self-confidence, and self-understanding, as well as social attitudes, social skills, and social roles, are familiar topics for psychologists who study adults. Increasingly, these same topics are central to researchers studying children, especially those looking at early child development. Between ages 1 and 6, children progress from a dawning awareness that they are independent individuals to a firm understanding of who they are and how their selfhood relates to others. In the course of this progression, children move from the first recognition of themselves in a mirror, to knowing their name, gender, and what belongs to them, to knowing what they need and want from their family and friends and how to get it.

Self-Concept and Social Awareness

The play years are filled with examples of an emerging self-concept, as preschoolers repeatedly explain who they are and who they are not ("I'm a big girl." "I'm not a baby.") and assiduously note which possessions are theirs (laying claim to everything from "my teacher" to "my mudpie"). Preschoolers' emerging self-concept is also evident in their relish of many forms of mastery play. As Erik Erikson pointed out (recall Chapter 2), young children's self-concept is largely defined by the expanding range of skills and competencies that demonstrate their independence and initiative, and preschoolers jump at almost any opportunity to show that "I can do it!" An emerging self-concept can also be seen in the initial social interaction between two preschoolers, which typically involves the children's telling each other their names and ages and showing off any interesting toy, garment, or skill they may have.

FIGURE 11.1 Peer play is an important arena for the growth of self-awareness. In its early stages, self-concept among peers is typically expressed in terms of what belongs to whom. This sets the stage for another important development in peer play—the art of negotiation.

During the play years, children gradually begin to perceive themselves not just in terms of their physical attributes ("I'm bigger than Natalie!"), or their characteristic behaviors or abilities ("I can run fast!"), but also in terms of their dispositions and traits, seeing themselves, for example, as friendly, shy, happy, or hardworking (Eder, 1989, 1990). By the late preschool years, children possess a self-concept that may include a recognition of certain psychological tendencies, as revealed in this exchange between a 5-year-old and two puppets (manipulated by an experimenter):

Puppet 1: My friends tell me what to do.
    Child: Mine don't.
Puppet 2: I tell my friends what to do.
    Child: I do too. I like to boss them around. [from Eder, 1990]

Nevertheless, preschoolers' psychological understanding of themselves and others is still very limited (Miller & Aloise, 1989). They do not grasp the complexity of personality or the variability of a person's competencies: they do not appreciate, for example, that a person can be mean to people but kind to animals, or can be good at math but poor in reading. Preschoolers also do not clearly distinguish the different psychological causes of their actions or skills, believing, for example, that ability is self-controlled and can always be changed through effort.

The growth of preschoolers' self-awareness is nowhere more apparent than in their negotiations with others. Just prior to the preschool years, parents typically find themselves dealing with a demanding, stubborn toddler, whose primary negotiating skills seem to be insistence and tantrums. But as children's theory of mind expands (see Chapter 10), giving them a better grasp of how they, and other people, think and feel, their negotiations with parents—over what they will wear, what they will eat, when they will go to bed, and so on—evolve from obstinant demands and defiance to bargaining, compromising, and rationalizing (Crockenberg & Litman, 1990; Kuczynski & Kochanska, 1990). Similar growth is seen in peer relationships. A very young child's first encounter with a new peer is likely to begin with assertions of self, such as "My ball" or "You can't have this." But as they mature and their friendships progress, older preschoolers negotiate and share decisions on everything from the theme for pretend play to the choice of a snack.

Self-Evaluation

For children of all ages, psychologists emphasize the importance of developing a positive self-concept. Unless their social world makes it impossible, preschoolers usually have no problem in this regard. Typically they form quite general, and quite positive, impressions of themselves. Indeed, much research, as well as anecdotal evidence, shows that preschool children regularly overestimate their own abilities. As every parent knows, the typical 3-year-old believes that he or she can win any race, skip perfectly, count accurately, and make up beautiful songs. In a laboratory test, even when preschoolers had just scored rather low on a game, they confidently predicted that they would do very well the next time (Stipek & Hoffman, 1980).

FIGURE 11.2 During the play years, pride in the final accomplishment generally overshadows any reasons for self-doubt or self-criticism—such as whether the skyscraper one has just built is recognizable as such to anyone else.

initiative versus guilt The third of Erikson's eight "crises" of psychosocial development, in which the preschool child eagerly begins new projects and activities—and feels guilt when efforts result in failure or criticism.

Only when it was specifically pointed out to them how poorly they had done did they revise their estimates downward (Stipek et al., 1984).

In addition, most preschoolers think of themselves as able in everything—competent at all physical skills as well as at all intellectual ones (Harter & Pike, 1984). This confidence is greatly different from the self-appraisal of school-age children, who make clear distinctions among their areas of competence, asserting, for example, that they are rather good in mathematical skills, particularly word problems, but poor in athletic ones, especially basketball (Harter, 1983).

Despite their sunny self-assessment, however, preschoolers become increasingly aware of, and concerned with, how others evaluate their behavior. In fact, the play years witness some important changes in how young children incorporate others' evaluations into their own self-assessment (Stipek et al., 1992). Toddlers seem to enjoy the sheer pleasure of accomplishing their goals, whether it involves mixing mashed potatoes with apple juice, chasing and catching the family dog, or discovering how to melt soap in water, and they rarely look to others for their approval or disapproval. At about age 2, however, young children begin to anticipate adults' reactions to their behavior, displaying great pleasure when adults applaud them, and seeking to avoid the disappointed or disapproving reactions of adults when they have failed or misbehaved, chiefly by denying their responsibility. As Erikson theorized, between toddlerhood and age 3, children are in the stage of autonomy versus shame and doubt (see p. 264), with the intensity of their feelings about their successes and failures depending largely on the reactions of adults.

Later in the play years, the anticipated adult reaction to the child's success or failure becomes the basis for the child's self-evaluation, as the young child begins to spontaneously appraise his or her behavior with the same standards as adults do. In many situations, for example, young children will respond with disappointment or shame when they fail at a task, such as completing a puzzle or tying their shoes, or when they cause some mishap, such as spilling a cup of juice, even when no adult is present (Cole et al., 1992; Lewis et al., 1992).

At this point, according to Erikson's theory, children are in the stage of **initiative versus guilt**. In this stage, which is closely tied to the child's developing sense of self and the awareness of the larger society, preschoolers eagerly take on new tasks and play activities and feel guilty when their efforts result in failure or criticism. Their readiness to take the initiative reflects preschoolers' desire to accomplish things, not simply to assert their autonomy as they did as toddlers. Thus, in a nursery-school classroom, the older preschoolers take the initiative to build impressive block towers, whereas younger children in the autonomy stage are more likely to be interested in knocking them down. The enthusiasm of older children to learn and master many things derives, in part, from their growing sense of membership in the larger culture and a desire to acquire the skills of citizen and worker as well as of family member.

According to Erikson, when initiative fails—when eager exploration leads to a broken toy, a crying playmate, or a criticizing adult—the result is guilt, an emotion that is beyond the scope of the infant because it depends on an internalized conscience and a sense of self (Campos et al., 1983).

Emotional Development in a Social Context

As young children begin to interact with the social world physically and symbolically—through language and reflection—their emotions grow in breadth and vitality and are aroused by a broader range of circumstances (Harris, 1989). Anger may arise from a peer's insult or a neighbor's meanness, as well as from a parent's punishment; anxiety may be created by the anticipation of a dental exam, or the thought of getting lost in a department store, as well as by the sight of one's own skinned knee; happiness may result from the contagious delight of a best friend at a birthday party or the prospect of a trip to the zoo, as well as from playing a new game with Dad.

Moreover, preschoolers also become more prone to experiencing empathy, as the involuntary "pull" of another's distress makes a child feel sad (Eisenberg et al., 1990). Preschool teachers often find that one child's anguished wails at a parent's departure soon brings on pouts and sniffles in the other children who are watching their distressed peer. For some young children, feelings of empathy for someone in distress precipitate actions to comfort and assist that person.

As their emotional experiences broaden, preschoolers also become increasingly adept at coping with their emotions (Garber & Dodge, 1991; Thompson, 1991). When distressed, newborn infants may cry inconsolably and toddlers may seek assistance from an adult. Preschoolers, on the other hand, may try to solve the problem directly, or they may talk about it with friends, or they may try to think themselves out of the distress (as we saw in the example of children's reactions to inoculation in Chapter 10). One research team observed 4½-year-olds at their day-care centers to see how they dealt with their anger when another child transgressed against them (Eisenberg et al., 1993, 1994; Fabes & Eisenberg, 1992). They discovered that the children used a variety of strategies for coping with their anger, including revenge (such as attacking the transgressor), resistance (such as trying to get back a toy that had been taken away), avoidance (such as leaving the area to be alone), "telling on" the transgressor, or venting emotion (such as sulking or throwing a tantrum). Children who had been rated by their teachers as the most socially competent and popular among their peers tended to use direct and positive means of coping (such as simply telling the transgressor to stop) that limited further conflict and damage to social relationships. Children rated as unpopular, on the other hand, tended to take revenge or go running to an adult.

Preschoolers' increasing ability to cope with their emotions comes about partly as a result of their greater understanding of the causes and consequences of emotion in other people. As we discovered in Chapter 10, young children are highly motivated to try to understand the feelings of others because their daily interactions with them often involve strong emotions. At home, at preschool, and elsewhere, young children frequently participate in or witness confrontations with other children over toys and friendship, disagreements between children and adults about rules and appropriate behavior, and arguments between adults over many different issues. At first, children's efforts to understand such events may be very limited. For example, when asked to explain why another child is feeling sad, or delighted, or angry, young children usually attribute the cause to something that was done to the child ("He's mad because she took his toy").

FIGURE 11.3 These 2-year-olds are clearly sympathetic to the baby's cries, although it looks as if they have different opinions regarding what to do about it. While these particular children may have an early advantage in responding to others' emotions because they are all in day care together, evidence of empathy is also apparent even in children who rarely play with others.

They are much less likely to cite internal causes, such as the child's goals ("He's mad because he can't finish the game"), thoughts ("She's mad because she thought it was her turn"), and dispositions ("He's mad because he's mean") (Fabes et al., 1991). With further growth in their theory of mind, children by age 4 or 5 begin to perceive emotions as arising from internal as well as situational causes (Gross & Ballif, 1991).

One factor that can help preschoolers understand emotions is family conversations about them (Brown & Dunn, 1992; Dunn & Brown, 1991, 1994). When a parent and child discuss a shared moment of pleasure, commiserate about the child's scraped elbow, or talk about why an older sibling seems upset, or unusually happy, young children learn much about emotion and its causes and consequences. One study found that 3-year-olds who had had more frequent conversations with their mothers about emotions were, at age 6, better at making judgments about the emotions of unfamiliar people and at understanding their feelings (Dunn et al., 1991). A related finding is that mothers who respond sympathetically to others, and who try to explain another person's emotional state to their child in terms of the child's own experiences, have children who are more likely to respond sympathetically to another's distress and to intervene to help that person (Eisenberg et al., 1992; Grusec, 1991).

Thus the basics of guided participation, described in Chapter 10 as they apply to physical and cognitive accomplishments, relate as well to the development of social skills and the growth of emotional understanding. Let us now look more specifically at the ways the social context can affect psychosocial development.

Relationships and Psychosocial Growth

The social world of the preschooler is considerably broader than that of the infant. During the play years, children often enter peer networks (in day care, in the neighborhood, or perhaps in a play group organized by parents) that bring them into contact with many new acquaintances and friends. They are also likely to know more adults—their immediate neighbors and others who live nearby, as well as people who play specific roles in their lives, such as the mail carrier, a favorite grocer, and the babysitter. In addition, many children take the initiative in conversing with unfamiliar adults they might encounter at religious services, at the supermarket, or on the street. And, of course, the preschooler's social world is expanded further by the media, as TV, movies, videotapes, and even computers expose them to an enormous variety of people, lifestyles, and social experiences.

Despite their broadening social world, however, psychosocial growth for most children during the play years remains fundamentally guided by the close relationships they share with their parents, siblings, and, secondarily, with peers. These relationships have such an impact because they are based upon a history of personal interaction that creates deep emotional ties and consolidates social expectations, allowing the child to anticipate, say, generosity or rambunctiousness from a close friend, or to rely on a parent for comfort when it is needed. Such long-standing close relationships also foster socioemotional skills (such as how to cheer up a sibling who is sad or how to avoid distracting a parent who is trying to concentrate on a task) and contribute to the growth of self-understanding by providing the child repeated encounters with those who know him or her well.

Developmentalists' awareness that psychosocial growth emerges mainly from experience in close relationships has led to the emergence of the **relationship perspective** (Dunn, 1993; Hartup, 1989; Hinde, 1987; Hinde & Stevenson-Hinde, 1987). With respect to early childhood, this perspective focuses on the ways variations in the quality of children's relationships—such as whether the parent-child relationship inspires security or uncertainty, or whether peer relationships are supportive or undermining—can profoundly affect the course of early psychosocial development. This perspective also highlights the mutual influences of these relationships, pointing out, for instance, that young children who have troubled family relationships are likely to have difficult peer relationships as well.

In Chapter 8, we learned how parent-infant attachment provides an important foundation for psychosocial growth in infancy, and in Chapter 10, we saw how cognitive growth occurs through a child's guided participation in developing new skills with a skilled mentor. We continue these themes by examining, during the play years, the relationships young children share with their parents, siblings, and peers.

The Parent-Child Relationship

The parent-child relationship is important to psychosocial development because of the myriad ways that parents guide the life experience of their offspring. From big decisions—such as what neighborhood the family lives in, whether or not the child attends preschool, and so on—to small ones—such as how to respond to a child's requests for more playtime, more information, or more dessert—parents' child-rearing choices affect the emotional well-being, intellectual growth, and social competence of their children. While it is also true that children profoundly affect the lives of their parents (indeed, simply having a child to care for is the most dramatic change that most adults experience after adolescence), there is probably no more significant influence on early psychosocial growth than parents' approach to parenting.

Styles of Parenting

What kinds of parenting help children to develop a positive sense of themselves, as well as to interact positively with others, and to be competent at school? This question has no simple, universal answer because, for several reasons that we will examine later, there is no guaranteed cause-and-effect relationship between how a parent rears a child and how a child turns out. Indeed, parents adopt many acceptable styles, from quite strict to very permissive, from intensely involved to rather relaxed, and a child reared in one type of family may not be markedly different from a child reared in another type. Conversely, children raised in the same household may differ quite notably in their response to the same parenting style.

However, twenty-five years of careful research have led to an important insight about the impact of certain parental styles—not that one style is always best, but that some styles are more likely to produce confident and competent children than others. The seminal study in this research was

FIGURE 11.4 Confronted with a conflict situation such as this, parents might react in a number of ways. Some, for example, might try to punish the initiator of the dispute; others might try to help both parties understand the consequences of their actions; others might leave the combatants to settle things for themselves. Each of these responses is indicative of specific parenting styles that have been identified by researchers.

relationship perspective Focuses on the diverse ways the quality of children's relationships affect the course of psychosocial development.

begun in the early 1960s, when Diana Baumrind set out to study 100 middle-class preschool children in California (Baumrind, 1967, 1971). She used many measures of behavior, several of them involving naturalistic observation. First, she observed the children in their nursery-school activities and, on the basis of their actions, rated their self-control, independence, self-confidence, and the like. She then interviewed both parents of each child, and observed parent-child interaction in two settings, at home and in the laboratory, in order to see if there was any relationship between the parents' behavior with the child and the child's behavior at school.

There were four features of parenting that stood out in Baumrind's observations and interviews. First, parents differed in their warmth, or *nurturance*, toward offspring. Second, they varied also in their strategies to *control* the child's actions through explanation, persuasion, and/or punishment. Third, parents also differed in the quality of *communication* with offspring. Fourth, and finally, they varied in their *maturity demands*—that is, in their expectations for age-appropriate conduct. On the basis of these features, Baumrind delineated three basic patterns of parenting.

authoritarian parenting A style of child-rearing in which standards for proper behavior are high, misconduct is strictly punished, and parent-child communication is low.

permissive parenting A style of child-rearing in which parents rarely punish, guide, or control their children but are nurturant and communicate well with their children.

authoritative parenting A style of child-rearing in which the parents set limits and provide guidance and are willing to listen to the child's ideas and make compromises.

1. **Authoritarian** The parents' word is law, not to be questioned, and misconduct brings strict punishment. Authoritarian parents seem aloof from their children, showing little affection or nurturance. Maturity demands are high, and parent-child communication is rather low.

2. **Permissive** The parents make few demands on their children, hiding any impatience they feel. Discipline is lax. Parents are nurturant, accepting, and communicate well with offspring. They make few maturity demands because they view themselves as available to help their children but not as responsible for shaping how offspring turn out.

3. **Authoritative** The parents in this category are similar in some ways to authoritarian parents, in that they set limits and enforce rules, but they are also willing to listen receptively to the child's requests and questions. Family rule is more democratic than dictatorial. Parents make high maturity demands on offspring, communicate well with them, and are nurturant.

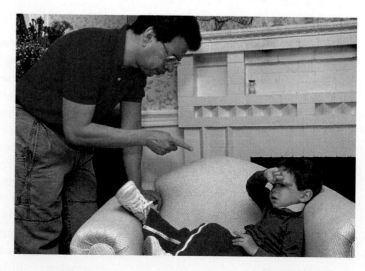

FIGURE 11.5 Both authoritarian and authoritative parents might sometimes scold a child. The difference is that the authoritarian parent tolerates no back talk, and is likely to use physical punishment in response to a display of disrespect. The authoritative parent, however, might listen to a child's response, paying close attention not only to the child's words but also to his or her gestures and body language.

Baumrind and others have continued and extended this research, following the original children as they grew into adulthood and studying hundreds of other children of various backgrounds and ages (Baumrind, 1989, 1991; Clark, 1983; Lamborn et al., 1991; Steinberg et al., 1989). The basic conclusions of the original studies have been confirmed: children whose parents are strict and aloof are likely to be obedient but not happy; those whose parents are quite lenient are likely to be even less happy and to lack self-control; those whose parents provide both love and limits are more likely to be successful, happy with themselves, and generous with others (Darling & Steinberg, 1993; Maccoby, 1992). In addition, the follow-up research has found that the initial advantages of the authoritative approach are likely to be even stronger over time (Steinberg et al., 1994). Authoritative parents, for example, "are remarkably successful in protecting their adolescents from problem drug use and in generating competence" (Baumrind, 1991).

Other Styles

The later research has also found that the original description of only three types of parenting was too limited. While various studies have proposed several new types—more than can be described here—three additional styles merit attention.

The permissive pattern, in particular, can take two distinct forms. While both forms are quite undemanding and uncoercive—that is, the parents rarely control, restrict, or punish the children unless health or safety are obviously jeopardized—some permissive parents are quite warm and responsive. They might best be called **democratic-indulgent**. Other permissive parents are quite cold and unengaged, and are called **rejecting-neglecting**. Although they fall far short of the extreme neglect that characterizes official maltreatment, rejecting-neglecting parents permit the child to do almost anything, and seem relatively uninvolved in, and even ignorant about, what the child actually does (Baumrind, 1991; Lamborn et al., 1991; Maccoby & Martin, 1983).

An example of the difference between the two types of permissive parenting might be that, while both would allow a 5-year-old to play unsupervised in the kitchen making a "cake" by mixing flour, sugar, water, baking soda, and cinnamon, the democratic-indulgent parent might taste the dough, pronounce it delicious, and bake it in the oven for the family dinner, whereas the rejecting-neglecting parent might simply pour the unappetizing mess into the garbage. Both of these reactions, of course, differ from nonpermissive parents: the authoritarian parent might not allow such a young child to be involved in any kind of food preparation, while the authoritative parent would likely be right beside the child, offering guidance, encouragement, and suggestions ("The batter looks a little bit thick, so maybe you should put in some more water." "Pepper usually doesn't taste good in cake.").

As Baumrind collected more information on parenting styles, she found another distinct type of parenting, which she called **traditional** (Baumrind, 1989). Parents in this category take somewhat old-fashioned male and female roles, the mother being quite nurturant and permissive, while the father is more authoritarian. In the cake-baking example, for in-

democratic-indulgent parenting
A style of parenting that is warm, responsive, and permissive.

rejecting-neglecting parenting
A style of parenting that is cold, detached, and permissive.

traditional parenting A style of parenting in which the parents take traditional male and female roles, the mother being primarily nurturant and permissive, while the father is more authoritarian.

stance, the mother might allow and even encourage the child's "creative cooking" (especially if the child is a daughter), but might warn that the mess must be cleaned up before Father gets home. Longitudinal research suggests that traditional and democratic-indulgent parenting are midway on the scale of successful parenting—less successful than consistently authoritative parenting but more successful than authoritarian or rejecting-neglecting parenting (Baumrind, 1989).

What can account for one parent's being authoritative, another's being authoritarian, and another's being traditional? Many factors play a role. Parenting style derives, in part, from the parent's specific child-rearing goals, as well as from his or her beliefs about the nature of children, the proper role of parents, and the best way to raise children (Goodnow & Collins, 1990; Murphey, 1992; Sigel et al., 1992). This combination of influences, which, themselves, are shaped by factors related to culture, religion, ethnicity, and gender, may cause one parent to use firm management to raise obedient, self-disciplined children who can accomplish their goals, while leading another parent to be nondirective, offering a range of opportunities and experiences from which children can choose.

A number of other influences also contribute to shaping parenting style. One of these is how parents remember their own upbringing (Ainsworth & Eichberg, 1991; Main & Hesse, 1990). Adults are sometimes astonished to find the legacy of their parents' parenting style affecting their interactions with their own offspring. Such a legacy often becomes apparent when particular admonishing phrases, or affectionate gestures, or modes of discipline, which seem to come to the parent naturally, even unconsciously, are suddenly recognized as virtually identical to what the parent experienced as a child. Another influence on parenting style is the family's economic well-being. Parents who are coping with the stress of poverty and related problems, for example, may not have the psychological energy to be authoritative parents and, instead, may demand obedience, use physical punishment to maintain control, and express less affection (Carter & Middlemiss, 1992; McLoyd,1990; McLoyd & Flanagan, 1990). Finally, the parent's personality—his or her quickness to anger, capacity for empathy with offspring, tendency toward optimism, and so forth—also influences parenting style (Dix, 1991).

Discipline

A critical task of parenting is to manage the child's behavior so that the child can grow up safely, competently, and securely. At first glance, the controlling, punishing style of authoritarian parenting might seem the most effective way to meet this challenge. One reason is that, initially, physical punishment seems to be effective: it usually stops the child from misbehaving at the moment and it provides an immediate outlet for a parent's anger or frustration (Kuczynski, 1984). However, physical punishment does not bring about the kind of long-term compliance and cooperation that most parents want from their children. Indeed, children who regularly experience physical punishment tend themselves to become hostile and aggressive (Weiss et al., 1992). (The effects of spanking are examined in the Research Report on p. 381.)

RESEARCH REPORT

The Effects of Spanking

More than 90 percent of today's American adults were spanked when they were young, and most consider themselves none the worse for it. Indeed, although the tide of public opinion is changing regarding physical abuse (see Chapter 9), most parents still believe that spanking is acceptable, legitimate, and necessary at times (Holden & Zambarano, 1992; Straus & Gelles, 1986). Nonetheless, history teaches that widespread acceptance of any child-rearing practice does not necessarily prove that it is good for children. Because of the demonstrated link between physical abuse in childhood and later violent aggression (Lewis et al., 1989), many developmentalists now wonder if children who are spanked learn to be more aggressive than children who are not spanked.

To try to answer this question, one research team (Strassberg et al., 1994) studied 273 children and their parents. The parents were from a full range of socioeconomic backgrounds, and roughly a third were single parents. The children were about evenly divided between boys and girls, and about three-fourths were European-American and one-fourth were African-American.

In the spring before their children entered kindergarten, the parents were asked how frequently they had spanked, hit, or beaten their children over the past year. Spanking was defined as involving "an open hand or an object on the child's buttocks in a controlled manner, whereas hitting involves the impulsive or spontaneous use of a fist or closed hand (or object) to strike the child more strongly than one would while spanking." Of the 408 parents surveyed, 9 percent did not use physical punishment at all, 72 percent spanked but did not use more violent punishment, and 19 percent hit or beat, as well as spanked, their preschool child.

Six months later, observers blind to the child's punishment history recorded each child's behavior in kindergarten, taking particular note of acts of aggression. In order to get an accurate snapshot of behavior, the observation was divided into twelve 5-minute segments occurring over several days. Within each segment, the observers recorded how many times the child engaged in one of three types of aggression:

1. *instrumental aggression*, used to obtain or retain a toy or other object;

2. *reactive aggression*, used in angry retaliation against an intentional or accidental act committed by a peer;

3. *bullying aggression*, used in an unprovoked attack on a peer.

Although it is sometimes difficult to differentiate these three types of aggression, the trained observers who independently watched each child agreed 96 percent of the time on the occurrence of aggression and 90 percent of the time on the type of aggression that had occurred.

Analysis of their data revealed that instrumental aggression was not much affected by the type of punishment a child experienced in the home. In other words, a kindergarten child was just as likely to fight over a toy whether he or she was spanked, hit, beaten, or not corporally punished at all. Bullying aggression, as expected, was clearly associated with being violently punished, particularly in the case of "a few extremely aggressive children," mostly boys who were frequently hit or beaten as well as spanked by both parents. Also as might have been expected, there was little association between bullying and either spanking or nonspanking.

The surprising finding was the clear relationship between spanking and reactive aggression. Compared to children who were not spanked, those children who were spanked were three times as likely to retaliate with an angry shove, punch, kick, or the like, to any wrong, real or imagined. In their analysis of the data, the researchers point out that while violent punishment seems to lead a child to be more aggressive under all circumstances, spanking does not seem to model the use of force in general. Rather, it seems to create a quite specific emotional-response pattern in the child—that is, a quick physical reaction to possible attacks. Because the "anger accompanying the spanking is highly salient to the child," the child models "the emotional behavior pattern and not the form of aggression, per se."

Note that this is a correlational study, and as has been pointed out on numerous occasions, correlation does not prove causation. It could be that spanking was more consequence than cause in this study. That is, it may have been that many of the children who were spanked "provoked" this response with angry and aggressive behavior in the home and that their hostile behavior merely carried through into kindergarten. However, several factors—including that girls were almost as likely to be spanked as boys even though they were half as aggressive—suggests that the parents' choice of punishment was related more to their own attitudes and temperament than to the actions of the child. Close analysis of all their data led the researchers to conclude that "in spite of parents' goals, spanking fails to promote prosocial development and, instead, is associated with higher rates of aggression toward peers."

In the long term, the most effective type of discipline is that typically associated with the authoritative parenting style—not because of the absence of punishment, but rather because of the authoritative parent's use of positive strategies for enlisting the child's cooperation and compliance. The affectionate quality of the parent-child relationship, together with the parent's respect for the child as an independent person, lead the parent quite naturally to use praise, encouragement, and other kinds of positive reinforcement for good behavior. They also lead the parent to use punishment that is designed to help the child follow certain consistent standards of behavior, and not to vent the parent's immediate anger. The open communication that typifies authoritative families encourages the parent to set clear standards in terms the child can understand. This open communication—in which the child is really listened to—also helps the parent to recognize when the child's failure to comply is for a good reason, such as a misunderstanding or a cognitive or psychological inability to act in an expected way.

Authoritative parents also provide a positive model for expected behavior, listening and considering before acting. This is in marked contrast to the model of aggressive behavior provided by the authoritarian parent, who spanks first and asks questions later, or not at all ("I don't want to hear any excuses"). Finally, authoritative parents are alert to ways to prevent trouble before it occurs: they may, for example, bring small toys to a restaurant if the child is going to endure a long wait; they dress the child in old clothes for outdoor play; they don't give the child so much responsibility that trouble is inevitable (Holden, 1983; Holden & West, 1989).

In a sense, therefore, a positive parent-child relationship helps to make the process of discipline somewhat easier. Such a relationship is like "money in the bank" (Maccoby & Martin, 1983), ready for use in later childhood. As one developmentalist explains, "If parents can do what is necessary early in the child's life to bring about a cooperative, trusting attitude in the child, that parent has earned the opportunity to become a nonauthoritarian parent" (Maccoby, 1984).

The Child's Influence

Any generalizations about the outcome of particular parenting styles—including the idea that authoritative parents produce the most competent children—must be interpreted with caution. In truth, parenting styles, and children's responses to them, are among the most complex aspects of family life. To begin with, children may influence parenting patterns as much as they are influenced by them. Hostile, unruly, or unreliable children, for example, may elicit overcontrolling behavior from adults, while children who are pleasant, self-reliant, and self-controlled may make it easy for parents to be relaxed and flexible in their approach to child-rearing. In fact, with experience, many parents tailor their child-rearing practices to fit their child's unique personality because they learn what works, what is ineffective, and what is overkill. A parent's pointed criticism, for example, may be taken in stride by a child who is assertive and outgoing but may wither one who is temperamentally fearful or inhibited (Kochanska, 1991, 1993).

Parenting style—whatever broad pattern it may follow—is also affected by the child's age. As children mature, for example, parents rely less on physical punishment to gain compliance than on verbal strategies, such as explanations, bargaining, and reprimands (Kuczynski et al., 1987). Most parents also believe that, with increasing age, children are better able to understand family rules and to exercise self-control, and thus should become more responsible for maintaining their own good behavior. Consequently, while the general trend is toward more authoritative parenting as children grow older, this trend is sometimes offset by the fact that parents are more upset with wrongdoing in older children. If the wrongdoing becomes prevalent as the child reaches school age, parents may adopt more authoritarian ways (Dix et al., 1986).

Children also perceive their relationships with parents differently as they themselves mature (Bretherton & Watson, 1990; Grusec & Goodnow, 1994). In one study, preschool and fifth-grade children were interviewed about what kind of punishment was appropriate for different kinds of wrongdoing. Whereas preschool children regarded severe physical punishment as warranted by almost any kind of transgression—whether it involved staying up past bedtime or stealing money—fifth-graders (like adults) were more discriminating in their judgments, believing that physical punishment should be reserved for the most serious wrongdoing and expecting greater flexibility from parents for nonserious mischief (Catron & Masters, 1993). These changing views of parents' proper disciplining influence how children respond to their parents' directives and methods of enforcement, and their response, in turn, affects the parents' demands and their enforcement of them.

Parenting in Context

The parent-child relationship obviously does not occur in a psychosocial vacuum. Each of its components is affected by other family members. As we will see later in this chapter, siblings—their number, age, and gender, as well as the nature of their mutual relationships—strongly influence each parent-child dyad. Each parent-child dyad is also influenced by the relationship between the parents and by the support—or lack of support—they provide each other for good parenting. Moreover, the interactions among all family members are also affected by broader cultural and economic processes that have an impact on each person. Thus, in order to understand how the parent-child relationship affects early psychosocial growth, we need to consider the overall family context and the social ecology in which the family lives.

The Marital Relationship

One of the truths to emerge from family research is that the relationship between husband and wife is a significant determinant of their parenting style. When the marriage is satisfying and mutually supportive, both parents tend to be authoritative or traditional, together setting high standards and responding with pleasure when their children meet them (Goldberg, 1990). On the other hand, when they are unhappy with each other, parents are more likely to be authoritarian, using threats and punishments to control their children's behavior and showing little patience when their children fail to obey. Parents are particularly likely to be rejecting and/or neglecting when the marriage is falling apart or is already dissolved (Baumrind, 1991).

RESEARCH REPORT

Television: A Dilemma for Parents

In virtually every home in the United States, a television is as familiar a fixture as a couch or refrigerator. Adults use TV for entertainment, information and, at times, for the simple comfort of a human voice in the same room. If they are parents, television additionally serves as a caretaker for offspring while parents are preparing meals or relaxing after a long day. For children, television is an equally compelling medium: it provides passive entertainment that is usually exciting and interesting. According to Nielsen Media Research, in 1990 children between the ages of 2 and 5 watched an average of 29 hours and 19 minutes of television each week, over 2 hours more than the 1984 average (and the highest of any age-group).

Because television serves so many different purposes in the average home, decisions about children's television viewing can be a frequent source of parent-child conflict. Compounding the difficulties parents may have making these decisions is the controversy over the potential effects of television viewing on the young. Many critics feel that the possible benefits of TV may be purchased at too high a price, and they cite three major problems: the effect of commercials, the content of programs, and the time that could be better spent.

Preschool children usually accept commercial messages uncritically because they have great difficulty recognizing when advertising techniques are bending the truth or exploiting fantasy in order to sell a product. Because young children believe much of what they see in commercials, they want almost everything they see in them. Parents are therefore placed in the position of resisting the constant demands of their children, or succumbing, buying everything from expensive toys that soon become boring or broken to sugared cereals and drinks that promote tooth decay.

An additional complaint about commercials is that they tend to reinforce certain social stereotypes. For one thing, a disproportionate number of the most active, competitive children in commercials are males. When girls do appear, they are usually shown in passive roles (Calvert & Huston, 1987). Similarly, minority children are typically among the cast of supporting characters—virtually never the leading characters.

The second major criticism of children's television is the amount of violence it portrays. Many psychologists maintain that TV violence promotes violence in children, primarily through example. The effect is interactive and cumulative: children who watch a lot of television are likely to be more aggressive than children who do not, and children who are aggressive are likely to watch a lot of TV violence (Friedrich-Cofer & Huston, 1986; Huston et al., 1989). Summing up the evidence for the relationship between television violence and aggression in children, Leonard Eron, head of the American Psychological Association's Commission on Violence and Youth, observes, "The evidence is overwhelming and longitudinal. The strength of the relationship is the same as for cigarettes causing lung cancer" (quoted in Mortimer, 1994).

Preschool children are even more likely to be influenced by violence on television than older children are, because they are uncritical television viewers. In television cartoons, which are designed primarily for young children, physical violence occurs an average of twenty-five times an hour (National Coalition on Television Violence, 1993). The good guys (Mighty Morphin Power Rangers, Teenage Mutant Ninja Turtles, Batman, etc.) do as much hitting, shooting, and kicking as the bad guys, yet the consequences of their violence are made comic or sanitized, never being portrayed as bloody or evil. In cartoonland, demolition, whether of people or things, is just plain fun (Potts & Henderson, 1991).

A related concern over the cumulative effects of watching repeated violence on television is that children will become desensitized to the fact and consequences of violence, a hypothesis with experimental support (Parke & Slaby, 1983). Children who see a lot of violence on television may thus become more passive when viewing actual violence in real life and may be more likely to regard violence as a "normal" part of everyday life. They are also more likely to become passive victims of, and bystanders to, violence (Slaby, 1994).

Many educators and parents have tried to reform children's television, their most successful efforts being through Action for Children's Television (ACT), begun in Boston in 1968. By 1972 ACT had helped to ban children's vitamin commercials and advertisements with a TV hero directly promoting a product. They have been less successful in reducing violence, however: not only did the role of violent acts increase in American children's television programs during the 1980s (Pearl, 1987), but many current TV heroes are more hostile and aggressive than those of past years (Pena et al., 1990). In 1991, for example, G.I. Joe rang up seventy-eight instances of violence per hour, and the Teenage Mutant Ninja Turtles, forty-three (National Coalition on Television Violence, 1993).

At the same time, public television has developed special educational programs, such as *Sesame Street* and *Mister Rogers' Neighborhood*, both of which are widely recognized for their successful teaching efforts. In many other countries, notably Japan, Great Britain, and Sweden, the government requires that at least an eighth of the total programming time be allotted to children's programs with an educational content (Lesser, 1984).

Nevertheless, a growing group of critics is concerned that even the best television does more harm than good because it robs children of play time, making them less creative, less verbal, and less independent (van der Voort & Valkenburg, 1994). Studies have shown that children who watch a lot of television tend to be lower achievers than children who watch only a little, partly owing to the way television competes with homework (Kubey & Csikszentmihalyi, 1990). In addition, television tends to cut off social communication, which, as we have seen, is essential for enhancing the social skills that children must develop. In contrast to social play, television watching is an essentially passive, noninteractive process, even when others are present.

Some support for these conclusions has come from experiments with certain families who voluntarily gave up television viewing. The parents of these families reported that their children played and read more, that siblings fought less, that family activities became more common, that mealtimes were longer, and that bedtimes were earlier (Chira, 1984; Winn, 1977). Unfortunately, these experiments lasted only a month and involved volunteers, so their value is limited.

What else can parents do? Some professionals, in fact,

Every parent quickly learns the advantages of television: it keeps children quiet and in place. However, this benefit might come at a high price—increased aggression, once the set is turned off.

recommend no television at all, especially for preschoolers. Others suggest that parents watch with their children, so that they can personalize the learning on educational programs and monitor or criticize the content of noneducational television. Many parents have found it easier to impose a simple rule—only an hour a day, or only before dinner, or only on Saturday—than to try to prohibit television completely or censor each program. Others try to foster children's critical thinking about television content by sensitizing them to advertising enticements or the actual consequences of violence portrayed on television. Although there is no clear consensus on how parents should control television viewing, one thing is certain: no psychologist who has studied the effects of children's television thinks parents should let their preschoolers watch whatever and whenever they want.

FIGURE 11.6 Marital stress can affect children in various ways—by heightening the likelihood that frustrated parents will act punitively with offspring, by increasing children's distress and anger when they hear their parents arguing, and by providing a salient model of conflict within the home. As a consequence, it is not surprising that when parents begin fighting, the rest of the family often erupts in conflict and anger as well.

Marital stress can also indirectly affect parenting practices through its effects on the children (Cummings & Davies, 1994; Grych & Fincham, 1990). In one experimental study, pairs of young children were observed playing while two adults simulated either a loud, angry argument, or a warm, friendly conversation, elsewhere in the room. Children who played against a backdrop of anger were significantly more distressed and aggressive toward each other than when adults were pleasantly conversing in the background. (Cummings et al., 1985). Similar reactions have been observed in children in the home, suggesting that children in a family beset by marital conflict are likely to be distressed, anxious, and/or misbehaving as a result of that conflict (Cummings, 1987; Cummings et al., 1984). They may also complicate marital disagreements by verbally or physically intervening in them (such as by hitting one parent) or otherwise choosing sides (Covell & Miles, 1992; Cummings et al., 1989; Grych & Fincham, 1993). These effects make authoritative parenting much more difficult, of course, since it is hard to be firm yet flexible, responsible yet responsive, when the children are crying, fighting, and out of control.

It should be noted that children who live in homes with persistent marital conflict do not "adjust" to it: they remain sensitive to their parents' disagreements and troubled by them. One reason is that marital conflict undermines the child's sense of emotional security at home (Davies & Cummings, 1994). As a consequence, marital conflict has not only immediate but long-term consequences for children who witness it: children from conflicted homes have been found to be more anxious, aggressive, and/or withdrawn many years later (Cummings, 1994; Katz & Gottman, 1993).

Cultural, Ethnic, and Community Context

Although authoritative parenting usually contributes to making children more confident, self-controlled, and successful, in some contexts other styles may be more effective (Darling & Steinberg, 1993; Maccoby, 1992). In single-mother homes with an adolescent son or daughter, for example, greater parental control and authority, in the direction of authoritarian parenting, is associated with reduced delinquency, probably because of the greater supervision it involves (Dornbusch et al., 1985). When adolescents from different ethnic groups are compared, those with the highest grades come from groups (for example, Asian-American) in which parents are more authoritarian, and less authoritative, than parents from other ethnic groups (Dornbusch et al., 1987; Steinberg et al., 1991, 1992). In a radically different context, characterized by a cultural emphasis on self-reliance, self-esteem, and shared caregiving, parents of the Aka Pygmy culture of the Central African Republic raise their children in a notably permissive fashion—and for the most part their children grow up cheerful, independent, and nonaggressive (Hewlett, 1992).

Examples like these—of which there are many—highlight the fact that culture, ethnicity, and community play important roles in parenting patterns, affecting not only parental goals and values but also the appropriateness and effectiveness of various parenting styles. In chaotic and dangerous environments, such as the urban ghettos of contemporary America, responsible parenthood in a particular family might well require a high level of parental control, whereas the same family in a more secure and stable setting might find a democratic-indulgent style to be preferable and more effective. In a culture like that of the Aka Pygmy, in which young children have already acquired considerable competence and self-reliance, a permissive style of parenting is consistent with children's independence and fosters greater competence rather than dependency. Thus, because parenting is embedded within a broader network of practices, beliefs, and supports from outside the family, the effects of parental style must always be regarded within the context of culture and community.

An Integrative View

Recognizing the importance of the overall social context, we are drawn to a new focus on the family. Rather than viewing it merely as an arena for child-rearing, we see, through the relationship perspective, that the family consists of multiple relationships that influence each other and which are, in turn, affected by the broader beliefs, supports, and demands of the social context in which the family lives. From the moment a child is conceived, the parents' relationship with each other shapes the emotional environment in which the child will live; and after the baby's birth, the marital relationship is continuously reshaped by the child's own contributions. Each family member is also buoyed and buffeted by economic, ecological, and interpersonal challenges from outside the home. In this sense, we might think of *family* development alongside our more traditional concern with individual development (Belsky et al., 1989; Cowan & Cowan, 1992; Cowan et al., 1992). Consider the following example of how families change and develop.

In the late 1980s, a group of researchers at Iowa State University began to study rural farm families, many of whom had been hard-hit by the decline in the agricultural economy during the preceding decade (Conger et al., 1990, 1992; Simons et al., 1992, 1993). Based on interviews with each family member, observations of family interaction, and other measures, the researchers learned that economic stress affected family relationships in various ways (see Figure 11.7). For parents, the inability to pay monthly bills often resulted in demoralization and depression as debts mounted. Although some spouses were mutually supportive during this difficult time, others experienced greater marital conflict. This difference, in turn, was re-

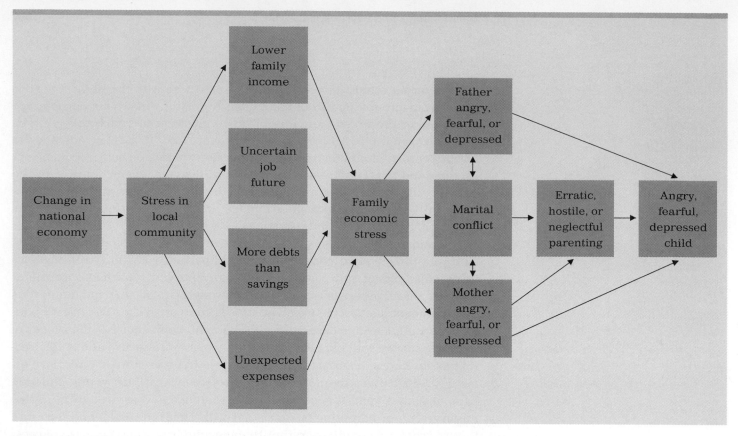

FIGURE 11.7 Can rising inflation and increased unemployment lead to psychological problems for a nation's children? The answer is yes, but, as shown here, the influence of these factors is indirect and is not inevitable. If, for instance, a given family had a steady income and job security, or if a particular couple responded to economic stress with increased emotional support for each other and their children, a downturn in the economy would be less likely to negatively affect the children's psychological health.

flected in parenting styles, as the couples in conflict became less nurturant and less positive toward their offspring and tended to use discipline more harshly and less consistently than did the mutually supportive couples. In older (seventh-grade) children, who were aware of the family's economic difficulties, and troubled by them, poor parenting contributed to adjustment problems, including greater depression and aggression toward others. By contrast, in families in which a supportive marital relationship contributed to more nurturant, involved parenting, children could cope more successfully with economic strain.

Whether positive or negative, all stories of family change point to the fact that child-rearing patterns, and their effects, are moderated by a host of complex and wide-ranging factors. Parental actions are embedded in community and family settings, influenced by children's temperament and age, shaped by prior parent-child and father-mother interactions, and subject to change as historical, economic, and social conditions change. While the authoritative style may represent the ideal for effective parenting in most circumstances, in actual, day-to-day child-rearing, the ideal balance between freedom and control is not always so clear.

Sibling Relationships

To a child, sibling relationships are unique, different from relationships with parents and peers. As they do with parents, siblings share lifelong relationships and common backgrounds and experiences. Like peers, however, siblings are closer (although usually not equal) in age, abilities, and outlook, and their interests are often different from those of parents. Perhaps for these reasons, siblings assume significant roles in a child's life. For a younger child, an older sibling is an enticing model, a source of learning, and occasionally a reservoir of comfort and security. For an older child, a

FIGURE 11.8 While hidden jealousy and open conflict between siblings are common, so are joint activity and obvious tenderness. Older siblings throughout the world can identify with these two sisters from the Yunnan region of China, who are quite delighted that baby brother accepts their offer of a drink.

younger sibling is an important benchmark of social comparison ("Mark can't jump rope, but *I* can!"), and permits the growth of new social skills related to nurturance and authority (Abramovich et al., 1979, 1982; Dunn, 1983, 1988).

Not surprisingly, the emotional quality of sibling relationships varies dramatically. Much attention, of course, has been given to sibling rivalry, and it is true that siblings are more likely to quarrel with each other than they are with nonrelated children. However, researchers have found that the flip side of sibling rivalry has been understressed: siblings are also more likely to have positive interactions with each other, showing more nurturance and cooperation than with an unrelated child (Howe & Ross, 1990). Consequently, *ambivalence* might be the best single word to describe the emotional quality of most sibling relationships.

Why do some siblings get along wonderfully, while others are in constant conflict? A prime reason may be the "goodness of fit" of their temperaments (Munn & Dunn, 1989; Stoneman & Brody, 1993). When one research team observed sibling interaction on two occasions—first when the younger sibling was 2 years old, and later when that child was 3—they found that what predicted levels of conflict between siblings at each age was the degree of difference between the siblings' temperament profiles. Siblings with similar profiles got along well, while those who were much different temperamentally tended to conflict. This correlation held especially for measures of emotional intensity and negative mood (Munn & Dunn, 1989).

As we would expect from the relationship perspective, sibling relationships are also affected by each parent-child relationship. Most notably, parents set the stage for sibling rivalry or cooperation by comparing one sibling unfavorably with another, for example, or by encouraging the children's collaborative play. Parental influences actually begin with the birth of the second child: one research group discovered that preschool-age siblings whose mothers frequently discussed the newborn sibling as a person with feelings and desires showed considerably greater interest in, and nurturance toward, the younger child (Dunn, 1988; see also Howe & Ross, 1990). Marital conflict and conflict between parents and children can also intensify sibling conflict by increasing tension and diminishing affection in the home (Brody et al., 1992; Volling & Belsky, 1992). And, of course, because siblings usually differ in age, personality, interests, and other characteristics, they share different kinds of relationships with each parent—and these can sometimes also lead to conflict. For example, the pleasant moments of reading time that one sib shares with a parent may anger another sib who dislikes this pastime and would rather be doing something active with the parent.

In fact, because each sibling has a unique position within the family, the home experiences of each child in a given family are quite different from those of the other children (Dunn, 1993). This helps explain a phenomenon that had, at first, puzzled researchers in behavioral genetics. Earlier researchers had assumed that, if two children from the same family were markedly different in personality, intelligence, and so forth, the differences must be genetic, since the environment within the home was similar for each. However, careful analysis finds that environmental variations within families are substantial (Plomin, 1990). Home is a quite different place for the first-born big brother than for the last-born baby sister (Dunn & Plomin, 1990; Hoffman, 1991).

While there are many reasons for marked experiential differences between siblings, one of the most important is the parents' different feelings toward, and different treatment of, their children. Even when well-intentioned and justifiable, these differences can fuel feelings of jealousy, anger, dominance, or inferiority (Daniels et al., 1985; McHale & Pawletko, 1992). Preschoolers, particularly, are very sensitive to social interactions between their parents and their siblings: they interrupt conversations, claim moral superiority when a sibling has transgressed, and make invidious comparisons, often to their own detriment (Dunn & Plomin, 1990). One example comes from a 2½-year-old, Andy, and Susie, his 14-month-old sister:

> Andy was a rather timid and sensitive child, cautious, unconfident, and compliant. His younger sister, Susie, was a striking contrast—assertive, determined, and a handful for her mother, who was nevertheless delighted by her boisterous daughter. In the course of an observation of Andy and his sister, Susie persistently attempted to grab a forbidden object on a high kitchen counter, despite her mother's prohibitions. Finally, she succeeded, and Andy overheard his mother make a warm affectionate comment on Susie's action: "Susie, you *are* a determined little devil!" Andy, sadly, commented to his mother, "*I'm* not a determined little devil!" His mother replied, laughing. "No! What are you? A poor old boy!" [Dunn, 1992]

Multiplied hundreds of times over during Andy's childhood, such feelings of inadequacy might spur him toward success or failure, bravery or timidity, but they certainly would not have neutral effects. Not all siblings are rivals, but almost all are reciprocally involved in ways that affect the personality and social understanding of both (Dunn & Plomin, 1990).

It is easy to see that, given the attentiveness they bring to their relationship, siblings might contribute more to the development of social skills than anyone else, since they are likely to guide, challenge, and encourage a child's social interactions more frequently and intimately than most others do. Very practical lessons in self-defense, sharing, and negotiation are part of every sibling's childhood.

The Only-Child

This raises questions about the child who is without brothers or sisters, the so-called only-child. How common are such children, and how does their family configuration affect their development? Actually, it is impossible to know for certain how many of today's children are true only-children, since many children spend a good part of their childhood as an only-child and then are joined by a younger sibling or a step-sibling. However, worldwide, the number of both true only-children and temporary only-children is clearly rising.

For example, in the United States the percentage of families with children with only one child under age 18 rose from 33 percent in 1971 to 40 percent in 1991. In fact, spending at least several years with no brothers or sisters at home is now a common experience for young American children: in 1991, about half of all children under age 6 were the only such child in their family (U.S. Bureau of the Census, 1972, 1992).

Family composition in many other nations of the world is likewise shifting from many children to only one or two. The example of this trend is most dramatic in China, where the government's strict "one-child policy" to combat overpopulation has resulted in many single-child families. Indeed, in 1991, 95 percent of the student body of most primary schools in Beijing consisted of only-children (Bakken, 1993).

Are only-children handicapped because they have no brothers or sisters? The general public still believes this to be the case. (In China, especially among the older generations, there is widespread prejudice against only-children, especially boys, who are stereotyped as lonely, spoiled, overly dependent on their parents, disrespectful "little emperors," and potential delinquents.) The truth is usually otherwise: only-children are more likely to benefit from increased parental attention than to suffer from lack of siblings (Falbo & Polit, 1986; Falbo & Poston, 1993; Mellor, 1990). Single-child status is particularly beneficial intellectually, with only-children being generally more verbal, more creative, and more likely to attain a college education than children who have one or more siblings. Only-children are particularly advantaged when compared to children from families with four or more children, even when the economic disadvantages of larger families are taken into account. These differences are apparent in China, in Europe, and in North America (Bakken, 1993; Blake, 1989).

The one area of development in which only-children might be disadvantaged is their social skills, particularly in the development of cooperative play, theory of mind, negotiation strategies, and self-assertion, which usually are enhanced through sibling interactions (Falbo & Poston, 1993). However, as preschool education and public day care become the rule rather than the exception in industrialized nations, most only-children develop social skills that are equal to those of their contemporaries with siblings.

Peer Relationships and Play

The play years are also a period for developing friendships outside the home. Whereas it was once typical for young children to spend most of their time at home (except for occasional forays with their mother to attend a play group or nursery school or to visit another child in the neighborhood), most children today spend a large portion of each weekday in a preschool program or day-care center. As we saw in the Chapter 10, high-quality day-care or preschool programs can have benefits for cognitive growth. The same is true of psychosocial development: children in well-run programs acquire a wide range of social skills, and become more socially competent as a result of their frequent interactions with other children of the same age (Hayes et al., 1990; Zaslow, 1991; Zigler & Lang, 1990). This can be a mixed blessing, however, for children in group day care may not only learn how to be more helpful and cooperative with peers and become more socially knowledgeable but may also become more assertive and aggressive than children without extensive day-care experience. Peer encounters in day care typically force children to learn to defend their interests, whether keeping their favorite toy or their place in line.

In fact, the play years witness the growth of many social skills (Howes, 1987). This is easy to see when we compare the 2-year-old, whose peer interactions consist mainly of simple cooperative games (like bouncing and

FIGURE 11.9 Peer relationships develop during the play years, enabling the cooperation, and the sheer pleasure, evidenced here.

catching a ball, or hiding and finding a partner) with the more sophisticated interactions of a 5-year-old, who has learned how to gain entry to a play group, can manage conflict through the use of humor, and has structured his or her peer world into friendships and acquaintanceships (Corsaro, 1985). Why peer relationships contribute to such psychosocial growth is fairly obvious. With peers, children are on a much more equal footing than they are with adults, and they must therefore assume greater responsibility for initiating and maintaining harmonious social interaction. In play with peers—whether learning how to share crayons or the sandbox, or how to include everybody in the construction of a spaceship, or how to respond to a friend's accusation that "it's not fair!"—children cannot rely on their partners to make all the effort, as they can in encounters with adults. Thus, peer encounters in early childhood afford crucial experiences that teach reciprocity, cooperation, and justice, experiences that would be hard for adults to provide (Eisenberg et al., 1985; Howes, 1987).

In their peer encounters, preschoolers also learn to distinguish among other children in terms of their cooperativeness, friendliness, and "likability" (Denham & Holt, 1993; Denham et al., 1990). As they learn about the characteristics of their peers, children develop friendships based, in part, on their peers' reputations for generosity, aggressiveness, and the like. This, in turn, helps to explain why friendships are remarkably consistent during the play years: young children tend to choose their friends as regular playmates, and their play together, in its complexity, self-disclosure, and reciprocity, becomes distinctively different from play with casual acquaintances (Hinde et al., 1985; Howes, 1983; Park et al., 1993).

What can account for differences in the "likeability" of children during the play years? One factor in this social dimension, as in others, is the nature of the parent-child relationship. Consistent with the relationship perspective, children who are most popular with their peers tend to have the most supportive parent-child relationships (Denham et al., 1991; Hart et al., 1992). For instance, young children whose parents used reasoning and explanations in their approach to discipline—typical of the authoritative parenting style—were found, in one study, to be their peers' most preferred playmates, probably because they were, as confirmed by observation, more cooperative and less aggressive when playing (Hart et al., 1992). Young children with supportive parents probably learn more readily how to interact congenially with others, and may approach encounters with age-mates expecting friendship rather than conflict. Parents can also shape early peer interactions more directly, by arranging informal play groups or after-school activities in their homes, or by coaching their offspring about how to take the initiative with another child (Ladd & Hart, 1992; Russell & Finnie, 1990).

Varieties of Play

Most developmentalists believe that play is the work of early childhood. Indeed, during the play years, play serves not only as a means of social interaction but also as an avenue for motor development, intellectual growth, and self-discovery. This is hardly surprising in light of the broad variety of types of play activity that can be observed among preschoolers (Garvey, 1990).

FIGURE 11.10 "Finger painting" frequently seems an understatement for sensorimotor work in this artistic medium, which often requires involvement of the whole arm, and more.

sensorimotor play Play that captures the pleasures of using the senses and one's motor abilities.

mastery play Any form of play that leads to a mastering of new skills, including motor skills as well as intellectual and language abilities.

Sensorimotor Play

Play that captures the pleasures of using the senses and motor abilities is called **sensorimotor play**. We have already seen that infants regularly engage in this kind of play, delighting in such things as watching a turning mobile or kicking the side of a bassinet. This pleasure in sensory experiences and motor skills continues throughout childhood. For example, given the chance, preschool children will happily explore the many sensory experiences that can be extracted from their food, feeling various textures as they mix noodles, meat, and gravy together with their hands, watching peas float after they put them in their milk, listening to the slurping sound they make as they suck in spaghetti, tasting unusual combinations such as cocoa sprinkled on lemonade. Children find similar opportunities for sensorimotor play in almost any context—in the sandbox, the bathtub, or a mud hole.

Mastery Play

Much of the physical play of childhood is **mastery play**, a term used to describe the play that helps children to master new skills. Children waste no opportunity to develop and practice their physical and intellectual skills. A simple walk down the block can become episode after episode of mastery play, as the child walks on top of a wall, then jumps over every crack in the sidewalk (so as not to "step on a crack and break your mother's back"), then skips, or walks backward, or races ahead. Along the way, there may be ice patches to slide across, or wind to run against, or puddles to jump over, or into. Similarly, making a snack, getting dressed, or singing along with music all are occasions for mastery play. Hand skills are also developed in mastery play, as when children intentionally tie knots in their shoelaces, put pegs in pegboards, or use a pair of scissors to make snippets of paper out of a single sheet.

Mastery play is most obvious when physical skills are involved, but it includes almost any skill the child feels motivated to learn. For instance, as children grow older, mastery play increasingly includes activities that are clearly intellectual, such as play with words or ideas. While the impulse to engage in mastery play comes naturally to preschool children, their parents' example and encouragement influence which skills a child will master.

FIGURE 11.11 Often the best way to recognize mastery play is not from the task or the result but from the child's facial expression while doing it. For these children, using their fine motor skills to make a collage is obviously mastery play.

Parents who enjoy throwing balls will find their children are much better catchers than the children of those who prefer spending their spare time watching TV (East & Hensley, 1985).

Rough-and-Tumble Play

Another type of physical play is called **rough-and-tumble play**. The aptness of its name is made clear by the following example:

> Jimmy, a preschooler, stands observing three of his male classmates building a sand castle. After a few moments he climbs on a tricycle and, smiling, makes a beeline for the same area, ravaging the structure in a single sweep. The builders immediately take off in hot pursuit of the hit-and-run phantom, yelling menacing threats of "come back here, you." Soon the tricycle halts and they pounce on him. The four of them tumble about in the grass amid shouts of glee, wrestling and punching until a teacher intervenes. The four wander off together toward the swings. [cited in Maccoby, 1980]

One distinguishing characteristic of rough-and-tumble play is its mimicry of aggression, a fact first noted in observations of young monkeys' wrestling, chasing, and pummeling of each other (Jones, 1976). The observers discovered that the key to the true nature of this seemingly hostile behavior was the monkeys' *play face*, that is, a mildly positive facial expression that seemed to suggest that the monkeys were having fun. The play face was an accurate clue, for only rarely, and apparently accidentally, did the monkeys actually hurt each other. (The same behaviors accompanied by a threatening expression usually meant a serious conflict was taking place.)

In human children, too, rough-and-tumble play is quite different from aggression, even though at first glance it may look the same. This distinction is important, for rough-and-tumble play is a significant part of the daily activities of many preschool children. In general, rough-and-tumble play, unlike aggression, is not only fun for children; it is also constructive, developing interactive skills as well as gross motor skills (Pellegrini, 1987). Adults who are unsure whether they are observing a fight that should be

rough-and-tumble play   Play such as wrestling, chasing, and hitting that mimics aggression but actually occurs purely in fun, with no intent to harm.

FIGURE 11.12 For many young children, especially boys who know each other well, rough-and-tumble play brings the most pleasure. Many developmentalists believe that this kind of play teaches social skills—such as how to compete without destroying a friendship—that are hard to learn any other way.

broken up or a social activity that should be allowed to continue may be helped by knowing that facial expression is as telltale in children as it is in monkeys: children almost always smile, and often laugh, in rough-and-tumble play, whereas they frown and scowl in real fighting.

Rough-and-tumble play is universal, occurring everywhere children play. It has been observed in Japan, Kenya, and Mexico, as well as in every income and ethnic group in North America, Europe, and Australia (Boulton & Smith, 1989). There are some cultural and situational differences, however. One of the most important is space and supervision: children are much more likely to instigate rough-and-tumble play when they have room to run and chase, and when adults are not directly nearby. In addition, rough-and-tumble play usually occurs among children who have had considerable social experience, often with each other. Not surprisingly, then, among children in nursery schools, newcomers, younger children, and only-children take longer to join in rough-and-tumble play than to participate in any other form of play (Garvey, 1976; Shea, 1981). Gender differences are also evident in rough-and-tumble play, and these, too, vary from culture to culture. In some cultures, such as traditional Moslem ones, girls almost never engage in rough-and-tumble play. Among North Americans, girls sometimes engage in such play, but not as often as boys do: one carefully controlled study found that boys spent three times as much time in rough-and-tumble play as girls did (DiPietro, 1981).

Sociodramatic Play

In **sociodramatic play**, children act out various roles and themes in stories of their own creation. Besides allowing children to have great fun, sociodramatic play provides a way for children to explore and rehearse the social roles they observe around them, and to examine personal concerns in a nonthreatening manner. This function of sociodramatic play is clearly apparent when children enact husband-and-wife stories, or scenarios involving sickness or death, or stories with monsters and superheroes.

The beginnings of sociodramatic play can be seen in a toddler's feeding, cuddling, or punishing a doll or stuffed animal. However, the frequency and complexity of sociodramatic play greatly increase between the ages of 2 and 6 (Howes, 1992; Rubin et al., 1983). One reason is that, as young children are expanding their theory of mind, or psychological understanding of other people (see Chapter 10), they practice what they are learning in their play scenarios (Goncu, 1993; Harris & Kavanaugh, 1993; Lillard, 1993a, 1993b, 1994). For instance, young children can use sociodramatic play to try out various means of managing emotions, whether it involves reenacting scary situations in the dark, or offering comfort to a frightened doll, or rehearsing courageous action in a difficult situation (Bretherton, 1989). In a sense, sociodramatic play is a testing ground for early psychological knowledge. Its growth is also related to the development of self-understanding in early childhood. In sociodramatic play, roles are assumed, and then discarded with ease, because of the child's underlying confidence in knowing who he or she is—and is not.

The nature and significance of sociodramatic play have been vividly documented in classic research by Catherine Garvey (1990), who found many examples of sociodramatic play when she studied forty-eight

FIGURE 11.13 Getting all dressed up to go grocery shopping is a form of sociodramatic play that combines elements of reality and fantasy for 3-year-old Lucy and Rachel. As they grow older, such play will typically become more creative and more dramatic, although not necessarily any more realistic.

sociodramatic play Pretend play in which children act out various roles and themes in stories of their own creation.

preschool children ranging in age from 2 years and 10 months to 5 years and 7 months. Each child was paired with a playmate the same age; then both children were placed in a well-equipped playroom to do whatever they wanted.

Many of these pairs, even some of the youngest, chose to engage in sociodramatic play. The 2- and 3-year-olds often played a simple mother-and-baby game; older children sometimes played a parent-child game or, if they were of different sexes, a husband-wife game (which tended to be a somewhat more complicated interaction, since it usually involved making some compromises about who did what). Older children created many other roles, including Hansel and Gretel, Dr. Jekyll and Dr. Hines (sic), and their own version of the latest TV shows. Although Garvey found that most sociodramatic play involves standard plots such as these, she also noted other types of scenarios, such as one player announcing that a child or pet is sick or dead and the other player automatically becoming the healer, administering food or medicine, or performing surgery, to restore life and health. In a third standard type of drama, one child announces a "sudden threat" (the appearance of a monster, for instance), then both children take the role of victim or defender, attacking or fleeing. The episode can end happily ("I got him!") or unhappily ("He ate me. I'm dead."), unfolding naturally yet without prearrangement.

As suggested by the last example, sociodramatic play is, for the most part, creative and fluid, with children making up and embellishing the drama as they go along. Yet underlying the seemingly improvisatory nature of this play are surprisingly complex rules and structures enabling children to smoothly coordinate their pretend activity (Garvey, 1990). Preceding the onset of play, for example, children negotiate the themes they will enact, the roles they will assume, and the imaginary setting. These joint decisions are provisional, however, and can be changed at a moment's notice by any actor ("Let's say this is a secret cave. OK?" "OK!"). Children use vocal inflections and other cues to signal when they are acting in-role or are instead providing out-of-role instructions or questions ("I'm feeling sick." "Really?" "No, pretend."). And preschoolers are quick to correct play partners who assume roles deemed inappropriate (such as an older boy wanting to play "mommy") or who play their roles inadequately (failing to "fall dead" when shot in a game of cops-and-robbers, for instance, or talking too much when playing the role of "baby").

Sociodramatic play such as this not only helps children try out and rehearse social roles; it also allows them to express their fears and fantasies and to learn to cooperate.

Gender Roles and Stereotypes

An important feature of self-understanding during the play years is the child's developing understanding of gender roles and personal gender identity. Gender preferences and play patterns emerge early in childhood. Not surprisingly, therefore, preschoolers have quite remarkable ideas about gender. Consider the following account by a leading researcher of gender identity, Sandra Bem (1989), concerning the day her young son Jeremy

FIGURE 11.14 Even in today's world, preschool boys and girls tend to engage in play that is gender-stereotyped, especially when playing with a good friend of the same sex. While some barriers have fallen, they have been more on the girls' side than the boys'. One could imagine these girls swordfighting, for example, but it seems unlikely that the boys would allow themselves to play patty-cake. The question, still unanswered with certainty, is why.

naively decided to wear barrettes to nursery school. Several times that day, another little boy insisted that Jeremy must be a girl because "only girls wear barrettes." After repeatedly asserting that "wearing barrettes doesn't matter; being a boy means having a penis and testicles," Jeremy finally pulled down his pants as a way of making his point more convincingly. The boy was not impressed. He simply said, "Everybody has a penis; only girls wear barrettes."

Children learn about gender very early (Huston, 1985). Most 2-year-olds know whether they are boys or girls, and can identify strangers as mommies or daddies. By age 3, children have a rudimentary understanding of the permanence of their own sex and can consistently apply gender labels (Fagot et al., 1992; Martin & Little, 1990). Further, children's behavior acknowledges traditional distinctions between boys and girls at a very early age. By age 2, children prefer to play with gender-typed toys (dolls versus trucks, for example) (Weinraub et al., 1984), and at age 3, they enact gender-typed roles (nurses versus soldiers) (Eisenberg-Berg et al., 1979; Huston, 1983, 1985; O'Brien et al., 1983). At these young ages, children also have definite ideas of typical male and female behavior and misbehavior, believing that girls are more likely than boys to clean the house and to "talk a lot" and that boys are more likely than girls to mow the lawn and to hit others (Kuhn et al., 1978; Weinraub et al., 1984).

By age 6, these notions become full-blown prejudices, as most children (even those from feminist homes) express stereotypic ideas of what each sex should do, wear, or feel (Huston, 1983; Martin et al., 1990). Indeed, by age 4, preschool girls and boys are quite judgmental about their peers' choice of gender-appropriate toys and play patterns (Lobel & Menashri, 1993; Roopnarine, 1984). The boy who wants to help the girls dress dolls or the girl who wants to be one of the space warriors is likely to be soundly criticized by his or her friends. And despite efforts from many quarters to promote the idea of gender equality, these preferences and stereotypes increase in strength and influence as children grow into the grade-school years and adolescence (Maccoby, 1990).

It is not surprising that a young child's awareness of gender roles and stereotypes emerges, in part, through interaction with other children. Indeed, consistent with the relationship perspective, a number of develop-

A CLOSER LOOK

Gender Distinctions in Play Patterns

Some differences between males and females, not only in body size and shape but also in motor skills and activity level, are apparent throughout childhood, as well as throughout the life span. Such differences have fascinating, but controversial, implications for other male-female differences that emerge in childhood, such as in accident rates, academic achievement, and, one we will examine here, play patterns. The basic question for social scientists is whether such differences are **sex differences**—arising from the differences between male and female chromosomes and hormones—or **gender differences**—arising from the special customs, values, and expectations that a particular culture attaches to one sex or the other.

In the preschool years, and indeed, throughout childhood, boys, compared with girls, typically spend more playtime outside, engaging in gross motor activities like running, climbing, and playing ball. Many, if not most, of boys' activities involve playful aggression and competition, as in rough-and-tumble play. Girls, by contrast, spend more time indoors, typically engaging in activities that demand fine motor coordination and a relatively lower activity level, such as arts and crafts, sewing, or dressing and undressing their dolls. When they do play outside, girls are more likely to engage in cooperative, turn-taking games (Beal, 1994; Crum & Eckert, 1985; Harper & Sanders, 1975). Take jump rope, for example, a girls' outdoor activity much more than a boys'. Two rope turners must synchronize their efforts with each other and with the jumpers, who, in turn, are not so much competing as displaying their skills—to the audience of other jumpers, who contribute by chanting rhythmic rhymes as they wait their turn.

Another distinction in children's play involves choice of playmates: as noted earlier, boys tend to play with boys, and girls, with girls (Beal, 1994; Maccoby, 1990). This preference for same-sex play partners, as well as the tendency for masculine play to be more aggressive and active than feminine play, is evident even in infancy (Maccoby, 1980) and becomes more apparent as children grow older (La Freniere et al., 1984). The same general trends are found in

every culture (Whiting & Edward, 1988), every historical period (Herron & Sutton-Smith, 1971), and—as you can easily confirm by observing the activities at your local playground—persist in the 1990s.

Are these sex differences or gender differences? Certainly there are some biological differences between the sexes that might help to explain their play differences. As noted in Chapter 9, for example, boys, on average, are slightly taller and more muscular, with less body fat, than girls, and their forearm strength is notably greater. In addition, boys' higher activity level, which is evident even in infancy, becomes increasingly apparent: by age 8, only about one girl in five is as active as the average boy (Eaton & Yu, 1989). Girls, on the other hand, mature more quickly than boys in a number of ways, including bone maturation and their dexterity and control in fine motor skills.

Thus if some children's innate activity level is high, and they are physically suited to activities involving arm strength, it seems quite natural that they (mostly boys) will want to engage in play that involves running, climbing, and throwing, as well as in rough-and-tumble play. On the other hand, if some children have a relatively low activity level, and if they are physically suited to activities involving fine motor skills more than strength, it seems equally natural that they (mostly girls) will enjoy sitting and working with their hands.

The fact is, however, that such physical differences as do exist between the sexes during the preschool years are slight. Until puberty, both sexes follow very similar paths of biological development, being about the same size, and able to do generally the same things, at the same age (Tanner, 1978). In those abilities in which one sex is more advanced or skilled than another, the advantage is small compared to the advantages of individual genetic endowment and/or repeated practice. This means that in every ability in which boys, in general, excel, most boys know several girls their age who are better than they are. The reverse is equally true.

This fact suggests that, if children played at whatever

mental theorists believe that gender differences are primarily displayed and intensified in the context of children's relationships, especially peer relationships (Maccoby, 1990). To begin with, given a group of age-mates, young children inevitably segregate into all-boy and all-girl groups because, in part, of the different styles of interaction that emerge in the peer groups of each sex. Boys' groups are larger, and are often oriented toward competition and dominance, with members using teasing, boasting, and exaggera-

sex differences Differences between males and females that arise from biological influences.

activities seemed within their capacity, many girls would be regularly engaged in "boys" games, and vice versa. In fact, this often occurs at home if a particular child has no playmates other than a sibling or neighbor of the other sex (Bloch, 1989). However, mixed-sex play is generally not the case, especially in public places such as school playgrounds. This suggests that social pressures add to, and foster, the biological differences that exist. Parents and other adults typically encourage children, directly and indirectly, to play with peers of their own sex. They also tend to give them "gender-appropriate" toys, thereby strengthening whatever physical differences there may actually be (Sutton-Smith, 1986).

In addition, children, as noted earlier, socialize each other into gender-typical play by playing in same-sex groups. The pattern becomes more distinct as preschoolers grow older. As one teacher notes:

> Kindergarten is a triumph of sexual self-stereotyping. No amount of adult subterfuge or propaganda deflects the five-year-old's passion for segregation by sex. Children of this age think they have invented the differences between boys and girls and, as with any new invention, must prove that it works. [Paley, 1984]

As this observation suggests, the intensity of children's gender stereotyping creates a great deal of social pressure for children to conform. Because of this, if a child wanted to spend a great deal of time in a particular activity favored by the other sex, he or she would probably hesitate, since his or her favorite playmates would be doing something else—not to mention the fact that girls rarely welcome the lone boy who wants to play hopscotch, and boys usually turn away the girl who wants to play football. By elementary school, when there are sufficient children of the same sex and age to play with, gender roles are firmly entrenched.

What, then, are the implications of sex differences in children's play patterns? Cross-cultural research finds that, in all societies, children are encouraged to engage in activities that teach them their culture's traditional adult roles. Indeed, in those societies where adults have quite distinct gender roles, girls and boys virtually never play together (Whiting & Edward, 1988). In modern technological societies, where adult roles are not so rigid, boys and girls do sometimes spontaneously play together, but usually in games where one sex teams up against the other. More significant, in modern societies, the gender-specific play of boys may serve to ready them for the largely male-dominated business world, where self-assertion and competitiveness lead to success. The activities of girls, by contrast, teach them cooperation, patience, and relative passivity, qualities that might help them in family life, but would handicap them in many careers.

This raises an important question for the future. Given that women are increasingly working outside the home, and that men are becoming more involved in family life, should preschool girls be urged to play rougher, more competitive games, and boys to spend more time in gentler, cooperative play? Should both sexes be encouraged, or even pushed, to play together? Or should parents and teachers remain neutral, allowing play patterns to emerge as they will?

Obviously, there is no easy answer. Not only is this a question on which it seems impossible to sort out the influences of nature and nurture; it is a question framed by a wide array of individual and cultural values. Some regard the two sexes as "opposites" and believe that gender differentiation should be encouraged; others believe that the sexes are much more similar than dissimilar, and that, as much as possible, gender distinctions should be obliterated. In the end, the emergence and consolidation of differences in play—and in a wide variety of other gender-typed behaviors—depend on the values of caregivers, of society, and, increasingly, of children themselves.

gender differences Differences between males and females that arise from the special customs, values, and expectations that a particular culture attaches to one sex or the other.

tion to establish themselves among their peers. By contrast, girls' groups are smaller and more exclusive, with members using cooperation and support to consolidate friendship. Consequently, children become increasingly comfortable with the interactional style of their same-sex groups, and increasingly avoid encounters with children of the other sex. Thus their friendships lead them to imitate, model, and mutually reinforce gender-typical behavior.

Three Theories of Gender-Role Development

We have already discussed the nature-nurture issue several times, and you are well aware that developmentalists disagree about what proportion of observed sex differences is biological—perhaps a matter of hormones, of brain structures, or of body size and musculature—and what proportion is environmental (Beal, 1994). (See A Closer Look on pp. 398–399 for an illustration of this controversy.) However, even for differences that seem most closely related to nurture, theorists hypothesize various reasons for their existence. Specifically, they ask: What is the origin of gender-role differences that children develop during the preschool years? The answers provided by three of the major psychological theories offer very different perspectives on how significant relationships shape this key component of psychosocial growth.

Psychoanalytic Theories

Freud (1938) called the period from about age 3 to 7 the *phallic stage*, because he believed its center of focus is the penis. At about age 3 or 4, said Freud, a boy becomes aware of his penis, beings to masturbate, and develops sexual feelings toward his mother, who has always been an important love object for him. These feelings make him jealous of his father—so jealous, in fact, that, according to Freud, every son secretly wants to replace his father. Freud called this phenomenon the **Oedipus complex**, after Oedipus, son of a king in Greek mythology. Abandoned as an infant and raised in a distant kingdom, Oedipus later returned to his birthplace, and, not realizing who they were, killed his father and married his mother. When he discovered what he had done, he blinded himself in a spasm of guilt.

According to Freud, little boys feel horribly guilty for having the feelings and thoughts that characterize the Oedipus complex and imagine that their father will inflict terrible punishments on them if he ever finds out about these thoughts. They cope with this guilt and fear by means of **identification**, a defense mechanism through which people imagine themselves to be like a person more powerful than themselves. In a sense, if they cannot replace the father, young boys strive to be *like* the father. As part of their identification with their father, boys copy their father's masculine behavior and adopt his moral standards. Through this process, they develop their superego, to control the forbidden impulses of the id (see page 44).

Freud offered two overlapping descriptions of the phallic stage as it occurs in little girls. One form, the **Electra complex**, follows the reverse pattern of the Oedipus complex: the little girl wants to get rid of her mother and become intimate with her father. In the other version, the little girl becomes jealous of boys because they have a penis, an emotion called *penis envy*. Somehow the girl decides that her mother is to blame for this state of affairs, so she becomes angry at her and decides the next best thing to having a penis of her own is to become sexually attractive so that someone with a penis, preferably her father, will love her (Freud, 1933/1965). (See A Closer Look, p. 401)

In both versions, the consequences of this stage are the same for girls as for boys: guilt and fear, which are resolved by the child's adopting gender-appropriate behavior and the moral code of his or her same-sex parent.

Oedipus complex In the phallic stage of psychosexual development, the sexual desire that boys have for their mother and the related hostility they have toward their father.

identification A defense mechanism that makes a person take on the role and attitudes of someone more powerful than himself or herself.

Electra complex In the phallic stage of psychosocial development, the female version of the Oedipus complex in which girls have sexual feelings for their father and accompanying hostility toward their mother.

A CLOSER LOOK

Professor Berger and Freud

As a woman, and as a mother of four daughters, I have always regarded Freud's theory of female sexual development as ridiculous, not to mention antifemale. I am not alone in this opinion. Psychologists generally agree that Freud's explanation of female sexual and moral development is one of the weaker parts of this theory, reflecting the values of middle-class Victorian society at the turn of the century more than any universal pattern. Many female psychoanalysts (e.g., Horney, 1967; Klein, 1957; Lerner, 1978) are particularly critical of Freud's idea of penis envy. They believe that girls envy, not the male's sexual organ, but the higher status the male is generally accorded. They also suggest that boys may experience a corresponding emotion in the form of womb and breast envy, wishing that they could have babies and suckle them.

However, my own view of Freud's theory as complete nonsense has been modified somewhat by the following experiences with my four daughters when each was in the age range of Freud's phallic stage. The first "Electra episode" occurred in a conversation with my oldest daughter, Bethany, when she was 4 or so.

Bethany: When I grow up, I'm going to marry Daddy.
   I: *But Daddy's married to me.*
Bethany: That's all right. When I grow up, you'll probably be dead.
   I: *(Determined to stick up for myself) Daddy's older than me, so when I'm dead, he'll probably be dead, too.*
Bethany: That's O.K. I'll marry him when he gets born again [Our family's religious beliefs, incidentally, do not include reincarnation.]

At this point, I couldn't think of a good reply. Bethany must have seen my face fall and taken pity on me.

Bethany: Don't worry Mommy. After you get born again, you can be our baby.

The second episode was also in a conversation, this time with my daughter Rachel, when she was about 5.

Rachel: When I get married, I'm going to marry Daddy.
   I: *Daddy's already married to me.*
Rachel: (With the joy of having discovered a wonderful solution) Then we can have a double wedding!

The third episode was considerably more graphic. It took the form of a "valentine" left on my husband's pillow by my daughter Elissa, who was about 8 at the time. It is reproduced in the next column.

Finally, by the time my youngest daughter, Sarah, turned 5, she also expressed the desire to marry my husband. Her response to my statement that she couldn't marry him because he is already married to me reveals one of the disadvantages of not being able to ban TV in our household: "Oh yes, a man can have two wives. I saw it on television."

I am not the only feminist developmentalist to find Freud's theories on this matter surprisingly perceptive. Nancy Datan (1986) writes about the Oedipal conflict: "I have a son who was once five years old. From that day to this, I have never thought Freud mistaken."

Obviously, these bits of "evidence" do not prove that Freud was correct. But Freud's description of the phallic stage seems not to be as bizarre as it first appears to be.

Theodore Lidz (1976), a respected developmental psychiatrist, offers a plausible explanation of the process evident in my daughters and in many other children. Lidz believes that all children must go through an Oedipal "transition," overcoming "the intense bonds to their mothers that were essential to their satisfactory pre-Oedipal development." As part of this process, children imagine becoming an adult and, quite logically, taking the place of the adult of their own sex whom they know best, their father or mother. This idea must be dispelled before the sexual awakening of early adolescence, otherwise an "incestuous bond" will threaten the nuclear family, prevent the child's extrafamilial socialization, and block his or her emergence as a well-adjusted adult. According to Lidz, the details of the Oedipal transition vary from family to family, but successful desexualization of parent-child love is essential for healthy maturity.

Learning Theories

Learning theorists take another view of gender-role development during early childhood. They believe that virtually all role patterns are learned, rather than inborn, and that parents, teachers, and society are responsible for whatever gender-role ideas and behaviors the child demonstrates.

Preschool children, according to learning theory, are reinforced for behaving in the ways deemed appropriate for their sex and punished for behaving inappropriately. In some ways, research bears this out. Parents, peers, and teachers are all more likely to reward "gender-appropriate" behavior than "gender-inappropriate behavior" (Fagot et al., 1992; Fagot & Hagen, 1991; Huston, 1983). Parents may commend their sons for not crying when hurt, for example, but caution their daughters more about the hazards of rough play. As noted earlier, this kind of learning may be strongest within sex-segregated peer groups, where, beginning in the early preschool years, children acquire gender-typical play styles and social skills, including strategies for influencing others (Maccoby, 1988, 1989).

Interestingly, boys are criticized more than girls for wanting to play with "gender-inappropriate" toys, and are rewarded more for playing with toys "for boys." Even between ages 1 and 5, boys are discouraged from wanting to play with dolls (Fagot & Hagen, 1991; Lytton & Romney, 1991). Furthermore, fathers are more likely to expect their girls to be "feminine" and their boys to be "masculine" than mothers are. As we saw in Chapter 8, fathers are more gentle with their daughters and are more likely to engage in rough-and-tumble play with their sons. Thus, in American society at least, gender-role conformity seems to be especially important for males.

Modeling

Social-learning theorists (Bandura, 1977; Mischel, 1970, 1979; Sears et al., 1965) say that children learn much of their gender and moral behavior by observing other people, especially people whom they perceive as nurturing, powerful, and similar to themselves. For all these reasons, parents are important models during childhood, although models in the neighborhood, at school or day care, and in the popular media are also very influential.

Social-learning theorists are not surprised when preschool children seem precociously and dogmatically conscious of gender roles, even when the parents espouse less traditional views. In this case, actions speak louder than words, and most adults are more gender-stereotyped, in their behaviors as well as self-concept, during the years when their children are young than at any other time in the life span (Feldman et al., 1981; Gutmann, 1975). Imagine a typical contemporary child-free couple who try to avoid traditional gender roles, both of them being employed and both sharing the housework. Then the wife becomes pregnant. The most likely sequel is that she will take a maternity leave, quit her job, or work part-time. This traditional pattern is reinforced by the biological fact that only the woman can breast-feed, the sociological fact that relatives and friends generally expect the woman to provide most infant care, and the economic fact that the man's salary is usually higher than the woman's. If the wife stays home, it is likely that she will do more than half the housework. If she does go back to work full-time, typically she will find another woman to care for her child, either at home or in a day-care center. In addition, influences from the broader society, including everything from who runs for president, to who

FIGURE 11.15 While parents almost all believe that they should, and that they do, treat their boys and girls the same, the fact is that in two-parent households, fathers share more activities with sons, and mothers share more activities than with daughters. If the parents divide household tasks in the typical way, with the yard, car, and garbage being the man's responsibility, and cooking, cleaning, and shopping the woman's, the children will most likely follow traditional gender roles.

FIGURE 11.16 Advertising images, interpreted by impressionable minds, may be part of the reason preschoolers tend to hold stereotypic ideas of male and female attributes, particularly regarding hairstyle, clothing, and behavior.

gender constancy The realization in children at age 4 or 5 that they are permanently male or female.

gender schemas The ways children organize their knowledge about people in terms of gender-based categories and evaluations.

does what in television commercials, to which characters take the initiative in children's books, teach children those behaviors that are considered gender-appropriate (Barnett, 1986; Beal, 1994; Huston, 1983).

Cognitive Theories

In explaining gender-identity and gender-role development, cognitive theorists focus on children's understanding of gender and male-female differences, and on how children's changing perceptions of gender motivate their efforts to behave consistently with their gender role. Two theories of gender identity have been proposed by cognitive theorists.

According to *cognitive-developmental theory* (Kohlberg, 1966, 1969), young preschoolers' understanding of gender is limited by their belief that sex differences depend on differences in appearance or behavior rather than on biology. Thus boys believe that they could become mommies; girls think they could be daddies; and children of both sexes think boys would be girls if they wore dresses and girls would be boys if they cut their hair very short. It is not until after age 4 or 5 that children realize that they are permanently male or female on the basis of their unchanging biology (Bem, 1989). This realization, called **gender constancy**, motivates, in turn, children's efforts to learn about gender roles and to adopt appropriate gender-role behavior.

There is strong evidence for the first part of this view. Lawrence Kohlberg and Dorothy Ullian (1974), for example, interviewed boys and girls between the ages of 3 and 18 and found that, by age 6, children understood that sex is a permanent characteristic and were pleased to be whatever sex they were. However, researchers have failed to confirm that an awareness of gender constancy underlies children's knowledge of gender-role behavior or their motivation to adopt appropriate behavior. Instead, children have a surprisingly sophisticated understanding of gender roles and behave in many sex-typed ways long before they have acquired an awareness of gender constancy (Fagot, 1985; Fagot & Leinbach, 1993; Huston, 1985; Martin, 1993; Martin & Little, 1990).

In response to this limitation of cognitive-developmental theory, researchers who support *gender-schema theory* (Bem, 1981, 1984; Martin & Halverson, 1981) argue that young children's motivation to behave in gender-appropriate ways derives instead from their **gender schemas**, that is, the ways they organize their knowledge about people in terms of gender-based categories and evaluations. A gender schema might dictate that women care for young children, for example, or that men do heavy labor. Children acquire gender schemas quite early in life because our society makes many gender-related distinctions between people that young children can easily comprehend. Thus, as soon as children start to become aware of gender schemas and can accurately label themselves as male or female, they try to conform to these schemas and use them to evaluate others' behavior. In support of this view, Levy and Carter (1989) found that children's accuracy in attributing gender stereotypes to others was related to development in their knowledge of gender schemas. Moreover, as children mature, they become increasingly *self*-socializing. Accordingly, their conformity to gender norms derives more from their own self-approval for doing so (or their anticipated self-criticism for failing to do so) than from the reactions of other people (Bussey & Bandura, 1992).

In a sense, each of the theories we have discussed points to different, but important, ingredients in gender-role development in early childhood and the role that close relationships play in this development. To psychoanalytic theorists, the emotional attachments to parents and identification with the same-sex parent are most significant. Learning theorists, by contrast, emphasize reinforcement and modeling processes that occur not just at home but in all the child's social environments. To cognitive theorists, in turn, the child's developing understanding of gender schemas is paramount, together with the characteristics that constitute these schemas in society at large. As we have seen, these theories vary also in the extent to which parents—who may or may not emphasize traditional gender roles at home—are viewed as the most significant influences on the gender-role development of their offspring. In this respect, learning and cognitive theorists point out what most parents themselves acknowledge: there is an overabundance of sources outside the family through which children learn about expected gender-role behavior.

A Different Goal: Androgyny

In recent years, many developmentalists, and many parents as well, have encouraged the concept of *androgyny*. As a biological term, of course, "androgyny" refers to an organism's having both male and female sexual characteristics. As developmentalists use the term, **androgyny** refers to a person's having a balance of what are commonly regarded as "male" and "female" psychological characteristics. The idea behind the emphasis on androgyny is to break through the restrictiveness of traditional gender roles and to encourage the individual to define himself or herself primarily as a human being, rather than as male or female. An additional goal has been to counter the misconception that masculinity and femininity are opposites.

Several measures of androgyny have been developed in which a person chooses from a list of adjectives those that most closely describe his or her personality (Bem, 1974; Spence & Helmreich, 1978). For instance, someone who scores high in instrumental characteristics such as aggression, dominance, competitiveness, and activity, and low in expressive characteristics such as gentleness, kindness, emotionality, and warmth, would be rated as typically masculine; someone with opposite scores would be rated typically feminine. A person who scored high in both sets of characteristics would be considered androgynous.

Thus, androgynous men and women share many of the same personality characteristics, instead of following the traditional gender-role patterns. For instance, traditional males rate significantly higher than traditional females on a personality trait labeled "dominant-ambitious," but androgynous males and females score about the same, because the men see themselves as less dominant than the traditional male does, while the women see themselves as more dominant than the traditional female does (Wiggins & Holzmuller, 1978). Androgynous people are nurturing as well as independent and try to be neither unemotional nor passive. They are more flexible in their sex roles, able to display the best qualities of both of the traditional stereotypes.

FIGURE 11.17 This daughter's evident delight in "driving" her daddy's fire truck mirrors her father's pleasure in her. It is worth noting, however, that our culture generally allows greater sex-role latitude to girls than to boys. Would this father be equally pleased if his son showed a strong interest in dressmaking?

androgyny Having the personality traits traditionally ascribed to both males and females.

Certainly in contemporary society, androgyny seems an admirable and highly functional goal. Yet comprehensive longitudinal research on the development and effects of an androgynous persona is lacking, and the research that is available shows mixed results—or at least different effects at different points in the life span. Much of the research on androgyny has shown that androgynous individuals are generally more competent and have a higher sense of self-esteem than people who follow traditional gender-role behavior (Bem, 1986; Spence, 1985). And while more recent research has generally found that androgynous college students, particularly, have higher self-esteem than more traditional young adults, at certain other stages of life, this does not seem to be the case. At age 16, for instance, those who consider themselves relatively traditional for their sex also tend to be high in self-esteem. This is particularly true for boys of average intellectual achievement, who take pride in having masculine qualities and in not having feminine ones (Allgood-Merten & Jean, 1991).

Overall, the fact that gender awareness and gender-role distinctions develop so early in a young child's life suggests that on some level young children welcome the simplistic clarity of a male-female dichotomy and resist the androgynous ideal. In fact, Sandra Bem (1986), one of the designers of an androgyny scale, recognizes that ideas about gender differences are useful to help young children organize their perceptions of the adult world. The problem comes, if at all, when children and their parents remain rigid in applying these schemas, causing the fixed stereotyping to stifle the full development of the child or the adult. Thus the child's gender-role concepts, like the child's definition of selfhood, mode of play, and all the other themes of this chapter, should change with exposure and maturity. These changes help the preschool child gradually become ready for the next stage of life, the school years, which are presented in the next trio of chapters.

SUMMARY

The Self and the Social World

1. An increasing sense of self-understanding helps children to increase their social understanding and to become more skilled in their relationships with others. In turn, social interaction helps young children to learn about who they are and contributes to their self-understanding and self-evaluation.

2. Emotional development during the preschool years includes not only the consolidation of self-conscious emotions like pride, shame, guilt, and embarrassment but also a greater understanding of the causes and consequences of emotion and a growing ability to cope with emotions.

Relationships and Psychosocial Growth

3. The relationship perspective holds that psychosocial growth emerges mainly from experience in close relationships, which can be mutually influential (such as when young children from troubled families have difficulties in their peer relationships).

4. Parent-child interaction is complex, with no simple answers about the best way to raise a child. However, in general, authoritative parents, who are warm and loving but willing to set and enforce reasonable limits, have children who are happy, self-confident, and competent. Highly punitive parents tend to produce aggressive children, while children with very lenient parents often lack self-control.

5. Although parenting style is an important element in shaping a child's development, it is only one of many such

elements, and its importance should not be overestimated. Often, children shape their parents' style of child-rearing as well as being shaped by it, chiefly through the effects of their temperament and their changing developmental needs. Parenting is also affected by the nature of the marital relationship, and the cultural, ethnic, socioeconomic, and community context of the family.

6. In many respects, children's relationships with their brothers and sisters are uniquely different from relationships with parents and peers. Although siblings may quarrel, they are also likely to show each other more nurturance and cooperation than they show others. One of the most important factors in shaping the relationship between siblings is the relationship each child shares with the parent.

7. Peer relationships are another important relational influence during the play years. In addition to providing an arena for developing their social skills, peer relationships help preschoolers learn about friendship.

8. Playing with other children requires preschoolers to take responsibility for maintaining social interaction through sharing and reciprocity. These features are evident whether the play concerns sensorimotor, mastery, rough-and-tumble, or sociodramatic play—the last of which also permits children to explore social roles, examine personal concerns, and learn to cooperate.

Gender Roles and Stereotypes

9. While developmentalists agree that children begin to learn gender roles and gender identity during early childhood, they disagree about how this process occurs. Psychoanalytic theorists stress the fears and fantasies that motivate children to identify with the same-sex parent; learning theorists emphasize the reinforcement and modeling that children experience at home and elsewhere; and cognitive theorists remind us that young children are slowly constructing an understanding of gender that motivates them to behave in gender-appropriate ways.

10. Androgynous individuals, who are less rigid in their gender roles and seem to have a high amount of both male and female characteristics, tend to be more confident and have a higher sense of self-esteem than those who follow more traditional gender-role behavior.

KEY TERMS

initiative versus guilt (374)	**mastery play** (393)
relationship perspective (377)	**rough-and-tumble play** (394)
authoritarian parenting (378)	**sociodramatic play** (395)
permissive parenting (378)	**sex differences** (398)
authoritative parenting (378)	**gender differences** (399)
democratic-indulgent parenting (379)	**Oedipus complex** (400)
	identification (400)
rejecting-neglecting parenting (379)	**Electra complex** (400)
	gender constancy (403)
traditional parenting (379)	**gender schemas** (403)
sensorimotor play (393)	**androgyny** (404)

KEY QUESTIONS

1. How does self-understanding grow during the play years? What difference does this make for young children's relationships with others?

2. How do family interactions contribute to the growth of emotional understanding in preschoolers?

3. What is the relationship perspective? What new insights does it provide for gaining an understanding of early social development?

4. Describe the three basic patterns of parenting, according to Baumrind's research.

5. What are some of the influences that contribute to the complexity of parenting?

6. How do children influence the nature of the parent-child relationship? How is this relationship affected in turn by social factors outside the family?

7. What word best describes sibling relationships, and why?

8. How do peer relationships change during the preschool years? What factors contribute to differences in the "likability" of children, in the view of their peers?

9. Distinguish among the four primary kinds of play. What are the benefits of sociodramatic play to preschoolers?

10. What are the similarities, and differences, in the views of psychoanalytic, learning, and cognitive theorists about the origins of gender roles in early childhood?

11. How do gender constancy and gender schemas contribute to the growth of gender-role behavior?

12. Describe the personality characteristics of androgynous individuals.

Biosocial Development

Cognitive Development

Psychosocial Development

Brain and Nervous System

The brain continues to develop faster than any other part of the body, attaining 00 percent of its adult weight by the time the child is 5 years old. Myelination proceeds at different rates in various areas of the brain, but the overall coordination between the two halves of the brain, as well as the child's ability to settle down and concentrate when necessary, gradually improves.

Motor Skills

As the child becomes stronger, and body proportions become more adultlike, gross motor skills, such as running and jumping, improve dramatically. Fine motor skills, such as writing and drawing, develop more slowly. Gender differences in motor skills become apparent.

Maltreatment

Child abuse and neglect, potential problems at every age, are particularly likely in homes with many children and few personal or community resources. During early childhood, home-visitation programs may be a useful preventive measure.

Cognitive Skills

Many cognitive abilities, including some related to number, memory, and problem solving, develop during early childhood. Throughout this period, children begin to develop a theory of mind, as they take into account the ideas and emotions of others. Social interaction, particularly in the form of guided participation, is both a cause and a consequence of this cognitive advancement. At the same time, however, child's thinking can be quite illogical.

Language

Language abilities develop rapidly; by the age of 6, the average child knows 10,000 words and demonstrates extensive grammatical knowledge. Children also learn to adjust their communication to their audience, and use language to help themselves learn. Specific contexts affect the particulars of what, and how much, children say and understand. Preschool education helps children develop language and express themselves.

Emotions and Personality Development

Self-concept emerges, usually with a positive slant. Children boldly initiate new activities, especially if they are praised for their endeavors. As their social and cognitive skills develop, children engage in ever more complex and imaginative types of play, sometimes by themselves and, increasingly, with others.

Parent-Child Interaction

As children become more independent and try to exercise control over their environment, supervising the child's activities becomes more difficult. Some parenting styles are more effective than others in encouraging the child to develop both autonomy and self-control. At the same time, parenting styles are influenced by cultural and community standards, various environmental pressures, and the characteristics of the child.

Gender Roles

Increasingly, children develop stereotypic concepts of sex differences in appearance and gender differences in behavior. The precise role of nature and nurture in this process is unclear.

PART IV The School Years

If someone asked you to pick the best years of the entire life span, you might choose the years from 7 to 11 and defend your choice persuasively. To begin with, physical development is usually almost problem-free, making it easy to master dozens of new skills. With regard to cognitive development, most children are able to learn quickly and think logically, providing the topic is not too abstract. Moreover, they are usually eager to learn, mastering new concepts, new vocabulary, and new skills with a combination of enthusiasm, perseverance, and curiosity that makes them a joy to teach.

Finally, the social world of middle childhood seems perfect, for most school-age children think their parents are helpful, their teachers fair, and their friends loyal. In addition, their moral reasoning and behavior have reached that state where right seems clearly distinguished from wrong, with none of the ambiguities that complicate moral issues for adolescents and adults. For most children, then, the future seems filled with promise.

However, school and friendships are so important at this age that two common events can seem crushing: failure in school and rejection by peers. Some lucky children escape these problems; others have sufficient self-confidence or family support to weather them when they arise; and some leave middle childhood with painful memories, feeling inadequate, incompetent, and inferior for the rest of their lives.

The next three chapters celebrate the joys, and commemorate the occasional tragedies, of middle childhood.

The School Years:

Biosocial Development

CHAPTER

12

For most children, the school years are a time of stable growth and notable improvement in both gross and fine motor abilities. For some, unfortunately, it is a time when disabilities first become evident, or become more pronounced in their consequences. In this chapter, we will examine the bodily changes and variations that are characteristic of middle childhood, as well as certain difficulties that sometimes occur in biosocial development during this period. The following questions reflect some of the topics we will consider in this chapter:

How is a child's physical growth affected by genetic and cultural patterns?

What effects does being overweight have on a school-age child?

Which games and sports are best suited to the skills of children in middle childhood?

How can the insights of normal development be used to help children who have psychophysiological disabilities?

What are some of the learning difficulties that hinder school achievement?

What are the causes of attention-deficit hyperactivity disorder, and how can this problem best be treated?

Compared with other periods of the life span, biosocial development in middle childhood seems, on the whole, to be relatively smooth and uneventful. For one thing, disease and death are rarer during these years than during any other period. For another, most children master new physical skills (everything from tree-climbing to roller-blading) easily and without much adult instruction, provided their bodies are sufficiently mature and they have an opportunity to practice these skills. In addition, sex differences in physical development and ability are minimal, and sexual urges are quiescent compared to what they will later be. Certainly when bodily development during these years is compared with the rapid and dramatic growth that occurs during infancy and adolescence, middle childhood seems a period of smooth progress and tranquility. Now let us look at some of the specifics, as well as at some of the special needs that may emerge during this period.

Size and Shape

Children grow more slowly during middle childhood than they did earlier or than they will in adolescence. Worldwide, the typical well-nourished child gains about 5 pounds (2¼ kilograms) and 2½ inches (6 centimeters) per year, and by age 10 weighs about 70 pounds (32 kilograms) and measures 54 inches (137 centimeters) (Lowrey, 1986).

During these years children generally seem slimmer, as they grow taller and their body proportions change. In addition, muscles become stronger, enabling the average 10-year-old, for instance, to throw a ball twice as far as the average 6-year-old. The capacity of the lungs also increases, so with each passing year children are able to run faster and exercise longer than before. These changes are accentuated in those children who take advantage of their increased strength and endurance and actually exercise.

Variations in Physique

In some regions of the world, most of the variation in children's height and weight is caused by malnutrition, with wealthier children being several inches taller than their impoverished contemporaries from the other side of town—whether the town is Hong Kong, Rio de Janeiro, or New Delhi. In developed countries, heredity is the main source of variation, since most children get enough food during middle childhood to grow as tall as their genes allow.

Genetic factors and nutrition affect not only size but rate of maturation as well. This is particularly noticeable at the end of middle childhood, as some 10- and 11-year-olds begin to undergo the changes of puberty, and may find that they are ahead of their peers not only in height but also in strength and endurance. Among Americans, those of African descent tend to mature somewhat more quickly (as measured by bone growth and loss of baby teeth) and to have longer legs than those of European descent, who, in turn, tend to be maturationally ahead of those with Asian ancestors. Such variations are quite normal and healthy.

Figure 12.1 During the school years, variations in children's size and rate of physical maturation are the result of genetic inheritance and nutrition, as well as of chronological age.

Figure 12.2 As you can see, growth is quite steady throughout middle childhood, except for those girls in the 90th percentile (the heaviest 10 percent). Typically, they begin puberty at about age 10, which accounts for their increasing rate of weight gain at ages 11 and 12.

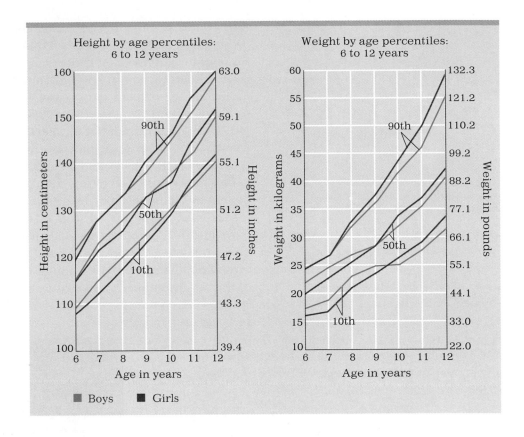

While it may be comforting for parents and teachers to know that healthy children come in many shapes and sizes, it is not always comforting to the children themselves. In elementary school, children compare themselves with one another, and those who are "behind" their classmates in areas related to physical maturation may feel deficient. Physical development during this period even affects friendships, which are based partly on physical appearance and competence (Hartup, 1983). Consequently, children who look "different," or who are noticeably lacking in physical skills, often become lonely and unhappy.

Childhood Obesity

One difference in size that, from middle childhood on, can seriously affect emotional as well as physical well-being is **obesity**. The precise point at which a particular child is not just chubby but actually obese varies, depending partly on the child's body type, partly on the proportion of fat to muscle, and partly on the culture's standards on this question. However, at least 10 percent of all American children are 20 pounds (9 kilograms) or more above the average weight for their age. By any criterion, they need to slim down. More exact measures of obesity, such as the thickness of fat on the triceps, find that the percentage of American children who are obese is higher than 10 percent and that this number has increased since 1960 (Gortmaker et al., 1987; Wolfe et al., 1994).

Obesity is a physical and medical problem at any stage of life, for the obese person runs a greater risk of serious illness (Lamb, 1984). In children,

obesity The condition of being significantly and unhealthily overweight.

orthopedic and respiratory problems are especially associated with obesity (Neumann, 1983). Being overweight is often a psychological problem as well. In middle childhood, fat children are often teased, picked on, and rejected. They know they are overweight, and they are more likely to experience diminished self-esteem, depression, and behavior problems as a result (Israel & Shapiro, 1985; Strauss et al., 1985). Obese children have fewer friends than other children (Strauss et al., 1985), and when they are accepted in a peer group, it is often at a high price, such as answering to nicknames like "Tubby" or "Blubber," and having to constantly suffer jokes about their shape. A vicious cycle of rejection, isolation, and low self-esteem leading to inactivity, compensatory overeating, and, in turn, to further rejection by peers, may cause obesity to persist in children. This, in turn, perpetuates psychological problems. Indeed, overweight adults who were obese as children tend to be more distressed and to have more psychophysiological problems than overweight adults who were of normal weight as children (Mills & Adrianopoulos, 1993).

Figure 12.3 Tug-of-war is one of the few competitive events in which this fifth-grader is likely to be the first one chosen for the team.

Causes of Obesity

Typically, no one explanation suffices for any particular case of obesity; rather, the problem is generally created through the interaction of a number of influences. Many of these influences usually begin in infancy, continue through childhood, and remain influential in adulthood.

1. *Heredity.* Body type, including the amount and distribution of fat, as well as height and bone structure, is inherited. So are individual differences in metabolic rate and activity level. Therefore, not everyone can be "average" in the ratio of height to weight. Indeed, research on adopted children shows that heredity is at least as strong as environmental factors in predisposing a person toward being overweight (Bray, 1989).

2. *Activity level.* Inactive people burn fewer calories and are more likely to be overweight than active people. This is even more true in infancy and childhood than during the rest of life. Activity level is influenced not only by heredity but also by the child's willingness to become involved in strenuous play and by the availability of safe places to play.

3. *Attitudes toward food.* In some families, parents take satisfaction when their children eat large quantities of food, and they frequently urge them to have another helping. The implied message seems to be that a father's love is measured by how much food he can provide; a mother's love, by how well she can cook; and a child's love, by how much he or she can eat. This is especially true when the parents or grandparents grew up in places where starvation was a real possibility. Further, some people consider food a symbol of love and comfort, and eat whenever they are upset. The pattern may begin in childhood, if parents use sweets as a reward or consolation, or as a substitute for emotional warmth (Lowrey, 1986).

4. *Types of food eaten.* Choice of food is important as well. Diets that emphasize fruits, vegetables, and grains do not lead to excess weight gain, whereas diets that are high in fat and sugar certainly do. Besides the obvious culprits, many other common foods, from breakfast cereals to ketchup, have sugar as a major ingredient. In addition, many snack foods contain large amounts of saturated fats, which the body metabolizes slowly. Unfortunately, but understandably, the diet of North American families who are below the poverty line tends to be high in fat, and to contain more fried than broiled or steamed foods. Ethnic and subcultural food preferences also affect fat intake. Traditional Chinese and Japanese foods, for example, include much more fiber and less fat than traditional northern and eastern European foods do. Research also shows that people develop tastes for certain types of foods, depending on what they have become accustomed to eating, especially in childhood (Bozin, 1990). Thus the "treats" and "junk food" that some parents regularly give their children may be creating dietary cravings that will lead directly to lifelong weight and health problems.

5. *Overfeeding in infancy and late childhood.* For most of life, the number of fat cells in a person's body remains relatively constant, no matter what that person eats. Adults become fatter because each fat cell becomes fuller, or thinner because each cell loses fat. However, in the prenatal period and the first two years of life, and again during early adolescence, when total body fat increases in anticipation of the rapid growth that follows, the number of fat cells is likely to increase. Malnutrition slows down the rate of cell multiplication, and overfeeding speeds it up (Bray, 1989). This is one more reason why fat babies and adolescents become adults who want more food and gain weight more easily than people who were not overfed as children. Even when these adults diet and lose weight, their bodies still contain those extra cells, just waiting to fill up with fat again, like sponges ready to soak up water.

6. *Television-watching.* In cultures where it is a regular pastime, television-watching correlates with obesity (Dietz & Gortmaker, 1985). Several factors make TV fattening. While watching television, children may be bombarded with, and swayed by, commercials for junk food. Indeed, 60 percent of the commercials during Saturday morning cartoons on U.S. television are for food products—almost all of them high-fat and high-sugar, shown being consumed by slim children who seem to be having a wonderful time because of what they are eating

(Ogletree et al., 1990). In addition, while watching TV, children tend to consume many snacks, and of course they burn fewer calories than they would if they were actively playing. In fact, they appear to burn fewer calories when watching TV than when doing *nothing*. A recent study found that when glued to the tube, children fall into a deeply relaxed state, akin to semiconsciousness, that lowers their metabolism below its normal at-rest rate—on average, 12 percent below normal in children of normal weight and 16 percent below normal in obese children (Klesges, 1993).

7. *Precipitating event.* For many children, the onset of obesity is associated with a critical event or traumatic experience—a hospitalization, a move to a new neighborhood, a parental divorce or death—that creates a sense of loss or diminished self-image and a corresponding need for an alternative source of gratification, in this case, food (Neumann, 1983).

8. *Physiological problems.* One more cause of obesity should be mentioned, even though it is rare. In a few instances, an abnormality in the growth process or in metabolism is to blame (Lowrey, 1986). In these cases, obesity is only one sign of a complex physiological problem that usually involves retardation of normal physical and mental growth. It must be stressed, however, that disorders of this type account for less than 1 percent of all cases of childhood obesity. Therefore, parents of the fat school-age child should, in all likelihood, be much more concerned about the child's diet and exercise than about the possibility of physiological disturbances.

Help for Overweight Children

Clearly, an overweight child needs emotional support for a bruised self-concept, as well as help in losing weight. But reducing is difficult, and psychological encouragement is often scarce, partly because obesity is usually fostered by entrenched family attitudes and habits that promote a fattening diet and, most likely, a sedentary lifestyle. Thus, changes in family patterns, as well as in the child's food intake, are essential to effective treatment. Unfortunately, when parents do try to get their child to eat a healthful, low-fat diet, they often make the mistake of using ultimatums ("You can't go and play until you eat your broccoli") or bribes ("Eat all your spinach and you can have dessert") that boomerang, reinforcing the child's dislike of the food or enhancing the attractiveness of sweets (Birch et al., 1982; Olvera-Ezzell et al., 1990).

Either at their parents' behest or on their own, obese children sometimes try crash diets, which make them irritable, listless, and even sick—adding to their psychological problems without accomplishing much long-term weight loss. The reason is that the body reacts to protect itself during periods of famine. The rate of metabolism becomes slower, enabling the body to maintain its weight with fewer calories, and after a certain amount of initial weight loss, additional pounds become much more difficult to lose (Wing, 1992). To make matters worse, strenuous dieting during childhood can be physically harmful, since cutting down on protein or calcium could hinder important brain and bone growth.

The best way to get children to lose weight is to increase their physical activity. However, exercise is hard for overweight children, and since they tend to move more slowly and with less coordination than other children (Hills, 1992), they are not often chosen to play on teams, and are likely to be teased and rebuffed when they try to join in group activities. Parents and teachers can help overweight children to do the kinds of exercise in which their size is not a disadvantage, such as walking to school rather than taking the bus, or bicycling around the neighborhood. Parents can also exercise with their children, not only making activity easier and providing a good model but bolstering the child's self-confidence as well. Children can share responsibility by monitoring their eating, recreation, television-watching, and other activities related to their weight. The importance of changing the child's eating and exercising patterns is apparent when one realizes that if the childhood weight problem reaches the point that the child is obese, and continues at that level throughout the childhood years, it is likely to last a lifetime. By one estimate, 60 percent to 80 percent of obese children become obese adults (Lucas, 1991). Treatment of obesity is more successful early in life, before the habits and attitudes contributing to weight gain jeopardize health as well as happiness throughout the life span.

Motor Skills

The fact that children grow more slowly during middle childhood may be part of the reason they become so much more skilled at controlling their bodies during these years. (Compare their self-control, for instance, with the clumsiness that typically accompanies sudden changes in body shape and size during toddlerhood or puberty.) School-age children can execute almost any motor skill, as long as it doesn't require very much power or judgment of speed and distance.

Figure 12.4 Sex differences in motor skills make boys slightly better at pulling themselves up with their arms—as illustrated by this smiling treeclimber—while girls, like these hopscotchers, are slightly better at bending and balancing. Most differences in play patterns are rooted in culture rather than physiology, however, which helps explain why girls may often be seen climbing trees but boys are seldom seen hopping around in little squares.

Of course, which particular skills a child masters depends, in part, on opportunity and encouragement. The skills of some North American 8- and 9-year-olds may include swinging a hammer well, sawing, using garden tools, sewing, knitting, drawing in good proportion, writing or printing accurately and neatly, cutting fingernails, riding bicycles, scaling fences, swimming, diving, roller-skating, ice-skating, jumping rope, and playing baseball, football, and jacks. Halfway around the world, in Indonesia, children master many of these same skills—though for environmental reasons, they do not learn to ice skate, for cultural reasons, they do not learn to play baseball or football, and, in Bali, for religious reasons, they do not learn to swim (water is considered to harbor evil) (Lansing, 1983). At the same time, Indonesian children learn skills not common among North American children, such as cutting wood with sharp knives and weaving intricate baskets.

Differences in Motor Skills

Boys and girls are just about equal in their physical abilities during the elementary-school years, except that boys have greater forearm strength and girls have greater overall flexibility. Consequently, boys have an advantage in sports like baseball, whereas girls have the edge in sports like gymnastics. But for most physical activities during middle childhood, sex is not as important as age and experience: boys can do cartwheels, and girls can hit home runs, if given an opportunity to learn these skills.

However, the maxim "Practice makes perfect" does not always hold true. Every motor skill is related to several other abilities, some depending on practice, but others relying on body size, brain maturation, or genetically based talent. For example, **reaction time**, the length of time it takes a person to respond to a particular stimulus, is tied to aspects of brain maturation that continue into adolescence. Not surprisingly, one study of reaction time in children aged 5 through 14 found that the older children were almost twice as fast as the younger ones (Southard, 1985). Thus in any sport in which reaction time is crucial, the average older child has a decided advantage over a younger one, and the average adult is quicker than the average child.

Other individual and age differences also come into play. Some are obvious, such as the advantage of height for basketball and of upper-body strength and size for tackle football. Other differences may not be so evident to the teacher or parent. For example, children vary in their ability to coordinate body movements, so some children are not able to aim a kick in soccer, or execute a leap in gymnastics, nearly as well as others. Individual differences in these characteristics derive from experience and training, and from one's heredity.

Looking closely at the sports that most American adults value reveals that few are well-suited for children, because they demand precisely those skills that are hardest for them to master. Even softball is much harder than one might think. Throwing with accuracy and catching both involve more distance judgment and eye-hand coordination than many elementary-school children possess. In addition, catching and batting depend on reaction time. Younger children are therefore apt to drop a ball even if it lands in their mitt, because they are slow to enclose it, and they are similarly likely to strike out by swinging the bat too late. Thus, a large measure of judgment, physical maturity, and experience is required for good ball-

reaction time The time it takes to respond to a particular stimulus.

Figure 12.5 The games that are well-suited for school-age children focus on the skills they can perform well, such as running and kicking. Not surprisingly, these are the activities that children themselves often choose, rather than the sports involving complex coordination and one-on-one competition commonly favored by adults.

playing. As always, of course, underlying differences among individuals are key. Some children will never be able to throw or kick a ball with as much strength and accuracy as others, a fact that parents, teachers, and teammates sometimes tend to forget.

Children with Special Needs

All parents witness the developing accomplishments of their offspring with pride and satisfaction, but for some, these feelings are mingled with worry and uncertainty as their child seems to experience unexplained difficulties in one area of development or another. Gradually these concerns build and deepen to the point that the parent suspects that the child might have a psychological disorder. Consider the experiences of this mother:

> Except for the fact that my daughter has always been a physically-active and strong-willed child, it was not until she entered the first grade that the problems seemed to start. She became very reluctant to attend school, which was very different from her excitement over kindergarten. The stomach aches that she had complained of since age 2 became more frequent and necessitated her going to the nurse's office at school at least once per day if not more often. She could not seem to complete her assignments—sometimes taking an hour to complete just one sentence. She did not seem to willfully refuse to do assignments but seemed preoccupied with daydreams and other, more interesting activities. She was not disruptive in class but did seem to go through a bout of pushing in line and there were some reports of aggressiveness. At home, I could not seem to get her moving in the morning—even to the point where I took her to the babysitter's home in her pajamas because she would not get up and get dressed. Kimberly also began to appear angry and frustrated, having more problems getting along with parents and peers. She had always had best friends, been very sociable, and friendly. She then started to verbalize that people didn't like her and no one wanted to play with her. She would often get very angry at the neighborhood children she played with. As a parent, I found myself constantly yelling and totally frustrated with how to handle my child. [Thompson, 1994]

What is a parent to do in such a situation? In this case, Kimberly's mother sought the advice of her daughter's teachers and school counselors, who had been equally perplexed that this intellectually above-average child seemed to have such difficulty paying attention in class and cooperating with others. Together, they also contacted developmental experts at a local child-guidance clinic who, after interviewing her mother, testing Kimberly, and observing her at school, diagnosed Kimberly's problem as attention-deficit hyperactivity disorder (ADHD), which you will read about later in this chapter. With treatment that included medication, parent-child therapy sessions, and structured school activities, Kimberly became a much happier, and more capable, child—although she still had lingering emotional difficulties and attention problems.

For many children like Kimberly—children with special needs—the development of new skills, closer friendships, and more mature ways of thinking is impaired by psychological disorders. Many such disorders originate in part, from physiological impairment in various structures of the brain. Others stem from the social and emotional consequences of disabilities such as deafness or paralysis. And others originate in the child's environment. Thus the learning-disabled child, the blind child, and the physically abused child are all children with special needs. The study of children with special needs is an integral part of developmental psychology because these children experience the same developmental needs that all children do—whether they involve forming attachments to caregivers, developing social skills with peers, or acquiring intellectual competence. Indeed, the view that children with psychological disorders are children first—with the developmental needs that all children share—and only secondarily children with special challenges is an organizing principle of a new branch of developmental study, developmental psychopathology.

The Developmental Psychopathology Perspective

In recent years, clinicians who study childhood psychological disorders have allied with developmental psychologists to create the new field of **developmental psychopathology**, which applies the insights from studies of normal development to the study and treatment of childhood disorders (Cicchetti, 1990, 1993; Sroufe & Rutter, 1984). The insights arising from this alliance have been mutually beneficial, for as developmental psychopathologists emphasize, "we can learn more about an organism's normal functioning by studying its pathology and likewise, more about its pathology by studying its normal condition" (Cicchetti, 1990). Indeed, as these developmentalists have discovered, when comparing abnormal and normal children, the distinction between the two often blurs and sometimes even disappears: most normal children, some of the time, act in ways that are decidedly unusual, and most children with psychological disorders are, in other respects, quite normal.

Further, taking a developmental perspective makes it clear that the manifestations of virtually any special problem a child might have will change as the child grows older: a child who seems severely handicapped by a disability at one stage of development may seem much less so at the next, or vice versa. Such shifts are not simply a matter of time passing, but, like all developmental changes, result from the interplay of changes within the individual and forces in the ecological setting (Berkson, 1993).

developmental psychopathology A field of psychology that applies the insights from studies of normal development to the study and treatment of childhood disorders.

From Perspective to Action

Because of its contextual approach, the developmental psychopathological perspective is of great benefit to the treatment of children with psychological disorders. Traditionally, clinicians treated disturbed children in the same way they treated disturbed adults: through individual therapy. But because developmentalists have come to recognize that the home, school, and community have a profound effect on normal children, developmental psychopathologists have broadened their treatment approach to include family members in group therapy and to enlist school personnel to design special educational programs for troubled children. They also marshal various community resources, such as the kind of home visitation (described in Chapter 9) that helps families reduce stress and better nurture their children.

In addition, the recognition of the interaction of various aspects of development in all children has led to treatments for children with special needs that simultaneously involve all three developmental domains. Today, treatment for most children like Kimberly is likely to involve a multidisciplinary team: a physician might prescribe medication to decrease the child's activity level, a resource-room teacher might teach the child specific academic skills, and a family therapist might assist in repairing a frayed parent-child relationship.

In addition to the disorders already mentioned, developmental psychopathologists study such childhood problems as aggression, anxiety, autism, conduct disorders, depression, Down syndrome, mental retardation, mutism, pervasive developmental delay—far too many to discuss here. Instead, we will focus in detail on three problems: autism, learning disabilities, and attention-deficit hyperactivity disorder. Each is particularly instructive about the development of all children.

Autism

One of the most severe disturbances of early childhood is called **autism**, from the prefix "auto-," meaning "self." The label "autism" was chosen in 1943 by an American physician, Leo Kanner, to describe children who have an "inability to relate themselves in an ordinary way to people . . . an extreme autistic aloneness that, whenever possible, disregards, ignores, shuts out anything that comes to the child from the outside." Kanner's term was apt: autistic individuals seem unusually restricted by their own perspective and their need for predictable routines, and they seem unable, unwilling, or uninterested in communicating with, or even understanding, others. Classical autism, described by Kanner as including such extreme asocial and uncommunicative behaviors that the person never learns normal speech or forms normal human relationships, is quite rare: it occurs in about 1 of every 2,000 children.

In highlighting the similarities between normal and abnormal behavior, however, the developmental psychopathological perspective has helped to show that many more individuals have less severe autistic symptoms. Such individuals are sometimes diagnosed as "high-functioning autistic," or as having "Asperger syndrome," named after a German psychiatrist who described a disorder in 1944 that he also called autism. (Because of World War II, Kanner and Asperger were unaware that they both were reaching

autism A disorder that is chiefly characterized by an inability or unwillingness to communicate with others.

similar conclusions and terminology.) Asperger's delineation of autism included some individuals who were quite intelligent and verbal, and his portrayal of autism is, on the whole, less extreme than that of the classical type described by Kanner.

Exactly how impaired must a child be before being diagnosed as autistic? Even today, there is no firm consensus, but experts agree that Kanner's original definition was too narrow, and that, when the entire spectrum of autistic disorders is taken into account, as many as 1 child in 100 shows autistic traits (Szatmari, 1992). Both the severe and less severe instances of the disorder are much more common in boys than in girls, generally in a ratio of 2 to 1 or higher.

The Developmental Path of Autism

Autism is truly a developmental disorder, because, although its origin is almost always congenital, its manifestations change markedly with age. As babies, many autistic children seem quite normal, and sometimes unusually "good." In early childhood, however, severe deficiencies appear in three areas: communication ability, social skills, and imaginative play.

The first noticeable symptom is usually the lack of spoken language. While they babble at a normal age, autistic children do not say their first words at about 12 months, or even at 2 years. As preschoolers, some autistic children continue to be mute, not talking at all, while others engage in a type of speech called *echolalia*, echoing, word for word, such things as advertising jingles or the questions put to them. If such a child is asked "Are you hungry?" the response is likely to be "Are you hungry?"

Social responsiveness of every kind is slow to develop. Indeed, in retrospect, some parents note that their autistic child was not a normal baby: he or she did not smile and laugh at peek-a-boo or patty-cake, and reacted to a soothing touch with increased distress rather than signs of being comforted.

By preschool, the deficit in social skills is more obvious: autistic children avoid eye contact and prefer to play by themselves rather than with other children. Their play patterns are unusual, characterized by repetitive rituals and a decided absence of spontaneous, imaginative play. One autistic adult, who has unusual verbal ability, remembers her childhood in the following manner:

> I also liked to sit for hours humming to myself and twirling objects or dribbling sand through my hands at the beach. I remember studying the sand intently as if I was a scientist looking at a specimen under the microscope. I remember minutely observing how the sand flowed, or how long a jar lid would spin when propelled at different speeds. My mind was actively engaged in these activities. I was fixated on them and ignored everything else. [Grandin & Scariano, 1986]

Although this woman's verbal abilities are atypical for autistic individuals, her childhood play was not. Autistic children tend to perform the same behaviors again and again: they can spend hours turning a visually attractive toy around and around in their hands or placing blocks in a particular, repeated pattern, or even banging their heads against a wall. Many seem unusually sensitive to noises and sights, and unusually insensitive to pain (Frith, 1989).

Later Childhood and Beyond

While autistic impairments in language and play patterns are pronounced and dysfunctional in early childhood, from the preschool years on, it is the lack of social understanding that often proves to be the most devastating problem. Autistic children appear to lack a theory of mind, an awareness of the thoughts, feelings, and intentions of other people (Holroyd & Baron-Cohen, 1993; Leslie & Frith, 1988). Consequently, to some autistic children, people seem of no greater interest than objects, because the child is unaware of the internal processes that make people unique and provocative.

At the same time, visible and loud expressions of anger and sadness can be confusing and disturbing to autistic children, precisely because they have no understanding of the reasons and consequences of such outbursts (Sigman, in press; Sigman et al., 1992). The everyday, noisy social interaction of other children can also be unsettling. Autistic adults sometimes remember school as a "horrifying experience," with classmates whose behavior seemed unpredictable and therefore frightening (Frith, 1989). In all forms of autism, this underlying problem with social understanding remains lifelong, but the degree to which it impairs functioning depends on the severity of the disorder, the intensity of the child's early education and treatment, the support offered by the overall social context, and the determination of the individual.

As developing persons with autism grow older, the variations among them can be quite marked. On intelligence tests, most young autistic individuals score in the mentally-retarded range, but a closer look at their intellectual performance on the various parts of the test often shows marked "scatter," with isolated areas of remarkable skill (such as memory for numbers, or for putting together puzzles). And while some autistic individuals never speak, or have only minimal verbal ability, many who were diagnosed as autistic at age 2 or 3 do learn to express themselves in language by age 6, and some of them demonstrate exceptional mastery of academic skills during the school years. Those in the last group may eventually live self-supporting adult lives, although they always will be less imaginative, more ritualistic, less communicative, and more socially isolated than most people. Indeed, occasionally, high-functioning autistic (or Asperger) individuals may be quite successful in professions in which their attention to routine, concentration on detail, and relative indifference to needless sentiment are an asset. One study of a small sample of individuals with Asperger traits found a dentist, a financial lawyer, a military historian, and a university professor among the group (Gilberg, 1991).

Causes of Autism

The precise cause of autism is not known, but genes certainly play a role (Hertzig & Shapiro, 1990; Volkman, 1991). For example, when one monozygotic twin is autistic, about 50 percent of the time the other twin is also autistic. In the remaining cases, the other twin, while not diagnosed as autistic, is nonetheless likely to have language disorders in childhood and social difficulties throughout life, particularly in forming close personal relationships. However, when one dyzygotic twin is autistic, it is quite unusual for the other to be autistic also, although that twin is more likely to have language and so-cial deficits compared to children with a normal sibling (Rutter, 1991).

Despite this strong evidence for a genetic origin for autism, genes are clearly not the whole story, as evidenced by the monozygotic twins who do not share the disorders with their autistic twin. In all likelihood, a genetic vulnerability in combination with some damage—either prenatal or early-postnatal—leads to autism. The role of environmental damage is suggested by the increased prevalence of abnormal neurological patterns, seizures, anoxia, previous exposure to viruses, and hearing abnormalities among children who have been diagnosed as autistic.

The specific link between genetic and environmental problems and autism is still not known. However, all current experts are agreed that the cause originally identified by Kanner—the parents' early child care—was terribly, damagingly wrong. Kanner saw the parents of autistic children as "emotional refrigerators," and proposed that it was their coldness toward their infants that produced autism. Now we know that this is clearly not the case, and one can only wonder what pain must have been felt by parents who needlessly blamed themselves for their child's plight. Most parents of autistic children are, in fact, devoted to them, despite the child's marked in-difference or resistance to signs of affection. Indeed, our understanding of the relationship perspective (see Chapter 11) helps us see that it is the inac-cessibility of the autistic child that often causes parents to develop ways of relating that appear to be unfeeling and distant.

Treatment

Taking a developmental view of autism is essential to its treatment. Since language skills normally develop most rapidly between ages 1 and 4, these are the crucial years for intervention. The most successful treatment meth-ods for autism combine individual attention with behavior techniques that shape particular skills. For example, the child is rewarded for making eye contact, for naming various parts of the face, for using pronouns appropri-ately, and so on. Each behavior is carefully taught, step by step, and rein-forcement is patiently delivered immediately after the child performs the behavior correctly. With such therapy, many autistic children can learn to talk, show appropriate social behaviors, and improve in other ways, with some making sufficient progress to enter normal schools and live normal lives (McEachin et al., 1993). The key seems to be early and very intensive treatment, with the goal of breaking through the communication barrier by age 6.

Again from a developmental psychopathological perspective, it is clear that family therapy is an important component of treatment for two reasons. For one thing, parents are the child's first special educators, and their continuing daily role as tutors, enacted virtually every waking hour, is critical. Equally important, however, is the realization that the family system is profoundly stressed by the presence of an autistic child, and therapy may be crucial to keeping the family from emotionally destroying itself.

Now let us look at a much less devastating but much more common problem, one that typically causes the most difficulty in the school years.

Figure 12.6 The prime prerequisite in breaking through the language barrier in a nonverbal autistic child, such as this 4-year-old, is to get the child to pay attention to another person's speech. Note that this teacher is sitting in a low chair to facilitate eye contact and is getting the child to focus on mouth movements—a matter of little interest to most children but intriguing to many autistic ones. Sadly, even such efforts were not enough: at age 13 this child was still mute.

Learning Disabilities

It is an obvious fact that children are not all equally adept at the skills required in school. For example, after a year or two of formal education, most 8-year-olds can sit attentively in class while they listen to the teacher's instructions, and can read simple books, add and subtract three-digit numbers, and write several sentences, as required. However, some children have extraordinary difficulty with one or another of these tasks.

In some children, these difficulties arise from an overall slowness in development: their thinking is like that of a normal child several years younger than their present chronological age, and thus they are considered to suffer **mental retardation**, that is, a pervasive delay in cognitive development. In others, however, such difficulties are in surprising contrast to their overall intelligence level. These children are said to have a **learning disability**, a failing in a specific cognitive skill that is not attributable to an overall intellectual slowness, to a specific physical handicap such as hearing loss, to a severely stressful living condition, or to a lack of basic education (Silver, 1991).

Children who are diagnosed as learning-disabled are markedly below the expected achievement in a particular academic area, such as reading, writing, or math. Typically, a teacher notices that a particular child is not learning as much as the other children in the class, and then recommends that the child see a psychologist for a series of diagnostic tests.

The key criterion for diagnosing a learning disability is a significant discrepancy between measures of overall aptitude and measures of performance in a particular area. For example, if a 9-year-old has an average IQ but reads at the first-grade level, that would indicate a learning disability in the area of reading. The actual process of diagnosis is more complex than this, and various experts use alternative definitions and measures (Aram et al., 1992; Fletcher et al., 1992).

Learning disabilities become more readily recognized as the child gets older. In the United States, about 1.5 percent of all 3- to 5-year-olds, about 7 percent of all 6- to 11-year-olds, and about 9 percent of all 12- to 17-year-olds have been diagnosed as learning-disabled. Interestingly, advantaged children—those who are middle-class, nonminority, in good health, and living in two-parent homes—are less likely to be learning-disabled than other children, but when they do have a disability, it is likely to be spotted later in their academic career, toward the end of elementary school or even later (Zill & Schoenborn, 1990). The reason for this late recognition is not known. It may be that teachers are less likely to notice the early difficulties of this group, or that parents are more likely to think that the child will grow out of them, or that the children themselves find better ways to hide their difficulties until the challenge of academic work becomes overwhelming.

The rate of recognized learning disabilities has increased dramatically over recent years, as indicated in part by the statistic that 5 percent of children in the United States were receiving special help for learning disabilities in 1989 compared to 1.8 percent in 1977 (U.S. Department of Education, 1991). In all likelihood, many more children and adults have undiagnosed learning disabilities that they have learned to hide or overcome.

Figure 12.7 One-on-one contact, literally, is helpful for many learning-disabled children who also benefit from explicit individualized instruction. In his special class, 7-year-old Alex receives both from his teacher. The one drawback with such special education is the limited opportunity it affords for learning social skills, a failing remedied when children with special needs *and* their teachers are included within a regular class.

mental retardation A pervasive delay in cognitive development.

learning disability A particular difficulty in mastering one or more basic academic skills, without apparent deficit in intelligence or impairment of sensory functions.

Problems in a Particular Academic Area

By definition, a learning-disabled child has unexpected difficulty in learning certain material. For example, a child might have **dyslexia**, which is a disability in reading. Dyslexic children may seem bright and happy in the early years of school, volunteering answers to some difficult questions, diligently completing their worksheets, sitting quietly and looking at their books. However, as time goes on, it becomes clear that they are not really reading: rather, they are guessing at simple words (occasionally making surprising mistakes) and explaining what they have just "read" by telling about the pictures.

Another common disability is **dyscalcula**, that is, great difficulty in math. This problem usually becomes apparent somewhat later in childhood, at about age 8, when even simple number facts, such as 3 + 3 = 6, are memorized one day and forgotten the next. Soon it becomes clear—especially with word problems—that the child is guessing at whether two numbers should be added or subtracted, and that almost everything the child knows about math is a matter of rote memory rather than understanding.

Other specific academic subjects that may reveal a learning disability are spelling and handwriting: a child might read at the fifth-grade level but repeatedly make simple spelling mistakes ("kum accros the rode") or take three times as long as any other child to copy something from the chalkboard and still produce a large, illegible scrawl. In addition, although they are not usually labeled as such and given special help, some children are learning-disabled in an underlying skill—such as spatial relations, sequential processing, memory, or attention span—that affects all intellectual areas (Rourke, 1989).

Causes of Learning Disabilities

None of these learning problems is caused by a lack of effort on the child's part, although, unfortunately, parents and teachers sometimes treat children who are learning-disabled as though they are not trying hard enough. In fact, the precise causes of learning disabilities are hard to pinpoint (Chalfant, 1989). Many professionals believe that the origin is often organic. It seems as if some parts of the learning-disabled child's brain do not function as well as they do in most people. In the case of dyslexia, for instance, various theories have focused on processes in the visual areas of the brain, such as those that enable the eye to scan from left to right, or to rapidly process small differences in the shape of letters, or to focus on one word and skip over another (Adams, 1990).

Interestingly, while it is quite logical to imagine that deficiencies in the visual part of the brain are the primary neurological culprit for dyslexia, according to a new hypothesis, the disability is more likely to originate in the auditory areas of the brain. One small area of the brain is dedicated to detecting the differences between sounds spoken very rapidly—such as *p* and *b*, which take less than a twentieth of a second to say—and longer sounds such as *a*, which lasts a full tenth of a second. Poor functioning in this area might affect the development of spoken language and language comprehension. The problem is unlikely to be noticed initially because social context and other cues from the environment would help the child to know, for

dyslexia A specific learning disability involving unusual difficulty in reading.

dyscalcula A specific learning disability involving unusual difficulty in arithmetic.

example, whether a parent had told him to pick up the "pail" or the "mail." But learning to read requires deciphering sounds without many contextual clues. Even when taught the elements of phonics, an affected child might still be lost, because he or she does not hear the difference between the various sounds.

This theory has received support from detailed studies of various areas of the brain, showing that dyslexic individuals have a different pattern of activity in the auditory areas than normal readers do. In addition, their brains contain fewer large cells in an area of the brain that controls the timing of auditory signals (Tallal et al., 1994). From this research, a possible clue to treatment emerges: teachers and parents can slow down their speech, and help the child strengthen the ability to hear subtle differences in speech sounds.

As detailed in Chapters 3 and 4, many prenatal factors can have a detrimental effect on brain functioning. Genetic inheritance is one of them, since learning disabilities tend to run in families (Oliver et al., 1991; Silver & Hagan, 1990). Teratogens, of course, are another factor, with maternal drug use, particularly of cigarettes, alcohol, and cocaine, being among the teratogenic influences that may be associated with later learning disabilities. Prenatal exposure to other toxins, notably mercury and PCBs, is clearly linked to learning disabilities (Jacobson et al., 1992), as is postnatal damage, such as that from convulsions caused by high fever, or from eating or inhaling leaded contaminants (Fergusson et al., 1993). The children most affected are those who are both genetically vulnerable and prenatally or postnatally exposed to insult. For a variety of reasons, the rate of learning disabilities is particularly high among children who were very-low-birthweight—as high as 28 percent, according to one study (Seigal et al., 1992).

However, every specialist cautions that the connection between organic damage and learning problems is not straightforward. Some children are learning-disabled even when nothing untoward occurred in their prenatal or early postnatal environment (Vandenberg et al., 1986), and some who experienced quite obvious insults, including prenatal exposure to cocaine and other illegal drugs, sometimes suffer no measurable deficits, especially if they are raised in a loving and stable family (Johnson et al., 1990; Robins & Mills, 1993).

Most important, even if a particular learning problem is of proven organic origin, that does not mean that it is impossible to ameliorate. In fact, no matter what the cause of learning disabilities, the way teachers and parents respond to a child who displays difficulties in learning can make an enormous difference to the child's chances of overcoming the problem. If teachers and parents recognize that a child with a learning disability is neither lazy nor stupid, they can help the child become a competent adult with patient, individual tutoring (see A Closer Look, p. 428). With such assistance, many children with learning disabilities develop into adults who are virtually indistinguishable from other adults in their educational and occupational achievements (Goodman, 1987).

In general, the earlier a learning-disabled child gets special help, and the more that help is tied to the particular problem (giving the child with dyscalcula targeted assistance and extra practice with number concepts or math strategies, or giving the dyslexic child direct tutoring with letter recognition or phonics), the better the child's future prospects are (Wilson &

A CLOSER LOOK

The Learning-Disabled Child in School

Learning-disabled children never have an easy time at school. However, their difficulties can be significantly lightened if everyone involved both knows why a particular child does not learn what other children seem to master quickly, and is motivated to help. Consider the experiences of two boys, Teddy and Pat.

Teddy is learning-disabled "in almost all modalities" (Osman, 1979), a fact that practically guarantees academic difficulties, and, eventually, behavior problems, if special help is not forthcoming from the home as well as from the school. Happily, Teddy never became disruptive or withdrawn, largely because he and his parents learned early how to cope with his difficulties.

His parents thought something was wrong as soon as Teddy began school, when he changed from a happy, cheerful preschooler to a cranky kindergartener who frequently complained that the "mean teacher" was giving him too much "hard work." He began having nightmares and wetting his bed almost every night. In first grade, he was shamed before the whole class when he was asked to read aloud and couldn't, and again when the teacher made everyone miss recess while the class waited for him to copy a sentence from the blackboard.

Soon after that, the school psychologist tested Teddy and diagnosed him as learning-disabled. Teddy remained in regular classes, but his teachers attempted to help him by structuring his assignments in ways that would make them easier for him to handle. Teddy also spent time each day in a resource room (his "haven"), where a special teacher gave him individual help. Finally, his parents became his support team, explaining Teddy's special needs to teachers and administrators before he became frustrated, embarrassed, or punished for not doing what he could not do.

Although this special help cushioned the psychological impact of Teddy's learning disabilities, he fell well behind his classmates. Consequently, at age 9, he was transferred into a class for learning-disabled children. He finally began to read, and, after three years, was considered ready for placement in a regular sixth-grade class in a middle school.

Although sympathetic, Teddy's middle-school teachers were not always prepared to help him. For example, his math teacher "wanted to help" but had no time, and, besides, felt that it would not be fair to give him individual attention, or to allow him to use a calculator to avoid computational errors. Even the resource-room teacher had no time to help, but she let Teddy use the tape library, which included cassettes of most of the textbooks. With special help from his parents, his tape recorder, and a tutor, Teddy managed to get through junior high.

Pat's first eight years of school were far more problematic—not because his learning problems were worse (in fact, he was dyslexic but not impaired in other areas)—but because no one recognized his problems as disabilities (Lamm & Fisch, 1982). Pat explains it well:

I wasn't good at reading. I was failing, but I was also one of the biggest kids in the class so no one called me stupid or dummy. . . . [The teachers] knew I couldn't do the work so they would send me on errands in the school. Pat, get this! Pat, get that! I felt dumb. I thought that I must have been absent the day they taught us how to read. I used to hate it. I didn't want to go to school but my mother said, "You have to go!" I'd say "I'm sick," and I came close to staying out.

The worse part was when I'd fail, and I'd have to bring a paper home to have my mother sign it. . . . [M]y mother would yell at me, that really hurt. My brothers who were in high school and my sisters would yell at me and say "What's wrong with you?" They had all gone to the same parochial school, and I was the only one having this trouble. My mother just couldn't take the school calling up all the time, and so she finally just left my sisters there and took me out and put me into public school . . . .

It was a school in which we did everything verbally at first. I felt good that I was finally coming home with good marks and my mother was happy. . . . Then after a while we sat down and started with the pencil and paper and books again, and that's when I started to fail all over again.

That's when they said that something was the matter. I'd just be sitting in class and they'd say, "Pat, go down to

Sindelar, 1991). In addition, attention should be given to social interaction, because social skills and self-esteem are often directly or indirectly affected by a learning disability, even where the problem is mild and the family and the school are supportive (Casey et al., 1992; Vaughn et al., 1993).

While the underlying problem is likely to remain lifelong (Spreen, 1988), training the child how to leapfrog, sidestep, or undercut the difficulty can minimize its effects, not only aiding the child in making and keeping friends but also helping with academic learning (McIntosh et al., 1991).

the office!" Well, I was used to that from the other school. I went down, took a test, and came back. The guidance counselor . . . told my mother that he would continue to test me but said I was being lazy. I asked my mother why I was being tested and she said, "Maybe you need glasses." . . . I thought that everyone was like me and had trouble reading. . . .

I stayed in that school for the fourth and fifth grade. They decided that junior high school was out and that they were going to have to find another program for me. Then fall came around and . . . they said, "How would you like to repeat the fifth grade?" I ended up doing *fifth*-grade work for another year.

Then around came fall again and . . . I was put in another school which had a special program . . . for the neurologically impaired. . . . The math was addition and the reading was words like "cat" that I had memorized years ago when I was a little kid. I never got in trouble. I never talked. . . . The other kids in the class made noise; some were retarded, some had emotional problems, and some were tough guys—behavior problems . . . I was absent a lot, but I would go in when they said that I had to pass a test for my report card . . . I hated that school . . . It was a total waste of time.

Fortunately, Pat's social isolation, withdrawal, and wasted learning time came to an end at this point, because he was tested and found to be dyslexic. Knowing this helped Pat with the difficult school years ahead:

I was dyslexic. I wasn't mentally disturbed, and I wasn't mentally retarded . . . since I had been messed around with for three years they promoted me, but to the eighth grade and that was tough. . . . School would be out at two-thirty, and I would stay there and work until four. Then I'd go home to work and I would do sixth and seventh grade work to catch up. . . . One teacher gave me a lot of help; she was there when I needed her. Last year I went to high school as a freshman in a regular class. . . .

For both Teddy and Pat, high school was difficult. However, Pat found that once he understood what his problem was, he had the confidence to cope with it:

I'm relaxed now, and I'm not shy. When a teacher asks me to stand up and read pages 101–103 during the class, I can say to her that I have trouble reading and I can't do that. I

never used to be able to say that. The teacher then says that she'll talk to me after class, and I explain it to her. I know what is wrong with me, and the people know what is wrong, so I don't have to worry. I know what I have to do to get around it and how to help myself.

Since Teddy had more problems than Pat, he found high school more difficult, but as his mother put it, he "wages his own battles now" (Osman, 1985). For example, he would tell each teacher at the start of the term that he is learning-disabled and ask not to be called on unless his hand was raised. He became particularly good in social studies, because the teachers let him tape their lectures. By his senior year, he had worked with the head of the department to create courses in American history, world history, and African and Asian history that were specially designed to provide learning-disabled students the same depth of coverage available in the regular courses.

What is to be learned from these two examples? First, many teachers and parents find it hard to accommodate a learning-disabled child. Second, even with special help, the problems do not go away. The task is to find ways to bypass some of them and to overcome others with special work. Finally, once the problem is recognized, and the learning-disabled child understands it, the child can gradually learn to compensate on his or her own. Many children like Teddy and Pat are making it through high school and can contemplate college and employment only "slightly more terrified than other kids" (as Teddy's mother put it). And, fortunately, some colleges have made adjustments to the specific difficulties of learning-disabled students, requiring no lesser mastery of the curriculum but allowing some flexibility with regard to such matters as time limits on exams and whether an oral report can supplement a written one. Surprisingly, some research shows learning-disabled college students outperforming many of their classmates academically, perhaps because they have developed better study skills and deeper determination (Vogel & Adelman, 1992).

Attention-Deficit Hyperactivity Disorder

attention-deficit hyperactivity disorder (ADHD) A behavior problem characterized by excessive activity, an inability to concentrate, and impulsive, sometimes aggressive, behavior.

One of the most puzzling and exasperating of childhood problems is **attention-deficit hyperactivity disorder,** or **ADHD,** in which the child has great difficulty concentrating for more than a few moments at a time and, indeed, is almost constantly in motion (Barkley, 1990; Weiss, 1991). Sitting down to do homework, for instance, an ADHD child might repeatedly look up, ask irrelevant questions, think about playing outside, get up to get a

Figure 12.8 In some children, actions like this may be an isolated instance of showing off or of outrageous mischief. In children with ADHD, they are commonplace. When such behavior is accompanied by aggression, the child may be at risk of developing a conduct disorder—possibly becoming the kind of stubborn, disobedient, daredevil who is constantly in trouble at home, at school, and in the neighborhood.

drink of water, and then get up again to get a snack. Often this urge for distraction and diversion is accompanied by excitability and impulsivity.

Many children with ADHD are also prone to aggression, which has led some researchers to propose *ADHDA—attention-deficit hyperactivity disorder with aggression—*as a subtype of this problem. Children who exhibit aggression with ADHD appear to be at increased risk for developing conduct disorders (Dykman & Ackerman, 1993). Attention-deficit disorder can also occur without hyperactivity or aggression. Children with this form of the problem, *ADD*, appear to be prone to anxiety and depression.

The crucial factor underlying ADHD (as well as the other forms of the attention-deficit problem) seems to be a neurological difficulty in screening out irrelevant and distracting stimuli, especially when trying to organize and communicate one's ideas (Riccio et al., 1993; Tannock et al., 1993). This deficit makes "paying attention" difficult, and therefore makes it hard for the child to focus on any one thought or experience long enough to process it. Thus a child might impulsively blurt out the wrong answer to a teacher's question, or might not have the patience to read and remember a passage in a school textbook. In addition to these difficulties, ADHD (as well as the other attention-deficit disorders) is often accompanied by further learning disabilities (Cantwell & Baker, 1991; Dykman & Ackerman, 1991).

Estimates of the prevalence of ADHD among school-age children vary, from about 1 percent to 5 percent, depending partly on diagnostic criteria, which vary by nation. British doctors, for example, are less likely to diagnose children as having ADHD than American doctors are, and are more likely to diagnose such children as having conduct disorders (Epstein et al., 1991; Rutter & Garmezy, 1983). Generally, however, the sex ratio of diagnosed ADHD children is four boys for every one girl (Bhatia et al., 1991).

Causes of Attention-Deficit Hyperactivity Disorder

When confronted with a school-age child who is considerably more active than other children and cannot concentrate very well, it is not easy to explain that child's behavior. However, researchers have identified at least six factors that are associated with, and may contribute to, attention-deficit hyperactivity disorder.

1. *Genetic differences.* Twin and adoption studies indicate that hereditary factors contribute to attention-deficit hyperactivity disorder. This genetic element may manifest itself in abnormal brain metabolism. A brain-scan study (Zametkin et al., 1990) of twenty-five adults who had had the disorder in childhood and who have at least one child with the disorder revealed that, on average, their overall rate of brain activity was 8 percent lower than that of a control group. More significant, the areas of lowest activity were in two areas of the brain that are associated with the control of attention and motor activity.

2. *Prenatal damage.* One precursor of this disorder is prenatal damage of some sort (Hartsough & Lambert, 1985). Thus, a person who was prenatally exposed to a teratogen may have escaped major harm but show minor problems in physical development and learning ability. Maternal drug use during pregnancy and pregnancy complications have both been implicated (Varley, 1984).

Figure 12.9 We do not know why this boy is crying. However, the lack of sympathy from his peers suggests that social rejection plays a part. Many children have disabilities that impair their interaction with others and would benefit from the same kind of skill training and practical assistance that children with more obvious academic disabilities often receive.

3. *Lead poisoning.* Lead poisoning in its early stages leads to impaired concentration and hyperactivity, as discussed in Public Policy, on page 432.

4. *Family influences.* Compared with other children, children diagnosed with attention-deficit hyperactivity disorder come from families who move often, are stressed, have fewer children, and are less concerned about the child's academic performance than about controlling the child's behavior. Obviously, each of these factors may be the result, rather than the cause, of the child's difficulties, or they might contribute to maintaining these difficulties once they have begun for other reasons.

5. *Environment.* The ecological niche in which some children find themselves may exacerbate attention-deficit hyperactivity disorder. The child is especially likely to "misbehave" in an exciting but unstructured situation (such as the typical birthday party) or in a situation with many behavioral demands (such as a long religious service, or dinner in a fancy restaurant). Children with no place to play, or who watch television hour after hour, may become restless, irritable, and aggressive.

6. *Food allergies.* Some children have allergies to certain foods or food additives that appear to be linked to ADHD. However, the once-popular notion that sugar and caffeine are possible contributors to ADHD has been discounted. Indeed, if anything, caffeine seems to slow some hyperactive children down (Ingersoll & Goldstein, 1993).

Help for Children with Attention-Deficit Hyperactivity Disorder

Not surprisingly, children with attention-deficit hyperactivity disorder are usually annoying to parents and teachers and are rejected by peers (Henker & Whalen, 1989). Many children with the disorder continue to have problems in adolescence, not only with hyperactivity but with academic demands and social skills as well (Barkley et al., 1991; Nussbaum et al., 1990). Many become disruptive and angry. In fact, more than half of all children with attention-deficit hyperactivity disorder have continuing problems as adults in pacing their work, controlling their temper, and developing patience. Some develop psychological disorders (such as antisocial personality) (Weiss, 1991). However, as they grow older, many people learn to cope with these problems, for example, by choosing occupations that suit their skills but that do not emphasize patience and control (Gittelman et al., 1985; Weiss & Hechtman, 1986). In childhood, the most effective forms of help are medication, psychological therapy, and changes in the family and school environments.

Drugs

The most frequent therapy for children with attention-deficit hyperactivity disorder is medication (Copeland et al., 1987). For reasons not yet determined, certain drugs that stimulate adults, such as amphetamines and methylphenidate (Ritalin), have a reverse effect on hyperactive children.

PUBLIC POLICY

Lead Poisoning

Taking a developmental view of learning disabilities helps not only in their treatment but, in some cases, in their prevention as well. One such case involves lead poisoning, which can cause specific learning disabilities, hyperactivity, and overall retardation. Although these symptoms are most notable in the school years, their origins are usually to be found in lead exposure that occurred in infancy or early childhood.

Most commonly, children are exposed to lead by breathing or ingesting lead residues, such as those in chips or dust from flaking lead-based paint or those in industrial pollutants. (Lead from automobile fuel, once a major source of childhood exposure, has been eliminated in most nations.) Since lead accumulates in the body, small amounts taken in over a period of time can produce toxicity.

Lead poisoning is diagnosed through blood analysis. If the lead level is above 70 milligrams per deciliter of blood, the toxic damage may include paralysis, permanent brain damage, and even death. If the level is between 25 and 70 milligrams per deciliter, many less obvious problems may result, including abnormally high activity level, poor concentration, and slow language development.

Whether lower levels, between 10 and 25 milligrams, are toxic is controversial. Some research finds an association between such levels of lead and developmental problems, and other research does not (Cooney et al., 1989; Silva et al., 1988). The controversy arises from confounding factors that make it difficult to draw firm conclusions. Looking at the same data, for example, two teams of American scientists both found a correlation between moderate lead levels and behavioral problems, but one team attributed this correlation directly to the effects of the lead (Bellinger & Needleman, 1985; Needleman et al., 1990), while the other team thought the deficits could be better explained by other factors (Ernhart et al., 1989). As the second team points out, for instance, elevated levels of lead are likely to be found in children who live in old houses with peeling paint or who play near the factories that pollute the air—in other words, in children who live in low-income neighborhoods. The proven hazards of poverty (such as troubled families, crowded schools, inadequate nutrition) may be the real culprit, not the hypothetical haz-

ard of low lead levels. Analyzing the data without taking such factors into account is "outrageous," according to noted developmental psychologist Sandra Scarr, partly because it shifts public attention away from reducing psychosocial risks to attending to purely biological ones (Palca, 1991).

Nevertheless, to be on the safe side, in 1991 the U.S. government lowered the level at which lead is considered toxic to 10 milligrams per deciliter. The Centers for Disease Control now recommends that all children under age 6 be tested for lead, and that when levels higher than 10 are found, precautions be taken. Obvious first steps include removal of any deteriorating lead-paint dust in the home, including lead-paint dust in window casements, eliminating lead contaminants from the yard, and keeping children from licking or eating anything that might contain lead (Hilts, 1991).

Fortunately, average blood-lead levels in the United States declined an average of 78 percent from about 1980 to 1990, primarily because all gasoline now sold is lead-free. In addition, less than 1 percent of all the food and soft-drink cans in the United States now use lead solder, compared to 47 percent in 1980. These changes have been particularly beneficial to children under age 6. In 1980, over 60 percent of children between the ages of 1 and 5 had blood-lead levels of 15 milligrams per deciliter or higher; in 1990, only 3 percent did. Nevertheless, there remain an estimated 1.7 million children—mostly low-income, city-dwelling children—whose blood-lead levels are at least 10 milligrams per deciliter. Although not all developmentalists agree that these children are necessarily at risk, most agree that lead testing of all young children and decreasing the pollutants in their environment—not just in their homes but also in the air and water—are wise public health precautions. When certain 3-year-olds consistently run rather than walk and jump up and down and fidget rather than ever being still, it would be reassuring to know that this high activity is age-related normal behavior that will improve in a few years, rather than a toxic reaction that might worsen, leaving the child disadvantaged when he or she is in elementary school and unable to learn as well as his or her classmates.

Figure 12.10 The use of psychoactive drugs to control mental disorders is controversial as well as complicated. However, those who assert that children should never be medicated to quiet their hyperactivity have not met Dusty Nash, age 7, or his mother. Without his daily Benzadrine, Dusty cannot concentrate or even sit quietly for a moment.

For many children, the results are remarkable, allowing them to sit still and concentrate for the first time in their lives. While this new ability to pay attention is a welcome relief to many children and parents, it does not necessarily produce gains in intelligence scores or achievement (Swanson et al., 1993).

Indeed, given the remarkable results that some ADHD children experience with psychoactive drugs, it needs to be emphasized that drug therapy is not a panacea. Unfortunately, drugs are sometimes prescribed for children without proper diagnosis or without follow-up examinations—an abuse that can harm the child. For instance, children are sometimes prescribed an excessively large dosage and become lethargic. Moreover, drugs do not aid all ADHD children. Further, by the time a child has become a candidate for psychoactive drugs, the child's behavior has usually created school, home, and personal problems that drugs alone cannot reverse. Psychoactive drugs should never be given as a one-step solution; instead, they should be part of an ongoing treatment program that involves the child's cognitive and psychosocial worlds (Wender, 1987).

Psychological Therapy

Usually, the child with attention-deficit hyperactivity disorder needs help overcoming a confused perception of the social world and a bruised ego, while the family needs help with their own management techniques and interaction. As noted in Chapter 2 (see Research Report, pp. 54–55), many families with difficult children unwittingly get caught in a vicious cycle of aggression and anger, in which the parents' and siblings' responses to the problem child perpetuate that child's problem behavior. Coercive family patterns seem especially apparent with ADHD children (Buhrmester et al., 1992). Typically, the child is told to behave in ways that are impossible for the child to follow ("sit still and be quiet") and then is confronted with anger and punishment when he or she fails to comply. Predictably, this unstructured and stressful situation leads to more out-of-control behavior by the child and by the adult.

Although some forms of therapy may work better with certain children than with others, the most effective types of therapy have generally been those developed from learning theory, such as teaching the parents how to use behavior-modification techniques with their child, guiding their efforts to organize and structure the child's environment in subdued and nondistracting ways, and helping the child see the effect of his or her own behavior (Anastopoulos et al., 1993; Henker & Whalen, 1989).

Teacher Response

Teachers are often the first professionals to suggest that a particular child might have attention-deficit hyperactivity disorder, for they are able to compare these children with their peers in a relatively structured setting. However, teachers, like parents, are often not aware that they themselves may be contributing to the child's difficulties. One study showed that some classroom environments, labeled **provocation ecologies**, made the problem worse, while others, called **rarefaction ecologies**, ameliorated the problem.

In provocation ecologies, structure was either unusually rigid or completely absent, and noise was either completely forbidden or tolerated to a distracting degree. In rarefaction ecologies, teachers who managed to diminish hyperactivity were flexible in their reactions to minor disruptions (for example, allowing children to ask questions of their neighbors as long as they did so quietly), but also provided sufficient structure so that the children knew what they should be doing and when (Whalen et al., 1979). Short periods of concentrated schoolwork in a quiet room alternating with opportunities for physical activity can also be helpful (Zadig & Meltzer, 1983). Often ADHD children have other learning disabilities. Once these are recognized and attended to, the child's other problems tend to diminish.

This is not to say that, with proper teaching, children with attention-deficit hyperactivity disorder suddenly quiet down and concentrate on their work. On the contrary, as with all physical handicaps and learning disabilities, no school, family, or community effort, no matter how structured or flexible, can make the problem disappear. However, like all children, children who have attention-deficit hyperactivity disorder can be greatly helped or harmed by the particular ecosystem of which they are a part.

It should be clear from our discussion of childhood psychopathology that physiological, educational, and social influences can interact to produce problems, and that all such influences must be understood before the impact of these problems can be reduced. Our focus on such problems should highlight the reality that the same interactional approach must characterize attempts to understand and meet the needs of all children. Further, as the developmental psychopathology perspective emphasizes, we must remember that each child has some of the strengths and liabilities typical of children in middle childhood, as well as capabilities and problems that few others share. This is, of course, true whether we are looking at biosocial development, as in this chapter, or at cognitive development, which we shall investigate in the next chapter.

provocation ecologies Classroom environments that provoke or exacerbate hyperactive behavior by imposing either an unusually rigid classroom structure or none at all.

rarefaction ecologies Classroom environments that ameliorate or diminish hyperactive behavior by providing sufficient classroom structure within a flexible individualized environment.

SUMMARY

Size and Shape

1. Children grow more slowly during middle childhood than at any other time until the end of adolescence. There is much variation in the size and rate of maturation of healthy North American children as a result of genetic as well as nutritional differences.

2. Overweight children suffer from peer rejection and low self-esteem. More exercise, rather than severe dieting, is the best solution, along with new attitudes toward food and recreation that are supported by family members.

3. Many influences interact to cause obesity. Hereditary factors, overfeeding in infancy and late childhood, and lack of exercise are among the chief contributors to this problem.

Motor Skills

4. School-age children can perform almost any motor skill, as long as it doesn't require much strength or refined judgment of distance or speed. The activities that are best for children are ones that demand only those skills that most children of this age can master.

Children with Special Needs

5. The developmental psychopathology perspective applies studies of normal development to an understanding of how children with psychological disorders cope with their particular difficulties. It emphasizes that they are children first—with the developmental needs that all children share—and, secondarily, are children with special challenges.

6. Autism is characterized by a lack of interest in people, delays in language and communication, and a deficiency in imagination that produces an insistence on sameness in the environment. Some researchers believe that autistic individuals lack a theory of mind to account for psychological processes in others. The severity and developmental outcome of autism vary enormously.

7. Children with problems such as a learning disability or attention-deficit hyperactivity disorder need special attention and help to learn to cope with their problems. They particularly need the support of adults who understand their special difficulties, and who can provide assistance so that these lifelong conditions do not become lifelong disabilities.

8. Some psychological disorders may originate in genetic or physical problems of some sort, but whether or not the cause is organic, many educational and psychological programs can help children with these disabilities. Psychoactive drugs also help some children, but these should be used carefully and cautiously.

KEY TERMS

obesity (413)
reaction time (418)
developmental psychopathology (420)
autism (421)
mental retardation (425)
learning disability (425)

dyslexia (426)
dyscalcula (426)
attention-deficit hyperactivity disorder (ADHD) (429)
provocation ecologies (434)
rarefaction ecologies (434)

KEY QUESTIONS

1. What are some of the causes of variation in physical growth in middle childhood?

2. How does obesity affect a child's development?

3. What are the causes of obesity?

4. What are some of the reasons for the notable improvement in children's motor skills during the school years?

5. How does the developmental psychopathology perspective view children with psychological disorders relative to children who develop normally?

6. What are the major characteristics of autism?

7. Why do some researchers believe that autistic individuals lack a theory of mind?

8. What are the symptoms of a learning disability? What are some of the more common types of learning disabilities?

9. What are the possible causes of attention-deficit hyperactivity disorder?

10. What are the arguments for and against the use of psychoactive drugs to control attention-deficit hyperactivity disorder?

11. What other types of treatment are helpful in controlling attention-deficit hyperactivity disorder?

The School Years:
Cognitive Development

During the school years, children's cognitive development enables them to focus their thinking less intuitively and more analytically on the facts and relationships that they perceive in the world. They become astute observers who have acquired "a sense of the game" of thinking. Growing language abilities complement these expanding cognitive skills, so older children can discuss and explain their world and themselves in ways no preschoolers can. These new abilities to investigate the world more objectively will be among the topics of this chapter, as will the questions that follow:

What are some of the factors that affect how school-age children remember and how well they learn new information?

What factors contribute to the growth of logical reasoning during middle childhood?

What factors may influence a child's success in learning a second language?

How does a child learn to communicate one way in the classroom and another on the playground?

What is the best approach to teaching children in the elementary school years?

How does culture affect education as well as the goals of instruction?

As we saw in Chapter 10, one of the major challenges of studying cognitive growth in the play years is to avoid underestimating the young child's competencies. Both scientific and casual observation of preschoolers in everyday activities can easily lead to the conclusion that the young child's cognitive skills are quite limited. It is only when preschoolers are observed in the context of carefully designed experiments, involving situations and stimuli that are meaningful and interesting to them, that their impressive cognitive abilities are more fully revealed.

By contrast, we rarely underestimate the cognitive competencies of school-age children. Their everyday skills are, in fact, obvious and quite remarkable, and expand every year. By age 11, for example, many children can figure out which brand and size of popcorn is the best buy, can multiply proper and improper fractions, can memorize a list of fifty new spelling words (or the batting averages of a favorite baseball team), and can use irony appropriately—accomplishments beyond virtually every preschooler.

The ability to plan and follow through on cognitive strategies further distinguishes older children from preschoolers. When faced with a homework assignment, whether it requires analyzing a science experiment performed in class, writing a story, or preparing for a geography test, most 11-year-olds know what they must do to succeed. It is, in fact, not just their skills but also their strategic knowledge that makes school-age children so educable—and accounts for why, upon entering middle childhood, children in most cultures are ushered into a formal educational system.

Our goal in this chapter is to understand the cognitive accomplishments of the school years, and, more important, to understand *why* these dramatic accomplishments occur. To do this, we will turn again to the insights provided by information-processing researchers, regarding how thinking becomes more organized and strategic, as well as to the views of Piaget and his followers, regarding how thinking becomes more systematic and logical. We will also discuss further growth in language and consider the impact of schooling on cognitive growth.

The Growth of Thinking, Memory, and Knowledge

Middle childhood witnesses many cognitive changes that make the school-age child a much different kind of thinker than the preschooler. Older children not only know more but are more resourceful in planning and using their cognitive resources when they must solve a problem, remember a piece of information, or increase their knowledge on a particular topic. In contrast to the fairly fragile cognitive accomplishments of the preschooler, school-age children can apply their thinking and reasoning skills to a variety of cognitive challenges—or can quickly figure out how to do so. In the words of John Flavell (1992), by the middle of childhood, most children have acquired "a sense of the game" of thinking. They know that good thinking entails consideration of all the evidence, planfulness, logic, formulation of alternative hypotheses, and consistency, and they try to incorporate these qualities into their own reasoning, as well as in their evaluation of the thinking of others (Flavell et al., 1993). Moreover, during the school years, children become more aware of intellectual strengths and weaknesses, recognizing that one can be "good at" certain things (like math and science) but not as proficient at others.

Information-processing researchers believe that these monumental advances in thinking occur because of basic changes in children's processing and analysis of information (Bjorklund, 1990; Klahr, 1992; Kuhn, 1992). As we will see, these changes are directly related to the growth of selective attention and memory skills, the enhancement of processing speed and capacity, the growth of knowledge, and, finally, the blossoming of "metacognition," or the ability to think about thinking.

Selective Attention

If you were to watch children in a kindergarten and then observe the students in a fifth-grade classroom, many of the differences you would find would be related to the growth of selective attention. In kindergarten, chil-

FIGURE 13.1 The ability to use selective attention to screen out distractions and focus on the task at hand makes fifth-graders, like this boy, much better students than younger children.

dren become easily distracted while listening to a story or printing alphabet letters: they chatter to each other, look around, fidget, and sometimes get up to visit friends or just wander around (further distracting their peers!). By contrast, fifth-graders are likely to be found working independently at their desks or in groups around a table, managing to read, write, discuss, and seek assistance from the teacher without distracting, or being distracted by, other children who are working on different assignments.

This ability to use **selective attention**—to screen out distractions and concentrate on relevant information—improves steadily during middle childhood. This advance was clearly revealed in a study in which children between the ages of 7 and 10 were presented with a large box consisting of twelve doors arranged in two rows. Behind each door was one of several pictures of either an animal or a household object. Which type of picture the door concealed was indicated on the front of the door by a logo of either a cage (indicating an animal) or a house (indicating a household object). Half the children were told to remember which specific animal was located behind which door, and the other half were told to do the same with the household objects. Then the children were given a study period during which they could open any of the doors as often as they wished. Obviously, the most efficient strategy was to open only the doors bearing the relevant logo, and this is what the older children tended to do. By contrast, the preschoolers were not selective: they usually opened all the doors, regardless of whether they were to remember animals or household objects (DeMarie-Dreblow & Miller, 1988; Miller, 1990; Miller et al., 1986). Not surprisingly, the older children were better at remembering the locations of the relevant pictures.

Selective attention is important not just for memory, but also for reasoning and problem solving. To complete a challenging problem, a person must first focus on the information that is likely to lead to a solution, and then proceed straightforwardly until a successful outcome is achieved. This is true whether one is figuring out the relative amounts of liquid in different containers or editing another child's writing for spelling and punctuation. Many preschoolers fail at simple problem solving, not because they are ignorant or lazy, but because their selective attention is inconsistent, and they become distracted on the way to the solution. Sometimes they even forget the problem itself! By contrast, older children are more methodical and strategic: they know when selective attention is called for and know how and where to focus their attention (Flavell et al., 1993; Miller, 1990).

selective attention The ability to concentrate on relevant information and ignore distractions.

Memory Strategies

If you wanted to remember some new information—the names of class-mates or former presidents, say—you could simply look at a list of the names for a while and hope it sinks into your memory. This ineffective approach (you might call it the "osmosis strategy") is precisely the one that most preschool children use.

During middle childhood, however, children's repertoire of procedures for retaining new information—their memory **storage strategies**—broadens significantly (Kail, 1990). This is especially true if, in the course of daily life, they are assigned things to remember and receive guidance from parents, teachers, and friends on how to do so. Typically, children first begin to use **rehearsal**, repeating the information to be remembered. Somewhat later, they also use **organization**, regrouping the information to make it more memorable. For example, to memorize the fifty states, one could learn them by region, or in alphabetical order. By early adolescence, children are capable of more complex storage strategies, such as associating information with personal experiences or hypothetical examples, and they have thus become quite skilled at knowing how to memorize.

FIGURE 13.2 How best to remember the names and locations of countries around the world? These boys know that any of a variety of memory strategies would be helpful—including simple rehearsal, grouping countries by region or in alphabetical order, or color-coding them on maps according to their location or other features.

storage strategies Procedures for holding information in memory, such as rehearsal (repeating the information to be remembered) and organization (regrouping the information to make it more memorable).

rehearsal A memory technique involving repetition of the material to be remembered.

organization In information-processing, a memory technique involving the regrouping of information to make it more memorable.

retrieval strategies Procedures for recollecting previously learned information, such as thinking of related information or trying to create a mental image of the thing to be remembered.

Once you have memorized something, of course, there remains the task of gaining access to this information when it is needed on a later occasion. Anybody who has had the frustrating experience of being unable to bring to mind a bit of information (a person's name, or an important term) that one knows is stored in memory realizes the importance of **retrieval strategies**, or procedures for accessing previously learned information. Although young children might know how to search their rooms to locate a misplaced toy, their limited grasp of mental processes (recall Chapter 10) makes them much less efficient at searching their memories. The ability to use retrieval strategies begins to emerge in middle childhood and improves steadily thereafter (Kail, 1990). For example, by fifth grade, children usually have a dawning awareness that if something can't initially be recalled, merely "taking a walk down memory lane"—that is, systematically searching one's recollections of other relevant events or information—might prove helpful (Flavell et al., 1993). Somewhat later, they become even more strategic in their retrieval efforts. For example, they try to jog their memories by thinking of clues to stimulate their recall (the first letter of a name or key term), or they attempt to visualize the experience they are trying to remember. By the seventh grade, many students would not panic in a geography test if they could not immediately remember the exact location of Bolivia or Bulgaria: they would try mentally visualizing a map of the world, or reconstructing the context of the last study session, to bring it to mind.

Taken together, storage strategies and retrieval strategies are called **mnemonics**, or memory aids. In contrast with preschoolers, whose aids to memory are limited to their scripts for familiar situations and careful questioning by adults, older children can use memory strategies spontaneously and skillfully, and are aware of the situations in which specific strategies can be most useful.

Processing Speed and Capacity

Another cognitive difference between younger and older children is that the latter are quicker thinkers (Hale, 1990; Kail, 1991a, 1991b). In fact, processing speed continues to improve from the preschool years through early adulthood (Kail, 1991b).

Processing speed affects more than just performance time. It also affects processing capacity: children who can think faster can also think about more things at once. In contrast with a preschooler who becomes easily befuddled when faced with complex tasks or simultaneous demands, the school-age child can mentally coordinate multiple ideas, thoughts, or strategies at the same time. A larger processing capacity means, for example, that an older sister can simultaneously listen to the dinner-table conversation of her parents, respond to the interruptions of her younger siblings, think about her weekend plans, and still remember to ask for her allowance.

Increased processing capacity also helps account for the stage differences that Piaget found in children's ability to conserve. In Piaget's famous conservation-of-liquid test, for example (see Chapter 10), increased processing capacity enables older children to mentally coordinate the height and width of a container to understand how changes in these dimensions affect the appearance of volume. This is in strong contrast to younger children, who, you will recall, tend to center their thinking on only one aspect of a situation at a time and are consequently misled by the volume's appearance.

An additional—and not always trivial—benefit of increased processing capacity is that older children can better predict whether an adult will think a joke is funny because they can consider multiple factors in advance, such as the person's preferences, values, and sense of humor, as well as the quality of the joke itself! By contrast, preschoolers are likely to believe that a joke is funny if *they* think it is.

Why do processing speed and capacity increase during middle childhood? Some researchers believe that neurological maturation helps to account for these changes, especially the myelination of nerve pathways and maturation of the frontal cortex (Bjorklund & Harnishfeger, 1990; Dempster, 1993; Kail, 1991b). Others, however, believe that processing becomes more efficient because children learn to use their cognitive resources better (Case, 1985; Flavell et al., 1993). Selective attention is an example: as older

FIGURE 13.3 This boy's concentration while heading the ball and simultaneously preparing to fall is a sign that he has practiced this maneuver enough times that he can perform it automatically. Not having to think about what to do on the way down, he can think about what to do when he gets up, such as pursuing the ball or getting back to cover his position.

mnemonics Memory aids, such as specific rhymes or mental associations, that facilitate the storage and retrieval of information.

children learn to focus their attention on only relevant information in a given task, their thinking becomes less "cluttered" with distractions, thereby enhancing their processing speed and capacity.

Another factor in improved processing is simple experience. Information processing becomes more efficient through **automatization**, the process in which familiar and well-rehearsed mental activities become routine and automatic. Recall when you were young how much concerted effort you needed to read words or to add numbers or to use a foreign vocabulary before you were fluent, or to hit the ball correctly when you first tried to play tennis, or baseball, or pool. As these activities became more familiar, well-practiced, and routine, less mental work was required to carry them out successfully, making it easier to devote your mental energies to other tasks. Consequently, you can now (most likely) comment to yourself mentally about what you are reading—even in a foreign language—or plot strategy while hitting a ball. As children mature and gain experience, more and more mental processes that initially required hard mental labor become automatized, and this increases processing speed and frees up processing capacity, enabling older children to think about many different things at once.

Knowledge Growth

Cognitive growth seems to follow the principle that the more one knows, the more one can learn. Having a body of knowledge or skills in a particular area—whether it concerns some aspect of history, the planets and stars, or the animal kingdom—makes it easier to learn new information in that area because it can be integrated with what is already known. Thus, one reason children become better learners in middle childhood is that they have expanded knowledge: they already know more about many different domains of knowledge.

An expanded knowledge base also improves memory ability. What has surprised developmental scientists, however, is *how much* of a difference one's knowledge can have for memory ability—independent of the maturity of thinking, reasoning, and other skills. It should not surprise you to discover, for example, that chess experts are able to remember the locations of chess pieces on the board better than novices are. But does this remain true even when the experts are children and the novices are adults? This question was explored by Michelene Chi (1978) in a study of young chess experts recruited from a local chess tournament. These children, who were from the third through the eighth grades, were compared on their recall of complex chess positions against a group of adults who were acquainted with the game but were not experts. The children were strikingly more accurate in their recall than were the adults, and their mental organization of the chess pieces into logical, interrelated memory "chunks" was also more efficient. By contrast, when the same children and adults were compared on a test of number recall—in which the children did not have expertise—the adults were more proficient (see Figure 13.4). The better memory skills of the children were apparent, therefore, only for those domains of thinking in which they had greater knowledge and experience.

Chi's findings are not a surprise to any parent who has been corrected by a 6-year-old dinosaur buff for mistaking a diplodocus for a brontosaurus. But the implications of this study may be surprising, since they suggest that

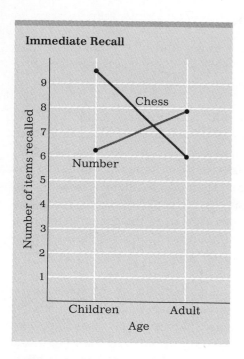

FIGURE 13.4 This graph shows the results of Michelene Chi's classic test of memory for chess positions. The fact that children who were expert at chess remembered the location of chess pieces better than adults who were novices—even though they did less well than the adults at remembering a series of random numbers—suggests the important role of knowledge in memory ability.

automatization The process by which familiar and well-rehearsed mental activities become routine and automatic.

adults are not always more cognitively competent than children. Many differences between schoolchildren's and adults' thinking and reasoning may be due, in fact, to the children's more limited knowledge and experience (Keil, 1984). As the child's storehouse of knowledge increases with age, concepts become more elaborated and interconnected with each other, the mental framework for organizing knowledge becomes more sophisticated, and the young learner can ask better questions to gain new understanding (Chi et al., 1989).

Metacognition

A final reason school-age children advance in learning and reasoning is their developing awareness of cognitive strategies. In essence, during the school years, children become aware that learning and problem solving require that they *do* something, and they increasingly understand *what* they must do to perform well. The ability to evaluate a cognitive task to determine how to best accomplish it—and to monitor one's performance—is called **metacognition**. In a sense, this "metacognition" means "thinking about thinking," and its development is related to the theory of mind children begin to acquire in the preschool years (see Chapter 10, pp. 344–346).

There are many indicators of developmental growth in metacognition (Flavell et al., 1993; Siegler, 1991). Preschoolers have difficulty judging whether a problem is easy or difficult and thus they devote equal effort to each kind. By contrast, children in the school years know how to identify challenging tasks and they devote greater effort to these challenges, with greater success. During the school years children also acquire a better grasp of which cognitive strategies are well-suited for which cognitive tasks: they might recognize, for example, that rehearsal is a good strategy for memorizing, but that for enhancing understanding, it is less effective than outlining (Lovett & Flavell, 1990).

Moreover, school-age children spontaneously monitor and evaluate their progress in a manner that is rare in preschoolers, so they are usually able to judge when they have adequately learned a set of spelling words or science principles. Older children are also more likely to use external aids—such as writing things down, or making lists—to enhance their memorization and problem-solving efforts. In short, older children approach cognitive tasks in a more strategic and planful manner. Their efforts are thus more comprehensive and exhaustive, because they have a heightened metacognitive awareness.

Not surprisingly, research on metacognition is relevant to education: children's learning can be improved if teachers can teach students more effective cognitive strategies (Kail, 1990; Weissberg & Paris, 1986). Children can be encouraged to analyze whether a problem is likely to be easy or difficult, select an appropriate learning or memory strategy, and monitor their progress throughout. One information-processing theorist, Robert Siegler (1983a, 1983b), has studied the intuitive strategies that children commonly employ in problem-solving situations, and he has noted that children learn most when they are shown the specific shortcomings in the strategies they use and are led to more advanced strategies. In general, children benefit from educational practices that not only impart knowledge but also foster cognitive strategies.

FIGURE 13.5 When younger children write an essay or a poem, their first thoughts become their first draft, which is also their final draft. With the advent of metacognition comes an appreciation that outlining, drafting, revising, redrafting, and checking spelling may all precede the final copy.

metacognition Thinking about thinking, including the ability to evaluate a cognitive task to determine how best to accomplish it and how to monitor one's performance.

Thinking Skills and Formal Education

As you can see, there are a variety of mental processes that develop during middle childhood in ways that enhance the child's learning, thinking, and problem-solving capabilities. It is no surprise, therefore, that formal education usually begins at the age that these capabilities start to unfold. Children become far more educable when they can deliberately use selective attention, mnemonics, and metacognition to assist their learning, and when they can benefit from expanded knowledge and enhanced processing capacity in their efforts to think and reason. In each of these ways, the older child can respond to formal instruction in ways the preschooler cannot.

To illustrate, consider the growth of two important skills that are taught during the elementary-school years, reading and mathematics. Reading requires the integration of a formidable variety of subprocesses, including the abilities to perceive and interpret both single letters and letter clusters; to understand the meanings of words; to remember chunks of text while deducing their meaning in relation to other chunks; and to monitor one's understanding of an entire text, returning, if necessary, to pertinent passages to fill in gaps in one's comprehension. Reading theorists believe that the growth of these reading skills during the school years is related to the information-processing advances we have discussed (Stanovich, 1990). As these subprocesses become well-practiced, for example, they gradually become automatized, enabling children to interpret letter clusters and word meanings more quickly and more efficiently. In turn, this expands their processing capacity, so they can do more things at once while reading a story—such as keeping track of the plot and gaining familiarity with the characters—rather than focusing exclusively on sounding out letters and words.

In addition, the growth of metacognition enables school-age children to use strategies suggested by their teachers, such as recognizing root stems when encountering unfamiliar words (the meanings of "joyful," "joyless," "joyride," and "joystick" are easy to deduce for the reader who knows the meaning of "joy" and the use of suffixes and compounds. Metacognition also allows children to monitor their understanding of what they have just read by relating it to what they already know about the topic. Finally, the growth of selective attention equips the older child to concentrate on using and integrating these complex subprocesses in a manner that is beyond the more distractable preschooler. For these reasons, literacy is gradually attained, skill by skill, until at about age 12, the entire process becomes automatic.

Similar information-processing skills are applied to the growth of mathematical understanding. As you know from Chapter 10, basic number concepts are understood by preschoolers and provide a basis for the school-age child's grasp of addition, subtraction, multiplication, and other mathematical operations. But *using* numbers competently is far more challenging than simply *knowing about* numbers. Indeed, using numbers requires almost as many subprocesses as reading does. To add or multiply, the school-age child must be able to, among other things, hold numbers in mind while mentally associating them, consistently apply the relevant mathematical rules (such as "borrowing" in subtraction), perform these subprocesses with sufficient speed that the overall operation is not "lost" before the problem is completed, and evaluate the solution to ensure that it is a reasonable one (Resnick, 1989). As you might guess, these subprocesses require considerable growth in processing capacity and speed, the knowledge base, and metacognition. Furthermore, when mathematical problems are in story form, the child must be able to exercise selective attention to ensure that only relevant information is included in the calculation. Like those necessary for reading, these skills are not easy to acquire, which is why formal schooling—building upon the growth of children's information-processing abilities—is important (although not necessarily essential, as we shall see) to their mastery.

Concrete Operational Thought

Another cognitive characteristic of older children that also contributes to their "educability" is that they are *logical* thinkers. Whereas preschoolers may invoke intuition and subjective insights to understand the results of a science experiment ("Maybe the caterpillar just felt like becoming a butterfly!"), school-age children seek explanations that are rational, internally consistent, and generalizable ("Does the caterpillar use the air temperature to know when it's time to begin a cocoon?"). This rationalizing process continues throughout middle childhood. Out on the playground, first-graders may argue over the rules of a game by using increasingly loud and assertive protests ("Is!" "Is not!" "*Is!*" "*Is not!*"), whereas fifth-graders temper their arguments with reason and justification ("That *can't* be right, because if it was, we'd have to score points differently!"). In academic and nonacademic contexts, logical thinking is crucial to understanding, to acquiring knowledge, and to communicating clearly with others.

As you know, Piaget was especially interested in the growth of logical reasoning skills during childhood. In his view, the most important cognitive achievement of middle childhood is the attainment of **concrete operational thought**, by which children can reason logically about the things and events they perceive. In Chapter 10 we saw that preschoolers, contrary to Piaget's expectations, sometimes show flashes of concrete operational thinking, as demonstrated in their ability to perform successfully on simplified, gamelike tests of conservation. But preschoolers' ability to think logically are fragile at best, and usually limited to tasks on which they have received special training. According to Piaget, between ages 7 and 11, children truly begin to understand logical principles, and are able to consistently apply them to concrete—that is specific, tangible—cases. They therefore become more systematic, objective, scientific—and educable—thinkers.

Logical Principles

To understand the importance of logical principles in the thinking of a concrete-operational child, consider the principle of identity. **Identity** is the idea that an object remains the same despite changes in its appearance. Just as infants early acquire an understanding that objects continue to exist even when they cannot be perceived, children who understand the principle of identity realize that superficial changes in an object's appearance do not alter its underlying substance or quantity. Mastery of this logical principle is one reason children become able to perform logical operations, such as those required in conservation tasks. In the conservation-of-liquids task (see pp. 60–61, 349–351), for example, an awareness of identity enables school-

concrete operational thought In Piaget's theory, the third period of cognitive development, characterized by the ability to apply logical processes to concrete problems.

identity In Piaget's theory, the logical principle that a given substance remains the same no matter what changes occur in its shape or appearance.

FIGURE 13.6 This science teacher and student are demonstrating the effects of static electricity. Such demonstrations turn on the logical abilities of concrete-operational children much better than the abstract descriptions of textbooks.

age children to realize that pouring the liquid contents of a particular container into a differently sized container does not change the amount of liquid.

Identity is also relevant to mathematical understanding. Once children have a firm grasp of identity, they know that the number 24 is always 24, whether it is arrived at by adding 14 and 10 or 23 and 1. This logical principle also enhances scientific understanding, whether it involves grasping the underlying oneness of the tadpole and frog or understanding the idea that a solid can be converted into a liquid. Identity can be applied in nonacademic ways as well, particularly in everyday social encounters. The principle of identity enables school-age children to understand—as most preschoolers cannot—that their mother was once a child and that a baby picture of their mother is, in fact, a picture of their mother (even though she looks quite changed). In all these ways, the underlying logical principle of identity contributes to more acute, and objective, understanding.

The same is true of two other logical principles, **reversibility** and **reciprocity**. These two principles relate to the fact that a transformation can be restored to its original state by reversing the transformation process or by performing another transformation that compensates for the effects of the original one. Equipped with these two principles in the conservation-of-liquids task, a child can argue that the amount of liquid in the second, differently sized container is the same as it was in the original container either by pouring the liquid back into the original container to demonstrate equivalence (reversibility) or by noting that the greater (or lesser) height of the liquid in the second container is attributable to that container's narrower (or wider) width (reciprocity). Such logical principles are also essential to understanding different mathematical operations, such as seeing subtraction as the reversing of addition (if $9 + 9 = 18$, then $18 - 9 = 9$) or understanding reciprocity in multiplication (that 4×3 and 3×4 both equal 12). Of course, reversibility and reciprocity also have everyday social relevance, such as when they are applied to social problem solving (as in "Let's start over and be friends again. OK?" or "I'll help you with math, if you teach me to dance").

Obviously a child who can consistently, and thoughtfully, apply logical principles is better equipped to carefully analyze problems, derive correct solutions, and ask follow-up questions that yield further understanding than is a more intuitive, haphazard thinker. The ability to apply logical principles

reversibility The logical principle that something that has been changed can be returned to its original state by reversing the process of change.

reciprocity The logical principle that a change in one dimension of an object can be compensated for by a change in another dimension.

also makes older children more objective thinkers, enabling them to distance themselves from their subjective impressions and personal experiences to derive a more reasoned judgment. Unlike preschoolers, they can arrive at assessments like "Maybe that's the way it seems to be, but really it's . . ." Moreover, as identity, reversibility, and other logical principles are generalized across different tasks and situations, they provide coherence and consistency to a child's thinking.

Limitations

Overall, Piaget's depiction of cognitive development tends to suggest that a child's movement from one stage to the next occurs fairly quickly once begun, and also occurs across the board in all domains. However, current researchers maintain that the child enters a new stage gradually, and that a certain type of reasoning might be apparent in one domain—say, math or science—but not in others, like social understanding.

Particularly in the case of concrete operational thought, these researchers believe that cognitive development is considerably more heterogeneous, or inconsistent, than Piaget's descriptions would suggest. According to Flavell (1982), two of the factors that account for this heterogeneity are the hereditary differences among individuals in their abilities and aptitudes and environmental differences in "cultural, educational, and other task-related experiential background." The sum of these differences, says Flavell, might well produce a great deal of cognitive heterogeneity:

> Imagine, for example, a child or adolescent who is particularly well-endowed with the abilities needed to do computer science, has an all-consuming interest in it, has ample time and opportunity to learn about it, and has an encouraging parent who is a computer scientist (whence much of the aptitude, interest, and opportunity, perhaps). The quality and sophistication of the child's thinking in this area might well be higher than that of most adults in any area. It would also likely be much higher in this area than in most other areas of the child's cognitive life. His level of moral reasoning or skill in making inferences about other people might be considerably less developed, for instance. The heterogeneity could be a matter of time constraints as well as a matter of differential aptitudes and interests: that is, time spent at the computer terminal is time not spent interacting with and learning about people.

Thus, while the overall thinking of a school-age child is definitely less intuitive and more logical than it was a few years earlier, how much so it is depends on the child, the topic, and the specific context.

Language

As you saw in Chapter 10, the preschool years are the time of a language explosion, in which children's vocabulary, grammar, and pragmatic language skills develop with marked rapidity. Language development between ages 6 to 11 is also remarkable, though much more subtle, as children consciously come to understand more about the many ways language is structured and can be used. This understanding gives them greater control in their comprehension and use of language, and, in turn, enlarges the range of their cognitive powers generally. Their understanding of language is a powerful key to a new understanding of themselves and their world.

Vocabulary

During middle childhood, children begin to really enjoy words, as they continue to fast-map new ones into their vocabularies. Indeed, by some estimates, the rate of school-age vocabulary growth exceeds that of the preschool years, with children acquiring as many as twenty words daily to achieve a vocabulary of nearly 40,000 words by the fifth grade (Anglin, 1993). Children's delight in verbal play—clearly demonstrated in the poems they write, the secret languages they create, and the jokes they tell—makes middle childhood a good time to explicitly help children expand their vocabularies, thus providing a foundation for more elaborate self-expression.

One of the most important language developments during middle childhood is a shift in the way children think about words. Gradually they become more analytic and logical in their processing of vocabulary, and less restricted to the actions and perceptual features directly associated with particular words (Holzman, 1983). When a child is asked to say the first word that comes to mind on hearing, say, "apple," the preschooler is likely to be bound to the immediate context of an apple, responding with a word that refers to its appearance ("red," "round") or to an action associated with it ("eat," "cook"). The older child, on the other hand, is likely to respond to "apple" by referring to an appropriate category ("fruit," "snack") or to other objects that logically extend the context ("banana," "pie," "tree"). Moreover, the older child can deduce the meanings of new words that have "apple" as their root (such as "applesauce" and "applecart"), and this ability also helps to account for rapid vocabulary growth (Anglin, 1993).

Similarly, when they define words, preschoolers tend to use examples, especially examples that are action-bound. For instance, while preschoolers understand that "under," "below," and "above" refer to relative position, they define these words with examples such as "Rover sleeps under the bed," or "Below is to go down under something." Older children tend to define words by analyzing their relationships to other words: they would be more likely to say, for instance, that "under" is the same as "below," or the opposite of "above" (Holzman, 1983).

Older children's more analytic understanding of words is particularly useful as children are increasingly exposed to words that may have no direct referent in their own personal experience. This understanding makes it possible for them to add to their conceptual framework abstract terms such as "mammal" (extracting the commonalities of, say, whales and mice) or foreign terms such as *yen* (relating this unit of currency to the dollar), and to differentiate among similar words such as "big," "huge," and "gigantic," or "jogging," "running," and "sprinting." Thus, the cognitive maturation of middle childhood, coupled with the school experiences that children have, enables children's vocabularies to increase exponentially.

Grammar

Similar progress occurs in grammar. Although many grammatical constructions of the child's native language are mastered before age 6, knowledge of syntax continues to develop throughout elementary school (Goodluck, 1991; Romaine, 1984). Children are increasingly able to use grammar to understand the implied connections between words, even if the usual clues, such as word order, are misleading.

FIGURE 13.7 With a language as irregular as English, it should be no surprise that many children (as well as adults) sometimes generate grammatical errors by applying logic to their language constructions.

For instance, children younger than age 6 often have trouble understanding the passive voice, because they know that the agent of an action in a sentence usually precedes the object that is being acted upon. By middle childhood, however, most children realize that the sentence "The truck was bumped by the car" does not state that the truck did the bumping (de Villiers & de Villiers, 1978). The increasing understanding of the passive voice is reflected in children's spontaneous speech as well as in research studies: compared with 6-year-olds, 8-year-olds use the passive voice two-and-a-half times as frequently, and 10-year-olds, three-and-a-half times as often (Romaine, 1984).

The school-age child's gradual understanding of logical relations helps in the understanding of other constructions, such as the correct use of comparatives ("longer," "deeper," "wider"), of the subjunctive ("If you were a millionaire . . ."), and of metaphors (that is, of how a person could be a dirty dog or a rotten egg) (Waggoner & Palermo, 1989). The ability to use these constructions depends on a certain level of cognitive development that typically occurs during elementary school. This is true even with languages in which the particular construction is relatively simple. For instance, the subjunctive form is much less complicated in Russian than in English, but Russian-speaking children master the subjunctive only slightly earlier than do English-speaking children, because the concept *if-things-were-other-than-they-are* must be understood before it can be expressed (de Villiers & de Villiers, 1978, 1992).

School-age children have another decided advantage over younger children when it comes to mastering the more difficult forms of grammar. Whereas preschool children are quite stubborn in clinging to their grammatical mistakes (remember the child in Chapter 10 who "holded" the baby bunnies?), school-age children are more teachable. They no longer judge correctness solely on the basis of their own speech patterns. Assuming that they have had ample opportunity to learn the correct grammar, by the end of middle childhood, children are able to apply the rules of proper grammar when asked to, even if they don't use them in their own everyday speech. Thus, even if they themselves say "Me and Suzy quarreled," they are able to understand that "Suzy and I quarreled" is considered correct.

Pragmatics

We have already seen that preschoolers have a grasp of some of the pragmatic aspects of language: they change the tone of their voice when talking to a doll, for instance, or when pretending to be a doctor. However, preschoolers are not very skilled at modifying vocabulary, sentence length, semantic content, and nonverbal cues to fit particular situations. The many skills of communicating improve markedly throughout middle childhood.

FIGURE 13.8 Next time you see a group of school-age children laughing at a friend's joke, you should be impressed with the young person's mastery of pragmatics. Telling a good story requires careful timing, exact vocabulary, and strategic nonverbal cues, as well as a knowledge of one's audience.

Communicating effectively requires, for instance, considering the needs and capacities of the listener. Although preschoolers show an early sensitivity to listener needs—by using simpler speech with a younger child, for example—these communications seldom take into account the specific listener's background or characteristics. In one study, Susan Sonnenschein (1986) asked first-grade and fourth-grade children to pretend that they were instructing a playmate on how to find a particular toy in their room at home. The playmate was either a best friend who was familiar with the toys in that room, or a child who was visiting for the first time. Sonnenschein found that although children at each age gave more instructions to the first-time visitor, only the fourth-graders' instructions were consistently well-suited to finding the toy: those of the first-graders included both helpful and irrelevant additional information.

One of the clearest demonstrations of schoolchildren's improved pragmatic skills is found in their joke-telling, which demands several skills not usually apparent in younger children—the ability to listen carefully; the ability to know what someone else will think is funny; and, hardest of all, the ability to remember the right way to tell a joke. Telling a joke is beyond most preschool children. If asked to do so, they usually just say a word (such as "pooh-pooh") or describe an action ("shooting someone with a water gun") that they think is funny. Even if they actually use a joke form, they often miss the point. One preschooler attempted a joke after listening to her older sisters tell jokes on a long car trip. "What happens when a car goes into a tunnel?" she asked. "What?" her sisters chorused. "It gets dark" came the punch line. By contrast, almost every 7-year-old can successfully tell a favorite joke upon request (Yalisove, 1978).

Further evidence of increased pragmatic skill is shown in children's learning the various forms of polite speech. School-age children realize that a teacher's saying "I would like you to put away your books now" is not a simple statement of preference but a command in polite form (Holzman, 1983). Similarly, compared with 5-year-olds, 7- to 9-year-olds are quicker to realize that when making requests of persons of higher status—particularly persons who seem somewhat unwilling to grant the request—they should use more polite phrases ("Could I please . . . ?") and more indirect requests ("It would be nice if . . . ") than when they are negotiating with their peers (Axia & Baroni, 1985).

Code-Switching

Changing from one form of speech to another is called **code-switching**. As we will see, children in middle childhood can engage in many forms of code-switching, from the relatively simple process of censoring profanity when they talk to their parents to switching back and forth from one language to another.

A very obvious example of code-switching is children's use of one manner of communicating when they are in the classroom and another when they are with friends outside of school. In general, the former style, called the **elaborated code**, is associated with conventional norms for correct language, while the latter style, called the **restricted code**, is more informal, abbreviated, and colloquial (Bernstein, 1971, 1973). The elaborated code is characterized by extensive vocabulary, complex syntax, and lengthy sentences: the restricted code, by comparison, has a much more limited use of vocabulary and syntax and relies more on gestures and intonation to convey meaning. The elaborated code is relatively context-free; the meaning of its statements is explicit. The restricted code tends to be context-bound, relying on the shared understandings and experiences of speaker and listener to provide some of the meaning. Switching from one code to another, a dispirited student might tell a teacher, "I am depressed today and I don't feel like doing anything," and later confide to a friend, "I feel crumby today, and school stinks." Research has shown that children of all social strata engage in this type of code-switching, and that their pronunciation, grammar, and slang all change in the process (Holzman, 1983; Rogers, 1976; Romaine, 1984; Yoon, 1992).

It seems clear that both elaborated and restricted codes have their place. It is important to be able to explain one's ideas in elaborate and formal terms when appropriate. In fact, two of the basic skills taught during these years, reading and writing, depend on the comprehension of language in a situation devoid of gestures and intonations. At the same time, it is useful to be able to express oneself informally with one's peers, using more emotive, colloquial, and inventive modes of communication than those of the standard, accepted code. While many adults rightly stress the importance of children's mastery of the elaborated code ("Say precisely what you mean in complete sentences, and no slang"), the code that is used with peers is also evidence of the child's pragmatic skill (Goodwin, 1990).

Nonstandard English

Another, more difficult type of code-switching is required of those whose ethnic or regional heritage includes vocabulary, grammar, and pronunciation quite distinct from "standard" English. To some degree, nonstandard English is pervasive: idiosyncrasies in speech patterns between one Canadian province and another, or one U.S. state and another, or even one side of town and another, are often strong enough to identify an individual's cultural and geographic origins (Wells, 1982). The Boston "r" (as in "Pahk the cah"), the Ontario "ou" (as in "Talk a'boot a lucky break"), the Mississippi "a" (as in "Cayan ya dayance?"), or the preferred regionalisms used for a "hero" / "hoagy" / "sub" / "grinder" / "dagwood" and a "soft drink" / "cola" / "pop"/ "soda" / "fizzy water" / "tonic" to wash it down are among the most obvious examples.

code-switching A pragmatic communication skill that involves a person's switching from one form of language, such as dialect or slang, to another.

elaborated code A form of language characterized by extensive and explicit vocabulary, complex syntax, and lengthy sentences.

restricted code A form of language characterized by limited use of vocabulary and syntax and a reliance on gestures, intonation, and shared experience for the communication of meaning.

FIGURE 13.9 In a multiethnic classroom, which is increasingly the norm in many nations, teachers need to appreciate each child's own linguistic voice while helping all the children master the culture's standard form of communication. If the facial expressions and the birthday chart on the wall are any indication, this classroom is a place where both diversity and commonality are respected.

For some groups, however, language differences form a distinct code. This is especially true for groups that are cohesive, geographically isolated, and culturally distinct, as reflected in the English spoken in Jamaica, Ireland, and Pakistan. Within the United States, the ethnic groups that are somewhat alienated from the mainstream culture tend to develop particular patterns of speech, including grammar and vocabulary.

Many users of standard English consider such variations simply wrong, a collection of mispronunciations, malapropisms, and grammatical mistakes that call for disdain or derision. Actually, however, each dialect has particular rules, rhythms, and phrases that survive because they hold communicative power beyond that of the standard language. Within the United States, the work of many African-American novelists, filmmakers, and rap artists is testimony to this power.

Both academic and social problems can arise, however, if a child's primary language is a nonstandard form, spoken by everyone at home and in the neighborhood. Success in school—and, quite often, in the broader community—requires learning to read and write standard English—a task that is made much more difficult if standard speech is unfamiliar. This task is further complicated if classmates tease the child for his or her unusual speech and if the teacher takes the stance that nonstandard English is incorrect, incomprehensible, and "illegitimate"—both responses representing an attack on the child's primary identity (Hemmings & Metz, 1990). Faced with such treatment, many children either become silent in the classroom or rebel, defiantly refusing to learn standard English, and often rejecting behavior codes and achievement expectations from the school as well. In addition, the school's reaction undercuts the merits of the child's own culture, causing a double blow to self-esteem.

Other teachers, taking the opposite tack, treat nonstandard English as legitimate, accepting it in classwork and speaking it with students (Hemmings & Metz, 1990). This reaction may unintentionally handicap the child's chances for advancement, not only in school and college, but also in the job market and the larger society, by impeding his or her ability to communicate clearly and comfortably with those in the mainstream culture (Delpit, 1988).

The best path is for the child to learn standard English as a distinct code, a task well-suited to middle childhood because of the systematic thinking and metacognition that characterize these years. Children are young enough to hear and notice the nuances of various codes and old enough to comprehend language rules and apply them logically. At the earlier stages of language learning, during toddlerhood and the preschool years, children seem to learn well by simply listening and talking, without specific correction, but during middle childhood, explicit language instruction that delineates the differences between the two codes is useful. For example, rather than merely criticizing, it is more helpful to point out that whereas double negatives in African-American dialect are used for emphasis (as in the spiritual "I Couldn't Hear Nobody Pray"), double negatives in standard English cancel each other. As long as they feel respected when using their usual speech forms, children are generally open to learning the pragmatics of code-switching and rule-changing, becoming competent in a standard code without being cut off from their original code. As we will see, the same general strategy applies to teaching children an entirely new language.

Learning a Second Language

Few nations are without a minority who speak a different language, and a majority of the citizens of the world are bilingual. Linguistically and culturally, and probably cognitively as well, it is an advantage for children to learn more than one language (Diaz, 1985). Although some critics of bilingualism have correctly noted that one language sometimes seems to interfere with verbal fluency in another, such interference seems to be either the result of poor teaching or else a temporary condition that ends when both languages are eventually separated in the child's mind (Cummins, 1991; McLaughlin, 1984). Moreover, bilingualism may actually enhance children's grasp of linguistic rules and concepts (Bialystok, 1988), as well as further their cognitive development in other ways (Diaz & Klinger, 1991).

Thus, from a developmental viewpoint, bilingualism is a goal to be sought, not a problem to be overcome. In the United States, the question is how to teach English to the approximately 4.5 million schoolchildren who have another native language, as well as how to help the English-speaking children learn at least one other language before adulthood (Hakuta, 1986; Rotberg, 1982). In Canada, the question is even more complex, since bilingualism is part of a cultural and political struggle that, for many, goes to the heart of Canadian identity.

FIGURE 13.10 Bilingual education can be exciting and successful when words are explained using two languages as well as pictures and actions that help students bridge the gap from one language to another.

RESEARCH REPORT

Bilingual Education

If there were some easy way to accomplish it, nearly everyone could benefit by being fluent in at least two languages. In addition to its practical value of enabling a person to communicate with a larger and more diverse group of people, bilingualism also enhances cognitive flexibility because it makes children aware that ideas can be expressed in many ways (McLaughlin, 1985; Genese, 1994).

Reaching this ideal is far from easy, however. The most effective approach is to begin in infancy, with the child hearing and speaking two languages, in the home and/or in day care. While such language mixing sometimes slows a child's early language learning, during the preschool years, the typical child's urge to be social and to communicate, coupled with relatively high self-esteem and little concern for social embarrassment, soon fosters rapid learning of every language the child hears, whether it be one, or two, or even three distinct tongues (McLaughlin, 1985; Goodz, 1994).

The same general success can occur in kindergarten, even for those children for whom the second language to be learned is the language of instruction. Most kindergarteners begin school already knowing such basics of communication as expressive gestures and turn-taking, as well as social and cognitive strategies for "getting along" in whatever language the other children speak (Saville-Troike et al., 1984). One study of Spanish-speaking children in an English-speaking kindergarten, for example, found eight distinct strategies:

Social Strategies

1. Join a group and act as if you know what is going on, even if you don't.

2. Give the impression, with a few well-chosen words, that you speak the language.

3. Count on your friends to help.

Cognitive Strategies

1. Assume that what people are saying is directly relevant to the situation at hand. GUESS.

2. Use some expression you understand and start talking.

3. Look for recurring parts in the formulas you know.

4. Make the most of what you've got.

5. Work on the big things first: save the details for later.

Obviously, the children need to feel fairly self-confident, and their peers need to be relatively receptive, before these strategies can be used effectively. Unfortunately, such is not always the case for many minority-language children, especially older children. In order for language learning to occur between one child and another

in elementary school, the teacher must encourage communication between the children, even if the result is not precisely what he or she would hope for. Indeed, in one study, many of the first phrases the children used would not be in any textbook: "Lookit," "All right you guys," "I wanna," "I don't wanna," "How do you do these [little tortillas/flowers/etc.] in English?" and "Shaddup your mouth."

The success of formal bilingual education, of course, varies greatly from child to child, teacher to teacher, and program to program (Wong Fillmore, 1987). One critical factor is the teacher's ability to create a social milieu that encourages all the children to make friends, to join conversations, and to feel free to guess (Wong Fillmore, 1976; 1987). The presence of this factor alone is the main reason that some young children pick up a second language much more quickly than others.

As children grow older and more self-conscious about making friends, it becomes harder to simply immerse them in a classroom and expect them to learn. One boy recalls his early experiences in a Toronto classroom:

> I did not know what to do when the other students spoke to me because I did not understand them. I was forced to use signs with my hands to communicate with people, just as if I were deaf and dumb. I hated the student who spoke with me . . . Sometimes there was a joke, and I had to laugh with the others even though I did not know what the joke was, because I was afraid of being laughed at. [quoted in Coelho, 1991]

For school-age children who do not speak the dominant school language, there are three general approaches to teaching them. One is the *second-language* approach (for instance, *ESL* or English as a second language), in which a group of children are taught the dominant language in much the same way native children might be taught a foreign language by an instructor who specifically focuses on language learning. Typically, such a group receives separate instruction in the second language all day, every day, and then soon joins the larger, dominant-language group, perhaps first in classes such as music and gym, then in math and science, and finally in English and social studies. Another approach is *bilingual-bicultural* education, in which the children are educated with others of their culture and are taught in their first language. Instead of focusing solely on learning the dominant language, they maintain their native language, learning various content areas in it, while studying the new language as an academic subject. Finally, there is *immersion*, in which the child is simply put in with students and teachers who use only the majority language. Each of these approaches has some advantages.

The second-language approach is quite practical, especially if there are children from many language groups in a school. However, in the process of learning the new language, children using this approach may come to feel ashamed of their native language, and may even refuse to speak it at home, except under duress. As a result, their relationship with their parents may be seriously strained and their cultural identity may falter (Mills and Mills, 1993). Further, children need to learn "in a context where they can voice their experiences." If they cannot use their native language, and they do not feel comfortable in the new language, their self-esteem, motivation, and education may suffer (Cummins, 1994).

The bilingual-bicultural approach attempts to remedy that problem by providing extensive instruction in both languages and cultures by teachers well-versed in each. This approach sounds ideal, but such programs are difficult to staff and fund, and too often the children feel themselves to be, and are seen as, a separate group. They tend not to socialize with the children from the dominant language group, and, since language is learned best in the context of social communication, this means they are slow to learn the new language and to feel comfortable in the second culture.

By contrast, in immersion programs, social communication among children is almost inevitable, especially if both languages and cultures are relatively high in status and the parents of the children are supportive. Such is the case in Quebec, where thousands of English-speaking children learn French through immersion that starts in kindergarten. By the fifth grade, they are almost as proficient in French as their classmates who are native French speakers. In addition, they do quite well on math, science, and history tests in either language. Similar results are found for Finnish children who are immersed in Swedish, especially if their knowledge of their native language is sound and they enter Swedish immersion in kindergarten or at about age 10. Entering immersion in the middle of elementary school, at about age 7, does not work as well (Paulston, 1992).

However, immersion programs fail if the child feels shy, stupid, or socially isolated. In the United States, many Latino children instructed only in English become slow learners who repeat a grade or two until they are old enough to drop out of school (McLaughlin, 1985). Typically, their poor performance is blamed on their deficit in English, rather than on the teachers and educational programs that fail to take into account their special language needs. Added to that, limited expectations held by everyone—students, parents, and teachers—are considered a major reason that Spanish-speaking children have the lowest rates of high school graduation—55 percent, compared with 73 percent for African-Americans and 87 percent for whites (U.S. Department of Education, 1993).

Failure for Latinos in immersion programs is, obviously, not inevitable. One notable case in point is that of Richard Rodriguez, a Mexican-American who entered an all-English school in kindergarten, and who eventually mastered the language so well that he studied English literature in graduate school at Berkeley and Columbia (Lucas et al., 1990). He and his family were determined that he would learn English, no matter what the cost. His teacher advised his parents to stop speaking Spanish to their children, and even though their understanding of English was minimal, they did so. Richard explains:

> As we children learned more and more English, we shared fewer and fewer words with our parents. Sentences needed to be spoken slowly when a child addressed his mother or father. (Often the parent wouldn't understand.) The child would need to repeat himself. (Still the parent misunderstood.) The young voice, frustrated, would end up saying "Never mind"—the subject was closed. Dinners would be noisy with the clinking of knives and forks against dishes. My mother would smile softly between her remarks; my father at the other end of the table would chew and chew his food, while he stared over the heads of his children.

In retrospect, Richard approves of his immersion:

> Without question, it would have pleased me to hear my teachers address me in Spanish when I entered the classroom. I would have felt much less afraid. I would have trusted them and responded with ease. But I would have delayed—for how long postponed?—having to learn the language of the public society.

However, Richard never learned to write Spanish, and as he grew older, he lost his ability to speak it as well. He found himself increasingly distant from his parents and their culture, a not uncommon consequence for immigrant children who succeed in the majority school. The latest wave of immigrants to suffer these consequences are from Southeast Asia. Many of the children in this group eventually become quite successful in school, but pay a high price—the loss of the ability to communicate with their parents (Wong Fillmore, 1991).

This raises a basic issue: What is the goal of language education? Virtually all programs and evaluations of bilingual education focus on one measure of success: how proficient children are in the new language. Other measures of school success, from math achievement to high school graduation, and measures of personal success, from self-esteem to social understanding, are often ignored (Hakuta & Garcia, 1989; McKeon, 1994). Obviously, school-age children need to learn the language of their society, but as the next chapter explains, they also need to develop their understanding of themselves and of others. Educational practices, including implicit attitudes regarding children's original language, can be instrumental in determining whether "the linguistic, cognitive, and sociocultural resources children bring to school" are used to achieve the larger goal—seeing that "the developing child becomes a fully functioning and valued member of the community" (Genesee, 1994).

Unfortunately, although this question has been one of intense concern and emotion, no simple answer is apparent. Almost every educational approach has been tried—from total **immersion**, in which the child's instruction occurs entirely in the second language, to "reverse immersion," in which the child is taught in his or her native language until most of childhood is over and the second language can be taught as a "foreign" language. Variations on these approaches present some topics of instruction in one language and other topics in the other language. However, few carefully controlled, longitudinal studies have been done to evaluate the effectiveness of the various approaches.

Of the research that is available, some of the most thorough comes from Canada, where both English and French are official languages that all children are expected to learn. Immersion programs seem to work best when children are young (Harley et al., 1987). In Canada, immersion has proven successful not only with immigrant children who speak neither English nor French, but also with English-speaking children who are taught exclusively in French in their first years of school and then are gradually given more instruction in English. These children eventually match their English-speaking English-taught peers in academic subjects, and surpass them in French (Genesse, 1983).

However, in most such instances of successful immersion, parents voluntarily placed their children in a special program designed to teach the second language. As the Research Report on pages 454–455 points out, variations in attitudes within the family and within the culture are often transmitted to the classroom, in some cases causing the child to cling steadfastly to his or her first language, in others helping the child to readily learn a second language, perhaps even to become truly bilingual and bicultural.

Thinking, Learning, and Schooling

The portrait of the school-age child sketched in this chapter is of someone who is thoughtful and eager to learn, able to focus attention, to master logical operations, to remember interrelated facts, and to speak in several linguistic codes. That portrait is universal, describing children aged 6 to 11 the world over.

Agreement on how best to direct and use that learning potential is not universal, however. While schooling of some sort during middle childhood is a feature of every community worldwide, the specifics of who receives instruction, in what, and how, vary enormously. Historically, boys and wealthier children were much more likely to be formally taught than girls or poor children, an inequality still apparent today. In 83 percent of developing countries, fewer girls than boys attend primary school, and although virtually every child in developed countries attends school, less is generally demanded of girls and poor children, particularly in math and science (Minuchin & Shapiro, 1983; UNICEF, 1990). For example, in the United States, more female and poor children drop out of school than do male and nonpoor, and of those who remain to graduate from high school, far fewer have taken algebra II, calculus, chemistry, and physics (U.S. Department of Education, 1989).

immersion An approach to learning a second language in which the learner is placed in an environment where only the second language is spoken.

Another critical variation is in the curriculum offered. Basic literacy is universally sought, but other curriculum elements—science, arts, health, and religion among them—are prominent in some schools and virtually absent in others. Pedagogical techniques vary widely as well, from the strict lecture method, in which students are forbidden to talk, whisper, or even move, to open education, in which students are encouraged to interact and to freely avail themselves of classroom resources, with the teacher acting more as an adviser, guide, and friend than as a knowledge authority and disciplinarian.

FIGURE 13.11 Educational curricula and methods reflect cultural values and national priorities. The children in this Koranic school in India and in this "classroom" in Somalia are mastering lessons quite different from those that are typically taught in North American, European, and Australian schools. To fairly evaluate any educational system, one must ask whether or not children are learning the skills they will need in their particular social setting.

Until fairly recently, such variations did not usually trouble the nations involved, because each culture's methods reflected traditions and a national ethos that were taken for granted. As the twenty-first century approaches, however, international economic competition—and the growing need for workers to be literate, skilled, and self-motivated—have intensified public concern about certain educational processes that now seem to be inadequate. This is particularly apparent in the United States, because achievement scores show American children behind their counterparts in most other industrialized countries, especially in math and science (Stevenson & Stigler, 1992; International Assignment of Educational Progress, 1989). The differences are most marked when children of the United States are compared with those from the Pacific-rim countries (Japan, Hong Kong, Korea, and the Republic of China). Significantly, while international comparisons generally find that children in countries on the Pacific rim do especially well in math and science and that, among industrialized nations, children in the United States, Italy, and Spain tend to be near the bottom in those subjects, a closer comparison reveals some interesting differences. For example, high school seniors in both the United States and Japan do better in physics than in biology, while in almost every other country the reverse is true. More fine-tuned analysis again reveals curious differences: Scottish 13-year-olds, for instance, rank among the lowest internationally in basic arithmetic, but among the highest in understanding statistics and probability, while Irish children are relatively good in arithmetic and poor in probability

FIGURE 13.12 An international comparison of the science achievement of 13-year-olds (Lapointe et al., 1992) shows the gap between the highest- and lowest-scoring countries narrowing compared to the scores in the early 1980s, when a child who was in the top 20 percent of U.S. students scored no better than the average South Korean student. However, the gap between the highest and lowest tenth of students reveals marked differences within nations in schooling and preparation. Spain and South Korea are the only countries where the lowest 10th percentile is less than 40 points below the highest 10th percentile.

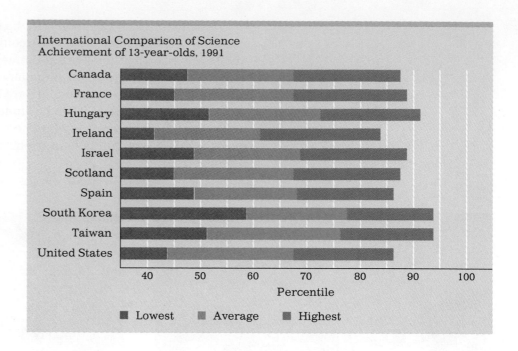

(National Science Foundation, 1992). In reading ability, especially among gifted children, the advantage of the Pacific-rim nations over the United States disappears (Stevenson et al., 1993a). Such comparisons suggest that international differences in achievement are not primarily the result of children's innate abilities or early nurturance but, rather, are related to specifics within the educational systems and social contexts during the school years (see Research Report, pp. 460–461).

As a result of these international differences, almost every aspect of the schooling process, from teacher selection to public financing, from ethnic diversity to religious instruction, from parental involvement to curriculum balance, has been the target of criticism. While most of the issues in these controversies are more appropriately discussed in a textbook on educational policies or political processes than here, research in cognitive development provides valuable insights into the basic question of how children learn best.

Cognitive Development and Classroom Learning

As we have seen, school-age children are active learners, eager to master logical principles and learning strategies, as well as to develop academic skills and accumulate knowledge. Further, their many skills, from mnemonic tricks to concrete operations, are most readily mastered through guided instruction and personal involvement. All this means that passive learning—such as sitting quietly and copying work from the blackboard—and piecemeal learning—such as memorization, by repetition and rote, of the sounds of the alphabet, of the sums of simple numbers, of the names of the continents, and so forth—are not the most appropriate means of instruction overall. Educators influenced by developmental theory, particularly Piaget's, have concluded that the classroom should always be a busy place, in which children's curiosity is met with an array of materials to explore and discuss, such as coins to count, objects to measure, books to read, stories to dramatize.

More recently, the information-processing perspective has led to a re-emphasis on explicit instruction, which was sometimes shunted aside in the initial excitement over the Piagetian idea of the child as a self-motivated explorer-scientist. However, the information-processing emphasis on specific skills and a solid knowledge base is quite different from that implicit in the workbooks and rote memorization of old. Student motivation, attention, and mastery of strategies and principles are the key, with the teacher at the ready to provide the necessary knowledge and skills whenever the child is prepared to open a new cognitive door.

An even more recent insight from developmental research has been a recognition of the importance, as highlighted by Vygotsky, of social interaction in the classroom, not only between teacher and student but also among the children themselves, and of the support for academic skills from home. Numerous studies have shown that if their task is structured to encourage cooperation, classmates can draw each other into the zone of proximal development (see pp. 353–354), expanding each other's knowledge as well as, and more often than, any one teacher can (Rogoff, 1990).

This fact was clearly demonstrated in an extensive experiment on the development of reading skills, in which teachers of 3,345 children in Hawaii followed a Vygotskiian model that emphasized social interaction within the zone of proximal development. Instead of the usual practice of having students read silently to themselves, with the teacher asking the entire class some simple comprehension questions, the teachers in this experiment used such strategies as having groups of children read a paragraph aloud together, and then collectively respond to a series of questions designed to elicit discussion as well as confirm understanding. Compared to a control group who received more conventional teaching within the same schools, the experimental children scored significantly higher on standard tests of reading achievement (Klein, 1988). A similar approach is being taken in many math classes, as workbooks, rote learning, and pure memorization are being replaced by instruction that involves "hands-on" materials and active discussion, both designed to elicit conceptual understanding, problem solving, and the ability to verbalize math concepts.

The importance of social interaction to cognitive growth is not limited to academic time in the classroom: a child's cognitive growth is also affected by the values shared with peers and family members. In elementary school, children tend to congregate in peer groups that have similar academic aspirations—ranging from those who take pride in "trying hard" in class to those who have little interest in schoolwork—and these groups influence the children's motivation and classroom achievement (Kindermann, 1993). At home, children may have parents who regularly offer encouragement and praise of the child's success, or who chronically criticize poor performance, or who show no interest at all in the child's education, and these responses can likewise affect the child's motivation and achievement (Ginsburg & Bronstein, 1993).

The social ecology contributes to cognitive growth in broader ways, as well. As revealed in the Research Report on pp. 460–461, the values that teachers, parents, and children assign to education are affected by the assumptions and values of the larger culture.

FIGURE 13.13 Children encourage and challenge each other to master new knowledge, often better than an adult can. All three children here—doctor, patient, and observer—are likely to remember the use of a stethoscope and the correct location of various organs.

RESEARCH REPORT

Education in the United States, Japan, and the Republic of China: A Cross-Cultural Comparison

The same international comparisons that find children in the United States close to the bottom in scholastic achievement find children in Japan, Korea, and the Republic of China (Taiwan) at the top (United States Department of Education, 1993; Suter, 1993). To understand these achievement differences, an international team of researchers headed by Harold Stevenson has spent the past fifteen years comparing the school achievement, leisure-time use, and academic attitudes of more than 5,000 children and their parents at sixty-four schools in three comparable cities, Minneapolis (USA), Taipei (the Republic of China), and Sendai (Japan) (Stevenson & Stigler, 1992; Stevenson et al., 1993). They found that children in the three cities were similar in aptitude, as measured by intelligence tests when they entered school and by tests of general knowledge when they were in the eleventh grade. However, as other researchers have also found, the Chinese and Japanese students outperformed the Americans in achievement tests, particularly in math and science, at every grade level and across every level of ability. Indeed, the performance of the top 10 percent of American students was only at the level of the average Asian student.

If it was not a matter of ability, why did these differences occur? One reason is the different number of hours the children in the three countries spend in schoolwork. In Japan and the Republic of China, for example, children go to school five and a half days a week, compared to five in the United States; the average school year is one-third longer than in the United States; and the children are in school more hours each day than American children are.

But according to these researchers, even more important than how much time children spend in the classroom is how they spend that time. American schoolchildren in the study devoted far less classroom time to academic activities than Japanese and Chinese students did, more frequently engaging in inappropriate activities (getting out of their seats, chatting with friends, and so on). By fifth grade, American students were spending 64 percent of the schoolday on academic work, whereas Japanese students were academically engaged 87 percent of the time.

One notable result of this difference in the use of classroom time was that American children spent an average of only three hours a week on math, whereas Japanese children spent an average of seven. Also, compared with Japanese and Chinese children, American children were more inclined to work alone than in groups. American teachers, in turn, worked more frequently with individual children or in small groups than with the class as a whole, while teachers in Japan and China strongly emphasized group instruction with every child actively participating. As a consequence, children from the Asian nations had greater overall opportunity to learn from their teachers in class.

Added to the difference in classroom time and work was a notable difference in the time that is devoted to homework. At grade 5, Americans averaged 4 hours per week studying at home, compared with 13 hours for Chinese children and 6 hours for the Japanese (Stevenson & Lee, 1990).

Education also involves the home environment, of course, and the most recent reports from these researchers reveals important differences in parental support and attitudes toward the child's educational progress. According to Stevenson and his colleagues, academic achievement was a much more central concern to Japanese and Chinese parents, who had higher expectations for their offspring and were more involved in fostering their children's success (Stevenson & Stigler, 1992; Stevenson et al., 1993). The Minneapolis mothers, according to these researchers, believed instead that "it is better for children to be bright than to be good students." Perhaps as a consequence, parents in Japan and the Republic of China were much more involved in the child's education, encouraging and supervising homework (91 percent of Japanese children had their own desk at home), maintaining high standards for academic work, and emphasizing the value and importance of hard work over innate capabilities. In addition, if a child shows signs of falling behind, it is common for Japanese parents to arrange for supplemental courses at special cram schools called *juku* (Rohlen, 1983). Another study, in the United States, revealed that the same family values help to account for the astonishing academic success of the children of immigrant families from Vietnam, Laos, and other Southeast Asia countries (Caplan et al., 1992).

In view of a decade's worth of publicity—often wildly exaggerated—claiming that schools in the United States are failing, that their graduates are ignorant, if not illiterate, and that U.S. industries are unable to compete in the international marketplace because they lack properly educated workers, one might think that American parents would have become at least somewhat concerned about the quality of their children's education. However, a 1990 survey found American parents to be far more satisfied with their children's progress and achievement than were parents in both Japan and the Republic of China, a contrast that, if anything, was even stronger than it was ten years earlier. Perhaps because of their parents' contentment with their achievement, American students spend more time doing nonschool activities than their Asian peers. This is particularly apparent in the eleventh grade, when 74 percent of American students have part-time jobs,

Japanese primary schools typically group children by age, not ability, and encourage cooperation among members of each table. The underlying belief is that all children can succeed at mastering quite complex material, as these sixth-graders in Tokyo seem to be doing.

compared with 21 percent of Asian students, and 85 percent are dating, compared with 37 percent of Asian students. Critics of the Asian emphasis on schooling have long maintained that Asian children, worn down by the constant grind and pressure to excel, are highly susceptible to depression and even suicide. In fact, American students are the ones who were more likely to feel stressed, depressed, and aggressive, as well as to be anxious about school (Stevenson et al., 1993).

As this research indicates, educational achievement entails a complex interaction involving a child's aptitude and motivation, the school environment, and support from the home. American parents tend to be most concerned about their child's progress during the preschool years, but then

> they abdicate some of these responsibilities to the teacher once the child enters school. This trend is opposite from that which occurs in Chinese and Japanese families . . . From the time that the child enters school, life for the Chinese and Japanese child becomes purposeful; the child, the parents, and the teachers begin the serious task of education. [Stevenson & Lee, 1990]

This difference is reflected in the political priorities of each culture as well. For example, in keeping with the culture's regard for education, Japanese teachers are highly trained, greatly esteemed, and well paid (their salary is 2.4 times the average Japanese salary, in contrast with that of American teachers, which is 1.7 times the national average). Similarly, Japanese schools are clean and very well equipped, with almost all having libraries, music rooms, and science laboratories, and 75 percent of them having swimming pools.

It is tempting, of course, to focus on one or two distinctive traits of successful education in another country and to consider them as solutions to domestic educational problems. However, an awareness of the importance of cultural context reminds us that no one national educational system can be transmitted, wholesale, to another. Even the easiest-seeming solutions, such as extending the school day, may contain hidden risks when lifted out of their overall context. As the researchers in the comparison study warn,

> increasing the amount of time spent in academic activities with out modifying the content of the curriculum and the manner of instruction might further depress American children's interest in school and increase their dislike of homework. Greater time on task is not the primary basis for the high achievement of Chinese and Japanese children. The answer lies instead in the high quality of experiences that fill this time . . . Chinese and Japanese elementary school classrooms, contrary to common stereotypes, are characterized by frequent interchange between teacher and students, enthusiastic participation by the students, and the frequent use of problems and innovative solutions. [Stevenson & Lee, 1990]

As you have just read, this is precisely the direction suggested by developmental theory, a direction that more and more educators in the United States, Canada, and elsewhere are pursuing. Perhaps combining more time on task and better instructional methods will soon boost American children's achievement. However, such a switch is not likely to occur without a change in the public's attitude, putting more financial resources, better professional training, and higher academic demands on teachers and students. As the researchers write:

> We conclude that the achievement gap is real, that it is persistent, and that it is unlikely to diminish until, among other things, there are marked changes in the attitudes and beliefs of American parents and students about education. American parents appeared to be no more likely in 1990 and 1991 than they were in 1980 to believe that there is an urgent need for educational reform. They did not seem to be incensed by the low levels of performance by American students. Rather they appeared to be pleased with their children's academic achievement, to be satisfied with the job their children's schools were doing, and to believe that children's innate abilities guide their course of progress through school. But the likelihood of improving the nation's competitive position through better education depends, at least in part, on changing such optimistic but ultimately self-defeating views. [Stevenson et al., 1993]

Evaluating Individual Differences in Cognitive Growth

The pace of cognitive development varies throughout the school years, of course, for reasons associated with heredity (Chapter 3) and early childhood education (Chapter 10), as well as with a variety of environmental incentives and opportunities. During the school years, teachers and parents become aware of, and may be troubled by, the differences in academic achievement among children. In many cultures, for example, schools send home report cards bearing grades and the teacher's comments on the child's current achievement and need for improvement. Educators use a wide range of tests and other measures to track children's progress and to assess how achievement in one classroom compares with that of other classes in the same school, in other local schools, in other states, and in other nations. One reason for this intense concern is that school experience has an important impact on intellectual growth (Ceci, 1991) and that academic achievement correlates with many indicators of individual adult success (such as job status and income). Similarly, a nation's educational level correlates with such measures of national success as economic well-being and mortality rates. Thus, as society invests in children's intellectual growth through formal schooling, policymakers likewise become interested in measures of educational success. Overall, this broad concern with individual differences in intellectual achievement means that a child's cognitive growth becomes increasingly monitored and evaluated, in ways that affect that child's current and future opportunities. One way this occurs is by achievement and aptitude testing.

Achievement tests, which are usually given every year in elementary school, are designed to measure actual learning—for example, how well a child reads, or adds, or understands science concepts. Typically, achievement tests focus on a particular subject and ask the child questions that are variously easy, average, and difficult. The child's score is then either compared with that of the typical child with the same amount of schooling or the same background, or it is measured against some objective standard. For instance, the reading achievement of a Latino fourth-grade boy in Denver, Colorado, might be compared to other fourth-graders in Denver or in the United States, or to other male Latino schoolchildren with the same level of fluency in Spanish, or to a general standard (such as being able to read and understand a basic vocabulary of 10,000 words). Ideally, achievement tests reveal not only what children have learned but also their weaknesses in specific skills or subject areas. Thus, a math achievement test might show that a child has good computation skills but a poor understanding of graphs.

Although achievement tests are sometimes used to determine whether students will be promoted to the next grade, they are more commonly used to group students according to achievement level within each class. Such tests are also used by administrators to evaluate the performance of individual teachers, or schools, or school systems. None of these uses is necessarily beneficial. Students who are held back in a grade are more likely to drop out than achieve, and grouping children by test scores reduces the achievement of the lowest-scoring students. There is also the danger that teachers may narrow their instructional goals to focus only on tasks that standardized tests measure (Armistead et al., 1992; Koretz, 1988; Toch, 1991).

achievement tests Tests designed to measure how much a person has learned in a specific subject area.

An additional problem in the various uses of achievement tests is that a child's performance on them can be affected by factors other than actual learning. Motivation to do well can be a very powerful factor in actual performance. This can be affected even by something as simple as the teacher's instructions right before the exam. In one study, school-age children about to take their usual standardized tests were randomly assigned either to an experimental group, who were told to do as well as possible for their parents, their teachers, and themselves, or to a control group, who were given only the usual instructions (such as to work steadily in the time allowed). Students in the experimental group performed significantly better, a result that held true for boys as well as girls, and older as well as younger children (Brown, 1993).

FIGURE 13.14 The fourth-graders taking this standardized achievement test in Walnut Creek, Texas, are being tested on more than their reading ability and vocabulary. Also being tested, indirectly, are their reading vision at 20 inches, their hand-eye coordination for filling in the proper circle with a dark-enough mark, their ability to concentrate and keep from looking out the window or at their neighbor, and their ability to control their anxiety. Another important factor that is being unintentionally tested is the children's motivation to do well. Given all this, it is no wonder that about one-fourth of children tested—mostly boys—seem to have difficulty.

Aptitude tests are designed to measure potential, such as how well and quickly a person could learn a new subject if given the chance. Their primary purposes are to predict school success and, at times, to diagnose learning problems. For example, aptitude tests can help teachers identify gifted children, as well as children with specific learning disabilities (see Chapter 12).

The most commonly used aptitude tests are intelligence tests, often called **IQ tests**, *IQ* being an abbreviation for "intelligence quotient." Originally, IQ scores were calculated as a quotient—the child's estimated mental age divided by the child's chronological age times 100. Thus, a child whose mental age was 12 and whose chronological age was 10 had an IQ score of 120.

The most widely used IQ tests are the Stanford-Binet and the Wechsler tests, each of which examines general knowledge, reasoning ability, mathematical skill, memory, vocabulary, and spatial perception. The Stanford-Binet can be used with individuals from 2 to 18 years of age. The Wechsler has special versions for preschoolers (the WPPSI), schoolchildren (the WISC-R), and adults (the WAIS-R). Depending on the age of the child, the questions posed by an examiner can determine general ability ("How many thumbs do you have?"), assess reasoning ("How are an elephant and a whale alike?"), test mathematical skill ("If a train traveling at 32 miles per hour takes three days to get from one place to another, how fast must a train go to travel the same distance in half a day?"), evaluate vocabulary ("What is a

aptitude tests Tests designed to measure potential, rather than actual, accomplishment.

IQ tests Aptitude tests designed to measure a person's intelligence, defined as mental age divided by chronological age (hence, Intelligence Quotient).

stanza?"), or ask the person to complete a puzzle, organize pictures into a sequence that tells a story, or arrange colored blocks to match a specific design.

In general, two-thirds of all children score within a year or two of their age-mates, achieving an IQ score somewhere between 85 and 115 (a score of 100 is average). Children scoring above 130 (typically only about 2 percent of the population) are considered gifted, while those in the 70–85 range are considered to be slow learners. Individuals below this range are considered mentally retarded. Of course, using a single test score to designate intelligence level seems contrary to everything you have learned about development, including the fact that children develop in various ways at various paces, depending on the family, school, and cultural contexts, as well as many other factors that can change from one year to the next. Therefore, any aptitude test, whether it is based on a general standard or is specific to a particular child, should be used with caution, for it is equivalent to a monochrome snapshot of a rapidly moving, multicolor target.

What, then, do IQ tests really measure? Although they are intended to be tests of intellectual potential, it is impossible to measure potential independent of current achievement, since IQ test scores reflect the child's knowledge of vocabulary, understanding of basic math, and familiarity with cultural ideas and artifacts—among other *learned* factors. In addition, performance on an IQ test inadvertently reflects other factors that bear on the child's score, including nonacademic competencies (such as the capacity to pay attention and concentrate, to verbally express one's thoughts clearly, and to ask questions if the instructions are unclear) and the effects of overall emotional stress, health, test-taking anxiety, and so on. It is particularly important to keep these factors in mind when comparing the IQ scores of children from significantly different cultural backgrounds or evaluating children from troubled families. Because it can be affected by so many "outside" variables, an IQ score may seriously underestimate the intellectual potential of disadvantaged children, or overestimate that of children from advantaged backgrounds.

Despite these limitations, however, IQ tests can be helpful. As part of a group of measures, they help predict a child's future school performance, and they are also useful in identifying learning problems (Rispens et al., 1991; Siegler & Richards, 1982; Snider & Tarver, 1989; Taylor, 1988). One reason for their success in these roles is that IQ tests are carefully administered by a highly trained professional who works individually with the child—in contrast with other aptitude and achievement tests that are often group-administered in pencil-and-paper format or that rely on teachers' impressions, which may miss some hidden potential in a shy or disturbed child. At their best, and if interpreted carefully and cautiously, IQ tests enable educators to do their jobs better by tailoring the child's academic challenges to the child's competencies. As a result, children who need additional time and assistance to master their lessons are not frustrated and discouraged by falling behind their classmates, while children who gain mastery quickly can be given new challenges before boredom sets in. At their worst—when they fail to take into account contextual factors or are interpreted too rigidly—IQ tests can unfairly judge and stigmatize certain individual children, certain groups of children, certain teachers, or certain schools.

Self-Perceptions of Cognitive Competence

Of course, teachers, parents, and policymakers are not the only ones who are interested in individual differences in children's intellectual achievement. During the school years, children become acute evaluators of their own intellectual strengths and weaknesses, as well as those of others. This causes them to be more realistic in estimating their skills, but it also poses risks for their self-confidence. Several studies have shown that children's perceptions of their intellectual competence decline steadily through the elementary-school years (Eccles et al., 1993; Phillips & Zimmerman, 1990). This is in striking contrast to the self-evaluations of preschoolers, who usually remain buoyantly optimistic and confident of their own abilities, even in the face of failure.

One reason for this difference in self-assessment is that preschoolers tend to evaluate their abilities through self-comparison, measuring their present competencies against what they were a year or two earlier. Consequently, they are bound to feel a sense of their own improvement (Stipek & MacIver, 1989). Older children, on the other hand, use **social comparison** to evaluate their competencies, comparing their abilities and attributes against those of their peers (Aboud, 1985; Ruble, 1983). Because there is always likely to be one or two children who surpass a particular child's abilities in a given area, social comparison makes older children more realistic in their self-evaluations, and also less confident. Another reason for developmental change in self-evaluation is that school-age children have begun to regard intellectual abilities as relatively enduring traits that can promote or limit success regardless of how hard one tries (Benenson & Dweck, 1986). They sometimes conclude, therefore, that they are "good at" certain subjects but just "can't do" others, regardless of the effort they put into their schoolwork. By contrast, preschoolers tend to think of intellectual ability as something that can be easily improved through practice and effort.

These changes in intellectual self-evaluation are illustrated in an observational study of children in kindergarten, first-, second-, and fourth-grade classrooms (Frey & Ruble, 1987). Observers made detailed ratings of the spontaneous comments that these children uttered during independent work, devoting particular attention to self-congratulatory comments ("Know how I did it? *Brains!*") and self-critical comments ("I missed a lot!"). They found that self-congratulatory comments peaked at first grade and then declined markedly by fourth grade, while self-critical comments increased steadily throughout this period. According to the researchers, these changes were due not only to the increasing self-criticism of the older children but also to their increased social sensitivity to classmates (which meant not bragging about one's academic success).

During the school years, of course, children vary notably in their self-evaluations. Some children remain self-confident even in the face of difficult challenges in math, science, or reading, while others experience self-doubt even when encountering familiar and manageable problems. Not surprisingly, children's self-perceptions of cognitive competence have motivational consequences. Carol Dweck (1991; Dweck & Leggett, 1988), for example, has distinguished students who approach schoolwork with a **mastery orientation** versus a **performance orientation**. Students with a mastery orientation believe that intellectual growth will occur through persistence and hard

social comparison The human tendency to assess one's abilities, achievements, social status, and the like by measuring them against those of others, especially those of one's peers.

mastery orientation An approach to schoolwork that is based on the belief that intellectual growth occurs through persistence and hard work. Students with this orientation accept challenging tasks and try harder when their initial efforts do not succeed.

performance orientation An approach to schoolwork that is based on the belief that a lack of academic success is a sign of a personal inadequacy that is unlikely to change. Students with this orientation tend to avoid challenges in which they might fail and give up easily in difficult situations.

work, and they tend to choose challenging tasks because they believe that they will learn from the experience even if they do not succeed. If they encounter failures, they persist and try harder, and if they never succeed, they attribute their failure to a lack of effort or other factors that can be managed in the future. By contrast, students with a performance orientation tend to shy away from challenges in which they might fail, regarding their lack of success as a sign of inadequacy that is unlikely to change. They give up more easily in difficult situations, and become self-critical and defensive rather than trying harder.

Although these different orientations appear to be a motivational prescription for success and failure in the classroom, Dweck and Leggett (1988) have noted that a performance orientation can be found among the brightest and most skilled students. In a sense, these high-ability students still have low self-confidence despite their academic success, perhaps owing to the lack of support they receive at home (Wagner & Phillips, 1992). Nevertheless, a performance orientation does not inspire optimism for a student's long-term success, partly because it resembles the beliefs of children who experience "learned helplessness"—the view that, in the end, one can do little to succeed (see p. 477).

Schooling and Culture

Developmental changes in how children view their intellectual competence are fostered by many factors, including the influence of peers and parents. And the classroom environment, of course, is key. As children get older, their educational experience typically grows more structured: their learning world becomes one of "right" and "wrong" answers, formal evaluations (such as letter grades instead of gold stars), the grouping of students according to ability, and frequent competition with classmates. In contrast to the preschool years, merely "trying hard" is no longer sufficient to win a teacher's praise. This shift reflects the traditional values of Western culture, where competition, individual achievement, and technical accuracy are highly regarded.

But not all cultures share these values, and not all cultures educate in this manner. In some cultures, the middle childhood years are demarcated not by the child's entrance into a formal educational system but rather by the child's transition from the home to the community, where skills related to hunting, farming, cooking, building, and other activities are cooperatively acquired from older mentors. In other cultures, as well as in some innovative schools and classrooms in Western cultures, the emphasis is on collaborative learning, group mastery, and respect for individual styles. These differences reveal that the goals and process of education are closely tied to the values and needs of the specific culture, as Vygotsky argued. Put differently, education is the acquisition of culturally approved skills, habits, and strategies.

As a consequence, the intellectual achievements of the middle childhood years depend, to a great extent, on the competencies required by the culture. Throughout this chapter, we have focused primarily on the skills emphasized by Western societies—and, most likely, that are part of your intellectual repertoire—associated with logical reasoning, systematic thinking, and the growth of cognitive strategies. By contrast, we have had little to

FIGURE 13.15 An important part of education is learning about one's cultural heritage. Children are fortunate if their grandparents are sufficiently patient, knowledgeable, and available to contribute to this fund of knowledge.

say about the growth of skills related to the construction of a brick-and-mortar hut, the estimation of when and how to plant and harvest, mathematical operations on an abacus, or other domains of knowledge more typically acquired during middle childhood in other cultures. Just as a child from a middle-class home in the United States would be culturally incompetent if asked to display the skills common to 11-year-olds from the Shui-jen community in southern China—a fishing culture that virtually lives on the water—so too would an 11-year-old from the Shui-jen community have great difficulty with many of the memory tasks, IQ assessments, and achievement tests routinely tackled by most American children.

Not surprisingly, then, cross-cultural studies show that children's ability on standard tests of vocabulary, memory, systematic thinking, and logical reasoning is associated with their formal schooling in the traditional Western mode (Cole, 1992; Rogoff & Morelli, 1989). Such schooling enables children, regardless of their cultural background, to acquire cognitive skills that can be applied impersonally and hypothetically, whether to solve story problems, math games, or remember and classify lists of unrelated terms. At the same time, middle childhood—irrespective of the amount of formal schooling it provides—also witnesses the growth of practical, culturally approved skills, transmitted by others in society, that may or may not require the thinking and reasoning skills commonly valued by Western society and taught in formal schools. This yields a constellation of abilities that helps make the child a competent member of his or her culture, as long as factors in that child's personal life do not seriously interfere with the ability to learn.

The acquisition of culturally approved skills during middle childhood can, in fact, sometimes yield surprising competencies. One of the most striking examples is the one cited in Chapter 2, in which a group of poor Brazilian street vendors—all in middle childhood, with little formal education—were interviewed to determine their grasp of mathematical concepts. When presented with standard math problems (such as 420 + 80) depicted in a pencil-and-paper manner, these children performed very poorly. When instead presented with oral problems involving fruit purchases and making change for a customer ("I'll take two coconuts that cost $40 apiece. Here's a $500 bill. What do I get back?"), children solved the problems far more quickly and successfully, often using unconventional but effective math strategies (Carraher et al., 1985; Carraher et al., 1988). In other words, though lacking the cognitive strategies necessary for hypothetical school-like math problems, these children, in learning the practical skills necessitated by their livelihood, had developed very sophisticated mathematical abilities. Cognitive growth is thus intimately connected to the ecologies of school, family, and culture in which children live. In the next chapter, we explore how these same ecologies influence psychosocial development.

SUMMARY

The Growth of Thinking, Memory, and Knowledge

1. Information-processing theorists seek to explain development in thinking, learning, memory, and problem solving during middle childhood in terms of the growth of selective attention, the broadening of memory strategies, an increase in processing speed and capacity, an expanding foundation of knowledge, and the acquisition of metacognitive awareness.

2. These cognitive skills have practical applications to the growth of reading, mathematics, and other abilities during middle childhood. Competent reading requires, for example, automatization of letter and word identification, metacognitive monitoring of understanding, and selective attention to focus on reading comprehension and avoid distractions.

Concrete Operational Thought

3. According to Piaget, beginning at about age 7 or 8, children begin to be able to use the logical operations of concrete operational thought. They can apply logical principles such as identity and reversibility to problems of conservation, mathematics, science, and social understanding, as well as to other aspects of knowledge.

4. While Piaget's theory captures some essential qualities of the reasoning of school-age children, most developmentalists believe that older children are not as consistently logical or objective as his theory portrayed.

Language

5. Language abilities continue to improve during middle childhood, partly because schools and families encourage this learning, and partly because increased cognitive development makes it easier to acquire new vocabulary, understand difficult grammatical constructions, and use language in everyday situations.

6. The ability to understand that language is a tool for communication makes the school-age child more capable of using different forms of language in different contexts. For example, a child can use African-American dialect on the playground and standard English in the classroom.

7. Teaching children a second language can be accomplished by a number of different methods, from total immersion in the new language to gradually increasing exposure over time. However, the most important factors seem to be the commitment from home and school.

Thinking, Learning, and Schooling

8. The typical school-age child is someone who is thoughtful and eager to learn and able to focus attention, use logical reasoning, remember interrelated facts, and speak in several linguistic codes. However, the manner in which these cognitive skills are fostered and shaped varies considerably in different school settings, nations, and cultures.

9. School-age children are active learners, which means that passive instruction is not the most appropriate means of teaching. Recent developmental research has shown the pedagogical benefits of greater classroom interaction, both between teachers and students and among the students themselves.

10. A growing interest in individual differences in intellectual achievement in the school years accounts for the use of achievement and aptitude tests, including intelligence tests, for school-age children. Achievement tests index how much a child has learned, while aptitude tests measure cognitive potential. Although their applications are controversial, the careful and cautious interpretation of the results of standardized tests can benefit students and teachers alike.

11. In middle childhood, students become more realistic and self-critical in evaluating their intellectual strengths and weaknesses. This can result in differences in self-confidence and in academic motivation.

12. Education is, in many respects, the acquisition of culturally approved skills. These may include the kinds of logical, systematic reasoning skills valued by Western societies, or practical skills related to hunting, building, and cooking, or both.

KEY TERMS

selective attention (439)
storage strategies (440)
rehearsal (440)
organization (440)
retrieval strategies (440)
mnemonics (441)
automatization (442)
metacognition (443)
concrete operational
   thought (445)
identity (445)
reversibility (446)

reciprocity (446)
code-switching (451)
elaborated code (451)
restricted code (451)
immersion (456)
achievement tests (462)
aptitude tests (463)
IQ tests (463)
social comparison (465)
mastery orientation (465)
performance orientation
   (465)

KEY QUESTIONS

1. How does selective attention distinguish the preschool from the grade-school child?

2. What specific memory strategies aid in older children's recall of specific information?

3. Why do processing speed and capacity seem to increase during the school years?

4. What are some of the logical operations, or principles, that enhance logical reasoning during middle childhood?

5. What are some of the language skills that develop in middle childhood?

6. What are the chief characteristics of the elaborated and restricted codes and in what general context is each code used?

7. What are some of the factors that facilitate learning of a second language?

8. What changes in curricular practices have resulted from a renewed appreciation of the cognitive abilities of middle childhood?

9. What does an IQ test measure?

10. What advice would you offer a teacher who was preparing to use an aptitude test to evaluate a student's academic potential?

11. What can account for the greater optimism of a preschooler encountering new cognitive challenges, compared with a grade-school child?

12. How is education shaped by culture? Should we expect that all school-age children master the same cognitive skills?

The School Years:

Psychosocial Development

CHAPTER

14

During the school years, emotional and social development occurs in a much more elaborate context than in the closely supervised and circumscribed arenas of the typical younger child. As school-age children explore the wider world of neighborhood, community, and school, independent of parental control, they experience new vulnerability, increasing competence, ongoing friendships, challenging and sometimes troubling rivalries, deeper social understanding, and conflicting moral values. Personality attributes, coping mechanisms, and future aspirations are all formed by their developing social cognition. This chapter describes their reaction to their expanding horizons, answering questions such as the following:

How does self-understanding—and understanding of others—evolve during the school years?

Why are friendships important to psychosocial growth?

How does moral understanding evolve throughout childhood?

What familial factors foster healthy development?

How does it affect a child to be poor or homeless?

What types of social support are most helpful to children who are experiencing serious stress?

As children between the ages of 6 and 11 become physically stronger and more capable, and cognitively wiser and more logical, their growing abilities serve as the foundation for remarkable psychological and social accomplishments. For example, as they become more independent, children also begin to make their own decisions and govern their own behavior, including everything from the mundane selection of which socks to wear, to the social choice of whom to befriend, to the moral decision about whether to lie or steal. In so doing, children increasingly experience the influence of other children and adults, as well as of the community as a whole.

This interplay between increasing competence and an expanding social world is the theme of psychosocial development in middle childhood, and thus the theme of this chapter. First let us look specifically at the psychosocial growth that characterizes these years, and then at some of the contexts, particularly those associated with family structure, that shape and propel that growth. Finally, we will look at the stresses that many school-age children confront, and at their ways of coping with those stresses.

An Expanding Social World

Throughout the world, school-age children are recognized as markedly more independent and more capable than younger children. As a result, children go to school, or outside to play, or off to work, out of their parents' view, meeting friends and strangers unknown to their families, and experiencing adventures and challenges that adults often know little about.

A Common Theoretical Thread

This new competence has been recognized by every developmental theorist who has attended to this period. Freud describes middle childhood as the period of **latency**, when children's emotional drives are quieter, their psychosexual needs are repressed, and their unconscious conflicts are submerged, features that make latency "a time for acquiring cognitive skills and assimilating cultural values as the child expands his world to include teacher, neighbors, peers" (Miller, 1983).

Erikson (1963) likewise agrees that middle childhood is a quiet period emotionally and that it is productive as well, as the child "becomes ready to apply himself to given skills and tasks." The specific crisis that Erikson sees for this developmental period is **industry versus inferiority**. According to Erikson, as children busily try to master whatever skills are valued in their culture, they develop views of themselves as either competent or incompetent, or, in Erikson's words, as either industrious and productive or inferior and inadequate.

Operating from quite different theoretical bases, developmentalists influenced by behaviorism or social learning theory, or by the cognitive or sociocultural perspectives, are less interested in the school-age child's convoluted emotional life and more concerned with the step-by-step acquisition of new cognitive abilities, and the steady unfolding of self-understanding, that characterize middle childhood. However, their overview of this period is quite similar to the psychoanalytic depiction: children during middle childhood meet the challenges of the outside world with an openness, insight, and confidence that few younger children possess. Middle childhood is seen as a time when many distinct competencies coalesce. The abilities to learn and to analyze, to express emotions, and to make friends have been in

FIGURE 14.1 The North American boy at his father's worktable and the Brazilian boy fashioning arrows in the Amazon jungle are both engaged in essentially the same task—attaining competence in their respective cultures, in accordance with the particulars of their social setting.

evidence from infancy, but now they come together in a much more focused and consistent manner, forming a much stronger, unified, and self-assured personality (Collins, 1984; Bryant, 1985; Bandura, 1981, 1989).

Now let us look at some of the specific manifestations of this developmental period.

Social Cognition

An integral key to the psychosocial development of school-age children is an advance in **social cognition,** that is, in the understanding of other people and groups. As we saw in Chapter 10, preschoolers first evidence social cognition in a simple theory of mind, when they begin to realize that other people's actions can be motivated by thoughts and emotions that are different from their own. But such theorizing is prone to error, because young children's grasp of the differences between subjective points of view is limited and fragile. During the school years, children's theory of mind evolves into a complex, multifaceted view of others. Children begin to understand human behavior not just as responses to specific thoughts or desires but as actions that are influenced, simultaneously, by diverse needs and emotions and by complex human relationships and motives (Arsenio & Kramer, 1992; Mc-Keough, 1992).

This developmental progression was shown explicitly in a very simple experiment in which children between the ages of 4 and 10 were shown pictures of various domestic situations and asked how the mother might respond and why (Goldberg-Reitman, 1992). In one scene, for example, a child curses while playing with blocks. As reflected in the following typical responses, in assessing what the mother might do, the 4-year-olds attended only to the immediate behavior, whereas older children recognized the implications and possible consequences of the behavior:

> Age 4: "The mother spanks her because she said a naughty word."

> Age 6: "The mother says 'Don't say that again' because it's not nice to say a bad word."

> Age 10: "The mother maybe hits her or something because she's trying to teach her . . . because if she grew up like that she'd get into a lot a trouble . . . she might get a bad reputation."

In a variety of similar research studies, as well as in everyday spontaneous examples, younger children are much more likely to focus solely on observable behavior, not on underlying motives, feelings, or social consequences: they know when an adult might protect, nurture, scold, or teach a child but not necessarily why. Older children tend not only to understand the motivational and affective origins of various behaviors but also to analyze the future impact of whatever action they might take.

This more complex social cognition is also shown in children's advancing realization that individuals differ in personality traits. Compare the following two descriptions from an extensive study (Livesley & Bromley, 1973) in which children aged 7 and older were asked to describe other children they knew:

> 7-year-old: Max sits next to me, his eyes are hazel and he is tall. He hasn't got a very big head, he's got a big pointed nose.

> 10-year-old; He smells very much and is very nasty. He has no sense of humor and is very dull. He is always fighting and he is cruel. He does silly things and is

latency Freud's term for the period between the phallic stage and the genital stage of psychosexual development. During latency, which lasts from about age 7 to age 11, children's psychosexual drives and unconscious emotional conflicts are relatively quiet, and children direct their attention and energies to the outside social world.

industry versus inferiority The fourth of Erickson's eight crises of psychosocial development, in which school-age children attempt to master many skills and develop a sense of themselves as either industrious and competent or incompetent and inferior.

social cognition A person's awareness and understanding of human personality, motives, emotions, intentions, and interactions.

very stupid. He has brown hair and cruel eyes. He is sulky and 11 years old and has lots of sisters. I think he is the most horrible boy in the class. He has a croaky voice and always chews his pencil and picks his teeth and I think he is disgusting.

As you can see, the 7-year-old's description focuses exclusively on physical characteristics. Children of this age are, in fact, aware of personality traits and can infer them from others' behavior (Berndt & Heller, 1985; Miller & Aloise, 1989), but they do not think of others primarily in terms of personality dispositions. Instead, they focus either on outward appearance or behavior that can be more easily observed and interpreted (Feldman & Ruble, 1988). Older children, by contrast, are aware of the importance of personality traits. They organize their perceptions of a person around the traits they observe in the individual and frequently use those traits as a basis for predicting the person's future behavior and emotional reactions (Gnepp & Chilamkurti, 1988).

During the school years, children's emotional understanding deepens in a number of other ways as well. They begin to appreciate, for example, that emotions have internal causes that can sometimes be personally redirected (such as thinking happy thoughts in a sad situation), and this enables children to better manage their emotions (Garber & Dodge, 1991; Thompson, 1994). Whereas a young child is likely to become distressed when confronting an older bully, school-age children can sometimes coach themselves into looking—and perhaps even feeling—unafraid. During the school years, moreover, children also realize that someone can feel several emotions simultaneously (and can thus have conflicting or ambivalent feelings), and that people sometimes disguise or mask their emotions to comply with social rules (such as looking delighted after opening a disappointing gift) (Harris, 1989; Harter & Whitesell, 1989; Saarni, 1989).

This expansion of emotional understanding has several important consequences for social interaction. It means that children are likely to become more sensitive to, and empathize with, the emotional experiences of others (Eisenberg, 1992; Hoffman, 1988). This heightened sensitivity influences children's willingness to be kind and helpful to others (Eisenberg et al., 1990; Eisenberg & Mussen, 1989). Another advance, for which adults may be grateful, is that older children are better able to recognize and rephrase or avoid potentially offensive statements to preserve the feelings of others (Johnson

FIGURE 14.2 This girl seems hesitant to proceed, perhaps in anticipation of getting a cold shock. However, because of the expanded emotional understanding that is typical of school-age children, she probably realizes that if she stalls much longer, she is bound to get teased. This greater emotional understanding may also help her to control her anxiety long enough for her to take the plunge.

et al., 1984). Thus the 11-year-old is much less likely than the 6-year-old to tell you that your stomach is too fat or to comment aloud on the silly-looking hat that a passerby is wearing.

Children's enhanced emotional understanding also increases their sensitivity to the social purposes of emotional expressions, and to the possibility that their own expressions—and those of other people—may not reflect what they truly feel. As a consequence, they are harder to fool: it is the school-age child who shrugs off a parent's sympathy by saying "You're just trying to make me feel better," or dismisses a parent's praise with "You have to say that because I'm your kid!" They also are more aware of the social situations in which it is appropriate to express emotions like anger—and when it is inappropriate to do so (Underwood et al., 1992).

Understanding Oneself

As we saw in Chapter 11, preschoolers have begun to develop a sense of themselves as persons with unique characteristics and dispositions, but their self-understanding lacks depth. Children's thoughts about themselves develop rapidly during middle childhood, however, as their cognitive abilities mature and their social experience widens. In the beginning of the school years, for example, children often explain their actions by referring to the events of the immediate situation; a few years later they more readily relate their actions to their personality traits and feelings (Higgins, 1981). Thus, whereas the 6-year-old might say that she hit him because he hit her, the 11-year-old might also explain that she was already upset because she had lost her bookbag and that, besides, he is always hitting people and getting away with it.

Moreover, because of their widening social networks, school-age children perceive themselves in terms of different roles (family member, teammate, student, etc.) and distinct skills (academic, athletic, social, and so forth). As their social networks widen, children also begin to become aware of their belonging to one or another ethnic, religious, or social group, and it is during the school years that children from minority groups begin to take pride in their ethnic identity (Aboud, 1987; Katz, 1987). For many, such pride "bolsters one's self-respect, exalts one's conception of oneself, and inures the individual against the pain incident to low status" (Spencer, 1987).

As children's self-understanding becomes more differentiated, it also becomes more integrated (Harter, 1983), enabling schoolchildren to view themselves in terms of several competencies at once. They might, for example, recognize themselves as weak at playing sports, good at playing a musical instrument, and a whiz at playing Nintendo. Similarly, they might feel that they are basically good at making friends, and are considerate of others, but that they have a quick temper that sometimes makes them do things that jeopardize their friendships. In sum, like their understanding of other people, children's self-understanding during the school years becomes psychologically more complex, more discriminating, and more richly textured.

Along with their developing self-understanding comes greater self-regulation, as children learn to control their reactions for strategic purposes. They know how to act in various social situations—whether at school, at a concert, or at a ballpark—and they have the self-control to act appropriately. They can use mental distraction to avoid becoming fidgety during a

RESEARCH REPORT

Paging for Feelings

Developmental researchers have long been interested in how the everyday emotional experiences of children change during the school years and early adolescence. Most theories predict significant changes as children enter what Freud called the latency period—a quieting of psychosexual urges and passions during the school years—and subsequently enter adolescence, with the reemergence of sexuality and emotional turmoil. Do these changes, in fact, occur?

To find out, Reed Larson and Claudia Lampman-Petraitis (1989) devised an inventive strategy. They equipped 473 children between the ages of 9 and 15 with electronic pagers and a booklet of emotional self-report forms, and asked the children to take them along wherever they went for one week. During the week, the children were signaled through their pagers seven times each day, at irregular intervals, between 7:30 a.m. and 9:30 p.m. On each occasion, they completed a self-report form, indicating their current emotional state on measures assessing their happiness, excitement, cheerfulness, and other emotions. Children were allowed to turn off the pager if they took a nap, slept late, or went to bed early, but otherwise kept the pager and rating booklet with them throughout the day.

Imagine, for a moment, the diverse circumstances in which children were suddenly interrupted by an imperative pager "beeping" them to complete another emotional self-report—in the midst of a boring class; while looking in the mirror; during an angry family dinner; while talking on

the phone with friends; during an evening out with somebody important. The possibilities are revealingly endless. This is, of course, what the "beeper methodology" was designed to accomplish: providing a detailed sampling of the daily emotional experience of children and youth.

When the self-ratings (from a total of 17,752 pager signals) were aggregated over the entire week, the results were surprising. Children at each age showed comparable fluctuations in emotional experience. In other words, the study provided no support for the idea that school-age children show greater emotional stability, and young adolescents greater moodiness: 10-year-olds were as likely to shift from a happy to sad mood—and back again—as 15-year-olds were. When average emotion ratings were compared, however, there were differences with age. On the whole, with increasing age, children reported themselves feeling less happy, friendly, and cheerful.

Thus these findings contradict one widely held view of development during later childhood—that, compared to adolescence, the school years are a period of greater emotional stability and fewer mood swings. However, the findings did confirm the equally prevalent notion that early adolescence is a period of diminished happiness and well-being. Taken together with other research discussed in this chapter, findings from the "beeper methodology" confirm that throughout the school years, advancing age leads to greater self-awareness, more social sensitivity, and, for some, diminished happiness with oneself.

boring concert, for example, and they know how to look attentive in class, even when they are not paying attention. The difference between how they act on the outside, and how they think or feel within, owes to the growth of self-understanding and self-regulation.

The Rising Tide of Self-Doubt

As their self-understanding sharpens, children gradually become more self-critical, and their self-esteem dips as they begin to see themselves more realistically, with weaknesses as well as strengths. One reason is that they more often evaluate themselves by comparing their skills and achievements with those of others. Further, as they mature, children are more likely to feel personally to blame for their shortcomings, and less likely to believe, as younger children often do, that it is bad luck that makes them do poorly (Powers & Wagner, 1984). Girls are especially likely to blame themselves for their difficulties (Stipek, 1984), a tendency apparent throughout childhood.

The rising tide of self-doubt is particularly evident at school, where, as you learned in the preceding chapter, children's perceptions of their intel-

FIGURE 14.3 The best antidote to learned helplessness is a competent and encouraging teacher. Given this girl's expression, her father has probably already begun to teach her some fundamentals of the game—rather than assuming that girls can't hit hard, throw straight, or catch—and to make her feel relaxed about messing up. In general, children learn much more from adults who believe that every child can become competent than from adults who think innate ability is the determining factor.

lectual competence decline steadily through the elementary-school years (Eccles et al., 1993; Phillips & Zimmerman, 1990). This is in striking contrast to the self-evaluations of preschoolers, who usually remain buoyantly optimistic and confident of their own abilities, even in the face of negative evaluations by others (Stipek, 1984; Stipek & MacIver, 1989).

This developmental change in self-confidence makes school-age children more vulnerable to **learned helplessness**—the view that, in the end, one can do little to succeed. Many children who experience learned helplessness attribute their failures—but not their success—to their ability. Consequently, they tend to lack self-confidence in challenging situations, and their performance deteriorates as a result: they use poor problem-solving strategies, their attention wanders, they feel that they are struggling for nothing. Thus learned helplessness leads to a self-fulfilling prophecy. Whereas children who believe in their ability will continue to work at a task they have not yet mastered—confident that their efforts will pay off—children experiencing learned helplessness "know" that they are bound to fail, and so give up trying. This is especially true if parents or teachers indicate that the child's failure was due to limited competence rather than to not trying hard enough—a message, by the way, that girls tend to receive more often than boys (Dweck et al., 1978; Eccles, 1993). As Erikson predicted when he described industry versus inferiority, a child with few successes may develop a sense of inferiority that leads to anticipation of continued failure and a lowering of self-esteem. Thus the child who experiences learned helplessness in middle childhood is likely to experience continuing social and/or academic problems unless parents and teachers can change how the child attributes successes and failures (Fincham et al., 1989).

However, as we will now see, in many respects, adults foster self-esteem and other aspects of psychosocial development in tandem with peer influences, which have their own unique role in psychosocial growth.

The Peer Group

Perhaps the most influential system in which the school-age child develops his or her self-esteem is the **peer group**, a group of individuals of roughly the same age and social status who play, work, and learn together. Acceptance in one's peer group can go a long way toward building a sense of competence, particularly in middle childhood, when frequency of contact with peers increases (Feiring & Lewis, 1989). Not surprisingly, children become increasingly dependent on their peers, not only for companionship but also for self-validation and advice (Nelson-Le Gall & Gumerman, 1984). Peer relationships also provide unique opportunities for the growth of both self-understanding and the ability to relate to others—partly because peer relationships, unlike adult-child relationships, involve partners who must learn to negotiate, compromise, share, and defend as equals (Hartup, 1989). Indeed, the peer group becomes a kind of separate society from that of adults.

The Society of Children

When groups of children play together, they develop particular patterns of interaction that regulate their play, distinguishing it from the activities of adult-organized society. Some social scientists call the peer group's subcul-

learned helplessness A fatalistic perception, based on past failures, that one can do nothing to improve one's performance or situation.

peer group A group of individuals of roughly the same age and social status who play, work, or learn together.

FIGURE 14.4 One expression of the society of children is its play behavior, including the rules, rituals, and chants of hide-and-seek, kick the can, and, as shown here, jump-rope. Double-dutch skills and jumping rhymes are passed down from slightly older children to younger ones, with each new cohort being likely to put its own distinctive twist on both.

ture the **society of children,** highlighting the distinctions between children's groups and the general culture (Davies, 1982; Knapp & Knapp, 1976; Opie & Opie, 1959).

The society of children typically has a special vocabulary, activities, dress codes, and rules of behavior that flourish without the approval, or even the knowledge, of adults. Its slang words and nicknames, for instance, are often ones adults would frown on (if they could understand them), and its activities—such as hanging out at the mall and long, meandering phone conversations—do not invite adult participation (Zarbatany et al., 1990). Its dress codes become known to adults only when they try to get a child to wear something that violates those codes—as when a perfectly fine pair of hand-me-down jeans is rejected because, by the standards of the dress code, they are an unfashionable color, or have the wrong label, or have legs that are too loose, or too tight, or too short, or too long. If parents find a certain brand and style of children's shoes on sale, they can bet that they are the very ones that their children would not be caught dead wearing. Sex differences in clothes, behavior, and play patterns and partners become increasingly salient as children move from kindergarten to the sixth grade (Furman, 1987; Hayden-Thompson et al., 1987).

The distinction between those who are "in" and those who are "out" is perhaps most obvious in children's spontaneous organization of clubs, in which much attention is given to details concerned with rules, officers, dress, and establishing a clubhouse, often deliberately distant from adult activity. Sometimes the club has no announced purpose, its only apparent function being the exclusion of adults and other children (especially those of the other sex). From a developmental perspective, however, such clubs serve many functions, including building self-esteem, sharpening social skills, and teaching social cooperation. As one researcher describes his club:

> I was a charter member of a second-grade club called the Penguins, whose two major activities were acquiring extensive information about penguins and standing outside in the freezing weather without a coat for as long as we could. Like most other groups of this sort, the Penguins did not last very long, but in the making and unmaking of such groups, children are conducting what may be informative experiments in social organization. [Rubin, 1980]

Many children instead gather in informal, loosely knit groups which provide a similar sense of solidarity and acceptance without the formal

society of children The social culture of children, including the games, vocabulary, dress codes, and rules of behavior that characterize their interaction.

trappings of a club. Unfortunately, for some children, youth gangs serve similar functions, with acceptance into them being dependent upon the child's willingness to engage in certain forms of tough talk and bravado, risk-taking, and flouting of conventions. All too often, it also requires a willingness to engage in criminal activities.

Even when it does not involve a specific club, gang, or group, the society of children entails general codes of behavior, many of which demand independence from adults. By age 10, if not before, children (especially boys) whose parents walk them to school or kiss them in public are pitied; "cry babies" and "teachers' pets" are ostracized; children who tattle or "rat" to adults are despised; and, as we shall see, children who are unduly aggressive—or those who do not defend themselves against aggression—are rejected. As they did at younger ages, school-age children (again, especially boys) engage in rough-and-tumble play but, observing the codes of their group, they become increasingly selective in when, where, and with whom they do it (Humphreys & Smith, 1987).

Aggression

Closely related to their increasing selectivity in friendly roughhousing is children's growing sensitivity to the norms for playful and nonplayful aggression—the teasing, insulting, and physical threatening that are at the edge of many episodes of children's social interaction. Indeed, a certain amount of aggression, counteraggression, and reconciliation is present in peer interactions beginning from early childhood, as conflict arises over favorite toys, preferred activities, and popular play partners (Ross & Conant, 1992). The social norms of the school years, however, mean that children often risk social isolation if they do not readily anticipate and defend themselves against sarcastic comments, implied insults, or direct verbal or physical attacks.

The specifics regarding when aggression is appropriate, in what forms, and to what degree depend, of course, on the specifics of the social context. A study in England, for example, found that children who were most socially accepted were those who "gave as much as they got," sometimes teasing and mocking each other and—girls as well as boys—coming to blows. In fact, reciprocity of aggression was such a part of peer-group acceptance that those who suffered attack without retaliating were rejected as "piss weak" (Davies, 1982). At the same time, arrogance beyond a certain limit was considered out of bounds, for children were quite critical of "getting the snobs, getting the cranks, . . . lying, showing off, getting too full of yourself, posing, . . . wanting everything your way, being spoilt . . ." (Davies, 1982).

A somewhat different distinction between proper and improper aggression was found in a study of first-grade African-American boys: instrumental aggression (e.g., fighting to get one's own way) did not enhance a boy's status, but relatively quick retaliation against an implied threat or insult or a show of force to establish dominance was likely to inspire admiration. As the boys grew older, aggression was less positively viewed, but it still did not undermine acceptance (Coie et al., 1991). Many of these boys viewed quick retaliation as a necessity for deterring threats and preventing future challenges (Graham et al., 1992; Herzberger & Hall 1993; Hudley & Graham, 1993).

As these examples suggest, variation in the norms for aggression can occur by age, by ethnic and economic group, by neighborhood, and by the specific social situation. In each context, there may be different rules about hitting someone smaller, or boys attacking girls, or girls using physical force, or the appropriate role of friends and bystanders—and different customs about which contacts (e.g., being bumped up against, being shoved, having one's shoe stepped on) or insults (directed at one's relatives, one's physical appearance, or one's intellect) should be ignored, reciprocated, or avenged. Friendship status also affects the norms for aggression. Friends disagree about as often as nonfriends do, but their conflicts lead to less hostility than those of nonfriends and more often result in compromises (Hartup, 1992; Hartup et al., 1988). Children recognize that a friend is "someone whom you fight with, but not forever" (Goodnow & Burns, 1988).

Even though conflict and aggression are normal features of peer interaction, however, a child who is unusually aggressive is likely to be rejected by peers, especially as those peers acquire other strategies to resolve conflict in the school years (Bryant, 1992; Perry et al., 1992). Moreover, children who are unusually aggressive are likely to gain an undesirable reputation among the peer group, further ensuring their social isolation (Hymel et al., 1990). This may be one reason why a child's exhibiting high levels of aggression with peers is one of the best predictors of dropping out of school or breaking the law in adolescence (Cairns et al., 1989; Kupersmidt & Coie, 1990; Kupersmidt et al., 1990). When children stay within the accepted bounds of conflict and aggression, peer relations remain supportive; when they exceed these limits, it usually reveals underlying psychosocial problems that need attention, lest they erupt in a more destructive form later on.

Prosocial Behavior

Peer relationships also provide a context for **prosocial behavior,** acts of sharing and caring that benefit others without the benefactor's expectation of personal reward. With their expanding understanding of other people during the school years, children become both more sensitive to the needs of others, and more competent and creative in their prosocial actions (Hoffman, 1988; Strayer & Schroeder, 1989). Noticing a classmate who forgot to bring her lunch to school, they may offer to share theirs; encountering a peer who is being picked on by a bully, they may come to the peer's defense. Children offer emotional as well as instrumental aid to friends, such as giving a pat on the back after a bad play, or sharing sympathy after the death of a pet. Their assistance often derives from "stepping into the shoes" of the other person—that is, thinking about the peer's feelings and needs (Eisenberg et al., 1987).

As their world widens during middle childhood, children also become more concerned about those they do not know personally, leading them to engage in such prosocial behavior as raising money to help the less fortunate or helping with clean-up efforts in a nearby community after a flood or tornado, or writing letters to impoverished children in distant countries. Their concern about people they do not know is accompanied by growth in their moral understanding, which, as we shall see, enables them to appreciate why a particular action is just or unjust, why people should help each other even when no personal gain is involved, and why war, racism, sexism, and poverty are wrong (Eisenberg et al., 1987).

prosocial behavior Any action, such as sharing, cooperating, or sympathizing, performed to benefit other people without the expectation of reward for oneself.

Prosocial behavior increases in middle childhood for other reasons also (Eisenberg, 1992). Younger children sometimes feel the impulse to help others but may hesitate to try because they are not sure what to do. Older children, on the other hand, are likely to have the knowledge and self-confidence to effectively give assistance, whether it entails comforting a distressed peer, cleaning up a sibling's accidental spill, or contributing hard-earned allowance money to combat world hunger. Moreover, older children are more likely to find themselves in situations requiring their assistance, whether at school, on the playground, or at a friend's home.

FIGURE 14.5 School-age children, such as this Girl Scout, are able to perform many useful prosocial tasks, and should be encouraged to do so. Although prosocial acts are performed without expectation of benefits to oneself, they can result in a very important one: a sense of connection to others and to the community at large.

However, because the motivation and the capacity for prosocial behavior increase during middle childhood does not mean that school-age children are always altruistic. Sometimes children's prosocial instincts remain dormant because they are concerned about doing the wrong thing, or because they are afraid of embarrassing the person in need or, worse, themselves (Eisenberg, 1992). In addition, during the school years, children tend to become more exclusive in giving help to those they know, offering assistance to friends but not to nonfriends, or to those they admire but not to those they dislike (Burelson, 1982; French, 1984).

Social Problem Solving

Children's deepening social understanding during the school years enhances their social problem-solving skills, which, in turn, makes their peer relations more intimate and sophisticated (Dodge, 1986; Rubin & Krasnor, 1986). Among preschoolers, peer conflict frequently results in retaliation, an appeal to an adult authority, or displays of distress. In the school years, however, children master a variety of alternative strategies for resolving conflict (Bryant, 1992). They can cajole the adversary, use bargaining, suggest compromise or cooperation (like turn-taking), and redirect conflict through humor. Children also acquire different strategies for accomplishing different social goals, such as gaining entry to a group, organizing cooperative activity, or getting to know an unfamiliar peer (Putallaz & Wasserman, 1990; Wentzel & Eroley, 1993). These problem-solving strategies enable children to become more sensitive and successful social partners.

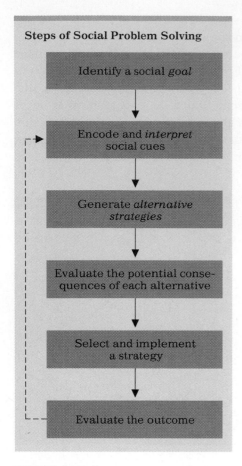

Steps of Social Problem Solving

Identify a social *goal*

↓

Encode and *interpret* social cues

↓

Generate *alternative strategies*

↓

Evaluate the potential consequences of each alternative

↓

Select and implement a strategy

↓

Evaluate the outcome

FIGURE 14.6 As you can see, solving social problems is no less complex than solving math or science problems. Partly because repeated efforts lead to repeated evaluations, most children steadily improve in their social problem-solving skills during middle childhood.

Social problem solving requires several steps (see Figure 14.6). Consider the following exchange between two third-graders who are building with blocks (Rubin & Krasnor, 1986):

Sarah: "Hey (reaches over). We can make it wider. Here, wanna do it?"
Lisa: *(no response)*
Sarah: "Don't you think it should be a bit wider?'
Lisa: *(no response)*
Sarah: "Yeah, let's make it wider."
Lisa: *(makes construction wider)*

Sarah's *goal* is to involve Lisa in her modified construction plan. She suggests to Lisa that they "make it wider" together because Lisa's previous social cues caused Sarah to *interpret* their relationship as cooperative. When this initial strategy fails, Sarah reinterprets the situation, and then devises two *alternative strategies* (a direct inquiry and a restatement of her goal) that eventually accomplish her goal.

As you can see, the social problem-solving flow chart shown in Figure 14.6 resembles an information-processing approach to social understanding (see Chapter 2). Using the information-processing perspective, researchers have begun to examine how specific skills at each step of social problem solving grow during the childhood years. Asking children to devise alternative strategies for resolving a conflict, for instance, they have found that older children, consistent with their more acute social understanding, offer a much wider range of creative strategies than younger children do (such as compromising, negotiating, or using humor to avoid conflict rather than merely retaliating). In addition, school-age children are much more skilled than preschoolers at evaluating the probable outcome of their strategies (such as realizing that using humor rather than retaliation may preserve a friendship) (Dodge, 1986; Dodge et al., 1986). To a large degree, children's overall social competence is linked to their developing skills in social problem solving. As we shall see shortly, children who have problems in their peer relationships often have difficulties with these skills (Perry et al., 1992).

Friendship

Throughout childhood, friendships become increasingly important, and children's understanding of friendship becomes increasingly abstract and complex, as children learn to balance honesty with protectiveness, mutual dependence with a respect for independence, and competition with cooperation, shared conversation, and shared actions (Berndt, 1989b; Rawlins, 1992). At the same time, older children perceive their friends in psychologically richer ways because of their deeper, more nuanced understanding of themselves (Parker & Gottman, 1989).

These changes are reflected in a study of hundreds of Canadian and Scottish children, from first grade through the eighth, who were asked what made their best friends different from other acquaintances. Children of all ages tended to say that friends did things together and could be counted on for help, but the older children were more likely to cite *mutual* help, whereas younger children simply said that their friends helped *them.* Further, the older children considered mutual loyalty, intimacy, and interests, as well as activities, to be part of friendship (Bigelow, 1977; Bigelow & La

FIGURE 14.7 These girls are having a "sleep over," a common occurrence among school-age children who enjoy the intimacy of staying overnight at each other's homes. Typically, sharing secrets, staying up late, and eating junk food are part of the event, bringing the friends closer together. Notice that all of these activities are much more possible for school-age children than for younger ones, who are more likely to get scared or have a quarrel when they try a sleep over.

Gaipa, 1975). Similarly, in a United States study (Berndt, 1981), children were asked "How do you know your best friend?" A typical kindergartner answered:

> I sleep over at his house sometimes. When he's playing ball with his friends he'll let me play. When I sleep over, he lets me get in front of him in 4-squares (a playground game). He likes me.

By contrast, a typical sixth-grader said:

> If you can tell each other things that you don't like about each other. If you get in a fight with someone else, they'd stick up for you. If you can tell them your phone number and they don't give you crank calls. If they don't act mean to you when other kids are around.

As suggested by the sixth-grader's account, older children increasingly regard friendship as a forum for self-disclosure, and expect that their intimacy will be reciprocated (Rotenberg & Mann, 1986; Rotenberg & Sliz, 1988). Partly because friendships become more intense and more intimate as children grow older, older children demand more of their friends, change friends less often, find it harder to make new friends, and are more upset when a friendship breaks up. They also are more picky: throughout childhood, children increasingly tend to choose best friends who are of the same sex, race, and economic background as themselves (Hartup, 1992).

As children become more choosy about their friends, their friendship groups become smaller. Whereas most 4-year-olds say that they have many friends (perhaps everyone in their nursery-school class, with one or two notable exceptions), most 8-year-olds have a small circle of friends, and by age 10, children often have one "best" friend to whom they are quite loyal. Although this trend toward an increasingly exclusive friendship network is followed by both sexes, it tends to be more apparent among girls. By the end of middle childhood, many girls have one and only one best friend on whom they depend (Gilligan et al., 1990).

Thus, as children grow older, friendship patterns become more rigidly set, so that by age 9 or so everyone knows who hangs out with whom, and few children would dare to try to break into an established group or a pair of close friends. With the changes of early puberty (at about age 10), some children come to be more advanced than others, disrupting former social patterns and wrecking many friendships. As one girl named Rachel put it:

Oh, I feel so horrible about friends. Everybody is deserting their best friend and everybody hates someone else and Paula Davis has been stranded with nobody—except me and Sarah. Cristine has run off with Liz and Joan has moved up from being an eleven-year-old . . . and, oh, well, I suppose it happens every year. [Rubin, 1980]

Lacking Acceptance Among Peers

All children feel left out or unwelcome among their peers on one occasion or another. As the children's ditty puts it, "Nobody likes me, everybody hates me . . . think I'll go out and eat some worms." But an estimated 10 percent of all schoolchildren are unpopular most of the time (Asher & Renshaw, 1981). Using procedures in which children are asked to nominate peers they especially like or dislike, researchers have identified several kinds of unpopular children (Coie & Dodge, 1983; Terry & Coie, 1991):

1. *rejected* children, who are actively disliked, some—*aggressive-rejected*—because of their aggressive, confrontational behavior, and others—*withdrawn-rejected*—because of their withdrawn, anxious demeanor (Bierman et al., 1993; Cillessen et al., 1992; Hymel et al., 1993);

2. *neglected* children, who are seldom nominated at all (either positively or negatively) because they are generally ignored by their peers;

3. *controversial* children, who receive a high number of both positive and negative peer nominations, reflecting ambivalence in how others regard them.

Many of these children have problems, especially rejected children. Withdrawn-rejected children are aware of their social isolation, making them lonely and unhappy, and their low self-esteem has a negative impact on their academic achievement and their family relationships. Aggressive-rejected children, on the other hand, remain oblivious to their lack of acceptance, and tend to overestimate their social competence (Hymel et al., 1993; Parkhurst & Asher, 1992). However, there is no doubt that their peers perceive them as argumentative, disruptive, and uncooperative—a perception that is confirmed by teachers' ratings and direct observations of their behavior with peers (Bierman et al., 1993; Dodge et al., 1990; Patterson et al., 1990).

FIGURE 14.8 Those most likely to reject the oddball are those who feel most vulnerable themselves, a truism for children as well as adults.

As rejected children get older, their problems get worse, because peers become more critical of each other as adolescence nears, and withdrawn or aggressive behavior becomes more self-defeating. Aggressive-rejected children are most likely to have adjustment problems—including heightened risk of psychological disorders—in adolescence and adulthood (Coie et al., 1992; Hymel et al., 1990; Parker & Asher, 1987).

Several studies have shown that children who are aggressive-rejected are impulsive and immature in their social cognition (Dodge & Feldman, 1990; Perry et al., 1992; Rabiner et al., 1990). Compared with other children, for instance, they tend to misinterpret social situations. They consider a friendly act to be hostile (Dodge et al., 1984; Graham et al., 1992; Hudley & Graham, 1993) or, especially when they feel anxious, interpret accidental harm as intentional (Dodge & Somberg, 1987). For example, they might interpret a compliment as sarcastic, or regard a request for a bite of candy as a demand, or assume that someone's inadvertently stepping on their shoe was intended as an insult. They also have difficulty in sharing and cooperating (Markell & Asher, 1984) and in understanding what other children's needs might be (Goetz & Dweck, 1980). Unfortunately, since the way most children develop their social understanding and skill is from normal give-and-take with peers, aggressive-rejected children are excluded from the very learning situations they need most.

The social competence of neglected and controversial children is mixed (Newcomb et al., 1993). Controversial children are often highly aggressive, but—by contrast with aggressive-rejected children—they compensate for this liability with strong, positive social skills. A controversial child may punch another child hard on the arm and then, just when the victim is about to explode, suggest playing a fun game together. By contrast, neglected children tend to be unaggressive but also unsociable, which may account for their being ignored by other children. Interestingly, however, these children are not necessarily lonely and they do not lack social skills. Often they merely prefer to play alone, and do not have long-term adjustment problems (Asher, 1983; Crick & Ladd, 1993; Parker & Asher, 1987; Parkhurst & Asher, 1992). This is useful information for parents and teachers who may otherwise believe that every child needs to have many friends all the time. Rather, it is the actively rejected child who most needs help.

Cause and Remedies

How do children come to behave in these ways? Consistent with the relationship perspective (see Chapter 11), children acquire social tendencies at home that may lead to popularity, or lack of acceptance, among peers (Parke & Ladd, 1992). For instance, the children of authoritarian parents (see pp. 377–383) tend to use domineering strategies themselves to get their way with peers—and not surprisingly, these children are very unpopular (Dekovic & Janssens, 1992; Hart et al., 1990). Rejected children generally—and aggressive-rejected children in particular—report feeling less companionship, affection, and support from their fathers than do other children, and their families experience more stress (Dishion, 1990; East, 1991; Patterson et al., 1990). By contrast, children whose parents are warm and affirming are likely to develop an orientation toward peers that is similarly positive

FIGURE 14.9 From this angle, it looks as though this boy is either *withdrawn-rejected*, experiencing problems with peers, or *neglected*, being overlooked by them. On the other hand, it may be that he simply enjoys being peacefully off by himself.

Enhancing Peer Acceptance

What can be done to assist children who lack acceptance among their peers, either because they are aggressive and disruptive or because they are passive and withdrawn? Several strategies have been used, each with a measure of proven success (Bierman & Furman, 1984; Coie & Koeppl, 1990; Hudley & Graham, 1993):

Social problem-solving approaches try to help children devise more thoughtful, creative—and ultimately successful—ways of resolving conflicts in their peer interactions. Using the framework of social problem-solving summarized in Figure 14.6, children participate in activities that enable them to find, and evaluate, alternative solutions to common dilemmas. For example, in a role-playing exercise, two children (or one child and a counselor) might act out a disagreement about what to do together on a free afternoon—with one person wanting to hang out at the mall, say, and the other wanting to go bowling. The child is then asked to come up with alternative strategies for resolving the disagreement (such as compromising on a third activity, or flipping a coin, or choosing the least expensive alternative.) Finally, the child and the counselor discuss the strengths and weaknesses of each strategy in order to help the child develop better skills for choosing among them. In another type of activity, a child might report on a personal experience in which his or her efforts to resolve a conflict with a peer failed. Then the child would discuss with a counselor (or another child) alternative approaches that might have worked better. By participating in these kinds of guided activities, children acquire problem-solving skills

that they can, and often do, apply in their everyday encounters with other children.

Attributional retraining encourages children to rethink their negative assumptions about other people's motives and intentions. Recall that rejected children tend to approach their peers suspiciously: they misinterpret friendly actions as hostile, such as perceiving a casual suggestion as criticism, or an accidental bump as malicious. Attributional retraining encourages children to interpret others' actions more benignly, with the expectation that this change in outlook will foster more positive social behavior. In one such exercise, for example, a child might watch a videotape of actors involved in an ambiguous social encounter—one person spilling milk on another in the lunchroom, for example. The child would then be asked to consider all the possible reasons for this event—that it might have been accidental, or deliberately provoked by the victim, or the result of another person's bumping into the lunch tray, and so on. A counselor would discuss with the child how to evaluate the spiller's true intent (by considering the person's facial expression, or relationship with the victim, or attitude after the event) and what to do when different motives are identified (such as being forgiving if the person is sincerely apologetic, or staying cool if the spill was intentional). Thus, through attributional retraining, children are encouraged to approach others less defensively and to give them the benefit of the doubt, assuming benign intent unless there is definite reason to think otherwise.

and affirmative (Putallaz & Heflin, 1990). Thus, children's experiences in their family relationships may lay the foundation for the social skills and social orientation that they bring to their peer relationships.

A rejected child's lack of acceptance can be exacerbated by the child's reputation in the school or peer group. For example, how teachers respond to a negative, disruptive child in the classroom can have a powerful effect on that child's peer status. In one study, young grade-school children who observed a teacher provide positive reinforcement for a disruptive child's good behavior ("Looks like Billy's paying attention. Good!") rated the child more positively themselves than when they witnessed the teacher focusing instead on the child's disruptive behavior and making derogatory comments ("Can't you ever be still?") (White & Kistner, 1992).

The rejected child's reputation within the peer group is also important in that it biases other children's attitudes and reactions to the child, creating a negative image that is hard to overcome. In the words of two experts,

Social-skills training teaches children specific behavior they can use to improve their peer relationships. By watching socially skilled children in action (either directly or through specially designed videotapes), or by participating in role-playing activities, children learn such things as how to comment positively on what another person has said, how to start a conversation with an unfamiliar person, how to ask appropriate questions while playing, how to use humor to defuse a disagreement, and other such strategies for effective social interaction. Typically the child rehearses these strategies (with a counselor, or with other children who have been enlisted into the therapy session) until he or she becomes familiar and comfortable with them. Of course, it is usually much less difficult to act positively in a supportive counseling session than it is in one's true peer environment—where a negative reputation can cause others to approach the child negatively and suspiciously. Consequently, the most effective social-skills training programs attempt to facilitate the child's generalization of these newly learned skills to his or her everyday encounters with peers.

Supportive interventions arise out of a recognition that children who are not accepted by their peers usually have other problems that further undermine their status within the peer culture. They are often poor students, they usually have bad reputations with other children, and they are often regarded negatively by their teachers as well. Consequently, well-designed programs often include supportive interventions that address these additional needs. Special academic tutoring may be provided to help these children perform better in the classroom (this approach can be especially beneficial when it includes the help of peer tutors). Teachers may be enlisted to help the child better understand and cooperate with classroom rules, as well as to help the child with classwork. Most important are interventions that attempt to change the peer group's perception of the child, since a negative reputation can undermine the child's best efforts to improve his or her standing with the peer group. This effort might include activities in which the child participates collaboratively with other children toward a particular goal, or in which the child is paired one-on-one with more popular children. When thoughtfully conceived, these kinds of interventions can create a more supportive context for the growth of social competence in children with low acceptance.

While it is impossible—and probably undesirable—to try to make all children popular among their peers, the long-term problems and personal unhappiness of many rejected children cry out for adult help, both to identify their particular social deficits and to design interventions that will assist them. Although there is no formula for instant social success, often it is the rejected child's own effort—usually motivated by an awareness of his or her poor standing with other children—that is the key predictor of the child's eventual acceptance into the peer group.

It is now clear that children who are rejected repeatedly by peers over time are confronted with consistently negative expectations, behavioral initiatives, and interpretations of their behavior by their peers. This group process contributes to the stability of the rejected child's poor social reputation. An important implication of these studies is that even if rejected children change their behavior, they still face a difficult time recovering accepted positions in the peer group. [Coie & Cillessen, 1993]

This means that any effort to improve the rejected child's social skills must not only target the child; it must also focus on the peer group to change the child's reputation so that it does not lead to a self-fulfilling prophecy even as the child is trying to develop better social skills (see A Closer Look above). Another element that is critical to changing the rejected child's plight is helping the child to find at least one friend. That friendship can go a long way toward remedying feelings of loneliness, and instilling the self-confidence that is an important ingredient to becoming, eventually, a welcomed part of the peer community (Parker & Asher, 1993).

Moral Development

The development of moral attitudes, arguments, and actions is lifelong, from the toddler's grabbing a toy and insisting "Mine!" (a primitive statement about individual property rights) to the elderly adult's revising provisions of a will (a complex statement about individual property rights involving an intricate balancing of individual desires, family and community values, and perhaps even religious faith). The first significant growth in this process occurs during the school years, for three reasons.

First, the prominence of peer relationships offers children a new arena for learning about moral values in the course of free give-and-take with other children. In contrast to learning about following the rule of authority in their relations in the home or classroom, children in their peer relationships must learn about negotiating, compromising, and determining fairness (as in "It's not fair!") with others of equal power. Second, the expanded cognitive skills of middle childhood, which enable the child to think more logically, rationally, and objectively, also advance the child's grasp of moral issues. The preschooler's morality is largely self-concerned, focusing on benefitting oneself, whether the issue involves who got more of something, whose turn it is, or who "started it." In the school years, this rudimentary sense of right and wrong is supplanted by an awareness of the needs and rights of other people, and of the importance of rationally balancing the conflicting priorities in a given issue so that everyone benefits. Finally, as their awareness of the world expands beyond the bounds of their own family, neighborhood, and country, school-age children begin to think about moral concerns (like war, hunger, and ecological harm) on a worldwide scale.

The development of moral values and behavior, especially as it occurs in children, has been charted and studied extensively for several decades. While many scholars have contributed to this research, the basic framework has been most clearly described by Lawrence Kohlberg.

Kohlberg's Stages of Moral Development

Building on Piaget's theories and research, Lawrence Kohlberg (1963, 1981) studied the development of moral reasoning by presenting children, adolescents, and adults with a set of hypothetical stories that pose ethical dilemmas. The stories were carefully designed to allow Kohlberg to examine how children conceived and reasoned about dilemmas that involved, among other things, the conflict between property rights and human need, and the value of human life. The most famous of these stories involves Heinz, a poor individual whose wife is dying of cancer. A local pharmacist has recently developed the only drug that can cure the disease but is charging thousands of dollars for it, far more than Heinz can pay and ten times what the drug costs to make:

> Heinz went to everyone he knew to borrow the money, but he could only get together about half of what it cost. He told the druggist that his wife was dying and asked him to sell it cheaper or let him pay later. But the druggist said "no." The husband got desperate and broke into the man's store to steal the drug for his wife. Should the husband have done that? Why?

Examining the responses to such dilemmas, Kohlberg found three levels of moral reasoning: preconventional, conventional, and postconventional—with two stages at each level.

FIGURE 14.10 In Kohlberg's scheme, a person's moral decisions can be motivated by reasoning at several possible levels. Many of these children may be demonstrating to save the whales because they want to please their parents or be thought well of by their teachers (stage three). Few, if any, would be demonstrating because they believe that it is everyone's responsibility to protect the environment (stage five).

I. **Preconventional** *Emphasis on getting rewards and avoidance of punishments.*

Stage 1: Might makes right (punishment and obedience orientation). At this stage the most important value is obedience to authority in order to avoid punishment, while still advancing self-interest.

Stage 2: Look out for number one (instrumental and relativist orientation). Each person tries to take care of his or her own needs. The reason to be nice to other people is so they will be nice to you. In other words, you scratch my back and I'll scratch yours.

II. **Conventional** *Emphasis on social rules.*

Stage 3: "Good girl" and "nice boy." Good behavior is considered behavior that pleases other people and wins their praise. Approval is more important than any specific reward.

Stage 4: "Law and order." Right behavior means being a dutiful citizen and obeying the laws set down by society.

III. **Postconventional** *Emphasis on moral principles.*

Stage 5: Social contract. One should obey the rules of society because they exist for the benefit of all, and are established by mutual agreement. If the rules become destructive, however, or if one party doesn't live up to the agreement, the contract is no longer binding.

Stage 6: Universal ethical principles. General universal principles determine right and wrong. These values (such as "Life is sacred") are established by individual reflection, and may contradict the egocentric or legal principles of earlier reasoning.

According to Kohlberg, *how* people reason morally, rather than what specific moral conclusions they reach, determines their stage of moral development. For example, moral reasoning at stage 3 might produce opposite conclusions—either that the husband should steal the drug (because people will blame him for not saving his wife) or that he should not steal it (because he has already done everything he could legally do, and people would call him a thief if he stole). But in both cases, the underlying moral precept is the same—that one should behave in ways that have the approval

preconventional moral reasoning
Kohlberg's term for the first two stages of moral thinking, in which the individual reasons in terms of his or her own welfare.

conventional moral reasoning
Kohlberg's term for the middle two stages of moral thinking, in which the individual considers social standards and laws to be the primary moral values.

postconventional moral reasoning
Kohlberg's term for the two highest stages of moral thinking, in which the individual follows moral principles that may supersede the standards of society or the wishes of the individual.

FIGURE 14.11 A longitudinal study (Colby et al., 1983) that compared individuals' moral reasoning between ages 10 and 36 reveals an overall decrease in preconventional reasoning and an increase in conventional reasoning. Note, however, that moral reasoning at the stage-five, postconventional level was rare.

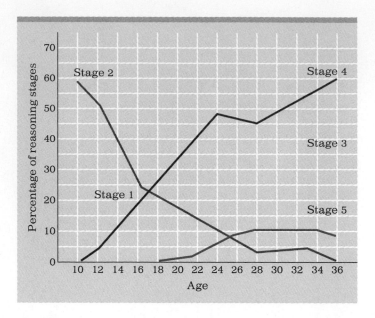

of others. In each of the other stages as well, what counts is the reasoning behind the person's response to Kohlberg's moral dilemmas.

According to Kohlberg's longitudinal research, people advance up his moral hierarchy as they become more mature, although their progress is slow. Kohlberg believed that most 10-year-olds reason morally no higher than stage 3, and that many adults never reach stages 5 and 6 (Colby et al., 1983; Kohlberg & Elfenbein, 1975). In fact, in a later reformulation of Kohlberg's scoring procedures for rating stages of moral judgment, stage 6 was dropped because only extraordinary people like Mahatma Gandhi and Martin Luther King, Jr., were found to reason consistently at this stage (Colby & Kohlberg, 1987; Colby et al., 1983).

Note, however, that Kohlberg's ratings are based on responses to hypothetical stories about adults, like Heinz, faced with extraordinary circumstances. Other research, using test cases that more closely reflect experiences children actually have, has found that children are somewhat more advanced in their moral thinking than Kohlberg had believed them to be. For example, moral reasoning about fairness and rule-making in games is often more advanced than reasoning about life-and-death dilemmas, partly because children and their friends have a personal stake in the outcome, partly because children know all the parties to the dispute, and partly because these conflicts (such as whether a new rule gives one side an unfair advantage) are resolved in group discussions that can enhance the quality of moral reasoning (Rest, 1983).

Kohlberg and His Critics

Originally, Kohlberg's ideas were the product of three sets of observations: Piaget's theory of cognitive development; various philosophers' delineations of ethical behavior; and Kohlberg's own research on a group of eighty-four boys, ages 10, 13, and 16, who provided Kohlberg with his original empirical data on the development of moral thinking. From these three elements, Kohlberg created and validated his moral dilemmas, his stages of moral thinking, and his theory of moral development.

His theory attracted a great deal of attention because many people had been searching for a way to clarify and focus their concern about moral education and growth. However, with this attention came criticism on a number of counts:

1. Kohlberg's "universal" stages seemed, generally, to reflect liberal, Western values (Miller, 1991; Reid, 1984). (In some cultures, serving the needs of kin may have a higher moral priority than observing principles that presumably apply to all of humankind.)

2. The structure of moral thinking is much less stagelike than Kohlberg implied, especially when practical rather than theoretical dilemmas are analyzed (Eisenberg, 1986).

3. Kohlberg's moral stages overemphasized rational thought and underrated religious faith (Lee, 1980; Wallwork, 1980). (Some people believe that divine revelation, rather than intellectual reasoning, provides the best standards for moral judgment.)

4. Kohlberg's original moral-dilemma scheme was validated only on males but was applied to females as well (Gilligan, 1982). (It may be that females and males are socialized to approach moral questions in different ways.)

Each of these criticisms has some validity, but, on balance, Kohlberg's scheme has withstood major attack. For example, cultural differences have been found, but not as many as critics predicted (Nisan, 1987; Snarey et al., 1985). Also, while individuals are much less rigid and stagelike in their moral reasoning than a strict interpretation of Kohlberg implies, they show a clear consistency in reasoning across various types of moral dilemmas (Denten et al., 1991; Walker, 1988). And instead of underrating religious faith, Kohlberg's ideas are often taught in religion courses, and have prompted one psychologist (Fowler, 1981) to delineate stages of faith that closely parallel Kohlberg's stages.

Gender Differences

Now let us consider one criticism in detail—that Kohlberg's stages of development are biased against females. The best-known expression of this position has come from Carol Gilligan (1982). According to Gilligan, girls and women tend to see moral dilemmas differently than boys and men do. In general, the characteristic male approach seems to be "Do not interfere with the rights of others"; the female approach, on the other hand, seems to be "Be concerned with the needs of others." Females give greater consideration to the context of moral choices, focusing on the human relationships involved. Gilligan contends that women are reluctant to judge right and wrong in absolute terms because they are socialized to be nurturant, caring, and nonjudgmental.

As evidence, Gilligan cites the responses of two bright 11-year-olds, Jake and Amy, to the dilemma of Heinz. Jake considered the dilemma "sort of like a math problem with humans," and he set up an equation that showed that life is more important than property. Amy, on the other hand, seemed to sidestep the issue, arguing that Heinz "really shouldn't steal the drug—but his wife shouldn't die either." She tried to find an alternative solution (a bank loan, perhaps) and then explained that stealing wouldn't be right because Heinz "might have to go to jail, and then his wife might get sicker again, and he couldn't get more of the drug."

While Amy's response may seem equally ethical, it would be scored lower than Jake's on Kohlberg's system. Gilligan argues that this is unfair, because what appears to be females' moral weakness—their hesitancy to take a definitive position based on abstract moral premises—is, in fact,

> inseparable from women's moral strength, an overriding concern with relationships and responsibilities. The reluctance to judge may itself be indicative of the care and concern that infuse the psychology of women's development. [Gilligan, 1982]

Of course, the difference between male and female moral thinking is not absolute, and some critics have argued that Gilligan provides a very traditional portrayal of gender differences in attitudes and beliefs (Mednick, 1989). Gilligan is aware that some women think about moral dilemmas the way men do, and vice versa. Nor does she believe that either way of reasoning is better than the other, or even in itself sufficient. If people stress human relationships too much, they may overlook the principles involved and may be unable to arrive at just decisions; if they stress abstract principles too much, they may blind themselves to the feelings and needs of the individuals affected by their decisions. The best moral thinking synthesizes both approaches (Gilligan, 1982; Murphy & Gilligan, 1980).

Gilligan maintains that Kohlberg's scoring system tends to devalue the female perspective. However, an exhaustive review of sex differences in moral reasoning (Walker, 1984) finds that there is no evidence that these differences systematically affect the scores on Kohlberg's dilemmas. Many studies in which males and females are compared find no gender differences at all. Those studies that do find differences confirm Gilligan's hypothesis to some degree: females do focus on interpersonal issues more than on moral absolutes—but the differences are not large (Gulotti et al., 1991; Walker et al., 1987).

Social Rules, Customs, and Values

While they are developing more refined skills of moral judgment, children are also becoming more aware of the **social conventions** of the larger society. They are realizing, in other words, that society is governed not only by moral values concerning honesty, obeying the law, and altruism, but also by customs concerning modes of dress, appropriate ways of eating, and suitable behavior in public places. This is shown in a series of studies by Elliot Turiel (Turiel, 1983; Turiel et al., 1991), who found that school-age children not only understand social conventions and moral values but can also distinguish between them.

For example, Turiel asked one typical 8-year-old what rules he knew. The boy cited a rule that the children in his house must clean up the mess that their guests make, and he explained that this rule could be easily changed if his parents decided to do so. He also knew another rule, that children should not steal, and he explained that this rule could *not* be changed because stealing is always wrong, whenever and wherever it occurs. He added, with an impressive sense of social justice, "People that don't have anything should be able to have something, but they shouldn't get it by stealing." In other words, this boy recognized that moral values are always obligatory, whereas social customs and conventions are subject to change.

social conventions The customs and traditions of a particular society, such as those regarding proper ways of dressing, eating, conversing, and behaving, especially in public places.

School-age children also understand that people sometimes obey customs more readily than they follow moral values. For example, Turiel (1983) found that 10-year-olds, but not 6-year-olds, were convinced that stealing an eraser is a more serious transgression than wearing pajamas to school, because stealing is wrong, while the question of appropriate clothing is simply a custom. However, the 10-year-olds also admitted that, personally, they would be more likely to commit a minor theft than to dress inappropriately!

Children's understanding of the distinctions between moral values and social conventions mirrors social reality. Many basic moral values—like those concerning the importance of human welfare, protection from harm, and justice—are widely shared across different cultures. By contrast, social conventions vary cross-culturally: standards for how people should dress, conduct themselves publicly, address their elders, and eat food depend, to a great extent, on whether the individuals in question are growing up in a Saudi Arabian city, a rural Indian community near the Pakistan border, an urban high-rise in Tokyo, a village in the People's Republic of China, or a middle-class suburban home in Kansas.

However, the distinction between moral values and social conventions is not always so clear, nor is it consistent across different cultures. In one study, school-age children from India and the United States were asked about the seriousness of various moral and conventional behaviors that could be found in either culture. Children from each culture agreed that it was wrong to break a promise, destroy another's picture, or kick harmless animals. However, consistent with their cultural and religious beliefs, children from India believed that eating beef, addressing one's father by his first name, and cutting one's hair and eating chicken after a father's death were far worse transgressions than did American children. By contrast, Indian children believed that inflicting serious corporal punishment and eating with one's hands were less serious offenses than did children in the United States (Schweder et al., 1990). In another study, Korean schoolchildren, consistent with the Confucian ethics of their culture, regarded a child's failure to greet an elder respectfully as a very serious offense—comparable to hitting or stealing (Song et al., 1987). Because of how cultural and religious values shape moral perception, what is merely conventional in one culture may have moral significance in another (Gabennesch, 1990; Schweder, 1990).

FIGURE 14.12 The setting is Israel; the group includes Jews and Muslims. In all probability, these boys are aware that their cooperative efforts are in accord with moral values that are contrary to the social customs prevailing around them.

Moral Behavior

The various findings of the research on moral development raise a crucial and very practical question. What is the relationship between moral thinking and moral behavior? A classic series of studies found that although most children can explain why honesty is right and cheating is wrong, most children cheat under certain circumstances, such as when their friends put pressure on them to do so, and when the chance of being caught is slim (Hartshorne et al., 1992). Often the conflict between human needs and the more abstract demands of justice presents children with challenging moral dilemmas in real life. In one study, for example, children were asked whether they would break a law to help their siblings or peers. The answer was, almost always, yes. In general, school-age children considered loyalty to siblings or peers, especially to a close friend, compelling reason to consider bending one's allegiance to impersonal standards of right action: many children said they would cheat, lie, or steal to help a needy friend (Smetana et al., 1991; Turiel et al., 1991). But children often experience a sense of violating their own moral standards, making them uncomfortable when doing so.

Indeed, while few children always follow their parents' moral standards, most studies have shown that moral thought can have a decided influence on action and vice versa (Eisenberg, 1986; Rest, 1983). Increasingly, as they grow older, children try to figure out what is the "right" thing to do, and feel guilty when they do "wrong." Significantly, juvenile delinquents generally score lower on tests of moral reasoning than do other adolescents their age (Nelson et al., 1990), suggesting that one reason they violate the norms of society is that they are less likely to consider those norms morally relevant. At the same time, of course, it is easier to recognize and condemn immorality and hypocrisy in others than in oneself. Many children who are quick to condemn another person's lying will exaggerate their own accomplishments and falsely accuse a sibling of wrongdoing without ever noticing the inconsistency.

We must not be too critical of such lapses, however. As young people become more aware of their social world, and better able to analyze it, they are increasingly confronted with problematic moral dilemmas, requiring some balance between their own self-interest, the codes of the peer group, the morality of their parents and teachers, the tenets of their religion, and the values of their culture. It takes substantial maturity and analytic ability to coordinate all these values—maturity and analytic ability that do not usually emerge until adolescence or later.

Family Structure and Child Development

Historically and cross-culturally, children have thrived robustly in many kinds of **family structure**, that is, in households composed of people connected to each other in various legal and biosocial ways. At mid-twentieth century, for example, a family of two biological parents living with their own two or three dependent children was both the cultural ideal and the reality for the great majority in most industrialized nations, including the United States. At the same time, the preferred family structure in most developing countries in Asia and Latin America was the large extended family, with

family structure　The legal and biological connections between members of a particular family.

grandparents and great-grandparents, and often cousins, aunts, and uncles, living within the same large household. Meanwhile in many African and Arab nations, a variety of family structures flourished, including the polygamous household, with each child growing up in the company of a dozen or more siblings and half-siblings.

Historical variations are apparent as well. In eighteenth- and nineteenth-century North America, both the extended family and the polygamous family existed, but were relatively rare. Much more common were other alternative family forms, usually necessitated by the death of young parents, especially of women in childbirth. These included single-parent and stepparent family structures, as well as households in which children were informally raised by relatives or neighbors (Uhlenberg, 1980). If for any reason parents divorced or separated, the father almost always was given custody of the children, since a woman was considered too weak to raise a family properly on her own.

As we approach the twenty-first century, of course, the traditional family form that predominated during most of America's history is becoming increasingly less common (Skolnick, 1991). If current trends continue, only a minority—about 40 percent—of children born in the United States in the 1990s will live with both biological parents from birth to age 18. Another 30 percent will begin life with married parents who will later divorce, while the remaining 30 percent will be born to an unmarried woman (Furstenberg & Cherlin, 1991). In addition, many children in the latter two groups will experience several changes in household composition—spending part of childhood living with a grandparent, or with a stepparent, or with a parent's live-in lover—and several marital transitions, from divorce to remarriage to divorce again.

Not all of the culture seems to have caught up to this reality. Common pejorative phrases such as "broken home," "fatherless household," and "illegitimate child" imply that every family structure except that headed by married biological parents (often termed the "natural" parents) is deviant and destructive of the child's well-being. However, current longitudinal research in the United States confirms the historical and international evidence: children can thrive in almost any family format. Specifics of family function or

FIGURE 14.13 For much of human history, the typical family contained three generations and several children, a pattern still followed in many cultures and by some families in the United States. An increasingly common alternative family arrangement today is one parent with one child, a family structure that can function well if the social milieu is supportive.

dysfunction, such as excessive conflict, overly authoritarian parenting, and coldness among family members, are much more crucial than specifics of family structure, such as whether the family is headed by one adult or two, and what the genetic or legal relationship among the household members might be (Demo, 1992; Hetherington, 1989; Rutter, 1982; Werner & Smith, 1982). We will now see that each structure can have particular advantages and liabilities.

Living with Both Biological Parents

According to large-scale surveys that compare various family structures, children living with both biological parents tend to fare best, having fewer physical, emotional, or learning difficulties from infancy throughout childhood than do children in other family structures. Further, at adolescence, they are less likely to abuse drugs or be arrested and more likely to graduate from high school. In adulthood, they are more likely to graduate from college and to continue to develop with self-confidence, social acceptance, and career success (Amato & Keith, 1991; Dawson, 1991; Zill, 1988; Emery, 1988).

Reasons for the Benefits

Two reasons for this seem clear. The most apparent is that two adults, both of whom have known and loved the child since birth, generally provide more complete caregiving than one. Not only can a mother and father together give an extra measure of the warmth, discipline, and attention that all children need (see Chapter 11), but they can also support each other, provide respite for each other, and try to compensate for each other's parental shortcomings and enhance each other's parental strengths (Pedersen, 1981; Zaslow et al., 1985).

Second, two-parent homes usually have a financial advantage over other forms—especially the single-parent home—enabling better health care, housing, nutrition, and education for their children. This advantage occurs, in part, because (1) most contemporary two-parent households have two wage-earners; (2) two parents are less likely than single parents to have to pay for various household and child-care services; and (3) couples who decide to marry and stay married tend to be those who already have an adequate and stable income. Thus there is a monetary advantage for matrimony, at least as far as the children involved are concerned. One indicator of this is that for two-parent homes in the United States in 1991, the median income was two to three times that for one-parent homes—$40,995 compared with $16,692 (U.S. Bureau of the Census, 1993).

Caveats

However, it is important not to conclude from such a broad overview that original two-parent homes are inevitably best, or that development is sure to falter in other family types. Many studies indicating an apparent advantage of original two-parent homes do not take sufficient account of other factors that affect child development (Demo & Acock, 1991). The most obvious one, which we have already touched on, is income: since a disproportionate number of one-parent families, for example, are also low-income families, economic stress and poverty may account for many of the difficulties these families experience.

Look, for instance, at the data correlating grade repetition and family structure (Figure 14.14). They seem to show a clear advantage for children in original two-parent families, who are only half as likely to be left back as children in other types of families. However, when the data on the same children are organized according to family income, it is apparent that economic factors interact with, and outweigh, the influence of family structure alone. If family income is below the poverty line (about $15,000 for a family of four in 1994), almost three times as many children repeat a grade as when family income is well above the poverty line (more than $45,000 for a family of four).

Other powerful factors including race, ethnic background, and religion also correlate with family structure as well as family functioning, and may underlie what at first looks like a link between family type and child outcome. For example, children of Mormons, or Mennonites, or Orthodox Jews are almost always raised in two-parent households *and* are almost never drug abusers, at least while still living at home. It would be an obvious mistake to ascribe their resistance to drugs primarily to their parents' marital status, ignoring the powerful influence of religious upbringing on abstinence (Jesser et al., 1992).

FIGURE 14.14 As you can see in the first chart, a child's likelihood of repeating a grade, whatever his or her ethnic background, is influenced by the family structure in which the child lives. However, as the second chart reveals, income is a more potent influence than either family structure or ethnicity, probably because the impact of income is more pervasive, affecting the quality of the neighborhood and the school as well as the home.

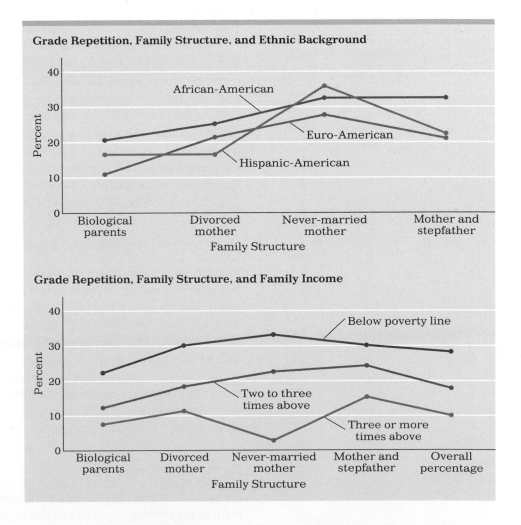

More important, in acknowledging that two parent-homes are generally best we should always bear in mind two important qualifications: (1) not every biological father or mother is a fit parent; and (2) not every marriage creates a nurturant household. As described in Chapter 9, some parents are so disturbed, addicted, or self-absorbed that they mistreat their children or undermine their partner's child-rearing efforts, causing harm that compromises the benefits usually associated with the presence of two parents in the home. Many others are adequate parents individually, but are caught in a marital relationship characterized by such frequent and open conflict that their children are at far greater risk of psychological harm than they would be in a tranquil one-parent home.

A review of cross-sectional and longitudinal research finds that, while all children are "harmed by intense conflict, whether or not their parents live together . . . children who live in intact families with persistently high levels of conflict are the most distressed of all" (Furstenberg & Cherlin, 1991). Such families are not the norm, but they are surprisingly common. Especially when the partners are under age 35 (and are likely to have young children), many couples disagree frequently, and in about one marriage in four that disagreement erupts in destructive ways. For example, when researchers asked a cross-section of Americans about their own behavior toward their mate, more than one spouse in four under age 35 admitted to engaging in nonphysical aggression—cursing, insulting, slamming doors—at least once a month, and in physical aggression—pushing, slapping, hitting—at least once a year (Gelles & Straus, 1988; Strauss & Sweet, 1992).

Most such couples fight for years before separating or getting help. In fact, most simply acclimate themselves to the tension, perhaps trying to avoid blow-ups but ultimately falling back into a pattern of mutual attack and counterattack, blaming each other and justifying themselves to the children. From the child's point of view, of course, the justification matters much less than the result—a home where blame and anger destroy the emotional safety that enables healthy growth (Cummings & Davies, 1994). Although adults may become impervious to conflict, young children do not: unless both parents find a better way to disagree, instead of staying together "for the sake of the kids," divorcing for the children's benefit may be best.

When the Two-Parent Family Breaks Down

The disruption and discord surrounding divorce almost always adversely affect the children for at least a year or two, even though many children eventually benefit from the end of an unhappy marriage. Immediately after divorce, children show signs of emotional pain, such as depression or rebellion, and symptoms of stress, such as having lower school achievement, poorer health, and fewer friends (Emery, 1988). Whether this distress is relatively mild and short-lived, or serious and long-lasting, depends primarily on three postdivorce factors: the harmony of the parents' ongoing relationship, the stability of the child's life, and the adequacy of the caregiving arrangement (Amato, 1993).

Harmony at Home

As already noted, the aspect of the parents' relationship that seems most critical for the development of children is the degree of harmony or discord between them. Unfortunately, even when the reason for divorce is to end long-standing hostility, the years immediately preceding and following the marital break-up are usually characterized by an escalation, not a cessation, of conflict. Most divorcing parents yell insults, exchange blows, destroy each other's property, or undermine each other's dignity and equanimity with greater intensity than ever before (Furstenberg & Cherlin, 1991; Peterson & Zill, 1986; Vaughn, 1987).

The more bitter and open the conflict, the more likely the children are to become depressed and angry, losing interest in schoolwork and in play, or becoming hostile with friends and teachers, as well as with both parents. Of course, this worsens the situation for everyone. Many parents find that, just when they need sympathy and cooperation, their children become more "aggressive, noncompliant, whining, nagging, dependent, and unaffectionate" than ever before. As one mother described it, she felt as though she was being bitten to death by ducks (Hetherington & Camara, 1984).

Relationships between siblings are likely to deteriorate as well, adding to the stress on parent-child relationships and removing a possible source of comfort for each child. Those exceptional children who do manage to maintain a close relationship with at least one brother or sister while their parents are at war are much more likely to escape serious emotional problems (Jenkins, 1992; MacKinnon, 1989).

Stability of Daily Life

The second critical factor determining the ease or difficulty of divorce for children is the stability of the child's life. One major source of instability is the child's being separated completely from a caregiver to whom he or she is highly attached, whether it be a parent, grandparent, or other relative. Another major source of instability is a reduction in household income, especially if it leads to a dramatic decline in the family's standard of living and/or unwelcome transitions such as a move to a less expensive neighborhood and entry into a different school. The need for more money may also dramatically reduce the time and energy the custodial parent has available for the children, because he or she must spend more time working—entering the job market for the first time, or taking full-time instead of part-time work, or seeking overtime or a second job.

Instability also commonly arises from the disorientation parents experience as they undergo the "eradication of the marital subworld," the habits and interactions that formed the structure of married life (Vaughn, 1987). Typically, a custodial mother is initially overwhelmed with the burden of having to run the household and care for the children while worrying about financial problems and coping with her own emotions and changes in self-esteem. Many women become depressed and withdrawn or, alternatively, try to find jobs, develop new skills, and expand their social lives just when their children need and demand even more attention than before. Correspondingly, mothers frequently become more strict, less playful, and more inconsistent in their disciplining (Hetherington, 1989; Spanier & Thompson, 1984; Wallerstein & Blakeslee, 1989).

Fathers also change, especially in the first year. Typically, if they are the noncustodial parent, they become more indulgent with their children. Many fathers also adopt a more "youthful" lifestyle, including dating a variety of women, often younger. Many change their appearance, adopting a new hairstyle or growing a beard, or taking on a new look in their wardrobe. All such changes, especially in combination, can greatly increase the child's sense of instability in his life or her life.

Even more stressful for children is that fathers, as noncustodial parents tend to visit their offspring less frequently and more inconsistently over time, and their children miss them (Thompson, 1994). A nationwide survey in 1989 found that only 25 percent saw their fathers at least once a week, while 33 percent saw their fathers no more than once a year (Seltzer, 1991). As low as this visitation rate is, it represents an improvement over the rate of a decade ago, when only 16 percent of children of divorce visited their fathers once a week, and almost half had not seen their fathers at all the previous year (Furstenberg & Nord, 1985).

Stability for Younger and Older Children

While the instability of divorce affects children at every age, the immediate disruptions of family life are generally harder on younger children, whose world is almost completely confined to the family attachments that they see disappearing in front of their eyes, and who have little understanding of why that world is changing so dramatically. The sense of dislocation may be particularly intense for children who must undergo new caregiving arrangements, entering day care for the first time because the custodial mother must work or switching from half-day, high-quality nursery school to less expensive, all-day family day care because of the financial pinch caused by the divorce. Children who themselves are in transition, such as when they are beginning kindergarten, also find divorce particularly hard (Allison & Furstenberg, 1989; Hetherington, 1989; Wallerstein & Blakeslee, 1989).

As children grow older, they are better able to absorb the immediate impact of divorce, because usually they have some understanding of what is happening and why. They also have areas of interest and emotional investment that lie outside the family, and they often have friends who can offer support because their own parents have divorced. Nevertheless, they too can be hard hit, especially when divorce coincides with, or requires, changes in the mainstays of middle childhood—neighborhood and school. In such circumstances, not only must children adjust to new family routines, patterns, and demands, but they must also leave old friends and enter a new society of children, something which is problematic even for children whose family is stable. In addition, as children enter their teens, the inevitable challenges of puberty, including defining one's identity and negotiating relationships with peers of the other sex, make early adolescence, overall, one of the worst times for children to experience divorce (Hetherington & Clingempeel, 1992). For older adolescents, the chief disruption of divorce is likely to be economic, as everything from clothing purchases and leisure expenditures to college plans and career aspirations are put on hold.

Custody and Caregiving

One aspect of divorce that has received a great deal of attention is how to best adjudicate custody to maintain adequate caregiving when a marriage ends (Maccoby & Mnookin, 1992). Until fairly recently, custody of children in a divorce was based almost exclusively on gender. Early in the nineteenth century, for example, custody nearly always went to the father, and for most

"Must I pick one of my parents? I'd rather live with Bill Cosby."

FIGURE 14.15 For many children, the problems of their own family life are in sharp contrast to the humor, affluence, and closeness they witness in typical "family fare" on television. Such a gap between reality and expectation may actually make coping with the difficulties brought on by their parents' divorce even harder.

of this century, it nearly always went to the mother. The current view of the judicial system, and of the general public, is that whoever was the most competent, involved parent before the divorce should continue to be the primary caregiver (Felner & Terre, 1987; Price & McHenry, 1988), a view that is supported by extensive research.

At the same time, children benefit when they can maintain ongoing contact with the noncustodial parent (Thompson, 1994). However, this is not as easy as many divorcing parents, and their offspring, expect. Simply coordinating the schedules and routines of everyone involved can be stressful and a source of conflict, and children may experience difficulty in adjusting to shuttling back and forth between homes that often have different rules, expectations, and emotional settings. These problems are compounded when the animosity of former spouses leads them—deliberately or unintentionally—to put the child in the middle of their battles.

Moreover, visits are sometimes actively opposed by a custodial parent who resents the other parent's failure to provide adequate child support or who wants to establish independence from his or her former spouse. Noncustodial parents may themselves resist visitation if they find it hard to maintain a fragmented relationship with their offspring or if they wish to start their life over with a new partner and stepchildren. These concerns, however, are usually not shared by children, who greatly miss the ongoing intimacy with two parents that they experienced in the intact (albeit troubled) predivorce family. Sadly, children often feel that in divorcing each other, their parents divorced them as well.

In general, the best situation for a child after a divorce is one in which parents can cooperate amiably on the child's behalf, and the child can continue an intimate, positive relationship with each parent. This is particularly true if the custodial parent provides both warmth and a stable structure for the child's daily life, and the noncustodial parent provides the child with ongoing support, psychological as well as financial (Amato, 1994; Amato & Rezac, in press). The worst situation for children is when postdivorce family life entails such ongoing bitterness and hostility between former spouses that the children suffer, rather than benefit, from relations with a noncustodial parent (Johnston, 1994; Johnston et al., 1989; Kline et al., 1989). In actuality, most families fall somewhere between these two extremes, and many children find that postdivorce life involves stress and demands that make them look back wistfully on their former family life, even as they recognize that they—and their parents—have benefitted from the divorce.

Single-Parent Households

The number of single-parent households has increased markedly over the past two decades in virtually every major industrialized nation except Japan (Burns, 1992) (see Figure 14.16). Although the specific reasons and consequences of this trend vary somewhat from nation to nation, worldwide this family structure tends to be blamed for all manner of developmental problems, from health problems to academic failure (Burns, 1992; National Center for Health Statistics, 1991; Roll, 1989; U.S. Department of Education, 1991). Such blanket condemnation often is linked to a grossly distorted stereotype—that of a single mother with little education, many neglected children, few conventional morals, and no ambition, spending her time collecting government checks and watching TV.

However, once we look at the data on single parenthood, we find that the reality is much more complex, both nationally and internationally (Burns, 1992; Roll, 1989). Even within the United States, it is not easy to generalize about single parenthood, partly because the reasons for it vary: divorce accounts for about 60 percent of single parents, death for about 8 percent, and out-of-wedlock birth for about 32 percent, with each of these patterns having different problems and strengths, and different consequences for children. Further, even within these categories, the functioning of families differs depending on ethnic, economic, and community patterns. For example, among Puerto Ricans living on the mainland, most "single" mothers are actually living with the father of their children, and have much more in common with married mothers than with truly single parents (Landale & Fennelly, 1992).

However, while it is not easy to generalize about single parenthood, it is easy to show that the above stereotype is false: in the United States in 1990, compared to married parents, single parents were *more* likely to be employed (e.g., 80 percent of divorced mothers compared to 68 percent of married mothers were in the labor force); their households had *fewer* children (half had only one child); and only a minority received government assistance of any kind, including welfare, unemployment, or Medicaid (Johnson et al., 1991; U.S. Bureau of the Census, 1991). No matter what nationality, ethnicity, or education a lone parent has, he or she is most likely to work hard to fill both the role of major income-producer and that of major caregiver, surrendering personal recreation, social life, and sleep to do so.

How do children actually develop in such households? All other things being equal (that is, taking into account differences in income and other factors), children frequently develop just as well living with one biological parent as with two (Adams et al., 1984). With the exception of children whose parents are recently divorced, children from single-parent families are usually on a par with other children, especially in three crucial areas: school achievement, emotional stability, and protection from serious injury. This

FIGURE 14.16 Beyond the obvious—that single-parent households are increasing worldwide—this chart also reflects a combination of two trends, liberalized divorce laws and increasing acceptance of never-married mothers. The country with the lowest rate of single parenthood, Japan, has experienced neither of these trends. The country that had the highest rate in the 1970s, Sweden, had already experienced both, and still has many adults who prefer to raise a family together without the bonds of marriage rather than to formalize their union and then risk divorce.

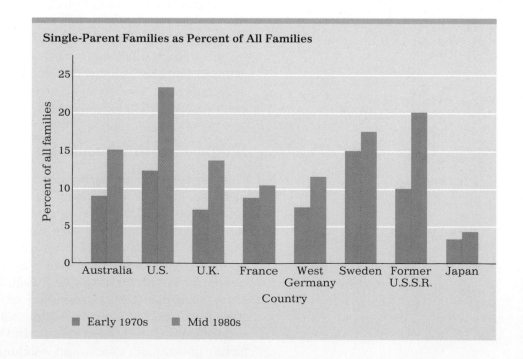

generality holds for preschoolers, school-age children, and adolescents (Dawson, 1991; Hawkins & Eggebeen, 1991; Milne et al., 1986; Smith, 1990).

If all factors are equal, then, the structure of single-parent households does not necessarily impair children's development. However, other factors are almost never equal, because single parents are vulnerable to many kinds of stress that can and do affect children. To begin with, most single parents suffer from "role overload," as they try to provide nurturance, discipline, and financial support all at the same time (Zill, 1983). Having a full-time job and a young family is not easy, no matter what one's marital status, but the single parent is particularly likely to be squeezed when a child is sick, when the job demands overtime, or when school holidays conflict with work obligations. These problems of the single parent increase markedly as family size increases: one child does not put nearly as much strain on the parent as two or more children do (Polit, 1984).

Another major problem is that the income of single-parent households is substantially lower than that of two-parent households, even when only one of those two parents is employed (McLanahan & Booth, 1991). Indeed, about a third of all American single parents are forced to rely on public assistance (at least temporarily), a solution that does not provide adequate income or self-respect. With or without government assistance, half of all American children living in single-parent households are living at or below the poverty line (U.S. Bureau of the Census, 1993).

Given these problems, how do single parents manage to cope as well as they do? Social support is often critical, as friends and relatives can relieve some of the single parent's stress by helping with child care, with overdue bills, and with low self-esteem. This may also explain another intriguing finding: regardless of ethnic group or income, children of widows and widowers generally develop as successfully as their peers with two living parents, perhaps because social support is generally much more freely given to widows than to divorcées or unwed mothers (Adams, 1984; Rutter, 1982).

Single Fathers

Most public discussion about single parents proceeds as though they are all mothers, but in the United States the number of single fathers is growing significantly (Meyer & Garasky, 1993). In 1970, there were only 341,000 single-father households; by 1980, this number had almost doubled to 616,000; and by 1992, it had reached 1,283,000—about 4 percent of all families (U.S. Bureau of the Census, 1993). Generally, children develop quite similarly in father-only homes as in mother-only homes (Thompson et al., 1992). In fact, if anything, children in father-headed homes fare better, especially if those children are boys, as they often are, since fathers are more likely to have custody of their sons than daughters.

Among the possible reasons for the father-advantage is that children sometimes respond better to a man's authority than to a woman's, and are thus likely to be less disruptive and destructive in father-headed households (Hetherington, 1989; Peterson & Zill, 1986; Santrock et al., 1982; Wallerstein & Blakeslee, 1989). In addition, since the father's having custody is still somewhat unusual, those fathers who seek and gain such arrangements are, on the whole, those who are likely to be suited for it, whereas mothers typically have custody whether they prefer it or not.

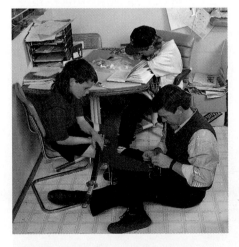

FIGURE 14.17 Can single fathers raise children well? Research finds that they can. In fact, some studies show that when the father chooses the custodial role, and when the community is supportive, and the children are aged 6 or older, offspring, particularly boys, thrive under paternal care.

Beyond the possible psychological benefits of a father-headed household, such families also have some practical advantages over mother-headed families. They are, on average, more secure financially (even though fathers are less likely to receive substantial child support from their former partners than mothers are). Fathers also get more child-care assistance from other people, particularly from women: former wives, childless women, and their own mothers tend to be more helpful to single fathers than former husbands, childless men, and their own fathers are to single mothers (Risman, 1987; Seltzer & Bianchi, 1988; Weitzman, 1985).

Blended Families

Most divorced parents remarry within a few years, and many unmarried parents eventually marry as well. When remarriage means less loneliness for the custodial parent, improved finances, less conflict with a former spouse, and more stable household organization, it eventually benefits all concerned. However, while the new partners are initially likely to be happy with the remarriage, such is almost never the case for the children, who must suddenly negotiate a new set of family relationships, not only with a stepparent but often also with stepsiblings, stepgrandparents, and so forth, most of whom they would not have chosen on their own (Coleman & Ganong, 1991).

The same factors affecting children in marriage and divorce—parental cooperation, stability, and adequacy of caregiving—affect children in step-families (Keshet, 1988; Kurdek, 1989). Even in the best of circumstances, however, harmony takes time to achieve, as the blended family must develop a new style and culture that all members can live with, each member making certain accommodations to the others. In the process, some members are more likely to benefit, especially younger boys from mother-headed families. Others are more likely to suffer, among them adolescent girls who are particularly likely to resent their new stepfathers, only-children who suddenly lose privacy to new siblings, and children who become indirect targets of the nonremarried parent's jealousy (Allison & Furstenberg, 1989; Giles-Sims & Crosbie-Burnett, 1989; Hetherington & Clingempeel, 1992; Vuchinich et al., 1991).

FIGURE 14.18 Some blended families, like this one, are fairly harmonious. Much depends on whether the parents are able to appreciate and help resolve the possible resentments between half-siblings.

While most remarriages eventually work out for the children as well as for the adults, many do not: the divorce rate is higher for second marriages than first marriages, and this is particularly true if there are young adolescent children involved. Overall, the stress of a second divorce adds disruption to the child's life as well as to the adult's, a fact that itself should caution any single parent hoping to marry primarily in order to give the children a two-parent home.

Grandparent Households

Grandparents often play an important role in parents' and children's adjustment to stresses of every kind—providing extra income, emotional support, continuity, and child care, all of which are especially needed during divorce and in single-parent homes (Thompson et al., 1992). However, when the child and a single parent move into a grandparent's household, notable stresses are likely to occur, as reflected in children's behavior. For example, one study comparing young children in various family structures found that those living with both grandparents had poorer language skills and more behavior problems, among them disobedience, dependence, and aggression, than children in any other kind of home (Hawkins & Eggebeen, 1991).

Interestingly, this effect was not seen for African-American children, who, in this study and others, appear to benefit by living with grandparents (Pearson et al., 1990; Taylor et al., 1991; Wilson, 1989). One suggested reason is that, among whites, the grandparent-headed household has traditionally been unusual, and thus is perceived as a sign of trouble or stress (Clemens & Axelson, 1985). Among nonwhites, however, extended family structures have always been more common, and more accepted, with established patterns of interaction to ease tensions when three generations share one roof. For example, traditional respect for the older generation among nonwhites may cause both the child and the parent to more readily defer to a grandparent in matters of child discipline than would their white counterparts, who may view grandparents' attempts to discipline a child as old-fashioned or intrusive.

This illustrates that the broader social context is a critical variable in the actual functioning of a family: if a particular family type is accepted and supported by ethnic, cultural, or community values, the chances are good that the adults will be able to nurture the children entrusted to them. Indeed, over the past thirty years, as social acceptance of nontraditional families in America has been increasing, the negative effects of alternative families on children have been decreasing (Amato & Keith, 1990; Demo, 1992).

Poverty in Middle Childhood

As you remember from Chapter 1, socioeconomic status affects developing persons throughout life, with low SES affecting development for the worse. The precise impact of poverty depends, of course, on many factors, among them the person's age, the specific developmental domain under consideration, and the public policies that soften or sharpen the blow (Huston et al., 1994). Each of these factors is relevant to understanding the effects of poverty during middle childhood.

The Biosocial Domain

For children of every age in every nation, poverty takes a toll on biosocial development: as SES decreases, the risk of health hazards—including malnutrition, disease, accidents, abuse, and neglect—increases (Pollitt, 1994). However, for two reasons, the specific toll of poverty on growth and health in middle childhood is blunted. First, their natural immunities, physical strengths, and growth patterns make school-age children relatively unlikely to suffer the most devastating consequences of malnutrition and disease. Second, their developing independence and reasoning ability make them better able to protect themselves against many kinds of dangers, from household fires to abusive parents. As a result, worldwide, poverty is less damaging biosocially in middle childhood than it is in infancy or early childhood.

The Cognitive Domain

As Chapter 13 detailed, school-age children depend on the particular lessons of formal education to fully develop their minds: the number of days and years a person attends school is directly reflected in the individual's tested intelligence and thinking ability, as well as in his or her proficiency at the specific tools of learning—including reading, writing, and math—that enhance further cognitive development (Ceci, 1991; Fiati, 1991). Of course, the quality of education is also crucial to the child's cognitive development. Since both the extent and the quality of education are in many ways tied to socioeconomic factors, poverty during the middle years can be particularly detrimental to intellectual growth.

FIGURE 14.19 After-school programs, such as this clown class in Oakland, California, can be instrumental in bolstering children's self-confidence and increasing their sense of connectedness with the school. This benefit may be of particular importance to economically disadvantaged children, who for a number of reasons are more prone to feeling alienated from the educational process.

In some nations, for example, an elementary school education must be paid for directly by the child's parents, including fees for tuition, uniforms, and books. As a result, poverty means little or no schooling for many children. By contrast, in other countries, a substantial portion of the national income is dedicated to providing free, quality education for all. Those nations devoting the highest proportion (about 7 percent) of their GNP to education are Canada, Sweden, Denmark, Norway, Israel, and Saudi Arabia (United Nations, 1990).

Still other countries are somewhere between these extremes, the United States, the United Kingdom, Australia, and New Zealand among them, spending about 5 percent of their GNP on education. In the United States, public schools are free, open to everyone, and are attended by 90 percent of the children between ages 6 and 16 (the other 10 percent attend private schools, mostly church-affiliated). However, the United States' method of supporting education makes poverty a particular liability. Because public school funding depends primarily on local property taxes, wide disparities in neighborhood wealth translate into per-pupil expenditures more than twice as high in rich districts as in poor ones, even within the same region of the same state (Kozol, 1991). While, in general, per-pupil expenditure is not *the* determining factor in quality of education, there comes a point at which the cumulative effects of substantially larger class size, lower salaries, less maintenance, and fewer new materials undercut teacher morale and seriously compromise student learning.

A case in point is one Chicago school, where many teachers are chronically late or absent, the building is crumbling, and

> there are no hoops on the basketball court and no swings in the playground. For 21 years . . . the school has been without a library. Library books, which have been piled and abandoned in the lunch room of the school have "sprouted mold" . . . Some years ago the school received the standard reading textbooks out of sequence: The second workbook in the reading program came to the school before the first. The principal, uncertain what to do with the wrong workbooks, was told by the school officials it was "all right to work backwards." [Kozol, 1991]

The attitudes and atmosphere in such an institution are antithetical to the ingredients for good learning reviewed in Chapter 13: dedicated teachers, age-appropriate curriculum, and structured materials that excite the children's intellectual curiosity. Not surprisingly, achievement scores in this school showed that, with each year of schooling, the children fell further behind their peers in better institutions.

The Psychosocial Domain

In middle childhood, the toll of poverty on psychosocial development, while harder to measure than biosocial or cognitive growth, may be the most devastating of all. Many children from low-income homes—especially those in dangerous neighborhoods—come to think of themselves as worthless and their futures as hopeless, and this makes them unmotivated, depressed, and angry (Garbarino et al., 1991).

One reason that poverty has such a debilitating effect during these years is that, being in the stage of concrete operational thinking, school-age children focus on the tangible and thus are highly susceptible to assessing individual and family worthiness in terms of material possessions. Unlike younger children, who do not recognize the difference between cheap and chic, or adults, who may esteem inner dignity and worth, school-age children are preoccupied with the status conveyed by consumer items, by advertised brands and "in" styles. Thus the child with tattered, ill-fitting clothes and a rusty second-hand bike becomes self-conscious, teased, and ashamed, as movingly illustrated by Shawn, a 10-year-old boy:

> Me and my brother are a little hard on shoes. This summer the only shoes we had were thongs and when church time came, the only shoes we had to wear were a pair of church shoes. The one that got them first got to wear them. The one that didn't had to wear a pair of my mom's tennis shoes or my sister's.
>
> Sometimes I pray that I won't be poor no more and sometimes I sit up at night and cry. But it didn't change anything. Crying just helps the hurt and the pain. It doesn't change anything.
>
> One day I asked my mom why the kids always tease me and she said because they don't understand but I do understand about being on welfare and being poor, and it can hurt. [Johnson et al., 1991]

One crucial factor in how psychologically debilitating poverty can be is in social comparison, a practice school-age children seem compelled to engage in, as they check each other out on everything from who got the highest grade and who has the coolest fad item to who gets the highest allowance and whose family has the hottest car. Realizing that one is at the bottom of the heap with respect to one's peers, or remembering better days—for instance, before the family income plummeted when Dad or Mom was laid off or left the family—can be emotionally destructive (Newman, 1988; Weitzman, 1985).

As children grow older, social comparison broadens to include not only one's immediate experience but also the somewhat larger community, depicted on television or observed as the child begins to travel outside the neighborhood. In the Chicago school described above, for instance, the first-graders seemed happy and quite eager to learn in their ill-equipped classrooms with unmotivated teachers; older children, however, were discouraged and bitter at the contrast between their schools and the local suburban schools they had seen, with landscaped lawns, computer laboratories, and well-prepared teachers (Kozol, 1991).

The personality attributes and coping methods nurtured by such discouraging comparisons are not constructive for later success. For example, the conviction that society does not care about them can lead some children to a general attitude of resignation and indifference and excite in others a penchant for dangerous, self-destructive actions. Overall, children who feel overlooked or cast aside by society are less likely to feel responsible for their own destiny, and to believe that their fate lies in the hands of luck or other people.

Neighborhood and Residence

Because school-age children are voyaging beyond the confines of their immediate home, developing an independent social life and devising their own adventures for the first time, the surrounding neighborhood has a powerful impact on them (Bryant, 1985). For many poor children, however, their surroundings make mastery of the normal skills of middle childhood very difficult. As Kenneth Keniston describes it, it is a

> dangerous world—an urban world of broken stair railings, of busy streets serving as playgrounds, of lead paint, rats and rat poisons, or a rural world where

families do not enjoy the minimal levels of public health . . . It is a world where even a small child learns to be ashamed of the way he or she lives. And it is frequently a world of intense social dangers, where many adults, driven by poverty and desperation, seem untrustworthy and unpredictable. Children who learn the skills for survival in that world, suppressing curiosity and cultivating a defensive guardedness toward novelty or a constant readiness to attack, may not be able to acquire the basic skills and values that are needed, for better or worse, to thrive in mainstream society. [Keniston, 1977]

The world of poverty has become even more dangerous since Keniston's analysis, as hard drugs and hand guns have flooded the inner cities. Newspapers, television, and especially the movies have given the public a sense of the dramatic danger of living in an urban environment where brutality, random violence, and drive-by killings punctuate daily life, but much less attention has been devoted to the ongoing emotional price paid by those struggling to maintain a normal life in the midst of such surroundings. Young children tend to internalize constant fear, sensing death around every corner. For older children, this premonition of mortality sometimes turns into malaise and indifference (Garbarino et al., 1992; Kotlowitz, 1991; Zinsmeister, 1990).

FIGURE 14.20 This drawing depicts 9 year-old Abdullah Abbar's memories of the summer of '91 in his Los Angeles neighborhood: flames, bullets, looting and death.

At this point in human history, poverty affects more children than adults, and because they are still developing, they are affected in more devastating ways. The percentage of children affected varies a great deal from nation to nation, from nearly 100 percent in the Indian subcontinent to less than 10 percent in northern Europe. Between those extremes is the United States, where in 1993 more than one child in five lived in a family with income below the poverty line (U.S. Bureau of the Census, 1994).

Homelessness

Between 50,000 and 100,000 American children are home-less each night, about half of them school-age (Jencks, 1994; Masten, 1992). Those literally without a roof over their heads are most often adolescent runaways or "throw-aways" whose parents have abused them or disowned them. Homeless children under age 12 usually live with their families in shelters. Although these children have, for the moment, the assurance of a bed and meals, they are troubled in many ways. As one report explains:

> By the time they arrive in a shelter, children may have ex-perienced many chronic adversities and traumatic events. More immediately, children may have gone hungry and lost friends, possessions, and the security of familiar places and people at home, at school, or in the neighbor-hood . . . Locations [of shelters] are usually undesirable, particularly with respect to children playing outside. Moreover, necessary shelter rules may strain a child and family life. For example, it is typical for no visitors to be al-lowed, and for children to be . . . accompanied at all times by a parent. [Masten, 1992]

Moreover, a shelter is a temporary solution to homeless-ness, requiring periodic upheaval as children move to al-ternate locations in the company of a parent who may be humiliated, depressed, and emotionally exhausted.

Comparing homeless children in middle childhood with their peers of equal SES finds that the homeless chil-dren have fewer friends, more fears, more fights, more chronic illnesses, more changes of school, and lower school attendance. They are also about fourteen months behind academically (Masten, 1992; Rafferty & Shinn, 1991). In terms of long-term development, the most chilling re-sult is a loss of faith in life's possibilities: compared even with other impoverished children, they have lower aspira-tions and less hope for the future or for their fellow hu-mans, expressing doubt that anyone will ever help them. Clinical depression is common, striking almost one home-less child in every three (Bassuk & Rosenberg, 1990). When such attitudes develop in a child, they may take a lifetime to reverse.

Under broader examination, homeless families are distinguished from other impoverished families by their lack of a personal support network to assist them in ob-taining food, shelter, and other necessities (Bassuk, 1989; Shinn et al., 1991). It is because of the inavailability, or un-willingness, of extended family members and friends to

Despite the anxiety evident in these children, this is a hopeful scene. The woman on the left, formerly homeless, is now living with her children in a stable, community residence and is also studying for her high school degree, with the help of a college student. With secure housing and education or job training, many homeless families can become functional again.

provide assistance that homeless families find themselves taking refuge at a city mission, a homeless shelter, or an isolated park. Most homeless families are headed by single mothers struggling to find affordable housing and provide for other family needs, often while trying to cope with the effects of having been physically or emotionally abused.

We have already seen that instability and conflict are the two most devastating home attributes for a child dur-ing middle childhood. Obviously, homeless children are overwhelmed by torrents of both. While the public may dis-agree about the root causes of, and the best solutions to, homelessness, it is apparent from a developmental per-spective that something must be done immediately for every homeless child. Every month of education that a homeless child loses, and every blow to self-esteem that he or she suffers, may take years—or perhaps a lifetime—to restore.

The growing numbers of poor children are especially troubling, since many of today's impoverished children must also cope with other problems, including learning difficulties, crowded households, and troubled parents (see Public Policy, pp. 510). Fortunately, as we will now see, even children growing up in such families sometimes find ways to survive, managing to develop normally despite their problems.

Coping with Life

As we have seen throughout these three chapters on middle childhood, the expansion of the child's social world sometimes brings with it new and disturbing problems. For example, the beginning of formal education forces any learning disabilities to the surface, making them an obvious handicap; playing with friends beyond the home may result in peer problems, such as rejection and attack that can take a serious toll; leaving the protection of the family can expose the child to social prejudices such as sexism, racism, and classism, in some cases causing shame, self-doubt, and loneliness. Such troublesome problems of middle childhood often piggyback on those chronic stresses that are detrimental at every age, such as living in an impoverished, overcrowded, or violent home, or having a parent who is emotionally disturbed, drug-addicted, or imprisoned. Because of problems such as these, many children fail at school, fight with their friends, fear the future, cry themselves to sleep. Indeed, the entire range of academic and psychiatric difficulties that school-age children sometimes display can be traced, in part, to psychosocial stresses (Anthony, 1987; Luthar & Zigler, 1991; Rutter, 1987).

Fortunately, although the potential stresses and hassles are many during middle childhood, so are the coping measures that children develop. As a result, between ages 6 and 11, the overall frequency of various psychological problems decreases while the number of evident competencies—at school, at home, and on the playground—increases (Achenbach et al., 1991). Two factors described in this chapter—the development of social cognition and an expanding social world—seem to combine to buffer school-age children against many of the stresses they encounter. According to some observers, many children seem "stress-resistant," even "invulnerable" and "invincible" (Garmezy, 1985; Murphy & Moriarty, 1976; Werner, 1992; Werner & Smith, 1992). Let us look more closely at how some children rise above problems that might seem potentially devastating.

Assessing Stress

The first important point to recognize in studying the effects of various stresses on children is that there is no simple correspondence between a given stress and a given result. Detailed longitudinal studies find that the likelihood that a given stress will produce psychological fallout depends on the number of stresses the child is experiencing concurrently and on their pervasiveness, that is, on the degree to which they affect the overall, long-term patterns of the child's daily life (Luthar & Zigler, 1991; Seifer & Sameroff, 1987).

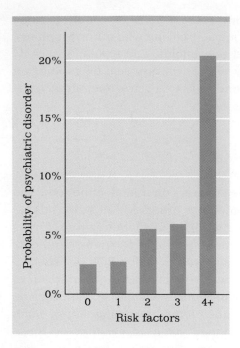

FIGURE 14.21 Rutter found that children who had to cope with one serious problem ran virtually as low a risk of suffering a psychiatric disorder as did children who faced no serious problems. However, when the child had two problems, the chances more than doubled. Four or more problems produced about ten times the likelihood of psychiatric disorders as one. About one child in five who experienced four or more serious stresses actually became emotionally disturbed.

Typical of this research is a study that found that children coping with one, and only one, serious, ongoing stress (e.g., poverty, large family size, criminal father, emotionally disturbed mother, frequent fighting between the parents) were no more likely to develop serious psychiatric problems than children with none of these liabilities. However, when there was more than one risk factor present, "the stresses potentiated each other so that the combination of chronic stresses provided very much more than a summation of the effects of the separate stresses considered singly" (Rutter, 1979). Indeed, the finding of a number of other studies is that, in general, a single chronic problem creates vulnerability in a child without causing obvious harm, but if that vulnerability is subjected to additional stresses—even mild ones that are more often termed "daily hassles" rather than "stressful events"—the child can suffer evident damage (Luthar & Zigler, 1991).

The underlying reason is that the impact of stresses depends on how they affect the moment-by-moment tranquillity of daily life. For example, living with an emotionally dysfunctional parent may mean that a child has to prematurely assume many of the responsibilities for his or her own daily care and school attendance, often in the midst of a chaotic household; and/or has to listen to an adult's confused, depressed, or irrational thinking; and/or has to supervise and discipline younger siblings. The net result is a child who never has a moment to play, to relax, to develop his or her own interests and skills.

Focus on Strengths

Particularly important to a child's ability to cope with problems is that child's competencies, especially well-developed social, academic, or creative skills. Each of these skills can help the child deflect or avoid many of the problems he or she may encounter at home or in the community.

There are several reasons why competence can more than compensate for disabling factors. One is self-esteem: if children feel confident in any area of their lives, they are better able to put the rest of their life in perspective. They believe, for example, that despite how others might reject or belittle them, they are not a worthless failure, and that despite the voices of despair within them, life is not hopeless.

More directly, children with better-developed cognitive and social skills are better able to employ various coping strategies, such as changing the conditions that brought about a problem in the first place, or restructuring their own reactions to the problem. This explains why older children may deal with the stresses of life better than children who are just beginning middle childhood. For example, when a peer is antagonistic, a 6-year-old is likely to dissolve into tears or to launch a clumsy counterattack, which merely brings further rejection. Older children, on the other hand, are more adept at finding ways to disguise their hurt, or at keeping a bully at bay, or at repairing a broken friendship, or at making new friends to replace the old ones (Compas et al., 1991).

Schools and teachers can obviously play a significant role in the development of competence. Even for children from seriously deprived backgrounds, school achievement can make it possible for them to aspire beyond the limited and constricting horizons that they may encounter in their daily lives.

Of course, much depends on the nature of the particular school the child attends. Even more important than the academic quality of the curriculum or the size of the classes is the overall emotional tone of the school. This was found in a study of twelve London schools that served low-SES children, many of whom came from crowded families that were headed by single parents or who had parents with serious psychological problems (Rutter, 1979). Some of these schools had markedly more students who passed higher-level exams, fewer students who dropped out, and lower rates of juvenile delinquency than would be expected on the basis of the students' backgrounds. One crucial factor that distinguished the more successful schools was that they cared about the children, as evidenced by such simple things as the students' work being displayed on the walls and the frequent expressions of praise from the teachers. Another factor was that the administration of these schools had high expectations of their teachers, who, in turn, had high expectations of their students. Apparently, in environments that expect and encourage competence, children tend to meet the challenge, overcoming home and community handicaps to do so.

Social Support

Another important element that helps children deal with problems is the social support they receive. The companionship and comfort provided by a grandparent, a sibling, or even a family pet can relieve some tension in a child's life (Furman & Buhrmester, 1992; Werner & Smith, 1992). In addition, one of the benefits of the expanding social world of middle childhood is that the child can venture forth to seek out many more potential sources of social support. For example, a child whose parents are fighting bitterly on their way to divorce may spend hours on the phone with a friend whose parents have successfully separated, or may frequently drop in for dinner at a neighbor's house where family harmony still prevails, or may devote himself or herself to helping a teacher, a coach, or a church group (Bryant, 1985; Hetherington & Clingempeel, 1992; Rutter, 1987).

An additional source of support for many children is religious faith and practice. Especially for children in difficult circumstances—such as the im-

FIGURE 14.22 Although the potential problems that beset children today are legion, including some their parents never knew, the best safeguard is an old-fashioned one—a supportive hand and an attentive ear from a caring adult.

poverished child in a single-parent family in a dangerous neighborhood—religious faith itself can be psychologically protective. School-age children, almost universally, develop their own theology—influenced by whatever formal religious education they might receive but by no means identical to it—that helps them structure life and deal with worldly problems (Coles, 1990; Hyde, 1990). Their view of a god figure is generally very personal, enabling troubled children to believe that they are being watched over and protected. One example is an 8-year-old African-American girl who, in the 1960s, was one of the first to enter a previously all-white school. She remembers walking past a gauntlet of adults yelling insults:

> I was all alone, and those people were screaming, and suddenly I saw God smiling, and I smiled. A woman was standing there, and she shouted at me "Hey you little nigger, what are you smiling at? I looked right up at her face, and I said 'At God.'" Then she looked up at the sky, and then she looked at me, and she didn't call me any more names. [quoted in Coles, 1990]

In a way, this example illustrates many aspects of children's coping abilities, for it was not only faith but also a measure of self-confidence, social understanding, and skill at deflecting her own emotional reactions that enabled this child to overcome a very real threat.

While adults may wish that all children could have an idyllic childhood, such is almost never the case. Nor is it necessary for healthy development: research on coping in middle childhood clearly suggests that, as they grow older, most children develop ways to deal with all sorts of stress, from the major traumatic events to minor hassles.

However, some children are at risk of developing serious psychological disturbances if they are faced with multiple problems that affect their daily routines. To help these children the best strategy may be not only to reduce their stress but also to increase their competencies and strengthen the social supports surrounding them. If the home situation is problematic, for instance, having access to anyone from a caring teacher to a best friend to a loving grandparent can make a critical difference. Or if a child has a severe reading difficulty, developing the child's talents in other areas, such as math and music, may be as important for the child's overall well-being as specific tutoring to overcome the dyslexia. Taking a wider view, measures to change the broader social context, such as making violent neighborhoods safer, or improving job opportunities in impoverished communities, or ensuring respect for families of every structure and culture, may benefit school-age children substantially, if indirectly.

We would like to bring our study of child development to a close with this thought. At the heart of all children's development is their way of perceiving themselves and the world at large, an individual view that shapes their daily interpretations, choices, and reactions to events. In a sense, the resiliency of some children, and the vulnerability of others, depends on whether they see themselves and the world in ways that inspire self-confidence, hopefulness, and trust in the future, or despair and self-denigration. We therefore hope that as you touch the lives of the young—as a parent, an educator, a practitioner, a caregiver, or a concerned citizen—you will keep this thought in mind, for in ensuring that children achieve what Erikson called "basic trust" through the love and support of others, you help to ensure that children learn to trust themselves and the world around them, and thereby help to ensure their future.

SUMMARY

An Expanding Social World

1. School-age children develop a multifaceted view of others, becoming increasingly aware of the complex personalities, motives, and emotions that underlie others' behavior. At the same time, they become better able to adjust their own behavior to interact appropriately with others.

2. Children also develop more sophisticated conceptions of themselves and their own behavior. As they become more knowledgeable about their personalities, emotions, abilities, and shortcomings, they evaluate themselves by comparing themselves with others, and this contributes to greater self-criticism and diminished self-esteem.

The Peer Group

3. Peer relationships provide opportunities for social growth because peers are on an equal footing with each other and must learn to adjust to each other accordingly. During the school years, children create their own subculture, with language, values, and codes of behavior that regulate aggression, prosocial behavior, and other activities.

4. Social problem-solving skills reflect the older child's enhanced ability to think through alternative solutions to social conflict and evaluate their potential results. Deficiencies in social problem-solving skills are observed in children who have problems in their relationships with peers.

5. Friendships become more selective and exclusive as children grow older. However, children may lack acceptance among their peers for various reasons, and this can have long-term consequences for psychosocial growth.

Moral Development

6. Moral reasoning becomes more complex during childhood and adolescence. Kohlberg proposed that this development occurs through six stages of increasing complexity, from the elemental "might makes right" to the recognition of universal ethical principles. Despite some criticisms leveled against it, Kohlberg's theory seems to be generally valid, and although males and females may analyze moral problems somewhat differently, neither sex is generally more competent at resolving moral dilemmas.

7. Children also better grasp the social conventions of the larger society, which, by contrast with moral values, vary and can be easily changed. However, various cultures may differ in the practices that are considered to be moral or merely conventional.

Family Structure and Child Development

8. Family functioning is far more crucial to children's well-being than family structure is. Whether a child lives in a two-parent, one-parent, or blended family is less important than whether the child's home situation is relatively stable, conflict-free, and supportive.

9. While family functioning is key, nonetheless certain family structures—especially single-parent, low-income homes and family arrangements that change unpredictably from year to year—tend to be more stressful for children. Transitions between different family structures can be difficult, especially when the detrimental effects are compounded by the stresses of parental conflict and low income. Support from extended kin, friends, and the community, on the other hand, can help ease the difficulty of such transitions.

Poverty in Middle Childhood

10. During middle childhood, poverty can be especially detrimental to cognitive and psychosocial development. One reason is that poverty is associated with family stress poor education and neighborhood danger that put children at risk. Another reason is that school-age children increasingly compare themselves with others, particularly in terms of visible signs of status, and this leads many children to feel ashamed and hopeless.

Coping with Life

11. Almost every child has some difficulties at home, at school, or in the community during middle childhood. Most children cope quite well, as long as the problems are limited in duration and degree.

12. How well particular children cope with the problems in their lives depends on the number and nature of the stresses they experience, the strengths of their various competencies, and the social support they receive.

KEY QUESTIONS

1. How does the child's understanding of other people change during the school years? What difference does this change make for how the child interacts with others?

2. How does a child's self-understanding change from the preschool years through middle childhood?

3. What factors typically cause children to become more self-critical during middle childhood?

4. Why are peer relationships important during the school years? Describe some of the characteristics of the society of children during middle childhood.

5. What are the steps of social problem solving? How are the skills of social problem solving different for children who are competent in their peer relationships, compared with those who have problems with peers?

6. What are some of the factors that may cause a child to lack acceptance among his or her peers? What can be done to provide assistance to such children?

7. What are the stages of moral development proposed by Kohlberg, and how do they differ in terms of the reasoning that typifies them?

8. What are some of the criticisms of Kohlberg's theory? Are they valid?

9. How do moral values differ from social conventions? How do children learn to tell the difference?

10. What are the advantages and possible disadvantages of a two-parent home?

11. What are some of the problems that are experienced in single-parent, blended, or grandparent households? What factors predict whether these families will be stressful, or beneficial, to a child?

12. How does socioeconomic status effect development in middle childhood?

13. What factors can help children cope more effectively with stress?

Biosocial Development

Growth

During middle childhood, children grow more slowly than they did during infancy and toddlerhood or than they will during adolescence. Increased strength and heart and lung capacity give children the endurance to improve their performance in skills such as swimming and running.

Skills

Slower growth contributes to children's increasing bodily control, and children enjoy exercising their developing skills of coordination and balance. Which specific skills they master depends largely on culture, gender, and inherited ability. Children with special needs typically require intensive education, but in many ways are similar to other children and benefit from interaction with them.

Cognitive Development

Thinking

During middle childhood, children become better able to understand and learn, in part because of growth in their processing capacity, knowledge base, and memory capacity. At the same time, metacognition techniques enable children to organize their learning. Beginning at about age 7 or 8, children also develop the ability to understand logical principles, including the concepts of identity, reciprocity, and reversibility.

Language

Children's increasing ability to understand the structures and possibilities of language enables them to extend the range of their cognitive powers and to become more analytical in their use of vocabulary. Most children develop proficiency in several language codes, and some become bilingual.

Education

Formal schooling begins worldwide, with the specifics of the curriculum depending on economic and societal factors. A child's actual learning also depends on the time allotted to each task and the attitudes of, and specific guided instruction from, teachers and parents.

Psychosocial Development

Emotions and Personality Development

The peer group becomes increasingly important to children as they become less dependent on their parents and more dependent on friends for help, loyalty, and sharing of mutual interests. A child's specific personality patterns can make peer acceptance or rejection an important aspect of life. Children are also increasingly aware of, and involved in, family life, as well as in the world outside the home, and therefore are more likely to feel the effects of family, economic, and political conditions. Moral judgments become sharper, with loyalty to friends often determining specific moral actions. Whether or not middle childhood will be stressful for a particular child will depend, in part, on the child's temperament, competence, and the social support provided by home and school. Economic factors, especially low SES, also become more influential.

Glossary

abuse All actions that are deliberately harmful to an individual's well-being. (308)

accommodation The process of shifting or enlarging current ideas, or schemes, in order to encompass new information. (61)

achievement tests Tests designed to measure how much a person has learned in a specific subject area. (462)

acquired immune deficiency syndrome (AIDS) The final, terminal stage of HIV degradation of the immune system, which typically appears as serious infections, specific cancers, and the like. (124)

activity level A measure of how much and how often a person moves his or her body. (301)

adaptation Cognitive processes that lead to adjustment of new and existing ideas and experiences. Adaptation takes two forms, assimilation and accommodation. (61)

additive pattern A common pattern of genetic inheritance in which each gene affecting a specific trait makes an active contribution to the final outcome. Skin color and height are additive. (83)

affordances The various opportunities for interaction that an object offers. These opportunities are perceived differently by each person depending on his or her past experiences and present needs. (213)

age of viability The age (usually between twenty and twenty-six weeks after conception) at which a fetus can possibly survive outside the mother's uterus if specialized medical care is available. (117)

alphafetoprotein (AFP) assay A blood test that reveals if a pregnant woman might have a fetus who has Down syndrome or defects in the central nervous system. (100)

amniocentesis A test that takes cells from amniotic fluid to be examined for chromosomal abnormalities. (100)

anal stage Freud's second stage of psychosexual development, in which the anus becomes the main source of bodily pleasure, and defecation and toilet training are therefore important activities. (44, 263)

androgyny Having the personality traits traditionally ascribed to both males and females. (404)

anoxia A temporary lack of fetal oxygen during the birth process; if prolonged, it can cause brain damage or even death. (148)

Apgar A test devised by Dr. Virginia Apgar to quickly assess the newborn's color, heart rate, reflex irritability, muscle tone, and respiratory effort. This simple method is used 1 minute and 5 minutes after birth to determine whether a newborn needs immediate medical care. (143)

aptitude tests Tests designed to measure potential, rather than actual, accomplishment. (463)

artificial insemination Alternative method to normal conception in which sperm is inserted with a syringe into a woman's vagina, either on or near the cervix. (112)

assimilation The process of including new information into already existing schemes. (61)

attachment The emotional connection between a person and other people, animals, or objects that produces a desire for consistent contact as well as feelings of distress during separation. (277)

attention-deficit hyperactivity disorder (ADHD) A behavior problem characterized by excessive activity, an inability to concentrate, and impulsive, sometimes aggressive, behavior. (429)

authoritarian parenting A style of child-rearing in which standards for proper behavior are high, misconduct is strictly punished, and parent-child communication is low. (378)

authoritative parenting A style of child-rearing in which the parents set limits and provide guidance and are willing to listen to the child's ideas and make compromises. (378)

autism A disorder that is chiefly characterized by an inability or unwillingness to communicate with others. (421)

automatization The process by which familiar and well-rehearsed mental activities become routine and automatic. (442)

autonomy versus shame and doubt Erikson's second stage of psychosocial development, in which the toddler struggles between the drive for self-control and feelings of shame and doubt about oneself and one's abilities. (265)

babbling Extended repetition of certain syllables, such as "ba, ba, ba," that begins at about 6 or 7 months of age. (239)

baby talk A term for the special form of language typically used by adults to speak with infants. Adults' baby talk is high-pitched, with many low-to-high intonations, is simple in vocabulary, and employs many questions and repetitions. (243)

behavioral teratogens Teratogens that tend to damage neural networks in the prenatal brain, affecting the future child's intellectual and emotional functioning. (121)

behaviorism A theory that emphasizes the systematic study of observable behavior, especially how it is conditioned. (49)

binocular vision The ability to use both eyes together to focus on a single object. (196)

biosocial domain Includes physical growth and development as well as the family, community, and cultural factors that affect that growth and development. (3)

blind Refers to researchers who are deliberately kept ignorant of the purpose of the research, or of relevant traits of the research subjects, in order to avoid biasing their data collection. (26)

Brazelton Neonatal Behavioral Assessment Scale (NBAS) A rating of twenty-six items of a newborn's behavior, such as responsiveness, strength of reflexes, and irritability. The NBAS is usually administered only when there is concern over the neonate's well-being, but the behaviors it elicits in healthy newborns reveals a surprising (to parents) repertoire of abilities. (160)

breathing reflex A reflex that ensures an adequate supply of oxygen and the discharge of carbon dioxide by causing the individual to inhale and exhale. (188)

breech position A birth in which the newborn emerges from the uterus buttocks-first instead of headfirst. About 3 percent of all births occur in the breech position. (154)

carrier An individual who has a recessive gene on his or her genotype that is not expressed on his or her phenotype. Carriers can pass the gene on to their children, who *will* express the gene if they receive a similar recessive gene from the other parent. (84)

case study A research method that focuses on the life history, attitudes, behavior, and emotions of a single individual. (32)

cephalo-caudal development The sequence of body growth and maturation that proceeds from head to foot. Human growth, from the embryonic period throughout early childhood, follows this pattern. (115)

Cesarean section A surgical procedure in which an obstetrician cuts open the abdomen and uterus to deliver the baby. This technique is used when the fetus or mother is in immediate danger or when the fetus is unable to travel safely through the birth canal. (156)

child maltreatment Includes all intentional harm to, or avoidable endangerment of, someone under age 18. (308)

childhood sexuality The Freudian idea that infants and children experience sexual fantasies and erotic pleasures. (44)

chromosome Molecules of DNA that carry the genes transmitted from parents to children. (79)

circular reaction Piaget's term for an action that an infant repeats because it triggers a pleasing response. (233)

classical conditioning The learning process in which a mean-ingful stimulus is linked to a neutral one, so that the latter elicits a response similar to that previously elicited by the former. (50)

code-switching A pragmatic communication skill that involves a person's switching from one form of language, such as dialect or slang, to another, such as formal or polite speech. (451)

cognitive domain Includes all the mental processes through which the individual thinks, learns, and communicates. (3)

cognitive theory The theory that the way people think and understand shapes their behavior and personality. (57)

cohort A group of people who, because they were born within a few years of each other, experience many of the same historical and social conditions. (9)

concrete operational thought In Piaget's theory, the third period of cognitive development, in which a child can reason logically about concrete events and problems but cannot reason about abstract ideas and possibilities. (58, 445)

conditioning The process of learning, either through the association of two stimuli or through reinforcement or punishment. (50)

conservation of liquids The concept that a given amount of liquid remains constant regardless of the shape of its container. (61)

continuity Refers to development that is gradual, steady, and predictable over time. (20)

control group Research subjects who are comparable to the experimental group in every relevant dimension except that they do not experience the special experimental conditions. (27)

control processes That part of the information-processing system that regulates the analysis and flow of information, including memory and retrieval strategies, selective attention, and rules or strategies for problem solving. (63)

conventional moral reasoning Kohlberg's term for the middle two stages of moral thinking, in which the individual considers social standards and laws to be the primary moral values. (489)

corpus callosum A network of nerves connecting the left and right hemispheres of the brain. (299)

correlation A statistical term that indicates a corresponding relation between two variables (when both variables either increase or decrease together, the correlation is positive; when one variable increases as the other decreases, the correlation is negative). (28)

crisis In Erikson's psychosocial theory, the central conflict of each developmental stage. (46)

critical period The period of prenatal development during which a particular organ or body part is most susceptible to teratogenic damage. In many cases the critical period occurs in the first eight weeks of development, when the basic organs and body structures are forming. (120)

cross-modal perception The ability to use information from one sensory modality to imagine something in another. (218)

cross-sectional research In the study of development, research that compares groups of people who are different in age but who are similar in other important ways. (33)

culture The set of shared values, attitudes, customs, and physical objects that are maintained by people in a specific setting as part of a design for living one's daily life. (10)

democratic-indulgent parenting A style of parenting that is warm, responsive, and permissive. (379)

dendrites Communication networks among the neurons in the brain (as well as those in the rest of the body). (184)

depth perception The ability to perceive where objects exist relative to each other in a three-dimensional world. (217)

dethronement Adjustment of an only-child to the arrival of a new sibling (the former little autocrat of the household having to suddenly relinquish his or her power). (167)

developmental psychopathology A field of psychology that applies the insights from studies of normal development to the study and treatment of childhood disorders. (420)

developmental theory A systematic set of hypotheses and principles that attempts to explain development and provide a framework for future research. (41)

differentiation The developmental process by which a relatively unspecified cell or tissue undergoes a progressive change to a more specialized cell or tissue. (111)

discontinuity Refers to development that is characterized by relatively abrupt, sudden, or surprising changes, often occurring in stages. (20)

disequilibrium Cognitive uncertainty and imbalance that arises when new information does not fit into existing schemes. (59)

dizygotic twins Twins formed when two separate ova are fertilized by separate sperm at roughly the same time. Such twins share about half of their genes, just like any other siblings. (82)

DNA (deoxyribonucleic acid) Molecules containing genetic information. (79)

dominant-recessive pattern A pattern of genetic inheritance in which one member of a gene pair (referred to as dominant) acts in a controlling manner, hiding the influence of the other (recessive) gene. (83)

dynamic perception Perception primed to focus on movement and change. (216)

dyscalcula A specific learning disability involving unusual difficulty in arithmetic. (426)

dyslexia A specific learning disability involving unusual difficulty in reading. (426)

eclectic perspective A view that, instead of adhering to a single perspective, incorporates what seems to be the best, or most useful, elements from various theories. (71)

ecological approach A perspective on development that takes into account the various physical and social settings in which development occurs. (4)

ectoderm The outer layer of the embryonic disk, which becomes the outer skin, the nails, part of the teeth, the lens of the eye, and the central nervous system. (114)

ego The part of the personality that attempts to deal, rationally and consciously, with reality. (45)

elaborated code A form of language characterized by extensive and explicit vocabulary, complex syntax, and lengthy sentences. (451)

Electra complex In the phallic stage of psychosexual development, the female version of the Oedipus complex in which girls have sexual feelings for their father and accompanying hostility toward their mother. (400)

electroencephalogram (EEG) A graphic recording of the waves of electrical activity that sweep across the brain's surface. These waves are measured by placing electrodes on the scalp. (185)

embryonic disk A flat inner structure of cells that, during the third week after conception, forms into three embryonic layers (the ectoderm, mesoderm, and endoderm). (114)

endoderm The inner layer of the embryonic disk, which becomes key elements of the digestive and respiratory systems. (115)

endometriosis A condition in which fragments of the uterine lining become implanted and grow on the surface of the ovaries or the Fallopian tubes, often causing fertility problems. (112)

environment All the nongenetic factors that can affect the individual's development—everything from the impact of the immediate cell environment on the genes themselves to the effects of nutrition, medical care, socioeconomic status, family dynamics, and the broader economic, political, and cultural contexts. (85)

episiotomy A small surgical incision that is made in the skin surrounding the vagina to allow the fetal head to emerge without tearing the vaginal opening. (156)

equilibrium Cognitive balance achieved through the assimilation and accommodation of conflicting experiences and perceptions. (59)

ethnic group A collection of people who share certain background characteristics, such as national origin, religion, upbringing, and language, and who, as a result, tend to have similar beliefs, values, and cultural experiences. (11)

ethology The scientific study of animal behavior in the natural environment, including its evolutionary origins and impact on survival. Ethological studies often shed light on human behavior. (250)

experiment A research method in which the scientist deliberately changes one variable and then observes the results in some other variable. (30)

experimental group Research subjects who experience special conditions or treatments that the control group does not experience. (27)

extrinsic reinforcer A reinforcer that comes from the environment, such as a word of praise (positive reinforcer) or the cessation of a disturbing noise (negative reinforcer). (52)

family structure The legal and biological connections between members of a particular family. (494)

fast mapping A way to grasp the essential meaning of new words by quickly connecting them to words and categories that are already understood. (355)

fetal alcohol syndrome (FAS) A cluster of birth defects, including abnormal facial characteristics, slow physical growth, and retarded mental development, that is caused by the mother's drinking excessive quantities of alcohol when pregnant. (126)

fetal monitor An electronic instrument that charts fetal heart rate, frequency of contractions, and other information. (154)

fine motor skills Physical skills involving small body movements, especially with the hands and fingers, such as picking up a coin and drawing. (191)

first stage of labor In the birth process, the period extending from the first regular uterine contraction to the full dilatation of the cervix to allow passage of the fetus's head through the vaginal canal. The first stage of labor usually lasts between eight and twelve hours in first births and between four and seven hours in subsequent births. (142)

folic acid A nutrient, found in dark-green leafy vegetables as well as certain fruits, grains, and organ meats, that helps protect against neural tube defects. (135)

forceps A large, spoonlike medical instrument sometimes used to facilitate or hasten birth. The forceps hold the fetal head and allow the fetus to be pulled through the birth canal. (156)

formal operational thought Piaget's term for the fourth period of cognitive development, characterized by hypothetical, logical, and abstract thought. (59)

foster care A legally sanctioned, publicly supported arrangement in which children are removed from their original parents and temporarily given to another caregiver. (321)

fragile-X syndrome A genetically based chromosomal abnormality in the twenty-third pair (sex chromosomes) that causes mental deficiency in about 30 percent of the women who carry it and in an even larger percentage of the men who carry it. (95)

gamete A reproductive cell, that is, a cell that can reproduce a new human being if it combines with a gamete from the other sex. Female gametes are called ova, or eggs; male gametes are called spermatozoa, or sperm. (78)

gender constancy The realization in children at age 4 or 5 that they are permanently male or female. (403)

gender differences Differences between males and females that arise from the special customs, values, and expectations that a particular culture attaches to one sex or the other. (399)

gender schemas The ways children organize their knowledge about people in terms of gender-based categories and evaluations. (403)

gene A basic unit of heredity. Genes, which number about 100,000 in humans, direct the growth and development of every living creature. (79)

genetic code The sequence of chemical bases in DNA and RNA that carries genetic information; referred to as a code because it determines the amino acid sequence in the enzymes and other protein molecules synthesized by the organism. (79)

genetic counseling Consultation and testing that enables couples to learn about their genetic heritage and to make decisions about childbearing. (97)

genital stage The final stage of psychosexual development, beginning at adolescence and continuing throughout adulthood, in which the primary source of sexual pleasure is in the genitals. (45)

genotype A person's entire genetic inheritance, including those characteristics carried by the recessive genes but not expressed in the phenotype. (82)

germinal period The first two weeks of development after conception, characterized by rapid cell division and the beginning of cell differentiation. (110)

goal-directed behavior Purposeful actions initiated by infants in anticipation of events that will fulfill their needs and wishes. (235)

goodness of fit The quality of the "match" between the child's temperament and the demands of the surrounding environment. (270)

gross motor skills Physical skills involving large body movements such as waving the arms, walking, and jumping. (189)

guided participation A learning process in which the child learns through social interaction with a "tutor" (a parent, a teacher, a more skilled peer), who offers assistance with difficult tasks, models problem-solving approaches, and provides explicit instruction when needed. (352)

habituation The process of becoming so familiar with a particular stimulus that it no longer elicits the physiological responses it did when it was originally experienced. (195)

holophrase A single word that expresses a complete thought. (241)

HOME A method that evaluates how well the home environment of a child fosters development. HOME looks at maternal responsiveness and involvement with the child, the child's freedom of movement, the play environment, the play materials, and the variety of activities in the child's day. (285)

Human Genome Project A worldwide effort to construct and decipher a chromosomal map of all 3 billion codes of the 100,000 human genes. (104)

human immunodeficiency virus (HIV) A viral disease agent that gradually overwhelms the body's immune responses, leaving the individual defenseless against a host of pathologies that eventually manifest themselves as AIDS. HIV is carried in the blood and certain other bodily fluids of an infected person and is transmitted chiefly through sexual or direct blood contact. (124)

id The part of the personality that contains unconscious sexual and aggressive impulses striving for immediate gratification. (45)

identification A defense mechanism that makes a person take on the role and attitudes of someone more powerful than himself or herself. (400)

identity In Piaget's theory, the logical principle that a given substance remains the same no matter what changes occur in its shape or appearance. (445)

immersion An approach to learning a second language in which the learner is placed in an environment where only the second language is spoken. (456)

implantation Beginning about a week after conception, the burrowing of the developing organism into the lining of the uterus, where it can be nourished and protected during growth. (111)

in vitro fertilization Alternative method to normal conception in which ova are removed from a woman and fertilized with sperm in a laboratory dish. After the resulting zygotes have begun normal cell division, they are inserted into a woman's uterus for implantation or are frozen for later use. (113)

industry versus inferiority The fourth of Erikson's eight crises of psychosocial development, in which school-age children attempt to master skills and develop a sense of themselves as either industrious and competent or incompetent and inferior. (473)

infertility Defined by medical doctors as failure to conceive a child after one year of trying. (112)

information-processing theory A theory of learning that focuses on the steps of thinking—such as sorting, categorizing, storing, and retrieving—that are similar to the functions of a computer. (61)

initiative versus guilt The third of Erikson's eight "crises" of psychosocial development, in which the preschool child eagerly begins new projects and activities—and feels guilt when efforts result in failure or criticism. (374)

injury control The implementation of educational and legal measures to reduce the risk and impact of childhood injuries. (305)

insecure attachment A troubled parent-child connection signaled by the child's overdependence on, or lack of interest in, the parent. Insecurely attached children are not readily comforted by the parent and are less likely to explore their environment than are children who are securely attached. (277)

intergenerational transmission The phenomenon of mistreated children growing up to become abusive or neglectful parents themselves, a phenomenon that is less common than is generally supposed. (318)

intermodal perception The ability to associate information from one sensory modality (like vision) with information from another (like hearing). (217)

interview A research method in which people are asked specific questions to discover their opinions or experiences. (31)

intrinsic reinforcer A reinforcer that comes from within the individual, such as a feeling of pride (positive reinforcer)

or the reduction of hunger pangs (negative reinforcer). (52)

IQ tests Aptitude tests designed to measure a person's intelligence, defined as mental age divided by chronological age (hence, Intelligence Quotient). (463)

knowledge base The part of memory that stores information over a long time, from minutes to decades. (Also called *long-term memory*.) (62)

kwashiorkor A disease resulting from protein-calorie deficiency in children. The symptoms include thinning hair, paleness, and bloating of the stomach, face, and legs. (204)

Lamaze method A childbirth technique involving breathing and relaxation exercises that reduce the pain of labor and allow the mother to help control the birth process. (162)

language acquisition device (LAD) Chomsky's term for the innate ability to acquire language, including an innate knowledge of basic aspects of grammar and an innate predisposition to attend to and remember the critical, unique aspects of the language. (243)

latency Freud's term for the period between the phallic stage and the genital stage of psychosexual development. During latency, which lasts from about age 7 to age 11, children's psychosexual drives and unconscious emotional conflicts are relatively quiet, and children direct their attention and energies to the outside social world. (45, 473)

launching event A habituation technique used to determine if a young infant understands the connection between causes and effects. (229)

learned helplessness A fatalistic perception, based on past failures, that one can do nothing to improve one's performance or situation. (477)

learning disability A particular difficulty in mastering one or more basic academic skills, without apparent deficit in intelligence or impairment of sensory functions. (425)

learning theory A theory that emphasizes the sequences and processes of conditioning that underlie most of human and animal behavior. (49)

longitudinal research In the study of development, research that follows the same people over time in order to measure both change and stability with age. (35)

low birthweight Birthweight of less than 2,500 grams (5½ pounds). (144) (See also *preterm infant* and *small for gestational age*.)

marasmus A disease that afflicts young infants suffering from severe malnutrition. Growth stops, the skin wrinkles, body tissues waste away, and death may eventually occur. (204)

markers In genetic testing, particular physiological characteristics or gene clusters that suggest that an individual is a carrier of a harmful gene. (100)

mastery orientation An approach to schoolwork that is based on the belief that intellectual growth occurs through persistence and hard work. Students with this orientation accept challenging tasks and try harder when their initial efforts do not succeed. (465)

mastery play Any form of play that leads to a mastering of new skills, including motor skills as well as intellectual and language abilities. (393)

mental combinations The mental playing out of a course of action before actually enacting it. (236)

mental retardation A pervasive delay in cognitive development. (425)

mesoderm The middle layer of the embryonic disk, which becomes muscles, bones, and the circulatory, excretory, and reproductive systems. (115)

metacognition Thinking about thinking, including the ability to evaluate a cognitive task to determine how best to accomplish it and how to monitor one's performance. (443)

mnemonics Memory aids, such as specific rhymes or mental associations, that facilitate the storage and retrieval of information. (441)

modeling The process in which one person learns from the example of another. (53)

monozygotic twins Twins who have identical genes because they were formed from one zygote that split into two identical organisms very early in development. (82)

multifactorial traits Characteristics produced by the interaction of several genetic and environmental influences. (82)

myelin A fatty insulating substance that coats the neurons, facilitating quicker, more efficient transmission of neural impulses. (184)

nature All the genetic influences on development, including those that affect physical characteristics as well as psychological traits, capacities, and limitations. (17)

negative reinforcer The removal of an unpleasant stimulus following a particular behavior, which removal increases the likelihood that the behavior will be repeated should the unpleasant stimulus recur. (51)

neglect A form of child maltreatment in which parents or caregivers fail to meet a child's basic needs. (308)

neonate A newborn baby. Infants are neonates from the moment of birth to the end of the first month of life. (143)

neural tube The fold of cells that appears in the embryonic disk about three weeks after conception, later developing into the central nervous system. (115)

neurons Nerve cells of the central nervous system. (184)

nonadditive pattern A pattern of genetic inheritance in which the outcome depends much more on the influence of one gene than of another. (83)

norms The overall usual, or average, standard for a particular behavior. Norms are generally established through research done on a large sample of a given population. (192)

nurture All the environmental influences on development, from prenatal influences on the embryo to the cultural context at death. (17)

obesity The condition of being significantly and unhealthily overweight. (413)

object permanence Piaget's term for the realization in infants, at about 8 months of age, that objects and people still exist even when they cannot be seen. (223)

observation The unobtrusive watching and recording of the behavior of subjects in certain situations, either in the laboratory or in natural settings. (24)

Oedipus complex In the phallic stage of psychosocial development, the sexual desire that boys have for their mother and the related hostility they have toward their father. (400)

operant conditioning The learning process in which a person or animal becomes more, or less, likely to perform a certain behavior because of past reinforcement or punishment for similar behavior. (Also called *instrumental conditioning*.) (50)

operational definition A precise definition of a research variable that is intended to make the variable easier to observe and measure. (26)

oral stage Freud's term for the first stage of psychosexual development, in which the infant gains erotic pleasure through sucking and biting. (44, 263)

organization In information-processing, a memory technique involving the regrouping of information to make it more memorable. (440)

organization In Piagetian theory, the process of synthesizing and analyzing perceptions and thoughts. (61)

overextension The application of a word to several objects that share a particular characteristic, such as the use of "doggie" to label all four-legged animals. (241)

overregularization The tendency to apply grammatical rules and structures when they are not called for, or when exceptions to them should be used. (360)

ovum (plural, ova) The reproductive cells of a female, which are present from birth in the ovaries. (78)

parent-infant bond The strong feelings of attachment between parents and newborns that are said to arise from their initial contact after birth. The long-term importance of this postpartem bond has been greatly, and dangerously, overblown by the popular media. (167)

peer group A group of individuals of roughly the same age and social status who play, work, or learn together. (477)

perception The mental processing of sensory information. (194)

perceptual constancy The awareness that the size and shape of an object remain the same despite changes in the object's appearance due to changes in viewing distance or perspective. (216)

performance orientation An approach to schoolwork that is based on the belief that a lack of academic success is a sign of a personal inadequacy that is unlikely to change. Students with this orientation tend to avoid challenges in which they might fail and give up easily in difficult situations. (465)

period of the embryo From approximately the third through the eighth week after conception, when the rudimentary forms of all anatomical structures develop. (110)

period of the fetus From the ninth week after conception until birth, when the organs grow in size and complexity. (111)

permissive parenting A style of child-rearing in which parents rarely punish, guide, or control their children but are nurturant and communicate well with their children. (378)

phallic stage The third stage of psychosexual development, occurring in early childhood, in which the penis becomes the focus of psychological concern as well as of physiological pleasure. (44)

phenotype An individual's observable characteristics that result from the interaction of the genes with each other and with the environment. (83)

physiological states Refers to various levels of physiological arousal, such as quiet sleep and alert wakefulness. (185)

placenta An organ made up of blood vessels that delivers oxygen and nutrients from the mother's bloodstream to the fetus and enables the fetus's waste products to be excreted through the mother's system. (115)

polygenic traits Characteristics produced by the interaction of many genes. (82)

positive reinforcer Anything (such as a reward or positive event) that follows a behavior and increases the likelihood that that behavior will occur again. (51)

postconventional moral reasoning Kohlberg's term for the two highest stages of moral thinking, in which the individual follows moral principles that may supersede the standards of society or the wishes of the individual. (489)

pragmatics A term for the practical aspects of communication, such as adjusting vocabulary and grammar to fit the specific situation and audience. (361)

preconventional moral reasoning Kohlberg's term for the first two stages of moral thinking, in which the individual reasons in terms of his or her own welfare. (489)

preoperational thought Piaget's term for the second period of cognitive development. In this period, which generally occurs from age 2 to 6, children are unable to grasp logical concepts such as conservation, reversibility, or identity. (58, 348)

preterm infant An infant born three or more weeks before the due date. (145)

primary circular reactions Piaget's term for circular reactions in which infants repeat actions that involve their bodies—for example, sucking their thumbs or kicking their legs. (233)

private speech The use of language to form thoughts and analyze ideas, either silently or by talking to oneself. (354)

Project Headstart A preschool educational program designed to give children advance preparation (a "head start") for the intellectual and social challenges of elementary school. (365)

prosocial behavior Any action, such as sharing, cooperating, sympathizing, performed to benefit other people without the expectation of reward for oneself. (480)

provocation ecologies Classroom environments that provoke or exacerbate hyperactive behavior by imposing either an unusually rigid classroom structure or none at all. (434)

proximo-distal development The sequence of body growth and maturation from the spine toward the extremities. Human growth, from the embryonic period through early childhood, follows this pattern. (115)

psychoanalytic theory A theory originated by Sigmund Freud that stresses unconscious forces that underlie human behavior. (43)

psychosexual stages A series of developmental stages, each originating in sexual interest in, and gratification through, a particular part of the body. (44)

psychosocial domain Includes emotions, personality characteristics, and relationships with other people. (3)

psychosocial theory A theory that stresses the interaction between internal psychological forces and external social influences. Erikson's theory is a psychosocial one. (47)

punishment An unpleasant event that follows from a particular behavior, making it less likely that the behavior will be repeated. (52)

rarefaction ecologies Classroom environments that ameliorate or diminish hyperactive behavior by providing sufficient classroom structure within a flexible individualized environment. (434)

reaction time The time it takes to respond to a particular stimulus. (418)

reciprocal determinism Refers to the idea that an individual's internal characteristics, environment, and behavior are mutually interactive in determining the individual's specific behaviors. (56)

reciprocity The logical principle that a change in one dimension of an object can be compensated for by a change in another dimension. (446)

reflexes Involuntary physical responses to stimuli. (188)

rehearsal A memory technique involving repetition of the material to be remembered. (440)

reinforcement The process whereby a particular behavior is strengthened, making it more likely that the behavior will be repeated. (51)

reinforcer Anything that increases the likelihood that a given response will occur again. (51)

rejecting-neglecting parenting A style of parenting that is cold, detached, and permissive. (379)

relationship perspective Focuses on the diverse ways the quality of personal relationships affects the course of psychosocial development. (377)

replicate To repeat, with a different population, the specific design and procedures of a previous scientific study in order to test the validity of that study's conclusions. (24)

report from secondary sources A research method in which the scientist obtains information about a research subject indirectly, usually from people who know the individual. (32)

representative sample A select group of research subjects who reflect the relevant characteristics of the larger population that is under study. (26)

repression A defense mechanism in which disturbing thoughts or impulses are excluded from consciousness. (46)

response Any behavior (either instinctual or learned) that is elicited by a specific stimulus. (49)

response generator A network of mental processes, involving the sensory register, working memory, and knowledge base, that organizes reactions to the environment. (62)

restricted code A form of language characterized by limited use of vocabulary and syntax and a reliance on gestures, intonation, and shared experience for the communication of meaning. (451)

retrieval strategies Procedures for recollecting previously learned information, such as thinking of related information or trying to create a mental image of the thing to be remembered. (440)

reversibility The logical principle that something that has been changed can be returned to its original state by reversing the process of change. (446)

risk analysis In teratology, the attempt to evaluate all the exacerbating and ameliorating factors surrounding exposure to teratogens, in order to assess the potential for prenatal damage. (119)

rooting reflex A reflex that helps babies find a nipple by causing them to turn their heads toward anything that brushes against their cheek and to attempt to suck on it. (188)

rough-and-tumble play Play such as wrestling, chasing, and hitting that mimics aggression but actually occurs purely in fun, with no intent to harm. (394)

rubella A form of measles, which, if contracted during pregnancy, can harm the fetus, including causing blindness, deafness, and damage to the central nervous system. (123)

sample size The number of individuals who are being studied in a research project. (26)

scaffold To sensitively structure a child's participation in learning encounters so that the child's learning is facilitated. (353)

scheme A general way of thinking about, or interacting with, objects and ideas in the environment. (59)

scientific method The sequence and procedures of scientific investigation (formulating questions, collecting data, testing hypotheses, and drawing conclusions) designed to reduce subjective reasoning, biased assumptions, and unfounded conclusions. (23)

scripts Skeletal outlines of the usual sequence of certain common recurrent events. Young children use such scripts to facilitate the storage and retrieval of memories related to specific episodes of these events. (336)

second stage of labor The period of the birth process during which the baby's head moves through the vaginal opening. The second stage of labor usually lasts less than an hour. (142)

secondary circular reactions Piaget's term for infants' tendency to repeat actions to produce responses from objects or people. (234)

secure attachment A healthy parent-child connection, signaled by the child's being confident when the parent is present, distressed at the parent's absence, and comforted by the parent's return. (277)

selective attention The ability to concentrate on relevant information and ignore distractions. (439)

self-awareness A person's sense of himself or herself as a being distinct from others, with particular characteristics. (259)

self-efficacy One's feelings of competency, capability, and effectiveness. (55)

sensation The response of a sensory system to a particular stimulus. (194)

sensitivity The capacity to notice and interpret the infant's signals appropriately and to respond to them in a nurturing way. (265)

sensorimotor intelligence Piaget's term for the first stage of cognitive development (from birth to about 2 years old). Children in this stage primarily use their senses and motor skills to explore and manipulate the environment. (58, 232)

sensorimotor play Play that captures the pleasures of using the senses and one's motor abilities. (393)

sensory register A memory system that functions for only a fraction of a second, retaining a fleeting impression of a stimulus on a particular sense organ. (62)

separation anxiety A child's fear of being left by the caregiver. This emotion emerges at about 8 or 9 months, peaks at about 14 months, then gradually subsides. (256)

separation-individuation Mahler's term to describe the child's gradual development of a sense of self, apart from the mother. This process begins at about 5 months of age and is completed at about 3 years. (265)

sex differences Differences between males and females that arise from biological influences. (398)

small for gestational age (SGA) A term applied to newborns who weigh substantially less than they should given how much time has passed since conception. (145)

social cognition A person's awareness and understanding of human personality, motives, emotions, intentions, and interactions. (473)

social comparison The tendency to assess one's abilities, achievements, social status, and the like by measuring them against those of others, especially those of one's peers. (465, 508)

social context The entire spectrum of social milieux—including the people, the customs, and the beliefs—that surround each developing person. (6)

social conventions The customs and traditions of a particular society, such as those regarding proper ways of dressing, eating, conversing, and behaving, especially in public places. (492)

social learning theory The theory that learning occurs through imitation of, and identification with, other people. (53)

social referencing Looking to trusted adults for emotional cues in interpreting a strange or ambiguous event. (258)

social smile An infant's smile in response to a human face or voice. In full-term infants, this smile first appears at about 6 weeks after birth. (253)

social support Emotional encouragement and practical assistance provided by other people, particularly friends and family, to a person in need. (137)

society of children The social culture of children, including the games, vocabulary, dress codes, and rules of behavior that characterize their interaction. (477)

sociocultural theory A theory that seeks to explain the growth of individual knowledge and competencies in terms of the guidance, support, and structure provided by the broader cultural context. (66)

sociodramatic play Pretend play in which children act out various roles and themes in stories of their own creation. (395)

socioeconomic status (SES) An indicator of social class that is based primarily on income, education, and occupation. (11)

sonogram A prenatal-screening technique, akin to an x-ray, that uses ultrasound waves to reveal the size and skeletal structure of the fetus. (100)

sperm The reproductive cells of a male, which begin to be produced in a young man's testicles at puberty. (78)

statistical significance A mathematical calculation, derived from such factors as sample size and differences between groups, that indicates the likelihood that a particular research result occurred by chance. (27)

stimulus Anything that elicits a response, such as a reflex or a voluntary action. (49)

storage strategies Procedures for holding information in memory, such as rehearsal (repeating the information to be remembered) and organization (regrouping the information to make it more memorable). (440)

Strange Situation An experimental condition devised by Mary Ainsworth to assess an infant's attachment. The infant's behavior is observed in an unfamiliar room while a caregiver (usually the mother) and a stranger move in and out of the room. (278)

stranger wariness Fear of unfamiliar people, first noticeable in infants at about 6 months of age and usually full-blown by 10 to 14 months. (256)

sucking reflex A reflex that causes newborns to suck anything that touches their lips. (188)

sudden infant death syndrome (SIDS) Death of a seemingly healthy baby who, without apparent cause, stops breathing during sleep. (180)

superego The part of the personality that is self-critical and judgmental and that internalizes the moral standards set by parents and society. (45)

surrogate motherhood Alternative method to normal conception in which sperm from the husband is inserted with a syringe into a woman who has agreed to bear the child for the infertile wife. (113)

survey A research method that collects interview information on a large number of people, either through written questionnaires or through personal interviews. (31)

symbolic thinking Thinking that involves the use of words, objects, or actions to represent ideas. (347)

synchrony Carefully coordinated interaction between infant and parent (or any other two people) in which each individual responds to and influences the other's movements and rhythms. (273)

syndrome A cluster of distinct characteristics that tend to occur together in a given disorder, although the number of characteristics exhibited, and their intensity, vary from individual to individual. (93)

temperament Inherent dispositions, such as activity level, intensity of reaction, emotionality, and sociability, that underlie and affect a person's responses to people and things. (265)

teratogens External agents, such as viruses, drugs, chemicals, and radiation, that can impair prenatal development and lead to abnormalities, disabilities, or even death. (119)

teratology The scientific study of birth defects caused by genetic or prenatal problems, or by birth complications. (119)

tertiary circular reactions Piaget's term for circular reactions that infants repeat with slight variations. (235)

thalidomide A tranquilizer—now banned in many countries—which, when taken early in pregnancy, causes malformations of the fetus's arms, legs, and ears. (125)

theory of mind An understanding of mental processes, that is, of one's own or another's emotions, perceptions, and thoughts. (344)

third stage of labor The expulsion of the placenta after a child is born. (143)

toddler A child, usually between the ages of 1 and 2, who has just begun to master the art of walking. (191)

toxoplasmosis A disease caused by a parasite present in uncooked meat, cat feces, and yard dirt. If a pregnant woman contracts this disease, her fetus may suffer eye or brain damage. (125)

traditional parenting A style of parenting in which the parents take traditional male and female roles, the mother being primarily nurturant and permissive, while the father is more authoritarian. (379)

transition The period of the birth process in which the fetus's head moves from the uterus through the birth canal to the vaginal opening. (142)

trimester One of the three-month periods in the nine months of pregnancy. (116)

trisomy-21 (Down syndrome) A chromosomal abnormality caused by an extra chromosome at the twenty-first pair. Individuals with this syndrome tend, with much variation, to have round faces, short limbs, and to be slow to develop. (93)

trust versus mistrust Erikson's first stage of psychosocial development, in which the infant experiences the world as either good and comfortable or as threatening and uncomfortable. (263)

twenty-third pair In humans, the chromosome pair that determines the person's sex. (80)

underextension The use of a word to refer to a narrower category of objects or events than the term signifies. (241)

vacuum extractor A special suction cup, used to facilitate or hasten birth, that fits over the top of the fetal head and allows the fetus to be pulled through the birth canal. (156)

variable Any factor or condition that can change or vary from one individual or group or situation to another and thus affect behavior. (28)

very low birthweight (VLBW) Birthweight of less than 1,500 grams (3½ pounds). (146)

working memory The part of memory that handles current, conscious mental activity. (Also called *short-term memory*.) (62)

X-linked genes Genes that are carried on the X chromosome. X-linked genes are more likely to appear on the phenotype of males, even though women are more likely to have them on their genotype. (84)

zone of proximal development Vygotsky's term for the difference between an individual's attained level of development and the person's potential level of development that might be reached with guidance. (68, 353)

zygote The single cell formed from the union of two gametes, a sperm and an ovum. (78)

Bibliography

Abel, E., & Sokol, R. (1987). Incidence of fetal alcohol syndrome and economic impact of FAS-related anomalies. *Drug and Alcohol Dependency, 19,* 51–70.

Aboud, F. (1985). Children's application of attribution principles to social comparisons. *Child Development, 56,* 682–688.

Aboud, F. (1987). The development of ethnic self-identification and attitudes. In J.S. Phinney & M.J. Rotheram (Eds.), *Children's ethnic socialization: Pluralism and development.* Newbury Park, CA: Sage.

Abramovitch, R., Corter, C., & Lando, B. (1979). Sibling interaction in the home. *Child Development, 50,* 997–1003.

Abramovitch, R., Pepler, D., & Corter, C. (1982). Patterns of sibling interaction among preschool children. In M. Lamb & B. Sutton-Smith (Eds.), *Sibling relationships.* Hillsdale, NJ: Erlbaum.

Achenbach, Thomas M., & Edelbrock, Craig S. (1981). Behavioral problems and competencies reported by parents of normal and disturbed children aged four through sixteen. *Monographs of the Society for Research in Child Development, 46* (Serial No. 188).

Achenbach, Thomas M., Howell, Catherine T., Quay, Herbert C., & Conners, C. Keith. (1991). *National survey of problems and competencies among four- to sixteen-year-olds, 56,* 3.

Adams, Edgar H., Gfroerer, Joseph C., & Bourse, Beatrice A. (1989). Epidemiology of substance abuse, including alcohol and cigarette smoking. In Donald Hutchings (Ed.), *Prenatal abuse of licit and illicit drugs.* New York: New York Academy of Sciences.

Adams, Marilyn Jager. (1990). *Beginning to read: Thinking and learning about print.* Cambridge, MA: MIT Press.

Adams, Paul L., Milner, Judith R., & Schrept, N.A. (1984). *Fatherless children.* New York: Wiley-Interscience.

Adams, Russell J. (1989). Newborns' discrimination among mid- and long-wavelength stimuli. *Journal of Experimental Child Psychology, 47,* 130–141.

Adams, Russell J. (1989). Obstetrical medication and the human newborn: The influence of alphaprodine hydrochloride on visual behavior. *Developmental Medicine and Child Neurology, 31,* 650–656.

Adams, Russell J., Maurer, D., & Davis, M. (1986). Newborns' discrimination of chromatic from achromatic stimuli. *Journal of Experimental Child Psychology, 41,* 267–281.

Ades, A.E., Newell, M.L., & Peckham, C.S. (1991). Children born to women with HIV-1 infection: Natural history and risk of transmission. *The Lancet, 337,* 253–260.

Adolph, K.E., Eppler, M.A., & Gibson, E.J. (1993). Development of perception of affordances. In C. Rovee-Collier & L.P. Lipsitt (Eds.), *Advances in infancy research* (Vol. 8). Norwood, NJ: Ablex.

Adolph, K.E., Eppler, M.A., & Gibson, E.J. (1993). Crawling versus walking infants' perception of affordances for locomotion over sloping surfaces. *Child Development, 64,* 1158–1174.

Ainsworth, Mary D. Salter. (1973). The development of infant-mother attachment. In Bettye M. Caldwell & Henry N. Ricciuti (Eds.), *Review of child development research* (Vol. III). Chicago: University of Chicago Press.

Ainsworth, Mary D. Salter. (1993). Attachment as related to mother-infant interaction. In C. Rovee-Collier & L.P. Lipsitt (Eds.), *Advances in infancy research* (Vol. 8). Norwood, NJ: Ablex.

Ainsworth, Mary D. Salter, & Bell, Silvia M. (1970). Attachment, exploration, and separation: Illustrated by the behavior of one-year-olds in a strange situation. *Child Development, 41,* 49–67.

Ainsworth, Mary D. Salter, & Eichberg, C. (1991). Effects of infant-mother attachment of mother's unresolved loss of an attachment figure, or other traumatic experience. In C. Murray Parkes, J. Stevenson-Hinde, & P. Marris (Eds.), *Attachment across the life cycle.* London: Routledge.

Akhtar, N., Dunham, F., & Dunham, P. (1991). Directive interactions and early vocabulary development: The role of joint attentional focus. *Journal of Child Language, 18,* 41–49.

Allen, E.M., Mitchell, E.H., Stewart, A.W., & Ford, R.P.K. (1993). Ethnic differences in mortality from sudden infant death syndrome in New Zealand. *British Medical Journal, 306,* 13–16.

Allgood-Merten, Betty, & Stockard, Jean. (1991). Sex role identity and self-esteem: A comparison of children and adolescents. *Sex Roles, 25,* 129–139.

Allison, Clara. (1985). Development direction of action programs: Repetitive action to correction loops. In Jane E. Clark & James H. Humphrey (Eds.), *Motor development: Current selected research.* Princeton, NJ: Princeton Book Company.

Allison, Paul D., & Furstenberg, Frank F. (1989). How marital dissolution affects children: Variations by age and sex. *Developmental Psychology, 25,* 540–549.

Altergott, Karen. (1993). *One world, many families.* Minneapolis, MN: National Council on Family Relations.

Amaro, Hortensia, Fried, Lise E., Cabral, Howard, & Zuckerman, Barry. (1990). Violence during pregnancy and substance use. *American Journal of Public Health, 80,* 575–579.

Amato, P.E., & Rezac, S.J. (in press). Contact with nonresidential parents, interparental conflict, and children's behavior. *Journal of Family Issues,* in press.

Amato, Paul R. (1993). Children's adjustment to divorce: Theories, hypotheses, empirical support. *Journal of Marriage and the Family, 55,* 23–38.

Amato, Paul R. (1994). Lifespan adjustment of children to their parents' divorce. *The Future of Children,* in press.

Amato, Paul R., & Keith, Bruce. (1991). Parental divorce and adult well-being: A meta-analysis. *Journal of Marriage and the Family, 53,* 43–58.

American College of Obstetrics and Gynecology. (1992). *Planning for pregnancy, birth and beyond.* New York: Dutton.

Ammerman, Robert T., & Hersen, Michel (Eds.). (1989). *Treatment of family violence.* New York: Wiley.`

Anastopoulos, Arthur D., Guevremont, David C., Shelton, Terri L., & DuPaul, George J. (1992). Parenting stress among families of children with attention deficit hyperactivity disorder. *Journal of Abnormal Child Psychology, 20,* 503–520.

Anderson, B. (1989). Effects of public day care: A longitudinal study. *Child Development, 60,* 857–866.

Anderson, Robert L., & Golbus, Mitchel S. (1989). Chemical teratogens. In Mark I. Evans, Alan O. Dixler, John C. Fletcher, & Joseph D. Schulman (Eds.), *Fetal diagnosis and therapy.* Philadelphia: Lippincott.

Andrich, David, & Styles, Irene. (1994). Psychometric evidence of intellectual growth spurts in early adolescence. *Journal of Early Adolescence, 14,* 328–344.

Angier, N. (1989, March). The gene dream. *American Health,* 103–108.

Anglin, Jeremy M. (1993). Vocabulary development: A morphological analysis. *Monographs of the Society for Research in Child Development, 58* (10, Serial No. 238).

Antell, S.E., & Keating, D.P. (1983). Perception of numerical invariance in neonates. *Child Development, 54,* 695–701.

Anthony, E.J. (1987). Risk, vulnerability, and resilience: An overview. In E.J. Anthony & B.J. Cohler (Eds.), *The invulnerable child.* New York: Guilford.

Apgar, Virginia. (1953). A proposal for a new method of evaluation in the newborn infant. *Current Research in Anesthesia and Analgesia, 32,* 260.

Appelbaum, Mark I., & McCall, Robert B. (1983). Design and analysis in developmental psychology. In Paul H. Mussen (Ed.), *Handbook of child psychology: Vol. I. History, theory, and methods.* New York: Wiley.

Apple, Rima D. (1988). *Mothers and medicine: A social history of infant feeding, 1890–1950.* Madison, WI: University of Wisconsin Press.

Aram, Dorothy M., Morris, Robin, & Hall, Nancy E. (1992). The validity of discrepancy criteria for identifying children with developmental language disorders. *Journal of Learning Disabilities, 25,* 549–554.

Arbuthnot, Jack, Gordon, Donald A., & Jurkovic, Gregory J. (1987). Personality. In Herbert C. Quay (Ed.), *Handbook of juvenile delinquency.* New York: Wiley.

Archer, Sally L., & Waterman, Alan S. (1990). Varieties of identity diffusions and foreclosures: An exploration of the subcategories of the identity statuses. *Journal of Adolescent Research, 5,* 96–111.

Arend, Richard, Gove, Frederick L., & Sroufe, L. Alan. (1979). Continuity of individual adaptation from infancy to kindergarten: A predictive study of ego-resiliency and curiosity in preschoolers. *Child Development, 50,* 950–959.

Armistead, Lisa, Kempton, Tracy, Lynch, Sean, Forehand, Rex, Nousiainen, Sarah, Neighbors, Bryan, & Tannenbaum, Lynne. (1992). Early retention: Are there long-term beneficial effects? *Psychology in the Schools, 29,* 342–347.

Arms, Suzanne. (1975). *Immaculate deception.* New York: Bantam.

Arnold, Elaine. (1982). The use of corporal punishment in child-rearing in the West Indies. *Child Abuse and Neglect, 6,* 141–145.

Arsenio, W.F., & Kramer, R. (1992). Victimizers and their victims: Children's conceptions of the mixed emotional consequences of moral transgressions. *Child Development, 63,* 915–927.

Asher, Steven R. (1983). Social competence and peer status: Recent advances and future directions. *Child Development, 54,* 1427–1434.

Asher, Steven R., & Renshaw, Peter D. (1981). Children without friends: Social knowledge and social skill training. In Steven R. Asher & John M. Gottman (Eds.), *The development of children's friendships.* Cambridge, England: Cambridge University Press.

Aslin, Richard N. (1987). Visual and auditory development in infancy. In Joy Doniger Osofsky (Ed.), *Handbook of infant development* (2nd ed.). New York: Wiley.

Aslin, Richard. (1988). Visual perception in early infancy. In Albert Yonas (Ed.), *Perceptual development in infancy.* Hillsdale, NJ: Erlbaum.

Astington, J.W., & Gopnik, A. (1988). Knowing you've changed your mind: Children's understanding of representational change. In J.W. Astington, P.L. Harris, & D.R. Olson (Eds.), *Developing theories of mind.* Cambridge, England: Cambridge University Press.

Axia, Giovanna, & Baroni, Rosa. (1985). Linguistic politeness at different age levels. *Child Development, 56,* 918–927.

Bachman, J.G., & Schulenberg, J. (1993). How part-time work intensity relates to drug use, problem behavior, time use, and satisfaction among high school seniors: Are these consequences or merely correlates? *Developmental Psychology, 29,* 220–235.

Bahrick, L.E. (1983). Infants' perception of substance and temporal synchrony in multimodal events. *Infant Behavior and Development, 6,* 429–451.

Bailey, J. Michael, Pillard, Richard C., & Knight, Robert. (1993). At issue: Is sexual orientation biologically determined? *CQ Researcher, 3,* 209.

Baillargeon, R. (1987). Object permanence in 3.5- and 4.5-month-old infants. *Developmental Psychology, 23,* 655–664.

Baillargeon, R. (1991). Reasoning about the height and location of a hidden object in 4.5- and 6.5-month-old infants. *Cognition, 38,* 13–42.

Baillargeon, R. (in press). The object concept revisited: New directions in the investigation of infants' physical knowledge. In C.E. Granrud (Ed.), *Carnegie-Mellon symposia on cognition: Vol. 23. Visual perception and cognition in infancy.* Hillsdale, NJ: Erlbaum.

Baillargeon, R., & DeVos, J. (1992). Object permanence in young infants: Further evidence. *Child Development, 62,* 1227–1246.

Baillargeon, R., Graber, M., Decops, J., & Black, J. (1990). Why do young infants fail to search for hidden objects? *Cognition, 36,* 255–284.

Bakeman, Roger, Adamson, Lauren B., Konner, Melvin, & Barr, Ronald G. (1990). !Kung infancy: The social context of object exploration. *Child Development, 61,* 794–809.

Baker-Ward, Lynne, Gordon, Betty N., Ornstein, Peter A., Larus, Deanna M., & Clubb, Patricia A. (1993). Young children's long-term retention of a pediatric examination. *Child Development, 64,* 1519–1533.

Bakken, B. (1993). Prejudice and danger: The only child in China. *Childhood, 1,* 46–61.

Bakker, D.J., & Vinke, J. (1985). Effect of hemispheric-specific stimulation on brain activity and reading in dyslexics. *Journal of Clinical Neuropsychology, 7,* 505–525.

Balfour-Lynn, Lionel. (1986). Growth and childhood asthma. *Archives of Diseases of Childhood, 60,* 231–235.

Ball, Jean A. (1987). *Reactions to motherhood.* New York: Cambridge University Press.

Bamford, F.N., Bannister, R., Benjamin, C.M., Hillier, V.F., Ward, B.S., & Moore, W.M.O. (1990). Sleep in the first year of life. *Developmental and Child Neurology, 32,* 718–734.

Bandura, Albert. (1977). *Social learning theory.* Englewood Cliffs, NJ: Prentice-Hall.

Bandura, Albert. (1986). *Social foundations of thought and action: A social cognitive theory.* Englewood Cliffs, NJ: Prentice-Hall.

Bandura, Albert. (1989). Social cognitive theory. In R. Vasta (Ed.), *Annals of child development* (Vol. 6). Greenwich, CT: JAI Press.

Barber, B.K. (1994). Cultural, family, and personal contexts of parent-adolescent conflict. *Journal of Marriage and the Family, 56,* 375–386.

Bardin, C. Wayne. (1986). The pituitary-testicular axis. In Samuel S.C. Yen & Robert B. Jaffe (Eds.), *Reproductive endocrinology: Physiology, pathophysiology, and clinical management* (2nd ed.). Philadelphia: W.B. Saunders.

Barinaga, Marcia. (1994). Surprises across the cultural divide. *Science, 263,* 1468–1472.

Barkley, R.A. (1990). Attention deficit disorders: History, definition, and diagnosis. In M. Lewis & S.M. Miller (Eds.), *Handbook of developmental psychopathology.* New York: Plenum.

Barkley, R.A., Anastopoulos, A.D., Guevremont, D.D., & Fletcher, K.E. (1991). Adolescents with ADHD. *Patterns of behavioral adjustment, academic functioning, and treatment utilization, 30,* 752–761.

Barnard, Kathryn E., & Bee, Helen L. (1983). The impact of temporally patterned stimulation on the development of pre-term infants. *Child Development, 54,* 1156–1167.

Barnett, D., Manley, J.T., & Cicchetti, D. (1993). Defining child maltreatment: The interface between policy and research. In D. Cicchetti & S.L. Toth (Eds.), *Advances in applied developmental psychology series: Vol. 8. Child abuse, child development, and social policy.* Norwood, NJ: Ablex.

Barnett, Mark A. (1986). Sex bias in the helping behavior presented in children's picture books. *Journal of Genetic Psychology, 147,* 343–351.

Barnett, W.S., & Escobar, C.M. (1987). The economics of early educational intervention: A review. *Review of Educational Research, 57,* 387–414.

Baron, J. (1989). *Teaching decision-making to adolescents.* Hillsdale, NJ: Erlbaum.

Barr, H.M., Streissguth, A.P., Darby, B.L., & Sampson, P.D. (1990). Prenatal exposure to alcohol, caffeine, tobacco, and aspirin: Effects on fine and gross motor performance in 4-year-old children. *Developmental Psychology, 26,* 339–348.

Barrett, Martyn D. (1986). Early semantic representations and early word-usage. In Stan A. Kuczaj & Martyn D. Barrett (Eds.), *The development of word meaning: Progress in cognitive developmental research.* New York: Springer-Verlag.

Bassuk, E.L. (1989). Homelessness: A growing American tragedy. *Division of Child, Youth, and Family Services Newsletter, 12,* 1–13.

Bassuk, E.L., & Rosenberg, L. (1990). Psychosocial characteristics of homeless children and children with homes. *Pediatrics, 85,* 257–261.

Bateman, David A., Ng, Stephen K.C., Hansen, Catherine A., & Heagarty, Margaret C. (1993). The effects of intrauterine cocaine exposure in newborns. *American Journal of Public Health, 83,* 190–193.

Bates, Elizabeth, & Carnevale, G.F. (1994). Developmental psychology in the 1990s: Research on language development. *Developmental Review,* in press.

Bates, Elizabeth, O'Connell, Barbara, & Shore, Cecilia. (1987). Language and communication in infancy. In Joy Doniger Osofsky (Ed.), *Handbook of infant development* (2nd ed.). New York: Wiley.

Bauer, H.H. (1992). *Scientific literacy and the myth of the scientific method.* Urbana: University of Illinois Press.

Bauer, P.J., & Hertsgaard, L.A. (1993). Increasing steps in recall of events: Factors facilitating immediate and long-term memory in 13.5- and 16.5-month-old children. *Child Development, 64,* 1204–1223.

Bauer, P.J., & Mandler, J.M. (1990). Remembering what happened next: Very young children's recall of event sequences. In R. Fivush & J.A. Hudson (Eds.), *Knowing and remembering in young children.* Cambridge, England: Cambridge University Press.

Bauer, P.J., & Mandler, J.M. (1992). Putting the horse before the cart: The use of temporal order in recall of events by one-year-old children. *Developmental Psychology, 28,* 441–452.

Bauman, K.E. (1980). *Predicting adolescent drug use: Utility structure and marijuana.* New York: Praeger.

Bauman, K.E., Fisher, L.A., Bryan, E.S., & Chenoweth, R.L. (1984). Antecedents, subjective expected utility, and behavior: A panel study of adolescent cigarette smoking. *Addictive Behaviors, 9,* 121–136.

Baumeister, R.F. (1990). Suicide as escape from self. *Psychological Review, 97,* 90–113.

Baumrind, Diana. (1967). Child-care practices anteceding three patterns of preschool behavior. *Genetic Psychology Monographs, 75,* 43–88.

Baumrind, Diana. (1971). Current patterns of parental authority. *Developmental Psychology, 4* (Monograph 1), 1–103.

Baumrind, Diana. (1982). Are androgynous individuals more effective persons and parents? *Child Development, 53,* 44–75.

Baumrind, Diana. (1987). A developmental perspective on adolescent risk-taking behavior. In C.E. Irwin (Ed.), *Adolescent social behavior and health.* San Francisco: Jossey-Bass.

Baumrind, Diana. (1989). Rearing competent children. In William Damon (Ed.), *New directions for child development: Adolescent health and human behavior.* San Francisco: Jossey-Bass.

Baumrind, Diana. (1991). Effective parenting during the early adolescent transition. In P.A. Cowan & E.M. Hetherington (Eds.), *Advances in family research* (Vol. 2). Hillsdale, NJ: Erlbaum.

Baumrind, Diana. (1991). The influence of parenting style on adolescent competence and substance use. *Journal of Early Adolescence, 11,* 56–95.

Baumrind, Diana. (1991). Parenting styles and adolescent development. In Jeanne Brooks-Gunn, Richard Lerner, & Anne C. Petersen (Eds.), *The encyclopedia of adolescence.* New York: Garland.

Baumrind, Diana. (1993). The average expectable environment is not good enough: A response to Scarr. *Child Development, 64,* 1299–1317.

Baynes, R.D., & Bothwell, T.H. (1990). Iron deficiency. *Annual Review of Nutrition, 10,* (Palo Alto: Annual Reviews), 133.

Beal, Carole R. (1988). Children's knowledge about representations of intended meaning. In J.W. Astington, P.L. Harris, & D.R. Olson (Eds.), *Developing theories of mind.* Cambridge, England: Cambridge University Press.

Beal, Carole R. (1994). *Boys and girls: The development of gender roles.* New York: McGraw-Hill.

Beal, Carole R., & Belgrad, S.L. (1990). The development of message evaluation skills in young children. *Child Development, 61,* 705–712.

Beal, S.M., & Finch, C.F. (1991). An overview of retrospective case control slides investigating the relationship between prone sleep positions and SIDS. *Journal of Paediatrics and Child Health, 27,* 334–339.

Beal, S.M., & Porter, C. (1991). Sudden infant death syndrome related to climate. *Acta Paediatrica Scandinavica, 80,* 278–287.

Becker, Joseph. (1989). Preschoolers' use of number words to denote one-to-one correspondence. *Child Development, 60,* 1147–1157.

Beckwirth, Leila, & Rodning, Carol. (1991). Intellectual functioning in children born preterm: Recent research. In Lynn Okagaki & Robert J. Sternberg (Eds.), *Directors of development: Influences on the development of children's thinking.* Hillsdale, NJ: Erlbaum.

Beecham, Clayton T. (1989). Natural childbirth: A step backward? *Female patient, 14,* 56–60.

Behrman, Richard E. (1992). *Nelson textbook of pediatrics.* Philadelphia: W.B. Saunders.

Beilin, H. (1992). Piaget's enduring contribution to developmental psychology. *Developmental Psychology, 28,* 191–204.

Bell, A.P., Weinberg, M.S., & Mammersmith, S. (1981). *Sexual preference: Its development in men and women.* Bloomington: University of Indiana Press.

Bell, M.A., & Fox, N.A. (1992). The relations between frontal brain electrical activity and cognitive development during infancy. *Child Development, 63,* 1142–1163.

Bellinger, David D., & Needleman, Herbert L. (1985). Prenatal and early postnatal exposure to lead: Developmental effects, correlations, and implications. *International Journal of Mental Health, 14,* 78–111.

Belsky, Jay. (1986). Infant day care: A cause for concern? *Zero to Three, 6,* 1–7.

Belsky, Jay. (1990). Infant day care, child development, and family policy. *Society, 27* (5), 10–12.

Belsky, Jay, Gilstrap, Bonnie, & Rovine, Michael. (1984). The Pennsylvania Infant and Family Development Project I: Stability and change in mother-infant and father-infant interaction in a family setting at one, three, and nine months. *Child Development, 55,* 692–705.

Belsky, Jay, & Rovine, Michael. (1987). Temperament and attachment security in the Strange Situation. *Child Development, 58,* 787–795.

Belsky, Jay, Rovine, M., & Fish, M. (1989). The developing family system. In M.R. Gunnar & E. Thelen (Eds.), *Minnesota symposia on child psychology: Systems and development.* Hillsdale, NJ: Erlbaum.

Belsky, Jay, Steinberg, Laurence, & Draper, Patricia. (1991). Childhood experience, interpersonal development, and reproductive strategy: An evolutionary theory of socialization. *Child Development, 62,* 647–670.

Belsky, Jay, & Vondra, Joan. (1989). Lessons from child abuse: The determinants of parenting. In Dante Cicchetti & Vicki Carlson (Eds.), *Child maltreatment: Theory and research on the causes and consequences of child abuse and neglect.* Cambridge, England: Cambridge University Press.

Bem, Sandra L. (1974). The measurement of psychological androgyny. *Journal of Consulting and Clinical Psychology, 42,* 155–162.

Bem, Sandra L. (1981). Gender schema theory: A cognitive account of sex typing. *Psychological Review, 88,* 354–364.

Bem, Sandra L. (1985). Androgyny and gender schema theory: A conceptual and empirical integration. In T.B. Sondegegger (Ed.), *Nebraska symposium on motivation 1984: Vol. 32. Psychology and gender.* Lincoln: University of Nebraska Press.

Bem, Sandra L. (1989). Genital knowledge and gender constancy in preschool children. *Child Development, 60,* 649–662.

Benbow, C.P., & Stanley, J.C. (1983). Sex differences in mathematical reasoning ability: More facts. *Science, 222,* 1029–1031.

Benedek, Elissa. (1989). Baseball, apple pie, and violence: Is it American? In Leah J. Dickerson & Carol Nadelson (Eds.), *Family violence: Emerging issues of national crisis.* Washington, DC: American Psychiatric Press.

Benenson, J.F., & Dweck, C.S. (1986). The development of trait explanations and self-evaluations in the academic and social domains. *Child Development, 57*, 1179–1187.

Bengston, Vern L. (1975). Generation and family effects in value socialization. *American Sociological Review, 40*, 358–371.

Bengston, Vern L., Reedy, Margaret N., & Gordon, Chad. (1985). Aging and self-conceptions: Personality processes and social contexts. In James E. Birren & K. Warner Schaie (Eds.), *Handbook of the psychology of aging* (2nd ed.). New York: Van Nostrand.

Benson, J.B., & Uzgiris, I.C. (1985). Effect of self-initiated locomotion on infant search activity. *Developmental Psychology, 21*, 923–931.

Benson, Peter L. (1993). *The troubled journey: A portrait of 6th–12th grade youth*. Minneapolis: Search Institute.

Bensur, Barbara, & Eliot, John. (1993). Case's developmental model and children's drawings. *Perceptual and Motor Skills, 76*, 371–375.

Beresford, Shirley A.A. (1994). Annotation: How do we get enough folic acid to prevent some neural tube defects? *American Journal of Public Health, 84*, 348–350.

Berger, Joseph. (1990, September 28). What students think about condom plan. *The New York Times*, B1, 4.

Bergstrom, Steffan, & Liljestrand, Jerker. (1988). Application to developing countries. In B.S. Lindblad (Ed.), *Perinatal nutrition*. San Diego, CA: Academic Press.

Berkson, Gershon. (1993). *Children with handicaps: A review of behavioral research*. Hillsdale, NJ: Erlbaum.

Berndt, Thomas J. (1981). Relations between social cognition, nonsocial cognition, and social behavior. In John H. Flavell & Lee Ross (Eds.), *Social cognitive development: Frontiers and possible futures*. Cambridge, England: Cambridge University Press.

Berndt, Thomas J. (1989). Friendships in childhood and adolescence. In William Damon (Ed.), *Child development today and tomorrow*. San Francisco: Jossey-Bass.

Berndt, Thomas J., & Heller, K.A. (1985). Measuring children's personality attributions: Responses to open-ended questions versus trait ratings and predictions of future behavior. In Stephen R. Yussen (Ed.), *The growth of reflection in children*. New York: Academic Press.

Berndt, Thomas J., & Savin-Williams, R.C. (1992). Peer relations and friendships. In P.H. Tolan & B.J. Kohler (Eds.), *Handbook of clinical research and practice with adolescents*. New York: Wiley.

Bernstein, Basil. (1971, 1973). *Class, codes, and control* (Vols. 1, 2). London: Routledge and Kegan Paul.

Bertenthal, Bennett I., & Campos, Joseph J. (1987). New directions in the study of early experience. *Child Development, 58*, 560–567.

Bertenthal, Bennett I., & Campos, Joseph J. (1990). A systems approach to the organizing effect of self-produced locomotion during infancy. In Carolyn Rovee-Collier & Lewis P. Lipsitt (Eds.), *Advances in infancy research* (Vol. 6). Norwood, NJ: Ablex.

Berzonsky, Michael D. (1989). Identity style: Conceptualization and measurement. *Journal of Adolescent Research, 4*, 268–282.

Besharov, Douglas J. (1992). A balanced approach to reporting child abuse. *Child, Youth, and Family Service Quarterly, 15* (1), 5–7.

Betancourt, Hector, & Lopez, Steven Regeser. (1993). The study of culture, ethnicity, and race in American psychology. *American Psychologist, 48*, 629–637.

Bettes, Barbara A. (1988). Maternal depression and motherese: Temporal and intonational features. *Child Development, 59*, 1089–1096.

Beunen, G.P., Malina, R.M., Van't Hof, M.A., Simons, J., Ostyn, M., Renson, R., & Van Gerven, D. (1988). *Adolescent growth and motor performance: A longitudinal study of Belgian boys*. Champaign, IL: Human Kinetics Books.

Beyth-Marom, Ruth, Austin, Laurel, Fischhoff, Baruch, & Palmgren, Claire. (1993). Perceived consequences of risky behaviors: Adults and adolescents. *Developmental Psychology, 29*, 539–548.

Bhatia, M.S., Nigam, V.R., Bohra, N., & Malik, S.C. (1991). Attention deficit disorder with hyperactivity among paediatric outpatients. *Journal of Child Psychology and Psychiatry and Allied Disciplines, 32*, 297–306.

Bialystok, E. (1988). Levels of bilingualism and levels of linguistic awareness. *Developmental Psychology, 24*, 560–567.

Bierman, Karen Lynn, & Furman, Wyndol. (1984). The effects of social skills training and peer involvement on the social adjustment of preadolescents. *Child Development, 55*, 151–162.

Bierman, Karen Lynn, Smoot, D.L., & Aumiller, K. (1993). Characteristics of aggressive-rejected, aggressive (nonrejected), and rejected (nonaggressive) boys. *Child Development, 64*, 139–151.

Bigelow, B.J. (1977). Children's friendship expectations: A cognitive developmental study. *Child Development, 48*, 246–253.

Bigelow, B.J., & La Gaipa, J.J. (1975). Children's written descriptions of friendship: A multidimensional analysis. *Developmental Psychology, 11*, 857–858.

Bijou, S.W. (1989). Behavior analysis. In R. Vasta (Ed.), *Annals of child development* (Vol. 6). Greenwich, CT: JAI Press.

Billingham, Robert E., & Sack, Alan R. (1986). Courtship and violence: The interactive status of the relationship. *Journal of Adolescent Research, 1*, 315–326.

Binder, Arnold, Geis, Gilbert, & Bruce, Dickson. (1988). *Juvenile delinquency: Historical, cultural and legal perspectives*. New York: Macmillan.

Bing, Elizabeth D. (1983). *Dear Elizabeth Bing: We've had our baby*. New York: Pocket Books.

Bingham, C. Raymond, Miller, Brent C., & Adams, Gerald R. (1990). Correlates of age at first sexual intercourse in a national sample of young women. *Journal of Adolescent Research, 5*, 7–17.

Birch, Leann L. (1990). Development of food acceptance patterns. *Developmental Psychology, 26*, 515–519.

Birch, Leann L., Birch, D., Marlin, D.W., & Kramer, L. (1982). Effects of instrumental consumption on children's food preference. *Appetite, 3*, 125–134.

Bittles, Alan H., Mason, William M., Greene, Jennifer, & Rao, N. Appagi. (1991). Reproductive behavior and health in consanguineous marriages. *Science, 252*, 789–794.

Bjorklund, D.F. (Ed.). (1990). *Children's strategies: Contemporary views of cognitive development*. Hillsdale, NJ: Erlbaum.

Bjorklund, D.F., & Bjorklund, B.R. (1992, August). "I forget." *Parents*, 62–68.

Bjorklund, D.F., & Harnishfeger, K.K. (1990). The resources construct in cognitive development: Diverse sources of evidence and a theory of inefficient inhibition. *Developmental Review, 10*, 48–71.

Blake, Judith. (1989). *Family size and achievement*. Berkeley: University of California Press.

Blank, Robert H. (1988). The challenge of emergent public policy issues in genetic counseling. In Susie Ball (Ed.), *Strategies in genetic counseling: The challenge of the future*. New York: Human Sciences Press.

Bloch, Marianne N. (1989). Young boys' and girls' play at home and in the community: A cultural ecological framework. In Marianne N. Bloch & Anthony D. Pellegrini (Eds.), *The ecological context of children's play*. Norwood, NJ: Ablex.

Bloom, L. (1973). *One word at a time: The use of single-word utterances before syntax*. The Hague: Mouton.

Bloom, L. (1991). *Language development from two to three*. New York: Cambridge University Press.

Bloom, L. (1993). *The transition from infancy to language: Acquiring the power of expression*. New York: Cambridge University Press.

Bloom, L., Merkin, S., & Wootten, Janet. (1982). Wh– questions: Linguistic factors that contribute to the sequence of acquisition. *Child Development, 53*, 1084–1092.

Bloomfield, L. (1933). *Language*. New York: Henry Holt.

Bolton, Frank G., Morris, Larry A., & MacEacheron, Ann E. (1989). *Males at risk: The other side of child sexual abuse*. Newbury Park, CA: Sage.

Bomba, P.C., & Siqueland, E.R. (1983). The nature and structure of infant form categories. *Journal of Experimental Child Psychology, 35*, 294–328.

Bornstein, Marc H. (1985). Habituation of attention as a measure of visual information processing in human infants: Summary, systematization, and synthesis. In Gilbert Gottlieb & Norman A. Krasnegor (Eds.), *Measurement of audition and vision in the first year of postnatal life: A methodological overview*. Norwood, NJ: Ablex.

Bornstein, M.H. (1989). Stability in early mental development: From attention and information processing in infancy to language and cognition in childhood. In M.H. Bornstein & N.A. Krasnegor (Eds.), *Stability and continuity in mental development: Behavioral and biological perspectives*. Hillsdale, NJ: Erlbaum.

Bornstein, Marc H., & Lamb, M.E. (1992). *Development in infancy* (3rd ed.). New York: McGraw-Hill.

Bornstein, Marc H., Tamis-LeMonda, C.S., Tal, J., Ludemann, P., Toda, S., Rahn, C.W., Pecheux, M.-G., Azuma, H., & Vardi, D. (1992). Maternal responsiveness to infants in three societies: The United States, France, and Japan. *Child Development, 63*, 808–821.

Borovsky, D., & Rovee-Collier, C. (1990). Contextual constraints on memory retrieval at six months. *Child Development, 61*, 1569–1583.

Bouchard, Thomas J. (1994). Genes, environment, and personality. Science, 264, 1700–1701.

Bouchard, Thomas J., Lykken, David T., McGue, Matthew, Segal, Nancy L., & Tellegen, Auke. (1990). Sources of human psychological differences: The Minnesota study of twins reared apart. *Science, 250*, 223–228.

Boulton, Michael, & Smith, Peter K. (1989). Issues in the study of children's rough-and-tumble play. In Marianne N. Bloch & Anthony D. Pellegrini (Eds.), *The ecological context of children's play*. Norwood, NJ: Ablex.

Bower, T.G.R. (1989). *The rational infant: Learning in infancy*. New York: Freeman.

Bowerman, Melissa. (1982). Reorganizational processes in lexical and syntactic development. In Eric Wanner & Lila R. Gleitman (Eds.), *Language acquisition: The state of the art*. Cambridge, England: Cambridge University Press.

Bowlby, John. (1969, 1973). *Attachment* (Vol. 1) and *Loss* (Vol. II). New York: Basic Books.

Boxer, Andrew M., Gershenson, Harold P., & Offer, Daniel. (1984). Historical time and social change in adolescent experience. *New Directions for Mental Health Services, 22*, 83–95.

Boyer, Debra, & Fine, David. (1992). Sexual abuse as a factor in adolescent pregnancy and child maltreatment. *Family Planning Perspectives, 24*, 4–11, 19.

Boysson-Bardies, B., Halle, P., Sagart, L., & Durand, C. (1989). A crosslinguistic investigation of vowel formants in babbling. *Journal of Child Language, 16*, 1–17.

Brackbill, Yvonne, McManus, Karen, & Woodward, Lynn. (1985). *Medication in maternity: Infant exposure and maternal information*. Ann Arbor: University of Michigan Press.

Brackbill, Yvonne, McManus, Karen, & Woodward, Lynn. (1988). *Medication in maternity: Infant exposure and maternal information*. Ann Arbor: University of Michigan Press.

Braddick, Oliver, & Atkinson, Janette. (1988). Sensory selectivity, attentional control, and cross-channel integration in early visual development. In Albert Yonas (Ed.), *Perceptual development in infancy*. Hillsdale, NJ: Erlbaum.

Bradley, Robert H. (1988). HOME measurement of maternal responsiveness. In M.H. Bornstein (Ed.), *Maternal responsiveness: Characteristics and consequences* (New Directions for Child Development, No. 43). San Francisco: Jossey-Bass.

Bradley, Robert H., & Caldwell, Bettye M. (1980). The relation of home environment, cognitive competence, and IQ among males and females. *Child Development, 51*, 1140–1148.

Bradley, Robert H., & Caldwell, Bettye M. (1984). The HOME inventory and family demographics. *Developmental Psychology, 20*, 315–320.

Bradley, R.H., Caldwell, B.M., Rock, S.I., Barnard, K.E., Gray, C., Hammond, M.A., Mitchell, S., Siegel, L., Ramey, C.T., Gottfried, A.W., & Johnson, D.L. (1988). Home environment and cognitive development in the first 3 years of life: A collaborative study involving six sites and three ethnic groups in North America. *Developmental Psychology, 25*, 217–235.

Bradley, Robert H., & Rock, Stephen L. (1985). The HOME inventory: Its relation to school failure and development of an elementary-age version. In William K. Frankenberg, Robert N. Emde, & Joseph W. Sullivan (Eds.), *Early identification of children at risk: An international perspective*. New York: Plenum.

Bray, G.A. (1989). Obesity: Basic considerations and clinical approaches. *Disease a Month, 35*, 449–537.

Brazelton, T. Berry. (1983). *Neonatal behavioral assessment scale* (2nd ed.). Philadelphia: Lippincott.

Brazelton, T. Berry. (1990). Saving the bathwater. *Child Development, 61,* 1661–1671.

Brazelton, T. Berry, Nugent, J.K., & Lester, B.M. (1987). Neonatal behavioral assessment scale. In Joy Doniger Osofsky (Ed.), *Handbook of infant development* (2nd ed.). New York: Wiley.

Breakey, G., & Pratt, B. (1991). Healthy growth for Hawaii's "Healthy Start": Toward a systematic statewide approach to the prevention of child abuse and neglect. *Zero to Three* (Bulletin of the National Center for Clinical Infant Programs), *11,* 16–22.

Bremner, J. Gavin. (1988). *Infancy.* Oxford, England: Basil Blackwell.

Bretherton, Inge. (1989). Pretense: The form and function of make-believe play. *Developmental Review, 9,* 383–401.

Bretherton, Inge. (1992). The origins of attachment theory: John Bowlby and Mary Ainsworth. *Developmental Psychology, 28,* 759–775.

Bretherton, Inge, & Beeghly, M. (1982). Talking about internal states: The acquisition of an explicit theory of mind. *Developmental Psychology, 18,* 906–921.

Bretherton, Inge, & Waters, Everett. (1985). Growing points of attachment theory and research. *Monographs of the Society for Research in Child Development, 50* (1–2, Serial No. 209).

Bretherton, I., & Watson, M.W. (Eds.). (1990). Children's perspectives on the family. *New Directions for Child Development, 48.* San Francisco: Jossey-Bass.

Briere, J.M., & Elliott, D.M. (1994). Immediate and long-term impacts of child sexual abuse. *The Future of Children, 4,* 54–69.

Bril, B. (1986). Motor development and cultural attitudes. In H.T.A. Whiting & M.G. Wade (Eds.), *Themes in motor development.* Dordrecht, Netherlands: Martinus Nijhoff Publishers.

Brody, G.H., Stoneman, Z., McCoy, J.K., & Forehand, R. (1992). Contemporaneous and longitudinal associations of sibling conflict with family relationship assessments and family discussions about sibling problems. *Child Development, 63,* 391–400.

Brody, Jane E. (1993, August 11). Personal health: Skipping vaccinations puts children at risk. *The New York Times.*

Brody, Jane E. (1994, April 6). The value of breast milk. *The New York Times.*

Bronfenbrenner, Urie. (1977). Toward an experimental ecology of human development. *American Psychologist, 32,* 513–531.

Bronfenbrenner, Urie. (1979). *The ecology of human development: Experiments by nature and design.* Cambridge, MA: Harvard University Press.

Bronfenbrenner, Urie. (1986). Ecology of the family as a context for human development research perspectives. *Developmental Psychology, 22,* 723–742.

Bronson, Gordon W. (1990). Changes in infants' visual scanning across the 2- to 14-week age period. *Journal of Experimental Child Psychology, 49,* 101–125.

Bronson, Wanda C. (1985). Growth in the organization of behavior over the second year of life. *Developmental Psychology, 21,* 108–117.

Bronstein, Phyllis. (1984). Differences in mothers' and fathers' behaviors toward children: A cross-cultural comparison. *Developmental Psychology, 20,* 995–1003.

Brooks-Gunn, Jeanne. (1991). Maturational timing variations in adolescent girls, antecedents of. In Richard M. Lerner, Ann C. Petersen, & Jeanne Brooks-Gunn (Eds.), *Encyclopedia of adolescence* (Vol. 2). New York: Garland.

Brooks-Gunn, Jeanne. (1991). Maturational timing variations in adolescent girls, consequences of. In Richard M. Lerner, Ann C. Petersen, & Jeanne Brooks-Gunn (Eds.), *Encyclopedia of adolescence* (Vol. 2). New York: Garland.

Brooks-Gunn, Jeanne, Attie, I., Burrow, C., Rosso, J.T., & Warren, M.P. (1989). The impact of puberty on body and eating concerns in athletic and nonathletic contexts. *Journal of Early Adolescence, 9,* 269–290.

Brooks-Gunn, Jeanne, Klebanov, P.K., Liaw, F., & Spiker, D. (1993). Enhancing the development of low-birthweight, premature infants: Changes in cognition and behavior over the first three years. *Child Development, 64,* 736–753.

Brooks-Gunn, Jeanne, & Reiter, Edward O. (1990). The role of pubertal processes. In Shirley S. Feldman & Glenn R. Elliott (Eds.), *At the threshold: The developing adolescent.* Cambridge, MA: Harvard University Press.

Brooks-Gunn, Jeanne, Warren, M.P., Samelson, M., & Fox, R. (1986). Physical similarity of and disclosure of menarchal status to friends: Effects of grade and pubertal status. *Journal of Early Adolescence, 6,* 3–14.

Brown, A.L., Kane, M.J., & Echols, K. (1986). Young children's mental models determine analogical transfer across problems with a common goal structure. *Cognitive Development, 1,* 103–122.

Brown, B.B. (1990). Peer groups and peer cultures. In S.S. Feldman & G.R. Elliott (Eds.), *At the threshold: The developing adolescent.* Cambridge, MA: Harvard University Press.

Brown, B.B, Lohr, Mary Jane, & McClenahan, Eben L. (1986). Early adolescents' perception of peer pressure. *Journal of Early Adolescence, 6,* 139–154.

Brown, B.B., Mounts, N., Lamborn, S.D., & Steinberg, L. (1993). Parenting practices and peer group affiliation in adolescence. *Child Development, 64,* 467–482.

Brown, Barry S., & Mills, Arnold R. (1987). *Youth at high risk for substance abuse.* Rockville, MD: National Institute on Drug Abuse.

Brown, J.R., & Dunn, J. (1992). Talk with your mother or your sibling? Developmental changes in early family conversations about feelings. *Child Development, 63,* 336–349.

Brown, Steven M. (1993). Motivational effects on test scores of elementary students. Journal of Educational Research, 86, 133–136.

Brown, W.T., Jenkins, E.C., Gross, A.C., Chan, C.B., Krawczun, M.S., Duncan, C.J., Sklower, S.L., & Fisch, G.S. (1987). Further evidence for genetic heterogeneity in the Fragile X syndrome. *Human Genetics, 75,* 311–321.

Bruch, Hilde. (1978). *The golden cage: The enigma of anorexia nervosa.* Cambridge, MA: Harvard University Press.

Bruck, M., Ceci, S.J., Francoeur, E., & Barr, R. (in press). "I hardly cried when I got my shot!": Influencing children's reports about a visit to their pediatrician. *Child Development.*

Bruner, Jerome S. (1982). The organization of action and the nature of adult-infant transaction. In M. von Cranach & R. Harre (Eds.), *The analysis of action.* Cambridge, England: Cambridge University Press.

Bryan, E. (1992). *Twins, triplets, and more.* New York: St. Martin's Press.

Bryant, B.K. (1985). The neighborhood walk: Sources of support in middle childhood. *Monographs of the Society for Research in Child Development, 50* (3, Serial No. 210).

Bryant, B.K. (1992). Conflict resolution strategies in relation to children's peer relations. *Journal of Applied Developmental Psychology, 13,* 35–50.

Bryant, Peter E. (1985). The distinction between knowing when to do a sum and knowing how to do it. *Educational Psychology, 5,* 207–215.

Buhrmester, D. (1990). Intimacy of friendship, interpersonal competence, and adjustment during preadolescence and adolescence. *Child Development, 61,* 1101–1111.

Buhrmester, D., Camparo, L., Christensen, A., Gonzalez, L.S., & Hinshaw, S.P. (1992). Mothers and fathers interacting in dyads and triads with normal and hyperactive sons. *Developmental Psychology, 28,* 500–509.

Buhrmester, D., & Furman, W. (1987). The development of companionship and intimacy. *Child Development, 58,* 1101–1113.

Burchinal, Margaret, Lee, Marvin, & Ramey, Craig. (1989). Type of day care and preschool intellectual development in disadvantaged children. *Child Development, 60,* 128–137.

Burelson, Brant R. (1982). The development of comforting communication skills in childhood and adolescence. *Child Development,* 1578–1588.

Burns, Alisa. (1992). Mother-headed families: An international perspective and the case of Australia. *Society for Research in Child Development: Social Policy Report, 6,* 1–22.

Bushnell, E.W., & Boudreau, J.P. (1993). Motor development and the mind: The potential role of motor abilities as a determinant of aspects of perceptual development. *Child Development, 64,* 1005–1021.

Buss, A.H. (1991). The EAS theory of temperament. In J. Strelau & A. Angleitner (Eds.), *Explorations of temperament.* New York: Plenum.

Buss, A.H., & Plomin, R. (1984). *Temperament: Early developing personality traits.* Hillsdale, NJ: Erlbaum.

Bussey, K., & Bandura, A. (1992). Self-regulatory mechanisms governing gender development. *Child Development, 63,* 1236–1250.

Butler, J., & Rovee-Collier, C. (1989). Contextual gating of memory retrieval. *Developmental Psychobiology, 22,* 533–552.

Butler, Robert N., & Golding, Jean. (1986). *From birth to five: A study of the health and behaviour of Britain's 5-year-olds.* Oxford: Pergamon.

Byne, William. (1994, May). The biological evidence challenged. *Scientific American, 270,* 50–55.

Byrne, Joseph, Ellsworth, Christine, Bowering, Elizabeth, & Vincer, Michael. (1993). Language development in low birth weight infants: The first two years. *Developmental and Behavioral Pediatrics, 14,* 21–27.

Byrnes, J.P. (1988). Formal operations: A systematic reformulation. *Developmental Review, 8,* 66–87.

Cairns, Robert B. (1983). The emergence of developmental psychology. In Paul H. Mussen (Ed.), *Handbook of child psychology: Vol. 1. History, theory, and methods.* New York: Wiley.

Cairns, Robert B., Cairns, B.D., & Neckerman, H.J. (1989). Early school dropout: Configurations and determinants. *Child Development, 60,* 1437–1452.

Caldwell, Bettye M., & Bradley, Robert H. (1984). *Home observation for the measurement of the environment.* New York: Dorsey.

Cameron, Judy L. (1990). Factors controlling the onset of puberty in primates. In John Bancroft & June Machover Reinisch (Eds.), *Adolescence and puberty.* New York: Oxford University Press.

Campbell, Frances A., & Ramey, Craig T. (1994). Effects of early intervention on intellectual and academic achievement: A follow-up study of children from low-income families. *Child Development, 65,* 684–698.

Campbell, Rona, & MacFarlene, Alison J. (1987). *Where to be born: The debate and the evidence.* England: National Perinatal Epidemiology Unit, National Infirmary.

Campos, Joseph J., Barrett, Karen C., Lamb, Michael L., Goldsmith, H. Hill, & Stenberg, Craig. (1983). Socioemotional development. In Paul H. Mussen (Ed.), *Handbook of child psychology: Vol. 2. Infancy and developmental psychobiology.* New York: Wiley.

Camras, L.A., & Sachs, V.B. (1991). Social referencing and caretaker expressive behavior in a day care setting. *Infant Behavior and Development, 14,* 27–36.

Cantwell, D., & Baker, L. (1987). *Developmental speech and language disorders.* New York: Guilford.

Caplan, M., Vespo, J., Pedersen, J., & Hay, D.F. (1991). Conflict and its resolution in small groups of one- and two-year-olds. *Child Development, 62,* 1513–1524.

Caplan, N., Choy, M.H., & Whitmore, J.K. (1992). Indochinese refugee families and academic achievement. *Scientific American,* 36–42.

Cappelleri, J.C., Eckenrode, J., & Powers, J.L. (1993). The epidemiology of child abuse: Findings from the Second National Incidence and Prevalence Study of Child Abuse and Neglect. *American Journal of Public Health, 83,* 1622–1624.

Carew, Jean V. (1980). Experience and the development of intelligence in young children at home and in day care. *Monographs of the Society for Research in Child Development, 45* (Serial No. 187).

Carey, S. (1985). *Conceptual change in childhood.* Cambridge, MA: MIT Press.

Carey, William B., & McDevitt, Sean C. (1978). Stability and change in individual temperament diagnoses from infancy to early childhood. *Journal of the American Academy of Child Psychiatry, 17,* 331–337.

Carlson, Bruce M. (1994). *Human embryology and developmental biology.* St. Louis: Mosby.

Carmen, Elaine. (1989). Family violence and the victim-to-patient process. In Leah J. Dickstein & Carol C. Nadelson (Eds.), *Family violence: Emerging issues of national crisis.* Washington, DC: American Psychiatric Press.

Carnegie Council on Adolescent Development. (1989). *Turning points: Preparing American youth for the 21st century.* New York: Carnegie Corporation.

Caron, Albert J., & Caron, Rose F. (1981). Processing of relational information as an index of infant risk. In S.L. Friedman & M. Sigman (Eds.), *Preterm birth and psychological development*. New York: Academic Press.

Caron, Albert J., Caron, Rose F., & MacLean, D.J. (1988). Infant discrimination of naturalistic emotional expressions: The role of face and voice. *Child Development, 59,* 604–616.

Carraher, T.N., Carraher, D.W., & Schliemann, A.D. (1985). Mathematics in the streets and in schools. *British Journal of Developmental Psychology, 3,* 21–29.

Carraher, T.N., Schliemann, A.D., & Carraher, D.W. (1988). Mathematical concepts in everyday life. In G.B. Saxe & M. Gearhart (Eds.), *New directions for child development: Vol. 41. Children's mathematics*. San Francisco: Jossey-Bass.

Carter, D.B., & Middlemiss, W.A. (1992). The socialization of instrumental competence in families in the United States. In J.L. Roopnarine & D.B. Carter (Eds.), *Annual advances in applied developmental psychology: Vol. 5. Parent-child socialization in diverse cultures*. Norwood, NJ: Ablex.

Case, Robbie. (1985). *Intellectual development: Birth to adulthood*. Orlando, FL: Academic Press.

Casey, Rosemary, Levy, Susan E., Brown, Kimberly, & Brooks-Gunn, J. (1992). Impaired emotional health in children with mild reading disability. *Journal of Developmental and Behavioral Pediatrics, 13,* 256–260.

Casey, R., & Rozin, Paul. (1989). Changing children's food preferences: Parent opinions. *Appetite, 12,* 171–182.

Caskey, C.T. (1992). DNA-based medicine: Prevention and therapy. In D.J. Kevles & L. Hood (Eds.), *The code of codes: Scientific and social issues in the Human Genome Project*. Cambridge, MA: Harvard University Press.

Caskey, C.T., Pizzuti, A., Fu, Y.-H., Fenwick, R.G., Jr., & Nelson, D.L. (1992). Triple repeat mutations in human disease. *Science, 256,* 784–789.

Caspi, Avshalom, Elder, Glen H., & Bem, Daryl J. (1988). Moving away from the world: Life-course patterns of shy children. *Developmental Psychology, 24,* 824–831.

Caspi, Avshalom, Elder, Glen H., & Herbener, Ellen S. (1990). Childhood personality and the prediction of life-course patterns. In Lee N. Robins & Michael Rutter (Eds.), *Straight and devious pathways from childhood to adulthood*. Cambridge, England: Cambridge University Press.

Caspi, A., & Moffitt, T.E. (1991). Individual differences are accentuated during periods of social change: The sample case of girls at puberty. *Journal of Personality and Social Psychology, 61,* 157–168.

Cassill, Kay. (1982). *Twins reared apart*. New York: Atheneum.

Catron, T.F., & Masters, J.C. (1993). Mothers' and children's conceptualizations of corporal punishment. *Child Development, 64,* 1815–1828.

Ceci, Stephen J. (1991). How much does schooling influence cognitive and intellectual development? *Developmental Psychology, 27,* 703–722.

Ceci, Stephen J. (1991). How much does schooling influence general intelligence and its cognitive components? *Developmental Psychology, 27,* 703–722.

Ceci, Stephen J., & Bruck, M. (1993). Child witnesses: Translating research into policy. *Social Policy Report of the Society for Research in Child Development, 7,* 1–30.

Ceci, Stephen J., & Bruck, M. (1993). The suggestibility of the child witness. *Psychological Bulletin, 113,* 403–439.

Ceci, Stephen J., Toglia, Michael P., & Ross, David F. (1990). The suggestibility of preschoolers' recollections: Historical perspectives on current problems. In Robyn Fivush & Judith A. Hudson (Eds.), *Knowing and remembering in young children*. Cambridge, England: Cambridge University Press.

Cefalo, Robert C., & Moos, Merry-K. (1988). *Preconceptual health promotion*. Rockville, MD: Aspen.

Centers for Disease Control. (1989, May 7). *AIDS weekly surveillance report*. Atlanta.

Centers for Disease Control. (1992). Selected behaviors that increase the risk for HIV infection among high school students—U.S. 1990. *Morbidity and Mortality Weekly Report, 41,* 231–240.

Centers for Disease Control. (1992). *Setting the national agenda for injury control in the 1990s*. Washington, DC: United States Department of Health and Human Services, Public Health Service.

Centers for Disease Control, Division of STD/HIV Prevention. (1992). *1991 Annual Report*. Atlanta.

Centers for Disease Control and Prevention. (1993, September 24). Summary of notifiable diseases, United States, 1992. *Morbidity and Mortality Weekly Report, 41*.

Centers for Disease Control and Prevention. (1993, December 31). Recommendations of the International Task Force for Disease Eradication. *Morbidity and Mortality Weekly Report, 42,* 17.

Centers for Disease Control and Prevention. (1994, January 28). General recommendations on immunization: Recommendations of the Advisory Committee on Immunization Practices. *Morbidity and Mortality Weekly Report, 43*.

Centers for Disease Control and Prevention. (1994, March 4). Health risk behaviors among adolescents who do and do not attend school: United States, 1992. *Morbidity and Mortality Weekly Report, 43,* 129–132.

Centers for Disease Control and Prevention. (1994, April 22). *Morbidity and Mortality Weekly Report, 43*.

Centers for Disease Control and Prevention, (1994, April 29). *Morbidity and Mortality Weekly Report, 43*.

Centers for Disease Control and Prevention. (1994, May 6). Monthly immunization table. *Morbidity and Mortality Weekly Report, 43,* 323.

Chalfant, J.C. (1989). Learning disabilities: Policy issues and promising approaches. *American Psychologist, 44,* 392–398.

Chandler, Lynette A. (1990). Neuromotor assessment. In Elizabeth D. Gibbs & Douglas M. Teti (Eds.), *Interdisciplinary assessment of infants*. Baltimore: Brookes.

Chandler, Michael. (1987). The Othello effect: Essay on the emergence and eclipse of skeptical doubt. *Human Development, 30,* 137–159.

Chappell, Patricia A., & Steitz, Jean A. (1993). Young children's human figure drawings and cognitive development. *Perceptual and Motor Skills, 76,* 611–617.

Charlish, Anne. (1991). *Birth-tech: Tests and technology in pregnancy and birth*. New York: Facts on File.

Chasnoff, Ira J. (1989). Drug use and women: Establishing a standard of care. In Donald Hutchings (Ed.), *Prenatal abuse of licit and illicit drugs*. New York: New York Academy of Sciences.

Chasnoff, Ira J., Chisu, G.M., & Kaplan, W.E. (1988). Maternal cocaine use and genitourinary tract malformations. *Teratology, 37*, 201–204.

Chen, S.-J., & Miyake, K. (1986). Japanese studies of infant development. In H. Stevenson, H. Azuma, & K. Hakuta (Eds.), *Child development and education in Japan*. New York: Freeman.

Chess, Stella, & Thomas, Alexander. (1990). Continuities and discontinuities in development. In Lee N. Robins & Michael Rutter (Ed.), *Straight and devious pathways from childhood to adulthood*. New York: Cambridge University Press.

Chess, Stella, Thomas, Alexander, & Birch, Herbert. (1965). *If your child is a person*. New York: Viking Press.

Chi, M.T.H. (1978). Knowledge structures and memory development. In R.S. Siegler (Ed.), *Children's thinking: What develops?* Hillsdale, NJ: Erlbaum.

Chi, M.T.H., Hutchinson, J.E., & Robin, A.F. (1989). How inferences about novel domain-related concepts can be constrained by structured knowledge. *Merrill-Palmer Quarterly, 35*, 27–62.

Children's Defense Fund. (1994). *The state of America's children yearbook 1994*. Washington, DC: Publications Department.

Chin, J., Sato, D.A., & Mann, J.M. (1990). Projections of HIV infections and AIDS cases to the year 2000. *Bulletin of the World Health Organization, 68*, 1–32.

Chira, Susan. (1984, February 11). Town experiment cuts TV. *The New York Times*.

Chomsky, Noam. (1968). *Language and mind*. New York: Harcourt, Brace, World.

Chomsky, Noam. (1980). *Rules and representations*. New York: Columbia University Press.

Christophersen, Edward R. (1989). Injury control. *American Psychologist, 44*, 237–241.

Cicchetti, Dante. (1990). The organization and coherence of socioemotional, cognitive, and representational development: Illustrations through a developmental psychopathology perspective on Down syndrome and child maltreatment. In R.A. Thompson (Ed.), *Nebraska symposium on motivation: Vol. 36. Socioemotional development*. Lincoln: University of Nebraska Press.

Cicchetti, Dante. (1991). Defining psychological maltreatment: Reflections and future directions (Editorial). *Development and Psychopathology, 3*, 1–2.

Cicchetti, Dante. (1993). Developmental psychopathology: Reactions, reflections, projections. *Developmental Review, 13*, 471–502.

Cicchetti, Dante, & Beeghly, Marjorie. (1990). *Children with Down Syndrome: A developmental perspective*. Cambridge, England: Cambridge University Press.

Cicchetti, Dante, & Carlson, Vicki. (Eds.). (1989). *Child maltreatment: Theory and research on the causes and consequences of child abuse and neglect*. Cambridge, England: Cambridge University Press.

Cicchetti, Dante, Toth, S.L., & Hennessy, K. (1993). Child maltreatment and school adaptation: Problems and promises. In D. Cicchetti & S.L. Toth (Eds.), *Advances in applied developmental psychology series: Vol. 8. Child abuse, child development, and social policy*. Norwood, NJ: Ablex.

Cillessen, A.H.N., van Ijzendoorn, H.W., van Lieshout, C.F.M., & Hartup, W.W. (1992). Heterogeneity among peer-rejected boys: Subtypes and stabilities. *Child Development, 63*, 893–905.

Clark, Eve V. (1982). The young word maker: A case study of innovation in the child's lexicon. In Eric Wanner & Lila R. Gleitman (Eds.), *Language acquisition: The state of the art*. Cambridge, England: Cambridge University Press.

Clark, E. (1990). On the pragmatics of contrast. *Journal of Child Language, 17*, 417–431.

Clark, Jane E., & Phillips, Sally J. (1985). A developmental sequence of the standing long jump. In Jane E. Clark & James H. Humphrey (Eds.), *Motor development: Current selected research*. Princeton, NJ: Princeton Book Company.

Clark, Robert D. (1983). *Family life and school achievement: Why poor black children succeed or fail*. Chicago: University of Chicago Press.

Clarke-Stewart, K. Alison. (1978). And daddy makes three: The father's impact on mother and young child. *Child Development, 49*, 466–478.

Clarke-Stewart, K. Alison. (1989). Infant day care: Maligned or malignant? *American Psychologist, 44*, 266–273.

Clarkson, Marsha G., & Berg, W. Keith. (1983). Cardiac orienting and vowel discrimination in newborns: Crucial stimulus parameters. *Child Development, 54*, 162–171.

Clarkson, Marsha G., Clifton, Rachel K., & Morrongiello, Barbara A. (1985). The effects of sound duration on newborns' head orientation. *Journal of Experimental Child Psychology, 39*, 20–36.

Clemens, Andra W. & Axelson, Leland J. (1985). The not-so-empty nest: The return of the fledgling adult. *Family Relations, 34*, 259–264.

Coe, Christopher, Kayashi, Kevin T., & Levine, Seymour. (1988). Hormones and behavior at puberty: Activation or concatenation? In Megan R. Gunnar & W. Andrew Collins (Eds.), *Development during the transition to adolescence*. Hillsdale, NJ: Erlbaum.

Coelho, Elizabeth. (1991). Social integration of immigrant and refugee children. In J. Porter (Ed.), *New Canadian voices*. Toronto: Wall and Emerson.

Cohen, L.B., & Oakes, L.M. (1993). How infants perceive a simple causal event. *Developmental Psychology, 29*, 421–433.

Cohn, Jeffrey F., Campbell, S.B., Matias, R., & Hopkins, J. (1990). Face-to-face interactions of postpartum depressed and nondepressed mother-infant pairs at 2 months. *Developmental Psychology, 26*, 15–23.

Cohn, Jeffrey F., & Tronick, Edward Z. (1983). Three-month-old infants' reaction to stimulated maternal depression. *Child Development, 54*, 185–193.

Cohn, Jeffrey F., & Tronick, Edward Z. (1987). Mother-infant face to face interaction: The sequence of dyadic states at 3, 6, and 9 months. *Developmental Psychology, 23*, 68–77.

Cohn, Lawrence D.S., & Adler, Nancy E. (1992). Female and male perception of ideal body shapes. *Psychology of Women Quarterly, 16*, 69–79.

Coie, John D., & Cillessen, A.H.N. (1993). Peer rejection: Origins and effects on children's development. *Current Directions in Psychological Science, 2,* 89–92.

Coie, John D., & Dodge, Kenneth A. (1983). Continuities and changes in children's social status: A five-year longitudinal study. *Merrill-Palmer Quarterly, 29,* 261–282.

Coie, John D., Dodge, Kenneth A., Terry, Robert, & Wright, Virginia. (1991). The role of aggression in peer relations: An analysis of aggression episodes in boys' play groups. *Child Development, 62,* 812–826.

Coie, John D., & Koeppl, G.K. (1990). Adapting intervention to the problems of aggressive and disruptive rejected children. In S.R. Asher & J.D. Coie (Eds.), *Peer rejection in childhood.* Cambridge, England: Cambridge University Press.

Coie, John D., Lochman, J.E., Terry, R., & Hyman, C. (1992). Predicting early adolescent disorder from childhood aggression and peer rejection. *Journal of Consulting and Clinical Psychology, 60,* 783–792.

Colby, Anne, & Kohlberg, Lawrence. (1987). *The measurement of moral judgment: Vol. 1. Theoretical foundations and research validation.* Cambridge, England: Cambridge University Press.

Colby, Anne, Kohlberg, Lawrence, Gibbs, John, & Lieberman, Marcus. (1983). A longitudinal study of moral development. *Monographs of the Society for Research in Child Development, 48* (1–2, Serial No. 200).

Cole, M. (1992). Culture in development. In M.H. Bornstein & M.E. Lamb (Eds.), *Developmental psychology: An advanced textbook* (3rd ed.). Hillsdale, NJ: Erlbaum.

Cole, P.M., Barrett, K.C., & Zahn-Waxler, C. (1992). Emotion displays in two-year-olds during mishaps. *Child Development, 63,* 314–324.

Coleman, J.C., & Hendry, L. (1990). *The nature of adolescence* (2nd ed.). London: Routledge.

Coleman, M., & Ganong, L.H. (1991). Remarriage and stepfamily research in the 1980s: Increased interest in an old family form. In A. Booth (Ed.), *Contemporary families: Looking forward, looking back.* Minneapolis: National Council on Family Relations.

Coles, Robert. (1990). *The spiritual life of children.* Boston: Houghton Mifflin.

Collins, W. Andrew. (1990). Parent-child relationships in the transition to adolescence: Continuity and change in interaction, affect, and cognition. In R. Montemayor, G. Adams, & T. Gullotta (Eds.), *From childhood to adolescence: A transitional period? Advances in adolescent development: Vol. 2. The transition from childhood to adolescence.* Beverly Hills, CA: Sage.

Collins, W. Andrew, & Russell, G. (1991). Mother-child and father-child relationships in middle childhood and adolescence: A developmental analysis. *Developmental Psychology, 11,* 99–136.

Colombo, J., Mitchell, D.W., Coldren, J.T., & Freeseman, L.J. (1991). Individual differences in infant visual attention: Are short lookers faster processors or feature processors? *Child Development, 62,* 1247–1257.

Compas, Bruce E., Banez, Gerard A., Malcarne, Vanessa, & Worsham, Nancy. (1991). Perceived control and coping with stress: A developmental perspective. *Journal of Social Issues, 47,* 23–34.

Condry, John. (1989). *The psychology of television.* Hillsdale, NJ: Erlbaum.

Conger, R.D., Conger, K.J., Elder, G.H., Jr., Lorenz, F.O., Simons, R.L., & Whitbeck, L.B. (1992). A family process model of economic hardship and adjustment of early adolescent boys. *Child Development, 63,* 526–541.

Conger, R.D., Elder, G., Lorenz, F., Conger, K., Simons, R., Whitbeck, L., Huck, S., & Melby, J. (1990). Linking economic hardship to marital quality and instability. *Journal of Marriage and the Family, 52,* 643–656.

Connor, J.M., & Ferguson-Smith, M.A. (1991). *Essential medical genetics.* Oxford, England: Blackwell Scientific Publications.

Consortium for Longitudinal Studies. (1983). *As the twig is bent: Lasting effects of preschool programs.* Hillsdale, NJ: Erlbaum.

Cook, Thomas D., Appleton, Hilary, Conner, Ross F., Shaffer, Ann, Tamkin, Gary, & Weber, Stephen J. (1975). *"Sesame Street" revisited.* New York: Russell Sage.

Cooney, George H., Bell, A., McBride, W., & Carter, C. (1989). Low-level exposures to lead: The Sydney Lead Study. *Developmental Medicine and Child Neurology, 31,* 640–649.

Cooper, R.O. (1993). The effect of prosody on young infants' speech perception. In C. Rovee-Collier & L.P. Lipsitt (Eds.), *Advances in infancy research* (Vol. 8). Norwood, NJ: Ablex.

Cooper, R.P., & Aslin, R.N. (1990). Preference for infant-directed speech in the first month after birth. *Child Development, 61,* 1584–1595.

Copeland, L., Wolraich, M., Lindgren, S., Milich, R., & Woolson, R. (1987). Pediatricians' reported practices in the assessment and treatment of attention deficit disorders. *Developmental and Behavioral Pediatrics, 8,* 191–197.

Corsaro, W.A. (1985). *Friendship and peer culture in the early years.* Norwood, NJ: Ablex.

Corse, S.J., Schmid, K., & Trickett, P.K. (1990). Social network characteristics of mothers in abusing and nonabusing families and their relationships to parenting beliefs. *Journal of Community Psychology, 18,* 44–59.

Coste, Joel, Job-Spira, Nadine, & Fernandez, Herve. (1991). Increased risk of ectopic pregnancy with maternal cigarette smoking. *American Journal of Public Health, 81,* 199–201.

Cotten, N.U., Resnick, J., Browne, D.C., Martin, S.L., McCarraher, D.R., & Woods, J. (1994). Aggression and fighting behavior among African-American adolescents: Individual and family factors. *American Journal of Public Health, 84,* 618–622.

Covell, Katherine, & Miles, Brenda. (1992). Children's beliefs about strategies to reduce parental anger. *Child Development, 63,* 381–390.

Cowan, C.P., & Cowan, P.A. (1992). *When partners become parents.* New York: Basic Books.

Cowan, C.P., Cowan, P.A., Heming, G., & Miller, N.B. (1992). Becoming a family: Marriage, parenting, and child development. In P.A. Cowan & M. Hetherington (Eds.), *Family transitions.* Hillsdale, NJ: Erlbaum.

Crick, N.R., & Ladd, G.W. (1993). Children's perceptions of their peer experiences: Attributions, loneliness, social anxiety, and social avoidance. *Developmental Psychology, 29,* 244–254.

Crittenden, Patricia M. (1992). The social ecology of treatment: Case study of a service system for maltreated children. *American Journal of Orthopsychiatry, 62,* 22–34.

Crockenberg, S., & Litman, C. (1990). Autonomy as competence in 2-year-olds: Maternal correlates of child defiance, compliance, and self-assertion. *Developmental Psychology, 26,* 961–971.

Cromer, B.A., Tarnowski, K.J., Stein, A.M., Harton, P., & Thornton, D.J. (1990). The school breakfast program and cognition in adolescents. *Journal of Developmental and Behavioral Pediatrics, 11,* 295–300.

Cromwell, Rue L. (1993). Searching for the origins of schizophrenia. *Psychological Science, 4,* 276–279.

Cross, W.W., Jr. (1991). *Shades of black: Diversity in African-American identity.* Philadelphia: Temple University Press.

Crowell, J.A., & Feldman, S.S. (1988). Mothers' internal models of relationships and children's behavioral and developmental status: A study of mother-child interaction. *Child Development, 59,* 1273–1283.

Crowell, J.A., & Feldman, S.S. (1991). Mothers' working models of attachment relationships and mother and child behavior during separation and reunion. *Developmental Psychology, 27,* 597–605.

Crum, Julie F., & Eckert, Helen M. (1985). Play patterns of primary school children. In Jane E. Clark & James H. Humphrey (Eds.), *Motor development: Current selected research.* Princeton, NJ: Princeton Book Company.

Csikszentmihalyi, M., & Larson, R. (1984). *Being adolescent.* New York: Basic Books.

Csikszentmihalyi, M., & Rathunde, K. (1993). The measurement of flow in everyday life: Toward a theory of emergent motivation. In J.E. Jacobs (Ed.), *Nebraska symposium on motivation: Vol. 40. Developmental perspectives on motivation.* Lincoln: University of Nebraska Press.

Csikszentmihalyi, M., Rathunde, K., & Whalen, S. (1993). *Talented teenagers: A longitudinal study of their development.* New York: Cambridge University Press.

Culotta, Elizabeth, & Koshland, Daniel E. (1993). P53 sweeps through cancer research. *Science, 262,* 1958–1961.

Cummings, E.M. (1987). Coping with background anger in early childhood. *Child Development, 58,* 976–984.

Cummings, E.M. (1994). Marital conflict and children's functioning. *Social Development, 3,* 16–36.

Cummings, E.M., & Davies, P. (1994). *Children and marital conflict: The impact of family dispute and resolution.* New York: Guilford.

Cummings, E.M., Hennessy, K.D., Rabideau, G.J., & Cicchetti, D. (1994). Responses of physically abused boys to interadult anger involving their mothers. *Development and Psychopathology, 6,* 31–41.

Cummings, E.M., Iannotti, R.J., & Zahn-Waxler, C. (1985). Influence of conflict between adults on the emotions and aggression of young children. *Developmental Psychology, 21,* 495–507.

Cummings, E.M., Zahn-Waxler, C., & Radke-Yarrow, M. (1984). Developmental changes in children's reactions to anger in the home. *Journal of Child Psychology and Psychiatry, 25,* 63–74.

Cummings, J.S., Pellegrini, D.S., Notarius, C.I., & Cummings, E.M. (1989). Children's responses to angry adult behavior as a function of marital distress and history of interparent hostility. *Child Development, 60,* 1035–1043.

Cummins, Jim. (1991). Interdependence of first- and second-language proficiency. In Ellen Bialystok (Ed.), *Language processing in bilingual children.* Cambridge, England: Cambridge University Press.

Cummins, Jim. (1994). Knowledge, power, and identity in teaching English as a second language. In Fred Genesee (Ed.), *Educating second-language children: The whole child, the whole curriculum, the whole community.* Cambridge, England: Cambridge University Press.

Curran, David K. (1987). *Adolescent suicidal behavior.* Washington, DC: Hemisphere Publishing.

Dalterio, S.L., & Fried, P.A. (1992). The effects of marijuana use on offspring. In T.B. Sonderegger (Ed.), *Perinatal substance abuse: Research, findings, and clinical implications.* Baltimore: Johns Hopkins University Press.

Daniels, Denise H., Dunn, Judy, Furstenberg, Frank, & Plomin, Robert. (1985). Environmental differences within the family and adjustment differences within pairs of adolescent siblings. *Child Development, 56,* 764–774.

Darling, N., & Steinberg, L. (1993). Parenting style as context: An integrative model. *Psychological Bulletin, 113,* 487–496.

Daro, Deborah. (1988). *Confronting child abuse.* New York: The Free Press.

Datan, Nancy. (1986). Oedipal conflict, platonic love: Centrifugal forces in intergenerational relations. In Nancy Datan, Anita L. Greene, & Hayne W. Reese (Eds.), *Life-span developmental psychology: Intergenerational relations.* Hillsdale, NJ: Erlbaum.

Davajan, Val, & Israel, Robert. (1991). Diagnosis and medical treatment of infertility. In Annette L. Stanton & Christine Dunkel-Schetter (Eds.), *Infertility.* New York: Plenum.

Davidson, Lucy. (1986, March 7). Is teenage suicide contagious? *Atlanta Constitution,* B1, B7–B9.

Davies, Bronwyn. (1982). *Life in the classroom and playground.* London: Routledge and Kegan Paul.

Davies, D.P., & Gantley, M. (1994). *Archives of Disease in Childhood, 70,* 349–353.

Davies, P.T., & Cummings, E.M. (1994). Marital conflict and child adjustment: An emotional security hypothesis. *Psychological Bulletin,* in press.

Davis, Janet M., & Rovee-Collier, Carolyn. (1983). Alleviated forgetting of a learned contingency in 8-week-old infants. *Developmental Psychology, 19,* 353–365.

Davis-Floyd, Robbie E. (1992). *Birth as an American rite of passage.* Berkeley: University of California Press.

Dawood, M. Yusoff. (1985). Overall approach to the management of dysmenorrhea. In M. Yusoff Dawood, John L. McGuire, & Laurence M. Demers (Eds.), *Premenstrual syndrome and dysmenorrhea.* Baltimore: Urban and Schwartzenberg.

Dawson, Deborah A. (1991). Family structure and children's health and well-being: Data from the 1988 national health interview study on child health. *Journal of Marriage and the Family, 53,* 573–584.

Dawson, G. (in press). Frontal electroencephalographic correlates of individual differences in emotional expression in infants. In N. Fox (Ed.), Emotion regulation: Behavioral and biological considerations. *Monographs of the Society for Research in Child Development.*

DeCasper, Anthony J., & Fifer, William P. (1980). Of human bonding: Newborns prefer their mothers' voices. *Science, 208,* 1174–1175.

DeCasper, Anthony J., & Spence, M.J. (1986). Prenatal maternal speech influences newborns' perception of speech sounds. *Infant Behavior and Development, 9,* 133–150.

Dekovic, M., & Janssens, J.M.A.M. (1992). Parents' child-rearing style and child's sociometric status. *Developmental Psychology, 28,* 925–932.

Delpit, L.D. (1988). The silenced dialogue: Power and pedagogy in educating other people's children. *Harvard Educational Review, 58,* 280–298.

DeMarie-Dreblow, D., & Miller, P. (1988). The development of children's strategies for selective attention: Evidence for a transitional period. *Child Development, 59,* 1504–1513.

Demo, David H. (1992). Parent-child relations: Assessing recent changes. *Journal of Marriage and the Family, 54,* 104–117.

Demo, David H., & Acock, A.C. (1991). The impact of divorce on children. In A. Booth (Ed.), *Contemporary families: Looking forward, looking back.* Minneapolis: National Council on Family Relations.

Denham, S.A., & Holt, R.W. (1993). Preschoolers' likability as cause or consequence of their social behavior. *Developmental Psychology, 29,* 271–275.

Denham, S.A., McKinley, M., Couchoud, E.A., & Holt, R. (1990). Emotional and behavioral predictors of preschool peer ratings. *Child Development, 61,* 1145–1152.

Denham, S.A., Renwick, S.M., & Hold, R.W. (1991). Working and playing together: Prediction of preschool social-emotional competence from mother-child interaction. *Child Development, 62,* 242–249.

DeParle, Jason. (1991, March 12). A state's fight to save babies enters round 2. *The New York Times,* A1, A20.

Depue, Richard A., Luciana, Monica, Arbisi, Paul, Collins, Paul, & Leon, Arthur. (1994). Dopamine and the structure of personality: Relation of agonist-induced dopamine activity to positive emotionality. *Journal of Personality and Social Psychology, 67,* 485–498.

de Villiers, Jill G., & de Villiers, Peter A. (1978). *Language acquisition.* Cambridge, MA: Harvard University Press.

de Villiers, Jill G., & de Villiers, Peter A. (1986). *The acquisition of English.* Hillsdale, NJ: Erlbaum.

de Villiers, Peter A., & de Villiers, Jill G. (1992). Language development. In M.H. Bornstein & M.E. Lamb (Eds.), *Developmental psychology: An advanced textbook* (3rd ed.). Hillsdale, NJ: Erlbaum.

Deyoung, Yolanda, & Zigler, Edward F. (1994). Machismo in two cultures: Relation to punitive child-rearing practices. *American Journal of Orthopsychiatry, 64,* 386–395.

Diamond, A. (1990). Neuropsychological insights into the meaning of object concept development. In S. Carey & R. Gelman (Eds.), *The epigenesis of mind: Essays on biology and cognition.* Hillsdale, NJ: Erlbaum.

Diamond, Marion Cleeves. (1988). *Enriching heredity.* New York: The Free Press.

Diaz, Rafael M. (1985). Bilingual cognitive development: Addressing three gaps in current research. *Child Development, 56,* 1376–1388.

Diaz, Rafael M. (1987). The private speech of young children at risk: A test of three deficit hypotheses. *Early Childhood Research Quarterly, 2,* 181–197.

Diaz, Rafael M., & Klinger, Cynthia. (1991). Toward an explanatory model of the interaction between bilingualism and cognitive development. In Ellen Bialystok (Ed.), *Language processing in bilingual children.* Cambridge, England: Cambridge University Press.

Dickerson, Leah J., & Nadelson, Carol (Eds.). (1989). *Family violence: Emerging issues of national crisis.* Washington, DC: American Psychiatric Press.

Dickinson, David K. (1984). First impressions: Children's knowledge of words gained from a single exposure. *Applied Psycholinguistics, 5,* 359–374.

Dick-Read, Grantly. (1972). *Childbirth without fear: The original approach to natural childbirth* (rev. ed.). Helen Wessel & Harlan F. Ellis (Eds.). New York: Harper & Row.

Dickstein, S., & Parke, R.D. (1988). Social referencing in infancy: A glance at fathers and marriage. *Child Development, 59,* 506–511.

DiClemente, Ralph J. (1990). The emergence of adolescents as a risk group for human immunodeficiency virus infection. *Journal of Adolescent Research, 5,* 7–17.

Dietz, William H., Jr., & Gortmaker, Steven L. (1985). Do we fatten our children at the television set? Obesity and television viewing in children and adolescents. *Pediatrics, 75,* 807–812.

DiPietro, Janet Ann. (1981). Rough and tumble play: A function of gender. *Developmental Psychology, 17,* 50–58.

Dishion, T.J. (1990). The family ecology of boys' peer relations in middle childhood. *Child Development, 61,* 874–892.

Dix, T. (1991). The affective organization of parenting: Adaptive and maladaptive processes. *Psychological Bulletin, 110,* 3–25.

Dix, T., Ruble, D.N., Grusec, J.E., & Nixon, S. (1986). Social cognition in parents. Inferential and affective reactions to children of three age levels. *Child Development, 57,* 879–894.

Dobbing, John (Ed.). (1987). *Early nutrition and later achievement.* London: Academic Press.

Dobkin, Leah. (1992). If you build it, they may not come. *Generations, 16* (2), 31–32.

Dockrell, J., Campbell, R., & Neilson, I. (1980). Conservation accidents revisited. *International Journal of Behavioral Development, 3,* 423–439.

Dodge, Kenneth A. (1986). A social information processing model of social competence in children. In M. Perlmutter (Ed.), *Minnesota symposia on child psychology: Vol. 18. Cognitive perspectives on children's social and behavioral development.* Hillsdale, NJ: Erlbaum.

Dodge, Kenneth A., Coie, J.D., Pettit, G.S., & Price, J.M. (1990). Peer status and aggression in boys' groups: Developmental and contextual analyses. *Child Development, 61,* 1289–1309.

Dodge, Kenneth A., & Feldman, E. (1990). Issues in social cognition and sociometric status. In S.R. Asher & J.D. Coie (Eds.), *Peer rejection in childhood.* Cambridge, England: Cambridge University Press.

Dodge, Kenneth A., Murphy, Roberta R., & Buchsbaum, Kathy. (1984). The assessment of intention-cue detection skills in children: Implications for developmental psychopathology. *Child Development, 55,* 163–173.

Dodge, Kenneth A., Pettit, Gregory S., & Bates, John E. (1994). Effects of physical maltreatment on the development of peer relations. *Development and Psychopathology, 6,* 43–55.

Dodge, Kenneth A., Pettit, Gregory S., McClaskey, C.L., & Brown, M.M. (1986). Social competence in children. *Monographs of the Society for Research in Child Development, 51* (2, Serial No. 213).

Dodge, Kenneth A., & Somberg, Daniel R. (1987). Hostile attributional biases among aggressive boys are exacerbated under conditions of threats to self. *Child Development, 58,* 213–224.

Dooley, David, & Catalano, R. (1988). Psychological effects of unemployment. *Journal of Social Issues, 44,* 1–191.

Dornbusch, S.M., Carlsmith, J.M., Bushwall, S.J., Ritter, P.L., Leiderman, H., Hastorf, A.H., & Gross, R.T. (1985). Single parents, extended households, and the control of adolescents. *Child Development, 56,* 326–341.

Dornbusch, S.M., Ritter, P.L., Leiderman, P.H., Roberts, D.F., & Fraleigh, M.J. (1987). The relation of parenting style to adolescent school performance. *Child Development, 58,* 1244–1257.

Dorris, Michael. (1989). *The broken cord: A family's ongoing struggle with fetal alcohol syndrome.* New York: Harper & Row.

Downs, A. Chris. (1990). The social biological constraints of social competency. In Thomas P. Gullotta, Gerald R. Adams, & Raymond R. Montemayor (Eds.), *Developing social competency in adolescence.* Newbury Park, CA: Sage.

Drotan, Dennis, Eckerle, Debby, Satola, Jackie, Pallotta, John, & Wyatt, Betsy. (1990). Maternal interactional behavior with nonorganic failure-to-thrive infants: A case comparison study. *Child Abuse and Neglect, 14,* 41–51.

Dryfoos, Joy. (1990). *Adolescents at risk: Prevalence and prevention.* New York: Oxford University Press.

Duany, Luis, & Pittman, Karen. (1990). *Latino youth at the crossroads.* Washington, DC: Children's Defense Fund.

Dubas, Judith Semon, Graber, Julia A., & Petersen, Anne C. (1991). A longitudinal investigation of adolescents' changing perceptions of pubertal timing. *Developmental Psychology, 27,* 580–586.

Duff, E. Marilyn Watson, & Cooper, Edward S. (1994). Neural tube defects in Jamaica following hurricane Gilbert. *American Journal of Public Health, 84,* 473–476.

Duggar, Celia W. (1991, March 9). Neighbors ask, how could parents let that baby starve? *The New York Times,* 25–26.

Duke-Duncan, Paula. (1991). Body image. In Richard M. Lerner, Ann C. Petersen, & Jeanne Brooks-Gunn (Eds.), *Encyclopedia of adolescence* (Vol. 1). New York: Garland.

Dunham, Roger G., & Alpert, Gregory P. (1987). Keeping juvenile delinquents in school: A prediction model. *Adolescence, 22,* 45–57.

Dunkel-Schetter, Christine, & Lobel, Marci. (1991). In Annette L. Stanton & Christine Dunkel-Schetter (Eds.), *Infertility.* New York: Plenum.

Dunn, Judy. (1983). Sibling relationships in early childhood. *Child Development, 54,* 787–811.

Dunn, Judy. (1985). *Sisters and brothers.* Cambridge, MA: Harvard University Press.

Dunn, Judy. (1988). *The beginnings of social understanding.* Cambridge, MA: Harvard University Press.

Dunn, Judy. (1992). Siblings and development. *Current Directions in Psychological Science, 1,* 6–9.

Dunn, Judy. (1993). *Young children's close relationships: Beyond attachment.* Newbury Park, CA: Sage.

Dunn, Judy, Bretherton, I., & Munn, P. (1987). Conversations about feeling states between mothers and their young children. *Developmental Psychology, 23,* 132–139.

Dunn, Judy, & Brown, J. (1991). Relationships, talk about feelings, and the development of affect regulation in early childhood. In G. Garber & K.A. Dodge (Eds.), *The development of emotion regulation and dysregulation.* New York: Cambridge University Press.

Dunn, Judy, & Brown, J. (1994). Affect expression in the family, children's understanding of emotions, and their interactions with others. *Merrill-Palmer Quarterly, 40,* 120–137.

Dunn, Judy, Brown, J., & Beardsall, L. (1991). Family talk about feeling states and children's later understanding of others' emotions. *Developmental Psychology, 27,* 448–455.

Dunn, Judy, Brown, J., Slomkowski, C., Tesla, C., & Youngblade, L. (1991). Young children's understanding of other people's feelings and beliefs: Individual differences and their antecedents. *Child Development, 62,* 1352–1366.

Dunn, Judy, & Kendrick, C. (1982). The speech of two- and three-year-olds to infant siblings: "Baby talk" and the context of communication. *Journal of Child Language, 9,* 579–595.

Dunn, Judy, & Munn, Penny. (1985). Becoming a family member: Family conflict and the development of social understanding in the second year. *Child Development, 56,* 480–492.

Dunn, Judy, & Plomin, Robert. (1990). *Separate lives: Why siblings are so different.* New York: Basic Books.

Du Randt, Ross. (1985). Ball-catching proficiency among 4-, 6-, and 8-year-old girls. In Jane E. Clark & James H. Humphrey (Eds.), *Motor development: Current selected research.* Princeton, NJ: Princeton Book Company.

DuRant, Robert H., Cadenhead, Chris, Pendergrast, Robert A., Slavens, Greg, & Linder, Charles W. (1994). *American Journal of Public Health, 84,* 612–617.

Dweck, Carol S., Davidson, W., Nelson, S., & Enna, B. (1978). Sex differences in learned helplessness, II: The contingencies of evaluative feedback in the classroom, and III: An experimental analysis. *Developmental Psychology, 14,* 268–276.

Dweck, Carol S., & Leggett, E.L. (1988). A social-cognitive approach to motivation and personality. *Psychological Review, 95,* 256–273.

Dykman, Roscoe, & Ackerman, Peggy T. (1991). Attention deficit disorder and specific reading disability: Separate but often overlapping disorders. *Journal of Learning Disabilities, 24,* 96–103.

Dykman, Roscoe, & Ackerman, Peggy T. (1993). Behavioral subtypes of attention deficit disorder. *Exceptional Children, 60,* 132–141.

East, P.L. (1991). The parent-child relationships of withdrawn, aggressive, and sociable children: Child and parent perspectives. *Merrill-Palmer Quarterly, 37,* 425–443.

East, Whitfield B., & Hensley, Larry D. (1985). The effects of selected sociocultural factors upon the overhand-throwing performance of prepubescent children. In Jane E. Clark & James

H. Humphrey (Eds.), *Motor development: Current selected research*. Princeton, NJ: Princeton Book Company.

Easterbrooks, M. Ann. (1989). Quality of attachment to mother and to father: Effects of perinatal risk status. *Child Development, 60*, 825–830.

Easterbrooks, M. Ann, & Goldberg, W.A. (1984). Toddler development in the family: Impact of father involvement and parenting characteristics. *Child Development, 55*, 740–752.

Eaton, Warren O., & Yu, Alice Piklai. (1989). Are sex differences in child motor activity level a function of sex differences in maturational status? *Child Development, 60*, 1005–1011.

Eaves, L.J., Eysenck, H.J., & Martin, N.G. (1989). *Genes, culture, and personality*. London: Academic Press.

Eccles, J.S. (1993). School and family effects on the ontogeny of children's interests, self-perceptions, and activity choices. In J.E. Jacobs (Ed.), *Nebraska symposium on motivation: Vol. 40. Developmental perspectives on motivation*. Lincoln: University of Nebraska Press.

Eccles, J.S., & Jacobs, J.E. (1986). Social forces shape math attitudes and performance. *Signs, 11*, 367–389.

Eccles, J.S., Midgley, C., Wigfield, A., Buchanan, C.M., Reuman, D., Flanagan, C., & Mac Iver, D. (1003). Development during adolescence: The impact of stage-environment fit on young adolescents' experiences in schools and in families. *American Psychologist, 48*, 90–101.

Eccles, J.S., Wigfield, A., Harold, R.D., & Blumenfeld, P. (1993). Age and gender differences in children's self- and task perceptions during elementary school. *Child Development, 64*, 830–847.

Eckenrode, J., Laird, M., & Doris, J. (1993). School performance and disciplinary problems among abused and neglected children. *Developmental Psychology, 29*, 53–62.

Eder, R.A. (1989). The emergent personologist: The structure and content of 3.5-, 5.5-, and 7.5-year-olds' concepts of themselves and other persons. *Child Development, 60*, 1218–1228.

Eder, R.A. (1990). Uncovering young children's psychological selves: Individual and developmental differences. *Child Development, 61*, 849–863.

Egeland, Byron, Carlson, Elizabeth, & Sroufe, L. Alan. (1993). Resilience as process. *Development and Psychopathology, 5*, 517–528.

Eichorn, Dorothy H. (1979). Physical development: Current foci of research. In Joy Doniger Osofsky (Ed.), *Handbook of infant development*. New York: Wiley.

Eiger, Marvin S. (1987). The feeding of infants and children. In Robert A. Hoekelman, Saul Blatman, Stanford B. Friedman, Nicholas M. Nelson, & Henry M. Seidel (Eds.), *Primary pediatric care*. St. Louis, MO: Mosby.

Eimas, Peter D., Siqueland, Einar R., Jusczyk, Peter, & Vigorito, James. (1971). Speech perception in infants. *Science, 171*, 303–306.

Eisenberg, N. (1986). *Altruistic emotion, cognition, and behavior*. Hillsdale, NJ: Erlbaum.

Eisenberg, N. (1992). *The caring child*. Cambridge, MA: Harvard University Press.

Eisenberg, N., Fabes, R.A., Bernzweig, J., Karbon, M., Poulin, R., & Hanish, L. (1993). The relations of emotionality and regulation to preschoolers' social skills and sociometric status. *Child Development, 64*, 1418–1438.

Eisenberg, N., Fabes, R.A., Carlo, G., Troyer, D., Speer, A.L., Karbon, M., & Switzer, G. (1992). The relations of maternal practices and characteristics to children's vicarious emotional responsiveness. *Child Development, 63*, 583–602.

Eisenberg, N., Fabes, R.A., Miller, P., Shell, R., & Plumlee, T. (1990). Sympathy and children's spontaneous prosocial behavior. *Merrill-Palmer Quarterly, 26*, 507–529.

Eisenberg, N., Fabes, R.A., Nyman, M., Bernzweig, J., & Pinuelas, A. (1994). The relations of emotionality and regulation to children's anger-related reactions. *Child Development, 65*, 109–128.

Eisenberg, N., Lunch, T., Shell, R., & Roth, K. (1985). Children's justifications for their adult and peer-direction compliant (prosocial and nonprosocial) behaviors. *Developmental Psychology, 21*, 325–331.

Eisenberg, N., & Mussen, P.H. (1989). *The roots of prosocial behavior in children*. Cambridge, England: Cambridge University Press.

Eisenberg, N., Shell, R., Pasternack, J., Lennon, R., Beller, R., & Mathy, R.M. (1987). Prosocial development in middle childhood: A longitudinal study. *Developmental Psychology, 23*, 712–718.

Eisenberg-Berg, Nancy, Boothby, Rita, & Matson, Tom. (1979). Correlates of preschool girls' feminine and masculine toy preferences. *Developmental Psychology, 48*, 1411–1416.

Eisenson, Jon. (1986). *Language and speech disorders in children*. New York: Pergamon.

Ekman, P., & Friesen, W. (1976). Measuring facial movement. *Environmental Psychology and Verbal Behavior, 1*, 56–75.

Ekman, P., & Friesen, W. (1978). *Facial action coding system*. Palo Alto, CA: Consulting Psychologists Press.

Ekman, P., Sorenson, E., & Friesen, W. (1969). Pancultural elements in the facial expression of emotion. *Science, 164*, 86–88.

Elder, Glen H., Jr., Nguyen, Tri Van, & Caspi, Avshalom. (1985). Linking family hardship to children's lives. *Child Development, 56*, 361–375.

Elkind, David. (1967). Egocentrism in adolescence. *Child Development, 38*, 1025–1034.

Elkind, David. (1978). *The child's reality: Three developmental themes*. Hillsdale, NJ: Erlbaum.

Elkind, David. (1984). *All grown up and no place to go*. Reading, MA: Addison-Wesley.

Ellis, Nancy Borel. (1991). An extension of the Steinberg accelerating hypothesis. *Journal of Early Adolescence, 11*, 221–235.

Ellsworth, C.P., Muir, D.W., & Hains, S.M.J. (1993). Social competence and person-object differentiation: An analysis of the still-face effect. *Developmental Psychology, 29*, 63–73.

Emde, Robert N. (1992). Individual meaning and increasing complexity: Contributions of Sigmund Freud and Rene Spitz to developmental psychology. *Developmental Psychology, 28*, 347–359.

Emde, Robert N., Biringen, Z., Clyman, R.B., & Oppenheim, D. (1991). The moral self of infancy: Affective core and procedural knowledge. *Developmental Review, 11*, 251–270.

Emde, Robert N., & Harmon, R.J. (1972). Endogenous and exogenous smiling systems in early infancy. *Journal of the American Academy of Child Psychiatry, 11*, 77–100.

Emde, Robert N., Plomin, R., Robinson, J., Corley, R., DeFries, J., Fulker, D.W., Reznick, J.S., Campos, J., Kagan, J., & Zahn-Waxler, C. (1992). Temperament, emotion, and cognition at fourteen months: The MacArthur Longitudinal Twin Study. *Child Development, 63,* 1437–1455.

Emery, Robert E. (1988). *Marriage, divorce, and children's adjustment.* Newbury Park, CA: Sage.

Enkin, Murray, Keirse, Marc J.N.C., & Chalmers, Iain. (1989). *Effective care in pregnancy and childbirth.* Oxford, England: Oxford University Press.

Enright, R.D., Lapsley, D.K., & Shukla, D.G. (1979). Adolescent egocentrism in early and late adolescence. *Adolescence, 14,* 687–695.

Epstein, M.A., Shaywitz, S.E., Shaywitz, B.A., & Woolston, J.L. (1991). The boundaries of attention deficit disorder. *Journal of Learning Disabilities, 2,* 78–86.

Erdrich, Louise. (1989). Foreward. In Michael Dorris (Ed.), *The broken cord: A family's ongoing struggle with fetal alcohol syndrome.* New York: Harper & Row.

Erikson, Erik H. (1963). *Childhood and society* (2nd ed.). New York: Norton.

Erikson, Erik H. (1968). *Identity, youth, and crisis.* New York: Norton.

Erikson, Erik H. (1975). *Life history and the historical moment.* New York: Norton.

Ernhart, Claire B., Sokol, Robert J., Ager, Joel W., Morrow-Tlucak, Mary, & Martier, Susan. (1989). Alcohol-related birth defects: Assessing the risk. In Donald Hutchings (Ed.), *Prenatal abuse of licit and illicit drugs.* New York: New York Academy of Sciences.

Eschenbach, David A. (1988). Infections and sexually transmitted diseases. In Dorothy Reycroft Hollingsworth & Robert Resnik (Eds.), *Medical counseling before pregnancy.* New York: Churchill Livingstone.

Evans, Mark I., Belsky, Robin L., Greb, Anne, Clementino, Nancy, & Snyer, Frank N. (1989). Prenatal diagnosis of congenital malformation. In Mark I. Evans, Alan O. Dixler, John C. Fletcher, & Joseph D. Schulman (Eds.), *Fetal diagnosis and therapy: Science, ethics, and the law.* Philadelphia: Lippincott.

Eveleth, Phillis B., & Tanner, James M. (1976). *Worldwide variation in human growth.* Cambridge, England: Cambridge University Press.

Ewing, Charles Patrick. (1990). *Kids who kill.* Lexington, MA: Lexington Books.

Eyer, D. (1992). *Maternal-infant bondings: A scientific fiction.* New Haven: Yale University Press.

Fabes, R.A., & Eisenberg, N. (1992). Young children's coping with interpersonal anger. *Child Development, 63,* 116–128.

Fabes, R.A., Eisenberg, N., Nyman, M., & Michealieu, Q. (1991). Young children's appraisals of others' spontaneous emotional reactions. *Developmental Psychology, 27,* 858–866.

Fagot, Beverly I. (1985). Changes in thinking about early sex role development. *Developmental Review, 5,* 83–98.

Fagot, Beverly I., & Hagan, R. (1991). Observations of parental reactions to sex-stereotyped behaviors: Age bind sex effects. *Child Development, 62,* 617–628.

Fagot, Beverly I., & Leinbach, M.D. (1993). Gender-role development in young children: From discriminating to labeling. *Developmental Review, 13,* 205–224.

Fagot, Beverly I., Leinback, M.D., & O'Boyle, C. (1992). Gender labeling, gender stereotyping, and parenting behaviors. *Developmental Psychology, 28,* 225–230.

Falbo, T., & Polit, D.F. (1986). Quantitative review of the only-child literature: Research evidence and theory development. *Psychology Bulletin, 1986,* 176–189.

Falbo, T., & Poston, D.L. (1993). The academic, personality, and physical outcomes of only children in China. *Child Development, 64,* 18–35.

Fantuzzo, J., DePaola, L., Lambert, L., Martino, T., Anderson, G., & Sutton, S. (1991). Effects of inter-parental violence on the psychological adjustment and competencies of young children. *Journal of Consulting and Clinical Psychology, 59,* 258–265.

Faroogi, S., Perry, I.J., & Beevers, D.G. (1993). Ethnic differences in infants. *Pediatric and Prenatal Epidemiology, 7,* 245–252.

Farrar, M.J. (1992). Negative evidence and grammatical morpheme acquisition. *Developmental Psychology, 28,* 90–98.

Farrar, M.J., & Goodman, G.S. (1990). Developmental differences in the relation between scripts and episodic memory: Do they exist? In R. Fivush & J.A. Hudson (Eds.), *Knowing and remembering in young children.* Cambridge, England: Cambridge University Press.

Farrington, David P. (1987). Epidemiology. In Herbert C. Quay (Ed.), *Handbook of juvenile delinquency.* New York: Wiley.

Feather, Norman T. (1980). Values in adolescence. In Joseph Adelson (Ed.), *Handbook of adolescent psychology.* New York: Wiley.

Featherstone, Helen. (1980). *A difference in the family.* New York: Basic Books.

Fein, Edith. (1991). Issues in foster family care: Where do we stand? *American Journal of Orthopsychiatry, 61,* 578–583.

Feinman, S. (1985). Emotional expression, social referencing, and preparedness for learning in infancy—Mother knows best, but sometimes I know better. In G. Ziven (Ed.), *The development of expressive behavior.* Orlando, FL: Academic Press.

Feiring, Candice, & Lewis, Michael. (1989). The social network of girls and boys from early through middle childhood. In Deborah Belle (Ed.), *Children's social networks and social supports.* New York: Wiley.

Feldman, L.H. (1991). Evaluating the impact of intensive family preservation services in New Jersey. In K. Wells & D.E. Biegel (Eds.), *Family preservation services: Research and evaluation.* Newbury Park, CA: Sage.

Feldman, Nina S., & Ruble, Diane N. (1988). The effect of personal relevance on psychological inference: A developmental analysis. *Child Development, 59,* 1339–1352.

Feldman, S. Shirley, Biringen, Zeynap C., & Nash, Sharon Churnin. (1981). Fluctuations of sex-related self-attributions as a function of stage of family life cycle. *Developmental Psychology, 17,* 24–35.

Feldman, S.S., & Gehring, T.M. (1988). Changing perceptions of family cohesion and power across adolescence. *Child Development, 59,* 1034–1045.

Felner, R.D., & Terre, L. (1987). Child custody dispositions and children's adaptation following divorce. In L.A. Weithorn (Ed.), *Psychology and child custody determinations*. Lincoln: University of Nebraska Press.

Ferguson, Charles A. (1977). Baby talk as a simplified register. In Catherine E. Snow & Charles A. Ferguson (Eds.), *Talking to children: Language input and requisition*. Cambridge, England: Cambridge University Press.

Fergusson, David M., Horwood, L. John, & Lynskey, Michael T. (1993). Early dentine lead levels and subsequent cognitive and behavioral development. *Journal of Child Psychology and Psychiatry and Applied Disciplines, 34*, 315–327.

Fernald, Anne. (1985). Four-month-old infants prefer to listen to motherese. *Infant Behavior and Development, 8*, 181–195.

Fernald, Anne. (1993). Approval and disapproval: Infant responsiveness to vocal affect in familiar and unfamiliar languages. *Child Development, 64*, 657–674.

Fernald, Anne, & Kuhl, P. (1987). Acoustic determinants of infant preference for motherese speech. *Infant Behavior and Development, 10*, 279–293.

Fernald, Anne, & Mazzie, Claudia. (1991). Prosody and focus in speech to infants and adults. *Developmental Psychology, 27*, 209–221.

Fiati, Thomas A. (1991). Cross-cultural variation in the structure of children's thought. In Robbie Case (Ed.), *The mind's staircase: Exploring the conceptual underpinning of children's thought and knowledge*. Hillsdale, NJ: Erlbaum.

Field, D. (1987). A review of preschool conservation training: An analysis of analysis. *Developmental Review, 7*, 210–251.

Field, Tiffany M. (1982). Individual differences in the expressivity of neonates and young infants. In R. Feldman (Ed.), *Development of nonverbal behavior in children*. New York: Springer-Verlag.

Field, Tiffany M. (1987). Affective and interactive disturbances in infants. In Joy Doniger Osofsky (Ed.), *Handbook of infant development* (2nd ed.). New York: Wiley.

Field, Tiffany M. (1991). Quality infant day-care and grade school behavior and performance. *Child Development, 62*, 863–870.

Field, Tiffany M., Gewirtz, Jacob L., Cohen, Debra, Garcia, Robert, Greenberg, Reena, & Kerry, Collins. (1984). Leavetakings and reunions of infants, toddlers, preschoolers, and their parents. *Child Development, 55*, 628–634.

Field, Tiffany M., Healy, B., Goldstein, S., Perry, S., Bendell, D., Schanberg, S., Zimmerman, E.A., & Kuhn, C. (1988). Infants of depressed mothers show "depressed" behavior even with non-depressed adults. *Child Development, 59*, 1569–1579.

Fincham, Frank D., Hokoda, Audrey, & Sanders, Reliford, Jr. (1989). Learned helplessness, test anxiety, and academic achievement: A longitudinal analysis. *Child Development, 60*, 138–145.

Fine, Michele. (1986). Why urban adolescents drop into and out of public high school. *Teachers' College Record, 87*, 393–409.

Finkelhor, David. (1990). Early and long-term effects of child sexual abuse: An update. *Professional Psychology: Research and Practice, 21*, 325–330.

Finkelhor, David. (1992). New myths about the child welfare system. *Child, Youth, and Family Service Quarterly, 15* (1), 3–5.

Finkelhor, David. (1994). Current information on the scope and nature of child sexual abuse. *The Future of Children, 4*, 31–53.

Finkelhor, David, & Strapko, N. (1992). Sexual abuse prevention education: A review of evaluation studies. In D.J. Willis, E.W. Holden, & M. Rosenberg (Eds.), *Prevention of child maltreatment: Developmental and ecological perspectives*. New York: Wiley.

Fischer, Judith L., Sollie, Donna L., & Morrow, K. Brent. (1986). Social networks in male and female adolescents. *Journal of Adolescent Research, 1*, 1–14.

Fischer, Kurt W. (1980). A theory of cognitive development: The control of hierarchies of skill. *Psychological Review, 87*, 477–531.

Fisher, Celia B. (1993). Integrating science and ethics in research with high-risk children and youth. *Society for Research in Child Development: Social Policy Report, 7* (4), 1–26.

Fisher, Celia B., & Brone, Ronald J. (1991). In Richard M. Lerner, Ann C. Petersen, & Jeanne Brooks-Gunn (Eds.), *Encyclopedia of adolescence* (Vol. 1). New York: Garland.

Fivush, R., & Hamond, N.R. (1990). Autobiographical memory across the preschool years: Toward reconceptualizing childhood amnesia. In R. Fivush & J.A. Hudson (Eds.), *Knowing and remembering in young children*. Cambridge, England. Cambridge University Press.

Flavell, John H. (1982). Structures, stages, and sequences in cognitive development. In W. Andrew Collins (Ed.), *Minnesota symposia on child psychology: Vol. 15. The concept of development*. Hillsdale, NJ: Erlbaum.

Flavell, John H. (1985). *Cognitive development* (2nd ed.). Englewood Cliffs, NJ: Prentice Hall.

Flavell, John H. (1992). Cognitive development: Past, present, and future. *Developmental Psychology, 28*, 998–1005.

Flavell, John H., Flavell, E.R., & Green, F.L. (1983). Development of the appearance-reality distinction. *Cognitive Psychology, 15*, 95–120.

Flavell, John H., Miller, P.H., & Miller, S.A. (1993). *Cognitive development* (3rd ed.). Englewood Cliffs, NJ: Prentice-Hall.

Fletcher, Jack M., Francis, David J., Rourke, Byron P., Shaywitz, Sally E., et al. (1992). The validity of discrepancy-based definitions of reading disabilities. *Journal of Learning Disabilities, 25*, 555–561.

Fletcher, John C. (1989). Ethics in experimental fetal therapy: Is there an early consensus? In Mark I. Evans, Alan O. Dixler, John C. Fletcher, & Joseph D. Schulman (Eds.), *Fetal diagnosis and therapy*. Philadelphia: Lippincott.

Fonagy, P., Steele, H., & Steele, M. (1991). Maternal representations of attachment during pregnancy predict the organization of infant-mother attachment at one year of age. *Child Development, 62*, 891–905.

Fordham, S., & Ogbu, J.U. (1986). Black students' school success coping with the burden of acting white. *Urban Review, 18*, 176–206.

Fowler, James W. (1981). *Stages of faith: The psychology of human development and the quest for meaning*. New York: Harper & Row.

Fox, N.A. (1991). If it's not left, it's right: Electroencephalograph asymmetry and the development of emotion. *American Psychologist, 46*, 863–872.

Fox, N.A., & Davidson, R.J. (1984). Hemispheric substrates of affect: A developmental model. In N.A. Fox & R.J. Davidson (Eds.), *The psychobiology of affective development*. Hillsdale, NJ: Erlbaum.

Fox, N.A., & Fitzgerald, H.E. (1990). Autonomic function in infancy. *Merrill-Palmer Quarterly, 36,* 27–51.

Fraiberg, Selma. (1959). *The magic years*. New York: Scribner.

Francis, P.L., & McCroy, G. (1983, April). Bimodal recognition of human stimulus configurations. Paper presented at the meeting of the Society for Research in Child Development. Detroit, MI.

Frankenburg, W.K., Frandel, A., Sciarillo, W., & Burgess, D. (1981). The newly abbreviated and revised Denver Developmental Screening Test. *Journal of Pediatrics, 99,* 995–999.

Franklin, Deborah. (1984). Rubella threatens unborn in vaccine gap. *Science News, 125,* 186.

Fraser, M.W., Pecora, P.J., & Haapala, D.A. (Eds.). (1991). *Families in crisis: The impact of intensive family preservation services*. New York: Aldine de Gruyter.

French, Doran C. (1984). Children's knowledge of the social functions of younger, older, and same-age peers. *Child Development, 55,* 1429–1433.

Freud, Sigmund. (1935). *A general introduction to psychoanalysis*. Joan Riviare (Trans.). New York: Modern Library.

Freud, Sigmund. (1938). *The basic writings of Sigmund Freud*. A.A. Brill (Ed. and Trans.). New York: Modern Library.

Freud, Sigmund. (1963). *Three case histories*. New York: Collier. (Original work published 1918).

Freud, Sigmund. (1964). *An outline of psychoanalysis: Vol. 23. The standard edition of the complete psychological works of Sigmund Freud*. James Strachey (Ed. and Trans.). London: Hogarth Press. (Original work published 1940).

Freud, Sigmund. (1965). *New introductory lectures on psychoanalysis*. James Strachey (Ed. and Trans.). New York: Norton. (Original work published 1933).

Freund, L.S. (1990). Maternal regulation of children's problem-solving behavior and its impact on children's performance. *Child Development, 61,* 113–126.

Frey, K.S., & Ruble, D.N. (1987). What children say about classroom performance: Sex and grade differences in perceived competence. *Child Development, 58,* 1066–1078.

Fried, Peter A., & Watkinson, Barbara. (1990). 36- and 48-month neurobehavioral follow-up of children prenatally exposed to marijuana, cigarettes, and alcohol. *Developmental and Behavioral Pediatrics, 11,* 49–58.

Friedman, Emanuel A., & Neff, Raymond K. *(1987). Labor and delivery: Impact on offspring*. Littleton, MA: PSG.

Friedrich-Cofer, Lynette, & Huston, Aletha C. (1986). Television violence and aggression: The debate continues. *Psychological Bulletin, 100,* 364–371.

Frisch, Rose E. (1983). Fatness, puberty, and fertility: The effects of nutrition and physical training on menarche and ovulation. In Jeanne Brooks-Gunn & Anne C. Petersen (Eds.), *Girls at puberty: Biological and psychosocial aspects*. New York: Plenum.

Frith, Uta. (1989). *Autism: Explaining the enigma*. Cambridge, England: Blackwell.

Frye, Douglas, Braisby, Nicholas, Lowe, John, Marouda, Cline, & Nicholls, Jon. (1989). Young children's understanding of counting and cardinality. *Child Development, 60,* 1158–1171.

Frye, Douglas, & Moore, C. (1991). *Children's theories of mind*. Hillsdale, NJ: Erlbaum.

Fuligni, A.J., & Eccles, J.S. (1993). Perceived parent-child relationships and early adolescents' orientation toward peers. *Developmental Psychology, 29,* 622–632.

Fullard, W., McDevitt, S.S., & Carey, W.B. (1984). Assessing temperament in one- to three-year-old children. *Journal of Pediatric Psychology, 9,* 205–217.

Furman, T., & Holmbeck, G.N. (in press). A contextual-moderator analysis of emotional autonomy and adjustment in adolescence. *Child Development,* in press.

Furman, Wyndol. (1987). Acquaintanceship in middle childhood. *Developmental Psychology, 23,* 563–570.

Furman, Wyndol, & Buhrmester, D. (1992). Age and sex differences in perceptions of networks of personal relationships. *Child Development, 63,* 103–115.

Furstenberg, Frank F., Brooks-Gunn, Jeanne, & Morgan, S. (1987). *Adolescent mothers in later life*. New York: Cambridge University Press.

Furstenberg, Frank F., & Cherlin, Andrew J. (1991). *Divided families: What happens to children when parents part*. Cambridge, MA: Harvard University Press.

Furstenberg, Frank F., Jr., & Nord, Christine Winquist. (1985). Parenting apart: Patterns of childbearing after marital disruption. *Journal of Marriage and the Family, 47,* 893–912.

Fuson, Karen C. (1988). *Children's counting and concepts of number*. New York: Springer-Verlag.

Fuson, Karen C., & Kwon, Youngshim. (1992). Korean children's understanding of multidigit addition and subtraction. *Child Development, 63,* 491–506.

Gabennesch, H. (1990). The perception of social conventionality by children and adults. *Child Development, 61,* 2047–2059.

Gaddis, Alan, & Brooks-Gunn, Jeanne. (1985). The male experience of pubertal change. *Journal of Youth and Adolescence, 14,* 61.

Gaensbauer, Theodore J. (1980). Anaclitic depression in a three-and-a-half month old child. *American Journal of Psychiatry, 137,* 841–842.

Galambos, N.L. (1992). Parent-adolescent relations. *Current Directions in Psychological Science, 1,* 146–149.

Gallaher, James J. 1990. The family as a focus for intervention. In Samuel J. Meisels & Jack P. Shonkoff (Eds.), *Handbook of early childhood intervention*. Cambridge, England: Cambridge University Press.

Galler, Janina. (1989). A follow-up study of the influence of early malnutrition on development: Behavior at home and at school. *Journal of the American Academy of Child and Adolescent Psychiatry, 28,* 254–261.

Galvin, Ruth Mehrtens. (1992). The nature of shyness. *Harvard Magazine, 94* (4), 40–45.

Gandour, M.J. (1989). Activity level as a dimension of temperament in toddlers: Its relevance for the organismic specificity hypothesis. *Child Development, 60,* 1092–1098.

Gantley, M., Davies, D.P., & Murcett, A. (1993). Sudden infant death syndrome: Links with infant care practices. *British Medical Journal, 306,* 16–20.

Garbarino, James. (1988). Preventing childhood injury: Developmental and mental health issues. *American Journal of Orthopsychiatry, 58,* 25–45.

Garbarino, James. (1989). An ecological perspective on the role of play in child development. In Marianne N. Bloch & Anthony D. Pellegrini (Eds.), *The ecological context of children's play.* Norwood, NJ: Ablex.

Garbarino, James. (1989). Troubled youth, troubled families: The dynamics of adolescent maltreatment. In D. Cicchetti & V. Carlson (Eds.), *Child maltreatment.* Cambridge, England: Cambridge University Press.

Garbarino, James, Dubrow, N., Kostelny, K., & Pardo, C. (1992). *Children in danger: Coping with the consequences of community violence.* San Francisco: Jossey-Bass.

Garbarino, James, Guttmann, Edna, & Seeley, James Wilson. (1986). *The psychologically battered child.* San Francisco: Jossey-Bass.

Garbarino, James, & Kostelny, Kathleen. (1992). Child maltreatment as a community problem. *Child Abuse and Neglect, 16,* 144–164.

Garbarino, James, Kostelny, Kathleen, & Dubrow, Nancy. (1991). *No place to be a child: Growing up in a war zone.* New York: Lexington Books.

Garber, J., & Dodge, K.A. (Eds.). (1991). *The development of emotional regulation and dysregulation.* Cambridge, England: Cambridge University Press.

Gardner, Howard. (1980). *Artful scribbles: The significance of children's drawings.* New York: Basic Books.

Gardner, Howard. (1983). *Frames of mind: The theory of multiple intelligences.* New York: Basic Books.

Gardner, William P. (1991). A theory of adolescent risk taking. In N. Bell (Ed.), *Adolescent and adult risk taking. The eighth Texas Tech symposium on interfaces in psychology.* Lubbock: Texas Tech University Press.

Garland, A.F., & Zigler, E. (1993). Adolescent suicide prevention: Current research and social policy implications. *American Psychologist, 48,* 169–182.

Garmezy, Norman. (1985). Stress-resistant children: The search for protective factors. In J. E. Stevenson (Ed.), *Recent research in developmental psychopathology.* Oxford, England: Pergamon.

Garrett, C.J. (1985). Effects of residential treatment on adjudicated delinquents. *Journal of Research on Crime and Delinquency, 22,* 287–308.

Garvey, Catherine. (1976). Some properties of social play. In Jerome S. Bruner, Alison Jolly, & Kathy Sylva (Eds.), *Play.* New York: Basic Books.

Garvey, Catherine. (1984). *Children's talk.* Cambridge, MA: Harvard University Press.

Garvey, Catherine. (1990). *Play* (2nd ed.). Cambridge, MA: Harvard University Press.

Garvey, Catherine, & Kramer, Thayer L. (1989). The language of social pretend play. *Developmental Review, 9,* 364–382.

Gaskin, Ina May. (1990). *Spiritual midwifery.* Summerton, TN: Book Publishers.

Gauvain, Mary. (1990). Review of Kathleen Berger, *The developing person through childhood and adolescence* (3rd ed.). New York: Worth.

Gazzaniga, Michael S. (1983). Right hemisphere language following brain bisection: A 20-year perspective. *American Psychologist, 43,* 184–188.

Gelles, Richard J. (1987). *Family violence* (2nd ed.). Newbury Park, CA: Sage.

Gelles, Richard J. (1988). *Intimate violence.* New York: Simon & Schuster.

Gelles, Richard J., & Straus, M.A. (1988). *Intimate violence.* New York: Simon & Schuster.

Gelman, R. (1982). Basic numerical abilities. In R.J. Sternberg (Ed.), *Advances in the psychology of human intelligence* (Vol. 1). Hillsdale, NJ: Erlbaum.

Gelman, Rochel, & Gallistel, C.R. (1978). *The child's understanding of number.* Cambridge, MA: Harvard University Press.

Gelman, Rochel, & Massey, Christine M. (1987). Commentary. In Geoffrey B. Saxe, Steven R. Guberman, & Maryl Gearhart, Social processes in early number development. *Monographs of the Society for Research in Child Development, 52.*

Genesse, Fred. (1983). Bilingual education of majority language children: The immersion experiments in review. *Applied Linguistics, 4,* 1–46.

Genesee, Fred. (1994). *Educating second-language children: The whole child, the whole curriculum, the whole community.* Cambridge, England: Cambridge University Press.

Genishi, Celie, & Dyson, Anne Haas. (1984). *Language assessment in the early years.* Norwood, NJ: Ablex.

Gesell, Arnold. (1926). *The mental growth of the pre-school child: A psychological outline of normal development from birth to the sixth year including a system of developmental diagnosis.* New York: Macmillan.

Gianino, A., & Tronick, Edward. (1988). The Mutual Regulation Model: The infant's self and interactive regulation and coping and defensive capacities. In T. Field, P. McCabe, & N. Schneiderman (Eds.), *Stress and coping* (Vol. 2). Hillsdale, NJ: Erlbaum.

Gibbs, N. (1993, July 19). In whose best interest? *Newsweek.*

Gibson, Eleanor. (1969). *Principles of perceptual learning and development.* New York: Appleton-Century-Crofts.

Gibson, Eleanor. (1982). The concept of affordances in development: The renascence of functionalism. In W. Andrew Collins (Ed.), *Minnesota symposia on child psychology: Vol. 15. The concept of development.* Hillsdale, NJ: Erlbaum.

Gibson, Eleanor. (1988). Levels of description and constraints on perceptual development. In Albert Yonas (Ed.), *Perceptual development in infancy.* Hillsdale, NJ: Erlbaum.

Gibson, Eleanor, & Walker, Arlene S. (1984). Development of knowledge of visual-tactile affordances of substance. *Child Development, 55,* 453–460.

Gibson, James J. (1979). *The ecological approach to visual perception.* Boston: Houghton-Mifflin.

Gilbert, Enid F., Arya, Sunita, Loxova, Renata, & Opitz, John M. (1987). Pathology of chromosome abnormalities in the fetus: Pathological markers. In Enid F. Gilbert & John M. Opitz (Eds.), *Genetic aspects of developmental pathology.* New York: Liss.

Gilbert, M.A., Bauman, K.E., & Udry, J.R. (1986). A panel study of subjective expected utility for adolescent sexual behavior. *Journal of Applied Social Psychology, 16,* 745–756.

Giles-Sims, Jean, & Crosbie-Burnett, Margaret. (1989). Adolescent power in stepparent families: A test of normative resource theory. *Journal of Marriage and the Family, 51,* 1065–1078.

Gillberg, Christopher. (1991). Clinical and neurobiological aspects of Asperger syndrome in six family studies. In Uta Frith (Ed.), *Autism and Asperger syndrome.* Cambridge, England: Cambridge University Press.

Gilligan, Carol. (1982). *In a different voice: Psychological theory and women's development.* Cambridge, MA: Harvard University Press.

Gilligan, Carol, & Belensky, M.F. (1980). A naturalistic study of abortion decisions. In R. Sleman & R. Yando (Eds.), *New directions for child development: Clinical developmental psychology.* San Francisco: Jossey-Bass.

Gilligan, Carol, Murphy, John M., & Tappan, Mark B. (1990). Moral development beyond adolescence. In Charles N. Alexander & Ellen J. Langer (Eds.), *Higher stages of human development.* New York: Oxford University Press.

Gilovich, Thomas. (1991). *How we know what isn't so.* New York: The Free Press.

Ginsburg, G.S., & Bronstein, P. (1993). Family factors related to children's intrinsic/extrinsic motivational orientation and academic performance. *Child Development, 64,* 1461–1474.

Gittelman, R., Mannuzza, S., Shenker, R., & Bonagura, N. (1985). Hyperactive boys almost grown up: Psychiatric status. *Archives of General Psychiatry, 42,* 937–947.

Gleason, Jean Berko. (1967). Do children imitate? *Proceedings of the International Conference on Oral Education of the Deaf, 2,* 1441–1448.

Gnepp, Jackie, & Chilamkurti, Chinni. (1988). Children's use of personality attributions to predict other people's emotional and behavioral reactions. *Child Development, 59,* 743–754.

Goedert, J.J., Mendez, H., Drummond, J.E., Robert-Guroff, M., Minkoff, H.L., Holman, S., Stevens, R., Rubinstein, A., Blattner, W.A., Willoughby, A., & Landesman, S.H. (1989). Mother-to-infant transmission of human immunodeficiency virus type I: Association with prematurity or low anti-gp120. *The Lancet, 335,* 1351–1354.

Goetz, T.E., & Dweck, Carol. (1980). Learned helplessness in social situations. *Journal of Personality and Social Psychology, 39,* 246–255.

Goldberg, W.A., & Easterbrooks, M.A. (1984). Role of marital quality in toddler development. *Developmental Psychology, 20,* 504–514.

Goldberg, Wendy A. (1990). Marital quality, parental personality, and spousal agreement about perceptions and expectations for children. *Merrill-Palmer Quarterly, 36,* 531–556.

Goldberg-Reitman, Jill. (1992). Young girls' conception of their mother's role: A neo-structural analysis. In Robbie Case (Ed.), *The mind's staircase: Exploring the conceptual underpinning of children's thought and knowledge.* Hillsdale, NJ: Erlbaum.

Goldenberg, Robert L. (1992). Prenatal care and pregnancy outcome. In Jonathan B. Kotch, Craig H. Blakely, Sarah S. Brown, & Frank Y. Wong (Eds.), *A pound of prevention: The case for universal maternity care in the U.S.* Washington, DC: American Public Health Association.

Goldfield, E.G., Kay, B.A., & Warren, W.H., Jr. (1993). Infant bouncing: The assembly and tuning of action systems. *Child Development, 64,* 1128–1142.

Goldin-Meadow, S. (1979). Structure in a manual communication system developed without a conventional language model: Language without a helping hand. In H. Whitaker & H.A. Whitaker (Eds.), *Studies in neurolinguistics* (Vol. 4). New York: Academic Press.

Goldman, Gail, Pineault, Raynald, Potvin, Louise, Blais, Regis, & Bilodeau, Henriette. (1993). Factors influencing the practice of vaginal birth after Cesarean section. *American Journal of Public Health, 83,* 1104–1108.

Goldsmith, H. Hill, Buss, A.H., Plomin, R., Rothbart, M. Klevjord, Thomas, A., Chess, S., Hinde, R.A., & McCall, R.B. (1987). Roundtable: What is temperament? Four approaches. *Child Development, 58,* 505–529.

Goldsmith, H. Hill, & Rothbart, M.K. (1991). Contemporary instruments for assessing early temperament by questionnaire and in the laboratory. In J. Strelau & A. Angleitner (Eds.), *Explorations in temperament.* New York: Plenum.

Goldsmith, H. Hill, & Rothbart, M.K. (1992). Laboratory temperament assessment battery (LAB-TAB): Locomotor version 2.0. Unpublished manuscript, University of Oregon.

Goldstein, Beth L. (1990). Refugee students' perception of curriculum differentiation. In Rebe Page & Linda Valli (Eds.), *Curriculum differentiation: Interpretive studies in U.S. secondary schools.* Albany: State University of New York Press.

Golinkoff, Roberta Michnick, & Hirsh-Pasek, Kathy. (1990). Let the mute speak: What infants can tell us about language acquisition. *Merrill-Palmer Quarterly, 36,* 67–91.

Golinkoff, Roberta Michnick, Hirsh-Pasek, Kathy, Bailey, Leslie M., & Wenger, Neill R. (1992). Young children and adult use lexical principles to learn new nouns. *Developmental Psychology, 28,* 99–108.

Golub, S. (1992). *Periods: From menarche to menopause.* Newbury Park, CA: Sage.

Golumb, C., & McLean, L. (1984). Assessing cognitive skills in pre-school children of middle and low income families. *Perceptual and Motor Skills, 58,* 119–125.

Goncu, A. (1993). Development of intersubjectivity in social pretend play. *Human Development, 36,* 185–198.

Goodluck, H. (1991). *Language acquisition: A linguistic introduction.* Oxford, England: Blackwell.

Goodman, G.S., Hirschman, J.E., Hepps, D., & Rudy, L. (1991). Children's memory for stressful events. *Merrill-Palmer Quarterly, 37,* 109–158.

Goodman, G.S., Rudy, L., Bottoms, B.L., & Aman, C. (1990). Children's concerns and memory: Issues of ecological validity in the study of children's eyewitness testimony. In Robyn Fivush & Judith A. Hudson (Eds.), *Knowing and remembering in young children.* Cambridge, England: Cambridge University Press.

Goodman, G.S., Taub, E.P., Jones, D.P.H., England, P., Port, L.K., Rudy, L., & Prado, L. (1992). Testifying in criminal court: Emotional effects on child sexual assault victims. *Monograph of the Society for Research in Child Development, 57* (Serial No. 229).

Goodman, N.C. (1987). Girls with learning disabilities and their sisters: How are they faring in adulthood? *Journal of Clinical Child Psychology, 16,* 290–300.

Goodnow, Jacqueline J., & Burns, A. (1988). *Home and school: Child's eye view.* Sydney: Allen & Unwin.

Goodnow, Jacqueline J., & Collins, W. Andrew. (1990). *Development according to parents: The nature, sources, and consequences of parents' ideas.* Hillsdale, NJ: Erlbaum.

Goodwin, M.H. (1990). *He-said-she-said: Talk as social organization among black children.* Bloomington: Indiana University Press.

Goodz, Naomi S. (1994). Interactions between parents and children in bilingual families. In Fred Genesee (Ed.), *Educating second-language children: The whole child, the whole curriculum, the whole community.* Cambridge, England: Cambridge University Press.

Gopnik, A., & Meltzoff, A. (1987). The development of categorization in the second year and its relation to other cognitive and linguistic developments. *Child Development, 58,* 1523–1531.

Gordon, Debra Ellen. (1990). Formal operational thinking: The role of cognitive-developmental processes in adolescent decision-making about pregnancy and contraception. *American Journal of Orthopsychiatry, 60,* 346–356.

Gortmaker, S.L., Dietz, W.H., Sobol, A.M., & Wehler, C.A. (1987). Increasing pediatric obesity in the United States. *American Journal of Diseases of Children, 141,* 535–540.

Gottesman, Irving I. (1991). *Schizophrenia genesis.* New York: Freeman.

Gottesman, Irving I., & Goldsmith, H.H. (1993). Developmental psychopathology of antisocial behavior: Inserting genes into its ontogenesis and epigenesis. In C.A. Nelson (Ed.), *Minnesota symposia on child psychology: Vol. 27. Threats to optimal development: Integrating biological, psychological, and social risk factors.* Hillsdale, NJ: Erlbaum.

Gottlieb, Gilbert, & Krasnegor, Norman. (1985). *Measurement of audition and vision in the first year of postnatal life: A methodological overview.* Cambridge, England: Cambridge University Press.

Gottlieb, Jay, & Leyser, Yona. (1981). Friendship between mentally retarded and nonretarded children. In Steven R. Asher & John M. Gottman (Eds.), *The development of children's friendships.* Cambridge, England: Cambridge University Press.

Gottman, John M. (1983). How children become friends. *Monographs of the Society for Research in Child Development, 48* (3, Serial No. 201).

Government Accounting Office. (1990). *Home visiting: A promising early intervention strategy for at-risk families.* Washington, DC: U.S. Government Printing Office.

Government Accounting Office. (1992). *Child abuse: Prevention programs need greater emphasis.* Washington, DC: U.S. Government Printing Office.

Goyent, Gregory L., Bottoms, Sidner F., Treadwell, Marjori C., & Nehra, Paul C. (1989). The physician factor in Cesarean birth rates. *New England Journal of Medicine, 320,* 706–709.

Graham, S., Hudley, C., & Williams, E. (1992). Attributional and emotional determinants of aggression among African-American and Latino young adolescents. *Developmental Psychology, 28,* 731–740.

Grandin, T., & Scariano, M. (1986). *Emergence labeled autistic.* TunbridgeWells: Costello.

Grant, James P. (1986). *The state of the world's children.* Oxford, England: Oxford University Press.

Gratch, Gerald, & Schatz, Joseph. (1987). Cognitive development: The relevance of Piaget's infancy books. In Joy Doniger Osofsky (Ed.), *Handbook of infant development* (2nd ed.). New York: Wiley.

Greenberger, E., & Goldberg, W.A. (1989). Work, parenting, and the socialization of children. *Developmental Psychology, 25,* 22–35.

Greenberger, E., & Steinberg, L. (1986). *When teenagers work.* New York: Basic Books.

Greenough, W.T. (1993). Brain adaptation to experience: An update. In M.H. Johnson (Ed.), *Brain development and cognition.* Oxford, England: Blackwell.

Greenough, W.T., Black, J.E., & Wallace, C.S. (1987). Experience and brain development. *Child Development, 58,* 539–559.

Gross, A.L., & Ballif, F. (1991). Children's understanding of emotion from facial expressions and situations: A review. *Developmental Review, 11,* 368–398.

Grossman, Frances K., Pollack, William S., & Golding, Ellen. (1988). Fathers and children: Predicting the quality and quantity of fathering. *Developmental Psychology, 24,* 82–91.

Grossman, John H. (1986). Congenital syphilis. In John L. Sever & Robert L. Brent (Eds.), *Teratogen update: Environmentally induced birth defect risks.* New York: Liss.

Grossman, K., Thane, K., & Grossman, K.E. (1981). Maternal tactile contact of the newborn after various postpartum conditions of mother-infant contact. *Developmental Psychology, 17,* 159–169.

Grotevant, Harold D., & Cooper, Catherine R. (1985). Patterns of interaction in family relationships and the development of identity exploration in adolescence. *Child Development, 56,* 415–428.

Grusec, J.E. (1991). Socializing concern for others in the home. *Developmental Psychology, 27,* 338–342.

Grusec, J.E. (1992). Social learning theory and developmental psychology: The legacies of Robert Sears and Albert Bandura. *Developmental Psychology, 28,* 776–786.

Grusec, J.E., & Goodnow, J.J. (1994). Impact of parental discipline methods on the child's internalization of values: A reconceptualization of current points of view. *Developmental Psychology, 30,* 4–19.

Grych, J.H., & Fincham, F.D. (1990). Marital conflict and children's adjustment: A cognitive-contextual framework. *Psychological Bulletin, 108,* 267–290.

Grych, J.H., & Fincham, F.D. (1993). Children's appraisals of marital conflict: Initial investigations of the cognitive-contextual framework. *Child Development, 64,* 215–230.

Guilleminault, C., Boeddiker, Margaret Owen, & Schwab, Deborah. (1982). Detection of risk factors for "near miss SIDS" events in full-term infants. *Neuropediatrics, 13,* 29–35.

Gustafson, G.E., & Harris, K.L. (1990). Women's responses to young infants' cries. *Developmental Psychology, 26,* 144–152.

Guthrie, Sharon R. (1991). Prevalence of eating disorders among intercollegiate athletes: Contributing factors and preventative measures. In David R. Black (Ed.), *Eating disorders among athletes.* Reston, VA: American Alliance for Health, Physical Education, Recreation and Dance.

Gutmann, David. (1975). Parenthood: Key to the comparative psychology of the life cycle. In Nancy Datan & L. Ginsberg (Eds.), *Life span developmental psychology.* New York: Academic Press.

Guttmacher Institute. (1994). *Sex and America's teenagers.* New York: Alan Guttmacher Institute.

Haas, Joel E., Taylor, James S., Bergman, Abraham B., & van Belle, Gerald. (1993). Relationship between epidemiologic risk factors and clinicopathologic findings in sudden infant death syndrome. *Pediatrics, 91,* 106–112.

Hack, M., Breslau, N., Aram, D., Weissmand, B., Klein, N., & Borawski-Clark, E. (1992). The effect of very low birth weight and social risk on neurocognitive abilities at school age. *Developmental and Behavioral Pediatrics, 13,* 412–420.

Haith, M. (1980). Progress in the understanding of sensory and perceptual processes in early infancy. *Merrill-Palmer Quarterly, 36,* 1–26.

Haith, M.M. (1980). *Rules that babies look by.* Hillsdale, NJ: Erlbaum.

Haith, M.M. (1990). Perceptual and sensory processes in early infancy. *Merrill-Palmer Quarterly, 36,* 1–26.

Haith, M.M. (1993). Preparing for the 21st century: Some goals and challenges for studies of infant sensory and perceptual development. *Developmental Review, 13,* 354–371.

Haith, M.M., Wentworth, N., & Canfield, R.L. (1993). The formation of expectations in early infancy. In C. Rovee-Collier & L.P. Lipsitt (Eds.), *Advances in infancy research* (Vol. 8). Norwood, NJ: Ablex.

Hakuta, K. (1986). *Mirror of language.* New York: Basic Books.

Hakuta, K., & Garcia, E. (1989). Bilingualism and education. *American Psychologist, 44,* 374–379.

Hale, S. (1990). A global developmental trend in cognitive processing speed. *Child Development, 61,* 653–663.

Halliday, M.A.K. (1979). One child's protolanguage. In Margaret Bullowa (Ed.), *Before speech: The beginning of interpersonal communication.* Cambridge, England: Cambridge University Press.

Hamer, Dean H., Hu, Stella, Magnuson, Victoria L., Hu, Nan, & Pattatucci, Angela M.L. (1993). A linkage between DNA markers on the X chromosome and male sexual orientation. *Science, 261,* 321–327.

Hamond, Nina R., & Fivush, Robyn. (1991). Memories of Mickey Mouse: Young children recount their trip to Disneyworld. *Cognitive Development, 6,* 433–448.

Hanna, E., & Meltzoff, A.N. (1993). Peer imitation by toddlers in laboratory, home, and day-care contexts: Implications for social learning and memory. *Developmental Psychology, 29,* 701–710.

Hans, Sydney L. (1989). Developmental consequences of prenatal exposure to methadone. In Donald Hutchings (Ed.), *Prenatal abuse of licit and illicit drugs.* New York: New York Academy of Sciences.

Hanson, David J., Conaway, Loren P. & Christopher, Jeanette Smitt. (1989). Victims of child physical abuse. In Robert T. Ammerman & Micheal Hersen (Eds.), *Treatment of family violence.* New York: Wiley.

Hanson, James W., Streissguth, Ann P., & Smith, David W. (1978). The effects of moderate alcohol consumption during pregnancy on fetal growth and morphogenesis. *Journal of Pediatrics, 92,* 457–460.

Hanson, Sandra L., Myers, David E., & Ginsberg, Alan L. (1987). The role of responsibility and knowledge in reducing teenage out-of-wedlock childbearing. *Journal of Marriage and the Family, 49,* 241–256.

Hardy, Janet B., Duggan, Anne K., Masnyk, Katya, & Pearson, Carol. (1989). Fathers of children born to young urban mothers. *Family Planning Perspectives, 21,* 159–163.

Harley, B., Allen, P., Cummins, Jim, & Swain, M. (1987). *Final report. The development of bilingual proficiency study.* Toronto: Ontario Institute for Studies in Education.

Harper, Lawrence V., & Sanders, Karen M. (1975). Preschool children's use of space: Sex differences in outdoor play. *Developmental Psychology, 11,* 119.

Harris, P.L. (1987). The development of search. In Philip Salapatek & Leslie Cohen (Eds.), *Handbook of infant perception: Vol. 2. From perception to cognition.* Orlando, FL: Academic Press.

Harris, P.L. (1989). *Children and emotion: The development of psychological understanding.* Oxford, England: Basil Blackwell.

Harris, P.L., & Kavanaugh, R.D. (1993). Young children's understanding of pretense. *Monographs of the Society for Research in Child Development, 58* (Serial No. 231).

Harrison, Algea O., Wilson, Melvin N., Pine, Charles J., Chan, Samuel Q., & Buriel, Raymond. (1990). Family ecologies of ethnic minority children. *Child Development, 61,* 347–362.

Harrison, James B. (1984). Warning: The male sex role may be dangerous to your health. In Janice M. Swanson & Katherine A. Forrest (Eds.), *Men's reproductive health.* New York: Springer-Verlag.

Hart, C.H., DeWolf, D.M., Wozniak, P., & Burts, D.C. (1992). Maternal and paternal disciplinary styles: Relations with preschoolers' playground behavioral orientations and peer status. *Child Development, 63,* 879–892.

Hart, Craig G., Ladd, Gary W., & Burelson, Brant R. (1990). Children's expectations of the outcomes of social strategies: Relations with sociometric status and maternal disciplinary styles. *Child Development, 61,* 127–137.

Hart, Stuart N., & Brassard, Marla R. (1991). Psychological maltreatment: Progress achieved. *Development and Psychopathology, 3,* 61–70.

Harter, Susan. (1983). Developmental perspectives on the self-system. In Paul H. Mussen (Ed.), *Handbook of child psychology: Vol. 4. Socialization, personality and social development.* New York: Wiley.

Harter, Susan. (1990). Causes, correlates, and the functional role of global self-worth: A life-span perspective. In R.J. Sternberg & J. Kolligian, Jr. (Eds.), *Competence considered.* New Haven: Yale University Press.

Harter, Susan. (1990). Processes underlying adolescent self-concept formation. In Raymond Montemayor, Gerald R. Adams, & Thomas P. Gullotta (Eds.), *From childhood to adolescence: A transitional period?* Newbury Park, CA: Sage.

Harter, Susan. (1990). Self and identity development. In S.S. Feldman & G.R. Elliott (Eds.), *At the threshold: The developing adolescent.* Cambridge, MA: Harvard University Press.

Harter, Susan. (1993). Visions of self: Beyond the me in the mirror. In J.E. Jacobs (Ed.), *Nebraska symposium on motivation: Vol. 40. Developmental perspectives on motivation.* Lincoln: University of Nebraska Press.

Harter, Susan, & Monsour, A. (1992). Developmental analysis of conflict caused by opposing attributes in the adolescent self-portrait. *Developmental Psychology, 28,* 251–260.

Harter, Susan, & Pike, Robin. (1984). The pictorial scale of perceived competence and social acceptance for young children. *Child Development, 55,* 1969–1982.

Harter, Susan, & Whitesell, N.R. (1989). Developmental changes in children's understanding of single, multiple, and blended emotion concepts. In C. Saarni & P.L. Harris (Eds.), *Children's understanding of emotion.* Cambridge, England: Cambridge University Press.

Hartshorne, Hugh, May, Mark A., & Maller, J.B. (1929). *Studies in service and self-control.* New York: Macmillan.

Hartsough, Carolyn S., & Lambert, Nadine M. (1985). Medical factors in hyperactive and normal children: Prenatal, developmental, and health history findings. *American Journal of Orthopsychiatry, 55,* 190–201.

Hartup, Willard W. (1983). Peer relations. In Paul H. Mussen (Ed.), *Handbook of child psychology: Vol. 4. Socialization, personality and social development.* New York: Wiley.

Hartup, Willard W. (1989). Social relationships and their developmental significance. *American Psychologist, 44,* 120–126.

Hartup, Willard W. (1992). Conflict and friendship relations. In C.U. Shantz & W.W. Hartup (Eds.), *Conflict in child and adolescent development.* Cambridge, England: Cambridge University Press.

Hartup, Willard W., Laursen, B., Stewart, M.I., & Eastenson, A. (1988). Conflict and the friendship relations of young children. *Child Development, 59,* 1590–1600.

Hashima, Patricia Y., & Amato, Paul R. (1994). Poverty, social support, and parental behavior. *Child Development, 65,* 394–403.

Haskett, Mary E., & Kistner, Janet A. (1991). Social interactions and peer perceptions of young physically abused children. *Child Development, 62,* 979–990.

Haskins, Ron. (1989). Beyond metaphor: The efficacy of early childhood education. *American Psychologist, 44,* 274–282.

Hauser, S.T., & Bowlds, M.K. (1990). Stress, coping, and adaptation. In S.S. Feldman & G.R. Elliott (Eds.), *At the threshold: The developing adolescent.* Cambridge, MA: Harvard University Press.

Haviland, J.M., & Lelwica, M. (1987). The induced affect response: 10-week-old infants' responses to three emotion expressions. *Developmental Psychology, 23,* 97–104.

Hawaii Department of Health. (1992). *Healthy Start: Hawaii's system of family support services.* Honolulu: Hawaii Department of Health.

Hawkins, Alan J., & Eggebeen, David J. (1991). Are fathers fungible? *Journal of Marriage and the Family.* 958–972.

Hawley, T.L., & Disney, E.R. (1992). Crack's children: The consequences of maternal cocaine abuse. *Social Policy Report of the Society for Research in Child Development, 6,* 1–22.

Hay, D.F., Caplan, M., Castle, J., & Stimson, C.A. (1991). Does sharing become increasingly "rational" in the second year of life? *Developmental Psychology, 27,* 987–993.

Hayden-Thompson, Laura, Rubin, Kenneth H., & Hymel, Shelley. (1987). Sex preferences in sociometric choices. *Developmental Psychology, 23,* 558–562.

Hayes, C. (Ed.). (1987). *Risking the future: Adolescent sexuality, pregnancy, and childbearing.* Washington, DC: National Academy Press.

Hayes, C.D., Palmer, J.L., & Zaslow, M.J. (Eds.). (1990). *Child care choices.* Washington, DC: National Academy Press.

Hayne, Harleen, Rovee-Collier, Carolyn, & Perris, Eve E. (1987). Categorization and memory retrieval by three-month-olds. *Child Development, 58,* 750–767.

Heap, Kari Killen. (1991). A predictive and follow-up study of abusive and neglectful families by case analysis. *Child Abuse and Neglect, 15,* 261–273.

Heibeck, Tracy H., & Markman, Ellen M. (1987). Word learning in children: An examination of fast mapping. *Child Development, 58,* 1021–1034.

Hein, Karen. (1993). "Getting real" about HIV in adolescents. *American Journal of Public Health, 83,* 492–494.

Hemmings, Annette, & Metz, Mary Haywood. (1990). Real teaching: How high school teachers negotiate societal, local community, and student pressures when they define their work. In Reba Page & Linda Valli (Eds.), *Curriculum differentiation: Interpretive studies in U.S. secondary schools.* Albany: State University of New York Press.

Henggeler, S.W. (1989). *Delinquency in adolescence.* Newbury Park, CA: Sage.

Henker, B., & Whalen, C.K. (1989). Hyperactivity and attention deficits. *American Psychologist, 44,* 216–223.

Herron, Robert E., & Sutton-Smith, Brian. (1971). *Child's play.* New York: Wiley.

Hertzig, M.E., & Shapiro, T. (1990). Autism and pervasive developmental disorders. In M. Lewis & S.M. Miller (Eds.), *Handbook of developmental psychopathology.* New York: Plenum.

Herzberger, S.D., & Hall, J.A. (1993). Consequences of retaliatory aggression against siblings and peers: Urban minority children's expectations. *Child Development, 64,* 1773–1785.

Hetherington, E. Mavis. (1989). Coping with family transitions: Winners, losers, and survivors. *Child Development, 60,* 1–14.

Hetherington, E. Mavis, & Camara, Kathleen A. (1984). Families in transition: The process of dissolution and reconstitution. In Ross D. Parke (Ed.), *Review of child development research* (Vol. 7). Chicago: University of Chicago Press.

Hetherington, E. Mavis, & Clingempeel, W. Glenn. (1992). Coping with marital transitions. *Monographs of the Society for Research in Child Development, 57* (2–3, Serial No. 227).

Hetherington, E. Mavis, Hagan, Margaret Stanley, & Anderson, Edward R. (1989). Marital transitions: A child's perspective. *American Psychologist, 44,* 303–312.

Hewlett, B.S. (1992). The parent-infant relationship and social-emotional development among Aka pygmies. In J.L. Roopnarine & D.B. Carter (Eds.), *Annual advances in applied developmental psychology: Vol. 5. Parent-child socialization in diverse cultures.* Norwood, NJ: Ablex.

Higgins, E. Tory. (1981). Role taking and social judgment: Alternative developmental perspectives and processes. In John H. Flavell & Lee Ross (Eds.), *Social cognitive development: Frontiers and possible futures.* Cambridge, England: Cambridge University Press.

Hill, John, & Holmbeck, G.N. (1987). Familial adaptation to biological change during adolescence. In Richard M. Lerner & Terry T. Foch (Eds.), *Biological-psychosocial interactions in early adolescence.* Hillsdale, NJ: Erlbaum.

Hills, Andrew P. (1992). Locomotor characteristics of obese children. *Child: Care, Health and Development, 18,* 29–34.

Hilts, Philip J. (1991, October 8). Lower lead limits are made official. *The New York Times,* C3.

Hinde, R.A. (1987). *Individuals, relationships, and culture.* Cambridge, England: Cambridge University Press.

Hinde, R.A. (1989). Ethological and relationships approaches. In R. Vasta (Ed.), *Annals of Child Development* (Vol. 6). Greenwich, CT: JAI Press.

Hinde, R.A. (1993). Ethology and child development. In Paul H. Mussen (Ed.), *Handbook of child psychology: Vol. 2. Infancy and developmental psychobiology.* New York: Wiley.

Hinde, R.A., & Stevenson-Hinde, J. (1987). Interpersonal relationships and child development. *Developmental Review, 7,* 1–21.

Hinde, R.A., Titmus, G., Easton, D., & Tamplin, A. (1985). Incidence of "friendship" and behavior toward strong associates versus nonassociates in preschoolers. *Child Development, 56,* 234–245.

Hirschberg, L.M., & Svejda, M. (1990). When infants look to their parents: I. Infants' social referencing of mothers compared to fathers. *Child Development, 61,* 1175–1186.

Hirschi, Travis. (1969). *Causes of delinquency.* Berkeley, CA: University of California Press.

Hochschild, Arlie. (1989). *The second shift: Working parents and the revolution at home.* New York: Viking.

Hoff-Ginsberg, E. (1986). Function and structure in maternal speech: Their relation to the child's development of syntax. *Developmental Psychology, 22,* 155–163.

Hoff-Ginsberg, E. (1990). Maternal speech and the child's development of syntax: A further look. *Journal of Child Language, 17,* 85–99.

Hoffman, L.W. (1991). The influence of the family environment on personality: Accounting for sibling differences. *Psychological Bulletin, 110,* 187–203.

Hoffman, M.L. (1988). Moral development. In M.H. Bornstein & M.E. Lamb (Eds.), *Developmental psychology: An advanced textbook* (2nd ed.). Hillsdale, NJ: Erlbaum.

Hoffman, Michelle. (1991). How parents make their mark on genes. *Science, 252,* 1250–1251.

Hoffman, S.D., Foster, E.M., & Furstenberg, F.F. (1993). Reevaluating the costs of teenage childbearing. *Demography, 30,* 1–13.

Holden, Constance. (1980). Identical twins reared apart. *Science, 207,* 1323–1328.

Holden, G.W. (1983). Avoiding conflict: Mothers as tacticians in the supermarket. *Child Development, 54,* 233–240.

Holden, G.W., & West, M.J. (1989). Proximate regulation by mothers: A demonstration of how differing styles affect young children's behavior. *Child Development, 60,* 64–69.

Holden, G.W., & Zambarano, R.J. (1992). The origins of parenting: Transmission of beliefs about physical punishment. In I.E. Sigel, A.V. McGillicuddy, & J.J. Goodnow (Eds.), *Parental belief systems: The psychological consequences for children* (2nd ed.). Hillsdale, NJ: Erlbaum.

Holmbeck, G.N., & O'Donnell, K. (1991). Discrepancies between perceptions of decision making and behavioral autonomy. In R.L. Paikoff (Ed.), *New directions for child development: No. 51. Shared views in the family during adolescence.* San Francisco: Jossey-Bass.

Holroyd, Sarah, & Baron-Cohen, Simon. (1993). Brief report: How far can people with autism go in developing a theory of mind? *Journal of Autism and Developmental Disorders, 23,* 379–385.

Holzman, Mathilda. (1983). *The language of children: Development in home and in school.* Englewood Cliffs, NJ: Prentice-Hall.

Holzman, Philip S., & Matthysse, Steven. (1990). The genetics of schizophrenia: A review. *Psychological Science, 1,* 279–286.

Honig, Alice Sterling. (1987). The shy child. *Young Children, 42,* 54–64.

Hopwood, N.J., Kelch, R.P., Hale, P.M., Mendes, T.M., Foster, C.M., & Beitins, I.Z. (1990). The onset of human puberty: Biological and environmental factors. In John Bancroft & June Machover Reinisch (Eds.), *Adolescence and puberty.* New York: Oxford University Press.

Horney, Karen. (1967). *Feminine psychology.* Harold Kelman (Ed.). New York: Norton.

Hornick, R., Risenhoover, N., & Gunnar, M. (1987). The effects of maternal positive, neutral, and negative affective communications on infant responses to new toys. *Child Development, 58,* 937–944.

Horowitz, F.D. (1992). John B. Watson's legacy: Learning and environment. *Developmental Psychology, 28,* 360–367.

Howard, Marion, & McCabe, Judith Blamey. (1990). Helping teenagers postpone sexual involvement. *Family Planning Perspectives, 22,* 21–26.

Howe, N., & Ross, H.S. (1990). Socialization, perspective-taking, and the sibling relationship. *Developmental Psychology, 26,* 160–165.

Howes, C. (1983). Patterns of friendship. *Child Development, 54,* 1041–1053.

Howes, C. (1987). Social competence with peers in young children: Developmental sequences. *Developmental Review, 7,* 252–272.

Howes, C. (1992). *The collaborative construction of pretend.* Albany: State University of New York Press.

Howes, C., & Hamilton, C.E. (1992). Children's relationships with caregivers: Mothers and child care teachers. *Child Development, 63,* 859–866.

Howes, C., Phillips, D.A., & Whitebook, M. (1992). Thresholds of quality: Implications for the social development of children in center-based child care. *Child Development, 63,* 449–460.

Howes, P.W., & Cicchetti, D. (1993). A family/relational perspective on maltreating families: Parallel processes across systems and social policy implications. In D. Cicchetti & S.L. Toth (Eds.), *Advances in developmental psychology: Vol. 8. Child abuse, child development, and social policy.* Norwood, NJ: Ablex.

Hsu, L.K. George. (1990). *Eating disorders.* New York: Guilford.

Hudley, C., & Graham, S. (1993). An attributional intervention to reduce peer-directed aggression among African-American boys. *Child Development, 64,* 124–138.

Hudson, J.A. (1990). The emergence of autobiographical memory in mother-child conversation. In R. Fivush & J.A. Hudson (Eds.), *Knowing and remembering in young children*. Cambridge, England: Cambridge University Press.

Hull, Valerie, Thapa, Shyam, & Pratomo, Hadi. (1990). Breastfeeding in the modern health sector in Indonesia: The mother's perspective. *Social Science and Medicine, 30,* 625–633.

Humphreys, Anne P., & Smith, Peter K. (1987). Rough and tumble, friendship, and dominance in schoolchildren: Evidence for continuity and change with age. *Child Development, 58,* 201–212.

Hunter, Fumiyo Tao. (1985). Adolescents' perception of discussion with parents and friends. *Developmental Psychology, 21,* 433–440.

Hunter, M. (1990). *Abused boys: The neglected victims of sexual abuse*. Lexington, MA: Lexington Books.

Hurrelmann, K., & Engel, W. (1989). *The social world of adolescents: International perspectives*. Berlin: Walter de Gruyter.

Huston, Aletha C. (1983). Sex-typing. In Paul H. Mussen (Ed.), *Handbook of child psychology: Vol. 4. Socialization, personality and social development*. New York: Wiley.

Huston, Aletha C. (1985). The development of sex-typing: Themes from recent research. *Developmental Review, 5,* 1–17.

Huston, Aletha C., & Alvarez, Mildred A. (1990). The socialization context of gender-role development in early adolescents. In Raymond Montemayor, Gerald R. Adams, & Thomas P. Gullotta (Eds.), *From childhood to adolescence: A transitional period?* Newbury Park, CA: Sage.

Huston, Aletha C., McLoyd, Vonnie C., & Coll, Cynthia Garcia. (1994). Children and poverty: Issues in contemporary research. *Child Development, 65,* 275–282.

Huston, Aletha C., Watkins, Bruca A., & Kunkel, Dale. (1989). Public policy and children's television. *American Psychologist, 44,* 424–433.

Hutchinson, J. (1991). What crack does to babies. *American Educator (Spring),* 31–32.

Huttenlocher, P.R. (1990). Morphometric study of human cerebral cortex development. *Neuropsychologia,* 517–527.

Hyde, Kenneth E. (1990). *Religion in childhood and adolescence: A comprehensive review of the research*. Birmingham, AL: Religious Education Press.

Hymel, S., Bowker, A., & Woody, E. (1993). Aggressive versus withdrawn unpopular children: Variations in peer and self-perceptions in multiple domains. *Child Development, 64,* 879–896.

Hymel, S., Rubin, K.H., Rowden, L., & LeMare, L. (1990). Children's peer relationships: Longitudinal prediction of internalizing and externalizing problems from middle to late childhood. *Child Development, 61,* 2004–2021.

Hymel, S., Wagner, E., & Butler, L.J. (1990). Reputational bias: View from the peer group. In S.R. Asher & J.D. Coie (Eds.), *Peer rejection in childhood*. Cambridge, England: Cambridge University Press.

Imbert, Michel. (1985). Physiological underpinnings of perceptual development. In Jacques Mehler & Robin Fox (Eds.), *Neonate cognition: Beyond the blooming confusion*. Hillsdale, NJ: Erlbaum.

Inch, Sally. (1984). *Birth-rights: What every parent should know about childbirth in hospitals*. New York: Pantheon.

Ingersoll, Barbara D., & Goldstein, Sam. (1993). *Attention deficit disorder and learning disabilities: Realities, myths and controversial treatments*. New York: Doubleday.

Ingleby, David. (1987). Psychoanalysis and ideology. In John M. Broughton (Ed.), *Critical theories of psychological development*. New York: Plenum.

Ingrassia, M., & Springen, K. (1994, March 24). She's not baby Jessica anymore. *Newsweek*.

Inhelder, Bärbel, & Piaget, Jean. (1958). *The growth of logical thinking from childhood to adolescence*. New York: Basic Books.

Institute for Social Research. (1994). High schoolers' jobs may "cost" too much. *Profiles: The ISR newsletter, 18,* 11.

International Assessment of Educational Progress. (1989). *A world of differences: An international assessment of math and science*.

Isabella, R.A. (1993). Origins of attachment: Maternal interactive behavior across the first year. *Child Development, 64,* 605–621.

Isabella, R.A., & Belsky, J. (1991). Interactional synchrony and the origins of infant-mother attachment: A replication study. *Child Development, 62,* 373–384.

Israel, A.C., & Shapiro, L.S. (1985). Behavior problems of obese children enrolling in a weight reduction program. *Journal of Pediatric Psychology, 10,* 449–460.

Izard, Carroll E. (1980). The maximally discriminative facial movement scoring system. Unpublished manuscript, University of Delaware.

Izard, Carroll E. (1991). *The psychology of emotions*. New York: Plenum.

Izard, Carroll E., & Malatesta, C.Z. (1987). Perspectives on emotional development I: Differential emotions theory of early emotional development. In Joy Doniger Osofsky (Ed.), *Handbook of infant development* (2nd ed.). New York: Wiley.

Izard, Carroll E., Hembree, E.A., & Huebner, R.R. (1987). Infants' emotional expressions to acute pain: Developmental change and stability of individual differences. *Developmental Psychology, 23,* 105–113.

Izard, Carroll E., Porges, Stephen W., Simons, Robert F., Haynes, O. Maurice, & Cohen, Ben. (1991). Infant cardiac activity: Developmental changes and relations with attachment. *Developmental Psychology, 27,* 432–439.

Jacklin, Carol Nagy, Wilcox, K.T., & Maccoby, Eleanor E. (1988). Neonatal sex-steroid hormone and intellectual abilities of six-year-old boys and girls. *Developmental Psychobiology, 21,* 567–574.

Jackson, Jacquelyne Faye. (1993). Human behavioral genetics, Scarr's theory, and her views on interventions: A critical review and commentary on their implications for African American children. *Child Development, 64,* 1318–1332.

Jackson, Sonia. (1987). Great Britain. In Michael E. Lamb (Ed.), *The father's role: Cross cultural perspectives*. Hillsdale, NJ: Erlbaum.

Jacobs, J.E., Bennett, M.A., & Flanagan, C. (1993). Decision–making in one-parent and two-parent families: Influence and information selection. *Journal of Early Adolescence, 13*, 245–266.

Jacobs, J.E., & Ganzel, A.K. (in press). Decision-making in adolescence: Are we asking the wrong question? In P.R. Pintrich & M.L. Maehr (Eds.), *Advances in achievement and motivation: Vol. 8. Motivation in adolescence.* Greenwich, CT: JAI Press.

Jacobs, P.A. (1991). The fragile X syndrome (Editorial). *Journal of Human Genetics, 28*, 809–810.

Jacobson, Joseph L., Boersma, David C., Fields, Robert B., & Olson, Karen L. (1983). Paralinguistic features of adult speech to infants and small children. *Child Development, 54*, 436–442.

Jacobson, Joseph L., & Jacobson, Sandra W. (1990). Methodological issues in human behavioral teratology. In Carolyn Rovee-Collier & Lewis P. Lipsitt (Eds.), *Advances in infancy research* (Vol. 6). Norwood, NJ: Ablex.

Jacobson, Joseph L., Jacobson, Sandra W., Fein, Greta G., Schwartz, Pamela M., & Dowler, Jeffrey K. (1984). Prenatal exposure to an environmental toxin: A test of multiple effects. *Developmental Psychology, 20*, 523–532.

Jacobson, Joseph L., Jacobson, Sandra W., Padgett, Robert J., Brummitt, Gail A., & Billings, Robin L. (1992). Effects of prenatal PCB exposure on cognitive processing efficiency and sustained attention. *Developmental Psychology, 28*, 297–306.

James, P.D. (1993). *The children of men.* New York: Knopf.

James, William. (1950). *The principles of psychology* (Vol. 1). New York: Dover. (Original work published 1890).

Jelliffe, Derrick B., & Jelliffe, E.F. Patrice. (1977). Current concepts in nutrition: "Breast is best": Modern meanings. *New England Journal of Medicine, 297*, 912–915.

Jencks, Christopher. (1994). *The homeless.* Cambridge, MA: Harvard University Press.

Jenkins, Jennifer. (1992). Sibling relationships in disharmonious homes: Potential difficulties and protective effects. In Fritz Boer & Judy Dunn (Eds.), *Children's sibling relationships: Developmental and clinical issues.* Hillsdale, NJ: Erlbaum.

Jessor, Richard. (1992). Risk behavior in adolescence: A psychosocial framework for understanding and action. *Developmental Review, 12*, 374–390.

Johnson, Charles D. (1992). Projecting unmet need for prenatal care. In Jonathan B. Kotch, Craig H. Blakely, Sarah S. Brown, & Frank Y. Wong (Eds.), *A pound of prevention: The case for universal maternity care in the U.S.* Washington, DC: American Public Health Association.

Johnson, Clifford M., Mirands, Leticia, Sherman, Arloc, & Weill, James D. (1991). *Child poverty in America.* Washington, DC: Children's Defense Fund.

Johnson, C. Merle. (1991). Infant and toddler sleep: A telephone survey of parents in the community. *Journal of Developmental and Behavioral Pediatrics, 12*, 108–114.

Johnson, Craig, & Connors, Mary E. (1987). *The etiology and treatment of bulimia nervosa: A biopsychosocial perspective.* New York: Basic Books.

Johnson, Dale L., Swank, Paul, Howie, Virgil M., Baldwin, Constance D., Owen, Mary, & Luttman, David. (1993). Does HOME add to the prediction of child intelligence over and above SES? *Journal of Genetic Psychology, 154*, 33–40.

Johnson, Edward S., & Meade, Ann C. (1987). Developmental patterns of spatial ability: An early sex difference. *Child Development, 58*, 725–740.

Johnson, Harold R., Gibson, Rose C., & Luckey, Irene. (1990). Health and social characteristics. In Zev Brown, Edward A. McKinney, & Michael Williams (Eds.), *Black aged.* Newbury Park, CA: Sage.

Johnson, Helen L., Glassman, Marc B., Fiks, Kathleen B., & Rosen, Tove S. (1990). Resilient children: Individual differences in developmental outcome of children born to drug users. *Journal of Genetic Psychology, 151*, 523–539.

Johnson, J., & Newport, E. (1989). Critical period effects in second language learning: The influence of maturational state on the acquisition of English as a second language. *Cognitive Psychology, 21*, 60–99.

Johnson, Russell R., Greenspan, Stephen, & Brown, Gwyn M. (1984). Children's ability to recognize and improve upon socially inept communications. *Journal of Genetic Psychology, 144*, 255–264.

Johnson, Tanya Fusco. (1991). *Elder mistreatment: Deciding who is at risk.* New York: Greenwood.

Johnston, J. (1994). High-conflict divorce. *The Future of Children*, in press.

Johnston, Janet R., Kline, Marsha, & Tschann, Jeanne. (1989). Ongoing post-divorce conflict in families contesting custody: Do joint custody and frequent access help? *American Journal of Orthopsychiatry, 59*, 576–592.

Johnston, Lloyd D., Bachman, Jerald G., & O'Malley, Patrick M. (1994). *Monitoring the future study: Preliminary report of 1993 findings* (University of Michigan News and Information Services Press Release, January 17, 1994). Ann Arbor: University of Michigan.

Johnston, Lloyd D., O'Malley, Patrick M., & Bachman, Jerald G. (1989). *Drug use, drinking, and smoking: National survey results from high school, college, and young adult populations, 1975–1988.* Rockville, MD: National Institute for Drug Abuse.

Johnston, Lloyd D., O'Malley, Patrick M., & Bachman, Jerald G. (1992). *Smoking, drinking, and illicit drug use among American secondary school students, college students, and young adults, 1975–1991.* NIH publication No. 93-3480. Rockville, MD: National Institute on Drug Abuse.

Jones, Celeste Pappas, & Adamson, Lauren B. (1987). Language use in mother-child and mother-child-sibling interactions. *Child Development, 58*, 356–366.

Jones, Mary Cover. (1957). The later careers of boys who were early- or late-maturing. *Child Development, 28*, 113–128.

Jones, Mary Cover. (1965). Psychological correlates of somatic development. *Child Development, 36*, 899–911.

Jones, Mary Cover, & Bayley, Nancy. (1950). Physical maturing among boys as related to behavior. *Journal of Educational Psychology, 41*, 129–248.

Jones, N. Burton. (1976). Rough-and-tumble play among nursery school children. In Jerome S. Bruner, Alison Jolly, & Kathy Sylva (Eds.), *Play.* New York: Basic Books.

Jones, Susan S., Smith, Linda B., & Landau, Barbara. (1991). Object properties and knowledge in early lexical learning. *Child Development, 62*, 499–516.

Juel-Nielsen, Neils. (1980). *Individual and environment: Monozygotic twins reared apart.* New York: International Universities Press.

Jurich, Anthony P., Polson, Cheryl J., Jurich, Julie A., & Bates, Rodney A. (1985). Family factors in the lives of drug users and abusers. *Adolescence, 20,* 143–159.

Kach, Nick, Mazurek, Kas, Patterson, Robert S., and DeFaveri, Ivan. (1991). *Essays on Canadian education.* Calgary, Alberta: Detselig.

Kagan, Jerome. (1981). *The second year.* Cambridge, MA: Harvard University Press.

Kagan, Jerome. (1989). Temperamental contributions to social behavior. *American Psychologist, 44,* 668–674.

Kagan, Jerome. (1992). Yesterday's premises, tomorrow's promises. *Developmental Psychology, 28,* 990–997.

Kagan, Jerome, & Snidman, Nancy. (1991). Infant predictors of inhibited and uninhibited profiles. *Psychological Science, 2,* 40–44.

Kagan, Jerome, & Snidman, Nancy. (1991). Temperamental factors in human development. *American Psychologist, 46,* 856–862.

Kagan, Jerome, Arcus, Doreen, & Snidman, Nancy. (1993). The idea of temperament: Where do we go from here? In Robert Plomin and Gerald E. McClearn (Eds.), *Nature, nurture, and psychology.* Washington, DC: American Psychological Association.

Kagan, Jerome, Reznick, J.S., & Snidman, Nancy. (1988). Biological bases of childhood shyness. *Science, 240,* 167–171.

Kahn, P.H., Jr. (1992). Children's obligatory and discretionary moral judgments. *Child Development, 63,* 416–430.

Kail, R. (1990). *The development of memory in children* (3rd ed.). New York: Freeman.

Kail, R. (1991). Developmental changes in speed of processing during childhood and adolescence. *Psychological Bulletin, 109,* 490–501.

Kail, R. (1991). Processing time declines exponentially during childhood and adolescence. *Developmental Psychology, 27,* 259–266.

Kaltenback, K., & Finnegan, L.P. (1992). Methadone maintenance during pregnancy: Implications for perinatal and developmental outcome. In T.B. Sonderegger (Ed.), *Perinatal substance abuse: Research findings and clinical implications.* Baltimore: Johns Hopkins University Press.

Kamerman, S.B., & Kahn, A.J. (1993). Home health visiting in Europe. *The Future of Children, 3,* 39–52.

Kanner, Leo. (1943). Autistic disturbances of affective contact. *Nervous Child, 2,* 217–250.

Kantrowitz, Barbara, Wingert, Pat, & Hager, Mary. (1988, May 16). Premies. *Newsweek.*

Kaplan, Cynthia, Heneghan, Randi J., Trunca, C., & Rochelson, B. (1987). Femoral cylinder index in the diagnosis of the Ullrich-Turner syndrome. In Enid F. Gilbert & John M. Opitz (Eds.), *Genetic aspects of developmental pathology.* New York: Liss.

Katchadourian, H. (1990). Sexuality. In S.S. Feldman & G.R. Elliott (Eds.), *At the threshold: The developing adolescent.* Cambridge, MA: Harvard University Press.

Katz, L.F., & Gottman, J.M. (1993). Patterns of marital conflict predict children's internalizing and externalizing behaviors. *Developmental Psychology, 29,* 940–950.

Katz, P.A. (1987). Developmental and social processes in ethnic attitudes and self-identification. In J.S. Phinney & M.J. Rotheram (Eds.), *Children's ethnic socialization: Pluralism and development.* Newbury Park, CA: Sage.

Kaufman, Joan, & Zigler, Edward. (1989). The intergenerational transmission of child abuse. In Dante Cicchetti & Vicki Carlson (Eds.), *Child maltreatment: Theory and research on the causes and consequences of child abuse and neglect.* Cambridge, England: Cambridge University Press.

Kaufman, K.L., Johnson, C.F., Cohn, D., & McCleery, J. (1992). Child maltreatment prevention in the health care and social service system. In D.J. Willis, E.W. Holden, & M. Rosenberg (Eds.), *Prevention of child maltreatment: Developmental and ecological perspectives.* New York: Wiley.

Kaye, Kenneth. (1982). *The mental and social life of babies: How parents create persons.* Chicago: University of Chicago Press.

Keating, D.P. (1990). Adolescent thinking. In S.S. Feldman & G.R. Elliott (Eds.), *At the threshold: The developing adolescent.* Cambridge, MA: Harvard University Press.

Keil, F. (1984). Mechanisms of cognitive development and the structure of knowledge. In Robert J. Sternberg (Ed.), *Mechanisms of cognitive development.* New York: Freeman.

Kendall-Tackett, K.A., Williams, L.M., & Finkelhor, D. (1993). Impact of sexual abuse on children: A review and synthesis of recent empirical studies. *Psychological Bulletin, 113,* 164–180.

Keniston, Kenneth, & The Carnegie Council on Children. (1977). *All our children: The American family under pressure.* New York: Harcourt, Brace, Jovanovich.

Kennell, J., Klaus, M., McGrath, S., Robertson, S., & Hinkley, C. (1991). Continuous emotional support during labor in a U.S. hospital. *Journal of the American Medical Association, 265,* 2197–2201.

Kenney, Asta M., Guardada, Sandra, & Brown, Lisanne. (1989). Sex education and AIDS education in the schools: What states and large school districts are doing. *Family Planning Perspectives, 21,* 56–64.

Keppel, Kenneth G., & Taffel, Selma M. (1993). Pregnancy-related weight gain and retention: Implications of the 1990 Institute of Medicine guidelines. *American Journal of Public Health, 83,* 1100–1103.

Kerr, Robert. (1985). Fitts' law and motor control in children. In Jane E. Clark & James H. Humphrey (Eds.), *Motor development: Current selected research.* Princeton, NJ: Princeton Book Company.

Keshet, Jamie. (1988). The remarried couple: Stresses and successes. In William R. Beer (Ed.), *Relative strangers.* Totowa, NJ: Rowman and Littlefield.

Kindermann, T.A. (1993). Natural peer groups as contexts for individual development: The case of children's motivation in school. *Developmental Psychology, 29,* 970–977.

Kirby, Douglas. (1984). *Sexuality education: An evaluation of programs and their effects.* Atlanta, GA: Bureau of Health Education, Centers for Disease Control.

Kirby, Douglas, Barth, Richard P., Leland, Nancy, & Fetro, Joyce V. (1991). Reducing the risk: Impact of a new curriculum on sexual risk-taking. *Family Planning Perspectives, 21,* 253–263.

Kitchener, K.S., & Fischer, Kurt S. (1990). A skill approach to the development of reflective thinking. In D. Kuhn (Ed.), *Developmental aspects of teaching and learning thinking skills: Vol. 21. Contributions to human development*. Basel, Switzerland: Karger.

Kitzinger, Sheila. (1989). *The complete book of pregnancy and childbirth*. New York: Knopf.

Klahr, D. (1989). Information-processing approaches. In R. Vasta (Ed.), *Annals of child development* (Vol. 6). Greenwich, CT: JAI Press.

Klahr, D. (1992). Information-processing approaches to cognitive development. In M.H. Bornstein & M.E. Lamb (Eds.), *Developmental psychology: An advanced textbook* (3rd ed.). Hillsdale, NJ: Erlbaum.

Klahr, D., & Wallace, J.G. (1976). *Cognitive development: An information-processing view*. Hillsdale, NJ: Erlbaum.

Klaus, Marshall H., & Kennell, John H. (1976). *Maternal-infant bonding: The impact of early separation or loss on family development*. St. Louis: Mosby.

Klaus, Marshall H., & Kennell, John H. (1982). *Parent-infant bonding*. St. Louis: Mosby.

Klebanoff, Mark A., Shiono, Patricia, & Rhoads, George G. (1990). Outcomes of pregnancy in a national sample of resident physicians. *New England Journal of Medicine, 323*, 1040–1045.

Klein, Melanie. (1957). *Envy and gratitude*. New York: Basic Books.

Klein, T.W. (1988). *Program evaluation of the Kaemhameha Elementary Education Program's reading curriculum in Hawaii public schools: The cohort analysis 1978–1986*. Honolulu: Center for Development of Early Education.

Kleinman, J.C., Fingerhut, L.A., & Prager, K. (1991). Differences in infant mortality by race, nativity status, and other maternal characteristics. *American Journal of the Diseases of Children, 145*, 194–199.

Klesges, Robert. (1993). Effects of television on metabolic rate: Potential implications for childhood obesity. *Pediatrics, 19* (2).

Kline, Marsha, Tschann, Jeanne M., Johnston, Janet R., & Wallerstein, Judith S. (1989). Children's adjustment in joint and sole physical custody families. *Developmental Psychology, 25*, 430–438.

Klinnert, M.D., Campos, J.J., Sorce, J.F., Emde, R.N., & Svejda, M. (1983). Emotions as behavior regulators: Social referencing in infancy. In R. Plutchik & H. Kellerman (Eds.), *Emotion: Theory, research, and experience: Vol 2. Emotions in early development*. New York: Academic Press.

Klopfer, P. (1971). Mother love: What turns it on? *American Scientist, 49*, 404–407.

Knapp, Mary, & Knapp, Herbert. (1976). *One potato, two potato: The secret education of American children*. New York: Morton.

Koch, Patricia Barthalow. (1988). The relationship of first intercourse to later sexual functioning concerns of adolescents. *Journal of Adolescent Research, 3*, 345–362.

Kochanska, G. (1991). Socialization and temperament in the development of guilt and conscience. *Child Development, 62*, 1379–1392.

Kochanska, G. (1993). Toward a synthesis of parental socializations and child temperament in early development of conscience. *Child Development, 64*, 325–347.

Koff, Elissa, & Rierdan, Jill. (1991). Menarche and body image. In Richard M. Lerner, Ann C. Petersen, & Jeanne Brooks-Gunn (Eds.), *Encyclopedia of adolescence* (Vol. 2). New York: Garland.

Koff, Elissa, Rierdan, Jill, & Stubbs, Margaret. (1990). Gender, body image, and self-concept during adolescence. *Journal of Early Adolescence, 10*, 56–68.

Kohlberg, Lawrence. (1963). Development of children's orientation towards a moral order (Part I). Sequencing in the development of moral thought. *Vita Humana, 6*, 11–36.

Kohlberg, Lawrence. (1966). A cognitive developmental analysis of children's sex-role concepts and attitudes. In Eleanor Maccoby (Ed.), *The development of sex differences*. Stanford, CA: Stanford University Press.

Kohlberg, Lawrence. (1969). Stage and sequence. The cognitive developmental approach to socialization. In D.A. Goslin (Ed.), *Handbook of socialization theory and research*. Chicago: Rand McNally.

Kohlberg, Lawrence. (1981). *Essays on moral development* (Vol. 1). New York: Harper & Row.

Kohlberg, Lawrence. (1981). *The philosophy of moral development*. New York: Harper & Row.

Kohlberg, Lawrence, & Elfenbein, Donald. (1975). The development of moral judgments concerning capital punishment. *American Journal of Orthopsychiatry, 45*, 614–640.

Kohlberg, Lawrence, & Ullian, Dorothy Z. (1974). Stages in the development of psychosexual concepts and attitudes. In Richard C. Friedman, Ralph M. Richart, & Raymond L. VandeWiele (Eds.), *Sex differences in behavior: A conference*. New York: Wiley.

Kolb, B. (1989). Brain development, plasticity, and behavior. *American Psychologist, 44*, 1203–1212.

Kondratas, A. (1991). Ending homelessness: Policy changes. *American Psychologist, 46*, 1226–1231.

Koonin, M.N., Smith, Jack C., & Ramick, Merrell. (1993, December 17). Abortion surveillance: United States, 1990. *Morbidity and Mortality Weekly Report, 42*.

Koopman, Peter, Gubbay, John, Vivian, Nigel, Goodfellow, Peter, & Lovell-Badge, Robin. (1991). Male development of chromosomally female mice transgenic for Sry. *Nature, 351*, 117–122.

Kopp, Clair B., & Kaler, Sandra R. (1989). Risk in infancy: Origins and implications. *American Psychologist, 44*, 224–230.

Korbin, J.E. (in press). Sociocultural factors in child maltreatment. In G.B. Melton & F. Barry (Eds.), *Safe neighborhoods: Foundations for a new national strategy on child abuse and neglect*. New York: Guilford.

Kornhaber, Arthur, & Woodward, Kenneth L. (1981). *Grandparents/grandchildren: The vital connection*. Garden City, NJ: Anchor.

Kotlowitz, Alex. (1991). *There are no children here*. New York: Doubleday.

Kozol, Jonathan. (1991). *Savage inequalities*. New York: Crown.

Kranichfeld, Marion L. (1987). Rethinking family power. *Journal of Family Issues, 8*, 42–56.

Kroger, Jane. (1989). *Identity in adolescence: The balance between self and other*. London: Routledge.

Kroger, Jane. (1993). Ego identity: an overview. In J. Kroger (Ed.), *Discussions on ego identity*. Hillsdale, NJ: Erlbaum.

Kropp, Joseph P., & Haynes, O. Maurice. (1987). Abusive and nonabusive mothers' ability to identify general and specific emotion signals of infants. *Child Development, 58,* 187–190.

Kuczaj, Stan A. (1986). Thoughts on the intentional basis of early object word extension: Evidence from comprehension and production. In Stan A. Kuczaj & Martyn D. Barrett (Eds.), *The development of word meaning: Progress in cognitive developmental research*. New York: Springer-Verlag.

Kuczynski, L. (1984). Socialization goals and mother-child interaction: Strategies for long-term and short-term compliance. *Developmental Psychology, 20,* 1061–1073.

Kuczynski, L., & Kochanska, G. (1990). Development of children's noncompliance strategies from toddlerhood to age 5. *Developmental Psychology, 26,* 398–408.

Kuczynski, L., Kochanska, G., Radke-Yarrow, M., & Girnius-Brown, O. (1987). A developmental interpretation of young children's noncompliance. *Developmental Psychology, 23,* 799–806.

Kuhl, P.K., & Meltzoff, A.N. (1988). Speech as an intermodal object of perception. In A. Yonas (Ed.), *Minnesota symposia on child psychology: Vol. 20. Perceptual development in infancy*. Hillsdale, NJ: Erlbaum.

Kuhl, P.K., Williams, K.A., Lacerda, F., Stevens, K.N., & Lindblom, B. (1992). Linguistic experience alters phonetic perception in infants by 6 months of age. *Science, 255,* 606–608.

Kuhn, D. (1989). Children and adults as intuitive scientists. *Psychological Review, 96,* 674–689.

Kuhn, D. (1991). *The skills of argument*. Cambridge, England: Cambridge University Press.

Kuhn, D. (1992). Cognitive development. In M.H. Bornstein & M.E. Lamb (Eds.), *Developmental psychology: An advanced textbook* (3rd ed.). Hillsdale, NJ: Erlbaum.

Kuhn, Deanna, Nash, Sharon Churnin, & Brucken, Laura. (1978). Sex role concepts of two- and three-year-olds. *Child Development, 49,* 445–451.

Kupersmidt, J.B., & Coie, J.D. (1990). Preadolescent peer status, aggression, and school adjustment as predictors of externalizing problems in adolescence. *Child Development, 61,* 1350–1362.

Kupersmidt, J.B., Coie, J.D., & Dodge, K.A. (1990). In S.R. Asher & J.D. Coie (Eds.), *Peer rejection in childhood* (pp. 274–305). Cambridge, England: Cambridge University Press.

Kurdek, Lawrence A. (1989). Relationship quality for newly married husbands and wives: Marital history, stepchildren, and individual difference predictors. *Journal of Marriage and the Family, 52,* 1053–1064.

Kurnit, D.M., Layton, W.M., & Matthyusse, Steven. (1987). Genetics, change and morphogenesis. *American Journal of Human Genetics, 41,* 979–995.

Ladd, G.W., & Hart, C.H. (1992). Creating informal play opportunities: Are parents' and preschoolers' initiations related to children's competence with peers? *Developmental Psychology, 28,* 1179–1187.

La Freniere, Peter, Strayer, F.F., & Gauthier, Roger. (1984). The emergence of same-sex affiliative preferences among preschool peers: A developmental/ethological perspective. *Child Development, 55,* 1958–1965.

Lamaze, Fernand. (1958). *Painless childbirth*. London: Burke.

Lamb, David R. (1984). *Physiology of exercise: Response and adaptation* (2nd ed.). New York: Macmillan.

Lamb, Michael E. (1981). The development of father-infant relationships. In Michael E. Lamb (Ed.), *Nontraditional families: Parenting and child development*. Hillsdale, NJ: Erlbaum.

Lamb, Michael E. (1982). Maternal employment and child development: A review. In Michael E. Lamb (Ed.), *Nontraditional families: Parenting and child development*. Hillsdale, NJ: Erlbaum.

Lamb, Michael E. (1987). *The father's role: Cross-cultural perspectives*. Hillsdale, NJ: Erlbaum.

Lamb, Michael E., & Easterbrooks, M.A. (1981). Individual differences in parental sensitivity: Origins, components, and consequences. In M.E. Lamb & L.R. Sherrod (Eds.), *Infant social cognition*. Hillsdale, NJ: Erlbaum.

Lamb, Michael E., & Malkin, C.M. (1986). The development of social expectations in distress-relief sequences: A longitudinal study. *International Journal of Behavioral Development, 9,* 235–249.

Lamb, Michael E., Thompson, R.A., Gardner, W.P., & Charnov, E.L. (1985). *Infant-mother attachment*. Hillsdale, NJ: Erlbaum.

Lamborn, Susie D., Mounts, Nina S., Steinberg, Laurence, & Dornbusch, Sanford M. (1991). Patterns of competence and adjustment among adolescents from authoritarian, authoritative, indulgent, and neglectful families. *Child Development, 62,* 1049–1065.

Lamborn, Susie D., & Steinberg, Laurence. (1993). Emotional autonomy redux: Revisiting Ryan and Lynch. *Child Development, 64,* 483–499.

Lamm, S.S., & Fisch, M.L. (1982). *Learning disabilities explained*. Garden City, NY: Doubleday.

Landale, Nancy S., & Fennelly, Katherine. (1992). Informal unions among mainland Puerto Ricans: Cohabitation or an alternative to legal marriage. *Journal of Marriage and the Family, 54,* 269–280.

Landry, S.H., Chapieski, M.L., Richarson, M.A., Palmer, J., & Hall, S. (1990). The social competence of children born prematurely: Effects of medical complications and parent behaviors. *Child Development, 61,* 1605–1616.

Lansing, L. Stephen. (1983). *The three worlds of Bali*. New York: Praeger.

Lapsley, D.K., Milstead, M., Quintana, S.M., Flannery, D., & Buss, R.R. (1986). Adolescent egocentrism and formal operations: Tests of a theoretical assumption. *Developmental Psychology, 22,* 800–807.

Larsen, Jean M., & Robinson, Clyde C. (1989). Later effects of preschool on low-risk children. *Early Childhood Research Quarterly, 4,* 133–144.

Larson, Reed, & Lampmann-Petraitis, Claudia. (1989). Daily emotional states as reported by children and adolescents. *Child Development, 60,* 1250–1260.

Larson, Reed, & Richards, M.H. (1991). Daily companionship in late childhood and early adolescence: Changing developmental perspectives. *Child Development, 62,* 284–300.

Lay, Keng-Ling, Waters, Everett, & Park, Kathryn A. (1989). Maternal responsiveness and child compliance: The role of mood as a mediator. *Child Development, 60,* 1405–1411.

Leach, Penelope. (1989). *Babyhood* (2nd ed.). New York: Knopf.

Leary, Warren E. (1994). Barriers to immunization peril children: Experts say. *The New York Times,* A24, A26.

Lee, James Michael. (1980). Christian religious education and moral development. In Brenda Munsey (Ed.), *Moral development, moral education and Kohlberg: Basic issues in philosophy, psychology, religion and education.* Birmingham, AL: Religious Education Press.

Lee, Thomas F. (1993). *Gene future: The promise and perils of the new biology.* New York: Plenum.

Lee, Valerie E., Brooks-Gunn, Jeanne, & Schnur, Elizabeth. (1988). Does Head Start work? A 1 year follow-up comparison of disadvantaged children attending Head Start, no preschool, and other preschool programs. *Developmental Psychology, 24,* 210–222.

Leibowitz, Sarah F., & Kim, Taewon. (1992). Impact of a galanin antagonist on exogenic galanin and natural patterns of fat ingestion. *Brain Research, 599,* 148.

Leifer, A.D., Leiderman, P.H., Barnett, C.R., & Williams, J.A. (1972). Effects of mother-infant separation on maternal attachment behavior. *Child Development, 43,* 1203–1218.

Leifer, Myra. (1980). *Psychological effects of motherhood: A study of first pregnancy.* New York: Praeger.

Lenneberg, Eric H. (1967). *Biological foundations of language.* New York: Wiley.

Leon, Gloria R. (1991). Bulimia nervosa in adolescence. In Richard M. Lerner, Ann C. Petersen, & Jeanne Brooks-Gunn (Eds.), *Encyclopedia of adolescence* (Vol. 1). New York: Garland.

Leon, Gloria R., Perry, Cheryl L., Mangelsdorf, Carolyn, & Tell, Grethe J. (1989). Adolescent nutritional and psychological patterns and risk for the development of an eating disorder. *Journal of Youth and Adolescence, 18,* 273–282.

Lerner, H.E. (1978). Adaptive and pathogenic aspects of sex-role stereotypes: Implications for parenting and psychotherapy. *American Journal of Psychiatry, 135,* 48–52.

Lerner, Jacqueline V., & Lerner, R.M. (1983). Temperament and adaptation across life: Theoretical and empirical issues. In P.B. Baltes & O.G. Brim, Jr. (Eds.), *Life-span development and behavior* (Vol. 5). New York: Academic Press.

Lerner, Richard A., Delaney, Mary, Hess, Laura E., Jovanovic, Jasna, & von Eye, Alexander. (1990). Adolescent physical attractiveness and academic competence. *Journal of Early Adolescence, 10,* 4–20.

Leslie, A.M. (1984). Spatiotemporal continuity and the perception of causality in infants. *Perception, 13,* 297–305.

Leslie, A.M., & Frith, U. (1988). Autistic children's understanding of seeing, knowing, and believing. *British Journal of Developmental Psychology, 6,* 315–324.

Leslie, A.M., & Keeble, S. (1987). Do six-month-olds perceive causality? *Cognition, 25,* 265–288.

Lesser, Gerald S. (1984). A world of difference. *Action for Children's Television Magazine, 13,* 8.

Lester, Barry M., Als, Heidelise, & Brazelton, T. Berry. (1982). Regional obstetric anesthesia and newborn behavior: A re-analysis toward synergistic effects. *Child Development, 53,* 687–692.

Lester, Barry M., Corwin, Michael J., Sepkoski, Carol, Seifer, Ronald, Peucker, Mark, McLauglin, Sarah, & Golub, Howard L. (1991). Neurobehavioral syndromes in cocaine-exposed newborn infants. *Child Development, 62,* 694–705.

Lester, Barry M., & Dreher, Melanie. (1989). Effects of marijuana use during pregnancy on newborn cry. *Child Development, 60,* 765–771.

Lester, Barry M., Hoffman, Joel, & Brazelton, T. Berry. (1985). The rhythmic structure of mother-infant interaction in term and preterm infants. *Child Development, 56,* 15–27.

LeVay, Simon, & Hamer, Dean H. (1994, May). Evidence for a biological influence in male homosexuality. *Scientific American, 270,* 43–49.

LeVine, Robert A. (1980). A cross-cultural perspective on parenting. In M.D. Fantini & R. Cardenas (Eds.), *Parenting in a multicultural society.* New York: Longman.

LeVine, Robert A. (1988). Human parental care: Universal goals, cultural strategies, individual behavior. In R.A. LeVine, P.M. Miller, & M.M. West (Eds.), *Parental behavior in diverse societies.* San Francisco: Jossey-Bass.

LeVine, Robert A. (1989). Cultural influences in child development. In William Damon (Ed.), *Child development today and tomorrow.* San Francisco: Jossey-Bass.

Levy, G.D., & Carter, D.B. (1989). Gender schema, gender constancy, and gender-role knowledge: The roles of cognitive factors in preschoolers' gender-role stereotype attributions. *Developmental Psychology, 25,* 444–449.

Lewin, Tamar. (1994). Births to young teenagers decline, agency says. *The New York Times,* A18.

Lewis, M. (1990). Social knowledge and social development. *Merrill-Palmer Quarterly, 36,* 93–116.

Lewis, M., Alessandri, S.M., & Sullivan, M.W. (1990). Violation of expectancy, loss of control, and anger expressions in young infants. *Developmental Psychology, 26,* 745–751.

Lewis, M., Alessandri, S.M., & Sullivan, M.W. (1992). Differences in shame and pride as a function of children's gender and task difficulty. *Child Development, 63,* 630–638.

Lewis, M., & Brooks, J. (1978). Self-knowledge and emotional development. In M. Lewis & L.A. Rosenblum (Eds.), *The development of affect.* New York: Plenum.

Lewis, M., & Michalson, L. (1983). *Children's emotions and moods.* New York: Plenum.

Lewis, M., Sullivan, M.W., Stanger, C., & Weiss, M. (1989). Self development and self-conscious emotions. *Child Development, 60,* 146–156.

Lidz, Theodore. (1976). *The person: His and her development throughout the life cycle* (rev. ed.). New York: Basic Books.

Lieberman, A.F. (1993). *The emotional life of the toddler.* New York: The Free Press.

Lieberman, A.F., Waston, D.R., & Pawl, J.H. (1991). Preventive intervention and outcome with anxiously attached dyads. *Child Development, 62,* 199–209.

Liebert, Robert M., Neale, John M., & Davidson, Emily S. (1973). *The early window: Effects of television on children and youth.* New York: Pergamon.

Lillard, A.S. (1993). Pretend play skills and the child's theory of mind. *Child Development, 64,* 348–371.

Lillard, A.S. (1993). Young children's conceptualization of pretense: Action or mental representational state? *Child Development, 64,* 372–386.

Lillard, A.S. (1994). Making sense of pretense. In C. Lewis & P. Mitchell (Eds.), *Children's early understanding of mind.* Hillsdale, NJ: Erlbaum.

Linde, Eleanor Vander, Morrongiello, Barbara A., & Rovee-Collier, Carolyn. (1985). Determinants of retention in 8-week-old infants. *Developmental Psychology, 21,* 601–613.

Lindsey, Duncan. (1991). Factors affecting the foster care placement decision: An analysis of national survey data. *American Journal of Orthopsychiatry, 61,* 272–281.

Lipsitt, Lewis P. (1990). Learning and memory in infants. *Merrill-Palmer Quarterly, 36,* 53–66.

Liston, Daniel P., & Zeichner, Kenneth M. (1991). *Teacher education and the social conditions of schooling.* New York: Routledge.

Livesley, W.J., & Bromley, D.B. (1973). *Person perception in childhood and adolescence.* London: Wiley.

Lobel, T.E., & Menashri, J. (1993). Relations of conceptions of gender-role transgressions and gender constancy to gender-typed toy preferences. *Developmental Psychology, 29,* 150–155.

Lockman, J.J., & Thelen, E. (1993). Developmental biodynamics: Brain, body, behavior connections. *Child Development, 64,* 953–959.

Loehlin, John C. (1992). *Genes and environment in personality development.* Newbury Park, CA: Sage.

Loehlin, John C., Willerman, Lee, & Horn, Joseph M. (1982). Personality resemblances between unwed mothers and their adopted-away offspring. *Journal of Personality and Social Psychology, 42,* 1089–1099.

Loehlin, John C., Willerman, Lee, & Horn, Joseph M. (1988). Human behavior genetics. *Annual Review of Psychology, 39,* 101–133.

Loevinger, J. (1976). *Ego development.* San Francisco: Jossey-Bass.

Loftus, Elizabeth F., & Wells, Gary L. (Eds.). (1984). *Eyewitness testimony: Psychological perspectives.* New York: Cambridge University Press.

Lovett, S.B., & Flavell, J.H. (1990). Understanding and remembering: Children's knowledge about the differential effects of strategy and task variables on comprehension and memorization. *Child Development, 61,* 1842–1858.

Lowrey, George H. (1986). *Growth and development of children* (8th ed.). Chicago: Year Book Medical Publishers.

Lozoff, Betsy. (1982). *Birth in non-industrial societies.* Johnson & Johnson Roundtable.

Lozoff, Betsy. (1989). Nutrition and behavior. *American Psychologist, 44,* 231–236.

Lucas, A.R. (1991). Eating disorders. In M. Lewis (Ed.), *Child and adolescent psychiatry: A comprehensive textbook.* Baltimore: Williams and Wilkins.

Lucas, Tamara, Hense, Rosemary, & Donato, Ruben. (1990). Promoting the success of Latino language-minority students: An exploratory study of six high schools. *Harvard Educational Review, 60,* 315–340.

Lujan, Carol, De Bruyn, Llemyra M., May, Philip A., & Bird, Michael E. (1989). Profile of abused and neglected American Indian children in the Southwest. *Child Abuse and Neglect, 13,* 449–461.

Lukeman, Diane, & Melvin, Diane. (1993). Annotation: The preterm infant: Psychological issues in childhood. *Journal of Child Psychology and Psychiatry, 34,* 837–849.

Luthar, Suniya S., & Zigler, Edward. (1991). Vulnerability and competence: A review of research on resilience in childhood. *American Journal of Orthopsychiatry, 61,* 6–22.

Lykken, D.T., McGue, M., Tellegen, A., & Bouchard, T.J., Jr. (1992). Emergenesis: Genetic traits that may not run in families. *American Psychologist, 47,* 1565–1577.

Lytton, Hugh, & Romney, D.M. (1991). Parents' differential socialization of boys and girls: A meta-analysis. *Psychological Bulletin, 109,* 267–296.

Lyytinen, Paula. (1991). Developmental trends in children's pretend play. *Child: Care, Health, and Development, 17,* 9–25.

Maccoby, Eleanor Emmons. (1980). *Social development: Psychological growth and the parent-child relationship.* New York: Harcourt Brace Jovanovich.

Maccoby, Eleanor Emmons. (1984). Socialization and developmental change. *Child Development, 55,* 317–328.

Maccoby, Eleanor Emmons. (1988). Gender as a social category. *Developmental Psychology, 24,* 755–765.

Maccoby, Eleanor Emmons. (1989, August). *Gender and relationships: A developmental account.* Distinguished Scientific Achievement Award address to the annual meeting of the American Psychological Association, New Orleans, LA.

Maccoby, Eleanor Emmons. (1990). Gender and relationships: A developmental account. *American Psychologist, 45,* 513–520.

Maccoby, Eleanor Emmons. (1992). The role of parents in the socialization of children: An historical overview. *Developmental Psychology, 28,* 1006–1017.

Maccoby, Eleanor Emmons, & Martin, John A. (1983). Socialization in the context of the family: Parent-child interaction. In Paul H. Mussen (Ed.), *Handbook of child psychology: Vol. 4. Socialization, personality and social development.* New York: Wiley.

Maccoby, Eleanor Emmons, & Mnookin, R.H. (1992). *Dividing the child: Social and legal dilemmas of custody.* Cambridge, MA: Harvard University Press.

MacDonald, A.D., McDonald, J. Corbett, Armstrong, B., Cherry, N.M., Nolin, A.D., & Robert, D. (1988). Prematurity and work in pregnancy. *British Journal of Industrial Medicine, 45,* 56–62.

MacDonald, Kevin, & Parke, Ross D. (1986). Parent-child physical play: The effect of sex and age of children and parents. *Sex Roles, 15,* 367–378.

Mackenzie, Thomas B., Collins, Nancy M., & Popkin, Michael E. (1982). A case of fetal abuse? *American Journal of Orthopsychiatry, 52,* 699–703.

MacKinnon, Carol E. (1989). An observational investigation of sibling interactions in married and divorced families. *Developmental Psychology, 25,* 36–44.

Maddox, John. (1993). Wilful public misunderstanding of genetics. *Nature, 364,* 281.

Magnusson, David, Stattin, Hakan, & Allen, Vernon L. (1985). Biological maturation and social development: A longitudinal study of some adjustment processes from mid-adolescence to adulthood. *Journal of Youth and Adolescence, 14,* 267–283.

Mahler, Margaret. (1968). *On human symbiosis and the vicissitudes of individuation.* New York: International Universities Press.

Mahler, Margaret S., Pine, Fred, & Bergman, A. (1975). *The psychological birth of the human infant: Symbiosis and individuation.* New York: Basic Books.

Main, Mary, & George, Carol. (1985). Responses of abused and disadvantaged toddlers to distress in agemates: A study in the day care setting. *Developmental Psychology, 21,* 407–412.

Main, Mary, & Goldwyn, R. (in press). Interview-based adult attachment classifications: Related to infant-mother and infant-father attachment. *Developmental Psychology,* in press.

Main, Mary, & Hesse, E. (1990). Parents' unresolved traumatic experiences are related to infant disorganized attachment status: Is frightened and/or frightening parental behavior the linking mechanism? In M.T. Greenberg, D. Cicchetti, & E.M. Cummings (Eds.), *Attachment in the preschool years.* Chicago: University of Chicago Press.

Main, Mary, Kaplan, N., & Cassidy, J. (1985). Security in infancy, childhood, and adulthood: A move to the level of representation. In I. Bretherton & E. Waters (Eds.), *Growing points of attachment theory and research. Monographs of the Society for Research in Child Development, 50* (Serial No. 209).

Main, Mary, & Solomon, J. (1986). Discovery of an insecure-disorganized/disoriented attachment pattern. In T.B. Brazelton & M.W. Yogman (Eds.), *Affective development in infancy.* Norwood, NJ: Ablex.

Malatesta, C.Z., Culver, C., Tesman, J.R., & Shepard, B. (1989). The development of emotional expression during the first two years of life. *Monographs of the Society for Research in Child Development, 54* (1–2), (Serial No. 219).

Malina, Robert M. (1990). Physical growth and performance during the transitional years (9–16). In Raymond Montemayor, Gerald R. Adams, & Thomas P. Gullotta (Eds.), *From childhood to adolescence: A transitional period?* Newbury Park, CA: Sage.

Malina, Robert M. (1991). Growth spurt, adolescent. In Richard M. Lerner, Ann C. Petersen, & Jeanne Brooks-Gunn (Eds.), *Encyclopedia of adolescence* (Vol. 1). New York: Garland.

Malina, Robert M., & Bouchard, Claude. (1991). *Growth, maturation, and physical activity.* Champaign, IL: Human Kinetics Books.

Malina, Robert M., Bouchard, Claude, & Beunen, G. (1988). Human growth: Selected aspects of current research on well-nourished children. *Annual Review of Anthropology, 17,* 187–219.

Mangelsdorf, S., Gunnar, M., Kestenbaum, R., Lang, S., & Andreas, D. (1990). Infant proneness-to-distress temperament, maternal personality, and mother-infant attachment: Associations and goodness of fit. *Child Development, 61,* 820–831.

Mann, L., Harmoni, R., & Power, C. (1989). Adolescent decision-making: The development of competence. *Journal of Adolescence, 12,* 265–278.

Marcia, James E. (1966). Development and validation of ego identity status. *Journal of Personality and Social Psychology, 3,* 551–558.

Marcia, James E. (1980). Identity in adolescence. In Joseph Adelson (Ed.), *Handbook of adolescent psychology.* New York: Wiley.

Markell, Richard A., & Asher, Steven R. (1984). Children's interactions in dyads: Interpersonal influence and sociometric status. *Child Development, 55,* 1412–1424.

Markman, E.M. (1989). *Categorization and naming in children: Problems of induction.* Cambridge, MA: MIT Press.

Markman, E.M. (1991). The whole object, taxonomic, and mutual exclusivity assumptions as initial constraints on word meanings. In J.P. Byrnes & S.A. Gelman (Eds.), *Perspectives on language and cognition.* Cambridge, England: Cambridge University Press.

Markus, H., & Nurius, P. (1986). Possible selves. *American Psychologist, 41,* 954–969.

Martin, C.L. (1993). New directions for investigating children's gender knowledge. *Developmental Review, 13,* 184–204.

Martin, C.L., & Halverson, C.F. (1981). A schematic processing model of sex-typing and stereotyping in children. *Child Development, 52,* 1119–1132.

Martin, C.L., & Little, J.K. (1990). The relation of gender understanding to children's sex-typed preferences and gender stereotypes. *Child Development, 61,* 1427–1439.

Martin, C.L., Wood, C.H., & Little, J.K. (1990). The development of gender stereotype components. *Child Development, 61,* 1891–1904.

Martin, J.C. (1992). The effects of maternal use of tobacco products or amphetamines on offspring. In T.B. Sonderegger (Ed.), *Perinatal substance abuse: Research findings and clinical implications.* Baltimore: Johns Hopkins University Press.

Marx, Jean L. (1991). Zeroing in on individual cancer risk. *Science, 252,* 612–626.

Masataka, N. (1992). Early ontogeny of vocal behavior of Japanese infants in response to maternal speech. *Child Development, 63,* 1177–1185.

Masten, Ann S. (1992). Homeless children in the United States: Mark of a nation at risk. *Current Directions in Psychological Science, 1,* 41–43.

Masten, Ann S., Best, K.M., & Garmezy, Norman. (1990). Resilience and development: Contributions from children who overcome adversity. *Development and Psychopathology, 2,* 425–444.

Matias, R., & Cohn, J.F. (1993). Are Max-specified infant facial expressions during face-to-face interaction consistent with differential emotions theory? *Developmental Psychology, 29,* 524–531.

Matute-Bianchi, M.E. (1986). Ethnic identities and patterns of school success and failure among Mexican-descent and Japanese-American students in a California high school: An ethnographic analysis. *American Journal of Education, 91,* 233–255.

Maughan, Barbara, & Pickles, Andres. (1990). Adopted and illegitimate children growing up. In Lee N. Robins & Michael Rutter (Eds.), *Straight and devious pathways from childhood to adulthood.* Cambridge, England: Cambridge University Press.

Mayes, L.C., Granger, R.H., Bornstein, M.H., & Zuckerman, B. (1992). The problem of prenatal cocaine exposure: A rush to judgment. *Journal of the American Medical Association, 267,* 406–408.

McCall, R.B. (1990). Infancy research: Individual differences. *Merrill-Palmer Quarterly, 36,* 141–157.

McCartney, Kathleen. (1984). Effect of quality of day care environment on children's language development. *Developmental Psychology, 20,* 244–260.

McCauley, Elizabeth, Kay, Thomas, Ito, Joanne, & Treder, Robert. (1987). The Turner Syndrome: Cognitive deficits, affective discrimination, and behavior problems. *Child Development, 58,* 464–473.

McClearn, Gerald E., Plomin, Robert, Gora-Maslak, Grazyna, & Crabbe, John C. (1991). The gene chase in behavioral science. *Psychological Science, 2,* 222–229.

McCurdy, Karen, & Daro, Deborah. (1994). *Current trends in child abuse reporting and fatalities: The results of the 1993 annual fifty-state survey.* Chicago: National Committee to Prevent Child Abuse.

McEachin, John J., Smith, Tristram, & Lovaas, O. Ivaf. (1993). Long-term outcome for children with autism who received early intensive behavioral treatment. *American Journal on Mental Retardation, 97,* 359–372.

McFadden, Robert D. (1990, June 19). Tragic end to adoption of crack baby. *The New York Times,* B1, B4.

McGarrigle, J., & Donaldson, Margaret. (1974). Conservation "accidents." *Cognition, 3,* 341–350.

McGee, Robin A., & Wolfe, David A. (1991). Psychological maltreatment: Toward an operational definition. *Development and Psychopathology, 3,* 3–18.

McGue, Matthew. (1993). From proteins to cognitions: The behavioral genetics of alcoholism. In *Nature, nurture, and psychology.* Washington, DC: American Psychological Association.

McGue, Matt, Bouchard, Thomas J., Jr., Iacono, William G., & Lykken, David T. (1993). Behavioral genetics of cognitive ability: A life-span perspective. In *Nature, nurture, and psychology.* Washington, DC: American Psychological Association.

McGue, Matt & Lykken, David T. (1992). Genetic influence on risk of divorce. *Psychological Science, 6,* 368–373.

McHale, Susan M., & Pawletko, Terese M. (1992). Differential treatment of siblings in two family contexts. *Child Development, 63,* 68–91.

Mcintosh, Ruth, Vaughn, Sharon, & Zaragoza, Nina. (1991). A review of social interventions for students with learning disabilities. *Journal of Learning Disabilities, 24,* 451–458.

McKenzie, Lisa, & Stephenson, Patricia A. (1993). Variation in Cesarean section rates among hospitals in Washington state. *American Journal of Public Health, 83,* 1109–1112.

McKeon, Denise. (1994). Language, culture, and schooling. In Fred Genesee (Ed.), *Educating second-language children: The whole child, the whole curriculum, the whole community.* Cambridge, England: Cambridge University Press.

McKeough, Anne. (1992). A neo-structural analysis of children's narrative and its development. In Robbie Case (Ed.), *The mind's staircase: Exploring the conceptual underpinning of children's thought and knowledge.* Hillsdale, NJ: Erlbaum.

McKusick, Victor A. (1990). *Mendelian inheritance in humans* (9th ed.) Baltimore: Johns Hopkins University Press.

McLanahan, S., & Booth, K. (1991). Mother-only families: Problems, prospects, and politics. In A. Booth (Ed.), *Contemporary families: Looking forward, looking back.* Minneapolis: National Council on Family Relations.

McLaughlin, Barry. (1984). *Second language acquisition in childhood: Vol. I. Preschool children* (2nd ed.). Hillsdale, NJ: Erlbaum.

McLaughlin, Barry. (1985). *Second language acquisition in childhood: Vol. II. School-age children* (2nd ed.). Hillsdale, NJ: Erlbaum.

McLoyd, V.C. (1990). The impact of economic hardship on black families and children: Psychological distress, parenting, and socioemotional development. *Child Development, 61,* 311–346.

McLoyd, V.C., & Flanagan, C. (Eds.). (1990). *New directions for child development: No. 46. Economic stress: Effects on family life and child development.* San Francisco: Jossey-Bass.

Mebert, C.J. (1991). Dimensions of subjectivity in parents' ratings of infant temperament. *Child Development, 62,* 352–361.

Mednick, M.T. (1989). On the politics of psychological constructs: Stop the bandwagon, I want to get off. *American Psychologist, 44,* 1118–1123.

Mellor, Steven. (1990). How do only children differ from other children. *Journal of Genetic Psychology, 151,* 221–230.

Melton, G.B. (1992). The improbability of prevention of sexual abuse. In D.J Willis, E.W. Holden, & M. Rosenberg (Eds.), *Prevention of child maltreatment: Developmental and ecological perspectives.* New York: Wiley.

Melton, G.B., & Russo, N. (1987). Adolescent abortion: Psychological perspectives on public policy. *American Psychologist, 42,* 69–72.

Melton, G.B., & Thompson, R.A. (1987). Getting out of a rut: Detours to less traveled paths in child witness research. In S.J. Ceci, M.P. Toglia, & D.F. Ross (Eds.), *Children's eyewitness memory.* New York: Springer-Verlag.

Meltzoff, A.N. (1988). Infant imitation and memory: Nine-month-old infants in immediate and deferred tests. *Child Development, 59,* 217–225.

Menken, Jane, Trussell, James, & Larsen, Ulla. (1986). Age and infertility. *Science, 233,* 1389–1394.

Mennuti, Michael T. (1989). Prenatal diagnosis—advances bring new challenges. *New England Journal of Medicine, 320,* 661–663.

Meny, Robert G., Carroll, John L., Carbone, Mary Therese, & Kelly, Dorothy H. (1994). Cardiovascular recordings from infants dying suddenly and unexpectedly at home. *Pediatrics, 93,* 44–49.

Meredith, Howard V. (1978). Research between 1960 and 1970 on the standing height of young children in different parts of the world. In Hayne W. Reese & Lewis P. Lipsitt (Eds.), *Advances in child development and behavior* (Vol. 12). New York: Academic Press.

Merewood, A. (1991). Sperm under siege. *Health,* 53–77.

Meyer, D.R., & Garasky, S. (1993). Custodial fathers: Myths, realities, and child support policy. *Journal of Marriage and the Family, 55,* 73–89.

Michelsson, Katarina, Rinne, Arto, & Paajanen, Sonja. (1990). Crying, feeding and sleeping patterns in 1- to 12-month-old infants. *Child: Care, Health, and Development, 116,* 99–111.

Midgley, Carol, Feldlauger, Harriet, & Eccles, Jacquelynne S. (1988). The transition to junior high school: Beliefs of pre- and post-transition teachers. *Journal of Youth and Adolescence, 17,* 543–562.

Miedzian, Miriam. (1991). *Boys will be boys: Breaking the link between masculinity and violence.* New York: Doubleday.

Miller, P.H. (1990). The development of strategies of selective attention. In D.F. Bjorklund (Ed.), *Children's strategies: Contemporary views of cognitive development.* Hillsdale, NJ: Erlbaum.

Miller, P.H. (1993). *Theories of developmental psychology.* New York: W.H. Freeman.

Miller, P.H., & Aloise, P.A. (1989). Young children's understanding of the psychological causes of behavior: A review. *Child Development, 60,* 257–285.

Miller, P.H., Haynes, V., DeMarie-Dreblow, D., & Woody-Ramsey, J. (1986). Children's strategies for gathering information in three tasks. *Child Development, 57,* 1429–1439.

Miller, Randi L. (1989). Desegregation experiences of minority students: Adolescent coping strategies in five Connecticut High Schools. *Journal of Adolescent Research, 4,* 173–189.

Mills, Jon K., & Andrianopoulos, Georgia D. (1993). The relationship between childhood onset obesity and psychopathology in adulthood. *Journal of Psychology, 127,* 547–551.

Mills, Richard W., & Mills, Jean. (1993). *Bilingualism in the primary school.* London: Routledge.

Millstein, S.G., & Litt, I.F. (1990). Adolescent health. In S.S. Feldman & G.R. Elliott (Eds.), *At the threshold: The developing adolescent.* Cambridge, MA: Harvard University Press.

Milne, Ann M., Myers, David E., Rosenthal, Alvin S., & Ginsburg, Alan. (1986). Single parents, working mothers, and the educational achievement of school children. *Sociology of Education, 59,* 125–139.

Milunsky, Aubrey. (1989). *Choices, not chances.* Boston: Little, Brown.

Minuchin, Patricia, & Shapiro, Edna K. (1983). The school as a context for social development. In Paul H. Mussen (Ed.), *Handbook of child psychology: Vol. 4. Socialization, personality and social development.* New York: Wiley.

Minuchin, Salvador, and Nichols, Michael P. (1993). *Family healing: Tales of hope and renewal from family therapy.* New York: The Free Press.

Mischel, Walter. (1970). Sex typing and socialization. In Paul H. Mussen (Ed.), *Carmichael's manual of child development* (Vol. 2). New York: Wiley.

Mischel, Walter. (1977). On the future of personality measurement. *American Psychologist, 32,* 246–254.

Mischel, Walter. (1979). On the interface of cognition and personality: Beyond the person-situation debate. *American Psychologist, 34,* 740–754.

Mitchell, Donald E. (1988). The recovery from early monocular visual deprivation in kittens. In Albert Yonas (Ed.), *Perceptual development in infancy.* Hillsdale, NJ: Erlbaum.

Mitchell, Donald E., & Timney, B. (1984). Postnatal development of function in the mammalian visual system. In J.M. Brookhart & V.D. Mountcastle (Eds.), *Handbook of physiology: The nervous system III.* Bethesda, MD: American Physiological Society.

Mitchell, E.A., Ford, R.P.K., Steward, A.W., & Taylor, B.J. (1993). Smoking and the sudden infant death syndrome. *Pediatrics, 91,* 893–896.

Mitchell, John J. (1986). *The nature of adolescence.* Calgary, Alberta: Detselig.

Mitchell, Sandra K., Bee, Helen L., Hammond, Mary A., & Barnard, Kathryn E. (1985). Prediction of school and behavior problems in children followed from birth to age eight. In William K. Frankenberg, Robert N. Emde, & Joseph W. Sullivan (Eds.), *Early identification of children at risk: An international perspective.* New York: Plenum.

Mitford, Jessica. (1992). *The American way of birth.* New York: Dutton.

MMWR *(Morbidity and Mortality Weekly Report):* See **Centers for Disease Control and Prevention.**

Moffit, T.E. (1990). Juvenile delinquency and attention deficit disorder: Boys' developmental trajectories from age 3 to age 15. *Child Development, 61,* 893–910.

Molfese, Dennis L., & Segalowitz, Sidney J. (Eds.). (1988). *Brain lateralization in children: Developmental implications.* New York: Guilford.

Monteiro, C.A., Zuniga, H.P. Pino, Benecio, M.H., & Victori, C.G. (1989). Better prospects for child survival. *World Health Forum, 10,* 222–227.

Montemayor, Raymond. (1986). Family variation in parent-adolescent storm and stress. *Journal of Adolescent Research, 1,* 15–31.

Moon, Christine, & Fifer, William P. (1990). Syllables as signals for 2-day-old infants. *Infant Behavior and Development, 13,* 377–390.

Moore, Keith L. (1988). *The developing human: Clinically oriented embryology* (4th ed.). Philadelphia: W.B. Saunders.

Moore, Keith L. (1989). *Before we are born: Basic embryology and birth defects* (3rd ed.). Philadelphia: W.B. Saunders.

Moore, Susan, & Rosenthal, Doreen. (1991). Adolescent invulnerability and perceptions of AIDS risk. *Journal of Adolescent Research, 6,* 164–180.

Morris, Edward K., & Braukmann, Curtis J. (Eds.). (1987). *Behavioral approaches to crime and delinquency: A handbook of applications, research, and concepts.* New York: Plenum.

Morrison, N.A., Qi, J.C., Tokita, A., Kelly, P.J., Crofts, L., Niguyen, T.V., Sambrook, P.N., & Eisman, J.A. (1994). Prediction of bone density from vitamin D receptor alleles. *Nature, 367,* 284–287.

Morrongiello, B.A., & Rocca, P.T. (1990). Infants' localization of sounds within hemifields: Estimates of minimum audible angle. *Child Development, 61,* 1258–1270.

Morton, Teru. (1987). Childhood aggression in the context of family interaction. In David H. Crowell, Ian M. Evans, & Clifford R. O'Donnell (Eds.), *Childhood aggression and violence: Sources of influences, prevention, and control.* New York: Plenum.

Moshman, D. (1990). The development of metalogical understanding. In W.F. Overton (Ed.), *Reasoning, necessity, and logic: Developmental perspectives.* Hillsdale, NJ: Erlbaum.

Moshman, D. (1993). Adolescent reasoning and adolescent rights. *Human Development, 36,* 27–40.

Moshman, D., & Franks, B.A. (1986). Development of the condept of inferential validity. *Child Development, 57,* 153–165.

Mueller, Edward, & Silverman, Nancy. (1989). Peer relations in maltreated children. In Dante Cicchetti & Vicki Carlson (Eds.), *Child maltreatment: Theory and research on the causes and consequences of child abuse and neglect.* Cambridge, England: Cambridge University Press.

Muller, J., Nielson, C. Thoger, & Skakkebaek, N.E. (1989). Testicular maturation and pubertal growth in normal boys. In I.M. Tanner & M.A. Preece (Eds.), *The physiology of human growth*. Cambridge, England: Cambridge University Press.

Munn, D., & Dunn, J. (1989). Temperament and the developing relationship between siblings. *International Journal of Behavioral Development, 12,* 433–451.

Murphey, D.A. (1992). Constructing the child: Relations between parents' beliefs and child outcomes. *Developmental Review, 12,* 199–232.

Murphy, John M., & Gilligan, Carol. (1980). Moral development in late adolescence and adulthood: A critique and reconstruction of Kohlberg's theory. *Human Development, 23,* 77–104.

Murphy, Lois Barclay, & Moriarty, Alice E. (1976). *Vulnerability, coping, and growth: From infancy to adolescence*. New Haven: Yale University Press.

Murray, Ann D., Dolby, Robyn M., Nation, Roger L., & Thomas, David B. (1981). Effects of epidural anesthesia on newborns and their mothers. *Child Development, 52,* 71–82.

Mussen, Paul Henry, & Jones, Mary Cover. (1957). Self-conceptions, motivations, and interpersonal attitudes of late- and early-maturing boys. *Child Development, 28,* 243–256.

Muuss, Rolf E. (1900). *Theories of adolescence*. New York. Random House.

Myers, B.J. (1987). Mother-infant bonding as a critical period. In M.H. Bornstein (Ed.), *Sensitive periods in development: Interdisciplinary perspectives*. Hillsdale, NJ: Erlbaum.

Myers, N.A., Clifton, R.K., & Clarkson, M.H. (1987). When they were very young: Almost-threes remember two years ago. *Infant Behavior and Development, 10,* 123–132.

Natagata, D. (1989). Japanese-American children and adolescents. In G.T. Gibbs & L.N. Huang (Eds.), *Children of color*. San Francisco: Jossey-Bass.

Natchigall, Robert, & Mehran, Elizabeth. (1991). *Overcoming infertility: A practical strategy for navigating the emotional, medical, and financial minefields of trying to have a baby*. New York: Doubleday.

National Center for Education Statistics. (1993). *The condition of education, 1993*. Washington, DC: U.S. Department of Education.

National Center for Health Statistics. (1991, June). Family structure and children's health: United States, 1988. *Vital and Health Statistics*, U.S. Department of Health and Human Services, Series 10, No. 178.

National Center for Health Statistics. (1993). *Vital statistics of the United States: Vol. 2. Mortality* (Part A). Washington, DC: U.S. Government Printing Office.

National Center for Health Statistics. (1993, August 31). *Monthly Vital Statistics Report, 42* (2). Centers for Disease Control and Prevention, U.S. Department of Health and Human Services.

National Center for Injury Prevention and Control. (1992). *Position papers from the third National Injury Control conference*. Centers for Disease Control.

National Center for Injury Prevention and Control. (1993). *Injury control in the 1990s: A national plan for action*. Centers for Disease Control and Prevention, U.S. Department of Health and Human Services.

National Center on Child Abuse and Neglect. (1988). *Study findings: Study of national incidence and prevalence of child abuse and neglect, 1988*. Washington, DC.

National Science Foundation. (1992). *Indicators of science and mathematics education, 1992*. Washington, DC.

Needleman, Herbert, Schell, Alan, Bellinger, David, Leviton, Alan, & Allred, Elizabeth N. (1990). The long-term effects of exposure to low doses of lead in childhood: An 11-year follow-up report. *New England Journal of Medicine, 322,* 83–89.

Nelson, Charles A. (1987). The recognition of facial expressions in the first two years of life: Mechanisms of development. *Child Development, 58,* 889–909.

Nelson, Charles A., & Horowitz, Frances Degen. (1987). Visual motion perception in infancy: A review and synthesis. In Philip Salapatek & Leslie Cohen (Eds.), *Handbook of infant perception: Vol. 2. From perception to cognition*. New York: Academic Press.

Nelson, J. Ron, Smith, Deborah, & Dodd, John. (1990). The moral reasoning of juvenile delinquents. *Journal of Abnormal Child Psychology, 18,* 231–239.

Nelson, K. (1981). Individual differences in language development: Implications for development and language. *Developmental Psychology, 17,* 171–187.

Nelson, K. (Ed.). (1986). *Event knowledge: Structure and function in development*. Hillsdale, NJ: Erlbaum.

Nelson, K. (1986). Preface. In K. Nelson (Ed.), *Event knowledge: Structure and function in development*. Hillsdale, NJ: Erlbaum.

Nelson, K., & Hudson, J. (1988). Scripts and memory: Functional relationships in development. In F.E. Weinert & M. Perlmutter (Eds.), *Memory development: Universal changes and individual differences*. Hillsdale, NJ: Erlbaum.

Nelson, Melvin D. (1992). Socioeconomic status and childhood mortality in North Carolina. *American Journal of Public Health, 82,* 1131–1133.

Nelson-Le Gall, Sharon A., & Gumerman, Ruth A. (1984). Children's perceptions of helpers and helper motivation. *Journal of Applied Developmental Psychology, 5,* 1–12.

Neumann, C.G. (1983). Obesity in childhood. In M.D. Levine, W.B. Carey, A.C. Crocker, & R.T. Gross (Eds.), *Developmental-behavioral pediatrics*. Philadelphia: W.B. Saunders.

Neuspiel, D.R., & Hamel, S.C. (1991). Cocaine and infant behavior. *Developmental and Behavioral Pediatrics, 12,* 55–64.

Newberger, Carolyn Moore, & White, Kathleen M. (1989). Cognitive foundations for parental care. In Dante Cicchetti & Vicki Carlson (Eds.), *Child maltreatment: Theory and research on the causes and consequences of child abuse and neglect*. Cambridge, England: Cambridge University Press.

Newcomb, A.F., Bukowski, W.M., & Pattee, L. (1993). Children's peer relations: A meta-analytic review of popular, rejected, neglected, controversial, and average sociometric status. *Psychological Bulletin, 113,* 99–128.

Newcomb, Michael D., & Bentler, Peter M. (1990). Antecedents and consequences of cocaine use: An eight-year study from early adolescence to young adulthood. In Lee N. Robbins & Michael Rutter (Eds.), *Straight and devious pathways from childhood to adulthood*. Cambridge, England: Cambridge University Press.

Newman, K. (1988). *Falling from grace: The experience of downward mobility in the American middle class.* New York: The Free Press.

Newton, Robert A. (1984). The medical work up: Male problems. In Miriam D. Mazor & Harriet F. Simons (Eds.), *Infertility: Medical, emotional, and social considerations.* New York: Human Sciences Press.

New York Times. (1980, September 19). Mistaken identity leads to surprising discovery. *The New York Times,* 17.

Nicholls, John G. (1989). *The competitive ethos and democratic education.* Cambridge, MA: Harvard University Press.

Nisan, Mordecai. (1987). Moral norms and social conventions: A cross-cultural comparison. *Developmental Psychology, 23,* 719–725.

Noller, Patricia, & Callan, Victor J. (1988). Understanding parent-adolescent interactions: Perceptions of family members and outsiders. *Developmental Psychology, 24,* 707–714.

Norbeck, J.S., & Tilden, V.P. (1983). Life stress, social pregnancy: A prospective multivariate study. *Journal of Health and Social Behavior, 24,* 30–46.

Nordio, S., Sormi, M., & deWonderweid, V. (1986). Neonatal intensive care: Policy, plans, services, and evaluation. In J.M.L. Phaff (Ed.), *Perinatal health services in Europe: Searching for better childbirth.* London: Croom Helm.

Nottelmann, Edith D., Inoff-Germain, Gale, Susman, Elizabeth J., & Chrousos, George P. (1990). Hormones and behavior at puberty. In John Bancroft & June Machover Reinisch (Eds.), *Adolescence in puberty.* New York: Oxford University Press.

Nottelmann, Edith D., & Welsh, C. Jean. (1986). The long and the short of physical stature in early adolescence. *Journal of Early Adolescence, 6,* 15–27.

Notzon, F.C. (1990). International differences in the use of obstetric interventions. *Journal of the American Medical Association, 263,* 3286–3291.

Nucci, L., Guerra, N., & Lee, J. (1991). Adolescent judgments of the personal, prudential, and normative aspects of drug usage. *Developmental Psychology, 27,* 841–848.

Nugent, J. Kevin. (1991). Cultural and psychological influences on the father's role in infant development. *Journal of Marriage and the Family, 53,* 475–485.

Nugent, J. Kevin, Lester, B.M., & Brazelton, T.B. (1989). *The cultural context of infancy* (Vol. 1). Norwood, NJ: Ablex.

Nussbaum, N.L., Grant, M.L., Roman, M.J., Poole, J.H., & Bigler, E.D. (1990). Attention deficit disorder and the mediating effect of age on academic and behavioral variables. *Developmental and Behavioral Pediatrics, 11,* 22–26.

Oakes, Jeanne. (1985). *Keeping track: How schools structure inequality.* New Haven: Yale University Press.

Oakes, Jeanne. (1986). *Educational indicators: A guide for policymakers.* Santa Monica, CA: The RAND Corporation.

Oakes, Jeanne, & Lipton, Martin. (1990). *Making the best of schools: A handbook for parents, teachers, and policymakers.* New Haven: Yale University Press.

Oakes, L.M., & Cohen, L.B. (1990). Infant perception of a causal event. *Cognitive Development, 5,* 193–207.

Oakley, Ann. (1980). *Women confined: Toward a sociology of childbirth.* Oxford, England: Martin Robertson.

Oberlé, I., Rousseau, F., Heitz, D., Kretz, C., Devys, D., Hanauer, A., Boule, J., Bertheas, M.F., & Mandel, J.L. (1991). Instability of a 550-base pair DNA segment and abnormal methylation in Fragile X syndrome. *Science, 252,* 1097–1102.

O'Brien, Marion, Huston, Aletha C., & Risley, Todd R. (1983). Sex-typed play of toddlers in a day care center. *Journal of Applied Developmental Psychology, 4,* 1–9.

O'Connor, Terence. (1989). Cultural voices and strategies for multi-cultural education. *Journal of Education, 171,* 57–74.

Offer, Daniel, & Offer, Judith. (1975). *From teenage to young manhood.* New York: Basic Books.

Ogletree, Shirley M., Williams, Sue W., Raffeld, Paul, Mason, Bradley, & Fricke, Kris. (1990). Female attractiveness and eating disorders: Do children's television commercials play a role? *Sex Roles, 22,* 791–797.

Ohr, P.S., Fagan, J.W., Rovee-Collier, C., Hayne, H., & Vander-Linde, E. (1989). Amount of training and retention by infants. *Developmental Psychobiology, 22,* 69–80.

Olds, D.L., & Henderson, C.R., Jr. (1989). The prevention of maltreatment. In D. Cicchetti & V. Carlson (Eds.), *Child maltreatment.* Cambridge, England: Cambridge University Press.

Olds, D.L., & Kitzman, H. (1990). Can home visitation improve the health of women and children at environmental risk? *Pediatrics, 86,* 108–116.

Olds, D.L., & Kitzman, H. (1993). Review of research on home visiting for pregnant women and parents of young children. *The Future of Children, 3,* 53–92.

O'Leary, Daniel S. (1990). Neuropsychological development in the child and the adolescent: Functional maturation of the central nervous system. In C.A. Hauert (Ed.), *Developmental psychology: Cognitive, perceptual-motor, and neuropsychological perspectives.* Amsterdam: North-Holland.

Oliver, J.M., Cole, Nancy Hodge, & Hollingsworth, Holly. (1991). Learning disabilites as functions of familial learning problems and developmental problems. *Exceptional Children, 57,* 427–440.

Oller, D. Kimbrough, & Eilers, Rebecca. (1988). The role of audition in infant babbling. *Child Development, 59,* 441–449.

Olsho, Lynne Werner, Harkins, Stephen W., & Lenhardt, Martin L. (1985). Aging and the auditory system. In James E. Birren & K. Warner Schaie (Eds.), *Handbook of the psychology of aging.* New York: Van Nostrand Reinhold.

Olsho, Lynn Werner, Koch, E.G., Carter, E.A., Halpin, C.F., & Spetner, N.B. (1988). Pure tone sensitivity in human infants. *Journal of the Acoustical Society of America, 84,* 1316–1324.

Olson, Heather Carmichael, Sampson, Paul D., Barr, Helen, Streissguth, Ann P., & Bookstein, Fred L. (1992). Prenatal exposure to alcohol and school problems in late childhood: A longitudinal prospective study. *Development and Psychopathology, 4,* 341–359.

Olson, L. (1988). *Crossing the schoolhouse border: Immigrant students and the California public schools.* San Francisco: California Tomorrow.

Olsho, Lynn Werner. (1984). Infant frequency discrimination. *Infant Behavior and Development, 7,* 27–35.

Olvera-Ezzell, Norma, Power, Thomas G., & Cousins, Jennifer H. (1990). Maternal socialization of children's eating habits: Strategies used by obese Mexican-American mothers. *Child Development, 61,* 395–400.

Opie, Iona, & Opie, Peter. (1959). *The lore and language of schoolchildren.* Oxford: Clarendon Press.

Osherson, Daniel N., & Markman, Ellen. (1974–1975). Language and the ability to evaluate contradictions and tautologies. *Cognition, 3,* 213–226.

Osman, B.B. (1979). *Learning disabilities: A family affair.* New York: Random House.

Osman, Patricia. (1985). Personal conversation with Kathleen Berger.

Oster, H., & Rosenstein, D. (in press). *Baby FACS: Analyzing facial movement in infants.* Palo Alto, CA: Consulting Psychologists Press.

Overton, William F. (1990). *Reasoning, necessity, and logic: Developmental perspectives.* Hillsdale, NJ: Erlbaum.

Pagal, Mark D., Smilksteign, Gabriel, Regan, Hari, & Montano, Dan. (1990). Psychosocial influences on newborn outcomes: A controlled prospective study. *Social Science and Medicine, 30,* 597–604.

Page, Reba. (1990). A "relevant" lesson: Defining the lower-track student. In Reba Page & Linda Valli (Eds.), *Curriculum differentiation: Interpretive studies in U.S. secondary schools.* Albany: State University of New York Press.

Page, Reba, & Valli, Linda (Eds.). (1990). *Curriculum differentiation: Interpretive studies in U.S. secondary schools.* Albany: State University of New York Press.

Paikoff, Roberta L. (1992). Attitudes toward consequences of pregnancy in young women attending a family planning clinic. *Journal of Adolescent Research.*

Paikoff, Roberta L., & Brooks-Gunn, Jeanne. (1991). Do parent-child relationships change during puberty? *Psychological Bulletin, 110,* 47–66.

Palca, Joseph. (1991). Get-the-lead-out guru challenged. *Science, 253,* 842–844.

Paley, V.G. (1984). *Boys and girls: Superheros in the doll corner.* Chicago: University of Chicago Press.

Palmer, Carolyn F. (1989). The discriminating nature of infants' exploratory actions. *Developmental Psychology, 25,* 885–893.

Panel on Research on Child Abuse and Neglect, National Research Council. (1993). *Understanding child abuse and neglect.* Washington, DC: National Academy Press.

Paneth, Nigel. (1992). The role of neonatal intensive care in lowering infant mortality. In Jonathan B. Kotch, Craig H. Blakely, Sarah S. Brown, & Frank Y. Wong (Eds.), *A pound of prevention: The case for universal maternity care in the U.S.* Washington, DC: American Public Health Association.

Park, K.A., Lay, K.-L., & Ramsay, L. (1993). Individual differences and developmental changes in preschoolers' friendships. *Developmental Psychology, 29,* 264–270.

Parke, Ross D. (1981). *Fathers.* Cambridge, MA: Harvard University Press.

Parke, Ross D., & Ladd, G.W. (Eds.). (1992). *Family-peer relationships: Modes of linkage.* Hillsdale, NJ: Erlbaum.

Parke, Ross D., & Slaby, Ronald G. (1983). The development of aggression. In Paul H. Mussen (Ed.), *Handbook of child psychology: Vol. 4. Socialization, personality and social development.* New York: Wiley.

Parke, Ross D., & Tinsley, Barbara R. (1981). The father's role in infancy: Determinants of involvement in caregiving and play. In Michael E. Lamb (Ed.), *The role of the father in child development* (2nd ed.). New York: Wiley.

Parker, Jeffrey G., & Asher, Steven R. (1987). Peer relations and later personal adjustment: Are low-accepted children at risk? *Psychological Bulletin, 102,* 357–389.

Parker, Jeffrey G., & Asher, Steven R. (1993). Friendship and friendship quality in middle childhood: Links with peer group acceptance and feelings of loneliness and social dissatisfaction. *Developmental Psychology, 29,* 611–621.

Parker, Jeffrey G., & Gottman, J.M. (1989). Social and emotional development in a relational context. In T.J. Berndt & G.W. Ladd (Eds.), *Peer relationships in child development.* New York: Wiley.

Parkhurst, J.T., & Asher, S.R. (1992). Peer rejection in middle school: Subgroup differences in behavior, loneliness, and interpersonal concerns. *Developmental Psychology, 28,* 231–241.

Parmelee, Arthur H., Jr., & Sigman, Marian D. (1983). Perinatal brain development and behavior. In Paul H. Mussen (Ed.), *Handbook of child psychology: Vol. 2. Infancy and developmental psychobiology.* New York: Wiley.

Pascarella, Ernest T., & Terenzini, Patrick T. (1991). *How college affects students: Findings and insights from twenty years of research.* San Francisco: Jossey-Bass.

Patel, Pragna, & Lupski, James R. (1991). DNA duplication associated with Charcot-Marie-Tooth Disease Type 1A. *Cell, 66,* 219–232.

Patterson, C.J., Kupersmidt, J.B., & Griesler, P.C. (1990). Children's perceptions of self and of relationships with others as a function of sociometric status. *Child Development, 61,* 1335–1349.

Patterson, Gerald R. (1980). Mothers: The unacknowledged victims. *Monographs of the Society for Research in Child Development, 45* (5), (Serial No. 186).

Patterson, Gerald R. (1982). *Coercive family processes.* Eugene, OR: Castalia Press.

Patterson, Gerald R., & Capaldi, D. (1991). Antisocial parents: Unskilled and vulnerable. In Paul E. Cowan & Mavis Hetherington (Eds.), *Family transitions.* Hillsdale, NJ: Erlbaum.

Patterson, Gerald R., DeBaryshe, Barbara D., & Ramsey, Elizabeth. (1989). A developmental perspective on antisocial behavior. *American Psychologist, 44,* 329–335.

Patterson, Gerald R., Littman, R.A., & Bricker, W. (1967). Assertive behavior in children: A step toward a theory of aggression. *Monographs of the Society for Research in Child Development, 32* (Serial No. 113).

Paulston, Christina Bratt. (1992). *Sociolinguistic perspectives on bilingual education.* Cleveden, England: Multilingual Matters.

Peak, L. (1991). *Learning to go to school in Japan: The transition from home to preschool life.* Berkeley: University of California Press.

Pearl, David. (1987). Familial, peer, and television influences on aggressive and violent behavior. In David H. Crowell, Ian M. Evans, & Clifford R. O'Donnell (Eds.), *Childhood aggression and violence: Sources of influence, prevention, and control.* New York: Plenum.

Pearson, Jane L., Hunter, Andrea G., Ensminger, Margaret E., & Kellam, Sheppard G. (1990). Black grandmothers in multi-generational households: Diversity in family structure and parenting involvement in the Woodlawn community. *Child Development, 61,* 434–442.

Pecora, P.J. (1991). Family-based and intensive family preservation services: A select literature review. In M.W. Fraser, P.J. Pecora, & D.A. Haapala (Eds.), *Families in crisis: The impact of intensive family preservation services.* New York: Aldine de Gruyter.

Pedersen, Frank A. (1981). Father influences viewed in a family context. In Michael E. Lamb (Ed.), *The role of the father in child development* (2nd ed.). New York: Wiley.

Pederson, Nancy L., Plomin, Robert, McClearn, Gerald E., & Friberg, L. (1988). Neuroticism, extraversion, and related traits in adult twins reared apart and reared together. *Journal of Personality and Social Psychology, 55,* 950–957.

Pellegrini, Anthony D. (1987). Rough and tumble play: Developmental and educational significance. *Educational Psychologist, 23–44.*

Pelton, L.H. (in press). The role of material factors in child abuse and neglect. In G.B. Melton & F. Barry (Eds.), *Safe neighborhoods: Foundations for a new national strategy on child abuse and neglect.* New York: Guilford.

Pena, Sally, Grench, Judy, & Doerann, Judy. (1990). Heroic fantasies: A cross-generational comparison of two children's television heroes. *Early Childhood Research Quarterly, 5,* 393–406.

Perris, Eve Emmanuel, Myers, Nancy Angrist, & Clifton, Rachel Kern. (1990). Long-term memory for a single infancy experience. *Child Development, 61,* 1796–1807.

Perry, D.G., Perry, L.C., & Kennedy, E. (1992). In C.U. Shantz & W.W. Hartup (Eds.), *Conflict in child and adolescent development.* Cambridge, England: Cambridge University Press.

Perry, William G., Jr. (1981). Cognitive and ethical growth: The making of meaning. In Arthur W. Chickering (Ed.), *The modern American college: Responding to the new realities of diverse students and a changing society.* San Francisco: Jossey-Bass.

Pertschuk, M., Collins, M., Kreisberg, J., & Rager, S. (1986). Psychiatric symptoms associated with eating disorders in a college population. *International Journal of Eating Disorders, 5,* 563–568.

Peters, S.D., Wyatt, G.E., & Finkelhor, David. (1986). Prevalence. In David Finkelhor (Ed.), *A sourcebook on child sexual abuse.* Beverly Hills, CA: Sage.

Peters-Martin, Patricia, & Wachs, Theodore D. (1984). A longitudinal study of temperament and its correlates in the first 12 months. *Infant Behavior and Development, 7,* 285–298.

Peterson, James L., & Zill, Nicholas. (1986). Marital disruption, parent-child relationships, and behavior problems in children. *Journal of Marriage and the Family, 48,* 295–307.

Peterson, Lizette, Ewigman, Bernard, & Kivlahan, Coleen. (1993). Judgments regarding appropriate child supervision to prevent injury: The role of environmental risk and child age. *Child Development, 64,* 934–950.

Petitto, Anne, & Marentette, Paula F. (1991). Babbling in the manual mode: Evidence for the ontogeny of language. *Science, 251,* 1493–1496.

Phaff, J.M.L. (Ed.). (1986). *Perinatal health services in Europe: Searching for better childbirth.* London: Croom Helm.

Phelps, LeAdelle, Johnston, Lisa Swift, Jimenez, Dayana P., Wilczenski, Felicia L., Andrea, Ronald K., & Healy, Robert W. (1993). Figure preference, body dissatisfaction, and body distortion in adolescence. *Journal of Adolescent Research, 8,* 297–310.

Phillips, D.A., & Zimmerman, M. (1990). The developmental course of perceived competence and incompetence among competent children. In R.J. Sternberg & J. Kolligian (Eds.), *Competence considered.* New Haven: Yale University Press.

Phinney, Jean S. (1993). Multiple group identities: Differentiation, conflict, and integration. In J. Kroger (Ed.), *Discussions on ego identity.* Hillsdale, NJ: Erlbaum.

Phinney, Jean S., Lochner, Bruce T., & Murphy, Rodolfo. (1990). Ethnic identity development and psychological adjustment in adolescence. In Arlene Rubin Stiffman & Larry E. Davis (Eds.), *Ethnic issues in adolescent mental health.* Newbury Park, CA: Sage.

Piaget, Jean. (1951). *Play, dreams, and imitation in childhood.* New York: Norton.

Piaget, Jean. (1952). *The child's conception of number.* London: Routledge and Kegan Paul.

Piaget, Jean. (1952). *The origins of intelligence in children.* Margaret Cook (Trans.). New York: International Universities Press.

Piaget, Jean. (1970). *The child's conception of movement and speed.* G.E.T. Holloway & M.J. Mackenzie (Trans.). New York: Basic Books.

Piaget, Jean. (1970). *The child's conception of time.* A.J. Pomerans (Trans.). New York: Basic Books.

Piaget, Jean. (1976). *The grasp of consciousness: Action and concept in the young child.* Susan Wedgewood (Trans.). Cambridge, MA: Harvard University Press.

Pianta, Robert, Egeland, Byron, & Ericson, Martha Farrell. (1989). The antecedents of maltreatment: Results of the mother-child interaction project. In Dante Cicchetti & Vicki Carlson (Eds.), *Child maltreatment: Theory and research on the causes and consequences of child abuse and neglect.* Cambridge, England: Cambridge University Press.

Pianta, Robert, Sroufe, L.A., & Egeland, Byron. (1989). Continuity and discontinuity in maternal sensitivity at 6, 24, and 42 months in a high-risk sample. *Child Development, 60,* 481–487.

Pick, H.L. (1992). Eleanor J. Gibson: Learning to perceive and perceiving to learn. *Developmental Psychology, 28,* 787–794.

Pickens, Jeffrey, & Field, Tiffany. (1993). Facial expressivity in infants of depressed mothers. *Developmental Psychology, 29,* 986–988.

Pinderhughes, Ellen E. (1991). The delivery of child welfare services to African-American clients. *American Journal of Orthopsychiatry, 61,* 599–605.

Pinker, S. (1984). *Language learnability and language development.* Cambridge, MA: Harvard University Press.

Pinker, S. (1987). The bootstrapping problem in language acquisition. In B. MacWhinney (Ed.), *Mechanisms of language acquisition.* Hillsdale, NJ: Erlbaum.

Pipp, S., Fischer, K.W., & Jennings, S. (1987). Acquisition of self- and mother knowledge in infancy. *Developmental Psychology, 23*, 86–96.

Pittman, Robert B. (1991). Social factors, enrollment in vocational/technical course, and high school dropout rates. *Journal of Educational Research, 84*, 288–295.

Pizzo, P. (1983). Slouching toward Bethlehem: American federal policy perspectives on children and their families. In E.F. Zigler, S.L. Kagan, & E. Klugman (Eds.), *Children, families, and government*. Cambridge, England: Cambridge University Press.

Pleck, J.H. (1985). *Working wives/working husbands*. Beverly Hills, CA: Sage.

Plomin, Robert. (1989). Environment and genes: Determinants of behavior. *American Psychologist, 44*, 105–111.

Plomin, Robert. (1990). *Nature and nurture: An introduction to human behavioral genetics*. Pacific Grove, CA: Brooks/Cole.

Plomin, Robert. (1990). The role of inheritance in behavior. *Science, 248*, 183–188.

Plomin, Robert, Emde, R.N., Braungart, J.M., Campos, J., Corley, R., Fulker, D.W., Kagan, J., Reznick, J.S., Robinson, J., Zahn-Waxler, C., & DeFries, J.C. (1993). Genetic change and continuity from fourteen to twenty months: The MacArthur Longitudinal Twin Study. *Child Development, 64*, 1354–1376.

Plomin, Robert, Lichtenstein, Paul, Pederson, Nancy L., McClearn, Gerald, & Nesselroade, John R. (1990). Genetic influence on life events during the last half of the life span. *Psychology and Aging, 5*, 25–30.

Poffenberger, Thomas. (1981). Child rearing and social structure in rural India: Toward a cross-cultural definition of child abuse and neglect. In Jill E. Korbin (Ed.), *Child abuse and neglect: Cross-cultural perspectives*. Berkeley: University of California Press.

Polansky, N.A., Gaudin, J.M., Ammons, P.W., & David, K.B. (1985). The psychological ecology of the neglectful mother. *Child Abuse and Neglect, 9*, 265–275.

Polit, Denise. (1984). The only child in single-parent families. In Toni Falbo (Ed.), *The single-child family*. New York: Guilford.

Polit, Denise F. (1989). Effects of a comprehensive program for teenage parents: Five years after project redirection. *Family Planning Perspectives, 21*, 164–169.

Pollack, William S., & Grossman, Frances K. (1985). Parent-child interaction. In L. L'Abate (Ed.), *The handbook of family psychology and therapy* (Vol. I). Homewood, IL: Dorsey Press.

Pollitt, E. (1994). Poverty and child development: Relevance of research in developing countries to the United States. *Child Development, 65*, 283–295.

Ponsoby, Anne-Louise, Dwyer, Terence, Gibbins, Laura E., Cochrane, Jennifer A., & Wang, Yon-Gan. (1993). Factors potentiating the risk of sudden infant death syndrome associated with the prone position. *New England Journal of Medicine, 329*, 377–382.

Pool, Robert. (1993). Evidence for the homosexuality gene. *Science, 261*, 291–292.

Pope, H.G., Hudson, J.I., Yurgelun-Todd, D., & Hudson, M.S. (1984). Prevalence of anorexia nervosa and bulimia in three student populations. *International Journal of Eating Disorders, 3*, 45–51.

Porges, S.W. (1991). Vagal tone: An autonomic mediator of affect. In J. Garber & K.A. Dodge (Eds.), *The development of emotional regulation and dysregulation*. Cambridge, England: Cambridge University Press.

Porter, R.H., Makin, J.W., Davis, L.B., & Christensen, K.M. (1992). Breast-fed infants respond to olfactory cues from their own mother and unfamiliar lactating females. *Infant Behavior and Development, 15*, 85–93.

Poussaint, Alvin F. (1990). Introduction. In Bill Cosby, *Fatherhood*. New York: Berkley Books.

Powers, Stephen, & Wagner, Michael J. (1984). Attributions for school achievement of middle school students. *Journal of Early Adolescence, 4*, 215–222.

Price, Sharon J., & McHenry, Patrick C. (1988). *Divorce*. Newbury Park, CA: Sage.

Purvis, George A., & Bartholmey, Sandra J. (1988). Infant feeding practices: Commercially prepared baby foods. In Reginald C. Tsang & Buford L. Nicholos (Eds.), *Nutrition during infancy*. Philadelphia: Hanley and Belfus.

Putallaz, Martha, & Heflin, A.H. (1990). Parent-child interaction. In Steven R. Asher & John David Coie (Eds.), *Peer rejection in childhood*. New York: Cambridge University Press.

Putallaz, Martha, & Wasserman, Aviva. (1990). Children's entry behavior. In Steven R. Asher & John David Coie (Eds.), *Peer rejection in childhood*. New York: Cambridge University Press.

Quay, Herbert C. (1987). Institutional treatment. In Herbert C. Quay (Ed.), *Handbook of juvenile delinquency*. New York: Wiley.

Quay, Lorene C., & Blaney, Robert L. (1992). Verbal communication, nonverbal communication, and private speech in lower and middle socioeconomic status preschool children. *Journal of Genetic Psychology, 153*, 129–138.

Quinn, P.C., & Eimas, P.D. (1988). On categorization in early infancy. *Merrill-Palmer Quarterly, 32*, 331–363.

Rabiner, D.L., Lenhart, L., & Lochman, J.E. (1990). Automatic versus reflective social problem solving in relation to children's sociometric status. *Developmental Psychology, 26*, 1010–1016.

Rafferty, Yvonne, & Shinn, Marybeth. (1991). The impact of homelessness on children. *American Psychologist, 46*, 1170–1179.

Rallison, Marvin L. (1986). *Growth disorders in infants, children, and adolescents*. New York: Wiley.

Ramey, C.T., Bryant, D.B., Wasik, B.H., Sparling, J.J., Fendt, K.H., & Levange, L.M. (1992). The Infant Health and Development Program for low birth weight, premature infants: Program elements, family participation, and child intelligence. *Pediatrics, 89*, 454–465.

Ramey, C.T., & Campbell, F.A. (1991). Poverty, early childhood education, and academic competence: The Abecedarian experiment. In A.C. Huston (Ed.), *Children in poverty: Child development and public policy*. Cambridge, England: Cambridge University Press.

Ramsey, P. (1976, August). The enforcement of morals: Nontherapeutic research on children. *Hastings Center Report*, 21–30.

Ramsey, P.G. (1987). Young children's thinking about ethnic differences. In J.S. Phinney & M.J. Rotheram (Eds.), *Children's ethnic socialization: Pluralism and development*. Newbury Park, CA: Sage.

Rank, Otto. (1929). *The trauma of birth*. New York: Harcourt Brace.

Rathunde, Kevin, & Csikszentmihalyi, M. (1991). Adolescent happiness and family interaction. In Karl Pillemer & Kathleen McCartney (Eds.), *Parent-child relations throughout life*. Hillsdale, NJ: Erlbaum.

Ratner, H.H., Smith, B.S., & Padgett, R.J. (1990). Children's organization of events and event memories. In R. Fivush & J.A. Hudson (Eds.), *Knowing and remembering in young children*. Cambridge, England: Cambridge University Press.

Rauste-von Wright, Maijaliisa. (1989). Body image satisfaction in adolescent girls and boys: A longitudinal study. *Journal of Youth and Adolescence, 18*, 71–83.

Rawlins, William K. (1992). *Friendship matters*. Hawthorne, NY: Aldine de Gruyter.

Read, Anne W., Prendiville, Walter J., Dawes, Vivienne P., & Stanley, Fiona J. (1994). Cesarean section and operative vaginal delivery in low-risk primiparous women, western Australia. *American Journal of Public Health, 84*, 37–42.

Reese, E., & Fivush, R. (1993). Parental styles of talking about the past. *Developmental Psychology, 29*, 596–606.

Reich, Peter A. (1986). *Language development*. Englewood Cliffs, NJ: Prentice-Hall.

Reid, B.V. (1984). An anthropological reinterpretation of Kohlberg's stages of moral development. *Human Development, 27*, 56–74.

Reid, Barbara Van Steenburgh. (1989). Socialization for moral reasoning: Maternal strategies of Samoans and Europeans in New Zealand. In Jaan Valsiner (Ed.), *Child development in cultural context*. Toronto: Hogrefe and Huber.

Resnick, L.B. (1989). Developing mathematical knowledge. *American Psychologist, 44*, 162–169.

Rest, James R. (1983). Morality. In Paul H. Mussen (Ed.), *Handbook of child psychology: Vol. 3. Cognitive development*. New York: Wiley.

Revkin, Andrew C. (1989, September). Crack in the cradle. *Discover, 10* (9), 62–69.

Riccio, Cynthia A., Hynd, George W., Cohen, Morris J., & Gonzalez, Jose J. (1993). Neurological basis of attention deficit hyperactivity disorder. *Exceptional Children, 60*, 118–124.

Ricciuti, Henry N. (1991). Malnutrition and cognitive development: Research policy linkages and current research directions. In Lynn Okagaki & Robert J. Sternberg (Eds.), *Directors of development*. Hillsdale, NJ: Erlbaum.

Rice, Mabel L. (1982). Child language: What children know and how. In Tiffany Field, Aletha Huston, Herbert C. Quay, Lillian Troll, & Gordon E. Finley (Eds.), *Review of human development*. New York: Wiley.

Rice, Mabel L. (1984). Cognitive aspects of communicative development. In Richard L. Schiefelbusch & Joanne Pickar (Eds.), *The acquisition of communicative competence*. Baltimore: University Park Press.

Rice, Mabel L. (1990). Preschoolers QUIL: Quick incidental learning of words. In G. Conti Ramsden & C. Snow (Eds.), *Children's language* (Vol. 7). Hillsdale, NJ: Erlbaum.

Rice, Mabel L., & Woodsmall, L. (1988). Lessons from television: Children's word learning when viewing. *Child Development, 59*, 420–429.

Richards, Maryse H., Boxer, Andrew M., Petersen, Anne C., & Albrecht, Rachel. (1990). Relation of weight to body image in pubertal girls and boys from two communities. *Developmental Psychology, 26*, 313–321.

Richman, Amy L., Miller, Patrice M., & LeVine, Robert A. (1992). Cultural and educational variations in maternal responsiveness. *Developmental Psychology, 28*, 614–621.

Rierdan, Jill, Koff, Elissa, & Stubbs, Margaret. (1987). Depressive symptomology and body image in adolescent girls. *Journal of Early Adolescence, 7*, 205–216.

Rierdan, Jill, Koff, Elissa, & Stubbs, Margaret. (1988). Gender, depression, and body image in early adolescents. *Journal of Early Adolescence, 8*, 109–117.

Riordan, Jan. (1983). *A practical guide to breastfeeding*. St. Louis: Mosby.

Risman, B.J. (1987). Intimate relationships from a microstructural perspective: Men who mother. *Gender and Society, 1*, 6–32.

Rispens, Jan, Van Ypern, Tom A., & Van Duijn, Gijs A. (1991). The irrelevance of IQ to the definition of learning disabilities: Some empirical evidence. *Journal of Learning Disabilities, 24*, 434–438.

Ritchie, Jane, & Ritchie, James. (1981). Child rearing and child abuse: The Polynesian context. In Jill E. Korbin (Ed.), *Child abuse and neglect: Cross-cultural perspectives*. Berkeley: University of California Press.

Roberts, K. (1988). Retrieval of a basic-level category in prelinguistic infants. *Developmental Psychology, 24*, 21–27.

Roberts, Laura R., & Petersen, Anne C. (1992). The relationship between academic achievement and social self-image during early adolescence. *Journal of Early Adolescence, 12*, 197–219.

Robins, Lee, & Mills, James L. (1993). Effects of in utero exposure to street drugs. *American Journal of Public Health, 83* (Supplement), 1–32.

Robins, Lee, & Rutter, Michael. (1990). *Straight and devious pathways from childhood to adulthood*. Cambridge, England: Cambridge University Press.

Robinson, J.L., Kagan, J., Reznick, J.S., & Corley, R. (1992). The heritability of inhibited and uninhibited behavior: A twin study. *Developmental Psychology, 28*, 1030–1037.

Rochat, Phillip. (1989). Object manipulation and exploration in 2- to 5-month-old infants. *Developmental Psychology, 25*, 871–884.

Rogan, Walter J. (1986). PCB's and Cola-colored babies: Japan 1968 and Taiwan 1979. In John J. Sever & Robert L. Brent (Eds.), *Teratogen update: Environmentally induced birth defect risks*. New York: Liss.

Rogers, Sinclair. (1976). The language of children and adolescents and the language of schooling. In Sinclair Rogers (Ed.), *They don't speak our language*. London: Edward Arnold.

Rogoff, Barbara. (1990). *Apprenticeship in thinking: Cognitive development in social context*. New York: Oxford University Press.

Rogoff, Barbara, & Mistry, Jayanthi. (1990). The social and functional context of children's remembering. In Robyn Fivush & Judith A. Hudson (Eds.), *Knowing and remembering in young children*. Cambridge, England: Cambridge University Press.

Rogoff, Barbara, Mistry, Jayanthi, Goncu, Artin, & Mosier, Christine. (1993). Guided participation in cultural activity by toddlers and caregivers. *Monographs of the Society for Research in Child Development, 58* (Serial No. 236).

Rogoff, Barbara, & Morelli, Gilda. (1989). Perspectives on children's development from cultural psychology. *American Psychologist, 44,* 343–348.

Rohlen, Thomas P. (1983). *Japan's high schools.* Berkeley: University of California Press.

Rohner, Ronald P. (1984). Toward a conception of culture for cross-cultural psychology. *Journal of Cross-cultural Psychology, 15,* 111–138.

Rohner, Ronald P., Kean, Kevin J., & Cournoyer, David E. (1991). Effects of corporal punishment, perceived caretaker warmth, and cultural beliefs on the psychological adjustment of children in St. Kitts, West Indies. *Journal of Marriage and the Family, 53,* 681–693.

Roll, J. (1989). *Lone parent families in the European community.* London: Family Policy Studies Center.

Romaine, Suzanne. (1984). *The language of children and adolescents: The acquisition of communication competence.* Oxford, England: Basil Blackwell.

Rona, R.J. (1981). Genetic and environmental factors in the control of growth in childhood. *British Medical Bulletin, 37,* 265–272.

Roopnarine, Jaipual L. (1984). Sex-typed socialization in mixed-age preschool classrooms. *Child Development, 55,* 1078–1084.

Rose, Susan A., & Feldman, J.F. (1990). Infant cognition: Individual differences and developmental continuities. In J. Colombo & J. Fagen (Eds.), *Individual differences in infancy: Reliability, stability, prediction.* Hillsdale, NJ: Erlbaum.

Rose, Susan A., & Ruff, Holly A. (1987). Cross-modal abilities in infants. In Joy Doniger Osofsky (Ed.), *Handbook of infant development* (2nd ed.). New York: Wiley.

Rosen, M.G. (1991). *Doula* at the bedwide of the patient in labor. *Journal of the American Medical Association, 265,* 2236–2237.

Rosen, W.D., Adamson, L.B., & Bakeman, R. (1992). An experimental investigation of infant social referencing: Mothers' messages and gender differences. *Developmental Psychology, 28,* 1172–1178.

Rosenberg, M. (1986). Self-concept from middle childhood through adolescence. In J. Suls & A.G. Greenwald (Eds.), *Psychological perspective on the self.* Hillsdale, NJ: Erlbaum.

Rosenblatt, Jay S. (1982). *Birth interaction and attachment.* Johnson & Johnson Roundtable.

Rosenblith, Judy F. (1992). *In the beginning: Development from conception to age two* (2nd ed.). California: Sage Newbury Park.

Rosenstein, Diana, & Oster, Harriet. (1988). Differential facial responses to four basic tastes. *Child Development, 59,* 1555–1568.

Ross, H.S., & Conant, C.L. (1992). The social structure of early conflict: Interaction, relationships, and alliances. In C.U. Shantz & W.W. Hartup (Eds.), *Conflict in child and adolescent development.* Cambridge, England: Cambridge University Press.

Rosser, Pearl L., & Randolph, Suzanne M. (1989). Black American infants: The Howard University normative study. In J. Kevin Nuegent, Barry M. Lester, & T. Berry Brazelton (Eds.), *The cultural context of infancy: Vol I. Biology, culture, and infant development.* Norwood, NJ: Ablex.

Rotberg, Iris C. (1982). Some legal and research considerations in establishing federal policy in bilingual education. *Harvard Educational Review, 52,* 149–168.

Rotenberg, Ken J., & Mann, Luanne. (1986). The development of the norm of reciprocity of self-disclosure and its function in children's attraction to peers. *Child Development, 57,* 1349–1357.

Rotenberg, Ken J., & Sliz, Dave. (1988). Children's restrictive disclosure to friends. *Merrill-Palmer Quarterly, 34,* 203–215.

Rothbart, M.K. (1981). Measurement of temperament in infancy. *Child Development, 52,* 569–578.

Rothbart, M.K. (1991). Temperament: A developmental framework. In J. Strelau & A. Angleitner (Eds.), *Explorations in temperament.* New York: Plenum.

Rothbart, M.K., & Derryberry, D. (1981). Development of individual differnces in temperament. In M.E. Lamb & A.L. Brown (Eds.), *Advances in developmental psychology* (Vol. 1). Hillsdale, NJ: Erlbaum.

Rothman, Barbara Katz. (1989). *Re-creating motherhood: Ideology and technology in patriarchal society.* New York: Norton.

Rourke, B.P. (1989). *Non-verbal learning disabilities: The syndrome and the model.* New York: Guilford.

Rovee-Collier, C. (1987). Learning and memory in infancy. In Joy Doniger Osofsky (Ed.), *Handbook of infant development* (2nd ed.). New York: Wiley.

Rovee-Collier, C.K. (1990). The "memory system" of prelinguistic infants. In A. Diamond (Ed.), *The development and neural bases of higher cognitive functions.* New York: New York Academy of Sciences.

Rovee-Collier, C.K., & Hayne, H. (1987). Reactivation of infant memory: Implications for cognitive development. In H.W. Reese (Ed.), *Advances in child development and behavior* (Vol. 20). New York: Academic Press.

Rubin, Kenneth H., Fein, Greata G., & Vandenberg, Brian. (1983). Play. In Paul H. Mussen (Ed.), *Handbook of child psychology: Vol. 4. Socialization, personality and social development.* New York: Wiley.

Rubin, Kenneth H., & Krasnor, L.R. (1986). Social-cognitive and social behavioral perspectives on problem solving. In M. Perlmutter (Ed.), *Cognitive perspectives on children's social and behavioral development: Minnesota symposia on child psychology* (Vol. 18). Hillsdale, NJ: Erlbaum.

Rubin, Zick. (1980). *Children's friendships.* Cambridge, MA: Harvard University Press.

Ruble, D. (1983). The development of social comparison processes and their role in achievement-related self-socialization. In E.T. Higgins, D.N. Ruble, & W.W. Hartup (Eds.), *Social cognition and social development.* Cambridge, England: Cambridge University Press.

Ruble, D., Boggiano, A., Feldman, N., & Loebl, J. (1980). A developmental analysis of the role of social comparison in self-evaluation. *Developmental Psychology, 16,* 105–115.

Ruff, Holly A. (1982). The development of object perception in infancy. In Tiffany M. Field, Aletha Huston, Herbert C. Quay, Lillian Troll, & Gordon E. Finley (Eds.), *Review of human development*. New York: Wiley.

Ruff, Holly A. (1984). An ecological approach to infant memory. In Morris Moscovitch (Ed.), *Infant memory*. New York: Plenum.

Rush, D., & Callaghan, K.R. (1989). Exposure to passive cigarette smoking and child development. In Donald Hutchings (Ed.), *Prenatal abuse of licit and illicit drugs*. New York: New York Academy of Sciences.

Russell, A., & Finnie, V. (1990). Preschool children's social status and maternal instructions to assist group entry. *Developmental Psychology, 26,* 603–611.

Rutherford, Andrew. (1986). *Growing out of crime*. Middlesex, England: Penguin.

Rutter, D.R., & Durkin, K. (1987). Turn-taking in mother-infant interaction: An examination of vocalization and gaze. *Developmental Psychology, 23,* 54–61.

Rutter, Michael. (1979). Protective factors in children's responses to stress and disadvantage. In Martha Whalen Kent & Jon E. Rolf (Eds.), *Primary prevention of psychopathology: Vol. III. Social competence in children*. Hanover, NH: University Press of New England.

Rutter, Michael. (1980). *Changing youth in a changing society: Patterns of development and disorder*. Cambridge, MA: Harvard University Press.

Rutter, Michael. (1982). Epidemiological-longitudinal approaches to the study of development. In W. Andrew Collins (Ed.), *Minnesota symposia on child psychology: Vol. 15. The concept of development*. Hillsdale, NJ: Erlbaum.

Rutter, Michael. (1982). Socio-emotional consequences of day care for preschool children. In E.F. Zigler & E.W. Gordon (Eds.), *Day care: Scientific and social policy issues*. Boston: Auburn House.

Rutter, Michael. (1984). Continuities and discontinuities in socioemotional development: Empirical and conceptual perspectives. In R.N. Emde & R.J. Harmon (Eds.), *Continuities and discontinuities in development*. New York: Plenum.

Rutter, Michael. (1987). Psychosocial resilience and protective mechanisms. *American Journal of Orthopsychiatry, 57,* 316–331.

Rutter, Michael. (1989). Intergenerational continuities and discontinuities. In Dante Cicchetti & Vicki Carlson (Eds.), *Child maltreatment: Theory and research on the causes and consequences of child abuse and neglect*. Cambridge, England: Cambridge University Press.

Rutter, Michael. (1991). Nature, nurture, and psychopathology: A new look at an old topic. *Development and Psychopathology, 3,* 125–136.

Rutter, Michael, Bailey, Anthony, Bolton, Patrick, & LeCouteru, Ann. (1993). Autism: Syndrome definition and possible genetic mechanisms. *Nature, Nurture, and Psychology*. Washington, DC: American Psychological Association.

Rutter, Michael, & Garmezy, Norman. (1983). Developmental psychopathology. In Paul H. Mussen (Ed.), *Handbook of child psychology: Vol. 4. Socialization, personality and social development*. New York: Wiley.

Rutter, Michael, & Giller, Henri. (1984). *Juvenile delinquency: Trends and perspectives*. New York: Guilford.

Ryan, R.M. (1993). Agency and organization: Intrinsic motivation, autonomy, and the self in psychological development. In J.E. Jacobs (Ed.), *Nebraska symposium on motivation: Vol. 40. Developmental perspectives on motivation*. Lincoln: University of Nebraska Press.

Ryan, R.M., & Lynch, J.H. (1989). Emotional autonomy versus detachment: Revisiting the vicissitudes of adolescence and young adulthood. *Child Development, 60,* 340–356.

Saarni, C. (1984). An observational study of children's attempts to monitor their expressive behavior. *Child Development, 55,* 1504–1513.

Saarni, C. (1989). Children's understanding of strategic control of emotional expression in social transactions. In C. Saarni & P.L. Harris (Eds.), *Children's understanding of emotion*. Cambridge, England: Cambridge University Press.

Sagi, A., & Lewkowicz, K.S. (1987). A cross-cultural evaluation of attachment research. In L.W.C. Tavecchio & M.H. van Ijzendoorn (Eds.), *Attachment in social networks*. Amsterdam: Elsevier Science.

Sagi, Abraham, van Ijzendoorn, Marinus H., & Koren-Karie, Nina. (1991). Primary appraisal of the Strange Situation: A cross-cultural analysis of preseparation episodes. *Developmental Psychology, 27,* 587–596.

Saigal, Saroj, Szatmari, Peter, & Rosenbaum, Peter. (1992). Can learning disabilities in children who were extremely low birth weight be identified at school entry? *Journal of Developmental and Behavioral Pediatrics, 13,* 356–362.

Salmi, L.R., Weiss, H.B., Peterson, P.L., Spengler, R.F., Sattin, R.W., & Anderson, H.A. (1989). Fatal farm injuries among young children. *Pediatrics, 83,* 267–271.

Salt, P., Galler, J.R., & Ramsey, F.C. (1988). The influence of early malnutrition on subsequent behavioral development. *Developmental and Behavioral Pediatrics, 9,* 15.

Salzinger, S., Feldman, R.S., Hammer, M., & Rosario, M. (1993). The effects of physical abuse on children's social relationships. *Child Development, 64,* 169–187.

Santrock, John W., Warshak, Richard A., & Elliott, Gary L. (1982). Social development and parent-child interaction in father-custody and stepmother families. In Michael E. Lamb (Ed.), *Non-traditional families: Parenting and child development*. Hillsdale, NJ: Erlbaum.

Saudino, Kimberly J., & Eaton, Warren O. (1989, July). *Heredity and infant activity level: An objective twin study*. Paper presented to the International Society for the Study of Behavioral Development, Jybaskyla, Finland.

Saville-Troike, Muriel, McClure, Erica, & Fritz, Mary. (1984). Communicative tactics in children's second language acquisition. In Fred R. Eckman, Lawrence H. Bell, & Diane Nelson (Eds.), *Universals of second language acquisition*. Rowley, MA: Newbury House.

Savin-Williams, R.C., & Berndt, T.J. (1990). Friendship and peer relations. In S.S. Feldman & G.R. Elliott (Eds.), *At the threshold: The developing adolescent*. Cambridge, MA: Harvard University Press.

Savin-Williams, R.C., & Demo, D.H. (1984). Developmental change and stability in adolescent self-concept. *Developmental Psychology, 20,* 1100–1110.

Savin-Williams, R.C., & Small, S.A. (1986). The timing of puberty and its relationship to adolescent and parent perceptions of family interactions. *Developmental Psychology, 22*, 342–347.

Savitz, David A., Whelan, Elizabeth A., & Kleckner, Robert C. (1989). Self-reported exposure to pesticides and radiation related to pregnancy outcome: Results from National Natality and Fetal Mortality Surveys. *Public Health Reports, 104*, 473–477.

Saxe, Geoffrey, Guberman, Steven R., & Gearhart, Maryl. (1987). Social processes in early number development. *Monographs of the Society for Research in Child Development, 52* (Serial No. 216).

Saywitz, K.J., Goodman, G.S., Nicholas, E., & Moan, S.F. (1991). Children's memories of a physical examination involving genital touch: Implications for reports of sexual abuse. *Journal of Consulting and Clinical Psychology, 59*, 682–689.

Scafidi, Frank A., Field, Tiffany, & Schanberg, Saul M. (1993). Factors that predict which preterm infants benefit most from massage therapy. *Journal of Developmental and Behavioral Pediatrics, 14*, 176–180.

Scarr, Sandra. (1985). Constructing psychology: Making facts and fables for our times. *American Psychologist, 40*, 499–512.

Scarr, Sandra. (1992). Developmental theories for the 1990s: Development and individual differences. *Child Development, 63*, 1–19.

Scarr, Sandra, & McCartney, Kathleen. (1983). How people make their own environments. A theory of genotype/environmental effects. *Child Development, 54*, 424–435.

Schaal, B. (1986). Presumed olfactory exchanges between mother and neonate in humans. In J. Le Camus & J. Cosnier (Eds.), *Ethology and psychology*. Toulouse, France: Private, I.E.C.

Schaffer, H. Rudolf. (1984). *The child's entry into a social world*. New York: Academic Press.

Schardein, James L. (1976). *Drugs as teratogens*. Cleveland: CRC Press.

Schauble, L. (1991). Belief revision in children: The role of prior knowledge and strategies for generating evidence. *Journal of Experimental Child Psychology, 49*, 31–57.

Scheper-Hughes, Nancy, & Stein, H. (1987). Child abuse and the unconscious in American popular culture. In N. Scheper-Hughes (Ed.), *Child survival*. Dordrecht, Netherlands: Reidel.

Schiefelbusch, Richard L. (1984). Assisting children to become communicatively competent. In Richard L. Schiefelbusch & Joanne Pickar (Eds.), *The acquisition of communicative competence*. Baltimore: University Park Press.

Schiff, Donald W. (1992). Health consequences of inadequate access to maternity and infant health care. In Jonathan B. Kotch, Craig H. Blakely, Sarah S. Brown, & Frank Y. Wong (Eds.), *A pound of prevention: The case for universal maternity care in the U.S.* Washington, DC: American Public Health Association.

Schlegal, Alice, & Barry, Herbert. (1991). *Adolescence: An anthropological inquiry*. New York: The Free Press.

Schneider, Anne L. (1990). *Deterrence and juvenile crime*. New York: Springer-Verlag.

Schneider-Rosen, Karen, & Cicchetti, Dante. (1991). Early self-knowledge and emotional development: Visual self-recognition and affect reactions to mirror self-images in maltreated and non-maltreated toddlers. *Developmental Psychology, 27*, 471–478.

Schnorr, T.M., Grajewski, B.A., Hornung, R.W., Thun, M.J., Egeland, G.M., Murray, W.E., Conover, D.L., & Halperin, W.E. (1991). Video display terminals and the risk of spontaneous abortion. *New England Journal of Medicine, 324*, 727–734.

Schoof-Tams, Karin, Schlaegel, Jürgen, & Walezak, Leonhard. (1976). Differentiation of sexual morality between 11 and 16 years. *Archives of Sexual Behavior, 5*, 353–370.

Schweder, R.A. (1990). In defense of moral realism: Reply to Gabennesch. *Child Development, 61*, 2060–2067.

Schweder, R.A., Mahapatra, M., & Miller, J.G. (1990). Culture and moral development. In J.W. Stigler, R.A. Schweder, & G. Herdt (Eds.), *Cultural psychology: Essays on comparative human development*. Cambridge, England: Cambridge University Press.

Schweinhart, Laurence J., & Weikart, David (Eds.). (1993). *Significant benefits: High/Scope Perry preschool study through age 27*. Ypsilanti, MI: High/Scope Press.

Sears, Robert R., Rau, Lucy, & Alpert, Richard. (1965). *Identification and child rearing*. Stanford, CA: Stanford University Press.

Seifer, R., & Sameroff, Arnold J. (1987). Multiple determinants of risk and invulnerability. In E.J. Anthony & B.J. Cohler (Eds.), *The invulnerable child*. New York: Guilford.

Seltzer, Judith A. (1991). Relationships between fathers and children who live apart: The father's role after separation. *Journal of Marriage and the Family, 53*, 79–102.

Seltzer, Judith A., & Bianchi, S.M. (1988). Children's contact with absent parents. *Journal of Marriage and the Family, 50*, 663–677.

Sena, Rhonda, & Smith, Linda B. (1990). New evidence on the development of the word Big. *Child Development, 61*, 1034–1052.

Shannon, Lyle W. (1988). *Criminal career continuity: Its social context*. New York: Human Sciences Press.

Shea, John D.C. (1981). Changes in interpersonal distances and categories of play behavior in the early weeks of preschool. *Developmental Psychology, 17*, 417–425.

Shedler, Jonathan, & Block, Jack. (1990). Adolescent drug use and psychological health: A longitudinal inquiry. *American Psychologist, 45*, 612–630.

Sherman, T. (1985). Categorization skills in infants. *Child Development, 53*, 183–188.

Shinn, M., Knickman, J.R., & Weitzman, B.C. (1991). Social relationships and vulnerability to becoming homeless among poor families. *American Psychologist, 46*, 1180–1187.

Shipp, E.E. (1985, November 4). Teen-agers taking risks: When pregnancy is the result. *The New York Times*, A16.

Shirley, Mary M. (1933). *The first two years: A study of twenty-five babies*. Institute of Child Welfare Monograph No. 8. Minneapolis: University of Minnesota Press.

Shneidman, Edwin S. (1978). Suicide. In Gardner Lindzey, Calvin S. Hall, & Richard F. Thompson, *Psychology* (2nd ed.). New York: Worth.

Shurkin, Joel N. (1992). *Terman's kids*. Boston: Little, Brown.

Shy, K.K., Luth, D.A., Bennett, F.C., Whitfield, M., Larson, E.B., van Belle, G., Hughes, J.P., Wilson, J.A., & Stenchever, M.A. (1990). Effects of electronic fetal-heart-rate monitoring, as compared with periodic auscultation, on the neurologic development of premature infants. *The New England Journal of Medicine, 322*, 588–594.

Siegler, Robert. (1976). Three aspects of cognitive development. *Cognitive Psychology, 8*, 481–520.

Siegler, Robert. (1983). Information processing approaches to development. In Paul H. Mussen (Ed.), *Handbook of child psychology: Vol. 1. History, theory, and methods*. W. Kessen (Vol. Ed.). New York: Wiley.

Siegler, Robert. (1983). Five generalizations about cognitive development. *American Psychologist, 38*, 263–277.

Siegler, Robert. (1991). *Children's thinking* (2nd ed.). Englewood Cliffs, NJ: Prentice-Hall.

Siegler, Robert, & Richards, D.D. (1982). The development of intelligence. In R.J. Sternberg (Ed.), *Handbook of human intelligence*. Cambridge, England: Cambridge University Press.

Sigel, I.E., McGillicuddy-DeLisi, A.V., & Goodnow, J.J. (Eds.). (1992). *Parent belief systems* (2nd ed.). Hillsdale, NJ: Erlbaum.

Sigler, Robert T. (1989). *Domestic violence: An assessment of community attitudes*. Lexington, MA: Lexington Books.

Sigman, M. (in press). What are the core deficits in autism? In S.H. Broman & J. Grafman (Eds.), *Atypical cognitive deficits in developmental disorders: Implications for brain function*. Hillsdale, NJ: Erlbaum.

Sigman, M.D., Kasari, C., Kwon, J.-H., & Yirmiya, N. (1992). Responses to the negative emotions of others by autistic, mentally retarded, and normal children. *Child Development, 63*, 796–807.

Silbereisen, Rainer K., & Kracke, Barbel. (1990). Variation in maturational timing and adjustment in adolescence. In Sandy Jackson & Hector Rodriguez-Tome (Eds.), *Adolescence and its social worlds*. Hove, England: Erlbaum.

Silbergeld, Ellen K., Mattison, Donald R., & Bertin, Joan E. (1989). Occupational exposures and female reproduction. In Mark I. Evans, Alan O. Dixler, John C. Fletcher, & Joseph D. Shulman (Eds.), *Fetal diagnosis and therapy: Science, ethics, and the law*. Philadelphia: Lippincott.

Silva, Phil A., Hughes, Pauline, Williams, Sheila, & Faed, James M. (1988). Blood lead, intelligence, reading attainment and behavior in eleven-year-old children in Dunedin, New Zealand. *Journal of Child Psychology and Psychiatry, 29*, 43–52.

Silver, A.A., & Hagin, R.A. (1990). *Disorders of learning in childhood*. New York: Wiley.

Silver, L.B. (1991). Developmental learning disorders. In M. Lewis (Ed.), *Child and adolescent psychiatry: A comprehensive textbook*. Baltimore: Williams and Wilkins.

Simmons, Roberta G., & Blyth, Dale A. (1987). *Moving into adolescence: The impact of pubertal change and school context*. New York: Aldine de Gruyter.

Simmons, Roberta G., Blyth, Dale A., & McKinney, Karen L. (1983). The social and psychological effects of puberty on white females. In Jeanne Brooks-Gunn & Anne C. Petersen (Eds.), *Girls at puberty: Biological and psychosocial aspects*. New York: Plenum.

Simmons, Roberta G., Burgeson, Richard, & Reef, Mary Jo. (1988). Cumulative change at entry to adolescence. In Megan R. Gunnar & W. Andrew Collins (Eds.), *Minnesota symposia on child psychology: Vol. 21. Development during the transition to adolescence*. Hillsdale, NJ: Erlbaum.

Simmons, Roberta G., Rosenberg, Florence, & Rosenberg, Morris. (1973). Disturbance in the self-image at adolescence. *American Sociological Review, 38*, 553–568.

Simon, Joseph E. (1992). Accidental injury and emergency medical services for children. In Richard E. Behrman, Robert M. Kliegman, Waldo E. Nelson, & Victor C. Vaughan (Eds.), *Nelson textbook of pediatrics* (14th ed.). Philadelphia: Harcourt Brace.

Simons, R.L., Lorenz, F.O., Conger, R.D., & Wu, C.-I. (1992). Support from spouse as mediator and moderator of the disruptive influence of economic strain on parenting. *Child Development, 63*, 1282–1301.

Simons, R.L., Lorenz, F.O., Wu, C.-I., & Conger, R.D. (1993). Social network and marital support as mediators and moderators of the impact of stress and depression on parental behavior. *Developmental Psychology, 29*, 368–381.

Simons, R.L., Whitbeck, L.B., Conger, R.D., & Wu, C.-I. (1991). Intergenerational transmission of harsh parenting. *Developmental Psychology, 27*, 159–171.

Simpson, J.A. (1990). Influence of attachment styles on romantic relationships. *Journal of Personality and Social Psychology, 59*, 971–980.

Sinclair, David. (1978). *Human growth after birth* (3rd ed.). London: Oxford University Press.

Skinner, B.F. (1953). *Science and human behavior*. New York: Macmillan.

Skinner, B.F. (1957). *Verbal behavior*. New York: Appleton-Century-Crofts.

Skinner, B.F. (1972). *Beyond freedom and dignity*. New York: Knopf.

Skolnick, A. (1990). Cocaine use in pregnancy: Physicians urged to look for problem where they least expect it. *Journal of the American Medical Association, 264*, 306–307.

Skolnick, A. (1991). *Embattled paradise: The American family in an age of uncertainty*. New York: Basic Books.

Slater, A., Cooper, R., Rose, D., & Morison, V. (1989). Prediction of cognitive performance from infancy to early childhood. *Human Development, 32*, 137–147.

Slavin, Robert E. (1987). Ability grouping and student achievement in elementary schools: A best evidence synthesis. *Review of Educational Research, 57*, 293–336.

Sloane, J.H., Kellerman, A.L., Reay, D.T., Ferris, J.A., Koepsell, T., & Rivara, F.P. (1988). Handgun regulation, crime, assault and homicide: A tale of two cities. *New England Journal of Medicine, 319*, 1256–1262.

Sloane, John Henry, Rivara, Frederick P., Reay, Donald T., Ferris, James A., Path, M.R.C., & Kellerman, Arthur. (1990). Firearm regulations and rates of suicide: A comparison of two metropolitan areas. *New England Journal of Medicine, 322*, 369–373.

Slobin, D.I. (1985). Crosslinguistic evidence for the language-making capacity. In D.I. Slobin (Ed.), *The crosslinguistic study of language acquisition: Vol. 2. Theoretical issues*. Hillsdale, NJ: Erlbaum.

Small, Stephen A., Eastman, Gay, & Cornelius, Steven. (1988). Adolescent autonomy and parental stress. *Journal of Youth and Adolescence, 17,* 377–391.

Smetana, Judith G. (1988). Adolescents' and parents' conceptions of parental authority. *Child Development, 59,* 321–335.

Smetana, Judith G. (1988). Concepts of self and social convention: Adolescents' and parents' reasoning about hypothetical and actual family conflicts. In M.R. Gunnar & W.A. Collins (Eds.), *Minnesota symposia on child psychology: Vol. 21. Development during the transition to adolescence.* Hillsdale, NJ: Erlbaum.

Smetana, Judith G., Killen, M., & Turiel, E. (1991). Children's reasoning about interpersonal and moral conflicts. *Child Development, 62,* 629–644.

Smetana, Judith G., Yau, Jenny, Restrepo, Angela, & Braeges, Judith L. (1991). Adolescent-parent conflict in married and divorced families. *Developmental Psychology, 27,* 1000–1010.

Smith, M. Brewster. (1983). Hope and despair: Keys to the socio-psychodynamics of youth. *American Journal of Orthopsychiatry, 53,* 388–399.

Smith, Thomas Ewin. (1990). Parental separation and the academic self-concepts of adolescents: An effort to solve the puzzle of separation effects. *Journal of Marriage and the Family, 52,* 107–118.

Snarey, John R., Reimber, Joseph, & Kohlberg, Lawrence. (1985). Development of social-moral reasoning among Kibbutz adolescents: A longitudinal cross-cultural study. *Developmental Psychology, 21,* 3–17.

Snider, Vicki E., & Tarver, Sara G. (1989). The relationship between achievement and IQ in students with learning disabilities. *Psychology in the Schools, 26,* 346–353.

Snow, Catherine E. (1984). Parent-child interaction and the development of communicative ability. In Richard L. Schiefelbusch & Joanne Pickar (Eds.), *The acquisition of communicative competence.* Baltimore: University Park Press.

Snyder, Dona J. (1985). Psychosocial effects of long-term antepartal hospitalization. In Manohar Rathi (Ed.), *Clinical aspects of perinatal medicine.* New York: Macmillan.

Snyder, James, Dishion, T.J., & Patterson, Gerald R. (1986). Determinants and consequences of associating with deviant peers during preadolescence and adolescence. *Journal of Early Adolescence, 6,* 29–43.

Society for Research in Child Development. (1990, Winter). SRCD ethical standards for research with children. *SRCD Newsletter,* 5–7.

Sokol, R.J., & Abel, E.L. (1992). Risk factors for alcohol-related birth defects: Threshold, susceptibility, and prevention. In T.B. Sonderegger (Ed.), *Perinatal substance abuse: Research findings and clinical implications.* Baltimore: Johns Hopkins University Press.

Sonenstein, Freya, Pleck, Joseph H., & Ku, Leighton C. (1989). Sexual activity, condom use, and AIDS awareness among adolescent males. *Family Planning Perspectives, 21,* 152–158.

Song, M.-J., Smetana, J.G., & Kim, S.Y. (1987). Korean children's conceptions of moral and conventional transgressions. *Developmental Psychology, 23,* 577–582.

Sonnenschein, Susan. (1986). Development of referential communication skills: How familiarity with a listener affects a speaker's production of redundant messages. *Developmental Psychology, 22,* 549–552.

Sosa, R., Kennell, J., Klaus, M., Robertson, S., & Urrutia, J. (1980). The effect of a supportive companion on perinatal problems, length of labor, and mother-infant interaction. *New England Journal of Medicine, 303,* 597–600.

Southard, B. (1985). Interlimb movement control and coordination in children. In Jane E. Clark & James H. Humphrey (Eds.), *Motor development: Current selected research.* Princeton, NJ: Princeton Book Company.

Spanier, Graham, & Thompson, Linda. (1984). *Parting: The aftermath of separation and divorce.* Beverly Hills, CA: Sage.

Spelke, Elizabeth. (1979). Perceiving bimodally specified events in infancy. *Developmental Psychology, 15,* 626–636.

Spelke, Elizabeth. (1987). The development of intermodal perception. In Philip Salapatek & Leslie Cohen (Eds.), *Handbook of infant perception: Vol. 2. From perception to cognition.* Orlando, FL: Academic Press.

Spelke, Elizabeth. (1988). Where perceiving ends and thinking begins: The apprehension of objects in infancy. In A. Yonas (Ed.), *Minnesota symposia on child psychology: Vol. 20. Perceptual development in infancy.* Hillsdale, NJ: Erlbaum.

Spelke, Elizabeth. (1991). Physical knowledge in infancy: Reflections on Piaget's theory. In S. Carey & R. Gelman (Eds.), *The epigenesis of mind: Essays on biology and cognition.* Hillsdale, NJ: Erlbaum.

Spence, Janet T. (1985). Achievement American style: The rewards and costs of individualism. *American Psychologist, 40,* 1285–1296.

Spence, Janet T., & Helmreich, Robert L. (1978). *Masculinity and femininity: Their psychological dimensions, correlates, and antecedents.* Austin: University of Texas Press.

Spencer, M.B. (1987). Black children's ethnic identity formation: Risk and resilience of castelike minorities. In J.S. Phinney & M.J. Rotheram (Eds.), *Children's ethnic socialization: Pluralism and development.* Newbury Park, CA: Sage.

Spencer, M.B. (1988). Self-concept development. In D.T. Slaughter (Ed.), *New directions for child development: No. 42. Black children and poverty: A developmental perspective.* San Francisco: Jossey-Bass.

Spencer, M.B., & Markstrom-Adams, C. (1990). Identity processes among racial and ethnic minority children in America. *Child Development, 61,* 290–310.

Spiker, Donna, Ferguson, Joan, & Brooks-Gunn, Jeanne. (1993). Enhancing maternal interactive behavior and child social competence in low birth weight premature infants. *Child Development, 64,* 754–768.

Spock, Benjamin. (1945). *The common sense book of baby and child care.* New York: Duell, Sloan and Pearce.

Spock, Benjamin. (1976). *Baby and child care.* New York: Pocket Books.

Springer, Sally P., & Deutsch, Georg. (1989). *Left brain, right brain.* New York: Freeman.

Sroufe, L. Alan. (1979). Socioemotional development. In Joy Doniger Osofsky (Ed.), *Handbook of infant development.* New York: Wiley.

Sroufe, L. Alan, & Fleeson, J. (1988). The coherence of family relationships. In R.A. Hinde & J. Stevenson-Hinde (Eds.), *Relationships within families.* Oxford, England: Clarendon Press.

Sroufe, L. Alan, Fox, Nancy E., & Pancake, Van R. (1983). Attachment and dependency in developmental perspective. *Child Development, 54,* 1615–1627.

Stafford, R.S. (1990). Alternative strategies for controlling rising Cesarean section rates. *Journal of the American Medical Association, 263,* 683–687.

Stambak, M., & Sinclair, H. (Eds.). (1993). *Pretend play among 3-year-olds.* Hillsdale, NJ: Erlbaum.

Stanhope, R. (1989). The endocrine control of puberty. In I.M. Tanner & M.A. Preece (Eds.), *The physiology of human growth.* Cambridge, England: Cambridge University Press.

Stanley, B., & Seiber, J.E. (Eds.). (1992). *Social research on children and adolescents: Ethical issues.* Newbury Park, CA: Sage.

Stanovich, K.E. (1990). Concepts in developmental theories of reading skill: Cognitive resources, automaticity, and modularity. *Developmental Review, 10,* 72–100.

Stein, N.L., & Levine, L.J. (1989). The causal organization of emotional knowledge: A developmental study. *Cognition and Emotion, 3,* 343–378.

Steinberg, Lawrence. (1988). Reciprocal relation between parent-child distance and pubertal maturation. *Developmental Psychology, 24,* 122–128.

Steinberg, Lawrence. (1990). Autonomy, conflict, and harmony in the family relationship. In S.S. Feldman & G.R. Elliott (Eds.), *At the threshold: The developing adolescent.* Cambridge, MA: Harvard Univesity Press.

Steinberg, Lawrence. (1990). Interdependency in the family: Autonomy, conflict, and harmony in the parent-adolescent relationship. In Shirley S. Feldman & G.R. Elliot (Eds.), *At the threshold: The developing adolescent.* Cambridge, MA: Harvard University Press.

Steinberg, Lawrence, & Dornbusch, Sanford M. (1991). Negative correlates of part-time employment during adolescence: Replication and elaboration. *Developmental Psychology, 27,* 304–313.

Steinberg, Lawrence, Dornbusch, Sanford M., & Brown, B.B. (1992). Ethnic differences in adolescent achievement: An ecological perspective. *American Psychologist, 47,* 723–729.

Steinberg, Lawrence, Elmen, J.D. & Mounts, N.S. (1989). Authoritative parenting, psychosocial maturity and academic success among adolescents. *Child Development, 60,* 1424–1436.

Steinberg, Lawrence, Fegley, Suzanne, & Dornbusch, Sanford M. (1993). Negative impact of part-time work on adolescent adjustment: Evidence from a longitudinal study. *Developmental Psychology, 29,* 171–180.

Steinberg, Lawrence, Lamborn, S.D., Dornbusch, Sanford M., & Darling, N. (1992). Impact of parenting practices on adolescent achievement: Authoritative parenting, school involvement, and encouragement to succeed. *Child Development, 63,* 1266–1281.

Steinberg, Lawrence, Mounts, Nina S., Lamborn, Susan D., & Dornbusch, Sanford M. (1991). Authoritative parenting and adolescent adjustment across various ecological niches. *Journal of Research on Adolescence, 1,* 19–36.

Stenberg, C.R., & Campos, J.J. (1990). The development of anger expressions in infancy. In N.L. Stein, B. Leventhal, & T. Trabasso (Eds.), *Psychological and biological approaches to emotion.* Hillsdale, NJ: Erlbaum.

Stern, Daniel. (1977). *The first relationship: Mother and infant.* Cambridge, MA: Harvard University Press.

Stern, Daniel N. (1985). *The interpersonal world of the infant.* New York: Basic Books.

Sternberg, Kathleen J., & Lamb, Michael E. (1991). Can we ignore context in the definition of child maltreatment? *Development and Psychopathology, 3,* 87–92.

Sternberg, Robert J. (1988). Intellectual development: Psychometric and information-processing approaches. In M.H. Bornstein & M.E. Lamb (Eds.), *Developmental psychology: An advanced textbook* (2nd ed.). Hillsdale, NJ: Erlbaum.

Stevenson, Harold W., Chen, Chuansheng, & Lee, Shin-Ying. (1993). Mathematics achievement of Chinese, Japanese, and American children: Ten years later. *Science, 259,* 53–58.

Stevenson, Harold W., & Lee, Shin-ying. (1990). Contexts of achievement: A study of American, Chinese, and Japanese children. *Monographs of the Society for Research in Child Development, 55* (1–2, Serial No. 221).

Stevenson, Harold W., & Stigler, Robert W. (1992). *The learning gap: Why our schools are failing and what we can learn from Japanese and Chinese education.* New York: Summit Books.

Stiles, Deborah A., Gibbons, Judith L., Hardardottir, Sara, & Schnellmann, Jo. (1987). The ideal man or woman as described by young adolescents in Iceland and the United States. *Sex Roles, 17,* 313–320.

Stipek, Deborah J. (1984). Young children's performance expectations: Logical analysis or wishful thinking? In J. Nicholls (Ed.), *The development of achievement motivation.* Greenwich, CT: JAI.

Stipek, Deborah J. (1992). The child at school. In M.H. Bornstein & M.E. Lamb (Eds.), *Developmental psychology: An advanced textbook* (3rd ed.). Hillsdale, NJ: Erlbaum.

Stipek, Deborah J., & Hoffman, J. (1980). Development of children's performance-related judgments. *Child Development, 51,* 912–914.

Stipek, Deborah J., & Mac Iver, D. (1989). Developmental change in children's assessment of intellectual competence. *Child Development, 60,* 521–538.

Stipek, Deborah J., Recchia, Susan, & McClintic, Susan. (1992). Self-evaluation in young children. *Monographs of the Society for Research in Child Development, 57* (Serial No. 226), 1–79.

Stipek, Deborah J., Roberts, Theresa A., & Sanborn, Mary E. (1984). Preschool-age children's performance expectations for themselves and another child as a function of the incentive value of success and the salience of past performance. *Child Development, 55,* 1983–1989.

Stoneman, Z., & Brody, G.H. (1993). Sibling temperaments, conflict, warmth, and role asymmetry. *Child Development, 64,* 1786–1800.

Strassberg, Zvi, Dodge, Kenneth A., Pettit, Gregory S., & Bates, John E. (1994). Spanking in the home and children's subsequent aggression toward kindergarten peers. *Development and Psychopathology, 6,* 445–462.

Straus, Murray A., & Gelles, Richard J. (1986). Societal change and change in family violence from 1975 to 1985 as revealed by two national surveys. *Journal of Marriage and the Family, 48,* 465–479.

Strauss, C.C., Smith, K., Frame, C., & Forehand, R. (1985). Personal and interpersonal characteristics associated with childhood obesity. *Journal of Pediatric Psychology, 10,* 337–343.

Strauss, M.S., & Curtis, L.E. (1984). Development of numerical concepts in infancy. In C. Sophian (Ed.), *Origins of cognitive skills.* Hillsdale, NJ: Erlbaum.

Strayer, J., & Schroeder, M. (1989). Children's helping strategies: Influences of emotion, empathy, and age. In N. Eisenberg (Ed.), *New directions for child development: No. 44. Empathy and related emotional responses.* San Francisco: Jossey-Bass.

Streissguth, Ann Pytkowicz, Barr, Helen M., Sampson, Paul D., Darby, Betty L., & Martin, Donald C. (1989). IQ at age 4 in relation to maternal alcohol use and smoking during pregnancy. *Developmental Psychology, 25,* 3–11.

Streitmatter, Janice L. (1988). Ethnicity as a mediating variable of early adolescent identity development. *Journal of Adolescence, 11,* 335–346.

Streitmatter, Janice L. (1989). Identity status development and cognitive prejudice in early adolescents. *Journal of Early Adolescence, 9,* 142–152.

Streri, A. (1987). Tactile discrimination of shape and intermodal transfer in 2- to 3-month-old infants. *British Journal of Developmental Psychology, 5,* 213–220.

Striegel-Moore, Ruth H., Silberstein, Lisa, & Rodin, Judith. (1986). Understanding of risk factors for bulimia. *American Psychologist, 41,* 246–263.

Super, C.M., & Harkness, S. (1982). The infant's niche in rural Kenya and metropolitan America. In L.L. Adler (Ed.), *Cross-cultural research at issue.* New York: Academic Press.

Super, C.M., Herrera, M.G., & Mora, J.O. (1990). Long-term effects of food supplementation and psychosocial intervention on the physical growth of Colombian infants at risk of malnutrition. *Child Development, 61,* 29–49.

Surbey, M. (1990). Family composition, stress, and human menarche. In F. Bercovitch & T. Zeigler (Eds.), *The socioendocrinology of primate reproduction.* New York: Liss.

Susman, Elizabeth J., & Dorn, Lorah D. (1991). Hormones and behavior in adolescence. In Richard M. Lerner, Ann C. Petersen, & Jeanne Brooks-Gunn (Eds.), *Encyclopedia of adolescence* (Vol. 2). New York: Garland.

Suter, Larry (Ed.). (1993). *Indicators of science and mathematics education, 1992.* Washington, DC: National Science Foundation.

Sutherland, David H., Olshen, Richard A., Biden, Edmund N., & Wyatt, Marilyn P. (1988). *The development of mature walking.* Philadelphia: Lippincott.

Sutton-Smith, Brian. (1986). *Toys as culture.* New York: Gardner Press.

Swanson, James M., McBurnett, Keith, Wigal, Tim, & Pfiffner, Linda J. (1993). Effect of stimulant medication on children with attention deficit disorder: "A review of reviews." *Exceptional Children, 60,* 154–161.

Szatmari, Peter. (1992). The validity of autistic spectrum disorders: A literature review. *Journal of Autism and Developmental Disorders, 22,* 583–600.

Szatmari, Peter, Saigal, Saroj, Rosenbaum, Peter, & Campbell, Dugal. (1993). Psychopathology and adaptive functioning among extremely low birthweight children at eight years of age. *Development and Psychopathology, 5,* 345–357.

Takanishi, R. (1978). Childhood as a social issue: Historical roots of contemporary child advocacy movements. *Journal of Social Issues, 34,* 8–28.

Tallal, Paula, Miller, S., & Fitch, R.H. (1993). Neurological basis of speech: A case for the preeminence of temporal processing. In Paula Tallal (Ed.), *Annals of the New York Academy of Sciences: Vol. 682. Temporal information processing in the nervous system: Special reference to dyslexia and aphasia.* New York: New York Academy of Sciences.

Tanner, James M. (1971). Sequence, tempo, and individual variation in the growth and development of boys and girls aged twelve to sixteen. *Daedalus, 100,* 907–930.

Tanner, James M. (1978). *Fetus into man: Physical growth from conception to maturity.* Cambridge, MA: Harvard University Press.

Tanner, James M. (1991). Growth spurt, adolescent. In Richard M. Lerner, Ann C. Petersen, & Jeanne Brooks-Gunn (Eds.), *Encyclopedia of adolescence* (Vol. 1). New York: Garland.

Tanner, James M. (1991). Menarche, secular trend in age of. In Richard M. Lerner, Ann C. Petersen, & Jeanne Brooks-Gunn (Eds.), *Encyclopedia of adolescence* (Vol. 2). New York: Garland.

Tannock, Rosemary, Purvis, Karen L., & Schachar, Russell J. (1993). Narrative abilities in children with attention deficit hyperactivity disorder and normal peers. *Journal of Abnormal Child Psychology, 21,* 103–117.

Tanzer, Deborah, & Block, Jean Libman. (1976). *Why natural childbirth? A psychologist's report on the benefits to mothers, fathers and babies.* New York: Schocken.

Taylor, H. Gerry. (1988). Neuropsychological testing: Relevance of assessing children's learning disabilities. *Journal of Consulting and Clinical Psychology, 56,* 795–800.

Taylor, R.J., Chatters, L.M., Tucker, M.B., & Lewis, E. (1991). Developments in research on black families: A decade review. In A. Booth (Ed.), *Contemporary families: Looking forward, looking back.* Minneapolis: National Council on Family Relations.

Terman, Lewis M., & Oden, Melita H. (1959). *Genetic studies of genius: Vol. 5. The gifted group at mid-life: Thirty-five years' follow-up of the superior child.* Stanford, CA: Stanford University Press.

Termine, N.T., & Izard, C.E. (1988). Infants' responses to their mothers' expressions of joy and sadness. *Developmental Psychology, 24,* 223–229.

Terry, R., & Coie, J.D. (1991). A comparison of methods for defining sociometric status among children. *Developmental Psychology, 27,* 867–880.

Tew, Marjorie. (1990). *Safer childbirth: A critical history of maternity care.* New York: Routledge, Chapman, and Hall.

Tharp, Roland G. (1989). Psychocultural variables and constants: Effect on teaching and learning in the schools. *American Psychologist, 44,* 349–359.

Tharp, Roland G., & Gallimore, Ronald. (1988). *Rousing minds to life: Teaching, learning, and schooling in social context.* Cambridge, England: Cambridge University Press.

Thelen, Esther. (1987). The role of motor development in developmental psychology: A view of the past and an agenda for the future. In Nancy Eisenberg (Ed.), *Contemporary topics in developmental psychology.* New York: Wiley.

Thelen, Esther, Corbetta, D., Kamm, K., Spencer, J.P., Schneider, K., & Zernicke, R.F. (1993). The transition to reaching: Mapping intention and intrinsic dynamics. *Child Development, 64,* 1058–1098.

Thelen, Esther, & Ulrich, Beverly D. (1991). Hidden skills. *Monographs of the Society for Research in Child Development, 56* (Serial No. 223).

Thoman, E.B., & Whitney, M.P. (1990). Behavioral states in infants: Individual differences and individual analyses. In J. Colombo & J. Fagen (Eds.), *Individual differences in infancy.* Hillsdale, NJ: Erlbaum.

Thomas, Alexander. (1981). Current trends in developmental theory. *American Journal of Orthopsychiatry, 51,* 580–609.

Thomas, Alexander, & Chess, Stella. (1977). *Temperament and development.* New York: Brunner/Mazel.

Thomas, Alexander, Chess, Stella, & Birch, Herbert G. (1963). *Behavioral individuality in early childhood.* New York: New York University Press.

Thomas, Alexander, Chess, Stella, & Birch, Herbert G. (1968). *Temperament and behavior disorders in children.* New York: New York University Press.

Thomas, Hoben. (1993). Individual differences in children, studies, and statistics: Application of an Empirical Bayes methodology. In Mark L. Howe & Robert Pasnak (Eds.), *Emerging themes in cognitive development: Vol. 1. Foundations.* New York: Springer-Verlag.

Thompson, Frances E., & Dennison, Barbara. (1994). Dietary sources of fats and cholesterol in U.S. children aged 2 through 5 years. *American Journal of Public Health, 84,* 799–806.

Thompson, Larry. (1994). *Correcting the code.* New York: Simon & Schuster.

Thompson, Linda, & Walker, Alexis J. (1989). Gender in families: Women and men in marriage, work, and parenthood. *Journal of Marriage and the Family, 5,* 845–871.

Thompson, R.A. (1990). Emotion and self-regulation. In R.A. Thompson (Ed.), *Nebraska symposium on motivation: Vol. 36. Socioemotional development.* Lincoln: University of Nebraska Press.

Thompson, R.A. (1990). *Social support and the prevention of child maltreatment.* Paper commissioned by the U.S. Advisory Board on Child Abuse and Neglect, Washington, DC.

Thompson, R.A. (1990). Vulnerability in research: A developmental perspective on research risk. *Child Development, 61,* 1–16.

Thompson, R.A. (1991). Attachment theory and research. In Melvin Lewis (Ed.), *Child and adolescent psychiatry: A comprehensive textbook.* Baltimore: Williams and Wilkins.

Thompson, R.A. (1991). Emotional regulation and emotional development. *Educational Psychology Review, 3,* 269–307.

Thompson, R.A. (1991). Infant day care: Concerns, controversies, choices. In Jacqueline V. Lerner & Nancy L. Galambos (Eds.), *Employed mothers and their children.* New York: Garland.

Thompson, R.A. (1992). Developmental changes in research risk and benefit: A changing calculus of concerns. In B. Stanley & J.E. Sieber (Eds.), *Social research on children and adolescents: Ethical issues.* Newbury Park, CA: Sage.

Thompson, R.A. (1994). Fatherhood and divorce. *The Future of Children,* in press.

Thompson, R.A. (in press). Emotional regulation: A theme in search of definition. In N.A. Fox (Ed.), *The development of emotional regulation and dysregulation: Biological and behavioral aspects. Monographs of the Society for Research in Child Development.*

Thompson, R.A. (in press). Social support and the prevention of child maltreatment. In G.B. Melton & F. Barry (Eds.), *Safe neighborhoods: Foundations for a new national strategy on child abuse and neglect.* New York: Guilford.

Thompson, R.A., & Frodi, A.M. (1984). The sociophysiology of infants and their caregivers. In W.M. Waid (Ed.), *Sociophysiology.* New York: Springer-Verlag.

Thompson, R.A., & Jacobs, Janis E. (1991). Defining psychological maltreatment: Research and policy perspectives. *Development and Psychopathology, 3,* 93–102.

Thompson, R.A., & Limber, S.P. (1990). "Social anxiety" in infancy: Stranger and separation anxiety. In H. Leitenberg (Ed.), *Handbook of social anxiety.* New York: Plenum.

Thompson, R.A., Lamb, M.E., & Estes, D. (1982). Stability of infant-mother attachment and its relationship to changing life circumstances in an unselected middle-class sample. *Child Development, 53,* 144–148.

Thompson, R.A., Scalora, M.J., Castrianno, L., & Limber, S.P. (1992). Grandparent visitation rights: Emergent psychological and psycholegal issues. In D.K. Kagehiro & W.S. Laufer (Eds.), *Handbook of psychology and law.* New York: Springer-Verlag.

Thornburg, Herschel D., & Aras, Ziya. (1986). Physical characteristics of developing adolescents. *Journal of Adolescent Research, 1,* 47–78.

Tisi, Gennaro M. (1988). Pulmonary problems: Smoking, obstructive lung disease, and other lung disorders. In Dorothy Reycroft Hollingsworth & Robert Resnik (Eds.), *Medical counseling before pregnancy.* New York: Churchill Livingstone.

Tobin, J.D., Wu, D.Y.H., & Davidson, D. (1989). *Preschool in three cultures.* New Haven: Yale University Press.

Tomasello, M. (1988). The role of joint attentional processes in early language development. *Language Sciences, 10,* 69–88.

Tomasello, M. (1992). The social bases of language acquisition. *Social Development, 1,* 67–87.

Tomkins, A.J., & Kepfield, S.S. (1992). Policy responses when women use drugs during pregnancy: Using child abuse laws to combat substance abuse. In T.B. Sonderegger (Ed.), *Perinatal substance abuse: Research findings and clinical implications.* Baltimore: Johns Hopkins University Press.

Tosignant, Marylou. (1993, November 6). When nursing moms go back to work: Logistics of breast-feeding are tough without a supportive employer. *The Washington Post,* A-1, 12, 13.

Tower, Roni Beth, Singer, Dorothy G., Singer, Jerome L., & Biggs, Ann. (1979). Differential effects of television programming on preschoolers' cognition, imagination, and social play. *American Journal of Orthopsychiatry, 49,* 265–281.

Trasler, Gordon. (1987). Biogenetic factors. In Herbert C. Quay (Ed.), *Handbook of juvenile delinquency.* New York: Wiley.

Treboux, Dominique, & Busch-Rossnagel, Nancy. (1990). Social network influences on adolescent sexual attitudes and behaviors. *Journal of Adolescent Research, 5,* 175–189.

Trehub, S.E., Schneider, B.A., Thorpe, L.A., & Judge, P. (1991). Observational measures of auditory sensitivity in early infancy. *Developmental Psychology, 27,* 40–49.

Treiber, F., & Wilcox, B. (1984). Discrimination of number by infants. *Infant Behavior and Development, 7,* 93–100.

Triandis, Harry C. (1994). *Culture and social behavior.* New York: McGraw-Hill.

Tronick, Edward Z. (1989). Emotions and emotional communication in infants. *American Psychologist, 44,* 112–119.

Tronick, Eward Z. (1992). Special section: Cross-cultural studies of development. *Developmental Psychology, 28,* 566–625.

Tronick, Edward Z., & Cohn, Jeffrey F. (1989). Infant-mother face-to-face interaction: Age and gender differences in coordination and the occurrence of miscoordination. *Child Development, 60,* 85–92.

Tronick, Edward Z., Cohn, Jeffrey, & Shea, E. (1986). The transfer of affect between mothers and infants. In T. Berry Brazelton & M.W. Yogman (Eds.), *Affective development in infancy.* Norwood, NJ: Ablex.

Tronick, Edward Z., Morelli, G.A., & Ivey, P.K. (1992). The Efe forager infant and toddler's pattern of social relationships: Multiple and simultaneous. *Developmental Psychology, 28,* 568–577.

Turiel, Elliot. (1983). *The development of social knowledge: Morality and convention.* Cambridge, England: Cambridge University Press.

Turiel, Elliot, Smetana, Judith G., & Killen, Melanie. (1991). Social context in social cognitive development. In William M. Kurtines & Jacob L. Gewirtz (Eds.), *Handbook of moral behavior and development: Vol. 2. Research.* Hillsdale, NJ: Erlbaum.

Uhlenberg, Peter. (1980). Death and the family. *Journal of Family History, 5,* 313–320.

Underwood, M.K., Coie, J.D., & Herbsman, C.R. (1992). Display rules for anger and aggression in school-age children. *Child Development, 63,* 366–380.

UNICEF. (1990). *Children and development in the 1990s: A UNICEF sourcebook.* New York: United Nations.

UNICEF. (1994). *The state of the world's children, 1994.* New York: Oxford University Press.

United Nations. (1990). *Human Development Report, 1990.* New York: United Nations Development Program.

United Nations. (1991). *Human Development Report, 1991.* New York: Oxford University Press.

United Nations. (1994). *The state of the world's children, 1994.* New York: Oxford University Press.

United States Advisory Board on Child Abuse and Neglect. (1993). *Neighbors helping neighbors: A new national strategy for the protection of children.* Washington, DC: U.S. Government Printing Office.

United States Bureau of the Census. (1972). *Statistical abstract of the United States, 1972* (92nd ed.). Washington, DC: United States Department of Commerce.

United States Bureau of the Census. (1991). *Statistical abstract of the United States, 1991* (111th ed.). Washington, DC: United States Department of Commerce.

United States Bureau of the Census. (1992). *Statistical abstract of the United States, 1992* (112th ed.). Washington, DC: United States Department of Commerce.

United States Bureau of the Census. (1993). *Statistical abstract of the United States, 1993* (113th ed.). Washington, DC: United States Department of Commerce.

United States Department of Education. (1989). *High school and beyond: 1987 transcript study.* Washington, DC: National Center for Educational Statistics.

United States Department of Education. (1991). *The condition of education, 1991: Vol 1. Elementary and secondary education.* Washington, DC: National Center for Educational Statistics.

United States Department of Justice. (1992). *Crime in the United States.* Washington, DC: Federal Bureau of Investigation.

Vandell, Deborah Lowe. (1987). Baby sister/baby brother. Reactions to the birth of a sibling and patterns of early sibling relations. *Journal of Children in Contemporary Society, 19* (3/4), 13–37.

Vandenberg, Steven G. (1987). Sex differences in mental retardation and their implications for sex differences in ability. In June Machover Reinisch, Leonard A. Rosenblum, & Stephanie A. Sanders (Eds.), *Masculinity/femininity: Basic perspectives.* New York: Oxford University Press.

Vandenberg, Steven G., Singer, Sandra Manes, & Paula, David L. (1986). *The heredity of behavior disorders in adults and children.* New York: Plenum.

van der Voort, T.H.A., & Valkenburg, P.M. (1994). Television's impact on fantasy play: A review of research. *Developmental Review, 14,* 27–51.

Van Ijzendoorn, M.H., & Kroonenberg, P.M. (1988). Cross-cultural patterns of attachment: A meta-analysis of the Strange Situation. *Child Development, 59,* 147–156.

van Loosbroek, E., & Smitsman, A.W. (1990). Visual perception of numerosity in infancy. *Developmental Psychology, 26,* 916–922.

Van Oeffelen, Michiel P., & Vos, Peter G. (1984). The young child's processing of dot patterns: A chronometric and eye movement analysis. *International Journal of Behavioral Development, 7,* 53–66.

Varley, C.K. (1984). Attention deficit disorder (the hyperactivity syndrome): A review of selected issues. *Developmental and Behavioral Pediatrics, 5,* 254–258.

Vaughn, Brian E. (1987). Maternal characteristics measured prenatally are predictive of ratings of temperamental "difficulty" on the Carey Infant Temperament Questionnaire. *Developmental Psychology, 23,* 152–161.

Vaughn, Brian E., Stevenson-Hinde, J., Waters, E., Kotsaftis, A., Lefever, G.B., Shouldice, A., Trudel, M., & Belsky, J. (1992). Attachment security and temperament in infancy and early childhood: Some conceptual clarifications. *Developmental Psychology, 28,* 463–473.

Vaughn, Sharon, Zaragoza, Nina, Hogan, Anne, & Walker, Judy. (1993). A four-year longitudinal investigation of the social skills and behavior problems of students with learning disabilities. *Journal of Learning Disabilities, 26,* 404–406.

Vega, W.A., Kolody, B., Hwang, J., & Noble, A. (1993). Prevalence and magnitude of perinatal substance exposures in California. *New England Journal of Medicine, 329,* 850–854.

Vogel, Susan A., & Adelman, Pamela B. (1992). The success of college students with learning disabilities: Factors related to educational attainment. *Journal of Learning Disabilities, 25,* 430–441.

Volkmar, F.R. (1991). Autism and the pervasive developmental disorders. In M. Lewis (Ed.), *Child and adolescent psychiatry: A comprehensive textbook.* Baltimore: Williams and Wilkins.

Volling, B.L., & Belsky, J. (1992). The contribution of mother-child and father-child relationships to the quality of sibling interaction: A longitudinal study. *Child Development, 63,* 1209–1222.

Volpe, E. Peter. (1987). *Test-tube conception: A blend of love and science.* Macon, GA: Mercer University Press.

Vondra, Joan I., Barnett, Douglas, & Cicchetti, Dante. (1990). Self-concept, motivation, and competence among children from maltreating and comparison families. *Child Abuse and Neglect, 14,* 525–540.

von Hofsten, Claes. (1983). Catching skills in infancy. *Journal of Experimental Psychology: Human Perception and Performance, 9,* 75–85.

Voyandoff, P., & Donnelly, B.W. (1990). *Adolescent sexuality and pregnancy.* Newbury Park, CA: Sage.

Vuchinich, S., Hetherington, E.M., Vuchinich, R.A., & Clingempeel, W.G. (1991). Parent-child interaction and gender differences in early adolescents' adaptation to stepfamilies. *Developmental Psychology, 27,* 618–626.

Vygotsky, Lev S. (1962). *Thought and language.* Cambridge, MA: MIT Press.

Vygotsky, Lev S. (1978). *Mind in society: The development of higher psychological processes.* Cambridge, MA: Harvard University Press.

Vygotsky, Lev S. (1987). *Thinking and speech.* N. Minick (Trans.). New York: Plenum.

Wachs, T.D., & Gruen, G.E. (1982). *Early experience and human development.* New York: Wiley.

Waggoner, J.E., & Palermo, D.S. (1989). Betty is a bouncing bubble: Children's comprehension of emotion-descriptive metaphors. *Developmental Psychology, 25,* 152–163.

Wagner, B.M., & Phillips, D.A. (1992). Beyond beliefs: Parent and child behaviors and children's perceived academic competence. *Child Development, 63,* 1380–1391.

Walden, T.A., & Ogan, T.A. (1988). The development of social referencing. *Child Development, 59,* 1230–1240.

Walker, Arlene S. (1982). Intermodal perception of expressive behaviors by human infants. *Journal of Experimental Child Psychology, 33,* 514–535.

Walker, Lawrence J. (1984). Sex differences in the development of moral reasoning: A critical review. *Child Development, 55,* 677–691.

Walker, Lawrence J. (1988). The development of moral reasoning. *Annals of Child Development, 55,* 677–691.

Walker, Lawrence J., de Vries, Brian, & Trevethan, Shelley D. (1987). Moral stages and moral orientations in real-life and hypothetical dilemmas. *Child Development, 58,* 842–858.

Walker-Andrews, A.S., Bahrick, L.E., Raglioni, S.S., & Diaz, I. (1991). Infants' bimodal perception of gender. *Ecological Psychology, 3,* 55–75.

Wallace, James R., Cunningham, Thomas F., & Del Monte, Vickie. (1984). Change and stability in self-esteem between late childhood and early adolescence. *Journal of Early Adolescence, 4,* 253–257.

Wallerstein, Judith S., & Blakeslee, S. (1989). *Second chances: Men, women, and children a decade after divorce.* New York: Ticknor & Fields.

Wallwork, Ernest. (1980). Morality, religion and Kohlberg's theory. In Brenda Munsey (Ed.), *Moral development, moral education and Kohlberg: Basic issues in philosophy, psychology, religion and education.* Birmingham, AL: Religious Education Press.

Wanner, Eric, & Gleitman, Lila R. (Eds.). (1982). *Language acquisition: The state of the art.* Cambridge, England: Cambridge University Press.

Ward, Nicholas, Sneddon, Joan, Densem, James, Frost, Christopher, & Stone, Rossana (The MRC Vitamin study research group). (1991). Prevention of neural tube defects: Results of the Medical Research Council vitamin study. *The Lancet, 138,* 131–136.

Wasik, B.H., Bryant, D.M., & Lyons, C.M. (1990). *Home visiting.* Newbury Park, CA: Sage.

Waterman, Alan S. (1985). Identity in the context of adolescent psychology. In Alan S. Waterman (Ed.), *Identity in adolescence: Processes and contents: Vol. 30. New directions in child development.* San Francisco: Jossey-Bass.

Waterson, E.J., & Murray-Lyon, Iain M. (1990). Preventing alcohol related birth damage: A review. *Social Science and Medicine, 30,* 349–364.

Watson, John B. (1924). *Behaviorism.* New York: Norton.

Watson, John B. (1927, March). What to do when your child is afraid (interview with Beatrice Black). *Children,* 25–27.

Watson, John B. (1928). *Psychological care of the infant and child.* New York: Norton.

Watson, John B. (1967). *Behaviorism* (rev. ed.). Chicago: University of Chicago Press. (Original work published 1930).

Watson, J.D. (1983). The Human Genome Project: Past, present, and future. *Science, 248,* 44–49.

Weddle, Karen D., McHenry, Patric C., & Leigh, Geoffrey K. (1988). Adolescent sexual behavior: Trends and issues in research. *Journal of Adolescent Research, 3,* 245–257.

Weil, Douglas S., & Hemenway, David. (1992). Loaded guns in the home: Analysis of a national random survey of gun owners. *Journal of the American Medical Association, 267,* 3033–3037.

Weinraub, M., Clemens, L.P., Sockloff, A., Ethridge, T., Gracely, E., & Myers, B. (1984). The development of sex role stereotypes in the third year: Relationships to gender labeling, gender identity, sex-typed toy preferences, and family characteristics. *Child Development, 55,* 1493–1503.

Weiss, B., Dodge, K.A., Bates, J.E., & Pettit, G.S. (1992). Some consequences of early harsh discipline: Child aggression and a maladaptive social information processing style. *Child Development, 63,* 1321–1335.

Weiss, G. (1991). Attention deficit hyperactivity disorder. In M. Lewis (Ed.), *Child and adolescent psychiatry: A comprehensive textbook.* Baltimore: Williams and Wilkins.

Weiss, Gabrielle, & Hechtman, Lily Trokenberg. (1986). *Hyperactive children grow up: Empirical findings and theoretical considerations.* New York: Guilford.

Weissberg, J.A., & Paris, S.G. (1986). Young children's remembering in different contexts: A reinterpretation of Istomina's study. *Child Development, 57,* 1123–1129.

Weitzman, Lenore J. (1985). *The divorce revolution: The unexpected social and economic consequences for women and children in America.* New York: The Free Press.

Wellman, H.M. (1990). *The child's theory of mind.* Cambridge, MA: MIT Press.

Wellman, H.M., & Gelman, S.A. (1992). Cognitive development: Foundational theories of core domains. *Annual Review of Psychology, 43,* 337–375.

Wells, J.C. (1982). *Accents of English* (Vols. 1–3). New York: Cambridge University Press.

Wells, K., & Biegel, D.E. (Eds.) (1991). *Family preservation services: Research and evaluation.* Newbury Park, CA: Sage.

Wells, K., & Biegel, D.E. (1992). Intensive family preservation services research: Current status and future agenda. *Social Work Research and Abstracts, 28,* 21–27.

Wender, Paul H. (1987). *The hyperactive child, adolescent and adult: Attention deficit disorder through the lifespan.* New York: Oxford.

Wentzel, K.R., & Erdley, C.A. (1993). Strategies for making friends: Relations to social behavior and peer acceptance in early adolescence. *Developmental Psychology, 29,* 819–826.

Werker, J.F. (1989). Becoming a native listener. *American Scientist, 77,* 54–59.

Werner, Emmy E. (1993). Risk resilience and recovery: Perspectives from Kauai longitudinal study. *Development and Psychopathology, 5,* 503–515.

Werner, Emmy E., & Smith, Ruth S. (1982). *Vulnerable but invincible: A study of resilient children.* New York: McGraw-Hill.

Werner, Emmy E., & Smith, Ruth S. (1992). *Overcoming the odds: High risk children from birth to adulthood.* Ithaca, NY: Cornell University Press.

Wertsch, J.V. (1985). *Vygotsky and the social formation of mind.* Cambridge, MA: Harvard University Press.

Wertsch, J.V., & Tulviste, P. (1992). L.S. Vygotsky and contemporary developmental psychology. *Developmental Psychology, 28,* 548–557.

West, M.M. (1988). Parental values and behavior in the outer Fiji islands. In R.A. LeVine, P.M. Miller, & M.M. West (Eds.), *New directions for child development: No. 40. Parental behavior in diverse societies.* San Francisco: Jossey-Bass.

Weston, Donna R., Ivins, Barbara, Zuckerman, Barry, Jones, Caryl, & Lopez, Richard. (1989). Drug-exposed babies: Research and clinical issues. *From Zero to Three, 9* (5), 1–7.

Whalen, C.K., Henker, B., Collins, B.E., Finck, D., & Dotemoto, S. (1979). A social ecology of hyperactive boys: Medication effects in systematically structured classroom environments. *Journal of Applied Behavioral Analysis, 12,* 65–81.

Wheale, Peter R., & McNally, Ruth M. (1988). *Genetic engineering: Catastrophe or utopia.* New York: St. Martin's Press.

While, Alison K. (1989). Early infant feeding practice: Socio-economic factors and health visiting support. *Child: Care, Health, and Development, 15,* 129–136.

Whitam, Frederick L., Diamond, Milton, Martin, James. (1993). Homosexual orientation in twins: A report on 61 pairs and three triplet sets. *Archives of Sexual Behavior, 22,* 187–206.

Whitbourne, Susan Krauss. (1985). *The aging body.* New York: Springer-Verlag.

Whitbourne, Susan Krauss. (1985). The psychological construction of the life span. In James E. Birren & K. Warner Schaie (Eds.), *Handbook of the psychosocial of aging* (2nd ed.). New York: Van Nostrand Reinhold.

White, K.J., & Kistner, J. (1992). The influence of teacher feedback on young children's peer preferences and perceptions. *Developmental Psychology, 28,* 933–940.

Whiten, A. (Ed.). (1991). *Natural theories of mind.* Oxford, England: Basil Blackwell.

Whiting, Beatrice Blyth, & Edwards, Carolyn Pope. (1988). *Children of different worlds: The formation of social behavior.* Cambridge, MA: Harvard University Press.

Whittaker, J.K., Kinney, J., Tracy, E.M., & Booth, C. (1990). *Reaching high-risk families: Intensive family preservation in human services.* New York: Aldinc de Gruyter.

Widholm, Olaf. (1985). Epidemiology of premenstrual tension syndrome and primary dysmenorrhea. In M. Yusoff Dawood, John L. McGuire, & Laurence M. Demers (Eds.), *Premenstrual syndrome and dysmenorrhea.* Baltimore: Urban and Schwartzenberg.

Widom, Cathy Spatz. (1991). The role of placement experience in mediating the criminal consequences of early childhood victimization. *American Journal of Orthopsychiatry, 61,* 195–209.

Wigfield, A., & Eccles, J.S. (1992). The development of achievement task values: A theoretical analysis. *Developmental Review, 12,* 265–310.

Wigfield, A., Eccles, J.S., Mac Iver, D., Reuman, D.A., & Midgley, C. (1991). Transitions during early adolescence: Changes in children's domain-specific self-perceptions and general self-esteem across the transition to junior high school. *Developmental Psychology, 27,* 552–565.

Wiggins, Jerry S., & Holzmuller, Ana. (1978). Psychological androgyny and interpersonal behavior. *Journal of Consulting and Clinical Psychology, 46,* 40–52.

Willatts, P. (1989). Development of problem-solving in infancy. In A. Slater & G. Bremner (Eds.), *Infant development.* Hove, United Kingdom: Erlbaum.

Williams, Terry, & Kornblum, William. (1985). *Growing up poor.* Lexington, MA: Lexington Books.

Willis, D.J., Holden, E.W., & Rosenberg, M. (Eds.). (1992). *Prevention of child maltreatment: Developmental and ecological perspectives.* New York: Wiley.

Wilson, B.L., & Corcoran, T.B. (1988). *Successful secondary schools.* New York: Falmer Press.

Wilson, C.L., & Sindelar, P.T. (1990). Direct instruction in math word problems: Students with learning disabilities. *Exceptional Children, 57,* 512–519.

Wilson, Geraldine S. (1989). Clinical studies of infants and children exposed prenatally to heroin. In Donald Hutchings (Ed.), *Prenatal abuse of licit and illicit drugs.* New York: New York Academy of Sciences.

Wilson, Geraldine S. (1992). Heroin use during pregnancy: Clinical studies of long-term effects. In T.B. Sonderegger (Ed.), *Perinatal substance abuse: Research findings and clinical implications.* Baltimore: Johns Hopkins University Press.

Wilson, James Q. (1983). Raising kids. *The Atlantic Monthly, 252* (4), 45–56.

Wilson, James Q., & Herrnstein, Richard J. (1985). *Crime and human nature.* New York: Simon & Schuster.

Wilson, Jerome. (1989). Cancer incidence and mortality differences of black and white Americans. In Lovell A. Jones (Ed.), *Minorities and cancer.* New York: Springer-Verlag.

Wilson, Melvin N. (1989). Child development in the context of the black extended family. *American Psychologist, 44,* 380–385.

Wilson, M.R. (1989). Glaucoma in Blacks: Where do we go from here? *Journal of the American Medical Association, 261,* 281–282.

Wilson, William J. (1987). *The truly disadvantaged.* Chicago: University of Chicago Press.

Wimmer, H., & Perner, J. (1983). Beliefs about beliefs: Representations and the constraining function of wrong beliefs in young children's understanding of deception. *Cognition, 13,* 103–128.

Wing, R.R. (1992). Weight cycling in humans: A review of the literature. *Annals of Behavioral Medicine, 14,* 113–119.

Winn, Marie. (1977). *The plug-in drug.* New York: Viking.

Wintemute, Garen J., Teret, Stephen P., Kraus, Jess F., Wright, Mona A., & Bradfield, Gretchen. (1987). When children shoot children: 88 unintended deaths in California. *Journal of the American Medical Association, 257,* 3107.

Wolfe, D.A. (in press). The role of intervention and treatment services in the prevention of child abuse and neglect. In G.B. Melton & F. Barry (Eds.), *Safe neighborhoods: Foundations for a new national strategy on child abuse and neglect.* New York: Guilford.

Wolfe, Wendy S., Campbell, Cathy C., Fongillo, Edward A., Haas, Jere D., & Melnick, Thomas A. (1994). Overweight schoolchildren in New York State: Prevalence and characteristics. *American Journal of Public Health, 84,* 807–813.

Wolff, P. (1969). The natural history of crying and other vocalizations in infancy. In B.M. Foss (Ed.), *Determinants of infant behavior* (Vol. IV). London: Methuen.

Wolfner, Glenn D., & Gelles, Richard J. (1993). A profile of violence toward children: A national study. *Child Abuse and Neglect, 17,* 197–212.

Wong Fillmore, Lily. (1976). *The second time around: Cognitive and social strategies in second language acquisition.* Doctoral dissertation, Stanford University. (Cited in McLaughlin, 1984).

Wong Fillmore, Lily. (1987, April 25). *Becoming bilingual: Social processes in second language learning.* Paper presented at the Society for Research in Child Development, Baltimore, MD.

Wong Fillmore, Lily. (1991). Second-language learning in children: A model of language learning in social context. In Ellen Bialystok (Ed.), *Language processing in bilingual children.* Cambridge, England: Cambridge University Press.

Wong Fillmore, Lily. (1991, April 20). *Asian-Americans and bilingualism.* Paper presented at the Society for Research in Child Development Biennial meeting, Seattle, WA.

Wood, D., Bruner, Jerome S., & Ross, G. (1976). The role of tutoring in problem solving. *Journal of Child Psychology and Psychiatry, 17,* 89–100.

Woodhead, Martin. (1991). Psychology and the cultural construction of "children's needs." In Martin Woodhead, Paul Light, & Ronnie Carr (Eds.), *Child development in social context: Vol. 3. Growing up in a changing society.* London: Routledge.

Wyatt, Gail Elizabeth. (1990). Changing influences on adolescent sexuality over the past forty years. In John Bancroft & June Machover Reinisch (Eds.), *Adolescence and puberty.* Oxford, England: Oxford University Press.

Wynn, K. (1992). Addition and subtraction by human infants. *Nature, 358,* 749–750.

Yasilove, Daniel. (1978). The effect of riddle-structure on children's comprehension and appreciation of riddles. Doctoral dissertation, New York University. *Dissertation Abstracts International, 36,* 6.

Yates, Alayne. (1989). Current perspectives on the eating disorders: I. History, psychological, and biological aspects. *Journal of the American Academy of Child and Adolescent Psychiatry, 28,* 813–828.

Yoon, Keumsil Kim. (1992). New perspective on intrasentential code-switching: A study of Korean-English switching. *Applied Psycholinguistics, 13,* 433–449.

Younger, B.A. (1990). Infant categorization: Memory for category-level and specific item information. *Journal of Experimental Child Psychology, 50,* 131–155.

Younger, B.A. (1993). Understanding category members as "the same sort of thing": Explicit categorization in ten-month-old infants. *Child Development, 64,* 309–320.

Youniss, James. (1989). Parent-adolescent relationships. In William Damon (Ed.), *Child development today and tomorrow.* San Francisco: Jossey-Bass.

Youniss, James, & Smollar, J. (1985). *Adolescent relations with mothers, fathers, and friends.* Chicago: University of Chicago Press.

Zadig, J.M., & Meltzer, L.J. (1983). Special education. In M.D. Levine, W.B. Carey, A.C. Crocker, & R.T. Gross (Eds.), *Developmental-behavioral pediatrics.* Philadelphia: W.B. Saunders.

Zahn-Waxler, C., Radke-Yarrow, M., Wagner, E., & Chapman, M. (1992). Development of concern for others. *Child Development, 28,* 126–136.

Zametkin, A.J., Nordahl, T.E., Gross, M., King, A.C., Semple, W.E., Rumsey, J., Hamburger, S., & Cohen, R.M. (1990). Cerebral glucose metabolism in adults with hyperactivity of childhood onset. *New England Journal of Medicine, 323,* 1361–1366.

Zarbatany, L., Hartmann, D.P., & Rankin, D.B. (1990). The psychological functions of preadolescent peer activities. *Child Development, 61,* 1067–1080.

Zaslow, Martha J. (1991). Variation in child care quality and its implications for children. *Journal of Social Issues, 47,* 125–138.

Zaslow, Martha J., Pederson, Frank A., Cain, Richard L., Suwalksy, Joan T.D., & Kramer, Eva L. (1985). Depressed mood in new fathers: Associations with parent-infant interaction. *Genetic, social, and general psychology monographs, 111,* 133–150.

Zedeck, Sheldon (Ed.). (1992). *Work, families, and organizations*. San Francisco: Jossey-Bass.

Zelazo, P.R. (1979). Infant reactivity to perceptual-cognitive events: Application for infant assessment. In Richard B. Kearsley & Irving E. Sigel (Eds.), *Infants at risk: Assessment of cognitive functioning*. Hillsdale, NJ: Erlbaum.

Zeskind, P.S., & Collins, V. (1987). Pitch of infant crying and caregiver responses in a natural setting. *Infant Behavior and Development, 10,* 501–504.

Zhang, Jun, & Ratcliffe, Jennifer, (1993). Paternal smoking and birthweight in Shanghai. *American Journal of Public Health, 83,* 207–210.

Zierler, Sally. (1994). Women, Sex, and HIV. *Epidemiology, 5,* 565–567.

Zigler, Edward, & Berman, Winnie. (1983). Discerning the future of early childhood intervention. *American Psychologist, 38,* 894–906.

Zigler, Edward, & Hall, Nancy W. (1989). Physical child abuse in America: Past, present, and future. In Dante Cicchetti & Vicki Carlson (Eds.), *Child maltreatment: Theory and research on the causes and consequences of child abuse and neglect*. Cambridge, England: Cambridge University Press.

Zigler, Edward, & Lang, M.E. (1990). *Child care choices*. New York: The Free Press.

Zigler, Edward, Styfco, Sally, & Gilman, Elizabeth. (1993). National Head Start program for disadvantaged preschoolers. In E. Zigler & Sally Styfco (Eds.), *Head Start and beyond: A national plan for extended childhood intervention*. New Haven: Yale University Press.

Zill, N. (1983). *Happy, healthy, and insecure*. New York: Doubleday.

Zill, Nicholas. (1988). Behavior, achievement, and health problems among children in stepfamilies: Findings from a national survey of child health. In E. Mavis Hetherington & Josephine D. Aresteh (Eds.), *Impact on divorce, single parenting, and stepparenting on children*. Hillsdale, NJ: Erlbaum.

Zill, Nicholas, & Schoenborn, Charlotte. (1990, November 16). Developmental, learning, and emotional problems: Health of our nation's children, United States, 1988. *Advance Data, 190.* U.S. Department of Health and Human Services.

Zinsmeister, K. (1990, June). Growing up scared. *Atlantic Monthly,* 49–66.

Zolbrod, Aline P. (1992). *Women and infertility: Intervention and treatment strategies*. New York: The Free Press.

Zuravin, Susan J., Benedict, Mary, & Somerfield, Mark. (1993). Child maltreatment in family foster care. *American Orthopsychiatric Association, 63,* 589–596.

Photo Acknowledgments

Part Openers

Part I p. 74–75 (reading left to right) Lennart Nilsson/Bonnier Fakta/Stockholm; Per Sundström/Gamma Liaison; Petit Format/Nestlé/Photo Researchers; S. J. Allen/International Stock Photo; Courtesy of Paul Hamilton. **Part II p. 172–173** (left to right) Petit Format/Photo Researchers; Michael Newman/PhotoEdit; Joe Epstein/Design Conceptions; Hazel Hankin/Stock, Boston; Susan Lapides/Design Conceptions; Adam Woolfitt/Woodfin Camp and Associates; Courtesy of Russ Thompson. **Part II Summary p. 291** Courtesy of Patrick Gagliardi; Courtesy of Robert DePalma; Sybil Shackman/Monkmeyer Press. **Part III p. 292–293** Laura Dwight; John Eastcott/The Image Works; Laura Dwight; Tom Prettyman/PhotoEdit; Laura Dwight. **Part III Summary p. 407** Courtesy of Guy Geraghty; Royce Bair/Monkmeyer Press; John Eastcott-Eva Momatiuk/Woodfin Camp and Associates. **Part IV p. 408–409** Paul Barton/The Stock Market; Gary Langley; Lawrence Migdale; Elizabeth Crews; David Young-Wolff/PhotoEdit; Joel Gordon. **Part IV Summary p. 517** Kaz Mori/The Image Bank; Tony Freeman/PhotoEdit; James Wilson/Woodfin Camp and Associates; Bill Gillette/ Stock, Boston; Bob Daemmrich/ Stock, Boston.

Chapter 1

Chapter Opener p. xxii Richard Hutchings/PhotoEdit; **p. 3** Tony Freeman/PhotoEdit; **p. 7** Joel Gordon; **p. 9** Library of Congress; **p. 10** (*left*) Paul Barton/The Stock Market; (*right*) J. Brignolo/The Image Bank; **p. 14** Michael McGovern/The Picture Cube; **p. 15** Joe Sohm/Chromosohm/The Stock Market; **p. 18** Ralph Dominguez/Globe Photos; **p. 23** Richard Hutchings/Photo Researchers; **p. 24** Jeff Greenberg/The Picture Cube; **p. 29** Bob Daemmrich/Stock, Boston; **p. 30** Lawrence Manning/Woodfin Camp and Associates; **p. 35** (*left*) Bob Daemmrich/The Image Works; (*right*) Ulrich Tutsch; **p. 36** Mark Antman/The Image Works.

Chapter 2

Chapter Opener p. 40 Uniphoto; **p. 42** (*left*) Erika Stone; (*right*) Camilla Smith/Rainbow; **p. 43** Archiv/Photo Researchers; **p. 45** Susan Lapides/Design Conceptions; **p. 46** UPI/Bettmann; **p. 48** (*top*) Evan Johnson/Jeroboam; (*bottom*) Richard Hutchings/PhotoEdit; **p. 50** Sovfoto; **p. 51** Sam Falk/Monkmeyer Press; **p. 52** (*top*) David R. Frazier/Photo Researchers; (*bottom*) Elizabeth Crews/The Image Works; **p. 53** (*left*) Elizabeth Crews; (*right*) Richard Hutchings/PhotoEdit; **p. 56** (*left*) William McCoy/Rainbow; (*right*) David C. Bitters/The Picture Cube; **p. 57** Yves Debraine/Black Star; **p. 59** (*left*) Sally Cassidy/The Picture Cube; (*center*) David Austen/Stock, Boston; (*right*) Lew Merrim/Monkmeyer Press; **p. 60** (*top and center*) Laura Dwight; (*bottom*) Julie O'Neil/The Picture Cube; **p. 61** Hazel Hankin; **p. 65** Anthony Jaladoni/Monkmeyer Press; **p. 67** (*top*) James Wilson/Woodfin Camp and Associates; (*bottom*) Courtesy of Dr. Michael Cole, Laboratory of Comparative Human Cognition.

Chapter 3

Chapter Opener p. 76 Lennart Nilsson/Bonnier Fakta/Stockholm; **p. 78** From Lennart Nilsson, *A Child Is Born*, 2nd ed., Delacorte Press, 1990 ©. Photograph courtesy Lennart Nilsson/Bonnier Fakta/Stockholm; **p. 80** CNRI/Science Photo Library/Photo Researchers; **p. 82** (*top*) Joel Gordon; (*bottom*) John Ficara/Woodfin Camp and Associates; **p. 83** Thomas Digory/Stockphotos/The Image Bank; **p. 88** Jack Solomon, P.C; **p. 89** Thomas J. Bouchard; **p. 93** Joel Gordon; **p. 96** Laura Dwight; **p. 97** Will and Deni McIntyre/Photo Researchers; **p. 110** Petit Fortmat/Science Source/Photo Researchers; **p. 100** DPA/The Image Works; **p. 103** Philippe Plailly/Eurelios/Science Photo Library/Photo Researchers.

Chapter 4

Chapter Opener p. 108 From Lennart Nilsson, *The Incredible Machine*, National Geographic Society, 1986 ©. Photograph courtesy of Lennart Nilsson/Bonnier Fakta/Stockholm; **p. 113** Hank Morgan/Photo Researchers; **p. 114** (*left, center left, and center right*) Petit Format/Nestlé/Science Source/Photo Researchers; (*right*) National Medical Slide/Custom Medical Stock Photo; **p. 116** Carolina Biological Supply; **p. 117** S. J. Allen/International Stock Photo; **p. 120** Carnegie Institute of Washington, Department of Embryology, David Division; **p. 124** Scott McKiernan/Gamma Liaison; **p. 127** George Steinmetz; **p. 128** Amy C. Etra/PhotoEdit; **p. 133** David Wells/The Image Works; **p. 135** Andrew Brilliant/The Picture Cube; **p. 136** (*left*) William Hubbell/Woodfin Camp and Associates; (*right*) Viviane Moos.

Chapter 5

Chapter Opener p. 140 Mark Richards/PhotoEdit; **p. 143** Henry Schleichkorn/Custom Medical Stock Photo; **p. 144** Laura Dwight; **p. 149** Dan McCoy/Rainbow; **p. 155** (*left*) Doug Goodman/Monkmeyer Press; (*right*) Viviane Moos; **p. 161** A. Glauberman/Science Source/Photo Researchers; **p. 163** (*top*) Joel Gordon; (*bottom*) J. T. Miller/The Stock Market; **p. 165** Jeffrey Reed/Medichrome; **p. 166** Elizabeth Crews.

Chapter 6

Chapter Opener p. 174 Lisl Dennis/The Image Bank; **p. 178** Stephen Fiorella/Gamma Liaison; **p. 182** L. K. Tai/Woodfin Camp and Associates; **p. 189** (*left and center*) Elizabeth Crews; (*right*) Petit Format/Photo Researchers; **p. 190** Laura Dwight; **p. 193** Michael Greenlar/The Image Works; **p. 195** Courtesy of A. Slater; **p. 196** Peter Menzel; **p. 197** Peter McLeod/Acadia University; **p. 199** and **p. 201** Laura Dwight; **p. 203** Barbara Alper/Stock, Boston; **p. 205** (*left*) John Bryson/The Image Bank; (*right*) Duclos, Van Der Stockt/Gamma Liaison; **p. 207** Michael Tchereukoff/The Image Bank.

Chapter 7

Chapter Opener p. 210 Superstock; **p. 214** Courtesy of Karen Adolph; **p. 215** Ulli Seer/The Image Bank; **p. 216** Courtesy of J. Campos, B. Bertenthal & R. Kermoinanan; **p. 222** Joel Gordon; **p. 223** Joseph McNally/Sygma; **p. 224** Elizabeth Crews/The Image Works; **p. 226** Michael Newman/PhotoEdit; **p. 232** Joe Epstein/Design Conceptions; **p. 234** and **p. 235** Laura Dwight; **p. 236** Elizabeth Crews; **p. 243** Hazel Hankin/Stock, Boston; **p. 246** Betty Press/Woodfin Camp and Associates.

Chapter 8

Chapter Opener p. 248 Kindra Clineff/The Picture Cube; **p. 251** Leong Ka Tai/Material World; **p. 253** Laura Dwight; **p. 254** and **p. 255** Carroll Izard; **p. 256** Susan Lapides/Design Conceptions; **p. 259** Courtesy of Bill Davis; **p. 260** Sybil Shackman/Monkmeyer Press; **p. 261** (*left*) Bruno Barbey/Magnum; (*right*) Michael Newman/PhotoEdit; **p. 263** Tom McCarthy/The Picture Cube; **p. 264** (*top*) Bill Ross/Woodfin Camp and Associates; (*bottom*) Robert Brenner/PhotoEdit; **p. 267** Corroon and Company/Monkmeyer Press; **p. 271** Leong Ka Tai/Material World; **p. 273** Anthony Edgeworth/The Stock Market; **p. 275** Laura Dwight; **p. 276** (*left*) Elizabeth Crews; (*right*) Laura Dwight; **p. 278** Courtesy of Mary Ainsworth; **p. 281** Lawrence Migdale; **p. 283** Hazel Hankin; **p. 288** Steve Starr/Stock, Boston.

Chapter 9

Chapter Opener p. 294 Lawrence Migdale; **p. 298** and **p. 300** Laura Dwight; **p. 302** (*left*) Andrea Brizzi/Brooklyn Image Group; (*right*) Adam Woolfitt/Woodfin Camp and Associates; **p. 303** Royce Bair/Monkmeyer Press; **p. 305** (*top*) Lew Merrim/Monkmeyer Press; (*center*) Renate Hiller/Monkmeyer Press; (*bottom*) Carol Palmer/The Picture Cube; **p. 307** Star Tribune/Stormi Greener; **p. 311** Wolfgang Kaehler; **p. 314** Porter Gifford/Gamma Liaison; **p. 320** Star Tribune/Stormi Greener; **p. 321** José R. Lopez/N.Y. Times; **p. 325** Courtesy of Hana Like Home Visitor Program, Hawaii.

Chapter 10

Chapter Opener p. 328 Barbara Campbell/Liaison International; **p. 334** Michael Nichols/Magnum; **p. 337** Elizabeth Crews; **p. 342** James Kamp/Life Magazine; **p. 344** John Eastcott/The Image Works; **p. 345** Laura Dwight; **p. 346** Photo Works/Monkmeyer Press; **p. 348** Laura Dwight; **p. 352** Dave Bartruff/Stock, Boston; **p. 353**, **p. 354**, and **p. 355** Laura Dwight; **p. 358** Elizabeth Crews; **p. 361** Mike Greenlar/The Image Works; **p. 362** John Eastcott-Eva Momatiuk/Woodfin Camp and Associates; **p. 365** (*left*) Tom Prettyman/PhotoEdit; (*right*) Fujifotos/The Image Works.

Chapter 11

Chapter Opener p. 371 Bob Daemmrich/Stock, Boston; **p. 372** Lawrence Migdale; **p. 374** Mel Digiacomo/The Image Bank; **p. 375** Elizabeth Crews; **p. 377** Joel Gordon; **p. 378** Robert Brenner/PhotoEdit; **p. 385** Tony Freeman/PhotoEdit; **p. 386** Dave Schaeffer; **p. 389** John Eastcott/The Image Bank; **p. 391** David M. Grossman; **p. 393** (*top*) Bob Kristi/Black Star; (*bottom*) Jim Harrison/Stock, Boston; **p. 394** Myrleen Ferguson/ PhotoEdit; **p. 395** Laura Dwight; **p. 397** (*left*) Erika Stone; (*right*) John Coletti/Stock, Boston; **p. 402** (*top*) Joel Gordon; (*bottom*) Spencer Grant/Photo Researchers; **p. 403** (*top*) Mike Mazzaschi/Stock, Boston; (*bottom*) Barbara Campbell/Liaison International; **p. 404** Joseph Schuyler/Stock, Boston.

Chapter 12

Chapter Opener p. 410 Elaine Rebman/Photo Researchers; **p. 412** Jeff Greenberg/Photo Researchers; **p. 414** Richard Orton/The Picture Cube; **p. 417** (*right*) Elizabeth Crews; (*left*) Ross Thompson; **p. 419** Jean-Claude Lejeune/Stock, Boston; **p. 424** Alan Carey/The Image Works; **p. 425** Elizabeth Crews; **p. 430** Nancy Acevedo/Monkmeyer Press; **p. 431** Hazel Hankin/Stock, Boston; **p. 433** José Azela/Aurora.

Chapter 13

Chapter Opener p. 436 Tony Freeman/PhotoEdit; **p. 439** HMS Images/The Image Bank; **p. 440** Elizabeth Crews; **p. 441** Kaz Mori/The Image Bank; **p. 443** Tony Freeman/PhotoEdit; **p. 446** Leif Skoogfors/Woodfin Camp and Associates; **p. 450** Joel Gordon; **p. 452** Lawrence Migdale; **p. 453** Paul Conklin/Monkmeyer Press; **p. 457** (*left*) John Elk/Stock, Boston; (*right*) Mike Yamashita/Woodfin Camp and Associates; **p. 459** Elizabeth Crews; **p. 461** Russell D. Curtis/Photo Researchers; **p. 463** Bob Daemmrich/Stock, Boston; **p. 467** Ken Lax/Photo Researchers.

Chapter 14

Chapter Opener p. 470 David Young-Wolff/PhotoEdit; **p. 472** (*left*) Victor Englebert/Photo Researchers; (*right*) Arnold John Kaplan/The Picture Cube; **p. 474** Ellis Herwig/Stock, Boston; **p. 477** David Lissy/The Picture Cube; **p. 479** and **p. 481** Joel Gordon; **p. 483** David Young-Wolff/PhotoEdit; **p. 485** Bob Daemmrich/Stock, Boston; **p. 489** S. Ferry/Gamma Liaison; **p. 493** Gary Langley; **p. 495** Bob Daemmrich/Stock, Boston; **p. 503** James Wilson/Woodfin Camp and Associates; **p. 504** Peter Byron/Monkmeyer Press; **p. 506** Elizabeth Crews; **p. 509** Alon Reininger/Woodfin Camp and Associates; **p. 510** Katherine McGlynn/The Image Works; **p. 513** Peter Chapman/Stock, Boston.

Name Index

Subject Index